CAMBRIDGE
UNIVERSITY PRESS

Core & Extended Mathematics

for Cambridge IGCSE™

COURSEBOOK

Karen Morrison & Nick Hamshaw

CAMBRIDGE
UNIVERSITY PRESS

Shaftesbury Road, Cambridge CB2 8EA, United Kingdom

One Liberty Plaza, 20th Floor, New York, NY 10006, USA

477 Williamstown Road, Port Melbourne, VIC 3207, Australia

314–321, 3rd Floor, Plot 3, Splendor Forum, Jasola District Centre, New Delhi – 110025, India

103 Penang Road, #05–06/07, Visioncrest Commercial, Singapore 238467

Cambridge University Press & Assessment is a department of the University of Cambridge.

We share the University's mission to contribute to society through the pursuit of education, learning and research at the highest international levels of excellence.

www.cambridge.org
Information on this title: www.cambridge.org/9781009297912

© Cambridge University Press & Assessment 2023

First published 2012
Second edition 2018
Third edition 2023

20 19 18 17

Printed in Poland by Opolgraf

A catalogue record for this publication is available from the British Library

ISBN   978-1-009-29791-2   Paperback with Cambridge Online Mathematics (2 Years)
ISBN   978-1-009-34367-1   Paperback with Digital Version (2 Years)
ISBN   978-1-009-29792-9   Cambridge Online Mathematics Course (1 Year)

Additional resources for this publication at www.cambridge.org/go

....

CAMBRIDGE DEDICATED TEACHER AWARDS
2022

Teachers play an important part in shaping futures. Our Dedicated Teacher Awards recognise the hard work that teachers put in every day.

Thank you to everyone who nominated this year; we have been inspired and moved by all of your stories. Well done to all of our nominees for your dedication to learning and for inspiring the next generation of thinkers, leaders and innovators.

Congratulations to our incredible winners!

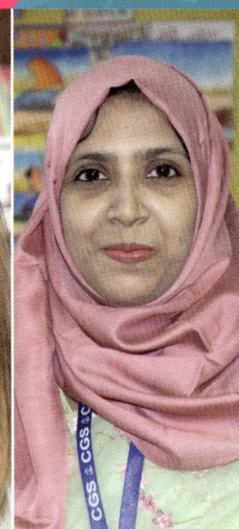

WINNER

Regional Winner Australia, New Zealand & South-East Asia	Regional Winner Europe	Regional Winner North & South America	Regional Winner Central & Southern Africa	Regional Winner Middle East & North Africa	Regional Winner East & South Asia
Mohd Al Khalifa Bin Mohd Affnan Keningau Vocational College, Malaysia	**Dr. Mary Shiny Ponparambil Paul** Little Flower English School, Italy	**Noemi Falcon** Zora Neale Hurston Elementary School, United States	**Temitope Adewuyi** Fountain Heights Secondary School, Nigeria	**Uroosa Imran** Beaconhouse School System KG-1 branch, Pakistan	**Jeenath Akther** Chittagong Grammar School, Bangladesh

For more information about our dedicated teachers and their stories, go to
dedicatedteacher.cambridge.org

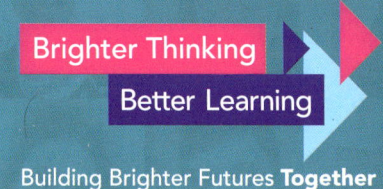

Brighter Thinking
Better Learning

Building Brighter Futures **Together**

Endorsement statement

Endorsement indicates that a resource has passed Cambridge International's rigorous quality-assurance process and is suitable to support the delivery of a Cambridge International syllabus. However, endorsed resources are not the only suitable materials available to support teaching and learning, and are not essential to be used to achieve the qualification. Resource lists found on the Cambridge International website will include this resource and other endorsed resources.

Any example answers to questions taken from past question papers, practice questions, accompanying marks and mark schemes included in this resource have been written by the authors and are for guidance only. They do not replicate examination papers. In examinations the way marks are awarded may be different. Any references to assessment and/or assessment preparation are the publisher's interpretation of the syllabus requirements. Examiners will not use endorsed resources as a source of material for any assessment set by Cambridge International.

While the publishers have made every attempt to ensure that advice on the qualification and its assessment is accurate, the official syllabus, specimen assessment materials and any associated assessment guidance materials produced by the awarding body are the only authoritative source of information and should always be referred to for definitive guidance. Cambridge International recommends that teachers consider using a range of teaching and learning resources based on their own professional judgement of their students' needs.

Cambridge International has not paid for the production of this resource, nor does Cambridge International receive any royalties from its sale. For more information about the endorsement process, please visit www.cambridgeinternational.org/endorsed-resources

❯ Contents

> Introduction

We have completely revised and updated the material to support the revised Cambridge IGCSE ™ and IGCSE (9-1) Mathematics syllabuses (0580/0980) for examination from 2025. As in previous editions, both Core and Extended topics are fully covered so that the book continues to offer a valuable resource for students and teachers. If you are following the Extended syllabus, you should also ensure you learn the Core content as you need to know this too. If you are following the Core syllabus, you can see the Extended material and use it if you are interested but you do not need to know this.

So, what is new?
Besides the updated content and fresh new design, we have increased the number of real-life applications and links to other subjects. You'll find these throughout the course.

To align with modern thinking about maths and maths teaching, and to develop problem-solving skills, we have added open-ended and open-middle problems, investigations and projects that encourage communication and collaboration around maths concepts and build thinking and reasoning into lessons.

We've increased the number of practice questions at the end of each chapter and updated the past paper questions that we have included so that you get many chances to apply your skills and make connections between different areas of mathematics as you work through structured and integrated problems.

In line with modern thinking about how people learn best, we've built in opportunities for different types of self- and peer- assessment. The feedback from these assessments will help you decide what revision or practice you can do to improve your understanding and/or performance.

There are also many opportunities for you to reflect on your own learning and to think about what you can do really well and to consider what you can learn from your mistakes. The reflection questions aim to encourage a growth mindset and develop positive attitudes towards learning maths.

We hope that you will enjoy working through the course and that you will find the material interesting, engaging and worthwhile.

Karen Morrison and Nick Hamshaw

〉How to use this book

Throughout this book, you will notice lots of different features that will help your learning. These are explained below.

IN THIS CHAPTER YOU WILL:

These set the scene for each chapter, help with navigation through the coursebook and indicate the important concepts in each topic.

Extended Content

Where content is intended for students who are studying the Extended content of the syllabus as well as the Core, this is indicated using the arrow and the bar, as on the left here.

GETTING STARTED

These boxes contain questions and activities on subject knowledge you will need before starting this chapter.

KEY WORDS

The key vocabulary appears in a box at the start of each chapter, and is highlighted in the text when it is first introduced. You will also find definitions of these words in the Glossary at the back of this Coursebook.

TIP

The information in this feature will help you complete the exercises, and give you support in areas that you might find challenging or confusing.

APPLY YOUR SKILLS

These activities give you an opportunity to apply your understanding of a concept to a real-world context. You can find answers to these questions in the digital version of the Coursebook.

Exercise 9.1

Appearing throughout the text, exercises give you a chance to check that you have understood the topic you have just learned about and practise the mathematical skills you have learned. You can find the answers to these questions in the digital version of the Coursebook on Cambridge GO.

INVESTIGATION/DISCUSSION

These boxes contain questions and activities that will allow you to extend your learning by investigating a problem, or by discussing it with classmates.

WORKED EXAMPLE 4

These boxes show you the step-by-step process to work through an example question or problem, giving you the skills to work through questions yourself.

LINK

This feature presents real-world examples and applications of the content in a chapter, encouraging you to look further into topics. Many of these examples, particularly ones that link to other syllabus subjects, extend beyond the syllabus and are presented solely for interest.

REFLECTION

These activities ask you to think about the approach that you take to your work, and how you might improve this in the future.

 This icon shows you where you should complete an exercise without using your calculator.

MATHEMATICAL CONNECTIONS

This feature will help you to link content in the chapter to what you have already learned, and highlights where you will use your understanding again in the course.

Practice Questions

Questions at the end of each chapter provide more demanding practice, some of which may require use of knowledge from previous chapters. Answers to these questions can be found in the digital version of the Coursebook on Cambridge GO.

SUMMARY

There is a summary of key points at the end of each chapter.

SELF/PEER ASSESSMENT

At the end of some exercises you will find opportunities to help you assess your own work, or that of your classmates, and consider how you can improve the way you learn.

 Projects from NRICH allow you to apply your learning from several chapters. They may give you the opportunity to extend your learning beyond the syllabus if you want to.

Past paper questions at the end of each unit give further practice in applying your learning from the previous chapters. Although all past paper questions were taken from calculator-based papers, we have marked some of the questions as non-calculator to indicate that you could try to answer these without your calculator for additional practice.

Answers to these questions can be found on Cambridge GO.

If a question asks you to complete a diagram/table/graph, you can find a printable copy of this in the Past Paper Questions Resource Sheets, which are available to download from Cambridge GO.

> How to use this series

This suite of resources supports learners and teachers following the Cambridge IGCSE™ and IGCSE (9–1) Mathematics syllabuses (0580/0980). Up-to-date metacognition techniques have been incorporated throughout the resources to meet the changes in the syllabus and develop a complete understanding of mathematics for learners. All of the components in the series are designed to work together.

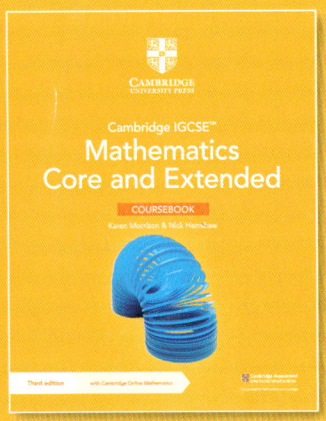

The coursebook contains six units that together offer complete coverage of the syllabus. We have worked with NRICH to provide a variety of project activities, designed to engage learners and strengthen their problem-solving skills. A new Mathematical Connections feature creates a holistic view of mathematics to help learners identify links between themes and topics. Each chapter contains opportunities for formative assessment, differentiation and peer and self-assessment offering learners the support needed to make progress. Cambridge Online Mathematics is available through the digital/ print bundle option or on its own without the print coursebook. Learners can review content digitally, explore worked examples and test their knowledge with practice questions and answers. Teachers benefit from the ability to set tests and tasks with the added auto-marking functionality and a reporting dashboard to help track learner progress quickly and easily.

The digital teacher's resource provides extensive guidance on how to teach the course, including suggestions for differentiation, formative assessment and language support, teaching ideas and PowerPoints. The Teaching Skills Focus shows teachers how to incorporate a variety of key pedagogical techniques into teaching, including differentiation, assessment for learning, and metacognition. Answers for all components are accessible to teachers for free on the Cambridge GO platform.

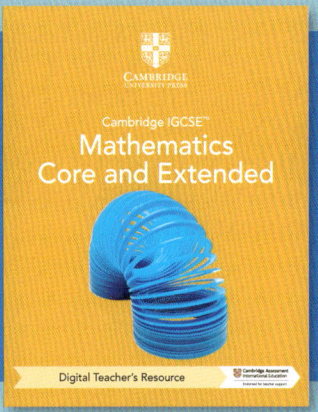

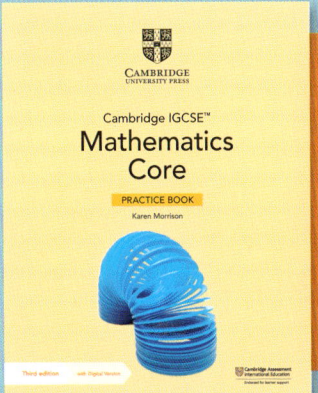

There are two practice books available, one for the core content of the syllabus and the other for learners studying extended content. These resources, which can be used in class or assigned as homework, provide a wide variety of extra maths activities and questions to help learners consolidate their learning and prepare for assessment. 'Tips' are also regularly featured to give learners extra advice and guidance on the different areas of maths they encounter. Access to the digital versions of the practice books is included, and answers can be found on the Cambridge GO platform.

› Acknowledgements

The authors and publishers acknowledge the following sources of copyright material and are grateful for the permissions granted. While every effort has been made, it has not always been possible to identify the sources of all the material used, or to trace all copyright holders. If any omissions are brought to our notice, we will be happy to include the appropriate acknowledgements on reprinting.

Cambridge International copyright material in this publication is reproduced under licence and remains the intellectual property of Cambridge Assessment International Education. Cambridge Assessment International Education bears no responsibility for the example answers to questions taken from its past question papers which are contained in this publication.

Thanks to the following for permission to reproduce images:

Cover **Wasan prunglampoo/GI**; *Inside* **Unit 1** Sean Gladwell/GI; Sander De Wilde/GI; Axel Heizmann/GI; **Unit 2** Jasmin Merdan/GI; Ultra.F/GI; **Unit 3** Michael Pasdzior/GI; Simon Mcgill/GI; David Holmes/GI; Anmbph/GI; Dinodia Photo/GI; Cooperphoto/GI; Kenishirotie/GI; **Unit 4** Courtneyk/GI; fizkes/GI; **Unit 5** Jill Newman/GI; Mattjeacock/GI; Daniel Viñé Garcia/GI; **Unit 6** Tetra Images/GI; **Unit 7** Stefan Cioata/GI; Shannonstent/GI; Bortonia/GI; Karl Hendon/GI; Nick Brundle Photography/GI; **Unit 8** Anusorn Nakdee/GI; Janiecbros/GI; Iropa/GI; Christian Adams/GI; Drazen Zigic/GI; **Unit 9** Thepalmer/GI; Mathisworks/GI; Mohamad Ridzuan Abdul Rashid/GI; **Unit 10** Victor Habbick Visions/GI; Sovfoto/GI; **Unit 11** Reklamlar/GI; Walstrom, Susanne/GI; Maravic/GI; Michael Burrell/GI; **Unit 12** Da-Kuk/GI; Solskin/GI; Chinnapong/GI; **Unit 13** Science Photo Library-NASA/GI; Sigrid Gombert/GI; AL Hedderly/GI; Jarama/GI; Nerthuz/GI; Stuart Westmorland/GI; Pal Teravagimov Photography/GI; maogg/GI; **Unit 14** Felix Cesare/GI; Barry Winiker/GI; **Unit 15** Enot-Poloskun/GI; **Unit 16** Inigo Cia/GI; James O'Neil/GI; Melanie Hobson/GI; Olaser/GI; **Unit 17** Randall Fung/GI; Oscar Wong/GI; AJ_Watt/GI; Peter Cade/GI; Hudiemm/GI; **Unit 18** Steve Satushek/GI; Mike Hill/GI; Norbert Schwaiger/GI; **Unit 19** Future Light/GI; Alikorkmaz/GI; Justin Paget/GI; Westend61/GI; **Unit 20** Antagain/GI; Monty Rakusen/GI; Andrea Pistolesi/GI; Yasser Chalid/GI; **Unit 21** PM Images/GI; Thomas Coex/GI; Cynoclub/GI; Sirapat Saeyang/GI; Carlos/GI; Steve Gschmeissner/GI; Ratnakorn Piyasirisorost/GI; Mellutto/GI; Ileximage/GI; **Unit 22** Stocktrek/GI; Darval/GI; Peter Dazeley/GI; Photograph By Hermann Platzer/GI; Rolfo Brenner/GI; **Unit 23** Alantobey/GI; Alexander Shelegov/GI; Miguel Vidal/GI; Creative-Touch/GI; Elizabeth Fernandez/GI; **Unit 24** Rodolfo Glcksberg/GI; Rosemary Calvert/GI; Erica Shires/GI; Yevgen Romanenko/GI

Key GI = Getty Images

Chapter 1

Review of number concepts

IN THIS CHAPTER YOU WILL:

- identify and classify different types of numbers
- find common factors and common multiples of numbers
- write numbers as products of their prime factors
- work with integers used in real-life situations
- calculate with powers and roots of numbers
- understand the meaning of indices
- use the rules of indices
- revise the basic rules for operating with numbers
- perform basic calculations using mental methods and with a calculator
- round numbers in different ways to estimate and approximate answers.

GETTING STARTED

1   A lot of the work in this chapter is revision. Look through the chapter to see what is covered.

   a   Are there any parts of this chapter that you could confidently skip? Explain why.

   b   If you only had to do three topics in this chapter, which would you choose? Why?

2   Look at this completed cross-number puzzle.

   a   Write a set of clues for the puzzle. Each clue should include at least one of the concepts from this chapter.

   b   Find the sum of the three greatest numbers. Write the answer in words.

3   Write each of the following using only numbers and brackets if needed.

   a   nine cubed

   b   twelve squared

   c   seven to the power of five

   d   the reciprocal of three to the power of two

   e   the reciprocal of three-quarters to the power of zero

   f   nine to the power of half

   g   fourteen billion, ten thousand and nineteen

4   Look at this decision diagram for problems involving calculation.

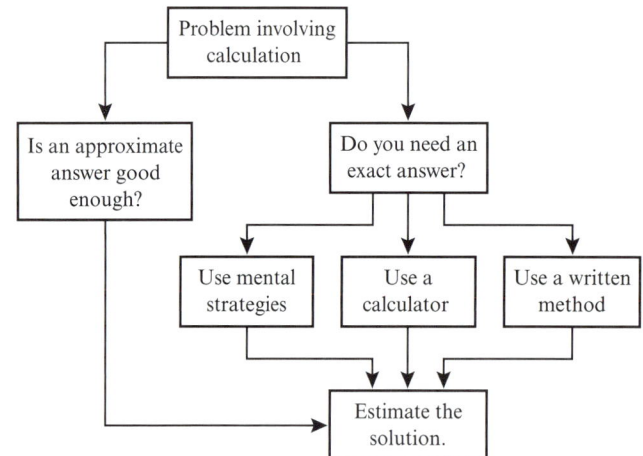

   a   Give an example of a problem where an approximate answer is good enough.

   b   How do you decide which method to use when an exact answer is needed?

   c   Estimates are useful for all of the methods in this decision tree. How could you convince someone that it is important to estimate even if you can use a calculator?

KEY WORDS

base

composite number

cube

cube root

exponent

factor

index

index notation

integer

irrational number

multiple

power

prime factor

prime number

rational number

reciprocal

square number

square root

The statue shown in the photograph is a replica of a 22 000-year-old bone found in the Congo Basin. The real bone is only 10 cm long and it is carved with groups of notches that represent numbers. One column lists the prime numbers from 10 to 20. It is one of the earliest examples of a number system using tallies. What do you think ancient civilisations used tallies for?

Our modern number system is called the Hindu-Arabic system because it was developed by Hindus and spread by Arab traders who brought it with them when they moved to different places in the world. The Hindu-Arabic system is decimal. This means it uses place value based on powers of ten. Any number at all, including decimals and fractions, can be written using place value and the digits from 0 to 9.

1.1 Different types of numbers

Make sure you know the correct mathematical words for the types of numbers in the table.

Number	Definition	Example
Natural number	Any whole number from 1 to infinity, sometimes called 'counting numbers'. 0 is not included.	1, 2, 3, 4, 5, …
Odd number	A whole number that cannot be divided exactly by 2.	1, 3, 5, 7, …
Even number	A whole number that can be divided exactly by 2.	2, 4, 6, 8, …
Integer	Any of the negative and positive whole numbers, including zero.	… −3, −2, −1, 0, 1, 2, 3, …
Prime number	A whole number greater than 1 which has only two factors: the number itself and 1.	2, 3, 5, 7, 11, …
Square number	The product obtained when an integer is multiplied by itself.	1, 4, 9, 16, …
Fraction	A number representing part of a whole number, written in the form $\frac{a}{b}$, where a and b are non-zero integers.	$\frac{1}{2}, \frac{1}{4}, \frac{1}{3}, \frac{1}{8}, \frac{13}{3}$
Decimal	A number that used place value and a decimal point to show a fraction.	0.5, 0.2, 0.08, 1.7

TIP

'Find the product' means 'multiply'. So, the product of 3 and 4 is 12, i.e. 3 × 4 = 12.

The set of real numbers is made up of **rational numbers** and **irrational numbers**.

Rational numbers can be written as fractions in the form $\frac{a}{b}$ where a and b are non-zero integers. The set of rational numbers includes all integers, all fractions, all terminating decimals and all recurring decimals.

Irrational numbers cannot be written as fractions. The set of irrational numbers consists of non-terminating, non-recurring decimals. The square root of a non-square number (such as $\sqrt{2}$), the cube root of a non-cube number (such as $\sqrt[3]{12}$) and π are all irrational numbers.

MATHEMATICAL CONNECTIONS

You will deal with rational and irrational numbers in more detail in Chapter 9.

LINK

Some numbers, for example $\sqrt{-1}$ and other roots of negative numbers, are not real numbers. They are neither rational nor irrational. Mathematicians call these imaginary numbers and you may learn about them if you study maths beyond Cambridge IGCSE.

Exercise 1.1

1   Here is a set of numbers: $\{-4, -1, 0, \frac{1}{2}, 0.75, 3, 4, 6, 11, 16, 19, 25\}$

List the numbers from this set that are:

a   natural numbers   b   even numbers   c   odd numbers

d   integers   e   negative integers   f   fractions

g   square numbers   h   prime numbers   i   neither square nor prime.

2   List:

a   the next four odd numbers after 107

b   four consecutive even numbers between 2008 and 2030

c   all odd numbers between 993 and 1007

d   the first five square numbers

e   four decimal fractions that are smaller than 0.5

f   four common fractions that are greater than $\frac{1}{2}$ but smaller than $\frac{3}{4}$.

3   State whether the following will be odd or even.

a   the sum of two odd numbers

b   the sum of two even numbers

c   the sum of an odd and an even number

d   the square of an odd number

e   the square of an even number

f   an odd number multiplied by an even number

INVESTIGATION

4   There are many other types of numbers. Find out what these numbers are and give an example of each.

a   Perfect numbers

b   Palindromic numbers

c   Narcissistic numbers (in other words, numbers that love themselves!)

MATHEMATICAL CONNECTIONS

You will learn much more about sets in Chapter 9. For now, just think of a set as a list of numbers or other items that are often placed inside curly brackets.

TIP

Remember that a 'sum' is the result of an addition. The term is often used for *any* calculation in early mathematics, but its meaning is very specific at this level.

TIP

Being able to communicate information effectively is a key 21st-century skill. As you work, think about what you are being asked to do in this task and how best to present your answers.

Using symbols to link numbers

Mathematicians use numbers and symbols to write mathematical information in the shortest, clearest way possible.

Exercise 1.2

1   Rewrite each of these statements using mathematical symbols.

   a   19 is less than 45

   b   12 plus 18 is equal to 30

   c   0.5 is equal to $\frac{1}{2}$

   d   0.8 is not equal to 8.0

   e -34 is less than 2 times -16

   f   therefore the number x equals the square root of 72

   g   a number (x) is less than or equal to negative 45

   h π is approximately equal to 3.14

   i   5.1 is greater than 5.01

   j   the sum of 3 and 4 is not equal to the product of 3 and 4

   k   the difference between 12 and -12 is greater than 12

   l   the sum of -12 and -24 is less than 0

   m   the product of 12 and a number (x) is approximately -40

2   Say whether these mathematical statements are true or false.

   a $0.599 > 6.0$

   b 5×1999 is approximately equal to 10 000

   c $8.1 = 8\frac{1}{10}$

   d $6.2 + 4.3 = 4.3 + 6.2$

   e $20 \times 9 \geqslant 21 \times 8$

   f $6.0 = 6$

   g $-12 > -4$

   h $19.9 \leqslant 20$

   i $1000 > 199 \times 5$

   j $\sqrt{16} = 4$

   k $35 \times 5 \times 2 \neq 350$

   l $20 \div 4 = 5 \div 20$

   m $20 - 4 \neq 4 - 20$

   n $20 \times 4 \neq 4 \times 20$

> **TIP**
>
> Remember:
> = is equal to
> ≠ is not equal to
> < is less than
> ≤ is less than or equal to
> > is greater than
> ≥ is greater than or equal to
> ∴ therefore
> √ the positive square root of

INVESTIGATION

3   Work with a partner.

   a   Look at the symbols used on the keys of your calculator. Say what each one means in words.

   b   List any symbols that you do not know. Try to find out what each one means.

1.2 Multiples and factors

Multiples

A **multiple** of a number is found when you multiply that number by a positive integer. You can think of the multiples of a number as the 'times table' for that number. For example, the multiples of 3 are $3 \times 1 = 3$, $3 \times 2 = 6$, $3 \times 3 = 9$ and so on. The first multiple of any number is the number itself.

WORKED EXAMPLE 1

a What are the first three multiples of 12?

b Is 300 a multiple of 12?

Answers

a	12, 24, 36	Multiply 12 by 1, 2 and then 3.
		$12 \times 1 = 12$
		$12 \times 2 = 24$
		$12 \times 3 = 36$
b	Yes, 300 is a multiple of 12.	Divide 300 by 12. If it goes exactly, then 300 is a multiple of 12.
		$300 \div 12 = 25$

Exercise 1.3

1 List the first five multiples of:

    a 12   **b** 3   **c** 5   **d** 8

    e 9   **f** 10   **g** 12   **h** 100

2 Use a calculator to find and list the first ten multiples of:

    a 29   **b** 44   **c** 75   **d** 114

    e 299   **f** 350   **g** 1012   **h** 9123

3 List:

    a the multiples of 4 between 29 and 53

    b the multiples of 50 less than 400

    c the multiples of 100 between 4000 and 5000.

4 Here are five numbers: 576, 396, 354, 792, 1164. Which of these are multiples of 12?

5 Which of the following numbers are not multiples of 27?

324	783	816	837	1116

The lowest common multiple (LCM)

The lowest common multiple of two or more numbers is the smallest number that is a multiple of all the given numbers.

WORKED EXAMPLE 2

Find the lowest common multiple of 4 and 7.

Answer

M_4 = 4, 8, 12, 16, 20, 24, **28**, 32	List several multiples of 4.
M_7 = 7, 14, 21, **28**, 35, 42	List several multiples of 7.
LCM = 28	Find the lowest number that appears in both sets. This is the LCM.

TIP

M_4 means the multiples of 4.

Exercise 1.4

1   Find the lowest common multiple of:

   a   2 and 5   **b**   8 and 10   **c**   6 and 4

   d   3 and 9   **e**   35 and 55   **f**   6 and 11

2   Is it possible to find the highest common multiple of two or more numbers? Give a reason for your answer.

MATHEMATICAL CONNECTIONS

Later in this chapter you will see how prime factors can be used to find LCMs.

Factors

A **factor** is a number that divides exactly into another number with no remainder. For example, 2 is a factor of 16 because it goes into 16 exactly 8 times. 1 is a factor of every number. The largest factor of any number is the number itself.

WORKED EXAMPLE 3

List the factors of:
a   12   **b**   25   **c**   110

Answers

a	F_{12} = 1, 2, 3, 4, 6, 12	Find pairs of numbers that multiply to give 12: 1 × 12 2 × 6 3 × 4
b	F_{25} = 1, 5, 25	Write the factors in numerical order. 1 × 25 5 × 5 Do not repeat the 5.
c	F_{110} = 1, 2, 5, 10, 11, 22, 55, 110	1 × 110 2 × 55 5 × 22 10 × 11

TIP

F_{12} means the factors of 12.

Exercise 1.5

1   List all the factors of:

a	4	b	5	c	8	d	11	e	18
f	12	g	35	h	40	i	57	j	90
k	100	l	132	m	160	n	153	o	360

2   Which number in each set is not a factor of the given number?

a   14   {1, 2, 4, 7, 14}   b   15   {1, 3, 5, 15, 45}

c   21   {1, 3, 7, 14, 21}   d   33   {1, 3, 11, 22, 33}

e   42   {3, 6, 7, 8, 14}

3   State true or false in each case.

a   3 is a factor of 313   b   9 is a factor of 99

c   3 is a factor of 300   d   2 is a factor of 300

e   2 is a factor of 122 488   f   12 is a factor of 60

g   210 is a factor of 210   h   8 is a factor of 420

4   What is the smallest factor and the largest factor of any number?

The highest common factor (HCF)

The highest common factor of two or more numbers is the highest number that is a factor of all the given numbers.

WORKED EXAMPLE 4

Find the highest common factor of 8 and 24.

Answer

$F_8 = \underline{1}, \underline{2}, \underline{4}, \underline{8}$ List the factors of each number.

$F_{24} = \underline{1}, \underline{2}, 3, \underline{4}, 6, \underline{8}, 12, 24$ Underline factors that appear in both sets.

$HCF = 8$ Pick out the highest underlined factor (HCF).

Exercise 1.6

1   Find the highest common factor of each pair of numbers.

a   3 and 6   b   24 and 16   c   15 and 40   d   42 and 70

e   32 and 36   f   26 and 36   g   22 and 44   h   42 and 48

2   Not including the factor provided, find two numbers less than 20 that have:

a   an HCF of 2   b   an HCF of 6

3   What is the highest common factor of two different prime numbers? Give a reason for your answer.

MATHEMATICAL CONNECTIONS

You will learn how to find HCFs using prime factors later in the chapter.

APPLY YOUR SKILLS

4 Simeon has two lengths of rope. One piece is 72 metres long and the other is 90 metres long. He wants to cut both lengths of rope into the longest pieces of equal length possible. How long will the pieces be?

5 Ms Sanchez has 40 canvases and 100 tubes of paint to give to the students in her art group. What is the largest number of students she can have if she gives each student an equal number of canvasses and an equal number of tubes of paint?

6 A jeweller has 300 blue beads, 750 red beads and 900 silver beads, which are used to make bracelets. Each bracelet must have the same number and colour of beads. What is the maximum number of bracelets that can be made with these beads?

TIP

Recognising the type of problem helps you to choose the correct mathematical techniques for solving it.

Word problems involving HCF usually involve splitting things into smaller pieces or arranging things in equal groups or rows.

1.3 Prime numbers

Prime numbers have exactly two different factors: one and the number itself.

Composite numbers have more than two factors.

The number 1 has only one factor so it is not prime and it is not composite.

MATHEMATICAL CONNECTIONS

Later in this chapter you will learn how to write integers as products of prime factors. One of the reasons why it is important for 1 to NOT be defined is prime is to make sure that the prime factorisation of any number is unique.

Finding prime numbers

Over 2000 years ago, a Greek mathematician called Eratosthenes made a simple tool for sorting out prime numbers. This tool is called the 'Sieve of Eratosthenes' and the diagram shows how it works for prime numbers up to 100.

~~1~~	(2)	(3)	~~4~~	(5)	~~6~~	(7)	~~8~~	~~9~~	~~10~~
(11)	~~12~~	(13)	~~14~~	~~15~~	~~16~~	(17)	~~18~~	(19)	~~20~~
~~21~~	~~22~~	(23)	~~24~~	~~25~~	~~26~~	~~27~~	~~28~~	(29)	~~30~~
(31)	~~32~~	~~33~~	~~34~~	~~35~~	~~36~~	(37)	~~38~~	~~39~~	~~40~~
(41)	~~42~~	(43)	~~44~~	~~45~~	~~46~~	(47)	~~48~~	~~49~~	~~50~~
~~51~~	~~52~~	(53)	~~54~~	~~55~~	~~56~~	~~57~~	~~58~~	(59)	~~60~~
(61)	~~62~~	~~63~~	~~64~~	~~65~~	~~66~~	(67)	~~68~~	~~69~~	~~70~~
(71)	~~72~~	(73)	~~74~~	~~75~~	~~76~~	~~77~~	~~78~~	(79)	~~80~~
~~81~~	~~82~~	(83)	~~84~~	~~85~~	~~86~~	~~87~~	~~88~~	(89)	~~90~~
~~91~~	~~92~~	~~93~~	~~94~~	~~95~~	~~96~~	(97)	~~98~~	~~99~~	~~100~~

Cross out 1, it is not prime.

Circle 2, then cross out other multiples of 2.

Circle 3, then cross out other multiples of 3.

Circle the next available number then cross out all its multiples.

Repeat until all the numbers in the table are either circled or crossed out.

The circled numbers are the primes.

Other mathematicians over the years have developed ways of finding larger and larger prime numbers. Until 1955, the largest known prime number had less than 1000 digits. Since the 1970s and the invention of more and more powerful computers, more and more prime numbers have been found. The graph below shows the number of digits in the largest known primes since 2000.

You should try to memorise the prime numbers between 1 and 100.

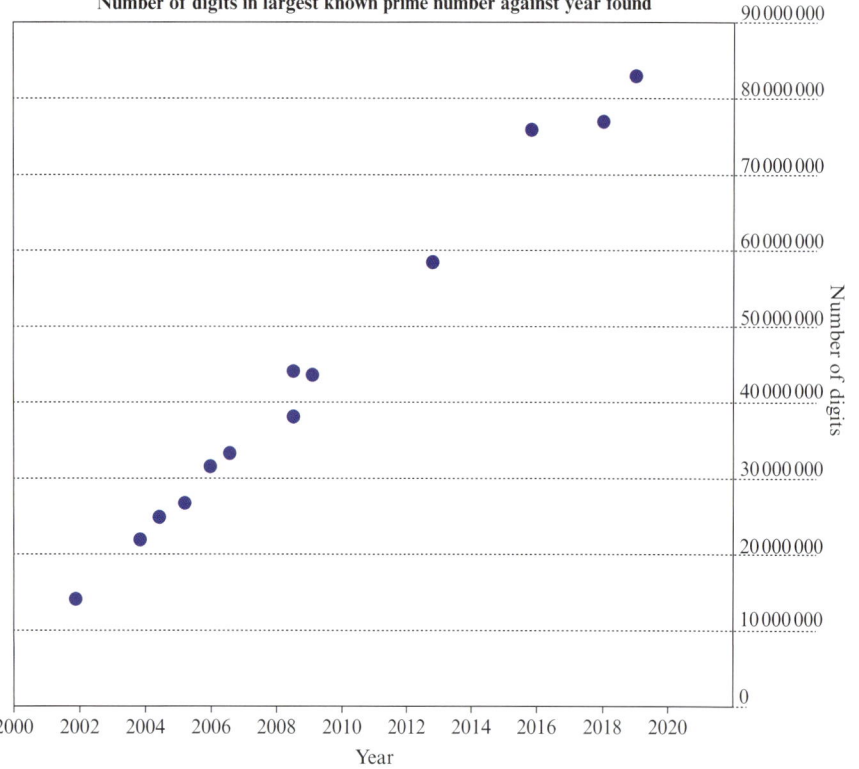

Number of digits in largest known prime number against year found

Source: https://www.mersenne.org/primes/

LINK

Today anyone can join the search for Mersenne prime numbers. This project links thousands of home computers to search continuously for larger and larger prime numbers while the computer processors have spare capacity.

INVESTIGATION

Why do mathematicians find prime numbers exciting?

One reason why prime numbers are interesting and intriguing is because there is a lot about them that we don't know and that mathematicians have not been able to prove.

1 Goldbach's conjecture (1742) is one of the oldest and best-known unsolved problems in number theory.

a What is Goldbach's strong conjecture?

b A Peruvian mathematician, Harald Helfgott, has published a largely accepted proof of Goldbach's weak conjecture. Find out more about this.

LINK

Prime numbers are used in codes and codebreaking. The larger the prime you use, the harder it is to break the code. This is why it is more and more important to find larger and larger primes.

INVESTIGATION CONTINUED

2   The Mersenne prime number search relies on massive computing power to find large primes. There is no other way to work out where the *n*th prime number will be or what the distance between large primes will be. Riemann's hypothesis (1859) claims you can accurately pinpoint the distribution of prime numbers. An Indian mathematician, Dr Kumar Eswaran published a proof for this hypothesis in 2016, but it has received mixed responses and is not yet fully accepted.

   a   Riemann built his ideas on the prime number theorem. Find out what this is and express it in simple language.

   b   Is there a proof for the existence of infinitely-many prime numbers?

3   And just for fun … What is an emirp? Find some examples to show what these are.

Exercise 1.7

1   Which is the only even prime number?

2   How many odd prime numbers are there that are less than 50?

3   **a**   List the composite numbers greater than four, but less than 30.

   b   Try to write each composite number on your list as the sum of two prime numbers. For example: 6 = 3 + 3 and 8 = 3 + 5.

4   Twin primes are pairs of prime numbers that differ by two. List the twin prime pairs up to 100.

5   Is 149 a prime number? Explain how you decided.

Prime factors

Prime factors are the factors of a number that are also prime numbers.

Every composite whole number can be broken down and written as the product of its prime factors. You can do this using tree diagrams or using division. Both methods are shown in Worked example 5.

TIP

Remember, a product is the answer to a multiplication. So to write a number as the product of its prime factors you write it like this:
$12 = 2 \times 2 \times 3$.

WORKED EXAMPLE 5

Write the following numbers as the product of prime factors.

a 36   **b** 48

Answers

Using a factor tree

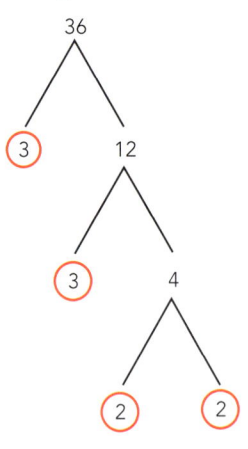
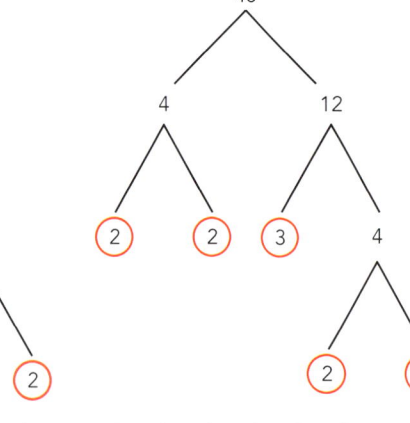

$36 = 2 \times 2 \times 3 \times 3$ $48 = 2 \times 2 \times 2 \times 2 \times 3$

Write the number as two factors.

If a factor is a prime number, circle it.

If a factor is a composite number, split it into two factors.

Keep splitting until you end up with two primes.

Write the primes in ascending order with × signs.

> **TIP**
>
> Prime numbers only have two factors: 1 and the number itself. As 1 is not a prime number, do not include it when expressing a number as a product of prime factors.

Using division

```
2 | 36          2 | 48
2 | 18          2 | 24
3 |  9          2 | 12
3 |  3          2 |  6
       1        3 |  3
                       1
```

$36 = 2 \times 2 \times 3 \times 3$ $48 = 2 \times 2 \times 2 \times 2 \times 3$

Divide by the smallest prime number that will go into the number exactly.

Continue dividing, using the smallest prime number that will go into your new answer each time.

Stop when you reach 1.

Write the prime factors in ascending order with × signs.

> **TIP**
>
> Choose the method that works best for you and stick to it. Always show your method when using prime factors.

Exercise 1.8

1   Express the following numbers as the product of prime factors.

a 30	**b** 24	**c** 100	**d** 225	**e** 360
f 504	**g** 650	**h** 1125	**i** 756	**j** 9240

> **TIP**
>
> When you write your number as a product of primes, group all occurrences of the same prime number together.

Using prime factors to find the HCF and LCM

When you are working with larger numbers you can determine the HCF or LCM by expressing each number as a product of its prime factors.

WORKED EXAMPLE 6

Find the HCF of 168 and 180.

Answer

$168 = \underline{2} \times \underline{2} \times 2 \times \underline{3} \times 7$	First express each number as a product of prime factors. Use tree diagrams or division to do this.
$180 = \underline{2} \times \underline{2} \times \underline{3} \times 3 \times 5$	Underline the factors common to both numbers.
$2 \times 2 \times 3 = 12$	Multiply these out to find the HCF.
HCF = 12	

WORKED EXAMPLE 7

Find the LCM of 72 and 120.

Answer

$72 = \underline{2 \times 2 \times 2} \times \underline{3 \times 3}$	First express each number as a product of prime factors. Use tree diagrams or division to do this.
$120 = 2 \times 2 \times 2 \times 3 \times \underline{5}$	Underline the largest set of multiples of each factor.
$2 \times 2 \times 2 \times 3 \times 3 \times 5 = 360$	List these and multiply them out to find the LCM.
LCM = 360	

MATHEMATICAL CONNECTIONS

You can also use prime factors to find the square and cube roots of numbers if you don't have a calculator. You will deal with this in more detail later in this chapter.

Exercise 1.9

1 Find the HCF of these numbers by using prime factors.

   a 48 and 108   b 120 and 216   c 72 and 90   d 52 and 78
   e 100 and 125   f 154 and 88   g 546 and 624   h 95 and 120

2 Use prime factorisation to determine the LCM of the following numbers.

   a 54 and 60   b 54 and 72   c 60 and 72   d 48 and 60
   e 120 and 180   f 95 and 150   g 54 and 90   h 90 and 120

3 Determine both the HCF and LCM of the following numbers.

   a 72 and 108   b 25 and 200   c 95 and 120   d 84 and 60

APPLY YOUR SKILLS

4   A radio station runs a phone-in competition for listeners. Every 30th caller gets a free airtime voucher and every 120th caller gets a free mobile phone. How many listeners must phone in before one receives both an airtime voucher *and* a free phone?

5   Li runs round a track in 12 minutes. Jaleel runs round the same track in 18 minutes. If they start together, how many minutes will pass before they both cross the start line together again?

6   The number p can be written as a product of the three prime numbers x, y and z, where x, y and z are all different.

   a   How many factors does the number p have?

   Another number q can be written as the product of four different primes.

   b   How many factors does q have?

   The number r can be written as a product of n different prime numbers.

   c   How many factors does r have?

TIP

Recognising the type of problem helps you to choose the correct mathematical techniques for solving it.

Word problems involving LCM usually include repeating events. You may be asked how many items you need to 'have enough' or when something will happen again at the same time.

1.4 Working with directed numbers

When you use numbers to represent real-life situations like temperatures, altitude, depth below sea level, profit or loss and directions (on a grid), you sometimes need to use the negative sign to indicate the direction of the number. For example, you can show a temperature of three degrees below zero as $-3\,°C$. Numbers like these, which have direction, are called directed numbers. So if a point 25 m above sea level is at $+25\,m$, then a point 25 m below sea level is at $-25\,m$.

TIP

Once a direction is chosen to be positive, the opposite direction is taken to be negative. So:
•   if up is positive, down is negative
•   if right is positive, left is negative
•   if north is positive, south is negative
•   if above 0 is positive, below 0 is negative.

Exercise 1.10

1 Express each of these situations using a directed number.

   a a profit of $100   **b** 25 km below sea level

   c a drop of 10 marks   **d** a gain of 2 kg

   e a loss of 1.5 kg   **f** 8000 m above sea level

   g a temperature of 10 °C below zero   **h** a fall of 24 m

   i a debt of $2000   **j** an increase of $250

   k a time two hours behind local time   **l** a height of 400 m

Calculating with directed numbers

In mathematics, directed numbers are also known as integers. You can represent the set of integers on a number line like this:

The further to the right a number is on the number line, the greater its value.

> **LINK**
>
> Directed numbers are important when describing temperatures. The Celsius (or centigrade) temperature scale places the temperature at which water freezes at zero. Positive temperatures indicate 'above freezing' and are warmer. Negative temperatures are 'below freezing' and are colder.

MATHEMATICAL CONNECTIONS

You will use similar number lines when solving linear inequalities in Chapter 14.

When you calculate with negative and positive integers, you need to pay attention to the signs and remember these rules:

- Adding a negative number is the same as subtracting the number. $3 + -5 = -2$
- Subtracting a negative number is the same as adding a positive number. $3 - -5 = 8$
- Multiplying or dividing the same signs gives a positive answer. $-3 \times -5 = 15$ and $-20 \div -4 = 5$
- Multiplying or dividing different signs gives a negative answer. $3 \times -5 = -15$ and $15 \div -3 = -5$.

TIP

Your calculator will have a [+/−] key that allows you to enter negative numbers. Make sure you know which key this is.

Exercise 1.11

1 Copy the numbers and fill in < or > to make a true statement.

   a 2 ☐ 8   **b** 4 ☐ 9   **c** 12 ☐ 3   **d** 6 ☐ −4

   e −7 ☐ 4   **f** −2 ☐ 4   **g** −2 ☐ −11   **h** −12 ☐ −20

   i −8 ☐ 0   **j** −2 ☐ 2   **k** −12 ☐ −4   **l** −32 ☐ −3

   m 0 ☐ −3   **n** −3 ☐ 11   **o** 12 ☐ −89   **p** −3 ☐ 0

2   Arrange each set of numbers in ascending order.

   a   −8, 7, 10, −1, −12   b   4, −3, −4, −10, 9, −8

   c   −11, −5, −7, 7, 0, −12   d   −94, −50, −83, −90, 0

3   Write down the missing integer in each of these calculations.

   a $7 + \square = 3$ b $-1.7 + \square = 8.3$ c $-7 + \square = -21$

   d $8 - \square = 11$ e $4 - \square = 6.7$ f $-8 - \square = -13$

   g $12 \div \square = -2$ h $-18 \div \square = 3$ i $\square \div 3 = -9$

   j $-3 \times \square = 12$ k $\square \times 4 = -16$ l $\square \times -4 = 20$

APPLY YOUR SKILLS

4   Study the temperature graph carefully.

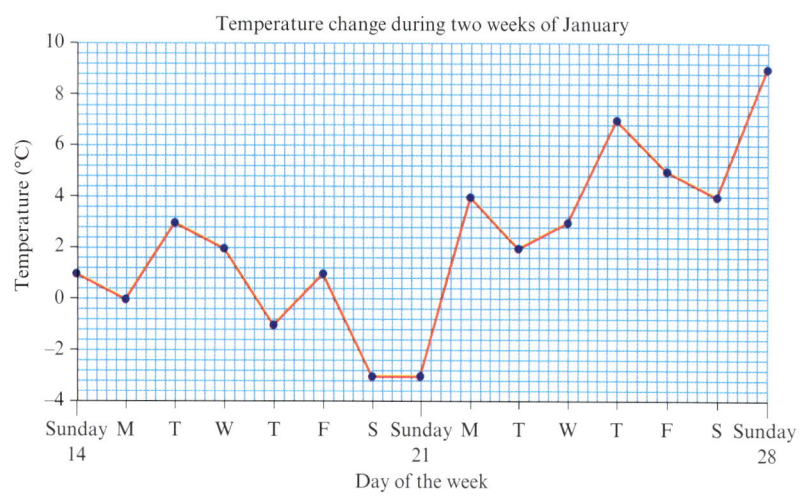

Temperature change during two weeks of January

> **TIP**
>
> The difference between the highest and lowest temperature is also called the range of temperatures.

   a   What was the temperature on Sunday 14 January?

   b   By how much did the temperature drop from Sunday 14 to Monday 15?

   c   What was the lowest temperature recorded?

   d   What is the difference between the highest and lowest temperatures?

   e   On Monday 29 January the temperature changed by −12 degrees. What was the temperature on that day?

5   Manu has a bank balance of $45.50. He deposits $15.00 and then withdraws $32.00. What is his new balance?

6   A bank account is $420 overdrawn.

   a   Express this as a directed number.

   b   How much money needs to be deposited for the account to have a balance of $500?

   c $200 is deposited. What is the new balance?

7   A diver 27 m below the surface of the water rises 16 m. At what depth is the diver now?

8   On a cold day in New York, the temperature at 6 a.m. was −5 °C. By noon, the temperature had risen by 8 °C. By 7 p.m. the temperature had dropped by 11 °C from its value at noon. What was the temperature at 7 p.m.?

9   Local time in Abu Dhabi is four hours ahead of local time in London. Local time in Rio de Janeiro is three hours behind local time in London.

   a   If it is 4 p.m. in London, what time is it in Abu Dhabi?

   b   If it is 3 a.m. in London, what time is it in Rio de Janiero?

   c   If it is 3 p.m. in Rio de Janeiro, what time is it in Abu Dhabi?

   d   If it is 8 a.m. in Abu Dhabi, what time is it in Rio de Janeiro?

10 A fuel tank at a workshop should be refilled when the gauge shows 0; however, there is a 100 litre reserve in the tank, so the level can drop below 0 if the tank is not filled on time.

   a   On 3 March, the gauge indicated 412 litres above the 0 mark. On 31 March the level had dropped to −66 litres. Calculate the mean rate of fuel use per day.

   b   On 1 April, the tank was topped up. The workshop owner estimates that this amount of fuel would be enough for 30 days, after which the level should be 0. How much fuel was added to the tank?

1.5 Powers, roots and laws of indices

You know that $2 \times 2 \times 2 \times 2 = 16$

You can write this in **index notation** as:

$2^4 = 16$

2 is the **base**

4 is the **index**

base $\longrightarrow 2^4 \longleftarrow$ index

The index is also called a **power** or an **exponent**.

Square numbers and square roots

A number is squared when it is multiplied by itself. For example, the square of 5 is $5 \times 5 = 25$. The symbol for squared is ^{2}. So you can write 5×5 as 5^2.

The **square root** of a number is the number that was multiplied by itself to get the square number. The symbol for square root is $\sqrt{}$.

You know that $25 = 5^2$, so $\sqrt{25} = 5$.

You also know that $-5 \times -5 = 25$. However, the mathematical convention is that the square root sign only refers to the positive square root. This is why if you enter $\sqrt{25}$ in your calculator you will always get the positive answer, 5.

If you want to indicate both the positive and negative square roots of 25 you need to write $\pm\sqrt{25}$.

Cube numbers and cube roots

A number is cubed when it is multiplied by itself and then multiplied by itself again. For example, the **cube** of 2 is $2 \times 2 \times 2 = 8$. The symbol for cubed is ^{3}. So $2 \times 2 \times 2$ can also be written as 2^3.

The **cube root** of a number is the number that was multiplied by itself twice to get the cube number. The symbol for cube root is $\sqrt[3]{}$. You know that $8 = 2^3$, so $\sqrt[3]{8} = 2$.

Finding powers and roots

You should know the squares of numbers from 1 to 15 (and their roots) and the cubes of numbers from 1 to 5 as well as the cube of 10. For other numbers, you can use your calculator to square or cube numbers quickly using the $\boxed{x^2}$ and $\boxed{x^3}$ keys or the $\boxed{x^\square}$ key. Use the $\boxed{\sqrt{}}$ or $\boxed{\sqrt[3]{}}$ keys to find the roots.

> **MATHEMATICAL CONNECTIONS**
>
> To solve equations like $x^2 = 25$, you need to find both the positive and negative square roots, so if $x^2 = 25$, then $x = \pm\sqrt{25} = 5$ and -5.

> **TIP**
>
> Not all calculators have exactly the same buttons. $\boxed{x^\square}$ $\boxed{x^y}$ and $\boxed{\wedge}$ all mean the same thing on different calculators. Make sure you know how to find powers and roots on your calculator.

> **WORKED EXAMPLE 8**
>
> Use your calculator to find:
>
> **a** 19^2 **b** 9^3 **c** $\sqrt{324}$ **d** $\sqrt[3]{512}$
>
> **Answers**
>
> **a** $19^2 = 361$ Enter $\boxed{1}$ $\boxed{9}$ $\boxed{x^2}$ $\boxed{=}$
>
> **b** $9^3 = 729$ Enter $\boxed{9}$ $\boxed{x^3}$ $\boxed{=}$
>
> **c** $\sqrt{324} = 18$ Enter $\boxed{\sqrt{}}$ $\boxed{3}$ $\boxed{2}$ $\boxed{4}$ $\boxed{=}$
>
> **d** $\sqrt[3]{512} = 8$ Enter $\boxed{\sqrt[3]{}}$ $\boxed{5}$ $\boxed{1}$ $\boxed{2}$ $\boxed{=}$

If you don't have a calculator, you can use the product of prime factors method to find square and cube roots of numbers. This method is shown in Worked example 9.

WORKED EXAMPLE 9

Without using a calculator find:

a $\sqrt{324}$ b $\sqrt[3]{512}$

Answers

a $324 = \underbrace{2 \times 2}_{2} \times \underbrace{3 \times 3}_{3} \times \underbrace{3 \times 3}_{3}$

Group the factors into pairs, and write down the square root of each pair.

$2 \times 3 \times 3 = 18$

Multiply the roots together to get the square root of 324.

$\sqrt{324} = 18$

b $512 = \underbrace{2 \times 2 \times 2}_{2} \times \underbrace{2 \times 2 \times 2}_{2} \times \underbrace{2 \times 2 \times 2}_{2}$

Group the factors into threes, and write the cube root of each group.

$2 \times 2 \times 2 = 8$

Multiply together to get the cube root of 512.

$\sqrt[3]{512} = 8$

Exercise 1.12

1   Write down the value of:

   a 3^2 b 7^2 c 11^2 d 12^2 e 100^2

   f 14^2 g 1^3 h 3^3 i 4^3 j 10^3

2   Calculate:

   a 21^2 b 19^2 c 32^2 d 68^2 e 6^3

   f 9^3 g 100^3 h 18^3 i 30^3 j 200^3

3   Find a value of x to make each of these statements true.

   a $x \times x = 25$ b $x \times x \times x = 8$ c $x \times x = 121$

   d $x \times x \times x = 729$ e $x \times x = 324$ f $x \times x = 400$

   g $x \times x \times x = 8000$ h $x \times x = 225$ i $x \times x \times x = 1$

   j $\sqrt{x} = 9$ k $\sqrt{1} = x$ l $\sqrt{x} = 81$

   m $\sqrt[3]{x} = 2$ n $\sqrt[3]{x} = 1$ o $\sqrt[3]{64} = x$

4   Use a calculator to find the following roots.

   a $\sqrt{9}$ b $\sqrt{64}$ c $\sqrt{1}$ d $\sqrt{4}$ e $\sqrt{100}$

   f $\sqrt{0}$ g $\sqrt{81}$ h $\sqrt{400}$ i $\sqrt{1296}$ j $\sqrt{1764}$

   k $\sqrt[3]{8}$ l $\sqrt[3]{1}$ m $\sqrt[3]{-27}$ n $\sqrt[3]{64}$ o $\sqrt[3]{1000}$

   p $\sqrt[3]{-216}$ q $\sqrt[3]{512}$ r $\sqrt[3]{729}$ s $\sqrt[3]{-1728}$ t $\sqrt[3]{5832}$

5   Use the given product of prime factors to find the square root of each number. Show your working.

   a $324 = 2 \times 2 \times 3 \times 3 \times 3 \times 3$

   b $225 = 3 \times 3 \times 5 \times 5$

   c $784 = 2 \times 2 \times 2 \times 2 \times 7 \times 7$

   d $2025 = 3 \times 3 \times 3 \times 3 \times 5 \times 5$

   e $19\,600 = 2 \times 2 \times 2 \times 2 \times 5 \times 5 \times 7 \times 7$

   f $250\,000 = 2 \times 2 \times 2 \times 2 \times 5 \times 5 \times 5 \times 5 \times 5 \times 5$

6   Use the given product of prime factors to find the cube root of each number. Show your working.

   a $27 = 3 \times 3 \times 3$

   b $729 = 3 \times 3 \times 3 \times 3 \times 3 \times 3$

   c $2197 = 13 \times 13 \times 13$

   d $1000 = 2 \times 2 \times 2 \times 5 \times 5 \times 5$

   e $15\,625 = 5 \times 5 \times 5 \times 5 \times 5 \times 5$

   f $32\,768 = 2 \times 2 \times 2 \times 2 \times 2 \times 2 \times 2 \times 2 \times 2 \times 2 \times 2 \times 2 \times 2 \times 2 \times 2$

7   Calculate:

   a $\left(\sqrt{25}\right)^2$ b $\left(\sqrt{49}\right)^2$ c $\left(\sqrt[3]{64}\right)^3$ d $\left(\sqrt[3]{32}\right)^3$

   e $\sqrt{9} + \sqrt{16}$ f $\sqrt{9 + 16}$ g $\sqrt{36} + \sqrt{64}$ h $\sqrt{36 + 64}$

   i $\sqrt{100 - 36}$ j $\sqrt{100} - \sqrt{36}$ k $\sqrt{25} \times \sqrt{4}$ l $\sqrt{25 \times 4}$

   m $\sqrt{9 \times 4}$ n $\sqrt{9} \times \sqrt{4}$ o $\sqrt{\dfrac{36}{4}}$ p $\dfrac{\sqrt{36}}{4}$

> **TIP**
>
> Brackets act as grouping symbols. Work out any calculations inside brackets before doing the calculations outside the brackets.
>
> Root signs work in the same way as a bracket. If you have $\sqrt{25 + 9}$, you must add 25 and 9 before finding the root.

8   Find the length of the edge of a cube with a volume of:

   a $1000\,\text{cm}^3$ b $19\,683\,\text{cm}^3$ c $68\,921\,\text{mm}^3$ d $64\,000\,\text{cm}^3$

9   If the symbol ★ means 'add the square of the first number to the cube of the second number', calculate:

   a $2 \star 3$ b $3 \star 2$ c $1 \star 4$ d $4 \star 1$ e $2 \star 4$

   f $4 \star 2$ g $1 \star 9$ h $9 \star 1$ i $5 \star 2$ j $2 \star 5$

You have covered many of the concepts in this chapter earlier in your study of mathematics.

* Which concepts did you remember really well?
* Why do you think you remembered these so well?
* Did you find any new ways of doing things or better ways of explaining things as you worked through this chapter? Share your ideas with a partner.

Other indices and roots

You have seen that square numbers are all raised to the power of two (5 squared = $5 \times 5 = 5^2$) and that cube numbers are all raised to the power of three (5 cubed = $5 \times 5 \times 5 = 5^3$). You can raise a number to any power. For example, $5 \times 5 \times 5 \times 5 = 5^4$. You read this as '5 to the power of 4'. The same principle applies to finding roots of numbers.

$5^2 = 25$ $\sqrt{25} = 5$

$5^3 = 125$ $\sqrt[3]{125} = 5$

$5^4 = 625$ $\sqrt[4]{625} = 5$

You can use your calculator to perform operations using any roots or squares.

The $\boxed{y^x}$ key calculates any power.

So, to find 7^5, you enter 7 $\boxed{y^x}$ 5 and get a result of 16 807.

The $\boxed{\sqrt[x]{}}$ key calculates any root.

So, to find $\sqrt[4]{81}$, you enter 4 $\boxed{\sqrt[x]{}}$ 81 and get a result of 3.

Make sure that you know which key is used for each function on your calculator and that you know how to use it. On some calculators these keys might be second functions.

MATHEMATICAL CONNECTIONS

You will work with higher powers and roots again when you deal with indices in algebra in Chapter 2, standard form in Chapter 5 and rates of growth and decay in Chapters 17 and 18.

Index notation and products of prime factors

Index notation is very useful when you have to express a number as a product of its prime factors because it allows you to write the factors in a short form.

WORKED EXAMPLE 10

Express these numbers as products of their prime factors in index form.

a 200   **b** 19 683

Answers

These diagrams are a reminder of the factor tree and division methods for finding the prime factors.

a

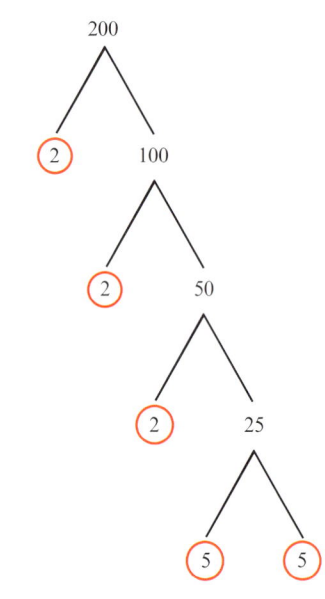

b

3	19 683
3	6561
3	2187
3	729
3	243
3	81
3	27
3	9
3	3
	1

$= 2 \times 2 \times 2 \times 5 \times 5$

$200 = 2^3 \times 5^2$

$= 3 \times 3 \times 3 \times 3 \times 3 \times 3 \times 3 \times 3 \times 3$

$19\,683 = 3^9$

Exercise 1.13

1 Evaluate.

     a $2^4 \times 2^3$ **b** $3^5 \times \sqrt[6]{64}$ **c** $3^4 + \sqrt[4]{256}$

     d $2^4 \times \sqrt[5]{7776}$ **e** $\sqrt[4]{625} \times 2^6$ **f** $8^4 \div \left(\sqrt[5]{32}\right)^3$

2 Which is greater and by how much?

     a $8^0 \times 4^4$ or $2^4 \times 3^4$ **b** $\sqrt[4]{625} \times 3^6$ or $\sqrt[6]{729} \times 4^4$

3 Express the following as products of prime factors, in index notation.

     a 64   **b** 243   **c** 400   **d** 1600   **e** 16 384

     f 20 736   **g** 59 049   **h** 390 625

4 Write several square numbers as products of prime factors, using index notation. What can you say about the index needed for each prime?

> **TIP**
>
> Remember that anything raised to the power of zero is equal to 1.

The laws of indices

The laws of indices are a set of mathematical rules that allow you to multiply and divide numbers written in index notation without having to write them in expanded form.

Make sure that you remember these three important rules.

To multiply different powers of the same number, add the indices.
For example, $3^2 \times 3^5 = 3^{2+5} = 3^7$ and $4^{-2} \times 4^3 = 4^{-2+3} = 4$.

To divide different powers of the same number, subtract the indices.
For example, $3^6 \div 3^2 = 3^{6-2} = 3^4$ and $\dfrac{4^3}{4^7} = 4^{3-7} = 4^{-4}$

To find the power of a power you multiply the indices.
For example, $(3^3)^2 = 3^{3 \times 2} = 3^6$ and $(4^2)^{-3} = 4^{2 \times -3} = 4^{-6}$

In general terms:

$$a^m \times a^n = a^{m+n} \qquad a^m \div a^n = a^{m-n} \qquad (a^m)^n = a^{mn}$$

Zero and negative indices

Do you remember how to work with zero and negative indices? Read through this information to refresh your memory.

In this table, each value is $\dfrac{1}{5}$ of the one to its left. For example, $5^4 \div 5 = 5^3$.

Power of 5	5^4	5^3	5^2	5^1	5^0	5^{-1}	5^{-2}	5^{-3}	5^{-4}
Value	625	125	25	5	1	$\dfrac{1}{5}$	$\dfrac{1}{25}$	$\dfrac{1}{125}$	$\dfrac{1}{625}$

$\div 5$

The pattern in the table shows that $5^0 = 1$. This is true for any number to the power of 0.

We can say $a^0 = 1$ (where a ≠ 0, because 0^0 is undefined.).

You can also see from the table that a number with a negative index is equal to its

reciprocal with a positive index. For example: $5^{-2} = \dfrac{1}{5^2}$.

This is true for all negative indices.

We can say $a^{-m} = \dfrac{1}{a^m}$ (where $a \neq 0$).

Exercise 1.14

1   Decide whether each statement is true or false. If it is false, work out the correct answer.

a $4^3 \times 4^5 = 4^8$ b $\dfrac{3^8}{3^2} = 3^4$ c $4^5 \div 4^2 = 4^3$ d $(8^3)^2 = 8^5$

e $34^0 = 1$ f $7^4 \times 7^3 = 7^7$ g $\dfrac{2^{10}}{2^5} = 2^5$ h $10^{10} \div 10^5 = 10^2$

i $(5^{-2})^4 = 5^2$ j $(-2^4)^2 = -2^6$ k $\dfrac{7^{-2}}{7^{-3}} = 7$ l $-(5^2)^0 = 1$

2 Simplify. Leave your answers in index notation.

a $10^3 \times 10^4$ b $3^{10} \times 3^{-5}$ c $2 \times 2^5 \times 2^{-1}$ d $10^0 \times 10^{-3}$

e $\dfrac{10^5}{10^4}$ f $\dfrac{12^6}{12^6}$ g $\dfrac{3^{-4}}{3^3}$ h $4^{-3} \div 4^4$

i $(3^4)^3$ j $(5^{-2})^2$ k $(4^2)^{-3}$ l $(4^3)^0$

3 Substitute $a = 2$, $b = 3$ and $c = \dfrac{1}{2}$ to find the value of each expression.

a $a^{-1} + b^{-1}$ b $(ab)^{-2}$ c $(a^2c)^{-1}$ d $a^{-1}b^{-1}c$

4 Evaluate.

a 3^{-1} b 4^{-1} c 2^{-1} d 4^{-2} e 2^{-4}

5 Express each value with a negative index.

a $\dfrac{1}{4}$ b $\dfrac{1}{5}$ c $\dfrac{1}{7}$ d $\dfrac{1}{3^3}$

e $\dfrac{1}{10^4}$ f $\dfrac{1}{2^8}$ g $\dfrac{1}{7^2}$ h $\dfrac{1}{2 \times 3^2}$

6 Evaluate.

a $\left(\dfrac{4}{9}\right)^{-2}$ b $8^0 \times 10^3$ c $12^2 \times 4^{-3}$ d $(2^3)^{-2}$

e $(-3)^2 \times \left(\dfrac{1}{2}\right)^{-2}$ f $\dfrac{(10-6)^3}{2^3}$ g $2^3 + \dfrac{3^2}{3} + 2$ h $(-3)^2 + \left(\dfrac{1}{2}\right)^{-3}$

7 Rewrite each expression in the form of 3^x (in other words, as a power of 3).

a 3 b 9 c 729 d $\dfrac{1}{27}$

e $\dfrac{1}{3}$ f 1 g $\dfrac{1}{243}$ h $-\sqrt{81}$

Fractional indices

Do you remember what a fractional index such as $5^{\frac{1}{2}}$ means?

You can use the laws of indices to show the meaning of fractional indices.

$5^{\frac{1}{2}} \times 5^{\frac{1}{2}} = 5^{\left(\frac{1}{2}+\frac{1}{2}\right)} = 5^1 = 5$

You also know that $\sqrt{5} \times \sqrt{5} = 5$

So, $5^{\frac{1}{2}} = \sqrt{5}$

$5^{\frac{1}{3}} \times 5^{\frac{1}{3}} \times 5^{\frac{1}{3}} = 5^{\left(\frac{1}{3}+\frac{1}{3}+\frac{1}{3}\right)} = 5^1 = 5$

And $\sqrt[3]{5} \times \sqrt[3]{5} \times \sqrt[3]{5} = 5$

So, $5^{\frac{1}{3}} = \sqrt[3]{5}$

In general terms, for unit fractions:

$a^{\frac{1}{2}} = \sqrt{a}$ $a^{\frac{1}{3}} = \sqrt[3]{a}$ $a^{\frac{1}{n}} = \sqrt[n]{a}$

> **LINK**
>
> Fractional indices and roots are used in many different financial calculations involving investments, insurance policies and economic decisions.

You can use the rule for finding the power of a power to show the meaning of fractional indices where the numerator is not 1 (non-unit fractions).

$$\left(4^{\frac{1}{4}}\right)^3 = 4^{\left(\frac{1}{4} \times \frac{3}{1}\right)} = 4^{\frac{3}{4}}$$

This shows that a number such as $5^{\frac{2}{3}}$ can be written with a unit fraction index as $\left(5^{\frac{1}{3}}\right)^2$.

You already know that you can write a unit fraction (such as $\frac{1}{3}$) as a root.

So $5^{\frac{2}{3}} = \left(5^{\frac{1}{3}}\right)^2 = \left(\sqrt[3]{5}\right)^2$

It is simpler to input the value in root form into your calculator than to enter $5^{\frac{2}{3}}$.

In general terms, for non-unit fractions:

$$a^{\frac{m}{n}} = \left(a^{\frac{1}{n}}\right)^m = \left(\sqrt[n]{a}\right)^m = \sqrt[n]{a^m}$$

> **TIP**
>
> Multiplication is commutative, so $\left(a^{\frac{1}{n}}\right)^m$ is the same as $(a^m)^{\frac{1}{n}} = \sqrt[n]{a^m}$

WORKED EXAMPLE 11

Work out the value of:

a $27^{\frac{2}{3}}$ **b** $25^{1.5}$

Answers

a $27^{\frac{2}{3}} = \left(\sqrt[3]{27}\right)^2$ $\frac{2}{3} = 2 \times \frac{1}{3}$, so you square the cube root of 27.

$\qquad\quad = (3)^2$

$\qquad\quad = 9$

b $25^{1.5} = 25^{\frac{3}{2}}$ Change the decimal to a fraction.

$\qquad\quad = \left(\sqrt{25}\right)^3$ $\frac{3}{2} = 3 \times \frac{1}{2}$, so you need to cube the

$\qquad\quad = (5)^3$ square root of 25.

$\qquad\quad = 125$

Exercise 1.15

1   Rewrite each expression using a root symbol.

   a $25^{\frac{1}{2}}$ **b** $3^{\frac{1}{3}}$ **c** $40^{\frac{1}{5}}$ **d** $6^{\frac{1}{2}}$

   e $3^{\frac{1}{8}}$ **f** $2^{\frac{3}{4}}$ **g** $12^{\frac{2}{3}}$ **h** $5^{\frac{2}{9}}$

2   Write each expression using index notation.

   a $\sqrt{5}$ **b** $\sqrt[3]{8}$ **c** $\sqrt[3]{13}$ **d** $\sqrt[4]{11}$

   e $\left(\sqrt[3]{9}\right)^2$ **f** $\left(\sqrt[3]{6}\right)^4$ **g** $\left(\sqrt[4]{32}\right)^3$ **h** $2\left(\sqrt[5]{12}\right)^7$

3   Use a calculator to evaluate.

   a $25^{\frac{1}{2}}$ **b** $27^{\frac{1}{3}}$ **c** $8^{\frac{2}{3}}$ **d** $16^{\frac{3}{4}}$

   e $216^{\frac{2}{3}}$ **f** $0.125^{\frac{1}{3}}$ **g** $46^{\frac{1}{2}}$ **h** $125^{-\frac{4}{3}}$

   i $32^{-\frac{1}{5}}$ **j** $8^{\frac{4}{3}}$ **k** $216^{\frac{2}{3}}$ **l** $256^{0.75}$

APPLY YOUR SKILLS

4 The number of calories a mammal uses when they are at rest can be worked out using the formula $C = 70 \times m^{\frac{3}{4}}$, where m is the mass of the animal in kilograms.

   a Express the formula using a root sign.

   b A cat has a mass of 5.5 kilograms. Work out how many calories it consumes while it is at rest.

   c How many calories would a 5000 kg elephant consume at rest?

1.6 Order of operations

At this level of mathematics you are expected to carry out calculations involving more than one operation ($+$, $-$, $\times$ and $\div$). When you do this you have to follow a sequence of rules so that there is no confusion about what operations you should do first. The rules for the order of operations are:

- complete operations in grouping symbols first
- deal with powers and roots next
- do division and multiplication next, working from left to right
- do addition and subtraction last, working from left to right.

Many people use the letters BODMAS to remember the order of operations. The letters stand for:

Brackets

Orders

Divide **M**ultiply

Add **S**ubtract

BODMAS indicates that indices (powers of) are considered after brackets but before all other operations.

Grouping symbols

The most common grouping symbols in mathematics are brackets. Here are some examples of the different kinds of brackets used in mathematics:

$(4 + 9) \times (10 \div 2)$

$[2(4 + 9) - 4(3) - 12]$

$\{2 - [4(2 - 7) - 4(3 + 8)] - 2 \times 8\}$

> **MATHEMATICAL CONNECTIONS**
>
> You will apply the order of operation rules to fractions, decimals and algebraic expressions as you progress through the course.

When you have more than one set of brackets in a calculation, you work out the innermost set first.

Other symbols used to group operations are:

- fraction bars, e.g. $\dfrac{5 - 12}{3 - 8}$

- root signs, such as square roots and cube roots, e.g. $\sqrt{9 + 16}$

WORKED EXAMPLE 12

Simplify.

a $7 \times (3 + 4)$ **b** $(10 - 4) \times (4 + 9)$ **c** $45 - [20 \times (4 - 3)]$

Answers

a $7 \times 7 = 49$ **b** $6 \times 13 = 78$ **c** $45 - [20 \times 1] = 45 - 20 = 25$

WORKED EXAMPLE 13

Calculate.

a $\dfrac{4 + 28}{17 - 9}$ **b** $\sqrt{36 \div 4} + \sqrt{100 - 36}$

Answers

a $(4 + 28) \div (17 - 9)$ **b** $\sqrt{36 \div 4} + \sqrt{100 - 36}$

$= 32 \div 8$ $= \sqrt{9} + \sqrt{64}$

$= 4$ $= 3 + 8$

$= 11$

Now that you know what to do with grouping symbols, you can apply the rules for order of operations to perform calculations with numbers.

Exercise 1.16

1 Calculate. Show the steps in your working.

  a $(4 + 7) \times 3$ **b** $(20 - 4) \div 4$ **c** $50 \div (20 + 5)$

  d $6 \times (2 + 9)$ **e** $(4 + 7) \times 4$ **f** $(100 - 40) \times 3$

  g $16 + (25 \div 5)$ **h** $19 - (12 + 2)$ **i** $40 \div (12 - 4)$

  j $100 \div (4 + 16)$ **k** $121 \div (33 \div 3)$ **l** $15 \times (15 - 15)$

2 Calculate.

  a $(4 + 8) \times (16 - 7)$ **b** $(12 - 4) \times (6 + 3)$ **c** $(9 + 4) - (4 + 6)$

  d $(33 + 17) \div (10 - 5)$ **e** $(4 \times 2) + (8 \times 3)$ **f** $(9 \times 7) \div (27 - 20)$

  g $(105 - 85) \div (16 \div 4)$ **h** $(12 + 13) \div 5^2$ **i** $(56 - 6^2) \times (4 + 3)$

3 Simplify. Show the steps in your working.

a $5 \times 10 + 3$

b $5 \times (10 + 3)$

c $2 + 10 \times 3$

d $(2 + 10) \times 3$

e $23 + 7 \times 2$

f $6 \times 2 \div (3 + 3)$

g $\dfrac{15 - 5}{2 \times 5}$

h $(17 + 1) \div 9 + 2$

i $\dfrac{16 - 4}{4 - 1}$

j $17 + 3 \times 21$

k $48 - (2 + 3) \times 2$

l $12 \times 4 - 4 \times 8$

m $15 + 30 \div 3 + 6$

n $20 - 6 \div 3 + 3$

o $10 - 4 \times 2 \div 2$

4 Simplify.

a $18 - 4 \times 2 - 3$

b $14 - (21 \div 3)$

c $24 \div 8 \times (6 - 5)$

d $42 \div 6 - 3 - 4$

e $5 + 36 \div 6 - 8$

f $(8 + 3) \times (30 \div 3) \div 11$

TIP

A bracket 'type' is always twinned with another bracket of the same type or shape. This helps mathematicians to understand the order of calculations even more easily.

5 Simplify. Remember to work from the innermost grouping symbols to the outermost.

a $4 + [12 - (8 - 5)]$

b $6 + [2 - (2 \times 0)]$

c $8 + [60 - (2 + 8)]$

d $200 - [(4 + 12) - (6 + 2)]$

e $200 \times \{100 - [4 \times (2 + 8)]\}$

f $\{6 + [5 \times (2 + 30)]\} \times 10$

g $[(30 + 12) - (7 + 9)] \times 10$

h $1000 - [6 \times (4 + 20) - 4 \times (3 + 0)]$

6 Calculate.

a $20 - 4 \div 2$

b $\dfrac{31 - 10}{14 - 7}$

c $\dfrac{100 - 40}{5 \times 4}$

d $\sqrt{100 - 36}$

e $\sqrt{8 + 8}$

f $\sqrt{90 - 9}$

7 State whether the following are true or false.

a $(1 + 4) \times 20 + 5 = 1 + (4 \times 20) + 5$

b $6 \times (4 + 2) \times 3 > (6 \times 4) \div 2 \times 3$

c $8 + (5 - 3) \times 2 < 8 + 5 - (3 \times 2)$

d $100 + 10 \div 10 > (100 + 10) \div 10$

8 Insert brackets into the following calculations to make them true.

a $3 \times 4 + 6 = 30$

b $25 - 15 \times 9 = 90$

c $40 - 10 \times 3 = 90$

d $14 - 9 \times 2 = 10$

e $12 + 3 \div 5 = 3$

f $19 - 9 \times 15 = 150$

g $10 + 10 \div 6 - 2 = 5$

h $3 + 8 \times 15 - 9 = 66$

i $9 - 4 \times 7 + 2 = 45$

j $10 - 4 \times 5 = 30$

k $6 \div 3 + 3 \times 5 = 5$

l $15 - 6 \div 2 = 12$

m $1 + 4 \times 20 \div 5 = 20$

n $8 + 5 - 3 \times 2 = 20$

o $36 \div 3 \times 3 - 3 = 6$

p $3 \times 4 - 2 \div 6 = 1$

q $40 \div 4 + 1 = 11$

r $6 + 2 \times 8 + 2 = 24$

9 Place the given numbers in the correct spaces to make a correct number sentence.

a $0, 2, 5, 10$ $\square - \square \div \square = \square$

b $9, 11, 13, 18$ $\square - \square \div \square = \square$

c $1, 3, 8, 14, 16$ $\square \div (\square - \square) - \square = \square$

d $4, 5, 6, 9, 12$ $(\square + \square) - (\square - \square) = \square$

Using your calculator

A calculator with algebraic logic will apply the rules for order of operations automatically. So, if you enter $2 + 3 \times 4$, your calculator will do the multiplication first and give you an answer of 14. (Check that your calculator does this!)

When the calculation contains brackets you must enter these to make sure your calculator does the grouped sections first.

WORKED EXAMPLE 14

Use a calculator to find:

a $3 + 2 \times 9$ b $(3 + 8) \times 4$ c $(3 \times 8 - 4) - (2 \times 5 + 1)$

Answers

a   21   Enter | 3 | + | 2 | × | 9 | = |

b   44   Enter | (| 3 | + | 8 |) | × | 4 | = |

c   9   Enter | (| 3 | × | 8 | − | 4 |) | − |
                   | (| 2 | × | 5 | + | 1 |) | = |

Experiment with your calculator by carrying out several calculations, with and without brackets. For example: $3 \times 2 + 6$ and $3 \times (2 + 6)$. Do you understand why these are different?

TIP

Your calculator might only have one type of bracket | (| and |) |. If there are two different shaped brackets in the calculation, such as $[4 \times (2 - 3)]$, enter the calculator bracket symbol for each type.

Exercise 1.17

1   Use your calculator to find the answers.

   a $10 - 4 \times 5$ b $12 + 6 \div 7 - 4$
   c $3 + 4 \times 5 - 10$ d $18 \div 3 \times 5 - 3 + 2$
   e $5 - 3 \times 8 - 6 \div 2$ f $7 + 3 \div 4 + 1$
   g $(1 + 4) \times 20 \div 5$ h $36 \div 6 \times (3 - 3)$
   i $(8 + 8) - 6 \times 2$ j $100 - 30 \times (4 - 3)$
   k $24 \div (7 + 5) \times 6$ l $[(60 - 40) - (53 - 43)] \times 2$
   m $[(12 + 6) \div 9] \times 4$ n $[100 \div (4 + 16)] \times 3$
   o $4 \times [25 \div (12 - 7)]$

2   Use your calculator to check whether the following answers are correct.
   If the answer is incorrect, work out the correct answer.

   a $12 \times 4 + 76 = 124$ b $8 + 75 \times 8 = 698$
   c $12 \times 18 - 4 \times 23 = 124$ d $(16 \div 4) \times (7 + 3 \times 4) = 76$
   e $(82 - 36) \times (2 + 6) = 16$ f $(3 \times 7 - 4) - (4 + 6 \div 2) = 12$

3   Each ★ represents a missing operation. Work out what they are.

   a $12 ★ (28 ★ 24) = 3$ b $84 ★ 10 ★ 8 = 4$
   c $3 ★ 7(0.7 ★ 1.3) = 17$ d $23 ★ 11 ★ 22 ★ 11 = 11$
   e $40 ★ 5 ★ (7 ★ 5) = 4$ f $9 ★ 15 ★ (3 ★ 2) = 12$

TIP

Some calculators have two '−' buttons: | − | and | (−) |. The first means 'subtract' and is used to subtract one number from another. The second means 'make negative'. Experiment with the buttons and make sure that your calculator is doing what you expect it to do!

4   Calculate.

   a $\dfrac{7 \times \sqrt{16}}{2^3 + 7^2 - 1}$

   b $\dfrac{5^2 \times \sqrt{4}}{1 + 6^2 - 12}$

   c $\dfrac{2 + 3^2}{5^2 + 4 \times 10 - \sqrt{25}}$

   d $\dfrac{6^2 - 11}{2(17 + 2 \times 4)}$

   e $\dfrac{3^2 - 3}{2 \times \sqrt{81}}$

   f $\dfrac{3^2 - 5 + 6}{\sqrt{4} \times 5}$

   g $\dfrac{36 - 3 \times \sqrt{16}}{15 - 3^2 \div 3}$

   h $\dfrac{-30 + [18 \div (3 - 12) + 24]}{5 - 8 - 3^2}$

5   Use your calculator to find the answer. Give your answers to 3 significant figures.

   a $\dfrac{0.345}{1.34 + 4.2 \times 7}$

   b $\dfrac{12.32 \times 0.0378}{\sqrt{16 + 8.05}}$

   c $\dfrac{\sqrt{16} \times 0.087}{2^2 - 5.098}$

6   Use your calculator to evaluate. Give your answers to 3 significant figures.

   a $\sqrt{64 \times 125}$

   b $\sqrt{2^3 \times 3^2 \times 6}$

   c $\sqrt[3]{8^2 + 19^2}$

   d $\sqrt{41^2 - 36^2}$

   e $\sqrt{3.2^2 - 1.17^3}$

   f $\sqrt[3]{1.45^3 - 0.13^2}$

   g $\dfrac{1}{4}\sqrt{\dfrac{1}{4} + \dfrac{1}{4} + \sqrt{\dfrac{1}{4}}}$

   h $\sqrt[3]{2.75^2 + \dfrac{1}{2} \times 1.7^3}$

7   Evaluate. Give your answer to 2 decimal places if necessary.

   a $\sqrt[3]{8} - \sqrt{1}$

   b $\sqrt[4]{16} \times 8^{-\frac{2}{3}}$

   c $(-3)^3 + 2^{-4}$

   d $\dfrac{15}{48 + 2\sqrt{7}}$

   e $\dfrac{77}{14} \times \dfrac{29}{11}$

   f $(0.467)^2 \times \sqrt{900}$

   g $\left(\dfrac{5}{6}\right)^2 + (\sqrt{144})^3$

   h $\sqrt[3]{205379} - 6(\sqrt{343})^2$

   i $\dfrac{19.23 \times 0.087}{2.45^2 - 1.03^2}$

SELF ASSESSMENT

Draw up a flow chart like this one to assess your own learning.

Some sentence stems are provided below each box to help you get started.

How do I describe my understanding?	What did I do well?	What can I improve?

I understood this easily because …
I struggled a bit with __ because …
I am still not sure of …
I am confident that I can …
I would give myself [   ] out of ten for this work.

I was very good at …
I was proud of …
My best work was …

To improve I can …
Next time I will …
I need to revise …

1.7 Rounding and estimating

In many calculations, particularly with decimals, you will not need to find an exact answer. Instead, you will be asked to give an answer to a stated level of accuracy. For example, you may be asked to give an answer correct to 2 decimal places, or to 3 significant figures.

LINK

We use 'rounding' in all subjects where numerical data is collected. Masses in physics, temperatures in biology, prices in economics: these all need to be recorded sensibly and will be rounded to a degree of accuracy appropriate for the situation.

WORKED EXAMPLE 15

Round 64.839906 to:

a   the nearest whole number
b   1 decimal place
c   3 decimal places.

Answers

a   6<u>4</u>.839906   4 is in the units place.

   64.839906   The next digit is 8, so you will round up to get 5.

   = 65 (to nearest whole number)   To the nearest whole number.

b   64.<u>8</u>39906   8 is in the first decimal place.

   64.8<u>3</u>9906   The next digit is 3, so the 8 will remain unchanged.

   = 64.8 (1 d.p.)   Correct to 1 decimal place.

c   64.83<u>9</u>906   9 is in the third decimal place.

   64.839<u>9</u>06   The next digit is 9, so you need to round up.

   = 64.840 (3 d.p.)   When you round 9 up, you get 10, so carry one to the previous digit and write 0 in the place of the 9.

                                Correct to 3 decimal places.

When a number has many digits or decimal places it is useful to round it to significant figures (s.f.). The first significant digit of a number is the first *non-zero* digit, when reading from left to right. The next digit is the second significant digit, the next the third significant and so on. All zeros *after* the first significant digit are considered significant.

If you are rounding to a whole number, write the appropriate number of zeros after the last significant digit as place holders to keep the number the same size.

TIP

Rounding to 1 significant figure does not mean you will only have one digit. When 13 432 is rounded to 1 significant figure it is 10 000 and not 1.

WORKED EXAMPLE 16

Round:

a 1.076 to 3 significant figures
b 0.00736 to 1 significant figure
c 23 512 435 to 2 significant figures

Answers

a 1.0*76*   The third significant figure is the 7. The next digit is 6, so round 7 up to get 8.

     = 1.08 (3 s.f.)   Correct to 3 significant figures.

b 0.007*3*6   The first significant figure is the 7. The next digit is 3, so 7 will not change.

     = 0.007 (1 s.f.)   Correct to 1 significant figure.

c 2*3* 512 475   The second significant figure is 3. The next digit is 5, so 3 will round up to 4.

     = 24 000 000 (2 s.f.) Include the zeros and state the level of accuracy.

Exercise 1.18

1 Round each number to 2 decimal places.

 a 3.185   **b** 0.064   **c** 38.3456   **d** 2.149   **e** 0.999

2 Round each number to the nearest 100.

 a 456   **b** 53 438   **c** 3012.567   **d** 38.299   **e** 10 060

3 Round each number to the nearest 10 000.

 a 629 534   **b** 100 999   **c** 9016   **d** 12 064   **e** 155 179

4 Express each number correct to:

 i 4 significant figures   **ii** 3 significant figures   **iii** 1 significant figure

 a 4512   **b** 12 305   **c** 65 238   **d** 320.55

 e 25.716   **f** 0.000765   **g** 1.0087   **h** 7.34876

 i 0.00998   **j** 0.02814   **k** 31.0077   **l** 0.0064735

5 Change $2\frac{5}{9}$ to a decimal using your calculator. Express the answer correct to:

 a 3 decimal places   **b** 2 decimal places

 c 1 decimal place   **d** 3 significant figures

 e 2 significant figures   **f** 1 significant figure

Estimating to get an approximate answer

To estimate the answer to a calculation, you need to round the numbers before you do the calculation. Although you can use any accuracy, often the numbers in the calculation are rounded to 1 significant figure:

3.9×2.1 is approximately equal to $4 \times 2 = 8$

Notice that $3.9 \times 2.1 = 8.19$, so the estimated value of 8 is not too far from the real value!

WORKED EXAMPLE 17

Estimate the value of:

a $\dfrac{4.6 + 3.9}{\sqrt{398}}$ b $\sqrt{42.2 - 5.1}$

Answers

a $\dfrac{4.6 + 3.9}{\sqrt{398}}$ is approximately equal to $\dfrac{5 + 4}{\sqrt{400}}$ Round the numbers to 1 significant figure.

$= \dfrac{9}{20} = \dfrac{4.5}{10} = 0.45$

Check the estimate: If you use a calculator you will find the exact value and see that the estimate was good.

$\dfrac{4.6 + 3.9}{\sqrt{398}} = 0.426$ (3 s.f.)

b $\sqrt{42.2 - 5.1}$ is approximately equal to $\sqrt{40 - 5}$ Begin by rounding each value to 1 significant figure.

$= \sqrt{35}$

is approximately equal to $\sqrt{36}$ Notice that if you round 35 up to 36 you get a square number and you can easily take the square root.

$= 6$

A good starting point for the questions in the Exercise 1.19 is to round the numbers to 1 significant figure. Remember that you can sometimes make your calculation even simpler by modifying your numbers again.

Exercise 1.19

1   The calculator displays show the answers that a student got for each calculation. Write an estimate for each calculation and say whether the calculator answer is sensible or not.

a $(7.1)^2 \div 9.9$ `0.509191919192`

b $4 \times \pi \times 3^2$ `75.39822369`

c 5×7.9 `395`

d 50×7.9 `395`

e 3×292.5 `87.75`

f $6.28 \times \sqrt{\dfrac{9.78}{0.53}}$ `26.97684374`

2   Estimate the value of each of the following. Show the rounded values that you use.

a $\dfrac{23.6}{6.3}$

b $\dfrac{4.3}{0.087 \times 3.89}$

c $\dfrac{7.21 \times 0.46}{9.09}$

d $\dfrac{4.82 \times 6.01}{2.54 + 1.09}$

e $\dfrac{\sqrt{48}}{2.54 + 4.09}$

f $(0.45 + 1.89)(6.5 - 1.9)$

g $\dfrac{23.8 + 20.2}{4.7 + 5.7}$

h $\dfrac{109.6 - 45.1}{19.4 - 13.9}$

i $(2.52)^2 \times \sqrt{48.99}$

j $\sqrt{223.8 \times 45.1}$

k $\sqrt{9.26} \times \sqrt{99.87}$

l $(4.1)^3 \times (1.9)^4$

> **TIP**
>
> When you are asked to estimate values, always show the rounded values that you use so anyone looking at your work knows what you have done.

3   Work out the actual answer for each part of question 2, using a calculator. How good were your estimates? How could you improve them?

INVESTIGATION

Making decisions about accuracy

There will be times when you have to decide how to round values to estimate. The place that you round to depends on the level of accuracy needed to solve each problem.

1   What would you round to in the following situations? Give reasons for your answers.

a   A real-life problem involving whole numbers, for example bricks or numbers of people.

b   Problems involving money amounts.

c   Calculations using numbers in the millions.

d   Scientific calculations with original values to four places.

e   Problems involving irrational numbers (such as π).

2   What have these students done to estimate?

Zaf 7.6×0.518 is approximately equal to $8 \times \dfrac{1}{2} = 4$

Marwan $\dfrac{\overset{2}{\cancel{11.75}} \times 5.7}{\underset{1}{\cancel{8.7}}}$ is approximately equal to $\dfrac{2 \times 6}{1} = 12$

a   Why is each strategy useful?

b   Why do you use the = symbol in some parts of the estimation but state 'is approximately equal to' in others?

3   What situations can you think of where it is helpful to make sure your estimate is:

a   an overestimate

b   an underestimate?

PEER ASSESSMENT

Tell … Ask … Give … (TAG) feedback is a way of assessing each other's work.

To use this method, read through your partner's answers to Exercise 1.19.

Use the guidelines in the table to help you give a TAG feedback on their work.

Tell your partner something they did well	Ask a constructive or thoughtful question	Give them a positive suggestion for improvement
I liked the way you … I could easily understand because you … The strongest part of your work was … You did … really well.	Why did you … Did you consider … Would it help if you … When does … Have you thought about …	One suggestion would be … Remember to … Think about … I'm confused by … If you … it might …

SUMMARY

Do you know …?

Numbers can be classified as natural numbers, integers, prime numbers and square numbers.

A multiple is obtained by multiplying a number by a natural number. The LCM of two or more numbers is the lowest multiple found in all the sets of multiples.

A factor of a number divides into it exactly. The HCF of two or more numbers is the highest factor found in all the sets of factors.

Prime numbers have only two factors, 1 and the number itself. The number 1 is not a prime number.

A prime factor is a number that is both a factor and a prime number.

All natural numbers that are not prime can be expressed as a product of prime factors.

Integers are also called directed numbers. The sign of an integer ($-$ or $+$) indicates whether its value is above or below 0.

When you multiply an integer (a) by itself you get a square number (a^2). If you multiply it by itself again you get a cube number (a^3).

The number you multiply to get a square is called the square root and the number you multiply to get a cube is called the cube root. The symbol for square root is $\sqrt{}$. The symbol for cube root is $\sqrt[3]{}$.

You can express numbers as powers of their factors using index notation. For example, 2^3 means $2 \times 2 \times 2$. The base is 2 and the index is 3.

Any number to the power of 0 is equal to 1: $a^0 = 1$.

A negative index can be written as a reciprocal fraction with a positive index: $a^{-m} = \dfrac{1}{a^m}$.

Fractional indices can be rewritten as roots: $a^{\frac{1}{n}} = \sqrt[n]{a}$.

For non-unit fractional indices: $a^{\frac{m}{n}} = (\sqrt[n]{a})^m = \sqrt[n]{a^m}$.

The laws of indices are: $a^m \times a^n = a^{m+n}$; $\dfrac{a^m}{a^n} = a^{m-n}$ and $(a^m)^n = a^{mn}$.

SUMMARY CONTINUED

Mathematicians apply a standard set of rules to decide the order in which operations must be carried out. Operations in grouping symbols are worked out first, then powers, then division and multiplication, then addition and subtraction.

Are you able to …?
identify rational numbers, irrational numbers, integers, square numbers and prime numbers
find multiples and factors of numbers and identify the LCM and HCF
write numbers as products of their prime factors using division and factor trees
work with integers used in real-life situations
apply the basic rules for operating with positive and negative numbers
perform basic calculations using mental methods and with a calculator
calculate squares, square roots, cubes and cube roots of numbers
apply the laws of indices to find the values of numbers written in index notation
round numbers to specified place to estimate and approximate answers.

Practice questions

 1 Find the difference between the sum of the three largest prime numbers smaller than 20 and the product of the three smallest prime numbers. [3]

 2 The product of two numbers is −36 and difference between the same two numbers is 13. Find the two possible pairs of numbers. [3]

 3 Find the number that is one fifteenth of its own square. [2]

 4 Find the highest common factor of

$2 \times 2 \times 2 \times 3 \times 3 \times 3 \times 3 \times 5 \times 7 \times 7 \times 11 \times 13$

and

$2 \times 2 \times 2 \times 3 \times 3 \times 3 \times 7 \times 11 \times 11 \times 13$ [3]

 5 The number 154.45ABC, where A, B and C represent the third, fourth and fifth decimal places in the number, is rounded to 4 decimal places and the answer is 154.4574. None of A, B or C are zero.

List all the possible sets of values of A, B and C. [4]

 6 By expressing 1080 as a product of prime factors, determine whether 1080 is a cube number. Explain your answer. [4]

7 **a** Find two numbers that have a sum of 94 and a product of 2013. [2]

   b Find two numbers have a difference of 19 and a product of 1170. [2]

 8 Simplify.

   a $6 \times 2 + 4 \times 5$ [2]   **b** $4 \times (100 - 15)$ [2]

   c $(5 + 6) \times 2 + (15 - 3 \times 2) - 6$ [2]   **d** $-3 \times 5 - 6 \times -8$ [2]

   e $-3 \times (-5 - 6) + 4 \times -6$ [2]   **f** $(-8 + 4)^3 + (-2)^4$ [2]

9   Insert +, −, × or ÷ into each blank square, to make the calculation work.

    a $5 \square 7 - 3 \square 8 = 11$ [2]

    b $(5 \square 3^2) \times 6 + 8 \square (-2) = -28$ [2]

 10   Add brackets to this statement to make it true.

    $7 + 14 \div 4 - 1 \times 2 = 14$ [2]

11   Use your calculator to find

$$\frac{5^3 - 3^2}{2^3 + 3^2 \times 11 - 2\sqrt{11}}$$

    Round your answer to 3 significant figures.   [2]

12   **a**   Without using a calculator, estimate the value of

$$\frac{4.8 - 5.1^2}{\sqrt{24.6}}$$
     [3]

    b   Use your calculator to find the difference between your estimate and the exact answer.   [2]

  13   Arrange the following numbers in order, starting with the smallest.

    A $4 \times (4 + 4 \times 4)$ B $\dfrac{4^3}{4 \times 4} + 4$

    C $\dfrac{4^2 - 4}{4} - 4$ D $4^2 - 4^2 \times 4 + \dfrac{4}{4}$ [3]

14   Find the exact values of

    a $\sqrt{98} + \sqrt{72}$ [2]   **b** $(3^{-2} + 2^{-3}) \times 216^{\frac{2}{3}}$ [3]   **c** $\left((\sqrt{2})^2 + 23\right)^{\frac{1}{2}}$ [2]

    d $\left(\dfrac{36}{25}\right)^{\frac{3}{2}}$ [2]   **e** $\left(\dfrac{16}{81}\right)^{-\frac{1}{4}}$ [2]

 15   **a**   Express 60 and 36 as products of primes.   [2]

    b   Hence find the LCM of 60 and 36.   [2]

    c   Planet Carceron has two moons, Anderon and Barberon. Anderon completes a full orbit of Carceron every 60 days, and Barberon completes a full single orbit of Carceron in 36 days. If Anderon, Barberon and Carceron lie on a straight line on 1 March 2023, on which date will this next be true?   [2]

 16   A code is developed as follows. Each letter of the alphabet is given a number, in order from 1 to 26. So A = 1, B = 2, C = 3, …, Z = 26.

    For any word with three letters, the numbers corresponding to its letters are written as powers of the prime numbers 2, 3 and 5 in order and the answers are multiplied together.

    Find the word with code 7500.   [4]

SELF ASSESSMENT

Use your answers to the practice questions to assess what you already know and to analyse your strengths and weaknesses.

What areas are you good at?

Which areas require more work?

What work will you do?

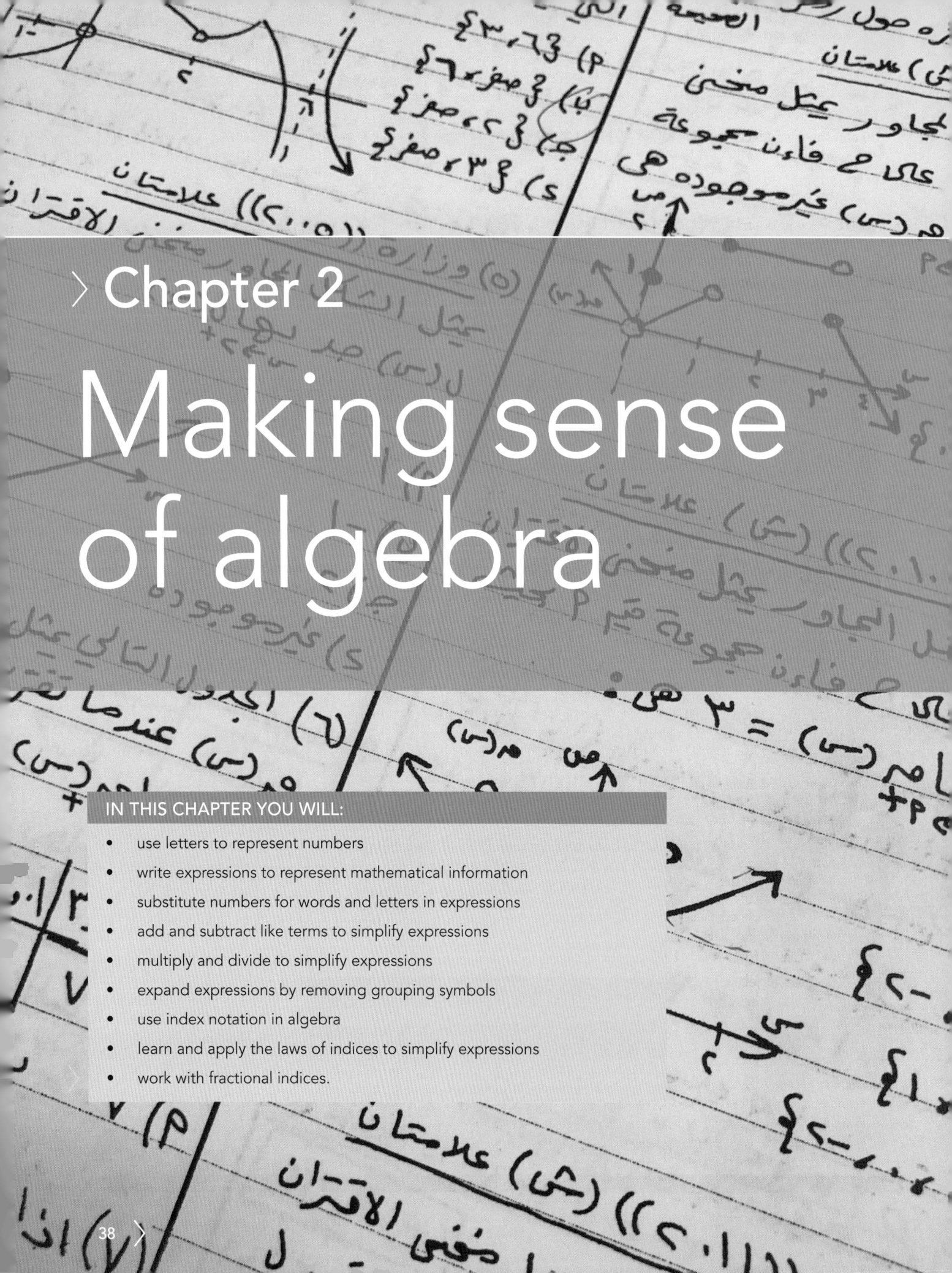

Chapter 2

Making sense of algebra

IN THIS CHAPTER YOU WILL:

- use letters to represent numbers
- write expressions to represent mathematical information
- substitute numbers for words and letters in expressions
- add and subtract like terms to simplify expressions
- multiply and divide to simplify expressions
- expand expressions by removing grouping symbols
- use index notation in algebra
- learn and apply the laws of indices to simplify expressions
- work with fractional indices.

You can think of algebra as the language of mathematics. When you learn a language, you have to learn its rules and structures. The language of algebra also has rules and structures. What are the students in the picture opposite trying to work out? What rules do you think these students are applying?

Algebra lets you describe and represent complex mathematical patterns in clear mathematical language. At school, and in the real world, you will use algebra in many ways. For example, you will use it to make sense of formulae and spreadsheets and you may use algebra to solve problems to do with money, building, science, agriculture, engineering, construction, economics, game design, animation and many other things.

KEY WORDS

coefficient

expression

formula

term

variable

GETTING STARTED

1 How do you write each of these using algebra? Choose A, B or C.

   a $a \times a$

      A 2^a B $2a$ C a^2

   b p multiplied by 5 and then added to 3.

      A $5p + 3$ B $5(p + 3)$ C $p + 15$

   c x cubed and then multiplied by 3.

      A $3x^3$ B $(3x)^3$ C $9x^3$

2 A class was asked to simplify four expressions containing indices. These are the answers:

   a   1   **b** a^{m-n} **c** a^{m+n} **d** a^{mn}

   Write an expression they could have simplified in each case.

3 These three examples contain some common mistakes that students make in algebra.

Example 1 Removing brackets	Example 2 Multiplying fractions	Example 3 Simplifying fractions
$3x - (x - 2) = 3x - x - 2$	$3\left(\dfrac{x+4}{5}\right) = \dfrac{3x+12}{15}$	$\dfrac{x+2}{2} = x$

   a   What is the error in each example?

   b   What is the correct answer?

4 Work in pairs or small groups. Consecutive numbers are those that follow each other, for example 4 and 5 are consecutive.

   a   Use algebra to show why the sum of two consecutive numbers will always be odd.

   b   Will the sum of three consecutive numbers always be even? Use algebra to justify your answer.

2.1 Using letters to represent unknown values

In primary school you used empty shapes to represent unknown numbers. For example, $2 + \square = 8$ and $\square + \diamond = 10$. If $2 + \square = 8$, the $\square$ can only represent 6. But if $\square + \diamond = 10$, then the $\square$ and the $\diamond$ can represent many different values. In puzzles, shapes are often used to represent unknown numbers. Sometimes the shape can only represent one number, for example if $2 + \square = 8$ then $\square$ must represent 6. Other times, the shapes can represent many different numbers, for example if $\square + \diamond = 10$, then the $\square$ and the $\diamond$ can represent many different values. When letters can represent many different values they are called **variables**.

Algebra uses letters to represent unknown numbers. You could write the number sentences above as: $2 + x = 8$ and $a + b = 10$. Number sentences like these are called equations. You can solve an equation by finding the values that make the equation true.

When you worked with area of rectangles and triangles in the past, you used algebra to make a general rule, or **formula**, for working out the area, A:

Area of a rectangle = length × width, so $A = lw$

Area of a triangle = $\frac{1}{2} \times$ base × height, so $A = \frac{1}{2}bh$ or $A = \frac{bh}{2}$

When two letters are multiplied together, you write them next to each other, e.g. for $l \times w$ you would write lw.

To use a formula you have to replace some or all of the letters with numbers. This is called substitution.

> **TIP**
>
> In an algebra problem, you must not change the 'case' of the letters being used. For example, '*n*' and '*N*' can represent *different* numbers in the *same* formula!

Writing algebraic expressions

An algebraic **expression** is a group of letters and numbers linked by operation signs. Each part of the expression is called a term.

Suppose the average height (in centimetres) of students in your class is an unknown number, h. A student who is 10 cm taller than the average will have a height of $h + 10$. A student who is 3 cm shorter than the average will have a height of $h - 3$.

$h + 10$ and $h - 3$ are algebraic expressions. Because the unknown value is represented by h, we say these are expressions in terms of h.

> **LINK**
>
> Algebra is used across all science subjects. For example, in Biology algebra is used to model biochemical networks, and linear relationships such as heart rate (bpm) and cardiac output (how much blood your heart pumps) can be graphed and compared. In chemistry, equations are important for expressing relationships between quantities (for example, density, mass and volume). Many situations in physics require motion or other physical changes to be described as an algebraic formula, such as $F = ma$, which describes the connection between the force, mass and acceleration of an object.

WORKED EXAMPLE 1

Use algebra to write an expression in terms of h (which represents average height) for:

a   a height 12 cm shorter than average
b   a height 2a taller than average
c   a height twice the average height
d   a height half the average height.

Answers

a $h - 12$ Shorter than means less than, so you subtract.

b $h + 2a$ Taller than means more than, so you add. 2a is unknown, but it can still be used in the expression.

c $2 \times h = 2h$ Twice means two times, so you multiply by two.

d $h \div 2 = \dfrac{h}{2}$ Half means divided by two.

Applying the rules

You should write algebraic expressions in the shortest, simplest possible way:

- $2 \times h$ is written as $2h$ and $x \times y$ is written as xy
- h means $1 \times h$, but you do not write the 1
- $h \div 2$ is written as $\dfrac{h}{2}$ and $x \div y$ is written as $\dfrac{x}{y}$
- when you have the product of a number and a variable, the number is written first, so $2h$ and not $h2$. Also, variables are normally written in alphabetical order, so xy and $2ab$ rather than yx and $2ba$
- $h \times h$ is written as h^2 (h squared) and $h \times h \times h$ is written as h^3 (h cubed). The ^{2} and the ^{3} are examples of a power or index
- the power only applies to the number or variable directly before it, so $5a^2$ means $5 \times a \times a$
- when a power is outside a bracket, it applies to everything inside the bracket, so $(xy)^3$ means $xy \times xy \times xy$.

> **TIP**
>
> Mathematicians write the product of a number and a variable with the number first to avoid confusion with powers. For example, you would write $x \times 5$ is as $5x$ and not as $x5$, which is easy to confuse with x^5.

WORKED EXAMPLE 2

Write expressions in terms of x to represent:

a   the number times four
b   the sum of the number and five
c   six times the number minus two
d   half the number.

Answers

a x times four   Let x represent 'the number'.

  $= x \times 4$ Replace 'times four' with $\times\ 4$.

  $= 4x$ Leave out the $\times$ sign, write the number before the variable.

WORKED EXAMPLE 2 CONTINUED

b Sum of x and five

  $= x + 5$

  Let x represent 'the number'.

  Sum of means +, replace five with 5.

c Six times x minus two

  $= 6 \times x - 2$

  Let x represent 'the number'.

  Times means × and minus means −, insert numerals.

  $= 6x - 2$

  Leave out the × sign.

d Half x

  $= x \div 2$

  $= \dfrac{x}{2}$

  Let x represent 'the number'.

  Half means $\times \dfrac{1}{2}$ or $\div 2$.

  Write the division as a fraction.

Exercise 2.1

1 Rewrite each expression in its simplest form.

  a $6 \times x \times y$

  b $7 \times a \times b$

  c $x \times y \times z$

  d $2 \times y \times y$

  e $a \times 4 \times b$

  f $x \times y \times 12$

  g $5 \times b \times a$

  h $y \times z \times z$

  i $6 \div x$

  j $4x \div 2y$

  k $(x + 3) \div 4$

  l $m \times m \times m \div m \times m$

  m $4 \times x + 5 \times y$

  n $a \times 7 - 2 \times b$

  o $2 \times x \times (x - 4)$

  p $3 \times (x + 1) \div 2 \times x$

  q $2 \times (x + 4) \div 3$

  r $(4 \times x) \div (2 \times x + 4 \times x)$

2 Let the unknown number be m. Write expressions for:

  a the sum of the unknown number and 13

  b a number that will exceed the unknown number by five

  c the difference between 25 and the unknown number

  d the unknown number cubed

  e a third of the unknown number plus three

  f four times the unknown number take away twice the number.

> **TIP**
>
> A 'sum' is the result of an addition and the 'difference' between two numbers is the result of a subtraction. The order of the subtraction matters.

3 Let the unknown number be x. Write expressions for:

  a three more than x

  b six less than x

  c ten times x

  d the sum of -8 and x

  e the sum of the unknown number and its square

  f a number which is twice x more than x

  g the fraction obtained when double the unknown number is divided by the sum of the unknown number and four.

4   A book and a pack of markers cost x dollars.

   a   If the book costs $10 what does the pack of markers cost?

   b   If the pack of markers is three times the price of the book, what does the book cost?

   c   If the book costs $(x − 15)$, what does the pack of markers cost?

5   A woman is m years old.

   a   How old will she be in ten years' time?

   b   How old was she ten years ago?

   c   Her son is half her age. How old is the son?

6   Three people win a prize of p.

   a   If they share the prize equally, how much will each receive?

   b   If one of the people wins three times as much money as the other two, how much will each receive?

MATHEMATICAL CONNECTIONS

Algebra allows you to translate information given in words to a clear and short mathematical form. This is a useful strategy for starting to solve many types of problems. You will use these skills throughout the course, and you will apply them to specific problems in Chapter 22.

LINK

Many people use spreadsheets to store and process numerical information. You can use formulae in spreadsheets to work out the number of one 'cell', based on what is in other cells. These formulae follow the same rules of algebra that you used here.

2.2 Substitution

Expressions have different values depending on what numbers you substitute for the variables. For example, imagine you are a waiter and you get paid $8 per hour. You can write an expression to represent your wages like this: $8h$, where h is the number of hours worked. If you work 1 hour, then you get paid $8 \times 1 = \$8$. So the expression $8h$ has a value of $8 in this case. If you work 6 hours, you get paid $8 \times 6 = \$48$. The expression $8h$ has a value of $48 in this case.

TIP

When you substitute values remember to write in the operation signs. $8h$ means $8 \times h$, so if $h = 1$, or $h = 6$, you cannot write this in numbers as 81 or 86.

WORKED EXAMPLE 3

Given that $a = 2$ and $b = 8$, evaluate:

a ab　　　**b**　$3b - 2a$　　　**c**　$2a^3$　　　**d**　$2a(a + b)$

Answers

a	ab	$= a \times b$	Put back the multiplication sign.
		$= 2 \times 8$	Substitute the values for a and b.
		$= 16$	Calculate the answer.

TIP

Evaluate means 'find the value of'.

WORKED EXAMPLE 3 CONTINUED

b $\quad 3b - 2a \quad = \quad 3 \times b - 2 \times a$ Put back the multiplication signs.

$\qquad\qquad\qquad = \quad 3 \times 8 - 2 \times 2$ Substitute the values for a and b.

$\qquad\qquad\qquad = \quad 24 - 4$ Use the order of operations rules ($\times$ before $-$).

$\qquad\qquad\qquad = \quad 20$ Calculate the answer.

c $\quad 2a^3 \quad = \quad 2 \times a^3$ Put back the multiplication signs.

$\qquad\qquad = \quad 2 \times 2^3$ Substitute the value for a.

$\qquad\qquad = \quad 2 \times 8$ Work out 2^3 first (grouping symbols first).

$\qquad\qquad = \quad 16$ Calculate the answer.

d $\quad 2a(a + b) \quad = \quad 2 \times a \times (a + b)$ Put back the multiplication signs.

$\qquad\qquad\qquad = \quad 2 \times 2 \times (2 + 8)$ Substitute the values for a and b.

$\qquad\qquad\qquad = \quad 4 \times 10$ In this case you can carry out two steps at the same time: multiplication outside the bracket, and the addition inside.

$\qquad\qquad\qquad = \quad 40$ Calculate the answer.

MATHEMATICAL CONNECTIONS

Always apply the order of operations rules you learned in Chapter 1.

LINK

You probably don't think about algebra when you watch animated cartoons, insert emojis in messages or play games on your phone or computer, but animators use complex algebra to programme all these items and to make objects move on screen.

WORKED EXAMPLE 4

Look at these three shapes.

a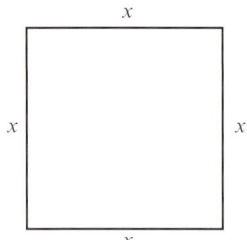

b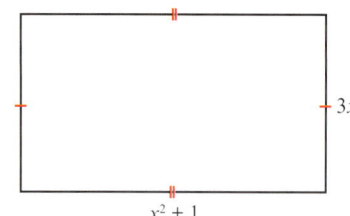

c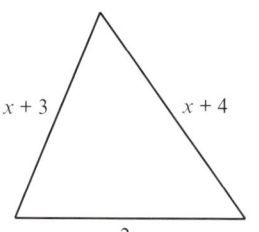

For each shape:

i   write an expression for the perimeter

ii   calculate the perimeter if $x = 4$ cm.

WORKED EXAMPLE 4 CONTINUED

Answers

a   i $x + x + x + x = 4x$ Add the four lengths together.

    ii $\begin{aligned} 4 \times x &= 4 \times 4 \\ &= 16 \text{ cm} \end{aligned}$ Substitute 4 into the expression.

b   i $3x + (x^2 + 1) + 3x + (x^2 + 1) = 2(3x) + 2(x^2 + 1)$ Add the four lengths together and simplify.

    ii $\begin{aligned} 2 \times (3 \times x) + 2 \times (x^2 + 1) &= 2 \times (3 \times 4) + 2 \times (4^2 + 1) \\ &= 2 \times 12 + 2 \times (16 + 1) \\ &= 24 + 2 \times 17 \\ &= 24 + 34 \\ &= 58 \text{ cm} \end{aligned}$ Substitute 4 into the expression.

c   i $x + 3 + x + 4 + 2x = 4x + 7$ Add the three lengths together and simplify

    ii $\begin{aligned} 4x + 7 &= 4 \times 4 + 7 \\ &= 16 + 7 \\ &= 23 \text{ cm} \end{aligned}$ Substitute 4 into the expression.

WORKED EXAMPLE 5

Complete this table of values for the formula $b = 3a - 3$.

a	0	2	4	6
b				

Answers

a	0	2	4	6
b	−3	3	9	15

Substitute in the values of a to work out b.

$3 \times 0 - 3 = 0 - 3 = -3$

$3 \times 2 - 3 = 6 - 3 = 3$

$3 \times 4 - 3 = 12 - 3 = 9$

$3 \times 6 - 3 = 18 - 3 = 15$

MATHEMATICAL CONNECTIONS

You will need to use tables of values similar to this one to find the (x, y) coordinates of different points so you can plot graphs in Chapter 10 and Chapter 18.

Exercise 2.2

1 Evaluate the following expressions for $x = 3$.

a $3x$

b $10x$

c $4x - 2$

d x^3

e $2x^2$

f $10 - x$

g $x^2 + 7$

h $x^3 + x^2$

i $2(x - 1)$

j $\dfrac{4x}{2}$

k $\dfrac{6x}{3}$

l $\dfrac{90}{x}$

m $\dfrac{10x}{6}$

n $\dfrac{(4x + 2)}{7}$

o $\dfrac{3(x + 2)}{7x + 9}$

MATHEMATICAL CONNECTIONS

You will learn more about algebraic fractions in Chapter 14.

2 What is the value of each expression when $a = 3$ and $b = 5$ and $c = 2$?

a abc

b $a^2 b$

c $4a + 2c$

d $3b - 2(a + c)$

e $a^2 + c^2$

f $4b - 2a + c$

g $ab + bc + ac$

h $2(ab)^2$

i $3(a + b)$

j $(b - c) + (a + c)$

k $(a + b)(b - c)$

l $\dfrac{3bc}{ac}$

m $\dfrac{4b}{a} + c$

n $\dfrac{4b^2}{bc}$

o $\dfrac{2(a + b)}{c^2}$

p $\dfrac{3abc}{10a}$

q $\dfrac{6b^2}{(a + c)^2}$

r $\left(\dfrac{1}{2} abc\right)^2$

s $\dfrac{8a}{\sqrt[3]{a + b}}$

t $\dfrac{6ab}{a^2} - 2bc$

u $(a^2 b c^3)^2$

TIP

Always show your substitution clearly. Write the formula or expression in its algebraic form but replace the letters with the appropriate numbers. This makes it clear to anyone marking your work that you have put the correct numbers in the right places.

3 Work out the value of y in each formula when:

i $x = 0$ ii $x = 3$ iii $x = 4$ iv $x = 10$ v $x = 50$

a $y = 4x$

b $y = 3x + 1$

c $y = 100 - x$

d $y = \dfrac{x}{2}$

e $y = x^2$

f $y = \dfrac{100}{x}$

g $y = 2(x + 2)$

h $y = 2(x + 2) - 10$

i $y = 3x^3$

APPLY YOUR SKILLS

4 A sandwich costs $3 and a drink costs $2.

a Write an expression to show the total cost of buying x sandwiches and y drinks.

b Find the total cost of:

i four sandwiches and three drinks

ii 20 sandwiches and 20 drinks

iii 100 sandwiches and 25 drinks.

---

5   The formula for finding the perimeter of a rectangle is $P = 2(l + w)$, where l represents the length and w represents the width of the rectangle.

Find the perimeter of a rectangle if:

a   the length is 12 cm and the width is 9 cm

b   the length is 2.5 m and the width is 1.5 m

c   the length is 20 cm and the width is half as long

d   the breadth is 2 cm and the length is the cube of the width.

6   a   Find the value of the expression $n^2 + n + 41$ when:

   i $n = 1$ ii $n = 3$ iii $n = 5$ iv $n = 10$

   b   What do you notice about all of your answers?

   c   Why is this different when $n = 41$?

> **MATHEMATICAL CONNECTIONS**
>
> Think back to Chapter 1 and the different types of number that you have already studied.

DISCUSSION

What is the point of algebra?

Students sometimes ask why they have to learn algebra because they cannot see how it is useful.

Work with a partner to prepare a short presentation to convince the rest of your class that algebra is valuable and useful.

- Choose one of the topics in this chapter (or another algebra topic you like and know well).
- Do research to find how this topic is useful in the real world.
- Prepare a slide show (or other presentation) to share what you find out. Include a description of the topic and how it is used. Provide at least three real-life examples.

2.3 Simplifying expressions

The parts of an algebraic expression are called **terms**. Terms are separated from each other by + or − signs. So $a + b$ is an expression with two terms, but ab is an expression with only one term and $2 + \dfrac{3a}{b} - \dfrac{ab}{c}$ is an expression with three terms.

The number in a term is called a **coefficient**. In the term $2a$, the coefficient is 2; in the term $-3ab$, the coefficient is -3. A term with only numbers is called a constant. So for example, in the expression $2a + 4$, the constant is 4.

> **TIP**
>
> Remember, terms are not separated by × or ÷ signs. A fraction line means divide, so the parts of a fraction are all counted as one term, even if there is a + or − sign in the numerator or denominator. So, $\dfrac{a + b}{c}$ is one term.

Collecting like terms

Terms with exactly the same variables are called like terms. $2a$ and $4a$ are like terms; $3xy^2$ and $-xy^2$ are like terms.

The variables and any indices attached to them have to be identical for terms to be like terms, so $2x^2y$ and $-3x^2y$ are like terms but $2x^2y$ and $-3xy$ are not. Variables in a different order mean the same thing, so xy and yx are like terms ($x \times y = y \times x$).

You can add and subtract like terms to simplify algebraic expressions. This is known as collecting like terms.

> **TIP**
>
> Any '+' or '−' that appears in an algebraic expression is attached to the term to its right. For example: $3x - 4y$ contains two terms: $3x$ and $-4y$. If a term has no symbol written before it, then you can assume that it is '+'.

WORKED EXAMPLE 6

Simplify.

a $4a + 2a + 3a$ b $4a + 6b + 3a$ c $5x + 2y - 7x$

d $2p + 5q + 3q - 7p$ e $2ab + 3a^2b - ab + 3ab^2$

Answers

a $4a + 2a + 3a$ Terms are all like.

   $= 9a$ Add the coefficients, write the term.

b $4a + 6b + 3a$ Identify the like terms ($4a$ and $3a$).

   $= 7a + 6b$ Add the coefficients of like terms.

                Write terms in alphabetical order.

c $5x + 2y - 7x$ Identify the like terms ($5x$ and $-7x$).

   $= -2x + 2y$ Subtract the coefficients, remember the rules.

                Write the terms.

                (You can also write this as $2y - 2x$.)

d $2p + 5q + 3q - 7p$ Identify the like terms ($2p$ and $-7p$; $5q$ and $3q$).

   $= -5p + 8q$ Add and subtract the coefficients.

                Write the terms.

e $2ab + 3a^2b - ab + 3ab^2$ Identify like terms; pay attention to terms that are squared because a and a^2 are not like terms.

   $= ab + 3a^2b + 3ab^2$ Remember that ab means $1ab$.

> **TIP**
>
> You can rearrange the terms as long as you move the '−' and '+' signs with the terms to their right. For example:
>
> $3x - 2y + 5z$
>
> $= 3x + 5z - 2y$
>
> $= 5z + 3x - 2y$
>
> $= -2y + 3x + 5z$

Exercise 2.3

1 Identify the like terms in each set.

   a $6x, -2y, 4x, x$ **b** $x, -3y, \frac{3}{4}, -5y$ **c** $ab, 4b, -4ba, 6a$

   d $2, -2x, 3xy, 3x, -2y$ **e** $5a, 5ab, ab, 6a, 5$ **f** $-1xy, -yx, -2y, 3, 3x$

2 Simplify by adding or subtracting like terms.

   a $2y + 6y$ **b** $9x - 2x$ **c** $10x + 3x$

   d $21x + x$ **e** $7x - 2x$ **f** $4y - 4y$

   g $9x - 10x$ **h** $y - 4y$ **i** $5x - x$

   j $9xy - 2xy$ **k** $6pq - 2qp$ **l** $14xyz - xyz$

   m $4x^2 - 2x^2$ **n** $9y^2 - 4y^2$ **o** $y^2 - 2y^2$

   p $14ab^2 - 2ab^2$ **q** $9x^2y - 4x^2y$ **r** $10xy^2 - 8xy^2$

3 Simplify.

   a $2x + y + 3x$ **b** $4y - 2y + 4x$ **c** $6x - 4x + 5x$

   d $10 + 4x - 6$ **e** $4xy - 2y + 2xy$ **f** $5x^2 - 6x^2 + 2x$

   g $5x + 4y - 6x$ **h** $3y + 4x - x$ **i** $4x + 6y + 4x$

   j $9x - 2y - x$ **k** $12x^2 - 4x + 2x^2$ **l** $12x^2 - 4x^2 + 2x^2$

   m $5xy - 2x + 7xy$ **n** $xy - 2xz + 7xy$ **o** $3x^2 - 2y^2 - 4x^2$

   p $5x^2y + 3x^2y - 2xy$ **q** $4xy - x + 2yx$ **r** $5xy - 2 + xy$

4 Simplify as far as possible.

   a $8y - 4 - 6y - 4$ **b** $x^2 - 4x + 3x^2 - x$ **c** $5x + y + 2x + 3y$

   d $y^2 + 2y + 3y - 7$ **e** $x^2 - 4x - x + 3$ **f** $x^2 + 3x - 7 + 2x$

   g $4xyz - 3xy + 2xz - xyz$ **h** $5xy - 4 + 3yx - 6$ **i** $8x - 4 - 2x - 3x^2$

5 Write an expression for the perimeter (P) of each of the following shapes and then simplify it to give P in the simplest possible terms.

<blockquote>
MATHEMATICAL CONNECTIONS

You will need to be very comfortable with simplifying algebraic expressions. It is a skill you will need throughout the course for solving equations and inequalities, and for simplifying expansions.
</blockquote>

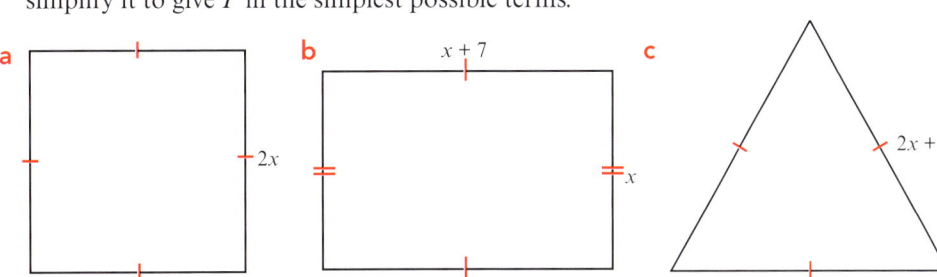

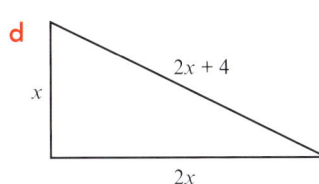

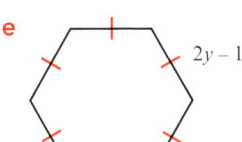

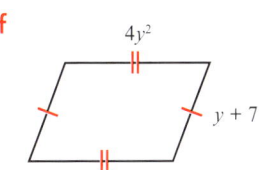

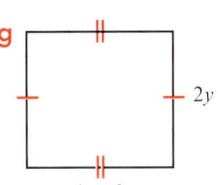

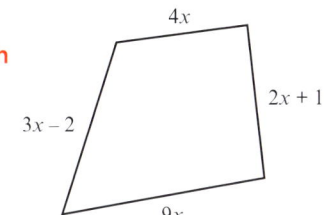

INVESTIGATION

Magic squares

In a magic square, the sum of each row, column and diagonal is the same.

1 Is this a magic square?

$5x + 2y$	$7y$	$7x + 8y$
$6x + 9y$	$4x + 5y$	$2x + y$
$x + 4y$	$8x + 3y$	$3x + 8y$

2 Copy and complete this magic square.

	a	
$a + b$	$a - b - c$	$a + c$

3 There are only four possible magic squares that use only the three terms: $x - 1$, x and $x + 1$
  a What are they?
  b Do you think the same applies to the terms $2x - 2$, $2x$ and $2x + 2$? Justify your answer.

REFLECTION

Think about how you worked on question 2 in the investigation.

- What steps did you follow to solve the problem? Could you work in a different order? If so, how?
- Could you solve the magic square using fewer steps? How?
- Will the strategies you used always work? Why?

Multiplying and dividing expressions

In Section 2.1 you learned how to write expressions in simpler terms when multiplying and dividing them. Make sure you understand and remember these important rules:

- $3x$ means $3 \times x$ and $3xy$ means $3 \times x \times y$
- xy means $x \times y$
- x^2 means $x \times x$ and x^2y means $x \times x \times y$ (only the x is squared)
- $\dfrac{2a}{4}$ means $2a \div 4$

WORKED EXAMPLE 7

Simplify.

a $4 \times 3x$ **b** $4x \times 3y$ **c** $4ab \times 2bc$ **d** $7x \times 4yz \times 3$

Answers

a $\begin{aligned} 4 \times 3x &= 4 \times 3 \times x \\ &= 12 \times x \\ &= 12x \end{aligned}$ Insert the missing $\times$ signs.
Multiply the numbers first.
Write in simplest form.

b $\begin{aligned} 4x \times 3y &= 4 \times x \times 3 \times y \\ &= 12 \times x \times y \\ &= 12xy \end{aligned}$ Insert the missing $\times$ signs.
Multiply the numbers.
Write in simplest form.

c $\begin{aligned} 4ab \times 2bc &= 4 \times a \times b \times 2 \times b \times c \\ &= 8 \times a \times b \times b \times c \\ &= 8ab^2c \end{aligned}$ Insert the missing $\times$ signs.
Multiply the numbers, then the variables.
Write in simplest form.

d $\begin{aligned} 7x \times 4yz \times 3 &= 7 \times x \times 4 \times y \times z \times 3 \\ &= 84 \times x \times y \times z \\ &= 84xyz \end{aligned}$ Insert the missing $\times$ signs.
Multiply the numbers.
Write in simplest form.

> **TIP**
>
> You can multiply numbers first and variables second because the commutative law ($ab = ba$) means that multiplication can be done in any order.

WORKED EXAMPLE 8

Simplify.

a $\dfrac{12x}{3}$ **b** $\dfrac{12xy}{3x}$ **c** $\dfrac{7xy}{70y}$ **d** $\dfrac{2x}{3} \times \dfrac{4x}{2}$

Answers

a $\dfrac{12x}{3} = \dfrac{\overset{4}{\cancel{12}}x}{\underset{1}{\cancel{3}}} = \dfrac{4x}{1} = 4x$ Divide both top and bottom by 3 (making the numerator and denominator smaller so that the fraction is in its simplest form is called cancelling).

b $\dfrac{12xy}{3x} = \dfrac{\overset{4}{\cancel{12}}xy}{\underset{1}{\cancel{3}x}} = \dfrac{4 \times y}{1} = 4y$ Cancel and then multiply.

> **MATHEMATICAL CONNECTIONS**
>
> You will learn more about cancelling and equivalent fractions in Chapter 5.

WORKED EXAMPLE 8 CONTINUED

c $\quad \dfrac{7xy}{70y} = \dfrac{\overset{1}{\cancel{7}}xy}{\underset{10}{\cancel{70}}y} = \dfrac{x}{10}$ Cancel.

d $\quad \dfrac{2x}{3} \times \dfrac{4x}{2} \quad = \quad \dfrac{2 \times x \times 4 \times x}{3 \times 2}$ Insert × signs and multiply.

$\qquad\qquad\quad = \quad \dfrac{\overset{4}{\cancel{8}}x^2}{\underset{3}{\cancel{6}}}$ Cancel.

$\qquad\qquad\quad = \quad \dfrac{4x^2}{3}$

or

$\dfrac{\overset{1}{\cancel{2}}x}{3} \times \dfrac{4x}{\underset{1}{\cancel{2}}} = \dfrac{1x}{3} \times \dfrac{4x}{1} = \dfrac{4x^2}{3}$ Cancel first, then multiply.

Exercise 2.4

1 Multiply.

a	$2 \times 6x$	b $\quad 4y \times 2$	c $\quad 3m \times 4$
d	$2x \times 3y$	e $\quad 4x \times 2y$	f $\quad 9x \times 3y$
g	$8y \times 3z$	h $\quad 2x \times 3y \times 2$	i $\quad 4xy \times 2xy$
j	$4xy \times 2x$	k $\quad 9y \times 3xy$	l $\quad 4y \times 2x \times 3y$
m	$2a \times 4ab$	n $\quad 3ab \times 4bc$	o $\quad 6abc \times 2a$
p	$8abc \times 2ab$	q $\quad 4 \times 2ab \times 3c$	r $\quad 12x^2 \times 2 \times 3y^2$

2 Simplify.

a	$3 \times 2x \times 4$	b $\quad 5x \times 2x \times 3y$	c $\quad 2x \times 3y \times 2xy$
d	$xy \times xz \times x$	e $\quad 2 \times 2 \times 3x \times 4$	f $\quad 4 \times 2x \times 3x^2y$
g	$x \times y^2 \times 4x$	h $\quad 2a \times 3ab \times 2c$	i $\quad 10x \times 2y \times 3$
j	$4 \times x \times 2 \times y$	k $\quad 9 \times x^2 \times xy$	l $\quad 4xy^2 \times 2x^2y$
m	$7xy \times 2xz \times 3yz$	n $\quad 4xy \times 2x^2y \times 7$	o $\quad 9 \times xyz \times 4xy$
p	$3x^2y \times 2xy^2 \times 3xy$	q $\quad 9x \times 2xy \times 3x^2$	r $\quad 2x \times xy^2 \times 3xy$

3 Simplify.

a $\dfrac{15r}{3}$	b $\dfrac{40r}{10}$	c $\dfrac{21r}{7}$	d $\dfrac{12rs}{2r}$
e $\dfrac{14rs}{2s}$	f $\dfrac{18r^2s}{9r^2}$	g $\dfrac{10rs}{40r}$	h $\dfrac{15r}{60rs}$
i $\dfrac{7rst}{14rs}$	j $\dfrac{6rs}{r}$	k $\dfrac{r}{4r}$	l $\dfrac{r}{9r}$

4   Simplify.

a $8x \div 2$ b $12xy \div 2x$ c $16x^2 \div 4xy$ d $24xy \div 3xy$

e $14x^2 \div 2y^2$ f $24xy \div 8y$ g $8xy \div 24y$ h $9x \div 36xy$

i $\dfrac{77xyz}{11xz}$ j $\dfrac{45xy}{20x}$ k $\dfrac{60x^2y^2}{15xy}$ l $\dfrac{100xy}{25x^2}$

5   Simplify these as far as possible.

a $\dfrac{a}{2} \times \dfrac{b}{3}$ b $\dfrac{a}{3} \times \dfrac{a}{4}$ c $\dfrac{ab}{2} \times \dfrac{5a}{3}$ d $\dfrac{2a}{3} \times \dfrac{5}{b}$

e $\dfrac{2a}{4} \times \dfrac{3b}{4}$ f $\dfrac{5a}{2} \times \dfrac{5a}{2}$ g $\dfrac{a}{b} \times \dfrac{2b}{a}$ h $\dfrac{ab}{3} \times \dfrac{a}{b}$

i $5b \times \dfrac{2a}{5}$ j $4 \times \dfrac{2a}{3}$ k $\dfrac{a}{6} \times \dfrac{3}{2a}$ l $\dfrac{5a}{2} \times \dfrac{4a}{10}$

2.4 Working with brackets

When an expression has brackets, you normally have to remove the brackets before you can simplify the expression. Removing the brackets is called expanding the expression.

To remove brackets you multiply each term inside the bracket by the number (and/or variables) outside the bracket. When you do this you need to pay attention to the positive and negative signs in front of the terms:

$x(y + z) = xy + xz$ $x(y - z) = xy - xz$

$-x(y + z) = -xy - xz$ $-x(y - z) = -xy + xz$

> **MATHEMATICAL CONNECTIONS**
>
> You will learn more about expanding expressions to remove brackets in Chapter 10.

> **TIP**
>
> Expanding brackets is really just multiplying, so the same rules you used for multiplication apply in these examples.

> **WORKED EXAMPLE 9**
>
> Expand the following expressions.
>
> a $2(2x + 6)$ b $4(7 - 2x)$ c $2x(x + 3y)$ d $xy(2 - 3x)$
>
> **Answers**
>
> a
>
> $2(2x + 6) = 2 \times 2x + 2 \times 6$
>
> $\qquad\qquad = 4x + 12$
>
> b
>
> $4(7 - 2x) = 4 \times 7 - 4 \times 2x$
>
> $\qquad\qquad = 28 - 8x$
>
> For parts (a) to (d) write out the expression, or do the multiplication mentally.
>
> Follow these steps when multiplying by a term outside a bracket:
>
> - Multiply the term on the left-hand inside of the bracket first – shown by the red arrow labelled i.
> - Then multiply the term on the right-hand side – shown by the blue arrow labelled ii.
> - Then add the answers together.

WORKED EXAMPLE 9 CONTINUED

c i

$$2x(x + 3y) = 2x \times x + 2x \times 3y$$
$$= 2x^2 + 6xy$$

d i

$$xy(2 - 3x) = xy \times 2 - xy \times 3x$$
$$= 2xy - 3x^2y$$

Exercise 2.5

1 Expand:

a	$2(x + 6)$	b	$3(x + 2)$	c	$4(2x + 3)$
d	$10(x - 6)$	e	$4(x - 2)$	f	$3(2x - 3)$
g	$5(a + 4)$	h	$6(4 + a)$	i	$9(a + 2)$
j	$7(2c - 2d)$	k	$2(3c - 2d)$	l	$4(c + 4d)$
m	$5(2x - 2y)$	n	$6(3x - 2y)$	o	$3(4y - 2x)$
p	$4(s - 4t^2)$	q	$9(t^2 - s)$	r	$7(4t + t^2)$

2 Remove the brackets to expand these expressions.

a	$2x(x + y)$	b	$3y(x - y)$	c	$2x(x + 2y)$
d	$4x(3x - 2y)$	e	$xy(x - y)$	f	$3y(4x + 2)$
g	$2ab(9 - 4b)$	h	$2a^2(3 - 2b)$	i	$3a^2(4 - 4b)$
j	$4a(9 - 2b)$	k	$5b(2 - a)$	l	$3a(4 - b)$
m	$2x^2y(y - 2x)$	n	$4xy^2(3 - 2x)$	o	$3xy^2(x + y)$
p	$x^2y(2x + y)$	q	$9x^2(9 - 2x)$	r	$4xy^2(3 - x)$

3 Given the formula for area, A = length × width, write an expression for A in terms of x for each of the following rectangles. Expand the expression to give A in simplest terms.

a

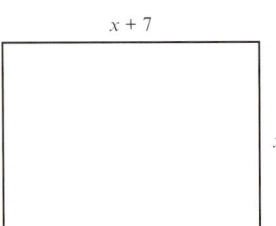

b

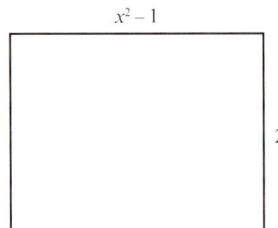

c

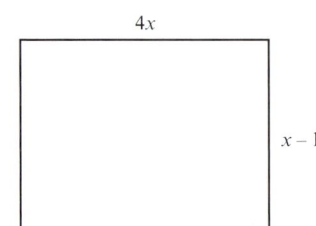

Maths jokes

If you do an internet search for 'maths jokes' you get about 12 million entries. What makes maths so funny?

Look at these examples of maths jokes.

> If I had ten dollars for every time algebra helped me, I'd have 10x dollars.

> • Expand 2(x + 3y)
> 2(x + 3y)
> = 2(x + 3y)
> = 2(x + 3y)

> Algebra wasn't very challenging in Ancient Rome because X was always equal to 10.

- What is the premise of each joke? In other words, what makes it funny?
- Find at least two more maths jokes that you think are funny. Tell your group why each one is amusing to you.

Expanding and collecting like terms

When you remove brackets and expand an expression you may end up with some like terms. When this happens, you collect the like terms together (add or subtract them) to write the expression in its simplest terms.

WORKED EXAMPLE 10

Expand and simplify where possible.

a　$6(x + 3) + 4$　　　　**b**　$2(6a + 1) - 2a + 4$　　　　**c**　$2x(x + 3) + x(x - 4)$

Answers

a　$6(x + 3) + 4 = 6x + 18 + 4$　　　　Remove the brackets.
　　　　　　　　　$= 6x + 22$　　　　Add like terms.

b　$2(6a + 1) - 2a + 4 = 12a + 2 - 2a + 4$　　　　Remove the brackets.
　　　　　　　　　　　　$= 10a + 6$　　　　Add or subtract like terms.

c　$2x(x + 3) + x(x - 4) = 2x^2 + 6x + x^2 - 4x$　　　　Remove the brackets.
　　　　　　　　　　　　　$= 3x^2 + 2x$　　　　Add or subtract like terms.

Exercise 2.6

1 Expand and simplify.

a $2(5 + x) + 3x$

b $3(y - 2) + 4y$

c $2x + 2(x - 4)$

d $4x + 2(x - 3)$

e $2t(4 + t) - 5$

f $4(x + 2) - 7$

g $6 + 3(x - 2)$

h $4x + 2(2x + 3)$

i $2x + 3 + 2(2x + 3)$

j $3(2h + 2) - 3h - 4$

k $6d + 2(d + 3)$

l $7y + y(x - 4) - 4$

m $2x(x + 4) - 4$

n $2y(2x - 2y + 4)$

o $2s(5 - 4s) - 4s^2$

p $3x(2x + 4) - 9$

q $3y(y + 2) - 4y^2$

r $2(x - 1) + 4x - 4$

2 Simplify these expressions by removing brackets and collecting like terms.

a $4(x + 40) + 2(x - 3)$

b $2(x - 2) + 2(x + 3)$

c $3(x + 2) + 4(x + 5)$

d $8(x + 10) + 4(3 - 2x)$

e $4(x^2 + 2) + 2(4 - x^2)$

f $4p(p + 1) + 2p(p + 3)$

g $3p(4q - 4) + 4(3pq + 4p)$

h $2x(5y - 4) + 2(6x - 4xy)$

i $3x(4 - 8y) + 3(2xy - 5x)$

j $3(6x - 4y) + x(3 - 2y)$

k $3x^2(4 - x) + 2(5x^2 - 2x^3)$

l $x(x - y) + 3(2x - y)$

m $4(s - 2) + 3s(4 - t)$

n $x(x + y) + x(x - y)$

o $2x(x + y) + 2(x^2 + 3xy)$

p $x(2x + 3) + 3(5 - 2x)$

q $4(2k - 3) + (k - 5)$

r $3(4xy - 2x) + 5(3x - xy)$

Expanding brackets with negative coefficients

So far the numbers in front of the brackets you expanded were positive. You expand brackets in the same way when there is a negative number before the bracket, but you have to make sure you use the correct signs.

The key is to remember that a '+' or a '−' is attached to the number immediately following it and should be included when you multiply out brackets.

WORKED EXAMPLE 11

Expand and simplify the following expressions.

a $-3(x + 4)$ b $4(y - 7) - 5(3y + 5)$ c $8(p + 4) - 10(9p - 6)$

Answers

a $-3(x + 4)$

$-3(x + 4) = -3x - 12$

$-3 \times x = -3x$ and $-3 \times 4 = -12$

Remember that the negative sign is attached to the 3.

b $4(y - 7) - 5(3y + 5) = 4y - 28 - 15y - 25$

Remember that both terms in the second bracket are multiplied by −5.

$= -11y - 53$

Collect like terms and simplify.

TIP

Remember:

$+ \times + = +$

$+ \times - = -$

$- \times - = +$

WORKED EXAMPLE 11 CONTINUED

c $8(p + 4) - 10(9p - 6) = 8p + 32 - 90p + 60$ Remove the brackets. Pay attention to the negative signs.

            $= -82p + 92$ Collect like terms and simplify.

Exercise 2.7

1   Expand each of the following and simplify your answers as far as possible.

   a $-10(3p + 6)$ b $-3(5x + 7)$ c $-5(4y + 0.2)$

   d $-3(q - 12)$ e $-12(2t - 7)$ f $-1.5(8z - 4)$

   g $-3(2x + 5y)$ h $-6(4p + 5q)$ i $-9(3h - 6k)$

   j $-2(5h + 5k - 8j)$ k $-4(2a - 3b - 6c + 4d)$ l $-6(x^2 + 6y^2 - 2y^3)$

2   Expand each of the following and simplify your answers as far as possible.

   a $2 - 5(x + 2)$ b $2 - 5(x - 2)$

   c $14(x - 3) - 4(x - 1)$ d $-7(f + 3) - 3(2f - 7)$

   e $3g - 7(7g - 7) + 2(5g - 6)$ f $6(3y - 5) - 2(3y - 5)$

   g $4x(x - 4) - 10x(3x + 6)$ h $14x(x + 7) - 3x(5x + 7)$

   i $x^2 - 5x(2x - 6)$ j $5q^2 - 2q(q - 12) - 3q^2$

   k $18pq - 12p(5q - 7)$ l $12m(2n - 4) - 24n(m - 2)$

> **TIP**
>
> Try not to carry out too many steps at once. Show every term of your expansion and then simplify.

3   Expand each expression and simplify your answers as far as possible.

   a $8x - 2(3 - 2x)$ b $11x - (6 - 2x)$

   c $4x + 5 - 3(2x - 4)$ d $7 - 2(x - 3) + 3x$

   e $15 - 4(x - 2) - 3x$ f $4x - 2(1 - 3x) - 6$

   g $3(x + 5) - 4(5 - x)$ h $x(x - 3) - 2(x - 4)$

   i $3x(x - 2) - (x - 2)$ j $2x(3 + x) - 3(x - 2)$

   k $3(x - 5) - (3 + x)$ l $2x(3x + 1) - 2(3 - 2x)$

2.5 Indices

Revisiting index notation

When you write a number using indices (powers) you have written it in index notation. Any number can be used as an index including 0, negative integers and fractions. The index tells you how many times the base has been multiplied by itself. So:

$3 \times 3 \times 3 \times 3 = 3^4$	3 is the base, 4 is the index
$a \times a \times a \times a \times a = a^5$	a is the base, 5 is the index

---

WORKED EXAMPLE 12

Write each expression using index notation.

a $x \times x \times x \times x \times x \times x$ **b** $x \times x \times x \times x \times y \times y \times y \times y$

Answers

a $x \times x \times x \times x \times x \times x = x^4$

Count how many times x is multiplied by itself to give you the index.

b $x \times x \times x \times x \times y \times y \times y \times y = x^3 y^4$

Count how many times x is multiplied by itself to get the index of x; then work out the index of y in the same way.

When you write a power out in full as a multiplication you are writing it in expanded form.

The laws of indices in algebra

The laws of indices are very important in algebra because they give you quick ways of simplifying expressions. You will use these laws over and over again as you learn more and more algebra, so it is important that you understand them and that you can apply them in different situations.

Multiplying the same base with different indices

Look at these two multiplications:

$3^2 \times 3^4$ $x^3 \times x^4$

In the first multiplication, 3 is the base and in the second, x is the base.

You already know you can simplify these by expanding them like this:

$3 \times 3 \times 3 \times 3 \times 3 \times 3 = 3^6$ $x \times x \times x \times x \times x \times x \times x = x^7$

In other words:

$3^2 \times 3^4 = 3^{2+4}$ and $x^3 \times x^4 = x^{3+4}$

When you multiply index expressions with the same base you can add the indices:
$$x^m \times x^n = x^{m+n}$$

> **MATHEMATICAL CONNECTIONS**
>
> In finance, when you apply interest to savings, the value increases by the same percentage each day, month or other fixed period of time. This involves repeated multiplication by the same number. You will see this when you study compound interest in Chapter 17.

WORKED EXAMPLE 13

Simplify.

a $x^2 \times x^3$ **b** $2x^2 y \times 3xy^4$

Answers

a $x^2 \times x^3 = x^{2+3} = x^5$

Add the indices.

b $2x^2 y \times 3xy^4 = 2 \times 3 \times x^{2+1} \times y^{1+4} = 6x^3 y^5$

Multiply the numbers first, then add the indices of like variables.

> **TIP**
>
> Remember, every letter or number has a power of 1 (usually not written). So x means x^1 and y means y^1.

Dividing the same base number with different indices

Look at these two divisions:

$3^4 \div 3^2$ and $x^6 \div x^2$

You already know you can simplify these by writing them in expanded form and cancelling like this:

$$\frac{3 \times 3 \times \cancel{3} \times \cancel{3}}{\cancel{3} \times \cancel{3}} \qquad \frac{x \times x \times x \times x \times \cancel{x} \times \cancel{x}}{\cancel{x} \times \cancel{x}}$$

$$= 3 \times 3 \qquad = x \times x \times x \times x$$

$$= 3^2 \qquad = x^4$$

In other words:

$3^4 \div 3^2 = 3^{4-2}$ and $x^6 \div x^2 = x^{6-2}$

When you divide index expressions with the same base you can subtract the indices:

$x^m \div x^n = x^{m-n}$

> **MATHEMATICAL CONNECTIONS**
>
> You will use the multiplication and division rules more when you study standard form in Chapter 5.

WORKED EXAMPLE 14

Simplify.

a $\dfrac{x^6}{x^2}$ **b** $\dfrac{6a^5}{3a^2}$ **c** $\dfrac{10x^3 y^2}{5xy}$

Answers

a $\dfrac{x^6}{x^2} = x^{6-2} = x^4$ Subtract the indices.

b $\dfrac{6a^5}{3a^2} = \dfrac{6}{3} \times \dfrac{a^5}{a^2}$ Divide (cancel) the coefficients.

$\qquad = \dfrac{2}{1} \times a^{5-2}$ Subtract the indices.

$\qquad = 2a^3$

c $\dfrac{10x^3 y^2}{5xy} = \dfrac{10}{5} \times \dfrac{x^3}{x} \times \dfrac{y^2}{y}$ Divide the coefficients.

$\qquad = \dfrac{2}{1} \times x^{3-1} \times y^{2-1}$ Subtract the indices.

$\qquad = 2x^2 y$

> **TIP**
>
> Remember: the coefficient is the number in the term.

The power 0

Any value divided by itself gives 1, so $3 \div 3 = 1$ and $x \div x = 1$ and $\dfrac{x^4}{x^4} = 1$.

If you use the law of indices for division you can see that $\dfrac{x^4}{x^4} = x^{4-4} = x^0$

So, you can see that $\dfrac{x^4}{x^4} = x^0 = 1$

Any value to the power 0 is equal to 1. So $x^0 = 1$.

Raising a power

Look at these two examples:

$$(x^3)^2 = x^3 \times x^3 = x^{3+3} = x^6 \qquad (2x^3)^4 = 2x^3 \times 2x^3 \times 2x^3 \times 2x^3 = 2^4 \times x^{3+3+3+3} = 16x^{12}$$

By writing in expanded form like this you can see that $(x^3)^2 = x^6$ and $(2x^3)^4 = 16x^{12}$

When you have to raise a power to another power you multiply the indices: $(x^m)^n = x^{mn}$

WORKED EXAMPLE 15

Simplify.

a $(x^3)^6$ **b** $(3x^4y^3)^2$ **c** $(p^3)^4 \div (p^6)^2$

Answers

a $(x^3)^6 = x^{3\times6}$ Multiply the indices.

$\quad\quad = x^{18}$

b $(3x^4y^3)^2$ Square each of the terms to remove the brackets and multiply the indices.

$\quad = 3^2 \times x^{4\times2} \times y^{3\times2}$

$\quad = 9x^8y^6$

c $(p^3)^4 \div (p^6)^2$ Expand the brackets first by multiplying the indices. Divide by subtracting the indices.

$\quad = p^{3\times4} \div p^{6\times2}$

$\quad = p^{12} \div p^{12}$

$\quad = p^{12-12}$

$\quad = p^0$

$\quad = 1$

> **TIP**
>
> A common error is to forget to take powers of the numerical terms. For example, in part (b) you need to square the '3' to give '9'.

Exercise 2.8

1 Simplify.

  a $x^2 \times x^6$ **b** $a^2 \times a^8$ **c** $y^2 \times y^0$ **d** $x^9 \times x^4$

  e $y^2 \times y^7$ **f** $y^3 \times y^4$ **g** $y \times y^5$ **h** $t \times t^4$

  i $3x^4 \times 2x^3$ **j** $3y^2 \times 3y^4$ **k** $2m \times m^3$ **l** $3s^3 \times 2s^4$

  m $5x^3 \times 3$ **n** $8x^4 \times x^3$ **o** $4z^6 \times 2z$ **p** $x^2 \times 4x^5$

2 Simplify.

  a $x^6 \div x^4$ **b** $g^{12} \div g^3$ **c** $y^4 \div y^3$ **d** $k^3 \div k$

  e $\dfrac{s^5}{s}$ **f** $\dfrac{x^6}{x^4}$ **g** $\dfrac{6x^5}{2x^3}$ **h** $\dfrac{9p^7}{3p^4}$

  i $\dfrac{12y^2}{3y}$ **j** $\dfrac{3x^4}{6x^3}$ **k** $\dfrac{15x^3}{5x^3}$ **l** $\dfrac{9b^4}{3b^3}$

  m $\dfrac{3x^3}{9x^4}$ **n** $\dfrac{16a^2b^2}{4ab}$ **o** $\dfrac{12xy^2}{12xy^2}$

3   Simplify.

a $(a^2)^2$ b $(v^2)^3$ c $(f^2)^6$ d $(y^3)^2$

e $(2x^2)^5$ f $(3c^2d^2)^2$ g $(x^4)^0$ h $(5x^2)^3$

i $(a^2b^2)^3$ j $(x^2y^4)^5$ k $(xy^4)^3$ l $(4gh^2)^2$

m $(3x^2)^4$ n $(xy^6)^4$ o $\left(\dfrac{x^2}{y}\right)^0$

4   Use the appropriate laws of indices to simplify these expressions.

a $2x^2 \times 3x^3 \times 2x$ b $4 \times 2x \times 3x^2y$ c $4k \times k \times k^2$

d $(x^2)^2 \div 4x^2$ e $11x^3 \times 4(a^2b)^2$ f $4x(x^2 + 7)$

g $x^2(4x - x^3)$ h $x^8 \div (x^3)^2$ i $7x^2y^2 \div (x^3y)^2$

j $\dfrac{(4x^2 \times 3x^4)}{6x^4}$ k $\left(\dfrac{a^4}{b^2}\right)^3$ l $\dfrac{x^8 \times (xy^2)^4}{(2x^2)^4}$

m $(8x^2)^0$ n $4x^2 \times 2x^3 \div (2x)^0$ o $\dfrac{(4x^2y^3)^2}{(2xy)^3}$

> **TIP**
>
> When there is a mixture of numbers and letters, deal with the numbers first and then apply the laws of indices to the letters in alphabetical order.

Negative indices

In Chapter 1 you learned how to use negative numbers as indices. You will now apply those rules to expressions containing letters.

Look at these two methods of working out.

Using expanded notation:

$$x^3 \div x^5 = \frac{x \times x \times x}{x \times x \times x \times x \times x}$$
$$= \frac{1}{x \times x}$$
$$= \frac{1}{x^2}$$

Using the law of indices for division:

$$x^3 \div x^5 = x^{3-5}$$
$$= x^{-2}$$

This shows that $\dfrac{1}{x^2} = x^{-2}$.

So, $x^{-m} = \dfrac{1}{x^m}$ (when $x \neq 0$)

> **LINK**
>
> Negative indices are often used in units in physics. For example, you often write 'kilometres per hour' as 'km h^{-1}'.

> **TIP**
>
> In everyday language you can say that when a number is written with a negative power, it is equal to '1 over' the number to the same positive power. Another way of saying '1 over' is reciprocal, so a^{-2} can be written as the reciprocal of a^2, i.e. $\dfrac{1}{a^2}$.

When an expression contains negative indices, you apply the same laws as for other indices to simplify it.

> **MATHEMATICAL CONNECTIONS**
>
> Both positive and negative indices are used in standard form. You will learn to use standard form to write very large or very small numbers in Chapter 5.

WORKED EXAMPLE 16

1 Write these with a positive index.

   a x^{-4} **b** y^{-3}

Answers

   a $x^{-4} = \dfrac{1}{x^4}$ **b** $y^{-3} = \dfrac{1}{y^3}$

2 Simplify. Give your answers with positive indices.

   a $\dfrac{4x^2}{2x^4}$ **b** $2x^{-2} \times 3x^{-4}$ **c** $(3y^2)^{-3}$

Answers

   a $\dfrac{4x^2}{2x^4} = \dfrac{4}{2} \times x^{2-4}$ **b** $2x^{-2} \times 3x^{-4} = \dfrac{2}{x^2} \times \dfrac{3}{x^4}$

   $\qquad\qquad = 2x^{-2}$ $\qquad\qquad\qquad\quad = \dfrac{6}{x^{2+4}}$

   $\qquad\qquad = \dfrac{2}{x^2}$ $\qquad\qquad\qquad\quad = \dfrac{6}{x^6}$

   c $(3y^2)^{-3} = \dfrac{1}{(3y^2)^3}$

   $\qquad\qquad\quad = \dfrac{1}{3^3 \times y^{2\times3}}$

   $\qquad\qquad\quad = \dfrac{1}{27y^6}$

The laws of indices can also help you find the value of an index in simple equations. For the same base, if $a^x = a^n$, then $x = n$.

For example, $2^x = 8$. You know that $2^3 = 8$, so $2^x = 2^3$ and $x = 3$.

WORKED EXAMPLE 17

If $2^x = 128$ find the value of x.

Answer

$2^x = 128$ Rewrite 128 as a power of 2. You might need to use trial
$2^7 = 128$ and improvement to do this.
$\therefore x = 7$

Exercise 2.9

1 State whether the following are true or false.

   a $4^{-2} = \dfrac{1}{16}$ **b** $8^{-2} = \dfrac{1}{16}$ **c** $x^{-3} = \dfrac{1}{3x}$ **d** $2x^{-2} = \dfrac{1}{x}$

2 Write each expression so it has only positive indices.

   a x^{-2} **b** y^{-3} **c** $(xy)^{-2}$ **d** $2x^{-2}$

   e $12x^{-3}$ **f** $7y^{-3}$ **g** $8xy^{-3}$ **h** $12x^{-3}y^{-4}$

3 Simplify. Write your answer using only positive indices.

a $b^{-3} \times b^4$ b $2x^{-3} \times 3x^{-3}$ c $4s^3 \div 12s^7$

d $\dfrac{h^{-7}}{h^4}$ e $(2x^2)^{-3}$ f $(c^{-2})^3$

g $x^{-3} \div x^{-4}$ h $\dfrac{x^{-2}}{x^3}$ i $a^4b^{-3} \times a^3b^{-2}$

j $(x^4y^{-2})^3 \times (xy^3)^{-2}$ k $\dfrac{2x^5y^3}{x^2y^{-4}} \times \dfrac{y^4}{x^7}$ l $\dfrac{m^3n^{-6}}{m^{-4}n^7} \div \dfrac{m^5n^{-9}}{m^{-2}n^4}$

m $\left(\dfrac{3m^4n^3}{2mn}\right)^2 \div \dfrac{3mn}{(2m^{-2}n^3)^4}$

4 Find the value of x in each equation.

a $3^x = 81$ b $2^x = 32$ c $4^{x-2} = 1$

d $5^x = \dfrac{1}{125}$ e $10^{1-x} = \dfrac{1}{100}$ f $2^x + 1 = 9$

g $4 \times 3^x = 36$ h $3 \times 3^x = 243$

Summary of index laws

$x^m \times x^n = x^{m+n}$ When multiplying terms, add the indices.

$x^m \div x^n = x^{m-n}$ When dividing, subtract the indices.

$(x^m)^n = x^{mn}$ When finding the power of a power, multiply the indices.

$x^0 = 1$ Any value to the power 0 is equal to 1.

$x^{-m} = \dfrac{1}{x^m}$ (when $x \neq 0$)

Fractional indices

The laws of indices also apply when the index is a fraction. Look at these examples carefully to remind yourself what fractional indices mean in algebra:

$x^{\frac{1}{2}} \times x^{\frac{1}{2}}$

$= x^{\frac{1}{2}+\frac{1}{2}}$ Use the law of indices and add the powers.

$= x^1$

$= x$

In order to understand what $x^{\frac{1}{2}}$ means, ask yourself: what number multiplied by itself will give x?

$\sqrt{x} \times \sqrt{x} = x$

So, $x^{\frac{1}{2}} = \sqrt{x}$

$y^{\frac{1}{3}} \times y^{\frac{1}{3}} \times y^{\frac{1}{3}}$

$= y^{\frac{1}{3}+\frac{1}{3}+\frac{1}{3}}$ Use the law of indices and add the powers.

$= y^1$

$= y$

What number multiplied by itself and then by itself again will give y?

$$\sqrt[3]{y} \times \sqrt[3]{y} \times \sqrt[3]{y} = y$$

So $y^{\frac{1}{3}} = \sqrt[3]{y}$

This shows that any root of a number can be written using fractional indices.

So, $x^{\frac{1}{m}} = \sqrt[m]{x}$.

WORKED EXAMPLE 18

1 Rewrite using root signs.

    a $y^{\frac{1}{2}}$ **b** $x^{\frac{1}{5}}$ **c** $x^{\frac{1}{y}}$

Answers

    a $y^{\frac{1}{2}} = \sqrt{y}$ **b** $x^{\frac{1}{5}} = \sqrt[5]{x}$ **c** $x^{\frac{1}{y}} = \sqrt[y]{x}$

2 Write in index notation.

    a $\sqrt{90}$ **b** $\sqrt[3]{64}$ **c** $\sqrt[4]{x}$ **d** $\sqrt[5]{(x-2)}$

Answers

    a $\sqrt{90} = 90^{\frac{1}{2}}$ **b** $\sqrt[3]{64} = 64^{\frac{1}{3}}$

    c $\sqrt[4]{x} = x^{\frac{1}{4}}$ **d** $\sqrt[5]{(x-2)} = (x-2)^{\frac{1}{5}}$

Dealing with non-unit fractions

Indices may contain non-unit fractions, for example $x^{\frac{2}{3}}$ or $y^{\frac{3}{4}}$. To find the rule for working with these, you have to think back to the law of indices for raising a power to another power. Look at these examples carefully to see how this works:

$$x^{\frac{2}{3}} = \left(x^{\frac{1}{3}}\right)^2 \qquad \frac{1}{3} \times 2 = \frac{2}{3}$$

$$y^{\frac{3}{4}} = \left(y^{\frac{1}{4}}\right)^3 \qquad \frac{1}{4} \times 3 = \frac{3}{4}$$

> **TIP**
>
> A non-unit fraction has a numerator that is not 1. For example, $\frac{2}{3}$ and $\frac{5}{7}$ are non-unit fractions.

You already know that a unit fraction gives a root. So you can rewrite these expressions using root signs like this:

$$\left(x^{\frac{1}{3}}\right)^2 = \left(\sqrt[3]{x}\right)^2 \text{ and } \left(y^{\frac{1}{4}}\right)^3 = \left(\sqrt[4]{y}\right)^3$$

So, $x^{\frac{2}{3}} = \left(\sqrt[3]{x}\right)^2$ and $y^{\frac{3}{4}} = \left(\sqrt[4]{y}\right)^3$.

> **TIP**
>
> You can reverse the order of calculations here and the result will be the same.
> $$x^{\frac{m}{n}} = x^{m \times \frac{1}{n}} = \left(x^{\frac{1}{n}}\right)^m = \left(\sqrt[n]{x}\right)^m$$

In general terms: $x^{\frac{m}{n}} = x^{m \times \frac{1}{n}} = \left(x^{\frac{1}{n}}\right)^m = \left(\sqrt[n]{x}\right)^m$

WORKED EXAMPLE 19

Simplify $\left(\sqrt[5]{a^2}\right)^{\frac{3}{2}} \times \left(\sqrt[3]{a^5}\right)^{\frac{1}{5}}$

Answer

$$\left(\sqrt[5]{a^2}\right)^{\frac{3}{2}} \times \left(\sqrt[3]{a^5}\right)^{\frac{1}{5}} = \left(a^{\frac{2}{5}}\right)^{\frac{3}{2}} \times \left(a^{\frac{5}{3}}\right)^{\frac{1}{5}}$$ Apply the rule $\sqrt[n]{a^m} = a^{\frac{m}{n}}$

$$= a^{\frac{3}{5}} \times a^{\frac{1}{3}}$$ Raise the powers. Simplify the fractions.

$$= a^{\frac{3}{5} + \frac{1}{3}}$$ Apply laws of indices.

$$= a^{\frac{9}{15} + \frac{5}{15}}$$ Form equivalent fractions and add them.

$$= a^{\frac{14}{15}}$$

In Exercise 2.9 you worked out the value of x when it was the exponent in an equation. An equation that requires you to find the exponent is called an exponential equation.

WORKED EXAMPLE 20

If $2^{x+3} = \dfrac{1}{16}$ find the value of x.

Answer

$2^{x+3} = \dfrac{1}{16}$ Rewrite the fraction as a power of 2 with a negative index.

$2^{x+3} = 2^{-4}$ Equate the indices.

$x + 3 = -4$

$x = -7$

Exercise 2.10

1 Simplify.

a $x^{\frac{1}{3}} \times x^{\frac{1}{3}}$ b $x^{\frac{1}{2}} \times x^{\frac{2}{3}}$ c $\left(\dfrac{y^4}{y^{10}}\right)^{\frac{1}{2}}$ d $\left(\dfrac{x^6}{y^2}\right)^{\frac{1}{2}}$

e $\dfrac{a^{\frac{6}{7}}}{a^{\frac{2}{7}}}$ f $\dfrac{7}{8}b^{\frac{1}{2}} \div \dfrac{1}{2}b^{-\frac{3}{2}}$ g $\dfrac{2x^{\frac{2}{3}}}{x^{\frac{8}{3}}}$ h $\dfrac{9k^{\frac{1}{3}}}{12k^{\frac{4}{3}}}$

i $3\left(\sqrt[4]{x^7}\right)$ j $\dfrac{1}{2}x^{\frac{1}{2}} \div 2x^2$ k $-\dfrac{1}{2}s^{\frac{3}{4}} \div -2s^{-\frac{1}{4}}$ l $\dfrac{3}{4}x^{\frac{1}{2}} \div \dfrac{1}{2}x^{-\frac{1}{4}}$

m $-\dfrac{1}{4}x^{\frac{3}{4}} \div -2x^{-\frac{1}{4}}$ n $\dfrac{1}{2}x^{\frac{1}{2}} \div 2x^2$ o $\sqrt[3]{x} \times \sqrt[4]{x^3}$ p $\dfrac{\sqrt[3]{x^2 y}}{\sqrt{xy^3}}$

2 Find the value of x in each of these equations.

a $2^x = 64$ b $196^x = 14$ c $x^{\frac{1}{5}} = 7$ d $(x-1)^{\frac{3}{4}} = 64$

e $3^x = 81$ f $4^x = 256$ g $2^{-x} = \dfrac{1}{64}$ h $3^{x-1} = 81$

i $9^{-x} = \dfrac{1}{81}$ j $3^{-x} = 81$ k $64^x = 2$ l $16^x = 8$

TIP

Remember, simplify means to write in its simplest form. So, if you were to simplify $x^{\frac{1}{5}} \times x^{-\frac{1}{2}}$ you would write:

$= x^{\frac{1}{5} - \frac{1}{2}}$

$= x^{\frac{2}{10} - \frac{5}{10}}$

$= x^{-\frac{3}{10}}$

$= \dfrac{1}{x^{\frac{3}{10}}}$

SELF ASSESSMENT

These are the stems of a 3 : 2 : 1 summary:

- 3 things I learned are:
- 2 questions I had were:
- 1 thing I understood really quickly was:

You can use a 3 : 2 : 1 summary to assess your own learning.

Here is an example of a student self assessment for this chapter.

3 things I learnt are:
- Indices in algebra work the same as in number
- You can write terms with negative indices as fractions to get positive indices
- Cube roots can be written using $\frac{1}{3}$ as the index

2 questions I had were:
- How do you work with fractions when the numerator isn't 1?
- Can you use your calculator to work with indices?

1 thing I understood really quickly was:
- How to use the laws of indices with letters.

Complete your own 3 : 2 : 1 summary to assess your learning in this chapter.

SUMMARY

Do you know …?
Algebra has special conventions (rules) that allow you to write mathematical information in short ways.
Letters in algebra are called variables, the number before a letter is called a coefficient and numbers on their own are called constants.
A group of numbers and variables is called a term. Terms are separated by + and − signs, but not by × or ÷ signs.
Like terms have exactly the same combination of variables and powers. You can add and subtract like terms. You can multiply and divide like and unlike terms.
The order of operations rules for numbers (BODMAS) apply in algebra as well.
Removing brackets (multiplying out) is called expanding the expression. Collecting like terms is called simplifying the expression.
Powers are also called indices. The index tells you how many times a number or variable is multiplied by itself. Indices only apply to the number or variable immediately before them.
The laws of indices are a set of rules for simplifying expressions with indices. These laws apply to positive, negative, zero and fractional indices.

SUMMARY CONTINUED

Are you able to …?
use letters to represent numbers
write expressions to represent mathematical information
substitute letters with numbers to find the value of an expression
add and subtract like terms to simplify expressions
multiply and divide to simplify expressions
expand expressions by removing brackets and getting rid of other grouping symbols
use and make sense of positive, negative and zero indices
apply the laws of indices to simplify expressions
work with fractional indices
solve exponential equations using fractional indices.

Practice questions

1   For a number, n, write an expression for:

    a   the sum of the number and 12   [1]

    b   twice the number minus four   [1]

    c   the number multiplied by x and then squared   [1]

    d   the square of the number cubed.   [1]

2   If n is any positive integer,

    a   Write an expression that is an even number for all possible values of n.   [1]

    b   Explain why $2n + 1$ is always an odd number.   [1]

    Every positive odd number p can be written in the form $p = 2n + 1$.

    c   Write an expression, in terms of n, for the next largest odd number after p.   [1]

    d   Use your answer to part (c) to show that any two consecutive odd numbers always add up to an even number.   [3]

3   Walls are made from bricks with algebraic expressions written on the sides.
    Each expression is made by adding the two expressions underneath, like this.

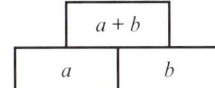

    a   Here is another wall. Write an expression for the brick at the top.   [2]

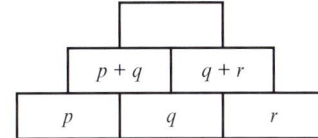

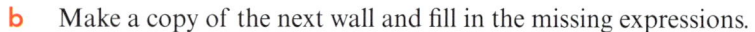
b Make a copy of the next wall and fill in the missing expressions. [3]

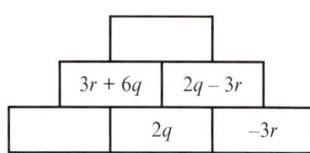

c Another wall is made with six bricks as before. The expressions in the bottom bricks are $2h$, j, and $2k$ reading left to right, where h, j and k are integers. Explain why the top brick always contains an even number. [4]

4 Simplify.

    a $9xy + 3x + 6xy - 2x$ [2]   **b** $6xy - xy + 3y$ [2]

5 Simplify.

    a $\dfrac{a^3b^4}{ab^3}$ [2]   **b** $2(x^3)^2$ [2]   **c** $3x \times 2x^3y^2$ [2]

    d $(4ax^2)^0$ [2]   **e** $4x^2y \times x^3y^2$ [2]   **f** $3x^{-4} \times 5x^6$ [2]

    g $\dfrac{3x^5}{7x^4} \div \dfrac{6x^{-6}}{14x^{-4}}$ [3]   **h** $(4x^{-5})^2$ [2]   **i** $\left(\dfrac{3x}{4y}\right)^3$ [3]

    j $\dfrac{4x^{12}y^{-3}}{12x^{-7}y^9}$ [3]   **k** $\dfrac{14p^5q^{-4}}{30p^4q^4} \times \dfrac{5pq^{-7}}{2p^{-4}q^5}$ [3]

6 Simplify $7x^3y^2 \times (2x)^3 - (4x^3y)^2 - 4xy^2 \times 10x^5$ [3]

 7 Find the value of $(x + 5) - (x - 5)$ when:

    a $x = 1$ [1]   **b** $x = 0$ [1]   **c** $x = 5$ [1]

 8 $s = \dfrac{1}{2}(u + v)t$

Without using a calculator find s if $u = \dfrac{2}{5}$, $v = 4\dfrac{1}{2}$, $t = 3$.

Write your answer as a simplified fraction. [3]

9 Expand each expression and simplify if possible.

    a $5(x - 2) + 3(x + 2)$ [3]   **b** $5x(x + 7y) - 2x(2x - y)$ [3]

10 a $m(m - n) - n(n - m)$ [3]

    b $x(y - z) + y(z - x) + z(x - y)$ [3]

11 Simplify and write the answers with positive indices only.

    a $x^5 \times x^{-2}$ [2]   **b** $\dfrac{8x^2}{2x^4}$ [2]   **c** $(2x^{-2})^{-3}$ [2]

12 Find the value of each unknown when:

    a $4^x = 64$ [2]   **b** $3^x - 5 = 22$ [2]   **c** $4 \times 6^p = 864$ [2]

 13 If $a = 3$, $b = 2$ and $c = -1$, find the value of $a^b - c^a + b^a$ [2]

14 Simplify.

a $3x^{\frac{1}{2}} \times 5x^{\frac{1}{2}}$ [2] b $(81y^6)^{\frac{1}{2}}$ [2] c $(64x^3)^{\frac{1}{3}}$ [2]

15 Find the value of x when:

a $\left(\frac{1}{2}\right)^x = 8$ [2] b $3^x = \frac{1}{27}$ [2] c $125^x = 5$ [2] d $125^x = \frac{1}{5}$ [2]

16 $p = 2^x$ and $q = 2^y$

Find, in terms of p and q:

a 2^{x+y} [2] b 2^{x+y-2} [2] c 2^{3x} [2]

17 Find the value of n for which:

a $n^{-1} = 2^{-2}$ [2] b $4^n = \left(\sqrt[4]{32}\right)^3$ [2]

SELF ASSESSMENT

Mark your answers to the practice questions.

Complete these statements in your book.

- I now know …
- I need to know more about …
- These things went well …
- I could do better if I …

Chapter 3

Lines, angles and shapes

IN THIS CHAPTER YOU WILL:

- use the correct terms to talk about points, lines, angles and shapes
- classify, measure and construct angles
- calculate unknown angles using angle relationships
- talk about the properties of triangles, quadrilaterals, circles and polygons
- construct triangles using a ruler and a pair of compasses.

The photo on the previous page shows buildings and the harbour promenade in Hamburg, Germany. The architects have made good use of lines to draw in the eye and curves to add interest to the design. What mathematical challenges can you see in the design of this building?

Geometry is one of the oldest known areas of mathematics. Farmers in Ancient Egypt knew about lines and angles, and they used them to mark out fields after floods. Builders in Egypt and Mesopotamia used knowledge of angles and shapes to build huge temples and pyramids.

Today construction workers, surveyors and architects use geometry to plan and build roads, bridges, houses and office blocks. Lines and angles are also used when reading maps and in the software of GPS devices. Artists use lines and angles to get the correct perspective in drawings, opticians use them to make spectacle lenses and tennis and snooker players use them to work out how to hit the ball. Can you think of any other sports where lines and angles play an important role?

GETTING STARTED

Spider diagrams like this one are useful for summarising information.

Copy the diagram into your book or work with a partner on a large sheet of paper.

Add bullet points or simple diagrams to each topic to show what you already know.

Add more bubbles if you need to.

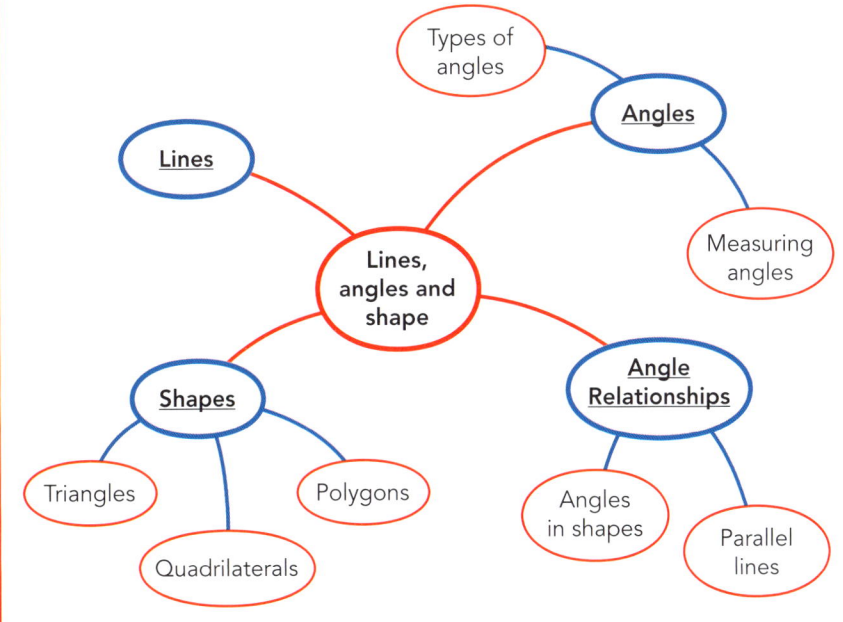

3.1 Lines and angles

Mathematicians use specific terms and definitions in geometry. You are expected to know what the terms mean and to use them correctly in your own work. Read through the table to remind yourself of the key terms and what they mean.

Terms used to talk about lines

Term	What it means	Examples
Point	A point is shown on paper using a dot (·) or a cross (×). Most often you will use the word 'point' to talk about where two lines meet. You will also talk about points on a grid (positions) and name these using ordered pairs of co-ordinates (x, y). Points are normally named using capital letters.	
Line	A line is a straight (one-dimensional) figure that extends to infinity in both directions. Normally though, the word 'line' is used to talk about the line segment that is the shortest distance between two points. Lines are named using starting point and end point letters.	line AB
Parallel	A pair of lines that are the same distance apart all along their length are parallel. The symbol $\parallel$ (or //) is used for parallel lines, e.g. $AB \parallel CD$. Parallel lines are marked with arrows on diagrams.	$AB \parallel CD$
Perpendicular	When two lines meet at right angles they are perpendicular to each other. The symbol $\perp$ is used to show that lines are perpendicular, e.g. $MN \perp PQ$.	$MN \perp PQ$

> **TIP**
>
> The shortest distance between a point and a line is the perpendicular distance from the point to the line.

The photo shows the Harpa Concert Hall in Reykjavik, Iceland.
The three-dimensional glass and steel bricks used to build the walls were inspired by the shape of basalt columns.

INVESTIGATION

Shapes and solids

1   Study the photograph of the Harpa Concert Hall. Try to find an example to illustrate each term in the table.

2   How many types of polygon can you find in the design of the walls?

3   Choose one of the 3D column-shaped bricks that you can see on the right-hand face of the building.

   a   What is the mathematical name for this type of shape?

   b   Can you work out how many faces the shape has? How?

4   The Harpa building was designed using 3D digital modelling. The model was shared online as people in different countries worked on the design. Discuss these questions in groups.

   a   How can a 3D model help an architect design structures, lights, ventilation, electrical wiring and plumbing?

   b   What advantages does 3D computer modelling have compared to plans drawn on paper?

LINK

Builders, designers, architects, engineers, artists and jewellers use shape, space and measure as they work and many of these careers use computer packages to plan and design various items. Most design work starts in 2D on paper or on screen and moves to 3D for the final representation. You need a good understanding of lines, angles, shape and space to use computer-aided design (CAD) packages.

Terms used to talk about angles

Term	What it means	Examples
Angle	When two lines meet at a point, they form an angle. The meeting point is called the vertex of the angle and the two lines are called the arms of the angle. Angles are named using three letters: the letter at the end of one arm, the letter at the vertex and the letter at the end of the other arm. The letter in the middle of an angle name always indicates the vertex.	 Angle ABC
Acute angle	An acute angle is >0° but <90°.	 $ABC < 90°$ $DEF < 90°$ $MNP < 90°$
Right angle	A right angle is exactly 90°. A right angle is formed between perpendicular lines. A right angle is represented by a square in the corner.	 $XYZ = 90°$; $XY \perp YZ$
Obtuse angle	An obtuse angle is >90° but <180°.	 $ABC > 90°$ $PQR > 90°$
Straight angle	A straight angle is 180°. A line is considered to be a straight angle.	 $MNO = 180°$ MO = straight line
Reflex angle	A reflex angle is >180° but <360°.	 $ABC > 180°$ $DEF > 180°$

> **TIP**
>
> Always take time to measure angles carefully. This is particularly important when you have to calculate using angles you've measured because a careless error can lead to several wrong answers.

Term	What it means	Examples
Revolution	A revolution is a complete turn: an angle of exactly 360°.	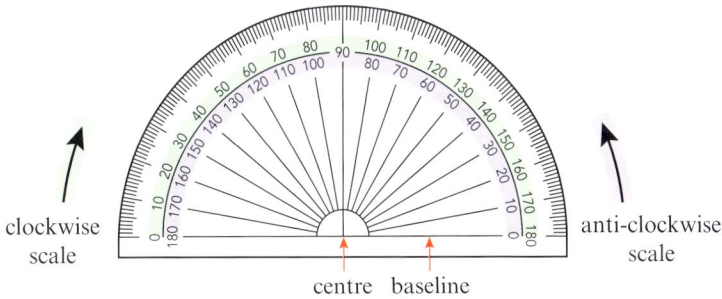 O 360°

Measuring and drawing angles

The size of an angle is the amount of turn from one arm of the angle to the other. Angle sizes are measured in degrees (°) from 0 to 360 using a protractor.

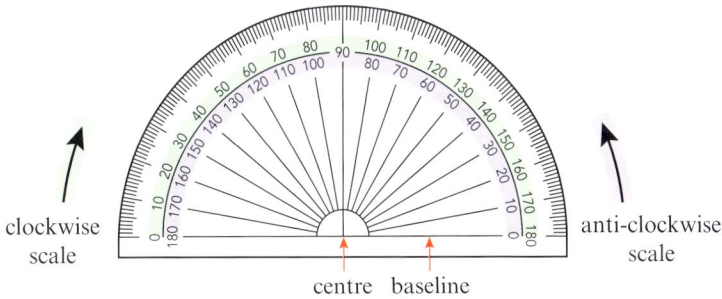

clockwise scale   anti-clockwise scale

centre baseline

A 180° protractor has two scales. You need to choose the correct one when you measure an angle.

MATHEMATICAL CONNECTIONS

You will use these skills when drawing pie charts in Chapter 4.

TIP

If the arm of the angle does not extend up to the scale, extend the arm past the scale. The length of the arms of the angle does not affect the size of the angle.

LINK

Geographers and other geoscientists use a piece of equipment called a 'clinometer' to measure angles and calculate the heights of cliffs on the coastline. A clinometer looks and behaves quite like a protractor, but it usually also has an eyepiece, so that you can easily line up with the top of the cliff. Geologists, engineers and surveyors also use clinometers to work out heights, for example of microwave towers and satellite dishes.

Measuring angles <180°

When an angle is smaller than 180° you can read the size from the scale on the protractor.

WORKED EXAMPLE 1

Measure angles *ABC* and *PQR*.

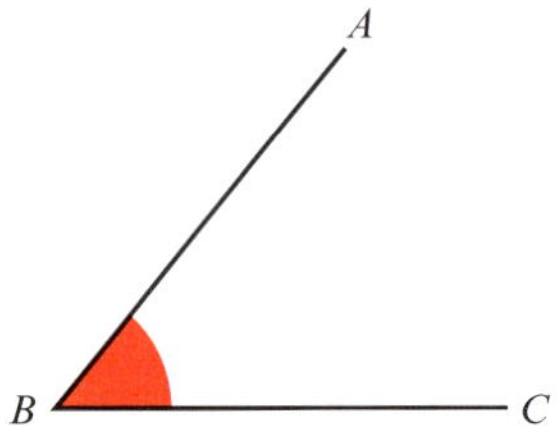

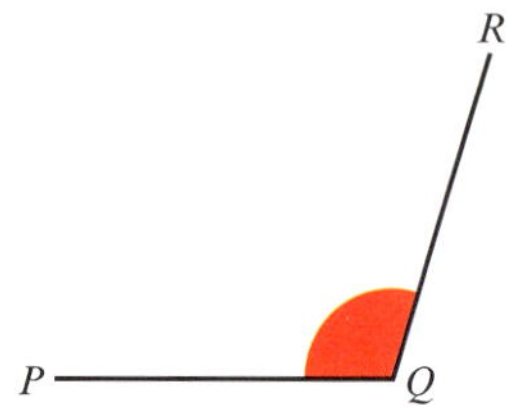

Answer

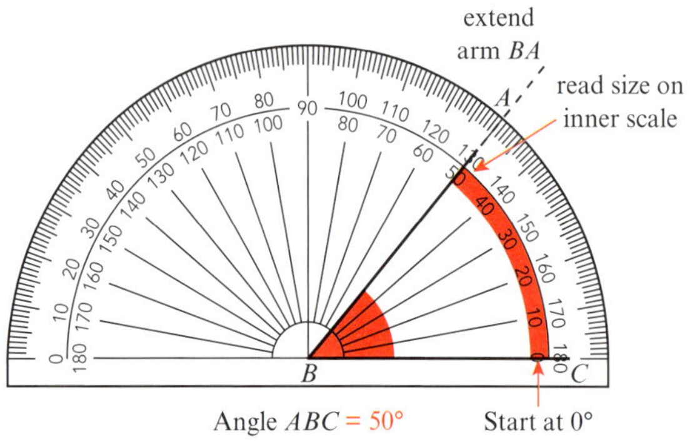

extend arm *BA*
read size on inner scale

read size on outer scale

Angle *ABC* = 50°   Start at 0°

Start at 0°   Angle *PQR* = 105°

Place the centre of the protractor at *B* and align the baseline so it sits on arm *BC*. Extend arm *BA* so that it reaches past the scale. Read the inner scale. Angle *ABC* = 50°

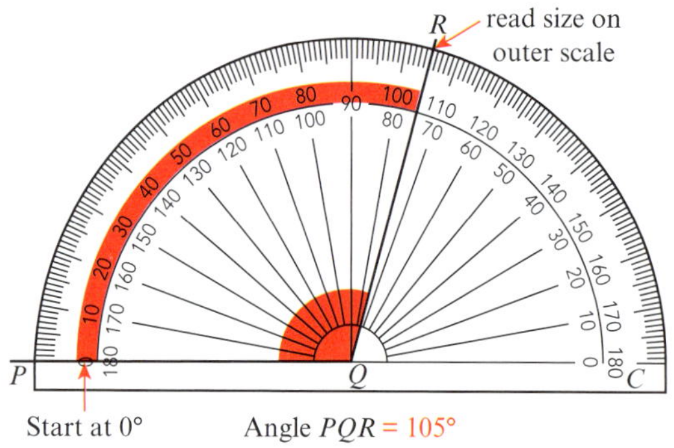

Put the centre of the protractor at *Q* and the baseline along *QP*. Start at 0° and read the outer scale. Angle *PQR* = 105°

Measuring angles >180°

Here are two different methods for measuring a reflex angle with a 180° protractor. Use the method that you find easier.

Suppose you had to measure the reflex angle *ABC*:

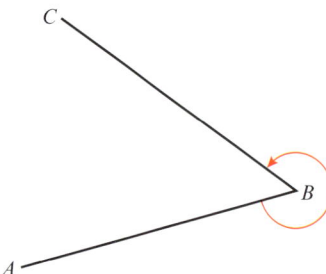

Angle *ABC* is >180°

TIP

If the word reflex is not included you can assume you are dealing with the angle between the two arms (acute, right or obtuse).

Method 1: Extend one arm of the angle to form a straight line (180° angle) and then measure the 'extra bit'. Add the 'extra bit' to 180° to get the total size.

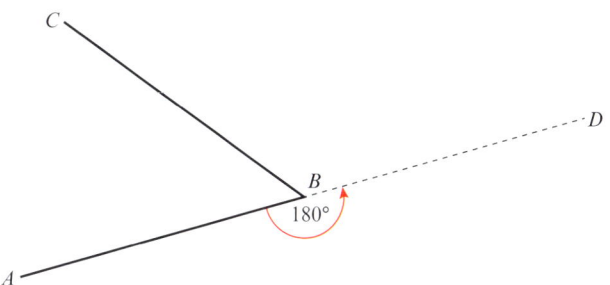

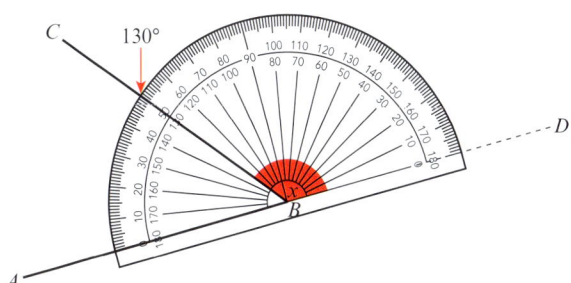

Extend AB to point D. You know the angle of a straight line is 180°. So $ABD = 180°$.

Measure the other piece of the angle DBC (marked x) and add this to 180° to find angle ABC.

$180° + 130° = 310°$

$\therefore ABC = 310°$

Method 2: Measure the inner (non-reflex) angle and subtract it from 360° to get the size of the reflex angle.

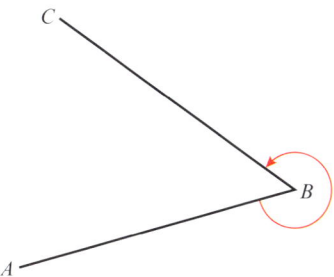

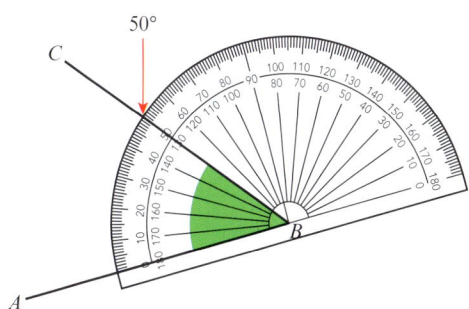

You can see that the angle ABC is almost 360°.

Measure the size of the angle that is <180° (non-reflex) and subtract from 360°.

$360° - 50° = 310°$

$\therefore ABC = 310°$

Exercise 3.1

1   For each angle listed:

   i   state what type of angle it is (acute, right or obtuse)

   ii estimate its size in degrees

   iii use a protractor to measure the actual size of each angle to the nearest degree.

   a BAC **b** BAD **c** BAE

   d CAD **e** CAF **f** CAE

   g DAB **h** DAE **i** DAF

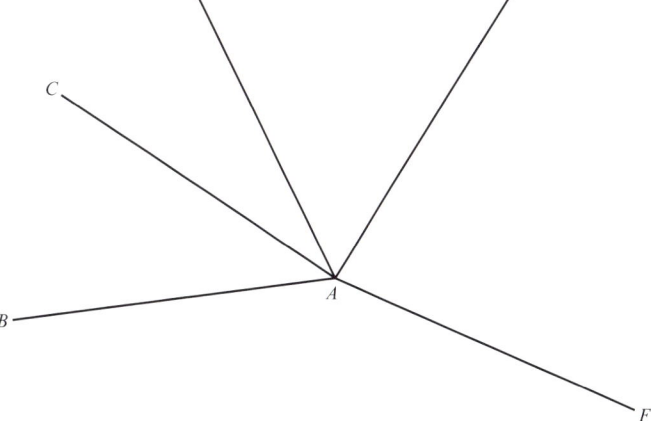

2   What is the size of reflex angle DAB in the diagram for question 1?

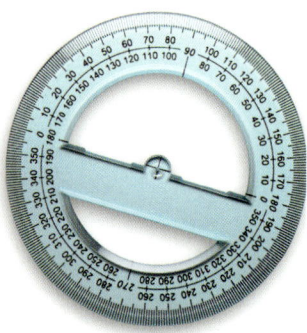

INVESTIGATION

3 This protractor is circular.

    a How is this different from the 180° protractor?

    b Write instructions to teach someone how to use a circular protractor to measure the size of an obtuse angle.

    c How would you measure a reflex angle with a circular protractor?

Drawing angles

You can draw an angle of any given size if you have a ruler, a protractor and a sharp pencil. Work through this example to remind yourself how to draw angles <180° and >180°.

WORKED EXAMPLE 2

Draw each angle:

a $ABC = 76°$ **b** $XYZ = 195°$.

Answers

a

Use a ruler to draw a line to represent one arm of the angle, make sure the line extends beyond the protractor.

Mark the vertex (B).

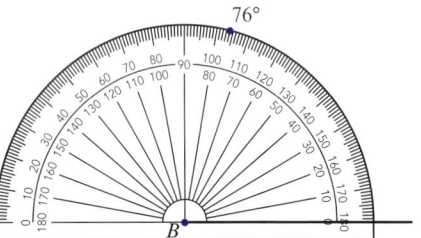

Place your protractor on the line with the centre at the vertex.

Measure the size of the angle you wish to draw and mark a small point.

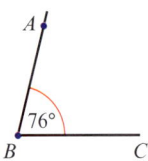

Remove the protractor and use a ruler to draw a line from the vertex through the point.

Label the angle correctly.

b

X Y

For a reflex angle, draw a line as in (a) but mark one arm (X) as well as the vertex (Y). The arm should extend beyond the vertex to create a 180° angle.

WORKED EXAMPLE 2 CONTINUED

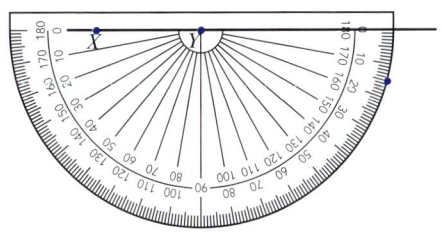

Calculate the size of rest the angle: 195° − 180° = 15°.

Measure and mark the 15° angle (on either side of the 180° line).

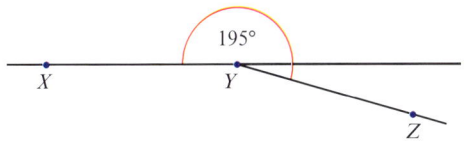

Remove the protractor and use a ruler to draw a line from the vertex through the third point.

Label the angle correctly.

> **TIP**
>
> To draw a reflex angle, you can also work out the size of the inner angle and simply draw that. 360° − 195° = 165°. If you do this, remember to mark the reflex angle on your sketch and not the inner angle!

Exercise 3.2

1 Use a ruler and a protractor to accurately draw the following angles:

a $ABC = 80°$ b $PQR = 30°$ c $XYZ = 135°$

d $EFG = 90°$ e $KLM = 210°$ f $JKL = 355°$

> **PEER ASSESSMENT**
>
> Exchange the angles you drew in Exercise 3.2 with a partner.
>
> 1 Use your protractor to measure each angle and give them a rating from 1 to 4 for accuracy (1 is not very accurate and 4 is extremely accurate).
>
> 2 What hints can you give people to help them draw angles as accurately as possible?

Angle relationships

Make sure you know the following angle facts:

Complementary angles

Angles in a right angle add up to 90°.

When the sum of two angles is 90° those two angles are **complementary angles**.

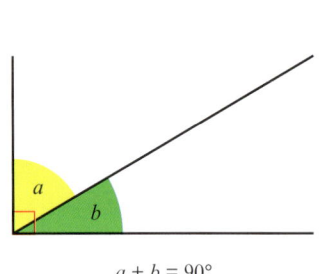

$a + b = 90°$

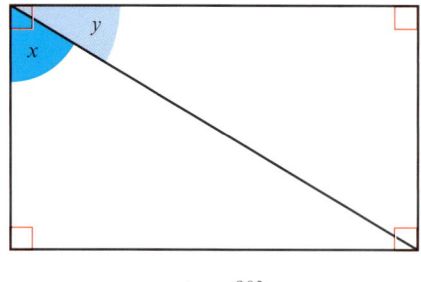

$x + y = 90°$

Supplementary angles

Angles on a straight line add up to 180°.

When the sum of two angles is 180° those two angles are **supplementary angles**.

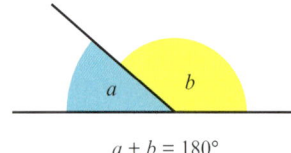

$a + b = 180°$

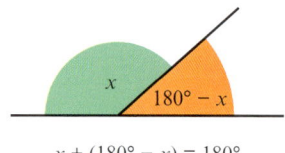

$x + (180° − x) = 180°$

Angles round a point

Angles at a point make a complete revolution.

The sum of the angles at a point is 360°.

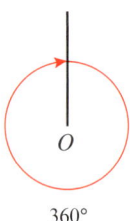

360°

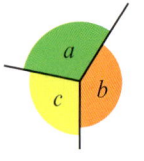

$a + b + c = 360°$

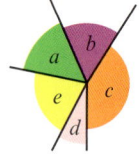

$a + b + c + d + e = 360°$

Vertically opposite angles

When two lines intersect, two pairs of **vertically opposite** angles are formed.

Vertically opposite angles are equal in size.

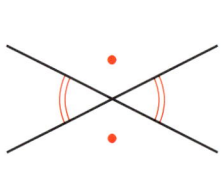

Two pairs of vertically opposite angles.

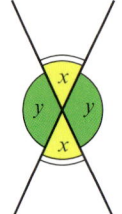

The angles marked x are equal to each other. The angles marked y are also equal to each other.

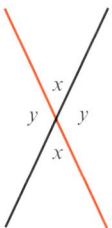

$x + y = 180°$

Using angle relationships to find unknown angles

You can use the relationships between angles to work out the size of unknown angles. To do this:

- identify the relationship
- make an equation
- give reasons for statements
- solve the equation to find the unknown value.

WORKED EXAMPLE 3

Find the size of the angle marked x in each of these figures. Give reasons.

Answers

a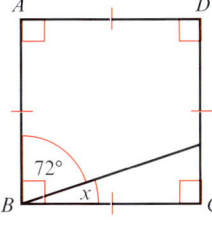

a $72° + x = 90°$
(angle $ABC = 90°$, comp angles)

$x = 90° - 72°$

$x = 18°$

You are told that angle ABC is a right angle, so you know that 72° and x are complementary angles. This means that $72° + x = 90°$, so you can solve to find the value of x.

b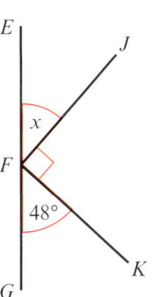

b $48° + 90° + x = 180°$
(angles on line)

$x = 180° - 90° - 48°$

$x = 42°$

You can see that 48°, the right angle and x are angles on a straight line. Angles on a straight line add up to 180°. So you can rearrange to make x the subject.

c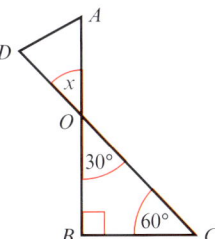

c $x = 30°$ (vertically opposite angles)

You know that when two lines intersect, the resulting vertically opposite angles are equal. x and 30° are vertically opposite, so $x = 30°$.

TIP

In geometry problems you need to present your reasoning in a logical and structured way.

You will usually be expected to give reasons when you are finding the size of an unknown angle. To do this, state the relationship that you used to find the unknown angle after your statements. You can use these abbreviations to give reasons:

- comp angles
- angles on line
- supp angles
- angles round point

Exercise 3.3

1 In the following diagram, name:

   a a pair of complementary angles   **b** a pair of equal angles

   c a pair of supplementary angles   **d** the angles on line *DG*

   e the complement of angle *EBF*   **f** the supplement of angle *EBC*.

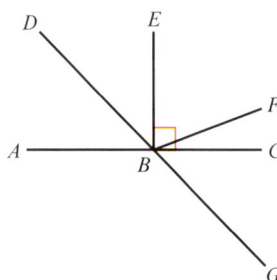

2 In each diagram, find the value of each angle marked with a letter.

  a
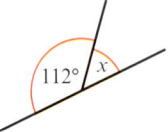
  b
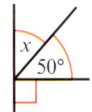
  c
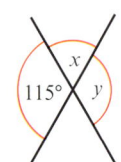
  d
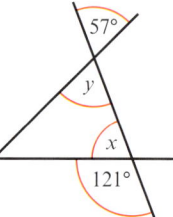

  e
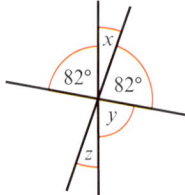
  f
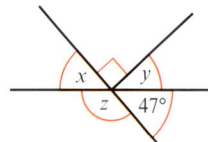
  g
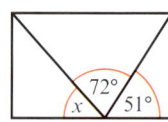

  h
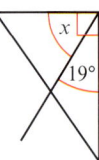
  i
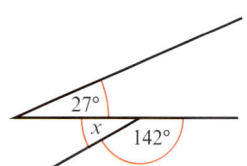

3 Find the value of *x* in each of the following diagrams.

  a
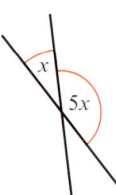
  b
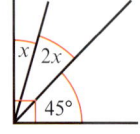
  c
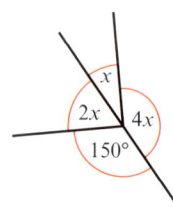

4 Two angles are supplementary. The first angle is twice the size of the second. What are their sizes?

5 One of the angles formed when two lines intersect is 127°. What are the sizes of the other three angles?

Angles and parallel lines

When two parallel lines are cut by a third line (the transversal) eight angles are formed. These angles form pairs which are related to each other in specific ways.

Corresponding angles ('F'-shape)

When two parallel lines are cut by a transversal four pairs of **corresponding angles** are formed. Corresponding angles are equal to each other.

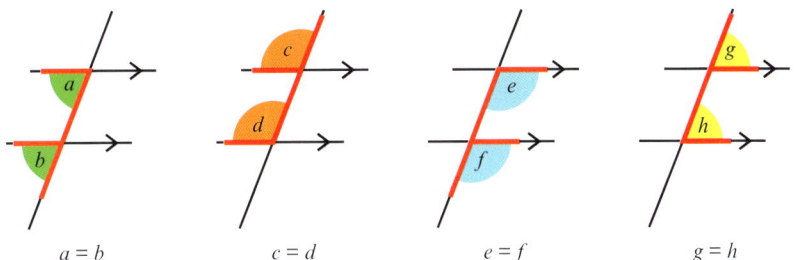

| $a = b$ | $c = d$ | $e = f$ | $g = h$ |

Alternate angles ('Z'-shape)

When two parallel lines are cut by a transversal two pairs of **alternate angles** are formed. Alternate angles are equal to each other.

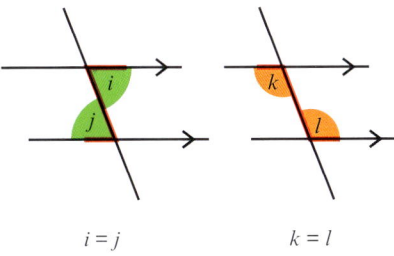

| $i = j$ | $k = l$ |

Co-interior angles ('C'-shape)

When two parallel lines are cut by a transversal two pairs of **co-interior angles** are formed. Co-interior angles are supplementary (together they add up to 180°).

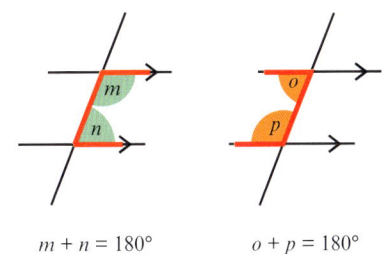

| $m + n = 180°$ | $o + p = 180°$ |

> **TIP**
>
> Although 'F', 'Z' and 'C' shapes help you to remember these properties, you must use the terms 'corresponding', 'alternate' and 'co-interior' to describe them when you answer a question.

> **MATHEMATICAL CONNECTIONS**
>
> You will use the angle relationships in this section again when you deal with triangles, quadrilaterals, polygons and circles later in this chapter.

> **TIP**
>
> 'Co-' means together. Co-interior angles are found together on the same side of the transversal.
>
> Co-interior angles will only be equal if the transversal is perpendicular to the parallel lines (when they will both be 90°).

The angle relationships around parallel lines and the other angle relationships from earlier in the chapter are very useful for solving unknown angles in geometry.

WORKED EXAMPLE 4

Find the size of angles *a*, *b* and *c* in this figure.

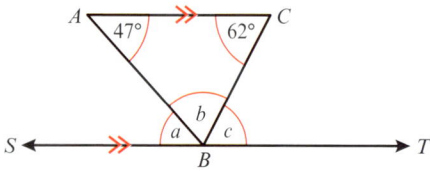

Answer

a = 47° (*CAB* alt *SBA*)

c = 62° (*ACB* alt *CBT*)

a + *b* + *c* = 180° (angles on line)

∴ *b* = 180° − 47° − 62°

  b = 71°

CAB and *SBA* are alternate angles and are equal. *ACB* and *CBT* are alternate angles and equal.
Angles on a straight line = 180°.

You know the values of *a* and *c*, so can use these to find *b*.

LINK

A clever application of alternate angles makes it possible to create a lifting platform like the one in the picture. The top platform must stay parallel to the ground as the platform lifts. Can you see how corresponding and alternate angles are involved?

Exercise 3.4

1   Calculate the size of all angles marked with letters in the following diagrams. Give reasons.

a

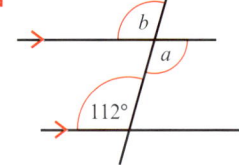

b

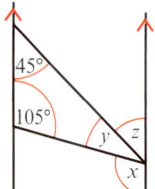

c

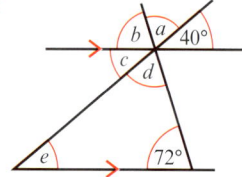

d

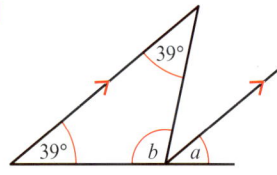

e

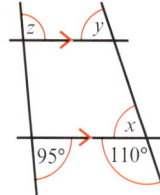

f

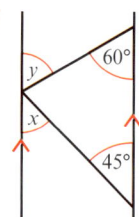

g

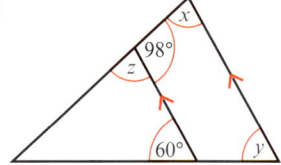

h

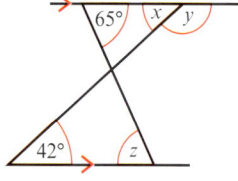

i

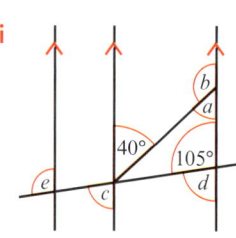

2   Decide whether $AB \parallel DC$ in each of these examples. Give a reason for your answer.

a

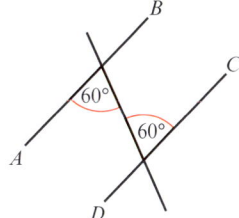

b

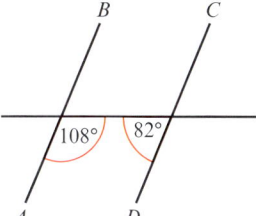

c

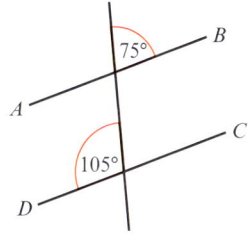

INVESTIGATION

General results

Mathematical reasoning doesn't always involve numbers. You can use letters and algebra to get results that will be true for any numbers. Results like these are called generalisations or proofs.

1   Work in pairs. Use your reasoning skills to answer these general questions.

    a   If $x + y = 180$, then $180 - x = [\ ]$?

    b   If $x + y = 180$, then $y = [\ ]$?

    c   If $y = 180 - x$ and $z = 180 - x$, what is y?

    d   If $x = y$ and $y = z$, what can you say about x and z?

2   How can you show in general terms that $x = y$ in each of these diagrams? Share your reasoning and proof with your group.

    a

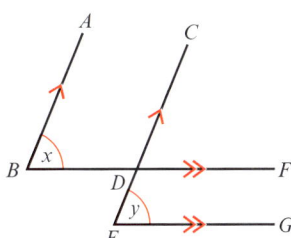

    b

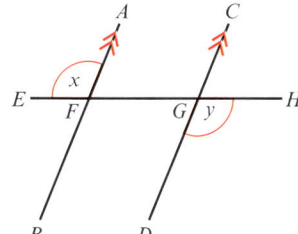

3.2 Triangles

A triangle is a plane shape with three sides and three angles.

Triangles are classified according to the lengths of their sides and the sizes of their angles (or both).

LINK

If you fix three straight sticks or rods together in a triangle it is not possible for the triangle to change its shape without breaking. This is why so many engineering structures use triangles for rigidity and strength.

Scalene triangle

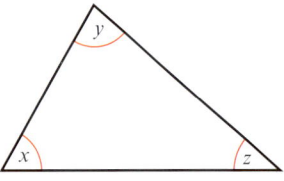

Scalene triangles have no sides of equal length and no angles that are of equal sizes.

Isosceles triangle

Isosceles triangles have two sides of equal length. The angles at the base of the equal sides are equal in size.

Equilateral triangle

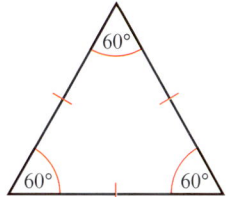

Equilateral triangles have three equal sides and three equal angles (each is 60°).

Other triangles

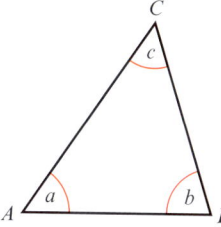

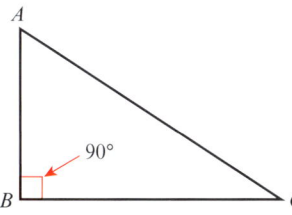

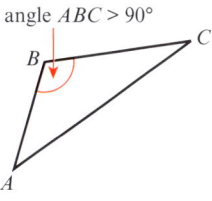

Acute-angled triangles have all angles <90°.

Right-angled triangles have one angle = 90°.

Obtuse-angled triangles have one angle >90°.

Angle properties of triangles

The three angles inside a triangle are called interior angles.

If you extend a side of a triangle you make another angle outside the triangle. Angles outside the triangle are called exterior angles.

Look at the following diagram carefully to see two important angle properties of triangles.

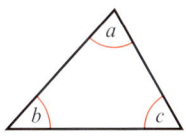

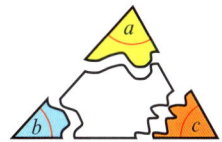

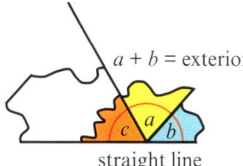

The diagram shows two things:

- the three interior angles of a triangle add up to 180°
- two interior angles of a triangle are equal to the opposite exterior angle.

If you try this yourself with any triangle you will get the same results. But why is this so? Mathematicians cannot just show things to be true, they have to prove them using mathematical principles. Read through the following two simple proofs that use the properties of angles you already know, to show that angles in a triangle will always add up to 180° and that the exterior angle will always equal the sum of the opposite interior angles.

Angles in a triangle add up to 180°

To prove this you can draw a line parallel to one side of the triangle.

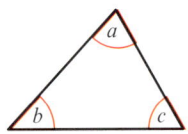 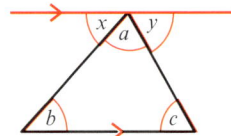

$x + a + y = 180°$ (angles on a line)

but:

$b = x$ and $c = y$ (alternate angles are equal)

so $a + b + c = 180°$

The exterior angle is equal to the sum of the opposite interior angles

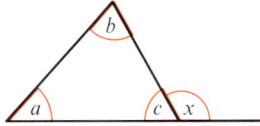

$c + x = 180°$ (angles on a line)

so, $c = 180° - x$

$a + b + c = 180°$ (angle sum of triangle)

$c = 180° - (a + b)$

so, $180° - (a + b) = 180° - x$

hence, $a + b = x$

These two properties allow you to find the missing angles in triangles and other diagrams involving triangles.

TIP

You don't need to know these proofs, but you do need to remember the rules associated with them.

MATHEMATICAL CONNECTIONS

Some of the algebraic processes used here are examples of the solutions to linear equations. You've done this before, but it is covered in more detail in Chapter 14.

WORKED EXAMPLE 5

Find the value of the unknown angles in each triangle. Give reasons for your answers.

Answers

a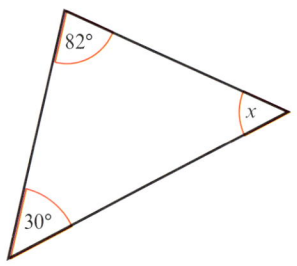

a $82° + 30° + x = 180°$ (angle sum of triangle)

$x = 180° - 82° - 30°$

$x = 68°$

b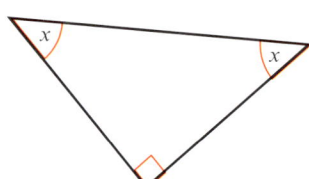

b $2x + 90° = 180°$ (angle sum of triangle)

$2x = 180° - 90°$

$2x = 90°$

$x = 45°$

WORKED EXAMPLE 5 CONTINUED

c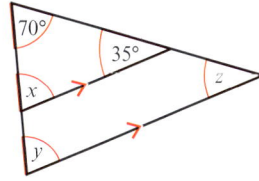

c $70° + 35° + x = 180°$ (angle sum of triangle)

$x = 180° − 105°$

$x = 75°$

$y = 75°$ (corresponding angles)

$70° + y + z = 180°$

$70° + 75° + z = 180°$ (angle sum of triangle)

$x = 180° − 75° − 70°$

$z = 35°$

or $z = 35°$ (corresponding angles)

MATHEMATICAL CONNECTIONS

Many questions on trigonometry require you to make calculations like the ones in Worked example 5 before you can move on to solve the problem.

WORKED EXAMPLE 6

Find the size of angle x, y and z.

Answers

a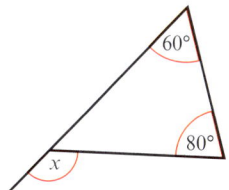

a $x = 60° + 80°$ (exterior angle of triangle)

$x = 140°$

b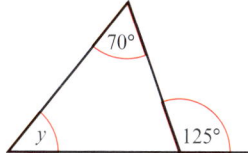

b $y + 70° = 125°$ (exterior angle of triangle)

$y = 125° − 70°$

$y = 55°$

c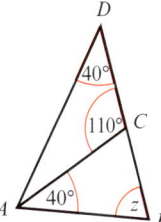

c $40° + z = 110°$ (exterior angle of triangle ABC)

$z = 110° − 40°$

$z = 70°$

> **TIP**
>
> The exterior angle of one triangle may be inside another triangle as in Worked example 6, part (c).

Worked examples 5 and 6 are straightforward, so you can see which rule applies. In most cases, you will be expected to apply these rules to find angles in more complicated diagrams. You will need to work out what the angle relationships are and combine them to find the solution.

WORKED EXAMPLE 7

Find the size of angle x.

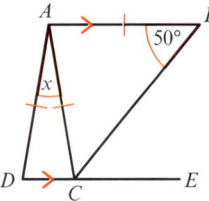

TIP

An isosceles triangle has two equal sides and two equal angles, so if you know that the triangle is isosceles you can mark the two angles at the bases of the equal sides as equal.

Answer

Angle ACB = 50°	(base angles isos triangle ABC)
∴ CAB = 180° − 50° − 50°	(angle sum of triangle ABC)
CAB = 80°	
Angle ACD = 80°	(alt angles)
∴ ADC = 80°	(base angles isos triangle ADC)
∴ x = 180° − 80° − 80°	(angle sum of triangle ADC)
x = 20°	

Exercise 3.5

1 Find the size of each marked angle. Give reasons.

a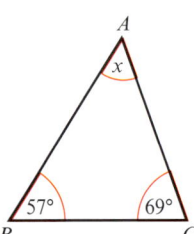

b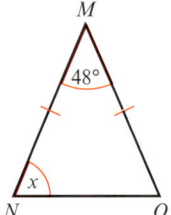

c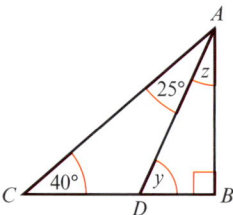

2 Calculate the value of x in each case. Give reasons.

a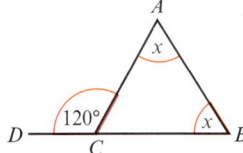

b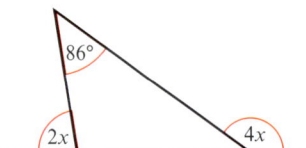

3 What is the size of the angle marked x in these figures? Show all steps and give reasons.

a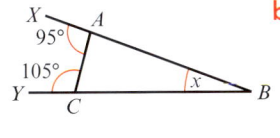

b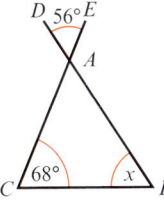

c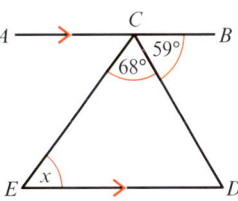

d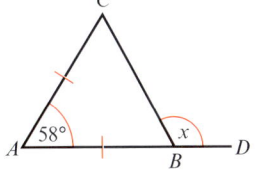

e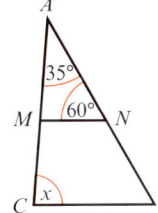

f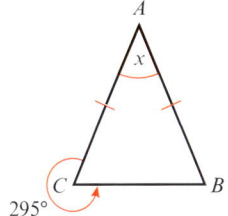

3.3 Quadrilaterals

Quadrilaterals are plane shapes with four sides and four interior angles. Quadrilaterals are named and classified according to their properties.

> **TIP**
>
> Some of these shapes are actually 'special cases' of others. For example, a square is also a rectangle because opposite sides are equal and parallel and all angles are 90°. Similarly, any rhombus is also a parallelogram. In both of these examples the converse is not true! A rectangle is not also a square. Which other special cases can you think of?

Type of quadrilateral	Examples	Summary of properties
Parallelogram		Opposite sides parallel and equal. Opposite angles are equal. Diagonals bisect each other.
Rectangle		Opposite sides parallel and equal. All angles = 90°. Diagonals are equal. Diagonals bisect each other.

Type of quadrilateral	Examples	Summary of properties
Square		All sides equal. All angles = 90°. Diagonals equal. Diagonals bisect each other at 90°. Diagonals bisect angles.
Rhombus	$a = c$ $b = d$	All sides equal in length. Opposite sides parallel. Opposite angles equal. Diagonals bisect each other at 90°. Diagonals bisect angles.
Trapezium		One pair of sides parallel.
Kite	$a = b$ $c = d$	Two pairs of adjacent sides equal. One pair of opposite angles is equal. Diagonals intersect at 90°.

TIP

Each diagonal on a square or rhombus is the perpendicular bisector of the other because they intersect at 90° and divide each other into two equal lengths.

The angle sum of a quadrilateral

All quadrilaterals can be divided into two triangles by drawing one diagonal.
You already know that the angle sum of a triangle is 180°. Therefore, the angle sum of a quadrilateral is 180° + 180° = 360°.

This is an important property and you can use it together with the other properties of quadrilaterals to find the sizes of unknown angles.

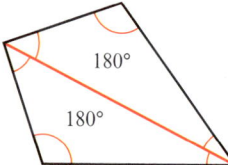
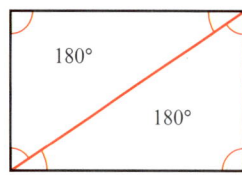
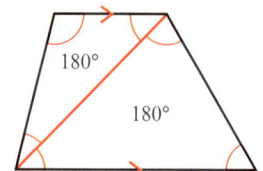

WORKED EXAMPLE 8

Find the size of each marked angle in each of these figures.

Answers

a Parallelogram

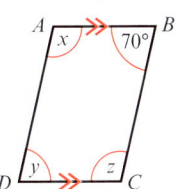

a $x = 110°$ (co-interior angles)

$y = 70°$ (opposite angles of ∥ gram)

$z = 110°$ (opposite angles of ∥ gram)

b Rectangle

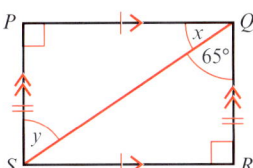

b $x + 65° = 90°$ (right angle of rectangle)

∴ $x = 90° - 65°$

$x = 25°$

$y = 65°$ (alt angles)

c Quadrilateral

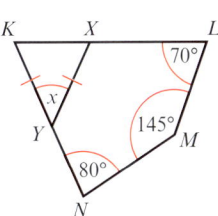

c Angle $XKY = 360° - 70° - 145° - 80°$ (angle sum of quad)

∴ Angle $XKY = 65°$

∴ $x = 180° - 65° - 65°$ (base angles isos triangle)

$x = 50°$ (angle sum of triangle KXY)

REFLECTION

When you are asked to calculate missing angles, there is often more than one way to do this.

How else could you find the unknown angles in Worked example 8?

Which way makes more sense to you? Why?

TIP

Another useful abbreviation is ∥ gram instead of parallelogram.

Exercise 3.6

1 A quadrilateral has two diagonals that intersect at right angles.

   a What quadrilaterals could it be?

   b The diagonals are not equal in length. What quadrilaterals could it NOT be?

2 Find the value of x in each of these figures. Give reasons.

a

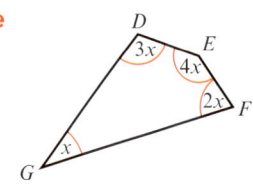

b

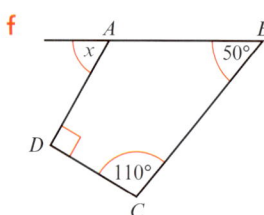

ABCD is a rectangle

c

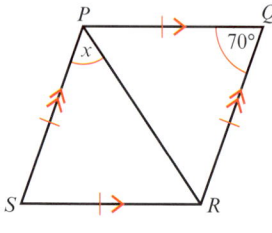

> **TIP**
>
> You may need to find some other unknown angles before you can find x. If you do this, write down the size of the angle that you have found and give a reason.

d

e

f

3 Find the value of x in each of these figures. Give reasons.

a

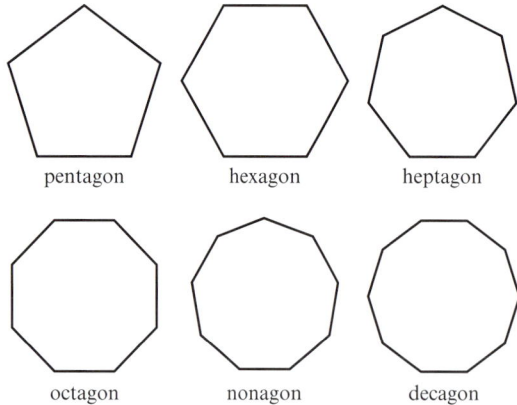

b

c

3.4 Polygons

A polygon is a plane shape with three or more straight sides. Triangles are polygons with three sides and quadrilaterals are polygons with four sides. Other polygons can also be named according to the number of sides they have. Make sure you know the names of these polygons:

pentagon   hexagon   heptagon

octagon   nonagon   decagon

A polygon with all its sides and all its angles equal is called a regular polygon.

If a polygon has any reflex angles, it is called a concave polygon.

All other polygons are convex polygons.

Angle sum of a polygon

By dividing polygons into triangles, you can work out the sum of their interior angles.

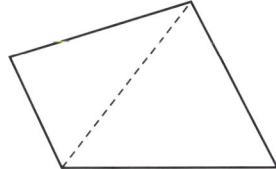 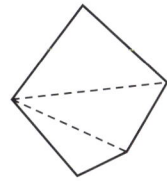 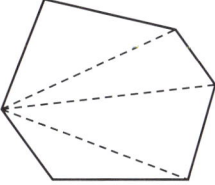

Can you see the pattern that is forming here?

The number of triangles you can divide the polygon into is always two less than the number of sides. If the number of sides is n, then the number of triangles in the polygon is $(n - 2)$.

The angle sum of the polygon is 180° × the number of triangles. So for any polygon, the angle sum can be worked out using the formula:

sum of interior angles = $(n - 2) \times 180°$

WORKED EXAMPLE 9

Find the angle sum of a decagon and state the size of each interior angle if the decagon is regular.

Answers

sum of interior angles	=	$(n - 2) \times 180°$	Sum of angles
	=	$(10 - 2) \times 180°$	A decagon has 10 sides, so $n = 10$.
	=	$1440°$	
	=	$\dfrac{1440}{10}$	A regular decagon has 10 equal angles.
	=	$144°$	Size of one angle.

WORKED EXAMPLE 10

A polygon has an angle sum of 2340°. How many sides does it have?

Answers

$2340°$	=	$(n - 2) \times 180°$	Put values into angle sum formula.
$\dfrac{2340}{180}$	=	$n - 2$	
13	=	$n - 2$	
$13 + 2$	=	n	Rearrange the formula to get n.
$\therefore 15$	=	n	So the polygon has 15 sides.

The sum of exterior angles of a convex polygon

The sum of the exterior angles of a convex polygon is always 360°, no matter how many sides it has. Read carefully through the following information about a hexagon to understand why this is true for every polygon.

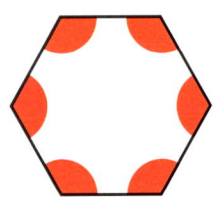

A hexagon has six interior angles.

The angle sum of the interior angles $\begin{aligned} &= (n-2) \times 180° \\ &= 4 \times 180° \\ &= 720° \end{aligned}$

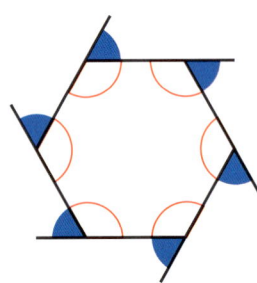

If you extend each side you make six exterior angles; one next to each interior angle.

Each pair of interior and exterior angles adds up to 180° (angles on line).

There are six vertices, so there are six pairs of interior and exterior angles that add up to 180°.

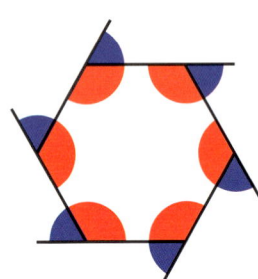

∴ sum of (interior + exterior angles) = 180° × 6

$= 1080°$

But, sum of interior angles = 720°

So, 720° + sum of exterior angles = 1080°

sum of exterior angles = 1080° − 720°

sum of exterior angles = 360°

This can be expressed as a general rule like this:

If I = sum of the interior angles, E = sum of the exterior angles and n = number of sides of the polygon

$I + E = 180n$

$E = 180n - I$

but $I = (n-2) \times 180$

so $E = 180n - (n-2) \times 180$

$\quad E = 180n - 180n + 360$

$\quad E = 360°$

TIP

You do not have to remember this proof, but you must remember that the sum of the exterior angles of any convex polygon is 360°.

Exercise 3.7

1   Copy and complete this table.

Number of sides in the polygon	5	6	7	8	9	10	12	20
Angle sum of interior angles								

2   Find the size of one interior angle for each of the following regular polygons.

  a   pentagon   **b**   hexagon

  c   octagon   **d**   decagon

  e   dodecagon (12 sides)   **f**   a 25-sided polygon

> **TIP**
>
> A regular polygon has all sides equal and all angles equal. An irregular polygon does not have all equal sides and angles.

3   A regular polygon has 15 sides. Find:

  a   the sum of the interior angles   **b**   the sum of the exterior angles

  c   the size of each interior angle   **d**   the size of each exterior angle.

4   A regular polygon has n exterior angles of 15°. How many sides does it have?

5   Find the value of x in each of these irregular polygons.

  a 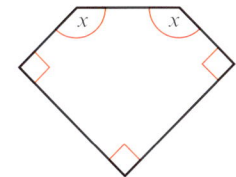   **b** 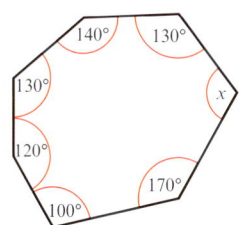   **c**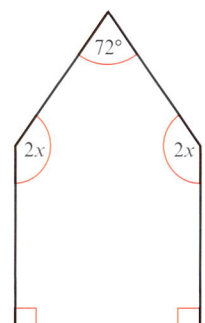

> **TIP**
>
> The rule for the sum of interior angles, and for the sum of exterior angles is true for both regular and irregular polygons. But with irregular polygons, you can't simply divide the sum of the interior angles by the number of sides to find the size of an interior angle: all interior angles may be different.

3.5 Circles

In mathematics, a circle is defined as a set of points which are all the same distance from a given fixed point. In other words, every point on the outside curved line around a circle is the same distance from the centre of the circle.

> **LINK**
>
> The shortest route between any two points on the surface of the Earth is part of a circle which has a centre at the centre of the Earth. These circles are called 'great circles'. If you find a globe and look at the cities of Brasilia and Copenhagen, try to trace what you think will be the shortest route between the two. Can you image the circle you are tracing? Airliners often fly along great circles, to make the distance travelled as short as possible.

Parts of a circle

Study the following diagrams carefully and then work through Exercise 3.8 to make sure you know and can use the names of circle parts correctly.

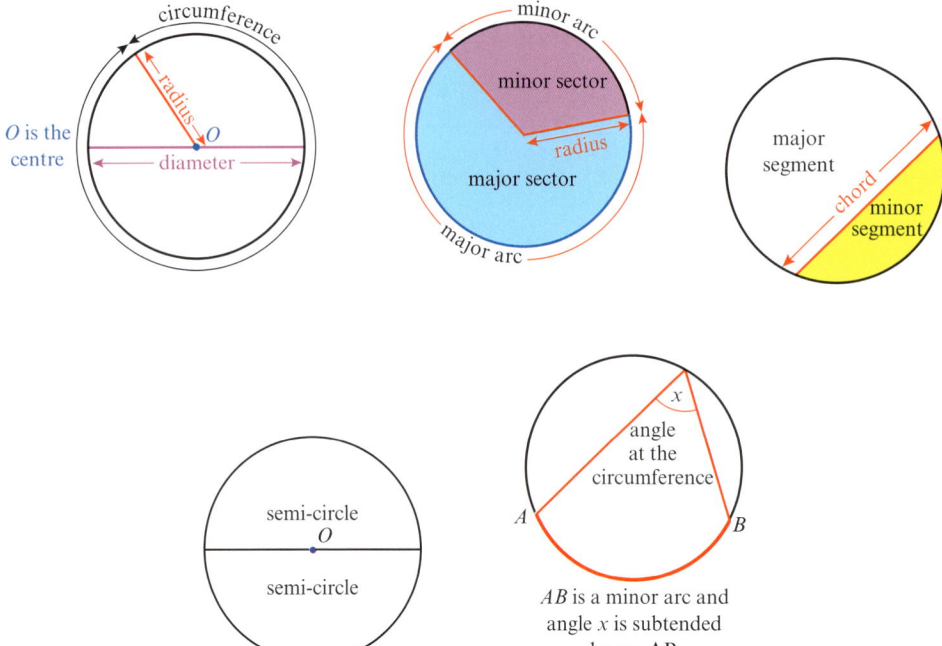

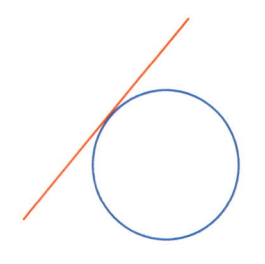

TIP

A line outside the circle that touches the circumference at just one point is called a tangent.

TIP

The angle x is subtended at the circumference. This means that it is the angle formed by two chords passing through the end points of the arc and meeting again at the edge of the circle.

Exercise 3.8

1   Name the circle parts shown in blue on these circles.

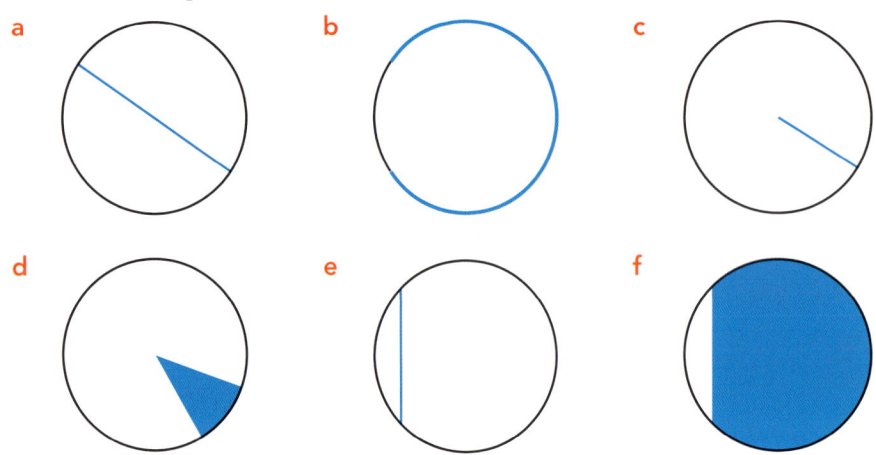

2 Draw four small circles. Use shading to show:

   a   a semi-circle

   b   a minor segment

   c   a tangent to the circle

   d   angle y subtended by a minor arc *MN*.

3 Circle 1 and circle 2 have the same centre (*O*). Use the correct terms or letters to copy and complete each statement.

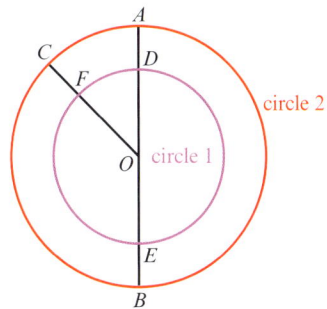

   a   *OB* is a __ of circle 2.

   b   *DE* is the __ of circle 1.

   c   *AC* is a __ of circle 2.

   d   __ is a radius of circle 1.

   e   *CAB* is a __ of circle 2.

   f   Angle *FOD* is the vertex of a __ of circle 1 and circle 2.

> **LINK**
>
> Look at the wheel of a bicycle as it travels along the road. You can see that the road forms a tangent to the circular wheel at all times.

> **TIP**
>
> The plural of radius is radii.

> **MATHEMATICAL CONNECTIONS**
>
> You will learn more about circles and the angle properties in circles when you deal with circle symmetry and circle theorems in Chapter 19.

3.6 Construction

In geometry, constructions are accurate geometrical drawings. You use mathematical instruments to construct geometrical drawings.

Using a ruler and a pair of compasses

A ruler (sometimes called a straight edge) and a pair of compasses are the most useful construction tools. You use the ruler to draw straight lines and the pair of compasses to measure and mark lengths, draw circles and construct triangles.

TIP

It is important that you use a sharp pencil and that your pair of compasses are tightened.

TIP

Once you can use a ruler and pair of compasses to measure and draw lines, you can construct triangles and other geometric shapes.

When you want to measure very accurately, you can use a pair of compasses to mark a given length. This method of drawing lines is useful in geometric construction.
This example shows how to construct line AB that is 4.5 cm long. (Because of printing, the following diagrams are NOT TO SCALE.)

- Use a ruler and sharp pencil to draw a straight line longer than the length you need. Mark point A on the line with a short vertical dash (or a dot).

- Open your pair of compasses to 4.5 cm by measuring against a ruler.

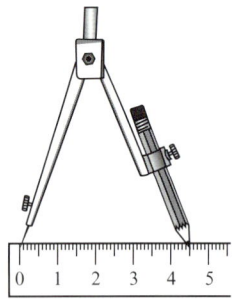

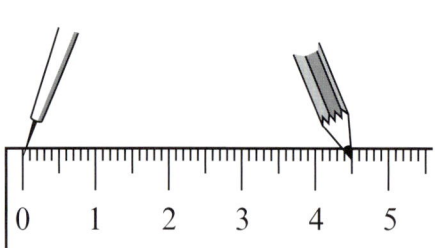

- Put the point of the pair of compasses on point A. Twist the pair of compasses lightly to draw a short arc on the line at 4.5 cm. Mark this as point B. You have now drawn the line AB at 4.5 cm long.

Constructing triangles

You can construct an accurate triangle if you know the length of three sides.

WORKED EXAMPLE 11

Construct triangle ABC with $AB = 5$ cm, $BC = 6$ cm and $CA = 4$ cm.

Answers

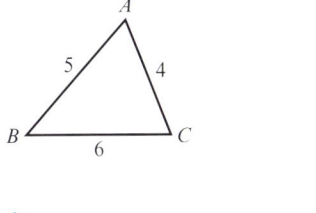

Always start with a rough sketch.

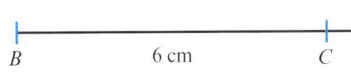

Draw the longest side ($BC = 6$ cm) and label it.

Set your pair of compasses at 5 cm. Place the point on B and draw an arc.

Set your pair of compasses at 4 cm. Place the point on C and draw an arc.

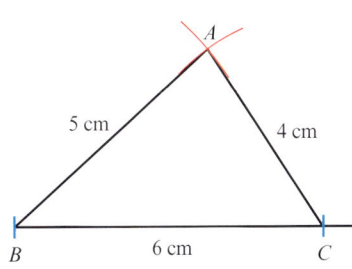

The point where the arcs cross is A. Join BA and CA.

> **TIP**
>
> It is a good idea to draw the line longer than you need it and then measure the correct length along it. When constructing a shape, it can help to mark points with a thin line to make it easier to place the point of the pair of compasses.

> **TIP**
>
> Note that these diagrams are NOT TO SCALE but when you are asked to construct a triangle, you must use the accurate measurements!

Exercise 3.9

1 Construct these lines.

   a $AB = 6\,\text{cm}$ **b** $CD = 75\,\text{mm}$ **c** $EF = 5.5\,\text{cm}$

2 Accurately construct these triangles.

   a 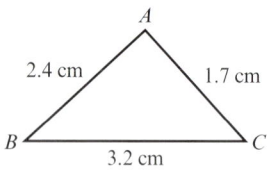   **b** 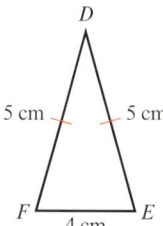   **c**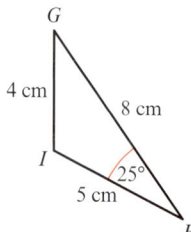

3 Construct these triangles.

   a   Triangle ABC with $BC = 8.5\,\text{cm}$, $AB = 7.2\,\text{cm}$ and $AC = 6.9\,\text{cm}$.

   b   Triangle XYZ with $YZ = 86\,\text{mm}$, $XY = 120\,\text{mm}$ and $XZ = 66\,\text{mm}$.

   c   Equilateral triangle DEF with sides of $6.5\,\text{cm}$.

   d   Isosceles triangle PQR with a base of $4\,\text{cm}$ and $PQ = PR = 6.5\,\text{cm}$.

4 The diagram shows a rough sketch for a logo design. AE and CE are straight lines and $AD = 8\,\text{cm}$.

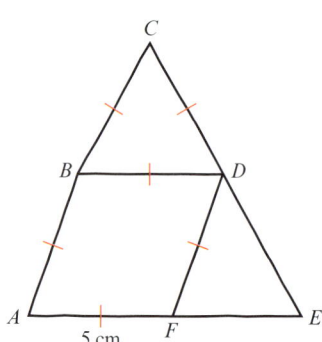

   a   Construct an accurate drawing using a ruler and a pair of compasses.

   b   Measure your diagram to find these lengths, to 1 decimal place.

      i   DE   **ii**   EF

REFLECTION

Read this statement about learning:

'The best way to learn something is to do it.'

a   Describe your experience of learning to construct accurate sketches.

b   What did you like best and what did you like least about the practical drawing work? Why?

c   Is the statement about learning true for you in the context of drawing accurate diagrams?

d   Is it true for you generally? Explain why or why not.

SELF ASSESSMENT

What criteria could you use to assess how successful your learning was in this chapter?

Success criteria describe how you will know when you have learnt something. They help you decide whether you have achieved the learning intentions for this chapter or not.

1   Draw a table like this one:

Success criteria	Evidence of success	Improvements

TIP

Success criteria are sometimes called 'what I'm looking for'.

2   Look back at the learning intentions at the start of this chapter. Use these to develop a list of criteria that you can use to decide whether you have met the learning intentions. For example:

I know all the key words and their meanings and I use them in my work.

3   Once you have your list, check your work against the success criteria.
   - Place a tick (✓) in the second column if you can find evidence that you have met each one. (You are looking for how your work shows you have achieved the criteria.)
   - If you cannot find evidence, write down what you can do to improve in that particular area.

4   Make any improvements that you need to over the next few days and then reassess your work using the same criteria.

SUMMARY

Do you know …?
A point is position and a line is the shortest distance between two points.
Parallel lines are the same distance apart along their length.
Perpendicular lines meet at right angles.
Acute angles are <90°, right angles are exactly 90°, obtuse angles are >90° but <180°. Straight angles are exactly 180°. Reflex angles are >180° but <360°. A complete revolution is 360°.
Scalene triangles have no equal sides, isosceles triangles have two equal sides and a pair of equal angles, and equilateral triangles have three equal sides and three equal angles.
Complementary angles have a sum of 90°. Supplementary angles have a sum of 180°.
Angles on a line have a sum of 180°.
Angles round a point have a sum of 360°.
Vertically opposite angles are formed when two lines intersect. Vertically opposite angles are equal.

SUMMARY CONTINUED

Do you know …?
When a transversal cuts two parallel lines various angle pairs are formed. Corresponding angles are equal. Alternate angles are equal. Co-interior angles are supplementary.
The angle sum of a triangle is 180°.
The exterior angle of a triangle is equal to the sum of the two opposite interior angles.
Quadrilaterals can be classified as parallelograms, rectangles, squares, rhombuses, trapeziums or kites according to their properties.
The angle sum of a quadrilateral is 360°.
Polygons are many-sided plane shapes. Polygons are named according to the number of sides they have, e.g. pentagon (5), hexagon (6), octagon (8) and decagon (10).
Regular polygons have equal sides and equal angles.
Irregular polygons have unequal sides and unequal angles.
The angle sum of a polygon is $(n - 2) \times 180°$, where n is the number of sides.
The angle sum of exterior angles of any convex polygon is 360°.

Are you able to …?
calculate unknown angles on a line and round a point
calculate unknown angles using vertically opposite angles and the angle relationships associated with parallel lines
calculate unknown angles using the angle properties of triangles, quadrilaterals and polygons
accurately measure and construct lines and angles
construct a triangle using given measurements.

Practice questions

1   a   Measure this line and construct AB the same length in your book using a ruler and compasses.   [3]

A _____ B

   b   At point A, measure and draw angle BAC, a 75° angle.   [2]

   c   At point B, measure and draw angle ABD, an angle of 125°.   [2]

2   Determine x in each figure. Give reasons.

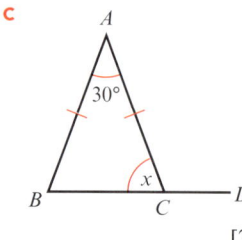

a   b   c

[3]   [2]   [2]

d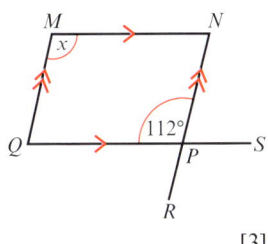

e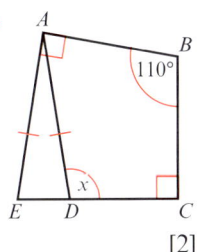

f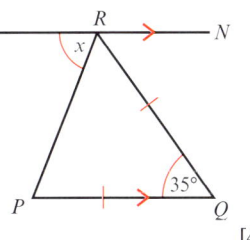

[3]   [2]   [4]

3   Study the triangle.

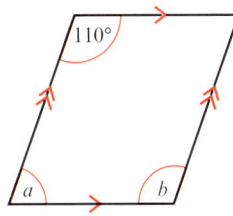

a   Explain why $x + y = 90°$.   [2]

b   Find y if $x = 37°$.   [1]

4   Calculate angles a, b and c.

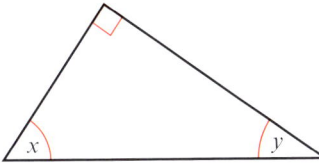

[4]

5   What is the sum of interior angles of a regular hexagon?   [4]

6   Prove that angle $NMQ = 3 ×$ angle MQN.

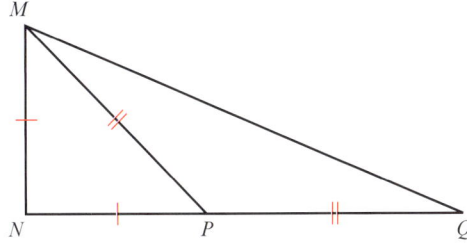

[4]

7   **a**   Find the sum of exterior angles of a convex regular polygon with 15 sides.   [4]

b   Determine the size of each exterior angle in this polygon.   [2]

c   Calculate the size of each interior angle.   [1]

8   Explain why $x = y$ in the following figures.

a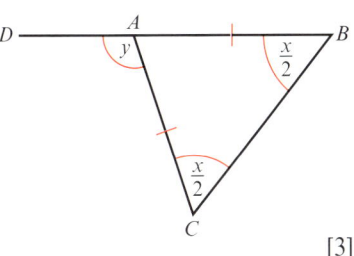

b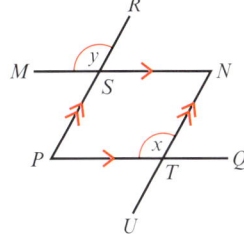

[3]   [3]

9 Construct triangle PQR with sides $PQ = 4.5\,\text{cm}$, $QR = 5\,\text{cm}$ and $PR = 7\,\text{cm}$. [3]

10 a Construct a triangle with sizes of length $5\,\text{cm}$, $7\,\text{cm}$ and $9\,\text{cm}$. [3]

    b Construct the perpendicular bisector of each of the three sides. What do you notice? [3]

    c Draw a circle with its centre at the point where the lines intersect and passing through each vertex of the triangle. [3]

    d Construct a different triangle and repeat **b** and **c** above. What do you notice? [3]

11 The sum of the interior angles of a convex polygon is 5400°. Work out how many sides the polygon has. [3]

12 The diagram shows a regular pentagon $ABCDE$.

    a Find x. [3]   **b** Find y. [3]

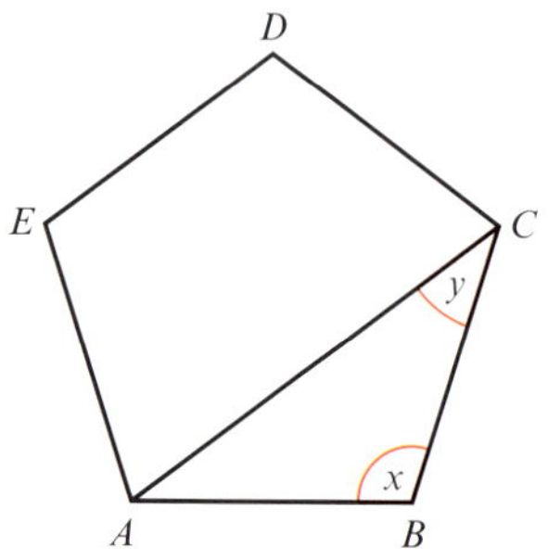

13 Regular polygon A has 10 sides and exterior angle $3x$. Regular polygon B has exterior angle $\frac{5}{3}x$.

Work out the number of sides polygon B has. [5]

14 The diagram shows a triangle and two parallel lines.

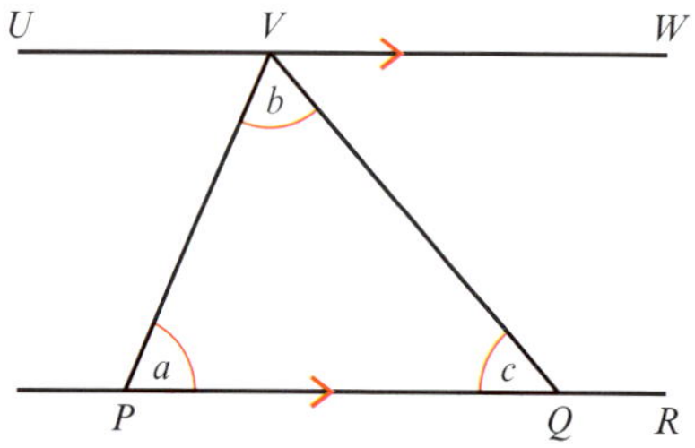

    a Write down angles UVP and WVQ in terms of a and c. Give reasons for your answers. [2]

    b Use your answer to **a** to prove that the sum of the interior angles of a triangle is 180 degrees. [3]

    c Write down the exterior angle RQV in terms of c. [1]

    d Use your answers to **b** and **c** to show that the exterior angle of a triangle is equal to the sum of the two opposite interior angles. [2]

SELF ASSESSMENT

Answer these questions about your work.

Did you…

- choose the right methods and strategies?
- show how you arrived at your solutions?
- give reasons for any statements you made?

> Chapter 4

Collecting, organising and displaying data

People collect information for many different reasons. With the right information we can answer questions, make decisions, predict what will happen in the future, compare ourselves with others and understand how things affect our lives. A scientist might collect information from experiments or tests to find out how well a new vaccine is working. A business owner might collect data from surveys to find out how well the business is performing. A teacher might collect test scores to see how well the students perform in an examination and an individual might collect data from magazines or the internet to decide which brand of shoes, jeans, phone or car to buy. The branch of mathematics that deals with collecting data is called statistics. In this chapter, you will focus on asking questions and then collecting information and organising or displaying it so that you can answer questions.

KEY WORDS

categorical data
class interval
continuous data
discrete data
numerical data
qualitative data
quantitative data
stem-and-leaf diagram
two-way table

GETTING STARTED

1   The person in the photo is doing a survey to find out whether people in a village know what health services are available to them. What other methods can you think of to collect data?

2   Look at these four graphs carefully. For each one, discuss:
   a   what the graph shows
   b   how you interpret and make sense of the data shown
   c   when each type of graph is useful and what type of data is suited to each graph
   d   how each type of graph can give a misleading or wrong impression of the data.

Number of gold medals

United States	●●●●●●●●●●●●◗
China	●●●●●●●●●◖
Russia	●●●●●●
Great Britain	●●●●●●◖
Germany	●●◖

Key	
●	= 4 Medals

GETTING STARTED CONTINUED

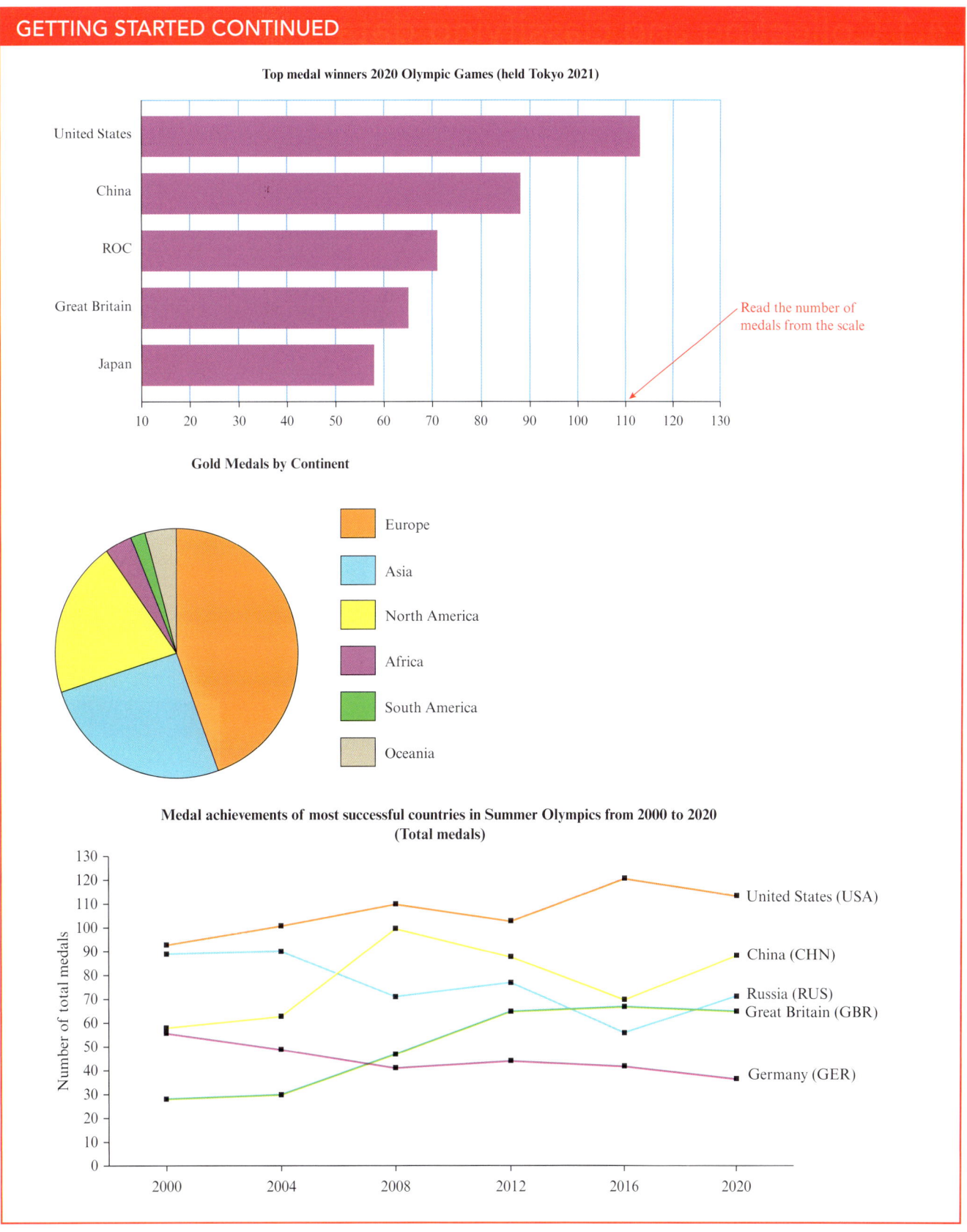

Top medal winners 2020 Olympic Games (held Tokyo 2021)

Read the number of medals from the scale

Gold Medals by Continent

- Europe
- Asia
- North America
- Africa
- South America
- Oceania

**Medal achievements of most successful countries in Summer Olympics from 2000 to 2020
(Total medals)**

Number of total medals

United States (USA)

China (CHN)

Russia (RUS)
Great Britain (GBR)

Germany (GER)

4.1 Collecting and classifying data

Data is a set of facts, numbers or other information. Statistics involves a process of collecting data and using it to try and answer a question. The flow diagram shows the four main steps involved in this process of statistical investigation:

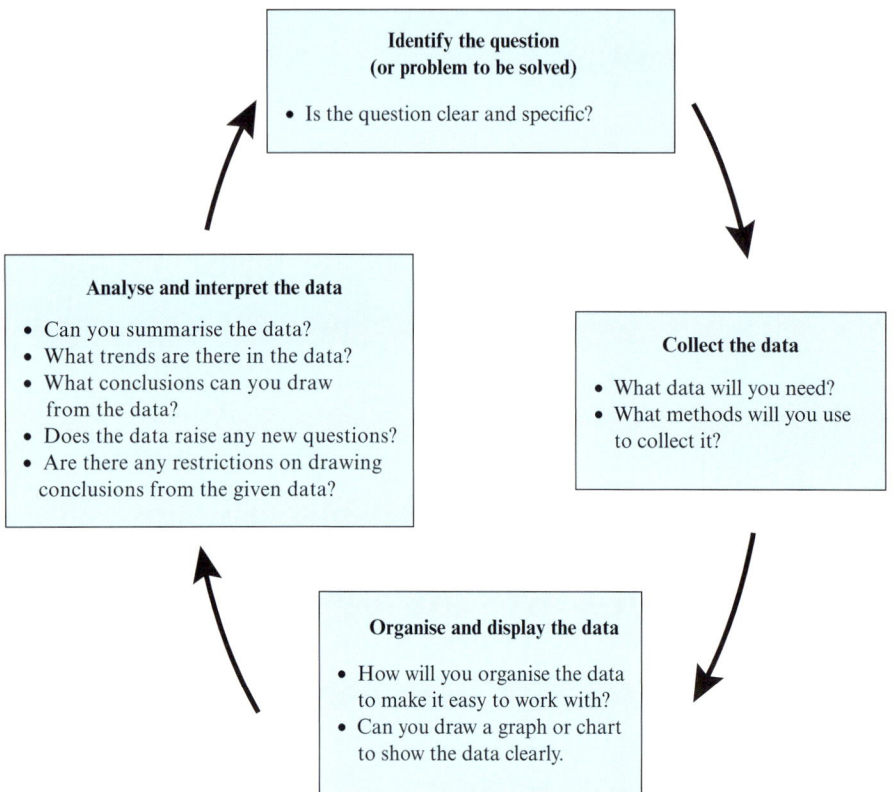

Identify the question (or problem to be solved)
- Is the question clear and specific?

Collect the data
- What data will you need?
- What methods will you use to collect it?

Organise and display the data
- How will you organise the data to make it easy to work with?
- Can you draw a graph or chart to show the data clearly.

Analyse and interpret the data
- Can you summarise the data?
- What trends are there in the data?
- What conclusions can you draw from the data?
- Does the data raise any new questions?
- Are there any restrictions on drawing conclusions from the given data?

Different types of data

Answer these two questions:
- Who is your favourite singer?
- How many people in your class wear glasses?

Your answer to the first question will be the name of a person. Your answer to the second question will be a number. Both the name and the number are types of data.

Categorical data is non-numerical data. It names or describes something without reference to number or size. Colours, names of people and places, yes and no answers, opinions and choices are all categorical. Categorical data is also called **qualitative data**.

Numerical data is data in number form. It can be an amount, a measurement, a time or a score. Numerical data is also called **quantitative data** (from the word quantity).

TIP

Data is actually the plural of the Latin word datum, but in modern English the word data is accepted and used as a singular form, so you can talk about a set of data, this data, two items of data or a lot of data.

TIP

The information that is stored on a computer hard-drive or your phone is also called data. In computer terms, data has nothing to do with statistics, it just means stored information.

LINK

All of this work is very important in the fields of human and social sciences, where scientists need to present data to inform their conclusions.

Numerical data can be further divided into two groups:

- **discrete data** – this is data that can only take certain values, for example, the number of students in a class, goals scored in a match or red cars passing a point. When you count things, you are collecting discrete data.

- **continuous data** – this is data that can take any value between two given values, for example, the height of a person who is between 1.5 m and 1.6 m tall could be 1.5 m, 1.57 m, 1.5793 m, 1.5793421 m or any other value between 1.5 m and 1.6 m depending on the degree of accuracy used. Heights, masses, distances and temperatures are all examples of continuous data. You normally collect continuous data by measuring.

> **LINK**
>
> Geographers and biologists use both discrete and continuous data. For example, they measure temperature or rainfall using continuous scales, but counting discrete numbers of people or animals in a particular place at a particular time.

> **TIP**
>
> One way to decide if data is continuous is to ask whether it is possible for the values to be fractions or decimals. If the answer is yes, the data is usually continuous. But be careful:
>
> - age may seem to be discrete, because it is often given in full years, but it is actually continuous because we are getting older all the time
> - shoe sizes are discrete, even though you can get shoes in half sizes, because you don't get shoes in size $7\frac{1}{4}$ or $7\frac{3}{4}$ or $7\frac{8}{9}$.

> **MATHEMATICAL CONNECTIONS**
>
> You will need to fully understand continuous data when you study histograms in Chapter 20.

Methods of collecting data

Data can be collected from primary sources by doing surveys or interviews, by asking people to complete questionnaires, by doing experiments or by counting and measuring. Data from primary sources is known as primary data.

Data can also be collected from secondary sources. This involves using existing data to find the information you need. For example, if you use data from an internet site or even from the pages of this book to help answer a question, to you this is a secondary source. Data from secondary sources is known as secondary data.

Exercise 4.1

1   Draw a table like this one.

Categorical data	Numerical data
Hair colour	*Number of people in household*

  a   Add five examples of categorical data and five examples of numerical data that could be collected about each student in your class.

  b   Look at the numerical examples in your table. Circle any that will give discrete data.

2   State whether the following data is discrete or continuous.

   a   Mass of each animal in a herd.

   b   Number of animals per household.

   c   Time taken to travel to school.

   d   Volume of water evaporating from a dam.

   e   Number of correct answers in a spelling test.

   f   Distance people travel to work.

   g   Foot length of each student in a class.

   h   Shoe size of each student in a class.

   i   Head circumference of new-born babies.

   j   Number of children per family.

   k   Number of TV programmes watched in the last month.

   l   Number of cars crossing a bridge per hour.

LINK

In 2021, a leading college foundation in the United States identified 'data scientist' as an important job with good prospects – the projected growth rate of jobs in this field is 16% (more than triple the 5% national growth rate for jobs in other fields). The use of computers in data collection and processing means that data collection, display and analysis have become more and more important to business and other organisations.

Stanford University is working with schools and education authorities to build data science into the maths curriculum at all levels. Their point of view is that this is much more important maths than many of the other traditional things taught in schools.

---

3   For each of the following questions state:

   i   one method you could use to collect the data

   ii   whether the source of the data is primary or secondary

   iii whether the data is categorical or numerical

   iv   for the numerical data, whether it is discrete or continuous.

   a   How many times will you get heads if you toss a coin 100 times?

   b   Which is the most popular TV show among your classmates?

   c   What are the lengths of the ten longest rivers in the world?

   d   What is the favourite sport of students in your school?

   e   How many books are taken out per week from the school library?

   f   Is it more expensive to drive to work than to use public transport?

   g   Is there a connection between shoe size and height?

   h   What is the most popular colour of car?

   i   What is the batting average of the national cricket team this season?

   j   How many pieces of fruit do you eat in a week?

4.2 Organising data

When you collect a large amount of data you need to organise it so that it is easy to read and use. Tables (tally tables, frequency tables and two-way tables) are the most commonly used methods of organising data.

Tally tables

A tally table is used to keep a record when you count things.

> **TIP**
>
> Remember each tally (|) shows one item. Tallies are grouped in fives (||||) to make it easier to get a total when you need one.

MATHEMATICAL CONNECTIONS

You will use and extend these methods of organising data in later chapters. Make sure that you understand them now.

WORKED EXAMPLE 1

Aisha wanted to find out what people thought about pop-up adverts on their social media feeds. She did a survey of 100 people. Each person chose an answer A, B C or D.

What do you think about this statement? Please choose one response.

Advertising should be strictly controlled on social media. Pop-up adverts should be banned from all social media feeds.

A   I strongly agree

B   I agree

C   I disagree

D   I strongly disagree

Aisha recorded these results:

A	B	A	C	A	C	C	D	A	C
C	C	D	A	D	D	C	C	C	A
B	B	A	C	D	B	B	A	C	C
A	B	C	A	D	B	C	D	A	B
A	C	C	D	A	C	C	C	D	A
D	D	C	C	C	A	B	B	A	C
D	C	C	D	A	C	A	B	D	B
C	C	D	A	D	D	C	C	C	A
B	B	A	C	D	B	B	C	C	C
A	B	C	A	D	B	C	D	A	B

a   Draw a tally table to organise the results.

b   What do the results of her survey suggest people think about pop-up advertising on social media?

WORKED EXAMPLE 1 CONTINUED

Answers

a

Response	Tally
A	卌 卌 卌 卌 IIII
B	卌 卌 卌 IIII
C	卌 卌 卌 卌 卌 卌 卌 II
D	卌 卌 卌 卌

Count each letter. Make a tally each time you count one.

It may help to cross the letters off the list as you count them.

Check that your tallies add up to 100 to make sure you have included all the scores. (It is more efficient to work across the rows or down the columns, putting a tally into the correct row in your table, rather than counting one letter at a time.)

b The results suggest that people generally don't think advertising should be banned on social media. 57 people disagreed or strongly disagreed. Only 24 of the 100 people strongly agreed with Aisha's statement.

By giving people a very definite statement and asking them to respond to it, Aisha has shown her own bias and that could affect the results of her survey. It is quite possible that people think some control is necessary, but not that adverts should be banned completely. However, they don't have that as an option when they answer. The people in the sample could also affect the responses, so Aisha will have to carefully consider any conclusions from this survey.

> **MATHEMATICAL CONNECTIONS**
>
> You will deal with restrictions on drawing conclusions in more detail in Chapter 12.

Exercise 4.2

1 Balsem recorded how many students left the classroom during a lesson for 50 lessons. Draw a tally table to organise this data.

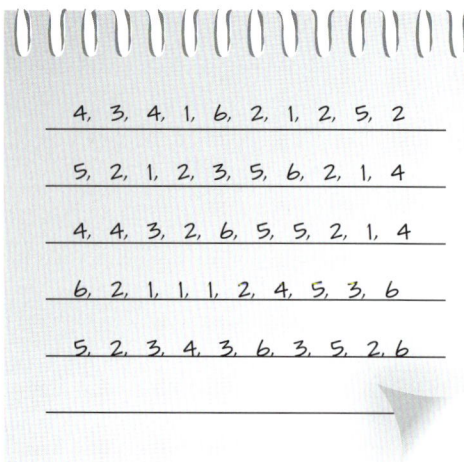

4, 3, 4, 1, 6, 2, 1, 2, 5, 2

5, 2, 1, 2, 3, 5, 6, 2, 1, 4

4, 4, 3, 2, 6, 5, 5, 2, 1, 4

6, 2, 1, 1, 1, 2, 4, 5, 3, 6

5, 2, 3, 4, 3, 6, 3, 5, 2, 6

2   Do a quick survey among your class to find out how many hours each person usually spends doing their homework each day. Draw your own tally table to record and organise your data.

3   Faizel threw two dice together 250 times and recorded the score he got using a tally table.

Score	Tally
2	IIII II
3	IIII IIII IIII
4	IIII IIII IIII IIII III
5	IIII IIII IIII IIII IIII IIII
6	IIII IIII IIII IIII IIII IIII III
7	IIII IIII IIII IIII IIII IIII IIII IIII I
8	IIII IIII IIII IIII IIII IIII IIII
9	IIII IIII IIII IIII IIII III
10	IIII IIII IIII IIII I
11	IIII IIII II
12	IIII I

a   Which score occurred most often?

b   Which two scores occurred least often?

c   Why do you think Faizel left out the score of one?

d   Why do you think he scored six, seven and eight so many times?

Frequency tables

A frequency table shows the totals of the tally marks. Some frequency tables include the tallies.

This frequency table shows the number of cars there were of each colour in a car park. It has a column for tallies and another column for the totals (frequencies) of the tallies.

Colour	Number of cars	Frequency
White	IIII IIII III	13
Red	IIII IIII IIII IIII I	21
Black	IIII IIII IIII IIII IIII IIII IIII II	37
Blue	IIII IIII IIII IIII IIII II	27
Silver	IIII IIII IIII IIII IIII IIII IIII IIII III	43
Green	IIII IIII IIII I	16
	Total	157

> **TIP**
>
> The frequency column tells you how often (how frequently) each result appears in the data.

The frequency table has space to write a total at the bottom of the frequency column. This helps you to know how many pieces of data were collected. In this example the student recorded the colours of 157 cars.

Most frequency tables will not include tally marks. Here is a frequency table without tallies. It was created by the staff at a clinic to record how many people were treated for different diseases in one week.

Illness	Frequency
Diabetes	30
HIV/AIDS	40
Tuberculosis (TB)	60
Other	50
Total	180

TIP

This data suggests that TB is the most common illness at this clinic. However, this does not mean that TB is the most common illness in the community. This data could have been collected during a week where there was a special TB clinic or when patients collected their medication. You need to think carefully about data and what you can or cannot conclude from it.

Grouping data in class intervals

Numerical data can be recorded in different groups. For example, if you collected test results for 40 students you might find that students scored between 40 and 84 (out of 100). If you recorded each individual score (and they could all be different) you would get a very large frequency table that is difficult to manage. To simplify things, you can arrange the collected data in groups called class intervals. A frequency table with results arranged in class intervals is called a grouped frequency table. Look at this example:

Points scored	Frequency
40–44	7
45–49	3
50–54	3
55–59	3
60–64	0
65–69	5
70–74	3
75–90	7
80–84	9
Total	40

The range of scores (40–84) has been divided into class intervals. Notice that the class intervals do not overlap so it is clear which data goes in what class.

MATHEMATICAL CONNECTIONS

You will use tables like these to construct bar charts and histograms. These diagrams give a clear, visual impression of the data.

Exercise 4.3

1   Sheldon did a survey to find out how many coins the students in a class had in their pockets or purses. These are the results:

0	2	3	1	4	6	3	6	7	2
1	2	4	0	0	6	5	4	8	2
6	3	2	0	0	0	2	4	3	5

a   Copy this frequency table and use it to organise Sheldon's data.

Number of coins	0	1	2	3	4	5	6	7	8
Frequency									

b   What is the highest number of coins that any person had?

c   How many people had only one coin?

d   What is the most common number of coins that people had?

e   How many people did Sheldon survey altogether? How could you show this on the frequency table?

2   Barkha works in a fast-food restaurant. These are the amounts (in dollars) spent by 25 customers during one shift.

43.55	4.45	17.60	25.95	3.75
12.35	55.00	12.90	35.95	16.25
25.05	2.50	29.35	12.90	8.70
12.50	13.95	6.50	39.40	22.55
20.45	4.50	5.30	15.95	10.50

a   Copy and complete this grouped frequency table to organise the data.

Amount ($)	0–9.99	10–19.99	20–29.99	30–39.99	40–49.99	50–59.99
Frequency						

b   How many people spent less than $20.00?

c   How many people spent more than $50.00?

d   What is the most common amount that people spent during Barkha's shift?

> **TIP**
>
> Note that currency (money) is discrete data because when you are paying for an item in dollars you cannot use a coin smaller than one cent.

3   Li records the length in minutes and whole seconds of each phone call he makes during one day. These are the results:

3 min 29 s	4 min 12 s	4 min 15 s	1 min 29 s	2 min 45 s
1 min 32 s	1 min 09 s	2 min 50 s	3 min 15 s	4 min 03 s
3 min 04 s	5 min 12 s	5 min 45 s	3 min 29 s	2 min 09 s
1 min 12 s	4 min 15 s	3 min 45 s	3 min 59 s	5 min 01 s

Use a grouped frequency table to organise the data.

Stem-and-leaf diagrams

A **stem-and-leaf diagram** allows you to organise and display grouped data using the actual data values. When you use a frequency table to organise grouped data you cannot see the actual data values, just the number of data items in each group. Stem-and-leaf diagrams are useful because when you keep the actual values, you can calculate the range and averages for the data.

> ### MATHEMATICAL CONNECTIONS
>
> You will work with stem-and-leaf diagrams again when you calculate averages and measures of spread in Chapter 12.

> ### LINK
>
> Sociologists and geographers sometimes draw population pyramids. These are sideways bar charts that show the numbers of people in various age categories. These charts look similar to stem-and-leaf diagrams.

In a stem-and-leaf diagram each data item is broken into two parts: a stem and a leaf. The final digit of each value is the leaf and the previous digits are the stem. The stems are written to the left of a vertical line and the leaves are written to the right of the vertical line. For example, a score of 13 is shown as:

Stem	Leaf
1	3

In this case, the tens digit is the stem and the units digit is the leaf.

A larger data value such as 259 is shown as:

Stem	Leaf
25	9

In this case, the stem represents both the tens and the hundreds digits while the units digit is the leaf.

To be useful, a stem-and-leaf diagram should have at least five stems. If the number of stems is less than that, you can split the leaves into two (or sometimes even five) classes. If you do this, each stem is listed twice and the leaves are grouped into a lower and higher class. For example, if the stem is tens and the leaves are units, you can make two classes like this:

Stem	Leaf
1	0 3 4 2 1
1	5 9 8 7 5 6

Values from 10 to 14 (leaves 0 to 4) are included in the first class, values from 15 to 19 (leaves 5 to 9) are included in the second class.

Stem-and-leaf diagrams are easier to work with if the leaves are ordered from smallest to greatest.

WORKED EXAMPLE 2

This data set shows the ages of customers in a café one lunchtime.

34	23	40	35	25	28	18	32
37	29	19	17	32	55	36	42
33	20	25	34	48	39	36	30

Draw a stem-and-leaf diagram to display this data.

Answers

Stem	Leaf
1	8 9 7
2	3 5 8 9 0 5
3	4 5 2 7 6 6 3 4 2 9 0
4	0 2 8
5	5

Key
1	7 represents 17

Group the ages in intervals of ten, 10–19; 20–29 and so on.

These are two-digit numbers, so the tens digit is the stem.

List the stems in ascending order down the left of the diagram.

Work through the data in the order it is given, writing the units digits (the leaves) in a row next to the appropriate stem. Space the leaves to make them easier to read.

If you need to work with the data, you can redraw the diagram, putting the leaves in ascending order.

Stem	Leaf
1	7 8 9
2	0 3 5 5 8 9
3	0 2 2 3 4 4 5 6 6 7 9
4	0 2 8
5	5

Key
1	7 represents 17

From this reorganised stem-and-leaf diagram you can quickly see that:

- the youngest person using the internet café was 17 years old (the first data item)
- the oldest person was 55 (the last data item)
- most users were in the age group 30–39 (the group with the largest number of leaves).

If you want to show two sets of data, you can use a back-to-back stem-and-leaf diagram. The second set of data is plotted against the same stem, but the leaves are written to the left.

Brand X		Brand Y
Leaf	Stem	Leaf
9 4 8 7 2	0	5 8
7 8 7 2 3	1	4 7 8 2
8 4 6 2 7 9 8	2	8 9 7 1 5
7 2	3	7 2 1 0
	4	2
	5	1

Key
Brand X 8	2 represents 28 hours
Brand Y 4	2 represents 42 hours

This stem-and-leaf diagram compares the battery life (between charges) of two different brands of mobile phone. You read the data for Brand X from right to left. The stem is still the tens digit.

Exercise 4.4

1 The masses of some Grade 10 students were measured and recorded to the nearest kilogram. These are the results:

| 45 | 56 | 55 | 68 | 53 | 55 | 48 | 49 | 53 | 54 |
| 56 | 59 | 60 | 63 | 67 | 49 | 55 | 56 | 58 | 60 |

Construct a stem-and-leaf diagram to display the data.

2 The numbers of pairs of running shoes sold each day for a month at different branches of 'Runner's Up Shoe Store' are given in the table.

Branch A	175, 132, 180, 134, 179, 115, 140, 200, 198, 201, 189, 149, 188, 179, 186, 152, 180, 172, 169, 155, 164, 168, 166, 149, 188, 190, 199, 200
Branch B	188, 186, 187, 159, 160, 188, 200, 201, 204, 198, 190, 185, 142, 188, 165, 187, 180, 190, 191, 169, 177, 200, 205, 196, 191, 193, 188, 200

a Draw a back-to-back stem-and-leaf diagram to display the data.

b Which branch had the most sales on one day during the month?

c Which branch appears to have sold the most pairs? Why?

APPLY YOUR SKILLS

3 A team of biologists wanted to investigate how pollution levels affect the growth of fish in a dam. In January, they caught a number of fish and measured their length before releasing them back into the water. The stem-and-leaf diagram shows the lengths of the fish to the nearest centimetre.

Length of fish (cm) January sample

```
1 | 2 4 4 6
2 | 0 1 3 3 4 5 8 9
3 | 3 5 6 6 6 7 8 9
4 | 0 2 5 7
5 | 2 7
```

Key
1 | 2 represents 12 cm

a How many fish did they measure?

b What was the shortest length measured?

c How long was the longest fish measured?

d How many fish were 40 cm or longer?

e How do you think the diagram would change if they did the same survey in a year and:

    i the pollution levels had increased and stunted the growth of the fish

    ii the conditions in the water improved and the fish increased in length?

APPLY YOUR SKILLS CONTINUED

4   This stem-and-leaf diagram shows the pulse rate of a group of people measured before and after exercising on a treadmill.

Pulse rate

Before exercise			After exercise
Leaf		Stem	Leaf
0 1 3 6 8 7 2		6	
3 4 1 2		7	
7 3 2 7 8		8	7 6 4 3
0		9	0 2 4 1 3
1		10	3 1 7 8 9
		11	8 2
		12	7
		13	
		14	2

Key	
Before exercise	2 | 6 represents 62 beats per minute
After exercise	8 | 7 represents 87 beats per minute

a   How many people had a resting pulse rate (before exercise) in the range of 60 to 70 beats per minute?

b   What was the highest pulse rate measured before exercise?

c   That person also had the highest pulse rate after exercise. What was it?

d   What does the stem-and-leaf diagram tell you about pulse rates and exercise in this group? How?

Two-way tables

A **two-way table** shows the frequency of certain results for two or more sets of data. Here is a two-way table showing how many people in cars were wearing their seat belts when they passed a check point.

	Wearing a seat belt	Not wearing a seat belt
Drivers	10	4
Passengers	6	3

The headings at the top of the table give you information about wearing seat belts. The headings down the side of the table give you information about drivers and passengers.

You can use the table to find out:

- how many drivers were wearing seat belts
- how many passengers were wearing seat belts
- how many drivers were not wearing seat belts
- how many passengers were not wearing seat belts.

You can also add the totals across and down to work out:

- how many drivers were surveyed
- how many passengers were surveyed
- how many people (drivers and passengers) were wearing seat belts or not wearing seat belts.

Here are two more examples of two-way tables:

Drinks and crisps sold at a school snack shop during lunch break

	Sweet chilli	Plain	Cheese and onion
Cola	9	6	23
Fruit juice	10	15	12

How often Grade 10 and Grade 11 students use the school group chat app

	Never use it	Use it sometimes	Use it every day
Grade 10	35	18	52
Grade 11	42	26	47

Exercise 4.5

1   A teacher did a survey to see how many students in two classes were left-handed. She drew this two-way table to show the results.

	Left-handed	Right-handed
Class 10 A	9	33
Class 10 B	6	42

   a   How many left-handed students are there altogether?

   b   How many of the students in Class 10 A are right-handed?

   c   Are the students in Class 10 B mostly left-handed or mostly right-handed?

   d   How many students are there in the two classes?

2   Do a quick survey in your own school to find out how many left- or right-handed students there are in two or more different classes. Draw a two-way table of your results.

3   Sima asked her friends whether they checked their email on their phone or on their computer. These are the responses:

Name	Checks on phone	Checks on computer
Sheldon		✓
Leonard	✓	✓
Raj	✓	
Penny		✓
Howard	✓	✓
Zarah		✓
Zohir	✓	✓
Ahmed	✓	
Jenny	✓	
Priyanka	✓	✓
Anne		
Ellen	✓	✓

a   Draw a two-way table using these responses.

b   Write a sentence to summarise what you can learn from the table.

Two-way tables in everyday life

Two-way tables are often used to summarise and present data in real-life situations. You need to know how to read these tables so that you can answer questions about them.

> **MATHEMATICAL CONNECTIONS**
>
> Make sure you understand how to draw and read a two-way table. You will use them again in Chapter 8 when you deal with probability.

WORKED EXAMPLE 3

This table shows population data for mid-2021 with estimated figures for 2025 and 2050.

Region	Population in mid-2021	Projected population 2035	Projected population 2050
World	7 837 000 000	8 848 000 000	9 688 000 000
Africa	1 373 000 000	1 890 000 000	2 529 000 000
North America	371 000 000	396 000 000	412 000 000
Latin America and the Caribbean	656 000 000	725 000 000	762 000 000
Asia	4 651 000 000	5 043 000 000	5 192 000 000
Europe	744 000 000	742 000 000	731 000 000
Oceania	43 000 000	53 000 000	62 000 000

Data from Population Reference Bureau.

WORKED EXAMPLE 3 CONTINUED

a What was the total population of the world in mid-2021?

b By how much is the population of the world expected to grow by 2035?

c What percentage of the world's population lived in Asia in mid-2021? Give your answer to the closest whole per cent.

d i Which region is likely to experience a decrease in population between 2021 and 2035?

   ii What is the population of this region likely to be in 2035?

   iii By how much is the population of this region expected to decrease by 2050?

Answers

a	7 837 000 000		Read this from the table.
b	8 848 000 000 − 7 837 000 000 = 101 100 000		Read the value for 2035 from the table and subtract the smaller figure from the larger.
c	$\dfrac{4\,651\,000\,000}{7\,837\,000\,000} \times 100 = 59.3467\,\% \approx 59\%$		Read the figures from the table and then calculate the percentage.
d	i	Europe	Look to see which numbers are decreasing across the row.
	ii	742 000 000	Read this from the table.
	iii	744 000 000 − 731 000 000 = 13 000 000	Read the values from the table and subtract the smaller figure from the larger.

Exercise 4.6

APPLY YOUR SKILLS

1 This distance table shows the flying distance (in miles) between some major world airports.

	Mumbai	Hong Kong	London	Montreal	Singapore	Sydney
Dubai	1199	3695	3412	6793	3630	7580
Hong Kong	2673		8252	10 345	1605	4586
Istanbul	2992	7016	1554	5757	5379	11 772
Karachi	544	3596	5276	8888	2943	8269
Lagos	5140	8930	3098	6734	7428	11 898
London	4477	8252		3251	6754	10 564
Singapore	2432	1605	6754	9193		3912
Sydney	6308	4586	10 564	12 045	3916	

a Find the flying distance from Hong Kong to:

   i Dubai   **ii** London   **iii** Sydney

b   Which is the longer flight: Istanbul to Montreal or Mumbai to Lagos?

c   What is the total flying distance for a return flight from London to Sydney and back?

d   If a plane flies at an average speed of 400 miles per hour, how long will it take to fly the distance from Singapore to Hong Kong to the nearest hour?

e   Why are there some empty blocks in this table?

4.3 Using charts to display data

Charts are useful for displaying data because you can see patterns and trends easily and quickly. You can also compare different sets of data easily. In this section you are going to revise what you already know about how to draw and make sense of pictograms, bar charts and pie charts.

Pictograms

Pictograms are fairly simple charts. Small symbols (pictures) are used to represent quantities. The meaning of the symbol and the amount it represents (a 'key') must be provided for the graph to make sense.

WORKED EXAMPLE 4

This pictogram shows the amount of time that five friends spent talking on their phones during one week.

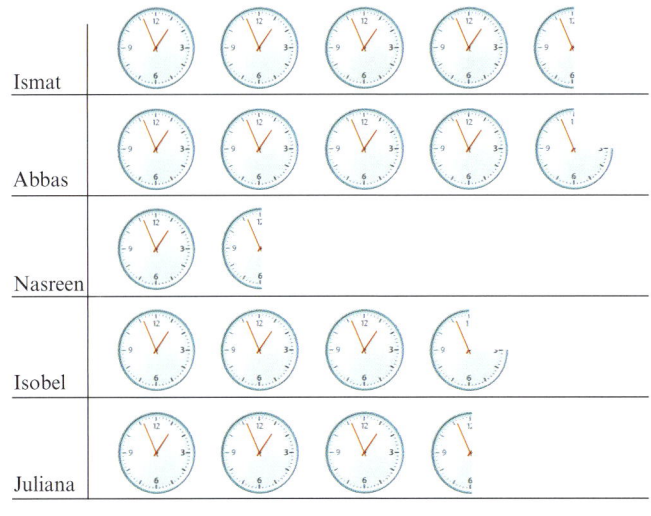
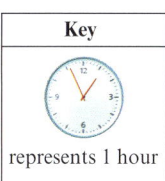

a   Who spent the most time on the phone that week?

b   How much time did Isobel spend on the phone that week?

c   Who spent $3\frac{1}{2}$ hours on the phone that week?

d   Draw the symbols you would use to show $4\frac{1}{4}$ hours.

WORKED EXAMPLE 4 CONTINUED

Answers

a   Anna   The person with the most clocks.

b $3\frac{3}{4}$ hours   There are three whole clocks; the key shows you that each one stands for 1 hour. The fourth clock is only three-quarters, so it must be $\frac{3}{4}$ of an hour.

c   Tara   She has three full clocks, each worth 1 hour, and one half clock.

d       Two full clocks to represent two hours, and a quarter of a clock to represent $\frac{1}{4}$ hours.

Exercise 4.7

1   A pictogram showing how many tourists visit the top five tourist destinations uses this symbol.

= 500 000 arrivals

How many tourists are represented by each of these symbols?

a   b   c   d

2   Here is a set of data for the five top tourist destination countries (2019). Use the symbol from question **1** with your own scale to draw a pictogram to show this data.

Top tourist destinations

Country	France	Spain	USA	China	Italy
Number of tourists	89 400 000	83 700 000	79 300 000	65 700 000	64 500 000

Source: https://worldpopulationreview.com/country-rankings/most-visited-countries

TIP

The number of arrivals represented by the key should be an integer that is easily divided into the data; you may also need to round the data to a suitable degree of accuracy.

LINK

Tourist numbers dropped dramatically in 2020 and 2021 as travel was severely restricted due to the COVID-19 pandemic. Data scientists predict that it may take years for the numbers to return to these 2019 levels.

3   This pictogram shows the number of fish caught by a fleet of five fishing boats
during one fishing trip.

Number of fish caught per boat

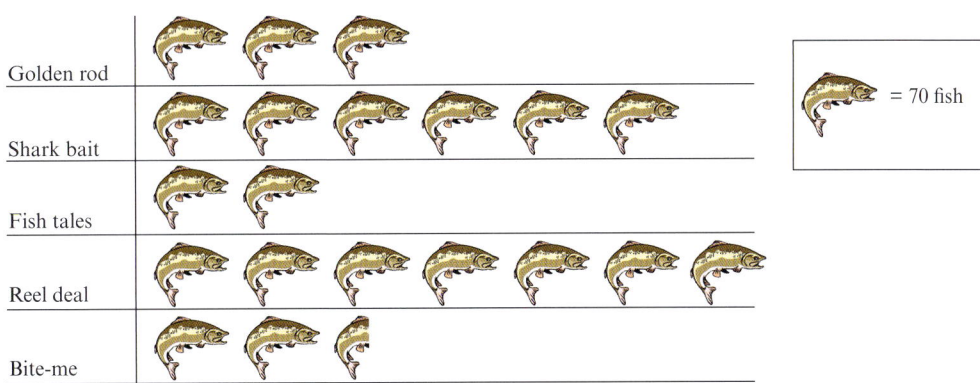

= 70 fish

a   Which boat caught the most fish?

b   Which boat caught the least fish?

c   How many fish did each boat catch?

d   What is the total catch for the fleet on this trip?

Bar charts

Bar charts are normally used to display discrete data. The chart shows information as a
series of bars plotted against a scale on the axis. The bars can be horizontal or vertical.

Number of days of rain

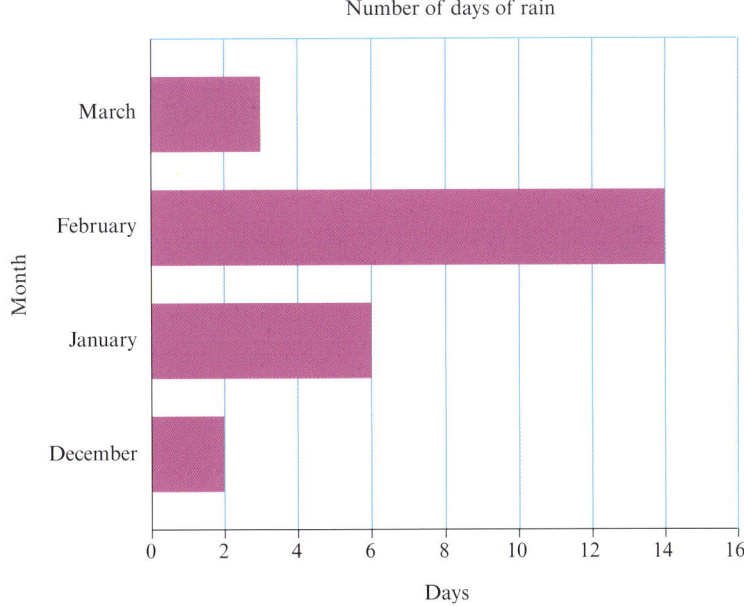

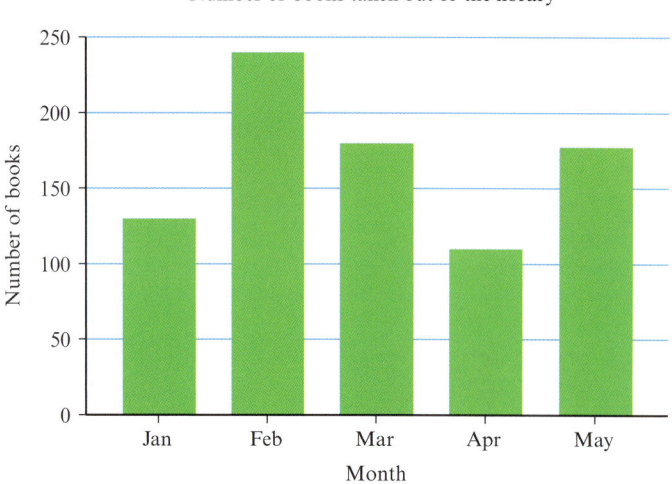

Number of books taken out of the library

There are different methods of drawing bar charts, but all bar charts should have:

- a title that tells you what data is being displayed
- a number scale or axis (so you can work out how many are in each class) and a label on the scale that tells you what the numbers stand for
- a scale or axis that lists the categories displayed
- bars that are equally wide and equally spaced
- bars that do not touch for qualitative of discrete data.

WORKED EXAMPLE 5

This frequency table shows the number of people who were treated for road accident injuries in the casualty department of a large hospital in the first six months of a year. Draw a bar chart to represent the data. Note that bar chart's frequency axis should start from zero.

| Patients admitted as a result of road accidents ||
Month	Number of patients
January	360
February	275
March	190
April	375
May	200
June	210

WORKED EXAMPLE 5 CONTINUED

Answer

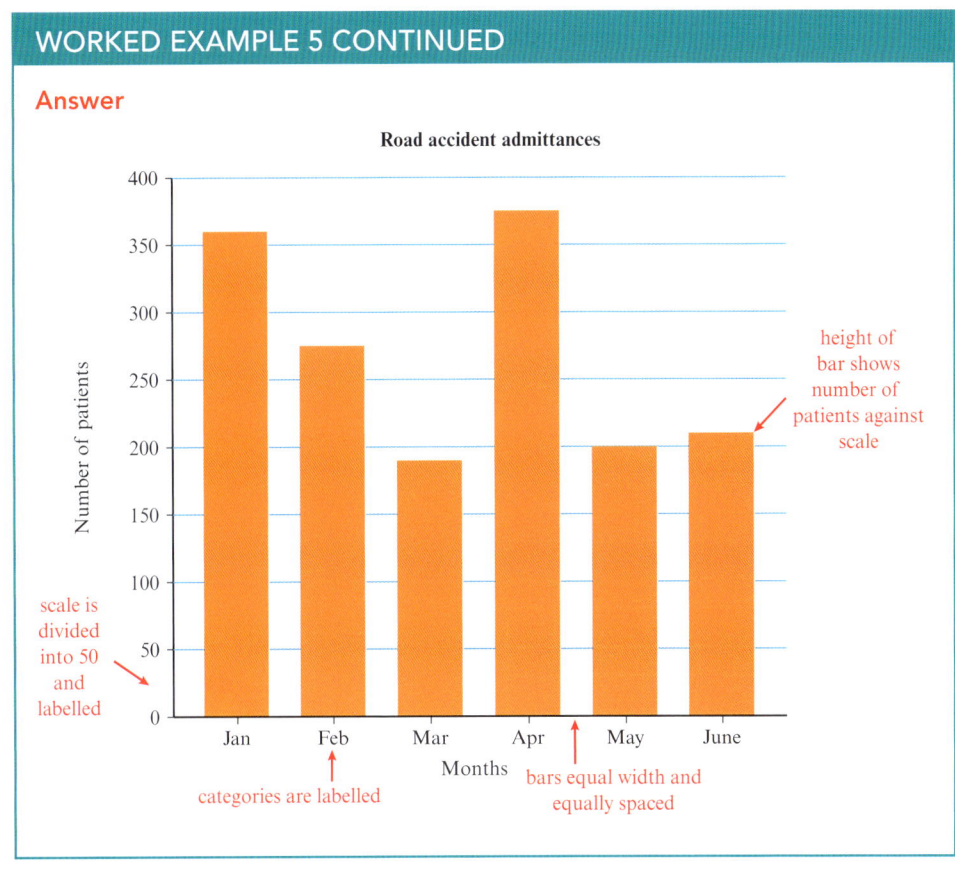

Road accident admittances

scale is divided into 50 and labelled

categories are labelled

Months

bars equal width and equally spaced

height of bar shows number of patients against scale

> **MATHEMATICAL CONNECTIONS**
>
> A bar chart is not the same as a histogram. A histogram is often used for continuous data. You will learn more about histograms in Chapter 20.

Dual bar charts

A dual bar chart displays two or more sets of data side-by-side on the same set of axes to make it easy to compare the data. This chart compares the percentage of Fortune 500 companies using different social media platforms in 2019 and 2020.

> **TIP**
>
> Fortune 500 is a yearly list of the 500 biggest companies (by revenue) in the USA. Many of the companies are multinationals that operate globally.

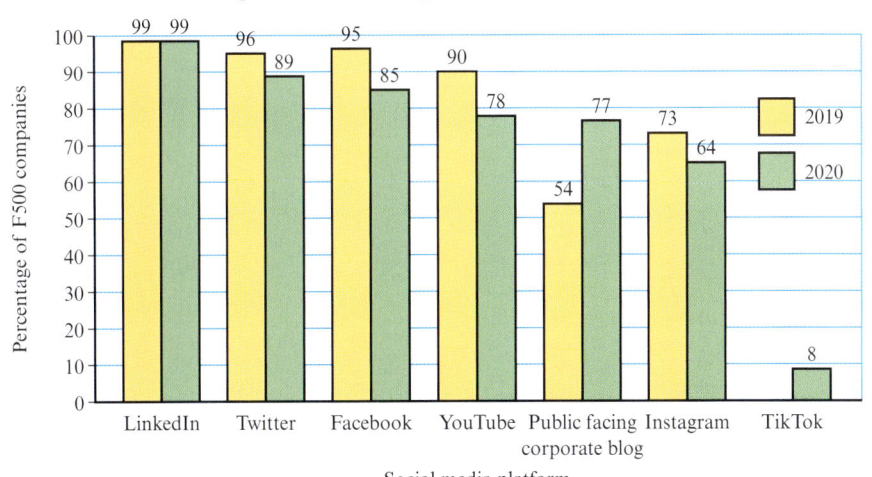

Percentage of Fortune 500 companies using different social media platforms

Data source: Center for Marketing Research, University of Massachusetts, Dartmouth

The graph shows that LinkedIn is the most popular platform, used by 99% of companies. Use of mainstream social media decreased slightly between 2019 and 2020, but public facing blog usage increased dramatically as companies needed to communicate with the public online during the COVID-19 pandemic. A few companies started to use TikTok in 2020 and analysts predict this will increase as companies target customers in the age groups that prefer this platform.

Composite bar charts

A composite (stacked) bar chart breaks the whole set of data shown on each bar into groups.

This composite bar graph shows the percentage of the total time that different athletes spend on three events in a triathlon. The bars are the same length because they all represent 100% of the time taken.

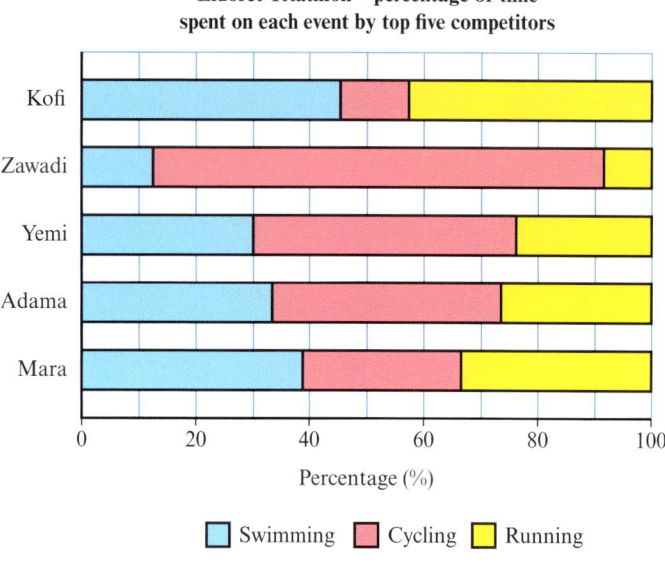

Eldoret Triathlon – percentage of time spent on each event by top five competitors

Percentage (%)

Swimming   Cycling   Running

The graph shows that Zawadi spent most of the time cycling (about 80%). By comparison, Kofi only spent about 10% of the time cycling.

This composite bar graph shows the number of students taking different computer programming courses. The bars are different heights because the total number of students increases over time.

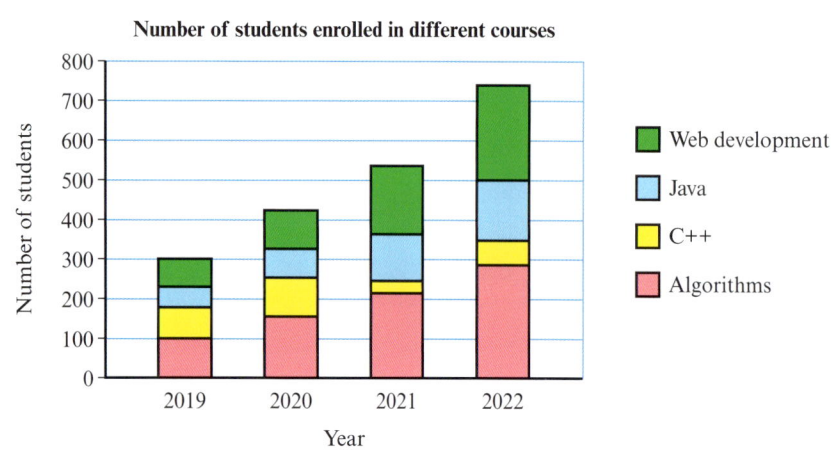

Number of students enrolled in different courses

Web development
Java
C++
Algorithms

Number of students

Year

> **TIP**
>
> Each colour section represents a share of the whole. You have to work out what that share is by counting along the scale from the start of each colour.

In 2019, 100 students enrolled in the Algorithms course. By 2022, this had increased to 290 students. In 2020, 100 students chose Web Development. This is an increase of 30 from the 70 students enrolled in that course in 2019.

Exercise 4.8

1   Draw a bar chart to show each of these sets of data.

a

Favourite take-away food	Burgers	Noodles	Fried chicken	Hot chips	Other
No. of people	40	30	84	20	29

b

African countries with the highest HIV/AIDS infection rates (2021 est)	
Country	% of adults (aged 15 to 49) infected
Eswatini	27.0
Botswana	20.7
Lesotho	22.8
Zimbabwe	12.8
South Africa	19.0
Namibia	11.6
Zambia	11.3
Malawi	8.9
Equatorial Guinea	7.3
Mozambique	10.6

(Data taken from https://aidsinfo.unaids.org and www.avert.org.)

LINK

HIV remains a global health issue, but it is now classified as an epidemic rather than a pandemic. In 2021, the organisation Avert reported that 37.7 million people worldwide were living with HIV. The vast majority of these people live in low- and middle-income countries. The countries of East and Southern Africa are the most affected by this disease and 20.6 million people in these countries are living with HIV. There has been an overall decrease in the rate of new infections in this region, largely due to awareness and education campaigns and the introduction of anti-retroviral medication on a large scale. (Source: www.Avert.org)

2   Here is a set of raw data showing the average summer temperature (in °C) for 20 cities in the Middle East during one year.

| 32 | 42 | 36 | 40 | 35 | 36 | 33 | 32 | 38 | 37 |
| 34 | 40 | 41 | 39 | 42 | 38 | 37 | 42 | 40 | 41 |

a   Copy and complete this grouped frequency table to organise the data.

Temperature (°C)	32–34	35–37	38–40	41–43
Frequency				

b   Draw a horizontal bar chart to represent this data.

MATHEMATICAL CONNECTIONS

Look at the earlier sections of this chapter to remind yourself about grouped frequency tables if you need to.

3   A tourism organisation on a Caribbean island recorded how many tourists visit from the region and how many tourists visit from international destinations. Here is the data for the first six months of the year.

	Jan	Feb	Mar	Apr	May	Jun
Regional visitors	12 000	10 000	19 000	16 000	21 000	2000
International visitors	40 000	39 000	15 000	12 000	19 000	25 000

Display this data using a:

a   dual bar chart   b   composite bar chart.

PEER ASSESSMENT

How can you decide whether another student's bar chart is correct or not?

One way of assessing a piece of work is to write a checklist. A checklist is an assessment tool. It is a list of statements that give the criteria you will use to measure skills or student success in a particular area. The answer to each statement is either 'yes' or 'no', or 'done' or 'not done'.

1   Work in small groups to write a checklist to assess whether someone can draw an accurate and clear bar chart.
   • Consider the learning outcomes for this work and what you have covered in the lessons.
   • Your statements should be clear, specific and easy to check. For example: The chart has a clear heading   [ ] yes   [ ] no
   • Leave space in your checklist to add comments. For example: Your heading has spelling mistakes in it.
      or
      The vertical scale needs to start at 0.

2   Use your checklist to assess another student's completed work in Exercise 4.8.

3   Use the checklist to suggest corrections, improvements or learning goals that still need to be met.

Think about your own academic performance as you worked through the material on bar charts and answer these questions.

- What new things did you learn? Why are these important?

- Were the strategies, skills and procedures that you knew or learned useful for completing the exercises? Explain why or why not.

- Did you come to each lesson prepared to learn? (Think about your attitude and the equipment you needed to bring.)

- Which activities helped you to learn the most? Why?

- Did you experience any difficulty or frustration in this work? What did you do about it?

Pie charts

A pie chart uses slices or sectors of a circle to show data. The circle represents the 'whole' set of data. For example, if you survey the favourite sports played by everyone in a school then the total number of students is represented by the circle. The sectors represent groups of students who prefer each sport.

Like other charts, pie charts should have a heading and a key.

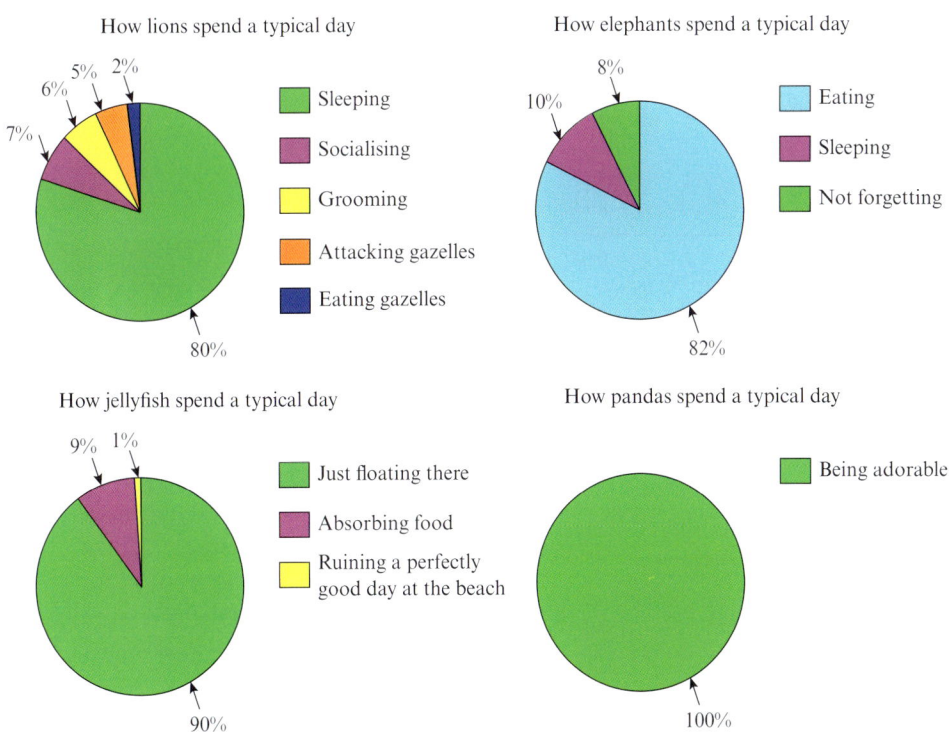

WORKED EXAMPLE 6

The table shows how a student spent one day.

Activity	School	Sleeping	Eating	Online	On the phone	Complaining about stuff
Number of hours	7	8	1.5	3	2.5	2

Draw a pie chart to show this data.

$7 + 8 + 1.5 + 3 + 2.5 + 2 = 24$ First work out the total number of hours.

Then work out each category as a fraction of the whole and convert the fraction to degrees:

	(as a fraction of 24)	(convert to degrees)
School	$= \dfrac{7}{24}$	$= \dfrac{7}{24} \times 360 = 105°$
Sleeping	$= \dfrac{8}{24}$	$\dfrac{8}{24} \times 360 = 120°$
Eating	$= \dfrac{1.5}{24} = \dfrac{15}{240}$	$\dfrac{15}{240} \times 360 = 22.5°$
Online	$= \dfrac{3}{24}$	$\dfrac{3}{24} \times 360 = 45°$
On the phone	$= \dfrac{2.5}{24} = \dfrac{25}{240}$	$\dfrac{25}{240} \times 360 = 37.5°$
Complaining about stuff	$= \dfrac{2}{24}$	$\dfrac{2}{24} \times 360 = 30°$

Answer

Activity	School	Sleeping	Eating	Online	On the phone	Complaining about stuff
Number of hours	7	8	1.5	3	2.5	2
Angle	105°	120°	22.5°	45°	37.5°	30°

- Draw a circle to represent the whole day.
- Use a ruler and a protractor to measure each sector.
- Label the chart and give it a title.

A student's day

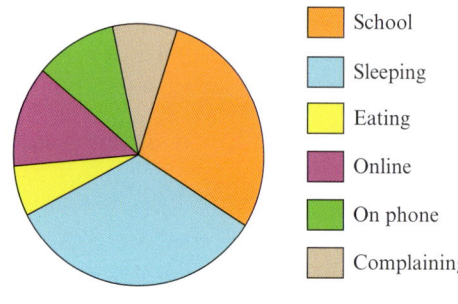

- School
- Sleeping
- Eating
- Online
- On phone
- Complaining

TIP

It is possible that your angles, once rounded, don't quite add up to 360°. If this happens, you can add or subtract a degree to or from the largest sector (the one with the highest frequency).

WORKED EXAMPLE 7

This pie chart shows how Javi spent one day of the school holidays.

Javi's day

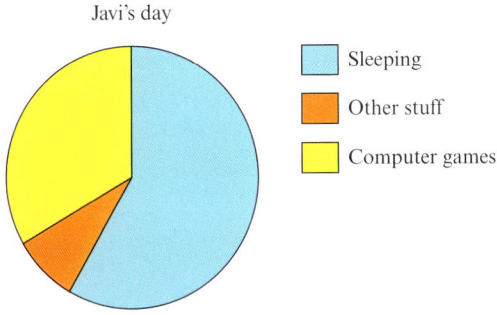

Sleeping

Other stuff

Computer games

a   What fraction of the day did Javi spend playing computer games?

b   How much time did Javi spend sleeping?

c   What do you think 'other stuff' involved?

Answers

a $\dfrac{120}{360} = \dfrac{1}{3}$

Measure the angle and convert it to a fraction. The yellow sector has an angle of 120°. Convert to a fraction by writing it over 360 and simplify.

b $\dfrac{210}{360} \times 24 = 14$ hours

Measure the angle, convert it to hours.

c   Things Javi didn't bother to list. Possibly eating, showering, getting dressed.

Exercise 4.9

1   The table shows the results of a survey carried out on a university campus to find out about the use of online support services among students. Draw a pie chart to illustrate this data.

Category	Number of students
Never used online support	160
Used online support in the past	110
Use online support at present	90

2   The table shows the home language of a number of people passing through an international airport. Display this data as a pie chart.

Language	Frequency
English	130
Spanish	144
Chinese	98
Italian	104
French	24
German	176
Japanese	22

3   The amount of land used to grow different vegetables on a farm is shown in the table. Draw a pie chart to show the data.

Vegetable	Squashes	Pumpkins	Cabbages	Sweet potatoes
Area of land (km²)	1.4	1.25	1.15	1.2

4   The nationalities of students in an international school are shown on this pie chart.

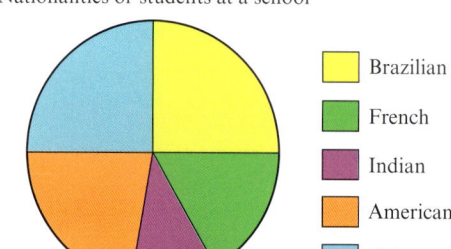

Nationalities of students at a school

- Brazilian
- French
- Indian
- American
- Chinese

a   What fraction of the students are Chinese?

b   What percentage of the students are Indian?

c   What proportion of the total students are Brazilian? Give your answer as a decimal.

d   If there are 900 students at the school, how many of them are:
    i   Chinese?   ii   Indian?   iii   American?   iv   French?

MATHEMATICAL CONNECTIONS

You will think about graphs that can be used for converting currencies or systems of units in Chapter 13. You will deal with graphs showing time, distance and speed in Chapter 21.

Line graphs

INVESTIGATION

Graphs can tell a story

Line graphs show changes over time.

1   Look at this generalised graph of noise levels in a classroom during
    a lesson.

    How does the shape of the graph and the slope of the lines tell a story
    even though there are no scales given on the axes?

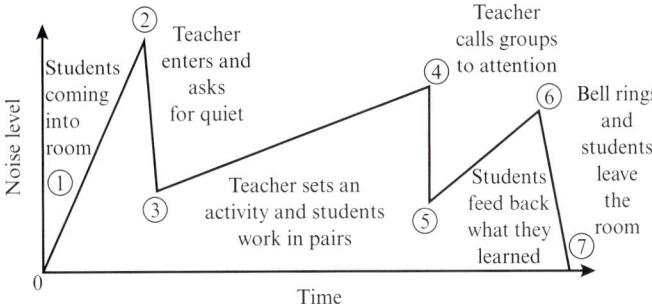

2   This graph shows the happiness levels of Team A's supporters during a
    football match. The final score in the match is 3 goals to 2, with Team A
    winning. Make up a story to fit the graph, describing the events that lead
    to changes in the graph.

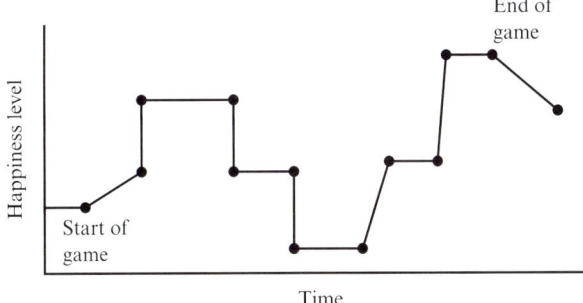

3   What would your happiness graph look like for a normal school day?
    Draw it and add notes giving the reasons or events that caused any
    changes in the graph.

Some data that you collect varies over time. For example, the average temperature each
month of the year, the number of cars each hour that park in a supermarket car park
or the amount of money in your bank account each week.

This line graph shows how the depth of water in a garden pond varies over a year. The graph shows that the water level is at its lowest between June and August.

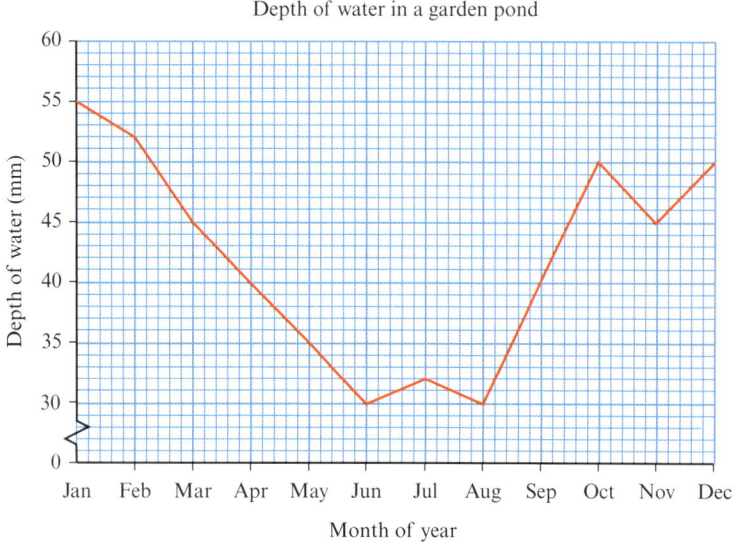

When time is one of your variables, you plot it on the horizontal axis.

Exercise 4.10

1 The table shows the temperature of water in a beaker as it is heated over a Bunsen burner. The line graph shows how the temperature changes over time.

Time (seconds)	0	30	60	90	120	150	180
Temperature (°C)	26	28	38	56	70	82	96

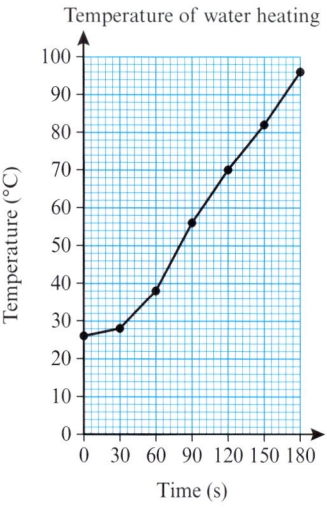

a Use the graph to estimate the temperature of the water after:

   i   45 seconds   ii   110 seconds.

b How long do you think it will take for the water to reach its boiling point (100 °C)? Give a reason for your answer.

2 The table shows the temperatures recorded at Jisan Forest Ski Resort in Icheon-si, South Korea on one day in February. The line graph shows this data.

Time	07:00	08:00	09:00	10:00	11:00	12:00	13:00	14:00	15:00	16:00
Temperature (°C)	−7	−5	−3	−3	0	1	3	3	1	−1

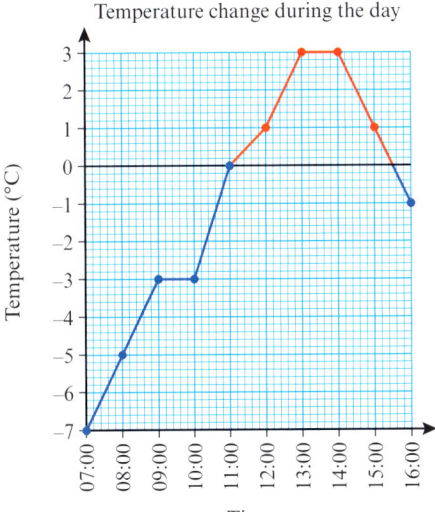

Temperature change during the day

a Estimate the temperature at 12:30.

b At what times was the temperature lower than −3 °C?

3 Nadia's fitness app produced this graph of her pulse rate before, during and after a run. Nadia did some exercises to warm up and then she stayed still for a few minutes while she waited for her running group so they could start their run together.

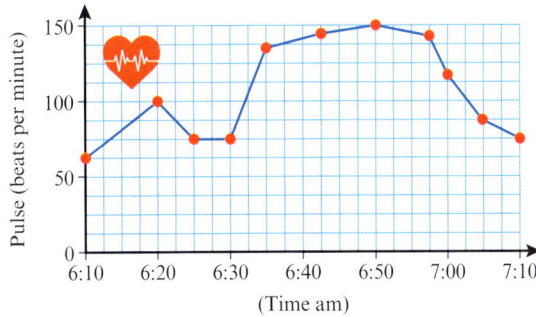

a What was Nadia's pulse rate before the warm-up exercises?

b At what time do you think they started running? Why?

c What was the highest pulse rate recorded? When was this recorded?

d The group stopped running at 6:55. What happened to Nadia's pulse after she stopped running?

SELF ASSESSMENT

Copy and complete this writing outline frame to assess your own learning in this chapter.
The notes at the side tell you what to include and why.

Use your own words. Write in short point form. For example, how to organise data; how to draw different graphs.

Identify any areas where you need help. For example, calculating percentages with large numbers.

Fill in when you will reassess yourself on this topic and how you will do that. For example, by trying some practice questions and rating my work.

Chapter _____ Date: _____

The main concepts we've been learning are:
-
-

The things I know well are:
-
-
-

I would like more help with:
-
-

I need more practice at:
-
-

I'll reassess myself on _____ by _____.

List what you know well, try to think of at least three things. For example, how to read graphs, how to draw bar charts.

Think of anything that you could improve by practising. For example, measuring in degrees, drawing pie charts.

SUMMARY

Do you know …?

In statistics, data is a set of information collected to answer a particular question.

Categorical (qualitative) data is non-numerical. Colours, names, places and other descriptive terms are all categorical.

Numerical (quantitative) data is collected in the form of numbers. Numerical data can be discrete or continuous. Discrete data takes certain values; continuous data can take any value in a given range.

Primary data is data you collect yourself from a primary source. Secondary data is data you collect from other sources (previously collected by someone else).

Unsorted data is called raw data. Raw data can be organised using tally tables, frequency tables, stem-and-leaf diagrams and two-way tables to make it easier to work with.

Data in tables can be displayed as graphs to show patterns and trends at a glance.

Pictograms are simple graphs that use symbols to represent quantities.

Bar charts have rows of horizontal bars or columns of vertical bars of different lengths. The bar length (or height) represents an amount. The actual amount can be read from a scale.

Dual bar charts display two or more sets of data side by side on the same set of axes.

Composite bar charts display groups within a set of data stacked on a single bar.

Pie charts are circular charts divided into sectors to show categories of data.

Line graphs use lines to plot changes in the data over time.

The type of graph you draw depends on the data and what you wish to show.

Are you able to …?

collect data to answer a statistical question

classify different types of data

use tallies to count and record data

draw a frequency table to organise data

use class intervals to group data and draw a grouped frequency table

construct single and back-to-back stem-and-leaf diagrams to organise and display sets of data

draw and use two-way tables to organise two or more sets of data

construct and interpret pictograms

construct and interpret bar charts, dual bar charts and composite bar charts

construct and interpret pie charts.

Practice questions

1 Salma is a quality control inspector. She randomly selects 40 packets of biscuits at a large factory. She opens each packet and counts the number of broken biscuits it contains. Her results are as follows:

0	0	2	1	3	0	0	2	3	1
1	1	2	3	0	1	2	3	4	2
0	0	0	0	1	0	0	1	2	3
3	2	2	2	1	0	1	2	1	2

a Explain whether this is primary or secondary data to Salma.   [2]

b Determine whether the data is discrete or continuous and explain your answer.   [2]

c Copy and complete this frequency table to organise the data.

No. of broken biscuits	Tally	Frequency
0		
1		
2		
3		
4		

[3]

d Draw a bar chart to represent this data.   [5]

2 The number of aircraft movements in and out of five main London airports in one month is summarised in the table.

Airport	Gatwick	Heathrow	London City	Luton	Stansted
Total flights	23 696	39 660	6380	10 697	15 397

a State which airport handled most aircraft movement.   [1]

b State how many aircraft moved in and out of Stansted Airport.   [1]

c Round each figure to the nearest thousand.   [2]

d Use the rounded numbers for all of the airports to draw a pictogram to show this data.   [4]

3 This table shows the percentage of people who own a laptop and a mobile phone in four different districts in a large city.

District	Own a laptop (%)	Own a mobile phone (%)
A	45	83
B	32	72
C	61	85
D	22	68

a   There are 6000 people in District A. Work out how many of them own
    a mobile phone.   [2]

b   One district is home to a University of Technology and several computer
    software manufacturers. Explain which district you think this is.   [2]

c   Draw a dual bar chart to display this data.   [5]

4   Study this pie chart and answer the questions that follow.

Sport played by students

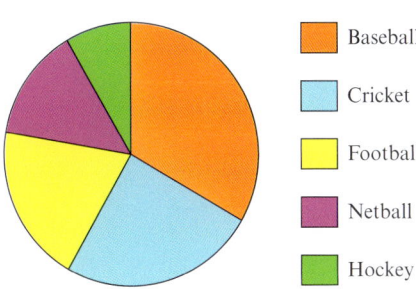

- Baseball
- Cricket
- Football
- Netball
- Hockey

The data was collected from a sample of 200 students.

a   Explain the type of data the chart shows.   [2]

b   Write down out many different categories of data there are.   [2]

c   Work out which is the most popular sport.   [2]

d   Work out the fraction of the students who play cricket.   [2]

e   Work out how many students play netball.   [2]

f   Work out how many students play baseball or hockey.   [2]

5   Study this graph carefully.

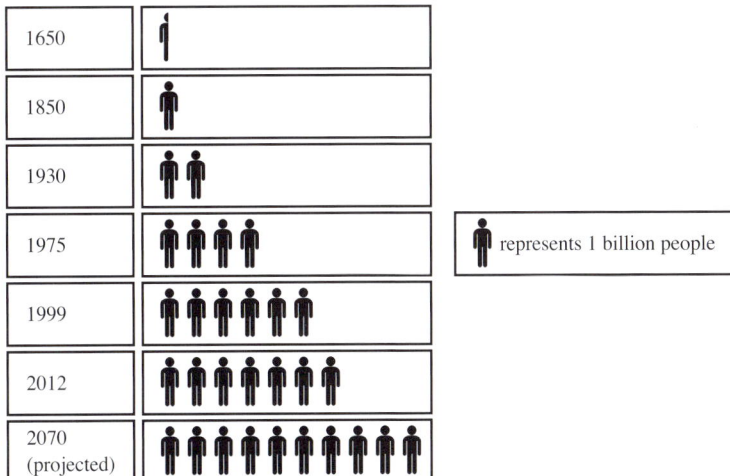

1650	
1850	
1930	
1975	
1999	
2012	
2070 (projected)	

represents 1 billion people

a   What type of graph is this?   [1]

b   What does each symbol represent?   [1]

c   What was the population of the world in 1650?   [2]

d   How long did it take the population to double after 1650?   [2]

e   When did the world's population reach 7 billion?   [2]

f   The United Nations predicts that the world's population will reach 9.2 billion in 2050. How would you show this on the graph?   [2]

6   Two neighbouring villages, Packthorpe and Rainbridge, decide to join together to form Football, Tennis and Bowling clubs. The table shows some information about 80 people who have joined the teams.

	Football	Tennis	Bowling	Total
Packthorpe		5		35
Rainbridge	21			45
Total	35	18		80

a   Copy and complete the table.   [3]

b   Draw a composite bar chart to show how many people take part in each sport from each village.   [5]

SELF ASSESSMENT

Use your answers to the practice questions to assess how well you are able to organise and display data.

List the question numbers.

Rate your work on each question using this scale:
- I'm starting to understand
- I mostly understand
- I understand
- I understand very well

Past paper questions

TIP

Unit 1 Past Paper Questions Resource Sheet is available on Cambridge GO.

1 Find the highest **odd** number that is a factor of 60 and a factor of 90. [1]

Cambridge IGCSE Mathematics (0580) Paper 11 Q8, June 2020

2 By rounding each number in the calculation correct to 1 significant figure, estimate the value of $\dfrac{38.7 \times 3.115}{20.3 - 4.1^2}$.

You must show all your working. [2]

Cambridge IGCSE Mathematics (0580) Paper 11 Q20, June 2021

3 a Write down the mathematical name for a polygon with 5 sides. [1]

b Work out the interior angle of a regular 18-sided polygon. [2]

Cambridge IGCSE Mathematics (0580) Paper 11 Q11, June 2021

4 a Write $\dfrac{1}{2 \times 2 \times 2 \times 2 \times 2}$ as a power of 2. [1]

b i $3^{18} \div 3^{t} = 3^{6}$

Find the value of t. $t = $ .... [1]

ii Simplify.

$8w^{10} \times 6w^5$ [2]

Cambridge IGCSE Mathematics (0580) Paper 11 Q17, June 2021

5

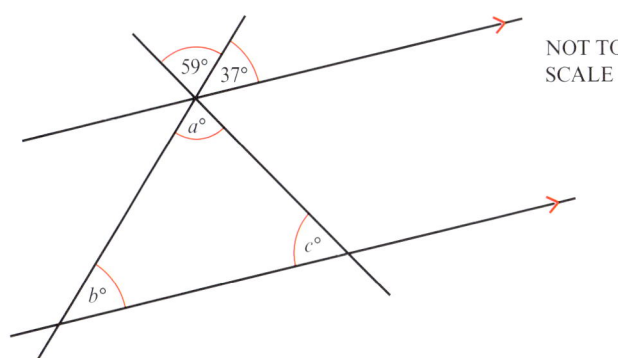

NOT TO SCALE

The diagram shows two parallel lines intersected by two straight lines.

Find the values of a, b and c

$a = $ ....

$b = $ ....

$c = $ .... [3]

Cambridge IGCSE Mathematics (0580) Paper 11 Q10, June 2021

6   Zachary asks the 30 students in his class which is their favourite sport.

The table shows the results.

Netball	Football	Hockey	Tennis
7	12	6	5

Complete the pictogram. [Using Figure 1 in the Unit 1 Past Paper Questions Resource Sheet.]

Netball	⊕ ◔
Football	
Hockey	
Tennis	

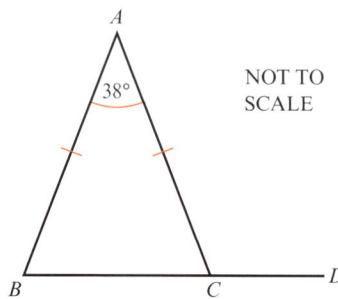

Key: ⊕ represents 4 people

[2]

Cambridge IGCSE Mathematics (0580) Paper 11 Q1, June 2021

7

NOT TO SCALE

In the triangle *ABC*, *AB* = *AC* and angle *BAC* = 38°.

BCD is a straight line.

Work out angle *ACD*.

Angle *ACD* = ... [3]

Cambridge IGCSE Mathematics (0580) Paper 11 Q5, June 2020

8   Simplify.

$4p^5q^3 \times p^2q^{-4}$

[2]

Cambridge IGCSE Mathematics (0580) Paper 11 Q15, June 2020

9   a   Using the integers from 60 to 75 only, find

   i   a multiple of 17,   [1]

   ii   the prime numbers.   [2]

   b   Find

   i   the square root of 4489,   [1]

   ii 4^3,   [1]

   iii $\sqrt[3]{274625}$,   [1]

   iv $2^{-3} \times 24^2$.   [1]

   c   Write down the reciprocal of 7.   [1]

   d   Write 3.72194 correct to 3 decimal places.   [1]

   e   Find the lowest common multiple (LCM) of 8 and 14.   [2]

   f   The average temperature at the North Pole is −23 °C in January and −11 °C in March.

   i   Find the difference between these temperatures.

                                                        .... °C   [1]

   ii   The average temperature in July is 28 °C higher than the average temperature in March.
        Find the average temperature in July.

                                                        .... °C   [1]

Cambridge IGCSE Mathematics (0580) Paper 31 Q5, June 2020

10 a   Simplify $(81y^{16})^{\frac{3}{4}}$.   [2]

   b $2^3 = 4^p$

   Find the value of p. $p =$ ....   [1]

Cambridge IGCSE Mathematics (0580) Paper 21 Q18, June 2019

❭ Unit 1 Project

Star polygons

Here is a five-pointed star:

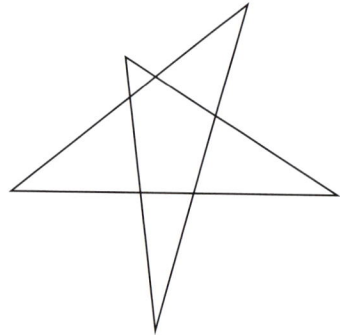

TIP

If you have access to the internet, you can find information to help you explain your findings on the NRICH website. Go to https://nrich.maths.org/11456 to do this.

Draw some five-pointed stars of your own. Make sure your lines are straight.

Measure the interior angles at the five points and add them together. What do you notice?

Here is a seven-pointed star:

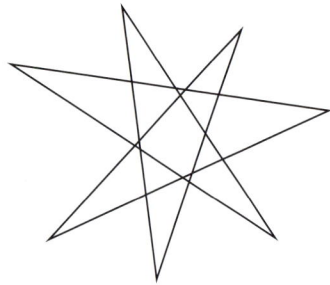

Draw some seven-pointed stars of your own.

Measure the interior angles at the seven points and add them together.

What do you notice? How can you explain your findings?

Try to state and prove similar results for a star with any number of points.

Chapter 5

Fractions, percentages and standard form

IN THIS CHAPTER YOU WILL:

- find equivalent fractions
- simplify fractions
- add, subtract, multiply and divide fractions and mixed numbers
- find fractions of numbers
- find a percentage of a number
- find one number as a percentage of another
- calculate percentage increases and decreases
- increase and decrease by a given percentage
- calculate reverse percentages (undoing increases and decreases)
- use standard form
- calculate with values in standard form.

Sea nettle jellyfish bodies on the previous page are $\frac{1}{20}$ protein, muscles and nerve cells – the rest is water. Work out what percentage of a jellyfish's body is water.

We use fractions and percentages on an almost daily basis, often without realising it. For example, we use fractions to answer questions like these:

- How far can you travel on half a tank of petrol?

- If you share $\frac{3}{4}$ of a cake between two people, how much will they each get?

- If three-fifths of a 100 km journey is complete, how far do you still have to travel?

- If a shop is offering a 25% discount, what will you pay for an item costing $120?

KEY WORDS

common denominator

denominator

equivalent fraction

fraction

lowest terms

mixed number

numerator

simplest form

standard form

GETTING STARTED

1 Match pairs of bubbles with the same value to find the one that has no matching value.

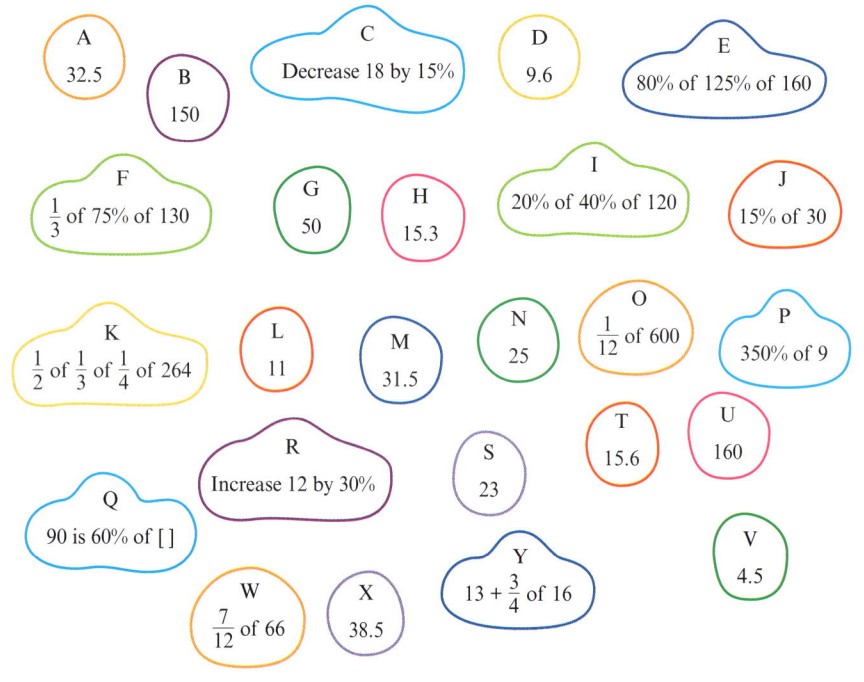

A 32.5

B 150

C Decrease 18 by 15%

D 9.6

E 80% of 125% of 160

F $\frac{1}{3}$ of 75% of 130

G 50

H 15.3

I 20% of 40% of 120

J 15% of 30

K $\frac{1}{2}$ of $\frac{1}{3}$ of $\frac{1}{4}$ of 264

L 11

M 31.5

N 25

O $\frac{1}{12}$ of 600

P 350% of 9

Q 90 is 60% of [ ]

R Increase 12 by 30%

S 23

T 15.6

U 160

V 4.5

W $\frac{7}{12}$ of 66

X 38.5

Y $13 + \frac{3}{4}$ of 16

2 Draw diagrams with labels or short notes to show why:

a a 50% increase followed by a 50% decrease does not get you back to where you started

b an increase of 40% followed by an increase of 50% is not equal to an increase of 90%.

5.1 Revisiting fractions

A **fraction** tells you what share or part of a whole amount you are working with. For example, $\frac{1}{2}$ of a pie means 1 of 2 equal parts of the pie and $\frac{7}{8}$ of the students means 7 out of every 8 students. The **mixed number** $2\frac{3}{4}$ means you are working with 2 wholes and 3 of 4 parts of another whole.

Proper fractions are written in the form $\frac{a}{b}$ where $a < b$. The number on the top, a, can be any number and is called the **numerator**. The number on the bottom, b, can be any number except 0 and is called the **denominator**.

When you multiply or divide both the numerator and the denominator by the same number you get a new fraction that has the same value as the original fraction. The new fraction is called an **equivalent fraction**.

For example, $\frac{2}{3} = \frac{2 \times 4}{3 \times 4} = \frac{8}{12}$ and $\frac{25}{35} = \frac{25 \div 5}{35 \div 5} = \frac{5}{7}$.

Notice in the second example that the original fraction $\left(\frac{25}{35}\right)$ was divided rather than multiplied to get $\frac{5}{7}$. The numbers 5 and 7 have no common factor other than 1 so the fraction cannot be divided any further. This means that $\frac{25}{35}$ is now in its **simplest form** as $\frac{5}{7}$. This is sometimes called the **lowest terms**.

> **TIP**
>
> Fractions were originally written with a slant line like this: 2/5. You will often find fractions written like this and when you enter fractions online you type them like that.

> **TIP**
>
> Remember, dividing the numerator and denominator by the same number simplifies the fraction.

MATHEMATICAL CONNECTIONS

Before you work through this section remind yourself about highest common factors (HCFs) in Chapter 1, but remember you can multiply or divide by **any** factor to make equivalent fractions, it does not have to be the HCF.

WORKED EXAMPLE 1

Express each fraction in its simplest form.

a $\frac{3}{15}$ **b** $\frac{16}{24}$ **c** $\frac{21}{28}$ **d** $\frac{5}{8}$

Answers

a $\frac{3}{15} = \frac{3 \div 3}{15 \div 3} = \frac{1}{5}$ **b** $\frac{16}{24} = \frac{16 \div 8}{24 \div 8} = \frac{2}{3}$ **c** $\frac{21}{28} = \frac{21 \div 7}{28 \div 7} = \frac{3}{4}$

d $\frac{5}{8}$ is already in its simplest form

(5 and 8 have no common factors other than 1).

> **TIP**
>
> Notice that in each case you divide the numerator and the denominator by their HCF.

WORKED EXAMPLE 2

Which two of $\frac{5}{6}$, $\frac{20}{25}$ and $\frac{15}{18}$ are equivalent fractions?

Answer

$\frac{5}{6}$ is already in its simplest form.

Simplify each of the other fractions:

$\frac{20}{25} = \frac{20 \div 5}{25 \div 5} = \frac{4}{5}$

$\frac{15}{18} = \frac{15 \div 3}{18 \div 3} = \frac{5}{6}$

So $\frac{5}{6}$ and $\frac{15}{18}$ are equivalent.

Alternative method

You could have written:

$\frac{^5\cancel{15}}{_6\cancel{18}} = \frac{5}{6}$

This is called cancelling and is a shorter way of showing what you have done.

Exercise 5.1

1   By multiplying or dividing both the numerator and denominator by the same number, find three equivalent fractions for each of the following.

   a $\frac{5}{9}$ b $\frac{3}{7}$ c $\frac{12}{18}$ d $\frac{18}{36}$ e $\frac{110}{128}$

2   Express each of the following fractions in its simplest form.

   a $\frac{7}{21}$ b $\frac{3}{9}$ c $\frac{9}{12}$ d $\frac{15}{25}$ e $\frac{500}{2500}$ f $\frac{24}{36}$ g $\frac{108}{360}$

INVESTIGATION

Fraction diagrams

1   Read this activity and look at the solutions from three students.

Draw two lines across each rectangle to divide it into fractional parts. Name the fractions you make.

Lines must go through a vertex and/or a dot, but they do not need to go all the way across the rectangle.

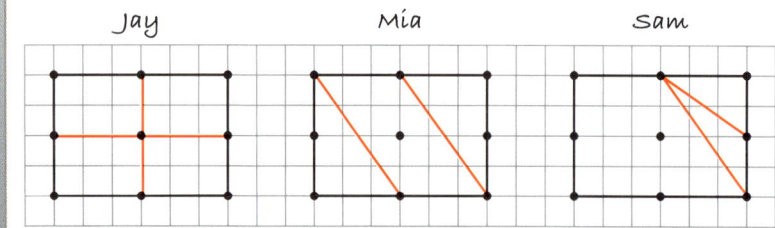

   a   What fractions did each student produce?

   b   Is it possible to do this and only produce two fractional parts? If so, how?

   c   What is the smallest fraction you can make in this task?

TIP

Work on squared or dotted paper to make it easier to draw the rectangles you need.

2   The second part of the task had the same instructions but used this rectangle with more dots on the sides.

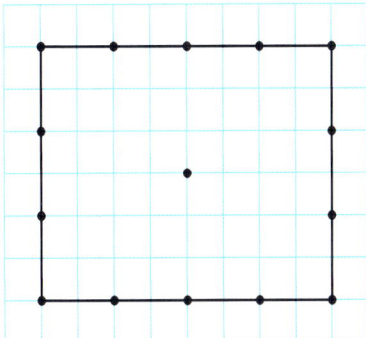

Work in pairs or small groups to investigate how many fractions you can make. Label your fractions.

5.2 Operations on fractions

Multiplying fractions

To multiply two or more fractions, multiply the numerators and then multiply the denominators. Sometimes you will need to simplify your answer.

WORKED EXAMPLE 3

Calculate.

a $\dfrac{3}{4} \times \dfrac{2}{7}$ b $\dfrac{5}{7} \times 3$ c $\dfrac{3}{8}$ of $4\dfrac{1}{2}$

Answers

a $\dfrac{3}{4} \times \dfrac{2}{7} = \dfrac{3 \times 2}{4 \times 7} = \dfrac{6}{28} = \dfrac{3}{14}$

Another method is to cancel before multiplying:

$\dfrac{3}{{}_{2}\!\cancel{4}} \times \dfrac{\cancel{2}^{1}}{7} = \dfrac{3 \times 1}{2 \times 7} = \dfrac{3}{14}$

Multiply the numerators to get the new numerator value. Do the same with the denominators. Then express the fraction in its simplest form.

Divide the denominator of the first fraction, and the numerator of the second fraction, by two.

b $\dfrac{5}{7} \times 3 = \dfrac{5 \times 3}{7 \times 1} = \dfrac{15}{7}$

15 and 7 do not have a common factor other than 1 and so cannot be simplified.

c $\dfrac{3}{8}$ of $4\dfrac{1}{2}$

$\dfrac{3}{8} \times 4\dfrac{1}{2} = \dfrac{3}{8} \times \dfrac{9}{2} = \dfrac{27}{16}$

You need to change the mixed number to an improper fraction. This allows you to complete the multiplication.

Notice that the word 'of' is replaced with the × sign.

TIP

To multiply a fraction by an integer you only multiply the numerator by the integer.
For example,
$\dfrac{5}{7} \times 3 = \dfrac{5 \times 3}{7} = \dfrac{15}{7}$.

TIP

An improper fraction is a fraction where the numerator is larger than the denominator.
To change a mixed number to a common fraction, multiply the whole number part (in this case 4) by the denominator and add it to the numerator.
So:
$4\dfrac{1}{2} = \dfrac{4 \times 2 + 1}{2} = \dfrac{9}{2}$.

Exercise 5.2

Evaluate each of the following.

1   **a** $\dfrac{2}{3} \times \dfrac{5}{9}$ **b** $\dfrac{1}{2} \times \dfrac{3}{7}$ **c** $\dfrac{1}{4} \times \dfrac{8}{9}$ **d** $\dfrac{2}{7} \times \dfrac{14}{16}$

2   **a** $\dfrac{50}{128} \times \dfrac{256}{500}$ **b** $1\dfrac{1}{3} \times \dfrac{2}{7}$ **c** $2\dfrac{2}{7} \times \dfrac{7}{8}$ **d** $\dfrac{4}{5}$ of $3\dfrac{2}{7}$

     e $1\dfrac{1}{3}$ of 24 **f** $5\dfrac{1}{2} \times 7\dfrac{1}{4}$ **g** $8\dfrac{8}{9} \times 20\dfrac{1}{4}$ **h** $7\dfrac{2}{3} \times 10\dfrac{1}{2}$

Adding and subtracting fractions

You can add or subtract fractions that have same denominators (**common denominator**). You can use equivalent fractions to make fractions with the same denominator.

This example shows how to use the lowest common multiple (LCM) of both denominators to find a common denominator.

> **MATHEMATICAL CONNECTIONS**
>
> You will use the LCM in this section. You learnt about this in Chapter 1.

WORKED EXAMPLE 4

Write each of the following as a single fraction in its simplest form.

a $\dfrac{3}{4} + \dfrac{5}{6}$ **b** $2\dfrac{3}{4} - 1\dfrac{5}{7}$

Answers

a $\dfrac{3}{4} + \dfrac{5}{6}$ Find the common denominator.

$= \dfrac{9}{12} + \dfrac{10}{12}$ The LCM of 4 and 6 is 12. Use this as the common denominator and find the equivalent fractions.

$= \dfrac{19}{12}$ Add the numerators.

$= 1\dfrac{7}{12}$ Change the improper fraction to a mixed number.

b $2\dfrac{3}{4} - 1\dfrac{5}{7} = \dfrac{11}{4} - \dfrac{12}{7}$ Change mixed numbers to improper fractions to make them easier to work with.

$= \dfrac{77}{28} - \dfrac{48}{28}$ The LCM of 4 and 7 is 28. Use this as the common denominator and find the equivalent fractions.

$= \dfrac{77 - 48}{28}$

$= \dfrac{29}{28}$ Subtract one numerator from the other.

$= 1\dfrac{1}{28}$ Change the improper fraction to a mixed number.

> **TIP**
>
> Once you have a common denominator, you only add the numerators. **Never** add the denominators.

> **TIP**
>
> Adding two fractions can result in an improper fraction. To write the fraction in its simplest form, rewrite it as a mixed number.

Exercise 5.3

Evaluate the following.

1 a $\frac{1}{3} + \frac{1}{3}$ b $\frac{3}{7} + \frac{2}{7}$ c $\frac{5}{8} - \frac{3}{8}$ d $\frac{5}{9} + \frac{8}{9}$

   e $\frac{1}{6} + \frac{1}{5}$ f $\frac{2}{3} - \frac{5}{8}$ g $2\frac{5}{8} - 1\frac{3}{4}$ h $5\frac{1}{8} - 3\frac{1}{16}$

2 a $4 - \frac{2}{3}$ b $6 + \frac{5}{11}$ c $11 + 7\frac{1}{4}$

   d $11 - 7\frac{1}{4}$ e $3\frac{1}{2} - 4\frac{1}{3}$ f $5\frac{1}{4} + 3\frac{1}{16} + 4\frac{3}{8}$

   g $5\frac{1}{8} - 3\frac{1}{16} + 4\frac{3}{4}$ h $1\frac{1}{3} + 2\frac{2}{5} - 1\frac{1}{4}$ i $\frac{3}{7} + \frac{2}{3} \times \frac{14}{8}$

   j $3\frac{1}{2} - 2\frac{1}{4} \times \frac{4}{3}$ k $3\frac{1}{6} - 1\frac{1}{2} + 7\frac{3}{4}$ l $2\frac{1}{4} - 3\frac{1}{3} + 4\frac{1}{5}$

> **TIP**
>
> Remember to use the correct order of operations (BODMAS) here.

INVESTIGATION

Fraction patterns

1 You can convert any fraction to a decimal number using your calculator.

For example, if you work out $\frac{1}{2}$ as a decimal by dividing 1 by 2 you will get the decimal 0.5.

Try converting the following fractions to decimals:

$$\frac{2}{5} \quad \frac{1}{3} \quad \frac{5}{8} \quad \frac{3}{7} \quad \frac{4}{9} \quad \frac{3}{16}$$

2 Which fractions in question 1 stop ('terminate') after a few decimal places and which seem to go on forever? Try some more fractions and decide which of these two groups they fall into.

3 Look at the dominators of the fractions that with decimals that terminate. What do they have in common? [Hint: what are the factors of the denominator each time?]

4 Now work out the decimals for:

$$\frac{1}{7} \quad \frac{2}{7} \quad \frac{3}{7} \quad \frac{4}{7} \quad \frac{5}{7}$$

Do the answers have anything in common?

Try the same thing with denominator 11. What about 13?

Explain any patterns that you see.

> **MATHEMATICAL CONNECTIONS**
>
> You will revisit multiplication, division, addition and subtraction of fractions in Chapter 14 when you deal with algebraic fractions.

Dividing fractions

To divide one fraction by another, you multiply the first fraction by the reciprocal of the second fraction.

To find the reciprocal of a fraction you invert it. So, the reciprocal of $\frac{3}{4}$ is $\frac{4}{3}$ and the reciprocal of $\frac{7}{2}$ is $\frac{2}{7}$.

The reciprocal of $\frac{1}{2}$ is $\frac{2}{1}$ or just 2 and the reciprocal of 5 is $\frac{1}{5}$.

When you multiply a fraction by its reciprocal the result is always 1. For example:

$$\frac{1}{3} \times \frac{3}{1} = 1, \qquad \frac{3}{8} \times \frac{8}{3} = 1 \qquad \text{and} \qquad \frac{a}{b} \times \frac{b}{a} = 1.$$

Look at the example below to understand why this method works.

$$\frac{5}{11} \div \frac{1}{2} = \frac{\frac{5}{11}}{\frac{1}{2}}$$

To get rid of the fraction $\left(\frac{1}{2}\right)$ in the denominator, multiply both the numerator and denominator by 2.

$$\frac{5}{11} \div \frac{1}{2} = \frac{\frac{5}{11} \times \frac{2}{1}}{\frac{1}{2} \times \frac{2}{1}} = \frac{\frac{10}{11}}{1} = \frac{10}{11}$$

If you invert the fraction you are dividing by and multiply, you will give the same answer with fewer steps:

$$\frac{5}{11} \div \frac{1}{2} = \frac{5}{11} \times \frac{2}{1} = \frac{10}{11}$$

WORKED EXAMPLE 5

Evaluate each of the following.

a $\frac{3}{4} \div \frac{1}{2}$ b $1\frac{3}{4} \div 2\frac{1}{3}$ c $\frac{5}{8} \div 2$ d $\frac{6}{7} \div 3$

Answers

a $\frac{3}{4} \div \frac{1}{2} = \frac{3}{24} \times \frac{2^1}{1}$ Multiply by the reciprocal of $\frac{1}{2}$.

$= \frac{3}{2}$ Use the rules you have learned about multiplying fractions.

$= 1\frac{1}{2}$

b $1\frac{3}{4} \div 2\frac{1}{3} = \frac{7}{4} \div \frac{7}{3}$ Convert the mixed fractions to improper fractions.

$= \frac{^1 7}{4} \times \frac{3}{7_1}$ Multiply by the reciprocal of $\frac{7}{3}$.

$= \frac{3}{4}$

WORKED EXAMPLE 5 CONTINUED

c $\dfrac{5}{8} \div 2 = \dfrac{5}{8} \div \dfrac{2}{1}$ Write 2 as an improper fraction.

$\qquad = \dfrac{5}{8} \times \dfrac{1}{2}$ Multiply by the reciprocal of $\dfrac{2}{1}$.

$\qquad = \dfrac{5}{16}$

d $\dfrac{6}{7} \div 3 = \dfrac{\overset{2}{\cancel{6}}}{7} \times \dfrac{1}{\underset{1}{\cancel{3}}}$

$\qquad = \dfrac{2}{7}$

> **TIP**
>
> To divide a fraction by an integer you can either multiply the denominator by the integer, *or* divide the numerator by the same integer.

Exercise 5.4

Evaluate each of the following.

1 $\dfrac{1}{7} \div \dfrac{1}{3}$

2 $\dfrac{2}{5} \div \dfrac{3}{7}$

3 $\dfrac{4}{9} \div 7$

4 $\dfrac{10}{11} \div 5$

5 $4\dfrac{1}{5} \div \dfrac{1}{7}$

6 $3\dfrac{1}{5} \div 5\dfrac{2}{3}$

7 $7\dfrac{7}{8} \div 5\dfrac{1}{12}$

8 $3\dfrac{1}{4} \div 3\dfrac{1}{2}$

9 a $\left(2\dfrac{1}{3} - 1\dfrac{2}{5}\right) \div 1\dfrac{1}{3}$ b $2\dfrac{1}{3} - 1\dfrac{2}{5} \div 1\dfrac{1}{3}$

Fractions with decimals

In some calculations either the numerator or the denominator, or both, might not be whole numbers. To express these fractions in their simplest forms:

- find an equivalent fraction where both the numerator and denominator are integers
- check that the equivalent fraction is in its simplest form.

WORKED EXAMPLE 6

Simplify each of the following fractions.

a $\dfrac{0.1}{3}$ b $\dfrac{1.3}{2.4}$ c $\dfrac{36}{0.12}$

Answers

a $\dfrac{0.1}{3} = \dfrac{0.1 \times 10}{3 \times 10}$ Multiply 0.1 by 10 to convert 0.1 to an integer.

$\qquad = \dfrac{1}{30}$ Make sure the fraction is equivalent by also multiplying the denominator (3) by 10.

WORKED EXAMPLE 6 CONTINUED

b $\dfrac{1.3}{2.4} = \dfrac{1.3 \times 10}{2.4 \times 10}$ Multiply both the numerator and denominator by 10 to get integers.

$\quad = \dfrac{13}{24}$ 13 and 24 do not have a HCF other than 1, so you cannot simplify the fraction.

c $\dfrac{36}{0.12} = \dfrac{36 \times 100}{0.12 \times 100}$ Multiply 0.12 by 100 to produce an integer.

$\quad = \dfrac{3600}{12}$ Remember to multiply the numerator by 100, so the fraction is equivalent.

$\quad = 300$ Simplify the final fraction by cancelling.

Exercise 5.5

Simplify each of the following fractions.

1 $\dfrac{0.3}{12}$ **2** $\dfrac{0.4}{0.5}$ **3** $\dfrac{6}{0.7}$ **4** $\dfrac{0.7}{0.14}$

5 $\dfrac{36}{1.5}$ **6** $0.3 \times \dfrac{5}{12}$ **7** $0.4 \times \dfrac{1.5}{1.6}$ **8** $\dfrac{2.8}{0.7} \times \dfrac{1.44}{0.6}$

> **TIP**
>
> Remember: a fraction that contains a decimal is not its simplest form.

Further calculations with fractions

You can use fractions to help you solve problems.

WORKED EXAMPLE 7

Suppose that $\dfrac{2}{5}$ of the students in a school wear glasses. If the school has 600 students, how many students wear glasses?

Answer

$\dfrac{2}{5}$ of $600 = \dfrac{2}{5} \times 600$

$\quad = \dfrac{2}{5} \times \dfrac{600^{120}}{1}$

$\quad = 2 \times 120 = 240$ students

> **TIP**
>
> Remember: in Worked example 3, you saw that 'of' is replaced by ×.

WORKED EXAMPLE 8

$\dfrac{2}{5}$ of the students in a school do not wear glasses. If 360 students do not wear glasses, how many students are there in the whole school?

Answer

$\dfrac{2}{5}$ of the total is 360, so $\dfrac{1}{5}$ of the total must be half of this, 180.

This means that the total $\left(\dfrac{5}{5}\right)$ is $5 \times 180 = 900$ students altogether.

Exercise 5.6

1 $\frac{3}{4}$ of the people at an auction bought an item. If there are 120 people at the auction, how many bought something?

2 An essay contains 420 sentences. 80 of these sentences contain typing errors. What fraction of the sentences contain errors? Write the fraction in its simplest form.

3 28 is $\frac{2}{7}$ of which number?

4 If $\frac{3}{5}$ of the people in a theatre buy a snack during the interval, and of those who buy a snack $\frac{5}{7}$ buy ice cream, what fraction of the people in the theatre buy ice cream?

5 Asma, Bashir and Candice are trying to save money for a party. If Asma saves $\frac{1}{4}$ of the total needed, Bashir saves $\frac{2}{5}$ and Candice saves $\frac{1}{10}$, what fraction of the cost of the party is left to pay?

6 A chef needs $6\frac{1}{2}$ cups of cooked rice for a recipe of Nasi Goreng.

If 2 cups of uncooked rice with $2\frac{1}{2}$ cups of water make $4\frac{1}{3}$ cups of cooked rice, how many cups of uncooked rice does the chef need?

How much water should the chef add?

REFLECTION

Which strategies, skills and procedures that you learned in your earlier studies were most useful for this work on fractions?

Did any of the activities on fractions in this chapter help you learn more than others? Why?

5.3 Percentages

Per cent means 'out of a hundred'. The percentage 40% means '40 out of every hundred'. You can see in the diagram that this is equivalent to 4 out of ten people:

$$\frac{4}{10} = \frac{40}{100} = 40\%$$

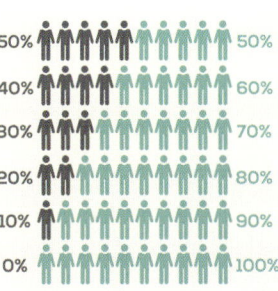

Equivalent percentages, fractions and decimals

Percentages, fractions and decimals are all ways of representing part of a whole.

To convert a percentage into a decimal, divide by 100. So, $45\% = \frac{45}{100} = 0.45$ and $3.1\% = \frac{3.1}{100} = 0.031$. (Notice that the digits move two places to the right.)

To convert a decimal to a percentage, multiply by 100. So, $0.65 = \frac{65}{100} = 65\%$ and $0.7 \times 100 = 70\%$. (Notice that the digits move two places to the left.)

To convert a percentage to a fraction, write the fraction with a denominator of 100 and simplify.

WORKED EXAMPLE 9

Convert each of the following percentages to fractions in their simplest form.

a 25% **b** 30% **c** 3.5%

Answers

a $25\% = \frac{25}{100} = \frac{1}{4}$ Write as a fraction with a denominator of 100, then simplify.

b $30\% = \frac{30}{100} = \frac{3}{10}$ Write as a fraction with a denominator of 100, then simplify.

c $3.5\% = \frac{3.5}{100} = \frac{35}{1000} = \frac{7}{200}$ Write as a fraction with a denominator of 100, then simplify.

To convert a fraction to a percentage, write it as an equivalent fraction with a denominator of 100.

WORKED EXAMPLE 10

Convert each of the following fractions into percentages.

a $\dfrac{1}{20}$ **b** $\dfrac{1}{8}$

Answers

a $\dfrac{1}{20} = \dfrac{1 \times 5}{20 \times 5}$ Find the equivalent fraction with a denominator of 100.

$\quad = \dfrac{5}{100}$

$\quad = 5\%$

b $\dfrac{1}{8} = \dfrac{1 \times 12.5}{8 \times 12.5}$ Find the equivalent fraction with a denominator of 100.

$\quad = \dfrac{12.5}{100}$

$\quad = 12.5\%$

You can convert any fraction into a percentage by multiplying by 100 and cancelling.

> **TIP**
>
> Remember to multiply both the numerator and denominator by the same number.

WORKED EXAMPLE 11

Convert the following fractions into percentages:

a $\dfrac{3}{40}$ **b** $\dfrac{8}{15}$ **c** $\dfrac{25}{4}$

Answers

a $\dfrac{3}{40} \times \dfrac{100}{1} = \dfrac{30}{4} = \dfrac{15}{2} = 7.5$, so $\dfrac{3}{40} = 7.5\%$

b $\dfrac{8}{15} \times \dfrac{100}{1} = \dfrac{160}{3} = 53.3$ (1 d.p.), so $\dfrac{8}{15} = 53.3\%$ (1 d.p.)

c $\dfrac{25}{4} \times \dfrac{100}{1} = \dfrac{2500}{4} = 625\%$

You can use a calculator to convert a fraction to a percentage. For example, to convert $\dfrac{3}{40}$ to a percentage you would enter:

Your display will show 7.5. This is the percentage.

> **TIP**
>
> You do not enter a percentage sign in this conversion calculation because the values you are entering are not percentages. The answer is a percentage.

Exercise 5.7

1   Convert each of the following percentages into fractions in their simplest form.

   a   70%   b   75%   c   20%   d   36%   e   15%   f   2.5%

   g   215%   h   132%   i   117.5% j   108.4% k   0.25%   l   0.002%

2   Express the following fractions as percentages.

   a $\dfrac{3}{5}$ b $\dfrac{7}{25}$ c $\dfrac{17}{20}$ d $\dfrac{3}{10}$ e $\dfrac{8}{200}$ f $\dfrac{50}{12}$

Percentage calculations

INVESTIGATION

Thinking about percentages

1   **Finding a percentage of an amount**
    13% of 500 is 65.

   a   Which of the following methods correctly find 13% of 500?

Method A	Method B	Method C	Method D	Method E
13×500	$\dfrac{500}{13} \times 65$	0.013×500	$\dfrac{13}{100} \times 500$	$\dfrac{13}{500} \times 100$

   b   Discuss why the other methods won't give the correct answer.

2   How does your calculator deal with percentages?

   a   Enter 2 5 % .
       What does your display show? Why?

   b   What do you need to enter on your calculator to work out that 12% of 650 is 78? Is there any other way to work this out using your calculator? Did you need to press the = key?

   c   When you converted between fractions, decimals and percentages, you did not use the % key. Why do you need to enter a % sign in these calculations?

   d   Compare how your calculator works with others in your group. Do all calculators work the same way?

3   **Using fraction or decimal equivalents** show how you can work out 15% of 500 using a fraction or a decimal (and no calculator).

Finding one number as a percentage of another

You can express one number as a percentage of another number. To do this, write the first number as a fraction of the second number then multiply by 100.

WORKED EXAMPLE 12

a   Express 16 as a percentage of 48.

Answer

$\dfrac{16}{48} \times 100 = 33.3\%$ (1 d.p.)   First, write 16 as a fraction of 48, then multiply by 100.

$\dfrac{16}{48} = \dfrac{1}{3}$ If you are working without a calculator, you may find it easier to write the fraction in its simplest form first.

$\dfrac{1}{3} \times 100 = 33.3\%$ (1 d.p.)

b   Express 15 as a percentage of 75.

Answer

$\dfrac{15}{75} \times 100 = \dfrac{1}{5} \times 100$ Write 15 as a fraction of 75, then simplify and multiply by 100. You know that 100 divided by 5 is 20, so you don't need a calculator.

$\qquad = 20\%$

c   Express 18 as a percentage of 23.

Answer

To calculate $\dfrac{18}{23} \times 100$ you can use your calculator. Enter:

| 1 | 8 | ÷ | 2 | 3 | × | 1 | 0 | 0 | = | 78.26% (2 d.p.)

d   Express 24 grams as a percentage of 15.

Answer

$\dfrac{24}{15} \times 100 = \dfrac{2400}{15} = 160\%$

Exercise 5.8

Where appropriate, give your answer to 3 significant figures.

1   Calculate:

   a   5% of 300   **b**   20% of 60   **c**   75% of 180

   d   120% of 300   **e**   7.5% of 1000   **f**   90% of 50 kg

   g   2.6% of 3 metres   **h** $\dfrac{1}{2}$% of 55 litres.

2   Express:

   a   14 as a percentage of 35   **b**   3.5 as a percentage of 14

   c   17 as a percentage of 63.

3   A factory that makes mobile phone batteries estimates that 2.4% of the batteries are not up to standard. If they produce 16 800 batteries, how many will be up to standard?

4   36 people live in a block of flats. 28 of these people jog around the park each morning. What percentage of the people living in the block of flats go jogging around the park?

5   Jaleel scores $\frac{19}{24}$ in a test. What percentage of the marks did Jaleel get?

6   Express 1.3 as a percentage of 5.2.

7   Express 0.13 as a percentage of 520.

8   One orange contains 53.2 mg of Vitamin C. The daily recommended amount for adults is 90 mg per day. Express the amount of Vitamin C in three oranges as a percentage of the daily recommended amount.

Percentage increases and decreases

The cost of a book increases from $12 to $15. The actual increase is $3. As a fraction of the original value, the increase is $\frac{3}{12} = \frac{1}{4}$. This is the fractional change and you can write this fraction as 25%. In this example, the value of the book increased by 25% of the original value. This is called the **percentage increase**. If the value reduces (for example if something is on sale in a shop) then it is a **percentage decrease**.

> **MATHEMATICAL CONNECTIONS**
>
> Percentages are used a lot in financial mathematics, where interest is added on a percentage basis to savings or debts. You will learn more about this in Chapter 17.

> **TIP**
>
> When increases or decreases are stated as percentages, they are always stated as percentages of the **original** value.

> **WORKED EXAMPLE 13**
>
> The value of a house increased from $120 000 to $124 800 between August and December. What percentage increase is this?
>
> **Answer**
>
> $124\,800 - \$120\,000 = \$4800$ First calculate the increase.
>
> $\% \text{ increase} = \dfrac{\text{increase}}{\text{original}} \times 100\%$ Write the increase as a fraction of the original and multiply by 100.
>
> $= \dfrac{4800}{120\,000} \times 100\%$ Then do the calculation (either in your head or using a calculator).
>
> $= 4\%$

Exercise 5.9

> **APPLY YOUR SKILLS**
>
> Where appropriate, give your answer to the nearest whole percent.
>
> **1**   Over a five-year period, the population of the state of Louisiana in the United States of America decreased from 4 468 976 to 4 287 768. Find the percentage decrease in the population of Louisiana in this period.
>
> **2**   Sunil streamed 38 series one year and 46 the next year. Find the percentage increase.

APPLY YOUR SKILLS CONTINUED

3   A theatre has 450 seats. After renovation it will have 480 seats. Find the percentage increase in the number of seats.

4   Sally works in an electrical component factory. On Monday she makes 363 components and on Tuesday she makes 432. Calculate the percentage increase.

5   Inter-Polation Airlines carried a total of 383 402 passengers in one year and 287 431 in the following year. Calculate the percentage decrease in passengers carried by the airline.

6   A liquid evaporates steadily. In one hour the mass of liquid in a container decreases from 0.32 kg to 0.18 kg. Calculate the percentage decrease.

Increasing and decreasing by a given percentage

If you know what percentage you want to increase or decrease an amount by, you can find the actual increase or decrease by finding a percentage of the original. If you want to know the new value, you either add the increase to, or subtract the decrease from, the original value.

You can also use a multiplier to increase or decrease amounts. An increase of 5% means you will end up with 105%. This is equivalent to $\frac{105}{100} = 1.05$, so you can multiply by 1.05 to work out the increased amount. A decrease of 5% will leave you with 95%. This is equivalent to $\frac{95}{100} = 0.95$ and you can use this to calculate the decreased amount.

WORKED EXAMPLE 14

Increase 56 by: **a** 10%   **b** 15%   **c** 4%

Answers

a $10\% \text{ of } 56 = \frac{10}{100} \times 56$ Calculate 10% of 56 to work out the size of the increase.

      $= \frac{1}{10} \times 56 = 5.6$ To increase the original by 10% add this to 56.

   $56 + 5.6 = 61.6$

b $1.15 \times 56 = 64.4$ A 15% increase means 115% of the original.

                     115% = 1.15

c $1.04 \times 56 = 58.24$ A 4% increase means 104% of the original.

                     104% = 1.04

TIP

Remember that you are always considering a percentage of the **original** value.

WORKED EXAMPLE 15

In a sale all items are reduced by 15%. If the normal price for a bicycle is $120 calculate the sale price.

Answer

100% − 15% = 85%

$\dfrac{85}{100} \times \$120 = \$102$

Or use a multiplier:

$0.85 \times \$120 = 102$

Reducing a number by 15% leaves you with 85% of the original. So, find 85% of the original value.

85% is equivalent to $\dfrac{85}{100} = 0.85$

You can draw a bar model to help you with percentage calculations.

WORKED EXAMPLE 16

A licence for anti-virus software normally costs $70.00. What would you pay for the software if you got 25% discount?

Answer

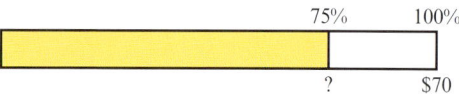

Draw a bar model.

A 25% discount means the software is now 75% of the original cost.

100% = $70 and you need to find 75%.

$1\% = \dfrac{\$70}{100} = \$0.7$

$75\% = \$0.7 \times 75 = \$52.50$

Divide $70 by 100 to find 1%

Multiply by 75 to find 75%

Exercise 5.10

1 Increase 40 by:

   a 10%   **b** 15%   **c** 25%   **d** 5%   **e** 4%

2 Increase 53 by:

   a 50%   **b** 84%   **c** 13.6%   **d** 112%   **e** $\frac{1}{2}$%

3 Decrease 124 by:

   a 10%   **b** 15%   **c** 30%   **d** 4%   **e** 7%

4 Decrease 36.2 by:

   a 90%   **b** 35.4%   **c** 0.3%   **d** 100%   **e** $\frac{1}{2}$%

APPLY YOUR SKILLS

5   Shajeen usually works 30 hours per week. He increases his working hours by 10% to earn enough to save for a holiday. How many hours per week will Shajeen work now?

6   12% sales tax is added to clothing sold in a certain shop. If a T-shirt is advertised for $12 before tax, what will it cost after tax is added?

7   In its first year, 21 300 people attended shows at the Oyler Theatre. The theatre decided to advertise more and this led to a 23% increase in its audience numbers for its second year. How many people attended shows in the second year?

8   The village of Trigville had 153 000 residents. A flood caused 17% of the residents to move away. What was the population of Trigville after the flood?

9   Anthea's screen time report said she spent 12 hours on screen during one week. The next week, this had reduced by 12%. How much time did she spend on screen in the second week? Give your answer in hours and minutes to the nearest minute.

10 A population of bacteria is increasing at a rate of 15% per hour. What is the percentage increase after 4 hours? Give your answer correct to 2 decimal places.

11 Due to surplus production, oil prices decrease by 12% in January and then by a further 12% in February. A newsreader reports that the price of oil has decreased by 24%. Is that correct? Justify your answer.

12 The number of passengers using a new ride-share service is increasing by x% each year and is expected to double in 5 years. What is the value of x correct to 1 decimal place?

DISCUSSION

13 Discuss these questions about percentage increases and decreases in small groups. Be prepared to explain your answers to the class.

   a   Two students start with the same number of points. Student A's points increase by 10% each day. Student B's points decrease by 10% each day. Will the original number of points have doubled and halved on the same day? Justify your answer.

   b   Which results in more points: doubling the original number or a 40% increase followed by a 50% increase? Why?

   c   Which of these offers gives cheaper data when you are buying airtime?

   •   50% discount from the price of data
   •   50% extra data free

PEER ASSESSMENT

Assess your partner's work in Exercise 5.10.

Provide feedback using these three headings:

- What went well?
- How could your work be better?
- What steps can you take to improve?

Some sentence starters that you can use for each heading are given in the table.

What went well?	How could your work be better?	Your next steps
The things that went well were …	To improve you can …	Your next step should be …
You are good at …	Try to …	To make this even better you can …
The best part of your work was …	Next time you need to …	It would be good if you could try to …
You can be proud of …	If you do this again you could …	
From your work I learned how to improve my own work by …	To help you understand this …	Ask for help on …
	Look at … in your coursebook to …	Focus on …

Reverse percentages

Sometimes you are given the value or amount of an item after a percentage increase or decrease and you need to work out what the original value was. To solve these reverse percentage questions, it is important to remember that you are always dealing with percentages of the original values.

WORKED EXAMPLE 17

A store is holding a sale in which every item is reduced by 10%. A jacket in this sale is sold for $108.

Calculate the original price of the jacket.

Answer

$\frac{90}{100} \times x = 108$ The new cost is 90% of the original.

$x = \frac{100}{90} \times 108$ To solve for x, multiply both sides of the equation by

Original price = $120   the reciprocal of $\frac{90}{100}$

It is important to remember that undoing a 10% decrease is not the same as increasing the reduced value by 10%.
If you increase the sale price of $108 by 10% you will get $\frac{110}{100} \times \$108 = \$118.80$, which is a different (and incorrect) answer.

You can use a bar model to help you with reverse percentage calculations.

WORKED EXAMPLE 18

A shop advertises a laptop for sale for $320 during a 20% off sale.
What was the original price of the laptop?

Answer

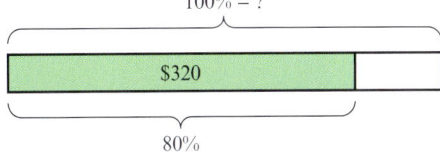

Draw a bar model.

20% has been taken off, so $320 is 80% of the original cost.

$1\% = \dfrac{\$320}{80} = \$4$

Divide $320 by 80 to find 1%

$100\% = \$4 \times 100 = \$400$

Multiply $4 by 100 to find 100%

Exercise 5.11

1   If 20% of an amount is 35, what is 100%?

2   If 35% of an amount is 127, what is 100%?

3   245 is 12.5% of an amount. What is the total amount?

4   The table gives the sale price and the per cent by which the price was reduced for a number of items. Copy the table and complete it by calculating the original prices.

Sale price ($)	% reduction	Original price ($)
52.00	10	
185.00	10	
4700.00	5	
2.90	5	
24.50	12	
10.00	8	
12.50	7	
9.75	15	
199.50	20	
99.00	25	

APPLY YOUR SKILLS

5   A shop keeper increases the cost price of items by 22% before selling them. The selling price (after the increase) of ten items are given below. For each item, work out the cost price.

   a $25.00   b $200.00   c $14.50   d $23.99   e $15.80

   f $45.80   g $29.75   h $129.20   i $0.99   j $0.80

6   Seven students were absent from a class on Monday. This is 17.5% of the class.

   a   How many students are there in the class in total?

   b   How many students were present on Monday?

7   A hat shop is holding a 10% sale. If Jay buys a hat for $18 in the sale, how much did the hat cost before the sale?

8   While Suresh is training for a race, he reduces his weight by 5% over a 3-month period. If Suresh weighs 76 kg at the end of three months, how much did he weigh before he started training?

9   The water in a pond evaporates at a rate of 12% per week. If the pond now contains 185 litres of water, approximately how much water was in the pond a week ago?

5.4 Standard form

- There are an estimated 1 000 000 000 000 000 000 000 000 stars in the universe.

- The star Betelgeuse has a mass of 21 880 000 000 000 000 000 000 000 000 000 kg.

- A single carbon atom has a mass of 0.000 000 000 000 000 000 000 000 019 9 kg.

It is clumsy and impractical to write out very large and very small numbers like this. You might make mistakes and add or miss out zeros in calculations. We use **standard form** to express very small and very large numbers as a number multiplied by a power of 10.

LINK

Very small and very large numbers occur often in chemistry; the carbon atom mass, given here, is just one example. The reason this happens a lot is because the subject usually deals with very small objects in very large numbers.

TIP

Standard form is also called scientific notation or exponential notation.

Writing numbers in standard form

You can write any number in standard form by writing it as a number between 1 and 10 multiplied by a suitable power of 10. In algebraic language we say that any number can be written in the form $A \times 10^n$, where $1 \leqslant A < 10$ and n is an integer.

The numbers at the start of this section can be written in standard form as 1×10^{24}, 2.188×10^{31} and 1.99×10^{-26}.

When a number is in standard form, the index (power of 10) tells you how many places the digits have moved and whether they have moved to the right or left.

WORKED EXAMPLE 19

Write 320 000 in standard form.

Answer

3.2 — Write the number with the decimal point after the first non-zero digit to get a number between 1 and 10.

$$
\begin{array}{c}
5\ \ 4\ \ 3\ \ 2\ \ 1 \\
3\ 2\ 0\ 0\ 0\ 0.0 \\
3.2
\end{array}
$$

Work out how many places the first digit needs to move to get back to its original place. In this case, the 3 needs to move five places to the left to get back to its original hundred thousands position.

$320\,000 = 3.2 \times 10^5$ — Work out the index (power of 10). In this case, the original number is bigger than 3.2 so the index will be positive.

In other words, to move the digit 3 back to its original position you would need to multiply by 10^5.

WORKED EXAMPLE 20

1 Write each of the following numbers in standard form.

   a 0.004   **b** 0.000 000 34

Answers

a
$$
\begin{array}{c}
1\ \ 2\ \ 3 \\
0.0\ 0\ 4 \\
4.0 \\
= 4 \times 10^{-3}
\end{array}
$$

Start with a number between 1 and 10, in this case 4.

Compare the position of the first digit: '4' needs to move three places to the right to get from the new number to the original number. In Worked example 19 you saw that moving five places to the *left* meant multiplying by 10^5, so moving three places to the *right* means multiply by 10^{-3}.

Notice also that the first non-zero digit in 0.004 is in the 3rd place after the decimal point and that the power of 10 is −3.

b $0.000\,000\,34 = 3.4 \div 10^7$
$$= 3.4 \times 10^{-7}$$

$$
\begin{array}{c}
1\ \ 2\ \ 3\ \ 4\ \ 5\ \ 6\ \ 7 \\
0.0\ 0\ 0\ 0\ 0\ 0\ 3\ 4 = 3.4 \times 10^{-7}
\end{array}
$$

The first non-zero digit in 0.000 000 34 is in the 7th place after the decimal point so the power of 10 is −7.

Exercise 5.12

1 Write each of the following numbers in standard form.

a	380	**b**	4 200 000	**c**	45 600 000 000
d	65 400 000 000 000	**e**	20	**f**	10
g	10.3	**h**	5	**i**	0.004
j	0.000 05	**k**	0.000 032	**l**	0.000 000 056 4

2 Write each of the following as an ordinary number.

a	2.4×10^6	**b**	3.1×10^8	**c**	1.05×10^7
d	9.9×10^3	**e**	7.1×10^1	**f**	3.6×10^{-4}
g	1.6×10^{-8}	**h**	2.03×10^{-7}	**i**	8.8×10^{-3}

APPLY YOUR SKILLS

3 A grain of rice has a mass of 25 mg.

    a Convert this to kilograms.

    b Write the mass in kilograms using scientific notation.

4 The closest star to our Sun is Proxima Centauri at a distance of 40 208 000 000 000 km. Express this in scientific notation.

5 A stack of 500 sheets of paper is 42 mm thick. Express the thickness of one sheet of paper using scientific notation.

TIP

When converting from standard form back to an ordinary number, the power of 10 tells you how many places the first digit moves, not how many zeros there are.

Your calculator and standard form

On modern scientific calculators you can enter numbers and calculations in standard form. Also, if an answer has too many digits to fit on the screen, your calculator will display it in standard form.

Calculators can display answers in standard form on one line like this:

`5.98ε-06`

This is 5.98×10^{-06}

or on two lines with the calculation and the answer, like this:

`6.23ε23*4.11`
`                2.56ε24`

This is 2.56×10^{24}

INVESTIGATION

Standard form on a calculator

1   How does your calculator deal with standard form?

    a   Find the $\boxed{\times 10^x}$ button or the $\boxed{\text{Exp}}$ or $\boxed{\text{EE}}$ button on your calculator. These are known as the exponent keys.

    b   Enter these calculations. Check that you get the correct answers.

        i 2.134×10^4 **ii** 3.124×10^{-6}

        Answers: **i**   21 340   **ii**   0.000 003 124

    c   Did you have to enter × 10? Why?

2   Here are ten calculator displays giving answers in standard form in different ways.

1.09 05	2.876 -06	4.012 09	1.89 07	8.124ε-11
3.123ε13	2.876ε-04	9.02ε15	8.076ε-12	5.0234 19

    a   Write out each answer in standard form.

    b   Arrange the ten numbers in order from smallest to largest.

> **TIP**
>
> Different calculators work in different ways and you need to understand how your own calculator works. Make sure you know what buttons to use to enter standard form calculations and how to interpret the display and convert your calculator answer into an ordinary number.

> **TIP**
>
> If you are asked to give your answer in standard form, you need to interpret the display and write the answer correctly. If you are asked to give your answer as an ordinary number then you need to apply the rules you already know to write the answer correctly.

Exercise 5.13

1   Enter each of these numbers into your calculator using the correct function key and write down what appears on your calculator display.

    a 4.2×10^{12} **b** 1.8×10^{-5} **c** 2.7×10^6

    d 1.34×10^{-2} **e** 1.87×10^{-9} **f** 4.23×10^7

    g 3.102×10^{-4} **h** 3.098×10^9 **i** 2.076×10^{-23}

2   Use your calculator. Give the answers in standard form correct to 5 significant figures.

    a 4234^5 **b** $0.0008 \div 9200^3$ **c** $(1.009)^5$

    d $123\,000\,000 \div 0.000\,76$ **e** $(97 \times 876)^4$ **f** $(0.0098)^4 \times (0.0032)^3$

    g $\dfrac{8543 \times 9210}{0.000034}$ **h** $\dfrac{9754}{(0.0005)^4}$

3   Use your calculator to find the answers correct to 4 significant figures.

    a $9.27 \times (2.8 \times 10^5)$ **b** $(4.23 \times 10^{-2})^3$ **c** $(3.2 \times 10^7) \div (7.2 \times 10^9)$

    d $(3.2 \times 10^{-4})^2$ **e** $231 \times (1.5 \times 10^{-6})$ **f** $(4.3 \times 10^5) + (2.3 \times 10^7)$

    g $\sqrt{3.24 \times 10^7}$ **h** $\sqrt[3]{4.2 \times 10^{-8}}$ **i** $\sqrt[3]{1.126 \times 10^{-9}}$

APPLY YOUR SKILLS

4   A hardware designer is trying to work out whether a small cuboid shaped chip will fit into the available space in a new smartwatch. The chip has a volume of 7.927×10^{-17} m. The space available is also a cuboid $0.000\,000\,3\,27$ m long. $0.000\,000\,2$ m wide and $0.000\,116$ m high. Will the chip fit into this space? Show your working.

5   Data storage (in computers) is measured in gigabytes. One gigabyte is 2^{30} bytes.

   a   Write 2^{30} in standard form correct to 3 significant figures.

   b   There are 1024 gigabytes in a terabyte. How many bytes is this? Give your answer in standard form correct to 1 significant figure.

Calculating in standard form without a calculator

Sometimes you may have to perform calculations using numbers written in standard form without using your calculator.

Multiplying and dividing

When numbers are written in standard form you can use the laws of indices to multiply and divide them without using a calculator.

> **MATHEMATICAL CONNECTIONS**
>
> The laws of indices are covered in Chapter 1 and revisited in Chapter 2.

WORKED EXAMPLE 21

Write each of the following in standard form.

a $(3 \times 10^5) \times (2 \times 10^6)$ b $(2 \times 10^3) \times (8 \times 10^7)$ c $(2.8 \times 10^6) \div (1.4 \times 10^4)$

Answers

a $(3 \times 10^5) \times (2 \times 10^6) = (3 \times 2) \times (10^5 \times 10^6)$ Rearrange the calculation.

$= 6 \times 10^{5+6}$ Use the laws of indices where appropriate.

$= 6 \times 10^{11}$ Write the number in standard form.

You may be asked to convert your answer to an ordinary number. 6.0×10^{11}

To convert 6×10^{11} into an ordinary number, the '6' needs to move 11 places to the left:

11 10 9 8 7 6 5 4 3 2 1

$= 6\,0\,0\,0\,0\,0\,0\,0\,0\,0\,0\,0.0$

b $(2 \times 10^3) \times (8 \times 10^7) = (2 \times 8) \times (10^3 \times 10^7)$ The answer 16×10^{10} is numerically correct but it is not in standard form because 16 is not between 1 and 10. You can change it to standard form by thinking of 16 as 1.6×10.

$= 16 \times 10^{10}$

$16 \times 10^{10} = 1.6 \times 10 \times 10^{10}$

$= 1.6 \times 10^{11}$

c $(2.8 \times 10^6) \div (1.4 \times 10^4) = \dfrac{2.8 \times 10^6}{1.4 \times 10^4}$

$= \dfrac{2.8}{1.4} \times \dfrac{10^6}{10^4}$

$= 2 \times 10^{6-4}$ Subtract the indices to divide the powers.

$= 2 \times 10^2$

Adding and subtracting

In Chapter 2 you learned that you can add and subtract like terms. In standard form, like terms are identical powers of 10. For example, 1.2×10^3 and 3×10^3 are like terms and you can add them to get 4.2×10^3.

The numbers 9×10^6 and 3×10^8 have different powers of 10, so these are not like terms and you cannot simply add them. Instead you can manipulate the expressions to make like terms. For example, you can write 3×10^8 as $3 \times 10^6 \times 10^2$ (because $10^6 \times 10^2 = 10^8$) and then you can write this as 300×10^6 and add it to 9×10^6.

> **TIP**
>
> If you are using a calculator you don't need to manipulate the expressions. You just enter the calculation correctly to get the answer.

> **WORKED EXAMPLE 22**
>
> Write each of the following in standard form.
>
> **a** $(9 \times 10^6) + (3 \times 10^8)$ **b** $(5 \times 10^{-3}) - (1.5 \times 10^{-4})$
>
> **Answers**
>
> **a** $(9 \times 10^6) + (3 \times 10^8) = 9 \times 10^6 + 3 \times 10^6 \times 10^2$ 3×10^8 is equivalent to $3 \times 10^6 \times 10^2$
> $$= 10^6(9 + 3 \times 10^2) \qquad \text{Remove the common factor.}$$
> $$= 10^6(9 + 300) \qquad \text{Calculate } 3 \times 10^2 = 300$$
> $$= 10^6(309) \qquad \text{Add the numbers.}$$
> $$= 3.09 \times 10^8 \qquad \text{Write the answer in standard form.}$$
>
> **b** $(5 \times 10^{-3}) - (1.5 \times 10^{-4}) = 50 \times 10^{-4} - 1.5 \times 10^{-4}$ 5×10^{-3} is equivalent to 50×10^{-4}
> $$= 10^{-4}(50 - 1.5) \qquad \text{Remove the common factor and}$$
> $$= 10^{-4}(48.5) \qquad \text{subtract the numbers.}$$
> $$= 4.85 \times 10^{-3} \qquad \text{Write the answer in standard form.}$$

You can also add or subtract numbers in standard form by rewriting them as ordinary numbers to add or subtract and then convert the answer back to standard form:

$9 \times 10^6 = 9\,000\,000$ and $3 \times 10^8 = 300\,000\,000$

So, $(9 \times 10^6) + (3 \times 10^8) = 9\,000\,000 + 300\,000\,000$
$$= 309\,000\,000$$
$$= 3.09 \times 10^8$$

> **TIP**
>
> When you solve problems in standard form you need to check your results carefully. Always check that your final answer is in standard form and make sure that the number part is between 1 and 10.

Exercise 5.14

1 Write each of the following in standard form.

a $(2 \times 10^{13}) \times (4 \times 10^{17})$
b $(1.4 \times 10^{8}) \times (3 \times 10^{4})$
c $(1.5 \times 10^{13})^{2}$
d $(12 \times 10^{5}) \times (11 \times 10^{2})$
e $(0.2 \times 10^{17}) \times (0.7 \times 10^{16})$
f $(9 \times 10^{17}) \div (3 \times 10^{16})$
g $(8 \times 10^{17}) \div (4 \times 10^{16})$
h $(1.5 \times 10^{8}) \div (5 \times 10^{4})$
i $(2.4 \times 10^{64}) \div (8 \times 10^{21})$
j $(1.44 \times 10^{7}) \div (1.2 \times 10^{4})$
k $\dfrac{(1.7 \times 10^{8})}{(3.4 \times 10^{5})}$
l $(4.9 \times 10^{5}) \times (3.6 \times 10^{9})$

2 Write each of the following in standard form.

a $(3 \times 10^{4}) + (4 \times 10^{3})$
b $(4 \times 10^{6}) - (3 \times 10^{5})$
c $(2.7 \times 10^{3}) + (5.6 \times 10^{5})$
d $(7.1 \times 10^{9}) - (4.3 \times 10^{7})$
e $(5.8 \times 10^{9}) - (2.7 \times 10^{3})$

3 Write each of the following in standard form.

a $(2 \times 10^{-4}) \times (4 \times 10^{-6})$
b $(1.6 \times 10^{-8}) \times (4 \times 10^{-4})$
c $(1.5 \times 10^{-6}) \times (2.1 \times 10^{-3})$
d $(11 \times 10^{-5}) \times (3 \times 10^{2})$
e $(9 \times 10^{17}) \div (4.5 \times 10^{-16})$
f $(7 \times 10^{-21}) \div (1 \times 10^{16})$
g $(4.5 \times 10^{8}) \div (0.9 \times 10^{-4})$
h $(11 \times 10^{-5}) \times (3 \times 10^{2}) \div (2 \times 10^{-3})$

> **TIP**
>
> When using standard form with negative indices, the power to which 10 is raised tells you the position of the first non-zero digit after (to the right of) the decimal point.

> **TIP**
>
> For some calculations, you might need to change a term into standard form before you multiply or divide.

4 Write each of the following in standard form.

a $(3.1 \times 10^{-4}) + (2.7 \times 10^{-2})$
b $(3.2 \times 10^{-1}) - (3.2 \times 10^{-2})$
c $(7.01 \times 10^{3}) + (5.6 \times 10^{-1})$
d $(1.44 \times 10^{-5}) - (2.33 \times 10^{-6})$

> **APPLY YOUR SKILLS**
>
> **5** Find the number of seconds in a day, giving your answer in standard form.
>
> **6** The speed of light is approximately 3×10^{8} metres per second. How far will light travel in:
>
> a 10 seconds? b 20 seconds? c 102 seconds?

> **REFLECTION**
>
> Think about the work you have done on standard form.
>
> - Did you find the examples clear and helpful? Explain why or why not.
> - Which class activity helped you learn the most? Why?
> - What do you think your teacher could have done differently to help you understand this work better?

SELF ASSESSMENT

How well do you understand standard form and how to calculate with numbers in standard form?

1   Use this scale to give yourself a rating of 1, 2, 3 or 4.

4	3	2	1
I know what we are trying to do.	I mostly know what we are trying to do.	I think I need more practice.	I really don't understand this at all.
I understand how to convert numbers to and from standard form.	I understand most of the work on converting numbers to and from standard form.	I get confused when I have to convert numbers to and from standard form.	I need help with all aspects of this work.
I can calculate using standard form.	I can do most of the calculations but find some of them confusing.	I cannot do many of the calculations.	
I can clearly explain this work to someone else.			

2   If you rated yourself 3, 2 or 1, write down the next step you will take to improve your rating.

SUMMARY

Do you know ...?

An equivalent fraction can be found by multiplying or dividing the numerator and denominator by the same number.

Fractions can be added or subtracted, but you must make sure that you have a common denominator first.

To multiply two fractions you multiply their numerators and multiply their denominators.

To divide by a fraction you find its reciprocal and then multiply.

Percentages are fractions with a denominator of 100.

Percentage increases and decreases are always percentages of the original value.

You can use reverse percentages to find the original value.

Standard form can be used to write very large or very small numbers quickly.

Are you able to ...?

find a fraction of a number

find a percentage of a number

find one number as a percentage of another number

calculate a percentage increase or decrease

find a value before a percentage change

do calculations with numbers written in standard form.

Practice questions

 1 Calculate $\dfrac{5}{6}\left(\dfrac{1}{4} + \dfrac{1}{8}\right)$ giving your answer as a fraction in its lowest terms. [4]

2 93 800 students took an examination.
19% received grade A.
24% received grade B.
31% received grade C.
10% received grade D.
11% received grade E.
The rest received grade U.

   a   Calculate the percentage of the students who received grade U. [2]

   b   Calculate the fraction of students who received a grade B?
       Give your answer in its lowest terms. [2]

   c   Work out how many students received grade A. [2]

3 During one summer there were 27 500 cases of *Salmonella* poisoning in Britain.
The next summer there was an increase of 9% in the number of cases.
Calculate how many cases there were in the second year. [3]

4 Abdul's height was 160 cm on his 15th birthday. It was 172 cm on his 16th
birthday. What was the percentage increase in his height? [3]

5 Timur's salary increases by 10% after one year and then another 20% after the
next year. Timur explains that his salary will have increased by a total of 30%
over the two years. Explain why Timur is incorrect and work out his actual
salary increase over that time. [3]

6 $n = \dfrac{ab}{a + b}$

If $a = 3 \times 10^8$ and $b = 2 \times 10^7$, determine the value of n. Give your answer in
standard form correct to 3 significant figures. [3]

7 A light year is the distance light travels in a year. The speed of light is 3.0×10^5
kilometres per second.

   a   Calculate, to the nearest kilometre, the number of kilometres in one
       light year. [2]

   b   Proxima Centauri is 4.0×10^{13} kilometres from our Sun. Work out how
       many light years there are in 4.0×10^{13} kilometres. Give your answer to
       3 significant figures. [2]

   c   There are approximately 0.625 miles in a kilometre. Calculate the speed
       of light in miles per second, giving your answer in standard form, to
       3 significant figures. [2]

8 Between January 2020 and January 2021, Mongolia's population increased by
1.6% to 3.352 million.
Calculate Mongolia's population in 2020, giving your answer to
the nearest 1000. [3]

9   $x = a \times 10^m$, $y = b \times 10^n$ and $100 < ab < 1000$
    Find xy in standard form.   [3]

10 The value of a car decreases by 12% per year. A car is two years old and its value
    is now $3875.
    a   What was the car's value when it was one year old?   [2]
    b   What was the original price of the car?   [2]
    c   If the value of a car decreases by x% per year and the original value of the
        car is $V, find a formula (in terms of x, V and n) for the value of the car
        after n years.   [3]

11 The value of a painting increases by 2% per year. The painting was bought on
    1 January 2021 for $1800. During which year will the painting first be worth
    more than $2500?   [3]

SELF ASSESSMENT

Analysing your mistakes can help you improve.

Consider any questions that you got wrong.

- Did you understand the question and know what to do? If not, what can you
  do about this?
- Did you make any errors in your calculations? If so, what can you do to avoid
  these errors in future?

> Chapter 6

Equations, factors and formulae

IN THIS CHAPTER YOU WILL:

- solve a linear equation
- solve equations where the unknown is a power
- factorise algebraic expressions
- rearrange a formula to change the subject.

Have you seen any of the equations in the image on the previous page before? What do they mean?

Equations are a used to easily record and manipulate mathematical problems. Drawing straight lines or curves can take a lot of time, but you can write their equations quickly, and formulae for calculating areas of shapes and volumes of solids can be recorded using a few easily remembered symbols.

You can use formulae to help you work out how long it takes to cook your dinner, how well your car is performing or how efficient the insulation is in your house.

GETTING STARTED

In each diagram, the numbers or expressions in any pair of circles add up to the number or expression in the square between them. Copy and complete each diagram by working out the missing numbers or expressions.

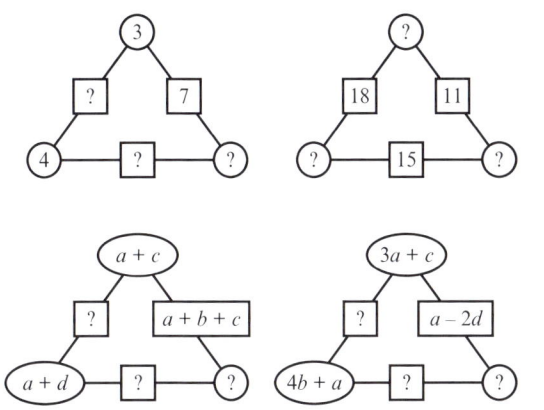

6.1 Solving equations

I think of a number, x. If I multiply my number by three and then add one, the answer is 13. What is my number?

To solve this problem you need to understand what is happening to x and then undo the operations in reverse order. This diagram (sometimes called a function machine) shows what is happening to x, with the reverse process written underneath. Notice how the answer to the problem appears quite easily:

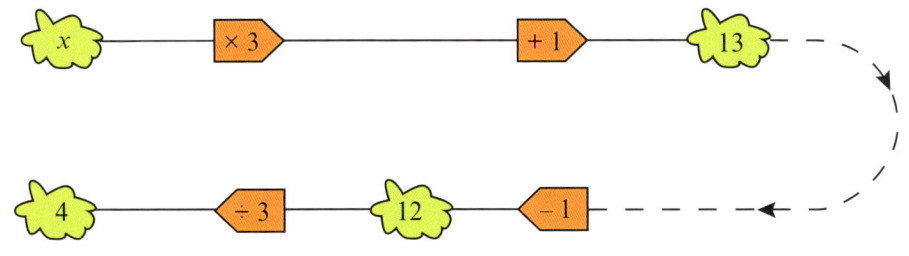

So $x = 4$.

MATHEMATICAL CONNECTIONS

The order of operations is very important here. You learnt about this in Chapter 1 and you can use the word BODMAS to help you remember the correct order.

You can reach the solution more efficiently using algebra. Follow the instructions in the question:

1	The number is x:	x
2	Multiply this number by three:	$3x$
3	Then add one:	$3x + 1$
4	The answer is 13:	$3x + 1 = 13$

This is called a **linear equation**. 'Linear' means there are no powers of x other than one.

> **LINK**
>
> Accounting uses a lot of mathematics. Accountants use computer spreadsheets to calculate and analyse financial data. Although the programs do the calculations, the user has to know which equations and formulae to insert to tell the program what to do. Most computer systems use the same rules for the order of operations.

> **MATHEMATICAL CONNECTIONS**
>
> You will study equations of straight lines in Chapter 10. Any equation in the form $y = mx + c$ is the equation of a straight line. This is why equations involving only the first power of x and constants are known as linear equations.

You can change the way an equation is written without changing the **solution** (the value of x for which the equation is true), as long as you do the same thing to both sides of the equation at the same time.

Follow the reverse process shown in the function machine on the previous page but carry out the instruction on both sides of the equation:

$3x + 1 = 13$

$3x + 1 - 1 = 13 - 1$ (subtract one from both sides)

$3x = 12$

$\dfrac{3x}{3} = \dfrac{12}{3}$ (divide both sides by three)

$x = 4$

> **TIP**
>
> Always line up the '=' signs because this makes your working much clearer.

> **TIP**
>
> Even if you can see what the solution is going to be easily you must show working.

Sometimes linear equations contain brackets, and sometimes they can also have unknown values (like x, though you can use any letter or symbol) on both sides of the equals sign.

Worked example 1 shows you how to solve some different types of linear equations.

WORKED EXAMPLE 1

An equation with x on both sides and all x terms with the same sign:

a   Solve the equation $5x - 2 = 3x + 6$

Answer

$$5x - 2 = 3x + 6$$
$$5x - 2 - 3x = 3x + 6 - 3x \qquad \text{Subtract } 3x \text{ from both sides.}$$
$$2x - 2 = 6$$
$$2x - 2 + 2 = 6 + 2 \qquad \text{Add 2 to both sides.}$$
$$2x = 8$$
$$\frac{2x}{2} = \frac{8}{2} \qquad \text{Divide both sides by 2.}$$
$$x = 4$$

TIP

You could subtract $5x$ from both sides instead, but this gives a negative coefficient of x which is clumsy to work with.

An equation with x on both sides and x terms with different signs:

b   Solve the equation $5x + 12 = 20 - 11x$

Answer

$$5x + 12 = 20 - 11x$$
$$5x + 12 + 11x = 20 - 11x + 11x \qquad \text{This time add } 11x \text{ to both sides, so}$$
$$16x + 12 = 20 \qquad \qquad \qquad \text{you have a positive number of } x\text{'s}$$
$$16x + 12 - 12 = 20 - 12 \qquad \text{Subtract 12 from both sides.}$$
$$16x = 8$$
$$\frac{16x}{16} = \frac{8}{16} \qquad \text{Divide both sides by 16.}$$
$$x = \frac{1}{2}$$

An equation with brackets on at least one side:

c   Solve the equation $2(y - 4) + 4(y + 2) = 30$

Answer

$$2y - 8 + 4y + 8 = 30 \qquad \text{Expand the brackets.}$$
$$6y = 30 \qquad \qquad \qquad \text{Collect like terms.}$$
$$\frac{6y}{6} = \frac{30}{6} \qquad \qquad \quad \text{Divide both sides by 6.}$$
$$y = 5$$

An equation that contains fractions:

d   Solve the equation $\frac{6}{7}p = 10$

Answer

$$\frac{6}{7}p \times 7 = 10 \times 7 \qquad \text{Multiply both sides by 7.}$$
$$6p = 70$$
$$\frac{6p}{6} = \frac{70}{6} \qquad \qquad \text{Divide both sides by 6.}$$
$$p = \frac{35}{3} \qquad \qquad \quad \text{Write the fraction in its simplest form.}$$

TIP

Unless the question asks you to give your answer to a specific degree of accuracy, you should leave it as a fraction.

WORKED EXAMPLE 1 CONTINUED

An equation with fractions and variables in the denominators

e Solve the equation $\dfrac{2}{3} + \dfrac{1}{3x} = \dfrac{4 - x}{6x}$

Answer

$$6x\left(\dfrac{2}{3} + \dfrac{1}{3x}\right) = 6x\left(\dfrac{4 - x}{6x}\right)$$ The lowest common denominator is $6x$, so multiply both sides by $6x$.

$$4x + 2 = 4 - x$$

$$4x + x = 4 - 2$$ Collect x terms on one side and numbers on the other.

$$5x = 2$$

$$x = \dfrac{2}{5}$$ Divide both sides by 5.

Leave your answer as a fraction.

MATHEMATICAL CONNECTIONS

You will deal with equations that have expressions containing unknowns in the denominator again in Chapter 10 and Chapter 14.

Some equations have an expression with x as the power. These types of equations are called exponential equations.

WORKED EXAMPLE 2

Solve each equation to find the value of x.

a $3^{3x + 1} = 81$ **b** $32^x = 2$ **c** $3^{x + 1} = 9^x$

Answers

a $3^{3x + 1} = 81$ Notice that 81 is the 4th power of 3.

$3^{3x + 1} = 3^4$

$3x + 1 = 4$ The powers must be the same.

$3x = 3$ Subtract 1 from both sides.

$x = 1$ Divide both sides by 3.

b $(2^5)^x = 2^1$ Write both terms as powers of 2.

$2^{5x} = 2^1$ Remove the brackets using the index laws.

$5x = 1$ Equate the indices.

$x = \dfrac{1}{5}$ Solve for x.

c $3^{x + 1} = (3^2)^x$ Write both terms with the same base (as powers of 3).

$3^{x + 1} = 3^{2x}$ Remove the brackets using the index laws.

$x + 1 = 2x$ Equate the indices.

$x = 1$ Solve for x.

Exercise 6.1

1   Solve the following equations.

a $4x + 3 = 31$

b $8x + 42 = 2$

c $6x - 1 = 53$

d $7x - 4 = -66$

e $9y + 7 = 52$

f $11n - 19 = 102$

g $12q - 7 = 14$

h $206t + 3 = 106$

2   Solve the following equations.

a $12x + 1 = 7x + 11$

b $6x + 1 = 7x + 11$

c $6y + 1 = 3y - 8$

d $11x + 1 = 12 - 4x$

e $8 - 8p = 9 - 9p$

f $\frac{1}{2}x - 7 = \frac{1}{4}x + 8$

3   Solve the following equations.

a $4(x + 1) = 12$

b $2(2p + 1) = 14$

c $8(3t + 2) = 40$

d $5(m - 2) = 15$

e $-5(n - 6) = -20$

f $-2(x + 2) = 4x + 9$

4   Solve for x.

a $7(x + 2) = 4(x + 5)$

b $4(x - 2) + 2(x + 5) = 14$

c $7x - (3x + 11) = 6 - (5 - 3x)$

d $3(x + 1) = 2(x + 1) + 2x$

e $4 + 2(2 - x) = 3 - 2(5 - x)$

f $2(p - 1) + 7(3p + 2) = 7(p - 4)$

g $2(p - 1) - 7(3p - 2) = 7(p - 4)$

h $3(2x + 5) - (3x + 2) = 10$

5   Solve for x.

a $\frac{2x + 1}{3} = 8$

b $\frac{2x}{3} + 1 = 8$

c $\frac{3}{5}x + 11 = 21$

d $\frac{x + 3}{2} = x$

e $\frac{2x - 1}{3} = 3x$

f $\frac{3x}{2} + 5 = 2x$

6   Solve the following equations.

a $\frac{3}{x} - 2 = \frac{1}{2} - \frac{9}{2x}$

b $\frac{2}{x} + \frac{3}{2x} = 7$

c $\frac{5 + 8}{x} = \frac{2(x + 4)}{x}$

d $\frac{x - 1}{3x} - \frac{1}{9} = \frac{x - 3}{9x}$

e $\frac{4}{3x} + \frac{1}{5} = \frac{4}{3} + \frac{1}{5x}$

f $\frac{4}{x + 1} = \frac{5}{x - 2}$

7   Solve the following equations for x.

a $3^{3x} = 27$

b $2^{3x+4} = 32$

c $8.1^{4x+3} = 1$

d $5^{2(3x+1)} = 625$

e $4^{3x} = 2^{x+1}$

f $9^{3x+4} = 27^{4x+3}$

6.2 Factorising algebraic expressions

You have already learnt how to expand brackets to simplify expressions and solve equations. It can sometimes be helpful to carry out the opposite process and put brackets back into an algebraic expression.

Consider the algebraic expression $12x - 4$. This expression is already simplified, but notice that 12 and 4 have a common factor. In fact the highest common factor (HCF) of 12 and 4 is 4.

Now, $12 = 4 \times 3$ and $4 = 4 \times 1$.

So, $12x - 4 = 4 \times 3x - 4 \times 1$
                      $= 4(3x - 1)$

Notice that the HCF has been 'taken out' of the bracket and written at the front. You find the terms inside by considering what you need to multiply by 4 to get $12x$ and -4.

The process of writing an algebraic expression using brackets in this way is called **factorisation**. The expression $12x - 4$ has been factorised to give $4(3x - 1)$.

Worked example 3 shows some factorisations that are not quite so simple.

> **MATHEMATICAL CONNECTIONS**
>
> You learnt how to find HCFs in Chapter 1.

WORKED EXAMPLE 3

Factorise each of the following expressions as fully as possible.

a $15x + 12y$ **b** $18mn - 30m$

c $36p^2q - 24pq^2$ **d** $15(x - 2) - 20(x - 2)^3$

e $6bx - 15cx + 10cy - 4by$ **f** $ax + by + atx + bty$

Answers

a $15x + 12y$ | The HCF of 12 and 15 is 3, but x and y have no common factors.

$15x + 12y = 3(5x + 4y)$ | Because $3 \times 5x = 15x$ and $3 \times 4y = 12y$

b $18mn - 30m$ | The HCF of 18 and 30 = 6 and the HCF of mn and m is m.

$18mn - 30m = 6m(3n - 5)$ | Because $6m \times 3n = 18mn$ and $6m \times -5 = -30m$.

c $36p^2q - 24pq^2$ | The HCF of 36 and 24 = 12 and p^2q and pq^2 have common factor pq.

$36p^2q - 24pq^2 = 12pq(3p - 2q)$ | Because $12pq \times 3p = 36p^2q$ and $12pq \times -2q = -24pq^2$.

Sometimes, the terms can have an expression in brackets that is common to both terms.

d $15(x - 2) - 20(x - 2)^3$ | The HCF of 15 and 20 is 5 and the HCF of $(x - 2)$ and $(x - 2)^3$ is $(x - 2)$.

$15(x - 2) - 20(x - 2)^3$
$= 5(x - 2)[3 - 4(x - 2)^2]$ | Because $5(x - 2) \times 3 = 15(x - 2)$ and $5(x - 2) \times 4(x - 2)^2 = 20(x - 2)^3$.

> **TIP**
>
> Make sure that you have taken out *all* the common factors (the highest common factor). If you don't, then your algebraic expression is not *fully* factorised.

> **TIP**
>
> Take care to put in all the bracket symbols.

> **WORKED EXAMPLE 3 CONTINUED**
>
> You also need to be able to factorise expressions in the form
> $ax + bx + kay + kby$.
>
> You can do this by collecting like terms and factorising the x and the y terms separately.
>
> **e** $6bx - 15cx + 10cy - 4by$
>
> $\quad = (6bx - 15cx) + (10cy - 4by)$ Collect like terms.
>
> $\quad = 3x(2b - 5c) + 2y(5c - 2b)$ Factorise the x and y terms separately.
>
> $\quad = 3x(2b - 5c) - 2y(2b - 5c)$ Take a common factor of -1. The bracket $(2b - 5c)$ is now a common factor.
>
> $\quad = (2b - 5c)(3x - 2y)$
>
> **f** $ax + by + atx + bty$
>
> $\quad = ax + atx + by + bty$ Collect like terms and factorise the x and y terms separately.
>
> $\quad = ax(1 + t) + by(1 + t)$ The HCF of ax and atx is ax and the HCF of by and bty is by.
>
> $\quad = (ax + by)(1 + t)$ The bracket $(1 + t)$ is a common factor.

Exercise 6.2

1   Factorise.

a $3x + 6$	**b** $15y - 12$	**c** $8 - 16z$	**d** $35 + 25t$
e $2x - 4$	**f** $3x + 7$	**g** $18k - 64$	**h** $33p + 22$
i $2x + 4y$	**j** $3p - 15q$	**k** $13r - 26s$	**l** $2p + 4q + 6r$

2   Factorise as fully as possible.

a $21u - 49v + 35w$	**b** $3xy + 3x$
c $3x^2 + 3x$	**d** $15pq + 21p$
e $9m^2 - 33m$	**f** $90m^3 - 80m^2$
g $36x^3 + 24x^5$	**h** $32p^2q - 4pq^2$

> **TIP**
>
> Once you have taken a common factor out, you may be left with an expression that needs to be simplified further.

3   Factorise as fully as possible.

a $14m^2n^2 + 4m^3n^3$	**b** $17abc + 30ab^2c$
c $m^3n^2 + 6m^2n^2(8m + n)$	**d** $\dfrac{1}{2}a + \dfrac{3}{2}b$
e $\dfrac{3}{4}x^4 + \dfrac{7}{8}x$	**f** $3(x - 4) + 5(x - 4)$
g $5(x + 1)^2 - 4(x + 1)^3$	**h** $6x^3 + 2x^4 + 4x^5$
i $7x^3y - 14x^2y^2 + 21xy^2$	**j** $x(3 + y) + 2(y + 3)$

4 For each of the following expressions, either state that it is fully factorised, or complete the factorisation

    a $4x + 12y$ **b** $3(15x + 5y)$ **c** $ab(3a^2 - 4ab)$

    d $51z^3 + 21x^2$ **e** $2x^2y^3(6xy - 10x^3y^2)$ **f** $52z^3 + 21x^2$

5 Factorise as fully as possible.

    a $3x + 4y + 6x + 8y$ **b** $3x - 4y + 6x - 8y$ **c** $4ax + 4ay + 6ax + 6ay$

    d $10x^5 - 15x^2 - 4x^3 + 6$ **e** $x^2 - 2x - y^2 - 2y$

    f $x^2 - 4m^2 + 4m - 1$ **g** $8ax + 10ay + 12bx + 15by$

    h $abx + bcy + abcx + bc^2y$ **i** $ax - by + kax - kby$

6 A rectangular field is 40 m long and $(12x + 30)$ metres wide.

    a   Find the perimeter of the field and factorise your answer as fully as possible.

    b   Find the area of the field and factorise your answer as fully as possible.

7 Two of the angles in a triangle are $3x$ and $4y$ degrees. Find an expression for the third angle and factorise your answer fully.

8 **a**   Given $a = 3 \times 10^m$ and $b = 9 \times 10^{m+3}$, find the value of $a + b$, factorising your answer completely.

    b   Why is this answer **not** in standard form?

    c   What would the answer be if written in standard form?

INVESTIGATION

Sums of consecutive numbers

1 Take any three consecutive positive whole numbers and add them up. Do this for at least four sets of numbers.

2 What do your answers all have in common?

3 Now let your first whole number be n.

    a   What would the next two whole numbers be?

    b   Add the three numbers up and factorise your answer. How does this relate to your answer for question 2?

4 Now repeat questions 1, 2 and 3 for sets of **five** consecutive whole numbers? What happens? What about **seven** consecutive numbers?

5 Now repeat questions 1 and 2 for sets of **four** consecutive whole numbers? What happens? What about **six** consecutive numbers?

6 Investigate this further by trying different numbers of consecutive integers.

6.3 Rearranging formulae

Formulae are very often expressed with one variable written alone on one side of the '=' symbol (usually on the left but not always). The variable that is written alone is called the **subject** of the formula. For example:

$s = ut + \frac{1}{2}at^2$ $\qquad$ (s is the subject)

$F = ma$ $\qquad$ (F is the subject)

$x = \dfrac{-b \pm \sqrt{b^2 - 4ac}}{2a}$ $\qquad$ (x is the subject)

Sometimes it is more helpful to have a different variable as the subject so you need to know how to change the subject of a formula. In the formula $v = u + at$ the subject is currently v, but you can change the subject by rearranging the formula.

For example, to make a the subject of this formula:

$v = u + at$ $\qquad$ Write down the starting formula.

$v - u = at$ $\qquad$ Subtract u from both sides (to isolate the term containing a).

$\dfrac{v - u}{t} = a$ $\qquad$ Divide both sides by t (notice that everything on the left is divided by t).

You now have a on its own and so now a is the subject of the formula.

Usually we rewrite this so the subject is on the left:

$a = \dfrac{v - u}{t}$

Notice how similar this process is to solving equations.

Make the variable shown in brackets the subject of the formula in each case.

> ## WORKED EXAMPLE 4
>
> **a** $\quad x + y = c$ (y) $\qquad$ **b** $\quad \dfrac{a - b}{c} = d$ (b)
>
> **c** $\quad \sqrt{x} + y = z$ (x)
>
> **Answers**
>
> **a** $\quad x + y = c$
>
> $\Rightarrow y = c - x$ $\qquad$ Subtract x from both sides.
>
> **b** $\quad \dfrac{a - b}{c} = d$
>
> $\Rightarrow a - b = cd$ $\qquad$ Multiply both sides by c to clear the fraction.
>
> $\Rightarrow a = cd + b$ $\qquad$ Make the number of b's positive by adding b to both sides.
>
> $\Rightarrow a - cd = b$ $\qquad$ Subtract cd from both sides.
>
> So, $b = a - cd$ $\qquad$ Rewrite so the subject is on the left.
>
> **c** $\quad \sqrt{x} + y = z$
>
> $\Rightarrow \sqrt{x} = z - y$ $\qquad$ Subtract y from both sides
>
> $\Rightarrow x = (z - y)^2$ $\qquad$ Square both sides.

MATHEMATICAL CONNECTIONS

You will learn more about rearranging formulae in Chapter 22.

TIP

Another word sometimes used for changing the subject is 'transposing'.

TIP

Remember that you must always do the same thing to both sides of a formula. This ensures that the formula you produce still represents the same relationship between the variables.

TIP

$\Rightarrow$ is a symbol that can be used to mean 'implies that'.

Exercise 6.3

Make the variable shown in brackets the subject of the formula in each case.

1 **a** $a + b = c$ (a) **b** $p - q = r$ (r) **c** $fh = g$ (h)

   d $ab + c = d$ (b) **e** $\dfrac{a}{b} = c$ (a) **f** $an - m = t$ (n)

2 **a** $an - m = t$ (m) **b** $a(n - m) = t$ (a) **c** $\dfrac{xy}{z} = t$ (x)

   d $\dfrac{x - a}{b} = c$ (x) **e** $x(c - y) = d$ (y) **f** $a - b = c$ (b)

3 **a** $p - \dfrac{r}{q} = t$ (r) **b** $\dfrac{x - a}{b} = c$ (b) **c** $a(n - m) = t$ (m)

   d $\dfrac{a}{b} = \dfrac{c}{d}$ (a) **e** $\dfrac{x - a}{b} = c$ (a) **f** $\dfrac{xy}{z} = t$ (z)

4 **a** $\sqrt{b} = c$ (b) **b** $\sqrt{ab} = c$ (b) **c** $a\sqrt{b} = c$ (b)

   d $\sqrt{b + c} = c$ (b) **e** $\sqrt{x - b} = c$ (b) **f** $\dfrac{x}{\sqrt{y}} = c$ (y)

APPLY YOUR SKILLS

5 The perimeter of a rectangle can be given as $P = 2(l + w)$, where l is the length and w is the width of the rectangle.

   a Make w the subject of the formula.

   b Find w if a rectangle has a length of 45 cm and a perimeter of 161 cm.

6 A small plane is about to take off from an aircraft carrier. The plane is pushed forwards using a steam device, so that it accelerates at a rate controlled by the ship's crew.

   The pilot knows that if u = initial speed, and v = speed at time t seconds, then:

   $v = u + at$

   where a is the acceleration and t is the time that has passed.

   a Rearrange the formula to make t the subject so the pilot can easily calculate the time for any given values of u, v and a.

   b Calculate the initial speed of the plane if the speed at 2 seconds is 78 m/s and the plane is accelerating at a rate of 33.64 m/s².

7 If the length of a pendulum is l metres, the acceleration due to gravity is g m s⁻² and T is the period of the oscillation in seconds then:

   $T = 2\pi \sqrt{\dfrac{l}{g}}$

   Rearrange the formula to make l the subject.

SELF ASSESSMENT

1   Three success criteria for this chapter are given in the table. For each one, write down how your work showed that you achieved that success criterion. One example has been given for each criterion.

Success criteria		How did my work show that I achieved this?
A	Derive and solve linear equations in one unknown.	I showed the inverse operations and got the correct solutions for almost all of the equations.
B	Factorise expressions by extracting common factors.	I worked out the HCF of coefficients correctly.
C	Change the subject of a formula.	I rearranged formulae to get the variable I wanted on its own on one side of the equals sign.

2   Write down two things that you understand and can do very well.

3   Write down two things that you can do to improve your work even further.

SUMMARY

Do you know …?

A variable is a letter or symbol used in an equation or formula that can represent many values.

A linear equation has no variable with a power greater than one.

Solving an equation with one variable means to find the value of the variable.

When solving equations, you must make sure that you always do the same thing to *both* sides of the equations.

Factorising is the reverse of expanding brackets.

A formula can be rearranged to make a different variable the subject.

Are you able to …?

solve a linear equation

factorise an algebraic expression by taking out any common factors

rearrange a formula to change the subject.

Practice questions

1   Given that $T = \dfrac{3p - 5}{2}$, calculate p when $T = 11$.   [3]

2   In mountaineering, in general, the higher you go, the colder it gets. This formula shows how the height (in metres) and temperature (in °C) are related.

$$\text{Temperature drop} = \frac{\text{height increase}}{200}$$

a The temperature at a height of $500\,\text{m}$ is $23\,°\text{C}$. Find the temperature when you climb to $1300\,\text{m}$. [3]

b Calculate how far you need to climb to experience a temperature drop of $5\,°\text{C}$. [3]

c Sabina wants to change the model so it can be used for a different season of the year. Sabina decides the model should be:

$$\text{Temperature drop} = \frac{\text{height increase} - 12}{q}$$

Sabina knows that the temperature drops by $13\,°\text{C}$ after a height increase of $700\,\text{m}$. Find the value of q, giving your answer to 1 decimal place. [3]

3 Rearrange $\dfrac{x}{y} = \dfrac{p}{q}$ to make y the subject. [2]

4 Factorise $x^4 y^3 + 7x^2 y - 3x^3 y^3$. [3]

5 My number is x.
3 more than 80% of my number is twice as large as 2 more than 60% of my number. Find my number. [4]

6 The sum of three consecutive *odd* numbers is 69. Find the smallest number. [3]

7 In a multiple choice test three marks are given for a correct answer and one mark is deducted for each incorrect answer. Jamal answers 14 questions and scores 22 marks. If n is the number of questions Jamal got right:

a Write down an expression for the number of questions Jamal got wrong. [1]

b Write down and simplify an expression for the number of points Jamal scored in the test.
Form and solve an equation to find how many questions Jamal got right. [3]

8 For a temperature F degrees Fahrenheit, the equivalent temperature T degrees Celsius is given by the formula:

$$T = \frac{5}{9}(F - 32)$$

a Rearrange the formula to make F the subject. [3]

b The temperature in Canada, one December morning is $-8\,°\text{C}$. Find this temperature in degrees Fahrenheit. [2]

c Find the temperature at which the Fahrenheit and Celsius measurements are the same. [3]

9

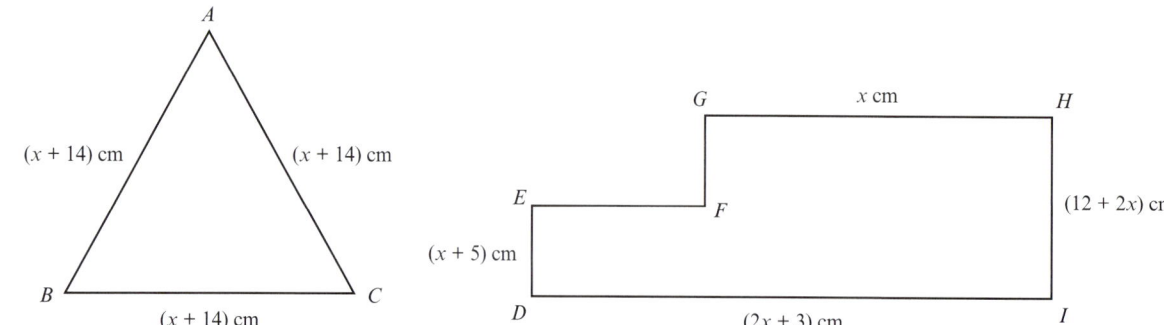

a Find the perimeter of triangle ABC. Simplify your answer as fully as possible. [2]

b Find the distance EF in terms of x. [2]

c   Find the distance FG in terms of x. [2]

d   Find the perimeter of shape $DEFGHI$ in terms of x.
Simplify your answer. [2]

e   You are given that the perimeters of both shapes are equal.
Form an equation and solve it for x. [3]

f   Find the perimeters of both shapes and the area of $DEFGHI$. [3]

10 The diagram shows a rectangle.
The dimensions are given in cm.

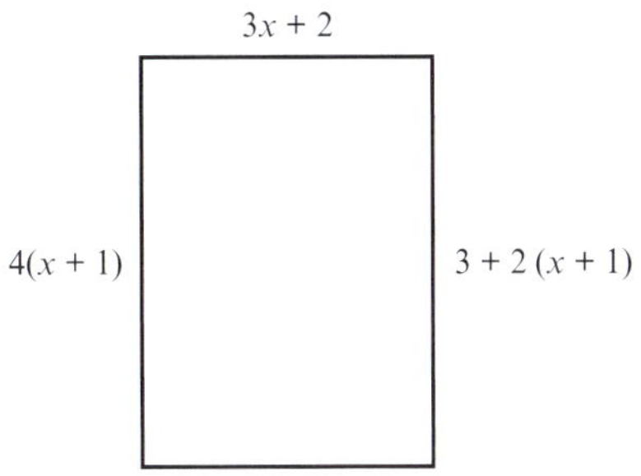

$3x + 2$

a   Find and simplify an expression for the
perimeter of the rectangle. [2]

$4(x + 1)$

$3 + 2(x + 1)$

b   Form and solve an equation to
find x. [3]

c   Find the perimeter of the rectangle. [2]

d   The area of the rectangle is 15% larger
than the area of a square.
Find the side length of the square, giving your answer to
2 decimal places. [3]

11 Rearrange $a + \dfrac{1}{\sqrt{b}} = c$ to make b the subject. [3]

12 Factorise completely $4p^3 q^4 + 8p^2 q + 2apq^3 + 4a$ [3]

13 Solve for x.
$4^{2x-3} = 2^{5+2(x-3)}$ [4]

SELF ASSESSMENT

List three things that you did well.

What could you improve?

What skills did you use here that you learned earlier or in other sections of work?

Chapter 7

Perimeter, area and volume

IN THIS CHAPTER YOU WILL:

- calculate areas and perimeters of two-dimensional shapes

- calculate areas and perimeters of shapes that can be separated into two or more simpler shapes

- calculate areas and circumferences of circles

- calculate areas and perimeters of circular sectors

- use nets for three-dimensional solids

- calculate volumes and surface areas of solids

- calculate volumes and surface area of pyramids, cones and spheres.

The glass pyramid at the entrance to the Louvre Art Gallery in Paris reaches to a height of 20.6 m. It is a beautiful example of a three-dimensional object. A smaller pyramid – suspended upside down – acts as a skylight in an underground mall in front of the museum.

Where have you seen pyramids or any other three-dimension objects used in architecture? Why do we need to know how to work out volumes and surface areas of these objects?

GETTING STARTED

Imagine you have six 1 cm by 1 cm square tiles. What fraction of each of the following shapes could you cover with the tiles without cutting or folding any of them and without the edges of any tile falling outside the shape? Simplify your answers as far as possible.

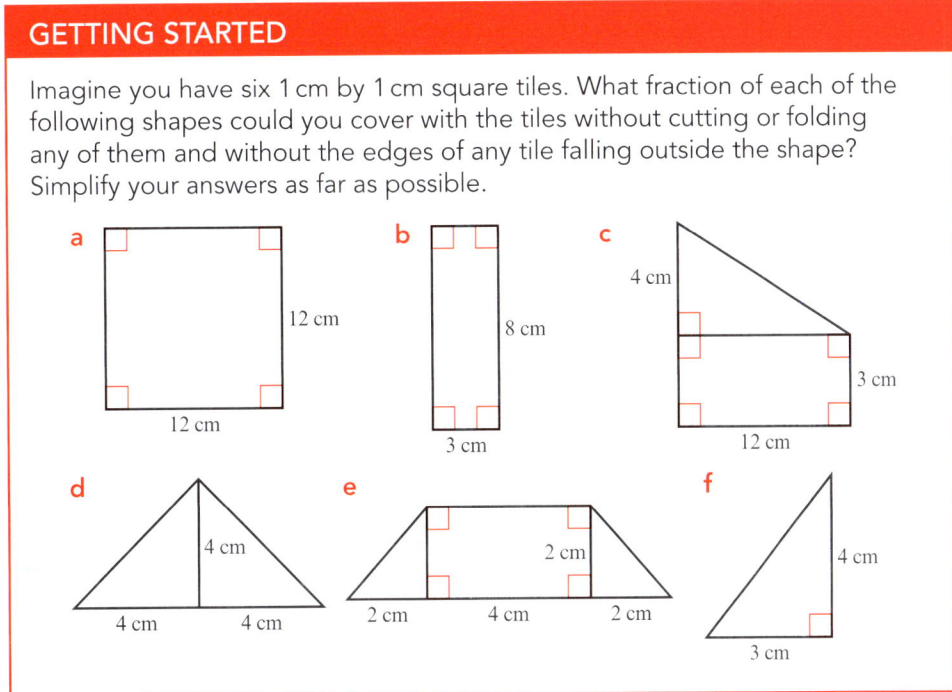

7.1 Perimeter and area in two dimensions

Perimeters appear everywhere in real life. Geographers may be interested in the length of an island's coastline. Gardeners may need to know the distance around the edge of a lawn, so they know how many border plants to order. A sports centre building a running track will need to work out the distance around the edge.

Polygons

A polygon is a flat (two-dimensional) shape with three or more straight sides. The perimeter of a polygon is the sum of the lengths of its sides. The perimeter measures the total distance around the outside of the polygon.

MATHEMATICAL CONNECTIONS

'Two-dimensional' means that you need two different pieces of information to find any given point on the shape. Usually you will use x- and y-coordinates for two dimensions, but you can also use a bearing and a distance, for example. You will learn about bearings in Chapter 15.

The area of a polygon measures how much space is contained inside it.

Two-dimensional shapes	Formula for area
Quadrilaterals with two pairs of parallel sides 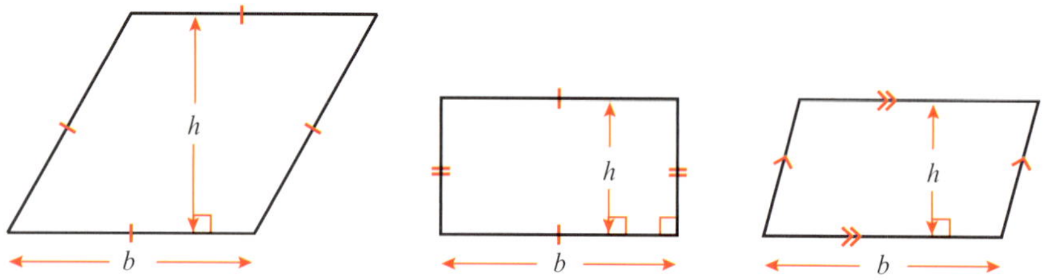 rhombus rectangle parallelogram	Area = bh
Triangles 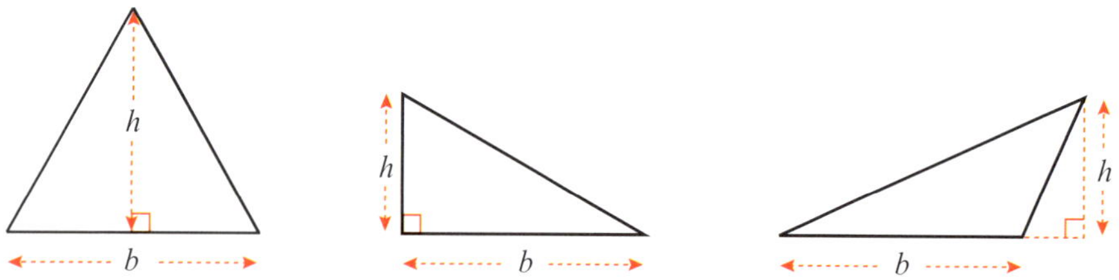	Area = $\frac{1}{2}bh$ or $\frac{bh}{2}$
Trapezium 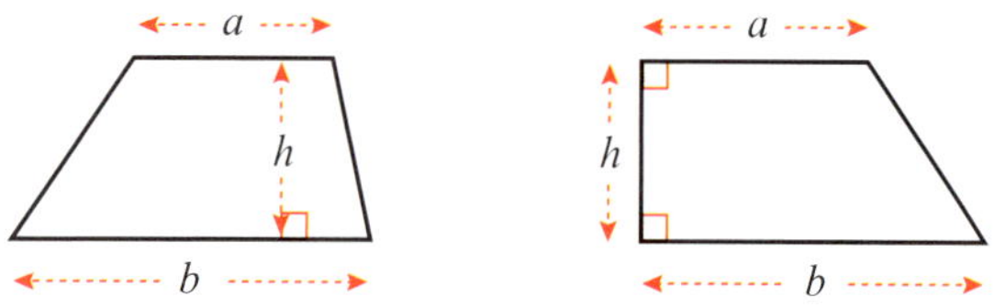	Area = $\frac{1}{2}(a + b)h$ or $\frac{(a + b)h}{2}$
Here are some examples of other two-dimensional shapes. 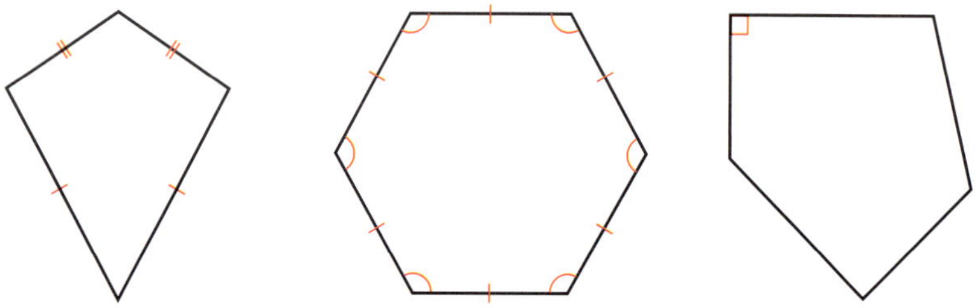 kite regular hexagon irregular pentagon	It is possible to find areas of other polygons such as those on the left by dividing the shape into other shapes such as triangles and quadrilaterals.

Units of area

If the dimensions of your shape are given in cm, then the units of area are square centimetres and this is written cm^2. For metres, m^2 is used and for kilometres, km^2 is used and so on. Area is always given in square units.

TIP

If an area is given in cm^2, this tells you the number of 1 cm × 1 cm squares you need to cover exactly the same area.

TIP

You will also see $A = l \times w$ for the area of a rectangle. The two formulae are equivalent, here the base, b, is equivalent to the length, l, and the height, h, is equivalent to the width, w.

WORKED EXAMPLE 1

a Calculate the area of the shape shown in the diagram.

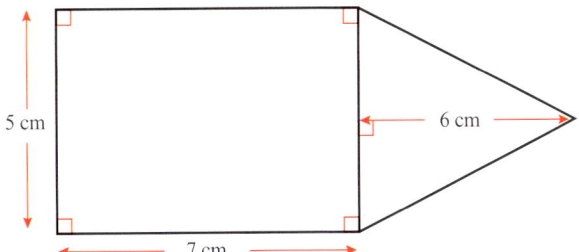

Answer

Divide the shape into two simple polygons: a rectangle and a triangle. Work out the area of each shape and then add them together.

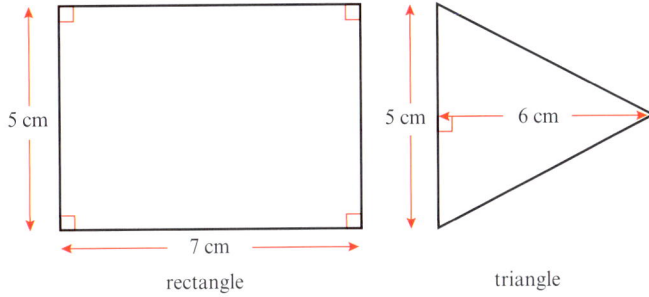

rectangle   triangle

Area of rectangle = bh = 7×5 = $35\,cm^2$ (substitute values in place of b and h)

Area of triangle = $\frac{1}{2}bh$ = $\frac{1}{2} \times 5 \times 6$ = $\frac{1}{2} \times 30$ = $15\,cm^2$

Total area = $35 + 15$ = $50\,cm^2$

b The area of a triangle is $40\,cm^2$. If the base of the triangle is $5\,cm$, find the height.

Answer

$A = \frac{1}{2} \times b \times h$ Use the formula for the area of a triangle.

$40 = \frac{1}{2} \times 5 \times h$ Substitute all values that you know.

$\Rightarrow 40 \times 2 = 5 \times h$

$\Rightarrow h = \dfrac{40 \times 2}{5} = \dfrac{80}{5} = 16\,cm$ Rearrange the formula to make h the subject.

c A square has area $36\,cm^2$. Find the perimeter of the square.

Answer

If x is the length of each side of the square, then:

$x^2 = 36$

$x = \sqrt{36} = 6\,cm$

There are four equal sides, so the perimeter is $4 \times 6 = 24\,cm$.

TIP

You do not usually have to redraw the separate shapes, but you might find it helpful.

TIP

You can write the formula for the area of a triangle in different ways:

$\frac{1}{2} \times b \times h = \dfrac{bh}{2}$

OR $= \left(\frac{1}{2}b\right) \times h$

OR $= b \times \left(\frac{1}{2}h\right)$

Make sure that you include the formula you use in your working.

TIP

You learnt how to rearrange and solve linear equations in Chapter 6.

TIP

It can be confusing to include units in all your working, but, where it is possible, always give units in your final answer.

Exercise 7.1

1 By measuring the lengths of each side and adding them together, find the perimeter of each of the following shapes.

a
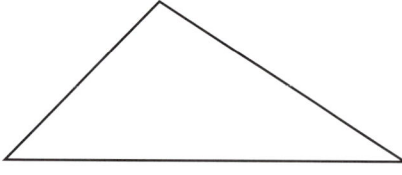

b
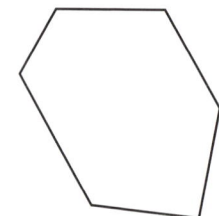

2 Calculate the perimeter of each of the following shapes.

a
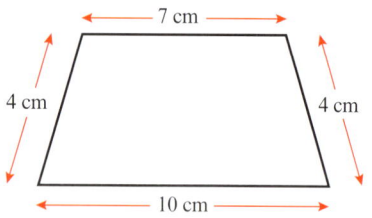

b
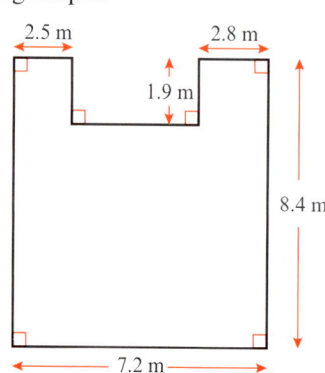

c
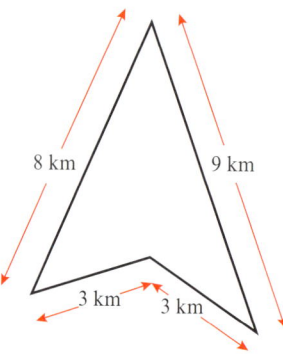

3 Calculate the area of each of the following shapes.

a
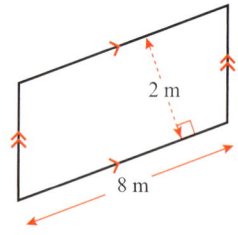

b
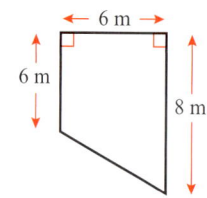

c
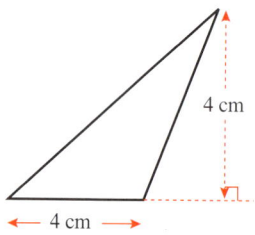

d
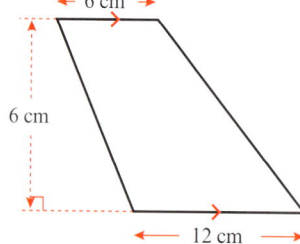

4 A triangular plate of glass forms part of a large stained-glass window.

a If the base of the plate is 45 cm and the height is 2.6 m, calculate the area of the glass plate, giving your answer in:

i cm^2 ii m^2

b Another triangular section of the window has area $0.54\,m^2$ and base 30 cm. Find the height of the section in cm.

5 The following shapes can all be divided into simpler shapes. In each case find the total area.

a
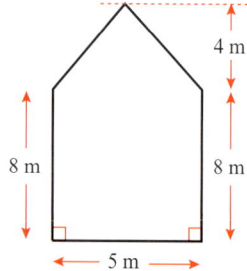

b
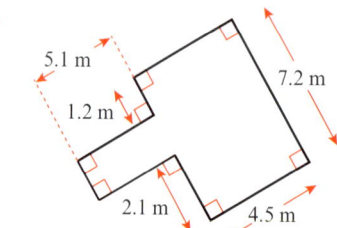

> **TIP**
>
> Draw the simpler shapes separately and then calculate the individual areas, as in Worked example 1.

c
4.9 cm
5.3 cm
8.2 cm

d
2.1 cm
5.4 cm
7.2 cm
3.4 cm
7.2 cm
7.8 cm

e
12 cm
12 cm
18 cm
2.4 cm

f
19.1 cm
38.2 cm
3.8 cm

g
1.82 cm
3.71 cm
8.53 cm
7.84 cm

6 For each of the following shapes you are given the area and one other measurement. Find the unknown length in each case.

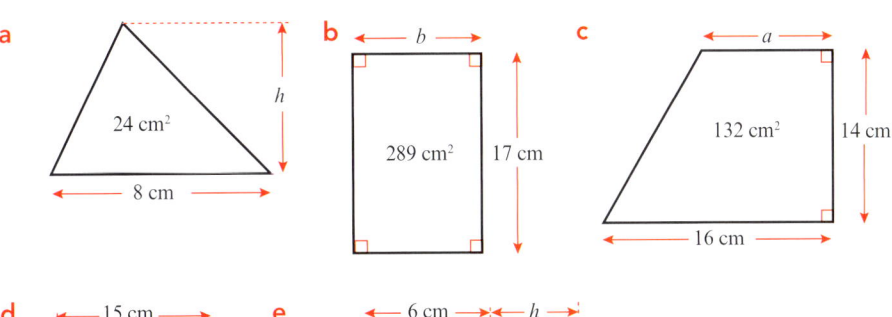

a
24 cm²
h
8 cm

b
b
289 cm²
17 cm

c
a
132 cm²
14 cm
16 cm

d
15 cm
75 cm²
b

e
6 cm
h
18 cm
200 cm²
6 cm

TIP

Write down the formula for the area in each case. Substitute into the formula the values that you already know and then rearrange it to find the unknown quantity.

APPLY YOUR SKILLS

7 How many 20 cm by 30 cm rectangular tiles do you need to tile the outdoor area shown?

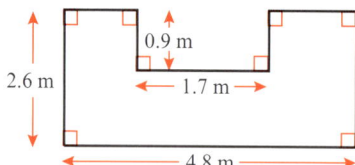

8 The image shows a tree decoration, made with three triangles of exactly the same shape but different sizes.

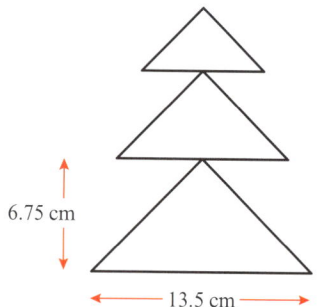

    a The dimensions of the middle triangle are $\frac{2}{3}$ of the dimensions of the bottom triangle, and the dimensions of the top triangle are $\frac{2}{3}$ of those of the triangle in the middle. Work out the area of the whole decoration, giving your answer to 1 decimal place.

    b Another decoration is made in the same way, but the base of the bottom triangle is x cm and the height is y cm. Find the area of the shape as a simplified fraction of xy.

9 Sanjay has a square mirror measuring 10 cm by 10 cm. Silvie has a square mirror which covers twice the area of Sanjay's mirror. Determine the dimensions of Silvie's mirror correct to 2 decimal places.

10 The flag of Guyana is rectangular, with some triangular patterns as shown.

    a The official flag of Guyana measures 152 cm by 91 cm. Find the area of the flag that is yellow or white. Give your answer in square metres.

    b What fraction is green?

    c Explain how you know that the black and red area is the same as the white and yellow area.

11 For each of the following, draw rough sketches and give the dimensions:

    a two rectangles with the same perimeter but different areas

    b two rectangles with the same area but different perimeters

    c two parallelograms with the same perimeter but different areas

    d two parallelograms with the same area but different perimeters.

12 Find the area and perimeter of the rectangle shown in the diagram.

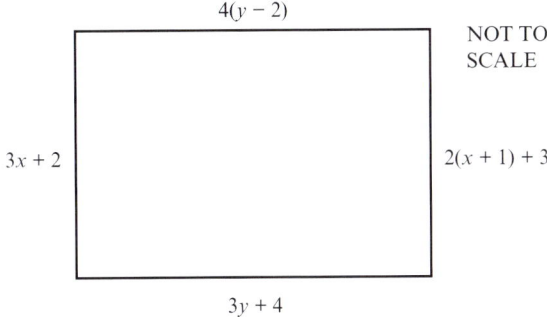

NOT TO SCALE

> **MATHEMATICAL CONNECTIONS**
>
> You will need to use some of the algebra from Chapter 6.

13 A trapezium has parallel sides of length a cm and $3a$ cm. The parallel sides are a distance a apart and the area of the trapezium is the same as the area of a triangle with base a cm and height a^2 cm. Find the area of the trapezium.

14 A rectangle is three times as long as it is wide. If the area of the rectangle is 243 cm², find the perimeter of the rectangle.

INVESTIGATION

Increasing areas

1 Calculate the area of a square of side 2 cm.

2 How many times larger than the area of a 2 cm × 2 cm square is the area of a 6 cm × 6 cm square?

3 How many times larger than the area of a 2 cm × 2 cm square is the area of a 10 cm × 10 cm square?

4 Find the areas of some more squares and try to work out what is happening to the area when you multiply the lengths of each side by the same number.

5 Now calculate the area of a right-angled triangle, with shorter sides 4 cm and 7 cm.

6 If the shorter sides double, triple or quadruple in length, what happens to the area each time?

> **MATHEMATICAL CONNECTIONS**
>
> You can continue this investigation for volumes later on in the chapter. What happens to the volume of a cube or cuboid if you double, triple or quadruple the lengths of the edges? This idea is continued in Chapter 11.

Circles

Circles appear in many places in our everyday lives, for example circular roundabouts, running tracks with semi-circular ends and circular markings on a basketball court.

MATHEMATICAL CONNECTIONS

You learnt the names of the parts of a circle in Chapter 3.

This diagram is a reminder of some of the parts.

A diameter is a line that passes through the centre of the circle.

Finding the circumference of a circle

Circumference is the word used to identify the perimeter of a circle. Note that the diameter = 2 × radius = $2r$. The Ancient Greeks knew that they could find the circumference of a circle by multiplying the diameter by a particular number. This number is now known as 'π', which is the Greek letter 'pi'. π is equal to 3.141592654… This is only the start of the number; π is an irrational number, so the decimal places go on forever and never repeat.

You can find the circumference of a circle using formulae that uses either the radius or the diameter:

Circumference = π × diameter

$\qquad\qquad$ = πd (where d = diameter)

$\qquad\qquad$ = $2\pi r$ (where r = radius)

Finding the area of a circle

There is a simple formula for calculating the area of a circle. Here is a method that shows how you can work out the formula:

Consider the circle shown in the diagram. It has been divided into 12 equal parts and these have been rearranged to give the diagram on the right.

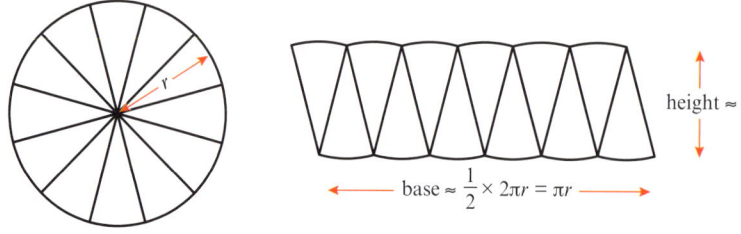

The parts of the circle are narrow, so the shape almost forms a rectangle with height equal to the radius of the circle and the length equal to half of the circumference.

The formula for the area of a rectangle is area = bh, so:

Area of a circle is approximately equal to

$\frac{1}{2} \times 2\pi r \times r$ (Using the base and height shown in the diagram on the previous page.)

$= \pi r^2$ (Simplify.)

If you try this yourself by dividing a circle into a greater number of parts that are even narrower, you will notice that the right-hand diagram will look even more like a rectangle.

This indicates (but does not prove) that the area of a circle is given by: $A = \pi r^2$.

You will now look at some examples so that you can see how to apply these formulae.

MATHEMATICAL CONNECTIONS

BODMAS in Chapter 1 tells you to calculate the square of the radius before multiplying by π.

WORKED EXAMPLE 2

For each of the following circles calculate the circumference and the area. Give each answer to 3 significant figures.

a
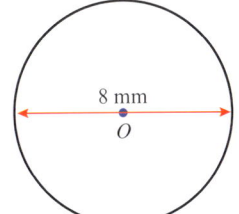

8 mm

O

b
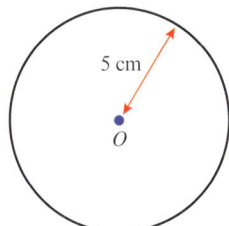

5 cm

O

TIP

Note that in (a), the diameter is given and in (b) the radius is given. Make sure that you look carefully at which measurement you are given and use the correct formula.

Answers

a   Circumference = πd

  = $\pi \times 8$

  = 25.1327…

is approximately equal to 25.1 mm (3 s.f.)

Area = πr^2

$r = \frac{d}{2}$

  = $\pi \times 4^2$

  = $\pi \times 16$

  = 50.265…

  = 50.3 mm² (3 s.f.)

b   Circumference = $2\pi r$

  = $2 \times \pi \times 5$

  = 31.415…

is approximately equal to 31.4 cm (3 s.f.)

Area = πr^2

  = $\pi \times 5^2$

  = $\pi \times 25$

  = 78.539…

  = 78.5 cm² (3 s.f.)

TIP

Your calculator should have a ⬜ π ⬜ button. If it does not, use the approximation 3.142, but make sure that you write this in your working. Make sure that you record the final calculator answer before rounding and then state what level of accuracy you rounded to.

WORKED EXAMPLE 3

Calculate the area of the shaded region in the diagram.

Answer

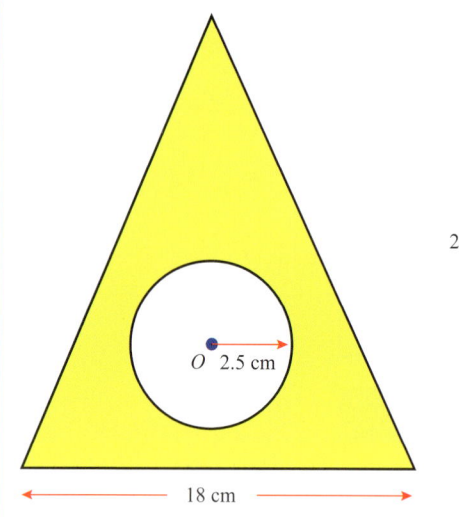

Shaded area
= area of triangle − area of circle.

Area = $\frac{1}{2}bh - \pi r^2$

= $\frac{1}{2} \times 18 \times 20 - \pi \times 2.5^2$

Substitute in values of b, h and r.

= 160.365…

= 160 cm² (3 s.f.)

Round the answer. In this case it has been rounded to 3 significant figures.

Exercise 7.2

1   Calculate the area and circumference in each of the following. Give your answers to 3 significant figures where necessary.

a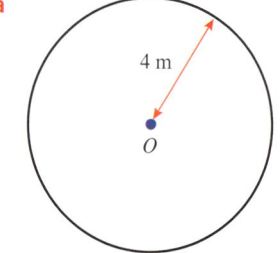

b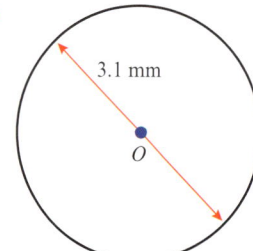

c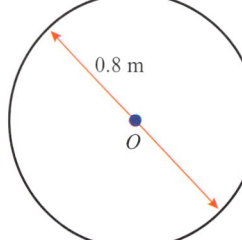

d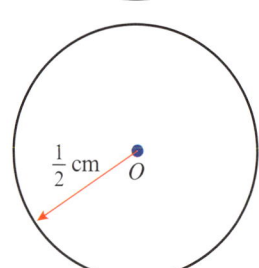

e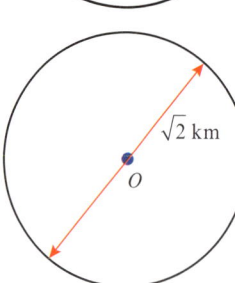

f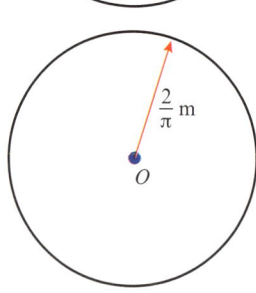

TIP

You should always try to use exact values in the calculation, rather than finding decimal approximations for the radius and diameter. This will mean you are not introducing rounding errors.

2   Calculate the area of the shaded region in each case. Give your answers to 3 significant figures where necessary.

a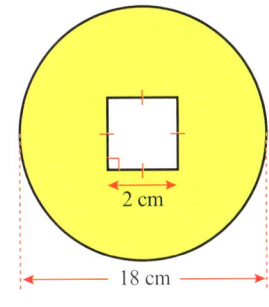

b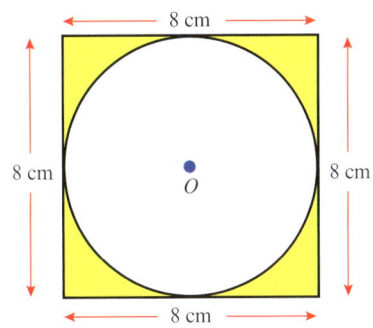

c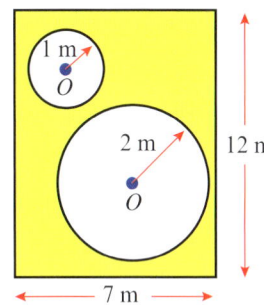

d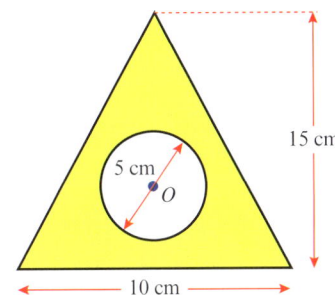

e

f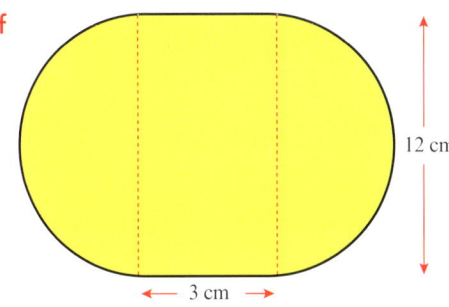

APPLY YOUR SKILLS

3   The diagram shows a plan for a rectangular garden with a circular pond. The part of the garden not covered by the pond is to be covered by grass. One bag of grass seed covers five square metres of lawn. Calculate the number of bags of seed that are needed.

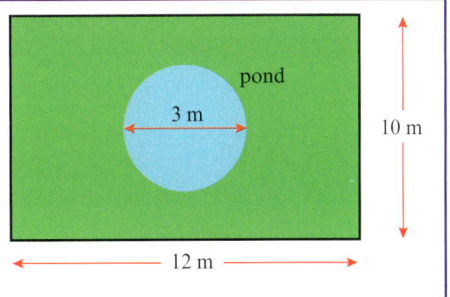

4   The diagram shows a road sign. If the triangle will be painted white and the rest of the sign will be painted red, calculate the area covered by each colour to 1 decimal place.

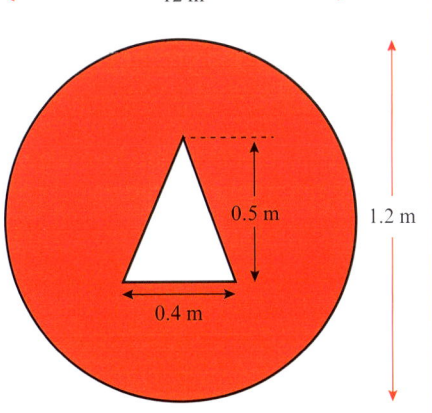

> **TIP**
>
> This is a good example of a problem in which you need to carry out a series of calculations. Set your work out in clear steps to show how you get to the solution.

5   Sixteen identical circles are to be cut from a square sheet of fabric with sides of 0.4 m. Find the area of the leftover fabric (to 2 d.p.) if the circles are made as large as possible.

APPLY YOUR SKILLS CONTINUED

6   Two friends usually order a large pizza to share. The large pizza has a diameter of 24 cm. This week they want to eat different things on their pizzas, so they decide to order two small pizzas. The small pizza has a diameter of 12 cm. They want to know if there is the same amount of pizza in two small pizzas as in one large. Work out the answer.

Exact answers as multiples of π

Pi is an irrational number so you cannot write out its exact value as a decimal. You can approximate it using a rounded decimal, or by using fractions that are similar in value, but none of these methods give the exact answer.

If you are asked to give an exact answer in any calculation that uses pi it means you have to give the answer in terms of pi. In other words, your answer will be a multiple of pi and the π symbol should be in the answer.

If the circumference or area of a circle is given in terms of π, you can work out the length of the diameter or radius by dividing by pi.

For example, if $C = 5\pi$ cm the diameter is 5 cm and the radius is 2.5 cm (half the diameter).

Similarly, if $A = 25\pi$ cm² then $r^2 = 25$ and $r = \sqrt{25} = 5$ cm.

WORKED EXAMPLE 4

For each calculation, give your answer as a multiple of π.

a   Find the circumference of a circle with a diameter of 12 cm.

b   What is the exact circumference of a circle of radius 4 mm?

c   Determine the area of a circle with a diameter of 10 m.

d   What is the radius of a circle of circumference 2.8π cm?

Answers

a $C = 12\pi$ cm   Multiply the diameter by 12 and remember
       $C = \pi d$ to write the units.

b $C = 2\pi r$ Use this version of the formula since you
       $C = 2 \times \pi \times 4 = 8\pi$ mm   have been told the radius.

c $A = \pi r^2$
       $r = 5$ m , so $A = \pi \times 5^2$
       $A = 25\pi$ m

d $C = 2\pi r$
       So, $r = \dfrac{C}{2\pi}$

       $r = \dfrac{2.8\pi}{2\pi} = 1.4$ cm

Exercise 7.3

1 Find the circumference and area of each shape.
Give each answer as a multiple of π.

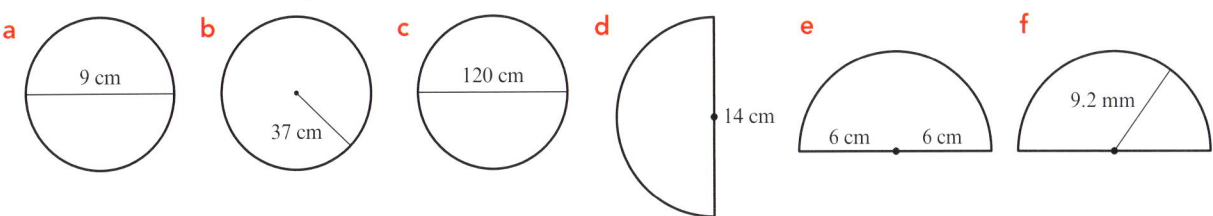

2 For each of the following, give the answer as a multiple of π.

a Calculate the circumference of a circle of diameter 10 cm.

b A circle has a radius of 7 mm. What is its circumference?

c What is the area of a circle of diameter 1.9 cm?

d The radius of a semicircle is 3 cm. What is the area of the semicircle?

3 A circle of circumference 12π cm is precision cut from a metal square as shown.

a What is the length of each side of the square?

b What area of metal is left after the circle has been cut out? Give your answer in terms of π.

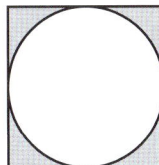

4 The diagram shows two concentric circles.
The inner circle has a circumference of 14π mm.
The outer circle has a radius of 9 mm.
Determine the exact area of the shaded portion.

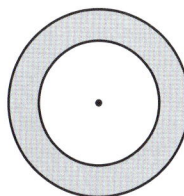

Arcs and sectors

The diagram shows a circle with two radii (plural of radius) drawn from the centre.

The region contained in-between the two radii is known as a sector.
Notice that there is a *major* sector and a *minor* sector.

A section of the circumference is known as an arc.

The Greek letter θ represents the angle subtended at the centre.

Notice that the minor sector is a fraction of the full circle. It is $\dfrac{\theta}{360}$ of the circle.

The area of a circle is πr^2. The sector is $\dfrac{\theta}{360}$ of the circle, so we can replace 'of' with '×' to give:

Sector area $= \dfrac{\theta}{360} \times \pi r^2$

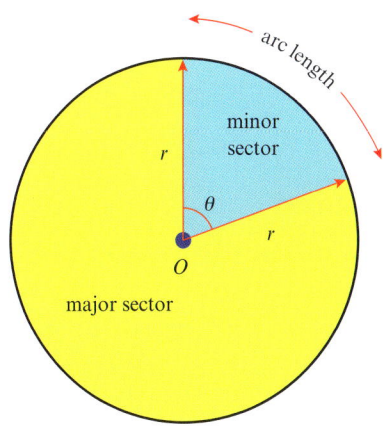

The circumference of a circle is $2\pi r$. The sector is $\dfrac{\theta}{360}$ of the circle, so the length of the arc of the sector is $\dfrac{\theta}{360}$ of the circumference. So:

Arc length $= \dfrac{\theta}{360} \times 2\pi r$

Make sure that you remember these two special cases:

- If $\theta = 90°$ then you have a quarter of a circle.

- If $\theta = 180°$ then you have a half of a circle. This is known as a semicircle.

WORKED EXAMPLE 5

Find the area and perimeter of the shapes. Give your answer to 3 significant figures.

a

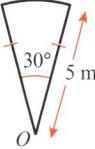

Answer

$$\text{Area} = \frac{\theta}{360} \times \pi r^2 = \frac{30}{360} \times \pi \times 5^2 = 6.544\ldots = 6.54\,\text{m}^2 \ \ (3\ \text{s.f.})$$

$$\text{Perimeter} = \frac{\theta}{360} \times 2\pi r + 2r = \frac{30}{360} \times 2 \times \pi \times 5 + 2 \times 5 = 12.617\ldots$$

$$= 12.6\,\text{m} \ \ (3\ \text{s.f.})$$

TIP

Note that for the perimeter you need to add 5 m twice because you need to include the two straight edges.

b

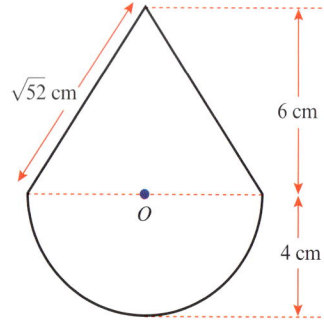

TIP

Note that the base of the triangle is the diameter of the circle. Remember to divide the circle area by two to find the area of the semicircle.

Answer

Total area = area of triangle + area of a semicircle

$$\text{Area} = \frac{1}{2}bh + \frac{1}{2}\pi r^2 = \frac{1}{2} \times 8 \times 6 + \frac{1}{2}\pi \times 4^2 = 49.132\ldots$$

is approximately equal to $49.1\,\text{cm}^2$ (3 s.f.)

$$\text{Perimeter} = \sqrt{52} + \sqrt{52} + \frac{1}{2} \times 2\pi \times 4 = 27.0\,\text{cm} \ \ (3\ \text{s.f.})$$

WORKED EXAMPLE 5 CONTINUED

c

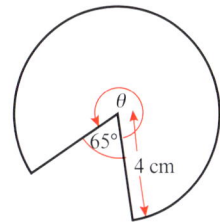

Answer

$$\text{Area} = \frac{\theta}{360} \times \pi r^2 = \frac{360 - 65}{360} \times \pi \times 4^2 = \frac{295}{360} \times \pi \times 16 = 41.189\ldots$$

is approximately equal to 41.2 cm²

$$\text{Perimeter} = \frac{\theta}{360} \times 2\pi r + 2r = \frac{295}{360} \times 2 \times \pi \times 4 + 2 \times 4 = 28.594\ldots$$

is approximately equal to 28.6 cm

Exercise 7.4

1   For each of the following shapes find both the area and the perimeter.
Give your answers to 3 significant figures.

a 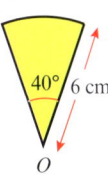   b 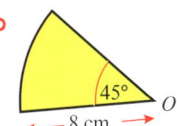   c 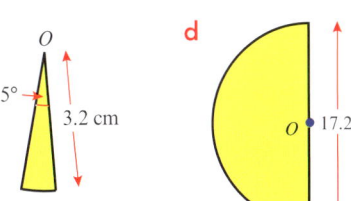   d

e 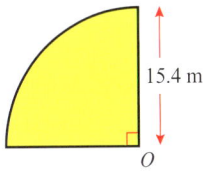   f 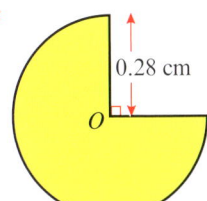   g 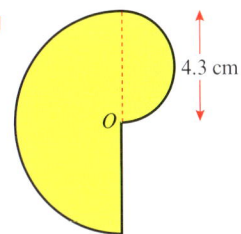   h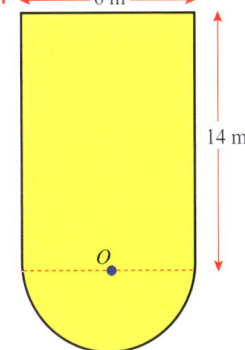

2   Find the area of the coloured region and find the arc length *l* in each of
the following. Give your answers to 3 significant figures.

a 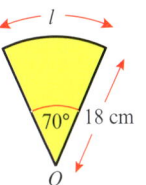   b 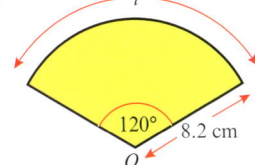   c 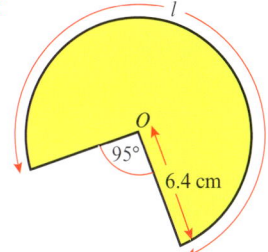   d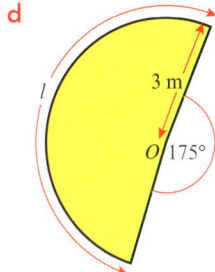

3   Find the area and perimeter of the following.
    Give your answers to 3 significant figures.

a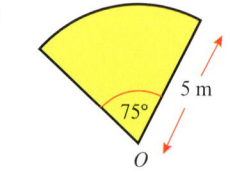

b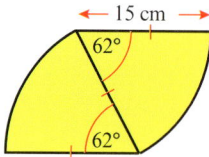

4   The diagram shows a circular sector, drawn from the centre of the Earth with an arc along the equator.

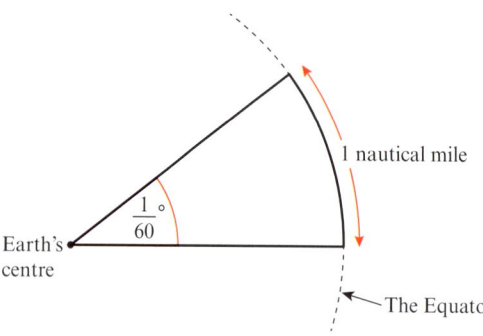

When the angle at the centre of the Earth is $\frac{1}{60}$ of a degree, the arc length along the equator is known as 1 nautical mile. Given that the Earth's diameter is approximately 12 760 km, find the length of 1 nautical mile in metres. Give your answer to the nearest metre.

5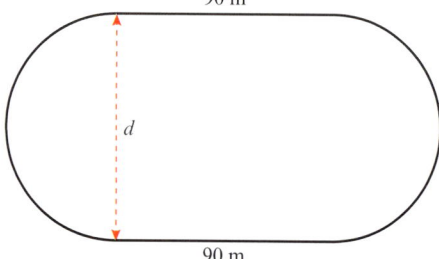

The diagram shows a running track of length 400 m. The two straight edges are both 90 m in length. Find the diameter, d, of the two semicircular sections. Give your answer to 1 decimal place.

6   Goro rolls pizza dough into a single circular pizza base of diameter 28 cm, but Huan asks for four identical, smaller pizza bases with the same thickness instead. Work out the diameter of each of the smaller pizza bases.

7   The diagram shows a slice of circular cake, seen from above. The radius of the cake is equal to the arc length and the area of the top of the slice is 40.5 cm². Find the radius of the cake.

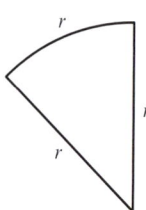

8   For each of the following find the area and perimeter of the coloured region.
Give your answer in terms of π.

a

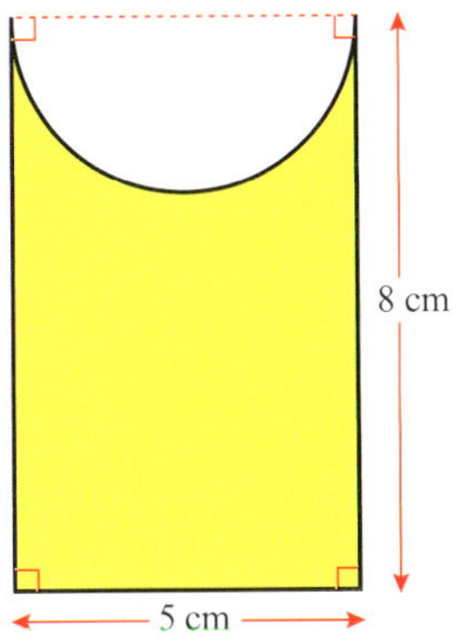

8 cm

5 cm

b

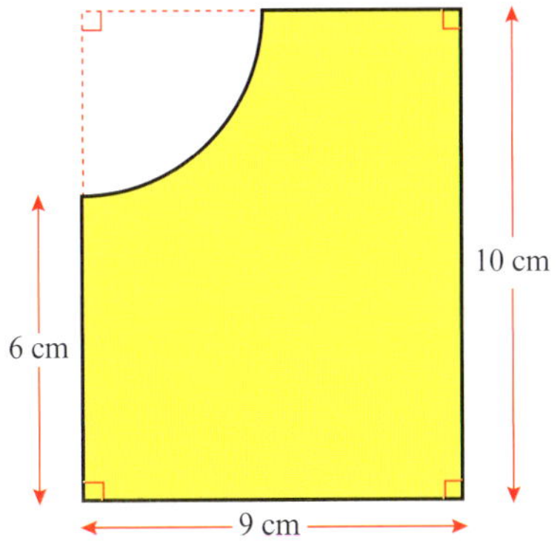

6 cm

10 cm

9 cm

c

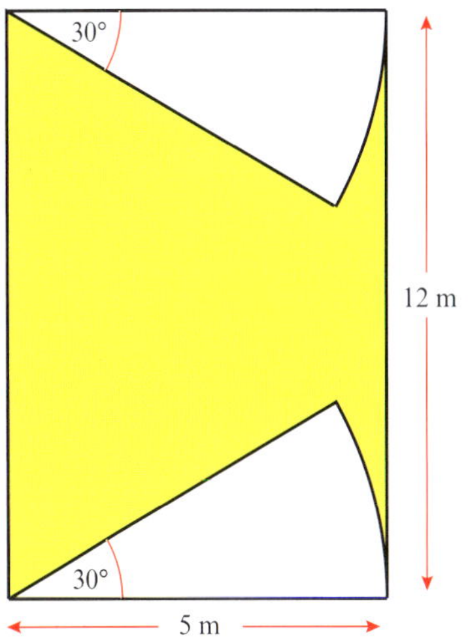

30°

12 m

30°

5 m

d

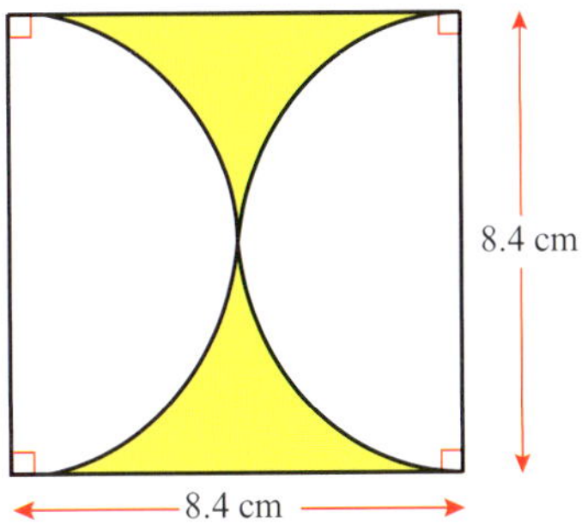

8.4 cm

8.4 cm

e

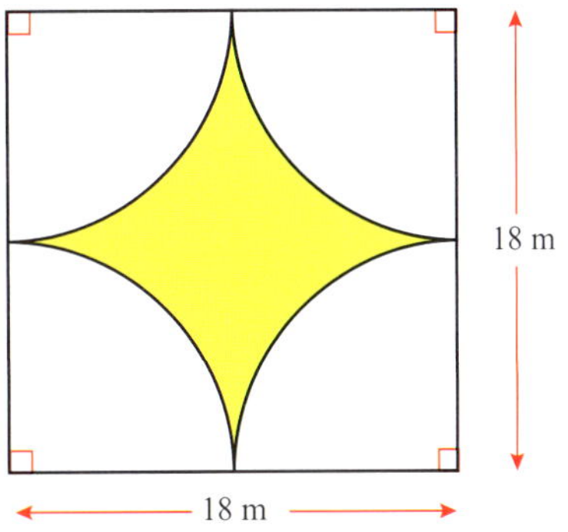

18 m

18 m

9   Find the perimeter and area of each shape. Give your answer to 3 significant figures.

a

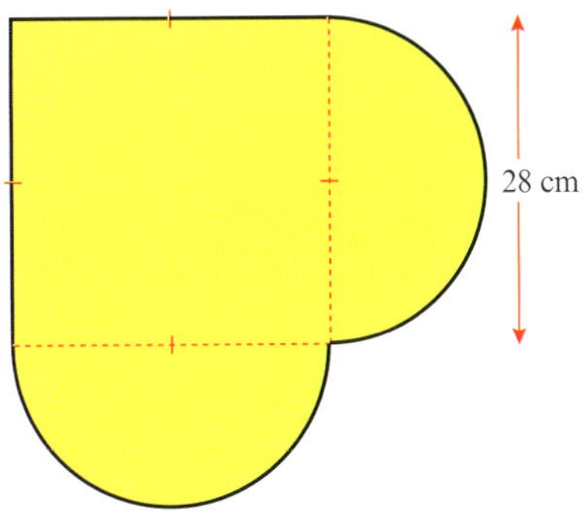

28 cm

b

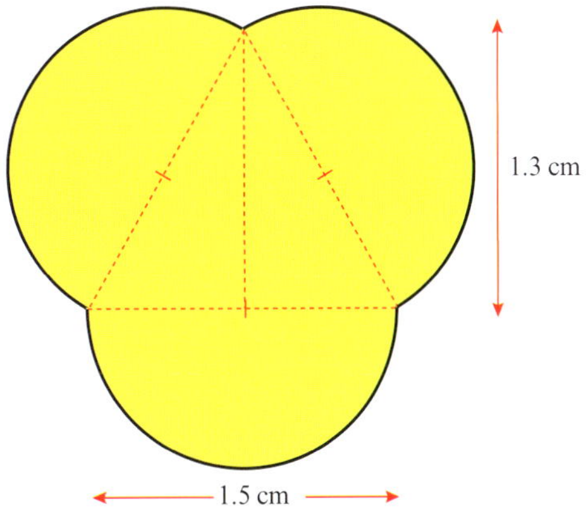

1.3 cm

1.5 cm

c

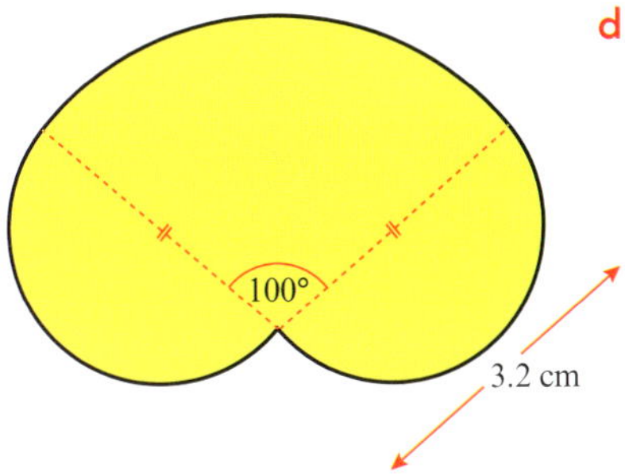

100°

3.2 cm

d

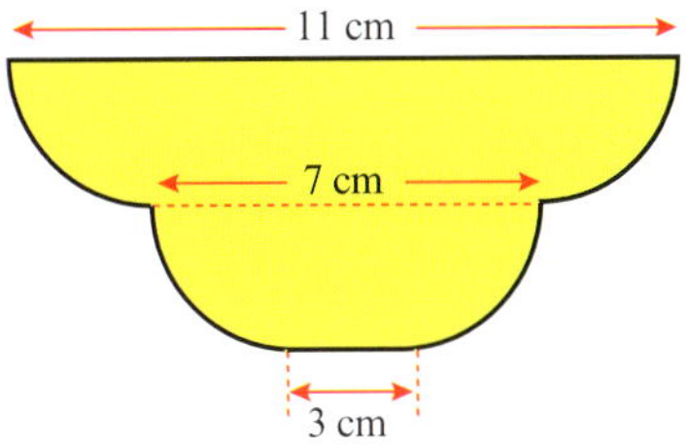

11 cm

7 cm

3 cm

e

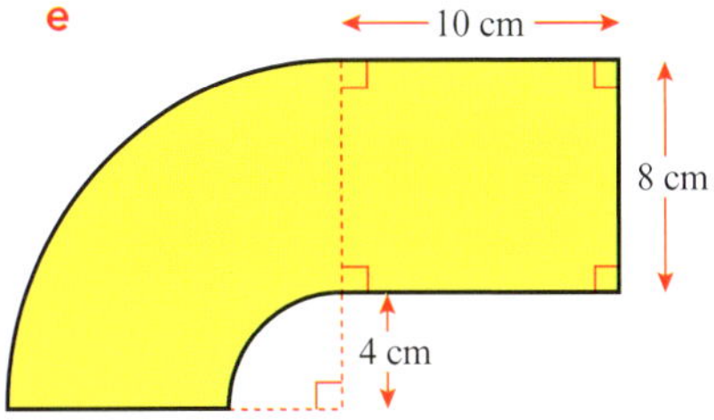

10 cm

8 cm

4 cm

10 Arjun has two designs for badges.

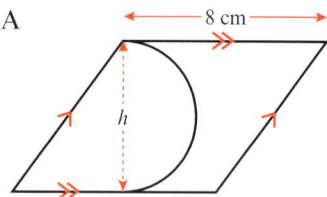
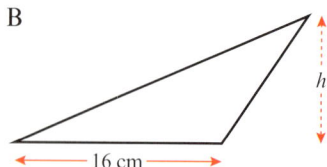

Badge A is a parallelogram. It is to be painted gold except for a semicircular section. The diameter of the semicircle is the same as the height of the parallelogram, h cm.

Badge B is a triangle with base 16 cm and height h cm. All of the triangle is to be painted gold. The area to be painted is 18 cm² more than the area to be painted on badge A.

Calculate the value of h. Give your answer to 3 significant figures.

7.2 Three-dimensional objects

The focus of the rest of this chapter is three-dimensional objects, but you will use many of the formulae for two-dimensional shapes in your calculations. A three-dimensional object is called a solid.

Nets of solids

A **net** is a two-dimensional shape that can be drawn, cut out and folded to form a three-dimensional solid.

This is the net of a solid that you should be quite familiar with.

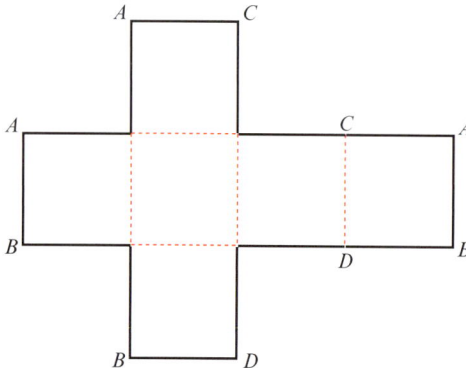

If you fold along the dotted lines and join the points with the same letters then you will form this cube.

You should try this yourself and look carefully at which edges (sides) and which **vertices** (points or corners) join up.

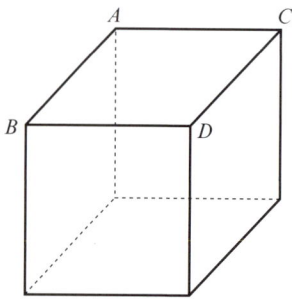

> **TIP**
>
> Cardboard boxes start out as a flat shape. The cardboard is then folded along carefully chosen lines, which become the edges of the box. Try unfolding a box to see how it was made.

Exercise 7.5

1   The diagram shows a cuboid. Draw a net for the cuboid.

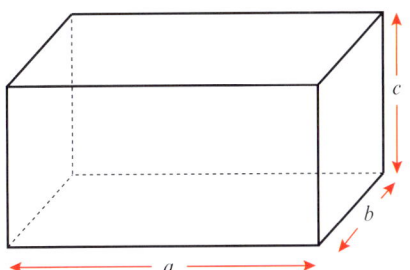

2   The diagram shows the net of a solid.

   a   Describe the solid in as much detail as you can.

   b   Which two points will join with point M when the net is folded?

   c   Which edges are equal in length to PQ?

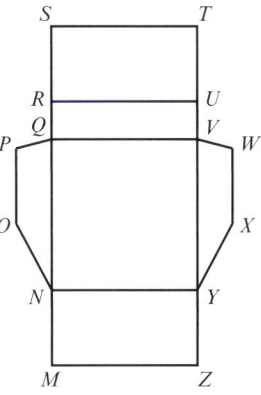

3   A teacher asked her class to draw the net of a cuboid cereal box. These are the diagrams that three students drew. Which of them is correct?

   a

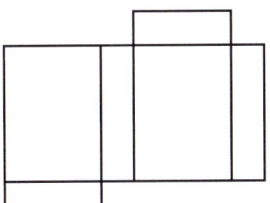

   b

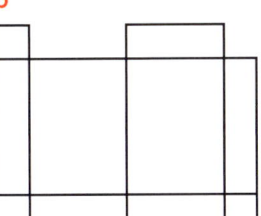

   c

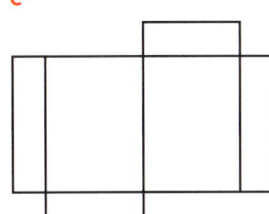

> **TIP**
>
> If you find it difficult to visualise the solution to problems like this, you can build models to help you.

4   How could you make a cardboard model of this numbered octahedron? Draw labelled sketches to show your solution.

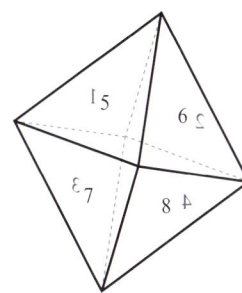

5 The diagram shows the net of a cuboid.

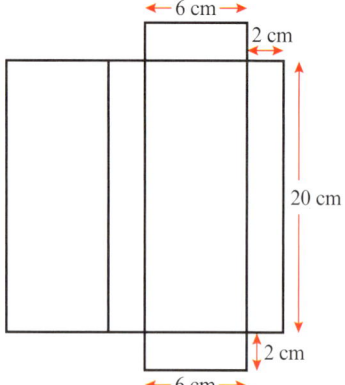

a Find the surface area of the cuboid in cm².

b Find the volume of the cuboid in m³.

7.3 Surface areas and volumes of solids

The flat, two-dimensional surfaces on the outside of a solid are called **faces**. You can find the area of each face using the techniques from earlier in this chapter. The total area of all the faces is the **surface area** of the solid.

The **volume** is the amount of space contained inside the solid. If the lengths are given in centimetres, then the volume is measured in cubic centimetres (cm³) and so on.

> **TIP**
>
> It can be helpful to draw the net of a solid when trying to find its surface area.

> **TIP**
>
> We measure the amount of water flowing over a waterfall in cubic metres per second. The maximum flow of water over the Iguazu Falls in South America was 45 700 cubic metres per second, on 9 June 2014. This is the equivalent to more than 18 standard Olympic swimming pools being emptied over the waterfall every second!

Cuboids

A cuboid has six rectangular faces, twelve edges and eight vertices.

If the length, width and height of the cuboid are *a*, *b* and *c* (respectively) then you can find the surface area by thinking about the areas of each rectangular face.

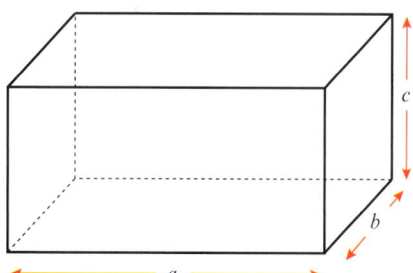

Notice that the surface area is exactly the same as the area of the cuboid's net.

Surface area of cuboid = 2($ab + ac + bc$)

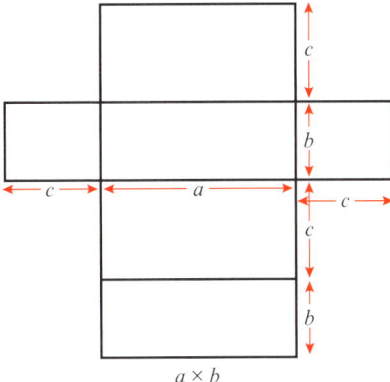

The volume of a cuboid is its length × width × height.

Volume of cuboid = $a\,b\,c$

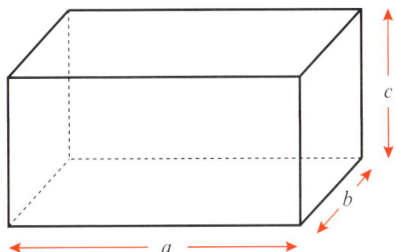

Prisms

A prism is a solid whose cross-section is the same all along its length. (A cross-section is the surface formed when you cut parallel to a face.)

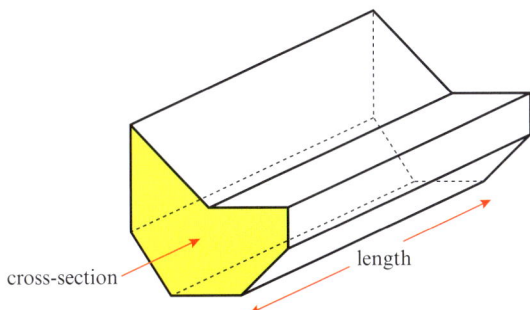

Prisms are often named according to the shape of their cross-section. For example, a triangular prism has a triangle cross-section, a pentagonal prism has a pentagon cross-section and so on.

A cuboid is a prism with a rectangular cross-section, so you may sometimes see it called a rectangular prism.

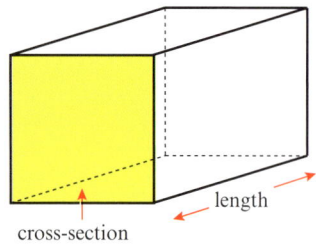 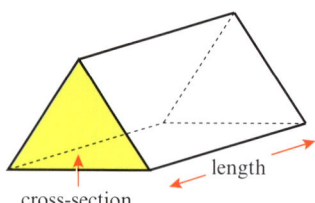

You can calculate the surface area of a prism by working out the area of each face and adding them together. There are two ends with area equal to the cross-sectional area. The remaining sides are all the same length, so their area is equal to the perimeter of the cross-section multiplied by the length:

Surface area of a prism = 2 × area of cross-section + perimeter of cross-section × length

You can calculate the volume of a prism by working out the area of the cross-section and multiplying this by the length.

Volume of a prism = area of cross-section × length

Cylinders

A cylinder is not a prism, because the cross section has curved edges. The cross section of a cylinder is a circle and is the same all along its length, so a cylinder is a 'tube'.

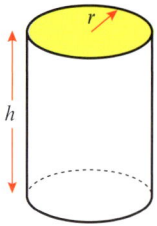 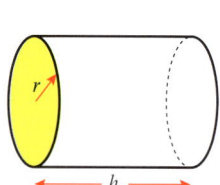

A cylinder can be 'unwrapped' to produce its net. The surface of the solid consists of two circular faces and a curved surface that can be flattened to make a rectangle.

Curved surface area of a cylinder = $2\pi rh$

and

Volume of a cylinder = $\pi r^2 h$

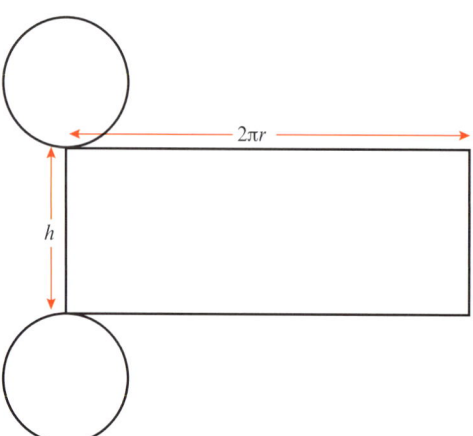

LINK

Deep sea divers carry tanks filled with compressed air on their backs. These tanks are usually shaped like cylinders, making it easy to calculate the volume and to work out how much air is left.

TIP

If questions ask for exact answers to surface area and volume calculations where π is part of the formula, you must give your answer as a multiple of π.

Exercise 7.6

1   Find the volume and surface area of the solid with the net shown in the diagram.

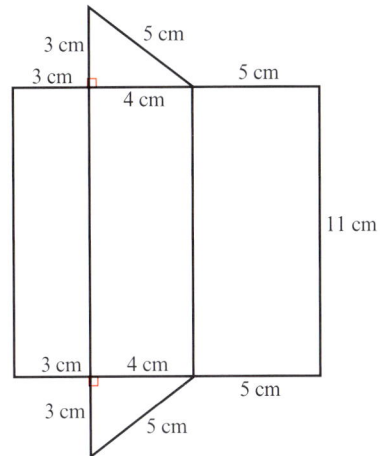

2   Find **(i)** the volume and **(ii)** the surface area of the cuboids with the following dimensions:

   a   length = 5 cm, width = 8 cm, height = 18 cm

   b   length = 1.2 mm, width = 2.4 mm, height = 4.8 mm

APPLY YOUR SKILLS

3   The diagram shows a bottle crate. Find the volume of the crate.

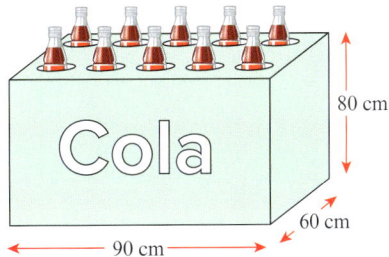

4   The diagram shows a pencil case in the shape of a triangular prism. Calculate its:

   a   volume   b   surface area.

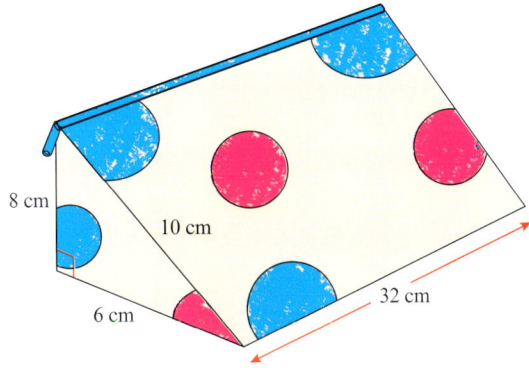

APPLY YOUR SKILLS CONTINUED

5   The diagram shows a cylindrical drain. Calculate the volume of the drain.

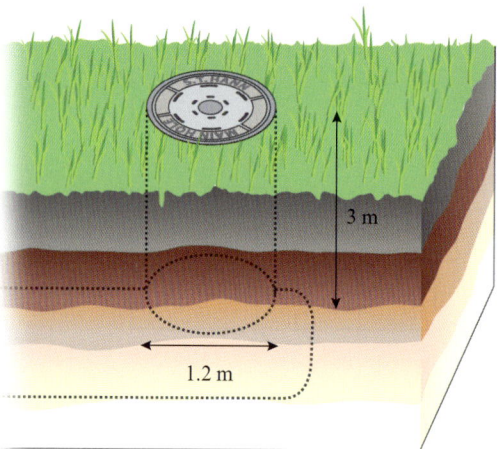

6   A 32 cm long cardboard cylinder has a radius of 2.5 cm.

   a   What is the exact volume of the cylinder?

   b   Some papers are rolled inside the cylinder and both ends are sealed
          What is the surface area of the sealed tube?

7   The diagram shows the solid glass case for a clock. The case is a cuboid
    with a cylinder removed (to fit the clock mechanism). Calculate the
    volume of glass required to make the clock case.

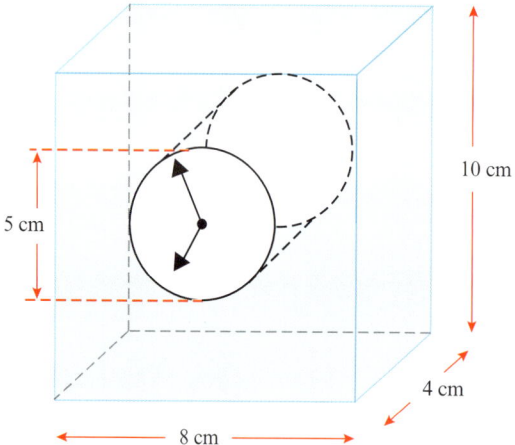

8   A storage company has a rectangular storage room 20 m long, 8 m wide
    and 2.8 m high.

   a   How many cardboard boxes with dimensions 1 m × 0.5 m × 2.5 m
          can fit into this storage room?

   b   What is the surface area of each cardboard box?

   c   When the maximum number of cardboard boxes are stored,
          what volume of empty space is left in the room?

9 Find the volume and surface area of this solid.

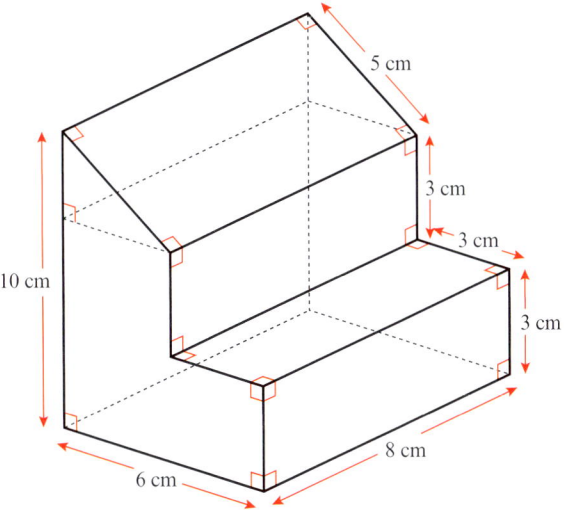

Pyramids

A pyramid is a solid with a polygon-shaped base and triangular faces that meet at a point called the **apex**.

You can find the surface area of a pyramid by finding the area of the base and the area of each of the triangles and adding them all together.

You can find the volume of a pyramid by using the following formula:

Volume = $\frac{1}{3}$ × base area × perpendicular height

The perpendicular height is the shortest distance from the base to the apex.

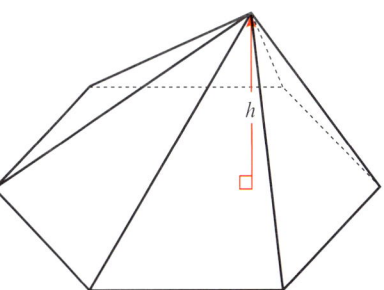

Cones

A cone is a not a pyramid, because it has a circular base and a curved surface. The length l is known as the **slant height** and h is the perpendicular height.

> **MATHEMATICAL CONNECTIONS**
>
> The slant height can be calculated using Pythagoras' theorem, which you will meet in Chapter 11.

The curved surface of the cone can be opened out and flattened to form a sector of a circle.

Curved surface area of cone = $\pi r l$

If you are asked for the total surface area of a cone, you must work out the area of the circular base and add it to the curved surface area.

> **TIP**
>
> In general, the perpendicular distance from a point to a line is the shortest distance to the line.

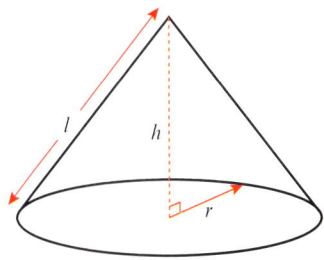

You can calculate the volume of a cone using the following formula:

Volume $= \frac{1}{3}\pi r^2 h$

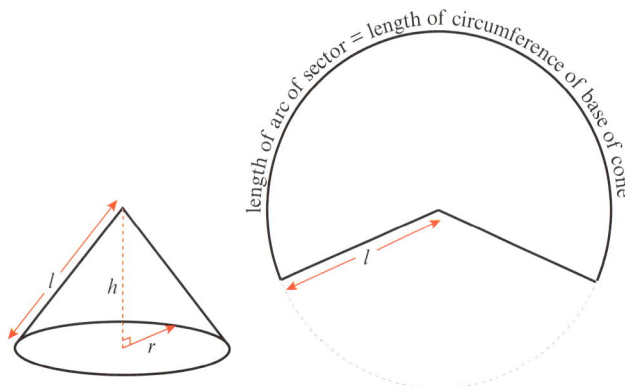

Spheres

The diagram shows a sphere with radius r.

Surface area of a sphere $= 4\pi r^2$

and

Volume of a sphere $= \frac{4}{3}\pi r^3$

A hemisphere is half a sphere.

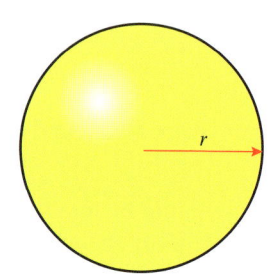

> **TIP**
>
> Remember, if you are asked for an exact answer you must give the answer as a multiple of π and you cannot use approximate values in the calculation.

> **REFLECTION**
>
> Questions on circles or spheres will involve either a radius or a diameter and you will need to remember to use the right one in the right formula. Have you made any errors? How can you use the letters in each formula to help you remember whether you use the radius or diameter?

Exercise 7.7

1   The diagram shows a beach ball. Giving your answers in terms of π, find:
    a   the surface area of the beach ball
    b   the volume of the beach ball.

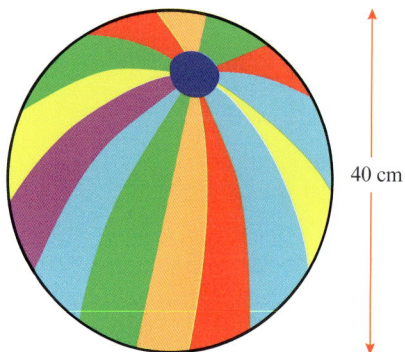

40 cm

2 The diagram shows a metal ball bearing that is completely submerged in a cylinder of water.

Find the volume of water in the cylinder.

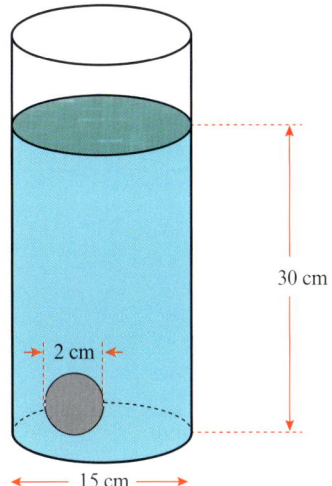

3 The Earth is roughly spherical with an approximate diameter of 12 800 km. What is the approximate volume of each hemisphere? Give your answer to 3 significant figures.

4 The Great Pyramid at Giza originally had a square base of side 230.6 m and perpendicular height 146.7 m. Assuming that the Great Pyramid is a true pyramid, find its original volume. Give your answer to 3 significant figures.

> **TIP**
>
> The equator divides the Earth into two halves called the northern hemisphere and the southern hemisphere.

> **LINK**
>
> The Great Pyramid – the largest and tallest of the Pyramids in Giza, Egypt – is one of the Seven Wonders of the Ancient World. It once stood at 146.6 m and the side length of the square base was 230.6 m. With the smooth stone casing now largely removed, the height has reduced to 138.5 m and the base length is approximately 230 m.

5 The diagram shows a rocket that consists of a cone placed on top of a cylinder. Giving your answers in terms of π, find:

a Find the surface area of the rocket

b Find the volume of the rocket.

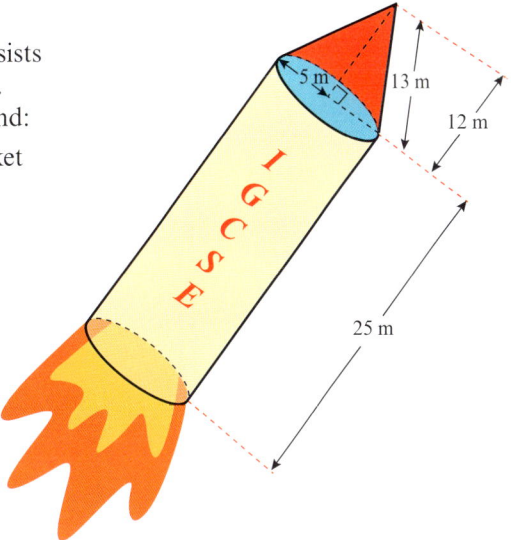

6   The diagram shows a glass pyramid ornament. The base is a regular hexagon.
Find the volume of the ornament. Give your answer to 3 significant figures.

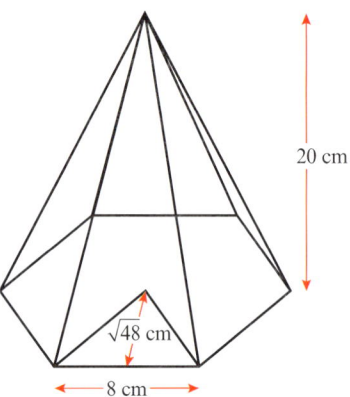

20 cm

$\sqrt{48}$ cm

8 cm

7   The diagram shows a child's toy. It is made by joining half of a sphere
to a cone.

   a   Find the volume of the toy.

   b   Find the surface area of the toy.

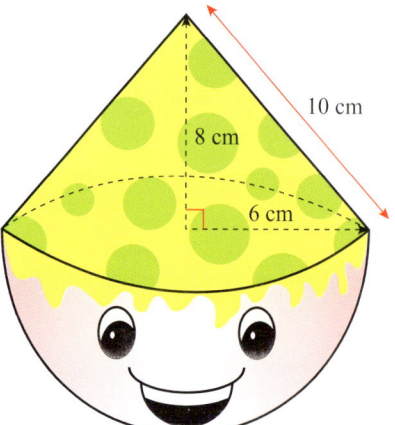

10 cm

8 cm

6 cm

8   The sphere and cone shown in the diagram have the same volume.
Find the radius of the sphere.

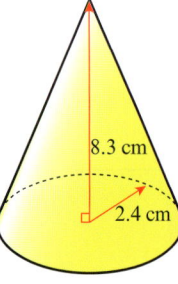

8.3 cm

2.4 cm

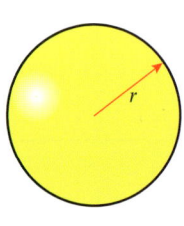

r

9   The volume of the larger sphere (of radius R) is twice the volume of the smaller
sphere (of radius r). Find an equation connecting r to R.

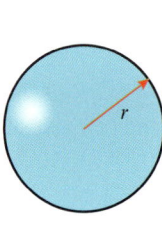

r

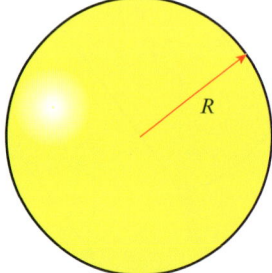

R

10 A hollow metal tube is made using a sheet of metal that is 5 mm thick. The tube is 35 cm long and has an exterior diameter of 10.4 cm.

   a   Draw a rough sketch of the tube and add its dimensions.

   b   Write down all the calculations you will have to make to find the volume of metal in the tube.

   c   Calculate the volume of metal in the tube.

   d   How could you find the total surface area of the outside plus the inside of the tube?

11 When a solid (usually a cone or a pyramid) is cut along a plane parallel to its base it is called a frustum. The frustum in this diagram was originally a pyramid with a vertical height of 15 cm. Calculate the volume of the frustum.

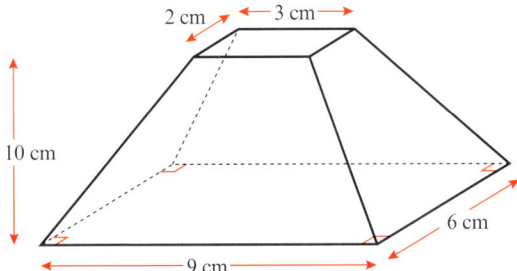

12 Amira want to make two open containers. These are the nets of the containers she will make.

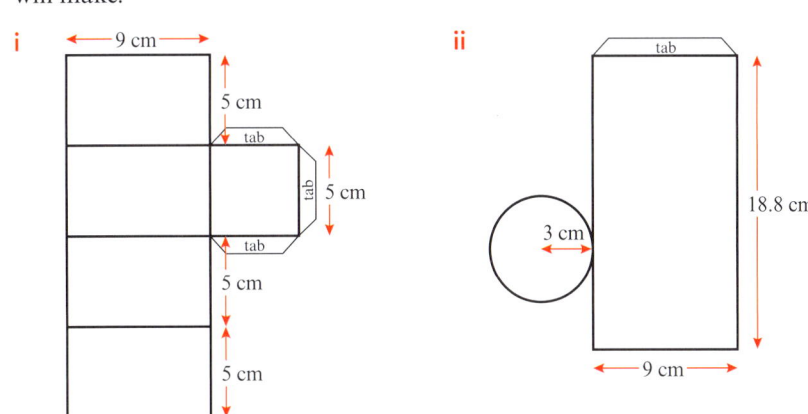

   a   Amira plans to paint the outside of each container. Use the information on each net to calculate the total area to be painted. Give your answer to 2 decimal places where necessary.

   b   Amira will use the containers to hold a sweet mix of seeds called mukhwas. Calculate the volume of mukhwas that each container can hold. Assume they are filled level with the opening.

SELF ASSESSMENT

Draw a flow chart like this one to assess your understanding of perimeter, area and volume.

How do I describe my understanding?		What did I do well?		What can I improve?
Perimeter: Area: Volume:	→		→	

TIP

Look back to Chapter 1 if you need some suggestions for sentence stems to get started.

SUMMARY

Do you know …?

The perimeter is the distance around the outside of a two-dimensional shape and the area is the space contained within the sides.

Circumference is the name for the perimeter of a circle.

If the units of length are given in cm then the units of area are cm^2 and the units of volume are cm^3. This relationship is also true if the lengths are measured in mm, m, km and so on.

A sector of a circle is the region contained in-between two radii of a circle. This splits the circle into a minor sector and a major sector.

An arc is a section of the circumference.

Prisms, pyramids, spheres, cubes and cuboids are examples of three-dimensional objects (or solids).

A net is a two-dimensional shape that can be folded to form a solid.

The net of a solid can be useful when working out the surface area of the solid.

Are you able to …?

recognise different two-dimensional shapes and find their areas

give the units of the area

calculate the areas of various two-dimensional shapes

divide a shape into simpler shapes and find the area

find unknown lengths when some lengths and an area are given

calculate the area and circumference of a circle

calculate the perimeter, arc length and area of a sector

recognise nets of solids

find the volumes and surface areas of cuboids, prisms and cylinders

find the volumes and surface areas of solids that can be broken into simpler shapes

find the volumes and surface areas of pyramids, cones and spheres.

Practice questions

1 A piece of rope is wound around a cylindrical pipe 18 times. If the diameter of the pipe is 600 mm, find the length of the rope. [4]

2 Find the perimeter and area of this shape.

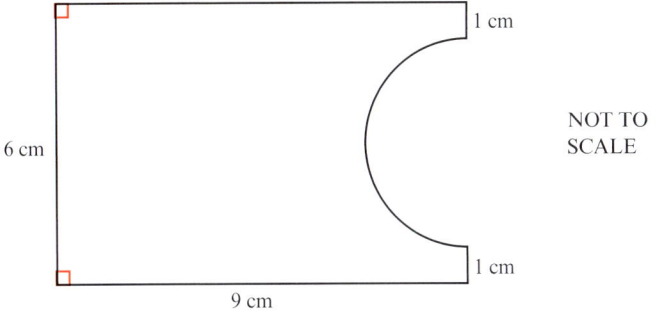

NOT TO SCALE

[4]

3 A cylindrical rainwater tank is 1.5 m tall with a diameter of 1.4 m. What is the maximum volume of rainwater it can hold? [3]

4 An ice cream maker likes to make perfect hemispherical shells of ice cream in perfect cones of wafer. If the gigantic cone is completely filled, calculate the total volume of ice cream used. Give your answer exactly, in terms of π.

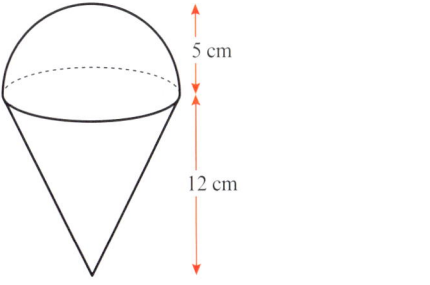

[5]

5 A beach umbrella consists of eight sectors of a circle of radius 1.2 m and angle at the centre of 40 degrees.

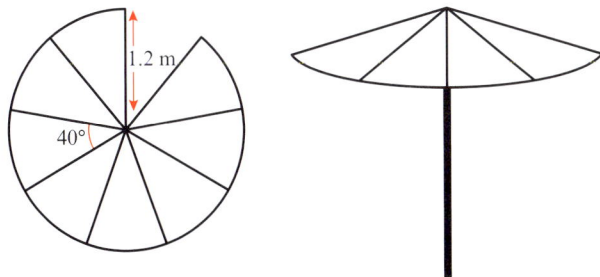

The sectors are all joined together to make an umbrella. Find the area of the top of the umbrella. [3]

6 A company logo is constructed from three identical circles.

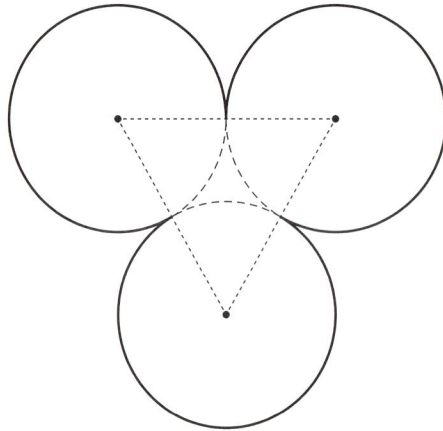

The centres of the circles are 8 cm apart.

a Calculate the perimeter of the logo. [3]

b Calculate the area of the logo. [3]

c For a new logo the distance between the centres of the circles is changed to 11 cm. Calculate the percentage increase in the perimeter. [3]

7 A wooden paperweight is made in the shape of a cuboid, with a triangular prism carved out.

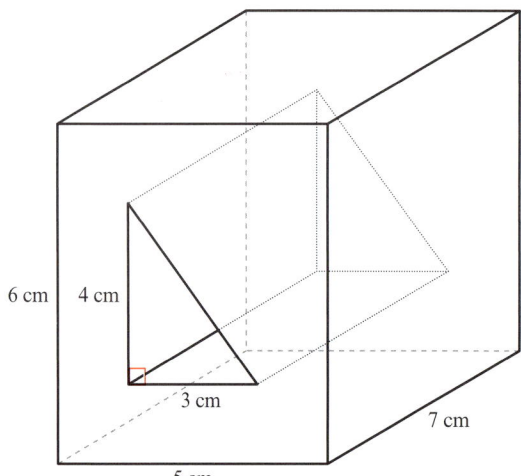

Calculate the volume of wood used to make the paperweight.
Give your answer in:

a cubic centimetres [4]

b cubic metres. [3]

8   This pyramid has a square base and four identical triangular sides.

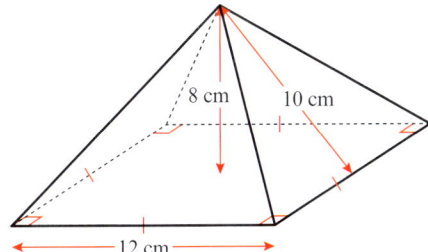

The perpendicular height is 8 cm.

The pyramid is cut in half parallel to its base to form a frustum of height 4 cm.
The sides of the square at the top of the frustum are all 6 cm.

Calculate the volume and the surface area of the frustum.   [6]

Chapter 8

Introduction to probability

IN THIS CHAPTER YOU WILL:

- express probabilities mathematically

- calculate probabilities associated with simple experiments

- use sample space diagrams to help you calculate the probability of combined events

- identify when events are independent

- identify when events are mutually exclusive.

Your genes are made up of DNA that determines the characteristics you are born with. The probability of two unrelated people having a matching DNA profile is very rare, approximately $\dfrac{1}{1\,000\,000\,000}$ or 0.000 0001%. Scientists can use the genetic profiles of parents to determine the probability of their children inheriting certain characteristics or conditions. For example, if a child's parents both carry the gene for a condition like cystic fibrosis or sickle cell anaemia, the probability that the child will be born with the condition is $\dfrac{1}{4}$ or 25%. Does this mean that a couple who have four children will have three children without the condition and one with it? Why?

GETTING STARTED

Most modern calculators are able to produce random numbers. Usually, there will be a number with the word 'ran' or 'ran#' written on it. For most, if you press this button and then press the = button, it will give you a random decimal between 0 and 1.

1   Try to work out how to use the random number button on your calculator.

2   Play a game of 'higher or lower' with yourself.

   • Start by getting a random number from your calculator.

   • Guess whether the next number will be 'higher' or 'lower'.

   • Find another random number and work out whether it was 'higher' or 'lower' than the previous number.

   • Were you correct?

   • If yes, take another go; if no, stop.

   • Write down the number of turns you take without getting it wrong.

3   Think about how you can maximise your chances of being correct. For which numbers would you most sensibly choose 'higher'? What about lower?

KEY WORDS

- bias
- combined events
- event
- experimental probability
- independent events
- mutually exclusive events
- outcomes
- probability
- relative frequency
- sample space
- sample space diagram
- theoretical probability
- trial

8.1 Understanding basic probability

Think about rolling dice. You cannot accurately predict what number you will roll, but you do know what the possible **outcomes** are. The set of all possible outcomes (1, 2, 3, 4, 5 or 6) is called the **sample space**. Any subset of the sample space is called an **event**. For example, rolling 2, 4 or 6 is an event. This can be described in words as getting an even number. We say that the event 'getting an even number' occurs if the outcome of rolling the dice is a 2, 4 or 6.

Probability is a measure of how likely an event is to happen. Something that is impossible has a value of zero and something that is certain has a value of one. The range of values from zero to one is called a probability scale. A probability cannot be negative, nor can it be greater than one.

The closer a probability is to zero, the less likely the event is to happen. The closer the probability is to one, the more likely the event is to happen.

Performing an experiment, such as rolling a dice, is called a **trial**. If you repeat an experiment, by carrying out a number of trials, you can find the **experimental probability** of an event happening. This fraction is often called the **relative frequency**.

$$P(A) = \frac{\text{number of times desired event happens}}{\text{number of trials}}$$

or, sometimes:

$$P(A) = \frac{\text{number of successes}}{\text{number of trials}}$$

TIP

Experimental probability is an estimate of how likely something is. The more data you collect in your experiment, the more accurate your probability estimate will be.

TIP

$P(A)$ means the probability of event A happening.

WORKED EXAMPLE 1

A person is blindfolded and asked to throw darts at a dartboard.

If they hit the dartboard 15 times out of 125 throws, estimate the probability they hit the dartboard on their next throw.

Answer

$$P(\text{six}) = \frac{\text{number times the person hits dartboard}}{\text{number of trials}}$$

$$= \frac{15}{125}$$

$$= 0.12$$

TIP

You can use fractions, decimals or percentages in probability, but fractions are often best (especially if the decimal is recurring). You should write fractions in their simplest form.

Relative frequency and expected occurrences

You can use relative frequency to work out how many times you expect something to occur over a large number of trials. For example, if you know that the relative frequency of rolling a four on particular dice is 18%, you can work out how many times you would expect to get a four when you roll the dice 80 or 200 times.

MATHEMATICAL CONNECTIONS

Remember that a percentage is a fraction with denominator of 100. If a probability is 18%, then it is $\frac{18}{100} = \frac{9}{50}$ when written as a fraction.

18% of 80 = 14.4 and 18% of 200 = 36, so if you rolled the same dice 80 times you would expect to get a four about 14 times and if you rolled it 200 times, you would expect to get a four 36 times.

Remember though, that even if you expected to get a four 36 times, this is not guaranteed and your actual results may be very different.

Theoretical probability

When you flip a coin you may be interested in the event 'getting a head' but this is only one possibility. When you flip a coin there are two possible outcomes: 'getting a head' or 'getting a tail.'

If all the possible outcomes are equally likely, you can calculate the **theoretical probability** of an event by counting the number of favourable outcomes and dividing by the number of possible outcomes. Favourable outcomes are any outcomes that mean your event has happened.

Using the example from the start of the chapter, if you roll an unbiased dice and want to find the probability of getting an even number, then the favourable outcomes are two, four or six. There are six possible outcomes and three of them are favourable.

If A is the event 'you get an even number', then:

$$P(A) = \frac{\text{number of favourable outcomes}}{\text{number of possible outcomes}} = \frac{3}{6} = \frac{1}{2}$$

Outcomes are equally likely because there is something about the experiment that makes them so. In the example of the dice, all of the faces on a fair dice are the same size and shape.

Of course, a dice may be weighted in some way, or imperfectly made, and this can be true of any object discussed in a probability question. Under these circumstances a dice, coin or other object is said to be **biased**. The outcomes will no longer be equally likely and you may need to use experimental probability.

> **TIP**
>
> In some countries, theoretical probability is referred to as 'expected probability'. This is a casual reference and does *not* mean the same thing as mathematical 'expectation'.

> **TIP**
>
> Questions will usually tell you whether an object or experiment is unbiased.

WORKED EXAMPLE 2

The numbers one to six are written on six identical cards. The cards are shuffled and placed face down on a table. If a card is selected at random, what is the probability of obtaining:

a   a three   **b**   an even number   **c**   a prime number?

Answers

a $P(3) = \dfrac{1}{6}$ There is only one way of picking a three, but six possible outcomes (you could select a 1, 2, 3, 4, 5, 6).

b $P(\text{even number}) = \dfrac{3}{6} = \dfrac{1}{2}$ There are three ways of picking an even number, giving three favourable outcomes.

c $P(\text{prime number}) = \dfrac{3}{6} = \dfrac{1}{2}$ The prime numbers you could pick are 2, 3 and 5, giving three favourable outcomes.

WORKED EXAMPLE 3

A card is drawn from an ordinary park of 52 cards. What is the probability that the card will be a king?

Answer

$P(king) = \dfrac{4}{52} = \dfrac{1}{13}$

Number of possible outcomes is 52.

Number of favourable outcomes is four, because there are four kings per pack.

TIP

A set of 52 playing cards four suits: hearts, diamonds, clubs and spades. Hearts and diamonds are red. Clubs and spades are black. Each suit is made up of numbers 2 to 10 and an ace, jack, queen and king.

WORKED EXAMPLE 4

Nasir has 20 socks in a drawer.

Eight socks are red, ten socks are blue and two socks are green. If a sock is drawn at random, what is the probability that it is green?

Answer

$P(green) = \dfrac{2}{20} = \dfrac{1}{10}$

Number of possible outcomes is 20.

Number of favourable outcomes is two.

WORKED EXAMPLE 5

Nine teams of painters were each given one letter from the word HOLLYWOOD to paint. Each painting team was given a letter at random. Find the probability that a team of painters was asked to paint:

a   the letter 'Y'

b   the letter 'O'

c   the letter 'H' or the letter 'L'

d   the letter 'Z'.

Answers

a $P(Y) = \dfrac{1}{9}$

Number of favourable outcomes is one (there is only one 'Y').

There are nine possible outcomes in total.

b $P(O) = \dfrac{3}{9} = \dfrac{1}{3}$

Number of favourable outcomes is three.

c $P(H \text{ or } L) = \dfrac{3}{9} = \dfrac{1}{3}$

Number of favourable outcomes = number of letters that are *either* 'H' or 'L' = 3, since there is one 'H' and two 'L's.

d $P(Z) = \dfrac{0}{9} = 0$

Number of favourable outcomes is zero (there are no 'Z's).

The probability that an event does not happen

Something may happen or it may not happen. The probability that an event happens will usually be different from the probability that the event does not happen, but the two combined probabilities will always add up to one.

If A is an event, then A' is the event that A does *not* happen and $P(A') = 1 - P(A)$

> **TIP**
>
> When you talk about A' you usually refer to it as 'not A'.
> Sometimes you may see $\bar{A}$ used instead of A'.

> **TIP**
>
> When the probability an event happens is equal to the probability the event does not happen, both probabilities must be equal to $\frac{1}{2}$.
> This probability is sometimes referred to as 'evens'.

WORKED EXAMPLE 6

The probability that Jas passes a driving test is $\frac{2}{3}$. What is the probability that Jas fails the driving test?

Answer

$P(\text{fails}) = 1 - \frac{2}{3} = \frac{1}{3}$ $P(\text{fails}) = P(\text{not passing}) = 1 - P(\text{passing})$

INVESTIGATION

Talking about probability

Many people try to use probability terms, but don't fully understand the statement they are making. How would you explain what is wrong with each of the following statements?

1   In a 'true or false' quiz with ten questions, you are certain to get five right if you guess.

2   In a rowing race a team can win, lose or draw, so the probability they win is $\frac{1}{3}$.

3   If you roll a dice ten times and get four sixes, the dice must be biased.

4   There are 16 red socks and 24 blue socks in a drawer. If you pull ten socks out of the drawer there will always be more blue socks than red socks.

5   The sign by the ice cream stall says that the probability of rain today is $\frac{1}{5}$, but it is raining, so the probability it rains today must have always been 1.

Exercise 8.1

1   A six-sided dice is thrown 100 times and the number five appears 14 times.

   a   Find the experimental probability of throwing a five, giving your answer as a fraction in its lowest terms.

   b   Write your answer to part (a) as a percentage.

> **TIP**
>
> Probabilities are most often given as decimals or fractions, but you can also use percentages. For example, you can write a probability of $\frac{1}{2}$ as 50% or a probability of 0.32 as 32%.

2   The diagram shows a spinner that is divided into exactly eight equal sectors.
Ryan spins the spinner 260 times and records the results in a table:

Number	1	2	3	4	5	6	7	8
Frequency	33	38	26	35	39	21	33	35

Calculate the experimental probability of spinning:

a   the number three

b   the number five

c   an odd number

d   a factor of eight.

3   A consumer organisation carried out tests to find the average lifetime of a new
brand of solar lamp. The results of the tests are summarised in the table.

Lifetime of lamp, L hours	$0 \leqslant L < 1000$	$1000 \leqslant L < 2000$	$2000 \leqslant L < 3000$	$3000 \leqslant L$
Frequency	30	75	160	35

a   Calculate the relative frequency of a lamp lasting for less than 3000 hours,
but more than 1000 hours.

b   If a hardware chain ordered 2000 of these lamps, how many would you
expect to last for more than 3000 hours?

4   A survey was carried out where people were asked to choose their favourite type
of film from five categories. The bar chart shows the results.

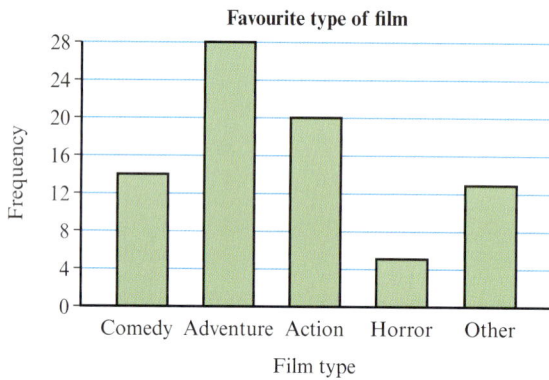

Favourite type of film

a   How many people took part in the survey?

b   Another person joins the group and is asked the same question. Estimate the
probability that the person chooses 'adventure'.

c   The survey was carried out in a village with a total population of 480.
If everyone in the village was asked the question, estimate the number of
people that would choose 'horror'.

5   Research shows that the probability of a person being right-handed is 0.77.
How many left-handed people would you expect in a population of 25 000?

6   A flower enthusiast collected 385 examples of a *Polynomialus mathematicus* flower
in Peru. Just five of the flowers were blue.
One flower is chosen at random. Find the probability that:

a   it is blue

b   it is not blue.

7   A bag contains nine equal sized balls. Four of the balls are blue and the remaining five balls are red.
What is the probability that, when a ball is taken from the bag:

a   it is blue

b   it is red

c   it neither blue nor red

d   it is either blue or red?

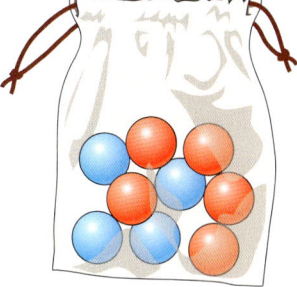

8   A bag contains 36 balls. The probability that a ball chosen at random is blue is $\frac{1}{4}$.
How many blue balls are there in the bag?

9   Liu shuffles an ordinary pack of 52 playing cards. If he draws a single card at random, find the probability that the card is:

a   a king

b   a spade

c   a black card

d   a prime-numbered card.

SELF ASSESSMENT

An exit ticket is a useful way of assessing how well you have understood the concepts covered in this section.

1   Complete the activities on this exit ticket.

Events	A Throwing a number greater than 2 on a regular dice.	B Drawing a red card from a set of 12 red, 12 white and 6 blue cards.	C Throwing a 7 using a regular dice.	D Getting heads 14 times when you toss a coin 20 times.

a   Which event has a probability of 0?

b   What is the probability of event B not happening?

c   Calculate the probability of A happening.

d   What type of probability is described in event D?

2   Which emoji best describes how you feel about this work?
Choose one of these or draw your own.

3   Write a sentence explaining why you chose that emoji.

8.2 Sample space diagrams

The probability space, or sample space, is the set of all possible outcomes. You can draw a **sample space diagram** to show all outcomes clearly and use it to work out the probability of different events.

TIP

In some countries, these might be called 'probability space diagrams'.

WORKED EXAMPLE 7

One red dice and one blue dice are thrown at the same time and the numbers showing on the dice are added together. Find the probability that:

a   the sum is 7

b   the sum is less than 5

c   the sum is greater than or equal to 8

d   the sum is less than 8.

Answers

Red

+	1	2	3	4	5	6
1	2	3	4	5	6	7
2	3	4	5	6	7	8
3	4	5	6	7	8	9
4	5	6	7	8	9	10
5	6	7	8	9	10	11
6	7	8	9	10	11	12

Blue

The diagram shows that there are 36 possible sums, so there are 36 equally likely outcomes in total.

a $P(7) = \dfrac{6}{36} = \dfrac{1}{6}$ There are six 7s in the grid, so six favourable outcomes.

b $P(\text{less than } 5) = \dfrac{6}{36} = \dfrac{1}{6}$ The outcomes that are less than 5 are 2, 3 and 4. There are six favourable outcomes for these numbers.

c $P(\text{greater than or equal to } 8) = \dfrac{15}{36}$ The outcomes greater than or equal to 8 (which includes 8) are 8, 9, 10, 11 or 12.

$= \dfrac{5}{12}$ These give 15 favourable outcomes.

d $P(\text{less than } 8) = 1 - \dfrac{5}{12} = \dfrac{7}{12}$ $P(\text{less than } 8) = P(\text{not greater than or equal to } 8)$
$= 1 - P(\text{greater than or equal to } 8)$

Exercise 8.2

1   An unbiased coin is thrown twice and the outcome for each is recorded as H (head) or T (tail). A sample space diagram can be drawn as shown.

   a   Copy and complete the diagram.

   b   Find the probability that:

   i   the coins show the same face

   ii   the coins both show heads

   iii   there is at least one head

   iv   there are no heads.

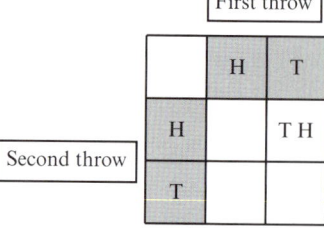

First throw

		H	T
	H		T H
Second throw	T		

2 Two unbiased dice are thrown and the product of the two numbers is recorded.

    a Draw a suitable sample space diagram to show all possible outcomes.

    b Find the probability that:

        i the product is 1

        ii the product is 7

        iii the product is less than or equal to 4

        iv the product is greater than 4

        v the product is a prime number

        vi the product is a square number.

3

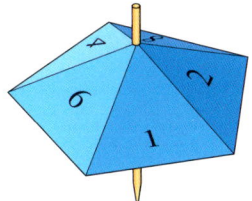 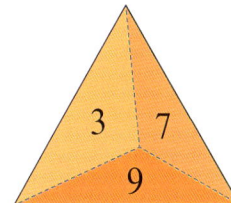

The diagram shows a spinner with five equal sectors numbered 1, 2, 4, 6 and 8, and an unbiased tetrahedral dice with faces numbered 3, 5, 7 and 9. The spinner is spun and the dice is thrown, and the greater of the two numbers is recorded. If both show the same number then that number is recorded.

    a Draw a sample space diagram to show the possible outcomes.

    b Calculate the probability that:

        i the greater number is even

        ii the greater number is odd

        iii the greater number is a multiple of 3

        iv the greater number is prime

        v the greater number is more than twice the smaller number.

4 An unbiased cubical dice has six faces numbered 4, 6, 10, 12, 15 and 24. The dice is thrown twice and the highest common factor (HCF) of the two scores is recorded.

    a Draw a sample space diagram to show the possible outcomes.

    b Calculate the probability that:

        i the HCF is 2

        ii the HCF is greater than 2

        iii the HCF is not 7

        iv the HCF is not 5

        v the HCF is 3 or 5

        vi the HCF is equal to one of the numbers thrown.

> **MATHEMATICAL CONNECTIONS**
>
> You learnt about highest common factors in Chapter 1.

> **LINK**
>
> Computer programming and software development uses probability to build applications (apps) such as voice activated dialling on a mobile phone. When you say a name to the phone, the app chooses the most likely contact from your contact list.

5 Two dice are thrown and the result is obtained by adding the two numbers.
Two sets of dice are available.
Set A: one dice has four faces numbered 1 to 4 and the other eight faces numbered 1 to 8.
Set B: each dice has six faces numbered 1 to 6.

a Copy and complete the sample space diagrams for each set.

Set A

+	1	2	3	4	5	6	7	8
1								
2								
3								
4								

Set B

+	1	2	3	4	5	6
1						
2						
3						
4						
5						
6						

b In an experiment with one of the sets of dice, the following results were obtained:

Dice score	Frequency
2	15
3	25
4	44
5	54
6	68
7	87
8	66
9	54
10	43
11	30
12	14

By comparing the probabilities and relative frequencies, decide which set of dice was used.

PEER ASSESSMENT

1 Work with a partner. Look at the sample space diagrams your partner has drawn in Exercise 8.2.

2 Use the following criteria to assess each other's sample space diagrams. Highlight any problematic areas and provide corrections or suggestions for improving the diagram.

Criteria:

- All possible outcomes are correctly indicated.
- The diagram is easy to read and interpret.
- You can find the probability of different events easily.

8.3 Combining independent and mutually exclusive events

Sometimes you will need to calculate the probability that two events happen, one after the other. You might also need to calculate the probability that either of two events happen. In this section you will learn some rules for calculating the probability of **combined events**.

Independent events

If you flip an unbiased coin once, the probability of it showing a head is 0.5. Whatever happened the first time, if you flip the coin a second time the probability of it showing a head will still be 0.5. The result of the first throw has no influence on the result of the second throw. Situations like this are called **independent events**.

Imagine you have a bag containing different coloured balls. If you choose a ball, note its colour, replace it and then choose another, the choice of the first ball does not influence the choice of the second ball. These events are also independent.

MATHEMATICAL CONNECTIONS

If you do not replace the first ball the events will not be independent. There is one ball less for the second choice so the probabilities will have changed. You will think about situations like this in Chapter 24.

You can calculate the probability that two independent events, A and B, both occur:

$P(A$ happens and then B happens$) = P(A) \times P(B)$

or

$P(A$ and $B) = P(A) \times P(B)$

For example, when flipping two coins,

$P(\text{flipping two heads}) = P(\text{Heads}) \times P(\text{Heads}) = \dfrac{1}{2} \times \dfrac{1}{2} = \dfrac{1}{4}$

> **TIP**
>
> Note that this formula is only true if A and B are independent.

Mutually exclusive events

If you throw a normal dice and let:

A = the event that you get an even number

and

B = the event that you get an odd number

then A and B cannot happen together because no number is both even and odd at the same time. You can say that A and B are **mutually exclusive** events.

> ## MATHEMATICAL CONNECTIONS
>
> When you throw a dice, the events 'get an even number' and 'get a number less than four' are not mutually exclusive because if you throw a two, both events occur at the same time. You will learn more about these sorts of events in Chapter 24.

For two mutually exclusive events A and B, you can calculate the probability that either A or B occurs:

$P(A \text{ or } B) = P(A) + P(B)$

For example, when rolling a normal dice,

$P(\text{even number or odd number}) = P(\text{even number}) + P(\text{odd number}) = \dfrac{1}{2} + \dfrac{1}{2} = 1$

Worked examples 8 and 9 demonstrate how you can use these simple formulae for independent and mutually exclusive events.

> **TIP**
>
> Note, this formula only works if A and B are mutually exclusive.

> ## WORKED EXAMPLE 8
>
> Noa and Sunja are both taking a music examination independently.
>
> The probability that Noa passes is $\dfrac{3}{4}$ and the probability that Sunja passes is $\dfrac{5}{6}$.
>
> What is the probability that:
>
> **a** both pass? **b** neither passes? **c** at least one passes?
>
> **d** either Noa or Sunja passes (but not both)?
>
> **Answers**
>
> **a** $P(\text{both pass}) = P(\text{Noa passes and Sunja passes})$
>
> $\qquad = \dfrac{3}{4} \times \dfrac{5}{6} = \dfrac{15}{24} = \dfrac{5}{8}$
>
> The outcomes are independent so use the formula:
> $P(A \text{ and } B) = P(A) \times P(B)$
>
> **b** $P(\text{neither passes}) = P(\text{Noa fails and Sunja fails}$
>
> $\qquad = \left(1 - \dfrac{3}{4}\right) \times \left(1 - \dfrac{5}{6}\right)$
>
> $\qquad = \dfrac{1}{4} \times \dfrac{1}{6}$
>
> $\qquad = \dfrac{1}{24}$
>
> $P(\text{fail}) = P(\text{not pass})$
> $\qquad = 1 - P(\text{pass})$

WORKED EXAMPLE 8 CONTINUED

c P(at least one passes) = $1 - P$(neither passes)

$$= 1 - \frac{1}{24} = \frac{23}{24}$$

d P(either Sunja or Noa passes)

= P(Noa passes and Sunja fails

or Noa fails and Sunja passes)

$$= \frac{3}{4} \times \frac{1}{6} + \frac{1}{4} \times \frac{5}{6}$$

$$= \frac{3}{24} + \frac{5}{24}$$

$$= \frac{8}{24}$$

$$= \frac{1}{3}$$

'Noa passes and Sunja fails' and, 'Noa fails and Sunja passes,' are mutually exclusive because they cannot both happen at the same time. So use the formula: $P(A \text{ or } B) = P(A) + P(B)$, where

A = Noa passes and Sunja fails

and

B = Noa fails and Sunja passes

TIP

It is not possible to pass and fail an exam at the same time. This is why the events are mutually exclusive.

WORKED EXAMPLE 9

Simone and Rami are playing basketball. The probability that Simone shoots the ball into the net is 0.1. The probability that Rami shoots the ball into the net is 0.2. Simone's success or failure at shooting the ball into the net is independent of Rami's and vice versa.

Simone and Rami take one shot each. Find the probability that:

a both shoot the ball into the net

b Simone shoots the ball into the net, but Rami does not

c exactly one ball is shot into the net.

Answers

a P(both shoot the ball into the net) = $0.1 \times 0.2 = 0.02$

b P(Simone shoots the ball into the net but Rami does not) = $0.1 \times (1 - 0.2)$
$= 0.1 \times 0.8 = 0.08$

c P(exactly one ball is shot into the net) = P(Simone shoots the ball into the net and Rami does not or Simone does not shoot the ball into the net and Rami does)

$= 0.1 \times 0.8 + 0.9 \times 0.2$

$= 0.08 + 0.18$

$= 0.26$

Exercise 8.3

 1   A standard six-sided dice is thrown twice. Calculate the probability that:

    a   two sixes are thrown

    b   two even numbers are thrown

    c   the same number is thrown twice

    d   the two numbers thrown are different.

 2   A bag contains 12 coloured balls. Five of the balls are red and the rest are blue. A ball is drawn at random from the bag. It is then replaced and a second ball is drawn. The colour of each ball is recorded.

    a   List the possible outcomes of the experiment.

    b   Calculate the following probabilities. Give your answers as percentages to 3 significant figures.

        i   The first ball is blue.

        ii   The second ball is red.

        iii   The first ball is blue and the second ball is red.

        iv   The two balls are the same colour.

        v   The two balls are a different colour.

        vi   Neither ball is red.

        vii   At least one ball is red.

3   Devin and Tej are playing cards. Devin draws a card, replaces it and then shuffles the pack. Tej then draws a card. Find the probability that:

    a   both draw an ace

    b   both draw the king of Hearts

    c   Devin draws a spade and Tej draws a queen

    d   exactly one of the cards drawn is a heart

    e   both cards are red or both cards are black

    f   the cards are different colours.

4   Kirti and Hussein are both preparing to take a driving test. They each learned to drive separately, so the results of the tests are independent. The probability that Kirti passes is 0.6 and the probability that Hussein passes is 0.4. Calculate the probability that:

    a   both pass the test

    b   neither passes the test

    c   Kirti passes the test, but Hussein does not pass

    d   at least one of Kirti and Hussein passes

    e   exactly one of Kirti and Hussein passes.

TIP

Usually 'AND' in probability means you will need to multiply probabilities. 'OR' usually means you will need to add them.

MATHEMATICAL CONNECTIONS

You will learn how to calculate probabilities for situations where objects are *not* replaced in Chapter 24.

SUMMARY

Do you know …?
Probability measures how likely something is to happen.
An outcome is the single result of an experiment.
An event is a collection of favourable outcomes.
Experimental probability can be calculated by dividing the number of favourable outcomes by the number of trials.
Favourable outcomes are any outcomes that mean your event has happened.
If outcomes are equally likely then theoretical probability can be calculated by dividing the number of favourable outcomes by the number of possible outcomes.
The probability of an event happening and the probability of that event not happening will always sum up to one. If A is an event, then A' is the event that A does not happen and $P(A) = 1 - P(A)$.
Independent events do not affect one another.
Mutually exclusive events cannot happen together.

Are you able to …?
find an experimental probability given the results of several trials
find a theoretical probability
find the probability that an event will not happen if you know the probability that it will happen
draw a sample space diagram
recognise independent and mutually exclusive events
do calculations involving combined probabilities.

Practice questions

1   A bowl of fruit contains three apples, four bananas, two pears and one orange.
A child chooses one piece of fruit at random. Find the probability that
they choose:

   a   a banana   [2]

   b   a pear or a banana   [2]

   c   a mango.   [1]

2   A shape is chosen at random from these quadrilaterals: square, rectangle, rhombus, parallelogram, trapezium and kite. Each shape is equally likely to be chosen.
Find the probability that:

   a   the chosen shape has four sides of equal length   [1]

   b   the chosen shape has three sides   [1]

   c   the chosen shape has at least one pair of parallel sides   [2]

   d   the angles in the chosen shape are all equal.   [2]

3   A four-sided dice has faces numbered 1, 2, 3 and 4. The dice is thrown on the table. The probabilities of each of the four faces landing flat on the table are as shown.

Face	1	2	3	4
Probability	$\frac{2}{9}$	$\frac{1}{3}$	$\frac{5}{18}$	$\frac{1}{6}$

   a   Copy the table and fill in the four empty boxes with the probabilities changed to fractions with a common denominator.   [3]

   b   Which face is most likely to finish flat on the table?   [2]

   c   What is the probability that face 3 does not finish flat on the table?   [2]

4   Josh and Soumik each take a coin at random out of their pockets and add them together to get an amount. Josh has two $1 coins, a 50c coin, a $5 coin and three 20c coins in his pocket. Soumik has three $5 coins, a $2 coin and three 50c pieces.

   a   Draw a probability space diagram to show all the possible outcomes for the sum of the two coins.   [4]

   b   Find the probability that the coins will add up to $6.   [2]

   c   Find the probability that the coins add up to less than $2.   [2]

   d   Find the probability that the coins will add up to $5 or more.   [3]

5   A six-sided dice is biased so that the probability of rolling a 5 is $\frac{1}{6}$, the probability of rolling a 6 is $\frac{1}{3}$ and the probabilities of rolling a 1, 2, 3 or 4 are all equal.

The dice is rolled twice and the result recorded each time.

   a   Calculate the probability of rolling a 3 on the first roll.   [2]

   b   Calculate the probability that the total of both rolls is 12.   [3]

   c   Calculate the probability that the product of both rolls is 12.   [3]

6   Two fair spinners, one in the shape of a square with sides numbered 1, 2, 3, 4, and one in the shape of a regular pentagon with sides numbered 1, 2, 3, 4, 5 are spun at the same time.

   a   Draw a sample space diagram to show all possible outcomes.
       Use a comma to separate the numbers on each spinner. For example, record the outcome 'a 3 on the square spinner and a 4 on the pentagon spinner' as 3, 4.   [3]

b   Event A is 'the total of the scores is 5'.
Event B is 'the scores have a difference of 1'.
Find the probability of the events:

    i A [2]

    ii B [2]

    iii A and B [3]

    iv A or B or both. [3]

c   **i**   Use your answer to part (b) to show that the result,
$P(A \text{ or } B) = P(A) + P(B)$, is not true for these events. [3]

    ii   Why is the result not true for these events? [2]

SELF ASSESSMENT

How well do you understand the work on probability?
Copy the headings. Write short points under each one.

- My strengths
- Evidence of my strengths
- My goals for the next set of practice questions
- My plan to reach the goals

Past paper questions

TIP

Unit 2 Past Paper Questions Resource Sheet is available on Cambridge GO.

1   Write these numbers in order, starting with the smallest.

$\dfrac{13}{201}$ 5.6%   0.065 $\dfrac{5}{89}$

[2]

Cambridge IGCSE Mathematics (0580) Paper 11 Q3, June 2020

 2   The probability that a train is late is 0.15.

Write down the probability that the train is not late.

[1]

Cambridge IGCSE Mathematics (0580) Paper 11 Q7, June 2021

3   A cone has radius 4.5 cm and height 10.4 cm.

Calculate, in terms of π, the volume of the cone.

[The volume, V, of a cone with radius r and height h is $V = \dfrac{1}{3}\pi r^2 h$.]

[2]

Cambridge IGCSE Mathematics (0580) Paper 11 Q11, June 2020

 4   Factorise completely.

$21a^2 + 28ab$

[2]

Cambridge IGCSE Mathematics (0580) Paper 11 Q13, June 2020

 5   A bag contains green balls and red balls only.

A ball is taken at random from the bag.

The probability of taking a green ball is 0.38.

Write down the probability of taking

a   a red ball,

[1]

b   a blue ball.

[1]

Cambridge IGCSE Mathematics (0580) Paper 11 Q4, June 2019

6 Write down the following numbers in standard form.

 a 640 000

[1]

 b 0.0006

[1]

Cambridge IGCSE Mathematics (0580) Paper 11 Q7, June 2019

7 A bag contains blue, red, yellow and green balls only.

A ball is taken from the bag at random.

The table shows some information about the probabilities.

Colour	Blue	Red	Yellow	Green
Probability	0.15	0.2		0.43

 a Complete the table. [Using Figure 1 in the Unit 2 Past Paper Questions Resource Sheet.]

[2]

 b Abdul takes a ball at random and replaces it in the bag.

He does this 200 times.

Find how many times he expects to take a red ball.

[1]

Cambridge IGCSE Mathematics (0580) Paper 21 Q4, June 2020

8 Work out $1.20 as a percentage of $16.

[1]

Cambridge IGCSE Mathematics (0580) Paper 11 Q2, June 2019

9 **a** Write the number 0.0605 in standard form.

[1]

 b Calculate $(1.63 \times 10^{12}) \times (2.47 \times 10^{-1})$.

Give your answer in standard form.

[1]

Cambridge IGCSE Mathematics (0580) Paper 11 Q16, June 2020

10 The diagram shows the net of a triangular prism on a 1 cm² grid.

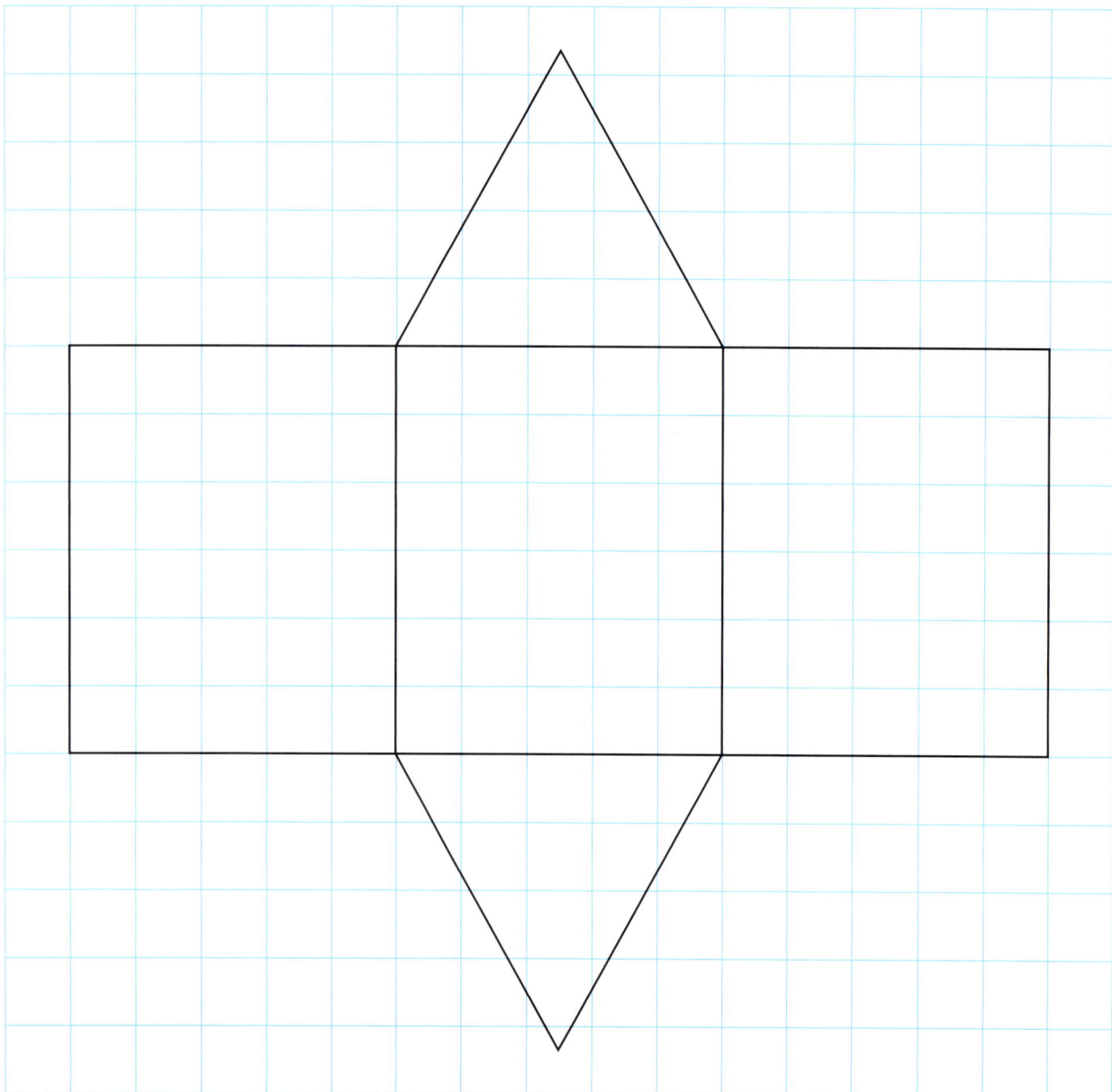

    a   Write down the mathematical name for the type of triangle shown on the grid.

[1]

b **i** Measure the perpendicular height of the triangle.

[1]

ii Calculate the area of the triangle.

[2]

iii Calculate the volume of the triangular prism.

[2]

Cambridge IGCSE Mathematics (0580) Paper 31 Q3, June 2020

11 **a** Simplify $8a + 3b - 2a + b$.

[2]

b Calculate the value of $4x^2 + xy$ when $x = 3$ and $y = -2$.

[2]

c Solve these equations.

i $\frac{x}{4} = 20$

[1]

ii $3x - 5 = 16$

[2]

iii $5(2x + 1) = 27$

[3]

d Make r the subject of this formula.

$p = 3r - 5$

[2]

Cambridge IGCSE Mathematics (0580) Paper 31 Q9, June 2019

12

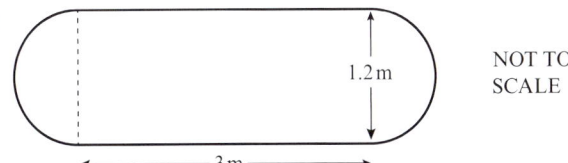

1.2 m

NOT TO
SCALE

3 m

The diagram shows the surface of a garden pond, made from a rectangle and two semicircles.

The rectangle measures 3 m by 1.2 m.

a Calculate the area of this surface.

[3]

b The pond is a prism and the water in the pond has a depth of 20 cm.
Calculate the number of litres of water in the pond.

[3]

c After a rainfall, the number of litres of water in the pond is 1007.
Calculate the increase in the depth of water in the pond.
Give your answers in centimetres.

[3]

Cambridge IGCSE Mathematics (0580) Paper 41 Q5, June 2019

13 a

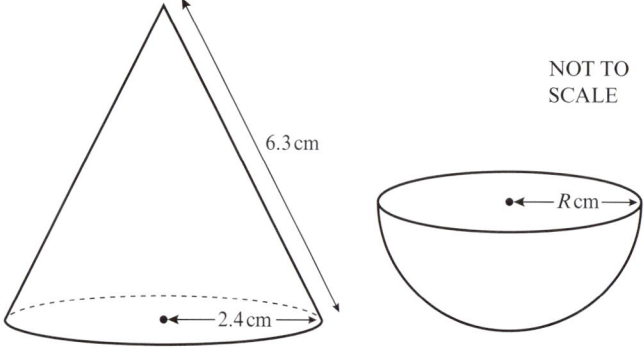

NOT TO SCALE

The diagram shows a solid cone and a solid hemisphere.

The cone has radius 2.4 cm and slant height 6.3 cm.

The hemisphere has radius R cm.

The **total** surface area of the cone is equal to the **total** surface area of the hemisphere.

Calculate the value of R.

[The curved surface area, A, of a cone with radius r and slant height l is $A = \pi rl$.]

[The curved surface area, A, of a sphere with radius r is $A = 4\pi r^2$.]

[4]

b

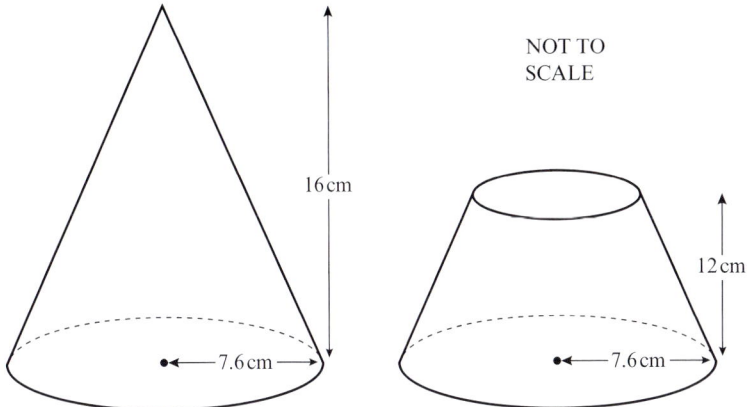

NOT TO
SCALE

16 cm

12 cm

7.6 cm

7.6 cm

The diagram shows a solid cone with radius 7.6 cm and height 16 cm.

A cut is made parallel to the base of the cone and the top section is removed.

The remaining solid has height 12 cm, as shown in the diagram.

Calculate the volume of the remaining solid.

[The volume, V, of a cone with radius r and height h is $V = \dfrac{1}{3}\pi r^2 h$.]

[4]

Cambridge IGCSE Mathematics (0580) Paper 41 Q3, June 2021

> Unit 2 Project

Odds and evens

This set of numbered balls is used to play a game:

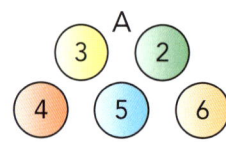

To play the game, the balls are mixed up and two balls are randomly picked out together. For example:

The numbers on the balls are added together: 4 + 5 = 9

If the total is even, you win.

If the total is odd, you lose.

How can you decide whether the game is fair?

Here are three more sets of balls:

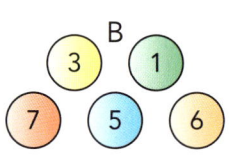 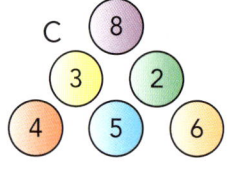 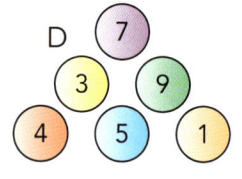

Which set would you choose to play with, to maximise your chances of winning? Why?

What proportion of the time would you expect to win with each set of balls? Explain your reasoning.

Can you find a set of balls where the chance of getting an even total is the same as the chance of getting an odd total?

- How many sets of balls with this property can you find?

- What do you notice about the number of odd and even balls in your sets?

> Chapter 9

Sequences, surds and sets

GETTING STARTED

1   Here is a number sequence.

27, 23, 19, 15 …

   a   In your own words, describe what a number sequence is.

   b   If T_1 means the first term in the sequence, what does T_n mean?

   c   What will the next term be? Why?

   d   It is possible to work out the value of the 20th term (or any term) without listing the numbers. How could you do this?

2   In everyday English, the word 'rational' means well thought out or logical and 'irrational' means going against reason or illogical.

   a   What do the words rational and irrational mean in maths?

   b   Why is π an irrational number?

   c   Why is 0.66666… rational even though its decimal part continues to infinity?

3   Read this information about the doctors on the Venn diagram.
   • Top left region is set A = {doctors that perform surgery}
   • Top right region is set B = {doctors that are specialists}
   • Bottom region is set C = {doctors that treat children}

   a   How many doctors perform surgery?

   b   How many doctors perform surgery or treat children?

   c   How many doctors are specialists who do not do surgery and who do not treat children?

   d   How many specialists treat children and perform surgery?

4   Consider the set of positive whole numbers less than 20. Draw a Venn diagram to show the relationship between even numbers and prime numbers.

KEY WORDS

- complement (of a set)
- consecutive
- element
- empty set
- exact value
- intersection
- rationalising the denominator
- recurring decimal
- sequence
- set
- set builder notation
- subscript notation
- subset
- surd
- term
- terminating decimal
- union
- universal set
- Venn diagram

This Venn diagram shows nine doctors in three overlapping sets. What properties could you use to put the doctors into sets? What do you know about the doctor in the dark grey region in the centre of the Venn diagram?

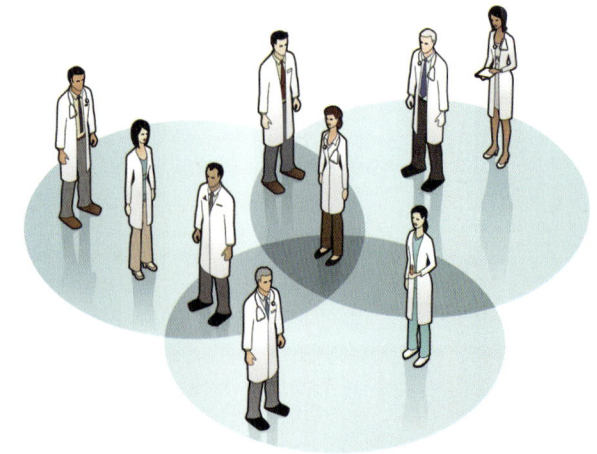

9.1 Sequences

A **sequence** is set of numbers (or a pattern) that follow a particular order. Each number in a sequence is called a **term**. Terms that follow each other in a sequence are called **consecutive** terms.

The position of a term is given using T, so T_1 is the first term, T_5 is the fifth term and T_n is any term.

The terms in a sequence usually follow a rule. You can use the rule for a sequence to work out which term comes next or the value of any term in the sequence.

There are different kinds of sequences.

Arithmetic sequences have a common (constant) difference between the terms. For example, the sequence 2, 6, 10, 14, … has a common difference of +4 and the sequence 100, 92, 84, 76, … has a common difference of −8. Arithmetic sequences are linear sequences.

Non-linear sequences do not have a common difference between the terms.

Geometric sequences involve multiplying or dividing by a common ratio. For example, each term in the sequence 3, 6, 12, 24, … is found by multiplying the previous term by 2 and the sequence 800, 400, 200, 100, … is formed by dividing the previous term by 2.

Some sequences involve powers:

- quadratic sequences involve square numbers. For example, 1, 4, 9, 16, …
- cubic sequences involve cube numbers. For example, 1, 8, 27, 64, …

LINK

Sequences of numbers are often used in cryptography, the science of codebreaking. In a simple code, the letters of the alphabet (which already form a clear sequence) can be matched to letters or numbers in another sequence. If you know the patterns defining the sequence, you can crack the codes.

The term-to-term rule

Here are some sequences with the rule that tells you how to keep the sequence going:

2, 8, 14, 20, 26, 32, … (get the next term by adding six to the previous term).

You can show this pattern by drawing it in this way:

$1, \dfrac{1}{2}, \dfrac{1}{4}, \dfrac{1}{8}, \dfrac{1}{16}, \ldots$ (divide each term by two to get the next term).

This diagram shows how the sequence progresses:

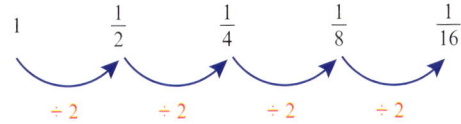

1, 2, 4, 8, 16, 32, … (multiply each term by two to get the next term).

In diagram form:

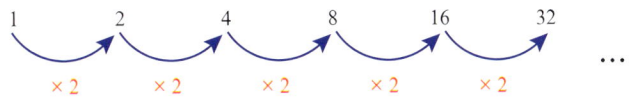

LINK

Chemists often need to understand how quantities change over time. An understanding of sequences can help chemists to understand how a reaction works and this allows them to predict what their results will be.

The rule that tells you how to generate the next term in a sequence is called the term-to-term rule. These rules are usually given in words and they tell you which operation to use to work out the next term.

Exercise 9.1

1   Draw a diagram to show how each of the following sequences continues and find the next three terms in each case.

a   5, 7, 9, 11, 13, …

b   3, 8, 13, 18, 23, …

c   3, 9, 27, 81, 243, …

d   0.5, 2, 3.5, 5, 6.5, …

e   8, 5, 2, −1, −4, …

f   13, 11, 9, 7, 5, …

g   6, 4.8, 3.6, 2.4, 1.2, …

h   2.3, 1.1, −0.1, −1.3, …

2   Find the next three terms in each of the following sequences and explain the rule that you used in each case.

a   1, −3, 9, −27, …

b   Mo, Tu, We, Th, …

c   a, c, f, j, o, …

INVESTIGATION

3   The first term (T_1) of a sequence is 5. The term-to-term rule for the sequence is 'add x'.

Find the value of x that will give you each of these sequences:

a   every second term is not an integer

b   every second term is a multiple of 10

c $T_2 < T_1$.

Relating a term to its position in the sequence

The term-to-term rule is useful for finding the next few terms in a sequence. However, if you are asked to find the 20th term or the 100th term it is not efficient to list all the terms. If you can work out an algebraic rule for generating the terms you can use it to find the value of a term in any position.

To find the rule you have to work systematically with the term number and the value of each term. Tables are very useful for doing this.

This table shows the term number and the value of the first five terms in a sequence.

Term number (n)	1	2	3	4	5
Term	5	8	11	14	17

You can see that the difference between the terms is 3. This tells you something about the algebraic rule.

If you multiply each term number (n) by 3, you get:

Term number (n)	1	2	3	4	5
Term	5	8	11	14	17
$3 \times n$	3	6	9	12	15

By comparing the value of each term with the value of $3n$, you can see that the term is 2 more than $3n$ each time.

This means that each term is $3 \times n + 2$ or $3n + 2$.

This is called a position-to-term rule.

An expression for the term in position n is called the nth term (or general term). So for this sequence the nth term $= 3n + 2$.

Notice that the common difference between each term in the sequence is the value that is multiplying n (the coefficient of n) in the nth term rule. This happens with any sequence for which you move from one term to the next by adding (or subtracting) a fixed number.

You can use this rule to find the term in any position by substituting the value of n into the rule. For example:

- the 45th term $= 3(45) + 2 = 137$
- the 90th term $= 3(90) + 2 = 272$.

WORKED EXAMPLE 1

a   Find the general rule for the nth term of this sequence.

$\qquad$ 2, 6, 10, 14, 18, 22, 26, …

b   Find the 40th term of the sequence.

c   Explain how you know that the number 50 is in the sequence and work out which position it is in.

d   Explain how you know that the number 125 is *not* in the sequence.

Answers

a
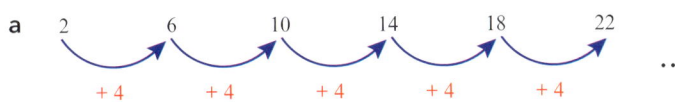

The common difference between terms is $+4$, so $4 \times n$ will appear in the rule.

Make a table to show the position of each term and include the values for $4n$.

n	1	2	3	4	5	6
Term	2	6	10	14	18	22
4n	4	8	12	16	20	24

Each term is 2 less than $4n$, so the rule for the nth term is $4n - 2$.

b   40th term $\therefore n = 40$ $\qquad$ To find the 40th term in the sequence substitute $n = 40$ into the nth term formula.

$\qquad 4 \times 40 - 2 = 158$

c $4n - 2 = 50$ $\qquad$ If the number 50 is in the sequence there must be a value of n for which $4n - 2 = 50$. Rearrange the rule to make n the subject.

$$
\begin{aligned}
4n - 2 &= 50 \\
4n &= 52 \qquad \text{Add 2 to both sides.} \\
n &= \frac{52}{4} = 13 \qquad \text{Divide both sides by 4.}
\end{aligned}
$$

WORKED EXAMPLE 1 CONTINUED

Since this has given a whole number, 50 must be the 13th term in the sequence.

d $4n - 2 = 125$ If the number 125 is in the sequence then there must be a value of n for which $4n - 2 = 125$. Rearrange to make n the subject.

$4n = 127$ Add 2 to both sides.

$n = \dfrac{127}{4} = 31.75$ Divide both sides by 4.

Since n is the position in the sequence it must be a whole number and it is not in this case. This means that 125 cannot be a number in the sequence.

TIP

There are other ways of knowing that 125 is not in the sequence. For example, you can see that $4n - 2$ is always an even number, but 125 is odd, so it cannot appear in the sequence. It is important, though, for you to understand how to use algebra to answer parts (c) and (d) because when sequences become more complicated you may have to use algebra.

Worked example 2 shows you how to find an expression for the nth term when there is no common difference between the terms.

WORKED EXAMPLE 2

Find an expression for the nth term of the sequence 2, 5, 10, 17, 26 …

Answer

Work out the difference between terms in the sequence. This is known as the first difference.

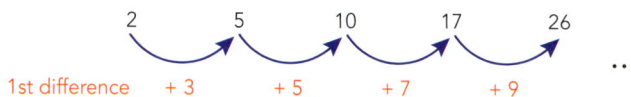

The first difference is not constant so work out the second difference:

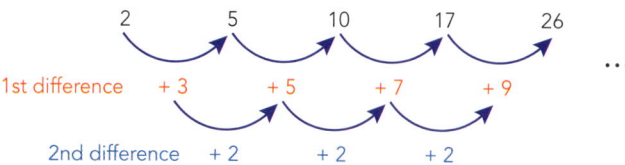

The second difference is constant. This means the sequence is quadratic and the rule will involve n^2.

TIP

You may recognise that the numbers in this sequence are all 1 greater than the sequence of square numbers and be able to answer the question by inspection.

WORKED EXAMPLE 2 CONTINUED

Make a table to show the position of each term and include a row for the values of n^2.

n	1	2	3	4	5
Term	2	5	10	17	26
n^2	1	4	9	16	25

Each term is 1 greater than the value of n^2, so the nth term is $n^2 + 1$.

All quadratic sequences have a constant second difference.
If the sequence is cubic it will have a constant third difference and the rule for the sequence will involve n^3.

The general term of a quadratic sequence is in the form $an^2 + bn + c$.

This table shows the first four terms in the general sequence and their first and second differences.

n	1	2	3	4
Term	$a + b + c$	$4a + 2b + c$	$9a + 3b + c$	$16a + 4b + c$
1st difference		$3a + b$	$5a + b$	$7a + b$
2nd difference			$2a$	$2a$

The table shows that for any quadratic sequence:

- the 1st term is $a + b + c$
- the 2nd term minus the 1st term ($T_2 - T_1$) is $3a + b$
- the 2nd difference is $2a$.

This gives us a way to work out the general term for complex quadratic sequences.

WORKED EXAMPLE 3

Find the nth term of the quadratic sequence 2, 8, 16, 26, 38 …

Answer

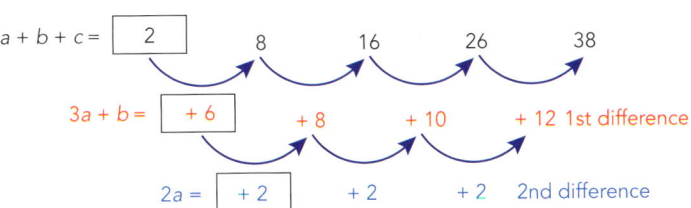

Once you have values for each expression you can make equations to find a, b and c.

$2a = 2$, so $a = 1$ Find the value of a first.

$3a + b = 6$ Find b by substituting the value of a.

$3(1) + b = 6$, so $b = 3$

TIP

If you are not told the sequence is quadratic, you will need to check that the second difference is constant before using this method.

> **WORKED EXAMPLE 3 CONTINUED**
>
> | | | |
> |---|---|---|
> | $a + b + c = 2$ | $1 + 3 + c = 2$ | Find c by substituting the values of a and b. |
> | $4 + c = 2$, so $c = -2$ | | |
>
> The nth term is $n^2 + 3n - 2$ Insert the values of a, b and c into the general term $an^2 + bn + c$.

Exponential sequences

Consider the sequence 20, 100, 500, 2500 …

You find each term by multiplying the previous term by 5. This type of sequence is called an exponential sequence and expression for the nth term will involve an exponent (in terms of n).

Listing the terms can help you find the rule:

T_2 20×5

T_3 $20 \times 5 \times 5 = 20 \times 5^2$

T_4 $20 \times 5 \times 5 \times 5 = 20 \times 5^3$

You can see that for each term the exponent is one less than the term number.

So for the nth term, the exponent will be $n - 1$:

T_n $20 \times 5^{n-1}$

In general terms, for any geometric sequence with a common ratio r and the first term a, we can say the nth term $= a \times r^{n-1}$.

> **MATHEMATICAL CONNECTIONS**
>
> You will work with these types of sequences involving real-life situations such as population growth, compound interest and depreciation when you deal with growth and decay in Chapter 17.

Combinations of sequences

If you add or subtract equivalent terms of two or more sequences together to form a new sequence then you can find the nth term of this new sequence by adding or subtracting the nth terms of the original sequences.

> **WORKED EXAMPLE 4**
>
> Complete this table of sequences.
>
> | Sequence | 1st term | 2nd term | 3rd term | 4th term | | nth term |
> |---|---|---|---|---|---|---|
> | A | 5 | 8 | 11 | | | |
> | B | 2 | 5 | 10 | | | |
> | C | 7 | 13 | 21 | | | |

WORKED EXAMPLE 4 CONTINUED

Answer

The terms in sequence A go up by 3 each time. It is a linear sequence with common difference 3 and *n*th term $3n + 2$.

The terms in sequence B are each 1 greater than the square number sequence. So the *n*th term is $n^2 + 1$.

In sequence C, each term is found by adding the equivalent terms of sequence A and B together: $5 + 2 = 7$, $8 + 5 = 13$, and so on. You can find the *n*th term in a similar way.

The completed table is:

Sequence	1st term	2nd term	3rd term	4th term		*n*th term
A	5	8	11	14		$3n + 2$
B	2	5	10	17		$n^2 + 1$
C	7	13	21	31		$n^2 + 3n + 3$

Exercise 9.2

1 Write down the next three terms in each of the following sequences.

   a   3   7   11   15   19   ...

   b   4   9   16   25   36   ...

   c   23   19   13   5   −5   ...

2 List the first three terms and find the 20th term of the number patterns given by the following rules, where T = term and *n* = the position of the term.

   a $T_n = 4 - 3n$ **b** $T_n = 2 - n$ **c** $T_n = \frac{1}{2}n^2$

   d $T_n = n(n + 1)(n - 1)$ **e** $T_n = \frac{3}{1 + n}$ **f** $T_n = 2n^3$

3 Find the (i) 15th and (ii) *n*th term for each of the following sequences.

   a   5, 7, 9, 11, 13, ...   **b**   3, 8, 13, 18, 23, ...

   c   3, 9, 27, 81, 243, ...   **d**   0.5, 2, 3.5, 5, 6.5, ...

   e   8, 5, 2, −1, −4, ...   **f**   13, 11, 9, 7, 5, ...

   g   6, 4.8, 3.6, 2.4, 1.2, ...   **h**   2, 8, 18, 32, 50, ...

4 Consider the sequence:

      4, 12, 20, 28, 36, 44, 52, ...

   a   Find the *n*th term of the sequence.

   b   Find the 500th term.

   c   Which term of this sequence has the value 236? Show full working.

   d   Show that 154 is not a term in the sequence.

> **TIP**
>
> In any sequence *n* must be a positive integer. There are no negative 'positions' for terms. For example, *n* can be 7 because it is possible to have a 7th term, but *n* cannot be −7 as it is not possible to have a −7th term.

5   The following information is given about a quadratic sequence.

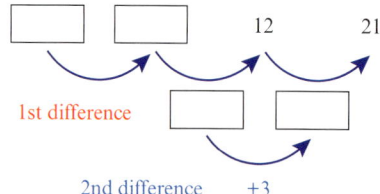

Copy the diagram and write the correct values in the empty boxes.

6   Consider the sequence:

3, 8, 15, 24, 35 …

a   Show that this is a quadratic sequence.

b   Determine the value of the 6th term.

c   Write an expression for the general term.

d   Work out the 20th term.

7   If $x + 1$ and $-x + 17$ are the second and sixth terms of a sequence with a common difference of 5, find the value of x.

8   If $x + 4$ and $x - 4$ are the third and seventh terms of a sequence with a common difference of -2, determine n when $T_n = x$.

9   a   Write down the first five terms in the sequence with nth term $2n^2$.

b   Use your answer to part (a) to find the nth term for each of the following sequences:

i	3	9	19	33	51
ii	4	16	36	64	100
iii	7	25	55	97	151

c   Now consider the sequence:

5   6   11   20   33

Copy and complete the table to show how the terms in this sequence compare to those in the sequence with nth term $2n^2$.

n	1	2	3	4	5
Sequence	5	6	11	20	33
$2n^2$	2			32	
Sequence $- 2n^2$	3			-12	

d   Find the nth term of the sequence of differences.

e   Use your answers to work out the nth term of the sequence:

5   6   11   20   33

10   Use the general from $an^2 + bn + c$ to find the nth term for each of the following sequences.

a   5, 12, 23, 38, 57, …   b   13, 17, 23, 31, 41, 53, …

11 Given the sequence $-4, -2, 4, 14, 28, 46, \ldots$

    a Show that this is a quadratic sequence.

    b Determine the next term, T_7.

    c Determine the nth term of the sequence.

    d Calculate T_{50}.

12 For the sequence $2, 6, 12, 20, \ldots$

    a Write down T_5 and T_6.

    b Write an expression for the nth term in this sequence.

    c Determine the value of T_{15}.

    d Which term has a value of 110?

13 An ancient myth involves the ruler putting a gold coin on the first square of a chessboard, two coins on the second square, four on the third square and continuing to double the number of coins up to the 64th square.

    a Write an expression for the number of coins on the nth square.

    b Determine the number of coins on the 64th square?

    c Write an expression for the number of coins on the nth square if the sequence changes to $1, 3, 9, 27, \ldots$

Some special sequences

You should be able to recognise the following patterns and sequences.

Sequence	Description
Square numbers $T_n = n^2$	A square number is the product of multiplying a whole number by itself. Square numbers can be represented using dots arranged to make squares. 1 4 9 16 25 Square numbers form the (infinite) sequence: $1, 4, 9, 16, 25, 36, \ldots$ Square numbers may be used in other sequences: $\frac{1}{4}, \frac{1}{9}, \frac{1}{16}, \frac{1}{25}, \ldots$ $2, 8, 18, 32, 50, \ldots$ (each term is double a square number)

Sequence	Description
Cube numbers $T_n = n^3$	A cube number is the product of multiplying a whole number by itself and then by itself again. Cube numbers form the (infinite) sequence: 1, 8, 27, 64, 125, …
Triangular numbers $T_n = \frac{1}{2}n(n + 1)$	Triangular numbers are made by arranging dots to form either equilateral or right-angled isosceles triangles. Both arrangements give the same number sequence. Triangular numbers form the (infinite) sequence: 1, 3, 6, 10, 15, …
Fibonacci numbers	Leonardo Fibonacci was an Italian mathematician who noticed that many natural patterns produced the sequence: 1, 1, 2, 3, 5, 8, 13, 21, … These numbers are now called Fibonacci numbers. They have the term-to-term rule 'add the two previous numbers to get the next term'.

INVESTIGATION

Fibonacci patterns

You can find Fibonacci patterns in flower petal arrangements, leaves on plant stems, pine cones, pineapples and the arrangement of seeds in a sunflower.

1 Look at this pine cone carefully.

    a Identify the clockwise and anti-clockwise spirals. Count and record how many there are of each.

    b Count sections from the centre. Can you identify the 1, 1, 2, 3, 5, … pattern?

2 Find another example to show Fibonacci patterns in nature. Your example could be a real object or a clear photograph or diagram.

3 The ratio between terms in the Fibonacci sequence gives an approximate value of 1.618. This value is known as the golden ratio.

    a Investigate where the golden ratio is used in art and architecture.

    b Provide a simple diagram and explanation of what the golden ratio means.

Generating sequences from patterns

The diagram shows a pattern using matches.

Pattern 1   Pattern 2   Pattern 3

The table shows the number of matches for the first five patterns.

Pattern number (n)	1	2	3	4	5
Number of matches	3	5	7	9	11

Notice that the pattern number can be used as the position number, n, and that the numbers of matches form a sequence, just like those considered in the previous section.

The number added on each time is two but you could also see that this was true from the original diagrams. This means that the number of matches for pattern n is the same as the value of the nth term of the sequence.

The nth term will therefore be: $2n \pm$ something.

Use the ideas from the previous section to find the value of the 'something'.

Taking any term in the sequence from the table, for example the first:

$n = 1$, so $2n = 2 \times 1 = 2$. But the first term is 3, so you need to add 1.

So, nth term $= 2n + 1$

Which means that, if you let 'm' be the number of matches in pattern n then,

$m = 2n + 1$.

WORKED EXAMPLE 5

The diagram shows a pattern made with squares.

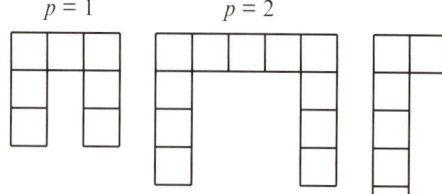

a   Construct a sequence table showing the first six patterns and the number of squares used.

b   Find a formula for the number of squares, s, in terms of the pattern number 'p'.

c   How many squares will there be in pattern 100?

Answers

a

Pattern number (p)	1	2	3	4	5	6
Number of squares (s)	7	11	15	19	23	27

WORKED EXAMPLE 5 CONTINUED

b 4p is in the formula

Notice that the number of squares increases by 4 from shape to shape. This means that there will be a term '4p' in the formula.

If $p = 1$ then $4p = 4$
$4 + 3 = 7$
so, $s = 4p + 3$

Now, if $p = 1$ then $4p = 4$. The first term is 7, so you need to add 3. This means that $s = 4p + 3$.

If $p = 5$ then
$4p + 3 = 20 + 3 = 23$,
the rule is correct.

Check: if $p = 5$ then there should be 23 squares, which is correct.

c For pattern 100, $p = 100$ and $s = 4 \times 100 + 3 = 403$.

Notice that 'p' has been used for the pattern number rather than 'n' here. You can use any letters that you like — it doesn't have to be n every time.

Exercise 9.3

For each of the following shape sequences:

i draw a sequence table for the first six patterns, taking care to use the correct letter for the pattern number and the correct letter for the number of shapes

ii find a formula for the number of shapes used in terms of the pattern number

iii use your formula to find the number of shapes used in the 300th pattern.

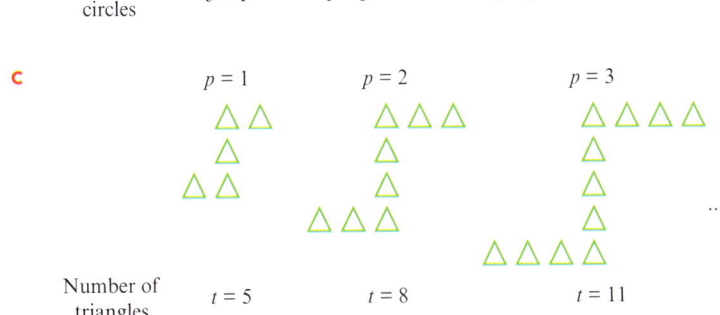

a

$n = 1$ $n = 2$ $n = 3$ ...

Number of matches $m = 4$ $m = 7$ $m = 10$

b

$p = 1$ $p = 2$ $p = 3$ ...

Number of circles $c = 1$ $c = 3$ $c = 5$

c

$p = 1$ $p = 2$ $p = 3$ ...

Number of triangles $t = 5$ $t = 8$ $t = 11$

d

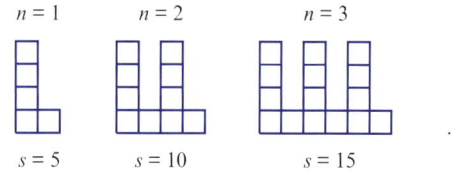

	$n = 1$	$n = 2$	$n = 3$	
Number of squares	$s = 5$	$s = 10$	$s = 15$	...

Subscript notation

The nth term of a sequence can be written as u_n. This is called **subscript notation** and u represents a sequence. You read this as 'u sub n'. Terms in a specific position (for example, the first, second and hundredth term) are written as u_1, u_2, u_{100} and so on.

Term-to-term rules and position-to-term rules may be given using subscript notation. You can work out the value of any term or the position of a term by substituting known values into the rules.

WORKED EXAMPLE 6

The position to term rule for a sequence is given as $u_n = 3n - 1$.

What are the first three terms of the sequence?

Answer

Substitute $n = 1$, $n = 2$ and $n = 3$ into the rule.

$u_1 = 3(1) - 1 = 2$ For the first term, $n = 1$

$u_2 = 3(2) - 1 = 5$

$u_3 = 3(3) - 1 = 8$

The first three terms are 2, 5 and 8.

WORKED EXAMPLE 7

The number 149 is a term in the sequence defined as $u_n = n^2 + 5$.

Which term in the sequence is 149?

Answer

$149 = n^2 + 5$ Find the value of n, when $u_n = 149$.

$149 - 5 = n^2$

$144 = n^2$ $n^2 = 144$ has solutions $n = 12$ and

$12 = n$ $n = -12$, but we cannot have a -12th term so $n = 12$.

149 is the 12th term in the sequence.

Exercise 9.4

1   Find the first three terms and the 25th term of each sequence.

   a $u_n = 4n + 1$ b $u_n = 3n - 5$ c $u_n = 5n - \dfrac{1}{2}$

   d $u_n = -2n + 1$ e $u_n = \dfrac{n}{2} + 1$ f $u_n = 2n^2 - 1$

   g $u_n = n^2$ h $u_n = 5 + 2^{n-1}$

2   The numbers 30 and 110 are found in the sequence $u_n = n(n - 1)$.
    In which position is each number found?

3   Which term in the sequence $u_n = 2n^2 + 5$ has a value of 167?

4   For the sequence $u_n = 2n^2 - 5n + 3$, determine:

   a   the value of the tenth term.

   b   the value of n for which $u_n = 45$.

5   The term-to-term rule for a sequence is given as $u_{n+1} = u_n + 2$.

   a   Explain in words what this means.

   b   Given that $u_3 = -4$, list the first five terms of the sequence.

9.2 Rational and irrational numbers

You already know about decimals and how they are used to write down numbers that are not whole. Some of these numbers can be expressed as fractions, for example:

$$0.5 = \frac{1}{2} \qquad 2.5 = \frac{5}{2} \qquad 0.125 = \frac{1}{8} \qquad 0.3333333\ldots = \frac{1}{3}$$

and so on.

Any number that can be expressed as a fraction is known as a rational number. If you cannot express the number as a fraction, it is an irrational number.

Notice that there are two types of rational number: **terminating decimals** (i.e. those with a decimal part that doesn't continue forever) and **recurring decimals** (the decimal part continues forever but repeats itself at regular intervals). Irrational numbers produce decimals that have non-repeating, non-terminating decimal parts.

Recurring decimals can be expressed by using a dot above the repeating digit(s):

$0.333333333\ldots = 0.\dot{3}$ $0.302302302302\ldots = 0.\dot{3}0\dot{2}$

$0.454545454\ldots = 0.\dot{4}\dot{5}$

> **TIP**
>
> At this level, it is fine to simply say that a rational number can be expressed as a fraction. However, when mathematicians use the definition of rational number to prove that some numbers are irrational, they need to say that the fraction is expressed in its lowest terms.

Exercise 9.5

1 Say whether each number is rational or irrational.

    a $\dfrac{1}{4}$ **b**   4   **c** -7 **d**   3.147

    e π **f** $\sqrt{3}$ **g** $\sqrt{25}$ **h**   0

    i   0.45   **j** -0.67 **k** -232 **l** $\dfrac{3}{8}$

    m   9.454 545 …   **n** $\sqrt{123}$ **o** 2π **p** $3\sqrt{2}$

2 Show that the following numbers are rational.

    a   6   **b** $2\dfrac{3}{8}$ **c**   0.427

    d $0.\dot{8}$ **e** $1.\dot{1}\dot{2}$ **f** $3.\dot{1}\dot{4}$

3 Find a number in the interval $-1 < x < 3$ so that:

    a x is rational   **b** x is a real number but not rational

    c x is an integer   **d** x is a natural number.

INVESTIGATION

4 Which set do you think has more members: rational numbers or irrational numbers? Why?

5 Mathematicians also talk about imaginary numbers. Find out what these are and give one example.

Converting recurring decimals to fractions

What can we do with a decimal that continues forever but *does* repeat?

Is this kind of number rational or irrational?

As an example we will look at the number $0.\dot{4}$.

We can use algebra to find another way of writing this recurring decimal:

Let

$x = 0.\dot{4} = 0.444444\ldots$

Then

$10x = 4.444444\ldots$

We can then subtract x from $10x$ like this:

$$
\begin{aligned}
10x &= 4.444444\ldots \\
x &= 0.444444\ldots \\
\hline
9x &= 4 \\
\Rightarrow x &= \frac{4}{9}
\end{aligned}
$$

This example shows that you can write the recurring decimal $0.\dot{4}$ as a fraction. This means that $0.\dot{4}$ is a rational number.

Remember that the dot above one digit means that you have a *recurring* decimal. If more than one digit repeats we place a dot above the first and last repeating digit. For example, $0.\dot{4}1\dot{8}$ is the same as $0.418418418418418…$ and $0.34\dot{2} = 0.3422222222…$.

Every recurring decimal is a rational number. It is always possible to write a recurring decimal as a fraction.

> **TIP**
>
> Sometimes you may see irrational numbers shown with a bar above the recurring digits. For example, $3.2\overline{65} = 3.265656565…$

WORKED EXAMPLE 8

Use algebra to write each of the following as fractions. Simplify your fractions as far as possible.

a $0.\dot{3}$ **b** $0.\dot{2}\dot{4}$ **c** $0.\dot{9}3\dot{4}$ **d** $0.52\dot{4}$

Answers

a

$x = 0.33333…$
$10x = 3.33333…$

Write your recurring decimal in algebra. It is easier to see how the algebra works if you write the number out to a handful of decimal places.

Subtract:

$10x = 3.33333…$
$x = 0.33333…$

Multiply by 10, so that the recurring digits still line up.

$9x = 3$

Subtract.

$\Rightarrow x = \dfrac{3}{9} = \dfrac{1}{3}$

Divide by 9.

b

$\text{Let } x = 0.242424…\quad(1)$
$\text{then, } 100x = 24.242424…\quad(2)$
$99x = 24.24 - 0.24$

Multiply by 100.

$99x = 24$

Subtract (2) − (1).

$\text{so, } x = \dfrac{24}{99} = \dfrac{8}{33}$

Divide both sides by 99.

Notice that you multiply by 100 to make sure that the 2s and 4s start in the correct place after the decimal point.

c

$x = 0.934934…$
$1000x = 934.934934…$

$1000x = 934.934934…$
$x = 0.934934…$

This time we have three recurring digits. To make sure that these line up we multiply by 1000, so that all digits move three places.

$999x = 934$

$\Rightarrow x = \dfrac{934}{999}$

Notice that the digits immediately after the decimal point for both x and $1000x$ are 9, 3 and 4 in the same order.

WORKED EXAMPLE 8 CONTINUED

d

$$x = 0.52444444\ldots$$
$$100x = 52.4444444\ldots$$
$$1000x = 524.444444\ldots$$

Multiply by 100 so that the recurring digits begin immediately after the decimal point.

$$1000x = 524.444444\ldots$$
$$100x = 52.4444444\ldots$$
$$\overline{}$$
$$900x = 472$$

Then proceed as in the first example, multiplying by a further 10 to move the digits one place.

$$\Rightarrow x = \frac{472}{900} = \frac{118}{225}$$

Subtract and simplify.

> **TIP**
>
> Once you have managed to get the recurring decimals to start immediately after the decimal point you will need to multiply again, by another power of 10. The power that you choose should be the same as the number of digits that recur. In part (c) the digits 9, 3 and 4 recur, so multiply by $10^3 = 1000$.

In this method you need to subtract two different numbers in such a way that the recurring part disappears. This means that sometimes you have to multiply by 10, sometimes by 100, sometimes by 1000, depending on how many digits repeat.

Exercise 9.6

1   Copy and complete each of the following by filling in the boxes with the correct number or symbol.

a   Let $x = 0.\dot{6}$

Then $10x =$

Subtracting:

$$10x =$$
$$-x = 0.\dot{6}$$
$$x =$$

So $x =$

Simplify: $x = \boxed{}$

b   Let $x = 0.\dot{1}\dot{7}$

Then $100x = \boxed{}$

Subtracting:

$$100x = \boxed{}$$
$$-x = 0.\dot{1}\dot{7}$$
$$\boxed{} \; x = \boxed{}$$

So, $x = \boxed{}$

2   Write each recurring decimal as a fraction in its lowest terms.

a	$0.\dot{5}$	**b**	$0.\dot{1}$	**c**	$0.\dot{8}$	**d**	$0.\dot{2}\dot{4}$
e	$0.6\dot{1}$	**f**	$0.3\dot{2}$	**g**	$0.6\dot{1}\dot{8}$	**h**	$0.\dot{2}3\dot{3}$
i	$0.\dot{2}0\dot{8}$	**j**	$0.0\dot{2}$	**k**	$0.1\dot{8}$	**l**	$0.03\dot{1}$
m	$2.4\dot{5}$	**n**	$3.\dot{1}0\dot{5}$	**o**	$2.5\dot{0}$	**p**	$5.\dot{4} + 4.\dot{5}$
q	$2.3\dot{6} + 3.6\dot{3}$	**r**	$0.\dot{1}\dot{7} + 0.\dot{7}\dot{1}$	**s**	$0.\dot{9}$	**t**	$99.\dot{9}$

INVESTIGATION

Recurring decimals

1   **a**   Write down the numerical value of each of the following:

    i $1 - 0.9$ **ii** $1 - 0.99$ **iii** $1 - 0.999$

    iv $1 - 0.999999999$

    b   Comment on your answers to (a). What happened to the answer as the number of digits in the subtracted number increased? What did the answer get closer to? Will it ever get there?

    c   Use algebra to express $0.\dot{6}$ and $0.\dot{2}$ as fractions in their simplest form.

    d   Express $0.\dot{6} + 0.\dot{2}$ as a recurring decimal.

    e   Use your answer to (c) to express $0.\dot{6} + 0.\dot{2}$ as a fraction in its lowest terms.

    f   Now repeat parts (c), (d) and (e) using the recurring decimals $0.\dot{4}$ and $0.\dot{5}$.

    g   Explain how your findings for part (f) relate to your answers in parts (a) and (b).

2   A teacher asked a class to find the greatest number that is less than 4.5. Jeevan gave the answer 4.4.

    a   Why is Jeevan not correct?

    Ryan then suggests that the answer is 4.49999.

    b   Why is Ryan not correct?

    Jamila then suggests the answer $4.49\dot{9}$.

    c   Is Jamila correct? Give full reasons for your answer, including any algebra that helps you to explain. Can you think of a better answer than Jamila's?

9.3 Surds

Some number have roots that can be written as rational numbers. For example, $\sqrt{4} = 2$, $\sqrt[3]{216} = 6$ and $\sqrt{2.25} = 1.5$.

Roots that cannot be written as rational numbers are called **surds**. $\sqrt{2}$, $\sqrt[3]{7}$ and $\sqrt{2.2}$ are all surds. For any root, if $\sqrt[n]{x}$ is an irrational number, the root is a surd.

A surd is an **exact value**. If you use a calculator to find $\sqrt{2}$ you get an approximate value of $1.414213562\ldots$ When you are asked for an exact value, you should leave your answer in surd form.

MATHEMATICAL CONNECTIONS

Surds are used to calculate exact values in trigonometry and you will re-use the skills you learn here in Chapter 15. Surds may also be useful in physics when you deal with resultant forces and velocities and in electronics for determining peak-to-peak voltages. The reality, however, is that for most real-world applications, people may use surds in calculations to avoid rounding errors, but in the end they will often work with an approximate number value rather than a surd.

WORKED EXAMPLE 9

Square *ABCD* has an area of 6 cm². Calculate:

a the exact length of each side

b the length of diagonal *AC* correct to 3 d.p.

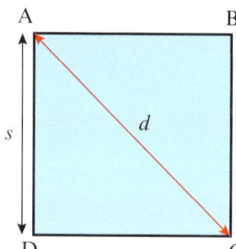

Answers

a Area = s^2, so $s = \sqrt{6}$ You are asked for an exact length, so leave the answer as a surd.

b $d^2 = s^2 + s^2$ *ABC* is a right-angled triangle, so use Pythagoras' theorem.

$d^2 = (\sqrt{6})^2 + (\sqrt{6})^2$

$d^2 = 6 + 6$

$d^2 = 12$

$d = \sqrt{12} = 3.464$ cm

The general rules that you already know for working with roots apply to surds as well.

General rule	Examples using numbers
$(\sqrt{x})^2 = x$	$(\sqrt{4})^2 = \sqrt{4} \times \sqrt{4} = 2 \times 2 = 4$ $(\sqrt{11})^2 = \sqrt{11} \times \sqrt{11} = 11$
$\sqrt{x^2} = x$	$\sqrt{6^2} = \sqrt{36} = 6$
$\sqrt{x} \times \sqrt{y} = \sqrt{xy}$	$\sqrt{4} \times \sqrt{16} = 2 \times 4 = 8$ This is the same as: $\sqrt{4} \times \sqrt{16} = \sqrt{4 \times 16} = \sqrt{64} = 8$
$\sqrt{x} \div \sqrt{y} = \sqrt{\dfrac{x}{y}}$	$\sqrt{64} \div \sqrt{4} = 8 \div 2 = 4$ $\sqrt{64} \div \sqrt{4} = \sqrt{\dfrac{64}{4}} = \sqrt{16} = 4$

You can apply these rules to simplify and manipulate surds so that you can solve problems involving exact values.

Simplifying surds

You can simplify a surd if the number under the root sign has factors that are square numbers.

To simplify a surd, use the fact that $\sqrt{xy} = \sqrt{x} \times \sqrt{y}$ to write the surd as a product of smaller roots, one of which is a perfect square.

TIP

Remember that $3\sqrt{7}$ is $3 \times \sqrt{7}$ written using algebraic conventions.
This is not the same as $\sqrt[3]{7}$, which is the cube root of 7.

WORKED EXAMPLE 10

Simplify each expression.

a $\sqrt{50}$ **b** $2\sqrt{18}$ **c** $-3\sqrt{80}$ **d** $3\sqrt{12} \times 2\sqrt{3}$

Answers

a   Factors of 50: 25 × 2   Find the factors of 50. One needs to be a square number.

       $\sqrt{50} = \sqrt{25} \times \sqrt{2}$ Write $\sqrt{50}$ as the product of two smaller roots.

           $= 5 \times \sqrt{2}$ Work out the root of the perfect square.

           $= 5\sqrt{2}$ Write the answer in simplest form.

b   Factors of 18: 9 × 2

       $2\sqrt{18} = 2 \times \sqrt{9} \times \sqrt{2}$ Write $\sqrt{18}$ as the product of two smaller roots.

           $= 2 \times 3 \times \sqrt{2}$ Work out the root of the perfect square.

                                     Multiply the integers.

           $= 6\sqrt{2}$ Write the answer in simplest form.

c   Factors of 80: 16 × 5

         $-3\sqrt{80} = -3 \times \sqrt{16} \times \sqrt{5}$ Write $\sqrt{80}$ as the product of two smaller roots.

           $= -3 \times 4 \times \sqrt{5}$ Work out the root of the perfect square.

                                     Multiply the integers.

           $= -12\sqrt{5}$ Write the answer in simplest form.

d   Factors of 12: 4 × 3   3 is prime, so you don't need to simplify $\sqrt{3}$.

       $3\sqrt{12} \times 2\sqrt{3} = 3 \times \sqrt{4} \times \sqrt{3} \times 2 \times \sqrt{3}$ Write $\sqrt{12}$ as a product of two smaller roots.

           $= 3 \times 2 \times \sqrt{3} \times 2 \times \sqrt{3}$ Simplify.

           $= 12 \times \sqrt{3} \times \sqrt{3}$ Multiply the integers.

           $= 12 \times 3$ Square the surds (remember $\sqrt{x} \times \sqrt{x} = x$).

           $= 36$

TIP

Choose factors that are perfect squares (4, 16, 25, 36, 49 …) and use the greatest possible square to have fewer steps in your simplifying.

You can see from part (a) in Worked example 10 that if you simplify $\sqrt{50}$, you get $5\sqrt{2}$.

You can use inverse operations to write simplified surds in the form of $\sqrt{n}$.

WORKED EXAMPLE 11

Write each expression in the form $\sqrt{n}$.

a $3\sqrt{7}$ **b** $4\sqrt{3}$

Answers

a $3\sqrt{7} = 3 \times \sqrt{7}$ which is equivalent to $\sqrt{9} \times \sqrt{7} = \sqrt{63}$

b $4\sqrt{3} = 4 \times \sqrt{3}$ which is equivalent to $\sqrt{16} \times \sqrt{3} = \sqrt{48}$

Adding and subtracting surds by collecting like terms

You already know that you can collect like terms to simplify expressions.

For example, $2 + 2a + a = 2 + 3a$ and $4x + 2y - x = 3x + 2y$.

You can simplify expressions containing like surds in the same way.

For example, $2\sqrt{5} + 3\sqrt{5} = 5\sqrt{5}$ and $5\sqrt{2} - 13\sqrt{2} = -8\sqrt{2}$.

You may need to simplify the surds before you can add or subtract like terms.

WORKED EXAMPLE 12

Simplify and collect like terms.

a $3\sqrt{5} + \sqrt{5}$ **b** $4\sqrt{5} - 2\sqrt{2} + 6\sqrt{5} - 3\sqrt{2}$ **c** $7\sqrt{5} - \sqrt{20}$

Answers

a $\quad 3\sqrt{5} + \sqrt{5} = 4\sqrt{5}$ Add the coefficients (remember $\sqrt{5}$ means $1 \times \sqrt{5}$).

b $\quad 4\sqrt{5} - 2\sqrt{2} + 6\sqrt{5} - 3\sqrt{2}$ Group like terms and add the coefficients.

$\quad = 10\sqrt{5} - 5\sqrt{2}$ Pay attention to the negative signs.

c $\quad 7\sqrt{5} - \sqrt{20} = 7\sqrt{5} - \sqrt{4} \times \sqrt{5}$ Simplify $\sqrt{20}$.

$\quad = 7\sqrt{5} - 2\sqrt{5}$ Take the root of the perfect square.

$\quad = 5\sqrt{5}$ Subtract the coefficients.

Exercise 9.7

1 Simplify.

    a $\sqrt{28}$ **b** $\sqrt{7}$ **c** $5\sqrt{12}$

    d $\sqrt{99}$ **e** $\sqrt{24}$ **f** $\sqrt{250}$

    g $3\sqrt{50}$ **h** $4\sqrt{72}$ **i** $-5\sqrt{63}$

    j $-4\sqrt{54}$ **k** $2\sqrt{98}$ **l** $-5\sqrt{60}$

2 Write each surd in the form $\sqrt{n}$.

   a $3\sqrt{6}$ **b** $2\sqrt{10}$ **c** $7\sqrt{2}$

   d $-2\sqrt{6}$ **e** $6\sqrt{3}$ **f** $-3\sqrt{8}$

3 How could you arrange each set of surds in descending order without using a calculator?

Set A $2\sqrt{5}, 3\sqrt{3}, 3\sqrt{5}$

Set B $3\sqrt{6}, \sqrt{24}, 4\sqrt{6}$

Set C $3\sqrt{6}, 2\sqrt{15}, 4\sqrt{3}$

   a   Use your method and write the surds in the correct order.

   b   Work with a partner. Discuss and compare the methods you used. Can you improve your method in any way? How?

4 Look at this student's homework. Both answers are incorrect.

   1   $5\sqrt{3} + 3\sqrt{2} + 6\sqrt{3} = 11\sqrt{6} + 3\sqrt{2}$

   2   $2\sqrt{5} + \sqrt{18} + \sqrt{20} - 2\sqrt{3} = \sqrt{2} + \sqrt{38}$

   a   What mistakes do you this student made in each calculation?

   b   Work out the correct answer for each calculation.

5 Use positive integer values of m and n to show that these rules are incorrect.

   a $\sqrt{m} + \sqrt{n} = \sqrt{m+n}$ **b** $\sqrt{m} - \sqrt{n} = \sqrt{m-n}$

6 Simplify by adding or subtracting. Give your answer in simplest form.

   a $2\sqrt{3} + 3\sqrt{7} + 3\sqrt{3}$ **b** $\sqrt{11} + 3\sqrt{5} + \sqrt{11}$

   c $-3\sqrt{2} + \sqrt{2} - 3\sqrt{5}$ **d** $4\sqrt{8} + 2\sqrt{7} - \sqrt{8} - 4\sqrt{7}$

   e $4\sqrt{5} - \sqrt{2} + 4\sqrt{5} - 3\sqrt{2}$ **f** $9\sqrt{3} + 3\sqrt{8} - \sqrt{3} + \sqrt{8}$

7 Simplify. Collect like terms where possible.

   a $\sqrt{20} + \sqrt{5}$ **b** $\sqrt{12} + \sqrt{27}$ **c** $4\sqrt{3} - 2\sqrt{27}$

   d $3\sqrt{8} + 2\sqrt{18}$ **e** $\sqrt{75} - 2\sqrt{48}$ **f** $3\sqrt{27} + 2\sqrt{12}$

8 Simplify.

   a $3 + 2\sqrt{3} - 2 + 3\sqrt{3}$ **b** $3 + 2\sqrt{3} - 4 + \sqrt{3}$

   c $2\sqrt{6} + 3 - 2(1 + \sqrt{6})$ **d** $3\sqrt{3} + 4 - (2\sqrt{3} - 1)$

   e $2(\sqrt{5} + 2) - 2(\sqrt{5} - 2)$ **f** $4(\sqrt{7} - \sqrt{2}) - (\sqrt{7} - \sqrt{2})$

> **TIP**
>
> Remove brackets as you would in any algebraic expression. Pay attention to the signs.

9 Calculate the exact perimeter of rectangle with sides $(2 + \sqrt{10})$ cm and $\sqrt{5}$ cm. Simplify the answer if possible.

10 Show that $x = 2\sqrt{7}$ in this rectangle.

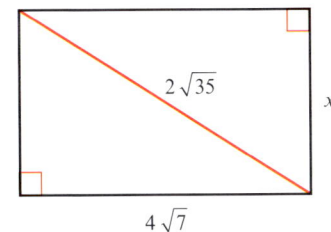

Multiplying and dividing surds

You can multiply and divide surds using general rules that you already know.

- $\sqrt{x} \times \sqrt{y} = \sqrt{xy}$
- $\sqrt{x} \times \sqrt{x} = x$
- $\sqrt{x} \div \sqrt{y} = \sqrt{\dfrac{x}{y}}$.

WORKED EXAMPLE 13

Simplify.

a $\sqrt{3} \times \sqrt{7}$ **b** $2\sqrt{3} \times 3\sqrt{5}$ **c** $\sqrt{21} \div \sqrt{3}$ **d** $\dfrac{8\sqrt{30}}{2\sqrt{6}}$

Answers

a $\sqrt{3} \times \sqrt{7} = \sqrt{3 \times 7}$

        $= \sqrt{21}$

Use $\sqrt{x} \times \sqrt{y} = \sqrt{xy}$.

b $2\sqrt{3} \times 3\sqrt{5} = 2 \times 3 \times \sqrt{3} \times \sqrt{5}$

               $= 6 \times \sqrt{15}$

               $= 6\sqrt{15}$

Multiply the whole numbers and multiply the surds.

c $\sqrt{21} \div \sqrt{3} = \sqrt{\dfrac{21}{3}}$

           $= \sqrt{7}$

Use $\sqrt{x} \div \sqrt{y} = \sqrt{\dfrac{x}{y}}$.

d $\dfrac{8\sqrt{30}}{2\sqrt{6}} = \dfrac{8}{2} \times \sqrt{\dfrac{30}{6}}$

         $= 4 \times \sqrt{5}$

         $= 4\sqrt{5}$

Divide the whole numbers and divide the surds.

Use algebraic rules to expand and simplify expressions with brackets.

WORKED EXAMPLE 14

Expand and simplify.

a $\sqrt{5}(\sqrt{2} + 3)$ **b** $-2(5 - \sqrt{7})$ **c** $4\sqrt{3}(2\sqrt{2} - \sqrt{3})$

Answers

a $\sqrt{5}(\sqrt{2} + 3) = \sqrt{5} \times \sqrt{2} + \sqrt{5} \times 3$

              $= \sqrt{10} + 3\sqrt{5}$

Multiply each term in the bracket by $\sqrt{5}$.

$\sqrt{5}\left(\sqrt{2} + 3\right)$

Remember $\sqrt{5} \times 3$ is written as $3\sqrt{5}$.

b $-2(5 - \sqrt{7}) = -10 + 2\sqrt{7}$

Multiply each term in the bracket by -2.

WORKED EXAMPLE 14 CONTINUED

c $\quad 4\sqrt{3}(2\sqrt{2} - \sqrt{3}) = 4\sqrt{3} \times 2\sqrt{2} + 4\sqrt{3} \times -\sqrt{3}$

Multiply each term in the bracket by $4\sqrt{3}$.

$$4\sqrt{3}\left(2\sqrt{2} - \sqrt{3}\right)$$

Multiply whole numbers and multiply surds.

$\qquad = 8\sqrt{6} - 4\sqrt{9}$

Remember: $-\sqrt{3}$ means $-1 \times \sqrt{3}$.

$\qquad = 8\sqrt{6} - 4 \times 3$

$\sqrt{9}$ can be simplified to 3.

$\qquad = 8\sqrt{6} - 12$

$8\sqrt{6}$ cannot be simplified further.

Rationalising the denominator

Here are two equivalent expressions:

$\dfrac{2}{\sqrt{3}} + \dfrac{1}{\sqrt{6} - \sqrt{3}}\quad$ and $\quad\dfrac{2\sqrt{3}}{3} + \dfrac{\sqrt{6} + \sqrt{3}}{3}$

Why is it easier to add the two terms in the second expression?

When the denominator of a fraction contains a surd, you can rewrite the fraction so that is has only rational numbers in the denominator. This is called **rationalising the denominator** and it means 'remove the roots from the denominator'.

Why do we do this? Rationalising the denominator is a mathematical convention, like writing a fraction in its simplest form. A fraction is not in simplest form if the denominator contains a surd. Also, if the denominators are integers it is easier to find and use common denominators.

You can use what you already know about equivalent fractions to remove surds from the denominator of an expression.

> **TIP**
>
> Remember that multiplying a fraction by $\dfrac{x}{x}$ doesn't change its value,
>
> so $\dfrac{1}{2} = \dfrac{1}{2} \times \dfrac{3}{3} = \dfrac{3}{6}$
>
> and $\dfrac{1}{\sqrt{2}} = \dfrac{1}{\sqrt{2}} \times \dfrac{\sqrt{2}}{\sqrt{2}}$
>
> $= \dfrac{\sqrt{2}}{2}$.

WORKED EXAMPLE 15

Write each fraction with a rational denominator.

a $\quad\dfrac{1}{\sqrt{10}}$
b $\quad\dfrac{3\sqrt{2}}{\sqrt{6}}$
c $\quad\dfrac{4}{3\sqrt{3}}$

Answers

a $\quad\dfrac{1}{\sqrt{10}} = \dfrac{1}{\sqrt{10}} \times \dfrac{\sqrt{10}}{\sqrt{10}}\qquad$ Multiply by $\dfrac{\sqrt{10}}{\sqrt{10}}$.

$\qquad = \dfrac{\sqrt{10}}{10}\qquad$ Remember: $\sqrt{x} \times \sqrt{x} = x$.

WORKED EXAMPLE 15 CONTINUED

b $\dfrac{3\sqrt{2}}{\sqrt{6}} = \dfrac{3\sqrt{2}}{\sqrt{6}} \times \dfrac{\sqrt{6}}{\sqrt{6}}$ 　　Multiply by $\dfrac{\sqrt{6}}{\sqrt{6}}$

$= \dfrac{3\sqrt{12}}{6}$ 　　Simplify by cancelling the whole numbers: $\dfrac{3}{6} = \dfrac{1}{2}$.

$= \dfrac{\sqrt{12}}{2}$ 　　$\sqrt{12}$ can be simplified further.

$= \dfrac{\sqrt{4 \times 3}}{2}$

$= \dfrac{2\sqrt{3}}{2} = \sqrt{3}$

c $\dfrac{4}{3\sqrt{3}} = \dfrac{4}{3\sqrt{3}} \times \dfrac{\sqrt{3}}{\sqrt{3}}$ 　　Multiply by $\dfrac{\sqrt{3}}{\sqrt{3}}$

$= \dfrac{4\sqrt{3}}{3 \times 3}$ 　　You only need to multiply by the irrational part of the denominator.

$= \dfrac{4\sqrt{3}}{9}$

> **TIP**
>
> Rationalising the denominator can help you simplify expressions when you are asked to give an exact answer. If you are asked for an approximate value, you can use a calculator to work with the surds and you don't need to rationalise the denominator.

You can also rationalise the denominator of expressions of the form $\dfrac{k}{a + \sqrt{b}}$ or $\dfrac{k}{a - \sqrt{b}}$.

$(\sqrt{a} + \sqrt{b}) \times (\sqrt{a} - \sqrt{b})$ gives $(\sqrt{a})^2 - (\sqrt{b})^2$, which is equal to $a - b$, since a and b are the squares of $\sqrt{a}$ and $\sqrt{b}$.

We call the two expressions $(\sqrt{a} + \sqrt{b})$ and $(\sqrt{a} - \sqrt{b})$ conjugate surds and we can use them to rationalise the denominator because their product does not contain any surd terms.

> **MATHEMATICAL CONNECTIONS**
>
> You will learn more about multiplying two pairs of brackets in Chapter 10.

WORKED EXAMPLE 16

Rationalise the denominator for each of the following expressions:

a $\dfrac{3}{2 + \sqrt{5}}$ 　　　　**b** $\dfrac{4 + \sqrt{2}}{3 - \sqrt{7}}$

Answers

a $\dfrac{3}{2 + \sqrt{5}} = \dfrac{3(2 - \sqrt{5})}{(2 + \sqrt{5})(2 - \sqrt{5})}$ 　　Multiply the numerator and denominator by $2 - \sqrt{5}$.

$= \dfrac{6 - 3\sqrt{5}}{2^2 - (\sqrt{5})^2}$ 　　Use $(\sqrt{a} + \sqrt{b})(\sqrt{a} - \sqrt{b}) = (\sqrt{a})^2 - (\sqrt{b})^2$.

$= \dfrac{6 - 3\sqrt{5}}{4 - 5}$ 　　Simplify.

$= \dfrac{6 - 3\sqrt{5}}{-1}$

$= 3\sqrt{5} - 6$ 　　Multiply the numerator and denominator by -1 to tidy it up.

WORKED EXAMPLE 16 CONTINUED

b $\dfrac{4 + \sqrt{2}}{3 - 2\sqrt{7}} = \dfrac{(4 + \sqrt{2})(3 + 2\sqrt{7})}{(3 - 2\sqrt{7})(3 + 2\sqrt{7})}$ Multiply the numerator and denominator by $3 + \sqrt{7}$.

$= \dfrac{12 + 3\sqrt{2} + 8\sqrt{7} + 2\sqrt{14}}{9 - 28}$ Simplify.

$= \dfrac{12 + 3\sqrt{2} + 8\sqrt{7} + 2\sqrt{14}}{-19}$

$= -\dfrac{12 + 3\sqrt{2} + 8\sqrt{7} + 2\sqrt{14}}{19}$

INVESTIGATION

Checking for errors

The circled letters show a student's answers to some multiple-choice questions. Two answers are incorrect.

a Find the two wrong answers and write the correct ones.

b What mistakes do you think the student made in each case?

What is the simplest form of each expression?
Circle the correct answer.

1 $4\sqrt{2} \times 5\sqrt{3} =$

   A $9\sqrt{6}$ **B** $20\sqrt{6}$ **C** $9\sqrt{5}$ **D** $20\sqrt{5}$

2 $3\sqrt{6} \times \sqrt{2} =$

   A $6\sqrt{3}$ **B** $3\sqrt{12}$ **C** $2\sqrt{3}$ **D** $3\sqrt{8}$

3 $\dfrac{6\sqrt{35}}{2\sqrt{5}} =$

   A $3\sqrt{7}$ **B** 21 **C** $4\sqrt{7}$ **D** $3\sqrt{30}$

4 $\dfrac{5}{\sqrt{2}}$ can be expressed with a rational denominator as:

   A $\dfrac{\sqrt{10}}{2}$ **B** $\dfrac{2\sqrt{5}}{5}$ **C** $\dfrac{5\sqrt{2}}{\sqrt{2}}$ **D** $\dfrac{5\sqrt{2}}{2}$

Exercise 9.8

1 Simplify.

   a $\sqrt{7} \times \sqrt{5}$ **b** $\sqrt{3} \times \sqrt{11}$ **c** $6\sqrt{3} \times 4\sqrt{2}$

   d $9\sqrt{10} \times \sqrt{3}$ **e** $-2\sqrt{5} \times 2\sqrt{6}$ **f** $9\sqrt{6} \times \sqrt{6}$

   g $2\sqrt{3} \times 3\sqrt{2}$ **h** $2\sqrt{3} \times \sqrt{6}$ **i** $-4\sqrt{2} \times -\sqrt{5}$

2 Simplify.

a $\sqrt{14} \div \sqrt{7}$

b $\sqrt{24} \div \sqrt{4}$

c $-\sqrt{30} \div \sqrt{3}$

d $\dfrac{\sqrt{5}}{\sqrt{10}}$

e $\dfrac{\sqrt{45}}{\sqrt{3}}$

f $\dfrac{\sqrt{2}}{\sqrt{18}}$

g $\dfrac{6\sqrt{33}}{\sqrt{11}}$

h $\dfrac{-2\sqrt{27}}{\sqrt{9}}$

i $\dfrac{12\sqrt{15}}{3\sqrt{5}}$

j $\dfrac{5\sqrt{30}}{15\sqrt{6}}$

k $\dfrac{3\sqrt{90}}{3}$

l $\dfrac{3\sqrt{27}}{\sqrt{12}}$

3 Multiply out the brackets and simplify each expression.

a $2(\sqrt{5} + 4)$

b $3(\sqrt{2} + 1)$

c $-2(4 + \sqrt{3})$

d $-4(6 + \sqrt{5})$

e $2(3\sqrt{11} - 2)$

f $4(1 - 2\sqrt{3})$

g $\sqrt{2}(2 + \sqrt{5})$

h $\sqrt{6}(\sqrt{2} + 3)$

i $-2(4 - \sqrt{5})$

j $4\sqrt{5}(1 + 2\sqrt{3})$

k $2\sqrt{3}(\sqrt{2} - 2\sqrt{7})$

l $5\sqrt{2}(\sqrt{5} - 2\sqrt{2})$

4 Simplify fully.

a $\dfrac{2\sqrt{6} \times 2\sqrt{3}}{4}$

b $\dfrac{4\sqrt{5} \times 2\sqrt{6}}{\sqrt{10}}$

c $\dfrac{4\sqrt{3} \times 3\sqrt{2}}{2\sqrt{3}}$

d $\dfrac{\sqrt{3} \times \sqrt{15}}{3\sqrt{5}}$

e $\dfrac{5\sqrt{7} \times \sqrt{3}}{\sqrt{28}}$

f $\dfrac{\sqrt{10} \times 3\sqrt{5}}{5\sqrt{2}}$

5 Write each expression in its simplest form with a rational denominator.

a $\dfrac{5}{\sqrt{3}}$

b $\dfrac{-2}{\sqrt{11}}$

c $\dfrac{\sqrt{3}}{\sqrt{5}}$

d $\dfrac{\sqrt{2} - 1}{\sqrt{2}}$

e $\dfrac{-3}{2\sqrt{5}}$

f $\dfrac{2\sqrt{2} + \sqrt{3}}{\sqrt{2}}$

g $\dfrac{\sqrt{10} - \sqrt{5}}{5\sqrt{10}}$

h $\dfrac{5 - 2\sqrt{5}}{-\sqrt{5}}$

i $\dfrac{3}{4 + \sqrt{3}}$

j $\dfrac{\sqrt{3}}{6 - \sqrt{3}}$

k $\dfrac{3 + \sqrt{7}}{3 - \sqrt{7}}$

l $\dfrac{2\sqrt{2}}{1 + 2\sqrt{3}}$

6 Write this expression as a single fraction with a rational denominator.

$$\dfrac{3 + 2\sqrt{7}}{\sqrt{7} - 2} + \dfrac{2 - \sqrt{7}}{\sqrt{12} + 3}$$

7 By first simplifying each surd in the fraction, or otherwise, rationalise the denominator for the expression $\dfrac{\sqrt{18} - \sqrt{8}}{2 + 3\sqrt{98}}$.

Work with a partner.

1   Write down three questions you could ask to check that someone understands the work in this exercise.

2   Get together with another pair and answer each other's questions.

3   After you have listened to the responses. Provide some feedback to the other students. For example, you could say things like:

   • It seems that you understand __ very well.

   • To understand __ better you could __

   • If you are finding __ difficult, it might help to __

Solving problems involving surds

When a problem involves surds, you need to combine your skills from this section with what you know from other topics to solve it.

WORKED EXAMPLE 17

What is the exact area of a circular disc of diameter $\sqrt{3}$ cm?

Answer

Area = πr^2

If the diameter is $\sqrt{3}$, then the radius is $\dfrac{\sqrt{3}}{2}$.

$A = \pi \left(\dfrac{\sqrt{3}}{2}\right)\left(\dfrac{\sqrt{3}}{2}\right)$

$\quad = \dfrac{3}{4}\pi \text{ cm}^2$ Include units in your answer.

> **MATHEMATICAL CONNECTIONS**
>
> You will do more work using Pythagoras' theorem in Chapter 11.

WORKED EXAMPLE 18

The lengths of the two shorter sides of a right-angled triangle are $\sqrt{6}$ and $\sqrt{18}$.

Calculate the exact length of the hypotenuse (h).

Answer

$h^2 = \left(\sqrt{6}\right)^2 + \left(\sqrt{18}\right)^2$ Use Pythagoras's theorem:

$\quad = 6 + 18$ The sum of the squares of the two shorter sides equals the square of the hypotenuse.

$\quad = 24$

        Use $\sqrt{x} \times \sqrt{x} = x$.

$h = \sqrt{24}$

$\quad = \sqrt{4} \times \sqrt{6}$ Simplify the surd.

$\quad = 2\sqrt{6}$ cm   Include the unit in your answer.

Exercise 9.9

1 What is the exact perimeter of a square with side lengths $(5 - \sqrt{7})$ cm?

2 **a** What is the exact length of AB in this triangle?

b If you made an accurate wire model of this triangle, what lengths would you make each side? Why?

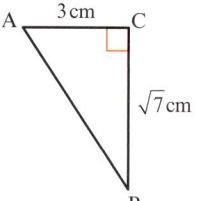

3 An engineer designed a round metal disk with an area of 236π mm².

a What is the exact diameter of the disk.

b What is the smallest square area from which the round disk could be cut?

4 A right-angled isosceles triangle has equal sides of length $\dfrac{6}{\sqrt{2}}$ cm.

a Show that the hypotenuse of this triangle is exactly 6 cm long.

b Calculate the exact perimeter of the triangle. Give your answer in simplest terms.

c Work out the area of the triangle.

5 Suri cut a circular hole of radius $\sqrt{7}$ mm from a metal plate with dimensions as shown on the diagram.

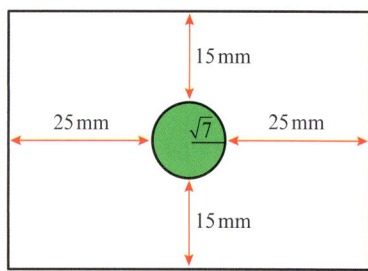

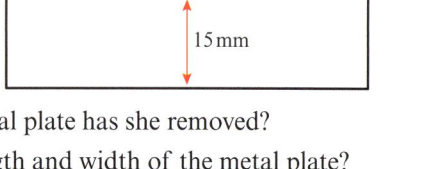

a What area of the metal plate has she removed?

b What is the exact length and width of the metal plate?

c Calculate the area of the rectangular metal plate Suri started with.

6 A sheet of A3 paper has sides in the ratio $1 : \sqrt{2}$. If the paper is 297 mm wide, calculate the exact length of its diagonal

> **TIP**
>
> Remember the rules for multiplying binomials:
>
> $(a + b)(a + b)$
> $\quad = a^2 + 2ab + b^2$
>
> $(a + b)(a - b)$
> $\quad = a^2 - b^2$

REFLECTION

There is quite a lot of debate (and some disagreement!) in online forums about whether or not surds are useful in real life. Many people do, however, agree that they are useful in maths because they help to develop mathematical thinking and improve your fluency in using and applying the rules of algebra.

- How does knowing rules of algebra help you to understand this section better?

- Does this section help you to understand any rules of algebra a bit better? How?

9.4 Sets

A **set** is a list or collection of objects that share one or more characteristics. The objects in a set can be anything from numbers, letters and shapes to names, places or paintings, but there is usually something that they have in common.

The list of members or **elements** of a set is placed inside a pair of curly brackets { }.

Some examples of sets are:

{2, 4, 6, 8, 10} − the set of all even integers greater than zero but less than 11

{a, e, i, o, u} − the set of vowels

{Red, Green, Blue} − the set containing the colours red, green and blue.

We use capital letters to name sets:

If A is the set of prime numbers less than 10, then: $A = \{2, 3, 5, 7\}$

If B is the set of letters in the word 'HAPPY', then: $B = \{H, A, P, Y\}$.

Two sets are equal if they contain exactly the same elements, even if the order is different, so:

$\{1, 2, 3, 4\} = \{4, 3, 2, 1\} = \{2, 4, 1, 3\}$ and so on.

The number of elements in a set is written as n(A), where A is the name of the set. For example, in the set $A = \{1, 3, 5, 7, 9\}$ there are five elements so n(A) = 5.

A set that contains no elements is known as the **empty set**. The symbol $\varnothing$ is used to represent the empty set.

For example:

{odd numbers that are multiples of two} = $\varnothing$ because no odd number is a multiple of two.

Now, if x is a member (an element) of the set A then it is written: $x \in A$.

If x is *not* a member of the set A, then it is written: $x \notin A$.

For example, if $H = \{Spades, Clubs, Diamonds, Hearts\}$, then:

Spades $\in H$ but   Turtles $\notin H$.

Some sets have a number of elements that can be counted. These are known as *finite* sets. If there is no limit to the number of members of a set then the set is *infinite*.

If $A = \{letters of the alphabet\}$, then A has 26 members and is finite.

If $B = \{positive integers\}$, then $B = \{1, 2, 3, 4, 5, 6, ...\}$ and is infinite.

So, to summarise:

- sets are listed inside curly brackets { }
- $\varnothing$ means it is an empty set
- $a \in B$ means a is an element of the set B
- $a \notin B$ means a is not an element of the set B
- n(A) is the number of elements in set A.

LINK

Sets are often used in advanced probability theory.

TIP

Remember the curly brackets on either side when you list a set.

TIP

Notice, for set B, that elements of a set are not repeated.

Exercise 9.10

1 List all of the elements of each set.

    a {days of the week}   **b** {months of the year}

    c {factors of 36}   **d** {colours of the rainbow}

    e {multiples of seven less than 50}   **f** {primes less than 30}

    g {ways of arranging the letters in the word 'TOY'}

2 List two more members of each set.

    a {rabbit, cat, parrot, ...}   **b** {carrot, potato, cabbage, ...}

    c {London, Paris, Stockholm, ...}   **d** {Nile, Amazon, Loire, ...}

    e {elm, pine, oak, ...}   **f** {tennis, cricket, football, ...}

    g {France, Germany, Belgium, ...}   **h** {Everest, Denali, Elbrus, ...}

    i {Beethoven, Mozart, Sibelius, ...}   **j** {rose, hyacinth, poppy, ...}

    k {3, 6, 9, ...}

    l {Hawksbill, Leatherback, Loggerhead, ...}

    m {Mercury, Venus, Saturn, ...}   **n** {happy, sad, angry, ...}

    o {German, Czech, Australian, ...}   **p** {hexagon, heptagon, triangle, ...}

3 Describe each set fully in words.

    a {1, 4, 9, 16, 25, ...}   **b** {Asia, Europe, Africa, ...}

    c {2, 4, 6, 8}   **d** {2, 4, 6, 8, ...}

    e {1, 2, 3, 4, 6, 12}

4 True or false?

    a If $A = \{1, 2, 3, 4, 5\}$ then $3 \notin A$

    b If $B = \{$primes less than 10$\}$, then $n(B) = 4$

    c If $C = \{$regular quadrilaterals$\}$, then square $\in C$

    d If $D = \{$paint primary colours$\}$, then yellow $\notin D$

    e If $E = \{$square numbers less than 100$\}$, then $64 \in E$

Universal sets

The following sets all have a number of things in common:

$M = \{1, 2, 3, 4, 5, 6, 7, 8\}$

$N = \{1, 5, 9\}$

$O = \{4, 8, 21\}$

All three are contained within the set of whole numbers. They are also all contained in the set of integers less than 22.

When you work with sets there is usually a 'largest' set which contains all of the sets that you are studying. This set can change according to the problem you are trying to solve.

Here, the set of integers contains all elements from M, N or O. But then so does the set of all positive integers less than 22.

Both these sets (and many more) can be used as a **universal set**. A universal set contains all possible elements that you would consider for a set in a particular problem. The symbol $\mathscr{E}$ is used to mean the universal set.

Complements

The **complement** of the set A is the set of all things that are in $\mathscr{E}$ but NOT in the set A. The symbol A' is used to denote the complement of set A.

For example, if $\mathscr{E}$ = {1, 2, 3, 4, 5, 6, 7, 8, 9, 10} and F = {2, 4, 6}

then the complement of F would be F' = {1, 3, 5, 7, 8, 9, 10}.

So, in summary:

* $\mathscr{E}$ represents a universal set

* A' represents the complement of set A.

Unions and intersections

The **union** of two sets, A and B, is the set of all elements that are members of A or members of B or members of both. The symbol $\cup$ is used to indicate union so, the union of sets A and B is written:

$A \cup B$

The **intersection** of two sets, A and B, is the set of all elements that are members of *both* A and B. The symbol $\cap$ is used to indicate intersection so, the intersection of sets A and B is written:

$A \cap B$

For example, if C = {4, 6, 8, 10} and D = {6, 10, 12, 14}, then:

$C \cap D$ = the set of all elements common to both = {6, 10}

$C \cup D$ = the set of all elements that are in C or D or both = {4, 6, 8, 10, 12, 14}.

> **TIP**
>
> Taking the union of two sets is like adding the sets together but remember you do not repeat elements within the set.

Subsets

You already know that a rectangle is a type of quadrilateral and that all rectangles are quadrilaterals. If set A is the set of all quadrilaterals and set B is the set of all rectangles, then every element of B is also a member of A and, therefore, B is completely contained within A. When this happens, you can say that B is a **subset** of A. You write this as $B \subseteq A$

You can reverse the $\subseteq$ symbol, but this does not change its meaning. $B \subseteq A$ means B is a subset of A, but so does $A \supseteq B$. If B is not a subset of A, you write $B \nsubseteq A$.

> **TIP**
>
> The symbol, $\subseteq$, has a open end and a closed end. The subset goes at the closed end.

So in summary:

* $\cup$ is the symbol for union
* $\cap$ is the symbol for intersection
* $B \subseteq A$ indicates that B is a subset of A
* $B \nsubseteq A$ indicates that B is not a subset of A.

WORKED EXAMPLE 19

If $W = \{4, 8, 12, 16, 20, 24\}$ and $T = \{5, 8, 20, 24, 28\}$.

a List the sets:

    i $W \cup T$ **ii** $W \cap T$

b Is it true that $T \subseteq W$?

Answers

a   **i** $W \cup T$ = set of all members of W or of T or of both = $\{4, 5, 8, 12, 16,$ $20, 24, 28\}$.

    ii $W \cap T$ = set of all elements that appear in both W and T = $\{8, 20, 24\}$.

b $5 \in T$ but $5 \notin W$. This means it is not true that every member of T is also a member of W, so T is not a subset of W.

Exercise 9.11

1 $A = \{2, 4, 6, 8, 10\}$ and $B = \{1, 3, 5, 6, 8, 10\}$.

    a   List the elements of:

        i $A \cap B$ **ii** $A \cup B$

    b   Find:

        i $n(A \cap B)$ **ii** $n(A \cup B)$

2 $C = \{a, b, g, h, u, w, z\}$ and $D = \{a, g, u, v, w, x, y, z\}$.

    a   List the elements of:

        i $C \cap D$ **ii** $C \cup D$

    b   Is it true that u is an element of $C \cap D$? Explain your answer.

    c   Is it true that g is not an element of $C \cup D$? Explain your answer.

3 $F = \{$equilateral triangles$\}$ and $G = \{$isosceles triangles$\}$.

    a   Explain why $F \subseteq G$.

    b   What is $F \cap G$? Can you simplify $F \cap G$ in any way?

4 $T = \{1, 2, 3, 6, 7\}$ and $W = \{1, 3, 9, 10\}$.

    a   List the members of the set:

        i $T \cup W$ **ii** $T \cap W$

    b   Is it true that $5 \notin T$? Explain your answer fully.

5   If $\mathscr{E} = \{$rabbit, cat, bird, emu, turtle, mouse, aardvark$\}$ and $H = \{$rabbit, emu, mouse$\}$ and $J = \{$cat, bird$\}$:

    a   list the members of H'

    b   list the members of J'

    c   list the members of $H' \cup J'$

    d   what is $H \cap J$?

    e   find $(H')'$

    f   what is $H \cup H'$?

TIP

Unions and intersections can be reversed without changing their elements, for example $A \cup B = B \cup A$ and $C \cap D = D \cap C$.

Venn diagrams

A **Venn diagram** is a graphical way of showing sets and how they relate to each other.

For example, if $\mathscr{E} = \{1, 2, 3, 4, 5, 6, 7, 8, 9, 10\}$, $A = \{1, 2, 3, 4, 5, 6, 7\}$ and $B = \{4, 5, 8\}$ then the Venn diagram looks like this:

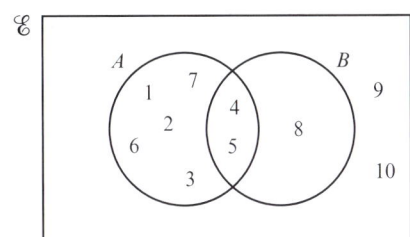

The universal set is shown by drawing a rectangle. Each set within the universal set is shown as a circle. The intersection of the sets A and B is contained within the overlap of the circles. The union is shown by the region enclosed by at least one circle. Here are some examples of Venn diagrams and shaded regions to represent particular sets:

MATHEMATICAL CONNECTIONS

You need to understand Venn diagrams well as you will need to use them to determine probabilities in Chapter 24.

TIP

Always remember to draw the box around the outside and mark it $\mathscr{E}$, to indicate that it represents the universal set.

The rectangle representing $\mathscr{E}$

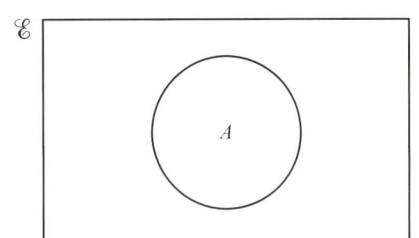

The circle representing set A.

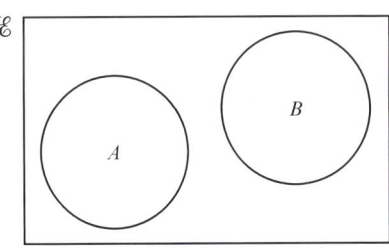

Set A and set B are disjoint, they have no common elements.

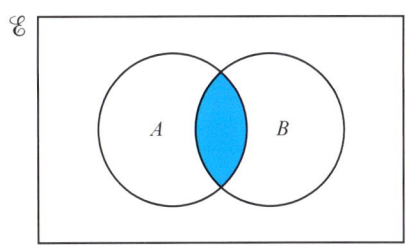

$A \cap B$ is the shaded portion.

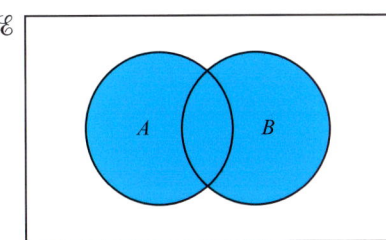

$A \cup B$ is the shaded portion.

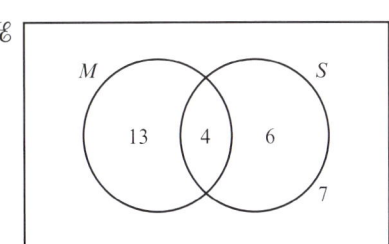

Venn diagrams can also be used to show the number of elements n(A) in a set.
In this case:
$M = \{$students doing Maths$\}$,
$S = \{$students doing Science$\}$.

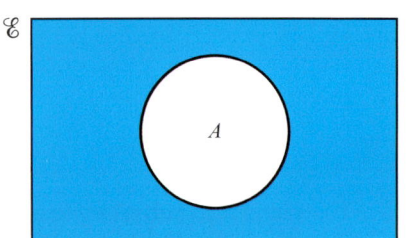

A' is the shaded portion.

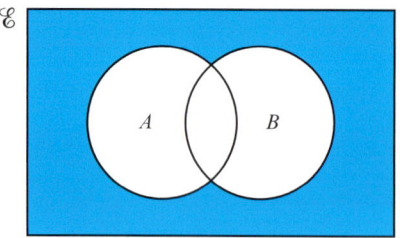

$(A \cup B)'$ is the shaded portion.

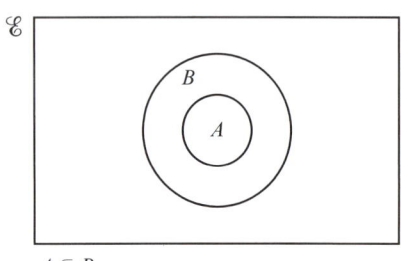

$A \subseteq B$

WORKED EXAMPLE 20

For the following sets:

$\mathscr{E}$ = {a, b, c, d, e, f, g, h, i, j, k}

A = {a, c, e, h, j}

B = {a, b, d, g, h}

a illustrate these sets in a Venn diagram

b list the elements of the set $A \cap B$

c find n($A \cap B$)

d list the elements of the set $A \cup B$

e find n($A \cup B$)

f list the set $A \cap B'$.

Answers

a

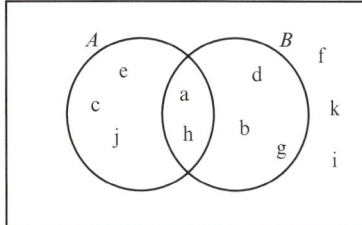

WORKED EXAMPLE 20 CONTINUED

b Look in the region that is contained within the overlap of both circles. This region contains the set {a, h}. So $A \cap B$ = {a, h}.

c $n(A \cap B) = 2$ as there are two elements in the set $A \cap B$.

d $A \cup B$ = set of elements of A or B or both = {a, b, c, d, e, g, h, j}.

e $n(A \cup B) = 8$

f $A \cap B'$ = set of all elements that are both in set A and not in set B = {c, e, j}.

Exercise 9.12

1 Use the given Venn diagram to answer the following questions.

    a List the elements of A and B.

    b List the elements of $A \cap B$.

    c List the elements of $A \cup B$.

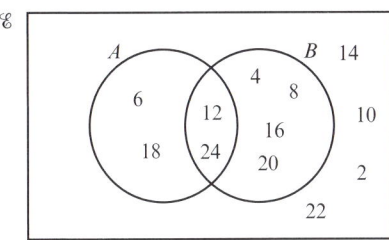

2 Use the given Venn diagram to answer the following questions.

    a List the elements that belong to:

        i P **ii** Q

    b List the elements that belong to both P and Q.

    c List the elements that belong to:

        i neither P nor Q **ii** P but not Q.

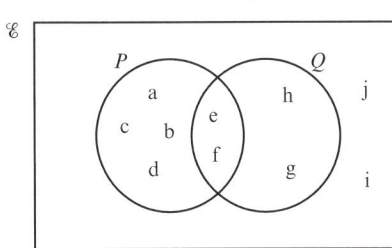

3 Draw a Venn diagram to show the following sets and write each element in its correct space.

    a The universal set is {a ,b, c, d, e, f, g, h}.

       A = {b, c, f, g} and B = {a, b, c, d, f}.

    b E = {whole numbers from 20 to 36 inclusive}.

       A = {multiples of four} and B = {numbers greater than 29}.

4   The universal set is: {students in a class}.

V = {students who like volleyball}

S = {students who play soccer}

There are 30 students in the class.

The Venn diagram shows numbers of students.

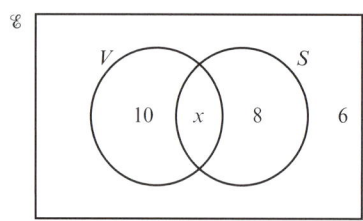

a   Find the value of x.

b   How many students like volleyball?

c   How many students in the class do not play soccer?

5   Copy the Venn diagram and shade the region which represents $A \cap B'$.

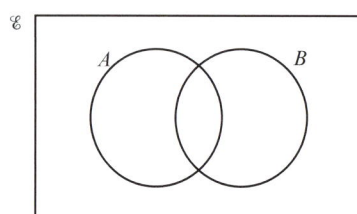

6   Make seven copies of this Venn diagram and shade the following sets:

a	$A \cup B$	**b**	$A \cup B \cup C$
c	$A \cup B'$	**d**	$A \cap (B \cup C)$
e	$(A \cup B) \cap C$	**f**	$A \cup (B \cup C)'$
g	$(A \cap C) \cup (A \cap B)$		

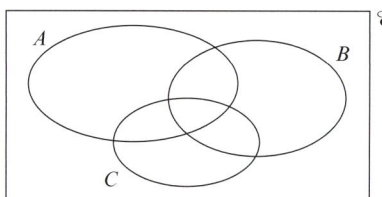

7   In a class of 30 students, 22 like classical music and 12 like Jazz. 5 like neither. Using a Venn diagram find out how many students like both classical and jazz music.

8   Students in their last year at a school must study at least one of the three main sciences: biology, chemistry and physics. There are 180 students in the last year, of whom 84 study biology and chemistry only, 72 study chemistry and physics only and 81 study biology and physics only. 22 pupils study only biology, 21 study only chemistry and 20 study only physics. Use a Venn diagram to work out how many students study all three sciences.

Set builder notation

So far, the contents of a set have either been given as a list of the elements or described by a rule (in words) that defines whether or not something is a member of the set. We can also describe sets using **set builder notation**. Set builder notation is a way of describing the elements of a set using the properties that each of the elements must have.

For example:

$A = \{x : x \text{ is a natural number}\}$

This means:

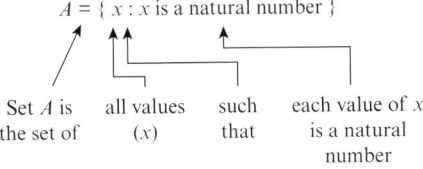

$A = \{\ x : x \text{ is a natural number } \}$

Set A is the set of — all values (x) — such that — each value of x is a natural number

In other words, this is the set: $A = \{1, 2, 3, 4, \ldots\}$.

Sometimes the set builder notation contains restrictions.

For example, $B = \{x : x \text{ is a letter of the alphabet}, x \text{ is a vowel}\}$.

In this case, set $B = \{a, e, i, o, u\}$.

Here is another example:

$A = \{\text{integers greater than zero but less than 20}\}$

In set builder notation this is:

$A = \{x : x \text{ is an integer}, 0 < x < 20\}$

This is read as: 'A is the set of all x such that x is an integer and x is greater than zero but less than 20'.

The following examples show how this notation is used.

WORKED EXAMPLE 21

List the members of the set C if $C = \{x: x \in \text{primes}, 10 < x < 20\}$.

Answer

Read the set as: 'C is the set of all x such that x is a member of the set of primes and x is greater than 10 but less than 20'.

The prime numbers greater than 10 but less than 20 are 11, 13, 17 and 19.

So, $C = \{11, 13, 17, 19\}$

WORKED EXAMPLE 22

Express the following set in set builder notation:

$D = \{\text{right-angled triangles}\}$

Answer

So, $D = \{x : x$ is a triangle, x has a right-angle$\}$

If D is the set of all right-angled triangles, then D is the set of all x such that x is a triangle and x is right-angled.

As you can see from this last example, set builder notation can sometimes force you to write more, but this isn't always the case, as you will see in the following exercise.

Exercise 9.13

1   Describe each of these sets using set builder notation.

   a   square numbers less than 101

   b   days of the week

   c   integers less than 0

   d   whole numbers between 2 and 10

   e   months of the year containing 30 days

2   Express each of the following in set builder notation.

   a $\{2, 3, 4, 5, 6, 7, 8\}$

   b $\{a, e, i, o, u\}$

   c $\{n, i, c, h, o, l, a, s\}$

   d $\{2, 4, 6, 8, 10, 12, 14, 16, 18, 20\}$

   e $\{1, 2, 3, 4, 6, 9, 12, 18, 36\}$

3   List the members of each of the following sets.

   a $\{x : x$ is an integer, $40 < x < 50\}$

   b $\{x : x$ is a regular polygon and x has no more than six sides$\}$

   c $\{x : x$ is a multiple of 3, $16 < x < 32\}$

4 If $A = \{x : x$ is a multiple of three$\}$ and $B = \{y : y$ is a multiple of five$\}$, express $A \cap B$ in set builder notation.

5 $\mathscr{E} = \{y : y$ is positive, y is an integer less than 18$\}$

$A = \{w : w > 5\}$ and $B = \{x : x \leqslant 5\}$

  a List the members of the set:

    i $A \cap B$ **ii** A' **iii** $A' \cap B$ **iv** $A \cap B'$ **v** $(A \cap B')'$

  b What is $A \cup B$?

  c List the members of the set in part (b).

6 Describe each set in words and say why it's not possible to list all the members of each set.

  a $A = \{x, y : y = 2x + 4\}$

  b $B = \{x : x^3$ is negative$\}$

TIP

Set builder notation is very useful when it isn't possible to list all the members of set because the set is infinite. For example, all the numbers less than -3 or all whole numbers greater than 1000.

SUMMARY

Do you know …?

A sequence is the elements of a set arranged in a particular order, connected by a rule.
A term is any number in a sequence.
If the position of a term in a sequence is given the letter n then a rule can be found to work out the value of the nth term.
A rational number is a number that can be written as a fraction.
An irrational number cannot be written as a fraction and will have a decimal part that continues forever without repeating.
Surds are exact values of irrational numbers written with a root sign.
A surd is in simplest form when it has no factors that are square numbers and when the denominator of a fraction with surds is a rational number.
A set is a list or collection of objects that share a characteristic.
An element is a member of a set.
A set that contains no elements is called the empty set ($\varnothing$).
A universal set ($\mathscr{E}$) contains all the possible elements appropriate to a particular problem.
The complement of a set is the elements that are not in the set ($'$).
The elements of two sets can be combined (without repeats) to form the union of the two sets ($\cup$).
The elements that two sets have in common is called the intersection of the two sets ($\cap$).
If the elements of a set A are all contained within set B, then A is a subset of B ($A \subset B$).
A Venn diagram is a pictorial method of showing sets.
A shorthand way of describing the elements of a set is called set builder notation.

Are you able to …?

continue sequences
describe a rule for continuing a sequence
find the nth term of a sequence

SUMMARY CONTINUED

use the *n*th term to find later terms
find out whether or not a specific number is in a sequence
generate sequences from shape patterns
find a formula for the number of shapes used in a pattern
write a recurring decimal as a fraction in its lowest terms
simplify surds • add and subtract surds by collecting like terms • multiply and divide surds using the rules of algebra • rationalise the denominator of a fraction that contains surds • solve problems involving surds
describe a set in words • find the complement of a set • represent the members of set using a Venn diagram • solve problems using a Venn diagram • describe a set using set builder notation.

Practice questions

1 Pattern 1   Pattern 2   Pattern 3

The first three patterns in a sequence are shown above.

a Copy and complete the table.

Pattern number (*n*)	1	2	3	4
Number of dots (*d*)	5			

[2]

b Find a formula for the number of dots, *d*, in the *n*th pattern. [3]

c Find the number of dots in the 60th pattern. [2]

d Find the number of the pattern that has 89 dots. [3]

2 The diagram below shows a sequence of patterns made from dots and lines.

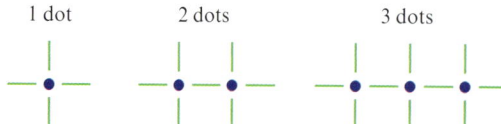

1 dot   2 dots   3 dots

a Draw the next pattern in the sequence. [2]

b Copy and complete the table for the numbers of dots and lines.

Dots	1	2	3	4	5	6
Lines	4	7	10			

[2]

c Find the number of lines in the pattern with 99 dots. [2]

d Find the number of lines are in the pattern with n dots. [3]

e Complete the following statement:

There are 85 lines in the pattern with … dots. [2]

3 Show that $5\sqrt{2} - 2\sqrt{8}$ is equivalent to $\sqrt{2}$. [3]

4 Simplify $\dfrac{3\sqrt{3} \times 5\sqrt{45}}{\sqrt{15}}$. [4]

5 Write $\dfrac{\sqrt{3}}{2} + \dfrac{7}{\sqrt{3}}$ as a single fraction with a rational denominator. [3]

6 The diagram shows a tile in the shape of a triangle. Find the area of the tile, giving your answer, as simply as possible, in the form $a\sqrt{b}$.

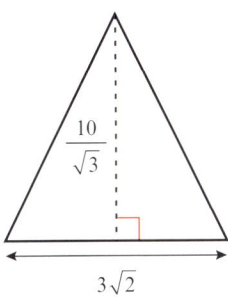

$\dfrac{10}{\sqrt{3}}$

$3\sqrt{2}$

[4]

7 **a** Find integers a and b, such that $(3 + 2\sqrt{5})^2 = a + b\sqrt{5}$. [3]

b Find integers p and q, such that $(3 + 2\sqrt{5})^2 = p + \dfrac{q}{\sqrt{45}}$. [3]

8 Write this expression as a single fraction with a rational denominator.

$\dfrac{3}{4 + \sqrt{7}} + \dfrac{7}{4 - \sqrt{7}}$ [4]

9

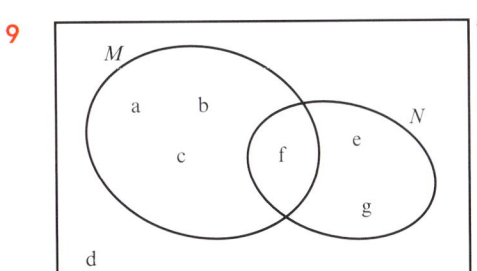

For the Venn diagram shown above, find:

a n(M ∩ N) [1] **b** n(N) [1] **c** M ∪ N [1] **d** M′ ∩ N [1]

e (M ∩ N)′ [1] **f** M ∪ N′ [1] **g** M′ ∪ N′ [1]

10 24 people live on Sport Street in Tennisville. 15 play cricket, 7 play rugby and 5 play neither. Find the number of Sports Street residents who play rugby but not cricket. [4]

11 Write $3.0\dot{2}0\dot{4}$ as a fraction in its lowest terms. [5]

12 Show that $0.\dot{9} = 1$. [4]

13 Simplify $0.\dot{3}00\dot{3} + 0.\dot{0}33\dot{0}$. [4]

14 107 students were asked how they travelled to school this morning:

- 53 had travelled by bus only
- 50 had not travelled on the bus
- 78 had travelled by either bus or car or both.

Draw a Venn diagram to illustrate this and hence find how many had:

a not travelled by car [2]

b travelled by car only [2]

c used neither bus nor car. [2]

15 $\mathscr{E} = \{\text{integers}\}$, $A = \{x : x \text{ is an integer and } -4 < x < 7\}$ and $B = \{x : x \text{ is a positive multiple of three}\}$.

a List the elements of set A. [2]

b Find $n(A \cap B)$. [3]

c Describe in words the set $(A \cap B)'$. [2]

16 Copy the diagram shown below twice and shade the sets indicated.

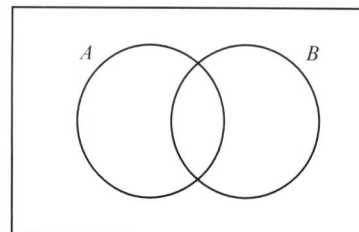

a $(A \cap B)'$ [2]

b $(A \cup B')' \cup (A \cap B)$ [3]

17 The rule for a sequence is given as $u_{n+2} = u_{n+1} + u_n$.

a Given that $u_1 = u_2 = 1$, list the first eight terms of this sequence. [2]

b What is the sequence called? [1]

c In which position is the number 233 in this sequence? [2]

18 For the sequence $u_n = \dfrac{1}{2}n(n + 1)$:

a list the first five terms [2]

b identify the special sequence of numbers [1]

c find the value of n for $u_n = 210$ [3]

d write an expression for u_{n-1}. [2]

SELF ASSESSMENT

Use the table to rate your understanding of the mathematical concepts needed in this section.

My work shows that I ...	Rating
understand all of the mathematical concepts needed to answer the questions	4
understand most of the mathematical concepts needed to answer the questions	3
understand some of the mathematical concepts needed to answer the questions	2
have limited understanding of the mathematical concepts needed to answer the questions	1

Chapter 10

Straight lines and quadratic equations

IN THIS CHAPTER YOU WILL:

- construct a table of values and plot points to draw graphs

- find the gradient of a straight line graph

- recognise and determine the equation of a line

- determine the equation of a line parallel to a given line

- calculate the gradient of a line using coordinates of points on the line

- find the gradient of parallel and perpendicular lines

- find the length of a line segment and the coordinates of its midpoint

- expand products of algebraic expressions

- factorise quadratic expressions

- solve quadratic equations by factorisation.

On 4 October 1957, the first artificial satellite, Sputnik, was launched. This particular satellite orbited the Earth, but many satellites that do experiments to study the upper atmosphere fly on short flights within the Earth's atmosphere. We can describe the flight path using the types of mathematical equations you will see in this chapter. This means scientists know where the rocket will be when it uses its parachute and where to recover the instruments. Similar equations can be used to describe any thrown projectile, including a ball!

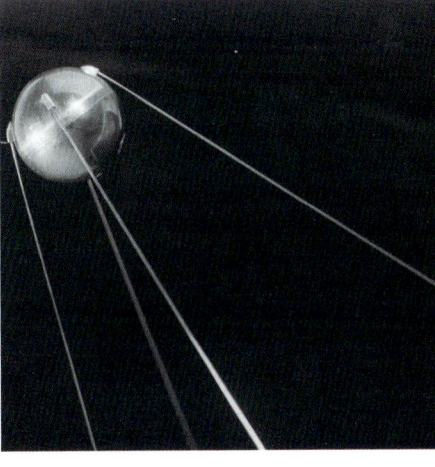

GETTING STARTED

1   A table of values gives a set of ordered pairs (x, y) that you can use to plot graphs on a coordinate grid.

x	−1	0	1	2
y	3	4	5	6

Plot these points and draw a line through them.

2   The standard equation of a straight line graph is $y = mx + c$

- m is the gradient (or steepness) of the graph.
- c is the point where the graph crosses the y-axis (the y-intercept).

a   What is the relationship between the x- and y-values in the table in question 1?

b   What equation could you use to describe the line you get when you plot the points?

3   *Look at the graph.* Calculate the gradient, find the y-intercept and use these to write the equation of the straight line.

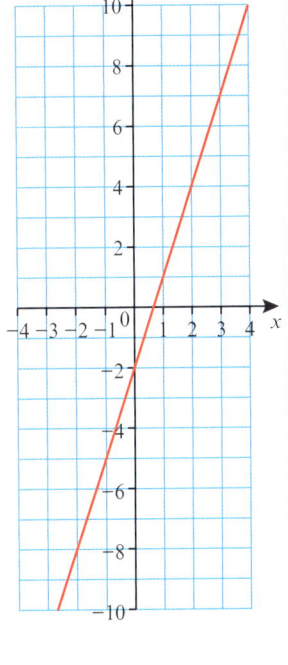

KEY WORDS

constant term

difference between two squares

equation of a line

expand

gradient

midpoint

quadratic equation

quadratic expression

10.1 Straight line graphs

We use straight line graphs in many situations, for example: to solve equations; to convert between different measures; to show the distance travelled by an object moving at a constant speed; and so on.

Using equations to plot lines

Keely owns a boat hire company. If Keely charges an initial fee of $40 to hire a boat and then $15 per hour, you can find a formula for the total cost $y after a hire time of x hours.

Total cost = initial fee + total charge for all hours

$y = 40 + 15 \times x$

or (rearranging)

$y = 15x + 40$

Now think about the total cost for a range of different hire times:

one hour: cost = 15 × 1 + 40 = $55

two hours: cost = 15 × 2 + 40 = $70

three hours: cost = 15 × 3 + 40 = $85

and so on.

If you put these values (and some more) into a table you can then plot a graph of the total cost against the number of hire hours:

Number of hours (x)	1	2	3	4	5	6	7	8	9
Total cost (y)	55	70	85	100	115	130	145	160	175

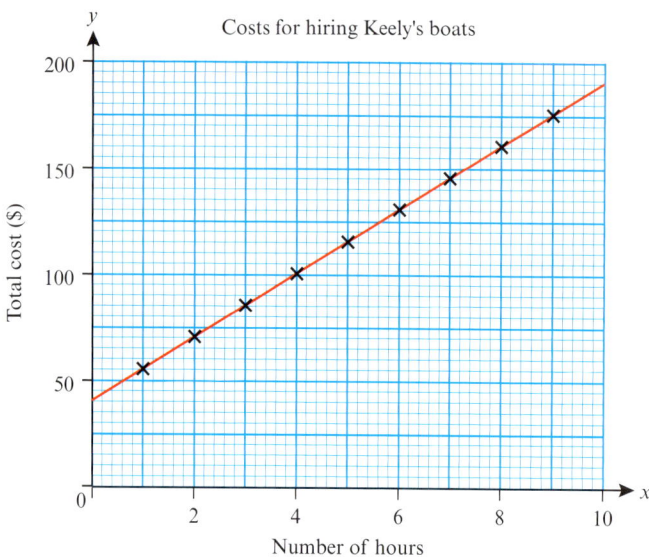

The graph shows the total cost of the boat hire (plotted on the vertical axis) against the number of hire hours (on the horizontal axis). Notice that the points all lie on a straight line.

The formula $y = 15x + 40$ tells you how the y-coordinates of all points on the line are related to the x-coordinates. This formula is called an **equation of the line**.

MATHEMATICAL CONNECTIONS

You will recognise that some of the formulae used to describe nth terms in Chapter 9 are very similar to the equations used in this chapter.

The following worked examples show you how some more lines can be drawn from given equations.

WORKED EXAMPLE 1

A straight line has equation $y = 2x + 3$. Construct a table of values for x and y and draw the line on a labelled pair of axes. Use integer values of x from -3 to 2.

Answer

Substituting the values -3, -2, -1, 0, 1 and 2 into the equation gives the values in the following table:

x	-3	-2	-1	0	1	2
y	-3	-1	1	3	5	7

Notice that the y-values range from -3 to 7, so your y-axis should allow for this.

Graph of $y = 2x + 3$

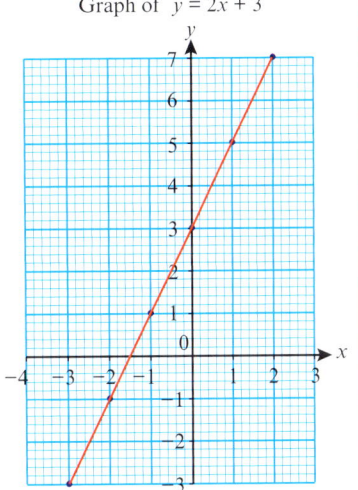

WORKED EXAMPLE 2

Draw the line with equation $y = -x + 3$ for x-values from -2 to 5.

Answer

The table for this line is:

x	-2	-1	0	1	2	3	4	5
y	5	4	3	2	1	0	-1	-2

Graph of $y = -x + 3$

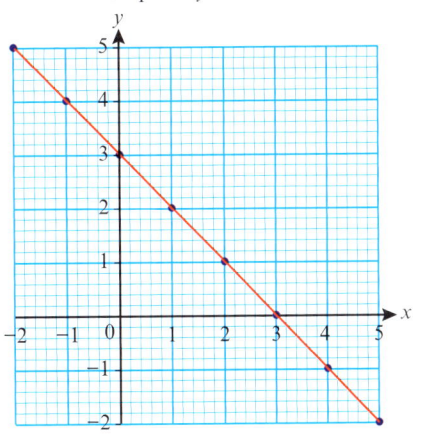

To draw a graph from its equation:

- construct a table of values and fill in the x- and y-coordinates of at least three points (although you may be given more)
- draw and label your set of axes for the range of y-values you have worked out
- plot each point on the number plane
- draw a straight line to join the points (use a ruler).

TIP

Before drawing your axes, always check that you know the range of y-values that you need to use.

Exercise 10.1

1   Make a table for x-values from -3 to 3 for each of the following equations.
    Plot the coordinates on separate pairs of axes and draw the lines.

    a $y = 3x + 2$ **b** $y = x + 2$ **c** $y = 2x - 1$ **d** $y = 5x - 4$

    e $y = -2x + 1$ **f** $y = -x - 2$ **g** $y = 6 - x$ **h** $y = 3x + \frac{1}{2}$

    i $y = \frac{1}{2}x + 1$ **j** $y = 4x$ **k** $y = -3$ **l** $y = -1 - x$

    m $x + y = 4$ **n** $x - y = 2$ **o** $y = x$ **p** $y = -x$

2   Plot the lines $y = 2x$, $y = 2x + 1$, $y = 2x - 3$ and $y = 2x + 2$ on the same pair of axes.
    Use x-values from -3 to 3. What do you notice about the lines that you have drawn?

3   For each of the following equations, construct a table of x-values for -3, 0 and 3.
    Complete the table of values and plot the graphs on the same set of axes.

    a $y = x + 2$ **b** $y = -x + 2$ **c** $y = x - 2$ **d** $y = -x - 2$

4   Use your graphs from question **3** above to answer these questions.

    a   Where do the graphs cut the x-axis?

    b   Which graphs slope up to the right?

    c   Which graphs slope down to the right?

    d   Which graphs cut the y-axis at (0, 2)?

    e   Which graphs cut the y-axis at (0, −2)?

    f   Does the point (3, 3) lie on any of the graphs? If so, which?

    g   Which graphs are parallel to each other?

    h   Compare the equations of graphs that are parallel to each other.
           How are they similar? How are they different?

Gradient

The **gradient** of a line tells you how steep the line is. For every one unit moved to the right, the gradient will tell you how much the line moves up (or down). When straight lines are parallel to each other, they have the same gradient.

Vertical and horizontal lines

Look at the two graphs shown in the following diagram:

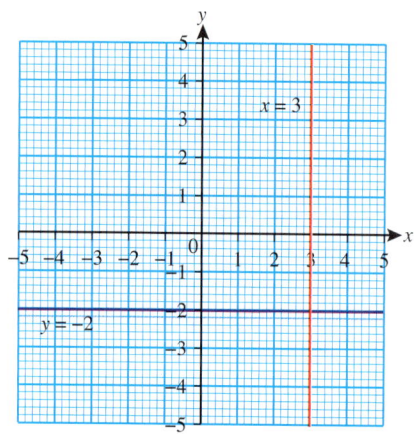

LINK

The word 'gradient' can also be used when creating art on a computer. A colour 'gradient' refers to a gradual change from one colour to another in the same image. The relationship with mathematical gradient comes from the idea of something changing gradually over time or distance.

Every point on the vertical line has x-coordinate = 3. So the equation of the line is simply $x = 3$.

Every point on the horizontal line has y-coordinate = −2. So the equation of this line is $y = -2$.

All vertical lines are of the form: x = a number.

All horizontal lines are of the form: y = a number.

The gradient of a vertical line is undefined because the graph does not move right or left.

The gradient of a horizontal line is zero (it does not move up or down when you move to the right).

LINK

It is not really sensible to talk about the gradient of a vertical line. When calculating gradients, you need to know how the y-values change with any change in x. The x values in a vertical line do not change! You will think about this idea in Chapter 18.

Exercise 10.2

1   Write down the equation of each line shown in the diagram.

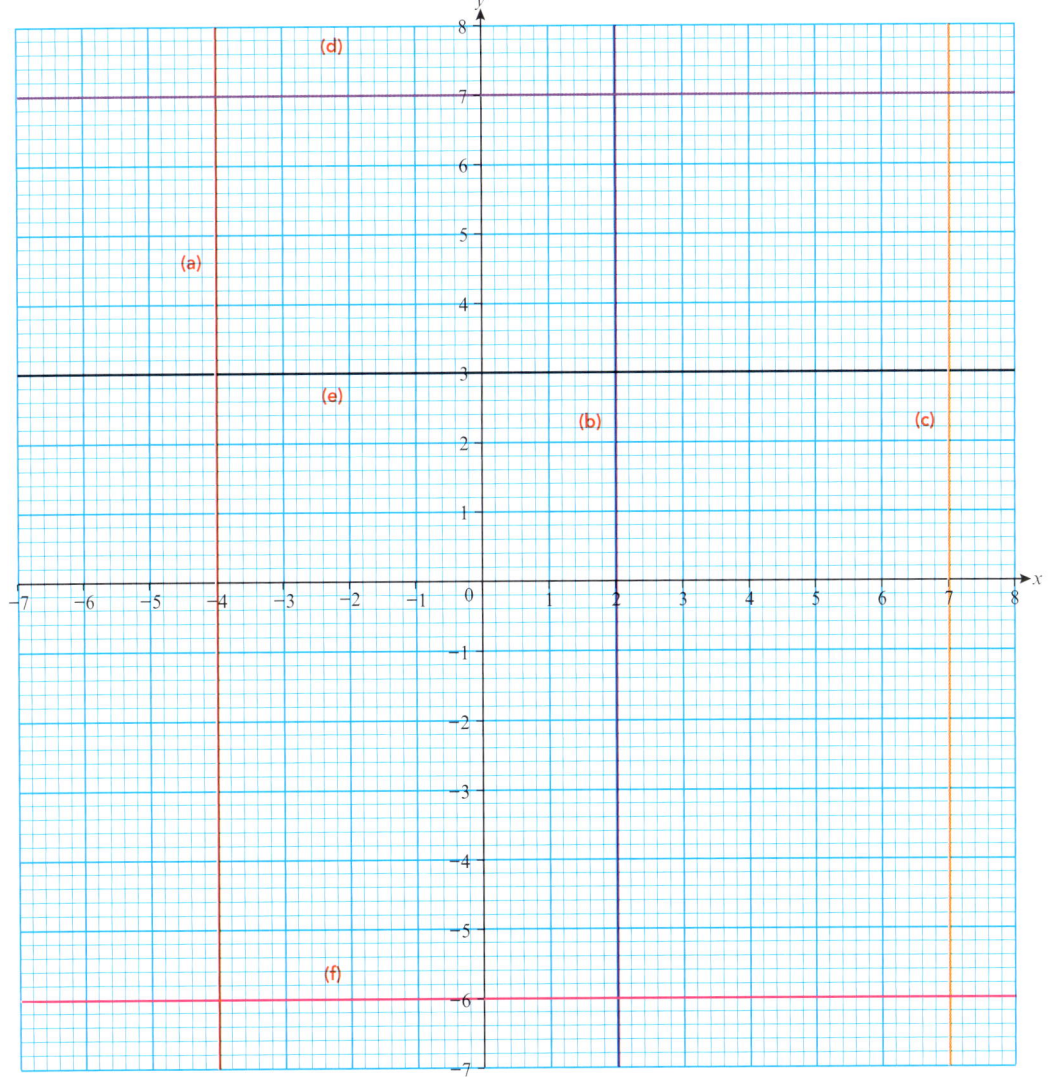

2   Draw the following graphs on the same set of axes without plotting points or drawing a table of values.

a $y = 3$ b $x = 3$ c $y = -1$ d $x = -1$

e $y = -3$ f $y = 4$ g $x = \dfrac{1}{2}$ h $x = -\dfrac{7}{2}$

i   A graph parallel to the *x*-axis which cuts the *y*-axis at (0, 4).

j   A graph parallel to the *y*-axis which goes through the point (−2, 0).

Lines that are neither vertical nor horizontal

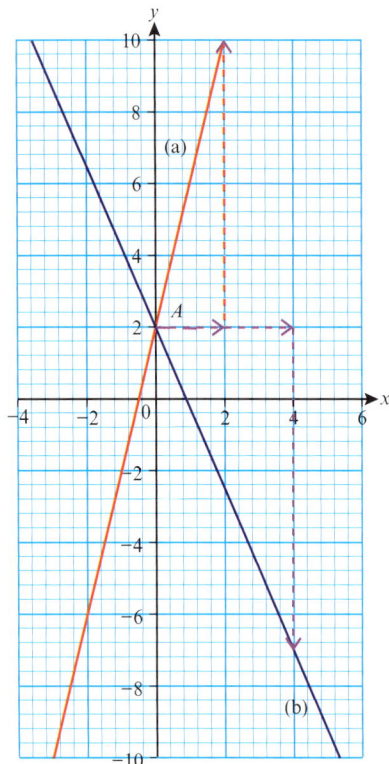

The diagram shows two different lines. If you take a point A on the line and then move to the right, then: on graph (a) you need to move up to return to the line; and on graph (b) you need to move down.

The gradient of a line measures how steep the line is. You calculate it by dividing the change in the *y*-coordinate by the *increase* in the *x*-coordinate:

$$\text{Gradient} = \frac{y\text{-change}}{x\text{-change}}$$

For graph (a): the *y*-change is 8 and the *x*-change is 2, so the gradient is $\dfrac{8}{2} = 4$.

For graph (b): the *y*-change is −9 (negative because you need to move *down* to return to the line) and the *x*-change is 4, so the gradient is $\dfrac{-9}{4} = -2.25$.

It is essential that you think about *x-changes* only. Whether the *y*-change is positive or negative tells you what the sign of the gradient will be.

> **MATHEMATICAL CONNECTIONS**
>
> You will deal with gradient as a rate of change when you work with kinematic graphs in Chapter 21.

> **TIP**
>
> Another good way to remember the gradient formula is $\dfrac{\text{'rise'}}{\text{'run'}}$. The 'run' must always be to the right (increase *x*).

> **TIP**
>
> When the *x*-increase is 0, the line is vertical and the gradient is undefined.

WORKED EXAMPLE 3

Calculate the gradient of each line. Leave your answer as a whole number or fraction in its lowest terms.

a

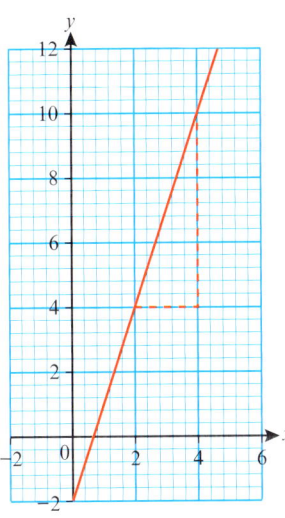

b

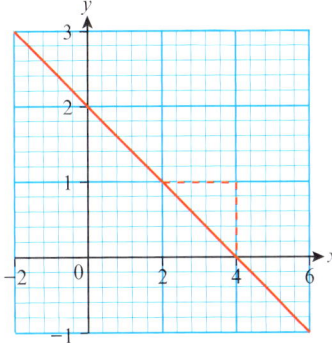

Answers

a   Notice that the graph passes through the points (2, 4) and (4, 10).

Gradient $= \dfrac{\text{y-change}}{\text{x-change}} = \dfrac{10 - 4}{4 - 2} = \dfrac{6}{2} = 3$

b   Notice that the graph passes through the points (2, 1) and (4, 0).

Gradient $= \dfrac{\text{y-change}}{\text{x-change}} = \dfrac{0 - 1}{4 - 2} = -\dfrac{1}{2}$

WORKED EXAMPLE 4

Calculate the gradient of the line that passes through the points (3, 5) and (7, 17).

Answer

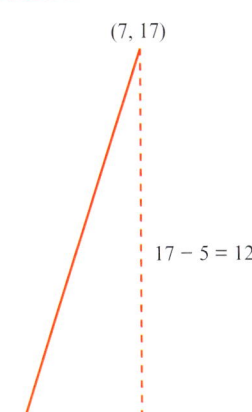

(7, 17)

17 − 5 = 12

(3, 5) 7 − 3 = 4

Think about where the points will be, in relation to each other, on a pair of axes. You don't need to draw this accurately, but the diagram will give you an idea of how the line may appear.

Gradient $= \dfrac{12}{4} = 3$

Exercise 10.3

1 Calculate the gradient of each line. Leave your answer as a whole number or a fraction in its lowest terms.

a
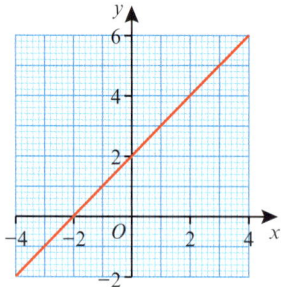

b
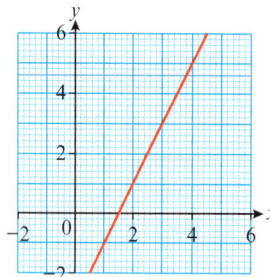

c
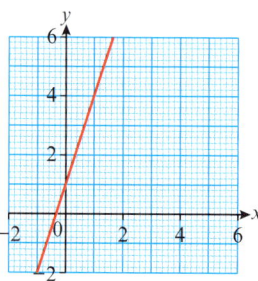

d
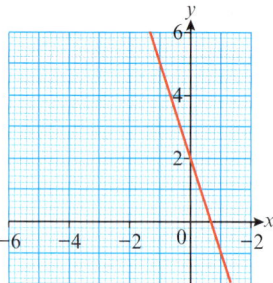

e
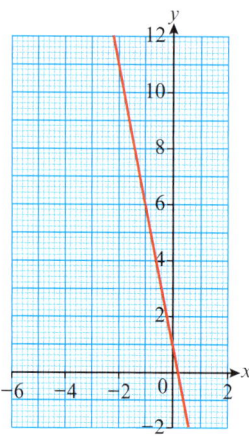

f
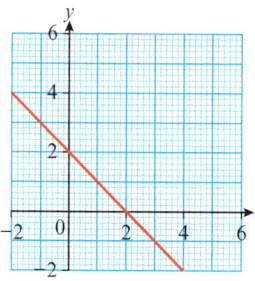

g
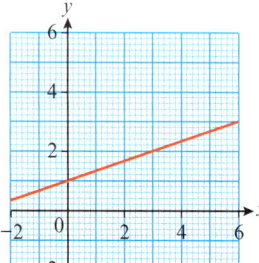

h
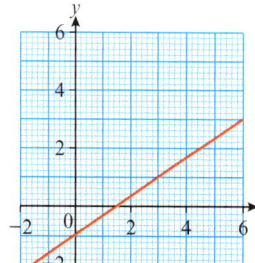

i
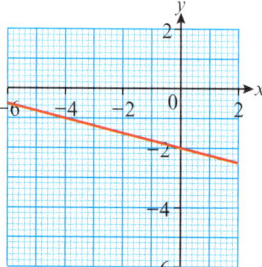

2 Calculate the gradient of the line that passes through each pair of points. Leave your answer as a whole number or a fraction in its lowest terms.

a $A(1, 2)$ and $B(3, 8)$

b $A(0, 6)$ and $B(3, 9)$

c $A(2, -1)$ and $B(4, 3)$

d $A(3, 2)$ and $B(7, -10)$

e $A(-1, -4)$ and $B(-3, 2)$

f $A(3, -5)$ and $B(7, 12)$

> **TIP**
>
> Think carefully about whether you expect the gradient to be positive or negative.

APPLY YOUR SKILLS

3 If the car climbs 60 m vertically, how far must the car have travelled horizontally?

REFLECTION

The formula for gradient involves fractions and subtractions. It is very easy to accidentally write the fractions 'upside down' or to calculate the wrong sign. How can you make sure you avoid making these mistakes?

INVESTIGATION

Before you read on, look at the gradients you calculated in Exercise 10.3. You should be able to work out the equation of a line by considering the connection between x- and y-coordinates of groups of points. Can you see a relationship between the gradient and the equation? You will look at this in more detail in the next section, but try to work it out before you read on.

Finding the equation of a line

Look at the three lines shown below.

a
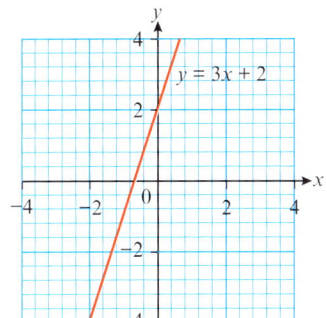

b
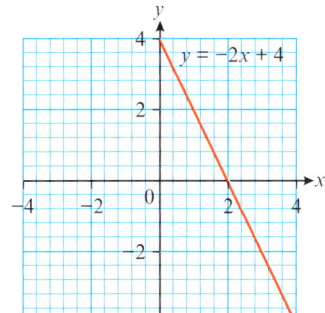

c
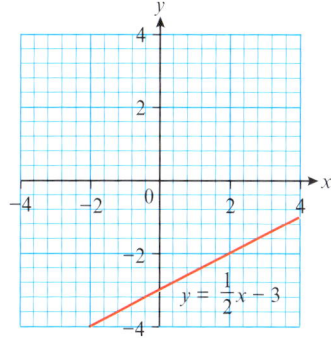

Check for yourself that the lines have the following gradients:

- gradient of line (a) = 3
- gradient of line (b) = −2
- gradient of line (c) = $\frac{1}{2}$

Notice that the gradient of each line is equal to the coefficient of x in the equation and that the point at which the line crosses the y-axis (known as the y-intercept) has a y-coordinate that is equal to the **constant term**.

In fact this is always true when y is the subject of the equation:

$$y \quad = \quad mx \quad + \quad c$$

y is the subject   gradient y-intercept
of the equation

In summary:

- Equations of a straight line graph can be written in the form $y = mx + c$.
- c (the constant term) tells you where the graph cuts the y-axis (the y-intercept).
- m (the coefficient of x) is the gradient of the graph; a negative value means the graph slopes down the to the right, a positive value means it slopes up to the right. The higher the value of m, the steeper the gradient of the graph.
- Graphs which have the same gradient are parallel to each other (therefore graphs that are parallel have the same gradient).

> **MATHEMATICAL CONNECTIONS**
>
> The coefficient of x is the number in front of x, in the expression. You met the word 'coefficient' in Chapter 2 and later on you will see that the number in front of x^2 in a quadratic expression is known at the 'coefficient of x^2' and so on.

WORKED EXAMPLE 5

Find the gradient and y-intercept of the lines given by each of the following equations.

a $y = 3x + 4$ **b** $y = 5 - 3x$ **c** $y = \frac{1}{2}x + 9$

d $x + y = 8$ **e** $3x + 2y = 6$

Answers

a $y = 3x + 4$

Gradient = 3   The coefficient of x is 3.

y-intercept = 4   The constant term is 4.

b $y = 5 - 3x$ Re-write the equation as $y = -3x + 5$.

Gradient = −3   The coefficient of x is −3.

y-intercept = 5   The constant term is 5.

c $y = \frac{1}{2}x + 9$

Gradient = $\frac{1}{2}$ The gradient can be a fraction.

y-intercept = 9

d $x + y = 8$ Subtract x from both sides to make y the

Gradient = −1   subject: $y = -x + 8$.

y-intercept = 8

e $3x + 2y = 6$ Make y the subject of the equation:

Gradient = $-\frac{3}{2}$ $3x + 2y = 6$

y-intercept = 3 $2y = -3x + 6$

$$y = -\frac{3}{2}x + \frac{6}{2}$$

$$y = -\frac{3}{2}x + 3$$

WORKED EXAMPLE 6

Find the equation of each line.

a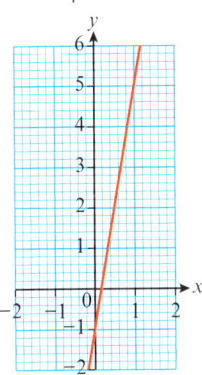

b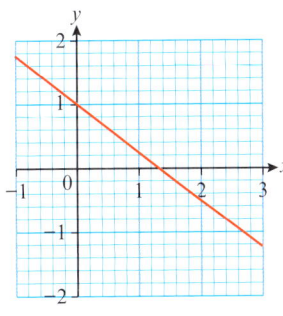

Answers

a   Gradient = 6 and the y-intercept = -1

So the equation is $y = 6x - 1$

Gradient = $\dfrac{6}{1} = 6$

Graph crosses y-axis at -1.

b   Gradient = $-\dfrac{3}{4}$ and the y-intercept = 1

So the equation is $y = -\dfrac{3}{4}x + 1$

Gradient = $-\dfrac{1.5}{2} = -\dfrac{3}{4}$

Graph crosses y-axis at 1.

> **TIP**
>
> You should always label your axes x and y when drawing graphs – even when they are sketches.

Exercise 10.4

1   Find the gradient and y-intercept of the lines with the following equations.
Sketch the graph in each case, taking care to show where the graph cuts the y-axis.

   a $y = 4x - 5$ **b** $y = 2x + 3$ **c** $y = -3x - 2$

   d $y = -x + 3$ **e** $y = \dfrac{1}{3}x + 2$ **f** $y = 6 - \dfrac{1}{4}x$

2   Sketch the graph of each equation. Show where the graph cuts the y-axis.

   a $x + y = 4$ **b** $x + 2y = 4$ **c** $x + \dfrac{y}{2} = 3$

   d $x = 4y - 2$ **e** $x = \dfrac{y}{4} + 2$ **f** $2x - 3y = -9$

3   Rearrange each equation so that it is in the form $y = mx + c$ and then find the gradient and y-intercept of each graph.

   a $2y = x - 4$ **b** $2x + y - 1 = 0$ **c** $x = \dfrac{y}{2} - 2$ **d** $2x - y - 5 = 0$

   e $2x - y + 5 = 0$ **f** $x + 3y - 6 = 0$ **g** $4y = 12x - 8$ **h** $4x + y = 2$

   i $\dfrac{y}{2} = x + 2$ **j** $\dfrac{y}{3} = 2x - 4$ **k** $\dfrac{x}{2} - 4y = 12$ **l** $-\dfrac{y}{3} = 4x - 2$

4 Find the equation (in the form $y = mx + c$) of a line which has:

    a a gradient of 2 and a y-intercept of 3

    b a gradient of -3 and a y-intercept of -2

    c a gradient of 3 and a y-intercept of -1

    d a y-intercept of -0.75 and a gradient of 0.75

    e a y-intercept of -2 and a gradient of 0

    f a gradient of 0 and a y-intercept of 4.

5 Find the equation (in the form $ax + by = c$) of a line which has:

    a a gradient of $-\dfrac{3}{2}$ and a y-intercept at $(0, -0.5)$

    b a y-intercept of 2 and a gradient of $-\dfrac{3}{4}$

    c a y-intercept of -3 and a gradient of $\dfrac{4}{8}$.

6 Find an equation for each line.

    a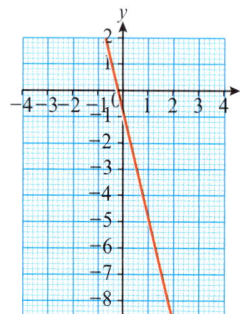
    b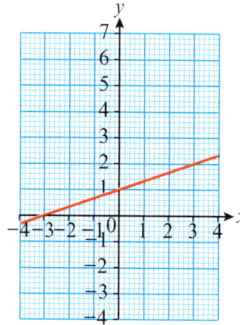
    c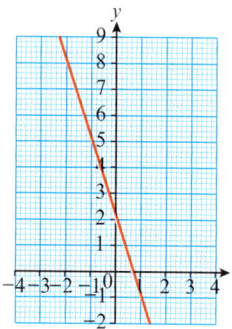

    d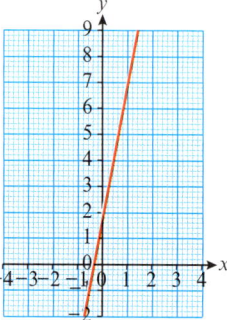
    e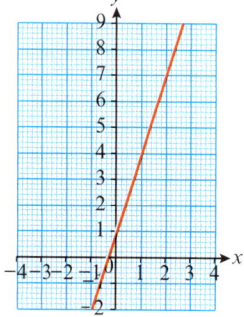
    f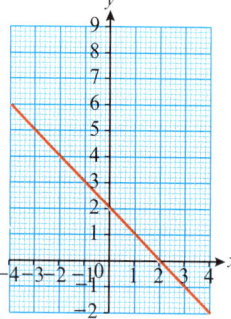

    g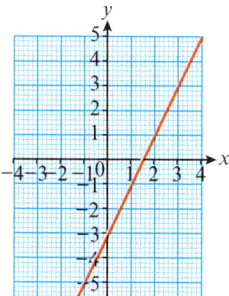
    h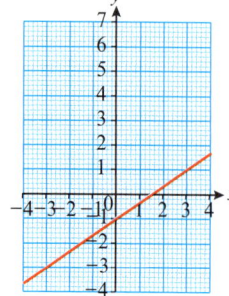
    i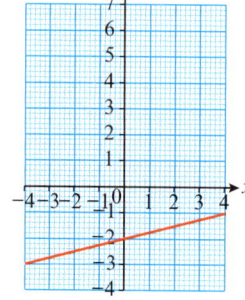

7 Find the equation of the line which passes through each pair of points.

    a $A(2, 3)$ and $B(4, 11)$ **b** $A(4, 5)$ and $B(8, -7)$

    c $A(-1, -3)$ and $B(4, 6)$ **d** $A(3, -5)$ and $B(7, 12)$

8 Write down the equation of a line that is parallel to:

    a $y = -3x$ **b** $y = 2x - 3$ **c** $y = \dfrac{x}{2} + 4$

    d $y = -x - 2$ **e** $x = 8$ **f** $y = -6$

9 Which of the following lines are parallel to $y = \dfrac{1}{2}x$?

    a $y = \dfrac{1}{2}x + 1$ **b** $y = 2x$ **c** $y + 1 = \dfrac{1}{2}x$

    d $2y + x = -6$ **e** $y = 2x - 4$

10 Find the equation of a line parallel to $y = 2x + 4$ which:

    a   has a y-intercept of -2 **b**   passes through the origin

    c   passes through the point $(0, -4)$ **d**   has a y-intercept of $\dfrac{1}{2}$.

11 A graph has the equation $3y - 2x = 9$.

    a   Write down the equation of one other graph that is parallel to this one.

    b   Write down the equation of one other graph that crosses the y-axis at the same point as this one.

    c   Write down the equation of a line that passes through the y-axis at the same point as this one and which is parallel to the x-axis.

Perpendicular lines

You have already seen that parallel lines have the same gradient and that lines with the same gradient are parallel.

Perpendicular lines meet at right angles. The product of the gradients is -1.

So, $m_1 \times m_2 = -1$, where m is the gradient of each line.

> **TIP**
>
> Remember that a product is the result of multiplying two numbers together.

The sketch shows two perpendicular graphs.

$y = -\dfrac{1}{3}x + 2$ has a gradient of $-\dfrac{1}{3}$

$y = 3x - 4$ has a gradient of 3

The product of the gradients is

$-\dfrac{1}{3} \times 3 = -1$.

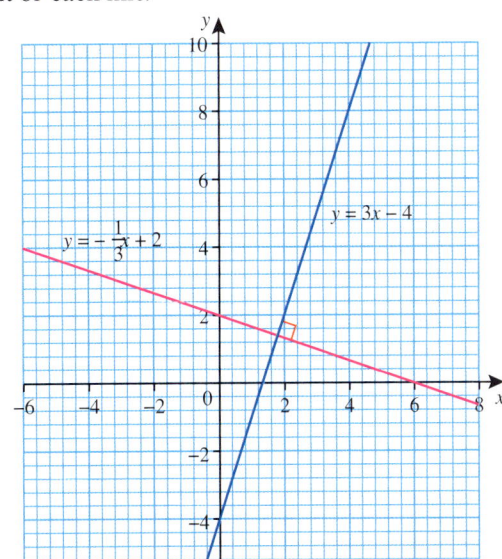

> **TIP**
>
> If the product of the gradients of two lines is equal to -1, it follows that the lines are perpendicular to each other.

INVESTIGATION

In two dimensions, straight lines that are not parallel always meet at one point. Is this true in three dimensions?

WORKED EXAMPLE 7

Given that $y = \frac{2}{3}x + 2$, determine the equation of the straight line that is:

a　perpendicular to this line and which passes through the origin

b　perpendicular to this line and which passes through the point $(-3, 1)$.

Answers

a　$y = mx + c$　　　　　　The gradient is the negative reciprocal

$m = -\frac{3}{2}$　　　　　　　of $\frac{2}{3}$.

$c = 0$

The equation of the line is

$y = -\frac{3}{2}x.$

b　$y = -\frac{3}{2}x + c$　　　　Using $m = -\frac{3}{2}$ from part (a).

$x = -3$ and $y = 1$　　　Substitute the values of x and y for the

$1 = -\frac{3}{2}(-3) + c$　　　given point to solve for c.

$1 = \frac{9}{2} + c$

$c = -3\frac{1}{2}$

$y = -\frac{3}{2}x - 3\frac{1}{2}$

Exercise 10.5

1　A line perpendicular to $y = \frac{x}{5} + 3$ passes through $(1, 3)$.

What is the equation of the line?

2　Show that the line through the points $A(6, 0)$ and $B(0, 12)$ is:

　a　perpendicular to the line through $P(8, 10)$ and $Q(4, 8)$

　b　perpendicular to the line through $M(-4, -8)$ and $N\left(-1, -\frac{13}{2}\right)$.

3　Given $A(0, 0)$ and $B(1, 3)$, find the equation of the line perpendicular to AB with a y-intercept of 5.

4　Find the equation of the following lines:

　a　perpendicular to $2x - y - 1 = 0$ and passing through $\left(2, -\frac{1}{2}\right)$

　b　perpendicular to $2x + 2y = 5$ and passing through $(1, -2)$.

5   Line A joins the points $(6, 0)$ and $(0, 12)$ and line B joins the points $(8, 10)$ and $(4, 8)$. Determine the gradient of each line and state whether line A is perpendicular to line B.

6   Show that points $A(-3, 6)$, $B(-12, -4)$ and $C(8, -5)$ cannot be the vertices of a rectangle $ABCD$.

7   Find the equation of the line that is the perpendicular bisector of the line joining the following points.

   a $(7, 4)$ and $(2, 5)$

   b $(3, -3)$ and $(1, -1)$

   c $(4, -2)$ and $(4, 4)$

> **TIP**
>
> The perpendicular bisector is the line that is perpendicular to the original line and passes through its midpoint.

8   A line is drawn from $P(1, 3)$ to $Q(-3, 5)$. Find the equation of line MN, the perpendicular bisector of PQ. Give your answer in the form $ax + by + c = 0$, where a, b and c are integers.

Intersection with the x-axis

So far you have only found the y-intercept, either from the graph or from the equation. There is, of course, an x-intercept too. The following sketch shows the line with equation $y = 3x - 6$.

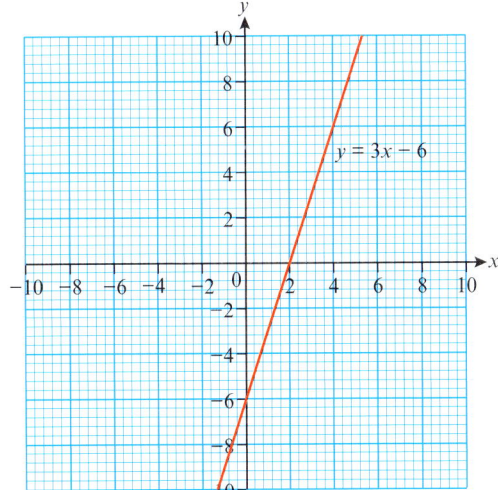

Notice that the line crosses the x-axis at the point where $x = 2$ and, importantly, $y = 0$. In fact, all points on the x-axis have y-coordinate $= 0$.

If you substitute $y = 0$ into the equation of the line:

$y = 3x - 6$

$0 = 3x - 6$ (put $y = 0$)

$3x = 6$ (add 6 to both sides)

$x = 2$ (divide both sides by 3)

This is exactly the answer that you found from the graph.

You can also find the *y*-intercept by putting $x = 0$. The following worked examples show calculations for finding both the *x*- and *y*-intercepts.

MATHEMATICAL CONNECTIONS

The *y*-intercept is also very important. You met it earlier in the chapter. The '*c*' in the equation $y = mx + c$ is the *y*-intercept.

WORKED EXAMPLE 8

Find the *x*- and *y*-intercepts for each of the following lines. Sketch the graph in each case.

a $y = 6x - 12$ **b** $y = -x + 3$

c $2x + 5y = 20$

Answers

a $y = 6x - 12$

$x = 0 \Rightarrow y = -12$

$y = 0 \Rightarrow 6x - 12 = 0$

$\Rightarrow x = 2$

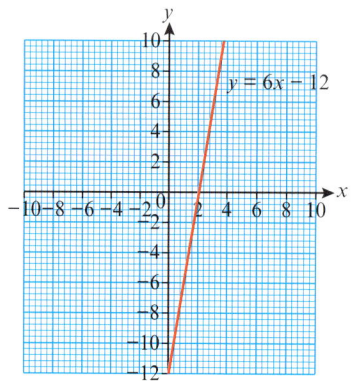

b $y = -x + 3$

$x = 0 \Rightarrow y = 3$

$y = 0 \Rightarrow -x + 3 = 0$

$\Rightarrow x = 3$

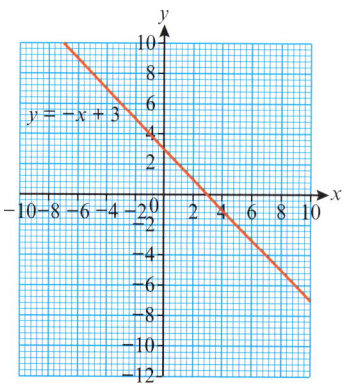

c $2x + 5y = 20$

$x = 0 \Rightarrow 5y = 20$

$\Rightarrow y = 4$

$y = 0 \Rightarrow 2x = 20$

$\Rightarrow x = 10$

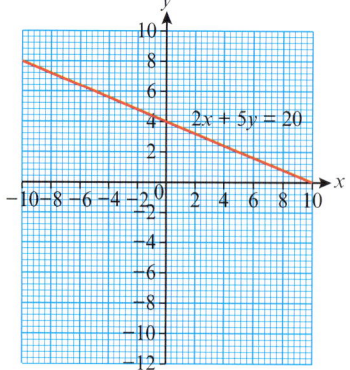

MATHEMATICAL CONNECTIONS

You will need to understand this method when solving simultaneous equations in Chapter 14.

Exercise 10.6

1   Find the x- and y-intercepts for each of the following lines. Sketch the graph in each case.

a $y = -5x + 10$

b $y = \dfrac{x}{3} - 1$

c $y = -3x + 6$

d $y = 4x + 2$

e $y = 3x + 1$

f $y = -x + 2$

g $y = 2x - 3$

h $y = \dfrac{2x}{3} - 1$

i $y = \dfrac{x}{4} - 2$

j $y - \dfrac{2x}{5} = +1$

k $-2 + y = \dfrac{x}{4}$

l $-\dfrac{y}{3} = 4x - 2$

2   For each equation the given point lies on the graph. Find each value of c.

a $y = 3x + c$ $(1, 5)$

b $y = 6x + c$ $(1, 2)$

c $y = -2x + c$ $(-3, -3)$

d $y = \dfrac{3}{4}x + c$ $(4, -5)$

e $y = \dfrac{1}{2}x + c$ $(-2, 3)$

f $y = c - \dfrac{1}{2}x$ $(-4, 5)$

g $y = c + 4x$ $(-1, -6)$

h $\dfrac{2}{3}x + c = y$ $(3, 4)$

Finding the length of a straight line segment

Although lines are infinitely long, you are usually only interested in a part of a line. Any section of a line joining two points is called a line segment.

> **MATHEMATICAL CONNECTIONS**
>
> The word 'segment' means 'part'. You have seen this word used in Chapter 3, where a segment of a circle is the part of a circle 'cut off' by a chord.

If you know the coordinates of the end points of a line segment you can use Pythagoras' theorem to calculate the length of the line segment.

WORKED EXAMPLE 9

Find the distance between the points (1, 1) and (7, 9).

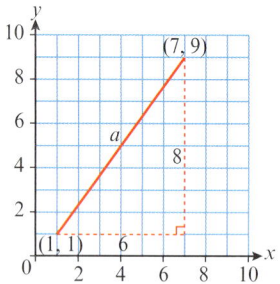

Answer

$a^2 = 8^2 + 6^2$	$a^2 = b^2 + c^2$ (Pythagoras' theorem)
$a^2 = 64 + 36$	Work out each expression.
$a^2 = 100$	
$\therefore a = \sqrt{100}$	Undo the square by taking the square root of both sides.
$a = 10$ units	

WORKED EXAMPLE 10

Given $A(3, 6)$ and $B(7, 3)$, find the length of AB.

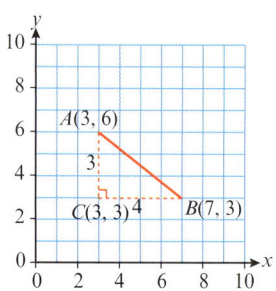

Answer

$AB^2 = AC^2 + CB^2$	$a^2 = b^2 + c^2$ (Pythagoras' theorem)
$AB^2 = 3^2 + 4^2$	Work out each expression.
$= 9 + 16$	
$= 25$	
$\therefore AB = \sqrt{25} = 5$ units	

MATHEMATICAL CONNECTIONS

Pythagoras' theorem is covered in more detail in Chapter 11. Remember though, that in any right-angled triangle the square on the hypotenuse is equal to the sum of the squares on the other two sides. You write this as $a^2 + b^2 = c^2$.

Midpoints

It is possible to find the coordinates of the **midpoint** of the line segment (i.e. the point that is exactly halfway between the two original points).

Consider the following line segment and the points $A(3, 4)$ and $B(5, 10)$.

If you add both x-coordinates and divide by two you get $\dfrac{(3 + 5)}{2} = \dfrac{8}{2} = 4$.

If you add both y-coordinates and divide by two you get $\dfrac{(4 + 10)}{2} = \dfrac{14}{2} = 7$.

This gives a new point with coordinates $(4, 7)$. This point is exactly halfway between A and B.

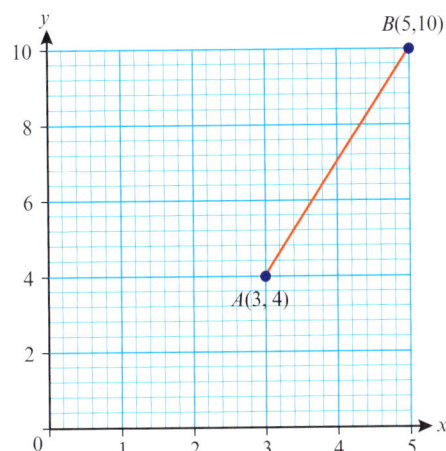

MATHEMATICAL CONNECTIONS

In Chapter 12 you will learn about the *mean* of two or more numbers. To find the midpoint you use the mean of the *x*-coordinates and the mean of the *y*-coordinates.

Exercise 10.7

1   Find the length and the coordinates of the midpoint of the line segment joining each pair of points.

a $(3, 6)$ and $(9, 12)$

b $(4, 10)$ and $(2, 6)$

c $(8, 3)$ and $(4, 7)$

d $(5, 8)$ and $(4, 11)$

e $(4, 7)$ and $(1, 3)$

f $(12, 3)$ and $(11, 4)$

g $(-1, 2)$ and $(3, 5)$

h $(4, -1)$ and $(5, 5)$

i $(-2, -4)$ and $(-3, 7)$

MATHEMATICAL CONNECTIONS

Check that you remember how to deal with negative numbers when adding.

2 Use the graph to find the length and the midpoint of each line segment.

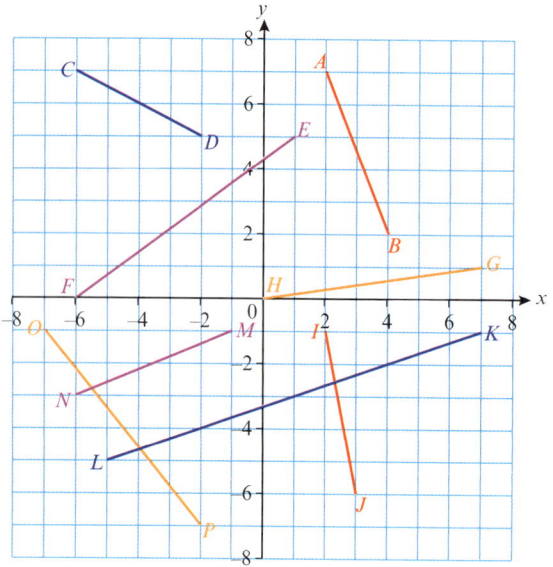

3 Find the distance from the origin to the point $(-3, -5)$.

4 Which of the points $A(5, 6)$ or $B(5, 3)$ is closer to point $C(-3, 2)$?

5 Which is further from the origin, $A(4, 2)$ or $B(-3, -4)$?

6 Triangle ABC has vertices at points $A(0, 0)$, $B(4, -5)$ and $C(-3, -3)$. Find the length of each side.

7 The midpoint of the line segment joining $(10, a)$ and $(4, 3)$ is $(7, 5)$. What is the value of a?

8 The midpoint of line segment DE is $(-4, 3)$. If point D has coordinates $(-2, 8)$, what are the coordinates of E?

MATHEMATICAL CONNECTIONS

There are several ways to find the 'centre' of a triangle. One of them is to join each vertex of the triangle to the midpoint of the opposite side. The resulting lines all cross at the same point. This point is called the 'centroid' and is the centre of gravity of the triangle if the mass is evenly spread over the whole area.

SELF ASSESSMENT

1 Look back at the learning intentions covering straight lines at the start of this chapter. Use these to write a list of criteria that you can use to decide whether you have met the learning intentions.

2 Once you have your list, check your work against the success criteria.

- Place a tick (✓) in the second column if you can find evidence that you have met each one. (You are looking for how your work shows you have achieved the criteria.)

- If you cannot find evidence, write down what you can do to improve in that particular area.

3 Make any improvements that you need to over the next few days and then reassess your work using the same criteria.

TIP

You learnt how to create a table of success criteria in Chapter 3. Read through that section again if you need to.

10.2 Quadratic expressions and equations

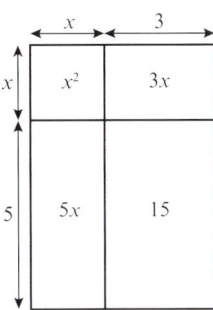

The diagram shows a rectangle of width $(x + 3)$ cm and length $(x + 5)$ cm that has been divided into smaller rectangles.

The area of the whole rectangle is equal to the sum of the smaller areas, so the area of whole rectangle $= (x + 3) \times (x + 5)$.

The sum of smaller rectangle areas: $x^2 + 3x + 5x + 15 = x^2 + 8x + 15$.

This means that $(x + 3) \times (x + 5) = x^2 + 3x + 5x + 15 = x^2 + 8x + 15$ and this is true for *all* values of x.

Notice what happens if you multiply every term in the second bracket by every term in the first:

$$(x + 3)(x + 5) \quad (x + 3)(x + 5) \quad (x + 3)(x + 5) \quad (x + 3)(x + 5)$$

$$\boxed{x^2} \qquad \boxed{5x} \qquad \boxed{3x} \qquad \boxed{15}$$

Notice that the four terms in boxes are exactly the same as the four smaller areas that were calculated before.

Another way to show this calculation is to use a grid:

	x	3
x	x^2	$3x$
5	$5x$	15

You will notice that this is almost the same as the areas method above but it can also be used when the constants are negative, as you will see in Worked example 11.

When you remove the brackets and rewrite the algebraic expression you are **expanding** or multiplying out the brackets. The resulting algebraic expression contains an x^2 term, an x term and a constant term. This is called a **quadratic expression**.

REFLECTION

How do you remember the difference between equations, expressions and formulae?

Write some short notes to help someone who finds this confusing.

The following worked example shows these methods and also a third method for expanding pairs of brackets. You should try each method when working through the next exercise and decide which you find easiest, though you will begin to notice that in fact they are all the same.

WORKED EXAMPLE 11

Expand and simplify.

a $(x + 2)(x + 9)$ **b** $(x − 7)(x + 6)$ **c** $(2x − 1)(x + 9)$

Answers

a $(x + 2)(x + 9)$

$x^2 + 9x + 2x + 18$
$= x^2 + 11x + 18$

In this version of the method you will notice that the arrows have not been included and the multiplication 'arcs' have been arranged so that they are symmetrical and easier to remember.

b

	x	$−7$
x	x^2	$−7x$
$+6$	$6x$	$−42$

$x^2 − 7x + 6x − 42$
$= x^2 − x − 42$

The grid method with a negative value.

c $(2x − 1)(x + 9)$

First: $2x × x = 2x^2$

Outside: $2x × 9 = 18x$

Inside: $−1 × x = − x$

Last: $−1 × 9 = −9$

$2x^2 + 18x − x − 9$
$= 2x^2 + 17x − 9$

A third method uses the mnemonic 'FOIL', which stands for First, Outside, Inside, Last. This means that you multiply the first terms in each bracket together, then the 'outside' pair together (i.e. the first term and last term), then the 'inside' pair together (i.e. the second term and third term) and finally the 'last' pair together (i.e. the second term in each bracket).

LINK

Quadratic expressions and formulae are useful for modelling situations that involve movement, including acceleration, stopping distances, velocity and distance travelled (displacement). These situations are studied in physics but they also have real-life applications in situations such as road or plane accident investigations.

The product of more than two sets of brackets

You can multiply in steps to expand three (or more) sets of brackets. Your answer may contain terms with powers of x greater than 2.

WORKED EXAMPLE 12

Expand and simplify $(3x + 2)(2x + 1)(x - 1)$.

Answers

$(3x + 2)(2x + 1)(x - 1)$

$= (6x^2 + 4x + 3x + 2)(x - 1)$ Expand the first two brackets.

$= (6x^2 + 7x + 2)(x - 1)$ Collect like terms.

$= 6x^3 + 7x^2 + 2x - 6x^2 - 7x - 2$ Multiply each term in the first bracket by each term in the second.

$= 6x^3 + x^2 - 5x - 2$ Collect like terms to simplify.

Exercise 10.8

1 Expand and simplify each of the following.

a $(x + 3)(x + 1)$	**b** $(x + 6)(x + 4)$	**c** $(x + 9)(x + 10)$
d $(x + 3)(x + 12)$	**e** $(x + 1)(x + 1)$	**f** $(x + 5)(x + 4)$
g $(x + 4)(x - 7)$	**h** $(x - 3)(x + 8)$	**i** $(x - 1)(x + 1)$
j $(x - 9)(x + 8)$	**k** $(x - 6)(x - 7)$	**l** $(x - 13)(x + 4)$
m $(y + 3)(y - 14)$	**n** $(z + 8)(z - 8)$	**o** $(t + 17)(t - 4)$
p $(h - 3)(h - 3)$	**q** $\left(g - \dfrac{1}{2}\right)(g + 4)$	**r** $\left(d + \dfrac{3}{4}\right)\left(d - \dfrac{3}{4}\right)$

> **MATHEMATICAL CONNECTIONS**
>
> You will need to remember how to multiply fractions. This was covered in Chapter 5.

2 Find the following products.

a $(4 - x)(3 - x)$	**b** $(3 - 2x)(1 + 3x)$	**c** $(3m - 7)(2m - 1)$
d $(2x + 1)(3 - 4x)$	**e** $(4a - 2b)(2a + b)$	**f** $(2m - n)(-3n - 4m)$
g $\left(x + \dfrac{1}{2}\right)\left(x + \dfrac{1}{4}\right)$	**h** $\left(2x + \dfrac{1}{3}\right)\left(x - \dfrac{1}{2}\right)$	**i** $(7 - 9b)(4b + 6)$
j $(3x - 3)(5 + 2x)$	**k** $(3x^2 + 1)(2x + 3)$	**l** $(5x^2 - 1)(3x^2 - 3)$

3 Expand and simplify each of the following.

a $(2x + 3)(x + 3)$	**b** $(3y + 7)(y + 1)$	**c** $(7z + 1)(z + 2)$
d $(t + 5)(4t - 3)$	**e** $(2w - 7)(w - 8)$	**f** $(4g - 1)(4g + 1)$
g $(8x - 1)(9x + 4)$	**h** $(20c - 3)(18c - 4)$	**i** $(2m - 4)(3 - m)$

> **MATHEMATICAL CONNECTIONS**
>
> Refer to Chapter 1 to remind yourself how to multiply different powers of the same number together.

4 Expand and simplify each of the following.

a $(2x^2 - 4y)(y - x^2)$	**b** $(x + y)(2y^2 - 4x^3)$	**c** $(3x^2 - y)(2x + 3y)$

5 Expand and simplify.

   a $(5x + 2)(3x - 3)(x + 2)$ b $(x - 5)(x - 5)(x + 5)$

   c $(4x - 1)(x + 1)(3x - 2)$ d $(x + 4)(2x + 4)(2x + 4)$

   e $(2x - 3)(3x - 2)(2x - 1)$ f $(3x - 2)^2(2x - 1)$

   g $(x + 2)^3$ h $(2x - 2)^3$

   i $(x^2y^2 + x^2)(xy + x)(xy - x)$ j $\left(\dfrac{1}{3} + \dfrac{x}{2}\right)\left(\dfrac{1}{9} - \dfrac{x^2}{4}\right)\left(\dfrac{1}{3} - \dfrac{x}{2}\right)$

6 The volume of a cuboid can be found using the formula $V = lwh$, where l is the length, w is the width and h is the height.

   A cuboid has length $\left(2x + \dfrac{1}{2}\right)$ m, width $(x - 2)$ m and height $(x - 2)$ m.

   a   Write an expression for the volume of the cuboid in factor form.

   b   Expand the expression.

   c   Determine the volume of the cuboid when $x = 2.2$ m.

> **REFLECTION**
>
> Many people make errors with negative signs when expanding brackets. List two things you can do to make sure you don't make those mistakes.

Squaring a binomial

$(x + y)^2$ means $(x + y)(x + y)$

To find the product, you can use the method you learnt earlier.

$(x + y)(x + y) = x^2 + xy + xy + y^2 = x^2 + 2xy + y^2$

However, you should be able to expand by just noticing that:

• the first term is the square of the first term (x^2)

• the middle term is twice the product of the middle terms $(2xy)$

• the last term is the square of the last term (y^2).

> **MATHEMATICAL CONNECTIONS**
>
> You already know from Chapter 1 that to 'square' a number means to multiply it by itself.

Exercise 10.9

1 Find the square of each binomial. Try to do this by inspection first and then check your answers.

   a $(x - y)^2$ b $(a + b)^2$ c $(2x + 3y)^2$ d $(3x - 2y)^2$

   e $(x + 2y)^2$ f $(y - 4x^2)^2$ g $(x^2 - y^2)^2$ h $(2 + y^3)^2$

   i $(-2x - 4y^2)^2$ j $\left(\dfrac{1}{2x} - \dfrac{1}{4y}\right)^2$ k $\left(\dfrac{3x}{4} - \dfrac{y}{2}\right)^2$ l $\left(a + \dfrac{1}{2}b\right)^2$

   m $(-ab - c^4)^2$ n $(3x^2y - 1)^2$ o $\left(\dfrac{2x}{3} + 4y\right)^2$ p $[-(x - 3)]^2$

2 Simplify.

   a $(x - 2)^2 - (x - 4)^2$ b $(x + 2)(x - 2) - (3 - x)(5 + x)$

   c $(y + 2x)^2 + (2x - y)(-y + 2x)$ d $\dfrac{1}{2}(3x - 2)\left(\dfrac{x}{3} + 2\right)$

   e $3(x + 2)(2x + 0.6)$ f $(\sqrt{2x} - y)(\sqrt{2x} + y) - (4x - y)^2$

   g $(x + 4)(x - 5) - 2(x - 1)^2$ h $(2x - y)^2 + (x - 2y)(x + 2y) - (x + 4y)^2$

   i $-2x(x + 1)^2 - (x - 5)(-3x)$ j $(3 + 2x)^2 - 5(5x + 2)$

3   Evaluate each expression when $x = 4$.

   a $(x + 7)(x - 7) - x^2$ **b** $x^2 - (x - 3)(x + 3)$

   c $(3 + 2x)^2 - (2x + 3)(2x - 3)$ **d** $(x + 2)^2$

   e $(x^2 + 3)(x - 4)$ **f** $(2x + 3)^2 - 4(x + 1)(2 - 3x)$

Factorising simple quadratic expressions

Look again at the expansion of $(x + 2)(x + 9)$, which gave $x^2 + 11x + 18$:

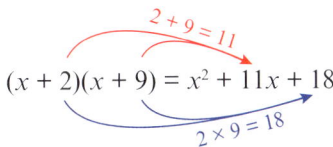

Here the two numbers add to give the coefficient of x in the final expression and the two numbers multiply to give the constant term.

This works whenever there is just one x in each bracket.

WORKED EXAMPLE 13

Expand and simplify.

a $(x + 6)(x + 12)$ **b** $(x + 4)(x - 13)$

Answers

a $(x + 6)(x + 12) = x^2 + 18x + 72$ $6 + 12 = 18$ and $6 \times 12 = 72$ so this gives $18x$ and 72.

b $(x + 4)(x - 13) = x^2 - 9x - 52$ $4 + -13 = -9$ and $4 \times -13 = -52$ so this gives $-9x$ and -52.

If you use the method in worked example 13 and work backwards you can see how to put a quadratic expression back into brackets. Note that the coefficient of x^2 in the quadratic expression must be 1 for this to work.

Consider the expression $x^2 + 18x + 72$ and suppose that you want to write it in the form $(x + a)(x + b)$.

From the worked example you know that $a + b = 18$ and $a \times b = 72$.

Now $72 = 1 \times 72$ but these two numbers don't add up to give 18.

However, $72 = 6 \times 12$ and $6 + 12 = 18$.

So, $x^2 + 18x + 72 = (x + 6)(x + 12)$.

The process of putting a quadratic expression back into brackets like this is called factorisation.

WORKED EXAMPLE 14

Factorise completely:

a $x^2 + 7x + 12$ **b** $x^2 - 6x - 16$

c $x^2 - 8x + 15$ **d** $2x^2 + 14x + 20$

Answers

a $12 = 1 \times 12$ You need two numbers that multiply to give 12 and add to give 7.

     $12 = 2 \times 6$ These don't add to give 7.

     $12 = 3 \times 4$ and $3 + 4 = 7$ These don't add to give 7.

     So, $x^2 + 7x + 12 = (x + 3)(x + 4)$ These multiply to give 12 and add to give 7.

b $-8 \times 2 = -16$ and $-8 + 2 = -6$ You need two numbers that multiply to give −16 and add to give −6.

     So, $x^2 - 6x - 16 = (x - 8)(x + 2)$ Since they multiply to give a negative answer, one of the numbers must be negative and the other must be positive. (Since they add to give a negative number, the larger of the two numbers must be negative.)

c $-5 \times -3 = 15$ and $-5 + -3 = -8$ You need two numbers that multiply to give 15 and add to give −8. Since they multiply to give a positive value but add to give a negative then both must be negative.

     So, $x^2 - 8x + 15 = (x - 3)(x - 5)$

d $2x^2 + 14x + 20$ There is a common factor of 2 in all the terms.

     $= 2(x^2 + 7x + 10)$ Remove this then find the factors that give 7 and 10.

     $= 2(x + 5)(x + 2)$ $5 \times 2 = 10$ and $5 + 2 = 7$

> **TIP**
>
> List the factor pairs of 12.
>
> (If you spot which pair of numbers works straight away then you don't need to write out all the other factor pairs.)

MATHEMATICAL CONNECTIONS

You have already seen in Chapter 1 that positive whole numbers are either prime or can be written as the product of two or more other numbers. The process of writing a number as a product like this is also known as 'factorisation'. In fact, factorisation is the process of writing something as the product of two or more factors in **any** context.

Exercise 10.10

1 Factorise each of the following.

a $x^2 + 14x + 24$ b $x^2 + 3x + 2$ c $x^2 + 7x + 12$

d $x^2 + 12x + 35$ e $x^2 + 12x + 27$ f $x^2 + 7x + 6$

g $x^2 + 11x + 30$ h $x^2 + 10x + 16$ i $x^2 + 11x + 10$

j $x^2 + 8x + 7$ k $x^2 + 24x + 80$ l $x^2 + 13x + 42$

2 Factorise each of the following.

a $x^2 - 8x + 12$ b $x^2 - 9x + 20$ c $x^2 - 7x + 12$

d $x^2 - 6x + 8$ e $x^2 - 12x + 32$ f $x^2 - 14x + 49$

g $x^2 - 8x - 20$ h $x^2 - 7x - 18$ i $x^2 - 4x - 32$

j $x^2 + x - 6$ k $x^2 + 8x - 33$ l $x^2 + 10x - 24$

3 Factorise each of the following.

a $y^2 + 7y - 170$ b $p^2 + 8p - 84$ c $w^2 - 24w + 144$

d $t^2 + 16t - 36$ e $v^2 + 20v + 75$ f $3x^2 + 21x + 36$

g $5x^2 - 5x - 10$ h $3x^2 - 9x - 30$ i $3x^2 - 6x + 3$

j $2x^2 - 14x - 36$ k $-2x^2 - 14x - 24$ l $x^2 - 100$

REFLECTION

When you look for your pair of integers, think about the factors of the constant term first. Then choose the pair that adds up to the x term in the right way. Write down a way to help you remember to do this.

Difference between two squares

The very last question in the previous exercise was a special kind of quadratic. To factorise $x^2 - 100$ you must notice that $x^2 - 100 = x^2 + 0x - 100$.

Now, continuing as in Worked example 14:

$10 \times -10 = -100$ and $-10 + 10 = 0$, so $x^2 + 0x - 100 = (x - 10)(x + 10)$.

Now think about a more general case in which you try to factorise $x^2 - a^2$.

Notice that $x^2 - a^2 = x^2 + 0x - a^2$.

Since $a \times -a = -a$ and $a + -a = 0$, this leads to:

$x^2 - a^2 = (x - a)(x + a)$

You must remember this special case. This kind of expression is called the **difference between two squares**.

LINK

Although the difference between two squares may seem like a very small part of quadratic expressions it is, in fact, a very important one. Beyond Cambridge IGCSE level, mathematicians use the difference between two squares to solve advanced problems in an area of mathematics known as 'complex numbers', where we start to understand the meaning of square roots of negative numbers!

TIP

Note that the difference 'between' two squares can also be called the difference 'of' two squares. It doesn't matter which you use.

WORKED EXAMPLE 15

Factorise the following using the difference between two squares:

a $x^2 - 49$ **b** $x^2 - \dfrac{1}{4}$ **c** $16y^2 - 25w^2$

Answers

a $49 = 7^2$

$x^2 - 49 = x^2 - 7^2$

$\qquad = (x - 7)(x + 7)$

Use the formula for the difference between two squares:
$x^2 - a^2 = (x - a)(x + a)$.
You know that $\sqrt{49} = 7$ so you can write 49 as 7^2. This gives you a^2. Substitute 7^2 into the formula.

b $\left(\dfrac{1}{2}\right)^2 = \dfrac{1}{4}$

$x^2 - \dfrac{1}{4} = x^2 - \left(\dfrac{1}{2}\right)^2$

$\qquad = \left(x - \dfrac{1}{2}\right)\left(x + \dfrac{1}{2}\right)$

$\sqrt{\dfrac{1}{4}}$ is $\dfrac{1}{2}$ so you can rewrite $\dfrac{1}{4}$ as $\left(\dfrac{1}{2}\right)^2$ and substitute it into the formula for the difference between two squares.

c $(4y)^2 = 4y \times 4y = 16y^2$

and

$(5w)^2 = 5w \times 5w = 25w^2$

$16y^2 - 25w^2 = (4y)^2 - (5w)^2$

$\qquad = (4y - 5w)(4y + 5w)$

$16y^2 = (4y)^2$

$25w^2 = (5w)^2$

Substitute in $(4y)^2$ and $(5w)^2$.

Perfect squares

Consider what happens when you expand expressions of the form $(a + b)^2$ and $(a - b)^2$.

$(a + b)^2 = (a + b)(a + b) = a^2 + 2ab + b^2$

$(a - b)^2 = (a - b)(a - b) = a^2 - 2ab + b^2$

Expressions in the form $(a + b)^2$ and $(a - b)^2$ are perfect squares.

You can use the results of the expansions in reverse to factorise expressions that follow this pattern.

WORKED EXAMPLE 16

Factorise:

a $x^2 + 8x + 16$ **b** $x^2 - 10x + 25$

Answers

a $x^2 + 8x + 16$

$= (x + 4)(x + 4)$

$= (x + 4)^2$

Check for the perfect square pattern.

Take the root of each square. Note the signs are both positive.

b $x^2 - 10x + 25$

$= (x - 5)(x - 5)$

$= (x - 5)^2$

Check for the perfect square pattern.

Take the root of each square. Note the signs are both negative.

Exercise 10.11

1 Factorise each of the following.

a	$x^2 - 36$	**b**	$p^2 - 81$	**c**	$w^2 - 16$	**d**	$q^2 - 9$
e	$k^2 - 400$	**f**	$t^2 - 121$	**g**	$x^2 - y^2$	**h**	$81h^2 - 16g^2$
i	$16p^2 - 36q^2$	**j**	$144s^2 - c^2$	**k**	$64h^2 - 49g^2$	**l**	$27x^2 - 48y^2$
m	$200q^2 - 98p^2$	**n**	$20d^2 - 125e^2$	**o**	$x^4 - y^4$	**p**	$xy^2 - x^3$

TIP

Where the numbers are not square, try taking a common factor out first.

2 Factorise each expression.

a	$x^2 + 6x + 9$	**b**	$x^2 + 4x + 4$	**c**	$x^2 - 14x + 49$
d	$x^2 - 18x + 81$	**e**	$36 + 12x + x^2$	**f**	$49 + 14x + x^2$
g	$4 - 4x + x^2$	**h**	$25 - 10x + x^2$	**i**	$4x^2 + 20x + 25$

3 Factorise and simplify $36^2 - 35^2$ without using a calculator.

4 Factorise and simplify $\left(6\frac{1}{4}\right)^2 - \left(5\frac{3}{4}\right)^2$ without using a calculator.

Using factors to solve quadratic equations

You can now use the factorisation method to solve some **quadratic equations**. A quadratic equation is an equation of the form $ax^2 + bx + c = 0$. The method is illustrated in Worked example 17.

WORKED EXAMPLE 17

Solve each of the following equations for x.

a $x^2 - 3x = 0$ **b** $x^2 - 7x + 12 = 0$

c $x^2 + 6x - 4 = 12$ **d** $x^2 - 8x + 16 = 0$

Answers

a $x^2 - 3x = 0$

$x(x - 3) = 0$

Now the key point:

If two or more quantities multiply to give zero, then at least one of the quantities must be zero.

So either $x = 0$ or $x - 3 = 0 \Rightarrow x = 3$.

Check: $0^2 - 3 \times 0 = 0$ (this works).

$3^2 - 3 \times 3 = 9 - 9 = 0$ (this also works)

In fact both $x = 0$ and $x = 3$ are solutions.

> Notice that both terms of the left-hand side are multiples of x so you can take out a common factor of x.

b $x^2 - 7x + 12 = 0$

$(x - 4)(x - 3) = 0$

Therefore either $x - 4 = 0 \Rightarrow x = 4$

or $x - 3 = 0 \Rightarrow x = 3$.

Again, there are two possible values of x.

> Use the factorisation method of Worked example 14 on the left-hand side of the equation.

TIP

When you solve quadratic equations, you should rearrange them so that a zero appears on one side, i.e. so that they are in the form $ax^2 + bx + c = 0$

TIP

There are still two solutions here, but they are identical. When a quadratic equation has solutions, there are always two of them, even if they are both the same!

> **WORKED EXAMPLE 17 CONTINUED**
>
> **c** $x^2 + 6x - 4 = 12$
>
> $\Rightarrow x^2 + 6x - 16 = 0$ (subtract 12 from both sides)
>
> Factorising, you get $(x + 8)(x - 2) = 0$
>
> So either $x + 8 = 0 \Rightarrow x = -8$
>
> or $x - 2 = 0 \Rightarrow x = 2$.
>
> **d** Factorise $\quad x^2 - 8x + 16 = 0$
>
> to give $\quad (x - 4)(x - 4) = 0$
>
> So either $x - 4 = 0 \Rightarrow x = 4$
>
> or $x - 4 = 0 \Rightarrow x = 4$.
>
> Of course these are both the same thing, so the only solution is $x = 4$.

When you rearrange some equations with fractions you get quadratic expressions and you may have to factorise those find the solutions.

> **WORKED EXAMPLE 18**
>
> Solve the equation $\dfrac{x}{x + 3} = \dfrac{8}{x + 6}$
>
> $x(x + 6) = 8(x + 3)$ Multiply both sides by $(x + 6)(x + 2)$.
>
> $x^2 + 6x = 8x + 24$ Expand the brackets. Note there is now a term with x^2.
>
> $x^2 - 2x = 24$ Subtract $8x$ from both sides.
>
> $x^2 - 2x - 24 = 0$ Subtract 24 from both sides.
>
> $(x - 6)(x + 4) = 0$ Factorise the quadratic expression.
>
> Either $\quad x - 6 = 0 \Rightarrow x = 6$
>
> Or $\quad\quad x + 4 = 0 \Rightarrow x = -4$

Exercise 10.12

1 Solve the following equations by factorisation.

  a $\quad x^2 - 9x = 0$ **b** $\quad x^2 + 7x = 0$ **c** $\quad x^2 - 21x = 0$

  d $\quad x^2 - 9x + 20 = 0$ **e** $\quad x^2 + 8x + 7 = 0$ **f** $\quad x^2 + x - 6 = 0$

  g $\quad x^2 + 3x + 2 = 0$ **h** $\quad x^2 + 11x + 10 = 0$ **i** $\quad x^2 - 7x + 12 = 0$

  j $\quad x^2 - 8x + 12 = 0$ **k** $\quad x^2 - 100 = 0$ **l** $\quad t^2 + 16t - 36 = 0$

  m $\quad y^2 + 7y - 170 = 0$ **n** $\quad p^2 + 8p - 84 = 0$ **o** $\quad w^2 - 24w + 144 = 0$

2 Simplify the fractions and solve each equation.

  a $\quad \dfrac{x + 3}{2} = \dfrac{5}{x}$ **b** $\quad \dfrac{1}{x} + \dfrac{5}{x + 4} = 2$ **c** $\quad \dfrac{4}{x + 2} - \dfrac{3}{x + 8} = 1$

  d $\quad \dfrac{x - 3}{7} = \dfrac{1}{x + 3}$ **e** $\quad \dfrac{6}{x + 5} = \dfrac{x}{6}$ **f** $\quad \dfrac{16}{x + 4} = \dfrac{x^2}{x + 4}$

  g $\quad \dfrac{1}{x + 1} = \dfrac{x - 2}{3x - 5}$ **h** $\quad \dfrac{1}{x} + \dfrac{1}{x - 8} = \dfrac{1}{3}$ **i** $\quad \dfrac{x}{x - 1} - \dfrac{2}{x} = \dfrac{1}{x - 1}$

MATHEMATICAL CONNECTIONS

Quadratic expressions and equations have a very special place in mathematics. At the start of the chapter you saw that the motion of satellites in the Earth's atmosphere follow paths that can be described using quadratic expressions. This is true for any object you might throw, where there is gravity. Quadratic expressions are also used to describe circles algebraically, and even the orbits of planets around the Sun can be described using expressions with quadratic terms.

SUMMARY

Do you know …?

The equation of a line tells you how the x- and y-coordinates are related for all points that sit on the line.

The gradient of a line is a measure of its steepness.

The x- and y-intercepts are where the line crosses the x- and y-axes respectively.

The value of m in $y = mx + c$ is the gradient of the line.

The value of c in $y = mx + c$ is the y-intercept.

The x-intercept can be found by substituting $y = 0$ and solving for x.

The y-intercept can be found by substituting $x = 0$ and solving for y.

Two lines with the same gradient are parallel.

The gradients of two perpendicular lines multiply to give -1.

Two brackets can be expanded by multiplying each term in the first bracket by each term in the second bracket.

Some quadratic expressions can be factorised to solve quadratic equations.

Sometimes the two solutions of a quadratic equation might be equal.

Are you able to …?

draw a line from its equation by constructing a table and plotting points

find the gradient, x-intercept and y-intercept from the equation of a line

calculate the gradient of a line from its graph

find the equation of a line if you know its gradient and y-intercept

find the equation of a vertical or horizontal line

calculate the gradient of a line from the coordinates of two points on the line

find the length of a line segment and the coordinates of its midpoint

expand double brackets

expand three or more sets of brackets

factorise a quadratic expression

factorise an expression that is the difference between two squares

solve a quadratic equation by factorising.

Practice questions

1 Expand and simplify each of the following.

    a $(3x - 2)(5x + 4)$ [3]   **b** $(x + 2)(x + 18)$ [3]

    c $(2x + 3)(2x - 3)$ [3]   **d** $(4y^2 - 3)(3y^2 + 1)$ [3]

2 Expand and simplify $\left(x - \dfrac{1}{x}\right)\left(x + \dfrac{1}{x}\right)$.   [3]

3 Expand and simplify.

    a $(2x - 5)^2$ [3]   **b** $(x + 2)^2 + (x - 2)^2$ [3]

4   **a** Expand and simplify $(2 + \sqrt{3})^2$.   [3]

    b Expand and simplify $(1 + \sqrt{3})^2$.   [3]

    c Use your answers to parts (a) and (b) to rationalise the denominator

        for $\dfrac{(2 + \sqrt{3})^2}{(1 + \sqrt{3})^2}$.   [4]

5 Find the equation of each line.

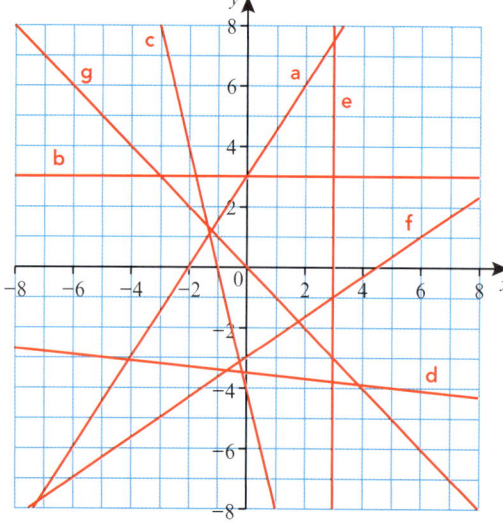

    [14]

6 Find the equation of a line that is:

    a parallel to the line with equation $y = 4x + 1$, and passes through the point $(3, 16)$ [3]

    b parallel to the line with equation $y = -3x + 5$, and passes through the point $(7, -8)$ [3]

    c parallel to the line with equation $y = 0.5x + 0.3$, and passes through the point $(3, 2.4)$.   [3]

7   Given that the vertices of a triangle are $A(2, 10)$, $B(9, 6)$ and $C(-6, -4)$,
show that the triangle is right angled.   [4]

8   **a**   Factorise $m^2 - n^2$.   [2]

   b   Write 9991 as the difference between two square numbers.   [2]

   c   Use your answer to b to write 9991 as a product of prime factors.   [2]

9   Factorise.

   a $x^2 - 15x - 34$ [2]   **b** $16x^2 - 49y^2$ [2]

10   Solve $x^2 + 12x = 28$.   [4]

11   Expand and simplify $(3x + 2)^3$.   [4]

12   **a**   Factorise each of the following.

   i $12x^2 - 6x$ [3]   **ii** $y^2 - 13y + 42$ [2]   **iii** $d^2 - 196$ [2]

   b   Solve the following equations.

   i $12x^2 - 6x = 0$ [3]   **ii** $y^2 - 13y + 30 = -12$ [3]   **iii** $d^2 - 196 = 0$ [3]

13   The diagram shows a square.
Given that the sides are measured in centimetres,
find the possible perimeters of the square.

$x^2 - 3x + 7$

$2x^2 + 3x - 9$ [4]

14   The points A and B have coordinates $(3, 4)$ and $(a, 3)$ respectively.
The length of the line segment AB is $\sqrt{2}$. Find the possible values of a.   [4]

15   Solve $5^{x(x+3)} = 25^{x^2-x-7}$.   [4]

16   **a**   Factorise the expression $x^2 - 50x + 609$.   [2]

   b   Hence or otherwise solve the equation $2x^2 - 100x + 1218 = 0$.
A farmer wants to use 100 m of fencing to build three sides of the rectangular
pen shown in the diagram:

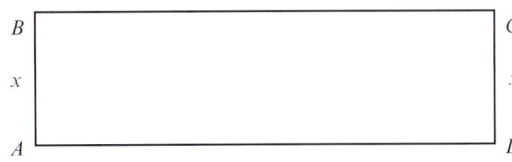

[2]

   c   Find an expression for the length AD in terms of x.   [2]

   d   Find an expression for the area of the pen in terms of x.   [1]

   e   The farmer wants the area of the pen to be exactly 609 square metres.
Using your answer to (d), find and solve an equation for x and determine
all possible dimensions of the pen.   [3]

17 The gradient of the line joining the points $A(3, 2)$ and $B(11, b)$ has gradient $\frac{1}{2}$.

    a   Find the value of b.   [3]

    b   Find the midpoint of A and B.   [2]

    c   Find the equation of a line that passes through the point A, but is perpendicular to the line passing through A and B.   [3]

The line joining A to B passes through the x-axis at the point C and the line perpendicular to AB, through A, passes through the x-axis at the point D.

    d   Find the area of triangle ACD.   [3]

SELF ASSESSMENT

After you have marked your work, consider what you wanted to achieve in this section.

- What were you aiming for?
- Where are you in relation to what you wanted to achieve?
- If you did not meet achieve what you wanted, what do you need to do?

Chapter 11

Pythagoras' theorem and similar shapes

IN THIS CHAPTER YOU WILL:

- use Pythagoras' theorem to find unknown sides of right-angled triangles

- use Pythagoras' theorem to solve problems

- decide whether or not triangles are mathematically similar

- use properties of similar triangles to solve problems

- find unknown lengths in similar figures

- use the relationship between sides and areas of similar figures to find missing values

- recognise similar solids

- calculate the volume and surface area of similar solids

- recognise whether shapes are congruent or not.

Pythagoras' theorem is very important in navigation. A pilot will need to use Pythagoras' theorem to calculate the distance to a landing place 300 km west and 200 km north. Similarly, a delivery driver looking for the most efficient route to make deliveries will often use software to work out the shortest possible distances. Pythagoras' theorem will be vital to that software.

GETTING STARTED

1 Calculations for Pythagoras' theorem involve lots of squares and square roots. Check you know how to use the $\sqrt{\ }$ button on your calculator by confirming the answers to these calculations.

a $\sqrt{9} = 3$ **b** $\sqrt{1.96} = 1.4$

c $\sqrt{2.34} = 1.53$ (to 2 d.p.)   **d** $\sqrt{9 + 16} = 5$

e $\sqrt{25 + 144} = 13$ **f** $\sqrt{6^2 + 8^2} = 10$

g $\sqrt{15 - 6} = 3$ **h** $\sqrt{10.3^3 - 8.6^2} = 5.67$ (to 2 d.p.)

i $\sqrt{1.44} + 3.5 = 4.7$

2 Calculate the following, giving your answers to 2 decimal places unless the answer is exact.

a $\sqrt{121}$ **b** $\sqrt{6.25}$ **c** $\sqrt{5.67}$

d $\sqrt{32 + 17}$ **e** $\sqrt{10^2 + 24^2}$ **f** $\sqrt{28.1^2 - 4.2^2}$

3 The answers to parts (d), (e) and (f) in question 1 are all positive integers. When three positive integers a, b and c satisfy $a^2 + b^2 = c^2$ they are called a *Pythagorean triple*. Do some research to find some others and try to learn to recognise some.

4 **a** Copy and complete this table by substituting different values of a into the expressions.

	a	$b = \dfrac{a^2 - 1}{2}$	$c = \dfrac{a^2 + 1}{2}$
i	3		
ii	5		
iii	7		
iv	9		

b Test whether the sets of numbers are Pythagorean triples.

c What happens for other odd values of a? What happens if $a = 1$?

KEY WORDS

congruent

hypotenuse

scale factor

similar

11.1 Pythagoras' theorem

Centuries before Pythagoras was alive, the Egyptians knew that if they tied knots in a rope at regular intervals, as in the diagram, they would produce a perfect right angle.

If you are given a right-angled triangle and asked to calculate the length of an unknown side, you can do this using Pythagoras' theorem if you know the lengths of the other two sides.

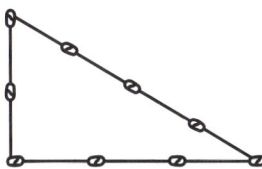

Learning the rules

Pythagoras' theorem describes the relationship between the sides of a right-angled triangle.

The longest side – the side that does not touch the right angle – is known as the **hypotenuse**.

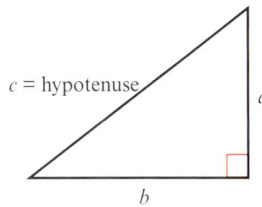

For this triangle, Pythagoras' theorem states that $a^2 + b^2 = c^2$.

In words this means that the square on the hypotenuse is equal to the sum of the squares on the other two sides. Notice that the square of the hypotenuse is the subject of the equation. This should help you to remember where to place each number.

> **TIP**
>
> You need to remember Pythagoras' theorem.

WORKED EXAMPLE 1

Find the value of x in each of these triangles. Give your answers to 1 decimal place where appropriate.

a
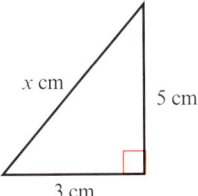

b
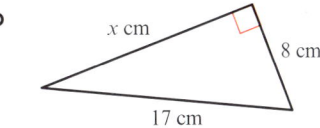

Answers

a $a^2 + b^2 = c^2$

$3^2 + 5^2 = x^2$

$9 + 25 = x^2$

$\Rightarrow x^2 = 34$

$x = \sqrt{34} = 5.8309\ldots$

is approximately equal to 5.8 cm (1 d.p.)   Round your final answer to 1 decimal place.

b $a^2 + b^2 = c^2$

$8^2 + x^2 = 17^2$

$64 + x^2 = 289$ You need to find a shorter side, so rearrange the formula to make x^2 the subject.

$x^2 = 289 - 64$

$x^2 = 225$

$x = \sqrt{225} = 15$ cm

Checking for right-angled triangles

You can also use Pythagoras' theorem to determine if a triangle is right angled or not. Substitute the values of a, b and c into the formula. If $a^2 + b^2$ does not equal c^2 then it is *not* a right-angled triangle.

MATHEMATICAL CONNECTIONS

At the start of this section, you read that the Ancient Egyptians used knots in a rope to create exact right angles. You can now see that this works because the number of knots on each side of the triangle satisfies Pythagoras' theorem.

WORKED EXAMPLE 2

Use Pythagoras' theorem to decide whether this triangle is right angled.

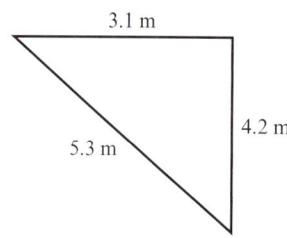

Answer

Check to see if Pythagoras' theorem is satisfied:

$c^2 = a^2 + b^2$

$a^2 + b^2 = 3.1^2 + 4.2^2 = 27.25$

$c^2 = 5.3^2 = 28.09 \neq 27.25$

Pythagoras' theorem is not satisfied, so the triangle is not right angled.

TIP

Notice here the theorem is written as $c^2 = a^2 + b^2$; you will see it written like this or as $a^2 + b^2 = c^2$, but it means the same thing.

TIP

The symbol '$\neq$' means 'does not equal'.

Exercise 11.1

For all the questions in this exercise, give your final answer correct to 3 significant figures where appropriate.

1   Find the length of the hypotenuse in each of the following triangles.

a
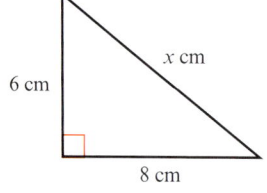

b
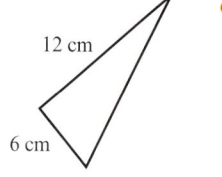

c
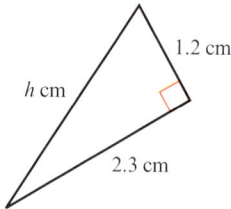

d
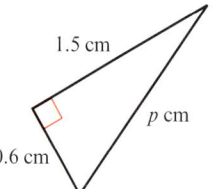

e
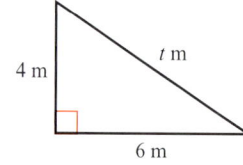

MATHEMATICAL CONNECTIONS

You will notice that some of your answers need to be rounded. Many of the square roots produce irrational numbers. You learnt about these in Chapter 9.

2   Find the values of the unknown lengths in each of the following triangles.

a
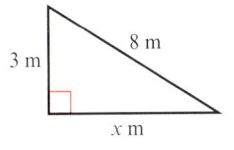
3 m, 8 m, x m

b
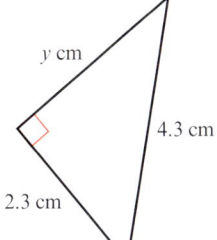
y cm, 4.3 cm, 2.3 cm

c
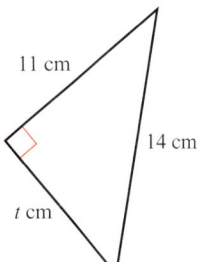
11 cm, 14 cm, t cm

d
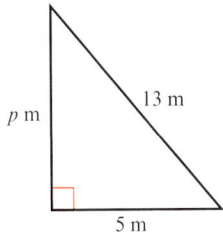
p m, 13 m, 5 m

e
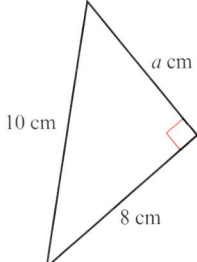
a cm, 10 cm, 8 cm

3   Find the values of the unknown lengths in each of the following triangles.

a
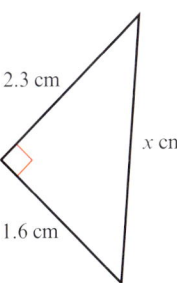
2.3 cm, x cm, 1.6 cm

b
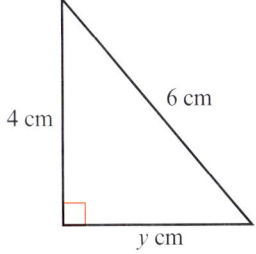
4 cm, 6 cm, y cm

c
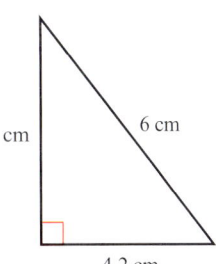
h cm, 6 cm, 4.2 cm

d
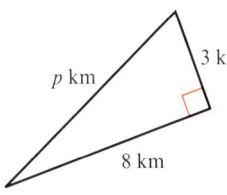
p km, 3 km, 8 km

e
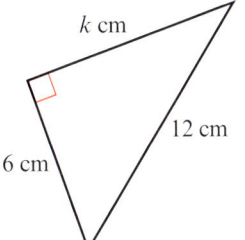
k cm, 12 cm, 6 cm

f
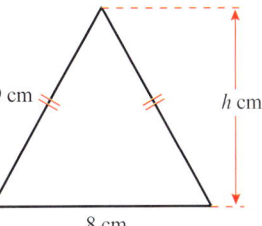
9 cm, h cm, 8 cm

g
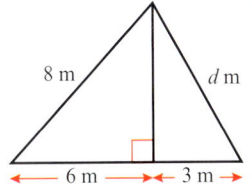
8 m, d m, 6 m, 3 m

h
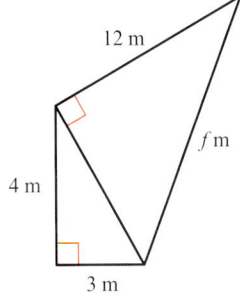
12 m, f m, 4 m, 3 m

4 Use Pythagoras' theorem to decide which of the following triangles are right angled.

a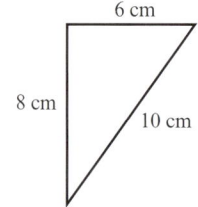

b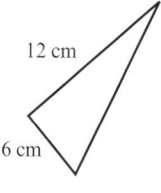

c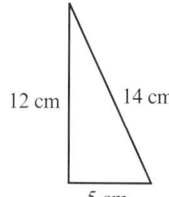

d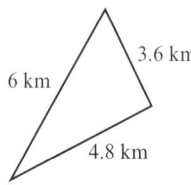

e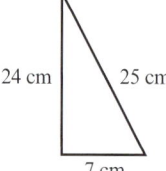

Applications of Pythagoras' theorem

You can use Pythagoras' theorem to solve real-life problems. In each case look carefully for right-angled triangles and draw them separately to show your working clearly.

LINK

Engineers and physicists use right-angled triangles a great deal to solve problems involving forces.

WORKED EXAMPLE 3

The diagram shows a bookcase that has fallen against a wall. The bookcase is 1.85 m tall and it touches the wall at a point 1.6 m above the ground. Calculate the distance of the foot of the bookcase from the wall. Give your answer to 2 decimal places.

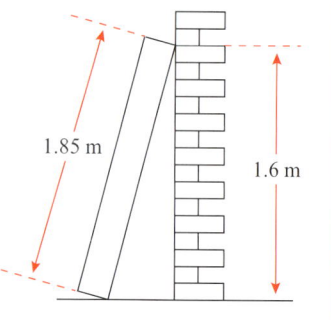

Answer

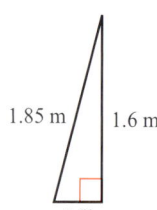

Apply Pythagoras' theorem:

$$a^2 + b^2 = c^2$$

$$x^2 + 1.6^2 = 1.85^2$$

$$x^2 = 1.85^2 - 1.6^2$$

$$= 3.4225 - 2.56$$

$$= 0.8625$$

$$x = \sqrt{0.8625} = 0.93 \text{ cm (2 d.p.)}$$

Think about the triangle that is formed and draw it. Label each side and substitute the side lengths into the formula.

TIP

It is often helpful to draw the triangle as part of your working.

WORKED EXAMPLE 4

Find the distance between the points $A(3, 5)$ and $B(5, 11)$.

Answer

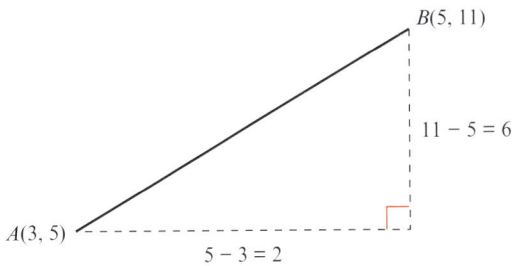

Draw a sketch showing the approximate position of points A and B.

Difference between the y-coordinates $= 11 - 5 = 6$

Difference between the x-coordinates $= 5 - 3 = 2$

$AB^2 = 6^2 + 2^2$

$\quad = 36 + 4$

$\quad = 40$

$AB = \sqrt{40}$

$\quad = 6.32$ units (3 s.f.)

Find the vertical and the horizontal distances.

Apply Pythagoras' theorem.

> **TIP**
>
> It is helpful to draw diagrams when you are given coordinates.

Exercise 11.2

1   The size of a television screen is usually given as the length of the diagonal. The diagram shows the length and width of a television set. Find the length of the diagonal.

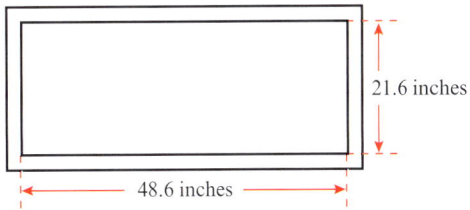

> **TIP**
>
> You won't usually be told to use Pythagoras' theorem to solve problems. You should always check for right-angled triangles in the context of the problem to see if you can use the theorem.

2   The diagram shows a ladder that is leaning against a wall. Find the length of the ladder.

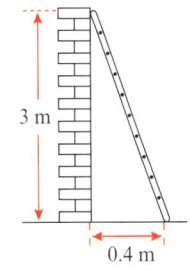

3   Sairda stands at the corner of a rectangular field. The field measures 180 m by 210 m. Sairda walks in a straight line to the opposite corner. How far does Sairda walk?

4   The diagram shows the side view of a shed.
    Calculate the height of the shed.

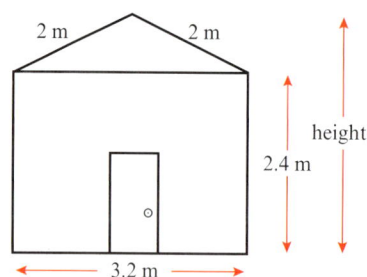

5   The diagram shows a bridge that can be lifted
    to allow ships to pass below. What is the
    distance AB when the bridge is lifted to the
    position shown in the diagram?

    (Note that the bridge divides exactly in half
    when it lifts open.)

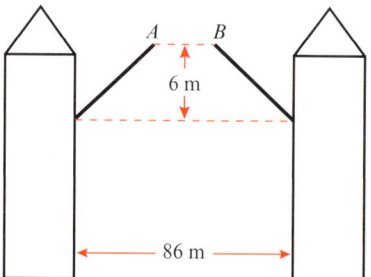

REFLECTION

Look at your answer to question 5. Did you get exactly the same answer as
shown in the answer pages? Sometimes you need to use a decimal answer
you just calculated to find another answer. If you round your first answer it can
mean the final answer isn't quite right. How can you use the memory functions
on your calculator to solve this problem?

6   Find the distance between the points A and B with coordinates:
    a $A(3, 2)$ $B(5, 7)$
    b $A(5, 8)$ $B(6, 11)$
    c $A(-3, 1)$ $B(4, 8)$
    d $A(-2, -3)$ $B(-7, 6)$

7   The diagonals of a square are 15 cm. Find the perimeter of the square.

8   The right-angled triangle ABC is drawn inside a
    circle, as shown in the diagram. The line AB is a
    diameter of the circle. Calculate the radius of the
    circle.

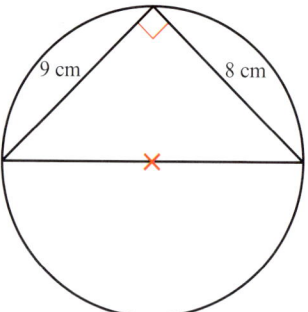

MATHEMATICAL CONNECTIONS

Any triangle drawn
inside a circle with
one side passing
through the centre
will always be right
angled. You will
explore this idea
in more depth in
Chapter 19.

9   An equilateral triangle has sides of length 16 cm. Find the triangle's vertical height
    and the area of the triangle.

APPLY YOUR SKILLS

10   Nasir rows a boat across a river that is 15 m wide. By the time Nasir reaches the other side, the current has carried the boat 18 m downstream. How far is Nasir from the starting point?

11   A membership badge for the *Archimedean Mathematical Society* is constructed by joining a right-angled triangle to a semicircle. Isha has enough paint to cover 50 cm^2 of the badge. Explain whether this is enough to cover the whole badge.

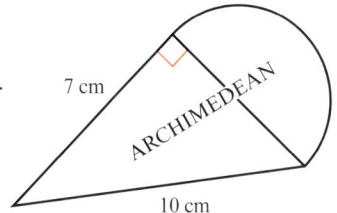

12   A birdhouse needs two 6 cm metal braces for it to be strong and stable. The ends of each brace should be fixed equal distances from the corner. How far from the corner is the end of each brace?

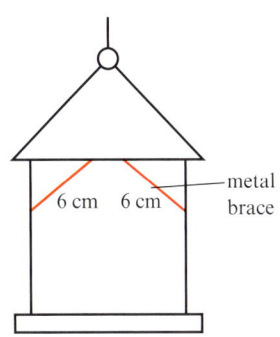

SELF ASSESSMENT

How well do you understand the work on Pythagoras' theorem and its applications?

1   Look back over your completed exercises.

2   Complete these sentences to summarise what went well:

   a   The things that went well were …

   b   I am good at …

   c   I am proud of …

   d   The best bit of my work was …

3   How could you improve your work? Complete these sentences about your own work:

   a   To improve my work I need to …

   b   Next time I work on Pythagoras's theorem I must remember to …

   c   I think I could improve if I focused on …

11.2 Understanding similar triangles

Two mathematically **similar** objects have exactly the same shape and proportions, but may be different in size.

When one shape is enlarged to produce the second shape, each part of the original will correspond to a particular part of the new shape. For triangles, corresponding sides join the same angles. The ratio that compares the measurements of two similar shapes is called the **scale factor**. The scale factor of lengths is the ratio that compares the length of corresponding sides.

All of the following are true for similar triangles:

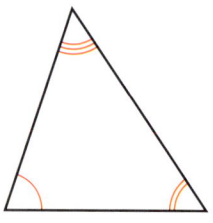 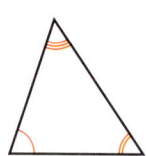

Corresponding angles are equal.

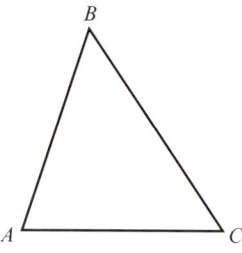 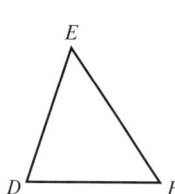

'Internal' ratios of sides are the same for both triangles. For example:

$$\frac{AB}{BC} = \frac{DE}{EF}$$

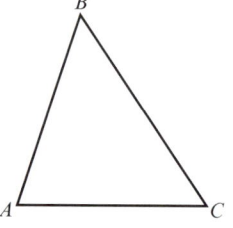 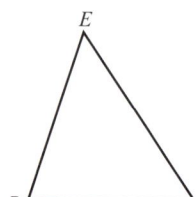

Ratios of corresponding sides are equal:

$$\frac{AB}{DE} = \frac{BC}{EF} = \frac{AC}{DF}$$

If any of these things are true about two triangles, then all of them will be true for both triangles.

INVESTIGATION

Gradients and triangles

You learnt about gradients of lines in Chapter 10.

1   Look back at Chapter 10 and use the ideas you learnt to plot the line with equation $y = 3x - 1$.

2   Mark the points $A(-1, -4)$, $B(1, 2)$ and $C(2, 5)$ on the line.

3   Draw a triangle on your graph, to show the gradient of the line AB and another to show the gradient BC. (Look back to Worked example 3 in Chapter 10 if you need a reminder.)

INVESTIGATION CONTINUED

4   Each of your triangles has two sides that form a right angle. Divide the length of the vertical side by the length of the horizontal side. What is the relationship and how does this relate to the equation of the line?

5   Draw more triangles to represent the gradient of the line and carry out the same calculations. What happens?

6   For each triangle, measure the length of the hypotenuse and divide it by the shortest side length. What do you notice?

7   Discuss with your partner how this shows that the triangles are all similar.

WORKED EXAMPLE 5

Explain why the two triangles shown in the diagram are similar and work out the lengths of x and y.

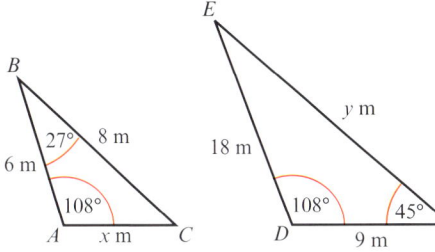

Answer

Angle $ACB = 180° − 27° − 108° = 45°$

Angle $FED = 180° − 45° − 108° = 27°$

Both triangles have exactly the same three angles, so they are similar.

Since the triangles are similar: $\dfrac{DE}{AB} = \dfrac{EF}{BC} = \dfrac{DF}{AC}$

So: $\dfrac{y}{8} = \dfrac{18}{6} = 3 \Rightarrow y = 24\,\text{m}$

and: $\dfrac{9}{x} = \dfrac{18}{6} = 3 \Rightarrow x = 3\,\text{m}$

> **MATHEMATICAL CONNECTIONS**
>
> You learnt that the angle sum in a triangle is always 180° in Chapter 3.

WORKED EXAMPLE 6

The diagram shows a tent that has been attached to the ground using ropes AB and CD. ABF and DCF are straight lines and the sides of the tent BG and CH are vertical. Find the height, EF, of the tent.

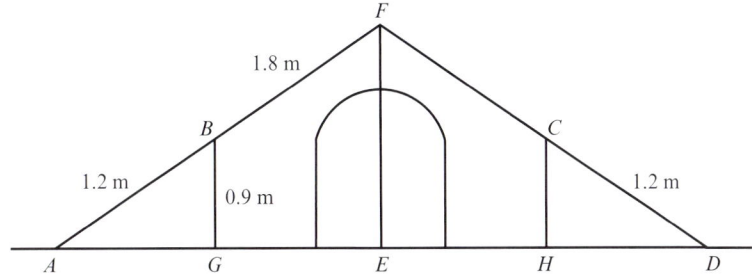

WORKED EXAMPLE 6 CONTINUED

Answer

Consider triangles *ABG* and *AEF*:

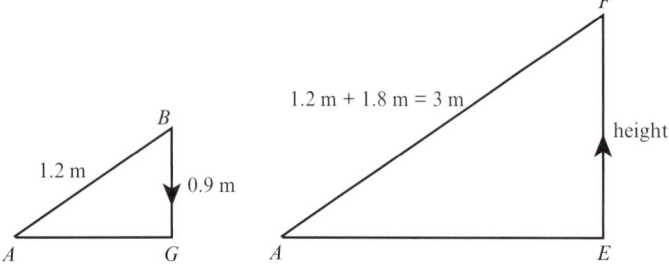

Angle *BAG* = *FAE*	Common to both triangles.
Angle *AGB* = *AEF* = 90°	
Angle *ABG* = *AFE*	*BG* and *FE* are both vertical, hence parallel lines. Angles correspond.

Therefore triangle *ABG* is similar to triangle *AEF*.

So: $\dfrac{\text{height}}{0.9} = \dfrac{3}{1.2} \Rightarrow \text{height} = \dfrac{0.9 \times 3}{1.2} = 2.25\,\text{m}$

Exercise 11.3

1 For each of the following decide whether or not the two triangles in each pair are similar in shape. You should explain your decisions fully.

a

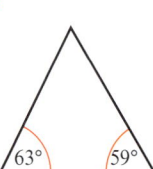

b

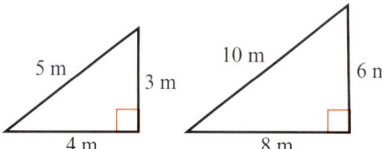

TIP

Always look for corresponding sides (sides that join the same angles).

c

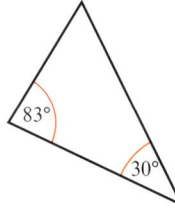

d

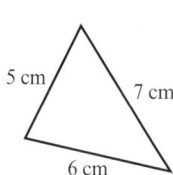

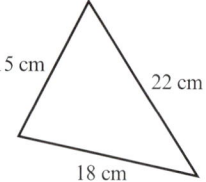

e

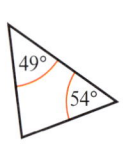

f

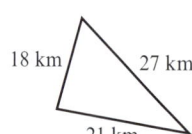

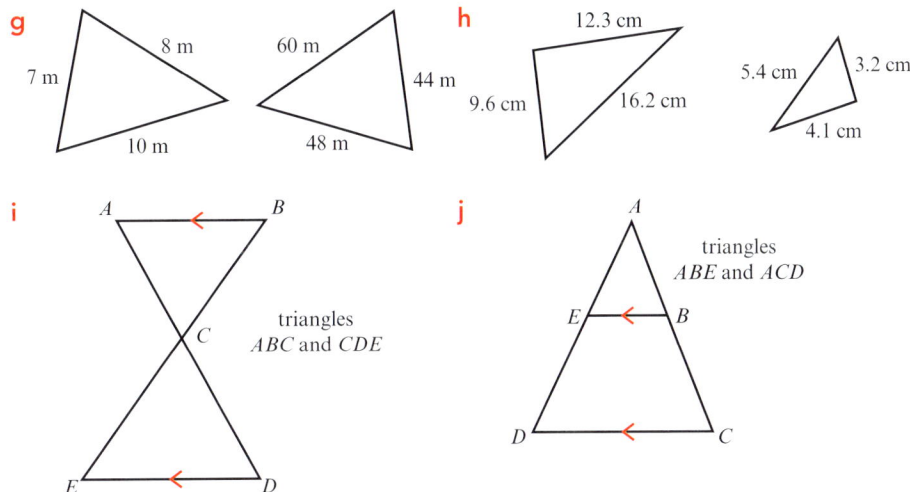

g   8 m   7 m   10 m   60 m   44 m   48 m

h   12.3 cm   9.6 cm   16.2 cm   5.4 cm   3.2 cm   4.1 cm

i   *A*   *B*   *C*   *E*   *D*   triangles *ABC* and *CDE*

j   *A*   *E*   *B*   *D*   *C*   triangles *ABE* and *ACD*

2   The two triangles in each pair in this question are similar. Calculate the unknown (lettered) length in each case.

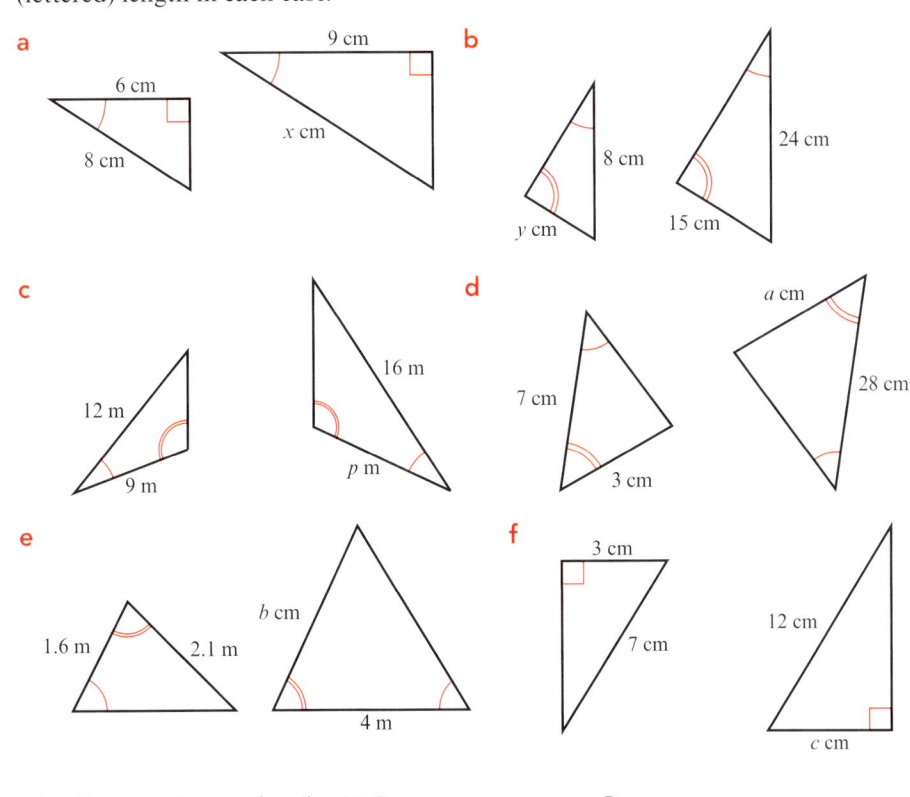

a   6 cm   8 cm   9 cm   *x* cm

b   8 cm   *y* cm   24 cm   15 cm

c   12 m   9 m   16 m   *p* m

d   7 cm   3 cm   *a* cm   28 cm

e   1.6 m   2.1 m   *b* cm   4 m

f   3 cm   7 cm   12 cm   *c* cm

3   The diagram shows triangle *ABC*. If *AC* is parallel to *EF*, find the length of *AC*.

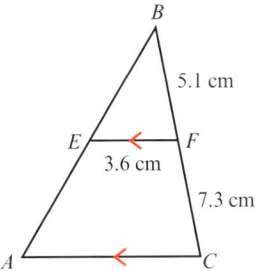

B   5.1 cm   *E*   *F*   3.6 cm   7.3 cm   *A*   *C*

4   In the diagram AB is parallel to DE.
    Explain why triangle ABC is mathematically
    similar to triangle DEC and find the length
    of CE.

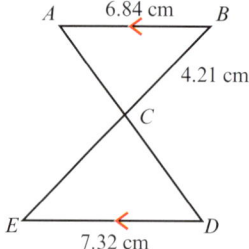

5   The diagram shows a part of a children's
    climbing frame. Find the length of BC.

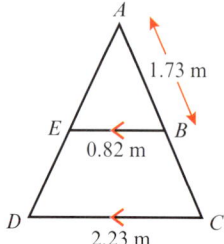

6   Swimmer A and boat B, shown in the diagram, are 80 m apart, and boat B is
    1200 m from the lighthouse C. The height of the boat is 12 m and the swimmer can
    just see the top of the lighthouse at the top of the boat's mast when his head is at
    sea level. What is the height of the lighthouse?

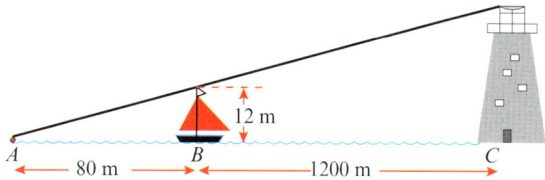

7   The diagram shows a circular cone that has been filled to a depth of 18 cm.
    Find the radius r of the top of the cone.

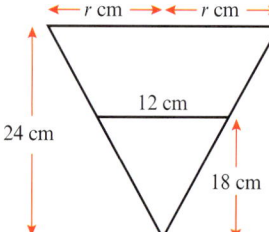

8   The diagram shows a step ladder that is held in place by an 80 cm piece of wire.
    Find x.

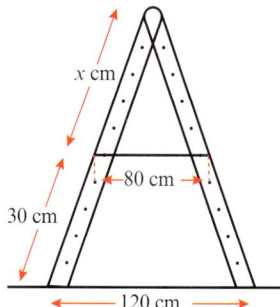

11.3 Understanding similar shapes

In the previous section you worked with similar triangles, but any shapes can be similar. A shape is similar if the ratio of corresponding sides is equal and the corresponding angles are equal. Similar shapes are therefore identical in shape, but can be different sizes.

You can use the ratio of corresponding sides to find unknown sides of similar shapes just as you did with similar triangles.

WORKED EXAMPLE 7

Ahmed has two rectangular flags. One measures 1000 mm by 500 mm, the other measures 500 mm by 350 mm. Are the flags similar in shape?

Answer

$\dfrac{1000}{500} = 2$ and $\dfrac{500}{350} = 1.43$ Work out the ratio of corresponding sides.

$\dfrac{1000}{500} \neq \dfrac{500}{350}$ The ratio of corresponding sides is not equal, therefore the shapes are not similar.

WORKED EXAMPLE 8

Given that the two shapes in the diagram are mathematically similar, find the unknown length x.

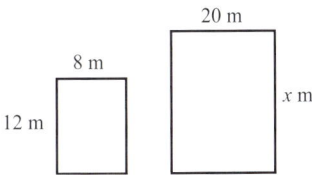

Answer

Using the ratios of corresponding sides: $\dfrac{x}{12} = \dfrac{20}{8} = 2.5$

$\Rightarrow x = 12 \times 2.5 = 30\,\text{m}$

Exercise 11.4

1   Determine whether the shapes in each pair of shapes are similar or not.
    Show your working.

a

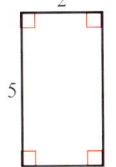

b

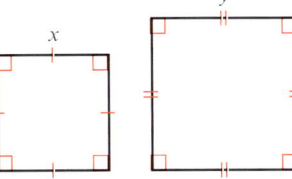

c
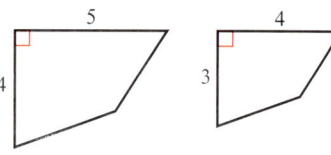

d
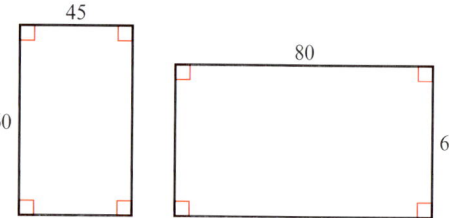

e
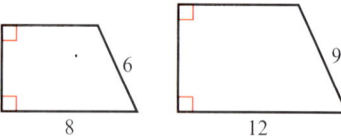

f
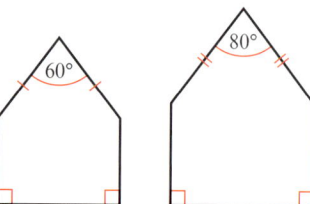

2 The shapes in each pair are mathematically similar to one another.
Calculate the unknown lengths in each case.

a
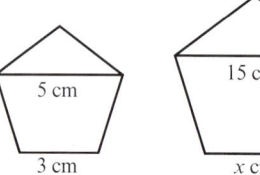

b
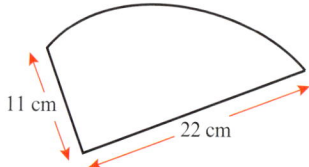

c
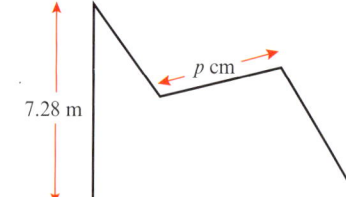

d
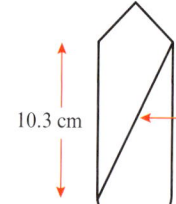
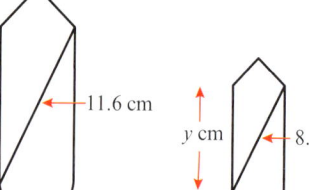

e
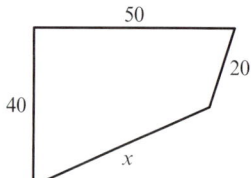

f
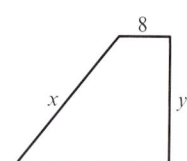
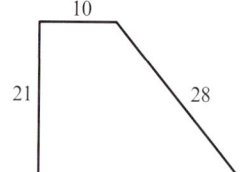

g
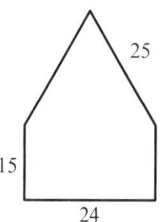

h
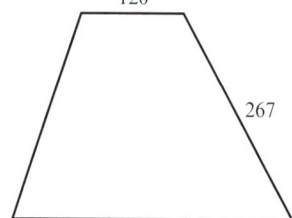
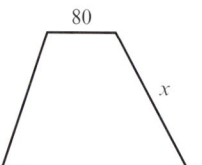

3   Determine the length of *ED*.

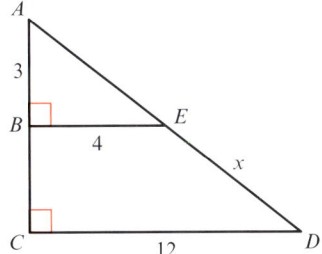

INVESTIGATION

4   **a**   All squares are similar to all other squares. Why is this the case?

b   Why are rectangles not always similar to all other rectangles?

c   Explain why circles are similar to all other circles.

d   You now know that circles are similar to all other circles and all squares are similar to all other squares. Are there any other shapes that behave like this?

REFLECTION

There are two types of similar shape problems:

- problems where you have to prove or decide whether a given set of shapes are similar
- problems where you have to calculate the missing angles and side lengths of similar shapes.

What do you need to do, or remember, to solve each type of problem?

PEER ASSESSMENT

1   If you had to explain similar shapes to someone else, what would you tell them?

Write a short statement or points (you can include simple diagrams) to explain similar shapes to another student.

2   Exchange statements with a partner.

a   Read each other's statements.

b   Tell your partner what you found helpful in their explanation.

c   Was there anything that was not helpful for you? Tell your partner why you found it unhelpful and suggest how they could improve it.

Area of similar shapes

The two shapes in each pair below are similar:

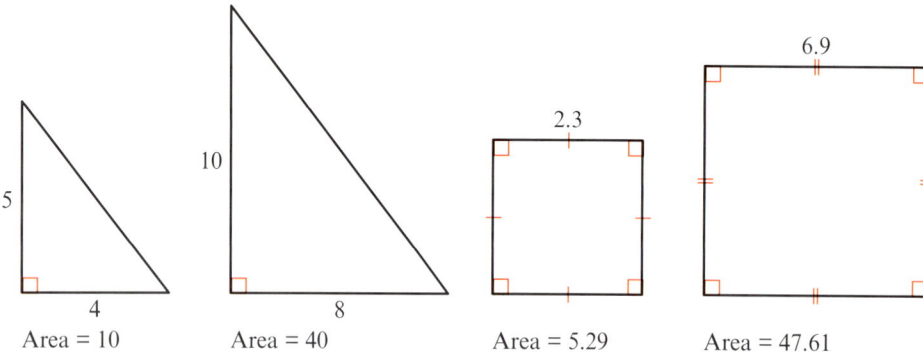

Area = 10   Area = 40   Area = 5.29   Area = 47.61

If you look at the diagrams and the dimensions you can see that there is a relationship between the scale factor for corresponding sides and the area factor.

In similar figures where the ratio of corresponding sides is $a : b$, the ratio of areas is $a^2 : b^2$.

In other words, scale factor of areas = (scale factor of lengths)^2.

WORKED EXAMPLE 9

These two rectangles are similar. What is the ratio of the smaller area to the larger?

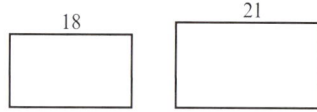

Answer

Ratio of sides = $18 : 21 = 6 : 7$ Simplify the ratio before squaring it.

Ratio of areas = $6^2 : 7^2$ Square the ratio of lengths.

            = $36 : 49$

WORKED EXAMPLE 10

Similar rectangles *ABCD* and *MNOP* have lengths in the ratio $3 : 5$. If rectangle *ABCD* has an area of 900 cm^2, find the area of *MNOP*.

Answer

$\dfrac{\text{Area } MNOP}{\text{Area } ABCD} = \dfrac{5^2}{3^2}$ Square the ratio of lengths.

$\dfrac{\text{Area } MNOP}{900 \text{ cm}^2} = \dfrac{25}{9}$ Simplify and substitute in any known values

$\text{Area } MNOP = \dfrac{25}{9} \times 900$ Solve the equation.

                = 2500 cm^2

The area of MNOP is 2500 cm^2.

WORKED EXAMPLE 11

The shapes below are similar. Given that the area of $ABCD = 48\,cm^2$ and the area of $PQRS = 108\,cm^2$, find the length of diagonal AC in $ABCD$.

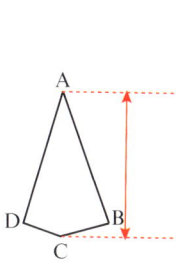
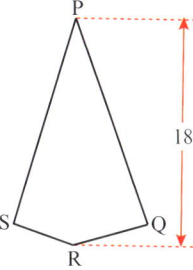

Answer

Let the length of the diagonal be x cm.

$$\frac{48}{108} = \frac{x^2}{18^2} \qquad \text{Square the ratio of lengths.}$$

$$\frac{48}{108} = \frac{x^2}{324}$$

$$\frac{48}{108} \times 324 = x^2 \qquad \text{Simplify and solve.}$$

$$x^2 = 144$$

$$x = 12$$

Diagonal AC is 12 cm long.

Exercise 11.5

1 In each part of this question, the two figures are similar. The area of one figure is given. Find the area of the other.

a

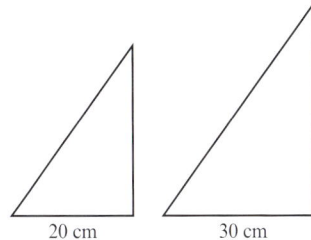

20 cm   30 cm

Area = 187.5 cm²

b

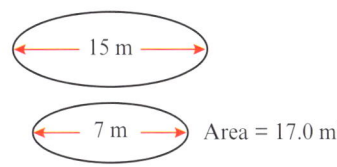

15 m

7 m   Area = 17.0 m²

c

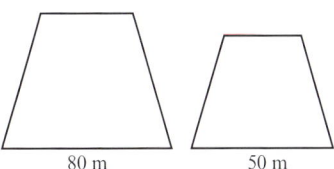

80 m   50 m

Area = 4000 m²

d

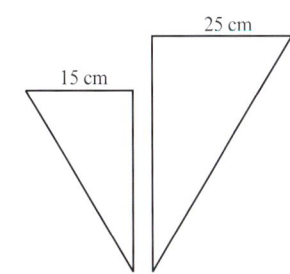

25 cm

15 cm

Area = 135 cm²

2   In each part of this question the areas of the two similar figures are given.
     Find the length of the side marked x in each.

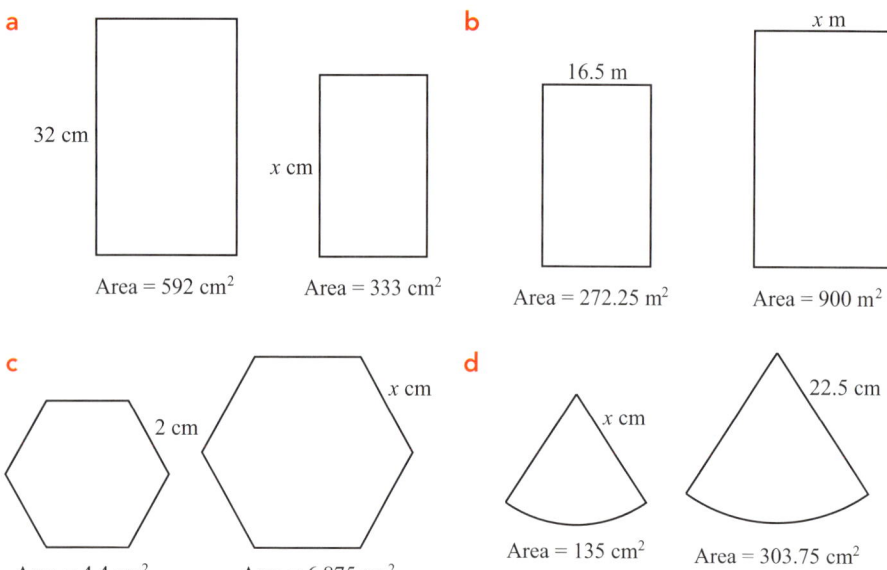

a

32 cm

x cm

Area = 592 cm²   Area = 333 cm²

b

16.5 m

x m

Area = 272.25 m²   Area = 900 m²

c

2 cm

x cm

Area = 4.4 cm²   Area = 6.875 cm²

d

x cm

22.5 cm

Area = 135 cm²   Area = 303.75 cm²

3   Mayumi is making a pattern using a regular pentagon. How will the area of the
     pentagon change if she:
     a   doubles the lengths of the sides?
     b   trebles the lengths of the sides?
     c   halves the lengths of the sides?

4   If the areas of two similar quadrilaterals are in the ratio 64 : 9, what is the ratio of
     matching sides?

Similar solids

Three-dimensional shapes (solids) can also be similar.

Similar solids have the same shape, their corresponding angles are equal and all
corresponding linear measures (edges, diameters, radii, heights and slant heights) are
in the same ratio. As with similar two-dimensional shapes, the ratio that compares the
measurements on the two shapes is called the scale factor.

Volume and surface area of similar solids

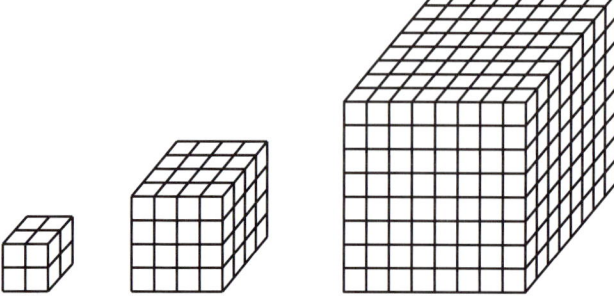

The following table shows the side length and volume of each of these cubes.

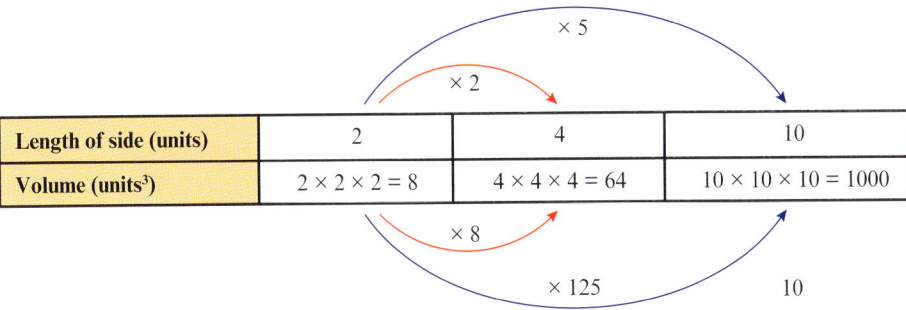

Length of side (units)	2	4	10
Volume (units³)	$2 \times 2 \times 2 = 8$	$4 \times 4 \times 4 = 64$	$10 \times 10 \times 10 = 1000$

Notice that when the side length is multiplied by 2 the volume is multiplied by $2^3 = 8$.

Here, the scale factor of lengths is 2 and the scale factor of volumes is 2^3.

Also, when the side length is multiplied by 5 the volume is multiplied by $5^3 = 125$.

This time the scale factor of lengths is 5 and the scale factor of volumes is 5^3.

In fact, this pattern is true in the general case:

Scale factor of volumes = (scale factor of lengths)³

By considering the surface areas of the cubes you can also see that the rule about the scale factor of areas is still true:

Scale factor of areas = (scale factor of lengths)²

In summary, if two solids (*A* and *B*) are similar:

- the ratio of their volumes is equal to the cube of the ratio of corresponding lengths (edges, diameter, radii, heights and slant heights). In other words:
  $\dfrac{\text{Volume } A}{\text{Volume } B} = \left(\dfrac{a}{b}\right)^3$ where *a* and *b* are corresponding lengths.

- the ratio of their surface areas is equal to the square of the ratio of corresponding linear measures. In other words: $\dfrac{\text{Surface area } A}{\text{Surface area } B} = \left(\dfrac{a}{b}\right)^2$

The following worked examples show how you can use these scale factors.

> **TIP**
>
> Sometimes you are given the scale factor of areas or volumes instead of the scale factor of lengths. You can use square roots or cube roots to find the scale factor of lengths.

WORKED EXAMPLE 12

The cones shown in the diagram are mathematically similar. The smaller cone has a volume of 40 cm³. Find the volume of the larger cone.

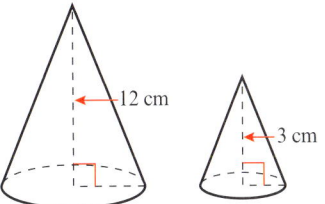

Answer

Scale factor of lengths = $\dfrac{12}{3} = 4$

$\Rightarrow$ Scale factor of volumes = $4^3 = 64$

So the volume of the larger cone = $64 \times 40 = 2560$ cm³.

WORKED EXAMPLE 13

The two shapes shown in the diagram are mathematically similar. If the area of the larger shape is 216 cm^2, and the area of the smaller shape is 24 cm^2, find the length x in the diagram.

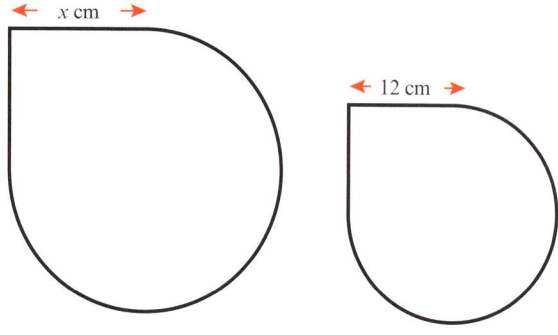

Answer

Scale factor of areas $= \dfrac{216}{24} = 9$

$\Rightarrow$ (Scale factor of lengths)^2 = 9

$\Rightarrow$ Scale factor of lengths = $\sqrt{9}$ = 3

So: $x = 3 \times 12 = 36$ cm

WORKED EXAMPLE 14

A shipping crate has a volume of 2000 cm^3. If the dimensions of the crate are doubled, what will its new volume be?

Answer

$\dfrac{\text{Original volume}}{\text{New volume}} = \left(\dfrac{\text{original dimensions}}{\text{new dimensions}}\right)^3$

$\dfrac{2000}{\text{New volume}} = \left(\dfrac{1}{2}\right)^3$

$\dfrac{2000}{\text{New volume}} = \dfrac{1}{8}$

New volume = 2000 × 8

New volume = 16 000 cm^3

WORKED EXAMPLE 15

The two cuboids A and B are similar. The larger cuboid has a surface area of 608 cm². What is the surface area of the smaller cuboid?

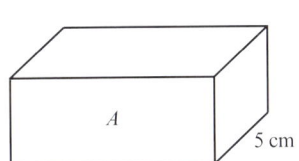 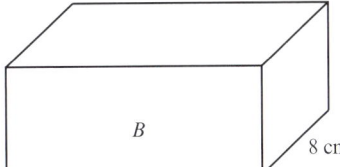

Answer

$$\frac{\text{Surface area } A}{\text{Surface area } B} = \left(\frac{\text{width } A}{\text{width } B}\right)^2$$

$$\frac{\text{Surface area } A}{608} = \left(\frac{5}{8}\right)^2$$

$$\frac{\text{Surface area } A}{608} = \frac{25}{64}$$

$$\text{Surface area } A = \frac{25}{64} \times 608$$

$$\text{Surface area } A = 237.5 \text{ cm}^2$$

Cuboid A has a surface area of 237.5 cm².

Exercise 11.6

1   Copy and complete the statement.

When the dimensions of a solid are multiplied by k, the surface area is multiplied by __ and the volume is multiplied by __.

2   Two similar cubes A and B have sides of 20 cm and 5 cm respectively.

   a   What is the scale factor of A to B?

   b   What is the ratio of their surface areas?

   c   What is the ratio of their volumes?

3   Pyramid A and pyramid B are similar. Find the surface area of pyramid A.

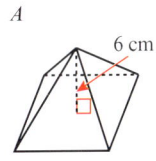   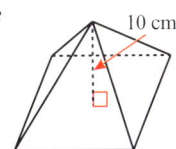

Surface area = 600 cm²

4   Yu has two similar cylindrical metal rods. The smaller rod has a diameter of 4 cm and a surface area of 110 cm². The larger rod has a diameter of 5 cm. Find the surface area of the larger rod.

5 Cuboid X and cuboid Y are similar. The scale factor X to Y is $\frac{3}{4}$.

    a If a linear measure in cuboid X is 12 mm, what is the length of the corresponding measure on cuboid Y?

    b Cuboid X has a surface area of 88.8 cm². What is the surface area of cuboid Y?

    c If cuboid X has a volume of 35.1 cm³, what is the volume of cuboid Y?

6 For each part of this question, the solids are similar. Find the unknown volume.

a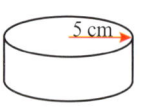

5 cm   12 cm

Volume = 288 cm³

b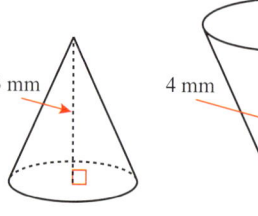

3 mm   4 mm

Volume = 9 mm³

c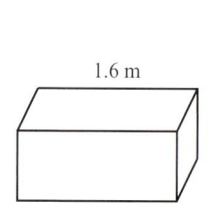

1.6 m   2 m

Volume = 0.384 m³

d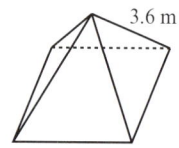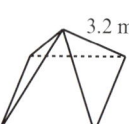

3.6 m   3.2 m

Volume = 80.64 m³

7 Find the unknown quantity for each of the following pairs of similar shapes.

a

3 cm   15 cm

Area = 21 cm²

Area = x cm²

b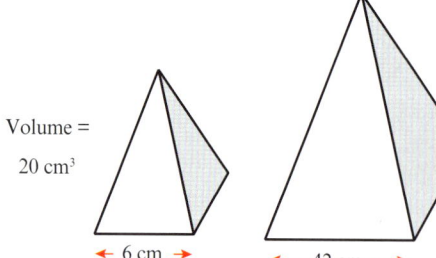

Volume = 20 cm³

Volume = y cm³

6 cm   42 cm

c

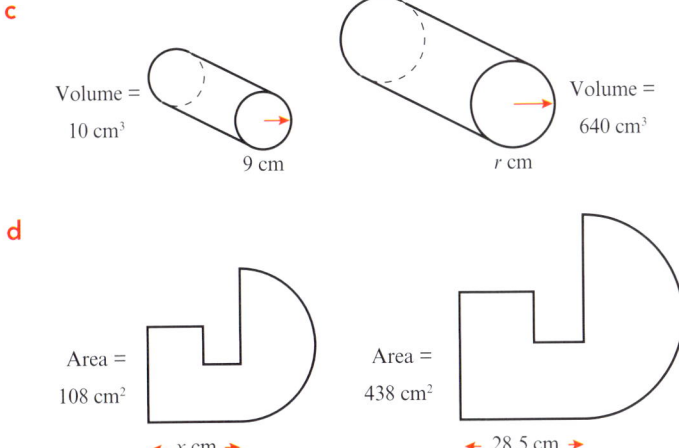

Volume = 10 cm³   9 cm

Volume = 640 cm³ r cm

d

Area = 108 cm²   ← x cm →

Area = 438 cm²   ← 28.5 cm →

APPLY YOUR SKILLS

8   Karen has this set of three dolls. The heights of the dolls are 13 cm, 11 cm and 9 cm. Draw a table to compare the surface area and volume of the three dolls in algebraic terms.

TIP

Organised tables and lists are a useful problem-solving strategy. Include headings for rows and/or columns to make sure your table is easy to understand.

9   A manufacturer is making pairs of weights from metal cones that have been cut along a plane parallel to the base. The diagram shows a pair of these weights.

If the volume of the larger (uncut) cone is 128 cm³ and the volume of the smaller cone cut off the top is 42 cm³ find the length x.

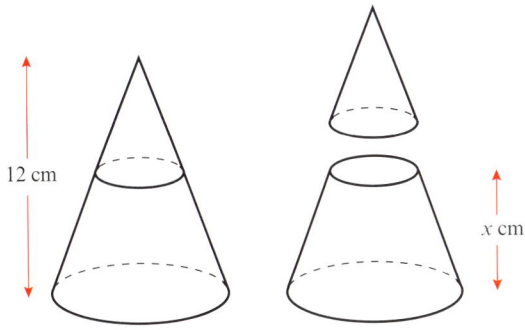

12 cm

x cm

TIP

A cone cut along a plane parallel to its base produces a smaller cone and a solid called a frustum.

11.4 Understanding congruence

Two shapes are **congruent** if they are the same shape and size.

MATHEMATICAL CONNECTIONS

You will meet rotations and reflections in Chapter 19. When an object is reflected or rotated its shape and size remain unchanged. The resulting object is congruent to the original.

If two shapes are congruent then:

- corresponding sides are equal in length
- corresponding angles are equal
- the shapes have the same area.

Look at these pairs of congruent shapes. The corresponding sides and angles on each shape are marked using the same colours and symbols.

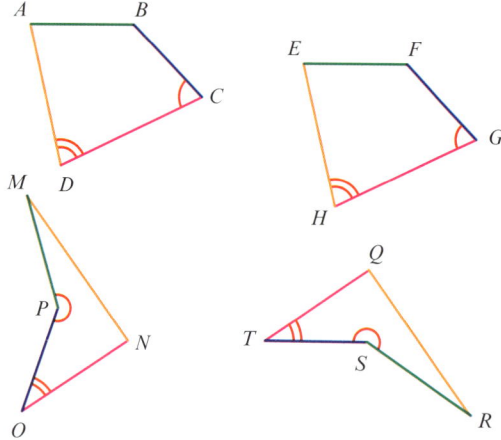

When you make a congruency statement, you name the shape so that corresponding vertices are in the same order.

For the shapes above:

- *ABCD* is congruent to *EFGH*
- *MNOP* is congruent to *RQTS*.

Exercise 11.7

1   These two figures are congruent.

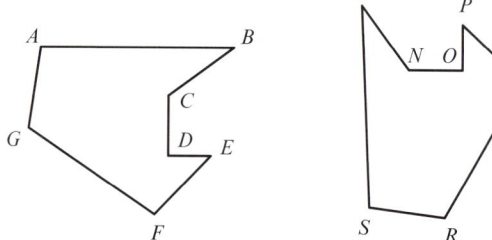

a Which side is equal in length to:

   i *AB*?   **ii** *EF*?   **iii** *MN*?

b Which angle corresponds with:

   i *BAG*?   **ii** *PQR*?   **iii** *DEF*?

c Write a congruency statement for the two figures.

2 Which of the shapes in the box are congruent to each shape given below?
Measure sides and angles if you need to.

a    **b**    **c**    **d**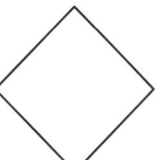

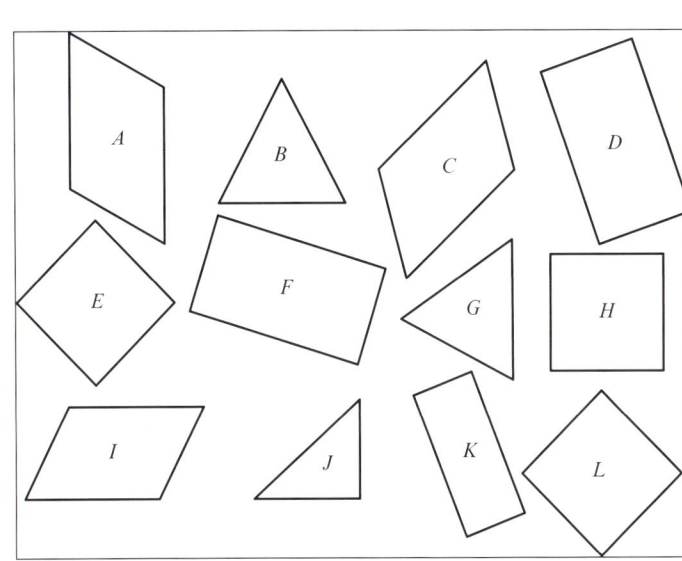

3 For each set of shapes, state whether any shapes are congruent or similar.

a

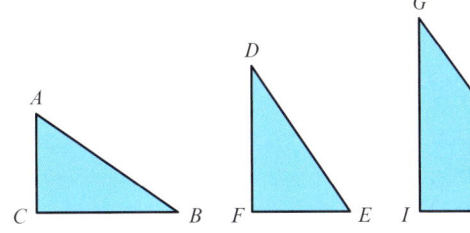

b

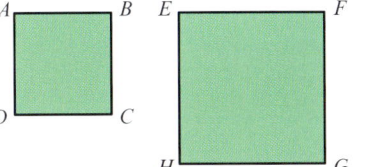 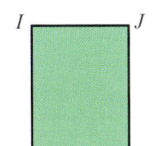

c

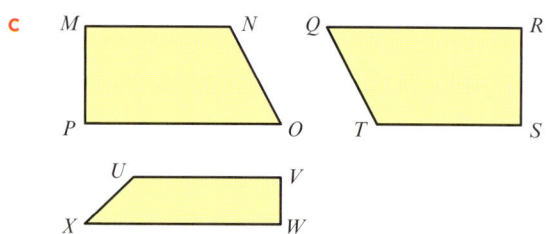

d

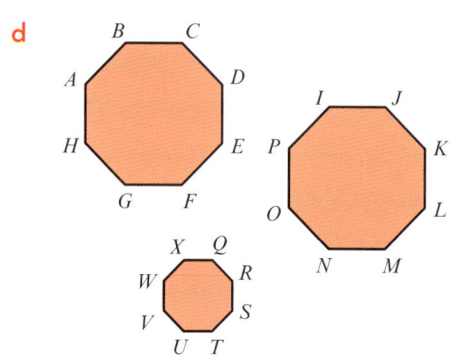

e

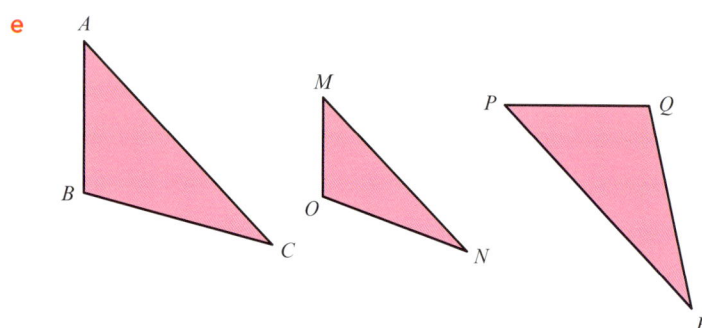

4   Figure *ABCDEF* has *AB* = *BC* = *CD* = *DE*.

Redraw the figure and show how you could split it into:

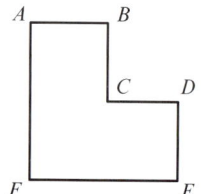

a   two congruent shapes

b   three congruent shapes

c   four congruent shapes.

5   Triangle *FAB* is congruent to triangle *FED*.
Prove that *BFDC* is a kite.

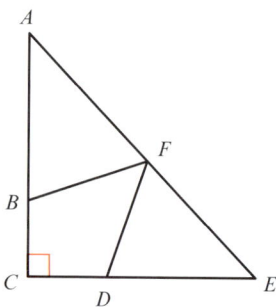

APPLY YOUR SKILLS

6   Two people in different parts of a park take a walk. They both walk in a straight line for 1000 metres, then they turn 110° right and continue to walk straight for a while before making a 120° turn to right. From there they walk back in a straight line to their starting point. Is it possible that they walked in congruent triangular paths? Explain your answer.

SUMMARY

Do you know …?

The longest side of a right-angled triangle is called the hypotenuse.

The square of the hypotenuse is equal to the sum of the squares of the two shorter sides of the triangle.

Similar shapes have equal corresponding angles and the ratios of corresponding sides are equal.

If shapes are similar and the lengths of one shape are multiplied by a scale factor of n:

*   then the areas are multiplied by a scale factor of n^2

*   and the volumes are multiplied by a scale factor of n^3.

Congruent shapes are exactly equal to each other.

Are you able to …?

use Pythagoras' theorem to find an unknown side of a right-angled triangle

use Pythagoras' theorem to solve real-life problems

decide whether or not two objects are mathematically similar

use the fact that two objects are similar to calculate:

*   unknown lengths

*   areas or volumes

recognise whether two shapes are congruent or not.

Practice questions

1   Habib takes a short cut from his home (H) to the bus stop (B) along a footpath HB.

How much further would it be for Habib to walk to the bus stop by going from H to the corner (C) and then from C to B?

Give your answer in metres.   [4]

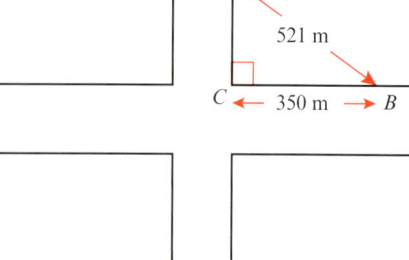

2   A ladder is standing on horizontal ground and rests against a vertical wall. The ladder is 4.5 m long and its foot is 1.6 m from the wall. Calculate how far up the wall the ladder will reach. Give your answer correct to 3 significant figures.   [3]

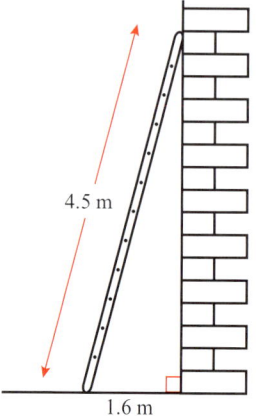

3   A rectangular box has a base with internal dimensions 21 cm by 28 cm, and an internal height of 12 cm. Calculate the length of the longest straight thin rod that will fit:

a   on the base of the box   [3]

b   in the box.   [3]

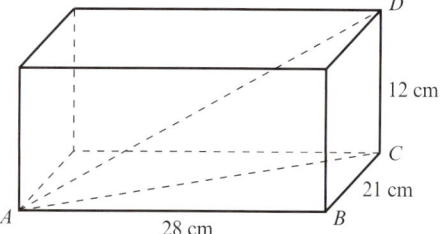

4   The right-angled triangle in the diagram has sides of length $7x$ cm, $24x$ cm and 150 cm.

a   Show that $x^2 = 36$.   [3]

b   Calculate the perimeter of the triangle.   [3]

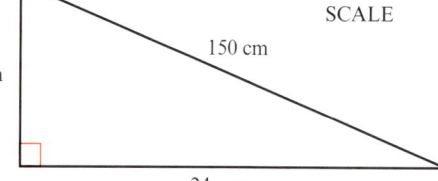

5   Josh and Sarah walk from the same point. Josh walks due west and Sarah walks due north.

After 1 hour, Josh is 4.2 km from the starting point and Sarah is 5.6 km from Josh in a straight line.

How far is Sarah from the starting point?   [3]

6   A plant feeder is shaped like a cone with height 12 cm.

When the plant feed is 8 cm deep, the diameter of the circular surface of the feed is 6 cm. Find the radius of the cone.   [3]

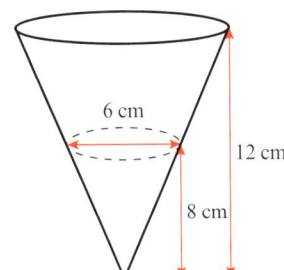

7   The diagram shows a right-angled triangle ABC.

   a   Explain why triangles ABC, CBD and ACD are similar.   [2]

   b   Show that $a^2 = ce$ and find an equivalent expression for b.   [3]

   c   Use your answers to prove that $a^2 + b^2 = c^2$.   [3]

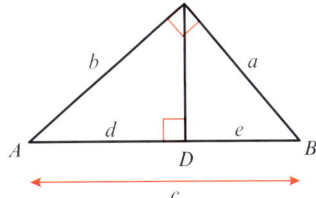

8   Chocolate bars come in a regular size that weighs 125 g and a giant size that weighs 343 g, the bars are similar in shape.

   a   If the regular bar is 12 cm long, find the length of the giant bar.   [3]

   b   The wrapper of the giant bar has a surface area of 201.6 cm², find the area of wrapping paper required for the regular bar. Give your answer to 3 s.f.   [3]

9   a   Show that if

$$a = uv$$

$$b = \frac{u^2 - v^2}{2}$$

$$c = \frac{u^2 + v^2}{2}$$

   then the triple (a, b, c) satisfies Pythagoras' theorem.   [4]

   b   Use the formulae given in part (a) to find a Pythagorean triple where the smallest integer in the triple is 17.   [3]

   c   Show that if a is prime and a is a member of a Pythagorean triple, then the other two numbers in the triple will differ by 1.   [3]

SELF ASSESSMENT

Look critically at your worked solutions to the practice questions.

Answer these questions about your work.

Did you …

*   choose the right methods and strategies?

*   show how you arrived at your solutions?

*   give reasons for any statements you made?

> Chapter 12

Averages and measures of spread

IN THIS CHAPTER YOU WILL:

- calculate the mean, median and mode of sets of data

- calculate and interpret the range as a measure of spread

- interpret the meaning of average and range, and use them to compare sets of data

- construct and use frequency distribution tables for grouped data

- calculate and work with quartiles

- divide data into quartiles and calculate the interquartile range

- identify the modal class from a grouped frequency distribution.

You can present statistical information in many different ways. If you choose a more complicated method, you increase the chance that another person will misinterpret the information. In the image on the previous page, several graphs are shown at once. Can you think when this might be helpful? When might it be unhelpful?

You do not always need to draw a diagram. Sometimes you present the information using a numerical summary. In this chapter you will explore different ways to present and compare data. Before you start, think about what statistical methods you already know.

GETTING STARTED

Rohan records the number of hours, to the nearest half hour, he spends reading each week for seven weeks:

    1.5   1.5   2   3.5   5   5.5   11.5

Rohan says to Jess, 'On average, I read for 3.5 hours per week.'

1 How has Rohan worked out 3.5 hours?

2 Do you agree with Rohan's claim?

3 What information is lost when Rohan makes his calculation?

  Jess records how long she spends reading for the next seven weeks:

    5.5   7   2.5   3   7.5   9.5   1

  Jess says to Rohan, 'On average, I read for 3 hours per week.'

4 Why is Jess incorrect?

5 What can you do to give a better answer?

  Rohan has made a mistake. His final value should be 14 and not 11.5

6 What will happen to Rohan's claim? Why?

7 What other ways do you know to calculate averages? Are they useful here?

12.1 Different types of average

The shoe sizes of 19 students in a class are:

| 4 | 7 | 6 | 6 | 7 | 4 | 8 | 6 | 8 | 11 | 6 | 8 | 6 | 3 | 5 | 6 | 7 | 6 | 4 |

How would you describe the shoe sizes in this class?

Sometimes you might want to represent a set of data with a single value. When you do this, you use an average value.

There are three main types of average used in statistics and you can use each of them to describe the shoe sizes for the class.

The **mode** is the value that occurs the most often. If you count how times each shoe size occurs in the class, you will find that the most common (most frequent) size is six, so in this example the mode is 6.

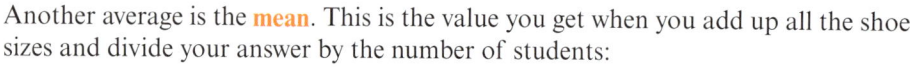
Another average is the **mean**. This is the value you get when you add up all the shoe sizes and divide your answer by the number of students:

$$\frac{\text{total of shoe sizes}}{\text{number of students}} = \frac{115}{19} = 6.05 \text{ (2 d.p.)}$$

The mean value tells you that the shoe sizes appear to be distributed in some way around the value 6.05. It also gives you a good impression of the general 'size' of the data. Notice that the value of the mean, in this case, is not a possible shoe size.

The third average is called the **median**. The median is the middle value when data is arranged in ascending order. So, putting the shoe sizes in order from smallest to largest gives:

| 3 | 3 | 4 | 4 | 4 | 5 | 6 | 6 | 6 | 6 | 6 | 6 | 7 | 7 | 7 | 8 | 8 | 8 | 11 |

To find the middle number you can think of the first and last values as one pair and cross them off. Then continue crossing off pairs until you are left with a single value in the middle.

| 3̶ | 3̶ | 4̶ | 4̶ | 4̶ | 5̶ | 6̶ | 6̶ | 6̶ | 6 | 6̶ | 6̶ | 7̶ | 7̶ | 7̶ | 8̶ | 8̶ | 8̶ | 11̶ |

For these shoe sizes, the median value is 6.

Crossing off numbers from each end can be difficult if you have a lot of data. If you count from the left, you find that the median is the 10th value. Adding one to the number of students and dividing the result by two, $\frac{(19 + 1)}{2}$, also gives 10 as the median position. You can use this method to find the position of the median whenever you have an odd number of data values.

But what if there had been 20 students in the class? For example, if there is an extra student with a shoe size of 11. Crossing off pairs gives this result:

| 3̶ | 3̶ | 4̶ | 4̶ | 4̶ | 5̶ | 6̶ | 6̶ | 6̶ | 6 | 6 | 6̶ | 7̶ | 7̶ | 7̶ | 8̶ | 8̶ | 8̶ | 11̶ | 11̶ |

You are left with a middle pair rather than a single value. If this happens then you need to find the mean of this middle pair: $\frac{(6 + 6)}{2} = 6$.

Notice that the position of the first value in this middle pair is $\frac{20}{2} = 10$. If you have an even number of data values, dividing the number by two will always give you the first value of the middle pair.

In summary:

Mode   The value that appears in the list more than any other. There can be more than one mode but if there are no values that occur more often than any other then there is no mode.

Mean   The value when you calculate $\frac{\text{total of all data}}{\text{number of values}}$.
The mean may not be one of the actual data values.

Median   1   Arrange the data into ascending numerical order.

2   If the number of data is n and n is odd, find $\frac{n + 1}{2}$.
This will give you the position of the median.

3   If n is even, then calculate $\frac{n}{2}$. This will give you the position of the first of the middle pair. Find the mean of this pair.

TIP

If you take the mean of n items and multiply it by n, you get the total of all n values.

The mean is sometimes referred to as a measure of 'central tendency' of the data.

LINK

Many people use averages in their work. Geographers use them to summarise numerical results for large populations, so they don't have to show every piece of numerical data they collect.

Medical scientists use means and medians to test whether or not a treatment makes a significant difference to the recovery of patients. They compare the average values for patients being tested with those of a 'control' group. The 'control' group is not given the same treatment, which means a fair comparison can take place.

Estate agents often list the median value of property sales in an area because the median price is not influenced by extreme values.

Dealing with extreme values

Sometimes your set of data may contain values that are extreme in some way. For example, if you measure the speeds of cars passing a certain point you may find that some cars are moving unusually slowly or unusually quickly. It is also possible that you may have made a mistake and measured a speed incorrectly or just written down the wrong number!

Imagine these are the speeds (in kilometres per hour) of six cars passing a certain point in a five-minute period:

| 67.2 | 58.3 | 128.9 | 65.0 | 49.0 | 55.7 |

The value 128.9 km/h seems much faster than any other car. How does this extreme value affect your averages?

You can check yourself that the mean of the above data *including* the extreme value is 70.7 km/h.

This average is *larger* than all but one of the values and is not representative of the data. This means that in this situation the mean might be a poor choice of average. If you discover that the highest speed was a mistake, you can exclude it from the calculation and get the much more realistic value of 59.0 km/h. (Try the calculation for yourself.)

If the extreme value is genuine and you cannot exclude it, then using the median is a better way to represent the main body of data. Start by writing the data in ascending order:

| 49.0 | 55.7 | 58.3 | 65.0 | 67.2 | 128.9 |

The median is the mean of 58.3 and 65.0. This is 61.7. Notice that if you remove the highest value, the median reduces to 58.3, so this doesn't change things very much.

There is no mode for these data.

TIP

The number of data values is even, so the median is the mean of the 3rd and 4th data points.

TIP

You could be asked to give reasons for choosing the mean or median as your average.

LINK

Most numerical quantities in physics are predictable, at least approximately, by using mathematical formulae to describe the situation. In these situations, extreme measurements that don't appear to follow a broad pattern need to be checked carefully. Any that are errors should be removed from the data. But remember, you can only remove the data if it really is incorrect.

WORKED EXAMPLE 1

After six tests, Gad has a mean average score of 48%. He takes a seventh test and scores 83%.

a   What is Gad's total score after six tests?

b   What is Gad's mean average score after seven tests?

Answers

a   Since $\text{mean} = \dfrac{\text{total of all data}}{\text{number of values}}$

then,   total of all data = mean × number of values

$$= 48 \times 6$$
$$= 288$$

b   Total of all seven scores = total of first six plus seventh

$$= 288 + 83$$
$$= 371$$

$$\text{mean} = \frac{371}{7} = 53\%$$

TIP

This is good example of where you need to think before you conclude that Gad is a typical student (scoring 53%). He may have had extra tuition and will get above 80% for all future tests.

Exercise 12.1

1   For each of the following data sets calculate:

   i   the mode   **ii**   the median   **iii**   the mean.

   a   12   2   5   6   9   3   12   13   10

   b   5   9   7   3   8   2   5   8   8   2

   c   2.1   3.8   2.4   7.6   8.2   3.4   5.6   8.2   4.5   2.1

   d   12   2   5   6   9   3   12   13   43

2   Look carefully at the data in parts (a) and (d) of question 1. What is different? How did your mean, median and mode change?

MATHEMATICAL CONNECTIONS

You can see from the contexts in some of these questions that averages can appear in just about any aspect of our lives, whether studying, reading the news or investigating behavioural patterns. Can you think of any ways that you use averages in your everyday life?

3   Ali and Bo decide to investigate their television watching patterns. They record the number of minutes that they watch television for eight days:

Ali:	38	10	65	43	125	225	128	40
Bo:	25	15	10	65	90	300	254	32

a   Find the median number of minutes spent watching television for:

   i   Ali   **ii**   Bo.

b   Find the mean number of minutes spent watching television for:

   i   Ali   **ii**   Bo.

4   Find a list of five numbers with a mean that is larger than all but one of the numbers.

5   A keen ten pin bowler plays five rounds in one evening. His scores are 98, 64, 103, 108 and 109. Which average (mode, mean or median) will he choose to report to his friends at the end of the evening? Explain your answer carefully, showing all your calculations clearly.

> **TIP**
>
> Think about whether the player will choose an average that helps them claim they are a good player or an average that is a fair representation of their scores.

> **LINK**
>
> Cricket players often talk about 'batting averages'. These usually refer to the mean number of runs per innings.

6   If the mean height of 31 children is 143.6 cm, calculate the sum of the heights used to calculate the mean.

7   The mean mass of 12 bags of potatoes is 2.4 kg. If a 13th bag containing 2.2 kg of potatoes is added, what will the new mean mass of the 13 bags be?

8   The mean temperature of 10 cups of coffee is 89.6 °C. The mean temperature of a different collection of 20 cups of coffee is 92.1 °C. What is the mean temperature of all 30 cups of coffee?

9   Find a set of five numbers with mean five, median four and mode four.

10   Find a set of five *different* whole numbers with mean five and median four.

11   The mean mass of a group of m green apples is X kg and the mean mass of a group of n red apples is Y kg. Find the mean mass of all the apples combined.

12.2 Making comparisons using averages and ranges

Now you know how to find an average value to represent your data, you can compare two or more sets of data. However, just comparing the averages can sometimes be misleading.

It can also be helpful to know how *consistent* the data is. You do this by thinking about how scattered – or spread – the values are. A simple measure of spread is the **range**.

Range = largest value − smallest value

The larger the range, the more spread out the data is and the less consistent the values are with one another.

WORKED EXAMPLE 2

Two groups of athletes want to compare their 100m sprint times. Each person runs once and records their time in seconds.

Team Pythagoras	14.3	16.6	14.3	17.9	14.1	15.7
Team Socrates	13.2	16.8	14.7	14.7	13.6	16.2

a   Calculate the mean 100m time for each team.

b   Which is the smaller mean?

c   What does this tell you about the 100m times for Team Pythagoras compared to those for Team Socrates?

d   Calculate the range for each team.

e   What does this tell you about the performance of each team?

Answers

a   Team Pythagoras:

$$\text{Mean} = \frac{14.3 + 16.6 + 14.3 + 17.9 + 14.1 + 15.7}{6} = \frac{92.9}{6} = 15.48 \text{ seconds}$$

Team Socrates:

$$\text{Mean} = \frac{13.2 + 16.8 + 14.7 + 14.7 + 13.6 + 16.2}{6} = \frac{89.2}{6} = 14.87 \text{ seconds}$$

b   Team Socrates have the smaller mean 100m time.

c   The smaller time means that Team Socrates are slightly faster as a team than Team Pythagoras.

d   Team Pythagoras' range = 17.9 − 14.1 = 3.8 seconds

Team Socrates' range = 16.8 − 13.2 = 3.6 seconds

e   Team Socrates are slightly faster as a whole and they are slightly more consistent.

TIP

When comparing means or ranges, make sure that you refer to the original context of the question. If you are comparing waiting times in queues at different airports, for example, your conclusions should mention waiting times in queues at different airports!

INVESTIGATION

Units for averages

You need to use the same units when comparing averages or ranges. There is no point in comparing one average or range measured in kilometres with another average or range measured in metres.

1   Calculate the mean and range of these lengths:

   3.2m   2.8m   4.1m   1.6m   4.4m

> **INVESTIGATION CONTINUED**
>
> **2**   Rewrite the lengths in centimetres. Calculate the mean and range of the new data. What do you notice?
>
> **3**   Try multiplying the original data by a fixed number and working out the mean and range again? What happens?
>
> **4**   Try to explain why this means you need to use the same units when comparing means or ranges.
>
> **5**   Investigate what happens if you add the same number to each value in your original data set. What happens to the mean? What about the range? Can you explain this?

Exercise 12.2

1   Two friends, Ru and Oli, are picking berries. The mass (in kg) of each box they fill is recorded.

Ru	0.145	0.182	0.135	0.132	0.112	0.155	0.189	0.132	0.145	0.201	0.139
Oli	0.131	0.143	0.134	0.145	0.132	0.123	0.182	0.134	0.128		

a   For each person calculate:

   i   the mean mass of berries collected per box

   ii   the range of masses.

b   Who collected more berries per box?

c   Who was more consistent when collecting the berries?

2   The marks out of 20 obtained by two classes in a mathematics test are shown in the table.

Class Archimedes	12	13	4	19	20	12	13	13	16	18	12
Class Bernoulli	13	6	9	15	20	20	13	15	17	19	3

a   Calculate the median score for each class.

b   Find the range of scores for each class.

c   Which class did better in the test overall?

d   Which class was more consistent?

3   Three shops sell light bulbs. A sample of 100 light bulbs is taken from each shop and the working life of each is measured in hours. The table shows the mean time and range for each shop.

Shop	Mean (hours)	Range (hours)
Brightlights	136	18
Footlights	145	36
Backlights	143	18

Which shop would you recommend to someone who is looking to buy a new light bulb and why?

SELF ASSESSMENT

1   Read through this activity that a class had to complete for homework. Think about how you would answer each question.

What mark do you think you would score out of 10 for this task? Why?

> A developer monitors how many people visited a new website each hour for the first two days that the site went live.
>
> These are the results arranged in order.
>
> 100, 105, 106, 106, 107, 107, 108, 110, 117, 118, 135, 137
>
> 145, 148, 148, 148, 153, 155, 157, 159, 162, 171, 171, 179
>
> 183, 183, 185, 185, 189, 199, 201, 203, 204, 209, 216, 220
>
> 223, 224, 224, 227, 229, 230, 231, 233, 234, 235, 237, 238
>
> 1 Calculate:
>
>   a   the mean, median and mode   [4]
>
>   b   the range   [1]
>
> 2 Company A owns the website and wants to sell advertising on it. What could they say about the number of visitors the site is receiving?   [2]
>
> 3 The developer compares the statistics for this website with those from a website run by Company B.
>
>   Company B
>
>   Mean number of visits per hour: 180
>
>   Median number of visits per hour: 140
>
>   Mode: 135 visits per hour
>
>   Range: 200
>
>   What could the developer say to compare the two sets of data?   [3]

SELF ASSESSMENT CONTINUED

2   Here is one student's answer to the homework activity.

What mark would you give this student out of 10? Why?

> 1 a   Mean = sum of values/number of values = 8394/48
>   = 174.88 visits per hour (2 d.p.)
>   Median = (179 + 183)/2 = 181 visits per hour
>   Mode = 148
>   b   Range = 238 − 100 = 138
> 2   The website consistently gets over 100 visits per hour with an average of 175 visits per hour.
> 3   The mean number of visits to Company B's website is a bit higher than Company A's but the median number of visits to Company B is much lower. This suggests that the mean of Company B is affected by a few high values and the usual number of visits is actually lower. The data for Company B has quite a wide range and this suggests that the data is spread out and the number of visits per hour is less consistent than for Company A.

3   The work above is an example of a model answer.

a   Did this student do anything differently to how you would have worked? What?

b   How can examples of good work like this one help you to improve your own work?

12.3 Calculating averages and ranges for frequency data

So far, you have calculated averages for quite small sets of data. When you have larger sets with more than 20 pieces of data, it is better to collect the data with the same value together and record it in a frequency distribution table.

> **TIP**
>
> Sometimes a frequency distribution table is simply called a frequency distribution.

Data shown in a frequency distribution table

If you throw a single dice 100 times, each of the six numbers will appear several times. You can record the number of times each number appears in a table:

Number showing on the upper face	1	2	3	4	5	6
Frequency	16	13	14	17	19	21

Mean

To calculate the mean, you first need to find the total of all 100 throws. There are sixteen 1s, which give a subtotal of $1 \times 16 = 16$, thirteen 2s giving a subtotal of $13 \times 2 = 26$ and so on. You can extend your table to show this:

TIP

You can add columns to a table given to you to help organise your calculations. In this case you need to swap the rows and columns to make it easier to use.

Number showing on the upper face	Frequency	Frequency × number on the upper face
1	16	$1 \times 16 = 16$
2	13	$2 \times 13 = 26$
3	14	$3 \times 14 = 42$
4	17	$17 \times 4 = 68$
5	19	$19 \times 5 = 95$
6	21	$21 \times 6 = 126$

The total of all 100 throws is the sum of all values in this third column:

Total score $= 16 + 26 + 42 + 68 + 95 + 126$

$\qquad = 373$

So the mean score per throw $= \dfrac{\text{total score}}{\text{total number of throws}} = \dfrac{373}{100} = 3.73$.

MATHEMATICAL CONNECTIONS

In Chapter 8 you studied the idea of 'experimental probability'. Notice that you also recorded data in frequency tables, so that you could estimate probabilities of different events.

Median

There are 100 throws, which is an even number, so the median will be the mean of a middle pair. The first of this middle pair is in position $\dfrac{100}{2} = 50$.

The values are all in order in the table. The first 16 are 1s, the next 13 are 2s and so on. If you add the first three frequencies, you get $16 + 13 + 14 = 43$. This means that the first 43 values are 1, 2 or 3. The next 17 values are all 4s, so the 50th and 51st values are both 4. The mean of two 4s is 4, so this is the median.

Mode

For the mode you simply need to find the value that has the highest frequency.
The number 6 occurs most often (21 times), so 6 is the mode.

Range

The highest and lowest values are known, so the range is $6 - 1 = 5$.

Data organised into a stem-and-leaf diagram

You can determine averages and the range from stem-and-leaf diagrams.

Mean

A stem-and-leaf diagram shows all the data values, so you find the mean by adding all the values and dividing them by the number of values in the same way you find the mean of any data set.

Median

You can use an ordered stem-and-leaf diagram to find the median. In an ordered stem-and-leaf diagram the leaves for each stem are arranged in order from smallest to greatest.

Mode

An ordered stem-and-leaf diagram allows you see which values are repeated in each row. You can compare these to find the mode.

Range

You can use the first and last value in an ordered stem-and-leaf diagram to find the range.

> **MATHEMATICAL CONNECTIONS**
>
> You learnt about stem-and-leaf diagrams in Chapter 4.

WORKED EXAMPLE 3

The ordered stem-and-leaf diagram shows the number of customers served at a supermarket checkout every half hour during an 8-hour shift.

Stem	Leaf
0	2 5 5 6 6 6 6
1	1 3 3 5 5 6 7 7
2	1

Key
0 | 2 represents 2 customers

a   What is the range of customers served?

b   What is the modal number of customers served?

c   Determine the median number of customers served.

d   How many customers were served altogether during this shift?

e   Calculate the mean number of customers served every half hour.

> **WORKED EXAMPLE 3 CONTINUED**
>
> **Answers**
>
> **a**   The lowest number is 2 and the highest number is 21.
>
>   The range is 21 − 2 = 19 customers.
>
> **b**   6 is the value that appears most often.
>
> **c**   There are 16 pieces of data, so the median is the mean of the 8th and 9th values:
>
> $$\frac{(11 + 13)}{2} = \frac{24}{2} = 12$$
>
> **d**   To calculate the total number of customers, find the sum of all the values. Find the total for each row and combine them to find the overall total:
>
>   Row 1: 2 + 5 + 5 + 6 + 6 + 6 + 6 = 36
>
>   Row 2: 11 + 13 + 13 + 15 + 15 + 16 + 17 + 17 = 117
>
>   Row 3: 21
>
>   36 + 117 + 21 = 174 customers in total
>
> **e**   Mean = $\dfrac{\text{sum of data values}}{\text{number of data values}}$ = $\dfrac{174}{16}$ = 10.875 customers per half hour

In summary:

- **Mode**   The value that has the highest frequency is the mode. If more than one value has the same highest frequency, then there is no single mode.

- **Mean** $\dfrac{\text{total of all data}}{\text{number of values}} = \dfrac{\text{sum of frequency} \times \text{value}}{\text{total frequency}}$

  (Remember to extend the table so that you can fill in a column for calculating frequency × value in each case.)

- **Median**   − If the number of data values is n and n is odd, then $\dfrac{n+1}{2}$ gives the position of the median. Add the frequencies until you reach the median position. The value in this position is the median.

  − If n is even, then $\dfrac{n}{2}$ gives the position of the first of the middle pair.

  Add the frequencies until you reach this position and then find the mean of the pair.

Exercise 12.3

1   Construct a frequency table for the following data and calculate:

   a   the mean   **b**   the median   **c**   the mode   **d**   the range.

3	4	5	1	2	8	9	6	5	3	2	1	6	4	7	8	1
1	5	5	2	3	4	5	7	8	3	4	2	5	1	9	4	5
6	7	8	9	2	1	5	4	3	4	5	6	1	4	4	8	

2   Tickets for a show were sold at the following prices: 180 at $6.50 each,
     215 at $8 each and 124 at $10 each.

     a   Present this information in a frequency table.

     b   Calculate the mean price of the tickets sold (give your answer to
          3 significant figures).

3   A receptionist kept count of the number of courier deliveries received each day
     over a period of 60 days. The results are shown in the table.

Number of deliveries per day	0	1	2	3	4	5
Frequency	28	21	6	3	1	1

     For this distribution, find:

     a   the mode   b   the median   c   the mean   d   the range.

4   A survey of the number of children in 100 families gave the following distribution:

Number of children in family	0	1	2	3	4	5	6	7
Number of families	4	36	27	21	5	4	2	1

     For this distribution, find:

     a   the mode   b   the median   c   the mean.

5   The distribution of marks obtained by students in a class is shown in the table.

Mark obtained	0	1	2	3	4	5	6	7	8	9	10
Number of students	1	0	3	2	2	4	3	4	6	3	2

     a   Find:

          i   the mode   ii   the median   iii   the mean.

     b   The class teacher is asked to report on the class's performance and wants to
          show they are doing as well as possible. Which average should the teacher
          include in the report and why?

6   The masses of 20 soccer players were measured to the nearest kilogram and this
     stem-and-leaf diagram was produced.

Stem	Leaf
4	6
5	4 0 0 7 8 9 5
6	3 0 1 1 3 2 6 8 6 9
7	4 0

Key
4 | 6 represents 64 kilograms

     a   Redraw the stem-and-leaf diagram to make an ordered data set.

     b   How many players have a mass of 60 kilograms or more?

     c   Why is the mode not a useful average for this data?

     d   What is the range of masses?

     e   What is the median mass of the players?

TIP

The question in part (c) could be asked slightly differently by asking 'Why is the mode not a useful statistic for this data?' The word 'statistic' means a calculation based on data you have collected. Averages and measures of spread are examples of statistics.

7 The number of electronic components produced by a machine every hour over a 24-period are:

143, 128, 121, 126, 134, 150, 128, 132, 140, 131, 146, 128

133, 138, 140, 125, 142, 129, 136, 130, 133, 142, 126, 129

    a Using two intervals for each stem, draw an ordered stem-and-leaf diagram of the data.

    b Determine the range of the data.

    c Find the median.

REFLECTION

What have you learnt about using averages in real-life situations in this section?

Has what you know about averages changed in any way? If so, how?

12.4 Estimating the mean and finding the modal class for grouped data

MATHEMATICAL CONNECTIONS

You learnt about discrete, continuous and **grouped data** in Chapter 4 and you used inequality notation to define the groups. You may find it helpful to review that work before continuing.

LINK

Real-world data can involve thousands of data points, so it is clear that grouping data, rather than recording a list of exact values is sensible.

When a government carries out a national census to collect numerical data about the population, the questions asked often involve ranges of ages, salaries and so on. It is not practical to record the individual details for every person, but a simple frequency or percentage for each class gives more than enough information.

When data is grouped in a frequency table you do not have the actual data points, so you have to work with the classes to estimate the mean and mode.

The following worked example shows how a grouped frequency table is used to find the estimated mean and the **modal class**.

WORKED EXAMPLE 4

The heights of 100 children were measured in cm and the results recorded in a table.

Height in cm (h)	Frequency (f)
$120 < h \leqslant 130$	12
$130 < h \leqslant 140$	16
$140 < h \leqslant 150$	38
$150 < h \leqslant 160$	24
$160 < h \leqslant 170$	10

Find:

a   an estimate for the mean height of the children

b   the modal class.

Answers

a   You don't know any of the children's heights exactly, so you use the midpoint of each class as the best estimate of the height of each child in that class. For example, the 12 children in the $120 \leqslant h < 130$ class have heights between 120 cm and 130 cm, but that is all that you know.

Halfway between 120 cm and 130 cm is $\dfrac{(120 + 130)}{2} = 125$ cm.

A good estimate of the total height of the 12 children in this class is 12×125 (frequency × midpoint).

Extend your table to include midpoints and totals for each class:

Height in cm (h)	Frequency (f)	Midpoint (x)	Frequency × midpoint (fx)
$120 < h \leqslant 130$	12	125	$12 \times 125 = 1500$
$130 < h \leqslant 140$	16	135	$16 \times 135 = 2160$
$140 < h \leqslant 150$	38	145	$38 \times 145 = 5510$
$150 < h \leqslant 160$	24	155	$24 \times 155 = 3720$
$160 < h \leqslant 170$	10	165	$10 \times 165 = 1650$

An estimate for the mean height of the children is:

$$\frac{1500 + 2160 + 5510 + 3720 + 1650}{12 + 16 + 38 + 24 + 10} = \frac{14\,540}{100} = 145.4 \text{ cm}$$

b   The class with the highest frequency is the modal class. In this case it is the class: $140 < h \leqslant 150$.

MATHEMATICAL CONNECTIONS

Histograms provide a clear way of representing grouped data in graphical form. You will study these in Chapter 20.

TIP

If a question asks you to explain why your calculations only give an estimate, remember that you don't have the exact data, only frequencies and classes.

Exercise 12.4

1   The table shows the heights of 50 sculptures in an art gallery.

   a   Find an estimate for the mean height of the sculptures.

   b   Which class contains the most sculptures?

Heights (h cm)	Frequency (f)
$130 < h \leqslant 135$	7
$135 < h \leqslant 140$	13
$140 < h \leqslant 145$	15
$145 < h \leqslant 150$	11
$150 < h \leqslant 155$	4
Total	$\Sigma f = 50$

> **TIP**
>
> The symbol Σ is the Greek letter capital 'sigma'. It is used to mean 'sum'.
> So, Σf simply means, 'the sum of all the frequencies'.

2   The table shows the lengths of 100 telephone calls.

Time (t minutes)	Frequency (f)
$0 < t \leqslant 1$	12
$1 < t \leqslant 2$	14
$2 < t \leqslant 4$	20
$4 < t \leqslant 6$	14
$6 < t \leqslant 8$	12
$8 < t \leqslant 10$	18
$10 < t \leqslant 15$	10

   a   Calculate an estimate for the mean length, in minutes, of a telephone call.

   b   Write your answer in minutes and seconds, to the nearest second.

   c   Identify the modal class for telephone call length.

3   The table shows the temperatures of several test tubes during a chemistry experiment.

Temperature (T °C)	Frequency (f)
$45 < T \leqslant 50$	3
$50 < T \leqslant 55$	8
$55 < T \leqslant 60$	17
$60 < T \leqslant 65$	6
$65 < T \leqslant 70$	2
$70 < T \leqslant 75$	1

Calculate an estimate for the mean temperature of the test tubes.

4   Two athletics teams – the *Hawks* and the *Eagles* – are about to compete in a race.
The masses of the team members are shown in the table below.

Hawks	
Mass (M kg)	**Frequency (f)**
$55 < M \leqslant 65$	2
$65 < M \leqslant 75$	8
$75 < M \leqslant 85$	12
$85 < M \leqslant 100$	3

Eagles	
Mass (M kg)	**Frequency (f)**
$55 < M \leqslant 65$	1
$65 < M \leqslant 75$	7
$75 < M \leqslant 85$	13
$85 < M \leqslant 100$	4

   a   Calculate an estimate for the mean mass of each team.

   b   Identify the modal class for the masses of each team.

5   The table shows the lengths of 50 pieces of wire used in a physics laboratory.
The lengths have been measured *to the nearest centimetre*. Find an estimate for the
mean length.

Length	26–30	31–35	36–40	41–45	46–50
Frequency (f)	4	10	12	18	6

6   The table shows the ages of the teachers in a secondary school to the nearest year.

Age in years	21–30	31–35	36–40	41–45	46–50	51–65
Frequency (f)	3	6	12	15	6	7

Calculate an estimate for the mean age of the teachers.

TIP

In this question ages are rounded to the nearest year. Someone who is 30 and a half is placed in the 31–35 class, because their age rounds up to 31 to the nearest year. In real life this person would say they are still 30.

LINK

Psychology relies heavily on statistics and if you do a psychology course you often need to complete a statistics module. Measurements (data) collected by psychologists include test scores (marks) as well as general properties in different population samples. Usually, a large amount of data is collected, so using estimated means and modal classes allow psychologists to develop ideas of what is usual and what is unusual and draw generalised conclusions from the data sets.

12.5 Quartiles

Quartiles are used to divide a data set into three groups. Quartiles are indicated by the symbols Q_1, Q_2 and Q_3.

You can use the following rules to estimate the positions of each quartile within a set of n items of ordered data:

Q_1 = **lower quartile** = value in position $\frac{1}{4}(n + 1)$

Q_2 = median (as calculated earlier in the chapter)

Q_3 = **upper quartile** = value in position $\frac{3}{4}(n + 1)$

If the position does not turn out to be a whole number, find the mean of the pair of numbers on either side. For example, if the position of the lower quartile turns out to be 5.25, then you find the mean of the 5th and 6th values.

Interquartile range

As with the range, the **interquartile range** gives a measure of how spread out or consistent the data is. The main difference is that the interquartile range (IQR) avoids using extreme data by finding the difference between the lower and upper quartiles. You are, effectively, measuring the spread of the central 50% of the data.

$$IQR = Q_3 - Q_1$$

If one set of data has a smaller IQR than another set, then the first set is more consistent and less spread out. This can be a useful comparison tool.

WORKED EXAMPLE 5

For each set of data calculate the median, upper quartile, lower quartile and the interquartile range.

a   13   12   8   6   11   14   8   5   1   10   16   12

b   14   10   8   19   15   14   9

Answer

a   First sort the data into ascending order:

   1   5   6   8   8   10   11   12   12   13   14   16

There are an even number of items (12). So, to find the median, find the mean of the middle pair. The first of the pair is in position $\frac{12}{2} = 6$, so the median is $\frac{(10 + 11)}{2} = 10.5$.

Calculate the position of the quartiles:

$$\frac{1}{4}(12 + 1) = 3.25 \text{ and } \frac{3}{4}(12 + 1) = 9.75$$

These are not whole numbers, so the lower quartile is the mean of the 3rd and 4th values, and the upper quartile is the mean of the 9th and 10th values.

$$Q_1 \frac{(6 + 8)}{2} = 7 \text{ and } Q_3 = \frac{(12 + 13)}{2} = 12.5$$

Then you know that the IQR = 12.5 − 7 = 5.5.

b   The ordered data is:

   8   9   10   14   14   15   19

There is an odd number of data values, so the median is in position $\frac{(7 + 1)}{2} = 4$.

The median is 14.

MATHEMATICAL CONNECTIONS

In Chapter 20 you will learn about cumulative frequency graphs. These allow you to calculate estimates for the median and quartiles when there are too many data points to put into order, or when you have grouped data.

WORKED EXAMPLE 5 CONTINUED

There are seven items, so the positions of the quartiles are: $\frac{1}{4}(7 + 1) = 2$ and $\frac{3}{4}(7 + 1) = 6$.

These are whole numbers so the lower quartile is in position two and the upper quartile is in position six.

So $Q_1 = 9$ and $Q_3 = 15$.

IQR = 15 − 9 = 6

WORKED EXAMPLE 6

Two companies sell sunflower seeds. In one year, seeds from Allbright produce flowers with a median height of 98 cm and IQR of 13 cm. In the same year seeds from Barstows produce flowers with a median height of 95 cm and IQR of 4 cm. Which seeds would you buy if you wanted to enter a competition for growing the tallest sunflower and why?

Answer

I would buy Barstows' seeds. Although Allbright sunflowers seem taller (with a higher median) they are less consistent. So, there is a chance of a very big sunflower, but there is also a good chance of a small sunflower. Barstows' sunflowers are a bit shorter, but are more consistent in their heights so you are more likely to get flowers around the height of 95 cm.

WORKED EXAMPLE 7

The back-to-back stem-and-leaf diagram shows the concentration of low-density lipoprotein (bad) cholesterol in the blood in 70 adults. Half of the adults are vegetarians and half are non-vegetarians. The data is measured in milligrams per 100 ml of blood (mg/dl).

Vegetarians		Non-vegetarians
Leaf	Stem	Leaf
8 0	9	
8 8 3 1	10	
9 9 8 8 6 5 2	11	2
9 9 8 7 7 0 0	12	0 1
9 6 5 1 1 1	13	0 2 3
4 2 2	14	1 3 5 6
8 2 1	15	0 4 5 5 9
6 5	16	0 1 4 7 8 9
3	17	2 3 6 8 8
	18	0 2 4 5
	19	1 6 8
	20	1
	21	5

Key

Vegetarians
  0 | 9 represents 90
Non-vegetarians
  11 | 2 represents 112

> **TIP**
> Remember to count the data in ascending order when you work with the left-hand side. The lowest values are closest to the stem in each row.

WORKED EXAMPLE 7 CONTINUED

a Determine the median for each group.

b Find the range for:

  i vegetarians   **ii** non-vegetarians.

c Determine the interquartile range for:

  i vegetarians   **ii** non-vegetarians.

d LDL levels of < 130 are desirable, levels of $130-160$ are considered borderline high and levels >160 are considered high risk. Using these figures, comment on what the distribution on the stem-and-leaf diagram suggests.

Answer

a The data is already ordered and there are 35 values in each set.

  $\frac{1}{2}(35 + 1) = 18$, so the median is the 18th value.

  i Median = 128 for vegetarians
  ii Median = 164 for non-vegetarians

b **i** Range = $173 - 90 = 83$ for vegetarians
  ii Range = $215 - 112 = 103$ for non-vegetarians

c Determine the position of Q_1 and Q_3.

  The lower quartile = $\frac{1}{4}(35 + 1) = $ 9th value

  The upper quartile = $\frac{3}{4}(35 + 1) = $ 27th value

  i IQR = $Q_3 - Q_1 = 142 - 116 = 26$ for vegetarians
  ii IQR = $Q_3 - Q_1 = 180 - 145 = 35$ for non-vegetarians

d For vegetarians the data is skewed toward the lower levels on the stem-and-leaf diagram. More than half of the values are in the desirable range, with only three in the high-risk range. For non-vegetarians, the data is more spread out. Only three values are in the desirable range, 12 are borderline high and 20 are in the high-risk category.

  This might suggest that non-vegetarians have higher levels of bad cholesterol in general. However, without considering other risk factors or medical history, you cannot say this for certain from one set of data.

Exercise 12.5

1 Find the median, quartiles and interquartile range for each set of data. Make sure that you show your method clearly.

  a 5   8   9   9   4   5   6   9   3   6   4

  b 12   14   12   17   19   21   23

  c 4   5   12   14   15   17   14   3   18   19   18   19   14   4   15

  d 3.1   2.4   5.1   2.3   2.5   4.2   3.4   6.1   4.8

  e 13.2   14.8   19.6   14.5   16.7   18.9   14.5   13.7   17.0   21.8   12.0   16.5

APPLY YOUR SKILLS

Try to think about what the calculations in each question tell you about each situation.

2 The area, in hectares, of 13 mango orchards in Sindh, Pakistan, were recorded as follows:

3.75	2.35	4.5	2.7	3.5	40.25	11.3
19.25	32.1	28.4	7.2	3.6	9.0	

   a Find the range of the areas.

   b Calculate the interquartile range.

   c Which value is more representative of the spread of the data? Why?

3 Members of a hiking group sometimes see a kingfisher when they walk in the park. Each week for 15 weeks they record the number of times they see a kingfisher.

5	7	5	8	4	2	9	9	4	7	6	4	6	12	4

Find the median, quartiles and interquartile range for this data.

4 Padmaja is conducting a survey into the traffic on a road. Every Monday for eight weeks in the summer Padmaja records the number of cars that pass an intersection between 08.00 a.m. and 09.00 a.m. Padmaja repeats the experiment during the winter. Both sets of results are shown in the table.

Summer:	18	15	19	25	19	26	17	13
Winter:	12	9	14	11	13	9	12	10

   a Find the median number of cars for each period.

   b Find the interquartile range for each period.

   c What differences do you notice? Try to explain why this might happen.

5 Julia and Aneesh are reading articles from different magazines. They count the number of words in a random selection of sentences from their articles and record the results:

Julia

(reading the *Statistician*):   23 31 12 19 23 13 24

Aneesh

(reading the *Algebraist*):   19 12 13 16 18 15 18 21 22

   a Calculate the median for each article.

   b Calculate the interquartile range for each article.

   c Aneesh claims that the editor of the *Algebraist* has tried to control the writing and seems to be aiming it at a particular audience. What do your answers from (a) and (b) suggest about this claim?

APPLY YOUR SKILLS CONTINUED

6 The fuel economy (km/ℓ of petrol) of 18 new car models was tested in both city traffic and open road driving conditions, and the following stem-and-leaf diagram was produced.

New car fuel economy (km/ℓ)

City traffic				Open road		
	Leaf	Stem	Leaf			
	0	8				
4 2 1		9				
5 3 1 1		10				
8 3 2		11	5 5 9			
7 6 4		12	1 1 2 7			
1		13	3 6			
5 2		14	5 6 7			
		15	2 7 9			
		16	0 1			
		17	4			

Key
0 | 8 represents 8.0 km/ℓ
11 | 5 represents 11.5 km/ℓ

a Find the range of the fuel economy (km/ℓ) of petrol for:

  i city traffic   **ii** open road driving.

b Find the median fuel economy for:

  i city traffic   **ii** open road driving.

c Determine the interquartile range for:

  i city traffic   **ii** open road driving.

d Compare and comment on the data for both city traffic and open road driving.

7 The table shows the marks that the same group of ten students received in three consecutive tests.

Test 1	34	45	67	87	65	56	34	55	89	77
Test 2	19	45	88	75	45	88	64	59	49	72
Test 3	76	32	67	45	65	45	66	57	77	59

a Calculate the range, interquartile range and median for each test.

b Use the values in part (a) to comment on the performance of this group of students in the three tests.

SUMMARY

Do you know ...?

Averages – the mode, median and mean – are used to summarise a collection of data.

Discrete data can be listed or arranged in a frequency distribution.

Continuous data can be listed or arranged into groups.

The mean is affected by extreme data.

The median is less affected by extreme data.

The lower quartile (Q_1) lies 25% of the way through the data.

The upper quartile (Q_3) lies 75% of the way through the data.

The interquartile range (IQR = $Q_3 - Q_1$) gives a measure of how spread out or consistent the central 50% of the data is.

The range is the difference between the largest and smallest values and also measures spread, but it is affected by extreme values and is used less often than the interquartile range.

Are you able to ...?

calculate the mean, median, mode and range of data given in a list

calculate the mean, median, mode and range of data given in a frequency distribution and a stem-and-leaf diagram

calculate an estimate for the mean of grouped data

find the modal class for grouped data

compare sets of data using summary averages and ranges

find the quartiles of data arranged in order

find the interquartile range for listed data.

Practice questions

1   A machine is set to make 15 g sweets, but in fact produces sweets that are *near* to 15 g. Jonah switches on the machine and makes 20 sweets, with a mean weight of 14.7 g.

   a   Find the total weight of the 20 sweets.   [2]

   b   Another 30 sweets are made, this time with a mean of 15.6 g. Find the mean weight of all 50 sweets.   [2]

   c   A final batch of sweets is made, with total weight 184 g, giving an overall mean of 17.2 g. Calculate the number of sweets in this last batch.   [2]

2   Residents on a Pacific island record how many earth tremors can be felt each year over 18 years. In the first 10 years of records, the mean number of tremors per year was recorded as 4.1. In the first 18 years, the mean number of tremors was recorded as 4.5. Calculate the mean number of tremors per year in the last 8 years of records.   [4]

3 A scientist collects insects in two different places: in the sunlight and in the shade. The stem-and-leaf diagram shows the masses of the bugs.

Leaf		Stem		Leaf					
Sunshine				**Shade**					
	4	0	6 3 2						
2 8 3 1		1	2 0 9 4 2 9 2						
8 3 1		2	5 9 0 8						
4 7 0 6 2 1		3	9 4						
5 4 3 9		4	5 9 5						
	1	5							

Key:
Sunshine $9 \mid 4$ represents 4.9 g
Shade $\quad 3 \mid 4$ represents 3.4 g

a State out how many insects were collected in total. [1]

b Draw an ordered stem-and-leaf diagram, using the same data. [5]

c Find the median mass of the insects collected in sunshine. [2]

d Find the median mass of the insects collected in shade. [2]

e Find the range of the masses of insects collected in the sunshine. [2]

f Find the range of the masses of insects collected in the shade. [2]

g Compare the masses of insects collected in the sunshine with the masses of those collected in the shade. [2]

h Find the interquartile range of the masses of insects collected in the sunshine. [2]

i Find the interquartile range of the masses of insects collected in the shade. [2]

j Explain why either the range or the interquartile range would be a suitable measure of spread for this data. [2]

4 The following data shows the shoe sizes of people who use a bouncy castle.

Shoe size	Frequency
2	21
3	11
4	2
5	n
6	5
7	2
8	1

a The median shoe size is known to be 3. Find the smallest and largest possible values of n. [3]

b Find the mean shoe size, giving your answer in terms of n. [2]

   c   The mean shoe size is known to be 3.5. Find the number of people with size 5 shoes. [3]

   d   State the modal shoe size. [1]

5   The temperature, $T\,°C$, in a hotel room is recorded several times in a single day.

Temp ($T\,°C$)	$25 < T \leqslant 30$	$30 < T \leqslant 35$	$35 < T \leqslant 40$	$40 < T \leqslant 45$
Frequency	16	5	2	1

   a   Find the number of times the temperature of the room was recorded. [2]

   b   State the modal class. [1]

   c   Calculate an estimate for the mean room temperature. [3]

SELF ASSESSMENT

Analysing your mistakes can help you improve.

Consider any questions that you got wrong.

- Did you understand the question and know what to do? If not, what can you do about this?

- Did you make any errors in your calculations? If so, what can you do to avoid these errors in future?

- Would doing corrections help you? If so, redo the questions you got wrong.

Past paper questions

TIP

Unit 3 Past Paper Questions Resource Sheet is available on Cambridge GO.

1 The *n*th term of a sequence is $6n - 4$.

   a Write down the first 3 terms in this sequence.

     [1]

   b The *k*th term of this sequence is 422.

     Work out the value of *k*.

     [2]

Cambridge IGCSE Mathematics (0580) Paper 11 Q12, June 2021

2 Expand and simplify.

$(x - 5)(x - 7)$

     [2]

Cambridge IGCSE Mathematics (0580) Paper 11 Q17, June 2020

3

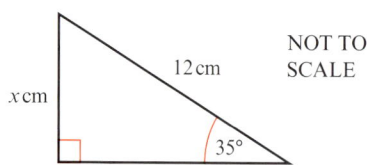

NOT TO SCALE

The diagram shows a right-angled triangle.

Calculate the value of *x*.

     [2]

Cambridge IGCSE Mathematics (0580) Paper 11 Q12, June 2019

4   The diagram shows a point P and a line L.

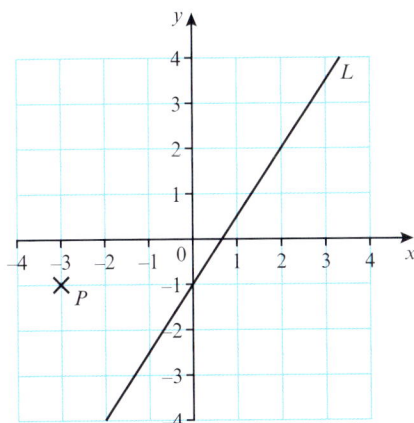

a   Write down the co-ordinates of point P.

[1]

b   Find the gradient of line L.

[2]

c   Write down the equation of line L in the form $y = mx + c$.

[2]

Cambridge IGCSE Mathematics (0580) Paper 11 Q22, June 2019

5

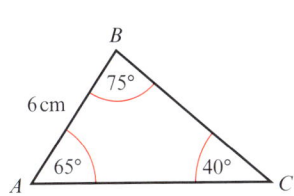   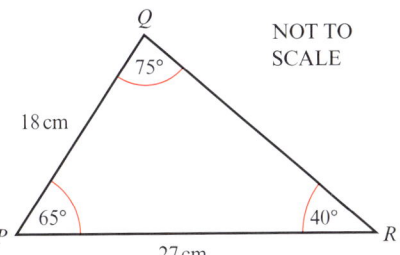

NOT TO SCALE

a   Explain why triangle ABC and triangle PQR are similar.

[1]

b   Find AC.

[2]

Cambridge IGCSE Mathematics (0580) Paper 11 Q17, June 2019

6 These are the first four terms of a sequence.

   5   8   11   14

   a Write down the next term.

   [1]

   b Find an expression, in terms of n, for the nth term.

   [2]

   Cambridge IGCSE Mathematics (0580) Paper 11 Q16, June 2019

7 The diagram shows a line L and two points, A and B, on a grid.

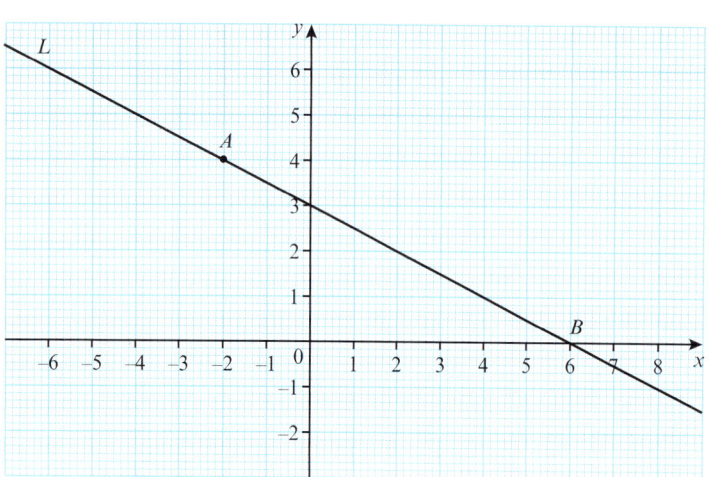

   a Write down the coordinates of point A.

   [1]

   b **i** Find the gradient of line L.

   [1]

   ii Write down the equation of line L in the form $y = mx + c$.

   [2]

   c **i** Draw a line that is perpendicular to line L and passes through the point A.
          [Using Figure 1 in the Unit 3 Past Paper Questions Resource Sheet.]

   [1]

   ii This line crosses the x-axis at point C.

          Mark point C on the grid and write down the coordinates of point C.
          [Using Figure 1 in the Unit 3 Past Paper Questions Resource Sheet.]

   [1]

   iii Find, by measuring, the perimeter of triangle ABC.

   [2]

   Cambridge IGCSE Mathematics (0580) Paper 31 Q4, June 2021

8 a On Monday, Main Street station sells 40 tickets.

There are four types of ticket: infant, child, adult and senior.

The bar chart shows the number of infant, child and adult tickets sold.

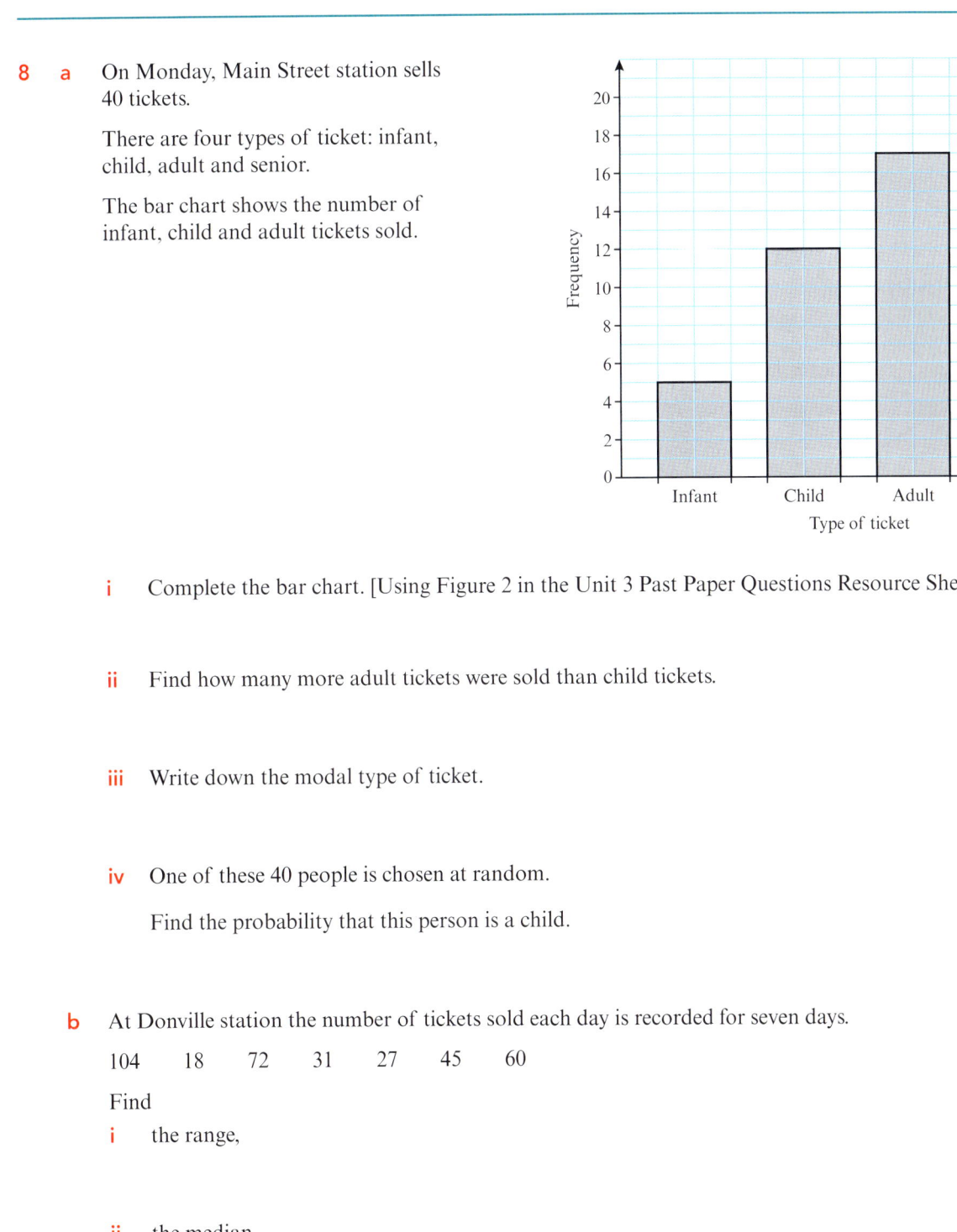

i Complete the bar chart. [Using Figure 2 in the Unit 3 Past Paper Questions Resource Sheet.]

[1]

ii Find how many more adult tickets were sold than child tickets.

[1]

iii Write down the modal type of ticket.

[1]

iv One of these 40 people is chosen at random.

Find the probability that this person is a child.

[1]

b At Donville station the number of tickets sold each day is recorded for seven days.

104   18   72   31   27   45   60

Find
i the range,

[1]

ii the median,

[2]

iii the mean.

[2]

Cambridge IGCSE Mathematics (0580) Paper 31 Q3, June 2019

9 **a** The nth term of a sequence is $n^2 + 3n$.

Find the first three terms of this sequence.

[2]

b These are the first five terms of a different sequence.

25   18   11   4   −3

Find the nth term of this sequence.

[2]

Cambridge IGCSE Mathematics (0580) Paper 21 Q6, June 2021

10 Write the recurring decimal $0.4\dot{7}$ as a fraction.

Show all your working.

[2]

Cambridge IGCSE Mathematics (0580) Paper 21 Q9, June 2019

11 A is the point $(5, -5)$ and B is the point $(9, 3)$.
  a Find the coordinates of the midpoint of AB.

[2]

  b Find the length of AB.

[3]

Cambridge IGCSE Mathematics (0580) Paper 21 Q9, June 2021

12 Factorise completely.
  a $21a^2 + 28ab$

[2]

  b $20x^2 - 45y^2$

[3]

Cambridge IGCSE Mathematics (0580) Paper 21 Q9, June 2020

13 a Find the size of an exterior angle of a regular polygon with 18 sides.

[2]

b

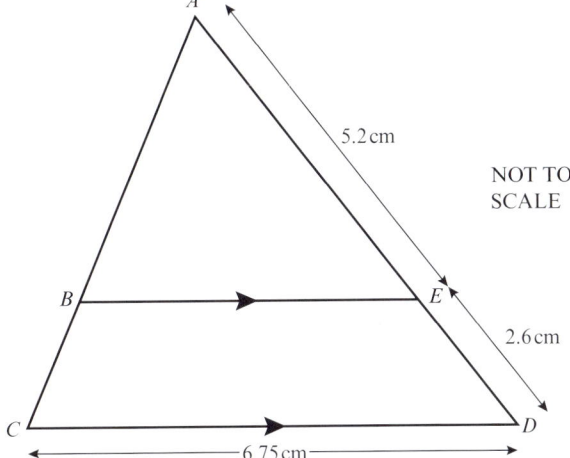

A

5.2 cm

NOT TO
SCALE

B   E

2.6 cm

C   D

6.75 cm

In triangle *ACD*, *B* lies on *AC* and *E* lies on *AD* such that *BE* is parallel to *CD*.

AE = 5.2 cm and *ED* = 2.6 cm.

Calculate *BE*.

[2]

c Two solids are mathematically similar.

The smaller solid has height 2 cm and volume 32 cm^3.

The larger solid has volume 780 cm^3.

Calculate the height of the larger solid.

[3]

Cambridge IGCSE Mathematics (0580) Paper 41 Q11a, b, c, June 2021

14 *x* is an integer.

$\mathscr{E} = \{x : 41 \leqslant x \leqslant 50\}$

$A = \{x : x$ is an odd number$\}$

$B = \{x : x$ is a multiple of 3$\}$

$C = \{x : x$ is a prime number$\}$

a Complete the Venn diagram to show this information. [Using Figure 3 in the Unit 3 Past Paper Questions Resource Sheet.]

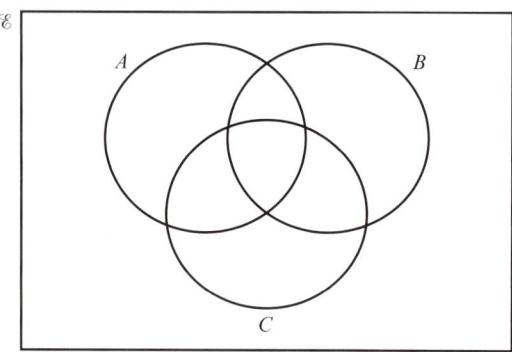

[3]

b List the elements of

i $A \cap C$,

[1]

ii $(B \cup C)'$.

[1]

c Find n$(A \cap B \cap C)$.

[1]

Cambridge IGCSE Mathematics (0580) Paper 41 Q5, June 2020

〉 Unit 3 Project

Litov's mean value theorem

Start with any two numbers, for example 8 and 2.

Generate a sequence where the next number is the mean of the previous two numbers.

- So the next number is half of (8 + 2), and the sequence continues: 8, 2, 5

- The next number is half of (2 + 5), and the sequence continues: 8, 2, 5, 3.5

What would happen if you continued this process indefinitely?

Choose a few pairs of starting numbers and repeat the process.

Each time, your sequence should get closer and closer to a value which we call the limit.

Can you find a relationship between your starting numbers and the limit of the sequence they generate?

Can you explain why this happens?

Investigate starting with three numbers

Generate a sequence where the next number is the mean of the previous three numbers.

- Check you agree that if we start with 4, 1, 10, the next number is 5, and the number after that is $\frac{16}{3}$.

What would happen if you continued this process indefinitely?

Choose some more sets of three starting numbers.

Can you find a relationship between your starting numbers and the limit of the sequence they generate?

Can you explain why this happens?

> **GO FURTHER**
>
> Explore what happens when you have n starting numbers and you generate a sequence where the next number is the mean of the last n numbers.

> # Chapter 13
Understanding
measurement

Meteorologists need to think about a very large number of measurements when predicting the path of a weather system such as a hurricane. These can include air temperature, sea temperature, air pressure and the area of land covered by the path of the hurricane. What other measurements might be useful?

All these different measurements mean that lots of small errors can combine to give a large total error, so there is always some uncertainty when trying to predict the likely path and power of a weather system.

GETTING STARTED

Units are often grouped together or subdivided into different units. If you want to convert between units you usually have to multiply or divide by powers of 10. For example, think about the relationship between metres, centimetres and millimetres:

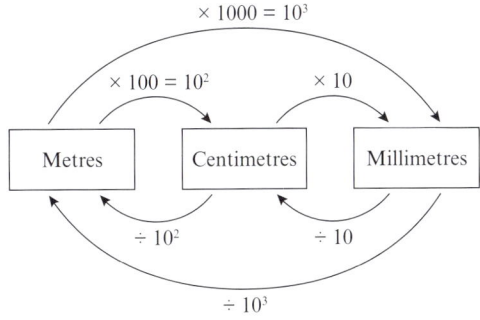

1   Draw a similar diagram for kilograms, grams and milligrams.

2   Find out what the prefixes kilo-, milli-, centi- mean.

3   Think about some other units and how to convert between them. Consider units of distance, mass and time. Draw some diagrams to represent the conversations.

13.1 Understanding units

Vishal has a $1\,m \times 1\,m \times 1\,m$ box and has collected a large number of $1\,cm \times 1\,cm \times 1\,cm$ building blocks. He decides to stack all the cubes neatly into the box.

Try to imagine a $1\,m \times 1\,m \times 1\,m$ box.

The length of each side is $1\,m = 100\,cm$. The total number of $1\,cm \times 1\,cm \times 1\,cm$ cubes that fit inside is $100 \times 100 \times 100 = 1\,000\,000$.

This means that one cubic metre is equivalent to one million cubic centimetres! So, you can see that if you change the units you measure with, the number of units can be very different.

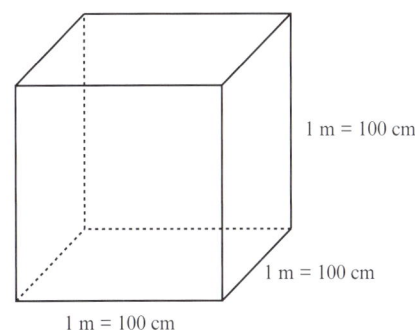

1 m = 100 cm
1 m = 100 cm
1 m = 100 cm

LINK

Almost all work in physics involves studying the relationships between different quantities we can measure. Physicists need to understand how units relate to one another. The way in which we express masses, speeds, temperatures and a vast array of other quantities can depend on the units used.

Measure	Units used	Equivalent to ...
Length – how long (or tall) something is.	Millimetres (mm) Centimetres (cm) Metres (m) Kilometres (km)	10 mm = 1 cm 100 cm = 1 m 1000 m = 1 km 1 km = 1 000 000 mm
Mass – the amount of material in an object.	Milligrams (mg) Grams (g) Kilograms (kg) Tonnes (t)	1000 mg = 1 g 1000 g = 1 kg 1000 kg = 1 t 1 t = 1 000 000 g
Capacity – the inside volume of a container; how much it can hold.	Millilitres (ml) Centilitres (cl) Litres (l)	10 ml = 1 cl 100 cl = 1 l 1 l = 1000 ml
Area – the amount of space taken up by a flat (two-dimensional) shape, always measured in square units.	Square millimetres (mm^2) Square centimetres (cm^2) Square metres (m^2) Square kilometres (km^2) Hectares (ha)	100 mm^2 = 1 cm^2 10 000 cm^2 = 1 m^2 1 000 000 m^2 = 1 km^2 1 km^2 = 100 ha 1 ha = 10 000 m^2
Volume – the amount of space taken up by a three-dimensional object, always measured in cubic units (or their equivalent liquid measurements, e.g. ml).	Cubic millimetres (mm^3) Cubic centimetres (cm^3) Cubic metres (m^3) Millilitres (ml)	1000 mm^3 = 1 cm^3 1 000 000 cm^3 = 1 m^3 1 m^3 = 1000 l 1 cm^3 = 1 ml

---

WORKED EXAMPLE 1

Express:

a   5 km in cm   b   3.2 cm in m   c   2 000 000 cm² in m².

Answers

a   1 km = 1000 m = 1000 × 100 cm = 100 000 cm

So, 5 km = 5 × 100 000 cm = 500 000 cm

b   100 cm = 1 m, so 1 cm = 0.01 m

So, 3.2 cm = 3.2 × 0.01 = 0.032 m

c   1 m² = 100 cm × 100 cm = 10 000 cm²

So, 2 000 000 cm² = $\dfrac{2\,000\,000}{10\,000}$ = 200 m²

Exercise 13.1

1   Express each quantity in the unit given in brackets.

   a   4 kg (g)   b   5 km (m)   c   35 mm (cm)

   d   81 mm (cm)   e   7.3 g (mg)   f   5760 kg (t)

   g   2.1 m (cm)   h   2 t (kg)   i   140 cm (m)

   j   2024 g (kg)   k   121 mg (g)   l   23 m (mm)

   m   3 cm 5 mm (mm)   n   8 km 36 m (m)   o   9 g 77 mg (g)

2   Arrange the following lengths in order of size, starting with the smallest.

   324 cm, 3.22 m, $3\dfrac{2}{9}$ m

3   Write the following volumes in order, starting with the smallest.

   $\dfrac{1}{2}$ litre, 780 ml, 125 ml, 0.65 litres

4   How many 5 ml spoonfuls are there in a bottle that contains 0.3 litres of medicine?

5   Express each quantity in the units given in brackets.

   a   14.23 m (mm, km)   b   19.06 g (mg, t)   c $2\dfrac{3}{4}$ litres (ml, cl)

   d   4 m² (mm², ha)   e   13 cm² (mm², ha)   f   10 cm³ (mm³, m³)

6   A cube has sides of length 3 m. Find the volume of the cube in:

   a   m³   b   cm³   c   mm³ (give your answer in standard form).

7   The average radius of the Earth is 6378 km. Assuming the Earth is a sphere, find the volume of the Earth, using each of the following units. Give your answers in standard form to 3 significant figures.

   The volume of a sphere = $\dfrac{4}{3}\pi r^3$

   a   km³

   b   m³

   c   mm³

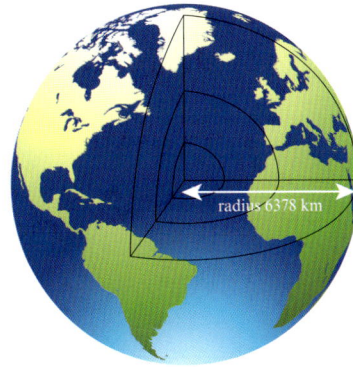

radius 6378 km

> **MATHEMATICAL CONNECTIONS**
>
> You learnt how to calculate volumes of three-dimensional shapes in Chapter 7. You also need to remember what you learnt about standard form in Chapter 5.

8 The dimensions of the cone shown in the diagram are given in cm.
Calculate the volume of the cone in:

   a cm^3 **b** mm^3 **c** km^3

Give your answers in standard form to 3 significant figures.

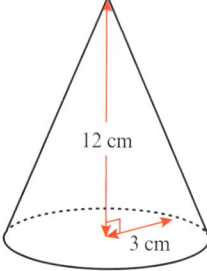

12 cm

3 cm

MATHEMATICAL CONNECTIONS

You learnt the formula for the volume of a cone in Chapter 7: volume $= \frac{1}{3}\pi r^2 h$.

APPLY YOUR SKILLS

9 A jar holds 200 grams of flour.

   a How many 30 gram measures can you take from the jar?

   b How much flour will be left over?

10 This is a lift in an office building.

The lift won't start if it holds more than 300 kg.

   a Tomas (105 kg), Shaz (65 kg), Sindi (55 kg), Rashied (80 kg) and Mandy (70 kg) are waiting for the lift. Can they all ride together?

   b Mandy says she will use the stairs. Can the others go safely into the lift?

   c Rashied says he will wait for the lift to come down again. Can the other four go together in the lift?

INVESTIGATION

11 **a** You may have seen the use of 'mega' and 'micro' in science. In Greek, 'mega' means 'large' and 'micro' means 'small'. Scientists use the word 'mega' to talk about 'millions' and 'micro' to talk about 'millionths'. Not everyone uses these words in quite the same way. Try to find out what 'mega' usually means in computing.

   b Try to find out about some more prefixes, like 'giga', 'terra', 'peta'. What others can you find?

13.2 Time

You have already learnt how to tell the time and you should know how to read and write time using the 12-hour and 24-hour systems.

WORKED EXAMPLE 2

Sara left home at 2.15 p.m. and returned at 3.50 p.m. How long was Sara away from home?

Answer

From 2.15 p.m. to 3.00 p.m. is 45 minutes	Start by counting on to the next whole hour.
From 3.00 p.m. to 3.50 p.m. is 50 minutes	
45 + 50 = 95 minutes	Add together the times in minutes.
= 1 hour and 35 minutes	Convert to hours and minutes.

INVESTIGATION

Babylonian mathematics

It may seem strange to have 60 as the number for converting units of time. This choice seems to have been made by the ancient Babylonians. They used 60 as their 'base' number, in the same way that use 10 for our most common number system. We call our number system a *decimal* system. The Babylonian system was a *sexagesimal* system!

1   Find all of the factors of the number 60.

2   Our decimal system is useful because we have 10 fingers and thumbs on our hands, divided into 2 lots of 5. Look at the factors of 60 and carry out some research to try to find out why the Babylonians might have chosen a sexagesimal system.

3   The Babylonians also seem to be the reason why we have 360 degrees in a full circle. What unit of time do you know that is divided into just over 360 units? How does this relate to a full turn of a circle?

The next example shows you how to calculate the duration of an event.

WORKED EXAMPLE 3

A train leaves at 05:35 and arrives at 18:20. How long is the journey?

Answers

You cannot simply calculate 18:20 − 05:35 because this does not take into account that time is not decimal. You can use the degrees, minutes and seconds function of a calculator to work with time. Look for the [DMS] key to do this.
To work out 18:20 − 05:35

Enter 18   Press [DMS]   Enter 20   Press [DMS]

Press the [−] key to subtract.

Enter 5   Press [DMS]   Enter 35   Press [DMS]

Press [=]

The display will show 12°45′00″

Write this as 12 hours and 45 minutes.

TIP

Calculators work differently, so learn how the time functions work on your calculator. Try to use your calculator to get the same answers as in the worked examples. You can also use this to check your answers in any exercises.

The methods you have seen in the examples so far are best used when you are dealing with time within the same day. But what happens when the time difference goes from one day to another day?

WORKED EXAMPLE 4

How much time passes from 19:35 on Monday to 03:55 on Tuesday?

Answer

19:35 to 24:00 is one part and 00:00 to 03:55 the next day is the other part.

A good way to start this problem is to divide the time into parts.

Part one:

19:35 to 20:00 is 25 minutes

20:00 to 24:00 is 4 hours

So, 19:35 to 24:00 is 4 h 25 min

Work out how much time passes to reach midnight.

Part two:

0:00 to 03:55 is 3 h 55 min

03:55 is 3 hours and 55 minutes past midnight.

4 h 25 min + 3 h 55 min = 7 h 80 min
                 = 8 h 20 min

The total time is 8 hours and 20 minutes.

Add the result of the two parts together.

80 minutes = 1 hour 20 minutes

Exercise 13.2

APPLY YOUR SKILLS

1   Aki has a satellite box that shows time in 24-hour format. He wants to set the machine to record some programmes.

   a   Write down the timer settings for starting and finishing each recording.

   i   10.30 p.m. to 11.30 p.m.

   ii   9.15 a.m. to 10.45 a.m.

   iii   7.45 p.m. to 9.10 p.m.

   b   Aki wants to record a tennis match being played in Melbourne. It starts at 4.30 p.m. in Melbourne. Aki is in Abu Dhabi, which is 7 hours behind Melbourne. At what time should he set the machine to start recording?

2   Imran started a marathon race at 9.25 a.m. He finished at 1.04 p.m. How long did he take? Give your answer in hours and minutes.

3   Lana records three songs. The songs last: 3 minutes 26 seconds; 3 minutes 19 seconds; and 2 minutes 58 seconds. She leaves a gap of two seconds between each of the songs. How long will it take to play the recording?

4   A journey started at 17:30 hours on Friday, 7 February, and finished 57 hours later. Write down the time, day and date when the journey finished.

5   Samuel works in a bookshop. This is his time sheet for the week.

Day	Mon	Tues	Wed	Thurs	Fri
Start	8:20	8:20	8:20	8:22	8:21
Lunch	12:00	12:00	12:30	12:00	12:30
Back	12:45	12:45	1:15	12:45	1:15
End	5:00	5:00	4:30	5:00	5:30
Total time worked					

   a   Calculate the values that go in the bottom row of the time sheet.

   b   How many hours in total did Samuel work in this week?

   c   Samuel is paid $5.65 per hour. Calculate how much he earned this week.

   d   This is how Samuel tried to work out the total time for Monday.

   'I start with 5:00 and subtract 12:45 to find the afternoon hours, then I use brackets to add on 12:00 minus 8:20.'

   i   Is his thinking mathematically correct?

   ii   He enters this into the calculator using the DMS key and gets the answer −4°5'00''. What did he do wrong?

Reading timetables

Most travel timetables are given as tables with columns representing journeys.
The 24-hour system is used to give the times.

Here is an example:

	SX	D	D	D	MO	D	SX
Anytown	06:30	07:45	12:00	16:30	17:15	18:00	20:30
Beecity	06:50	08:05	12:25	16:50	17:35	18:25	20:50
Ceeville	07:25	08:40	13:15	17:25	18:15	19:05	21:25

D – daily including Sundays, SX – daily except Saturdays, MO – Mondays only

Make sure you can see that each column represents a journey. For example, the first
column shows a bus leaving at 06:30 every day except Saturday (six times per week).
It arrives at the next town, Beecity, at 06:50 and then goes on to Ceeville, where it
arrives at 07:25.

Exercise 13.3

APPLY YOUR SKILLS

1   The timetable for evening trains between Mitcham's Place and Crosswell
    is shown below.

Mitcham's Place	18:29	19:02	19:32	20:02	21:04
Ninesides	18:40	19:13	19:43	20:13	21:15
Pentlands	19:01	19:31	20:01	20:31	21:33
Crosswell	19:17	19:47	20:17	20:47	21:49

a   Shaheeda wants to catch a train at Mitcham's Place and get to
    Pentlands by 8.45 p.m. What is the time of the latest train she
    should catch?

b   Calculate the time the 19:02 train from Mitcham's Place takes to
    travel to Crosswell.

c   Thabo arrives at Ninesides station at 6.50 p.m. How long will he have
    to wait for the next train to Crosswell?

2   The timetable for a bus service between Aville and Darby is shown below.

Aville	10:30	10:50	and	18:50
Beeston	11:05	11:25	every	19:25
Crossway	11:19	11:39	20 minutes	19:39
Darby	11:37	11:57	until	19:57

a   How many minutes does a bus take to travel from Aville to Darby?

b   Write down the timetable for the first bus on this service to leave
    Aville after the 10:50 bus.

c   Arjun arrives at Beeston bus station at 2.15 p.m. What is the time of
    the next bus to Darby?

APPLY YOUR SKILLS CONTINUED

3   The tides for a two-week period are shown on this tide table.

February	High tide		Low tide	
	Morning	**Afternoon**	**Morning**	**Afternoon**
1 Wednesday	12:13	--	05:18	18:00
2 Thursday	00:17	12:57	06:14	18:49
3 Friday	01:09	13:32	07:00	19:30
4 Saturday	01:52	14:04	07:40	20:04
5 Sunday	02:29	14:34	08:15	20:38
6 Monday	03:03	15:05	08:48	21:11
7 Tuesday	03:36	15:37	09:22	21:43
8 Wednesday	04:11	16:10	09:57	22:15
9 Thursday	04:48	16:44	10:30	22:45
10 Friday	05:28	17:18	11:04	23:16
11 Saturday	06:14	17:57	11:40	23:54
12 Sunday	07:06	18:45	12:22	--
13 Monday	08:08	19:48	00:41	13:15
14 Tuesday	09:17	21:11	01:41	14:25

a   What is the earliest high tide in this period?

b   How long is it between high tides on day 2?

c   How long is it between the first high tide and the first low tide on day 7?

d   Tatsuo likes to go surfing an hour before high tide.

   i   What time will this be on Sunday 5 February?

   ii   Explain why it is unlikely to be at 01:29.

e   Sandra owns a fishing boat.

   i   She cannot go out in the mornings if the low tide occurs between 5 a.m. and 9 a.m. On which days does this happen?

   ii   Sandra takes her boat out in the afternoons if high tide is between 11 a.m. and 2.30 p.m. On which days can she go out in the afternoons?

13.3 Limits of accuracy – upper and lower bounds

Measurements are always given to a certain level of accuracy. The limits of accuracy of any measurement depends on the instruments used to measure it, but even with very accurate scientific measuring devices, quantities cannot be measured exactly because they are continuous values.

MATHEMATICAL CONNECTIONS

You learnt to round numbers in Chapter 1. Make sure that you remember how rounding works before continuing with this section.

The way we round numbers means that all measurements have to be between certain limits. These limits depend on the level of accuracy that was used to round the measurement.

The smallest value a measurement can take is called the **lower bound**. The greatest value it can take is called the **upper bound**. The difference between the upper and lower bounds is called the error interval – a measurement can fall anywhere within this interval.

Read through the next example to see how these bounds apply in real life.

Raeman operates a crane at a building site. The manufacturer states that the crane can safely lift a maximum of 6.2 tonnes. Raeman needs to move some 1.2 tonne blocks, where the mass of each block is given to 1 decimal place. He starts by calculating how many 1.2 tonne blocks make 6.2 tonnes in total. $\frac{6.2}{1.2} = 5.17$ blocks, so Raeman decides he can safely lift 5 blocks.

But, the mass of the blocks has been rounded to 1 decimal place. What if the blocks all weigh 1.245 tonnes? They all round to 1.2 tonnes to 1 decimal place, but the total mass of 5 blocks is now:

$5 \times 1.245 = 6.225$ tonnes.

This is more than the crane can lift safely.

How can Raeman work out the maximum number of blocks he can lift safely?

LINK

The Hubble Space Telescope, launched into space in 1990, was originally made with a 1 mm error in the shape of the lens. This caused many of the images to be blurred and a repair had to be made in 1993. Even a small error can completely ruin scientific instruments that rely on precise measurement.

Finding the greatest and least possible values of a rounded measurement

In the crane example 1.2 tonnes is rounded to 1 decimal place. It can be useful to work out the greatest and least possible values of the actual measurement.

If you place 1.2 on a number line, you can see much more clearly what the range of possible values are:

At the upper end, the range of possible values stops at 1.25. If you round 1.25 to 1 decimal place you get 1.3. Although 1.25 does not round to 1.2 (to 1 decimal place), it is still used as the upper value. However, you should understand that the actual value can be anything up to *but not including* 1.25. The largest possible value is called the upper bound. Similarly, the lowest possible value is called the lower bound.

> **TIP**
>
> To find the limits think about what 1 decimal place means. One decimal place is 0.1. If you divide 0.1 by 2 you get 0.05. Add 0.05 to find the upper limit and subtract 0.05 to find the lower limit. Write the boundaries as an inequality.
>
> $$1.15 \leqslant \overset{\textcircled{+0.05}}{\underline{\qquad}} 1.2 \overset{\textcircled{+0.05}}{\underline{\qquad}} < 1.25$$

If *m* represents the mass (in tonnes) of the block, then you can express the error interval as:

$1.15 \leqslant m < 1.25$

This is called inequality notation and it shows that the true value of *m* lies between 1.15 (including 1.15) and 1.25 (not including 1.25).

> ## WORKED EXAMPLE 5
>
> Find the upper and lower bounds of the following, taking into account the level of rounding shown in each case.
>
> **a**   10 cm, to the nearest cm
> **b**   22.5, to 1 decimal place
> **c**   128 000, to 3 significant figures
> **d**   120, to the nearest 20
>
> **Answers**
>
> **a**   Show 10 cm on a number line.
>
> The real value will be closest to 10 cm if it lies between the lower bound of 9.5 cm and the upper bound of 10.5 cm.
>
> **b**   Look at 22.5 on a number line.
>
> The real value will be closest to 22.5 if it lies between the lower bound of 22.45 and the upper bound of 22.55.
>
> **c**   128 000 is shown on a number line.
>
> 128 000 lies between the lower bound of 127 500 and the upper bound of 128 500.
>
> **d**   120 is shown on a number line.
>
> 120 lies between the lower bound of 110 and the upper bound of 130.

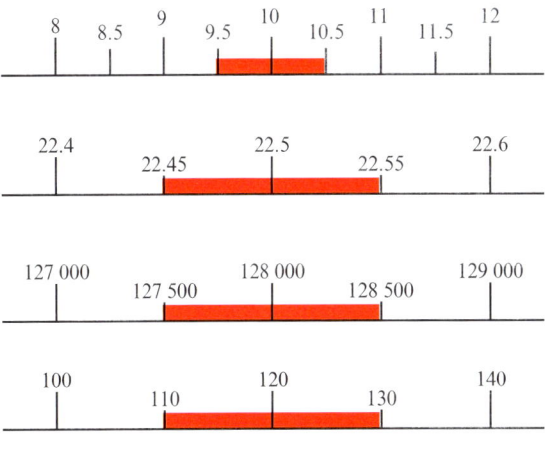

Exercise 13.4

1 Each of the following numbers is given to the nearest whole number. Find the lower and upper bounds of the numbers.

    a 12   **b** 8   **c** 100

    d 9   **e** 72   **f** 127

2 Each of the following numbers is correct to 1 decimal place. Write down the lower and upper bounds of the numbers.

    a 2.7   **b** 34.4   **c** 5.0

    d 1.1   **e** −2.3   **f** −7.2

3 Each of the following numbers has been rounded to the degree of accuracy shown in brackets. Find the upper and lower bounds in each case.

    a 132 (nearest whole number)   **b** 300 (nearest one hundred)

    c 405 (nearest five)   **d** 15 million (nearest million)

    e 32.3 (1 d.p.)   **f** 26.7 (1 d.p.)

    g 0.5 (1 d.p.)   **h** 12.34 (2 d.p.)

    i 132 (3 s.f.)   **j** 0.134 (3 s.f.)

APPLY YOUR SKILLS

4 Anne estimates that the mass of a lion is 300 kg. Her estimate is correct to the nearest 100 kg. Between what limits does the actual mass of the lion lie?

5 In a race, Nomatyala ran 100 m in 15.3 seconds. The distance is correct to the nearest metre and the time is correct to 1 decimal place. Write down the lower and upper bounds of:

    a the actual distance Nomatyala ran   **b** the actual time taken.

6 The length of a piece of thread is 4.5 m to the nearest 10 cm. The actual length of the thread is L cm. Find the range of possible values for L, giving your answer in the form $\dots \leqslant L < \dots$

Problem-solving with upper and lower bounds

Some calculations use more than one rounded value. You can use the upper and lower bounds of each value to find the upper and lower bounds for the calculated answer, but you need to work carefully.

TIP

If you get confused when dealing with upper and lower bounds, draw a number line to help you.

WORKED EXAMPLE 6

The dimensions of a rectangular rug are given as 14 m × 2 m, correct to the nearest metre.

Find the greatest and smallest values for the area of this rug.

Answer

$13.5 \leqslant L < 14.5$	Find the upper and lower bounds of each measurement.
$1.5 \leqslant W < 2.5$	
Smallest possible area:	Multiply the lower bounds of the measurements to find the smallest possible area.
$13.5 \times 1.5 = 20.25\,\text{m}^2$	
Greatest possible area:	Multiply the upper bounds of the measurements to find the greatest possible area.
$14.5 \times 2.5 = 36.25\,\text{m}^2$	

WORKED EXAMPLE 7

An antelope runs across a riverbed that is 380 m wide (to the nearest 10 metres) at a speed of 3.9 metres per second (to 1 decimal place).

What is the least and greatest possible time it will take to run this distance?

Answer

Start by finding the upper and lower bounds of each measurement.

Draw a two-way table to relate the measurements.

Divide the distance in each column by each speed.

Distance Speed	375	385
3.85	97.40	100
3.95	94.94	97.47

The greatest possible time is 100 seconds. The least possible time is 94.94 seconds (correct to 2 decimal places).

> **TIP**
>
> Time = $\dfrac{\text{distance}}{\text{speed}}$

WORKED EXAMPLE 8

If $a = 3.6$ (to 1 d.p.) and $b = 14$ (to the nearest whole number), find the upper and lower bounds for each of the following:

a $a + b$ **b** ab **c** $b - a$ **d** $\dfrac{a}{b}$ **e** $\dfrac{a + b}{a}$

Answers

First, find the upper and lower bounds of a and b:

$3.55 \leqslant a < 3.65$ and $13.5 \leqslant b < 14.5$

a Upper bound for $(a + b)$ = upper bound of a + upper bound of b

$= 3.65 + 14.5$

$= 18.15$

Lower bound for $(a + b)$ = lower bound for a + lower bound for b

$= 3.55 + 13.5$

$= 17.05$

You can write this as: $17.05 \leqslant (a + b) < 18.15$

b Upper bound for ab = upper bound for a × upper bound for b

$= 3.65 \times 14.5$

$= 52.925$

Lower bound for ab = lower bound of a × lower bound of b

$= 3.55 \times 13.5$

$= 47.925$

You can write this as: $47.925 \leqslant ab < 52.925$

c Think carefully about $b - a$. To find the upper bound you need to subtract the smallest possible number from the largest possible number. So:

Upper bound for $(b - a)$ = upper bound for b − lower bound for a

$= 14.5 - 3.55$

$= 10.95$

For the lower bound, subtract the largest possible number from the smallest possible number:

Lower bound for $(b - a)$ = lower bound for b − upper bound for a

$= 13.5 - 3.65$

$= 9.85$

You can write this as: $9.85 \leqslant (b - a) < 10.95$

d To find the upper bound of $\dfrac{a}{b}$ you need to divide the largest possible value of a by the smallest possible value of b:

Upper bound $= \dfrac{\text{upper bound for } a}{\text{lower bound for } b} = \dfrac{3.65}{13.5} = 0.2703\ldots = 0.270$ (3 s.f.)

Lower bound $= \dfrac{\text{lower bound for } a}{\text{upper bound for } b} = \dfrac{3.55}{14.5} = 0.2448\ldots = 0.245$ (3 s.f.)

You can write this as: $0.245 \leqslant \dfrac{a}{b} < 0.270$

WORKED EXAMPLE 8 CONTINUED

e Upper bound of $= \dfrac{a+b}{a} = \dfrac{\text{upper bound for } a+b}{\text{lower bound for } a} = \dfrac{18.15}{3.55}$

$$= 5.1126\ldots = 5.11 \text{ (3 s.f.)}$$

Lower bound of $= \dfrac{a+b}{a} = \dfrac{\text{lower bound for } a+b}{\text{upper bound for } a} = \dfrac{17.05}{3.65}$

$$= 4.6712\ldots = 4.67 \text{ (3 s.f.)}$$

You can write this as: $4.67 \leqslant \dfrac{a+b}{a} < 5.11$

REFLECTION

Do you think the worked examples have improved your skills in working with upper and lower bounds? Explain why or why not.

Are there any ideas that you are still not sure about? If so, what can you do to develop more confidence in this topic?

Exercise 13.5

1 Each of these values has been rounded to the degree of accuracy in brackets:

$a = 5.6$ (to 1 d.p.) $b = 24.1$ (to 1 d.p.) $c = 145$ (to 3 s.f.) $d = 0.34$ (to 2 d.p.)

Calculate the upper and lower bounds for each of the following to 3 significant figures.

a a^2 **b** b^3 **c** $c\,d^3$ **d** $a^2 + b^2$ **e** $\dfrac{c}{b^2}$

f $\dfrac{ab}{cd}$ **g** $\dfrac{c}{a} - \dfrac{b}{d}$ **h** $\dfrac{a}{d} \div \dfrac{c}{b}$ **i** $dc + \sqrt{\dfrac{a}{b}}$ **j** $dc - \sqrt{\dfrac{a}{b}}$

APPLY YOUR SKILLS

2 12 kg of sugar are removed from a container holding 50 kg. Each measurement is correct to the nearest kilogram. Find the lower and upper bounds of the mass of sugar left in the container.

3 The dimensions of a rectangle are 3.61 cm and 2.57 cm, each correct to 3 significant figures.

    a Write down the upper and lower bounds for each dimension.

    b Find the upper and lower bounds of the area of the rectangle.

    c Write down the upper and lower bounds of the area correct to 3 significant figures.

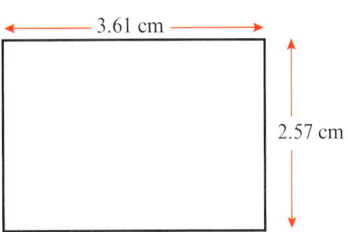

APPLY YOUR SKILLS CONTINUED

4 The mean radius of the Earth is 6378 km, to the nearest km.
Assume that the Earth is a sphere.
Find upper and lower bounds for:

    a the surface area of the Earth in km²

    b the volume of the Earth in km³.

5 A cup holds 200 ml to the nearest ml, and a large container holds
86 litres to the nearest litre. What is the largest possible number of
cups of water needed to fill the container? What is the smallest possible
number of cups?

6 A straight road slopes steadily upwards. If the road rises 8 m (to the
nearest metre) over a horizontal distance of 120 m (to the nearest 10 m),
what is the maximum possible gradient of the road? What is the minimum
possible gradient? Give your answers to 3 significant figures.

7 The two short sides of a right-angled
triangle are 3.7 cm (to the nearest mm)
and 4.5 cm (to the nearest mm).
Calculate upper and lower bounds for:

    a the area of the triangle

    b the length of the hypotenuse.

Give your answers to the nearest mm.

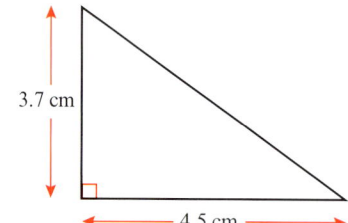

8 The angles in a triangle are $x°$, 38.4° (to 1 d.p.) and 78.1° (to 1 d.p.).
Calculate upper and lower bounds for x.

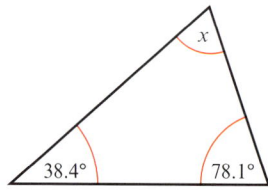

9 Quantity x is 45 to the nearest integer. Quantity y is 98 to the nearest
integer. Calculate upper and lower bounds for x as a percentage of y to 1
decimal place.

10 The following five masses are given to 3 significant figures.

138 kg	94.5 kg	1090 kg	345 kg	0.354 kg

Calculate upper and lower bounds for the mean of these masses.

MATHEMATICAL CONNECTIONS

There are several
connections to other
topics in this exercise.
Look back at earlier
chapters if you need
to remind yourself
of anything.

In all real-life situations
you will need to
be careful when
rounding. What other
real-life situations can
you think of where
rounding makes
a difference?

APPLY YOUR SKILLS CONTINUED

11 Gemma is throwing a biased dice. The probability that she throws a five is 0.245 to 3 decimal places. If Gemma throws the dice exactly 480 times, calculate upper and lower bounds for the number of fives Gemma *expects* to throw. Give your answer to 2 decimal places.

12 A cuboid of height, h, has a square base of side length, a.

a In an experiment, a and h are measured as 4 cm and 11 cm respectively, to the nearest cm.
What are the minimum and maximum possible values of the volume in cm^3?

b In another experiment, the volume of the block is found to be 350 cm^3, measured to the nearest 50 cm^3, and its height is measured as 13.5 cm, to the nearest 0.5 cm.

i What are the maximum and minimum possible values of the length a, in centimetres?

ii How many significant figures should you use to give a reliable answer for the value of a?

13 In a physics experiment a trolley is timed as it runs down a ramp 1.000 m long (to the nearest millimetre) to find its estimated speed. The speed in metres per second is calculated using $v = \dfrac{d}{t_1 - t_2}$. At the start of the experiment (t_1), the stopwatch shows 0.2 s and at the end (t_2) it shows 1.4 seconds (both correct to the nearest 0.1 second).
Find the upper and lower bounds for v, giving your answer correct to 3 significant figures.

SELF ASSESSMENT

A learning log is a useful tool that can help you identify what revision you need to do to improve your understanding and performance.

Here is an example of a completed learning log for the work on limits of accuracy.

I learnt …	Measurements are not ever exact.
	Any measurement will fall between limits called the upper and lower bound.
	You can write a measurement as an inequality that shows the error interval (what the measurement could be).
	When you use approximate measurements in calculations you combine small errors to get a bigger error and the answer will be less accurate than if you only round the final answer.

SELF ASSESSMENT CONTINUED

I still need to learn more about …	Finding upper and lower bounds when there are different degrees of accuracy. Understanding when a problem involves upper and lower bounds.
My next steps will be …	To do some of the exercises in the Practice Book. Watch an online tutorial on this topic.
I need some help with …	Problem solving where upper and lower bounds are given for more than one measurement.
In general, I feel __ about this section of work.	Reasonably confident.

Copy the headings and make your own learning log for the work on limits of accuracy.

13.4 Conversion graphs

So far in this chapter, you have seen that it is possible to convert between different units in the metric system. Another measuring system is the imperial system. Sometimes you might need to convert a measurement from one system to the other. Similarly, different countries use different currencies, for example dollars, yen, pounds and euros. When trading, it is important to accurately convert between currencies.

You can use **conversion** graphs when you need to convert from one measurement to another, for example from miles (imperial) to kilometres (metric) or from dollars to yen.

- Eight kilometres is approximately equal to five miles.

- If you travel no distance in kilometres then you also travel no distance in miles.

These two facts mean you can draw a graph for converting between miles and kilometres.

If you extend the line far enough you can read higher values. Notice, for example, that the line passes through the point with coordinates (25, 40). This means that 25 miles is approximately 40 km.

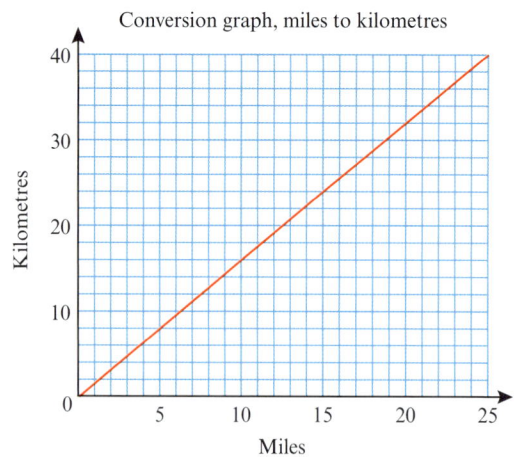
Conversion graph, miles to kilometres

MATHEMATICAL CONNECTIONS

You learned about line graphs and how to draw them in Chapter 4.

LINK

Imperial units are still used in some countries. For example, the United States and United Kingdom often give road distances in miles and speed limits in miles per hour. In Europe, distances are in kilometres and speeds in kilometres per hour. Many cars have speedometers that show the speed in both systems, so it is easier to obey speed limits wherever you drive.

Check for yourself that you can see that the following are true:

10 miles is roughly 16 km

12 miles is roughly 19 km

20 km is roughly 12.5 miles, and so on.

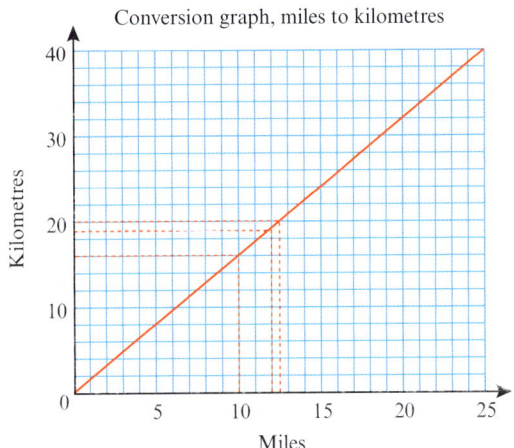

Conversion graph, miles to kilometres

Exercise 13.6

APPLY YOUR SKILLS

1 The graph shows the relationship between temperature in degrees Celsius (°C) and degrees Fahrenheit (°F).

Use the graph to convert:

a 60 °C to °F

b 16 °C to °F

c 0 °F to °C

d 100 °F to °C.

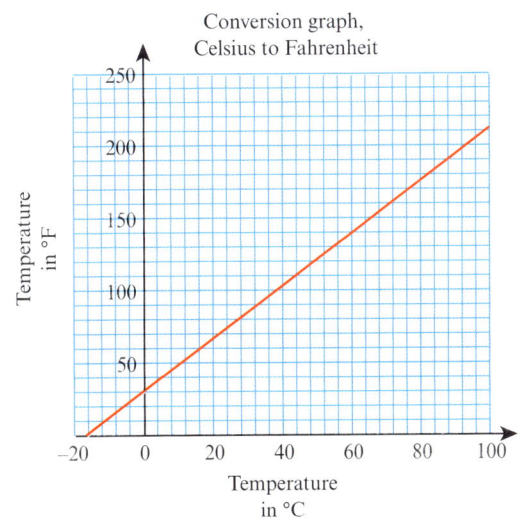

Conversion graph, Celsius to Fahrenheit

2 The graph is a conversion graph for kilograms and pounds.

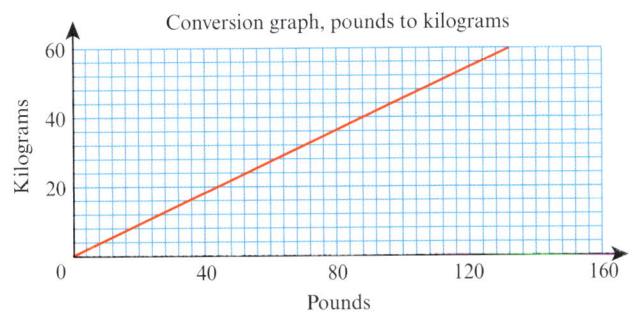

Conversion graph, pounds to kilograms

TIP

The unit symbol for the imperial mass, pounds, is lb.

APPLY YOUR SKILLS CONTINUED

a   What does one small square on the horizontal axis represent?

b   What does one small square on the vertical axis represent?

c   Change 80 pounds to kilograms.

d   According to the Amateur International Boxing Association, the minimum mass to qualify of as amateur lightweight boxer is 60 kg. What is this in pounds?

e   Which of the following conversions are incorrect? What should they be?

   i   30 kg = 66 pounds   ii   18 pounds = 40 kg
   iii   60 pounds = 37 kg   iv   20 pounds = 9 kg

3   The graph shows the conversion between UK pounds (£) and US dollars ($), as shown on a particular website in February 2022.

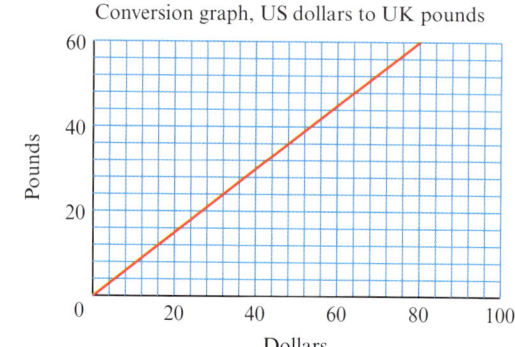

Conversion graph, US dollars to UK pounds

Use the graph to convert:

a   £12 to $

b   £48 to $

c $44 to £

d $32 to £.

4   The cooking time (in minutes) for a joint of meat (in kilograms) can be calculated by multiplying the mass of the joint by 40 and then adding 30 minutes. The graph shows the cooking time for different masses of meat.

Use the graph to answer the following questions.

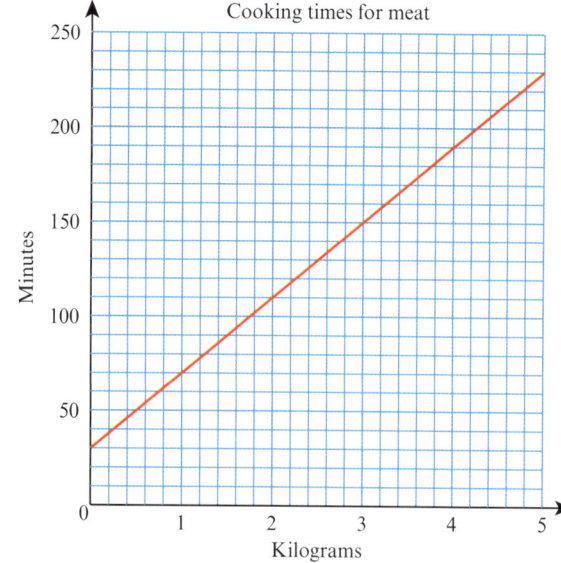

Cooking times for meat

APPLY YOUR SKILLS CONTINUED

   a If a joint of this meat has a mass of 3.4 kg, approximately how long will it take to cook?

   b If a joint of meat needs to be cooked for 220 minutes, approximately how much is its mass?

   c By calculating the mass of a piece of meat that takes only 25 minutes to cook, explain carefully why it is not possible to use this graph for every possible joint of meat.

5 You are told that Mount Everest is approximately 29 000 ft high, and that this measurement is approximately 8850 m.

   a Draw a conversion graph for feet and metres on graph paper.

   b You are now told that Mount Snowdon is approximately 1085 m high. What is this measurement in feet? Use your graph to help you.

   c A tunnel in the French Alps is 3400 feet long. Approximately what is the measurement in metres?

6 Mount Rubakumar, on the planet Ktorides is 1800 *squidges* high. This measurement is equivalent to 3450 *splodges*.

   a Draw a conversion graph for *squidges* and *splodges*.

   b If Mount Otsuki, also on planet Ktorides, is 1200 *splodges* high, what is this measurement in *squidges*?

   c There are, in fact, 80 *ploggs* in one *splodge*. If Mount Adil on planet Ktorides is 1456 *squidges* high, what is the measurement in *ploggs*?

TIP

ft is the abbreviation for the imperial unit foot (plural, feet). One foot is a little over 30 cm.

13.5 Exchanging currencies

You have used graphs to convert from one currency to another. However, if you know the exchange rate, then you can convert between currencies without a graph.

Calculating money involves working with decimals, because most currencies are decimals. Remember though, when you calculate with money you need to include the units ($ or cents) in your answers.

The money a country uses is called its currency. Each country has its own currency and most currencies work on a decimal system (100 small units are equal to one main unit). The following table shows you the currency units of a few different countries.

Country	Main unit	Smaller unit
USA	Dollar ($)	= 100 cents
Japan	Yen (¥)	= 100 sen
UK	Pound (£)	= 100 pence
Germany	Euro (€)	= 100 cents
India	Rupee (₹)	= 100 paise

WORKED EXAMPLE 9

Convert £50 into Botswanan pula, given that £1 = 15.63 pula.

Answer

£1 = 15.63 pula

£50 = 15.63 pula × 50 = 781.50 pula

TIP

You can write currency exchange rates using ratios, For example:

British pounds : Botswanan pula = 1 : 15.63

Botswanan pula : British pounds = $1 : \dfrac{1}{15.63}$

WORKED EXAMPLE 10

Convert 803 Mexican pesos into British pounds at a rate of £1 = 27.63 pesos.

Answer

27.63 pesos = £1

So 1 peso = £$\dfrac{1}{27.63}$

803 pesos = £$\dfrac{1}{27.63}$ × 803 = £29.06

LINK

Currency conversion rates change constantly. You can find up-to-date conversion factors as well as currency conversion apps and calculators on the internet. When you use a debit or credit card to pay for items in a different currency, the bank will convert the price using the rate at the time of the transaction.

Exercise 13.7

APPLY YOUR SKILLS

1   Find the total cost of eight apples at 50c each, three oranges at 35c each and 5 kg of bananas at $2.69 per kilogram.

2   How much would you pay for: 240 textbooks at $15.40 each, 100 pens at $1.25 each and 360 erasers at 95c each?

3   If 1 Bahraini dinar = £1.99, convert 4000 dinar to pounds.

4   If US $1 = £0.7802, how many dollars can you buy with £300?

APPLY YOUR SKILLS CONTINUED

5   An American tourist visits South Africa with $3000. The exchange rate when she arrives is $1 = R15.84. She changes all her dollars into rands and then spends R900 per day for seven days. She changes the rands she has left back into dollars at a rate of $1 = R15.92. How much does she get in dollars?

6   Convert 450 Peruvian Nuevo Sol into US Dollars given that $1 = 3.95540 Nuevo Sols.

TIP

There is no special symbol for Rands, you just use the letter R.

REFLECTION

What have you learnt from this work on currencies?

When converting between currencies you sometimes multiply and sometimes divide. Did you make any mistakes when choosing whether to multiply or divide? How can you make sure you choose the correct operation?

PEER ASSESSMENT

Assess your partner's work in Exercise 13.7. You can find the answers online if you need them.

Provide feedback using these three headings:
*   What went well?
*   How could your work be better?
*   What steps can you take to improve?

TIP

There are some starter sentences for this method of peer assessment in Chapter 5 if you need some guidance.

SUMMARY

Do you know ...?
There are several measuring systems; the most common are metric and imperial.
Time is measured in different units, so you have to consider the conversion factors when you work with time.
Every measurement quoted to a given accuracy has a lower bound and an upper bound. The actual value of a measurement is greater than or equal to the lower bound, but strictly less than the upper bound.
You can draw a graph to help convert between different systems of units.
Countries use different currencies and you can convert between them if you know the exchange rate.

SUMMARY CONTINUED

Are you able to …?
convert between various metric units
convert between units of time and solve problems involving times in different formats (with and without a calculator)
calculate upper and lower bounds for numbers rounded to a specified degree of accuracy
calculate upper and lower bounds when more than one rounded number is used in a problem
draw a conversion graph
use a conversion graph to convert between different units
convert between currencies when given the exchange rate.

Practice questions

1   The graph shows the relationship between speeds in mph and km/h.

Use the graph to estimate:

a   the speed, in km/h, of a car travelling at 65 mph   [2]

b   the speed, in mph, of a train travelling at 110 km/h.   [2]

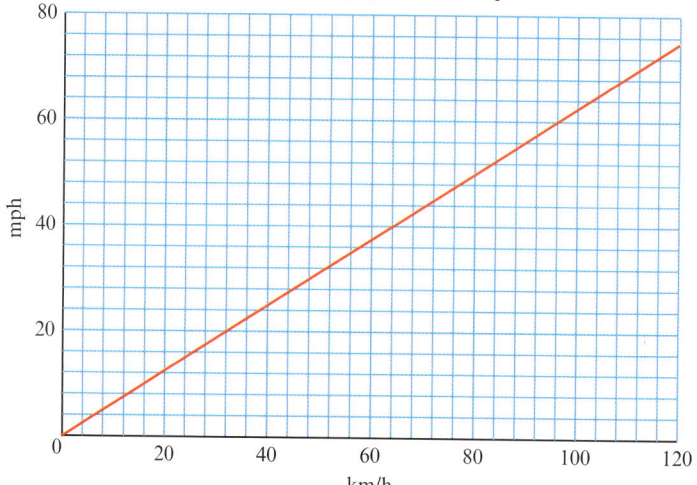

Conversion graph, km/h to mph

2   This time-card records a worker's start time and finish times and the length of their lunch break each day for a week.

Day	Time in	Time out	Lunch	Hours worked
Monday	8.15 a.m.	5.25 p.m.	45 mins	
Tuesday	8.17 a.m.	5.30 p.m.	30 mins	
Wednesday	8.23 a.m.	5.50 p.m.	45 mins	
Thursday	8.22 a.m.	6.00 p.m.	60 mins	
Friday	7.58 a.m.	7.00 p.m.	45 mins	

a Calculate the hours worked for each day. [3]

b Calculate the total hours worked for the week. [2]

c This person earns $8.95 per hour. Calculate how much they earned in this week. [2]

d The employer has to deduct 12% tax from the earnings. How much will be paid after deductions? [2]

3 Each of the following numbers has been rounded to the degree of accuracy shown in the brackets. Find the upper and lower bounds in each case.

a 34 (nearest unit) [2]

b 600 (1 s.f.) [2]

c 12.69 (2 d.p.) [2]

d 670 (nearest 10) [2]

4 A child is weighed at a clinic and their mass is recorded to the nearest half kilogram as 12.5 kg.

What is the greatest and least possible mass of this child? [3]

5 These exchange rates are displayed at a hotel reception desk in Mumbai.

Currency	Rate (Indian Rupees)
US $	75.40
UK £	98.97
Euro (€)	82.82
Australian $	56.79
UAE Dirham (Dhs)	20.53
Saudi Riyal (SR)	20.10

a Use the table to convert these amounts of money to Indian Rupees.

i US$100 [2]

ii €600 [2]

iii Dhs450 [2]

iv SR1265 [2]

b An Australian visitor booked a room for five nights at a rate of Rs14 000 per night. What is the cost of the accommodation in Australian dollars? [2]

6 Japan has an area of 378,000 km², to the nearest 1000 km².

a Work out the area of Japan in m², giving your answer in standard form, correct to 3 significant figures. [3]

b Calculate the upper and lower bounds for the area of Japan in km². [2]

c We calculate population density, in people per square kilometre, using the formula:

$$\text{Population density} = \frac{\text{population}}{\text{area}}.$$

If the population of Japan is 126 million, to the nearest million, calculate the upper bound of Japan's population density. Give your answer to 3 significant figures. [3]

7   The diagram shows a conversion graph for gallons to litres.

    a   Use the graph to convert 4 gallons into litres.   [2]

    b   Use the graph to convert 27 litres into gallons.   [2]

    c   If L is the number of litres and G is the number of gallons, find an approximate formula for L in terms of G. Explain why the formula is not necessarily exact.   [2]

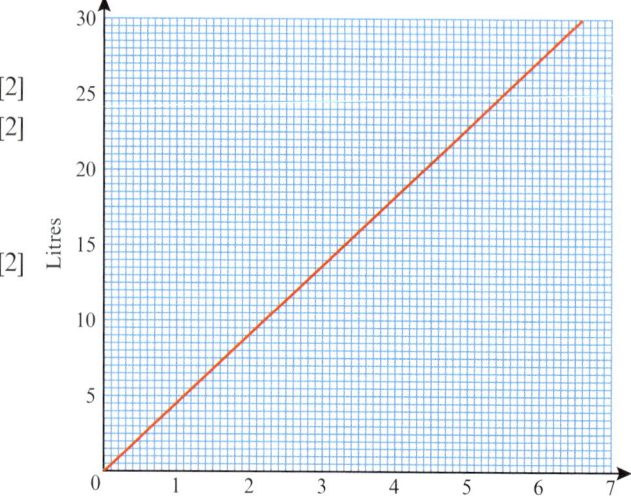

8   Given that $a = 2.5$, $b = 4.3$ and $c = 8.5$, all given to 1 decimal place, calculate the upper bounds of each expression, giving your answer to 2 decimal places.

    a $a + b - c$ [4]   **b** $\dfrac{a^2}{b}$ [4]   **c** $\dfrac{a}{(c - b)}$ [4]

9   A cuboid has dimensions 14.5 cm, 13.2 cm and 21.3 cm. These dimensions are all given to 1 decimal place.
    Calculate the upper and lower bounds for the volume of the cuboid in:

    a cm^3 [2]   **b** mm^3 [2]

    Give your answers in standard form.

10 The lengths in the diagram are given to 1 decimal place.

    Giving your answers to 2 decimal places:

    a   find the lower bound for the area of the triangle   [3]

    b   find the upper bound for the length AB [3]

    c   find the maximum possible gradient of the line AB.   [3]

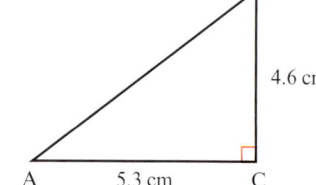

11 A cuboid of height, h, has a square base of side length, a.

    a   In an experiment, a and h are measured as 7 cm and 13 cm, to the nearest cm, respectively. Calculate the maximum possible value of the volume in cm^3.   [3]

    b   In another experiment, the volume of the block is found to be 300 cm^3, measured to the nearest 50 cm^3, and its height is measured as 13.5 cm, to the nearest 0.5 cm. Calculate the maximum and minimum possible values of the length a, in centimetres.   [4]

SELF ASSESSMENT

Use your answers to the practice questions to assess of your own understanding of measurement.

List the question numbers.

Rate your work on each question using this scale:

- Circle the question number if you understand the concept well.
- Underline the question number if you need to revise the concept.

> # Chapter 14

Further solving of equations and inequalities

IN THIS CHAPTER YOU WILL:

- derive and solve simultaneous linear equations graphically and algebraically
- use number lines to represent and interpret inequalities
- solve linear inequalities algebraically
- derive linear inequalities and find regions in a plane
- solve quadratic equations by completing the square
- solve quadratic equations by using the quadratic formula
- factorise quadratics where the coefficient of x^2 is not 1
- simplify algebraic fractions.

Think about a number of boats leaving and entering a port. They are all on separate paths and there are no markings in the ocean to guide them. Understanding how to find the meeting points of different paths can help port controllers guide vessels and avoid collisions.

Think about how to work out where a ship is at any given time. What do you need to know? Why is this more complicated than a problem with two cars moving along a road?

GETTING STARTED

1   In this chapter you need to be good at plotting straight lines from their equations. Draw a pair of axes, with x-values from -2 to 6 and y-values from -6 to 5, as shown in the diagram.

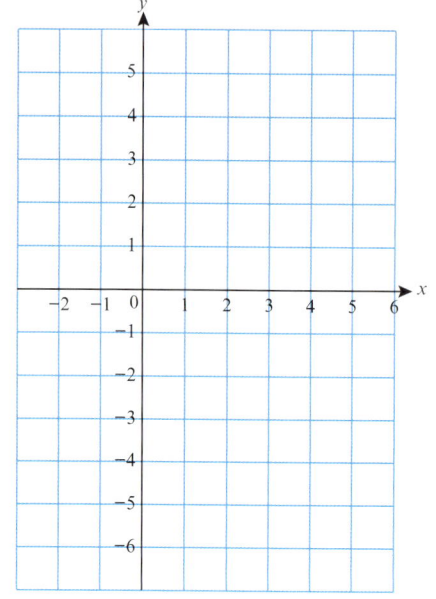

2   On the same pair of axes, plot the lines with the following equations:

$y = 1$
$x = 4$
$3x + 2y = 8$

3   Find the area of triangle 1 formed by these lines.

4   Now plot the line with the equation $3x + 2y = 2$.

5   Find the area of triangle 2 formed by this new line and the lines $y = 1$ and $x = 4$.

6   Another triangle is drawn with an area, A, that is greater or equal to the area of triangle 1 but smaller than the area of triangle 2.
Write an inequality to show the possible values of A.

14.1 Simultaneous linear equations

Graphical solution of simultaneous linear equations

Miguel enjoys walking and has two favourite walks. One is into the hills and is 4 km long. The other is along the river and is 2 km long. Miguel takes one of the walks each day for eight days and walks a total of 26 km. How many of each walk did Miguel take?

If you let x be the number of walks into the hills and y be the number of walks along the river, you can use the total number of walks to see that $x + y = 8$.

The total distance walking in the hills will be $x \times 4 = 4x$ and the total distance walking along the river will be $y \times 2 = 2y$. So the total distance walked is $4x + 2y$, which must equal 26.

This gives two equations:

$x + y = 8$

$4x + 2y = 26$

The information has two unknown values and you can use it to form two different equations. The equations are both linear equations and you can plot them on the same pair of axes. There is only one point where the values of x and y are the same for both equations – this is where the lines cross (the intersection). This is the **simultaneous** solution.

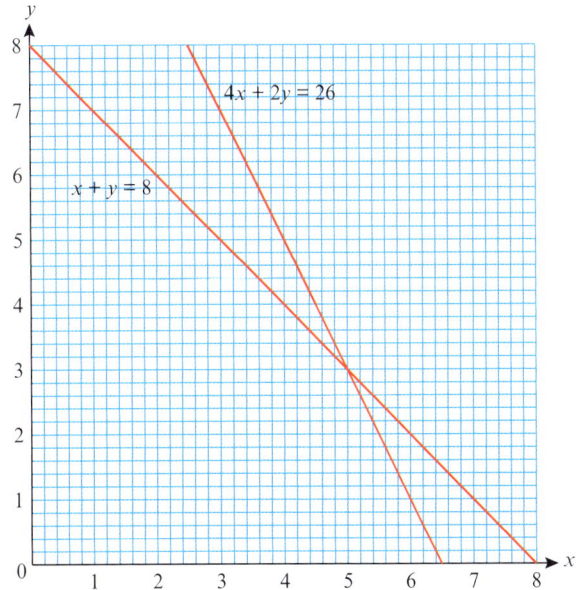

> **TIP**
>
> Simultaneous means, 'at the same time'. When you draw graphs of simultaneous linear equations you are looking for the point where two lines cross. The coordinates of this point give the x and y values which are solutions for both equations.

Notice that the point with coordinates (5, 3) lies on *both* lines so, $x = 5$ and $y = 3$ satisfy *both* equations. You can check this by substituting the values into the equations:

$x + y = 5 + 3 = 8$

and

$4x + 2y = 4(5) + 2(3) = 20 + 6 = 26$

This means that there were five walks into the hills and three walks by the river.

> **TIP**
>
> It is important that you remember to work out *both* unknowns. Every pair of simultaneous linear equations will have a pair of solutions.

LINK

Many problems in economics involve formulae containing several variables. When we try to answer financial questions – for example finding when a business venture breaks even or an investment gives the maximum return – we end up with several equations and several unknown values. This gives a set of simultaneous equations to solve.

WORKED EXAMPLE 1

By drawing the graphs of each of the following equations on the same pair of axes, find the simultaneous solutions to the equations.

$x - 3y = 6$

$2x + y = 5$

Answer

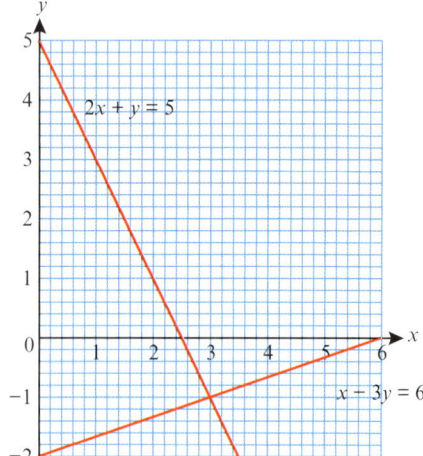

For the first equation:

if $x = 0$, $-3y = 6 \Rightarrow y = -2$

and, if $y = 0$, $x = 6$

So this line passes through the points $(0, -2)$ and $(6, 0)$.

For the second equation:

if $x = 0$, $y = 5$

and, if $y = 0$, $2x = 5 \Rightarrow x = \dfrac{5}{2}$

So this line passes through the points $(0, 5)$ and $\left(\dfrac{5}{2}, 0\right)$.

Plot the pairs of points and draw lines through them.

Notice that the two lines meet at the point with coordinates $(3, -1)$.

So, the solution to the pair of equations is $x = 3$ and $y = -1$.

Exercise 14.1

1 Draw the lines for each pair of equations and then use the point of intersection to find the simultaneous solution. The axes that you should use are given in each case.

    a $x + 2y = 11$

          $2x + y = 10$ (x from 0 to 11 and y from 0 to 10)

    b $x - y = -1$

          $2x + y = 4$ (x from -2 to 3 and y from 0 to 4)

    c $5x - 4y = -1$

          $2x + y = 10$ (x from -1 to 5 and y from 0 to 10)

MATHEMATICAL CONNECTIONS

Throughout this chapter you will need to solve basic linear equations as part of the method. Look back to Chapter 6 if you need to remind yourself how to do this.

2 Use the graphs shown to find the solutions to the following pairs of simultaneous equations.

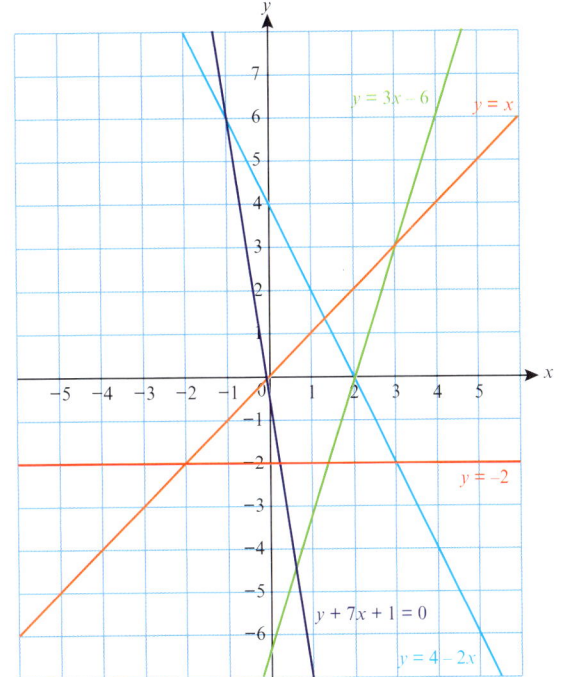

a $y = x$
    $y = -2$

b $y = x$
    $y = 3x - 6$

c $y = 4 - 2x$
    $y = -2$

d $y = 4 - 2x$
    $y + 7x + 1 = 0$

e $y = -2$
    $y + 7x + 1 = 0$

f $y = x$
    $y = 4 - 2x$

3 For each pair of equations, find three points on each line and draw the graphs. Use your graphs to estimate the solution of each pair of simultaneous equations.

a $3y = -4x + 3$
    $x = 2y + 1$

b $2 - x = -y$
    $8x + 4y = 7$

c $4x = 1 + 6y$
    $4x - 4 = 3y$

d $3x + 2y = 7$
    $4x = 2 + 3y$

4 a Explain why the graphical method does not always give an accurate and correct answer.

b How can you check whether a solution you obtained graphically is correct or not?

INVESTIGATION

When is there a solution?

1   Plot the following lines on the same pair of axes:
    $3x + 2y = 7$
    $6x + 4y = -2$

2   Why is it not possible to solve these equations simultaneously?

3   Is there any way that you can tell, from the equations, that there are no solutions?

4   (Challenge!) If you have the following pair of equations, what needs to be true for there to be a solution?
    $ax + by = 3$
    $cx + dy = 4$

Algebraic solution of simultaneous linear equations

The graphical method for solving simultaneous equations is suitable for whole number solutions but it can be slow and, for non-integer solutions, may not be as accurate as you need. You have already learnt how to solve linear equations with one unknown using algebraic methods. A pair of simultaneous equations gives information about two unknowns. You have to solve the equations together to find the solutions.

You are going to learn two methods of solving simultaneous equations:

- solving by substitution
- solving by elimination.

Solving by substitution

You can solve simultaneous equations by substitution by writing one of the equations in the form '$y = \dots$' or '$x = \dots$' and substituting into the other equation. The method is explained in the following worked example.

WORKED EXAMPLE 2

Solve simultaneously by substitution.

$3x - 2y = 29$ [1]

$4x + y = 24$ [2]

Answer

$4x + y = 24$	Solve equation [2] for y.
$y = 24 - 4x$ [3]	Label the new equation [3].
$3x - 2y = 29$ [1]	
$3x - 2(24 - 4x) = 29$	Substitute [3] into [1] by replacing y with $24 - 4x$.
$3x - 48 + 8x = 29$	Remove brackets.
$3x + 8x = 29 + 48$	Add 48 to both sides.
$11x = 77$	Add like terms.
$x = 7$	Divide both sides by 11.
So, $x = 7$	
$y = 24 - 4(7)$	Now, substitute the value of x into any of the equations to find y. Equation [3] will be easiest, so use this one.
$y = 24 - 28$	
$y = -4$	
$x = 7$ and $y = -4$	Write out the solutions.

TIP

You should always number the equations so you can identify each equation quickly and easily.

MATHEMATICAL CONNECTIONS

The substitution method involves rearranging formulae to make one of the variables the subject. You learnt how to do this in Chapter 6.

Solving by elimination

You can also solve simultaneous equations by eliminating (getting rid of) one of the variables.

WORKED EXAMPLE 3

Solve the following pair of equations using elimination:

$x - y = 4$ [1]

$x + y = 6$ [2]

Answer

$x - y = 4$ [1]   You can add the two equations together by adding the
$\underline{x + y = 6}$ [2]   left-hand sides and adding the right-hand sides.

$2x \quad = 10$

$2x = 10$ Notice that the equation that comes from this addition

$\Rightarrow x = \dfrac{10}{2}$ no longer contains a 'y' term, so you can now solve to find the value of x.

$x = 5$

$x + y = 6$ [2]   You now need to find the y-value that goes with this

$\Rightarrow 5 + y = 6$ value of x. Substitute x into equation [2].

$y = 1$

$x - y = 5 - 1 = 4$ Check that these values for x and y work in equation [1].

Both equations are satisfied by the pair of values $x = 5$ and $y = 1$.

The following worked examples look at different cases where you may need to subtract the equations, instead of adding, or where you need to multiply one or both equations before you add or subtract.

WORKED EXAMPLE 4

Solve the following pairs of simultaneous equations:

$2x - 3y = -8$ [1]

$5x + 3y = 1$ [2]

Answer

$2x - 3y = -8$ Notice that both equations have the same
                        coefficient of y, though the signs are different.
$\underline{5x + 3y = 1}$ If you add the equations together, you make use

$7x \quad\quad = -7$ [1] + [2]   of the fact that $-3y + 3y = 0$

$\Rightarrow x = -1$

TIP

Always 'line up' 'x's with 'x's, 'y's with 'y's and '=' with '='.

It will make your method clearer.

WORKED EXAMPLE 4 CONTINUED

$2x - 3y = -8$

$\Rightarrow 2(-1) - 3y = -8$ Substitute in [1]

$6 - 3y = 0$

$3y = 6$

$y = 2$

Now you know the value of x, you can substitute this into either equation and solve for y.

$5x + 3y = 5(-1) + 3(2)$

$= -5 + 6 = 1$

Check your values in equation [2] to be sure.

The second equation is also satisfied by these values, so $x = -1$ and $y = 2$.

MATHEMATICAL CONNECTIONS

If you need to remind yourself about working with directed numbers, look back to Chapter 1. In particular, make sure you are confident subtracting negative numbers.

WORKED EXAMPLE 5

Solve simultaneously:

$4x + y = -1$ [1]

$7x + y = -4$ [2]

Answer

$7x + y = -4$ [2] − [1]

$\underline{4x + y = -1}$

$3x \quad = -3$

$\Rightarrow x = -1$

The y-values have the same coefficient again, but this time they have the same sign. Use the fact that $y - y = 0$ and *subtract* one equation from the other. There are more 'x's in equation [2] so, consider [2] − [1].

$4x + y = -1$ [1]

$\Rightarrow 4(-1) + y = -1$

$y = 3$

Substitute into equation [1].

$7x + y = 7(-1) + 3$

$= -7 + 3 = -4$

Check that the values $x = -1$ and $y = 3$ work in equation [2].

Equation [2] is also satisfied by these values, so $x = -1$ and $y = 3$.

> **TIP**
>
> Always make it clear which equation you have chosen to subtract from which.
>
> Here, you have used the fact that $-4 - (-1) = -3$.

Manipulating equations before solving them

Sometimes you need to manipulate or rearrange one or both of the equations before you can solve them simultaneously by elimination. Worked examples 6 to 8 show you how this is done.

WORKED EXAMPLE 6

Solve simultaneously:

$2x - 5y = 24$ [1]

$4x + 3y = -4$ [2]

Answer

$2 \times$ [1]:
$4x - 10y = 48$ [3]

Here, neither the coefficients of x nor the coefficients of y match. But, if you multiply equation [1] by 2, you can make the coefficient of x the same in each.

Call this new equation [3].

$4x + 3y = -4$ [2]
$4x - 10y = 48$ [3]

Equations [2] and [3] have the same coefficient of x, so write these equations together and solve as before.

$4x + 3y = -4$ [2] − [3]
$\underline{4x - 10y = 48}$
      $13y = -52$
$\Rightarrow y = -4$

$2x - 5y = 24$
$\Rightarrow 2x - 5(-4) = 24$
$2x + 20 = 24$
$x = 2$

Substitute $y = -4$ into equation [1].

$4x + 3y = 4(2) + 3(-4)$
$= 8 - 12 = -4$

Check using equation [2].

So the pair of values $x = 2$ and $y = -4$ satisfy the pair of simultaneous equations.

WORKED EXAMPLE 7

Solve simultaneously:

$2x - 21 = 5y$

$3 + 4y = -3x$

Answer

Before you can work with these equations you need to rearrange them so they are in the same form.

$2x - 5y = 21$ [1]
$3x + 4y = -3$ [2]

In this pair, you cannot make the coefficients of x or y match by multiplying just one equation.

WORKED EXAMPLE 7 CONTINUED

$4 \times$ [1]:

$\quad 8x - 20y = 84 \qquad$ [3]

$5 \times$ [2]:

$\quad 15x + 20y = -15 \quad$ [4]

Here, you need to multiply each equation by a different value so that the coefficient of x or the coefficient of y match. It is best to choose to do this for the 'y' terms here because they have different signs and it is simpler to add equations rather than subtract!

$\quad 8x - 20y = 84 \qquad$ [3] + [4]

$\underline{15x + 20y = -15}$

$23x \qquad = 69$

$\Rightarrow x = 3$

$\quad 2x - 5y = 21$

$\Rightarrow 2(3) - 5y = 21$

$\quad 6 - 5y = 21$

$\quad\quad 5y = -15$

$\quad\quad y = -3$

Substitute for x in equation [1].

$3x + 4y = 3(3) + 4(-3)$

$\quad = 9 - 12 = -3$

Check using equation [2].

So $x = 3$ and $y = -3$ satisfy the pair of simultaneous equations.

WORKED EXAMPLE 8

Solve simultaneously:

$\dfrac{3x - 4y}{2} = 10 \quad$ [1]

$\dfrac{3x + 2y}{4} = 2 \quad$ [2]

Answer

$3x - 4y = 20$

In this pair of equations it makes sense to remove the fractions before you work with them. Multiply both sides of equation [1] by 2.

$3x + 2y = 8$

Multiply both sides of equation [2] by 4.

WORKED EXAMPLE 8 CONTINUED

$3x - 4y = 20$	$[3] - [4]$	Subtract equation [4] from equation [3].
$\underline{3x + 2y = 8}$		
$-6y = 12$		
$y = -2$		

$3x - 4(-2) = 20$ Substitute the value for y into equation [3].

$3x + 8 = 20$

$3x = 12$

$x = 4$

$3(4) + 2(-2) = 12 - 4 = 8$ Check using equation [4].

So $x = 4$ and $y = -2$ satisfy the pair of simultaneous equations.

Exercise 14.2

MATHEMATICAL CONNECTIONS

Remember from Chapter 1 that adding a negative is the same as subtracting a positive.

1   Solve for x and y by substitution. Check each solution.

    a $y + x = 7$ **b** $y = 1 - x$ **c** $2x + y = -14$
          $y = x + 3$ $x - 5 = y$ $y = 6$

    d $x - 8 = 2y$ **e** $3x - 2 = -2y$ **f** $3x + y = 6$
          $x + y = -2$ $2x - y = -8$ $9x + 2y = 1$

    g $4x - 1 = 2y$ **h** $3x - 4y = 1$
          $x + 1 = 3y$ $2x = 4 - 3y$

2   Solve for x and y by elimination. Check each solution.

    a $2x - y = 4$ **b** $-3x + 2y = 6$ **c** $2x + 5y = 12$
          $5x + y = 24$ $3x + 5y = 36$ $2x + 3y = 8$

    d $5x - 2y = 27$ **e** $x + 2y = 11$ **f** $-2x + 5y = 13$
          $3x + 2y = 13$ $x + 3y = 15$ $2x + 3y = 11$

    g $4x + y = 27$ **h** $4x - y = 16$ **i** $6x - 5y = 9$
          $3x - y = 15$ $6x - y = 26$ $2x + 5y = 23$

    j $6x - y = 18$ **k** $x + y = 12$ **l** $4x + 3y = 22$
          $4x - y = 10$ $5x - y = 24$ $4x + y = 18$

TIP

Remember that you need either the same coefficient of x or the same coefficient of y.

If both have the *same* sign, you should then subtract one equation from the other. If they have a *different* sign, then you should add them.

3 Solve simultaneously. Use the method you find easiest. Check all solutions.

a $5x + 3y = 22$
$10x - y = 16$

b $4x + 3y = 25$
$x + 9y = 31$

c $-3x + y = 5$
$-6x + 5y = -20$

d $x + y = 10$
$3x + 5y = 40$

e $5x + y = 11$
$-2x + 2y = 1$

f $4x - 3y = 11$
$5x - 9y = -2$

g $6x + 2y = 9$
$7x + 4y = 12$

h $12x - 13y = 34$
$3x - 26y = 19$

i $5x - 17y = -3$
$25x - 19y = -45$

j $3x - 3y = 13$
$4x - 12y = -6$

k $10x = 2 - 2y$
$2y = -7x - 1$

l $-2y = 1 - 7x$
$4x = 4 + 2y$

m $x = 12 + y$
$2x = 3 - y$

n $3x + 4y = -1$
$3x + 10 = 2y$

o $2x + y = 7$
$11 + x = 2y$

> **REFLECTION**
>
> As you work through the rest of the exercise, think about which methods you use. Why do you choose a particular method? Does it depend on the question or do you always choose the same method? Why?

4 Solve simultaneously.

a $3x + 7y = 37$
$5x + 6y = 39$

b $2x - 5y = -16$
$3x - 5y = -14$

c $-7x + 4y = 41$
$-5x + 6y = 45$

d $7x + 4y = 54$
$2x + 3y = 21$

e $2x - y = 1$
$3x + 5y = 34$

f $3x - 4y = 25$
$x - 3y = 15$

g $7x - 4y = 23$
$4x + 5y = 35$

h $3x - y = 2$
$3x + 5y = 26$

i $2x + 7y = 25$
$x + y = 5$

j $x + 3 = y$
$4x + y = -7$

k $3x + 11 = -y$
$-2x + y = 4$

l $y = 6x - 1$
$4x - 3y = -4$

m $2x + 3y - 8 = 0$
$4x + 5 = y$

n $y = \frac{2}{3}x + 6$
$2y - 4x = 20$

o $8x - 5y = 0$
$13x = 8y + 1$

5 Solve each pair of equations simultaneously.

a $3x + \frac{2y}{3} = 0$
$2x - \frac{y}{4} = 14$

b $4y + x + 5 = 0$
$y = x - 5$

c $3y - \frac{3x}{8} = -3$
$y - \frac{x}{2} = 2$

d $2x + \frac{y}{2} = 3$
$6x = -2y$

e $y = 3x - 6$
$2x + \frac{3y}{7} = -5$

f $\frac{3x}{7} - \frac{2y}{13} = 5$
$x + \frac{1}{3}y = \frac{3}{5}$

> **TIP**
>
> If an equation contains fractions, clear the fractions by multiplying each term by a suitable number (a common denominator).

6   Form a pair of simultaneous equations for each situation, and use them to solve the problem. Let the unknown numbers be x and y.

   a   The sum of two numbers is 120 and one of the numbers is 3 times the other. Find the value of the numbers.

   b   The sum of two numbers is −34 and their difference is 5. Find the numbers.

   c   A pair of numbers has a sum of 52 and a difference of 11. Find the numbers.

   d   The combined ages of two people is 34. If one person is 6 years younger than the other, find their ages.

7   A computer store sold 4 hard drives and 10 pen drives for $200, and 6 hard drives and 14 pen drives for $290. Find the cost of a hard drive and the cost of a pen drive.

8   A large sports stadium has 21 000 seats. The seats are organised into blocks of either 400 or 450 seats. There are three times as many blocks of 450 seats as there are blocks of 400 seats. How many blocks are there in total?

DISCUSSION

9   Work with a partner to create some more problems like those in questions 6–8. Set questions for each other and try solving them. Explain clearly what the two answers represent.

REFLECTION

Think carefully about these problems. How can you recognise problems involving simultaneous equations if you are not told to use this method to solve them?

SELF ASSESSMENT

How well do you understand simultaneous equations and the methods used to solve them?

1   Mark your own answer to questions 1 to 5 in Exercise 14.2.

2   Use this scale to give yourself a rating of 1, 2, 3 or 4.

4	3	2	1
I know what we are trying to do. I understand how to use algebra to solve a pair of simultaneous equations. I can look at the equations and decide which method is best to use to solve them. I can clearly explain this work to someone else.	I mostly know what we are trying to do. I understand most of the work on simultaneous equations. I can find most of the solutions, but I find some questions confusing.	I think I need more practice. I get confused and am not sure what method to use to solve the equations. I cannot do many of the calculations.	I really don't understand this at all. I need help with all aspects of this work.

3   If you rated yourself 3, 2 or 1, write down the next step you will take to improve your rating.

14.2 Linear inequalities

When you solve linear equations you end up with a single solution for a single variable. Sometimes, however, there are situations where there are a range of possible solutions. This section extends your earlier work on linear equations to look at **linear inequalities**.

Number lines

Imagine you are told that $x < 4$. You already know this means that each possible value of x must be less than 4. Therefore, x can be 3, 2, 1, 0, -1, -2, … but that is not all. 3.2 is also less than 4, as is 3.999, 2.43, -3.4, -100, …

If you draw a number line, you can use an arrow to represent the set of numbers less than 4:

LINK

You are already familiar with the idea of a number line. Both the x- and y-axes are examples of number lines.

Any kind of regular scale like a thermometer or tape measure used in a long jump pit, for example, is really a kind of number line.

This allows you to show the possible values of x neatly without writing them all down. (In fact, there is an infinite number of values, so you can't write them all down!) Notice that the 'open circle' above the four is not filled in. This symbol is used because it is **not** possible for x to be equal to four.

Now imagine that $x \geqslant -2$. This means that x can be greater than, or equal to -2. You can show that x can be equal to -2 by 'filling in' the circle above -2 on the number line:

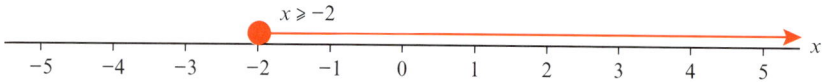

MATHEMATICAL CONNECTIONS

Remind yourself how you used inequality symbols for grouped data in Chapter 12.

You will use inequalities again when you describe intervals and label histograms in Chapter 20.

WORKED EXAMPLE 9

a   Show the set of values that satisfy each of the following inequalities on a number line.

   i $x > 3$ **ii** $4 < y < 8$ **iii** $-1.4 < x \leqslant 2.8$

b   List all integers that satisfy the inequality $4.2 < x \leqslant 10.4$

Answers

a   **i**   The values of x have to be larger than 3. x cannot be equal to 3, so do not fill in the circle. 'Greater than' means 'to the right' on the number line.

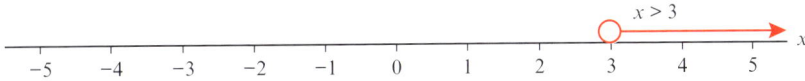

   ii   Notice that y is now being used as the variable and this should be clearly labelled on your number line. Also, two inequality symbols have been used. In fact there are two inequalities, and *both* must be satisfied.

      $4 < y$ means that y is greater than (but not equal) to 4.

      $y < 8$ means that y is less than (but not equal to) 8.

      So, y lies between 4 and 8 (not inclusive):

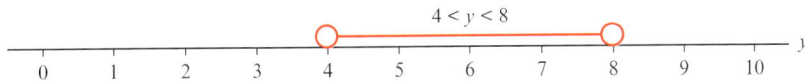

   iii   This example has two inequalities that must both be satisfied. x is greater than (but not equal to) -1.4, and x is less than or equal to 2.8:

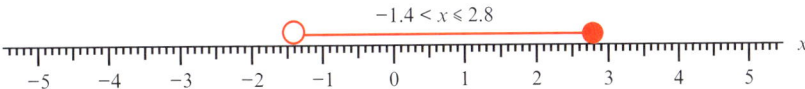

b x must be greater than, but not equal to 4.2, so the smallest possible value of x is 5. x must also be less than or equal to 10.4, so the largest possible value of x is 10.

   The possible integer values of x are 5, 6, 7, 8, 9 or 10.

Exercise 14.3

1   Draw a number line to represent the possible values of the variable in each case.

   a $x < 5$ **b** $x > 2$ **c** $p \leqslant 6$

   d $y > -8$ **e** $q \geqslant -5$ **f** $x < -4$

   g $1.2 < x < 3.5$ **h** $-3.2 < x \leqslant 2.9$ **i** $-4.5 \leqslant k \leqslant -3.1$

2   Write down all the *integers* that satisfy each of the following inequalities.

   a $3 < b < 33$ **b** $7 < h \leqslant 19$ **c** $18 \leqslant e \leqslant 27$

   d $-3 \leqslant f < 0$ **e** $-3 \leqslant f \leqslant 0$ **f** $2.5 < m < 11.3$

   g $-7 < g \leqslant -4$ **h** $\pi < r < 2\pi$ **i** $\sqrt{5} < w < \sqrt{18}$

Solving inequalities algebraically

Consider the inequality $3x > 6$.

Now, suppose that $x = 2$, then $3x = 6$ but this doesn't quite satisfy the inequality! However, any value of x that is **larger** than 2 *will* work. For example:

If $x = 2.1$, then $3x = 6.3$, which *is* greater than 6.

In the same way that you could divide both sides of an equation by 3, both sides of the inequality can be divided by 3 to get the solution:

$$3x > 6$$
$$\frac{3x}{3} > \frac{6}{3}$$
$$x > 2$$

Notice that this solution is a range of values of x rather than a single value. Any value of x that is greater than 2 is a solution.

You can solve any linear inequality in a similar way to how you would solve a linear equation. But there are important exceptions, which are described in the 'warning' section after Worked example 10. Most importantly, you should remember that what you do to one side of the inequality you must do to the other.

> **MATHEMATICAL CONNECTIONS**
>
> There is a clear relationship between this method and how you solved equations in Chapter 6.

WORKED EXAMPLE 10

Find the set of values of x which satisfy each of the following inequalities.

a $3x - 4 < 14$ **b** $4(x - 7) \geqslant 16$ **c** $5x - 3 \leqslant 2x + 18$

d $4 - 7x \leqslant 53$ **e** $-10 \leqslant 3x - 2 < 4$

Answers

a $3x - 4 < 14$

$\quad 3x < 18$ Add 4 to both sides.

$\quad \frac{3x}{3} < \frac{18}{3}$ Divide both sides by 3.

So, $x < 6$

b $4(x - 7) \geqslant 16$

$\quad 4x - 28 \geqslant 16$ Expand the brackets.

$\quad 4x \geqslant 44$ Add 28 to both sides.

$\quad \frac{4x}{4} \geqslant \frac{44}{4}$ Divide both sides by 4.

So, $x \geqslant 11$

$\quad 4(x - 7) \geqslant 16$ You can also solve this inequality by dividing both sides by 4 at the beginning:

$\quad x - 7 \geqslant 4$ Divide both sides by 4.

$\quad x \geqslant 11$ Add 7 to both sides to get the same answer as before.

WORKED EXAMPLE 10 CONTINUED

c
$$5x - 3 \leqslant 2x + 18$$
$$5x - 3 - 2x \leqslant 2x + 18 - 2x$$
Subtract the smaller number of 'x's from both sides (2x).

$$3x - 3 \leqslant 18$$
Simplify.

$$3x \leqslant 21$$
Add 3 to both sides.

$$x \leqslant 7$$
Divide both sides by 3.

d $4 - 7x \leqslant 53$

$$4 \leqslant 53 + 7x$$
Add 7x to both sides

$$-49 \leqslant 7x$$
Subtract 53 from both sides.

$$-7 \leqslant x$$
Divide both sides by 7.

The x is on the right-hand side of the inequality in this answer. This is acceptable. You can reverse the entire inequality to place the x on the left without changing its meaning, but remember to reverse the actual inequality symbol!

And, $x \geqslant -7$

e $-10 \leqslant 3x - 2 < 4$
There are three parts to this inequality.

$$-10 \leqslant 3x - 2 \quad \text{and} \quad 3x - 2 < 4$$

$$-8 \leqslant 3x \qquad\qquad 3x < 6$$
Split into two inequalities.

$$-\frac{8}{3} \leqslant x \qquad\qquad x < 2$$
Solve each part.

$$-\frac{8}{3} \leqslant x < 2$$
Recombine the solutions.

A warning

Before working through the next exercise you must understand and apply one further rule. Think about this inequality:

$$3 - 5x > 18$$

$$\Rightarrow -5x > 15$$

If you divide both sides by -5 it *appears* that the solution will be,

$$x > -3$$

This is satisfied by any value of x that is greater than -3, for example $-2, -1, 2.4, 3.5, 10 \dots$

If you calculate the value of $3 - 5x$ for each of these values you get $13, 8, -9, -14.5, -47 \dots$ and not one of these works in the original inequality as they are all smaller than 18.

Here is an alternative solution:

$$3 - 5x > 18$$

$$\Rightarrow \qquad 3 > 18 + 5x$$

$$-15 > 5x$$

$$-3 > x$$

Or, $x < -3$

This is a correct solution, and the final answer is very similar to the 'wrong' one above. The only difference is that the inequality symbol has been reversed.

Why does this happen? When you multiply both sides by a negative value, the side that was greater will end up being a 'bigger' negative number, which actually means it is now less than the other side!

You need to remember the following:

If you multiply or divide both sides of an inequality by a *negative* number then you must *reverse* the direction of the inequality.

If you can avoid negatives, by adding or subtracting terms, then try to do so.

REFLECTION

Have you completely understood this warning? How will you make sure you remember to reverse the inequality symbol at the right moment each time?

Exercise 14.4

In this exercise, give your answers as fractions in their simplest form where appropriate.

1   Solve these inequalities.

a $18x < 36$

b $13x > 39$

c $15y \leqslant 14$

d $7y > -14$

e $4 + 8c \geqslant 20$

f $\frac{1}{2}(x + 5) \leqslant 2$

g $\frac{x}{3} < 2$

h $5p - 3 > 12$

i $\frac{x}{3} + 7 > 2$

j $12g - 14 \geqslant 34$

k $22(w - 4) < 88$

l $10 - 10k > 3$

2   Solve these inequalities.

a $\frac{y + 6}{4} > 9$

b $\frac{y + 6}{4} \leqslant 9$

c $\frac{z - 2}{3} - 7 > 13$

d $\frac{3k - 1}{7} - 7 > 7$

e $\frac{r}{2} + \frac{1}{3} < 2$

3   Solve these inequalities.

a $10q - 12 < 48 + 5q$

b $3g - 7 \geqslant 5g - 18$

c $3 - 7h \leqslant 6 - 5h$

d $3(h - 4) > 5(h - 10)$

e $2(y - 7) + 6 \leqslant 5(y + 3) + 21$

f $6(n - 4) - 2(n + 1) < 3(n + 7) + 1$

g $5(2v - 3) - 2(4v - 5) \geqslant 8(v + 1)$

h $\frac{2e + 1}{9} > 7 - 6e$

i $2t - \frac{2t + 1}{3} > 12$

j $\frac{2}{3}t - \frac{2t + 1}{9} > 12$

k $\frac{2}{7}t - \frac{2t + 1}{9} > 12$

4   Solve these inequalities.

a $5 < 1 - 2x < 12$

b $0 < x + 3 \leqslant 12$

c $0 < x - 6 \leqslant 7$

d $18 < 3x + 2 \leqslant 23$

e $12x + 6 \leqslant -5x + 2 < 18$

5   The reserve price at an auction is the lowest price that will be accepted. The reserve price of a sculpture is $1 700 000.

   a   Represent all the possible selling prices (p) on a number line.

   b   Write the inequality that represents this.

6   The sign in a goods elevator says the maximum weight allowed is 630 kilograms. A delivery person has to load boxes of books (b) each with a mass of 28 kg. Given the delivery person weighs 78 kilograms, write an inequality to represent this situation and solve it to find the largest number of boxes that can be safely loaded into the elevator.

14.3 Regions in a plane

So far, you have only looked at inequalities involving a single variable. Now you will look at what happens when there are two variables connected with an inequality. In these situations you need to think about a **region**, which is a set of points in the coordinate plane.

LINK

You will often hear the word 'region' used in geography. It refers to a section of land or sea contained within a boundary. The region might be a whole continent, a collection of countries or even a national park or shipping lane. These regions are often marked with clear boundaries on a map, or they may be shaded in different colours.

The diagram shows a broken line that is parallel to the x-axis. Every point on the line has a y-coordinate of 3. This means that the equation of the line is $y = 3$.

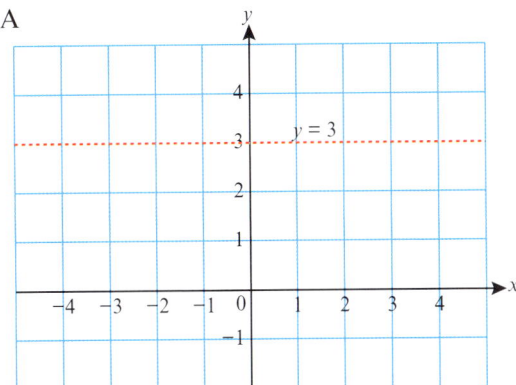

All of the points above the line $y = 3$ have y-coordinates that are greater than 3. The region above the line represents the inequality $y > 3$. Similarly, the region below the line represents the inequality $y < 3$.

The regions $y > 3$ and $y < 3$ are shown on this diagram.

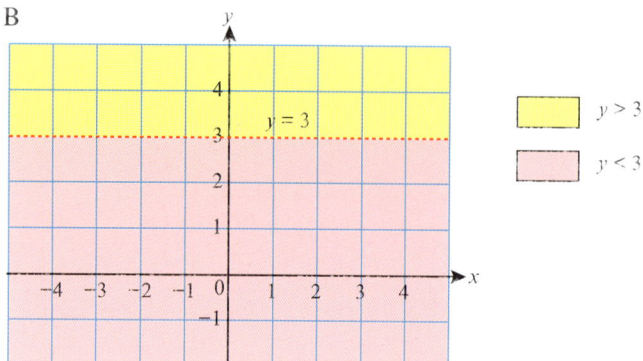

In the diagram below, the graph of $y = 2x + 1$ is shown as a broken line. Every point on the line has coordinates (x, y) which satisfy $y = 2x + 1$.

Q is a point on the line. Point P has a y-coordinate that is greater than the y-coordinate of Q. P and Q have the same x-coordinate. This means that for any point P in the region above the line, $y > 2x + 1$.

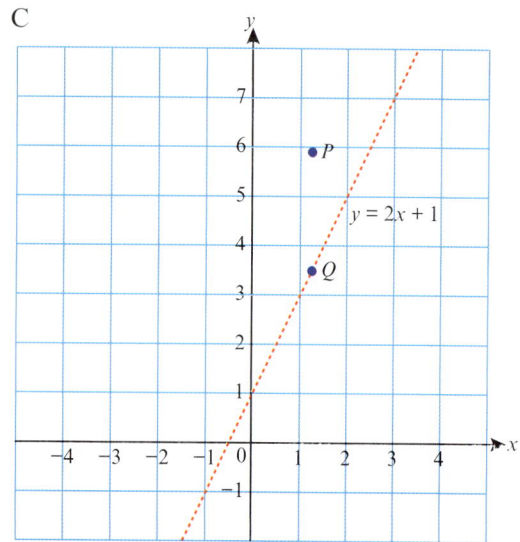

The region above the line represents the inequality $y > 2x + 1$.

Similarly, the region below the line represents the inequality $y < 2x + 1$.

You can see this on the following diagram.

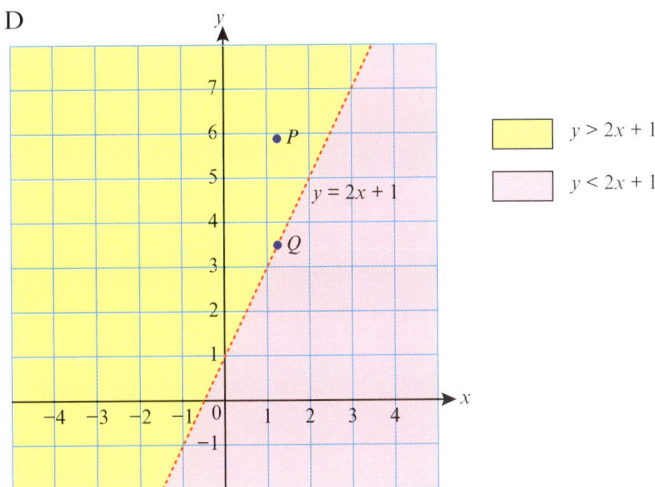

If the equation of the line is in the form $y = mx + c$, then:

- the inequality $y > mx + c$ is above the line
- the inequality $y < mx + c$ is below the line.

If the equation is not in the form $y = mx + c$, you have to find a way to check which region represents which inequality.

WORKED EXAMPLE 11

On a diagram, show the regions that represent the inequalities $2x - 3y < 6$ and $2x - 3y > 6$.

Answer

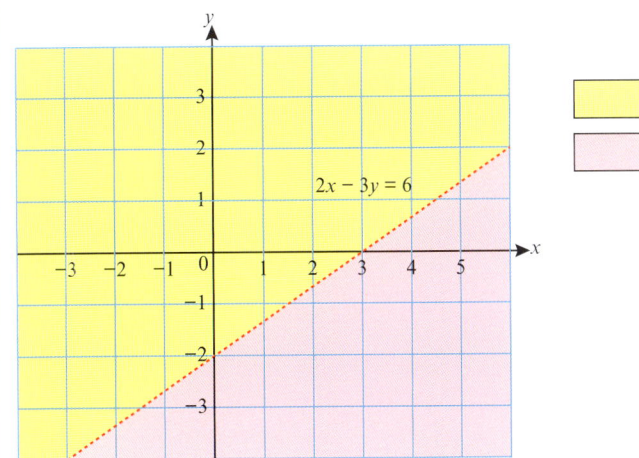

The boundary between the two required regions is the line $2x - 3y = 6$.

This line crosses the x-axis at $(3, 0)$ and the y-axis at $(0, -2)$. It is shown as a broken line in the diagram.

Consider any point in the region above the line. The easiest point to use is the origin $(0, 0)$. When $x = 0$ and $y = 0$, $2x - 3y = 0$. Since 0 is less than 6, the region above the line represents the inequality $2x - 3y < 6$.

Rules for boundaries and shading of regions

You have already seen inequalities are not always $<$ or $>$. They may also be $\leqslant$ or $\geqslant$. Graphical representations have to show the difference between these variations.

When the inequality includes equal to ($\leqslant$ or $\geqslant$), the boundary line must be included in the graphical representation. It is therefore shown as a solid line.

When the inequality does not include equal to ($<$ or $>$), the boundary line is not included in the graphical representation, so it is shown as a broken line.

> **TIP**
>
> Sometimes it is better to shade out the *unwanted* region.

WORKED EXAMPLE 12

By shading the *unwanted* region, show the region that represents the inequality $3x - 5y \leqslant 15$.

Answer

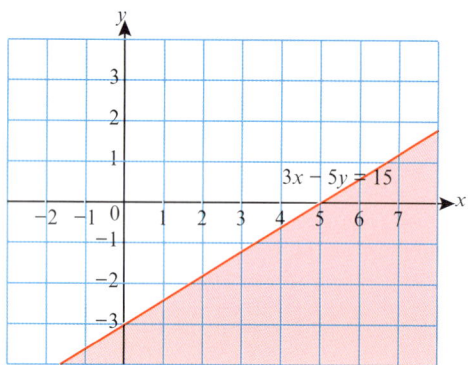

The boundary line is $3x - 5y = 15$ and it is included in the region (because the inequality includes **equal** to).

This line crosses the x-axis at (5, 0) and crosses the y-axis at (0, −3). It is shown as a solid line in the diagram.

When $x = 0$ and $y = 0$, $3x - 5y = 0$. Since 0 is less than 15, the origin (0, 0) is in the required region.

(Alternatively, rearrange $3x - 5y \leqslant 15$ to get $y \geqslant \frac{3}{5}x - 3$ and deduce that the required region is above the line.)

The unshaded region in this diagram represents the inequality $3x - 5y \leqslant 15$.

WORKED EXAMPLE 13

By shading the *unwanted* region, show the region that represents the inequality $3x - 2y \geqslant 0$.

Answer

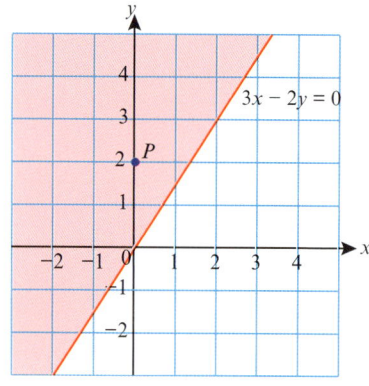

You cannot take the origin as the checking point because it lies on the boundary line. Instead take the point $P(0, 2)$, which is *above* the line. When $x = 0$ and $y = 2$, $3x - 2y = -4$, which is less than 0. Hence P is *not* in the required region.

The boundary line is $3x - 2y = 0$ and it is included in the region. It is shown as a solid line in the diagram.

WORKED EXAMPLE 14

Find the inequality that is represented by the *unshaded* region in this diagram.

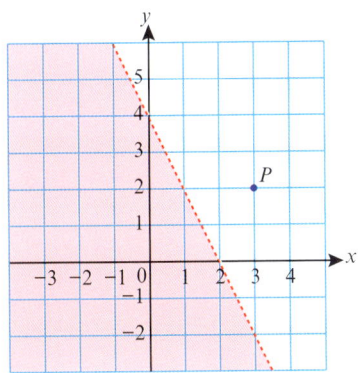

Answer

First find the equation of the boundary. Its gradient $= \dfrac{-4}{2} = -2$ and its intercept on the y-axis is $y = 4$. Therefore the boundary line is $y = -2x + 4$. This can be rewritten as $y + 2x = 4$. Take $P(3, 2)$ in the unshaded region as the check-point: $2 + 6 = 8$. Note that 8 is greater than 4 and hence the *unshaded* region represents $y + 2x > 4$. As the boundary is a broken line, it is not included, and so the sign is not $\geqslant$.

Exercise 14.5

For questions 1 to 3, show your answers on a grid with x- and y-axes running from -3 to $+4$.

1   By shading the unwanted region, show the region that represents the inequality $2y - 3x \geqslant 6$.

2   By shading the unwanted region, show the region that represents the inequality $x + 2y < 4$.

3   By shading the unwanted region, show the region that represents the inequality $x - y \geqslant 0$.

4   Shade the region that represents each inequality.

    a $y > 3 - 3x$ **b** $3x - 2y \geqslant 6$ **c** $x \leqslant 5$ **d** $y > 3$

    e $x + 3y \leqslant 10$ **f** $-3 < x < 5$ **g** $0 \leqslant x \leqslant 2$

5   Copy and complete these statements by choosing the correct option:

    a   If $y < mx + c$, shade the unwanted region **above/below** the graph of $y = mx + c$.

    b   If $y > mx + c$, shade the unwanted region **above/below** the graph of $y = mx + c$.

    c   For $y < m_1x + c_1$ and $y > m_2x + c_2$, shade the unwanted region **above/below** the graph of $y = m_1x + c_1$ **and/or above/below** the graph of $y = m_2x + c_2$.

6   For each of the following diagrams, find the inequality that is represented by the *unshaded* region.

a

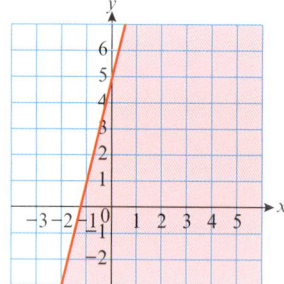

b

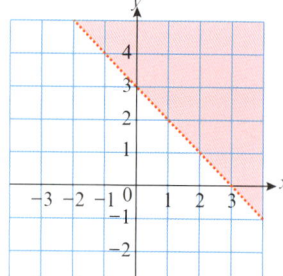

c

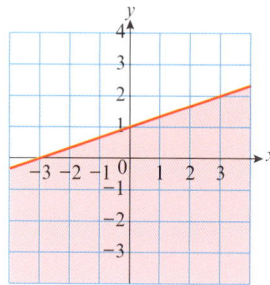

d

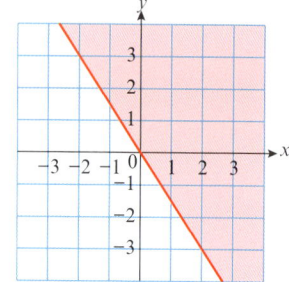

Representing simultaneous inequalities

When two or more inequalities have to be satisfied at the same time, they are called simultaneous inequalities. These can also be represented graphically. On the diagram in Worked example 15 the inequalities are represented by regions on the same diagram. The unwanted regions are shaded or crossed out. The unshaded region will contain all the coordinates (x, y) that satisfy all the inequalities simultaneously.

MATHEMATICAL CONNECTIONS

You studied simultaneous equations at the start of this chapter, and you saw that the solution was where two lines intersected. In this section, simultaneous inequalities show where two or more *regions* intersect.

WORKED EXAMPLE 15

By shading the unwanted regions, show the region defined by the set of inequalities $y < x + 2$, $y \leqslant 4$ and $x \leqslant 3$.

Answer

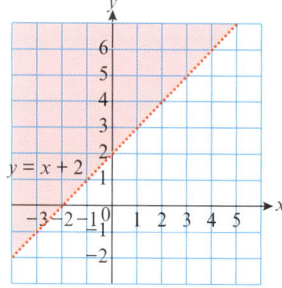

The boundaries of the required region are $y = x + 2$ (broken line), $y = 4$ (solid line) and $x = 3$ (solid line).

Start by drawing the line $y = x + 2$.

$y < x + 2$ so shade the unwanted region above the line.

WORKED EXAMPLE 15 CONTINUED

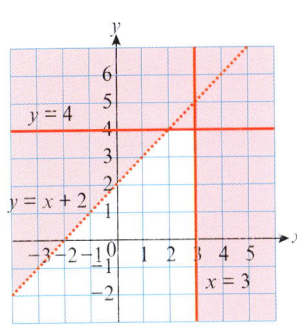

Continue drawing the other boundary lines and shading the unwanted regions.

The unshaded region in the diagram represents the set of inequalities

$y < x + 2$, $y \leqslant 4$ and $x \leqslant 3$.

Notice that this region does not have a finite area – it is not 'closed'.

INVESTIGATION

Shading the wanted region

In the questions you have seen so far, you were asked to shade *unwanted* regions. Try working through Worked example 15 again, but shade the *wanted* regions instead. What happens?

Exercise 14.6

1   By shading the unwanted regions, show the region defined by the set of inequalities $x + 2y \geqslant 6$, $y \leqslant x$ and $x < 4$.

2   By shading the unwanted regions, show the region defined by the set of inequalities $x + y \geqslant 5$, $y \leqslant 2$ and $y \geqslant 0$.

3   a   On a grid, draw the lines $x = 4$, $y = 3$ and $x + y = 5$.

   b   By shading the unwanted regions, show the region that satisfies all the inequalities $x \leqslant 4$, $y \leqslant 3$ and $x + y \geqslant 5$. Label the region R.

4   Write down the three inequalities that define the unshaded triangular region R.

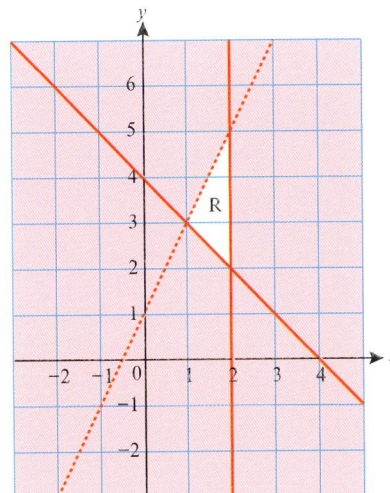

5 The unshaded region in the diagram represents the set of inequalities $y \geqslant 0$, $y + 2x \geqslant 2$ and $x + y < 4$. Write down the pairs of integers (x, y) that satisfy all the inequalities.

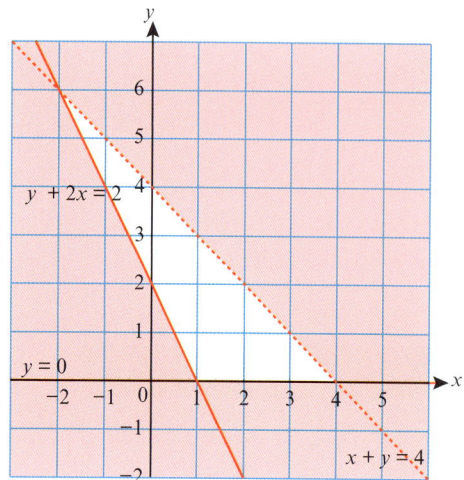

6 Draw graphs to show the region that satisfies all of these inequalities: $y \leqslant 4$, $y \geqslant x + 2$ and $3x + y \geqslant 4$. Write down the integer coordinates (x, y) that satisfy all the inequalities in this case.

14.4 Completing the square

Compare these two quadratic expressions:

$x^2 + 6x + 9$

$x^2 + 6x - 7$

You should recognise from your work in Chapter 10 that the first expression is a perfect square and that it factorises to give two identical factors:

$x^2 + 6x + 9 = (x + 3)(x + 3) = (x + 3)^2$.

The second quadratic is not the square of a single bracket, but you can use a similar idea to write it in a different way that does involve a square bracket. This is useful when you cannot factorise the expression but need to solve an equation. It is also very useful when learning about the symmetry of quadratic graphs in Chapter 18.

Compare the two expressions again and write the second quadratic using a squared bracket:

$x^2 + 6x + 9 = (x + 3)^2$

$x^2 + 6x - 7 = (x + 3)^2 - 16$ Subtract 16 from both sides to get the -7 you need.

TIP

Notice that the two quadratics are very similar. The only difference is that the constant term in the second one is 16 less than in the first.

Notice that the coefficient of x in the original expression is twice the constant inside the bracket. The coefficient of x is **always** twice the constant inside the bracket you are squaring, because:

$(x + a)^2 = (x + a)(x + a) = x^2 + 2ax + a^2$

The method of rewriting a quadratic expression in the form $(x + p)^2 + q$ is called **completing the square**.

> **TIP**
>
> You will usually be told when to use completing the square.

WORKED EXAMPLE 16

Rewrite the expression $x^2 - 4x + 11$ in the form $(x + p)^2 + q$.

Answer

The coefficient of x is -4. Half of this is -2.
So start by thinking about $(x - 2)^2 = x^2 - 4x + 4$.
You need to add 7 to make the constant equal to 11, so
$x^2 - 4x + 11 = (x - 2)^2 + 7$.

WORKED EXAMPLE 17

a   Write the expression $x^2 + 4x - 6$ in the form $(x + p)^2 + q$

b   Hence solve $x^2 + 4x - 6 = 0$, giving your answers to 2 decimal places.

Answers

a   Try $(x + 2)^2 = x^2 + 4x + 4$ The coefficient of x in $x^2 + 4x - 6$ is 4. Half of this is 2.

$(x + 2)^2 - 10 = x^2 + 4x + 4 - 10$ Subtract 10 from both sides to make the constant term -6.
$\qquad\qquad\quad = x^2 + 4x - 6$

b $x^2 + 4x - 6 = 0$

$(x + 2)^2 - 10 = 0$ Rewrite the quadratic expression in completed square form.

$(x + 2)^2 = 10$

$x + 2 = \pm\sqrt{10}$ Solve for x.

$x = -2 \pm\sqrt{10}$

$x = 1.16$ or $x = -5.16$ Give your answers to 2 decimal places.

> **TIP**
>
> The square root symbol means only the *positive* square root. There are two different numbers that square to give 10. These are $\sqrt{10}$ and $-\sqrt{10}$. You must include the $\pm$ symbol so that you find both solutions.

Exercise 14.7

1   Write each of the following expressions in the form $(x + p)^2 + q$.

a $x^2 + 6x + 14$	**b** $x^2 + 8x + 1$	**c** $x^2 + 12x + 20$
d $x^2 + 6x + 5$	**e** $x^2 - 4x + 12$	**f** $x^2 - 2x + 17$
g $x^2 + 5x + 1$	**h** $x^2 + 7x - 2$	**i** $x^2 - 3x - 3$
j $x^2 + 7x - 8$	**k** $x^2 - 13x + 1$	**l** $x^2 - 20x + 400$

2   Solve the following quadratic equations using the method of completing the square. Give your final answer to 2 decimal places.

a $x^2 + 6x - 5 = 0$	**b** $x^2 + 8x + 4 = 0$	**c** $x^2 - 4x + 2 = 0$
d $x^2 + 5x - 7 = 0$	**e** $x^2 - 3x + 2 = 0$	**f** $x^2 - 12x + 1 = 0$

3 Solve each equation by completing the square.

    a $x^2 - x - 10 = 0$ **b** $x^2 + 3x - 6 = 0$ **c** $x(6 + x) = 1$

    d $x^2 + 2x = 8$ **e** $5x = 10 - \dfrac{1}{x}$ **f** $x - 5 = \dfrac{2}{x}$

    g $(x - 1)(x + 2) - 1 = 0$ **h** $(x - 4)(x + 2) = -5$ **i** $x^2 = x + 1$

INVESTIGATION

4   You can use a formula to complete the square if that works better for you.

$x^2 + bx + c$ can be written as $\left(x + \dfrac{b}{2}\right)^2 - \left(\dfrac{b}{2}\right)^2 + c$

Choose five of the questions in the exercise that you found challenging and try to use this formula to complete the square. Which method are you more comfortable with? How can you make sure you remember the formula correctly?

REFLECTION

Think back to your earlier work on quadratic expressions.

Which ideas from there did you use in this exercise?

Mathematics often involves building new ideas on earlier ones. What difficulties might you have learning new ideas if there are earlier ideas that you do not fully understand?

Completing the square when the coefficient of x is not 1

Sometimes you will need to write an expression in completed square form when the coefficient of x is not equal to 1. This means that you will need a number other than 1 in front of the squared bracket. Read through Worked example 18 to see how to do this.

WORKED EXAMPLE 18

Write these expressions in the form $a(x + p)^2 + q$

a $2x^2 + 8x - 3$ **b** $3x^2 + 5x - 2$

Answers

a $2x^2 + 8x - 3$

$= 2(x^2 + 8x) - 3$	Take the coefficient of x^2 out of the first two terms only.
$= 2\{(x + 2)^2 - 4\} - 3$	Complete the square on the expression inside the bracket.
$= 2(x + 2)^2 - 8 - 3$	Expand the outer bracket.
$= 2(x + 2)^2 - 11$	Simplify.

WORKED EXAMPLE 18 CONTINUED

b $3x^2 + 5x - 2$

$= 3\left(x^2 + \dfrac{5}{3}x\right) - 2$

Take the coefficient of x^2 out of the first two terms only.

$= 3\left\{\left(x + \dfrac{5}{6}\right)^2 - \left(\dfrac{5}{6}\right)^2\right\} - 2$

Complete the square on the expression inside the bracket.

$= 3\left(x + \dfrac{5}{6}\right)^2 - 3\left(\dfrac{25}{36}\right) - 2$

Expand the outer bracket.

$= 3\left(x + \dfrac{5}{6}\right)^2 - \dfrac{25}{12} - 2$

$= 3\left(x + \dfrac{5}{6}\right)^2 - \dfrac{25}{12} - \dfrac{24}{12}$

$= 3\left(x + \dfrac{5}{6}\right)^2 - \dfrac{49}{12}$

Simplify fully.

> **TIP**
>
> Remember that half of $\dfrac{5}{3}$ is $\dfrac{5}{6}$.

Exercise 14.8

1   Write each of the following expressions in the form $a(x + p)^2 + q$.

a	$3x^2 + 6x + 14$	**b**	$2x^2 + 8x + 1$	**c**	$6x^2 + 12x + 20$
d	$2x^2 + 6x + 5$	**e**	$4x^2 - 8x + 11$	**f**	$2x^2 - 4x + 17$
g	$5x^2 + 10x + 1$	**h**	$3x^2 + 7x - 2$	**i**	$2x^2 - 3x - 3$
j	$5x^2 + 7x - 8$	**k**	$2x^2 - 13x + 1$	**l**	$3x^2 - 20x + 400$

2   Solve the following quadratic equations using the method of completing the square. Give your final answer to 2 decimal places.

a	$2x^2 + 6x - 5 = 0$	**b**	$4x^2 + 8x - 3 = 0$	**c**	$2x^2 - 4x - 3 = 0$
d	$3x^2 + 5x - 7 = 0$	**e**	$2x^2 - 3x + 2 = 0$	**f**	$5x^2 - 12x + 1 = 0$

3   Write $ax^2 + bx + c$ in the form $(x + p)^2 + q$ and hence show that provided $b^2 - 4ac \geqslant 0$, the equation $ax^2 + bx + c = 0$ has solutions $x = \dfrac{-b \pm \sqrt{b^2 - 4ac}}{2a}$.

14.5 Quadratic formula

If you complete the square for the general form of a quadratic equation $(ax^2 + bx + c = 0)$, the following result is produced:

If $ax^2 + bx + c = 0$ then $x = \dfrac{-b \pm \sqrt{b^2 - 4ac}}{2a}$

This is known as the quadratic formula.

Notice the '$\pm$' symbol. This tells you that you should calculate two values: one with a '+' and one with a '−' in the position occupied by the '$\pm$'. You can use the quadratic formula to solve any quadratic equation even if you cannot factorise the quadratic expression.

The advantage of the quadratic formula over completing the square is that you don't have any extra steps to include when the coefficient of x^2 is not 1.

TIP

If you are asked to give solutions to a number of decimal places or significant figures or to leave the answer in surd form it is a good indication that you cannot factorise the expression and you should use the formula or complete the square instead.

DISCUSSION

By starting with $ax^2 + bx + c = 0$ and dividing every term by a it is possible to use completing the square to get the formula above. Work with a partner or your teacher to see if you can get to the formula from the original quadratic equation.

MATHEMATICAL CONNECTIONS

You saw in Chapter 2 that the coefficient of a variable is the number that multiplies it. This is still true for quadratic equations: a is the coefficient of x^2 and b is the coefficient of x. c is the constant term.

WORKED EXAMPLE 19

Solve the following quadratic equations, giving your answers to 3 significant figures.

a $x^2 + 4x + 3 = 0$ b $x^2 - 7x + 11 = 0$ c $3x^2 - 2x - 1 = 0$

Answers

a Compare the quadratic equation $x^2 + 4x + 3 = 0$ with $ax^2 + bx + c = 0$. From this you can see that $a = 1$, $b = 4$ and $c = 3$.

$$x = \frac{-b \pm \sqrt{b^2 - 4ac}}{2a} = \frac{-4 \pm \sqrt{4^2 - 4 \times 1 \times 3}}{2 \times 1}$$

$$= -4 \pm \frac{\sqrt{16 - 12}}{2}$$

$$= \frac{-4 \pm \sqrt{4}}{2}$$

$$= \frac{-4 \pm 2}{2}$$

So, $x = \dfrac{-4 + 2}{2} = \dfrac{-2}{2} = -1$ or $x = \dfrac{-4 - 2}{2} = \dfrac{-6}{2} = -3$

Notice that the original quadratic equation can be factorised to give $(x + 1)(x + 3) = 0$ and the same solutions. If you can factorise the quadratic then you should because the method is much simpler.

TIP

Here you need to take particular care. BODMAS always applies and you should check the order of your working, and your solution, carefully.

WORKED EXAMPLE 19 CONTINUED

b $x^2 - 7x + 11 = 0$, so $a = 1$, $b = -7$ and $c = 11$.

$$x = \frac{-(-7) \pm \sqrt{(-7)^2 - 4 \times 1 \times 11}}{2 \times 1} = \frac{7 \pm \sqrt{49 - 44}}{2}$$

$$= \frac{7 \pm \sqrt{5}}{2}$$

So, $x = \dfrac{7 + \sqrt{5}}{2} = 4.6180\ldots$ or $x = \dfrac{7 - \sqrt{5}}{2} = 2.3819\ldots$

x is approximately equal to 4.62 or 2.38 (3 s.f.)

c $3x^2 - 2x - 1 = 0$, so $a = 3$, $b = -2$ and $c = -1$.

$$x = \frac{-(-2) \pm \sqrt{(-2)^2 - 4 \times 3 \times (-1)}}{2 \times 3} = \frac{2 \pm \sqrt{4 + 12}}{6}$$

$$= \frac{2 \pm \sqrt{16}}{6}$$

$$= \frac{2 \pm 4}{6}$$

So, $x = \dfrac{2 + 4}{6} = \dfrac{6}{6} = 1$ or $x = \dfrac{2 - 4}{6} = \dfrac{-2}{6} = \dfrac{-1}{3}$

TIP

Notice that there are brackets around the -7. If you miss these the calculation becomes $-7^2 = -49$ rather than $+49$.

If b is negative **always** use brackets to make sure that you square it correctly.

WORKED EXAMPLE 20

Use the quadratic formula to find the exact solutions, in surd form, to this equation:

$-3x^2 - 12x - 7 = 0$

Answer

$$x = \frac{-(-12) \pm \sqrt{(-12)^2 - 4 \times (-3) \times (-7)}}{2 \times (-3)} = \frac{12 \pm \sqrt{60}}{-6}$$

$$= \frac{12 \pm 2\sqrt{15}}{-6}$$

$$= \frac{6 \pm \sqrt{15}}{-3}$$

So, $x = \dfrac{6 + \sqrt{15}}{-3}$ or $x = \dfrac{6 - \sqrt{15}}{-3}$

TIP

It is more accurate to leave your answer in surd form than to convert to a decimal. Surds are exact, but decimals are approximations.

MATHEMATICAL CONNECTIONS

You learnt how to work with surds in Chapter 9. Review that work if you need to.

LINK

Artificial intelligence (AI) engines allow computer programmes such as Mathematica and Wolfram Alpha to do almost all complex calculations (including solving quadratic equations) faster than most people can do by hand. Stephen Wolfram is a physicist who developed these programmes to do the maths he needed (and struggled to do). Programmes like this are able to carry out standard calculations much more quickly than humans can. This mean that we can spend more time on higher level thinking instead of time-consuming calculations.

Exercise 14.9

1   Each of the following quadratics will factorise. Solve each of them by factorisation and then use the quadratic formula to show that you get the same answers with both methods.

a $x^2 + 7x + 12 = 0$ b $x^2 + 8x + 12 = 0$ c $x^2 + 11x + 28 = 0$

d $x^2 + 4x - 5 = 0$ e $x^2 + 6x - 16 = 0$ f $x^2 + 12x - 160 = 0$

g $x^2 - 6x + 8 = 0$ h $x^2 - 3x - 28 = 0$ i $x^2 - 5x - 24 = 0$

j $x^2 - 12x + 32 = 0$ k $x^2 - 2x - 99 = 0$ l $x^2 - 9x - 36 = 0$

m $x^2 - 10x + 24 = 0$ n $x^2 - 12x + 35 = 0$ o $x^2 + 9x - 36 = 0$

2   Solve each of the following equations by using the quadratic formula. Round your answers to 3 significant figures where necessary. These quadratic expressions do not factorise.

a $x^2 + 6x - 1 = 0$ b $x^2 + 5x + 5 = 0$ c $x^2 + 7x + 11 = 0$

d $x^2 + 4x + 2 = 0$ e $x^2 - 3x - 1 = 0$ f $x^2 - 4x + 2 = 0$

g $x^2 - 8x + 6 = 0$ h $x^2 - 2x - 2 = 0$ i $x^2 - 6x - 4 = 0$

j $x^2 - 8x - 2 = 0$ k $x^2 - 9x + 7 = 0$ l $x^2 + 11x + 7 = 0$

3   Solve each of the following equations by using the quadratic formula. Round your answers to 3 significant figures where necessary. Take particular note of the coefficient of x^2.

a $x^2 - 4x + 1 = 0$ b $x^2 - 3x - 1 = 0$ c $4x^2 + 2x - 5 = 0$

d $-2x^2 + 3x + 4 = 0$ e $-2x^2 - 2x + 1 = 0$ f $5x^2 + x - 3 = 0$

TIP

You must make sure that your equation takes the form of a quadratic expression *equal to zero*.

If it does not, then you will need to collect all terms on to one side so that a zero appears on the other side!

4   Solve each of the following equations by using the quadratic formula. Round your answers to 3 significant figures where necessary.

a $x^2 - x + 6 = 4x + 5$ b $7x^2 - 3x - 6 = 3x - 7$ c $x(6x - 3) - 2 = 0$

d $0.5x^2 + 0.8x - 2 = 0$ e $(x + 7)(x + 5) = 9$ f $\frac{1}{x} + x = 7$

5   Find the exact solution of each equation using the quadratic formula.

a $x^2 - 5x + 1 = 0$ b $2x^2 + 3x - 7 = 0$ c $3x^2 - 5x - 1 = 0$

d $x^2 + 4x = -1$ e $9 + x^2 + 8x = 0$ f $2x^2 + 5 = 10x$

6   A rectangle has area $12\,\text{cm}^2$. If the length of the rectangle is $(x + 1)\,\text{cm}$ and the width of the rectangle is $(x + 3)\,\text{cm}$, find the possible value(s) of x.

7 A biologist claims that the average height, h metres, of trees of a certain species after t months is given by $h = \frac{1}{5}t^{\frac{2}{3}} + \frac{1}{3}t^{\frac{1}{3}}$.

For this model:

a find the average height of trees of this species after 64 months

b find the number of months that the trees have been growing when the model predicts an average height of 10 metres. Give your answer to 3 significant figures.

TIP

Let $x = t^{\frac{1}{3}}$.

Form and solve a quadratic in x.

REFLECTION

Did you make any mistakes with negative coefficients of x? How did you correct them and how will you avoid making the same mistake in the future?

14.6 Factorising quadratics where the coefficient of x^2 is not 1

The quadratic equation in part (c) of Worked example 19 gave two solutions that could have been obtained by factorisation. It turns out that $(x - 1)(3x + 1) = 3x^2 - 2x - 1$ (you can check this by expanding the brackets).

In general, if the coefficient of x^2 in a quadratic is a number other than 1 you need to carry out more steps to factorise the expression.

WORKED EXAMPLE 21

Factorise each of the following expressions:

a $2x^2 + 3x + 1$

b $3x^2 - 14x + 8$

c $6x^2 + 14x - 12$

d $10x^2 + 11x - 8$

Answers

a $2x^2 + 3x + 1$

$2x^2 + 3x + 1 = (2x\ \ )(x\ \ )$

The only way to produce the term $2x^2$ is to multiply $2x$ and x. Place these two terms at the front of each bracket. There are blank spaces in the brackets because you don't yet know what else needs to be included. The clue lies in the constant term at the end, which is obtained by multiplying these two unknown values together.

The constant term is 1, so the only possible values are $+1$ or -1. Since the constant term is positive, the unknown values must be either both -1 or both $+1$.

Try each of these combinations systematically:

$(2x - 1)(x - 1) = 2x^2 - 3x + 1$ The coefficient of x is wrong.

$(2x + 1)(x + 1) = 2x^2 + 3x + 1$ This is correct.

So, $2x^2 + 3x + 1 = (2x + 1)(x + 1)$

WORKED EXAMPLE 21 CONTINUED

b $3x^2 - 14x + 8$

Start by writing $3x^2 - 14x + 8 = (3x\ \ )(x\ \ )$.

The two unknown terms must multiply to give 8. Since the constant term is positive, the unknowns must have the same sign. The possible pairs are:

  8 and 1   2 and 4 -8 and -1 -2 and -4

Try each pair in turn, remembering that you can reverse the order:

$(3x + 8)(x + 1) = 3x^2 + 3x + 8x + 8 = 3x^2 + 11x + 8$ Incorrect

$(3x + 1)(x + 8) = 3x^2 + 24x + x + 8 = 3x^2 + 25x + 8$ Incorrect

$(3x + 2)(x + 4) = 3x^2 + 12x + 2x + 8 = 3x^2 + 14x + 8$ Incorrect

This last one is very close. You just need to change the sign of the 'x' term. This can be done by jumping to the last pair: -2 and -4.

$(3x - 2)(x - 4) = 3x^2 - 12x - 2x + 8 = 3x^2 - 14x + 8$ Correct

So, $3x^2 - 14x + 8 = (3x - 2)(x - 4)$

c $6x^2 + 14x - 12 = 2(3x^2 + 7x - 6)$ Take out the common factor first.

Write the pair of brackets; the factors have to be $3x$ and x:

$6x^2 + 14x - 12 = 2(3x\ \ )(x\ \ )$

The two unknown terms must multiply to give -6, because you have taken out the common factor 2. The possible pairs are:

  2 and -3 3 and -2 6 and -1 -6 and 1

Test the pairs until you find the correct combination.

You will find that:

$6x^2 + 14x - 12 = 2(3x - 2)(x + 3)$

d $10x^2 + 11x - 8$

This question requires more thought because there is more than one way to multiply two expressions to get $10x^2$:

  $2x$ and $5x$ or $10x$ and x.

Each possibility needs to be tried.

Start with $10x^2 + 11x - 8 = (10x\ \ )(x\ \ )$.

Factor pairs that multiply to give -8 are:

  -8 and 1   8 and -1 2 and -4 -2 and 4

Remember that you will need to try each pair with the two values in either order.

For this particular quadratic you will find that none of the eight possible combinations works!

Instead, you must now try: $10x^2 + 11x - 8 = (5x\ \ )(2x\ \ )$.

Trying the above set of pairs once again you will eventually find that:

$10x^2 + 11x - 8 = (5x + 8)(2x - 1)$

Exercise 14.10

1   Factorise each of the following expressions.

a $3x^2 + 14x + 8$ b $2x^2 + x - 3$ c $6x^2 + x - 2$

d $3x^2 + 14x + 16$ e $2x^2 - x - 10$ f $16x^2 + 32x - 9$

g $3x^2 + 16x + 5$ h $8x^2 + 2x - 1$ i $2x^2 - x - 6$

j $2x^2 + 9x + 9$ k $3x^2 + 2x - 16$ l $10x^2 - x - 3$

m $5x^2 + 6x + 1$ n $2x^2 - 19x + 9$ o $12x^2 + 8x - 15$

Here is another method for factorising a quadratic like those in the previous exercise.

WORKED EXAMPLE 22

Factorise $10x^2 + 11x - 8$.

Answer

$10 \times -8 = -80$	Multiply the coefficient of x^2 by the constant term.
$-1, 80$ (no)	List the factor pairs of -80 until you obtain a pair that totals the coefficient of x, which is 11.
$-2, 40$ (no)	(Note that as 11 is positive and -80 is negative, the larger number of the pair must be positive and the other negative.)
$-4, 20$ (no)	
$-5, 16$ (yes)	
$10x^2 - 5x + 16x - 8$	Rewrite the x term using this factor pair.
$5x(2x - 1) + 8(2x - 1)$	Factorise pairs of terms. (Be careful with signs here so that the second bracket is the same as the first bracket.)
$(5x + 8)(2x - 1)$	Factorise, using the bracket as the common term.

Exercise 14.11

1   Go back to Exercise 14.10 and try to factorise the expressions using this new method.

2   Factorise each expression completely. Remember to remove any common factors before factorising.

a $6x^2 - 5x - 21$ b $-2x^2 - 13x - 15$ c $4x^2 + 12xy + 9y^2$

d $6x^2 - 19xy - 7y^2$ e $x^3 - 13x^2 + 36x$ f $6x^2 - 38xy + 40y^2$

g $6x^2 + 7x + 2$ h $3x^2 - 13x + 12$ i $3x^2 - 39x + 120$

j $px^2 + 7px + 12p$ k $5x^3 - 16x^2 + 12x$ l $48x - 24x^2 + 3x^3$

m $(x + 1)^2 - 5(x + 1) + 6$ n $(2x + 1)^2 - 8(2x + 1) + 15$

o $3(2x + 5)^2 - 17(2x + 5) + 10$

14.7 Algebraic fractions

You will now use several of the techniques covered so far in this chapter to simplify complex algebraic fractions.

You already know that you can simplify fractions by dividing the numerator and denominator by a common factor. This can also be done with algebraic fractions.

MATHEMATICAL CONNECTIONS

You revised highest common factors (HCFs) in Chapter 1.

WORKED EXAMPLE 23

Simplify each of the following fractions as far as possible:

a $\dfrac{3x}{6}$ **b** $\dfrac{y^2}{y^5}$ **c** $\dfrac{12p^3}{16p^7}$ **d** $\dfrac{x^2 - 4x + 3}{x^2 - 7x + 12}$

Answers

a $\dfrac{3x}{6}$

$\dfrac{3x}{6} = \dfrac{3x \div 3}{6 \div 3} = \dfrac{x}{2}$

The highest common factor (HCF) of 3 and 6 is 3.

b $\dfrac{y^2}{y^5}$

$\dfrac{y^2}{y^5} = \dfrac{y^2 \div y^2}{y^5 \div y^2} = \dfrac{1}{y^3}$

The HCF of y^2 and y^5 is y^2.

c $\dfrac{12p^3}{16p^7}$

$\dfrac{12p^3}{16p^7} = \dfrac{3p^3}{4p^7}$

$= \dfrac{3}{4p^4}$

Consider the constants first.

The HCF of 12 and 16 is 4, so you can divide both 12 and 16 by 4.

The HCF of p^3 and p^7 is p^3. You can divide both the numerator and the denominator by this HCF.

d $\dfrac{x^2 - 4x + 3}{x^2 - 7x + 12}$

$\dfrac{x^2 - 4x + 3}{x^2 - 7x + 12} = \dfrac{(x - 3)(x - 1)}{(x - 3)(x - 4)}$

$= \dfrac{\cancel{(x - 3)}(x - 1)}{\cancel{(x - 3)}(x - 4)}$

$= \dfrac{(x - 1)}{(x - 4)}$

Notice that you can factorise both the numerator and the denominator.

$(x - 3)$ is a factor of both the numerator and the denominator, so you can cancel this common factor.

MATHEMATICAL CONNECTIONS

You might need to recap the laws of indices that you learned in Chapter 2.

Exercise 14.12

Simplify each of the following fractions by dividing both the numerator and the denominator by their HCF.

1 **a** $\dfrac{2x}{4}$ **b** $\dfrac{3y}{12}$ **c** $\dfrac{5x}{x}$ **d** $\dfrac{10y}{y}$ **e** $\dfrac{6t}{36}$

   f $\dfrac{9u}{27}$ **g** $\dfrac{5t}{50}$ **h** $\dfrac{4y}{8}$ **i** $\dfrac{15z}{20}$ **j** $\dfrac{16t}{12}$

2   a $\dfrac{5xy}{15}$ b $\dfrac{3x}{12y}$ c $\dfrac{17ab}{34ab}$ d $\dfrac{9xy}{18x}$ e $\dfrac{25x^2}{5x}$

   f $\dfrac{21b^2}{7b}$ g $\dfrac{14x^2}{21xy}$ h $\dfrac{12ab^2}{4ab}$ i $\dfrac{20de}{30\,d^2e^2}$ j $\dfrac{5a}{20ab^2}$

3   a $\dfrac{7a^2b^2}{35ab^3}$ b $\dfrac{(ab)^2}{ab}$ c $\dfrac{18abc}{36ac}$ d $\dfrac{13a^2bc}{52ab}$ e $\dfrac{12a^2b^2c^2}{24abc}$

   f $\dfrac{36(ab)^2c}{16a^2bc^2}$ g $\dfrac{(abc)^3}{abc}$ h $\dfrac{9x^2y^3}{12x^3y^2}$ i $\dfrac{20x^3y^2z^2}{15xy^3z}$ j $\dfrac{(3y)^3}{3y^3}$

4   a $\dfrac{18(xy)^2z^3}{17(xyz^3)^2}$ b $\dfrac{334x^4y^7z^3}{668xy^8z^2}$ c $\dfrac{249u(vw)^3}{581u^3v^2w^7}$ d $\dfrac{x^2+3x}{x^2+4x}$

   e $\dfrac{x^2+3x}{x^2+7x+12}$ f $\dfrac{y^3+y^4}{y^2+2y+1}$ g $\dfrac{x^2-8x+12}{x^2-6x+8}$ h $\dfrac{x^2+9x+20}{x^2+x-12}$

   i $\dfrac{24x^2+8x}{3x^2+x}$ j $\dfrac{3x^2-10x-8}{3x^2-14x+8}$ k $\dfrac{x^2-9}{x^2+5x-24}$ l $\dfrac{2x^2-x-3}{x^2+2x+1}$

   m $\dfrac{7x^2-29x+4}{x^2-8x+16}$ n $\dfrac{10y^2-3y-4}{2y^2-13y-7}$ o $\dfrac{6x^2-11x-7}{10x^2-3x-4}$

5   a $\dfrac{6x^2-35x+36}{14x^2-61x-9}$ b $\dfrac{(x^2)^2-(y^2)^2}{(x-y)(x+y)}$ c $\dfrac{\sqrt{x}}{(\sqrt{x})^3}$ d $\dfrac{x^4+2x^2+1}{x^2+1}$

   e $\dfrac{(x^2+7x+12)(x^2+8x+12)}{(x^2+9x+18)(x^2+6x+8)}$ f $\dfrac{\left(\sqrt{x^3+y^3}\right)^3}{x^3+y^3}$

Multiplying and dividing algebraic fractions

MATHEMATICAL CONNECTIONS

You learned how to multiply and divide numerical fractions in Chapter 5.

Consider the following multiplication: $\dfrac{x}{y^2}\times\dfrac{y^4}{x^3}$.

You already know that the numerators and denominators can be multiplied in the

usual way: $\dfrac{x}{y^2}\times\dfrac{y^4}{x^3}=\dfrac{xy^4}{y^2x^3}$.

Now you can see that the HCF of the numerator and denominator is xy^2. If you divide

through by xy^2 you get: $\dfrac{x}{y^2}\times\dfrac{y^4}{x^3}=\dfrac{y^2}{x^2}$.

The following worked example will help you to understand the process for slightly more complicated multiplications and divisions.

WORKED EXAMPLE 24

Simplify each of the following.

a $\dfrac{4}{3x^2} \times \dfrac{14x^3}{16y^2}$
   b $\dfrac{3(x+y)^3}{16z^2} \times \dfrac{12z}{9(x+y)^7}$
   c $\dfrac{14x^4y^3}{9} \div \dfrac{7x^2y}{18}$

Answers

a $\dfrac{4}{3x^2} \times \dfrac{14x^3}{16y^2}$

$\dfrac{4}{3x^2} \times \dfrac{14x^3}{16y^2} = \dfrac{4 \times 14x^3}{3x^2 \times 16y^2} = \dfrac{56x^3}{48x^2y^2} = \dfrac{7x}{6y^2}$

Multiply the numerators and the denominators and then simplify using the methods you have just learnt.

b $\dfrac{3(x+y)^3}{16z^2} \times \dfrac{12z}{9(x+y)^7}$

$\dfrac{3(x+y)^3}{16z^2} \times \dfrac{12z}{9(x+y)^7} = \dfrac{36(x+y)^3 z}{144(x+y)^7 z^2} = \dfrac{1}{4(x+y)^4 z}$

c $\dfrac{14x^4y^3}{9} \div \dfrac{7x^2y}{18}$

$\dfrac{14x^4y^3}{9} \div \dfrac{7x^2y}{18} = \dfrac{14x^4y^3}{9} \times \dfrac{18}{7x^2y} = \dfrac{14x^4y^3 \times 18}{9 \times 7x^2y} = 4x^2y^2$

REFLECTION

The multiplication or division was carried out before any simplification in these examples, but you have already seen that it is possible to cancel first. Try the worked example questions for yourself, but cancel before multiplying or dividing and see if you can get the same answer.

Which method makes more sense to you? Why?

Exercise 14.13

Write each of the following as a single fraction in its lowest terms.

1 **a** $\dfrac{2x}{3} \times \dfrac{3x}{8}$
   b $\dfrac{3y}{4} \times \dfrac{2y}{7}$
   c $\dfrac{2z}{7} \times \dfrac{3z}{4}$

   d $\dfrac{5t}{9} \times \dfrac{9t}{15}$
   e $\dfrac{2x^2}{5} \times \dfrac{5}{2x^2}$
   f $\dfrac{7x^2}{12} \times \dfrac{4}{14x^2}$

   g $\dfrac{12e^2}{11f} \times \dfrac{33f^2}{24e^3}$
   h $\dfrac{18g^4}{16h^2} \times \dfrac{h^4}{36g^3}$
   i $\dfrac{3y}{4} \div \dfrac{3y}{8}$

   j $\dfrac{3y}{8} \div \dfrac{3y^3}{4}$
   k $\dfrac{4cd}{7} \div \dfrac{16c^2}{8}$
   l $\dfrac{8pq}{r} \div \dfrac{16p^2q^2}{r^2}$

2 **a** $\dfrac{24z\,t^3}{x^2} \div \dfrac{8xt}{z}$

b $\dfrac{8}{12} \times \dfrac{x^3}{t^2} \times \dfrac{t^3}{x^2}$

c $\dfrac{9}{27} \times \dfrac{3x^2}{12y^3} \times \dfrac{81}{27} \times \dfrac{9y^2}{3x^3}$

d $\left(\dfrac{3}{8} \times \dfrac{64\,t^3 y^2}{27t}\right) \div \left(\dfrac{3}{8} \times \dfrac{y^2}{t^3} \times \dfrac{t}{y^4}\right)$

e $\dfrac{(x+y)^2}{(x-y)^3} \times \dfrac{33(x-y)^2}{44(x+y)^7}$

f $\dfrac{3(a+b)(a-b)}{(a+b)^2} \div \dfrac{12(a-b)^2}{(a+b)}$

g $\dfrac{\sqrt{x^2+y^2}}{24\sqrt{z^2+t^2}} \times \dfrac{(z^2+t^2)^2}{18\left(\sqrt{x^2+y^2}\right)^3}$

h $\dfrac{3(x+y)^{10}}{18(z-t)^{19}} \times \dfrac{10(x+y)(z-t)^4}{12(x+y)^3(z-y)} \times \dfrac{108(x+y)^2(z-t)^{20}}{15(z-t)^4(x+y)^{10}}$

Adding and subtracting algebraic fractions

You can use common denominators to add or subtract algebraic fractions, just as you do with ordinary fractions.

WORKED EXAMPLE 25

Write as a single fraction in its lowest terms, $\dfrac{1}{x} + \dfrac{1}{y}$

Answer

$\dfrac{1}{x} + \dfrac{1}{y} = \dfrac{y}{xy} + \dfrac{x}{xy} = \dfrac{y+x}{xy}$ The lowest common multiple of x and y is xy.
This will be the common denominator.

WORKED EXAMPLE 26

Write as a single fraction in its lowest terms, $\dfrac{1}{x+1} + \dfrac{1}{x+2}$

Answer

The lowest common multiple of $(x+1)$ and $(x+2)$ is $(x+1)(x+2)$.

$\dfrac{1}{x+1} + \dfrac{1}{x+2} = \dfrac{x+2}{(x+1)(x+2)} + \dfrac{x+1}{(x+1)(x+2)}$

$= \dfrac{x+2+x+1}{(x+1)(x+2)}$

$= \dfrac{2x+3}{(x+1)(x+2)}$

WORKED EXAMPLE 27

Write as a single fraction in its lowest terms, $\dfrac{3x + 4}{x^2 + x - 6} - \dfrac{1}{x + 3}$

Answer

First you should factorise the quadratic expression:

$$\frac{3x + 4}{x^2 + x - 6} - \frac{1}{x + 3} = \frac{3x + 4}{(x + 3)(x - 2)} - \frac{1}{(x + 3)}$$

The two denominators have a common factor of $(x + 3)$, and the lowest common multiple of these two denominators is $(x + 3)(x - 2)$:

$$\frac{3x + 4}{x^2 + x - 6} - \frac{1}{x + 3} = \frac{3x + 4}{(x + 3)(x - 2)} - \frac{1}{(x + 3)}$$

$$= \frac{3x + 4}{(x + 3)(x - 2)} - \frac{(x - 2)}{(x + 3)(x - 2)}$$

$$= \frac{3x + 4 - (x - 2)}{(x + 3)(x - 2)}$$

$$= \frac{3x + 4 - x + 2}{(x + 3)(x - 2)}$$

$$= \frac{2x + 6}{(x + 3)(x - 2)}$$

This may appear to be the final answer, but if you factorise the numerator you will find that more can be done!

$$\frac{3x + 4}{x^2 + x - 6} - \frac{1}{x + 3} = \frac{2x + 6}{(x + 3)(x - 2)}$$

$$= \frac{2(x + 3)}{(x + 3)(x - 2)}$$

$$= \frac{2}{(x - 2)}$$

TIP

Always check to see if your final numerator can be factorised. If it can, then there may be more stages to go.

Exercise 14.14

Write each of the following as a single fraction in its lowest terms.

1 a $\dfrac{y}{2} + \dfrac{y}{4}$ b $\dfrac{t}{3} + \dfrac{t}{5}$ c $\dfrac{u}{7} + \dfrac{u}{5}$ d $\dfrac{z}{7} - \dfrac{z}{14}$

e $\dfrac{(x + y)}{3} + \dfrac{(x + y)}{12}$ f $\dfrac{2x}{3} + \dfrac{5x}{6}$ g $\dfrac{3y}{4} + \dfrac{5y}{8}$ h $\dfrac{2a}{5} - \dfrac{3a}{8}$

i $\dfrac{2a}{7} + \dfrac{3a}{14}$ j $\dfrac{x}{9} + \dfrac{2y}{7}$

2 a $\dfrac{5(x + 1)^2}{7} - \dfrac{3(x + 1)^2}{8}$ b $\dfrac{10pqr}{17} - \dfrac{3pqr}{8}$ c $\dfrac{3p}{5} + \dfrac{3p}{7} + \dfrac{3p}{10}$

d $\dfrac{2x}{3} + \dfrac{3x}{7} - \dfrac{x}{4}$ e $\dfrac{8x^2}{9} + \dfrac{3x^2}{7} - \dfrac{x^2}{3}$ f $\dfrac{5 - x}{2} - \dfrac{3 - x}{3} + \dfrac{3 - x}{9}$

3 **a** $\dfrac{x}{a} + \dfrac{3}{a}$ **b** $\dfrac{2}{3a} + \dfrac{5}{4a}$ **c** $\dfrac{3x}{2y} + \dfrac{5x}{3y}$

   d $\dfrac{3}{a} + \dfrac{2}{a^2}$ **e** $\dfrac{3}{2x} + \dfrac{4}{3x}$ **f** $\dfrac{5}{4e} + \dfrac{3}{20e}$

4 **a** $\dfrac{1}{x+1} + \dfrac{1}{x+4}$ **b** $\dfrac{3}{x-2} + \dfrac{2}{x-1}$ **c** $\dfrac{5}{x+2} + \dfrac{2}{x+7}$

   d $\dfrac{3}{x} - \dfrac{1}{2x}$ **e** $\dfrac{5}{2xy} - \dfrac{4}{3xy}$ **f** $\dfrac{2}{x} + x$

   g $\dfrac{x+1}{2} + \dfrac{2}{x+1}$ **h** $\dfrac{3(x^2-1)}{7y} - \dfrac{2(x^2-1)}{9y^2}$ **i** $\dfrac{1}{x^2} - \dfrac{x}{2y}$

   j $\dfrac{x+1}{3z^2} - \dfrac{y+z}{12xy}$ **k** $\dfrac{1}{(x+2)} - \dfrac{1}{(x+3)(x+2)}$ **l** $\dfrac{2}{x+1} - \dfrac{2}{x^2+3x+2}$

SUMMARY

Do you know …?

Simultaneous means at the same time.

The intersection of two straight lines is the simultaneous solution of their equations.

Simultaneous linear equations can be solved graphically or algebraically.

Inequalities represent a range of solutions.

Inequalities in one variable can be represented on a number line and inequalities in two variables as a region on a plane.

A quadratic expression, $x^2 + bx + c$ can be written in the completed square form as $\left(x + \dfrac{b}{2}\right)^2 - \left(\dfrac{b}{2}\right)^2 + c$.

Quadratic equations that do not factorise can be solved by completing the square or by using the quadratic formula.

If $ax^2 + bx + c = 0$ then $x = \dfrac{-b \pm \sqrt{b^2 - 4ac}}{2a}$.

Complex algebraic fractions can be simplified by factorising and cancelling like terms.

Are you able to …?

solve simultaneous linear equations graphically

solve simultaneous linear equations algebraically

show an inequality in one variable on a number line

show an inequality in two variables as a region in the x–y plane

show a region in the x–y plane that satisfies more than one inequality

rewrite a quadratic expression in completed square form

solve a quadratic equation using the completed square or the quadratic formula

simplify complex algebraic fractions.

Practice questions

SELF ASSESSMENT

Answer these questions before you work through the practice questions:

- What do I aim to achieve?
- What do I already know or am able to do well?
- How will I know if I have met my aims?

Answer these questions once you have completed the practice questions.

- What evidence shows that I have achieved my aims?
- What did I do well?
- What can I improve on?

1 Solve the following pair of simultaneous equations.

$6x - 5y = -3$

$5x + 4y = 22$ [4]

2 A rectangle has sides of length $3x + 1$ cm and $6x - 3$ cm. The perimeter of the rectangle is less than 88 cm.

a Form an solve an inequality for x. [4]

b Given that x is an integer, find the largest possible area of the rectangle. [3]

3 Represent the inequality $4 < x \leqslant 12$ on a number line. [2]

4 Two straight lines are defined by the equations

$x + y = 9$

$2x + y = 13$

a Copy and complete the table of values for $x + y = 9$

x	0	3	
y			0

[2]

b Copy and complete the table of values for $2x + y = 13$

x	0	1	
y			3

[2]

c Plot the lines with equations $x + y = 9$ and $2x + y = 13$ on the same pair of axes.
The x-axis should go from 0 to 10 and the y-axis should go from 0 to 14. [4]

d Use your graph to find the solution to the pair of simultaneous equations. [2]

5 The of the first n numbers in the sequence 1, 2, 3, 4, … is given by the formula $S = \frac{1}{2}n(n + 1)$. Work out how many numbers must be added to give the sum 105. [3]

6 100 m fencing is used to make a rectangular sheep enclosure. The enclosure is x m long.

    a Find, in terms of x, the width of the enclosure. [2]

    b Find and expand an expression for the area of the enclosure. [3]

    c By completing the square on your answer to b, find the value of x for which the area is a maximum. [3]

    d Find the maximum area. [2]

7 Write $x^2 + 8x - 17$ in the form $(x + p)^2 + q$. Hence solve the equation $x^2 + 8x - 17 = 0$. [4]

8 Use the quadratic formula to solve $x^2 + 5x - 9 = 0$. [4]

9 Find the set of all integers that satisfy both $\frac{1}{4}(3x - 2) > 2$ and $3x - 12 < 17$. [6]

10 Simplify $\frac{4x}{3y} \div \frac{2x^3}{9y^4}$. [4]

11 A piece of cable of length 1 m is cut into two parts. Each part is then bent into the shape of a square. The sum of the areas of both squares is 325 cm². Let x cm be the length of one part of the wire.

    a Find the length of the other piece of the wire in cm. [2]

    b Find the area of each square in terms of x. [2]

    c Using the fact that the combined area of both squares is 325 cm², write down and solve an equation for x. [3]

    d Find the perimeter of the smaller square. [3]

12 a Factorise $3x^2 - 7x + 2$. [2]

    b By first factorising $x^2 - y^2$ and $2yz - 2xz$, factorise $x^2 - y^2 - 2xz + 2yz$. [3]

13 Write as a single fraction, giving your answer as simply as possible.

$\frac{3}{x^2 - 4} + \frac{1}{x - 2}$ [4]

14 Write $5x^2 - 30x + 51$ in the form $a(x + p)^2 + q$ and explain why $5x^2 - 30x + 51$ is always positive. [4]

15 Simplify.

$\frac{x^2 - 7x + 12}{x^2 + 3x - 28} \times \frac{x^2 - 49}{x^2 - 9}$ [5]

16 A coin is biased and for any flip, $P(\text{Heads}) = p$.

    a Write down $P(\text{Tails})$ for this coin. [1]

    The coin is flipped twice.

    b Find, in terms of p the probability of flipping heads and then tails. The probability of flipping heads and then tails is now known to be $\frac{3}{16}$. [2]

    c Find the possible values of p. [3]

    d Using the larger value of p find the probability of at least one head in two flips of the coin. [3]

17 The quadratic equation $x^2 - 5x - 3 = 0$ has solutions a and b. Find the value of:

    i $a - b$ [3]

    ii $a + b$ [3]

    Leave your answers in exact form.

18 **a**   By shading the unwanted regions on a diagram, show the region that satisfies all the inequalities $y \geqslant \frac{1}{2}x + 1$, $5x + 6y \leqslant 30$ and $y \leqslant x$.   [5]

    b   Given that x and y satisfy these three inequalities, find the greatest possible value of $x + 2y$.   [3]

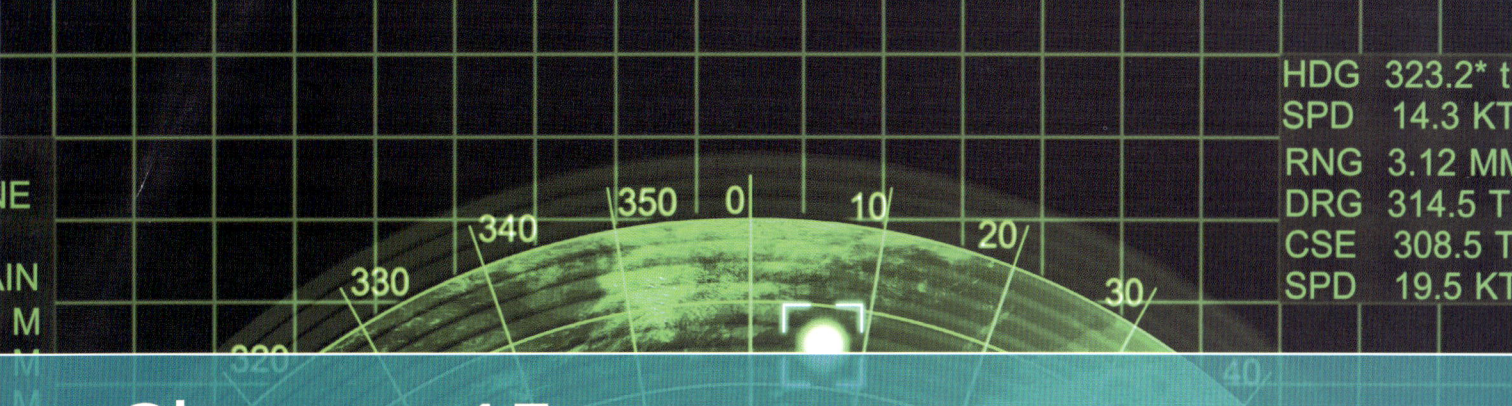

HDG   323.2* t
SPD   14.3 KT
RNG   3.12 MM
DRG   314.5 T
CSE   308.5 T
SPD   19.5 KT

> # Chapter 15

Scale drawings, bearings and trigonometry

IN THIS CHAPTER YOU WILL:

- interpret scale drawings

- calculate bearings

- calculate sine, cosine and tangent ratios for right-angled triangles

- use sine, cosine and tangent ratios to calculate the angles and lengths of sides of right-angled triangles

- solve trigonometric equations, finding all the solutions between 0° and 360°

- apply the sine and cosine rules to calculate unknown sides and angles in triangles that are not right-angled

- calculate the area of a triangle that is not right-angled using the sine ratio

- use the sine, cosine and tangent ratios, together with Pythagoras' theorem in three-dimensions

- use exact sine, cosine and tangent ratios for certain angles.

To 'get your bearings' means to find out where you are and the direction you need to move in. Satnavs and the Global Positioning System (GPS) can make it much easier to work out where you are going. Their software uses the mathematical principles of calculating angles that you will learn about in this chapter.

The image on the previous page shows a 'radar' screen. If you imagine the centre of the screen represents your position, you can then start to work out how far away other objects are and in which direction. How do you think the diagram works?

GETTING STARTED

1   The scale on a map is 1:50 000. The measured distance between two points on the map is 3.9 cm.

   A class is asked to work out the actual distance between the two points in kilometres. Here are three students' solutions:

Student A	Student B	Student C
$\dfrac{1}{50\,000} \times \dfrac{3.9}{1}$ $= 0.000\,058$ cm $= 0.58$ km	Map distance $= 39$ mm Scale $= 1:50\,000$ Real distance $\quad = 39 \times 50\,000$ $\quad = 1\,950\,000$ mm $\quad = 19.5$ km	$3.9 \times 50\,000 = 195\,000$ The distance is: $190\,000$ cm $\div 100 = 1950$ m $\div 1000 = 1.95$ km

   a   Which student has worked it out correctly?

   b   What mistakes did the other two make?

2   The City of Mahlerville is building a new concert hall with 3000 seats inside. The architects create a 1:500 scale model of the hall. How many seats will the model have?

3   A tiny insect is 0.32 mm long and 0.08 mm wide. A biologist is making a scale model of the insect. If the model is 14.4 cm wide, how long will it be?

15.1 Scale drawings

Later in this chapter you will learn how to use the trigonometric ratios to accurately calculate missing angles and sides. For this you will need to use a calculator. Missing lengths and angles can also be found using scale drawings; although this is less accurate, it is still valid. For scale drawings you will need a ruler, a protractor and a sharp pencil.

Sometimes you have to draw a diagram to represent something that is much bigger than you can fit on the paper or so small that it would be very difficult to make out any detail. Examples include a plan of a building, a map of a country or the design of a microchip. These accurate diagrams are called scale drawings.

The lines in the scale drawing are all the same fraction of the lines they represent in reality. This fraction is called the **scale** of the drawing. The scale of a diagram, or a map, may be given as a fraction or a ratio such as $\dfrac{1}{50\,000}$ or 1:50 000.

A scale of $\frac{1}{50\,000}$ means the length of every line in the diagram is $\frac{1}{50\,000}$ of the length of the line that it represents in real life. So, 1 cm in the diagram represents 50 000 cm in real life. In other words, 1 cm represents 500 m, or 2 cm represents 1 km.

MATHEMATICAL CONNECTIONS

Some of the construction skills from Chapter 3 will be useful for scale drawings.

LINK

Scale drawings are often used to plan the production of items in design technology subjects. Many problems that involve fitting together different shapes can be solved by using a good quality scale drawing. Maps in geography are also scale drawings and allow us to represent the real world in a conveniently sized diagram.

WORKED EXAMPLE 1

A rectangular field is 100 m long and 45 m wide. A scale drawing of the field is made with a scale of 1 cm to 10 m. What are the length and width of the field in the drawing?

Answer

10 m is represented by 1 cm

$\therefore$ 100 m is represented by $(100 \div 10)\,\text{cm} = 10\,\text{cm}$

and 45 m is represented by $(45 \div 10)\,\text{cm} = 4.5\,\text{cm}$

So, the dimensions on the drawing are: length = 10 cm and width = 4.5 cm.

LINK

Today most draughtspeople, architects and designers use computers to generate accurate scale diagrams and plans, but most of these designs start with hand-drawn sketches using pencils, rulers and compasses. Often the changes to plans will be accurately drawn over the computer designs before a final design is reached.

Exercise 15.1

1   On the plan of a house, the living room is 3.4 cm long and 2.6 cm wide. The scale of the plan is 1 cm to 2 m. Calculate the actual length and width of the room.

2   The actual distance between two villages is 12 km. Calculate the distance between the villages on a map whose scale is:

a   1 cm to 4 km   b   1 cm to 5 km.

3 A car ramp is 28 m long and makes an angle of 15° with the horizontal.
A scale drawing is made of the ramp using a scale of 1 cm to 5 m.

a How long is the ramp on the drawing?

b What angle does the ramp make with the horizontal on the drawing?

Angle of elevation and angle of depression

Scale drawing questions often involve observations of objects that are higher than
you or lower than you, for example, the top of a building, an aeroplane or a ship in a
harbour. In these cases, the angle of elevation or depression is the angle between the
horizontal and the line of sight of the object.

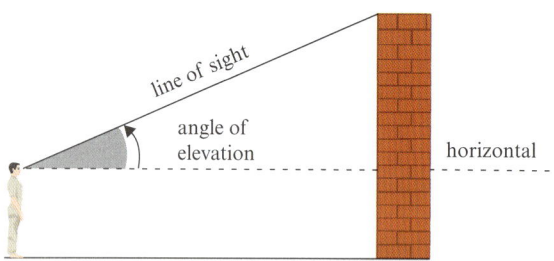

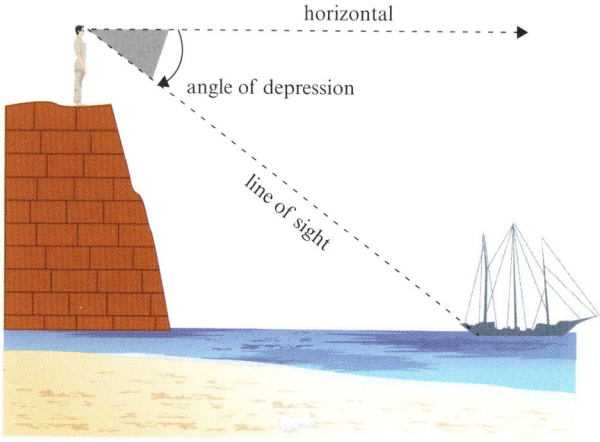

TIP

Angles of elevation are *always* measured from the *horizontal*.

Drawing a scale diagram

Here are some steps for drawing diagrams to scale:

- Draw a rough sketch, showing all details as given in the question.

- If you are told to use a particular scale you must use it! If you are not given a
  scale, try to choose one that will make your diagram fit neatly onto a page.

- Make a clean, tidy and accurate scale drawing using appropriate geometrical
  instruments. Show on it the given lengths and angles. Write the scale next to
  the drawing.

- Measure lengths and angles on the drawing to the answer the problem. Remember
  to change the lengths to full size using the scale. Remember that the full size
  angles are the same as the angles in the scale drawing.

MATHEMATICAL CONNECTIONS

A scale drawing is similar to the real object, so the sides are in proportion and
corresponding angles are equal. You learned about similar shapes in Chapter 11.

Exercise 15.2

1   The diagram is a rough sketch of a field *ABCD*.

   a   Using a scale of 1 cm to 20 m, make an accurate scale drawing of the field.

   b   Find the sizes of angle *BCD* and angle *ADC* at the corners of the field.

   c   Find the length of the side *CD* of the field.

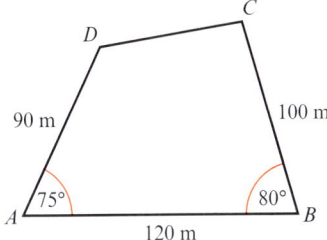

2   A ladder of length 3.6 m stands on horizontal ground and leans against a vertical wall at an angle of 70° to the horizontal (see diagram).

   a   What is the size of the angle that the ladder makes with the wall (*a*)?

   b   Draw a scale drawing using a scale of 1 cm to 50 cm, to find how far the ladder reaches up the wall (*b*).

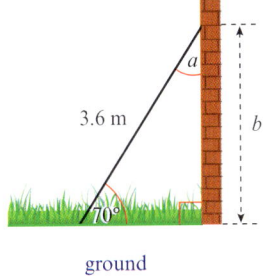

ground

3   The scale diagram represents the vertical wall *TF* of a building that stands on horizontal ground. It is drawn to a scale of 1 cm to 8 m.

   a   Find the height of the building.

   b   Find the distance from the point *A* to the bottom (*B*) of the building.

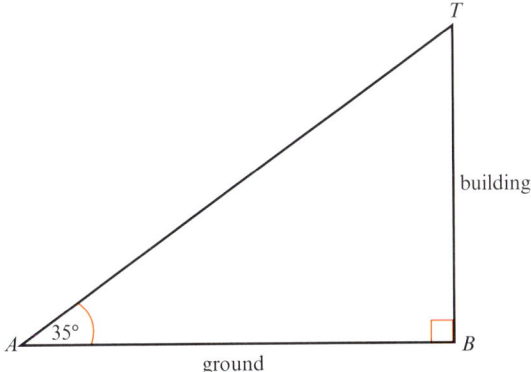

REFLECTION

What advice would you give to a student who finds this work difficult?

15.2 Bearings

You have now used scale drawings to find distances between objects and to measure angles. When you want to move from one position to another, you not only need to know how far you have to travel but you need to know the direction. One way of describing a direction is the **bearing**. This description is used around the world.

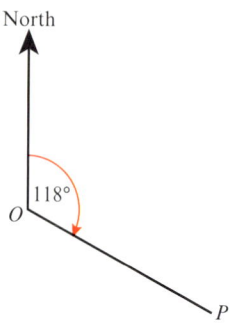

The angle 118°, shown on the right, is measured clockwise from the north direction. Such an angle is called a bearing.

All bearings are measured clockwise from the north direction.

Here the bearing of *P* from *O* is 118°.

> ## MATHEMATICAL CONNECTIONS
>
> One degree of bearing does not seem like a lot but it can represent a huge distance in the real world. This is why you need to use the trigonometry you will learn later in this chapter to calculate angles accurately.

If the angle is less than 100° you still use three figures so that it is clear that you mean to use a bearing.

Here the bearing of *Q* from *O* is 040°.

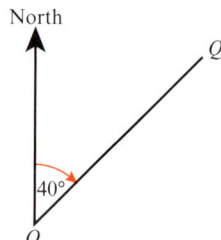

Since you *always* measure clockwise from north it is possible for your bearing to be a reflex angle.

Here the bearing of *R* from *O* is 315°.

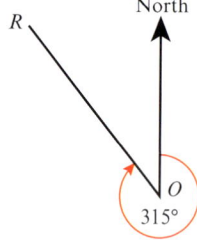

> ## MATHEMATICAL CONNECTIONS
>
> You saw in Chapter 3 that a reflex angle is >180° but <360°.

You may sometimes need to use angle properties from previous chapters to solve bearings problems.

WORKED EXAMPLE 2

The bearing of town *B* from city *A* is 048°. What is the bearing of city *A* from town *B*?

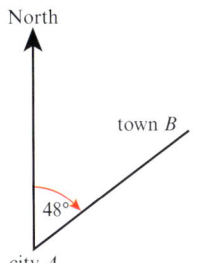 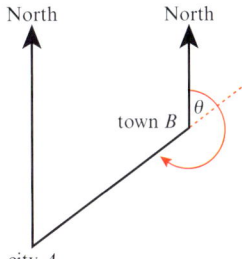

Answer

In the second diagram, the two north lines are parallel. Hence angle $\theta = 48°$ (using the properties of corresponding angles).

The bearing of city *A* from town *B* = 48° + 180° = 228°.

Notice that the difference between the two bearings (48° and 228°) is 180°.

TIP

Always make sure that you draw a clear diagram and mark all north lines clearly. Bearings should always be measured from north.

TIP

This is an example of a 'back' bearing. If you know the bearing of point *X* from point *Y* then, to find the bearing to return to point *Y* from point *X*, you add 180° to the original bearing (or subtract 180° if adding would give a value greater than 360°).

MATHEMATICAL CONNECTIONS

You should remind yourself how to deal with alternate and corresponding angles from Chapter 3.

Exercise 15.3

1   Give the three-figure bearing corresponding to:

   a   west   **b**   south-east   **c**   north-east.

2   Write down the three figure bearings of *B* from *A* for each of the following:

   a 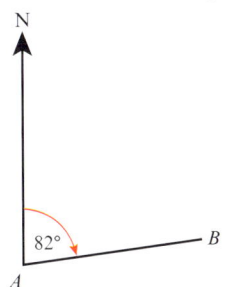   **b**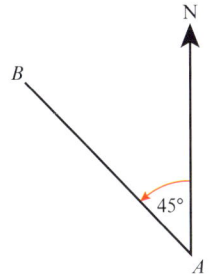

3   Use the map of Southern Africa to find the three-figure bearing of:

   a   Johannesburg from Windhoek

   b   Johannesburg from Cape Town

   c   Cape Town from Johannesburg

   d   Lusaka from Cape Town

   e   Kimberley from Durban.

4   Townsville is 140 km west and 45 km north of Beeton. Using a scale drawing with a scale of 1 cm to 20 km, find:

   a   the bearing of Beeton from Townsville

   b   the bearing of Townsville from Beeton

   c   the direct distance from Beeton to Townsville.

5   Village Q is 7 km from village P on a bearing of 060°. Village R is 5 km from village P on a bearing of 315°. Using a scale drawing with a scale of 1 cm to 1 km, find:

   a   the direct distance from village Q to village R

   b   the bearing of village Q from village R.

6   A hiker walks 400 m east from a parking area and then turns south and walks 250 m to the starting point for the hike.

   a   Use a scale diagram to work out on the bearing of the starting point from the parking area.

   b   How far south-east is the start of the hike from the parking lot? Give your answer in metres, correct to one tenth of a metre.

SELF ASSESSMENT

Write a short social media post about your own understanding of bearings and scale diagrams.

There are some sentence stems at the side to get you started.

Add a hashtag to describe what you learned or something memorable from this section of work.

I found it easy to …

I struggled most with …

I improved my understanding by …

@ _____

_____

- I found it easy to …
- I struggled most with …
- I improved my understanding by …

15.3 Understanding the tangent, cosine and sine ratios

In trigonometry you will use ratios of side lengths in a right-angled triangle to calculate angles or the lengths of other sides. The techniques covered in the following sections will help you to make much more precise calculations with bearings.

Throughout the remainder of this chapter you must make sure that your calculator is set in degrees mode. A small letter 'D' will usually be displayed. If this is not the case, or if your calculator displays a 'G' or an 'R', then please consult your calculator manual.

Labelling the sides of a right-angled triangle

You already know that the longest side of a right-angled triangle is called the hypotenuse. If you take one of the two non right-angles in the triangle for reference then you can also 'name' the two shorter sides:

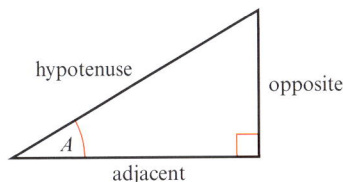

> **MATHEMATICAL CONNECTIONS**
>
> The hypotenuse was introduced with the work on Pythagoras' theorem in Chapter 11.

Notice that the **adjacent** is the side of the triangle that touches the angle A, but is not the hypotenuse. The third side does not meet with angle A at all and is known as the **opposite**. Throughout the remainder of the chapter, we will use opp(A) to mean the length of the opposite side, and adj(A) to mean the length of the adjacent. The hypotenuse does not depend upon the position of angle A, so is just written as 'hypotenuse' (or hyp).

Exercise 15.4

1   For each of the following triangles write down the letters that correspond to the length of the hypotenuse and the values of opp(A) and adj(A).

a
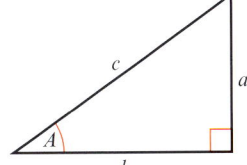

b
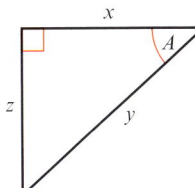

c
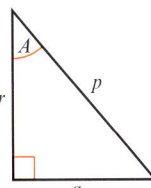

d
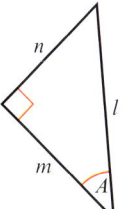

e
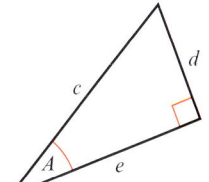

f
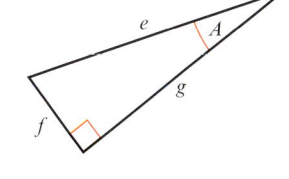

2 For each of these, copy and complete the statements written underneath the triangle.

a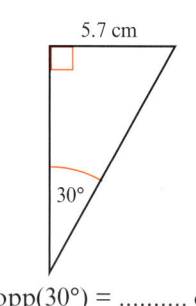

opp(30°) = ... cm

b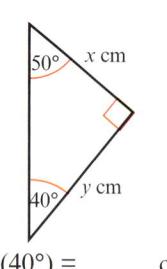

opp(40°) = ... cm
adj(50°) = ... cm

c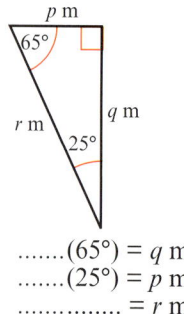

.......(65°) = q m
.......(25°) = p m
.... = r m

INVESTIGATION

Lengths and angles in triangles

You will now explore the relationship between the opposite, adjacent and hypotenuse and the angles in a right-angled triangle.

For this investigation, draw four *different* scale copies of this diagram. Draw the angles as accurately as possible, and all four triangles should be different sizes.

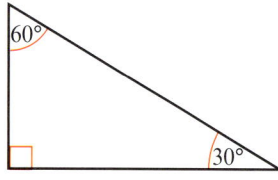

1 Label opp(30°), adj(30°) and hypotenuse clearly.

2 Measure the length of opp(30°) and write it down.

3 Measure the length of adj(30°) and write it down.

4 Calculate $\dfrac{\text{opp}(30°)}{\text{adj}(30°)}$ in each case.

5 What do you notice about your answers?

6 Compare your answers with those of a partner. What do you notice?

7 Now repeat the investigation using another right-angled triangle with different angles. Write down any observations that you make.

8 Does the same happen if you divide another pair of sides for each triangle?

> **MATHEMATICAL CONNECTIONS**
>
> You will need to use the skills you learnt for constructing accurate drawings of triangles in Chapter 3.

Tangent ratio

It turns out that $\dfrac{\text{opp}(A)}{\text{adj}(A)}$ is constant for any given angle A. $\dfrac{\text{opp}(A)}{\text{adj}(A)}$ depends on the angle only, and not the actual size of the triangle. The ratio $\dfrac{\text{opp}(A)}{\text{adj}(A)}$ is called the **tangent ratio** and you write:

$$\tan A = \dfrac{\text{opp}(A)}{\text{adj}(A)}$$

> **MATHEMATICAL CONNECTIONS**
>
> Look back at the work on calculating gradients in Chapter 10 and compare it with the tangent ratio. What connection do you notice?

Your calculator can work out the tangent ratio for any given angle and you can use this to help work out the lengths of unknown sides of a right-angled triangle.

For example, if you wanted to find the tangent of the angle 22° you enter:

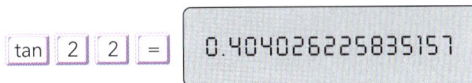

Notice that the answer has many decimal places. When using this value you must make sure that you don't round your answers too soon.

Now, consider the right-angled triangle shown.

You can find the *unknown side*, x cm, by writing down what you know about the tangent ratio:

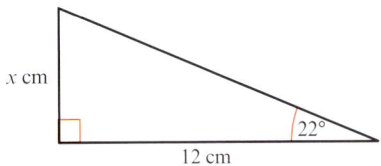

$$\tan 22° = \frac{\text{opp}(22°)}{\text{adj}(22°)} = \frac{x}{12}$$

$\Rightarrow x = 12 \tan(22°)$

$\therefore \ x = 4.848314…$

$\quad x \approx 4.8\,\text{cm} \ (1 \text{ d.p.})$

WORKED EXAMPLE 3

Calculate the value of:

a $\tan 40°$ **b** $\tan 15.4°$

Answers

a

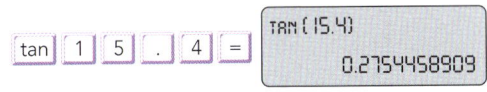

b

WORKED EXAMPLE 4

Find the value of x in the diagram. Give your answer to the nearest mm.

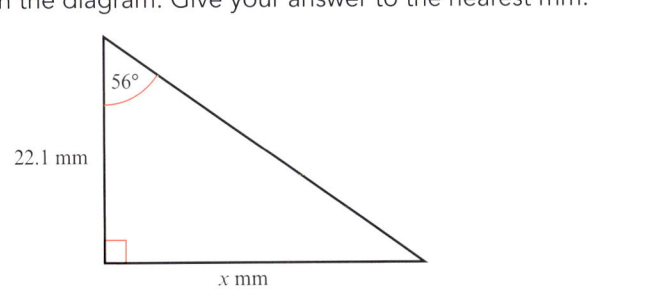

WORKED EXAMPLE 4 CONTINUED

Answer

opp(56°) = x

adj(56°) = 22.1 mm

$\tan 56° = \dfrac{x}{22.1}$

$\Rightarrow x = 22.1 \tan(56°)$

$\quad = 32.76459\ldots$

$\quad \approx 33$ mm (nearest mm)

MATHEMATICAL CONNECTIONS

If you need a reminder of how to deal with equations that involve fractions, look back to Chapter 6 and Chapter 10.

WORKED EXAMPLE 5

The angle of approach of an airliner should be 3°. If a plane is 305 metres above the ground, how far should it be from the airfield?

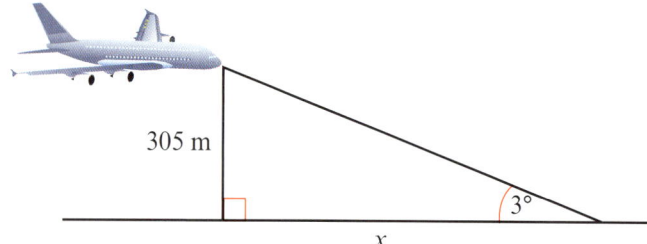

Answer

$\tan 3° = \dfrac{305}{x}$

$\Rightarrow x \tan 3° = 305$

$\Rightarrow x = \dfrac{305}{\tan 3°}$

$\quad = 5819.74\ldots$

$\quad \approx 5820$ (nearest metre)

Exercise 15.5

1 Calculate the value of these tangent ratios, giving your answers to 3 significant figures where necessary.

  a tan 35°   b tan 46°   c tan 18°   d tan 45°

  e tan 15.6°   f tan 17.9°   g tan 0.5°   h tan 0°

2   For each of the following triangles find the required tangent ratio as a fraction in the lowest terms.

a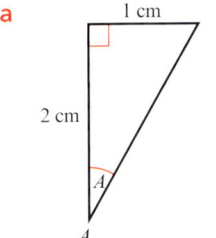

b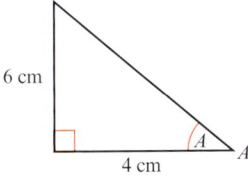

c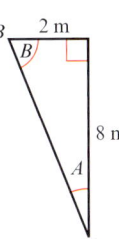

d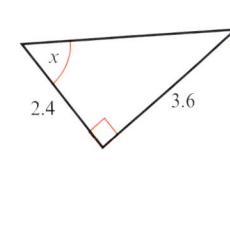

e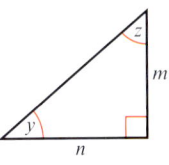

f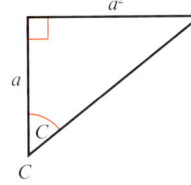

g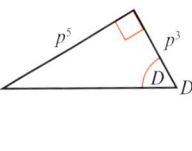

3   Find the length of the lettered side in each triangle. Give your answers to 3 significant figures where necessary.

a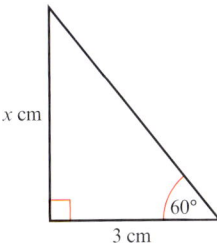

b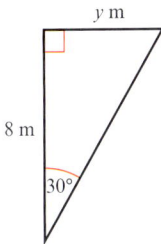

c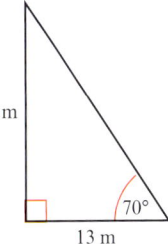

d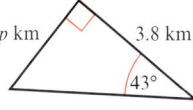

e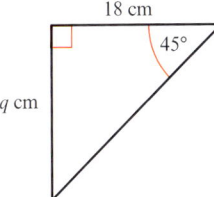

f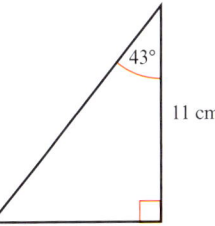

4   Calculate the lettered length in each triangle. Be careful when substituting lengths into the tangent ratio formula.

a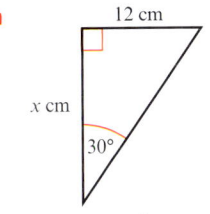

b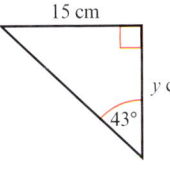

c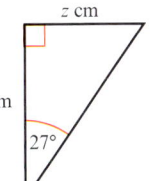

d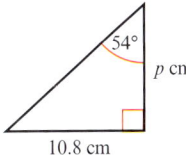

e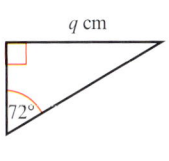

f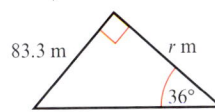

g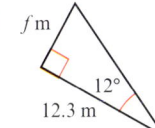

h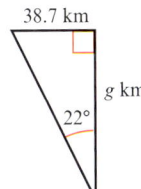

i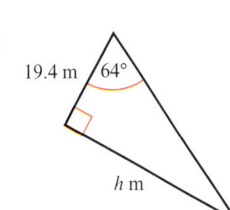

5

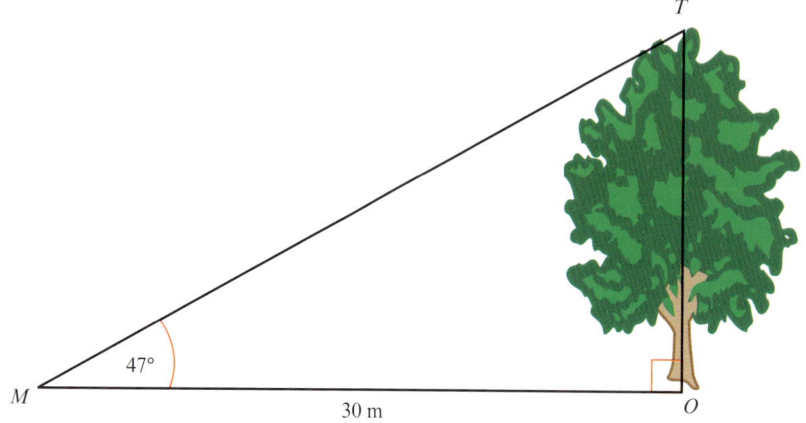

a Use your calculator to find the value of $\tan 47°$ correct to 4 decimal places.

b The diagram shows a vertical tree, OT, whose base, O, is 30 m horizontally from point M. The angle of elevation of T from M is 47°. Calculate the height of the tree.

APPLY YOUR SKILLS

6   Melek wants to estimate the width of a river which has parallel banks. He starts at point A on one bank directly opposite a tree on the other bank. He walks 80 m along the bank to point B and then looks back at the tree. He finds that the line between B and the tree makes an angle of 22° with the bank. Calculate the width of the river.

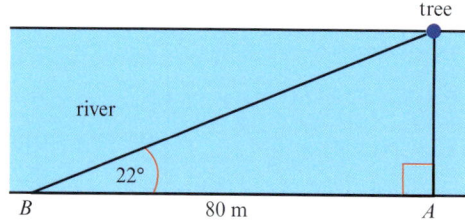

7   The right-angled triangle ABC has angle $BAC = 30°$. Taking the length of BC to be one unit:

a work out the length of AC

b use Pythagoras' theorem to obtain the length of AB.

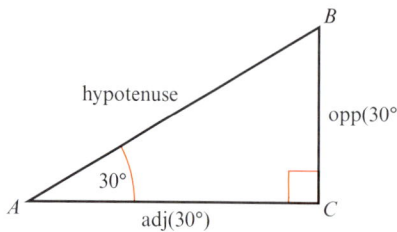

APPLY YOUR SKILLS CONTINUED

8   The diagram shows a ladder leaning against a brick wall. If the angle between the ladder and the floor is 82°, and the ladder reaches 3.2 m up the wall, find the distance d m of the bottom of the ladder from the bottom of the wall. Give your answer to the nearest cm.

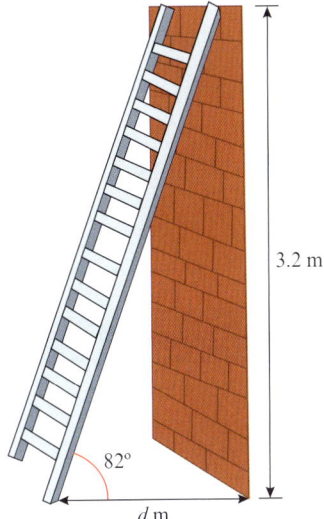

3.2 m

82°

d m

TIP

You need to be able to work out whether you can solve a problem using trigonometry or whether you can use Pythagoras' theorem.

9   A person at the top of a building can see two bus stops (A and B) at ground level. The top of the building is 60 m vertically above ground level. The angle of depression from the top of the building to bus stop A is 25° and the angle of depression to bus stop B is 20°. Assuming ground level is perpendicular to the building, how far apart are the bus stops?

Calculating angles

Your calculator can also 'work backwards' to find the *unknown angle* associated with a particular tangent ratio. You use the inverse tangent function $\boxed{\tan^{-1}}$ on the calculator. Generally this **inverse function** uses the same key as the tangent ratio, but is placed above. If this is the case you will need to use $\boxed{\text{2ndF}}$ or $\boxed{\text{shift}}$ before you press the tan button.

MATHEMATICAL CONNECTIONS

'Functions' are dealt with more thoroughly in Chapter 22.

WORKED EXAMPLE 6

Find the acute angle with the following tangents, correct to 1 decimal place:

a   0.1234   b   5   c   2.765

WORKED EXAMPLE 6 CONTINUED

Answers

a

shift tan . 1 2 3 4 =   TAN⁻¹ 0.1234   7.034735756   So the angle is 7.0°

b

shift tan 5 =   TAN⁻¹ 5   78.69006753   So the angle is 78.7°

c

shift tan 2 . 7 6 5 =   TAN⁻¹ 2.765   70.11678432   So the angle is 70.1°

WORKED EXAMPLE 7

Calculate, correct to 1 decimal place, the lettered angles.

a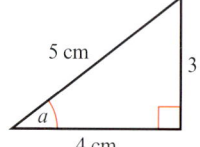

b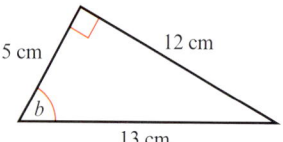

c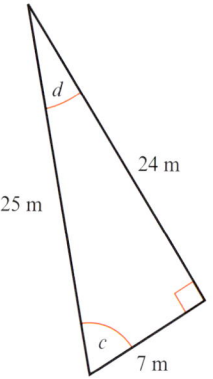

Answers

a $\tan a = \dfrac{\text{opp}(a)}{\text{adj}(a)} = \dfrac{3}{4} = 0.75$

  $a = \tan^{-1}(0.75)$

   $= 36.869897...$

  $a = 36.9°$ (1 d.p.)

b $\tan b = \dfrac{\text{opp}(b)}{\text{adj}(b)} = \dfrac{12}{5} = 2.4$

  $b = \tan^{-1}(2.4)$

   $= 67.380135...$

  $b = 67.4°$ (1 d.p.)

WORKED EXAMPLE 7 CONTINUED

c $\tan c = \dfrac{\text{opp}(c)}{\text{adj}(c)} = \dfrac{24}{7}$

$c = \tan^{-1}\left(\dfrac{24}{7}\right)$

$\quad = 73.739795\ldots$

$c = 73.7°$ (1 d.p.)

To find the angle d, you could use the fact that the angle sum in a triangle is 180°. This gives $d = 180° - (90° + 73.7°) = 16.3°$.

Alternatively, you could use the tangent ratio again but with the opp and adj reassigned to match this angle:

$\tan d = \dfrac{\text{opp}(d)}{\text{adj}(d)} = \dfrac{7}{24}$

$d = \tan^{-1}\left(\dfrac{7}{24}\right)$

$\quad = 16.260204\ldots$

$d = 16.3°$ (1 d.p.)

Exercise 15.6

1   Find, correct to 1 decimal place, the acute angle that has the tangent ratio:

   a   0.85   b   1.2345   c   3.56   d   10.0

2   Find, correct to the nearest degree, the acute angle that has the tangent ratio:

   a $\dfrac{2}{5}$ b $\dfrac{7}{9}$ c $\dfrac{25}{32}$ d $2\dfrac{3}{4}$

3   Find, correct to 1 decimal place, the lettered angles in these diagrams.

a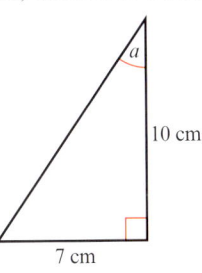

b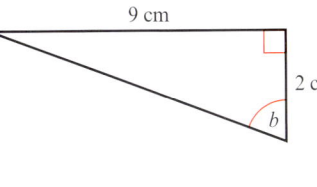

c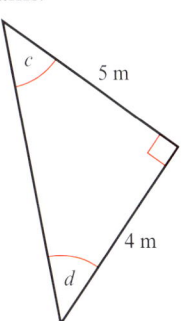

d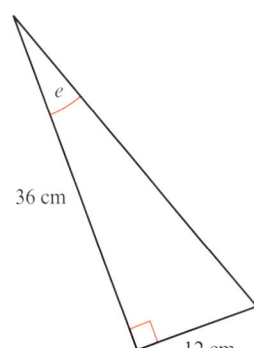

e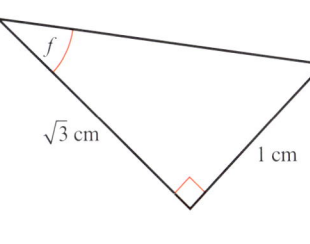

4   A ladder stands on horizontal ground and leans against a vertical wall. The bottom of the ladder is 2.8 m from the base of the wall and the ladder reaches 8.5 m up the wall. Calculate the angle the ladder makes with the ground.

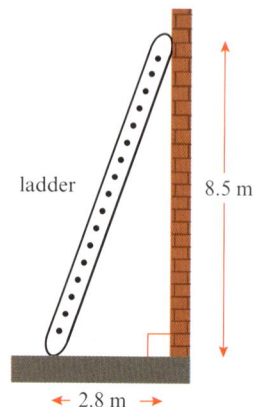

ladder   8.5 m

← 2.8 m →

5   The top of a vertical cliff is 68 m above sea level. A ship is 175 m from the bottom of the cliff. Calculate the angle of elevation of the top of the cliff from the ship.

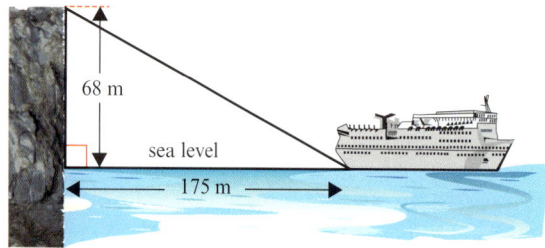

68 m

sea level

175 m

6   O is the centre of a circle with $OM = 12$ cm.

   a   Calculate AM.   b   Calculate AB.

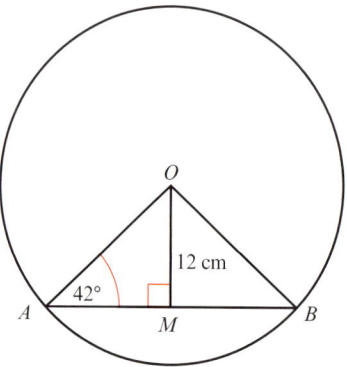

O

12 cm

42°

A M B

7   The right-angled triangle ABC has hypotenuse $AC = 7$ cm and side $BC = 3$ cm. Calculate the length AB and hence the angle ACB.

TIP

Draw a clear diagram.

Sine and cosine ratios

You will have noticed that the tangent ratio only makes use of the opposite and adjacent sides. What happens if you need to use the hypotenuse? In fact, there are three possible pairs of sides that you could include in a ratio:

*   opposite and adjacent (already used with the tangent ratio)
*   opposite and hypotenuse
*   or adjacent and hypotenuse.

This means that you need two more ratios:

- the **sine ratio** is written as $\sin(A) = \dfrac{\text{opp}(A)}{\text{hyp}}$

- the **cosine ratio** is written as $\cos(A) = \dfrac{\text{adj}(A)}{\text{hyp}}$

As with the tangent ratio, you can use the sin and cos keys on your calculator to find the sine and cosine ratios associated with given angles. You can also use the shift sin or sin⁻¹ and shift cos or cos⁻¹ 'inverse' functions to find angles.

Before looking at some worked examples you should note that with three possible ratios you need to know how to pick the right one! 'SOHCAHTOA' might help you to remember:

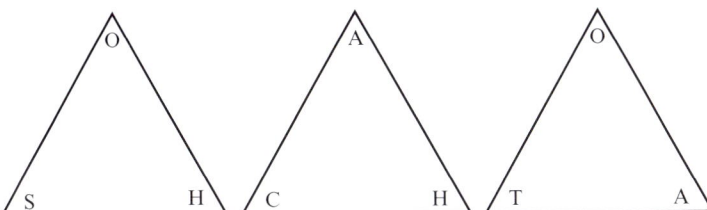

> **TIP**
>
> S = sine
> O = opposite
> H = hypotenuse
> C = cosine
> A = adjacent
> T = tan

The letters 'SOHCAHTOA' can be divided into three triangles of letters, each representing one of the three trigonometric ratios. The first letter in each trio tells you which ratio it represents (sine, cosine or tangent), the second letter (at the top) tells you which side's length goes on the top of the ratio, and the third letter tells you which side's length goes on the bottom.

For example, if a problem involves the opposite and hypotenuse, you simply need to find the triangle of letters that includes 'O' and 'H': SOH.

The 'S' tells you that it is the sine ratio, the 'O' at the top of the triangle sits on top of the fraction, and the lower 'H' sits on the bottom.

The use of 'SOHCAHTOA' is shown clearly in the following worked examples. The tangent ratio has been included again in these examples to help show you how to decide which ratio should be used.

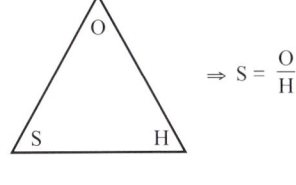

WORKED EXAMPLE 8

Find the length of the sides lettered in each of the following diagrams.

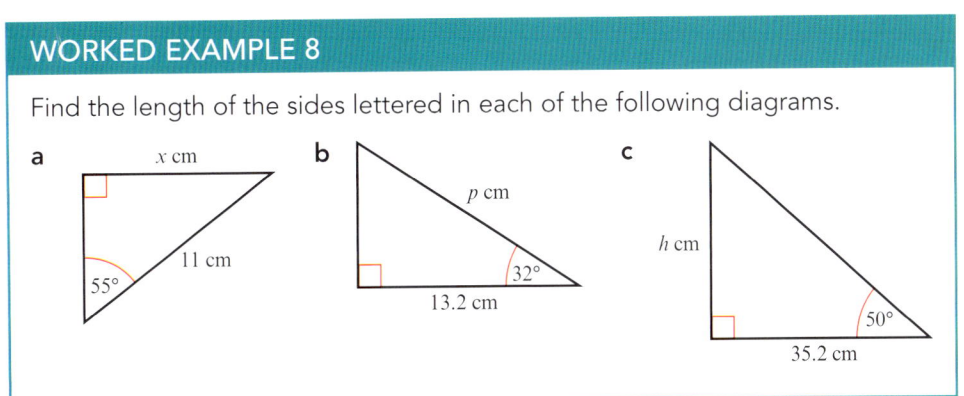

WORKED EXAMPLE 8 CONTINUED

Answers

a opp(55°) = x

hyp = 11 cm

So $\sin 55° = \dfrac{\text{opp}(55°)}{\text{hyp}} = \dfrac{x}{11}$

$\Rightarrow x = 11 \sin 55°$

$\Rightarrow x = 9.0\,\text{cm}$ (to 1 d.p.)

Identify the sides that you are going to consider clearly:

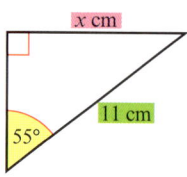 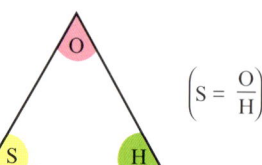

$\left(S = \dfrac{O}{H}\right)$

b adj(32°) = 13.2 cm

hyp = p cm

So $\cos 32° = \dfrac{\text{adj}(32°)}{\text{hyp}} = \dfrac{13.2}{p}$

$\Rightarrow p \cos 32° = 13.2$

$\Rightarrow p = \dfrac{13.2}{\cos 32°}$

$\Rightarrow p = 15.6\,\text{cm}$ (to 1 d.p.)

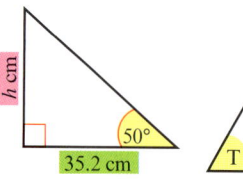 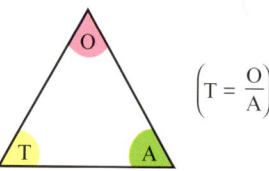

$\left(C = \dfrac{A}{H}\right)$

c opp(50°) = h cm

adj(50°) = 35.2 cm

So $\tan 50° = \dfrac{\text{opp}(50°)}{\text{adj}(50°)} = \dfrac{h}{35.2}$

$\Rightarrow h = 35.2 \tan 50°$

$\Rightarrow h = 41.9\,\text{cm}$ (to 1 d.p.)

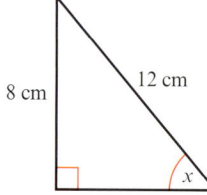 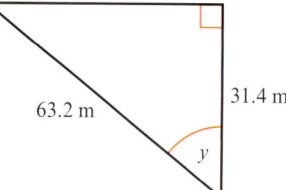

$\left(T = \dfrac{O}{A}\right)$

WORKED EXAMPLE 9

Find the size of the lettered angles in each of the following diagrams.

a

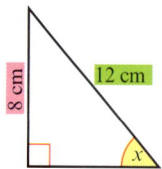

b

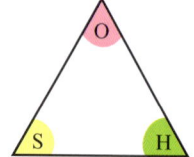

Answers

a opp(x) = 8 cm

hyp = 12 cm

So $\sin x = \dfrac{\text{opp}(x)}{\text{hyp}} = \dfrac{8}{12}$

$\Rightarrow x = \sin^{-1}\left(\dfrac{8}{12}\right)$

$\Rightarrow x = 41.8°$ (1 d.p.)

Once again, clearly identify the sides and ratio to be used:

WORKED EXAMPLE 9 CONTINUED

b   adj(y) = 31.4 m

hyp = 63.2 m

So $\cos y = \dfrac{\text{adj}(y)}{\text{hyp}} = \dfrac{31.4}{63.2}$

$\Rightarrow y = \cos^{-1}\left(\dfrac{31.4}{63.2}\right)$

$\Rightarrow y = 60.2°$ (1 d.p.)

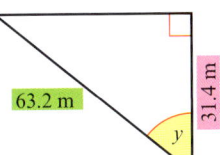
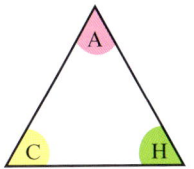

WORKED EXAMPLE 10

A ladder 4.8 m long leans against a vertical wall and on horizontal ground. The ladder makes an angle of 70° with the ground.

a   How far up the wall does the ladder reach?

b   How far is the bottom of the ladder from the wall?

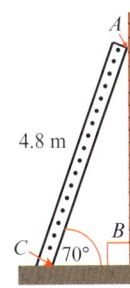

Answers

a   In the diagram, AC is the hypotenuse of the right-angled triangle *ABC*. *AB* is the distance that the ladder reaches up the wall.

opp(70°) = *AB*

hyp = 4.8 m

So $\sin 70° = \dfrac{\text{opp}(70°)}{\text{hyp}} = \dfrac{AB}{4.8}$

$\Rightarrow AB = 4.8 \sin 70°$

$\Rightarrow AB = 4.5$ m (1 d.p.)

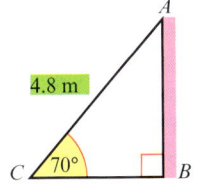
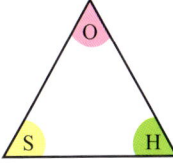

So the ladder reaches 4.5 m up the wall.

b   The distance of the bottom of the ladder from the wall is *BC*.

adj(70°) = *BC*

hyp = 4.8 m

So $\cos 70° = \dfrac{\text{adj}(70°)}{\text{hyp}} = \dfrac{BC}{4.8}$

$\Rightarrow BC = 4.8 \cos 70°$

$\Rightarrow BC = 1.64$ m (2 d.p.)

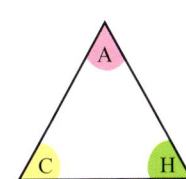

The bottom of the ladder is 1.64 m from the wall.

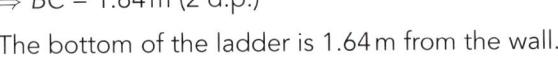

Exercise 15.7

1 For each of the following triangles write down the value of:

    i $\sin A$ **ii** $\cos A$ **iii** $\tan A$

a 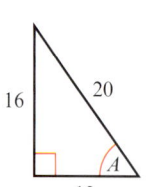   **b** 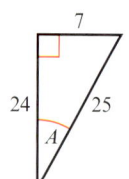   **c** 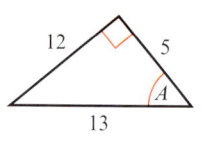   **d**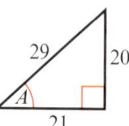

e 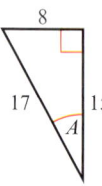   **f** 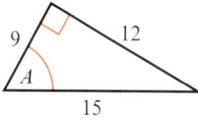   **g**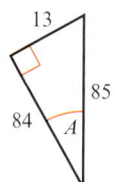

2 Use your calculator to find the value of each of the following. Give your answers to 4 decimal places.

    a $\sin 5°$ **b** $\cos 5°$ **c** $\sin 30°$ **d** $\cos 30°$

    e $\sin 60°$ **f** $\cos 60°$ **g** $\sin 85°$ **h** $\cos 85°$

3 For each of the following triangles, use the letters of the sides to write down the given trigonometric ratio.

a 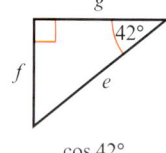   **b** 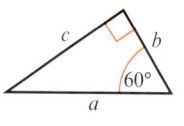   **c** 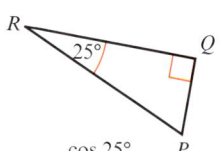   **d**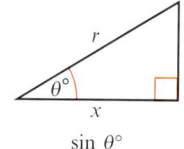
$\cos 42°$ $\sin 60°$ $\cos 25°$ $\sin \theta°$

e 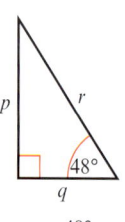   **f** 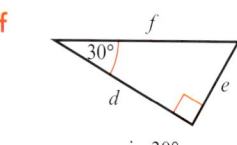   **g** 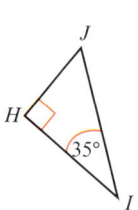   **h**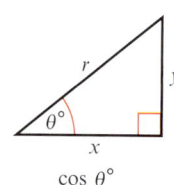
$\cos 48°$ $\sin 30°$ $\cos 35°$ $\cos \theta°$

4 For each of the following triangles find the length of the unknown, lettered side. (Some questions that require the tangent ratio have been included. If you use SOHCAHTOA carefully you should spot these quickly!)

a 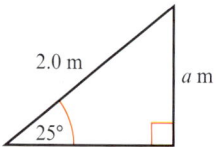   **b** 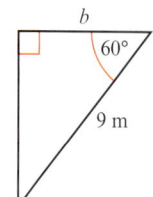   **c** 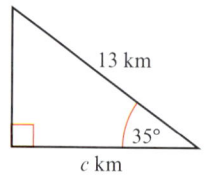   **d**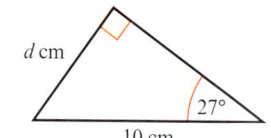

e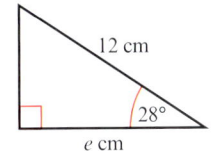

f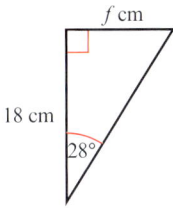

g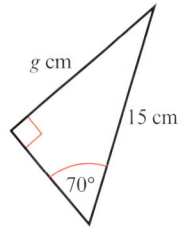

h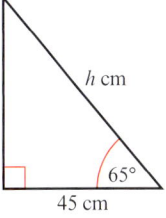

i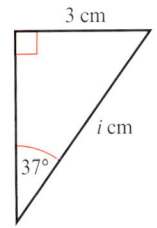

j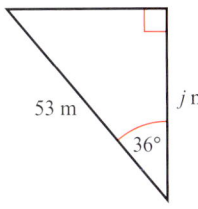

k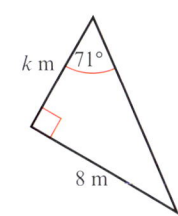

l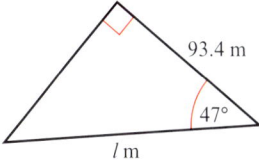

5 Use your calculator to find, correct to 1 decimal place:

   a   an acute angle whose sine is 0.99

   b   an acute angle whose cosine is 0.5432

   c   an acute angle whose sine is $\frac{3}{8}$

   d   an acute angle whose cosine is $\frac{\sqrt{3}}{2}$.

6 Find, to 1 decimal place, the lettered angle in each of the following triangles.

a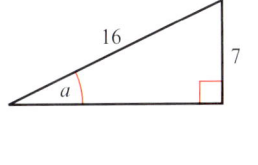

b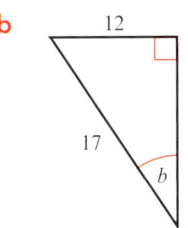

c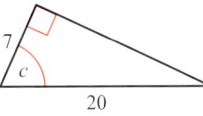

d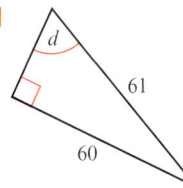

e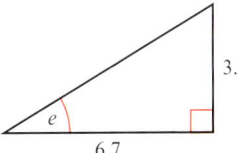

f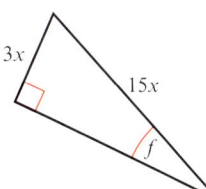

7 The diagram shows a ramp, *AB*, which makes an angle of 18° with the horizontal. The ramp is 6.25 m long. Calculate the difference in height between *A* and *B* (this is the length *BC* in the diagram).

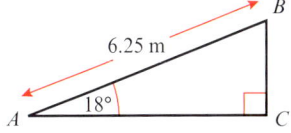

8 Village *Q* is 18 km from village *P*, on a bearing of 056°.

   a   Calculate the distance *Q* is north of *P*.

   b   Calculate the distance *Q* is east of *P*.

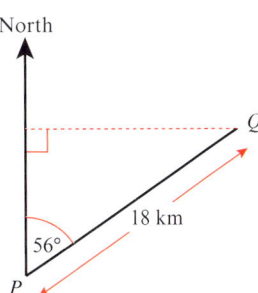

APPLY YOUR SKILLS

9 A trail runner runs 5 km on a bearing of 025° from the start of the run to the first water point. The runner then continues on a bearing of 078° for another 6 km to the second water point.

    a How far east of the starting point is the first water point?

    b How far east of the first water point is the runner at the second water point?

    c What is the direct bearing from the starting point to the second water point?

    d What distance east of the starting point is the runner at the second water point?

10 a A surf-skier paddles 600 m on a bearing of 038°. Draw a sketch to show this journey and work out how far north the surf-skier is from their starting point.

    b Another surf-skier paddles in a straight line on a bearing of 070° before changing direction. How far has the surf-skier travelled if the direction change is 550 m north of the starting point?

11 A 15 m beam is resting against a wall. The base of the beam forms an angle of 70° with the ground.

    a At what height is the top of the beam touching the wall?

    b How far is the base of the beam from the wall?

12 A mountain climber walks 380 m along a slope that is inclined at 65° to the horizontal, and then a further 240 m along a slope inclined at 60° to the horizontal. Calculate the total vertical distance through which the climber travels.

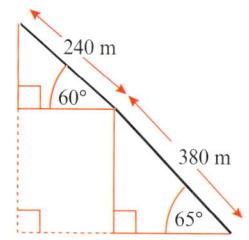

13 Calculate the unknown, lettered side(s) in each of the following shapes. Give your answers to 2 decimal places where necessary.

a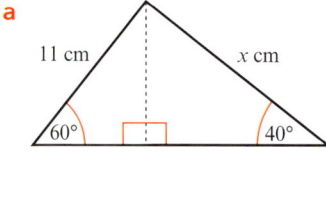

b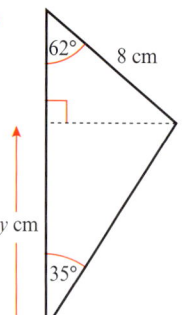

c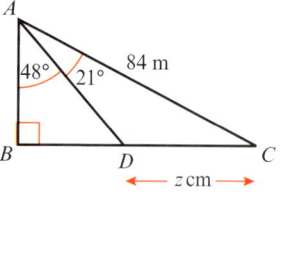

d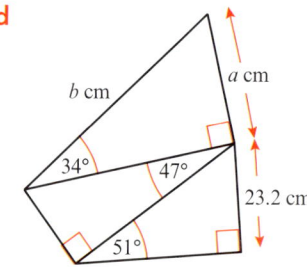

14 For each of the following angles calculate:

    i $\tan x$ **ii** $\dfrac{\sin x}{\cos x}$

    a $x = 30°$ **b** $x = 48°$ **c** $x = 120°$ **d** $x = 194°$

What do you notice?

15 **a**   Calculate.

  i $(\sin 30°)^2 + (\cos 30°)^2$

  ii $(\sin 48°)^2 + (\cos 48°)^2$

  b   Choose another angle and repeat the calculation.

  c   What do you notice?

INVESTIGATION

16   Using trigonometry is sometimes called triangulation. Investigate how triangulation is used in surveying and how this is used to locate satellites in a GPS system. Make a poster or slide show to present your findings.

15.4 Exact trigonometric ratios

You saw in Chapter 3 that some angles arise naturally in familiar shapes. Here are some important examples.

Equilateral triangles contain three 60° angles:

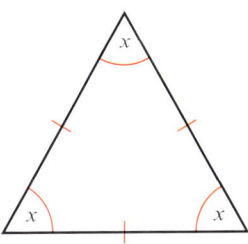

Isosceles right-angled triangles contain one 90° angle and two 45° angles:

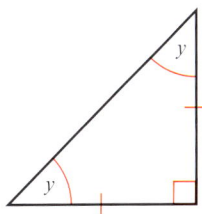

$x + x + x = 180°$

$\Rightarrow \quad 3x = 180°$

$\qquad x = \dfrac{180°}{3} = 60°$

$y + y + 90° = 180°$

$\Rightarrow \qquad 2y = 90°$

$\Rightarrow \qquad y = \dfrac{90°}{2} = 45°$

Think about an isosceles right-angled triangle, where the two shorter sides are both 1 cm long.

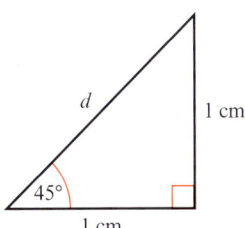

By Pythagoras' theorem:

$d^2 = 1^2 + 1^2 = 2$

$\Rightarrow d = \sqrt{2}$

This means that d is the exact length of the hypotenuse, which you can now use to find the exact values of some trigonometric ratios:

$$\sin 45° = \frac{\text{opposite}}{\text{hypotenuse}} = \frac{1}{\sqrt{2}} \qquad \cos 45° = \frac{\text{adjacent}}{\text{hypotenuse}} = \frac{1}{\sqrt{2}} \qquad \tan 45° = \frac{\text{opposite}}{\text{adjacent}} = \frac{1}{1} = 1$$

$$= \frac{1}{\sqrt{2}} \times \frac{\sqrt{2}}{\sqrt{2}} = \frac{\sqrt{2}}{2} \qquad\qquad = \frac{1}{\sqrt{2}} \times \frac{\sqrt{2}}{\sqrt{2}} = \frac{\sqrt{2}}{2}$$

MATHEMATICAL CONNECTIONS

You learnt about irrational numbers in Chapter 9. Surds such as $\sqrt{2}$ and recurring decimals such as $\frac{2}{3}$ are irrational numbers and cannot be written exactly in decimal form.

When a question asks for an answer in exact form, you need to leave surds in root form and recurring decimals as fractions.

You can also use an equilateral triangle, with side 2 cm, to find exact trigonometric ratios for the sine, cosine and tangent of 30° and 60°.

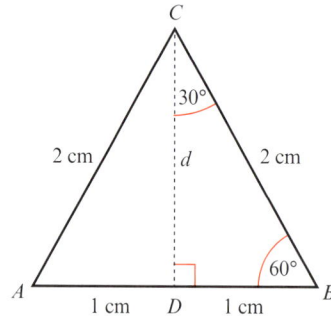

By Pythagoras' theorem:

$d^2 + 1^2 = 2^2$

$\Rightarrow \quad d^2 = 4 - 1 = 3$

$\Rightarrow \quad d = \sqrt{3}$

If you think about the angle 60° shown in the diagram. Side CD is the opposite, BD is the adjacent and BC is the hypotenuse.

$$\sin 60° = \frac{\text{opposite}}{\text{hypotenuse}} \qquad \cos 60° = \frac{\text{adjacent}}{\text{hypotenuse}} \qquad \tan 60° = \frac{\text{opposite}}{\text{adjacent}}$$

$$= \frac{\sqrt{3}}{2} \qquad\qquad\qquad = \frac{1}{2} \qquad\qquad\qquad = \frac{\sqrt{3}}{1} = \sqrt{3}$$

If you think about the angle marked 30° instead, then BD becomes the opposite, CD becomes the adjacent and BC remains the hypotenuse.

$$\sin 30° = \frac{\text{opposite}}{\text{hypotenuse}} \qquad \cos 30° = \frac{\text{adjacent}}{\text{hypotenuse}} \qquad \tan 30° = \frac{\text{opposite}}{\text{adjacent}} = \frac{1}{\sqrt{3}}$$

$$= \frac{1}{2} \qquad\qquad\qquad = \frac{\sqrt{3}}{2} \qquad\qquad\qquad = \frac{1}{\sqrt{3}} \times \frac{\sqrt{3}}{\sqrt{3}} = \frac{\sqrt{3}}{3}$$

It is important to notice that you can write the exact values of fractions involving surds in more than one way. Mathematicians usually prefer to use the version that contains an integer in the denominator.

MATHEMATICAL CONNECTIONS

You learnt how to rationalise the denominator in Chapter 9. It is almost always better to rationalise the denominator where possible in trigonometry; if you need to use your answer to calculate something else, the algebra that follows is much easier.

This table summarises the results worked out on the previous page and adds trigonometric ratios for 0° and 90°. You can check these using your calculator.

	$\sin x$	$\cos x$	$\tan x$
0°	0	1	0
30°	$\dfrac{1}{2}$	$\dfrac{\sqrt{3}}{2}$	$\dfrac{1}{\sqrt{3}}$ or $\dfrac{\sqrt{3}}{3}$
45°	$\dfrac{1}{\sqrt{2}}$ or $\dfrac{\sqrt{2}}{2}$	$\dfrac{1}{\sqrt{2}}$ or $\dfrac{\sqrt{2}}{2}$	1
60°	$\dfrac{\sqrt{3}}{2}$	$\dfrac{1}{2}$	$\sqrt{3}$
90°	1	0	Doesn't exist

WORKED EXAMPLE 11

Find the exact area of the triangle shown in the diagram.

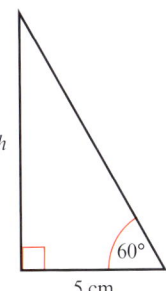

Answer

First, find the height of the triangle, h.

$\tan 60° = \dfrac{h}{5}$

$\Rightarrow h = 5\tan 60°$

$h = 5\sqrt{3}$ cm, using the exact value of $\tan 60°$.

Area $= \dfrac{1}{2} \times$ base $\times$ height

$= \dfrac{1}{2} \times 5 \times 5\sqrt{3}$

$= \dfrac{25\sqrt{3}}{2}$ cm^2

Exercise 15.8

1 Calculate the exact length of the unknown side in each triangle.

a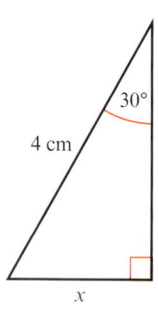

b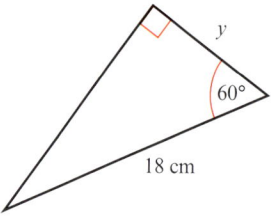

c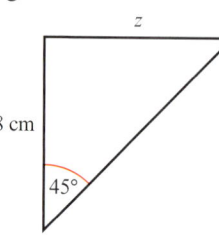

2 Calculate the exact length of the unknown side in each triangle.

a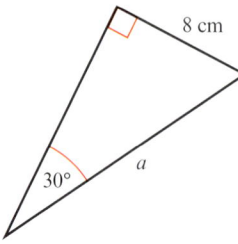

b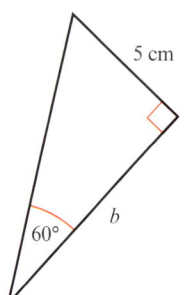

c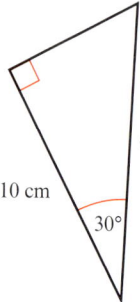

3 Find the exact area of triangle *ACD*.

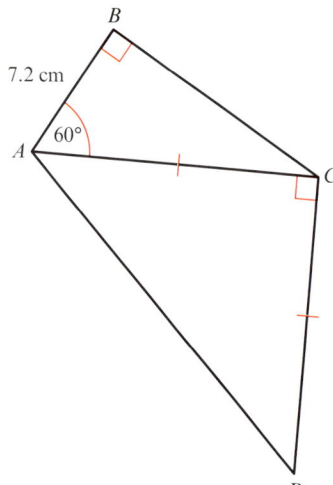

4 The angle of elevation of the top of a flagpole, (*C*), seen from point *A* is 30°.
The angle of elevation of the top of the same flagpole, seen from point B is 60°.
The flagpole is 18 m high. Work out the exact distance between the
points *A* and *B*.

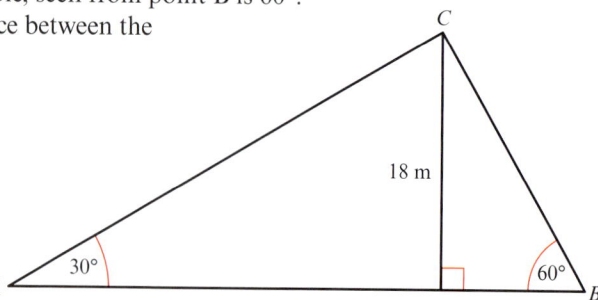

15.5 Solving problems using trigonometry

You may need to use more than one trigonometric ratio when you solve problems that involve right-angled triangles. To make it clear which ratio to use and when, you should follow these guidelines.

- If the question does not include a diagram, draw one. Make it clear and large.
- Identify any right-angled triangles that may be useful to you.
- Draw each triangle separately and clearly label any sides and angles that you already know.
- Write down which of the opposite, adjacent and hypotenuse you are going to use, and then use SOHCAHTOA to help you decide which ratio to use.
- Write down the ratio and solve, either for an angle or a side.
- If you need to use a side or angle that you have calculated for another part of a question, try to use the unrounded value that you have in your calculator memory. This will help to avoid rounding errors later on.

> **MATHEMATICAL CONNECTIONS**
>
> It will be useful to remind yourself about general angle properties of triangles from Chapter 3.

Calculating distances

In mathematics, when you are asked to calculate the distance from a point to a line you are expected to find the shortest distance between the point and the line. This distance is equal to the length of a perpendicular from the point to the line.

In this diagram, the distance from P to the line AB is 5 units.

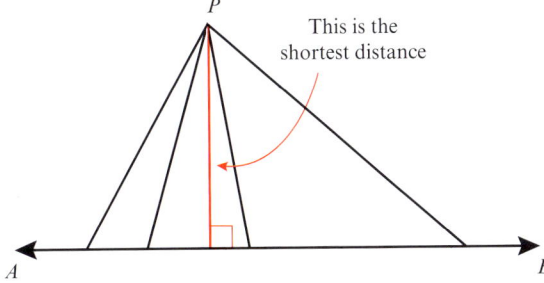

This is the shortest distance

Any other line from the point to the line creates a right-angled triangle and the line itself becomes the hypotenuse of that triangle. Any hypotenuse must be longer than the perpendicular line, so, all the other distances from P to the line are longer than 5 units.

There are different ways of working out the distance between a point and a line. The method you choose will depend on the information you are given. For example, if you are asked to find the distance between point A and line BD given the information on the diagram on the right, you could draw in the perpendicular and use trigonometry to find the lengths of the other sides of the triangle.

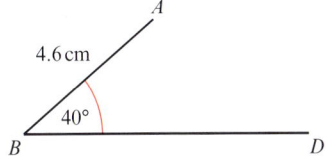

MATHEMATICAL CONNECTIONS

You will use the distance between a point and a line again when you deal with circles in Chapter 19.

Worked example 12 shows you how to use trigonometry to find the distance between point A and the line BD and then how to use it to solve the problem given. It also shows you how you can set out the solution to a trigonometry problem.

WORKED EXAMPLE 12

The diagram shows an isosceles trapezium $ABDC$. Calculate the area of the trapezium.

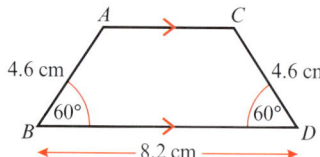

Answer

The area of a trapezium = (mean of the parallel sides) × (perpendicular distance between them).

In this diagram, perpendiculars have been added to form right-angled triangles so that trigonometry can be used.

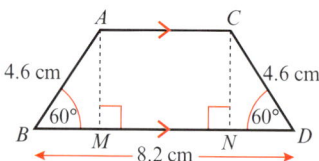

$AC = MN$ and you can find the length of MN if you calculate the lengths of BM and ND.

In triangle ABM, $\sin 60° = \dfrac{\text{opp}(60°)}{\text{hyp}} = \dfrac{AM}{4.6}$ and $\cos 60° = \dfrac{\text{adj}(60°)}{\text{hyp}} = \dfrac{BM}{4.6}$

Hence, $AM = 4.6 \times \sin 60°$ and $BM = 4.6 \times \cos 60°$

$AM = 3.983716\ldots$ cm and $BM = 2.3$ cm

By symmetry, $ND = BM = 2.3$ cm

and $\therefore MN = 8.2 - (2.3 + 2.3) = 3.6$ cm

Hence, $AC = 3.6$ cm and $AM = CN = 3.983716\ldots$ cm

The area of $ABDC = \left(\dfrac{AC + BD}{2}\right) \times AM$

$\qquad = \left(\dfrac{3.6 + 8.2}{2}\right) \times 3.983716\ldots$ cm²

$\qquad = 23.503929\ldots$ cm²

Area of $ABDC = 23.5$ cm² (to 3 s.f.)

TIP

Give your answer to 3 significant figures if no degree of accuracy is specified.

LINK

Trigonometry is used to work out lengths and angles when they can't really be measured. For example in navigation, surveying, engineering, construction and even the placement of satellites and receivers.

WORKED EXAMPLE 13

The span between the towers of Tower Bridge in London is 76 m. When the arms of the bridge are raised to an angle of 35°, how wide is the gap between their ends?

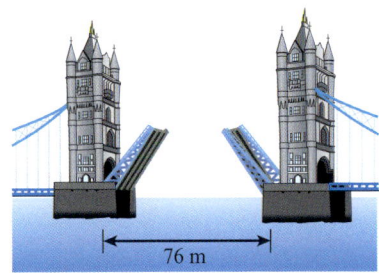

76 m

Answer

Here is a simplified labelled drawing of the bridge, showing the two halves raised to 35°.

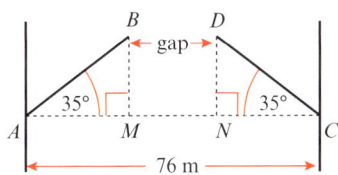

The gap = BD = MN and MN = AC − (AM + NC).

The right-angled triangles ABM and CDN are congruent, so AM = NC.

When the two halves are lowered, they must meet in the middle.

$\therefore AB = CD = \dfrac{76}{2} = 38$ m

In triangle ABM, $\cos 35° = \dfrac{\text{adj}(35°)}{\text{hyp}} = \dfrac{AM}{38}$

$AM = 38 \times \cos 35°$

$\quad = 31.1277... \text{m}$

$\therefore MN = 76 − (31.1277... + 31.1277...)$

$\quad = 13.744... \text{m}$

The gap BD = 13.7 m (to 3 s.f.)

TIP

Drawing a clear, labelled sketch can help you work out what mathematics you need to do to solve the problem.

Exercise 15.9

APPLY YOUR SKILLS

1 The diagram represents a ramp *AB* for a lifeboat. *AC* is vertical and *CB* is horizontal.

   a Calculate the size of angle *ABC* correct to 1 decimal place.

   b Calculate the length of *BC* correct to 3 significant figures.

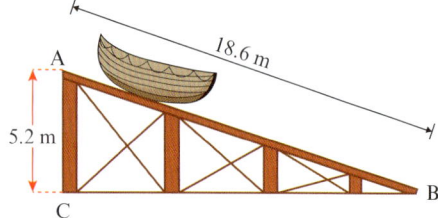

2 *AB* is a chord of a circle, centre *O*, radius 8 cm. Angle *AOB* = 120°. Calculate the length of *AB*.

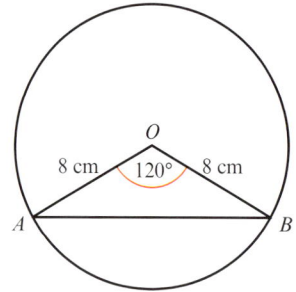

3 The diagram represents a tent in the shape of a triangular prism. The front of the tent, *ABD*, is an isosceles triangle with *AB* = *AD*. The width, *BD*, is 1.8 m and the supporting pole *AC* is perpendicular to *BD* and 1.5 m high. The tent is 3 m long. Calculate:

   a the angle between *AB* and *BD*

   b the length of *AB*

   c the capacity inside the tent (i.e. the volume).

> **MATHEMATICAL CONNECTIONS**
>
> Look at Chapter 7 and remind yourself about the formula for the volume of a prism.

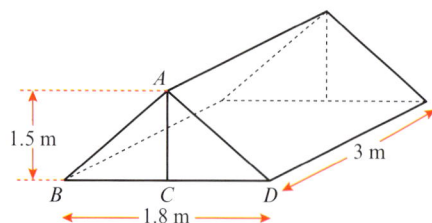

APPLY YOUR SKILLS CONTINUED

4   Calculate the angles of an isosceles triangle that has sides of length 9 cm, 9 cm and 14 cm.

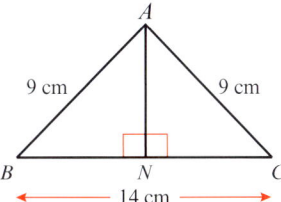

5   The sketch represents a field *PQRS* on level ground.
    The sides *PQ* and *SR* run due east.

    a   Write down the bearing of *S* from *P*.

    b   Calculate the perpendicular (shortest) distance between *SR* and *PQ*.

    c   Calculate, in square metres, the area of the field *PQRS*.

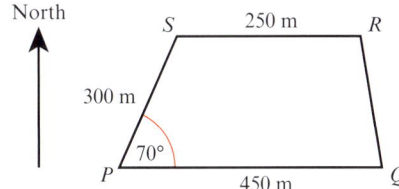

6   In the isosceles triangle *DEF*, angle *E* = angle *F* = 35° and side *EF* = 10 m.

    a   Calculate the perpendicular (shortest) distance from angle *D* to *EF*.

    b   Calculate the length of the side *DE*.

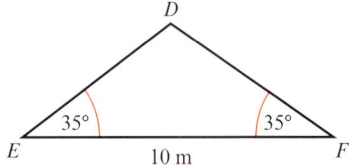

7   Find the length of a diagonal (*QT*) of a regular pentagon that has sides of length 10 cm. Give your answer to the nearest whole number.

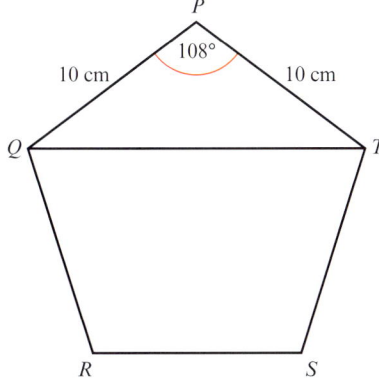

8 The diagram shows a regular pentagon with sides of 2 cm. *O* is the centre of the pentagon.

    a Find angle *AOE*.

    b Find angle *AOM*.

    c Use trigonometry on triangle *AOM* to find the length *OM*.

    d Find the area of triangle *AOM*.

    e Find the area of the pentagon.

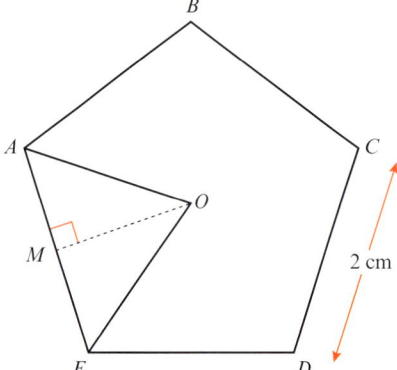

9 Using a similar method to that described in question 8 find the area of a regular octagon with sides of 4 cm.

10 Find the area of a regular pentagon with sides of 2*a* metres.

11 Find the area of a regular polygon with *n* sides, each of length 2*a* metres.

MATHEMATICAL CONNECTIONS

Areas of two-dimensional shapes were covered in Chapter 7.

REFLECTION

Some students find applications of trigonometry confusing and difficult to understand.

Did you find anything in this exercise confusing or difficult? If so, which parts?

Do you draw diagrams to understand the angles and trigonometric ratios? How can this help?

Choose at least one idea in trigonometry that you would you like to understand better. Describe three things you could do to achieve better understanding of this idea.

15.6 Sines, cosines and tangents of angles greater than 90°

You have now seen that we can find the sine, cosine or tangent of an angle in a triangle by using your calculator.

It is possible to find sines, cosines and tangents of angles of any size.

INVESTIGATION

Relationships between sines, cosines and tangents

Use a calculator to find each of the following:

$\sin 30°$ and $\sin 150°$

$\sin 10°$ and $\sin 170°$

$\sin 60°$ and $\sin 120°$

$\sin 5°$ and $\sin 175°$

What did you notice? What is the relationship between the two angles in each pair?

Now do the same for these pairs:

$\cos 30°$ and $\cos 330°$	$\tan 30°$ and $\tan 210°$
$\cos 60°$ and $\cos 300°$	$\tan 60°$ and $\tan 240°$
$\cos 50°$ and $\cos 310°$	$\tan 15°$ and $\tan 195°$
$\cos 15°$ and $\cos 345°$	$\tan 100$ and $\tan 280°$

The pattern is different for each of sine, cosine and tangent.

Try plotting the value of $\sin \theta$, $\cos \theta$ and $\tan \theta$ against θ for several values of θ. You can find a graph plotting website on the internet, using a search.

In the rest of this section you will explore the graphs of $y = \sin \theta$, $y = \cos \theta$ and $y = \tan \theta$ in more detail.

The graph of $y = \sin \theta$

If you plot several values of $\sin \theta$ against θ you will get the following:

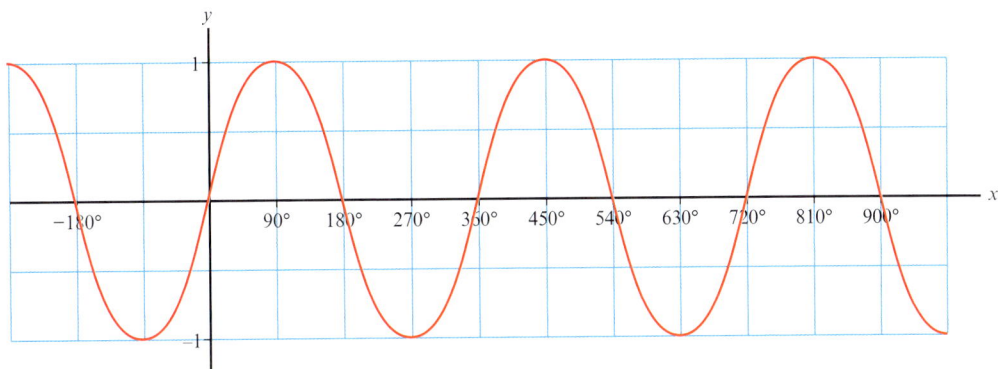

The graph repeats itself every 360° in both the positive and negative directions.

Notice that the section of the graph between 0 and 180° has reflection symmetry, with the line of reflection being $\theta = 90°$. This means that $\sin\theta = \sin(180° - \theta)$, exactly as you should have seen in the investigation.

It is also very important to notice that the value of $\sin\theta$ is never larger than 1 nor smaller than −1.

MATHEMATICAL CONNECTIONS

$\sin\theta$, $\cos\theta$ and $\tan\theta$ are actually functions. Functions take input values and give you a numerical output. For example, if you use your calculator to find $\sin 30°$ you will get the answer $\frac{1}{2}$. Your calculator takes the input 30°, finds the sine of this angle and gives you the output $\frac{1}{2}$. You will learn more about functions in Chapter 22.

The graph of $y = \cos\theta$

If you plot several values of $\cos\theta$ against θ you will get a similar shape, but the line of symmetry is in a different place:

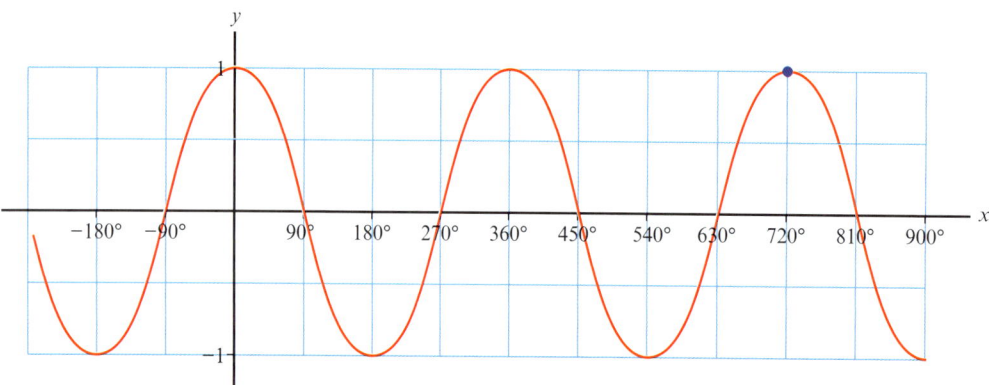

The graph repeats itself every 360° in both the positive and negative directions.

Here the graph is symmetrical from 0 to 360°, with the reflection line at $\theta = 180°$. This means that $\cos\theta = \cos(360° - \theta)$, again you should have seen this in the investigation. By experimenting with some angles you will also see that $\cos\theta = -\cos(180° - \theta)$

It is also very important to notice that the value of $\cos\theta$ is never larger than 1 nor smaller than −1.

The graph of $y = \tan \theta$

Finally, if you plot values of $\tan \theta$ against θ you get this graph:

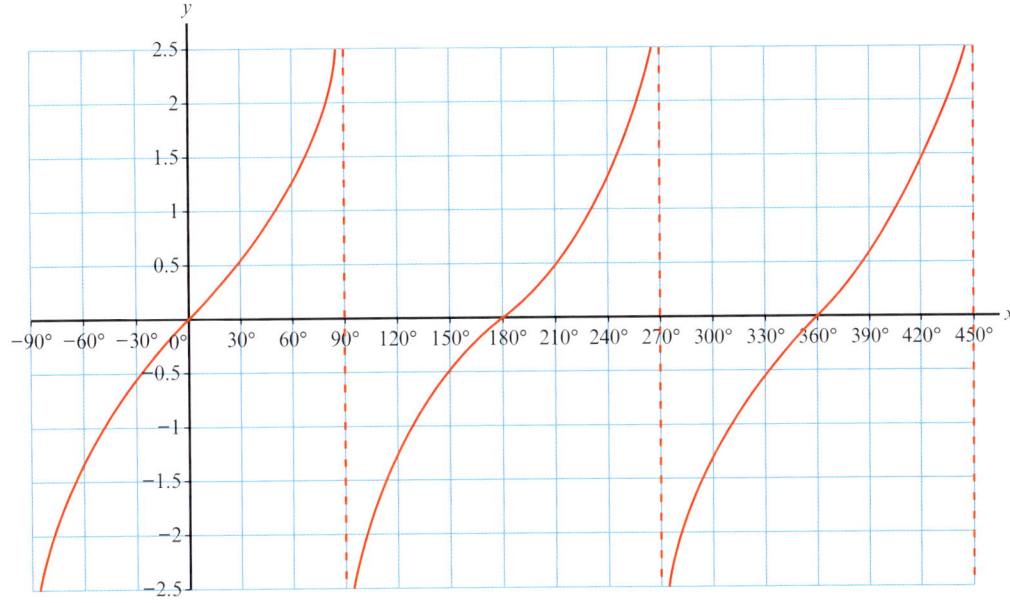

The graph approaches the vertical dotted lines, but it never touches nor crosses them.

Notice that this graph has no reflection symmetry, but it does repeat every 180°. This means that $\tan \theta = \tan(180° + \theta)$.

Note that, unlike $\sin \theta$ and $\cos \theta$, $\tan \theta$ is not restricted to being less than 1 or greater than -1.

The shapes of these three graphs means that equations involving sine, cosine or tangent will have multiple solutions. The following examples show you how you can find these.

MATHEMATICAL CONNECTIONS

A line that is approached by a graph in this way is known as an *asymptote*. You will learn more about asymptotes in Chapter 18.

WORKED EXAMPLE 14

Which acute angle has the same sine as 120°?

Answer

$\sin(180° - \theta) = \sin \theta$ The graph of $\sin \theta$ gives this relationship.

$\sin(180° - 120°) = \sin 120°$ Let $\theta = 120°$ and subtract to find another angle

$\sin 60° = \sin 120°$ with the same sine value.

WORKED EXAMPLE 15

Express each of the following in terms of another angle between 0° and 180°.

a cos 100°

b −cos 35°

Answers

a $\cos(180° − θ) = −\cos θ$ Start with the general relationship.

 $\cos(180° − 100°) = −\cos 100°$ Let $θ = 100°$ and subtract.

 $\cos 80° = −\cos 100°$

 So, $\cos 100° = −\cos 80°$ Rearrange to find another value equal to
                               cos 100°

b $−\cos θ = \cos(180° − θ)$

 $−\cos 35° = \cos 145°$

WORKED EXAMPLE 16

Solve the following equations, giving all possible solutions in the range 0 to 360 degrees.

a $\sin θ = \dfrac{1}{\sqrt{2}}$

b $\tan θ = 3$

c $\cos x = −\dfrac{1}{2}$

Answers

a Use your calculator to find one solution: $\sin^{-1}\left(\dfrac{1}{\sqrt{2}}\right) = 45°$.

 Now mark $θ = 45$ degrees on a sketch of the graph $y = \sin θ$ and draw the
 line $y = \dfrac{1}{\sqrt{2}}$ like this:

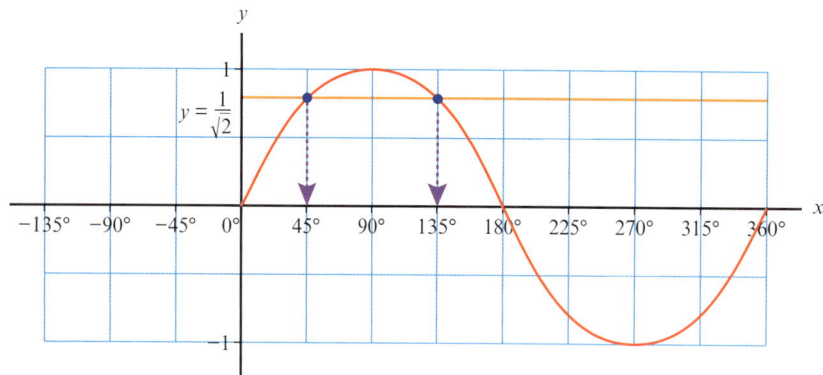

> **TIP**
>
> As well as $θ$, other variables can be used to represent the angle. In part (c) of the example, x is used. You work in exactly the same way whatever variable is used.

Using the symmetry of the graph, you can see that there is another
solution at $θ = 135°$.

Use your calculator to check that $\sin 135° = \dfrac{1}{\sqrt{2}}$.

Notice that $135° = 180° − 45°$. You can use this rule, but drawing a sketch
graph always makes it easier to understand *why* there is a
second solution.

> **TIP**
>
> This only needs to be a sketch and doesn't need to be accurate. It should be just enough for you to see how the symmetry can help.

WORKED EXAMPLE 16 CONTINUED

b   Use your calculator to find one solution: $\tan^{-1}(3) = 71.6°$. As before, mark this on a sketch of the graph $y = \tan\theta$ and draw the line $y = 3$.

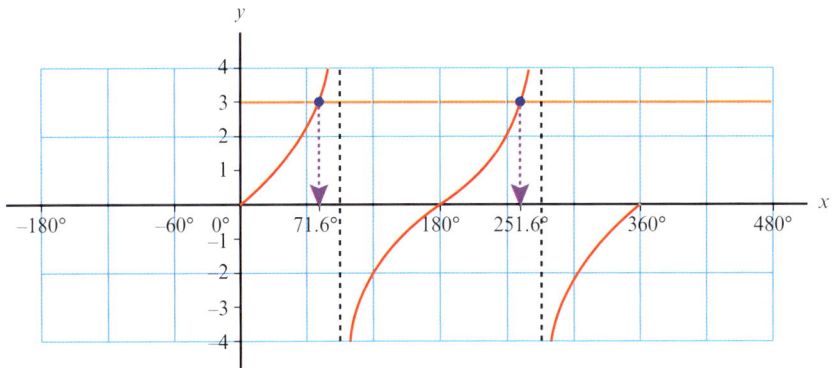

You can see that the second solution is $180° + 71.6° = 251.6°$.
More solutions can be found by adding 180 degrees over and over, but these will all be larger than 360 degrees, so they are not in the range that you want.

c   Use your calculator to find one solution: $\cos^{-1}\left(-\dfrac{1}{2}\right) = 120°$.
Draw a sketch and mark the values:

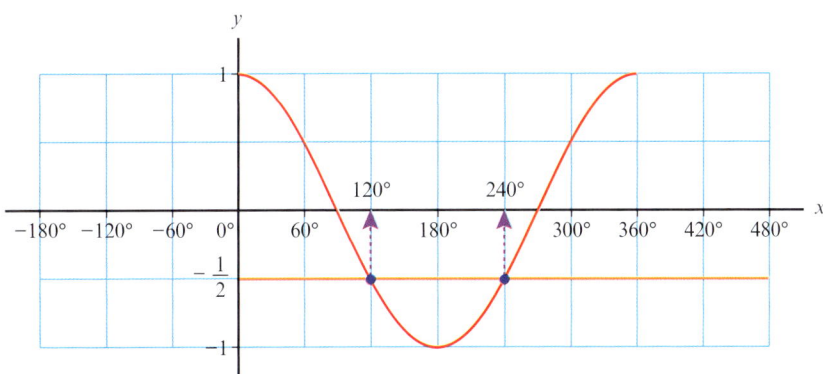

You can now see that the second solution will be at $360° - 120° = 240°$.

Exercise 15.10

1   Express each of the following in terms of the same trigonometric ratio of another angle between 0° and 180°.

    a $\cos 120°$ **b** $\sin 35°$ **c** $\cos 136°$ **d** $\sin 170°$ **e** $\cos 88°$

    f $-\cos 140°$ **g** $\sin 121°$ **h** $\sin 99°$ **i** $-\cos 45°$ **j** $-\cos 150°$

2   Solve each of the following equations, giving all solutions between 0 and 360 degrees.

    a $\sin\theta = \dfrac{1}{2}$ **b** $\sin\theta = 1$ **c** $\cos\theta = \dfrac{\sqrt{2}}{2}$

    d $\tan\theta = 5$ **e** $\cos\theta = -\dfrac{\sqrt{3}}{2}$ **f** $\sin\theta = -0.2$

    g $\cos\theta = -\dfrac{1}{3}$ **h** $\tan\theta = \sqrt{3}$ **i** $\tan\theta = -4$

3 For each of the following find the smallest positive value of x for which:

   a $\sin x = \sin 135°$ **b** $\cos x = \cos 120°$ **c** $\tan x = \tan 235°$

   d $\cos x = \cos(-45°)$ **e** $\sin x = \sin 270°$ **f** $\tan x = \tan 840°$

   g $\sin(x - 30°) = \sin 240$ **h** $\cos(2x) = \cos(540°)$ **i** $\tan\left(\dfrac{x}{6}\right) = \tan(-476°)$

4 Solve, giving all solutions between 0 and 360 degrees:

$$(\sin x)^2 = \frac{1}{4}$$

5 Solve each of the following equations, giving all solutions between 0 and 360 degrees.

   a $2\sin x - 1 = 0$ **b** $\cos x = 5\cos x + 2$

   c $3(\tan x + 2) = 7$ **d** $3\sin x - 2 = 4\sin x + 4$

   e $(\cos x + 1)^2 = \dfrac{9}{4}$ **f** $(2\sin x - 1)(2\cos x - \sqrt{3}) = 0$

> **TIP**
>
> Write $\cos x = y$ and try to factorise.

6 Solve, giving all solutions between 0 and 360 degrees:

$$8(\cos x)^2 - 10\cos x + 3 = 0$$

15.7 The sine and cosine rules

The sine and cosine ratios are not only useful for right-angled triangles. To understand the following rules you must first look at the standard way of labelling the angles and sides of a triangle. Look at the triangle shown in the diagram.

Notice that the sides are labelled with lower case letters and the angles are labelled with upper case letters. The side that is placed opposite angle A is labelled 'a', the side that is placed opposite angle B is labelled 'b' and so on.

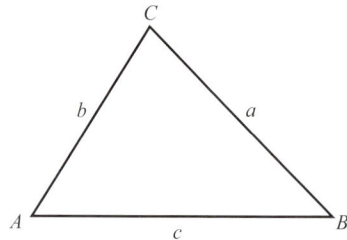

The sine rule

For the triangle shown on the right, the following are true:

$$\frac{\sin A}{a} = \frac{\sin B}{b} \quad \text{and} \quad \frac{\sin A}{a} = \frac{\sin C}{c} \quad \text{and} \quad \frac{\sin B}{b} = \frac{\sin C}{c}$$

These relationships are usually expressed in one go:

$$\frac{\sin A}{a} = \frac{\sin B}{b} = \frac{\sin C}{c}$$

This is the **sine rule**. This version of the rule, with the sine ratios placed on the tops of the fractions, is normally used to calculate angles.

The formulae can also be turned upside down when you want to calculate lengths:

$$\frac{a}{\sin A} = \frac{b}{\sin B} = \frac{c}{\sin C}$$

> **TIP**
>
> Remember, the sine rule is used when you are dealing with pairs of opposite sides and angles.

You should remember that this represents *three* possible relationships.

Notice that in each case, both the upper and lower case form of each letter is used. This means that each fraction that you use requires an angle and the length of its opposite side.

WORKED EXAMPLE 17

In $\triangle ABC$, $A = 80°$, $B = 30°$ and side $BC = 15\,\text{cm}$.

Calculate the size of C and the lengths of the sides AB and AC.

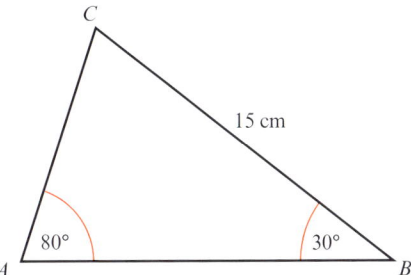

Answer

To calculate the angle C, use the fact that the sum of the three angles in a triangle is always $180°$.

So, $C + 80 + 30 = 180 \Rightarrow C = 180 - 30 - 80 = 70°$

Now think about the side AB. AB is opposite the angle C (forming an 'opposite pair') and side BC is opposite angle A, forming a second 'opposite pair'.

So, write down the version of the sine rule that uses these pairs:

$$\frac{a}{\sin A} = \frac{c}{\sin C} \Rightarrow \frac{BC}{\sin A} = \frac{AB}{\sin C}$$

So, $\dfrac{15}{\sin 80°} = \dfrac{AB}{\sin 70°} \Rightarrow AB \dfrac{15}{\sin 80°} \times \sin 70° = 14.3\,\text{cm}$ (3 s.f.)

Similarly:

AC forms an opposite pair with angle B, so once again use the pair BC and angle A:

$$\frac{a}{\sin A} = \frac{b}{\sin B} \Rightarrow \frac{BC}{\sin A} = \frac{AC}{\sin B}$$

So, $\dfrac{15}{\sin 80°} = \dfrac{AC}{\sin 30°} \Rightarrow AC \dfrac{15}{\sin 80°} \times \sin 30° = 7.62\,\text{cm}$ (3 s.f.)

The ambiguous case of the sine rule

The special properties of the sine function can lead to more than one possible answer. Worked example 18 demonstrates how this may happen.

TIP

The word 'ambiguous' means that there is more than one way to interpret the question being asked. Here the ambiguous case arises because there are two possible answers.

WORKED EXAMPLE 18

In triangle DEF, $DF = 10\,cm$, $EF = 7\,cm$ and angle $EDF = 34°$.

Calculate, to the nearest degree, the possible size of:

a   angle DEF **b**   angle DFE.

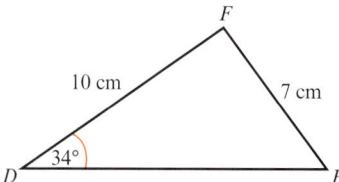

Answers

a   Angle DEF is opposite a side of length 10 cm. This forms one pair.

     Angle EDF is opposite a side of length 7 cm. This forms the second pair.

     You are trying to find an angle, so choose the version of the sine rule with the value of sine ratios in the numerators:

$$\frac{\sin 34°}{7} = \frac{\sin E}{10} \Rightarrow \sin E = 10 \times \frac{\sin 34°}{7}$$

     So, angle $DEF = \sin^{-1}\left(10 \times \frac{\sin 34°}{7}\right) = 53.0°$

     But there is actually a second angle DEF such that $\sin E = 10 \times \frac{\sin 34°}{7}$.

     You can see this if you consider the sine graph. The values of both $\sin x$ and $\cos x$ repeat every $360°$. This property of both functions is called 'periodicity', i.e., both $\sin x$ and $\cos x$ are *periodic*. The periodicity of the function tells you that the second possible value of angle DEF is $180° - 53.0° = 127.0°$.

     Both of these are possible values of angle DEF because there are two ways to draw such a triangle.

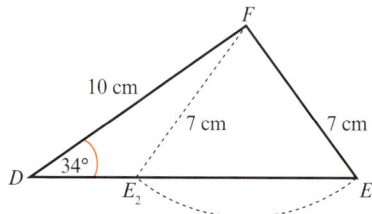

b   Of course, the answers to part (a) must lead to two possible answers for part (b).

     If angle $DEF = 127.0°$, then angle $DFE = 180° - 127° - 34° = 19°$ (shown as E_1 in the diagram).

     If angle $DEF = 53.0°$, then angle $DFE = 180° - 53° - 34° = 93°$ (shown as E_2 in the diagram).

     (If you had been asked for the length DE, there would also have been two possible solutions.)

     You must always take care to check that all possible answers have been calculated. Bear this in mind as you work through the following exercise.

Exercise 15.11

1   Find the value of x in each of the following equations.

a $\dfrac{x}{\sin 50} = \dfrac{9}{\sin 98}$ b $\dfrac{x}{\sin 25} = \dfrac{20}{\sin 100}$ c $\dfrac{20.6}{\sin 50} = \dfrac{x}{\sin 70}$ d $\dfrac{\sin x}{11.4} = \dfrac{\sin 63}{16.2}$

2   Find the length of the side marked x in each of the following triangles.

a   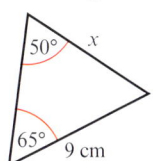   b   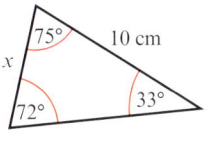   c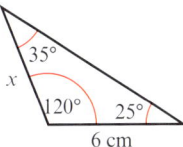

d   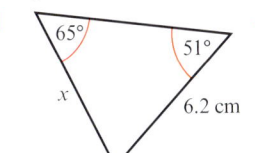   e   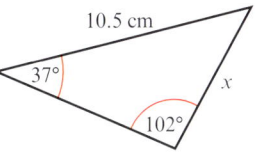   f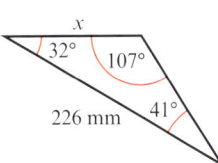

3   Find the size of the angle marked θ in the following triangles. Give your answers correct to 1 decimal place.

a   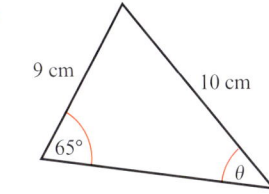   b   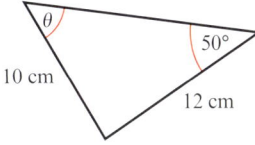   c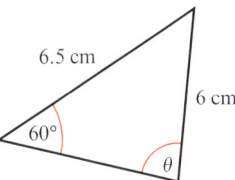

d   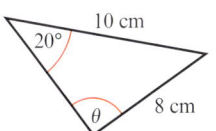   e   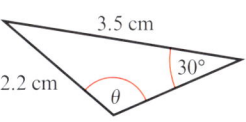   f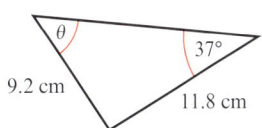

4   In triangle ABC, $A = 72°$, $B = 45°$ and side $AB = 20$ cm.
Calculate the size of C and the lengths of the sides AC and BC.

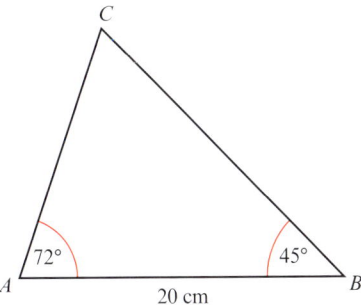

5   In triangle DEF, $D = 140°$, $E = 15°$ and side $DF = 6$ m.
Calculate the size of F and the lengths of the sides DE and EF.

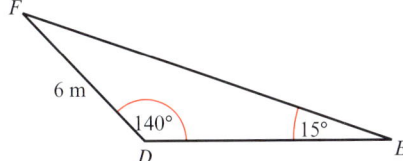

6 In triangle PQR, $Q = 120°$, side $PQ = 8$ cm and side $PR = 13$ cm. Calculate the size of R, the size of P, and the length of side QR. Give your answers to the nearest whole number.

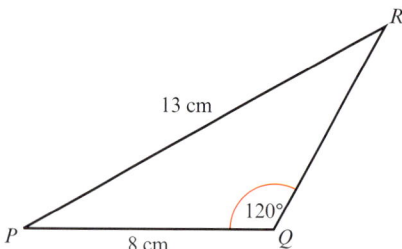

7 In triangle XYZ, $X = 40°$, side $XZ = 12$ cm and side $YZ = 15$ cm.

   a Explain why Y must be less than $40°$.

   b Calculate, correct to 1 decimal place, Y and Z.

   c Calculate the length of the side XY.

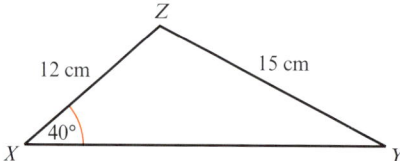

8 $ABCD$ is a parallelogram with $AB = 32$ mm and $AD = 40$ mm and angle $BAC = 77°$.

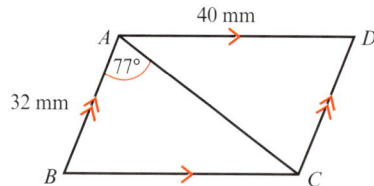

   a Find the size of angle BCA (to the nearest degree).

   b Find the size of angle ABC (to the nearest degree).

   c Find the length of diagonal AC correct to 2 decimal places.

Cosine rule

For the **cosine rule**, consider a triangle labelled in exactly the same way as that used for the sine rule.

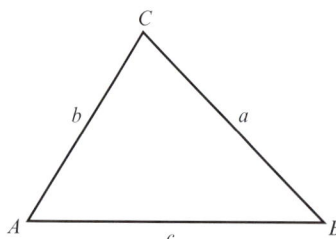

The cosine rule is stated as a single formula:

$$a^2 = b^2 + c^2 - 2bc \cos A$$

Notice that all three sides are used in the formula, and just one angle. The side whose square is the subject of the formula is opposite the angle used (here a and A). This form of the cosine rule is used to find unknown sides. You can use equivalent versions of the rule to find sides labelled b or c:

$$b^2 = a^2 + c^2 - 2ac\cos B \quad \text{or} \quad c^2 = a^2 + b^2 - 2ab\cos C$$

Notice, also, that you can rearrange any version of the formula to make the cosine ratio the subject.

This version can be used to calculate angles:

$$a^2 = b^2 + c^2 - 2bc\cos A$$

$$\Rightarrow a^2 + 2bc\cos A = b^2 + c^2$$

$$\Rightarrow 2bc\cos A = b^2 + c^2 - a^2$$

$$\Rightarrow \cos A = \frac{b^2 + c^2 - a^2}{2bc}$$

> ### MATHEMATICAL CONNECTIONS
>
> You learned how to rearrange a formula in Chapter 6.

TIP

Remember, if you know all three sides of a triangle, you can use the cosine rule to find any angle. If you know two sides, and the unknown side is opposite a *known* angle, then you can use the cosine rule to calculate the unknown side.

WORKED EXAMPLE 19

In triangle ABC, $B = 50°$, side $AB = 9\,$cm and side $BC = 18\,$cm.

Calculate the length of AC.

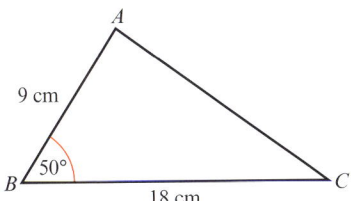

Answer

Notice that $AC = b$ and you know that $B = 50°$.

Use the cosine rule in the form, $b^2 = a^2 + c^2 - 2ac\cos B$.

$b^2 = 9^2 + 18^2 - (2 \times 9 \times 18 \times \cos 50°)$

$\quad = 81 + 324 - (208.2631...)$

$\quad = 196.7368...$

$\therefore b = \sqrt{196.7368...}$

$\quad = 14.0262...$

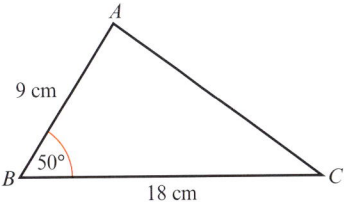

Length of $AC = 14.0\,$cm (to 3 s.f.)

WORKED EXAMPLE 20

In triangle DEF, $F = 120°$, side $EF = 25\,m$ and side $FD = 34\,m$.

Calculate the length of side DE.

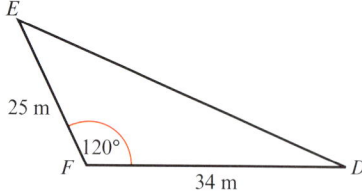

Answer

$DE = f$, so use the cosine rule in the form, $f^2 = d^2 + e^2 - 2de\cos F$.

$f^2 = 25^2 + 34^2 - (2 \times 25 \times 34 \times \cos 120°)$

$ = 625 + 1156 - (-850)$ (notice that $\cos 120°$ is negative)

$ = 625 + 1156 + 850$

$ = 2631$

$\therefore f = \sqrt{2631}$

$ = 51.2932\ldots$

Length of $DE = 51.3\,m$ (to 3 s.f.)

Combining the sine and cosine rules

The following worked examples show how you can combine the sine and cosine rules to solve problems.

WORKED EXAMPLE 21

In triangle PQR, $R = 100°$, side $PR = 8\,cm$ and side $RQ = 5\,cm$.

a   Calculate the length of side PQ.

b   Calculate, correct to the nearest degree, P and Q.

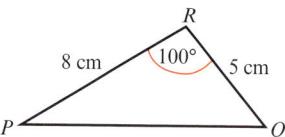

Answers

a $PQ = r$, so use the cosine rule in the form, $r^2 = p^2 + q^2 - 2pq\cos R$.

$ r^2 = 5^2 + 8^2 - (2 \times 5 \times 8 \times \cos 100°)$

$ = 25 + 64 - (-13.8918\ldots)$ (notice that $\cos 100°$ is negative)

$ = 102.8918\ldots$

$ \therefore r = \sqrt{102.8918\ldots}$

$ = 10.1435\ldots$

Length of $PQ = 10.1\,cm$ (to 3 s.f.)

WORKED EXAMPLE 21 CONTINUED

b   Now you know the value of r as well as the value of R, you can use the sine rule:

$$\frac{\sin P}{p} = \frac{\sin Q}{q} = \frac{\sin R}{r}$$

$$\frac{\sin P}{5} = \frac{\sin Q}{8} = \frac{\sin 100°}{10.1435\ldots}$$

Using the first and third fractions, $\sin P = \dfrac{5 \times \sin 100°}{10.1435\ldots} = 0.4853\ldots$

R is obtuse so P is acute, and $P = 29.0409\ldots°$

$P = 29°$ (to the nearest degree)

To find Q you can use the angle sum of a triangle $= 180°$:

$Q = 180° - (100° + 29°)$

$\therefore Q = 51°$ (to the nearest degree)

> **TIP**
>
> If you need to use a previously calculated value for a new problem, leave unrounded answers in your calculator to avoid introducing rounding errors.

WORKED EXAMPLE 22

a   Change the subject of the formula $c^2 = a^2 + b^2 - 2ab\cos C$ to $\cos C$.

b   Use your answer to part (a) to find the smallest angle in the triangle which has sides of length 7 m, 8 m and 13 m.

Answers

a $c^2 = a^2 + b^2 - 2ab\cos C$

$2ab\cos C = a^2 + b^2 - c^2$

$\cos C = \dfrac{a^2 + b^2 - c^2}{2ab}$

b   The smallest angle in a triangle is opposite the shortest side. In the given triangle, the smallest angle is opposite the 7 m side. Let this angle be C.

Then $c = 7$ and take $a = 8$ and $b = 13$.

Using the result of part (a):

$$\cos C = \frac{8^2 + 13^2 - 7^2}{2 \times 8 \times 13}$$

$$= \frac{64 + 169 - 49}{208}$$

$$= \frac{184}{208}$$

$$C = \cos^{-1}\frac{184}{208}$$

$$= 27.7957\ldots°$$

The smallest angle of the triangle $= 27.8°$ (to 1 d.p.)

Exercise 15.12

1 In triangle *ABC*, *B* = 45°, side *AB* = 10 cm and side *BC* = 12 cm.
   Calculate the length of side *AC*.

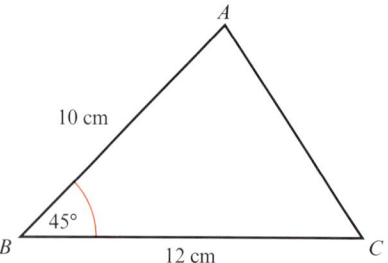

2 In triangle *DEF*, *F* = 150°, side *EF* = 9 m and side *FD* = 14 m.
   Calculate the length of side *DE*.

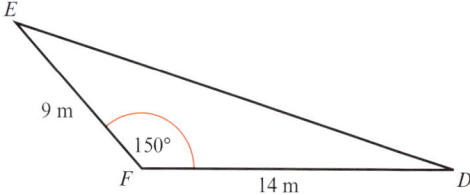

3 In triangle *PQR*, side *PQ* = 11 cm, side *QR* = 9 cm and side *RP* = 8 cm.
   Calculate the size of *p* correct to 1 decimal place.

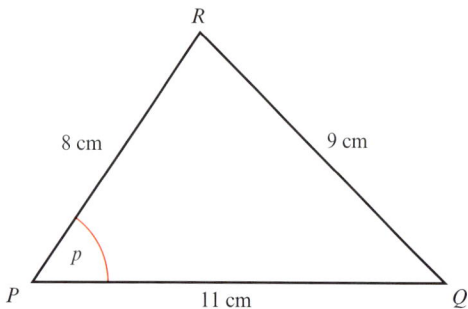

4 In triangle *STU*, *S* = 95°, side *ST* = 10 m and side *SU* = 15 m.
   a Calculate the length of side *TU*.
   b Calculate *U*.
   c Calculate *T*.

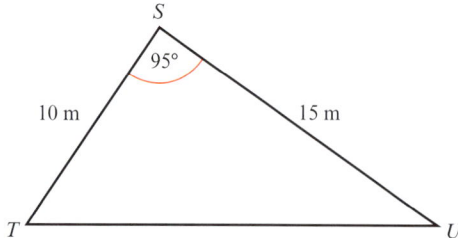

5   In triangle XYZ, side $XY = 15\,$cm, side $YZ = 13\,$cm and side $ZX = 8\,$cm.
Calculate the size of:

a X **b** Y **c** Z.

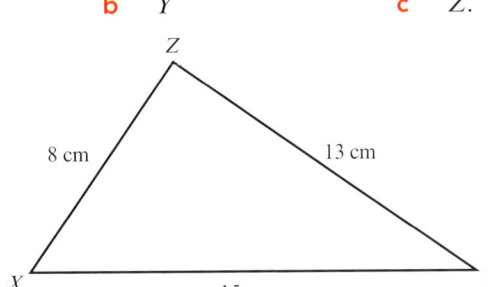

6   A boat sails in a straight line from Aardvark Island on a bearing of 060°. When
the boat has sailed 8 km it reaches Beaver Island and then turns to sail on a
bearing of 150°. The boat remains on this bearing until it reaches Crow Island,
12 km from Beaver Island. On reaching Crow Island the boat's pilot decides to
return directly to Aardvark Island.
Calculate:

a   the length of the return journey

b   the bearing on which the pilot must steer the boat to return to
Aardvark Island.

7   Jason stands in the corner of a very large field. He walks a distance of d metres on
a bearing of 030°. Jason then changes direction and walks twice as far on a new
bearing of 120°. At the end of the walk Jason calculates both the distance he must
walk and the bearing required to return to his original position. Given that the
total distance walked is 120 metres, what answers will Jason get if he is correct?

PEER ASSESSMENT

Work with a partner. Check each other's answers for Exercise 15.12.

Provide oral or written feedback using the TAG feedback cues you learnt in
Chapter 1:

• **Tell** your partner something they did well.

• **Ask** a thoughtful question about their work

• **Give** a positive suggestion to improve their work.

15.8 Area of a triangle

You already know that the area of a triangle is given
by the following formula:

This method can be used if you know both the
length of the base and perpendicular height,
but if you don't have these values you need
to use another method.

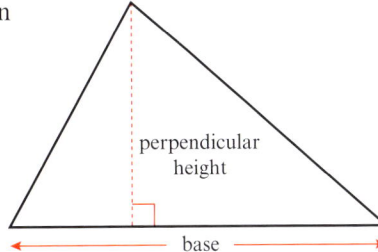

You can calculate the area of any triangle by
using trigonometry.

Look at the triangle ABC shown in the diagram:

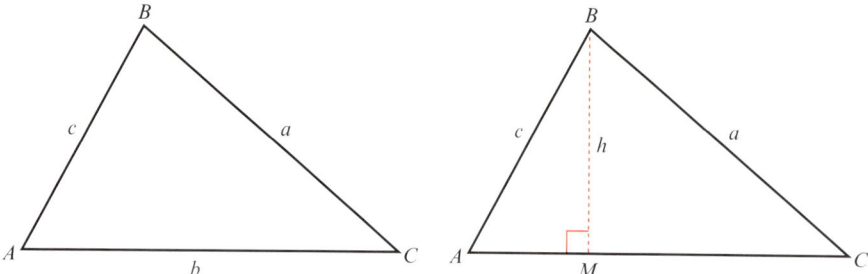

The second copy of the triangle is drawn with a perpendicular height that you don't yet know, but if you draw the right-angled triangle BCM separately, you can use basic trigonometry to find the value of h.

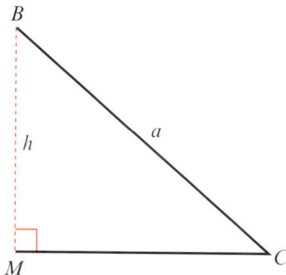

Now note that $\text{opp}(C) = h$ and the hypotenuse $= a$.

Using the sine ratio: $\sin C = \dfrac{h}{a} \Rightarrow h = a \sin C$

This means that you now know the perpendicular height and can use the base length b to calculate the area:

$\text{Area} = \dfrac{1}{2} \times \text{base} \times \text{perpendicular height}$

$\qquad = \dfrac{1}{2} \times b \times a \sin C$

$\text{Area} = \dfrac{1}{2} ab \sin C$

In fact you could use any side of the triangle as the base and draw the perpendicular height accordingly. This means that the area can also be calculated with:

$\text{Area} = \dfrac{1}{2} ac \sin B \quad \text{or} \quad \text{Area} = \dfrac{1}{2} bc \sin A$

In each case the sides used meet at the angle that has been included.

WORKED EXAMPLE 23

Calculate the areas of each of the following shapes.

a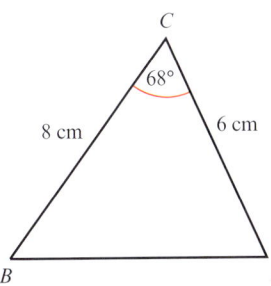

b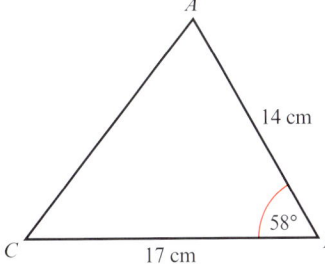

Answers

a   Area $= \dfrac{1}{2}ab\sin C$

   $= \dfrac{1}{2} \times 8 \times 6 \times \sin 68°$

   $= 22.3\,\text{cm}^2$ (to 1 d.p.)

b   Area $= \dfrac{1}{2}ac\sin B$

   $= \dfrac{1}{2} \times 17 \times 14 \times \sin 58°$

   $= 100.9\,\text{cm}^2$ (to 1 d.p.)

WORKED EXAMPLE 24

The diagram shows a triangle with area $20\,\text{cm}^2$.

Calculate the size of angle F.

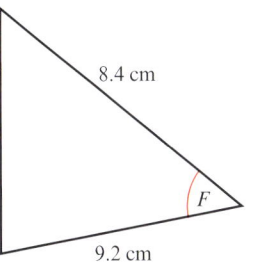

Answer

Notice that the area $= \dfrac{1}{2} \times 8.4 \times 9.2 \times \sin F = 20$

$\sin F = \dfrac{2 \times 20}{8.4 \times 9.2}$

So $F = \sin^{-1}\left(\dfrac{2 \times 20}{8.4 \times 9.2}\right)$

   $= 31.2°$ (to 1 d.p.)

Exercise 15.13

1   Find the area of each triangle.

a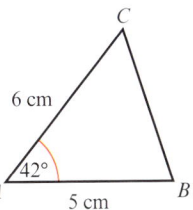

b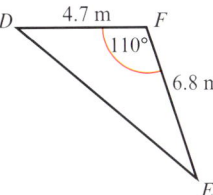

c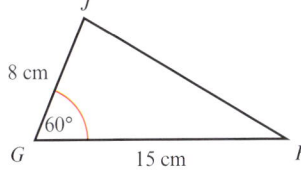

d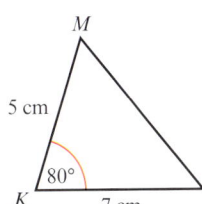

e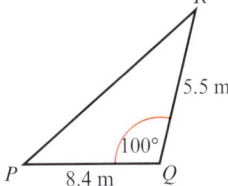

f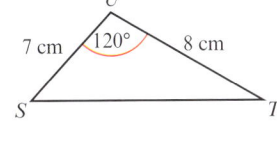

2 Find the area of the parallelogram shown in the diagram.

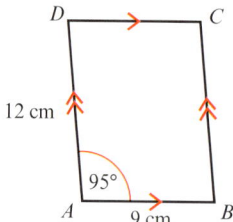

3 The diagram shows the dimensions of a small herb garden. Find the area of the garden.
Give your answer correct to 2 decimal places.

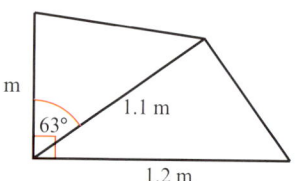

4 Find the area of $PQRS$.

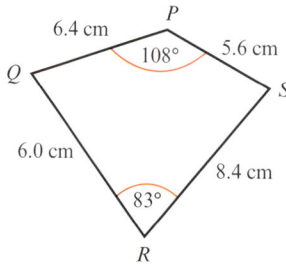

5 Find the area of each polygon. Give your answers to 1 decimal place.

a

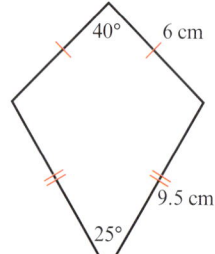

b

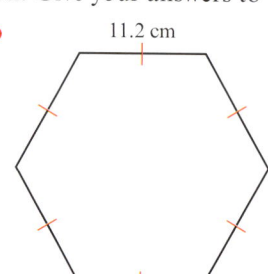

c

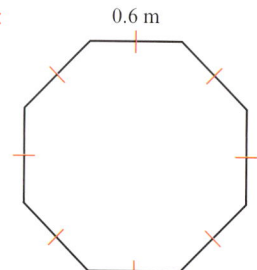

6 The diagonals of a parallelogram bisect each other at an angle of 42°.
If the diagonals are 26 cm and 20 cm long, find:

a the area of the parallelogram

b the lengths of the sides.

7

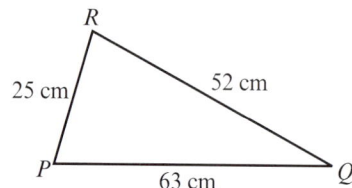

The diagram shows triangle PQR, which has an area of 630 cm².

a Use the formula area $= \frac{1}{2}pr\sin Q$ to find Q correct to 1 decimal place.

b Find P correct to 1 decimal place.

REFLECTION

How does this work relate to everyday situations?

Which ideas in this section make most sense to you? Why?

15.9 Trigonometry in three dimensions

You can also use the trigonometry ratios to solve problems in three dimensions.
With problems of this kind you must draw and label each triangle as you use it.
This will help you to organise your thoughts and keep your solution tidy.

When you work with solids you may need to calculate the angle between an edge, or a
diagonal, and one of the faces. This is called the angle between a line and a plane.

Consider a line PQ, which meets a plane $ABCD$ at point P. Through P draw lines PR_1,
PR_2, PR_3, … in the plane and consider the angles QPR_1, QPR_2, QPR_3 …

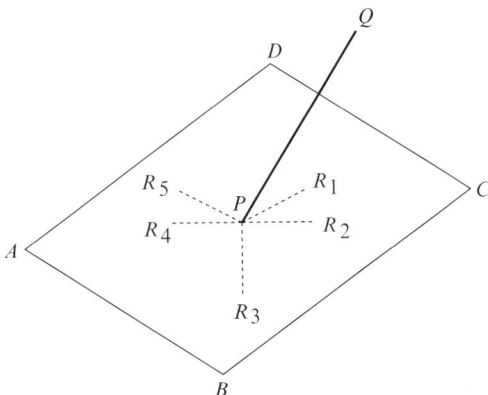

- If PQ is perpendicular to the plane, all these angles will be right angles.

- If PQ is not perpendicular to the plane, these angles will vary in size.

- It is the smallest of these angles which is called the angle between the line PQ and
  the plane $ABCD$.

To identify this angle, do the following:

- From Q draw a perpendicular to the plane. Call the foot of this perpendicular R.

- The angle between the line PQ and the plane is angle QPR.

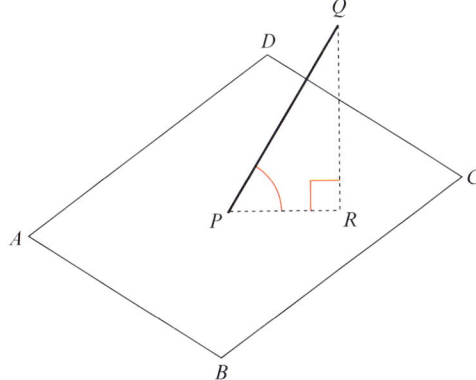

PR is called the **projection** of PQ on the plane $ABCD$.

The following worked example shows how you might work through a problem in
three dimensions.

WORKED EXAMPLE 25

The diagram represents a room which has the shape of a cuboid. $AB = 6\,m$, $AD = 4\,m$ and $AP = 2\,m$. Calculate the angle between the diagonal BS and the floor $ABCD$.

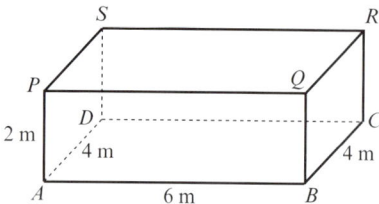

Answer

First identify the angle required. B is the point where the diagonal BS meets the plane $ABCD$.

SD is the perpendicular from S to the plane $ABCD$ and so DB is the projection of SB onto the plane.

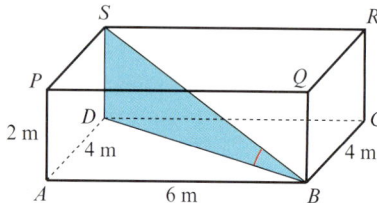

The angle required is SBD.

You know that triangle SBD has a right angle at D and that $SD = 2\,m$ (equal to AP).

To find angle SBD, you need to know the length of DB or the length of SB. You can find the length of BD by using Pythagoras' theorem in triangle ABD.

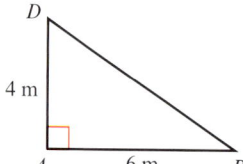

$BD^2 = 6^2 + 4^2 = 36 + 16 = 52$

$BD = \sqrt{52}$

So, using right-angled triangle SBD:

$$\tan B = \frac{\text{opp}(B)}{\text{adj}(B)} = \frac{SD}{BD} = \frac{2}{\sqrt{52}}$$

Angle $SBD = \tan^{-1}\left(\dfrac{2}{\sqrt{52}}\right) = 15.5013\ldots$

The angle between diagonal BS and the floor $ABCD = 15.5°$ (to 1 d.p.)

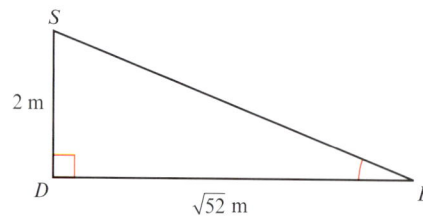

TIP

It can be helpful to use colour or shading in diagrams involving 3D situations.

Exercise 15.14

1   The diagram represents a triangular prism. The rectangular base, $ABCD$, is horizontal. $AB = 20$ cm and $BC = 15$ cm.
The cross-section of the prism, BCE, is right-angled at C and angle $EBC = 41°$.

   a   Calculate the length of AC.

   b   Calculate the length of EC.

   c   Calculate the angle which the line AE makes with the horizontal.

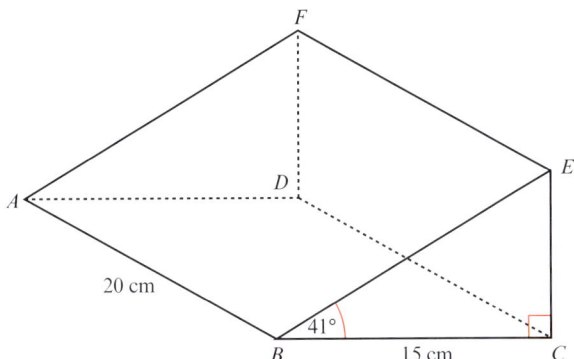

2   The cube shown in the diagram has sides of 5 m.

   a   Use Pythagoras' theorem to calculate the distance EG. Leave your answer in exact form.

   b   Use Pythagoras' theorem to calculate the distance AG. Leave your answer in exact form.

   c   Calculate the angle between the line AG and the plane $EFGH$. Give your answer to 1 decimal place.

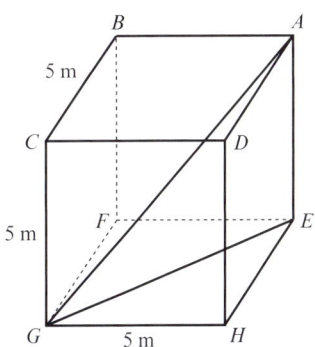

3   The diagram shows a tetrahedron $ABCD$. M is the midpoint of CD. $AB = 4$ m, $AC = 3$ m, $AD = 3$ m. Calculate:

   a   the angle ACB

   b   the length of BC

   c   the length of CD

   d   the length of BM

   e   the angle BCD.

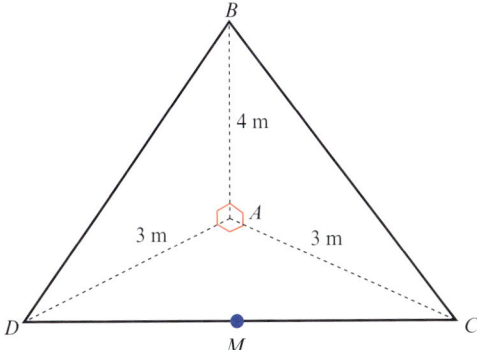

4   A cuboid is 14 cm long, 5 cm wide and 3 cm high. Calculate:

   a   the length of the diagonal on its base

   b   the length of its longest diagonal

   c   the angle between the base and the longest diagonal.

5   $ABCD$ is a tetrahedral drinks carton. Triangle ABC is the base and B is a right angle. D is vertically above A. AB is x, BC is y and AD is z. Calculate the following in terms of the appropriate lettered side(s):

   a   the length of AC

   b   the size of angle DAB

   c   the length of BD

   d   the length of DC.

REFLECTION

What are the most important things you need to remember when you are solving problems involving 3D situations?

Does using different colours and marking up diagrams help you to understand these problems better? Explain why or why not.

SUMMARY

Do you know …?

A scale drawing is an accurate diagram to represent something that is much bigger, or much smaller.
An angle of elevation is measured upwards from the horizontal.
An angle of depression is measured downwards from the horizontal.
The ratio of any two lengths in a right-angled triangle depends on the angles in the triangle: $\sin A = \dfrac{\text{opp}(A)}{\text{hyp}}$ $\cos A = \dfrac{\text{adj}(A)}{\text{hyp}}$ $\tan A = \dfrac{\text{opp}(A)}{\text{adj}}$
Bearings are measured clockwise from north.
You can use these trigonometric ratios to calculate an unknown angle from two known sides.
You can use these trigonometric ratios to calculate an unknown side from a known side and a known angle.
The sine, cosine and tangent function can be extended beyond the angles in triangles.
The sine, cosine and tangent functions can be used to solve trigonometric equations.
The sine and cosine rules can be used to calculate unknown sides and angles in triangles that are not right-angled.
The sine rule is used for calculating an angle from another angle and two sides, or a side from another side and two known angles. The sides and angles must be arranged in opposite pairs.
The cosine rule is used for calculating an angle from three known sides, or a side from a known angle and two known sides.
You can calculate the area of a non right-angled triangle by using the sine ratio.

SUMMARY CONTINUED

Are you able to …?

calculate angles of elevation
calculate angles of depression
use trigonometry to calculate bearings
identify which sides are the opposite, adjacent and hypotenuse
calculate the sine, cosine and tangent ratio when given lengths in a right-angled triangle
use the sine, cosine and tangent ratios to find unknown angles and sides
solve more complex problems by extracting right-angled triangles and combining sine, cosine and tangent ratios
use the sine and cosine rules to find unknown angles and sides in right-angled triangles
work with exact values of trigonometric ratios
use the sine, cosine and tangent functions to solve trigonometric equations, finding all the solutions between 0 and 360°
use sine and cosine rules to find unknown angles and sides in triangles that are not right-angled
use trigonometry in three dimensions
find the area of a triangle that is not right-angled.

Practice questions

1   A scale drawing is made of a church window. The scale of the drawing is 1 cm to 150 cm. The window measures 2.5 m by 3.5 m. Calculate the length of the diagonal of the scale drawing.   [3]

2   The diagram shows the cross-section of the roof of Mr Haziz's house. The house is 12 m wide, angle $CAB = 35°$ and angle $ACB = 90°$. Calculate the lengths of the two sides of the roof, AC and BC.

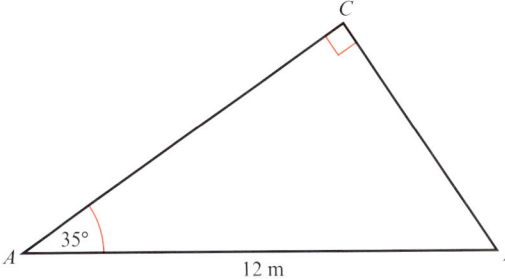

[4]

3   The diagram shows a trapezium $ABCD$ in which angles $ABC = BCD = 90°$. $AB = 90$ mm, $BC = 72$ mm and $CD = 25$ mm. Calculate the angle DAB.

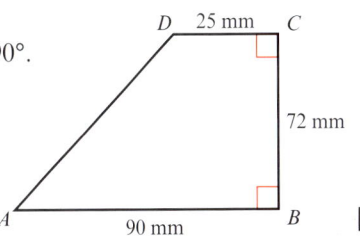

[3]

4 A child, whose eyes are 1.5 m above the ground, stands 12 m away from a tall chimney. She has to raise her eyes 35° upwards from the horizontal to look directly at the top of the chimney. Calculate the height of the chimney.

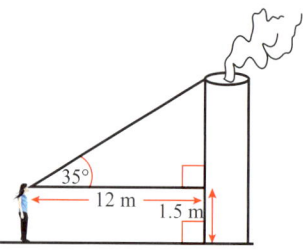

[3]

5 The diagram shows the cross-section, *PQRS*, of a cutting made for a road. *PS* and *QR* are horizontal. *PQ* makes an angle of 50° with the horizontal.

   a Calculate the horizontal distance between *P* and *Q* (marked *x* in the diagram). [3]

   b Calculate the angle which *RS* makes with the horizontal (marked *y* in the diagram).

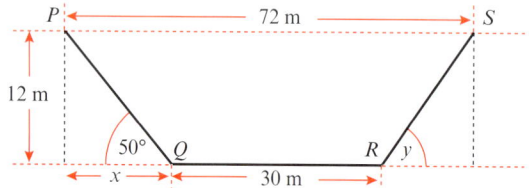

[3]

6 A game warden is standing at a point *P* alongside a road which runs north–south. There is a marker post at the point *X*, 60 m north of his position. The game warden sees a lion at *Q* on a bearing of 040° from him and due east of the marker post.

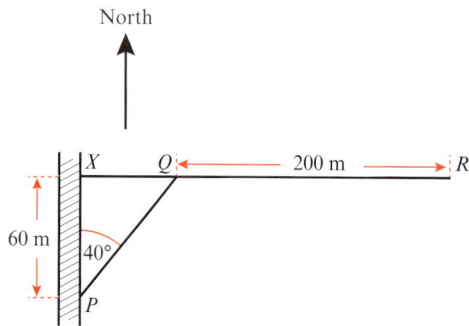

   a **i** Show by calculation that the distance, *QX*, of the lion from the road is 50.3 m, correct to 3 significant figures. [3]

      ii Calculate the distance, *PQ*, of the lion from the game warden. [3]

   b Another lion appears at *R*, 200 m due east of the first one at *Q*.

      i Write down the distance *XR*. [1]

      ii Calculate the distance, *PR*, of the second lion from the game warden. [3]

      iii Calculate the bearing of the second lion from the game warden, correct to the nearest degree. [3]

7   In the triangle OAB, angle $AOB = 15°$, $OA = 3\,$m and $OB = 8\,$m.
    Calculate, correct to 2 decimal places:

    a   the length of AB [3]

    b   the area of triangle OAB.   [3]

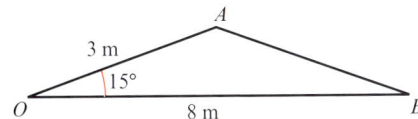

8   A pyramid, $VPQRS$, has a square base, $PQRS$, with sides of length $8\,$cm.
    Each sloping edge is $9\,$cm long.

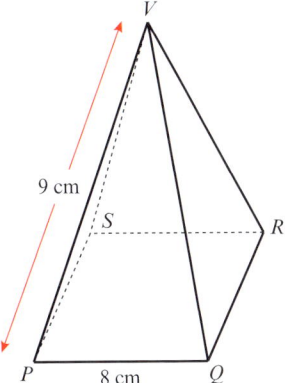

    a   Calculate the perpendicular height of the pyramid.   [4]

    b   Calculate the angle the sloping edge VP makes with the base. [3]

9   The diagram shows the graph of $y = \sin x$ for $0 \leq x \leq 360$.

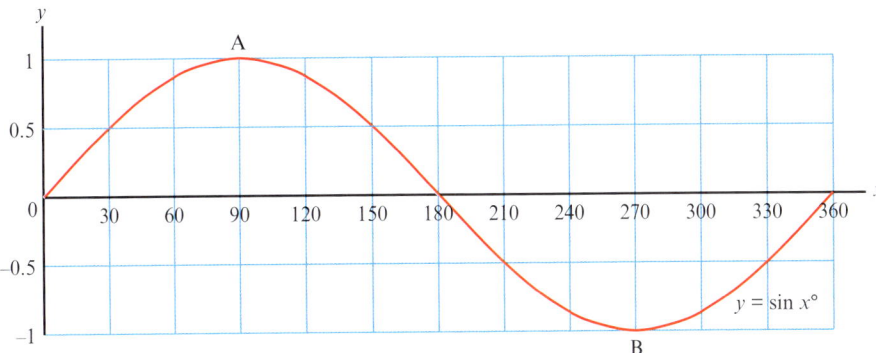

    a   Write down the coordinates of A, the point on the graph where $x = 90°$.   [2]

    b   Find the value of $\sin 270°$.   [1]

    c   By considering the line $y = -\dfrac{1}{2}$ for $0 \leq x \leq 360$, find the number of solutions
        there are for the equation $\sin x = -\dfrac{1}{2}$ for $0 \leq x \leq 360$.   [2]

10 Solve the equation $\sin x° = \cos 300°$ for $0 \leq x \leq 360$.   [3]

11 Two ships leave port P at the same time. One ship sails 60 km on a bearing of 030° to position A. The other ship sails 100 km on a bearing of 110° to position B.

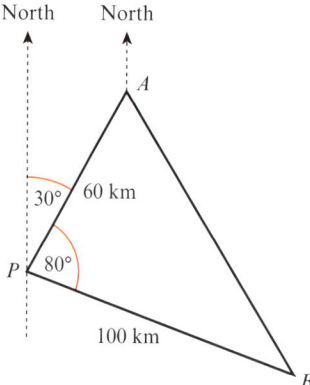

a Calculate:

    i   the distance AB [3]

    ii   angle PAB [3]

    iii   the bearing of B from A.   [3]

b Both ships took the same time, t hours, to reach their positions. The speed of the *faster* ship was 20 km/h. For an object travelling at a constant speed, $\text{speed} = \dfrac{\text{distance}}{\text{time}}$.

Write down:

    i   the value of t [2]

    ii   the speed of the slower ship.   [2]

12 Simplify $\dfrac{\sin(30°)}{\tan(60°)} \times \dfrac{(\cos(45°))^2}{\tan(45°)}$. You must show all of your working and use exact values only.   [5]

13 Solve these equations for $0° \leqslant x \leqslant 180°$.

    a $2\cos x - \sqrt{3} = 0$ [3]   **b** $\tan x = 3\tan x - 72$ [3]

    c $4 + 2(\tan x + 2) = 7$ [3]   **d** $3\cos x + 3 = 4\cos x + 4$ [3]

    e $(\tan x)^2 = \dfrac{1}{3}$ [3]   **f** $6(\sin x)^2 - 7\sin x + 2 = 0$ [4]

SELF ASSESSMENT

You can get good marks in mathematics by clearly showing your working and methods even if you get the final answer incorrect.

Evaluate your answers to the practice questions.

- Did you show your working?
- Is your working clearly laid out and systematic?
- Does your working show that you understood the question and give evidence that you know how to answer it?
- Do you think you would get part marks for any questions where you got the incorrect answer? Support your opinion.

Chapter 16

Scatter diagrams and correlation

IN THIS CHAPTER YOU WILL:

- draw scatter diagrams for bivariate data

- identify whether or not there is a positive or negative correlation between the two variables

- decide whether a correlation is strong or weak

- draw a line of best fit

- use a line of best fit to make predictions

- decide how reliable your predictions are

- recognise the common errors that are often made with scatter diagrams.

Mount Everest, the highest mountain on Earth, stands 8849 metres above mean sea level. Even close to the mountain there are big changes in the height of the land, but other things change too. How does the depth of snow at the top of the mountain compare to the snow cover much further down? Why do you think this happens? How can scientists display data, so that they can predict the depths of snow at different heights?

KEY WORDS

bivariate data

correlation

dependent variable

extrapolation

line of best fit

negative correlation

positive correlation

scatter diagram

zero correlation

GETTING STARTED

You should already be familiar with scatter diagrams and correlation.

Positive correlation	Negative correlation	Zero correlation
Points clustered around a 'line' sloping up to the right.	Points clustered around a 'line' sloping down to the right.	Points are not in a line.

1   If you plot the depth of snow against the height above sea level at several places on the slopes of Mount Everest, which of these diagrams is likely to be closest to the graph you draw? Why is the real data not likely to be exactly the same as the diagram you choose?

2   Think of some other situations where you can compare pairs of measurements using a scatter diagram. Which situations do you think will show positive, negative or zero correlation? Try to find at least three examples of each.

3   A scientist plots the number of shark attacks on Australian beaches against the profit reported by the top three Australian ice cream manufacturers during each month in 2016, 2017, 2018 and 2019. She finds that there is a strong positive correlation, showing that as ice cream sales increase, so do shark attacks. The scientist concludes that those people who eat ice cream are more likely to be attached by a shark. Explain what might be wrong with this conclusion.

16.1 Introduction to bivariate data

In earlier chapters you have seen how to summarise data and draw conclusions based on your calculations. So far the data has been a collection of single measurements, but sometimes you can make more than one calculation in the same situation.

MATHEMATICAL CONNECTIONS

You learnt how to summarise data and draw conclusions from it in Chapters 4 and 12.

Read through this example. A shop sells ice creams throughout the year and the manager wants to look into how sales change as the daily temperature rises or falls. The manager chooses 10 days at random and records both the temperature and the total sales from ice cream for each day. The results are shown in the table:

Day	A	B	C	D	E	F	G	H	I	J
Temperature (°C)	4	18	12	32	21	−3	0	10	22	31
Total sales ($)	123	556	212	657	401	23	45	171	467	659

Notice that two measurements are taken on each day and are recorded as pairs. This type of data is known as **bivariate data**. You can see this data much more clearly and explore any **correlation** if you plot the values on a **scatter diagram**.

Drawing a scatter diagram

When you plot a scatter diagram, the variable you plot on the vertical axis is called the **dependent variable**. If one variable clearly depends on the other, then use this as your dependent variable. Otherwise, unless you are told what to do, you can choose which way round you plot the variables.

DISCUSSION

Think about your answers to question 2 in the *Getting started* activity, where you thought about pairs of variables you could plot on a scatter diagram. For which pairs is there no obvious dependent variable and for which pairs is the dependent variable clear?

LINK

Correlations are used to investigate possible relationships between variables in many subjects where measurements are taken. For example, a biologist might think about the relationship between the length of a particular bone and the height of a person. Economists may need to consider the relationship between profit and working hours for employees. Geographers can use graphs to investigate any relationship between the heights of cliffs and the maximum gradients of the cliff faces.

TIP

If you are told to plot A against B, then you should plot A on the vertical axis and B on the horizontal axis.

In the example of the ice cream shop, it seems sensible that the total sales will depend on the temperature, so plot the sales on the vertical axis.

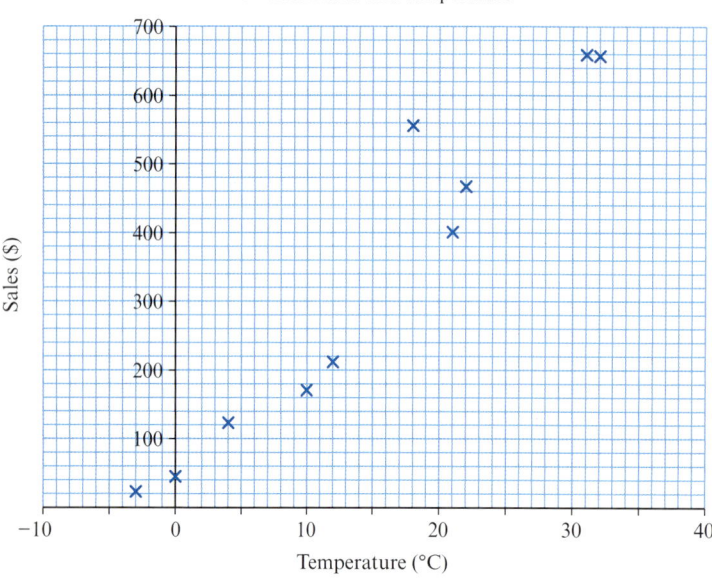

Scatter diagram showing the relationship between ice cream sales and temperature

Notice that there seems to be a relationship between the ice cream sales and the temperature. In fact, the sales rise as the temperature rises. This is called a **positive correlation**. The trend seems to be that the points roughly run from the bottom left of the diagram to the top right.

If the points been placed from the top left to bottom right you would conclude that the sales decrease as the temperature increases. Under these circumstances you would have a **negative correlation**. If there is no obvious pattern then you have **zero correlation**.

The clearer the pattern is and the closer the points are to a straight line, the stronger the correlation. These graphs show different 'strengths' of correlation:

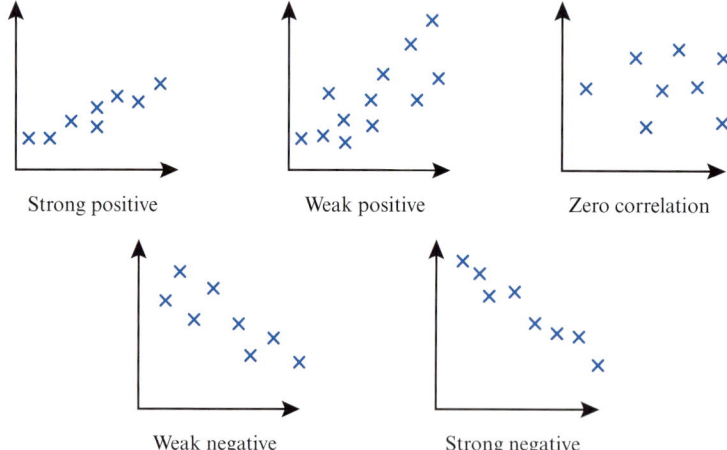

Strong positive   Weak positive   Zero correlation

Weak negative   Strong negative

You should always be ready to state whether a correlation is positive, negative, strong or weak.

Notice on the graph of ice cream sales that one of the results seems to lie outside the general pattern. Unusually high sales were recorded on one day. This may have been a special event or it may have been an error. When you see points like this you should pay attention and investigate them.

Drawing a line of best fit

You can also show the general trend by drawing a **line of best fit**. In the diagram a line has been drawn so that it passes as close to as many points as possible.

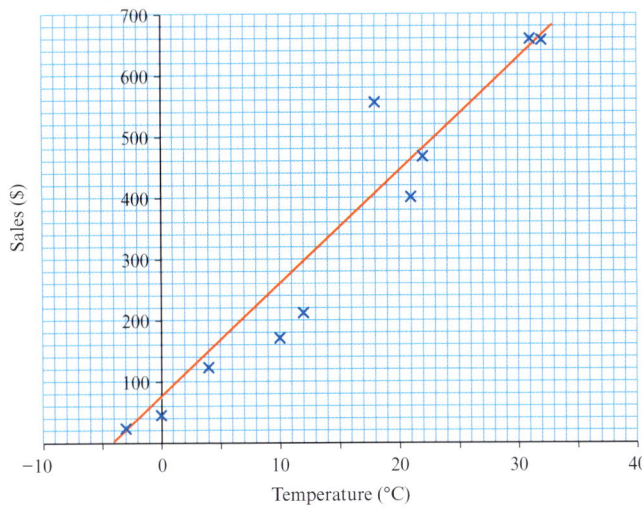

Scatter diagram showing the relationship betweenice cream sales and temperature

This is the line of best fit and you can use it to make predictions based on the collected data.

For example, if you want to try to predict the ice cream sales on a day with a temperature of 27 °C, you carry out the following steps:

1   Locate 27 °C on the temperature axis.
2   Draw a clear line vertically from this point to the line of best fit.
3   Draw a horizontal line from the point on the line of best fit to the sales axis.
4   Read the sales value from the graph.

The diagram now looks like this and the estimated value for the sales is approximately $575.

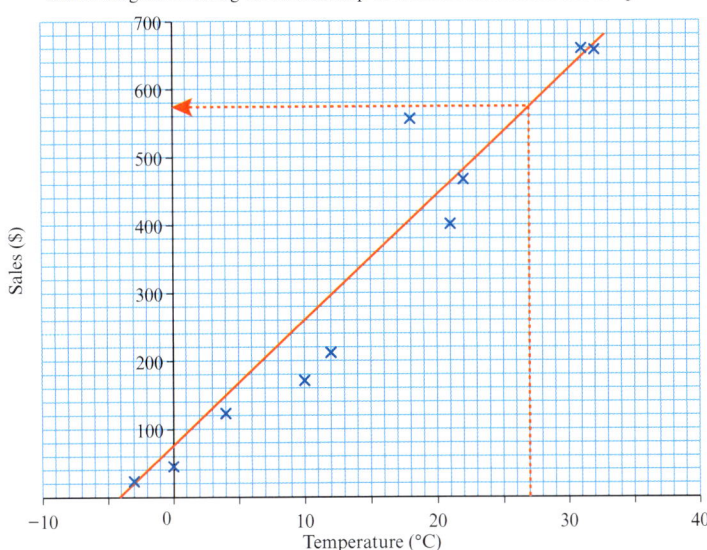

Scatter diagram showing the relationship between ice cream sales and temperature

WORKED EXAMPLE 1

The manager of a shoe shop claims that a person's height can give a very good idea of the length of their foot. To investigate this claim, the manager collects the heights and foot lengths, in cm, of ten people and records the results in a table:

Person	A	B	C	D	E	F	G	H	I	J
Height (cm)	156.2	182.4	165.3	155.1	165.2	122.9	176.3	183.4	163.0	143.1
Foot length (cm)	28.2	31.1	22.5	28.6	25.4	13.2	29.9	33.4	22.5	19.4

a Draw a scatter diagram, with height on the horizontal axis and foot length on the vertical axis.

b State what type of correlation the diagram shows.

c Draw a line of best fit.

d Estimate the foot length of a person with height 164 cm.

e Estimate the height of a person with foot length 17 cm.

f Comment on the likely accuracy of your estimates in parts (d) and (e).

Answers

a

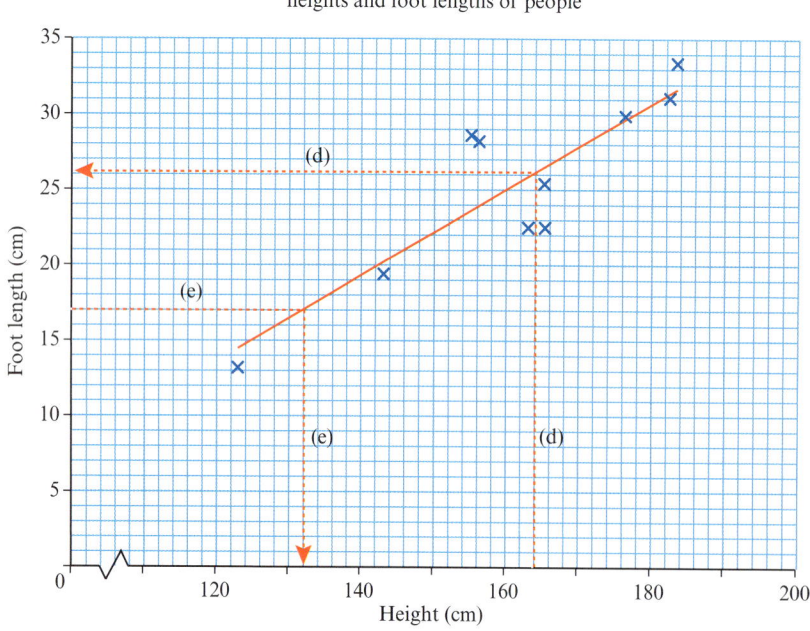

Scatter diagram showing the relationship between heights and foot lengths of people

WORKED EXAMPLE 1 CONTINUED

b   This is a strong positive correlation because foot length generally increases with height. We can make good predictions of foot length from someone's height and good predictions of someone's height from their foot length.

c   The line of best fit is drawn on the diagram. The line should extend across the entire data set and there should be approximately equal numbers of points on either side of the line.

d   The appropriate lines are drawn on the diagram. A height of 164 cm corresponds to a foot length of approximately 26 cm.

e   A foot length of 17 cm corresponds to a height of approximately 132 cm.

f   Most points are reasonably close to the line, so the correlation is fairly strong. This means that the line of best fit will allow a good level of accuracy when estimates are made.

> **TIP**
>
> If you are asked to comment on a prediction that you have made, always keep in mind the strength of the correlation as shown in the diagram. If the correlation is weak you should say that your prediction may not be very reliable.

Extrapolation

Before you draw and interpret some scatter diagrams for yourself you should be aware that there may be problems with making predictions outside the range of the collected data.

In Worked example 1, the data does not include any heights above 183.4 cm. The trend may not continue or it may look different for greater heights. So, for example, you should not try to predict the foot length for a person of height 195 cm without collecting more data.

The process of extending the line of best fit beyond the collected data is called **extrapolation**.

> **TIP**
>
> If you do need to use the diagram to make predictions outside of the range of your data, you must explain how uncertain you are about the result. You should always comment on how unreliable the result is when you do this.

Exercise 16.1

APPLY YOUR SKILLS

1   What is the correlation shown by each of the following scatter diagrams? In each case you should comment on the strength of correlation.

a
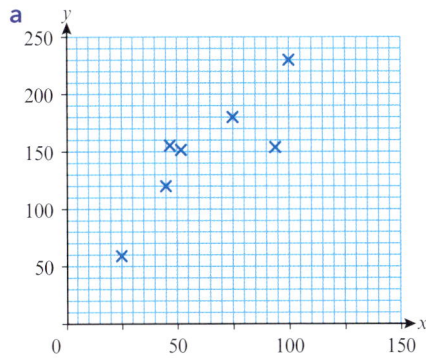

b
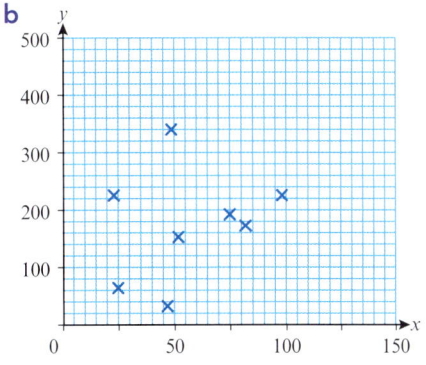

APPLY YOUR SKILLS CONTINUED

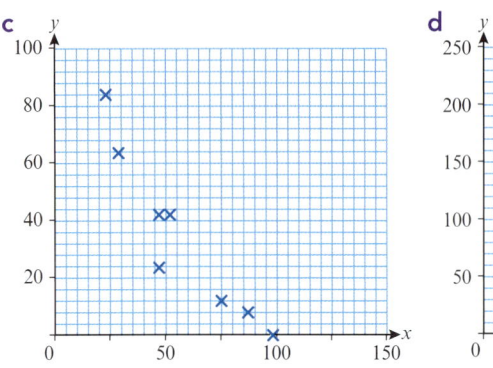

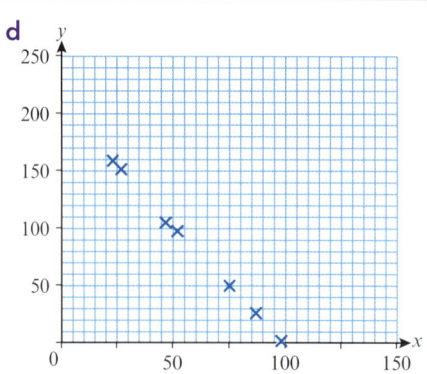

2 The widths and lengths of leaves (measured in cm) on a particular tree are recorded in the table.

Width (cm)	14	25	67	56	26	78	33	35	14	36	13	36	25	62	25
Length (cm)	22	63	170	141	76	201	93	91	24	91	23	67	51	151	79

a Draw a scatter diagram for this data with the lengths of the leaves shown on the vertical axis.

b Comment on the strength of correlation.

c Draw a line of best fit for this data.

d Estimate the length of a leaf that has width 20 cm.

3 Emma is conducting a survey into the masses of dogs and the duration of their morning walk in minutes. The results are shown in the table.

Duration of walk (min)	23	45	12	5	18	67	64	15	28	39
Mass (kg)	22	5	12	32	13	24	6	38	21	12

a Draw a scatter diagram to show the mass of each dog against the duration of the morning walk in minutes. (Plot the mass of the dog on the vertical axis.)

b How strong is the correlation between the masses of the dogs and the duration of their morning walks?

TIP

When we say 'plot A against B' we mean 'plot A on the vertical axis and B on the horizontal axis'.

APPLY YOUR SKILLS CONTINUED

4   A shopper is investigating the relationship between the number of sales assistants working in a department store and the length of time (in seconds) spent waiting in a queue to be served. The results are shown in the table.

Number of sales assistants	12	14	23	28	14	11	17	21	33	21	22	13	7
Waiting time (seconds)	183	179	154	150	224	236	221	198	28	87	77	244	266

a   Draw a scatter diagram to show the length of time spent waiting and the number of sales assistants working in the store.

b   Describe the correlation between the number of sales assistants and the time spent queuing.

c   Draw a line of best fit for this data.

d   In a very large department store there are 45 sales assistants. What happens when the shopper tries to extend and use the scatter diagram to predict the queuing time in this store?

5   Eyal is investigating the relationship between the amount of time spent watching television during a week and the score on a maths test taken a week later. The results for 12 students are shown on the scatter diagram.

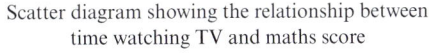

Scatter diagram showing the relationship between time watching TV and maths score

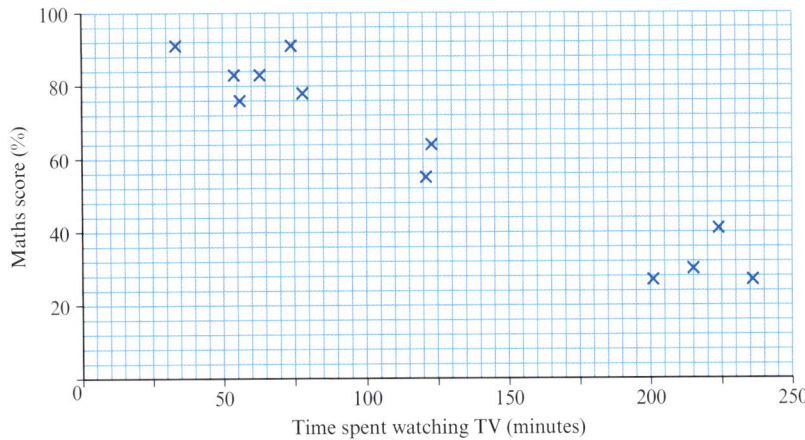

APPLY YOUR SKILLS CONTINUED

The table shows some of Eyal's results, but it is incomplete.

TV watching (min)	A	34	215	54	C	78	224	236	121	74	63	E
Maths score (%)	64	B	30	83	76	78	41	D	55	91	83	27

a Use the scatter diagram to find the missing values A to E.

b Comment on the correlation between the length of time spent watching television and the maths score.

c Copy the diagram and draw a line of best fit.

d Aneesh scores 67% on the maths test. Estimate the amount of time that Aneesh spent watching television.

e Comment on the likely accuracy of your estimate in part (d).

REFLECTION

How has the work in this chapter improved your understanding of correlation?

Are there any ideas that you are still not sure about?

What will you do about those?

SELF ASSESSMENT

Copy and complete this outline to assess your own learning in this chapter. Look back to the guidelines in Chapter 4 if you have forgotten how to complete a form like this one.

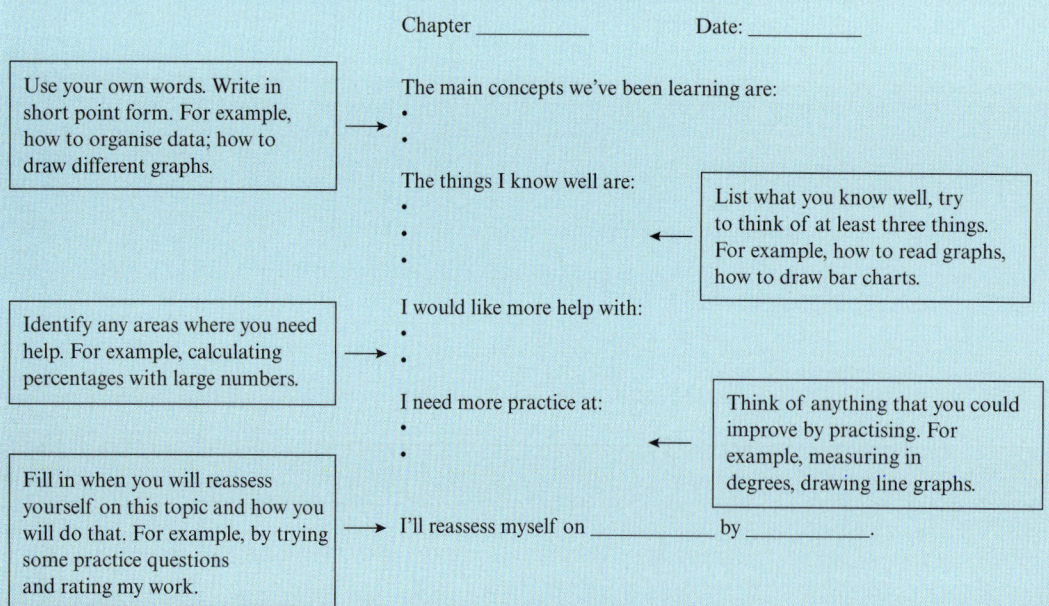

Chapter _____   Date: _____

Use your own words. Write in short point form. For example, how to organise data; how to draw different graphs.

The main concepts we've been learning are:
•
•

The things I know well are:
•
•
•

List what you know well, try to think of at least three things. For example, how to read graphs, how to draw bar charts.

Identify any areas where you need help. For example, calculating percentages with large numbers.

I would like more help with:
•
•

I need more practice at:
•
•

Think of anything that you could improve by practising. For example, measuring in degrees, drawing line graphs.

Fill in when you will reassess yourself on this topic and how you will do that. For example, by trying some practice questions and rating my work.

I'll reassess myself on _____ by _____.

SUMMARY

Do you know ...?

You can use a scatter diagram to investigate the strength of any relationship between two variables.
If one of the variables generally increases as the other variable increases, then you say that there is a positive correlation.
If one of the variables generally decreases as the other variable increases, then you say that there is a negative correlation.
The clearer the relationship, the stronger the correlation.
You can draw a line of best fit if the points seem to lie close to a straight line.
You can use the line of best fit to predict values of one variable from values of the other.
You should only make predictions using a line of best fit that has been drawn within the range of the data.

Are you able to ...?

draw a scatter diagram
describe the relationship between the variables shown
use a scatter diagram to make predictions.

Practice questions

1   The table shows the sizes (in square metres) and prices (in US dollars) of 15 paintings on display in a gallery.

Painting	A	B	C	D	E	F	G	H
Painting area (m²)	1.4	2.3	0.8	0.1	0.7	2.2	3.4	2.6
Price ($)	2400	6565	1800	45	8670	4560	10150	8950

Painting	I	J	K	L	M	N	O
Painting area (m²)	1.1	1.3	3.7	1.5	0.4	1.9	0.6
Price ($)	3025	4560	11230	4050	1450	5420	1475

a   Draw a scatter diagram for this data. The price should be represented by the vertical axis.   [4]

b   Identify the painting that is unusually expensive.
Explain your answer clearly.   [2]

c   Assuming that the unusually expensive painting is **not** to be included, draw a line of best fit for this data.   [2]

d   A new painting is introduced to the collection. The painting measures 1.5 m by 1.5 m. Use your graph to estimate the price of the painting.   [2]

e   Another painting is introduced to the collection. This painting measures 2.1 m by 2.1 m. Explain why you should not try to use your scatter diagram to estimate the price of this painting.   [2]

2 A particular type of printing machine has been sold with a strong recommendation that regular maintenance takes place even when the machine appears to be working properly.

Several companies are asked to provide the machine manufacturer with two pieces of information: the number of hours spent maintaining the machine in the first year and the number of minutes required for repair in the second year. The results are shown in the table.

Maintenance hours	42	71	22	2	60	66	102
Repairs in second year (minutes)	4040	2370	4280	4980	4000	3170	940

Maintenance hours	78	33	39	111	45	12
Repairs in second year (minutes)	1420	3790	3270	500	3380	4420

a Draw a scatter diagram to show this information. You should plot the second year repair times on the vertical axis. [4]

b Describe the correlation between maintenance time in the first year and repair time needed in the second year. [2]

c Draw a line of best fit on your scatter diagram. [2]

d Another company schedules 90 hours of maintenance for the first year of using their machine. Use your graph to estimate the repair time that will be needed in the second year. [2]

e Another company claims that they will schedule 160 hours of maintenance for the first year. Describe what happens when you try to predict the repair time for the second year of machine use. [2]

f You are asked by a manager to work out the maintenance time that will reduce the repair time to zero. Use your graph to suggest a maintenance time and comment on the reliability of your answer. [2]

SELF ASSESSMENT

Mark your answers to the practice questions.

Complete these statements in your book.

- I now know …
- I need to know more about …
- These things went well …
- I could do better if I …

Past paper questions

TIP

Unit 4 Past Paper Questions Resource Sheet is available on Cambridge GO.

1 The length, *l* metres, of a piece of rope is 5.67 m, correct to the nearest centimetre.

Copy and complete this statement about the value of *l*.

…………………… $\leq l <$ ……………………

Adapted from Cambridge IGCSE Mathematics (0580) Paper 11 Q15, June 2021

2 Solve the simultaneous equations.

You must show all your working.

$2x + y = 3$

$x - 5y = 40$

[3]

Cambridge IGCSE Mathematics (0580) Paper 11 Q21, June 2021

3 Fourteen students each take two tests in French, a speaking test and a written test.

The table shows the scores.

Speaking test	10	13	48	30	35	18	41	40	22	28	20	44	37	46
Written test	24	44	51	39	45	29	56	20	39	49	33	52	44	52

a Complete the scatter diagram. [Using Figure 1 in the Unit 4 Past Paper Questions Resource Sheet.]

The first ten points have been plotted for you.

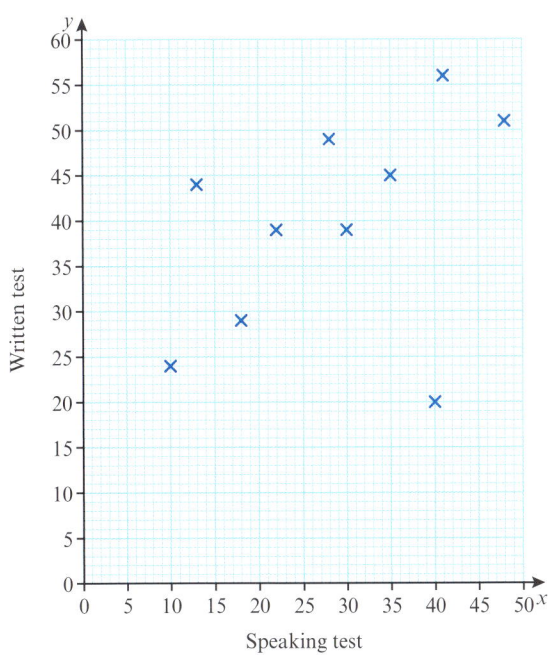

[2]

b What type of correlation is shown in this scatter diagram?

[1]

c One student has a high score in the speaking test and a low score in the written test.

On the scatter diagram, put a ring around the point. [Using Figure 1 in the Unit 4 Past Paper Questions Resource Sheet.]

[1]

d On the scatter diagram, draw a line of best fit. [Using Figure 1 in the Unit 4 Past Paper Questions Resource Sheet.]

[1]

e Use your line of best fit to estimate a score in the written test for a student who scored 25 in the speaking test.

[1]

Cambridge IGCSE Mathematics (0580) Paper 31 Q6, June 2019

4 Point B is 36 km from point A on a bearing of 140°.

a Using a scale of 1 centimetre to represent 4 kilometres, mark the position of B. [Using Figure 2 in the Unit 4 Past Paper Questions Resource Sheet.]

North

A

Scale: 1 cm to 4 km

[2]

b **i** Point C is 28 km from A and 20 km from B.

The bearing of C from A is less than 140°.

Using a ruler and compasses only, construct triangle ABC.

Show all your construction arcs.

[3]

ii Measure angle ACB.

[1]

Cambridge IGCSE Mathematics (0580) Paper 31 Q10, June 2020

5 **a** Simplify $3c - 5d - c + 2d$.

[2]

b Solve the equation $12x - 7 = 23$.

[2]

c   Multiply out.

$9(3 - x)$

[1]

d $A = \dfrac{(a + b)h}{2}$

Work out the value of h when $A = 38.64$, $a = 5.5$ and $b = 3.7$.

[3]

e   Alphonse is x years old and Beatrice is y years old.

Three times Alphonse's age is equal to 5 times Beatrice's age.

Twice Beatrice's age is 4 years more than Alphonse's age.

i   Use this information to write down two equations in x and y.

[2]

ii   Find the age of Alphonse and the age of Beatrice.

[3]

Cambridge IGCSE Mathematics (0580) Paper 31 Q8, June 2020

6   $P = 2(w + h)$

$w = 12$ correct to the nearest whole number.

$h = 4$ correct to the nearest whole number.

Work out the upper bound for the value of P.

[2]

Cambridge IGCSE Mathematics (0580) Paper 21 Q18, June 2020

7   $x^2 + 4x - 9 = (x + a)^2 + b$

Find the value of a and the value of b.

[3]

Cambridge IGCSE Mathematics (0580) Paper 21 Q13, June 2019

8   On a map, a lake has an area of $32\,cm^2$.

The scale of the map is $1 : 24\,000$.

Calculate the actual area of the lake.

Give your answer in km^2.

[2]

Cambridge IGCSE Mathematics (0580) Paper 21 Q13, June 2021

9 Write as a single fraction in its simplest form.

$$\frac{1}{x+2} - \frac{2}{3x-1}$$

[3]

Cambridge IGCSE Mathematics (0580) Paper 21 Q20, June 2019

10 a Sketch the graph of $y = \tan x$ for $0° \leqslant x \leqslant 360°$. [Using Figure 3 in the Unit 4 Past Paper Questions Resource Sheet.]

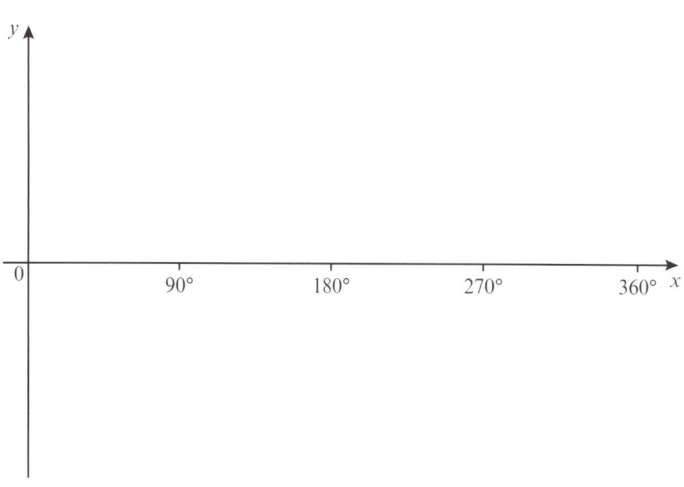

[2]

b Solve the equation $5 \tan x = 1$ for $0° \leqslant x \leqslant 360°$.

[2]

Cambridge IGCSE Mathematics (0580) Paper 21 Q19, June 2021

11

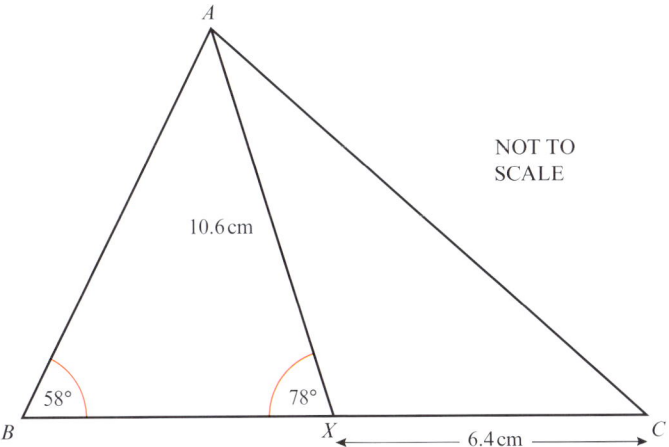

NOT TO SCALE

The diagram shows triangle *ABC*.

X is a point on *BC*.

AX = 10.6 cm, *XC* = 6.4 cm, angle *ABC* = 58° and angle *AXB* = 78°.

a   Calculate *AC*.

[4]

b   Calculate *BX*.

[4]

c   Calculate the area of triangle *ABC*.

[3]

Cambridge IGCSE Mathematics (0580) Paper 41 Q5, June 2021

12

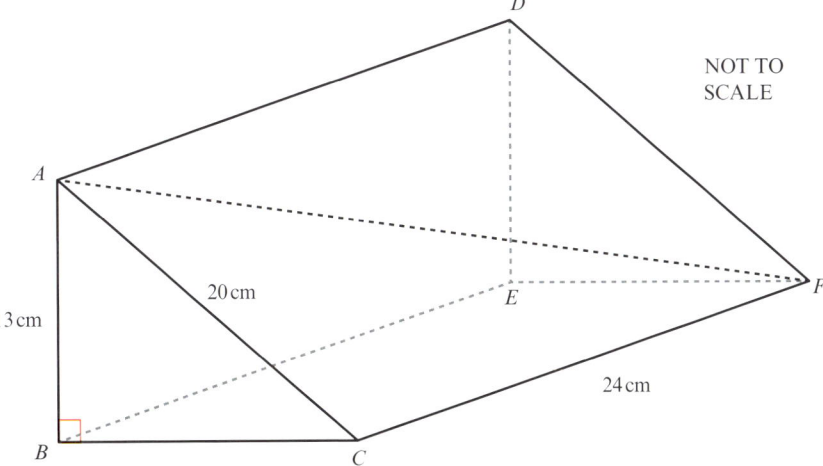

NOT TO SCALE

The diagram shows a prism, *ABCDEF*.

AB = 13 cm, *AC* = 20 cm, *CF* = 24 cm and angle *ABC* = 90°.

a Calculate the total surface area of the prism.

[6]

b Calculate the volume of the prism.

[1]

c Calculate the angle that *AF* makes with the base *BCFE*.

[4]

Cambridge IGCSE Mathematics (0580) Paper 41 Q9, June 2021

13 a $s = ut + \dfrac{1}{2}at^2$

Find the value of s when $u = 5.2$, $t = 7$ and $a = 1.6$.

[2]

b Simplify.

i $3a - 5b - a + 2b$

[2]

ii $\dfrac{5}{3x} \times \dfrac{9x}{20}$

[2]

c Solve.

i $\dfrac{15}{x} = -3$

[1]

ii $4(5 - 3x) = 23$

[3]

d Simplify.

$(27x^9)^{\frac{2}{3}}$

[2]

e Expand and simplify.

$(3x - 5y)(2x + y)$

[2]

Cambridge IGCSE Mathematics (0580) Paper 41 Q3, June 2020

14

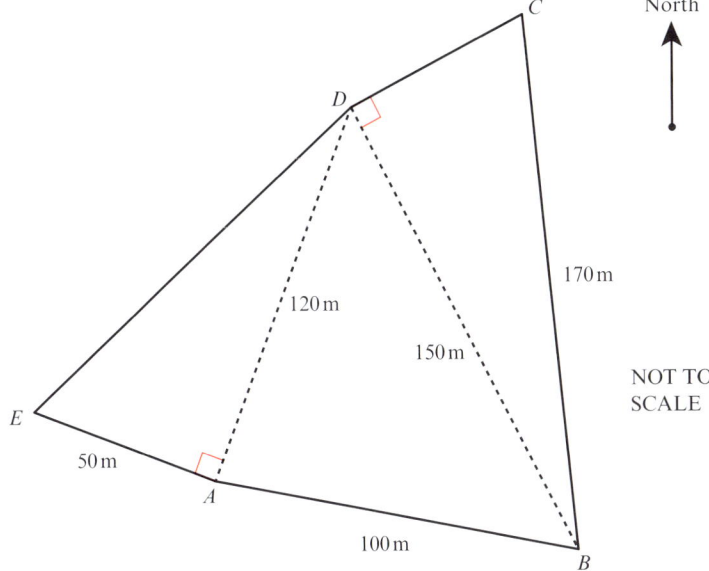

North

NOT TO
SCALE

The diagram shows a field *ABCDE*.

a   Calculate the perimeter of the field *ABCDE*.

[4]

b   Calculate angle *ABD*.

[4]

c   **i**   Calculate angle *CBD*.

[2]

   ii   The point *C* is due north of the point *B*.
      Find the bearing of *D* from *B*.

[2]

d   Calculate the area of the field *ABCDE*.
   Give your answer in hectares.
   [1 hectare = 10 000 m²]

[4]

Cambridge IGCSE Mathematics (0580) Paper 41 Q3, June 2019

> Unit 4 Project

Marbles in a box

Consider an imaginary three-dimensional game where two players take it in turn to place different coloured marbles into a box.

The box is made from 27 transparent unit cubes arranged in a 3-by-3-by-3 array.

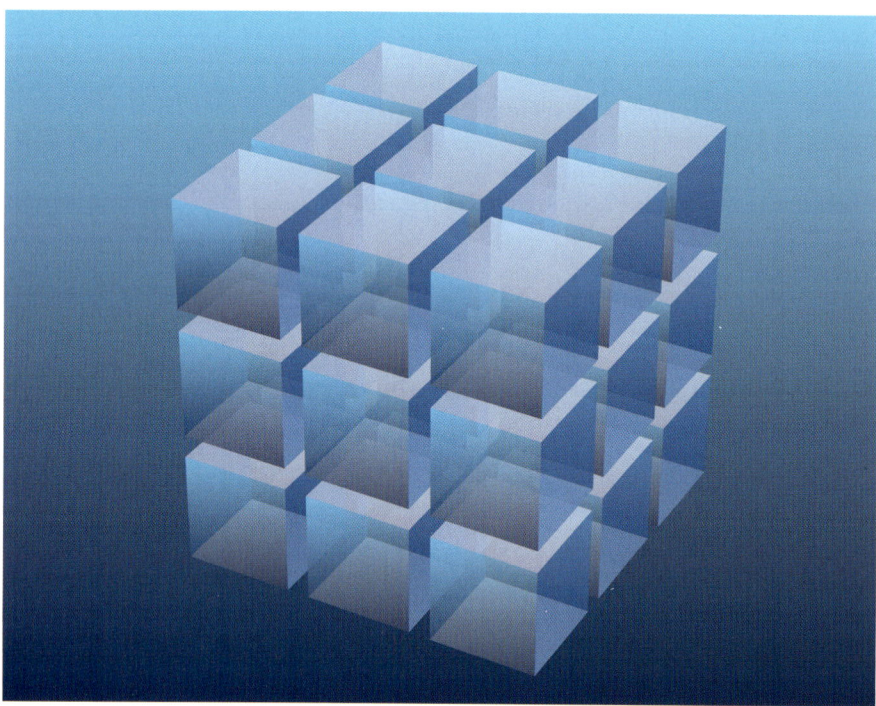

The aim of the game is to make a winning row of three of your own marbles. Rows can be horizontal, vertical or diagonal.

This diagram shows the placement of one winning row. The marbles are on three levels and the row is diagonal.

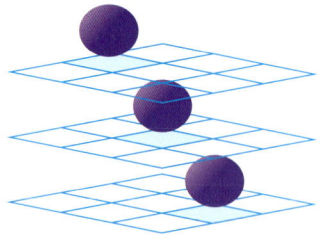

How many different ways are there to make a winning row?

Explain clearly how you got to your answer.

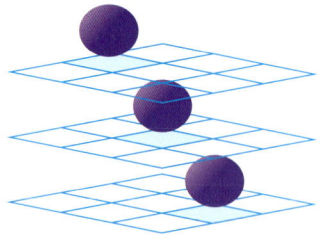

TIP

Take note that in this diagram the edges of the cubes are not shown, just the placement of the marbles on each level.

> # Chapter 17

Managing money

IN THIS CHAPTER YOU WILL:

- calculate earnings (wages and salaries) in different situations
- use and manipulate formulae to calculate simple and compound interest
- solve problems related to simple and compound interest
- apply what you already know about percentages to work out discounts, profit and loss in everyday contexts
- use a calculator effectively to perform financial calculations
- read and interpret financial data provided in tables and charts
- use exponential growth and decay in relation to finance.

Smartphone technology has changed how many people bank and manage their money as well as how people receive and make payments in everyday life. What banking and money apps do you know of? How do they work? What makes them safe to use?

In a survey, a leading business magazine found that 63% of adults agreed that financial skills should be taught in schools. Personal financial skills are important for everyone and they become more important as you get older and have to manage your own money. How well (or poorly) you understand the basics of budgeting, saving, debt and investing will affect many aspects of your life. Good financial skills can often be the difference between wealth and poverty.

In this chapter you will apply some of the maths skills you already know to solve finance-related problems. You will use your calculator to find the answers quickly and efficiently.

GETTING STARTED

1   The box contains some of the terms people use to talk about money and finance.

earnings	wages	salary	commission	deductions
net income	gross income	simple interest		
compound growth	investment	cost price	selling price	
profit	loss	mark up	discount	principal amount
rate of interest	appreciation	depreciation		
inflation rate	annually	credit	debit	transaction

KEY WORDS

compound interest

cost price

discount

interest

interest rate

loss

principal

profit

selling price

simple interest

a   Copy this table.

I've never heard this before	I have heard this but I am not sure what it means	I know what this means and can explain it to others

b   Write the terms from the box in the appropriate columns.

c   Work in pairs. Find the meanings of any words you wrote in the first two columns. If you can, explain the words you know to each other. If not, find out what they mean in financial contexts.

2   How would you:

a   increase $40 by 5%?   b   decrease $40 by 10%?

3   The formula for simple interest is $I = \dfrac{PRT}{100}$. Use what you learned in Chapter 6 to change the subject of this formula to:

a P b R c T

17.1 Earning money

When people are employed they are paid for their work. Earnings can be worked out in different ways:

- Wages – pay based on a fixed number of hours worked, usually paid weekly. Extra hours of work are called overtime and these are usually paid at a higher rate.
- Salary – pay based on a fixed yearly amount, usually paid monthly. Overtime may be paid, or workers may be given time off in exchange for extra time spent at work.
- Piece work – pay based on the number of items produced.
- Commission – pay is based on a percentage of sales made; sometimes a low wage, called a retainer, is paid as well as commission.

WORKED EXAMPLE 1

Emmanuel makes beaded necklaces. He is paid in South African rand at a rate of R24.50 per completed necklace. He is able to make 55 necklaces per week. Calculate his weekly earnings from the sale of necklaces.

Answer

Earnings = 55 × 24.50   Multiply items produced by the rate paid.

= R1347.50

WORKED EXAMPLE 2

Sanjay works as a sales representative for a company that sells mobile phones in the United Arab Emirates. He is paid a retainer of 800 Dhs (dirhams) per week plus a commission of 4.5% of all sales.

a   How much would he earn in a week if he made no sales?

b   How much would he earn if he sold four phones at 3299 Dhs each in a week?

Answers

a   800 Dhs   If he made no sales, he would earn no commission, only his retainer.

b   Commission = 4.5% of (3299 × 4)   Calculate 4.5% of the total sales Sanjay made.

= 0.045 × 13196

= 593.82 Dhs

Earnings = retainer + commission   Add this to the retainer of 800 Dhs.

= 800 Dhs + 593.82 Dhs

= 1393.82 Dhs

> **MATHEMATICAL CONNECTIONS**
>
> You learnt about the decimal equivalents of percentages in Chapter 5.

WORKED EXAMPLE 3

Josh's hourly rate of pay is $12.50. He is paid 'time-and-a-half' for work after hours and on Saturdays and 'double-time' for Sundays and Public Holidays.

One week he worked 5.5 hours on Saturday and 3 hours on Sunday. How much overtime pay would he earn?

Answer

Saturday overtime	= 1.5 × $12.50 × 5.5	(time-and-a-half = 1.5 × normal time)
	= $103.13	
Saturday overtime	= 2 × $12.50 × 3	(double-time = 2 × normal time)
	= $75	
Total overtime	= $103.13 + $75.00	
	= $178.13	

Exercise 17.1

APPLY YOUR SKILLS

1   A waiter earns $8.25 per hour.
    How much would she earn for a six-hour shift?

2   How much would a receptionist earn for working a 35-hour week if the rate of pay is $12.25 per hour?

3   Calculate the hourly rate for each of the following payments:

    a $67.50 for five hours

    b $245.10 for a 38-hour week

    c $126.23 for 13.5 hours

    d $394.88 for five $6\frac{1}{2}$ hour shifts

    e $71.82 for working five hours and 15 minutes.

4   Truck drivers are paid $15.45 per tonne of wood pulp delivered to a factory in Malaysia. If the drivers deliver 135 tonnes to the factory, how much will they earn?

5   A team of workers in a factory is paid $23.25 per pallet of goods produced. If a team of five workers produces 102 pallets in a shift, how much will each person in the team have earned that shift?

6   An estate agent is paid a retainer of $150 per week plus a commission on sales. The rate of commission is 2.5% on sales up to $150 000 and 1.75% on amounts above that. How much would she earn in a week if she sold a house for $220 000 and an apartment for $125 000?

TIP

Commissions like these are on a sliding scale. So if the agent had sales of $160 000, she would be paid 2.5% of $150 000 and 1.75% of the $10 000 that is above this threshold.

7   Here is the time sheet for five workers in a factory. Calculate each person's income for the week if their standard rate of pay is $8.40 per hour.

Worker	Normal hours worked	Hours overtime at time-and-a-half	Hours overtime at double-time
Annie	35	2	0
Bonnie	25	3	4
Connie	30	1.5	1.75
Donny	40	0	4
Elizabeth	20	3.75	2

Deductions from earnings

Gross income (earnings) is the total amount a person earns.

Deductions, such as income tax, pension contributions, unemployment and health insurance, and union dues are often taken from the gross earnings before the person is paid. The amount that is left over after deductions is called the net income.

Net income = gross income − deductions

Exercise 17.2

1   For each person shown in the table:

   a   calculate their net income

   b   calculate their net income as a percentage of their gross income. Give your answers to the nearest whole percent.

Employee	Gross weekly earnings ($)	Tax ($)	Other deductions ($)
B Willis	675.90	235.45	123.45
M Freeman	456.50	245.20	52.41
J Malkovich	1289.00	527.45	204.35
H Mirren	908.45	402.12	123.20
M Parker	853.30	399.10	90.56

2   Use the gross weekly earnings of the employees in question 1 to work out:

   a   the mean weekly earnings

   b   the median weekly earnings

   c   the range of earnings.

TIP

Gross earnings, deductions and net income are normally shown on a payment advice (slip) which is given to each worker when they get paid.

MATHEMATICAL CONNECTIONS

In Chapter 5 you learnt how to write one number as a percentage of another number – look back if you need to remind yourself.

APPLY YOUR SKILLS

3   Study the following two pay advice slips. For each worker, calculate:
   a   the difference between gross (excluding medical and car allowances) and net income
   b   the percentage of gross income that each takes home as net income.

Poovan's Plastics Pty Ltd PAYMENT ADVICE				
EMPLOYEE DETAILS			**SEPTEMBER**	
M Badru			Income tax no	0987654321A
Employee no: MBN 0987			Bank details	Big Bucks Bank
			Account no.	9876598
EARNINGS			**DEDUCTIONS**	
Details	Taxable amount	Payable amount	Description	Amount
Salary	12 876.98	12 876.98	Unemployment Insurance Fund (UIF)	89.35
Medical	650.50	0.00	First aid course fees	
Car allowance	1 234.99	0.00	Group life insurance	9.65
			Union membership	132.90
			PAYE	32.00
				3 690.62
	14 762.47	12 876.98		3 954.52
			NET PAY:	**8 922.46**

Nehru–Kapoor Network Services		Employee name:	B Singh	ID number:	630907000000
		Job title:	Clerk		
Hours/Days		**Earnings**		**Deductions**	
Normal hours	84.00	Wages	1402.80	Income tax	118.22
O/time @ 1.5 hours	11.00	Overtime @ 1.5	275.55	UIF	18.94
				Pension fund	105.21
				Loan	474.00
				Sick pay	8.42
Year-to-date					
Taxable	22 881.40				
Benefits	0.00				
Tax paid	509.30				
Current period		TOTAL EARNINGS		TOTAL DEDUCTIONS	
Company contributions 358.12			1678.35		724.79
				NET PAY	953.56

LINK

If you study business or economics you will need a good understanding of financial mathematics as well as the ability to apply formulae, draw and interpret graphs and calculate rates of change using percentages and real money amounts.

INVESTIGATION

Types of tax

Income tax is a form of direct taxation. Carry out some research of your own to find out about each type of tax below, who pays this tax, how it is paid, and the rate/s at which it is charged in your country.

a   Value added tax

b   General sales tax

c   Customs and excise duties

d   Capital gains tax

e   Estate duties

f   Property taxes

g   Air passenger tax

h   Corporate tax

Information from tax tables

In most countries, employers deduct taxes from earnings and pay them over to the tax authority. The tax authority publishes a table of tax rates every year so that employers can work out how much tax to deduct. Here is a portion of a tax table:

TAXABLE INCOME (in $)	RATES OF TAX
0–132 000	18% of each $1
132 001–210 000	$23 760 + 25% of the amount above $132 000
210 001–290 000	$43 260 + 30% of the amount above $210 000
290 001–410 000	$67 260 + 35% of the amount above $290 000
410 001–525 000	$109 260 + 38% of the amount above $410 000
525 001 and above	$152 960 + 40% of the amount above $525 000

TIP

In some Islamic countries, tax is not deducted from earnings. Instead people pay a portion of their earnings as a religious obligation (*zakat*).

WORKED EXAMPLE 4

Mr Smit's taxable income is $153 772.00 per annum. How much tax must he pay:

a   per year?

b   per month?

Answers

a   To work out the yearly tax, find his tax bracket on the table. His income is in row two because it is between $132 001 and $210 000.

He has to pay $23 760 + 25% of his earnings above $132 000.

$153 772 − $132 000 = $21 772

25% of $21 772 = $5443

Tax payable = $23 760 + $5443 = $29 203 per year

b $29 203 ÷ 12 = $2433.58   To find the monthly tax, divide the total from part (a) by 12.

TIP

Per annum means each year or annually. It is often abbreviated to p.a.

Exercise 17.3

APPLY YOUR SKILLS

1   Use the tax table on the previous page to work out the annual tax payable and the monthly tax deductions for each of the following taxable incomes.

   a $98 000   **b** $120 000   **c** $129 000

   d $135 000   **e** $178 000

2   Use the following tax table to answer the questions that follow.

Single person (no dependants)	
Taxable income	**Income tax payable**
$0–$8375	10% of the amount over $0
$8375–$34 000	$837.50 plus 15% of the amount over $8375
$34 000–$82 400	$4681.25 plus 25% of the amount over $34 000
$82 400–$171 850	$16 781.25 plus 28% of the amount over $82 400
$171 850–$373 650	$41 827.25 plus 33% of the amount over $171 850
$373 650+	$108 421.25 plus 35% of the amount over $373 650

   a Li-Gon has a taxable income of $40 000 for this tax year. He tells his friends that he is in the 25% tax bracket.

   i   Is this correct?

   ii Does it mean that he pays $10 000 in income tax? Explain why or why not.

   iii When Li-Gon checks his tax return, he finds that he only has to pay $6181.25 income tax. Show how this amount is calculated by the revenue services.

   b How much tax would a person earning $250 000 pay in this tax year?

   c Cecelia earned $30 000 in taxable income in this year. Her employer deducted $320.25 income tax per month from her salary.

   i   Will Cecelia have to pay any additional tax at the end of the tax year or will she be due for a tax refund as a result of overpayment?

   ii How much is the amount due in part (i)?

17.2 Borrowing and investing money

When you borrow money or you buy things on credit, you are normally charged **interest** for the use of the money. Similarly, when you save or invest money, you are paid interest by the bank or financial institution in return for allowing them to keep and use your money.

Simple interest

Simple interest is a fixed percentage of the original amount borrowed or invested. In other words, if you borrow $100 at an **interest rate** of 5% per year, you will be charged $5 interest for every year of the loan.

Simple interest involves adding the interest amount to the original amount at regular intervals. The formula used to calculate simple interest is:

$I = \dfrac{PRT}{100}$, where:

P = the **principal**, which is the original amount borrowed or saved

R = the interest rate

T = the time (in years).

LINK

In Islam, interest (*riba*) is forbidden so Islamic banks do not charge interest on loans or pay interest on investments. Instead, Islamic banks charge a fee for services which is fixed at the beginning of the transaction (*murabaha*). For investments, the bank and its clients share any profits or losses incurred over a given period in proportion to their investment (*musharaka*). Many banks in Islamic countries have the responsibility of collecting *zakat* on behalf of the government. *Zakat* is a religious tax which Muslims who earn above a threshold amount (*nisab*) are obliged to pay. It is usually calculated at about 2.5% of yearly personal wealth. *Zakat* is intended to help the less prosperous and to uplift communities in need.

WORKED EXAMPLE 5

$500 is invested at 10% per annum simple interest. How much interest is earned in three years?

Answer

10% of $500 = $\dfrac{10}{100} \times 500 = \$50$ The interest rate is 10% per annum.

The interest every year is $50.

So after three years, the interest is:

$3 \times \$50 = \$150$ Multiply by the number of years.

WORKED EXAMPLE 6

Sam invested $400 at 15% per annum for three years. How much money would the investment be worth at the end of the period?

Answer

At the end of the period he would have $P + I$ (the principal plus the interest paid).

$I = \dfrac{PRT}{100}$ and $P = 400$, so:

$P + I = 400 + \dfrac{(400 \times 15 \times 3)}{100}$

$ = 400 + 180$

$ = \$580$

WORKED EXAMPLE 7

How long will it take for $250 invested at the rate of 8% per annum simple interest to grow to $310?

Answer

Amount = principal + interest

Interest = amount − principal

∴ Interest = $310 − $250 = $60

Rate = 8% per annum = $\dfrac{8}{100} \times 250 = \$20$

So the interest per year is $20.

Total interest (60) ÷ annual interest (20) = 3

So it will take three years for $250 to grow to $310 at the rate of 8% per annum simple interest.

WORKED EXAMPLE 8

Calculate the rate of simple interest if a principal of $250 grows to $400 in three years.

Answer

Interest paid = $400 − $250 = $150

$I = \dfrac{PRT}{100}$

$100I = PRT$

$R = \dfrac{100I}{PT} = \dfrac{100 \times 150}{250 \times 3} = 20$

Change the subject of the formula to R to find the rate.

So, the interest rate = 20%

TIP

You can manipulate the formula to find any of the values:

$I = \dfrac{PRT}{100}$

$P = \dfrac{100I}{RT}$

$R = \dfrac{100I}{PT}$

$T = \dfrac{100I}{PR}$

Exercise 17.4

1 Calculate the simple interest earned on each amount.

	Principal amount ($)	Interest rate (%)	Time invested
a	500	1	3 years
b	650	0.75	$2\frac{1}{2}$ years
c	1000	1.25	5 years
d	1200	4	$6\frac{1}{2}$ years
e	875	5.5	3 years
f	900	6	2 years
g	699	7.25	3.75 years
h	1200	8	9 months
i	150 000	$9\frac{1}{2}$	18 months

2 Calculate how much would have to be repaid in total for each of the following loans.

	Principal amount ($)	Interest rate (%)	Time invested
a	500	4.5	2 years
b	650	5	2 years
c	1000	6	2 years
d	1200	12	18 months
e	875	15	18 months
f	900	15	3 years
g	699	20	9 months
h	1200	21.25	8 months
i	150 000	18	$1\frac{1}{2}$ years

3 $1400 is invested at 4% per annum simple interest. How long will it take for the amount to reach $1624?

4 The simple interest on $600 invested for five years is $210. What is the rate percentage per annum?

APPLY YOUR SKILLS

5 If you invest a sum of money at a simple interest rate of 6%, how long will it take for your original amount to treble?

6 Jessica spends $\frac{1}{4}$ of her income from odd jobs on books, $\frac{1}{3}$ on transport and $\frac{1}{6}$ on clothing. She saves the rest.

    a If she saves $8 per month, how much is her income each month?

    b How much does she save in a year at a rate of $8 per month?

    c She deposits one year's savings into an account that pays 8.5% interest for five years.

        i How much interest will she earn?

        ii How much will she have altogether in the end?

7 Ms Mazumder took a personal loan of $8000 over three years. She repaid $325 per month in that period.

    a How much did she repay in total?

    b How much interest did she pay in pounds?

    c At what rate was simple interest charged over the three years?

Hire purchase

Many people buy items such as TVs, furniture and cars on a system of payment called hire purchase (HP).

On HP you pay a part of the price as a deposit and the remainder in a certain number of weekly or monthly instalments. Interest is charged on outstanding balances. It is useful to be able to work out what interest rate is being charged on HP as it is not always clearly stated.

TIP

In HP agreements, the deposit is sometimes called the down-payment.

When interest is calculated as a proportion of the amount owed it is called a flat rate of interest. This is the same as simple interest.

WORKED EXAMPLE 9

The cash price of a car is $20 000. The hire purchase price is $6000 deposit and instalments of $700 per month for two years. How much more than the cash price is the hire purchase price?

Answer

Deposit = $6000

One instalment = $700

24 instalments = $700 × 24 = $16 800 (once per month over two years is 24 monthly instalments)

Total HP price = deposit + 24 instalments

               = $6000 + $16 800

               = $22 800

The hire purchase price is $2800 more than the cash price.

WORKED EXAMPLE 10

A person bought a car for $30 000 on hire purchase. The deposit was 20% and interest on the outstanding balance for the period of repayment is at 10% per annum. If the balance is to be paid in 12 equal instalments, calculate each instalment.

Answer

Cash price = $30 000

Deposit of 20% = $\dfrac{20}{100} \times 30\,000 = \$6000$

Outstanding balance = $30\,000 - \$6000 = \$24\,000$

Interest of 10% = $\dfrac{10}{100} \times 24\,000 = \$2400$

Amount to be paid by instalments	= outstanding balance + interest
	= $24\,000 + \$2400$
	= $26\,400$

Each instalment = $\dfrac{26\,400}{12} = \$2200$ (divide by total number of instalments)

Exercise 17.5

APPLY YOUR SKILLS

1   A shopkeeper wants 25% deposit on a bicycle costing $400 and charges 20% interest on the remaining amount. How much is:

    a   the deposit?   **b**   the interest?   **c**   the total cost of the bicycle?

2   A person paid 30% deposit on a fridge costing $2500 and the balance in one year with interest of 20% per year. How much did the person actually pay for the fridge?

3   A student bought a laptop priced at $1850. She paid 20% deposit and 12 equal monthly instalments. The interest rate is 15% per annum on the outstanding balance.

    a   How much was each monthly instalment?

    b   What was the total cost of buying the laptop on HP?

4   A large flat screen TV cost $999. Josh agreed to pay $100 deposit and 12 monthly payments of $100.

    a   How much interest will Josh pay?

    b   What rate of interest was he charged?

5   A second-hand car is advertised for $15 575 cash or $1600 deposit and 24 monthly payments of $734.70.

    a   What is the difference between the cash price and the HP price?

    b   What annual rate of interest is paid on the HP plan?

Compound interest

Simple interest is calculated on the original amount saved or borrowed. It is more common, to earn or to be charged **compound interest**. With a loan where you are charged compound interest, the interest is added to the amount you owe at regular intervals so the amount you owe increases for the next period. When you invest money for a fixed period, you can earn compound interest. In this case, the interest earned is added to the amount each period and you then earn interest on the amount plus the interest for the next period.

One way of doing compound interest calculations is to view them as a series of simple interest calculations. This method is shown in Worked example 11.

LINK

When a virus is out of control in a population of animals, it is often true that the number of cases starts to increase by a similar percentage each day. The mathematics that describes this kind of growth is very similar to compound interest. Both start with an initial value – the investment in financial mathematics and the original population in biology – and then a fixed percentage increase occurs at regular intervals.

WORKED EXAMPLE 11

Priya invested $100 at a rate of 10%, compounded annually. How much is the investment worth after three years?

Answer

Year 1

$$I = \frac{PRT}{100} = \frac{100 \times 10 \times 1}{100} = \$10$$ Use the formula for simple interest.

$P + I = \$100 + \$10 = \$110$

Year 2

$$I = \frac{PRT}{100} = \frac{110 \times 10 \times 1}{100} = \$11$$ P for year 2 is $110; T is one year as you are only finding the interest for year 2.

$P + I = 110 + 11 = \$121.00$

Year 3

$$I = \frac{PRT}{100} = \frac{121 \times 10 \times 1}{100} = \$12.10$$ P for year 3 is $121; T remains one year.

$P + I = \$133.10$

TIP

When the principal, rate and time are the same, compound interest will be higher than simple interest. The exception is when the interest is only calculated for one period (for example one year), in that case, the compound interest and the simple interest will be the same.

This table and graph compare the value of two $100 investments. The first is invested at 10% simple interest, the second at 10% compound interest.

Year (T)	Total $ 10% simple interest	Total $ 10% interest compounded annually
1	110	110
2	120	121
3	130	133.10
4	140	146.41
5	150	161.05
6	160	177.16
7	170	194.87
8	180	214.36
9	190	235.79
10	200	259.37

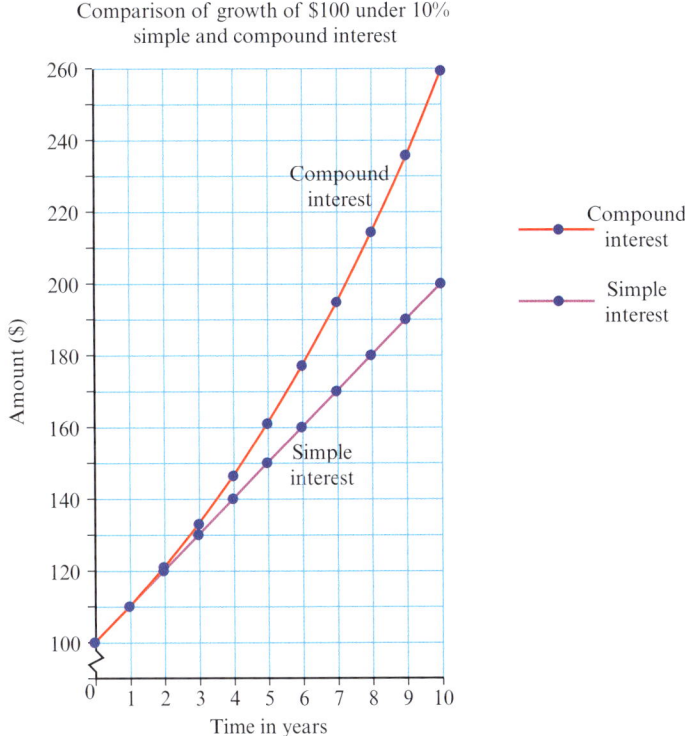

Comparison of growth of $100 under 10% simple and compound interest

It is clear that choosing a compound interest rate is to the advantage of the investor. Remember, though, that the same effect is felt with borrowing – the outstanding debt increases each period as the interest is compounded.

You can also calculate compound interest using a multiplier. The calculations in the third column of the table show how this is done.

Year (T)	Total $ 10% interest compounded annually	Working using a multiplier
1	110	$100 \times 1.1 = 110$
2	121	$100 \times 1.1 \times 1.1 = 121$
3	133.10	$100 \times 1.1 \times 1.1 \times 1.1 = 133.10$
4	146.41	$100 \times (1.1)^4 = 146.41$
5	161.05	$100 \times (1.1)^5 = 161.05$
6	177.16	$100 \times (1.1)^6 = 177.16$
7	194.87	$100 \times (1.1)^7 = 194.87$
8	214.36	$100 \times (1.1)^8 = 214.36$
9	235.79	$100 \times (1.1)^9 = 235.79$
10	259.37	$100 \times (1.1)^{10} = 259.37$

> **MATHEMATICAL CONNECTIONS**
>
> You learnt about indices in Chapters 1 and 2.

- Add the annual interest rate to 100 to get a percentage increase (subtract for a decrease): $100\% + 10\% = 110\%$

- Express this as a decimal: $\dfrac{110}{100} = 1.1$

- Multiply the principal by a power of the decimal using the number of years as the power. So, for five years: $100 \times (1.1)^5$

You can also insert values into a formula to calculate the value (V) of an investment when it is subject to compound interest.

$V = P\left(1 + \dfrac{r}{100}\right)^n$, where

P is the amount invested

r is the percentage rate of interest

n is the number of years of compound interest.

> **TIP**
>
> Multiply the decimal by itself the same number of times as the number of years. For three years it would be $1.1 \times 1.1 \times 1.1$ or $(1.1)^3$ not 1.1×3.

> **TIP**
>
> You are expected to know this formula.

WORKED EXAMPLE 12

$1500 is invested at 5% p.a. compound interest. What will the investment be worth after five years?

Answer

$\begin{aligned} V &= P\left(1 + \dfrac{r}{100}\right)^n \\ &= 1500\,(1 + 0.05)^5 \\ &= \$1914.42 \end{aligned}$

Insert values in the formula and then use your calculator.

WORKED EXAMPLE 13

A sum of money is invested at a rate of 5% interest, compounded yearly. After five years it grows to $2500. What was the initial sum invested?

Answer

$$V = P\left(1 + \frac{r}{100}\right)^n$$

$$2500 = P\left(1 + \frac{5}{100}\right)^5 \qquad \text{Substitute values for } V, r \text{ and } n.$$

$$= P \times 1.05^5$$

$$P = \frac{2500}{1.05^5} \qquad \text{Rearrange to solve for } P.$$

$$= \$1958.82$$

Exercise 17.6

1   Calculate the total amount owing on a loan of $8000 after two years at an interest rate of 12%:

   a   compounded annually   **b**   calculated as a flat rate.

2   Calculate the total amount owing on a housing loan of $60 000 after ten years if the interest rate is 4% compounded annually.

3   Suyin bought an apartment in Manila for (US)$320 000 as an investment. If the value of the apartment appreciates (grows) at an average rate of 3.5% per annum, what will it be worth in five years' time?

4   How much would you have to repay on a credit card debt of $3500 after two years if the interest rate is:

   a   19.5% compounded annually?

   b   19.5% compounded half-yearly (the interest rate will be half of 19.5 for half a year)?

REFLECTION

Look back at the three methods of working out compound interest.

- Which method makes most sense to you? Why?
- What are the main advantages of working with the formula?
- What are the most important things that you need to remember when you use the compound interest formula?
- What can you do to remember the formula and how to use it?

Exponential growth and decay

When a quantity increases (grows) in a fixed proportion (normally a percentage) at regular intervals, we say that the growth is exponential. Similarly, when the quantity decreases (decays) by a fixed percentage over regular periods of time, it is called exponential decay.

Increasing exponential functions produce curved graphs that slope steeply up to the right. Decreasing exponential functions produce curved graphs that slope steeply down to the right.

Exponential growth and decay can be expressed using formulae.

For growth: $y = a(1 + r)^n$

For decay: $y = a(1 - r)^n$

Where a is the original value or principal, r is the rate of change expressed as a decimal and n is the number of time periods.

MATHEMATICAL CONNECTIONS

When financial investments increase or decrease in value at an exponential rate we talk about appreciation (growth) and depreciation. When the number of individuals in a population increase or decrease exponentially over time, we usually talk about growth or decay.

You will deal with exponential curves in more detail in Chapter 18.

17 Managing money

WORKED EXAMPLE 14

$100 is invested subject to compound interest at a rate of 8% per annum. Find the value of the investment correct to the nearest cent after a period of 15 years.

Answer

Value = $a(1 + r)^n$

    = $100(1 + 0.08)^{15}$

    = $100(1.08)^{15}$

    = 317.2169114

Value of investment is $317.22 (correct to the nearest cent).

Use the formula for exponential growth and substitute the given values.

WORKED EXAMPLE 15

The value of a new computer system depreciates by 30% per year. If it cost $1200 new, what will it be worth after two years?

Answer

Value = $a(1 - r)^n$

    = $1200(1 - 0.3)^2$

    = $1200(0.7)^2$

    = 588

Value after two years is $588.

Use the formula for exponential decay and substitute the given values.

Exercise 17.7

APPLY YOUR SKILLS

1 In December 2021 there were approximately 7.874 billion people on Earth. The annual growth rate was estimated to be 1.04%. Assuming this growth rate continues, estimate the population of the world in December:

    a 2025   **b** 2030   **c** 2050.

2 In 2021 there were an estimated 1800 giant pandas in China. Calculate the likely panda population in 2030 if there is:

    a an annual growth in the population of 0.5%

    b an annual decline in the population of 0.5%.

569

APPLY YOUR SKILLS

3   A population of microbes in a laboratory doubles every day. At the start of the period, the population is estimated to be 1 000 000 microbes.

a   Copy and complete this table to show the growth in the population.

Time (days)	0	1	2	3	4	5	6	7	8
Total number of microbes (millions)	1	2	4						

b   Draw a graph to show growth in the population over 8 days.

c   Use the graph to determine the microbe population after:

   i   2.5 days   ii   3.6 days.

d   Use the graph to determine how long it will take the microbe population to reach 20 million.

TIP

This is essentially the same as the compound interest formula.

4   This graph shows how a radioactive substance loses its radioactivity over time.

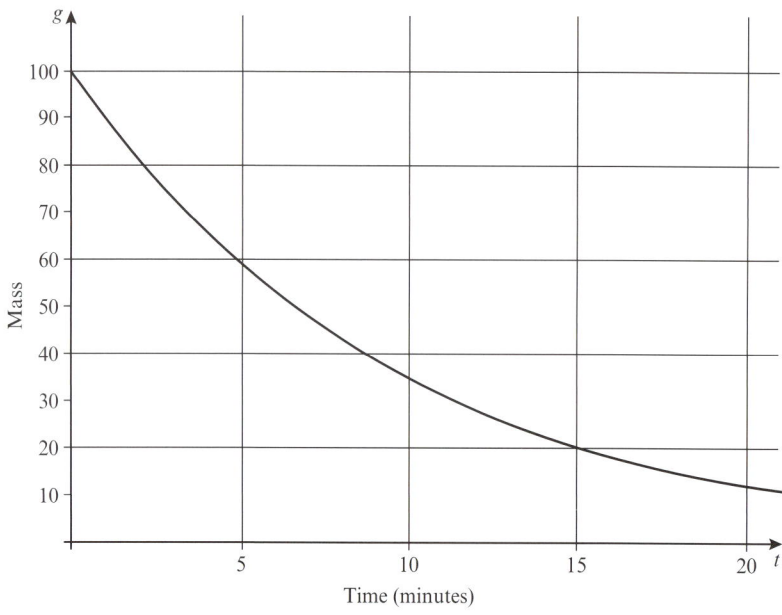

a   The half life of the substance is how long it takes to decay to half its original mass. What is the half life of this substance?

b   What mass of the substance is left after 20 minutes?

5   Ms Singh owns a small business. She borrows $18 500 from the bank to finance some new equipment. She repays the loan in full after two years. If the bank charged her compound interest at the rate of 21% per annum, how much did she repay after two years?

APPLY YOUR SKILLS CONTINUED

6 The value of a car depreciates each year by 8%. A new small car is priced at $11 000. How much will this car be worth in:

a 1 year?   **b** 3 years?   **c** 8 years?   **d** n years?

7 Nils invests his savings in an account that pays 6% interest compounded half yearly. If he puts $2300 into his account and leaves it there for two years, how much money will he have at the end of the period?

8 The total population of a developed country is decreasing at a rate of 0.6% per year. In 2022, the population of the country was 7.4 million people.

a What is the population likely to be in 2028 if it decreases at the same rate?

b How long will it take for the population to drop below 7 million people?

9 A colony of bacteria grows by 5% every hour. How long does it take for the colony to double in size?

INVESTIGATION

Is it worth it?

Sal says he would never buy a brand new car because it would lose value as soon as he drove it out of the dealership.

a Sal is correct about cars depreciating. Do your own research to find out how much new cars depreciate in the first year and then every year after that.

b A motoring magazine says that most cars lose between 15–30% of their value annually. This is quite a large range. What factors might affect the rate at which a new car depreciates?

c Once you have driven 150 000 km, your car is worth approximately 30% of its initial price. What would a car that cost $42 000 when new be worth at this stage?

d Given what you have found out, what advice would you give a young person about to buy their first car?

17.3 Buying and selling

When people trade, they buy goods, mark them up (decide on a price) and then sell them.

The price the trader pays for goods is called the **cost price**.

The price the goods are sold at is called the **selling price**.

If the selling price is higher than the cost price, the goods are sold at a **profit**.

If the selling price is lower than the cost price, the goods are sold at a **loss**.

Profit = selling price − cost price

Loss = cost price − selling price

Percentage profit and loss

Profit and loss are normally calculated as percentages of the cost price.

The following formulae are used to calculate percentage profit or loss:

$$\text{Percentage profit} = \frac{\text{profit}}{\text{cost price}} \times 100\%$$

$$\text{Percentage loss} = \frac{\text{loss}}{\text{cost price}} \times 100\%$$

> **MATHEMATICAL CONNECTIONS**
>
> Notice the similarity with percentage increases and decreases in Chapter 5.

WORKED EXAMPLE 16

A shopkeeper buys an article for $500 and sells it for $600. What is the percentage profit?

Answer

Profit = selling price − cost price

$\quad$ = $600 − $500

$\quad$ = $100

$$\text{Percentage profit} = \frac{\text{profit}}{\text{cost price}} \times 100\%$$

$$= \frac{\$100}{\$500} \times 100\%$$

$$= 20\%$$

WORKED EXAMPLE 17

A person buys a car for $16 000 and sells it for $12 000. Calculate the percentage loss.

Answer

Loss = cost price − selling price

$\quad$ = $16 000 − $12 000

$\quad$ = $4000

$$\text{Percentage loss} = \frac{\text{loss}}{\text{cost price}} \times 100\%$$

$$= \frac{\$4000}{\$16 000} \times 100\%$$

$$= 25\%$$

Exercise 17.8

1 For each of the following, find

   i   the profit

   ii the percentage profit.

Use an appropriate degree of accuracy where needed.

a   Cost price $20, selling price $25

b   Cost price $500, selling price $550

c   Cost price $1.50, selling price $1.80

d   Cost price 30 cents, selling price 35 cents

2   For each of the following, find
    i   the loss
    ii   the percentage loss.
    Use an appropriate degree of accuracy where needed.
    a   Cost price $400, selling price $300
    b   Cost price 75c, selling price 65c
    c   Cost price $5.00, selling price $4.75
    d   Cost price $6.50, selling price $5.85

3   A market trader buys 100 oranges for $30. She sells them for 50 cents each.
    Calculate the percentage profit or loss she made.

PEER ASSESSMENT

1   Exchange your answers to Exercise 17.8 with another student.

    Check and mark each other's work.

    Rate the work using the following scale:

4	3	2	1
You know what we are trying to do. You understand how to calculate percentage profit and loss. You can calculate percentages with and without using a calculator. You could clearly explain this work to someone else.	You mostly know what we are trying to do. You understood most of the work on percentage profit and loss. You could do most of the calculations but you made mistakes in some of them.	You need more practice. You got confused when you had to calculate with percentages. You could not do many of the calculations.	You really don't understand this at all. You need help with all aspects of this work.

2   If you rated the work 3, 2 or 1, write down the next step/s your partner could take to improve their rating.

Calculating the selling price, cost price and mark up

People who sell goods have to decide how much profit they want to make. In other words, they have to decide by how much they will mark up the cost price to make the selling price.

Cost price + % mark up = selling price

The cost price is always 100%. If you add 10% mark up, the selling price will be 110%.

WORKED EXAMPLE 18

At a market, a trader makes a profit of $1.08 on an item selling for $6.48. What is his percentage profit?

Answer

Cost price = $6.48 − $1.08 = $5.40   Subtract the profit from the selling price to find the cost price of the item.

$$\text{Percentage profit} = \frac{\text{profit}}{\text{cost price}} \times 100$$

$$= \frac{1.08}{5.40} \times 100$$

$$= 20\%$$

WORKED EXAMPLE 19

Find the selling price of an article bought for $400 and sold at a loss of 10%.

Answer

Cost price = $400

Loss = 10% of $400

$$= \frac{10}{100} \times 400$$

$$= \$40$$

Selling price = cost price − loss

$$= \$400 - \$40$$

$$= \$360$$

WORKED EXAMPLE 20

A trader sells her product for $39. If her mark up is 30%, what is the cost price of the product?

Answer

Cost price + mark up = selling price

Selling price = 130% of the cost price

So, $39 = 130% × selling price

To find 100%:

$\frac{39}{130} \times 100 = \$30$ Divide by 130 to find 1% and then multiply by 100 to find 100% (which is the cost price).

The cost price is $30.

Exercise 17.9

1   Find the price that each of each of the following items sold for:

   a   cost price $130, profit 20%

   b   cost price $320, profit 25%

   c   cost price $399, loss 15%

   d   cost price $750, loss $33\frac{1}{3}$%.

2   Find the selling price of an article that was bought for $750 and sold at a profit of 12%.

3   Calculate the selling price of a car bought for $3000 and sold at a profit of 7.5%.

4   Hakim bought a computer for $500. Two years later he sold it at a loss of 28%. What was his selling price?

5   An article costing $240 is sold at a loss of 8%. Find the selling price.

6   Kwame makes jewellery and sells it to her friends. Her costs to make ten rings are $377. She wants to sell them and make a 15% profit. What should she charge?

7   Tim sells burgers for $6.50 and makes a profit of $1.43 on each one. What is his percentage profit on cost price?

APPLY YOUR SKILLS

8   VAT at a rate of 17% is added *each* time an item is sold on. The original cost of an item is $112.00. The item is sold to a wholesaler, who sells it on to a retailer. The retailer sells it to the public.

   a   How much tax will the item have incurred?

   b   Express the tax as a percentage of the original price.

Discount

If items are not being sold as quickly as a shop would like or if they want to clear stock as new fashions come out, then goods may be sold at a **discount**.

Discount can be treated in the same way as percentage change (loss) as long as you remember that the percentage change is always calculated as a percentage of the original amount.

WORKED EXAMPLE 21

During a sale, a shop offers a discount of 15% on a pair of jeans originally priced at $75. What is the sale price?

Answer

$$\text{Discount} = 15\% \text{ of } \$75$$
$$= \frac{15}{100} \times 75$$
$$= \$11.25$$

$$\text{Sale price} = \text{original price} - \text{discount}$$
$$= \$75 - 11.25$$
$$= \$63.75$$

You can also work out the price by considering the sale price as a percentage of 100%.

100 − 15 = 85, so the sale price is 85% of $75:

$$\frac{85}{100} \times 75 = \$63.75$$

Exercise 17.10

1   Copy and complete the following table.

Original price ($)	% discount	Savings ($)	Sale price ($)
89.99	5		
125.99	10		
599.00	12		
22.50	7.5		
65.80	2.5		
10 000.00	23		

2 Calculate the percentage discount given on the following sales. Round your answer to the nearest whole per cent.

Original price ($)	Sale price ($)	% discount
89.99	79.99	
125.99	120.00	
599.00	450.00	
22.50	18.50	
65.80	58.99	
10 000.00	9500.00	

SELF ASSESSMENT

Choose emojis to reflect your thinking at the start of this chapter and your progress as you worked through the topics in this chapter.

Explain why you chose each emoji.

SUMMARY

Do you know …?

People in employment earn money for the work they do. This money can be paid as wages, salaries, commission or as a fee per item produced (piece work).

Gross earnings refers to how much you earn before deductions. Gross earnings − deductions = net earnings. Net earnings are what you actually receive as payment.

Companies are obliged by law to deduct tax and certain other amounts from earnings.

Simple interest is calculated per time period as a fixed percentage of the original amount (the principal).

The formula for finding simple interest is $I = \dfrac{PRT}{100}$.

Compound interest is interest added to the original amount at set intervals. This increases the principal and further interest is compounded. Most interest in real life situations is compounded.

The formula for calculating compound interest is $V = P\left(1 + \dfrac{r}{100}\right)^n$.

Hire purchase (HP) is a method of buying goods on credit and paying for them in instalments which include a flat rate of interest added to the original price.

When goods are sold at a profit they are sold for more than they cost. When they are sold at a loss they are sold for less than they cost. The original price is called the cost price. The price they are sold for is called the selling price. If goods are sold at a profit, selling price − cost price = profit. If they are sold at a loss, cost price − selling price = loss.

A discount is a reduction in the usual price of an item. A discount of 15% means you pay 15% less than the usual price.

SUMMARY CONTINUED

Are you able to …?
use given information to solve problems related to wages, salaries, commission and piece work
read information from tables and charts to work out deductions and tax rates
calculate gross and net earnings given the relevant information
use the formula to calculate simple interest
manipulate the simple interest formula to calculate the principal amount, rate of interest and time period of a debt or investment
solve problems related to HP payments and amounts
calculate compound interest over a given time period and solve problems related to compound interest
use exponential growth and decay in relation to finance and population changes
calculate the selling price, percentage profit or loss and actual mark up using given rates and prices
calculate the cost price using given rates and prices
work out the actual price of a discounted item and calculate the percentage discount given the original and the new price.

Practice questions

1 Kolo is paid $10.48 per hour for a standard 36-hour week. He is paid 'time-and-a-half' for all overtime worked. Calculate:

   a   his gross weekly earnings if he works $4\frac{3}{4}$ hours overtime   [3]

   b   the hours overtime worked if he earns $420.75 for the week.   [3]

2 Ahmed bought a book for $15. He sold it to Barbara, making a 20% loss.

   a   Calculate how much Barbara paid for it.   [3]

   b   Barbara later sold the book to Luvuyo. She made a 20% profit.

       Calculate how much Luvuyo paid for it.   [3]

3 Last year, Salma's wages were $94 per week. Her wages are now $102 per week. Calculate the percentage increase.   [3]

4 Yasmin is making iced lollies to sell outside her house on a hot day. She spends $25.55 on the ingredients. Yasmin uses all of the ingredients to sell 35 lollies at $1.25 each. Calculate:

   a   the total profit made   [2]

   b   the percentage profit.   [2]

5 Calculate the simple interest on $160 invested at 7% per year for three years. [2]

6 Senor Vasquez invests $500 in a Government Bond, at 9% compound interest per year. Calculate the value of the Bond after three years. [3]

7 Simon's salary has increased by 6% p.a. over the past three years. It is now $35 730.40 p.a.

   a Calculate Simon's salary per year three years ago. [3]

   b Find Simon's gross monthly salary at the present rate. [2]

   c The deductions each month amount to 22.5% of the gross salary. Calculate Simon's net pay per month. [2]

8 A new car cost $14 875. Three years later, the insurance company valued it at $10 700. Calculate the percentage reduction in value over the three years. [3]

9 Exercise equipment advertised at $2200 is reduced in a sale to $1950. Calculate the percentage discount. [3]

10 A motor dealer tries to sell a car at 35% above the $18 000 which he paid to a supplier.

   a Calculate the dealer's selling price. [3]

   b Calculate the percentage reduction the dealer can now apply before making a loss. [3]

11 The value of an asset, currently priced at $100 000, is expected to increase by 20% per year.

   a Find its value in ten years' time. [3]

   b After how many years will it be worth more than $1 million? [3]

12 The temperature of a cup of water is decreasing. The temperature, $T°C$, is recorded t minutes after the water is left to cool. The results are shown in the table.

t (minutes)	2	4	6	8	10	12	14
T (°C)	96	80.6	67.7	56.9	47.8	40.1	33.7

   a By calculating the percentage change in temperature from one calculation to the next, show that this is exponential decay. [3]

   b Plot a graph to show the data in the table. [4]

   c Estimate the time in minutes after the water was left to cool that the temperature reached 60 °C. [2]

SELF ASSESSMENT

Find any errors in your work.

For each one, decide what type of error you made:

- **careless** (writing the wrong number, not following instructions, forgetting to give reasons, not showing steps in calculation)
- **computational** (miscalculating a value using the basic operations)
- **precision** (mistakes with signs, decimal places, forgetting brackets or order of operations, missing units, incorrect notation)
- **mathematical** (not using properties or rules, not completing all the steps needed to solve the problem).

Write down three suggestions to help yourself avoid these errors in the future.

> Chapter 18

Curved graphs

The Adelie penguins in the photograph are diving off an iceberg into the water. Their height above and below the water can be graphed against time. What would you expect the shape of the graph to look like? Why?

In Chapter 10 you saw that many problems can be represented by linear equations and straight line graphs. Real-life problems, such as those involving area; the path of a moving object; the shape of a bridge or other structure; the growth of bacteria; and variation in speed, can only be solved using non-linear equations. Graphs of non-linear equations are curves.

In this chapter you are going to use tables of values to plot a range of curved graphs. Once you understand the properties of the different graphs, you will use these to sketch the graphs (rather than plotting them). You will also learn how to interpret curved graphs and how to find the approximate solution of equations from graphs.

GETTING STARTED

1   The graph shows the first stages of a penguin's dive from an iceberg into the ocean.

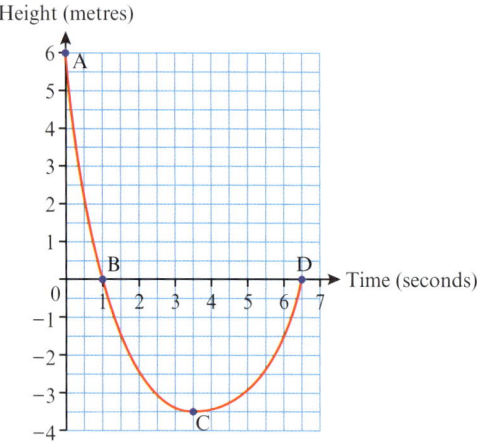

a   Explain what is happening to the penguin from A to B, B to C and C to D.

b   From what height did the penguin dive?

c   How long did it take for the penguin to enter the water?

d   What is the greatest depth the penguin reaches during this dive?

e   How much time did the penguin spend under the surface of the water?

f   What do you think the graph would look like if you continued it to the right? Why?

KEY WORDS

asymptote

derivative of function

differentiation

exponential

hyperbola

maximum

minimum

parabola

stationary point

turning point

2   Here are three sets of quadratic graphs.

Set A

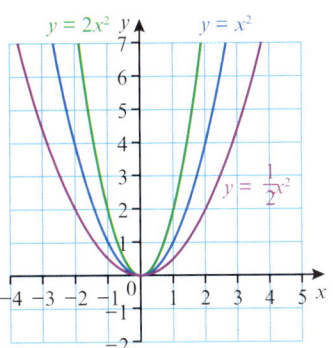

Set B

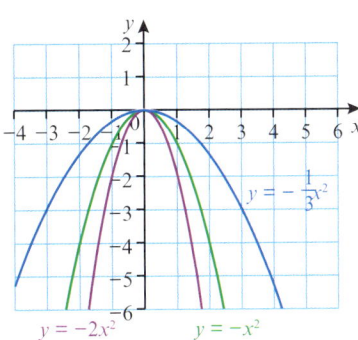

Set C

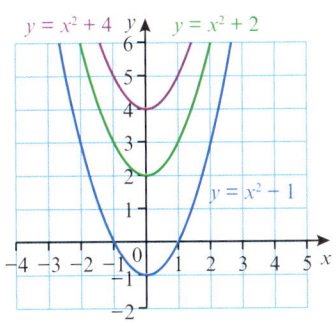

a   How are the graphs in each set similar?

b   How are they different?

c   Describe in your own words the effect that the coefficient of the x^2 term has on the shape of the graph.

d   The general equation for the graphs in set C is $y = x^2 + a$.

   i   What does a tell you about a quadratic graph?

   ii   What effect does the value of a have on the graph?

18.1 Review of quadratic graphs (the parabola)

In Chapter 10 you learnt that quadratic equations have an x^2 term as their highest power. The simplest quadratic equation for a quadratic graph is $y = x^2$.

Here is a table showing the values for $y = x^2$ from $-3 \leqslant x \leqslant 3$.

x	−3	−2	−1	0	1	2	3
$y = x^2$	9	4	1	0	1	4	9

You can use these points to plot and draw a graph just as you did with linear equations. The graph of a quadratic relationship is called a **parabola**.

Here is the table of values for $y = -x^2$ from $-3 \leqslant x \leqslant 3$.

x	−3	−2	−1	0	1	2	3
$y = -x^2$	−9	−4	−1	0	−1	−4	−9

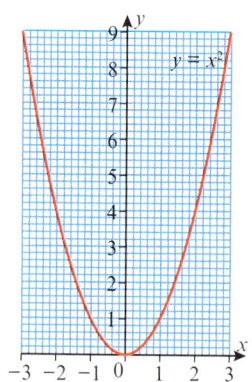

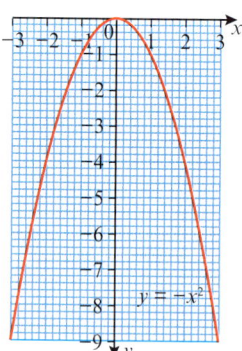

When you plot these points and draw the parabola you can see that the negative sign in front of the x^2 has the effect of turning the graph so that it faces downwards.

If the coefficient x^2 of in the equation is positive, the parabola is a 'valley' shaped curve.

If the coefficient of x^2 in the equation is negative, the parabola is a 'hill' shaped curve.

The axis of symmetry and the turning point

The axis of symmetry is the line which divides the parabola into two symmetrical halves. In the two graphs on the previous page, the y-axis ($x = 0$) is the axis of symmetry.

The **turning point** or vertex of the graph is the point at which it changes direction. For both of the graphs, $y = x^2$ and $y = -x^2$, the turning point is at the origin $(0, 0)$.

> **TIP**
>
> For most graphs, a turning point is a local minimum or maximum value of y. For a parabola, if the x^2 term is positive the turning point will be a minimum. If the x^2 term is negative, the turning point will be a maximum.

Exercise 18.1

1   Complete the following tables of values and plot the graphs on the *same* set of axes. Use values of -8 to 12 on the y-axis.

> **TIP**
>
> Remember that if you square a negative number the result will be positive. If using your calculator, place brackets round any negative numbers.

a

x	−3	−2	−1	0	1	2	3
y = x² + 1							

b

x	−3	−2	−1	0	1	2	3
y = x² + 3							

c

x	−3	−2	−1	0	1	2	3
y = x² − 2							

d

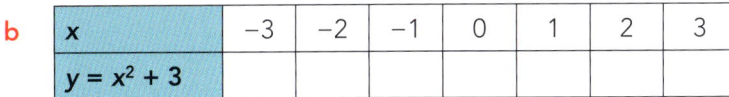

x	−3	−2	−1	0	1	2	3
y = −x² + 1							

e

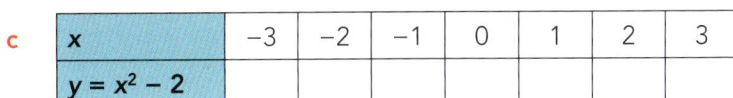

x	−3	−2	−1	0	1	2	3
y = 3 − x²							

f   What happens to the graph when the value of the constant term changes?

> **LINK**
>
> If you throw an object and ignore any air resistance, the path of the object can be described using a quadratic curve. The symmetry and overall shape of the curve makes it possible to work out things like the maximum height and the distance the object will travel horizontally.

2   Match each of the five parabolas shown here to its equation.

   a $y = 4 - x^2$

   b $y = x^2 - 4$

   c $y = x^2 + 2$

   d $y = 2 - x^2$

   e $y = -x^2 - 2$

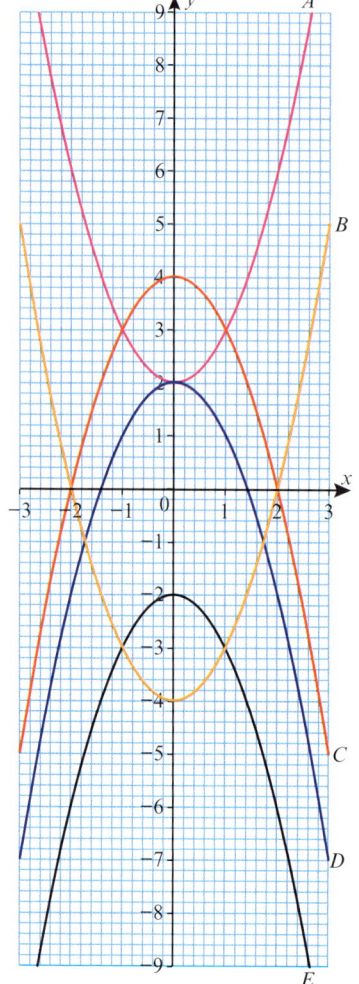

TIP

These equations are all of the form $y = -x^2 + c$, where c is the constant term. The constant term is the y-intercept of the graph in each case.

REFLECTION

Students sometimes convince themselves that they understand a concept once they have successfully done a few examples and memorised the processes.

Do you ever do that?

This approach is counter-productive and doesn't help you master key concepts. Explain why, and suggest two things you can do to focus on fully understanding what you are learning.

Equations of the form $y = x^2 + ax + b$

You can construct a table of values to plot graphs of quadratic equations of the form $y = x^2 + ax + b$. For these tables, you usually work out each term on a separate row and then add them to find the value of y. Read through the two worked examples carefully to make sure you understand this.

WORKED EXAMPLE 1

Construct a table of values for $y = x^2 + 2x - 1$ for values $-4 \leqslant x \leqslant 2$.

Plot the points to draw the graph.

Answer

x	−4	−3	−2	−1	0	1	2
x^2	16	9	4	1	0	1	4
2x	−8	−6	−4	−2	0	2	4
−1	−1	−1	−1	−1	−1	−1	−1
$y = x^2 + 2x - 1$	7	2	−1	−2	−1	2	7

In this table, you work out each term separately.

Add the terms of the equation in each column to get the totals for the last row (the y-values of each point).

To draw the graph:

*   plot the points and join them to make a smooth curve
*   label the graph with its equation.

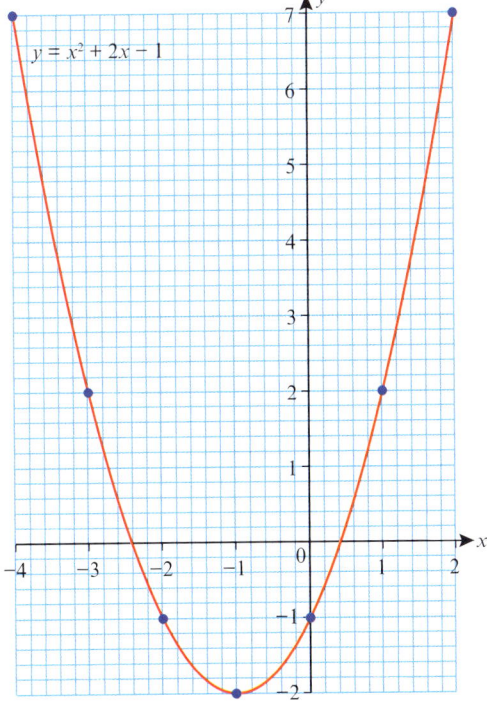

$y = x^2 + 2x - 1$

WORKED EXAMPLE 2

Draw the graph of $y = 6 + x - x^2$ for values of x from -3 to 4.

Answer

x	−3	−2	−1	0	1	2	3	4
6	6	6	6	6	6	6	6	6
+x	−3	−2	−1	0	1	2	3	4
−x²	−9	−4	−1	0	−1	−4	−9	−16
y = 6 + x − x²	−6	0	4	6	6	4	0	−6

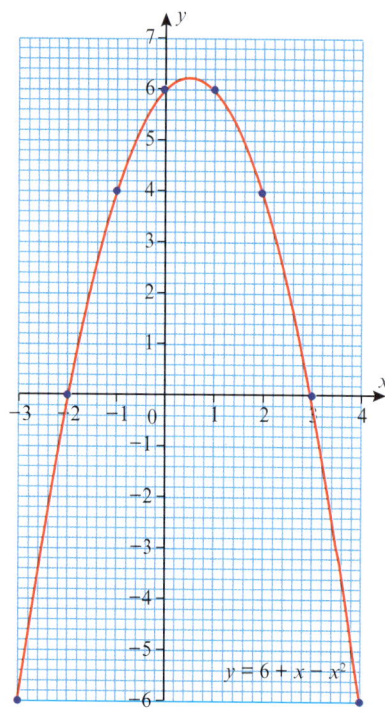

To plot the graph of a quadratic relationship:
- complete a table of values (often some of the values will be given)
- draw the axes with a ruler and label them
- plot the (x, y) values from the table of values
- join the points with a smooth curve.

LINK

Parabolas are part of a family of curves called 'conic sections'. These curves include parabolas, hyperbolas and ellipses. You can make each of them by cutting a cone in different directions. The conic sections also describe the possible paths of planets, comets and meteorites in the solar system.

TIP

Some calculators have an in-built function to create tables of values. These can help you avoid errors provided you use them correctly. However, make sure that you can still do the calculations without the table function.

Exercise 18.2

1   Construct a table of values for $y = x^2 - 2x + 2$ for $-1 \leqslant x \leqslant 3$ and use the (x, y) points from the table to plot and draw the graph.

2   Copy and complete this table of values and then draw the graph of $y = x^2 - 5x - 4$.

x	−2	−1	0	1	2	3	4	5	6
x^2	4								
$-5x$	10								
−4	−4	−4	−4	−4	−4	−4	−4	−4	−4
y									

3   Construct a table of values for $y = x^2 + 2x - 3$ from $-3 \leqslant x \leqslant 2$. Plot the points and join them to draw the graph.

4   Using values of x from 0 to 4, construct a table of values and use it to draw the graph of $y = -x^2 - 4x$.

5   Using values of x from −6 to 0, construct a table of values and use it to draw the graph of $y = -x^2 - 6x - 5$.

APPLY YOUR SKILLS

6   People who design water displays (often set to music) need to know how high water will rise from a jet and how long it will take to return to the pool. This graph shows the height (in metres) of a water arc from a fountain over a number of seconds.

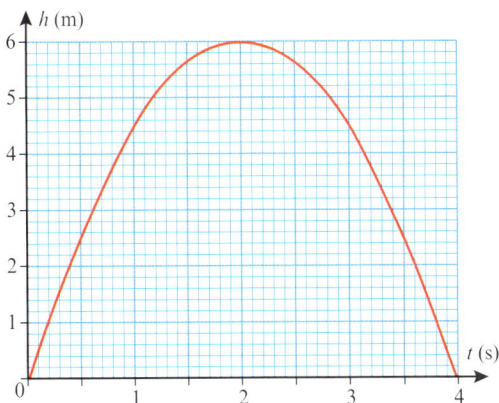

a   What was the greatest height reached by the water arc?

b   How long did it take the water to reach the greatest height?

c   For how long was the water arc above a height of 2.5 m?

d   How far did the water rise in the first second?

e   Why do you think this graph shows only positive values of height?

Sketching quadratic functions

You can use the characteristics of the parabola to sketch a graph without drawing up a table of values. Your sketch should show the general features of the graph but it does not have to be accurately plotted on graph paper.

Sketching simple quadratic functions

When the equation is of the form $y = ax^2$ or $y = ax^2 + c$:

- Check the sign of a to decide whether the graph is ∪ or ∩ shaped. If a is positive the graph will be ∪ shaped, if a is negative the graph will be ∩ shaped.

- Find the y-intercept by making $x = 0$ in the equation. The coordinates of the y-intercept are $(0, c)$.

- Calculate the x-intercepts by substituting $y = 0$ into the equation. If the graph has no x-intercepts, you must work out the coordinates of one point on the graph.

- Mark the values you have worked out on the axis and draw a smooth curve to complete the graph. Remember to label the graph with its equation.

WORKED EXAMPLE 3

Sketch the graph of $y = 2x^2$.

Answer

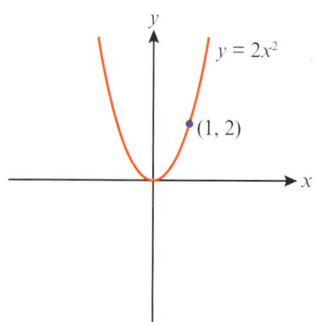

The coefficient of x is $+2$, so the graph is ∪ shaped.

There is no constant, c, so the y-intercept is 0 and the graph goes through the origin.

When $y = 0$, $x = 0$, so there is only one solution for x and you need to find a point on the graph.

Using $x = 1$ substitute into the equation: $y = 2(1)^2 = 2$. So $(1, 2)$ is a point on the graph.

Sketch and label the graph.

TIP

Graphs of the form $y = ax^2 + c$ are symmetrical about the y-axis and the turning point is on the y-axis.

WORKED EXAMPLE 4

Sketch and label the graph of $y = -x^2 + 4$.

Answer

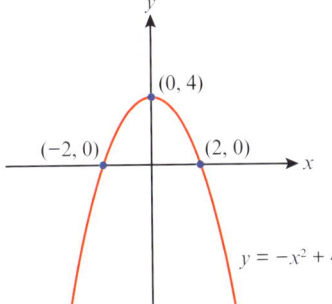

The coefficient of x is -1, so the graph is $\cap$ shaped.

The constant, c is 4, so the y-intercept is $(0, 4)$.

When $y = 0$,
$-x^2 + 4 = 0$

$\Rightarrow x^2 - 4 = 0$

$\Rightarrow x^2 = 4$

$\Rightarrow x = \pm\sqrt{4}$

So $x = -2$ or 2

The x-intercepts are $(-2, 0)$ and $(2, 0)$.

Sketch and label the graph.

Turning points

To find the coordinates of the turning point of a parabola, you need to find the axis of symmetry.

When the equation is in standard form $y = ax^2 + bx + c$, you can find the axis of symmetry using $x = -\dfrac{b}{2a}$. This gives the x-coordinate of the turning point.

You can then find the y-coordinate of the turning point by substituting the value of x into the original equation. This y-value is the **minimum** or **maximum** value of the graph.

> **TIP**
>
> The turning point of a parabola is the minimum or maximum point of the graph. For the graph $y = ax^2 + bx + c$, the turning point is a maximum if a is negative and a minimum if a is positive.

Sketching quadratic functions of the form $y = ax^2 + bx + c$

When the equation is in the standard form $y = ax^2 + bx + c$:

* Identify the shape of the graph. If the x^2 term is positive the graph is $\cup$ shaped; if the x^2 term is negative, the graph is $\cap$ shaped.
* Find the y-intercept by making $x = 0$. The coordinates of the y-intercept are $(0, c)$.
* Calculate the x-intercepts by substituting $y = 0$ into the equation and solving for x. If there is only one intercept then the graph just touches the x-axis.
* Find the axis of symmetry and the coordinates of the turning point.
* Use what you know about the shape of the graph and its symmetry to draw a smooth curve. Label the graph.

WORKED EXAMPLE 5

Sketch the graph of $y = x^2 + 2x - 3$.

Answer

x^2 is positive, so the graph is ∪ shaped.

y-intercept = $(0, -3)$ Remember that there is only ever one y-intercept.

To find the x-intercepts make $y = 0$, so
$x^2 + 2x - 3 = 0$
$(x + 3)(x - 1) = 0$
$x = -3$ or $x = 1$
So, $(-3, 0)$ and $(1, 0)$ are the x-intercepts.

The axis of symmetry is $x = -\dfrac{b}{2a} = -\dfrac{2}{2(1)} = -1$.

Substitute $x = -1$ to find the turning point: $(-1, -4)$.

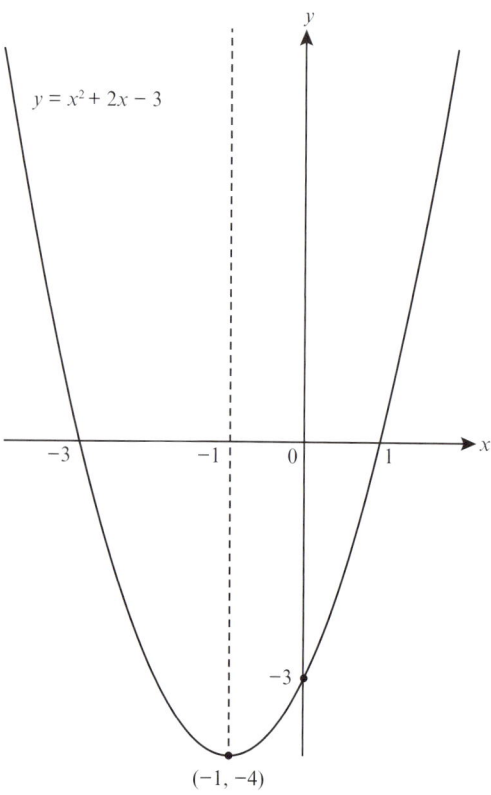

TIP

The graph is symmetrical about the vertical line halfway between the x-intercepts. This gives another way to find the line of symmetry. Halfway between $x = -3$ and $x = 1$ is $x = -1$.

WORKED EXAMPLE 6

Sketch the graph $y = -2x^2 - 4x + 6$.

Answer

$a = -2$, so the graph is $\cap$ shaped.

The y-intercept $= (0, 6)$

Find the x-intercepts:

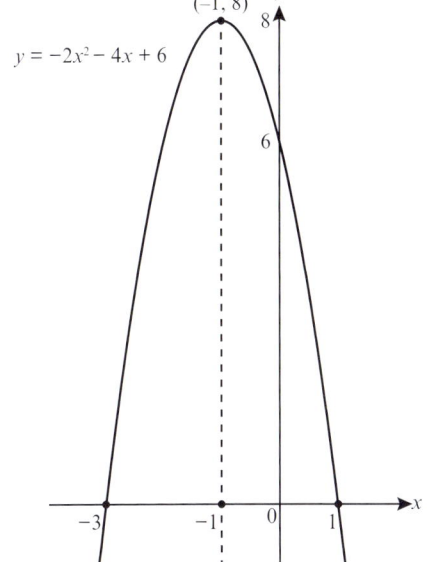

$-2x^2 - 4x + 6 = 0$ Divide both sides by common factor -2.

$x^2 + 2x - 3 = 0$

$(x - 1)(x + 3) = 0$ Factorise the trinomial.

$x = 1$ or $x = -3$ Solve for x.

$(1, 0)$ and $(-3, 0)$ are the x-intercepts.

Find the axis of symmetry using $x = -\dfrac{b}{2a}$.

$x = \dfrac{4}{2(-2)} = -1$ Remember this is the x-coordinate of the turning point.

Substitute $x = -1$ into the equation to find the y-coordinate of the turning point.

$y = -2(-1)^2 - 4(-1) + 6 = 8$

The turning point is at $(-1, 8)$ and is a maximum because a is negative.

Sketch the graph and label all the important features.

Find the turning point by completing the square

You can find the coordinates of the turning point of a parabola algebraically by completing the square. This involves changing the quadratic equation from the form $y = ax^2 + bx + c = 0$ to the form $y = a(x + p)^2 + q$. In this form, the turning point of a parabola has the coordinates $(-p, q)$.

Consider the equation $y = x^2 + 4x - 5$.

You can rewrite this in completed square form as $y = (x + 2)^2 - 9$.

Squaring any value gives an answer that is either positive or 0. So, for any value of x, the smallest possible value of $(x + 2)^2$ is 0.

This means that the minimum value of $(x + 2)^2 - 9$ is -9 and that this occurs when $x = -2$.

The turning point of the graph $y = (x + 2)^2 - 9$ has the coordinates $(-2, -9)$.

> **MATHEMATICAL CONNECTIONS**
>
> You learned how to solve quadratic equations by completing the square in Chapter 14. Revise that section now if you've forgotten how to do this.

WORKED EXAMPLE 7

a Determine the equation of the axis of symmetry and the turning point of $y = x^2 - 8x + 13$ by completing the square.

b Sketch the graph.

Answers

a $y = x^2 - 8x + 13$ First complete the square.

    $y = (x - 4)^2 - 16 + 13$ Half of 8 is four, but $(x - 4)^2 = x^2 - 8x + 16$ so you have to subtract 16 to keep the equation balanced.

    $y = (x - 4)^2 - 3$ Simplify your solution.

    Turning point: $(4, -3)$

    Axis of symmetry: $x = 4$

b To sketch the graph, you must find the intercepts.

    y-intercept $= (0, 13)$ You can read this from the original equation.

    To find the x-intercept(s), let $y = 0$ and solve.

    $0 = (x - 4)^2 - 3$

    $3 = (x - 4)^2$

    $x - 4 = \pm\sqrt{3}$ Remember that there is a negative and a positive root.

    $x = \pm\sqrt{3} + 4$

    $x = 5.7$ or 2.3

    Sketch the graph and label it.

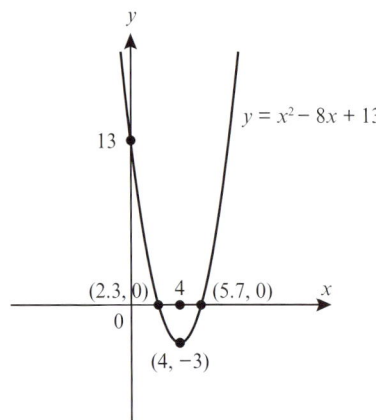

Exercise 18.3

1   Sketch the following graphs. Indicate the y-intercept. Label the x-intercepts where they exist or give the position of one point on the graph.

   a $y = -3x^2$ **b** $y = 3x^2$ **c** $y = \frac{1}{2}x^2$

   d $y = x^2 - 4$ **e** $y = -x^2 + 9$ **f** $y = 3x^2 - 12$

   g $y = -2x^2 + \frac{1}{2}$

2   Sketch the following graphs. Indicate the axis of symmetry and the coordinates of the turning point on each graph.

   a $y = x^2 + 6x - 5$ **b** $2x^2 + 4x = y$

   c $y = 3 - (x + 1)^2$ **d** $y = 4 - 2(x + 3)^2$

   e $y = 17 + 6x - x^2$ **f** $y = 5 - 8x + 2x^2$

   g $y = 1 + 2x - 2x^2$ **h** $y = -(x + 2)^2 - 1$

3   Nadia sketched the following graphs and forgot to label them. Use the information on the sketch to determine the equation of each graph.

a

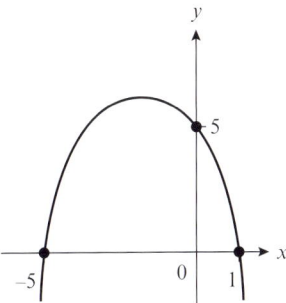

b

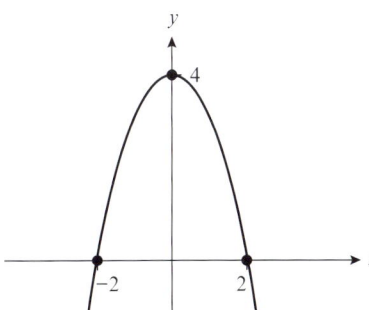

c

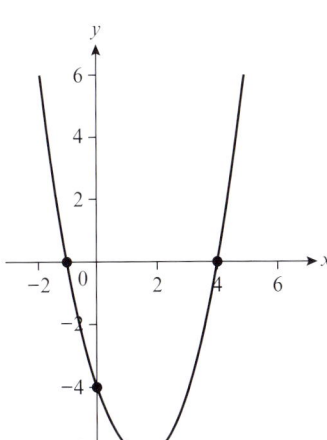

d

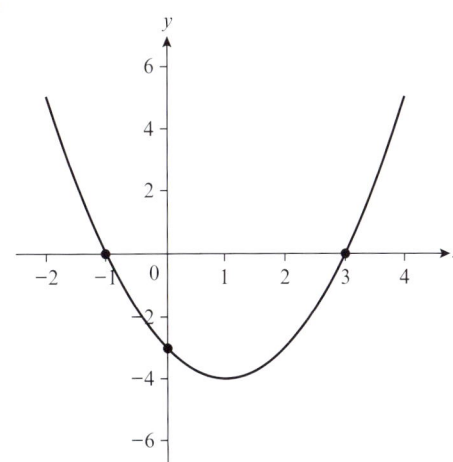

4   The equation for the curved supporting arch of a bridge (shown in red on the diagram) is given by $h = -\dfrac{1}{40}(x - 20)^2$, where h m is the distance below the base of the bridge and x m is the distance from the left side.

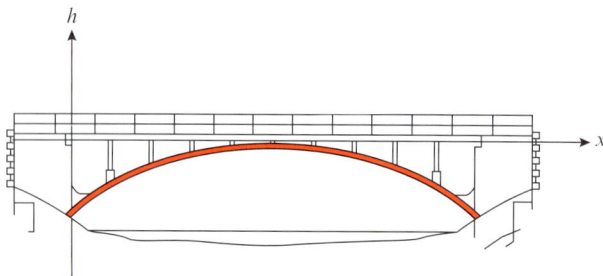

   a   Determine the turning point of the graph of the relationship.

   b   What are the possible values for x?

   c   Determine the range of values of h.

   d   Sketch a graph of the equation within the possible values.

   e   What is the width of the supporting arch?

   f   What is the maximum height of the supporting arch?

Maths often builds on key concepts from earlier learning. Explain how a firm foundation and understanding of earlier concepts allows you to move on to mastery of more complex ideas and problems

18.2 Drawing reciprocal graphs (the hyperbola)

Equations of the form $y = \dfrac{a}{x}$ (where a is a whole number) are called reciprocal equations. Graphs of reciprocal equations are called **hyperbolas**. These graphs have a very characteristic shape. Although it is one graph, it consists of two non-connected curves that are mirror images of each other, drawn in opposite quadrants.

Here is a table of values for $y = \dfrac{6}{x}$.

x	−6	−5	−4	−3	−2	−1	1	2	3	4	5	6
$y = \dfrac{6}{x}$	−1	−1.2	−1.5	−2	−3	−6	6	3	2	1.5	1.2	1

> **TIP**
>
> Include at least five negative and five positive values in the table of values to draw a hyperbola because it has two separate curves.

When you plot these points, you get this graph.

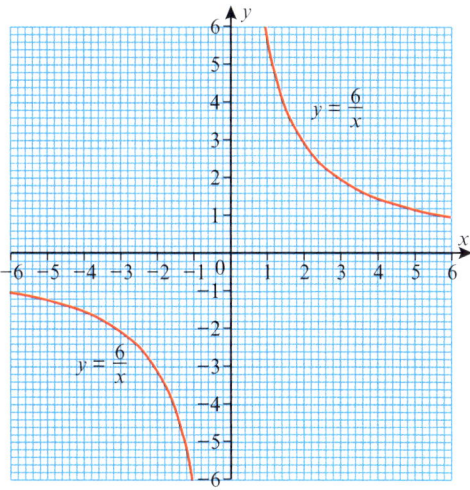

Notice the following about the graph:

* it has two parts which are the same shape and size, but in opposite quadrants
* the curve is symmetrical
* the curve approaches the axes, but it will never touch them
* there is no value of y for $x = 0$ and no value of x for $y = 0$.

An **asymptote** is a line that a graph approaches but never intersects. When the equation is of the form $y = \frac{a}{x}$, the curve approaches both axes and gets closer and closer to them without ever touching them.

For other reciprocal equations, the asymptotes may not be the axes, in these cases, they are normally shown on the graph using dotted lines.

MATHEMATICAL CONNECTIONS

Reciprocal graphs occur in inverse proportion problems. You will study inverse proportion in Chapter 21.

WORKED EXAMPLE 8

Construct a table of values and then draw a graph of $xy = -12$ ($x \neq 0$) for $-12 \leqslant x \leqslant 12$.

Answer

$xy = -12$ is the same as $y = -\frac{12}{x}$.

You do not need all 24 points to draw the graph, so work out every second value.

x	−12	−10	−8	−3	−4	−2	2	4	6	8	10	12
$y = -\frac{12}{x}$	1	1.2	1.5	4	3	6	−6	−3	−2	−1.5	−1.2	−1

WORKED EXAMPLE 8 CONTINUED

Plot the points to draw the graph.

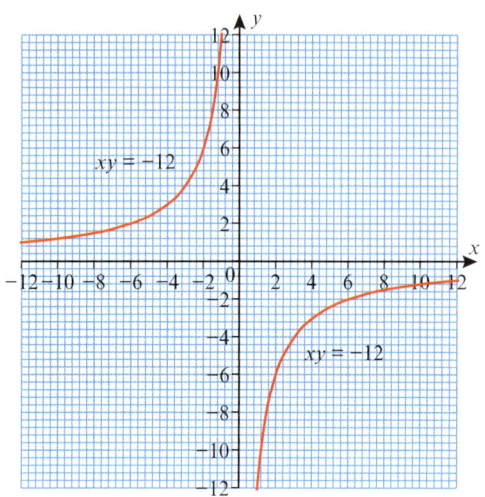

Notice that the graph of $xy = -12$ is in the top left and bottom right quadrants.

This is because the value of the constant term $\left(a \text{ in the equation } y = \dfrac{a}{x} \right)$ is negative.

When a is a positive value, the hyperbola will be in the top right and bottom left quadrants.

TIP

The quadrants are labelled in an anti-clockwise direction. The coordinates of any point in the first quadrant will always be positive.

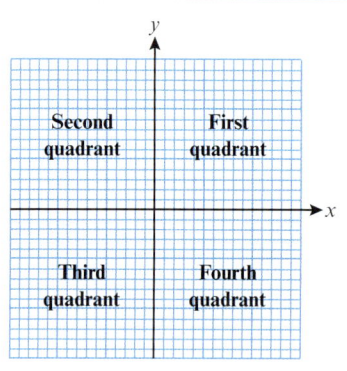

To plot the graph of a reciprocal relationship:

- complete a table of values (often some of the values will be given)
- draw the axes with a ruler and label them
- plot the (x, y) values from the table of values
- join the points with a smooth curve
- write the equation on both parts of the graph.

Sketching graphs of reciprocal functions

As with the parabola, you can use the features of the hyperbola (reciprocal function) to sketch the graph.

When the equation is in standard form $y = \frac{a}{x} + q$ $(x \neq 0)$ follow these steps to sketch the graph.

Step 1: Identify the shape of the graph.

The value of a determines where the curves will be on the graph.

If $a > 0$, the y-values are positive for positive x-values and negative for negative x.

If $a < 0$, the y-values are negative for positive x-values and positive for negative x.

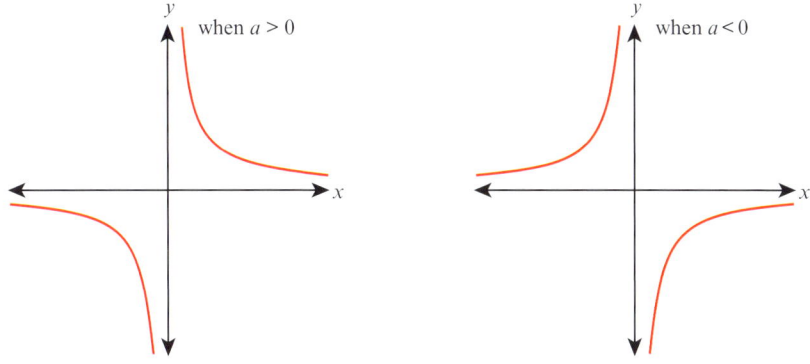

Step 2: Work out whether the graph intercepts the x-axis using q. If $q \neq 0$, the graph will have one x-intercept. Make $y = 0$ to find the value of the x-intercept.

$0 = \frac{a}{x} + q$

So, $-q = \frac{a}{x}$

$-qx = a$

$x = -\frac{a}{q}$

Step 3: Determine the asymptotes. One asymptote is the y-axis (the line $x = 0$). The other is the line $y = q$.

Step 4: Using the asymptotes and the x-intercept, sketch and label the graph.

> **TIP**
>
> If $q = 0$, the x-axis is the other asymptote.

WORKED EXAMPLE 9

Sketch and label the graph of $y = \dfrac{3}{x} + 3$.

Answer

Position of the curves:

$a = 3$, so $a > 0$

Asymptotes:

$x = 0$

$y = 3$

x-intercept:

$0 = \dfrac{3}{x} + 3$

$-3 = \dfrac{3}{x}$

$x = -1$

x-intercept $(-1, 0)$

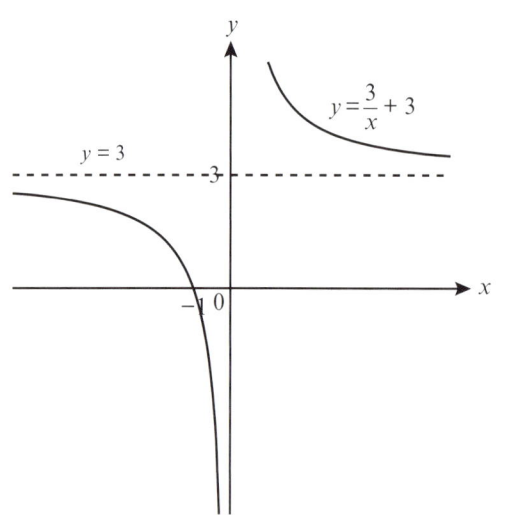

Exercise 18.4

1   Copy and complete the following tables giving values of y correct to 1 decimal place. Use the points to plot each graph on a separate set of axes.

a

x	−6	−4	−3	−2	−1	1	2	3	4	6
$y = \dfrac{2}{x}$										

b

x	−5	−4	−3	−2	−1	1	2	3	4	5
$y = -\dfrac{1}{x}$										

c

x	−6	−4	−3	−2	−1	1	2	3	4	6
$y = -\dfrac{6}{x}$										

d

x	−6	−4	−3	−2	−1	1	2	3	4	6
$y = \dfrac{4}{x}$										

2   Sketch and label the following graphs on separate sets of axes.

a $y = \dfrac{3}{x}$

b $xy = -4$

c $y = \dfrac{1}{x} + 3$

d $2y = \dfrac{4}{x} + 7$

e $y = \dfrac{4}{x} + 2$

f $y = -\dfrac{9}{x} - 3$

TIP

Rewrite the equation in standard form before you sketch the graph.

APPLY YOUR SKILLS

3   A person makes a journey of 240 km. The average speed is x km/h and the time the journey takes is y hours.

   a   Complete the table of corresponding values for x and y.

x	20	40	60	80	100	120
y	12		4			2

   b   On a set of axes, draw a graph to represent the relationship between x and y.

   c   Write down the relationship between x and y in its algebraic form.

INVESTIGATION

4   Investigate what happens when the equation of a graph is $y = \dfrac{1}{x^2}$.

   a   Copy and complete the table of values for x-values between -4 and 4.

x	-4	-3	-2	-1	$-\dfrac{1}{2}$	$\dfrac{1}{2}$	1	2	3	4
y										

   b   Plot the points to draw the graph.

   c   How is your graph different from the hyperbola?

   d   Why do we not use $x = 0$ in the table of values?

   e   What are the asymptotes of the graph you have drawn?

   f   As with the hyperbola, the standard form $y = \dfrac{1}{x^2} + q$ can be used to work out the asymptotes. Given $y = \dfrac{1}{x^2} + 3$, what will the asymptotes be?

   g   Use what you have learned in your investigation to sketch the following graphs.

   i $y = -\dfrac{1}{x^2}$ **ii** $y = x^{-2} + 2$

   h   Explain in your own words how a graph in the general form $y = ax^{-1}$ is different from $y = ax^{-2}$. (Consider negative and positive values of a.)

LINK

The reciprocal of a square appears in the formula Isaac Newton developed for the force of gravity between two masses placed a distance r metres apart:

$F = \dfrac{G m_1 m_2}{r^2}$.

18.3 Using graphs to solve quadratic equations

Suppose you were asked to solve the equation $x^2 - 3x - 1 = 0$.

To do this, you would need to find the value or values of x that make $x^2 - 3x - 1$ equal to 0.

You can try to do this by trial and error, but you will find that the value of x you need is not a whole number (in fact, it lies between the values of 3 and 4).

It is much quicker and easier to draw the graph of the equation $y = x^2 - 3x - 1$ and to use that to find a solution to the equation. Here is the graph:

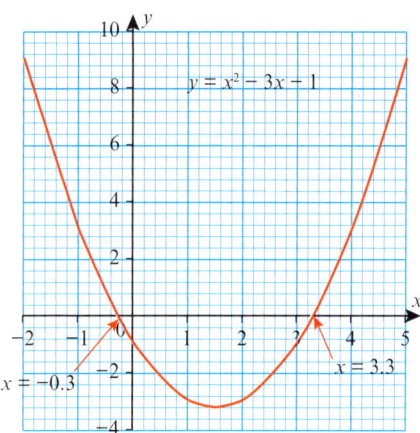

The solution to the equation is the point (or points) where $y = 0$, in other words you are looking for the value of x where the graph crosses the x-axis.

If you look at the graph you can see that it crosses the x-axis in two places. The value of x at these points is 3.3 and -0.3.

These two values are sometimes referred to as the roots of the equation $x^2 - 3x - 1 = 0$.

You can use the graph to find the solution of the equation for different values of x. Work through Worked example 10 carefully to see how to do this.

WORKED EXAMPLE 10

This is the graph of $y = x^2 - 2x - 7$. Use the graph to solve the following equations.

a $x^2 - 2x - 7 = 0$

b $x^2 - 2x - 7 = 3$

c $x^2 - 2x = 1$

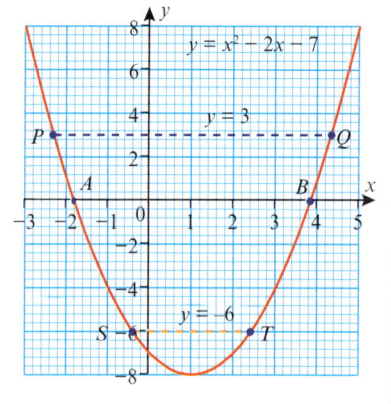

WORKED EXAMPLE 10 CONTINUED

Answers

a   Since this is the graph of $y = x^2 - 2x - 7$ simply find the points on the curve that have a y-coordinate of 0 (i.e. where the curve cuts the x-axis).

There are two such points marked A and B on the graph.

The x-coordinates of these points are -1.8 and 3.8, so the solutions of the equation $x^2 - 2x - 7 = 0$ are $x = -1.8$ and $x = 3.8$.

b   Find the points on the curve that have a y-coordinate of 3. (Draw in the horizontal line $y = 3$ to help with this.)

There are two such points, marked P and Q, on the graph.

The x-coordinates of these points are -2.3 and 4.3, so the solutions of the equation $x^2 - 2x - 7 = 3$ are $x = -2.3$ and $x = 4.3$.

c   Rearrange the equation $x^2 - 2x = 1$ so that the left-hand side matches the equation of the graph you are using.

Subtracting 7 from both sides gives $x^2 - 2x - 7 = 1 - 7$, that is $x^2 - 2x - 7 = -6$.

You can now proceed as you did in parts (a) and (b).

Find the points on the curve that have a y-coordinate of -6; they are marked S and T on the graph.

The x-coordinates of these points are -0.4 and 2.4.

The solutions of the equation $x^2 - 2x = 1$ are $x = -0.4$ and $x = 2.4$.

In summary, to solve a quadratic equation graphically:
* read off the x-coordinates of any points of intersection for the given y-values
* you may need to rearrange the original equation to do this.

Exercise 18.5

1   Use this graph of the relationship $y = x^2 - x - 2$ to solve the following equations.

   a $x^2 - x - 2 = 0$

   b $x^2 - x - 2 = 6$

   c $x^2 - x = 6$

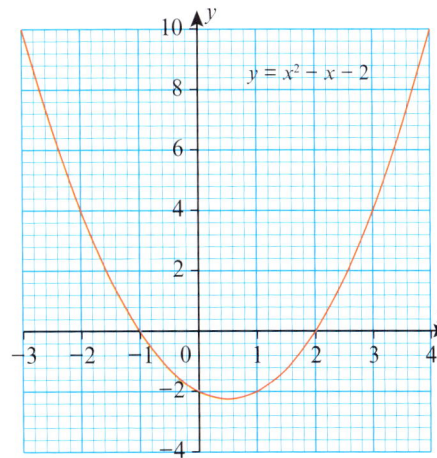

2 **a** Construct a table of values for $y = -x^2 - x + 1$ for values $-3 \leqslant x \leqslant 2$.

b Plot the points on a grid and join them with a smooth curve.

c Use your graph to solve the equation $-x^2 - x + 1 = 0$. Give your answer correct to 1 decimal place.

3 Solve the following equations by drawing suitable graphs over the given intervals.

a $x^2 - x - 3 = 0 \ (-3 \leqslant x \leqslant 4)$

b $x^2 + 3x + 1 = 0 \ (-4 \leqslant x \leqslant 1)$

4 **a** Use an interval of $-2 \leqslant x \leqslant 4$ to draw the graph $y = 4 - x^2 + 2x$.

b Use the graph to solve the following equations.

i $0 = 4 - x^2 + 2x$ **ii** $0 = -x^2 + 2x$

5 **a** Draw the graph of $y = x^2 - 2x - 4$ for values of x from -2 to 4.

b Use your graph to find approximate solutions to the following equations.

i $x^2 - 2x - 4 = 0$ **ii** $x^2 - 2x - 4 = 3$ **iii** $x^2 - 2x - 4 = -1$

SELF ASSESSMENT

Develop a set of success criteria to assess your understanding of curved graphs.

1 Draw a table like this one:

Success criteria	Evidence of success	Improvements

> **TIP**
>
> Success criteria are sometimes called 'what I'm looking for'. Refer back to Chapter 3 for guidance on this type of self assessment.

2 Look back at the learning intentions at the start of this chapter. Use these to develop a list of criteria that you can use to decide whether you have met the learning intentions for graphs of quadratic and reciprocal functions. For example:

I can use a table of values to plot graphs of equations of the form $y = x^2 + ax + b$.

3 Once you have your list, check your work against the success criteria.

- Place a tick (✓) in the second column if you can find evidence that you have met each one. (You are looking for how your work shows you have achieved the criteria.)

- If you cannot find evidence, write down what you can do to improve in that particular area.

4 Make any improvements that you need to over the next few days and then reassess your work using the same criteria.

18.4 Simultaneous linear and non-linear equations

As you did with linear equations, you can use graphs to solve a linear and a non-linear equation, or two non-linear equations simultaneously.

MATHEMATICAL CONNECTIONS

In Chapter 14 you learnt how to use the point of intersection of two straight lines to find the solutions to simultaneous linear equations. Revise that section now if you cannot remember how to do this.

WORKED EXAMPLE 11

The graphs of $y = 2 + x$ and $y = x^2 - 3x + 4$ have been drawn on the same set of axes. Use the graphs to find the x-values of the points of intersection of the line and the curve.

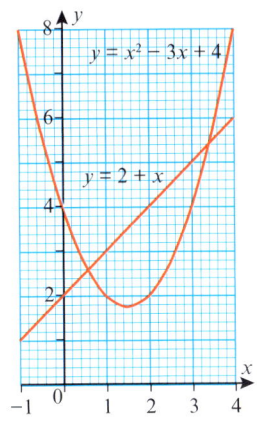

Answer

The coordinates of the two points of intersection are approximately (0.6, 2.6) and (3.4, 5.4), so the x-values of the points of intersection are $x = 0.6$ and $x = 3.4$.

TIP

You might also be asked for the y-values, so it is important to pair up the correct x-value with the correct y-value. When $x = 0.6$, $y = 2.6$ and when $x = 3.4$, $y = 5.4$.

WORKED EXAMPLE 12

The diagram shows the graphs of $y = \dfrac{8}{x}$ and $y = x$ for positive values of x.

a Use the graph of $y = \dfrac{8}{x}$ to solve the equation $\dfrac{8}{x} = 5.7$.

b Find a value of x such that $\dfrac{8}{x} = x$.

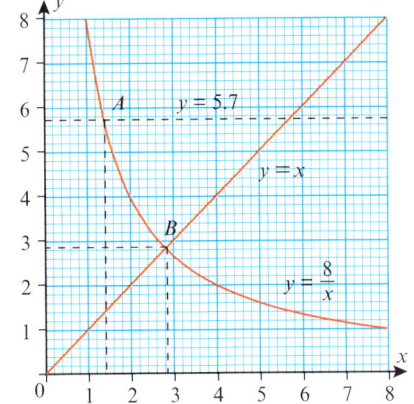

Answers

a You have to find a point on the curve that has a y coordinate of 5.7. Draw the line $y = 5.7$ to help find this it will be where the line cuts the curve.

The point is marked A on the diagram. Its x-coordinate is 1.4, so the solution of the equation $\dfrac{8}{x} = 5.7$ is $x = 1.4$.

b The straight line $y = x$ crosses the curve $y = \dfrac{8}{x}$ at the point B on the diagram.

Its x-coordinate is 2.8. Hence, a value of x such that $\dfrac{8}{x} = x$ is 2.8.

Algebraic solutions of simultaneous linear and non-linear equations

As with simultaneous linear equations, you can also use an algebraic method to find the solution of simultaneous linear and non-linear equations.

You can use a substitution method by first rearranging the linear equation to isolate one of the variables and then substituting this into the quadratic equation and solving.

> **TIP**
>
> You can solve the quadratic equation using any method you like.

WORKED EXAMPLE 13

Solve simultaneously:

$y = 2x^2 - x + 3$ [1]

$4x - 2y + 10 = 0$ [2]

Answer

$4x - 2y + 10 = 0$	
$y = 2x + 5$ [3]	Rearrange the linear equation to the form $y = \ldots$
$2x + 5 = 2x^2 - x + 3$	Substitute [3] into [2] by replacing y by $2x + 5$.
$2x^2 - 3x - 2 = 0$	Solve the quadratic equation. This one factorises.
$(2x + 1)(x - 2) = 0$	
$x = -\dfrac{1}{2}$ and $x = 2$	These are the x-values of the solutions.
$y = 2\left(-\dfrac{1}{2}\right) + 5 = 4$ and $y = 2(2) + 5 = 9$	Substitute each value of x into [3] to find the corresponding y-values.

So the solutions are:

$x = -\dfrac{1}{2}$ and $y = 4$ and

$x = 2$ and $y = 9$

WORKED EXAMPLE 14

Find the points of intersection of these graphs by solving the equations algebraically. Give your answers in exact form.

$2y = 10x - x^2 - 2$ [1]

$x + y = 6$ [2]

WORKED EXAMPLE 14 CONTINUED

Answer

$x + y = 6$

$y = 6 - x$ [3]   Rearrange the linear equation to the form $y = \ldots$

$2(6 - x) = 10x - x^2 - 2$ Substitute [3] into [2].

$12 - 2x = 10x - x^2 - 2$

$x^2 - 12x + 14 = 0$

$x = \dfrac{12 \pm \sqrt{12^2 - 4(1)(14)}}{2(1)}$ Use the quadratic formula to find the values of x.

$= \dfrac{12 \pm \sqrt{88}}{2}$

$= \dfrac{12 \pm 2\sqrt{22}}{2}$

So, $x = 6 + \sqrt{22}$ and $x = 6 - \sqrt{22}$ Find the corresponding y-values.

$y = 6 - \left(6 + \sqrt{22}\right) = -\sqrt{22}$

and $y = 6 - \left(6 - \sqrt{22}\right) = \sqrt{22}$

The points of intersection are:

$\left(6 + \sqrt{22},\ -\sqrt{22}\right)$ and $\left(6 - \sqrt{22},\ \sqrt{22}\right)$ Write your answers as pairs of coordinates.

Exercise 18.6

1   Find the points of intersection of the graphs and thus give the solution to the simultaneous equations.

a

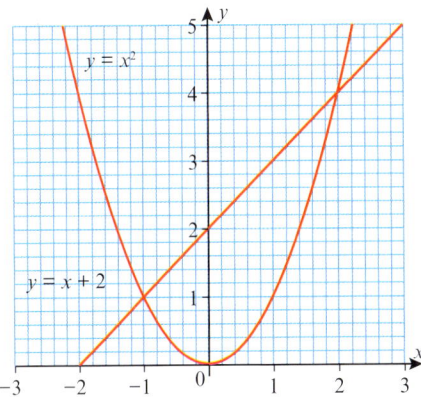

b

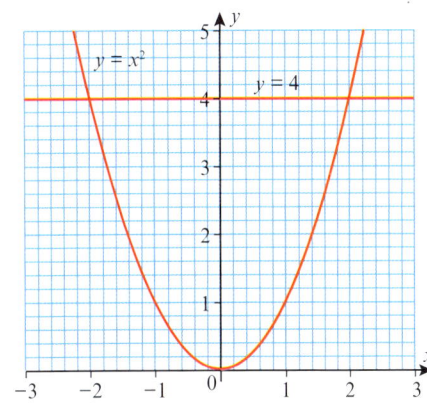

c 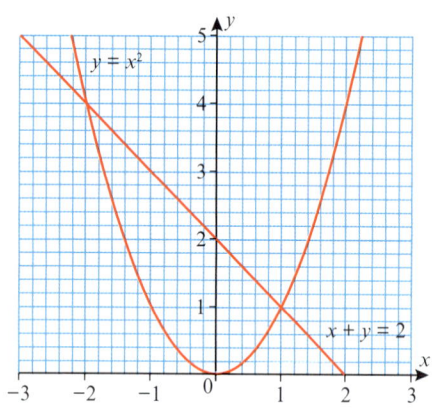   d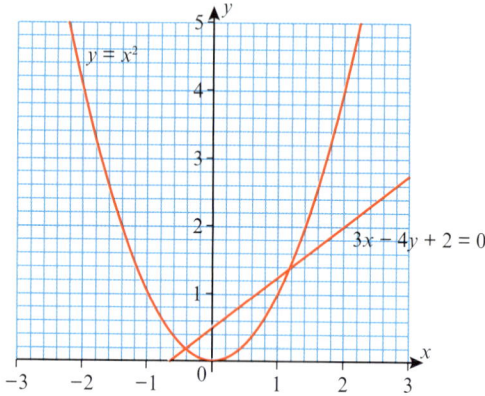

2   Find the points of intersection of the following graphs by drawing the graphs.
   a $y = x^2$ and $y = 3x$
   b $y = x$ and $y = \dfrac{2}{x}$
   c $y = 2 - x$ and $y = x^2 - 5x + 6$

3   Use a graphical method to solve each pair of simultaneous equations.
   a $y = x^2 - 8x + 9$ and $y = 2x + 1$
   b $y = x^2 - x - 6$ and $y = 2 + x$
   c $y = 4x + 4$ and $y = 2x - 3 + x^2$

4   Show graphically that there is no value of x which satisfies the pair of equations
   $y = -4$ and $y = x^2 + 2x + 3$ simultaneously.

5   Solve each pair of simultaneous equations algebraically. Give your answers to
   2 decimal places where necessary.
   a $y = x^2 - 5x + 3$ and $y - x - 10 = 0$
   b $y = 2x^2 + x - 4$ and $y = 2x + 3$
   c $y - 1 = 5x - x^2$ and $2y - 6 = 2x$

6   Find the points of intersection of the following graphs by solving the
   equations algebraically. Give your answers in exact form.
   a $y = x^2 - 4x + 9$ and $y = 2x + 4$
   b $y = 3x^2 - 5x - 2$ and $3y = 8 - 15x$
   c $y - 4 = 2x$ and $2y = 3x - 3 + x^2$

> **TIP**
>
> If a straight line is a tangent to the quadratic curve, there will be only one pair of solutions because the line and curve meet only at one point.

18.5 Other non-linear graphs

So far you have learnt how to construct a table of values and draw three different kinds of graphs:

*   linear graphs (straight lines of equations of the form $y = mx + c$)

*   quadratic graphs (parabolas of equations of the form $y = ax^2 + bx + c$)

*   reciprocal graphs (hyperbolas of equations of the form $y = \dfrac{a}{x} + c$).

In this section you are going to apply what you already know to plot and draw graphs formed by higher order equations (cubic equations) and graphs formed by equations that have combinations of linear, quadratic, reciprocal and cubic terms.

Plotting cubic graphs

MATHEMATICAL CONNECTIONS

In this section you will plot cubic graphs using a table of values. Later in the chapter you will learn how to sketch the graph of a cubic function by using differentiation to find the stationary (turning) points.

A cubic equation has a term with an index of three as the highest power of x. In other words, one of the terms is ax^3. For example, $y = 2x^3$, $y = -x^3 + 2x^2 + 3$ and $y = 2x^3 - 4x$ are all cubic equations. The simplest cubic equation is $y = x^3$.

Cubic equations produce graphs called cubic curves. The graphs you draw will have two main shapes:

If the coefficient of the x^3 term is positive, the graph will take one of these shapes.

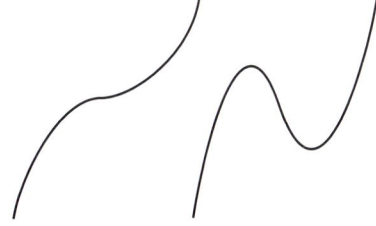

If the coefficient of the x^3 term is negative, the graph will be take one of these shapes.

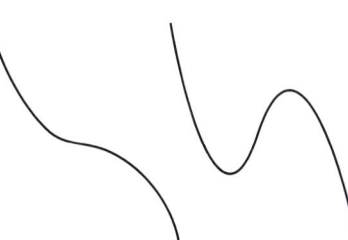

LINK

Geophysicists use equations and graphs to process measurements (such as the rise or pressure of magma in a volcano) and use these to generalise patterns and make predictions.

WORKED EXAMPLE 15

Complete the tables of values and plot the points to draw the graphs on the same set of axes.

a

x	−2	−1	0	1	2
$y = x^3$					

b

x	−2	−1	0	1	2
$y = -x^3$					

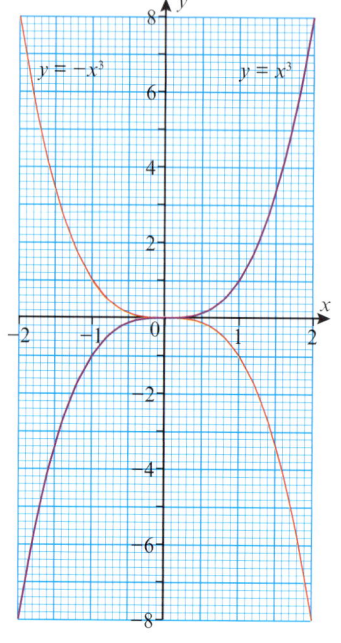

Answer

a

x	−2	−1	0	1	2
$y = x^3$	−8	−1	0	1	8

b

x	−2	−1	0	1	2
$y = -x^3$	8	1	0	−1	−8

TIP

As the value of x increases, the value of x^3 increases quickly and it becomes difficult to fit them onto the graph. If you have to construct your own table of values, stick to low numbers and, possibly, include the half points (0.5, 1.5, etc.) to find more values that will fit onto the graph.

WORKED EXAMPLE 16

Draw the graph of the equation $y = x^3 - 6x$ for $-3 \leqslant x \leqslant 3$.

Answer

Construct a table of values for whole number values of x first.

Put each term in a separate row.

Add the columns to find $y = x^3 - 6x$. (Remember not to add the top row when calculating y.)

x	−3	−2	−1	0	1	2	3
x^3	−27	−8	−1	0	1	8	27
$-6x$	18	12	6	0	−6	−12	−18
$y = x^3 - 6x$	−9	4	5	0	−5	−4	9

WORKED EXAMPLE 16 CONTINUED

Plot the points and join them with a smooth curve.

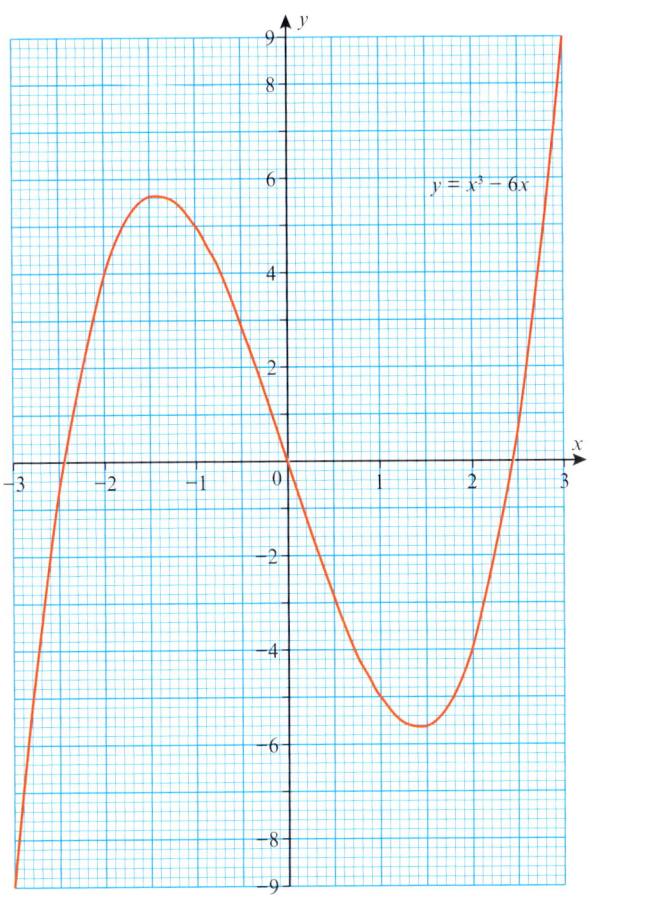

$y = x^3 - 6x$

INVESTIGATION

Sketching simple cubic graphs

You need to recognise the shape and be able to plot cubic graphs of the form $ax^3 + d$, where a and d are rational numbers.

Use an online graph plotter to investigate these graphs for different values of a and d.

Summarise your findings using sketches and notes to explain the key features of the graph and what happens to its shape for different values of a and d.

Using graphs to solve higher order equations

You can use cubic graphs to find approximate solutions to equations. Worked example 17 shows how to do this.

WORKED EXAMPLE 17

a   Draw the graph of the equation $y = x^3 - 2x^2 - 1$ for $-1 \leqslant x \leqslant 3$.

b   Use the graph to find the approximate solutions to the following equations.

   i $x^3 - 2x^2 - 1 = 0$ ii $x^3 - 2x^2 = -1$ iii $x^3 - 2x^2 - 5 = 0$

Answers

a   Construct a table of values of y for whole and half values x.

x	−1	−0.5	0	0.5	1	1.5	2	2.5	3
x^3	−1	−0.125	0	0.125	1	3.375	8	15.625	27
$-2x^2$	−2	−0.5	0	−0.5	−2	−4.5	−8	−12.5	−18
-1	−1	−1	−1	−1	−1	−1	−1	−1	−1
$y = x^3 + 2x^2 - 1$	−4	−1.625	−1	−1.375	−2	−2.125	−1	2.125	8

b   Plot the points on the axes and draw the curve.

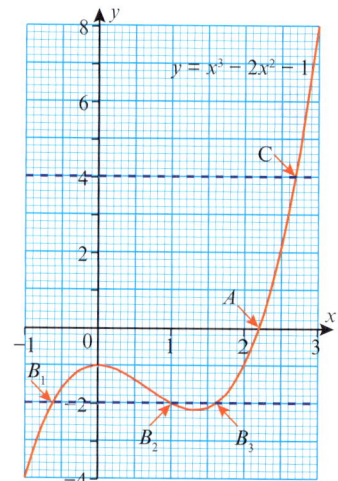

   i   To solve $x^3 - 2x^2 - 1 = 0$, find the point(s) on the curve that have a y-coordinate of 0.

   There is only one point (A on the graph).

   The x-coordinate of A is 2.2, so the approximate solution of $x^3 - 2x^2 - 1 = 0$ is $x = 2.2$.

   ii   To solve $x^3 - 2x^2 = -1$, rearrange the equation so that the left-hand side is the same as the equation shown by the graph.

   Subtracting 1 from both sides gives $x^3 - 2x^2 - 1 = -2$.

   Now find the point(s) on the curve that have a y-coordinate of −2.

   There are three points (B_1, B_2 and B_3 on the graph).

   The x-coordinates of these points are the solutions of the equation.

   So the approximate solutions of $x^3 - 2x^2 = -1$ are $x = -0.6$, $x = 1$ and $x = 1.6$.

   iii   Rearrange the equation $x^3 - 2x^2 - 5 = 0$ so that you can use the graph of $y = x^3 - 2x^2 - 1$ to solve it.

   Adding 4 to both sides of the equation gives $x^3 - 2x^2 - 1 = 4$.

   Find the point(s) on the curve that have a y-coordinate of 4.

   There is only one point (C on the graph).

   At C the x-coordinate is 2.7.

   The approximate solution is, therefore, $x = 2.7$.

Exercise 18.7

1   Construct a table of values from $-3 \leqslant x \leqslant 3$ and plot the points to draw graphs of the following equations.

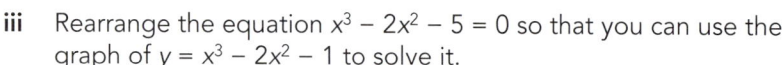

   a $y = 2x^3$
   b $y = -3x^3$
   c $y = x^3 - 2$
   d $y = 3 + 2x^3$
   e $y = x^3 - 2x^2$
   f $y = 2x^3 - 4x + 1$
   g $y = -x^3 + x^2 - 9$
   h $y = x^3 - 2x^2 + 1$

TIP

Before drawing the axes, check the range of y-values required from your table.

2 a Copy and complete the table of values for the equation $y = x^3 - 6x^2 + 8x$.
(You may want to add more rows to the table as in the worked examples.)

x	−1	−0.5	0	0.5	1.5	1	2.5	3	3.5	4	4.5	5
$y = x^3 - 6x^2 + 8x$	−15	−5.6										

b On a set of axes, draw the graph of the equation $y = x^3 - 6x^2 + 8x$ for $-1 \le x \le 5$.

c Use the graph to find the approximate solutions to the following equations.

i $x^3 - 6x^2 + 8x = 0$

ii $x^3 - 6x^2 + 8x = 3$

3 a Draw the graphs of $y = \dfrac{x^3}{10}$ and $y = 6x - x^2$ for $-4 \le x \le 6$.

b Use the graphs to find the approximate solutions to the equation
$\dfrac{x^3}{10} + x^2 - 6x = 0$.

INVESTIGATION

4 Graphs of the form $y = ax^n$ may have fractional values of n, for example
$y = ax^{\frac{1}{2}}$ and $y = ax^{-\frac{1}{2}}$.

$y = x^{\frac{1}{2}}$ is the function $y = \sqrt{x}$. This is sometimes called the square root function. The table of values and the graph of $y = \sqrt{x}$ is shown here.

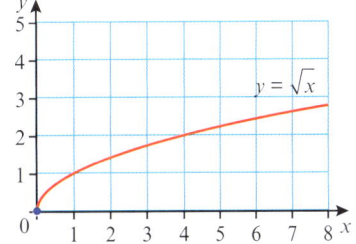

x	0	1	2	3	4
y	0	1	1.4	1.7	2

> **TIP**
>
> It is not practical to plot points with more than 1 decimal place when you are drawing graphs, so it makes sense to round the values to 1 decimal place.

a Explain why you cannot use negative values of x for this function.

b Use an online graph plotter to investigate the following functions.

$$y = 2x^{\frac{1}{2}} \qquad y = 3x^{\frac{1}{2}} \qquad y = 4x^{\frac{1}{2}}$$

i Sketch graphs of the functions on the same set of axes.

ii How does the value of a in the function $y = ax^{\frac{1}{2}}$ affect the shape of the graph?

iii What happens if the value of a is negative?

c Use an online graph plotter to investigate functions of the form $y = ax^{-\frac{1}{2}}$ for different values of a. Draw some sketches and write some notes to explain what you find out.

Graphs of equations with combinations of terms

When you have to plot graphs of equations with a combination of linear, quadratic, cubic, reciprocal or constant terms you need to construct a table of values with at least eight values of x to get a good indication of the shape of the graph.

WORKED EXAMPLE 18

Complete this table of values for the equation $y = 2x + \dfrac{1}{x}$ for $0.5 \leqslant x \leqslant 7$ and draw the graph.

x	0.5	1	2	3	4	5	6	7
2x	1	2	4	6	8	10	12	14
$\dfrac{1}{x}$								
$y = 2x + \dfrac{1}{x}$								

Answer

x	0.5	1	2	3	4	5	6	7.14
2x	1	2	4	6	8	10	12	14
$\dfrac{1}{x}$	2	1	0.5	0.33	0.25	0.2	0.17	0.14
$y = 2x + \dfrac{1}{x}$	3	3	4.5	6.3	8.33	10.2	12.2	14.1

Round the y-values in the last row to 1 decimal place to make the points easier to plot.

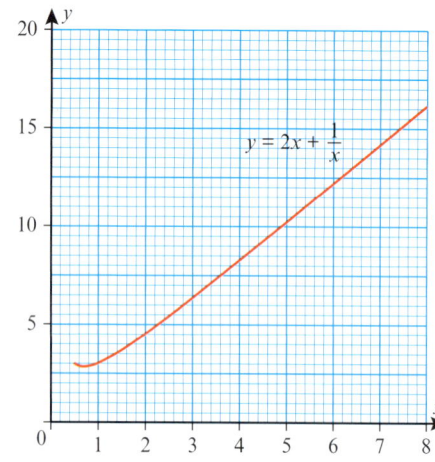

WORKED EXAMPLE 19

Complete this table of values and plot the graph of $y = x^3 - \dfrac{1}{x}$ for $0.2 \leqslant x \leqslant 3$.

x	0.2	0.5	1	1.5	2	2.5	3
x^3	0.008		1		8		27
$-\dfrac{1}{x}$							
$y = x^3 - \dfrac{1}{x}$							

Answer

x	0.2	0.5	1	1.5	2	2.5	3
x^3	0.008	0.125	1	3.375	8	15.625	27
$-\dfrac{1}{x}$	−5	−2	−1	−0.667	−0.5	−0.4	−0.33
$y = x^3 - \dfrac{1}{x}$	−5.0	−1.9	0	2.7	7.5	15.2	26.7

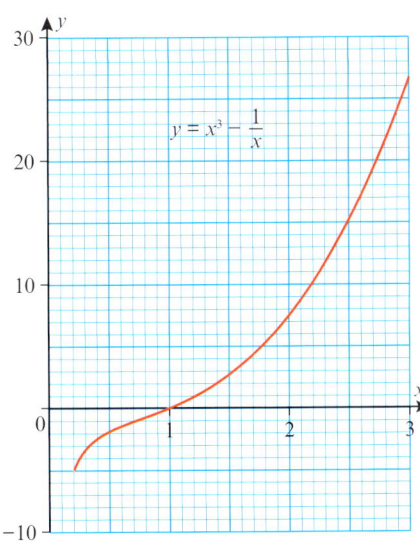

Exercise 18.8

1 Construct a table of values for $-3 \leqslant x \leqslant 3$ (including negative and positive values of 0.5 and 0.2) for each equation and draw the graph.

a $y = 3 + x^2 - \dfrac{2}{x}$

b $y = 3x - \dfrac{1}{x}$

c $y = -x + x^2 + \dfrac{2}{x}$

d $y = -x^3 - 2x + 1$ (omit the fractional values in this case)

Exponential graphs

Exponential growth is found in many real-life situations where a quantity increases by a constant percentage in a particular time: population growth and compound interest are both examples of exponential growth.

> ## MATHEMATICAL CONNECTIONS
>
> You learnt about exponential growth and decay and applied a formula to calculate growth in Chapter 17.

Equations in the general form $y = a^x$ (where a is a positive integer) are called exponential equations.

The shape of $y = a^x$ is a curve which rises rapidly as it moves from left to right; this is exponential growth. As x becomes more negative, the curve gets closer and closer to the x-axis but never crosses it. The x-axis is an asymptote.

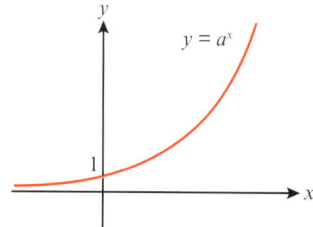

> ## TIP
>
> An exponential graph of the form $y = a^x$ will always intersect the y-axis at the point (0, 1) because $a^0 = 1$ for all values of a.
>
> (You should remember this from the laws of indices.)

The shape of $y = a^{-x}$ is a curve which falls as it moves from left to right; this is exponential decay. The x-axis is also an asymptote for $y = a^{-x}$. As x becomes more positive the curve gets closer and closer to the x-axis.

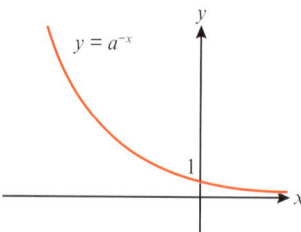

> ## LINK
>
> If you leave money in a bank account that earns a fixed percentage of interest every year, then the balance of the account will increase exponentially. The growth gets larger the more money is in the account, so it pays to wait before withdrawing anything!

WORKED EXAMPLE 20

a   Complete the table of values for $y = 2^x$ for $-2 \leqslant x \leqslant 4$ and draw the graph.

x	−2	−1.5	−1	−0.5	0	1	2	3	3.5
$y = 2^x$									

b   Use the graph to find the value of $2^{2.5}$ and check your result using the fact that $2^{2.5} = 2^{\frac{5}{2}} = \sqrt{2^5}$.

Answers

a

x	−2	−1.5	−1	−0.5	0	1	2	3	4
$y = 2^x$	0.25	0.35	0.5	0.71	1	2	4	8	16

Plot the points to draw the graph.

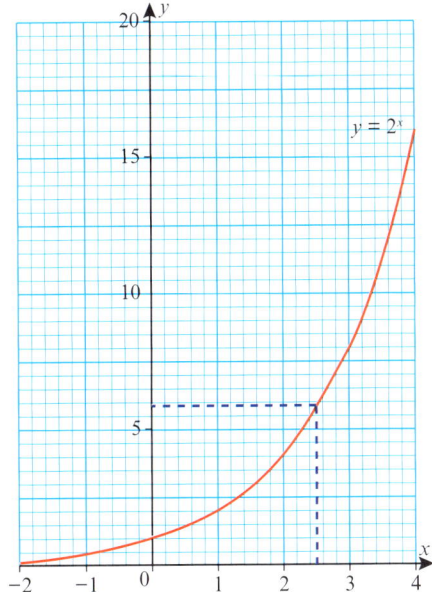

b   From the graph you can see that when $x = 2.5$ the value of y is 5.7, so, $2^{2.5} \approx 5.7$.

Check: $2^{2.5} = 2^{\frac{5}{2}} = \sqrt{2^5} = \sqrt{32} = 5.656...$

Exercise 18.9

1   a   Draw the graph of $y = 3^x$ for x-values between −2 and 3. Give the values to 2 decimal places where necessary.

b   On the same set of axes draw the graph of $y = 3^{-x}$ for x-values between −3 and 2. Give the values to 2 decimal places where necessary.

c   What is the relationship between the graph $y = 3^x$ of and $y = 3^{-x}$?

2 The graph of $y = 10^x$ for $-0.2 \leqslant x \leqslant 1.0$ is shown here.

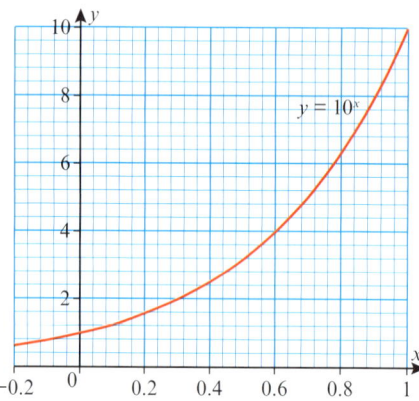

a Use the graph to find the value of:

i $10^{0.3}$ **ii** $10^{-0.1}$

ii Copy the diagram using tracing paper and draw a straight line graph that will allow you solve the equation $10^x = 8 - 5x$.

APPLY YOUR SKILLS

3 Bacteria multiply rapidly because a cell divides into two cells and then those two cells divide to each produce two more cells and so on. The growth rate is exponential and you can express the population of bacteria over time using the formula $P = 2^t$ (t is the period of time).

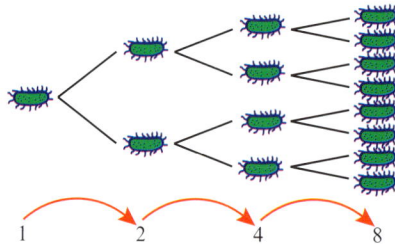

The graph shows the increase in bacteria numbers in a six-hour period.

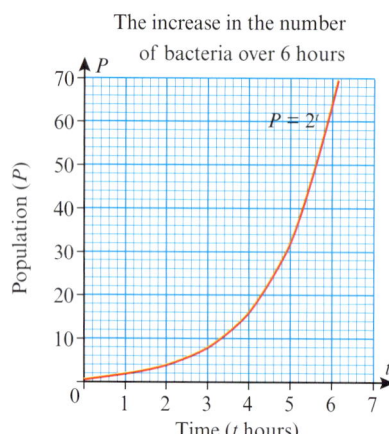

The increase in the number of bacteria over 6 hours

APPLY YOUR SKILLS CONTINUED

a   How many bacteria are there after one hour?

b   How long does it take for the number of bacteria to exceed 40 cells?

c   How many cells will there be after six hours?

d   When would you expect the population to exceed one million bacteria if it continued to grow at this rate?

4   The temperature of metal in a smelting furnace increases exponentially as indicated in the table. Draw a graph to show this data.

Time (min)	0	1	2	3	4
Temp (°C)	5	15	45	135	405

5   The population of bedbugs in New York City is found to be increasing exponentially. The changes in population are given in the table.

Time (months)	0	1	2	3	4
Population	1000	2000	4000	8000	16 000

a   Plot a graph to show the population increase over time.

b   When did the bedbug population reach 10 000?

c   What will the bedbug population be after six months if it continues to increase at this rate?

> **TIP**
>
> These values are given by the exponential equation $T = 5 \times 3^t$, where T is the temperature and t is the time in minutes.

INVESTIGATION

6   Mae finds the following explanation on the internet.

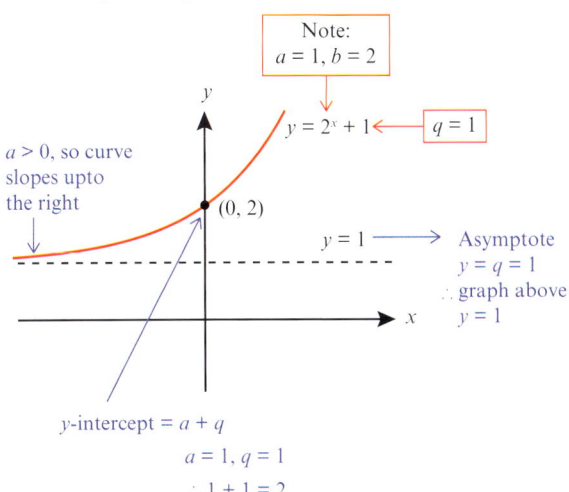

Understanding exponential graphs
standard equation: $y = ab^x + q$ $(b > 0, b \neq 1)$

Note:
$a = 1, b = 2$

$y = 2^x + 1$ ← $q = 1$

$a > 0$, so curve slopes upto the right

$(0, 2)$

$y = 1$ → Asymptote
$y = q = 1$
∴ graph above
$y = 1$

y-intercept $= a + q$
$a = 1, q = 1$
∴ $1 + 1 = 2$

INVESTIGATION CONTINUED

a Read the information carefully and write a step-by-step set of instructions for sketching an exponential graph.

b Sketch and label the following graphs.

    i $y = -3^x$ **ii** $y = 3^x - 4$ **iii** $y = -2^x + 1$

c Consider the blank exponential function:

$y = \square \times \square^{(x + \square)} + \square$

y-intercept $= \square$

    i   Use integer values from −9 to 9 (using any digit at most twice) to write an exponential growth function and its y-intercept.

    ii   Using the same conditions, write a function with the greatest possible y-intercept.

MATHEMATICAL CONNECTIONS

Look again at calculating gradients in Chapter 10. Make sure you understand how to do this before moving onto this section.

18.6 Finding the gradient of a curve

This simple graph of height against distance shows the route followed by a mountain biker on a trail.

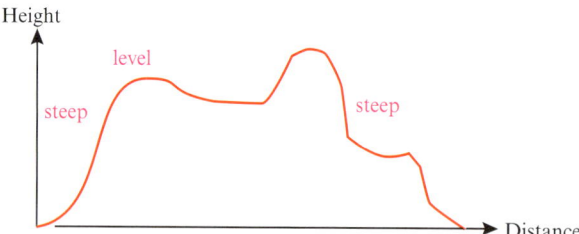

Height against distance

Some parts of the trail have a steep positive gradient, some have a gradual positive gradient, some parts are level and other parts have a negative gradient. It should be clear from this graph, that a curved graph never has a single gradient like a straight line has.

You cannot find the gradient of a whole curve but you can find the gradient of a point on the curve by drawing a tangent to it.

The gradient of a curve at a point is the gradient of the tangent to the curve at that point. Once you have drawn the tangent to a curve, you can work out the gradient of the tangent just as you would for a straight line $\left(\text{gradient} = \dfrac{y\text{-change}}{x\text{-change}} \right)$.

Look at the graph to see how this works.
BC is the tangent to the curve at
point *A*.

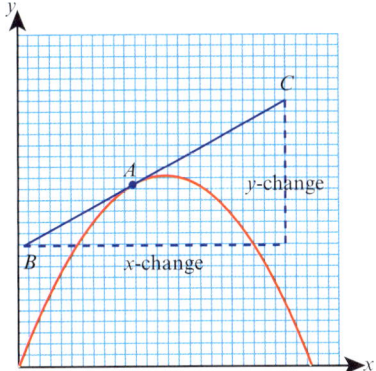

How to draw the tangent

Mark a point on the curve (*A*).

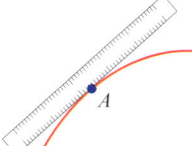

Place your ruler against the
curve so that it touches it only
at point *A*.

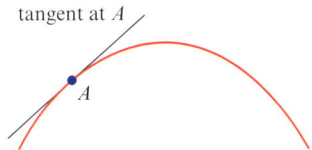

Use a pencil to draw the tangent.

> **TIP**
>
> If you extend your tangent, it may touch the curve again at a completely
> different point, but this is not a problem.
>
> If the tangent is rising from left to right, its gradient is positive. If the tangent
> is falling from left to right, its gradient is negative.
>
> Upwards = positive
>
> Downwards = negative

Calculating the gradient of a tangent

Mark two points, *P* and *Q*, on the tangent. Try to make the horizontal distance
between *P* and *Q* a whole number of units (measured on the *x*-axis scale).

Draw a horizontal line through *P* and a
vertical line through *Q* to form a right-angled
triangle *PNQ*.

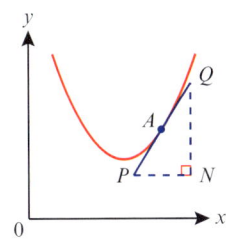

> **TIP**
>
> You must measure
> *NQ* and *PN* according
> to the scales on the
> *y*-axis and *x*-axis
> respectively. One of
> the most common
> mistakes is not doing
> this!

Gradient of the curve at *A*   =   gradient of the tangent *PAQ*

$$= \frac{\text{distance } NQ \text{ (measured on the } y\text{-axis scale)}}{\text{distance } PN \text{ (measured on the } x\text{-axis scale)}}$$

WORKED EXAMPLE 21

The graph of the equation $y = 5x - x^2$ is shown in the diagram. Find the gradient of the graph:

a at the point (1, 4)

b at the point (3, 6).

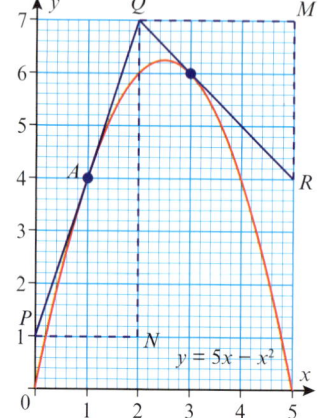

Answers

a At the point A(1, 4),

$$\text{gradient} = \frac{NQ}{PN} = \frac{6}{2} = 3.$$

b At the point B(3, 6),

$$\text{gradient} = \frac{MR}{QM} = -\frac{3}{3} = -1.$$

WORKED EXAMPLE 22

The graph shows the height of a tree (y metres) plotted against the age of the tree (x years). Estimate the rate at which the tree was growing when it was four years old.

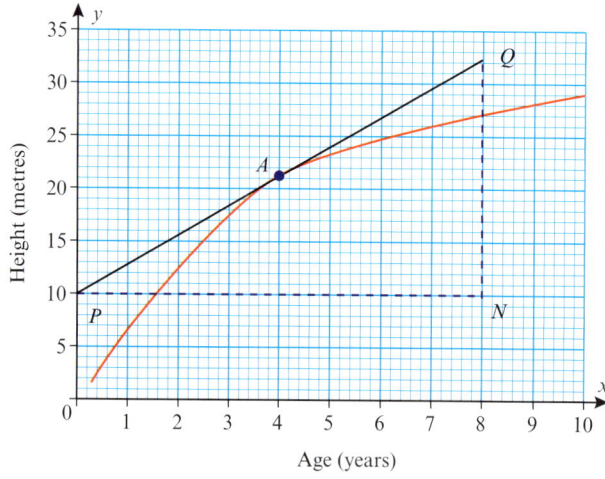

Age (years)

TIP

Remember, the gradient can be used to determine rates of change.

Answer

The rate at which the tree was growing when it was four years old is equal to the gradient of the curve at the point where $x = 4$.

Draw the tangent at this point (A).

Gradient at $A = \dfrac{NQ}{PN} = \dfrac{22.5}{8} = 2.8$

The tree was growing at a rate of 2.8 metres per year.

Exercise 18.10

1   The graph of $y = x^2$ is shown in the diagram.

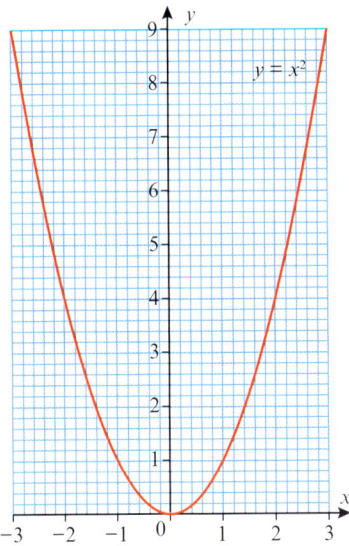

a   Copy the graph using tracing paper and find the gradient of the graph at the points:

   i   (2, 4)   ii   (−1, 1).

b   The gradient of the graph at the point (1.5, 2.25) is 3. Write down the coordinates of the point at which the gradient is −3.

2   The graph shows how the population of a village has changed since 1930.

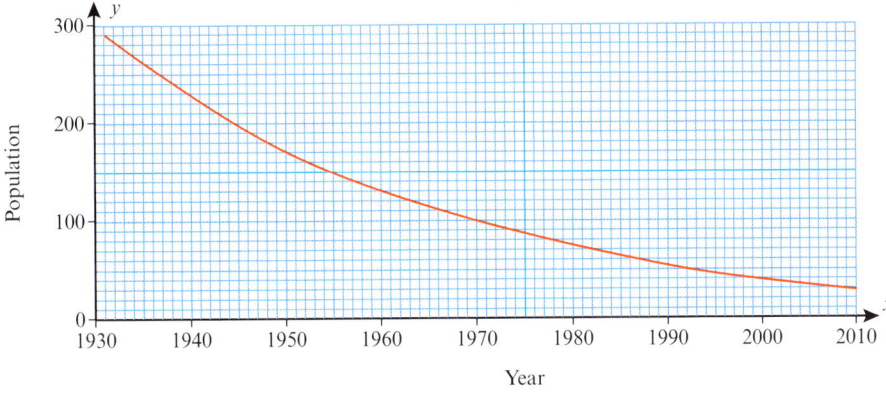

a   Copy the graph using tracing paper and find the gradient of the graph at the point (1950, 170).

b   What does this gradient represent?

3   a   Draw the graph of the curve $y = x^3 + 1$ for values $-2 \leqslant x \leqslant 2$.

   b   Find the gradient of the curve at the point $A(1, 2)$.

18.7 Derivatives of functions

As well as drawing a tangent, you can calculate the gradient at any point by using the equation of the curve.

INVESTIGATION

Gradients of tangents

1 In Exercise 18.10 you considered the gradient of the curve with equation $y = x^2$ at the points with x-coordinates 2, −1 and −1.5. You should have noticed that the gradient is twice the value of the x-coordinate at any given point.

Now use the diagram or a larger copy, to draw tangents at the points (1, 1), (−2, 4), (3, 9) and (−3, 9). Compare the gradient of each tangent to the x-coordinate of the point you have used. You should notice that the gradients are twice the x-coordinate in each case.

2 Here is the curve with equation $y = x^3$.

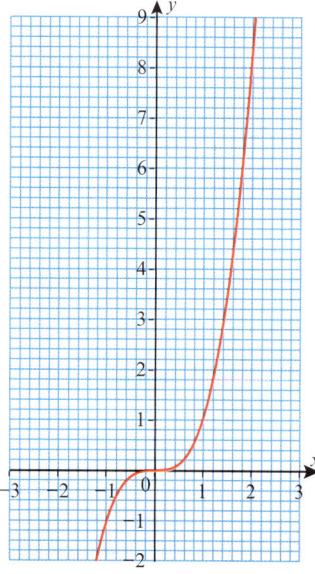

Copy the graph using tracing paper and draw tangents to find the gradient of the graph at the points (1,1), (2, 8) and (−1, −1).

Copy and complete the table and compare the gradient to the value of x^2 in each case.

x-coordinate	x^2	Gradient of tangent
1	1	
2	4	
−1	1	

What do you notice?

Try some other points on the curve, where the x-coordinates are not integers. Do you get the same result?

Differentiation

You should have found that the gradient at any point on the curve $y = x^2$ is $2x$.
It is helpful to write this as $2x^1$ for reasons that you will see shortly.

You should also have found that the gradient at any point on the curve $y = x^3$ is $3x^2$.

$2x$ and $3x^2$ are known as **derivatives of functions** and the process used to find them is called **differentiation**.

Using the notation $\dfrac{dy}{dx}$ to stand for the derivative of function:

if $y = x^2$ then $\dfrac{dy}{dx} = 2x^1$

if $y = x^3$ then $\dfrac{dy}{dx} = 3x^2$

In both cases, to find the derivative of function you multiply the original equation by the power and reduce the power by 1.

If $y = x^n$ then, differentiating, $\dfrac{dy}{dx} = nx^{n-1}$.

Sometimes there is already a number in front of the power of x. When this happens you still follow the rule and multiply everything by the power before reducing the power by 1.

If $y = ax^n$ then, differentiating, $\dfrac{dy}{dx} = n \times ax^{n-1} = anx^{n-1}$.

TIP

It was useful to write the power of 1 in the case $y = x^2$ of to make it easy to see that the power of 2 had been reduced by 1 as the rule suggests.

TIP

This rule always works for any power of x, even if it is negative or a fraction.

WORKED EXAMPLE 23

Find $\dfrac{dy}{dx}$ for curves with the following equations.

a $y = x^7$ b $y = x^8$ c $y = 4x^5$ d $y = -6x^3$

Answers

a $\dfrac{dy}{dx} = 7x^6$ — Multiply the expression by the power. Then reduce the power by 1.

b $\dfrac{dy}{dx} = 8x^7$ — Multiply by 8 and then subtract 1 from the power, 8.

c $\dfrac{dy}{dx} = 4 \times (5 \times x^4)$ — You need to multiply the whole expression by 5. Then subtract 1 from the power.
$= 20x^4$

d $\dfrac{dy}{dx} = 3 \times (-6x^2)$ — The rule is the same for positive and negative terms.
$= -18x^2$

WORKED EXAMPLE 24

Find the gradient of the curve with equation $y = 4x^3$ at the point (2, 32).

Answer

The derivative of function tells you the gradient at the point where the x-coordinate is x. To find the gradient at a particular point, substitute the value of x into the derivative of function.

$\dfrac{dy}{dx} = 12x^2$ — Multiply by the power and subtract 1 from the power.

$\dfrac{dy}{dx}$ at $x = 2$ is $12 \times 2^2 = 48$ — Substitute $x = 2$ to find the gradient at the point where the x-coordinate is 2.

The gradient of the curve at the point (2, 32) is 48.

Exercise 18.11

1 For each of the following, find $\dfrac{dy}{dx}$.

a $y = x^4$ b $y = x^6$ c $y = x^9$

d $y = 4x^3$ e $y = 12x^2$ f $y = 7x^7$

g $y = -4x^4$ h $y = 7x^{12}$ i $y = -16x^5$

2 Find the gradient of each of the following curves at the given point.

a $y = x^2$ at the point (3, 9)   b $y = x^3$ at the point (1, 1)

c $y = x^4$ at the point (2, 16)   d $y = 4x^2$ at the point (−1, 4)

e $y = -3x^3$ at the point (2, −24)   f $y = -5x^6$ at the point (−2, −320)

3 Find the coordinates of the point at which the curve with equation $y = 3x^2$ has gradient 18.

TIP

Remember that you will need to use the x-coordinate in each case. Look back at Worked example 24 if you need help.

Differentiating sums and differences

The equation of a curve may involve more than one term and you may be asked to differentiate expressions like $y = x^2 + x^4$ or $y = 3x^2 - 4x$.

To do this, you differentiate each term independently.

You can see this by differentiating $y = 4x^3$ and then rewriting the answer as a sum of separate terms:

$y = 4x^3$

$\Rightarrow \dfrac{dy}{dx} = 12x^2$

You can rewrite $12x^2$ as the sum:

$\dfrac{dy}{dx} = 3x^2 + 3x^2 + 3x^2 + 3x^2$

Compare this to the original equation, also written as a sum of separate terms:

$y = x^3 + x^3 + x^3 + x^3$.

You can see that each term has been differentiated independently.

So we have the rule:

If $y = ax^m + bx^n$ then $\dfrac{dy}{dx} = amx^{m-1} + bnx^{n-1}$.

You can extend this rule to adding any number of terms together and it also works for subtraction.

WORKED EXAMPLE 25

Find $\dfrac{dy}{dx}$ for each of the following.

a $y = 4x^7 + 3x^6$ **b** $y = \dfrac{8}{3}x^2 - 4x^5$

Answers

a $\dfrac{dy}{dx} = 28x^6 + 18x^5$ Differentiate each term separately then add them together.

b $\dfrac{dy}{dx} = \dfrac{16}{3}x - 20x^4$ Differentiate each term separately and then subtract.

Exercise 18.12

1 Find $\dfrac{dy}{dx}$ for each of the following.

a $y = x^4 + x^5$ **b** $y = 3x^3 - 5x^4$ **c** $y = 7x^6 + 9x^2$

d $y = \dfrac{1}{3}x^3 - 4x^7$ **e** $y = 6x^5 - \dfrac{8}{11}x^4$ **f** $y = -7x^2 + 3x^6$

g $y = 12x^3 + \dfrac{2}{3}x^8$ **h** $y = -10x^{12} - 8x^{10}$ **i** $y = 4x^2 - 12x^3 + 5x^4$

j $y = -\dfrac{8}{11}x^4 + \dfrac{2}{7}x^3 - \dfrac{3}{4}x^2$

2 Find the gradient of each curve at the point with the given x-coordinate.

a $y = 3x^3 + 2x^2$ at $x = 3$
b $y = -2x^4 + 3x^2$ at $x = -2$
c $y = 3x^4 + 6x^3 - 3x^2$ at $x = -1$

3 Find the coordinates of the point where the curve with equation $y = 2x^3 + 3x^2$ has gradient 12.

MATHEMATICAL CONNECTIONS

You may need to revise the different methods for solving quadratic equations that you learnt in Chapter 14.

---

4 Find the coordinates of the points where the curve with equation $y = \dfrac{1}{4}x^4 - \dfrac{3}{2}x^2$ has gradient zero.

Special cases

Sometimes the equation of a curve will contain a multiple of x or a constant term. In the case of a multiple of x the rule still applies, for example:

$$y = 5x = 5x^1 \Rightarrow \frac{dy}{dx} = 5x^0 = 5$$

So, if $y = kx$, then $\frac{dy}{dx} = k$.

If your equation involves a constant term, you need to think about what the graph of $y = constant$ looks like. You know from Chapter 10 that this is a horizontal line and has gradient zero.

So, if $y = $ constant then $\frac{dy}{dx} = 0$.

> **MATHEMATICAL CONNECTIONS**
>
> You will need to remember that $x^1 = x$ and $x^0 = 1$.

> **TIP**
>
> This should not be a surprise, because the 'curve' with equation $y = kx$ is in fact a straight line with gradient k all the way along its length.

> **MATHEMATICAL CONNECTIONS**
>
> It is possible to differentiate an expression like this without expanding the brackets, but this is beyond the requirements of the syllabus.

WORKED EXAMPLE 26

Find $\frac{dy}{dx}$ if $y = (2x + 3)^2$.

Answer

$y = (2x + 3)^2 = (2x + 3)(2x + 3)$ Begin by expanding the brackets.

$\quad = 4x^2 + 6x + 6x + 9$

$\quad = 4x^2 + 12x + 9$ Now you can differentiate:

$\frac{dy}{dx} = 8x + 12 + 0$ $4x^2$ is differentiated to give $8x$

$\quad = 8x + 12$ $12x$ is differentiated to give 12

    9 is differentiated to give 0

Exercise 18.13

1   Differentiate each of the following.

   a $y = 5x$ b $y = -4x$ c $y = 4$

   d $y = 7x - 6$ e $y = -3x + 6$ f $y = 4x^2 - 4x + 1$

   g $y = 7x^3 + 2x - 4$ h $y = \frac{1}{3}x^3 + \frac{1}{2}x^2 + \frac{1}{4}$

   i $y = mx + c$, where m and c are constants

2   Differentiate each of the following.

   a $y = x(x + 2)$ b $y = x^3(x^2 + 2x)$

   c $y = (x + 2)(x - 3)$ d $y = (x - 4)(x - 5)$

   e $y = 4x^3(x + 2)$ f $y = -5x(x - 4)$

   g $y = (2x + 1)(x + 2)$ h $y = (3x + 2)(x - 3)$

   i $y = (4x + 1)(3x + 5)$ j $y = (2x - 7)(3x + 4)$

k $y = (3x - 5)(7x - 3)$ **l** $y = (x + 3)^2$

m $y = (2x + 1)^2$ **n** $y = (3x - 2)^2$

o $y = \dfrac{1}{5}x^2(x + 3)$ **p** $y = \dfrac{2}{3}x^6\left(x + \dfrac{1}{4}\right)$

q $y = 5(x + 3)(x - 7)$ **r** $y = (x + 3)(x - 3)$

3   Find the gradient of the curve with equation $y = (3x - 2)(4x + 1)$ at the point with coordinates $(3, 91)$.

4   Find the point at which the gradient of the curve with equation $y = 3x^2 - 4x + 1$ is zero.

5   Find the coordinates of the point on the curve with equation $y = 3x^2 - 4x - 2$ where the curve is parallel to the line with equation $y = -2x + 1$.

6   Find the coordinates of both points on the curve with equation $y = 2x^3 - 9x^2 + 12x$ where the curve is parallel to the x-axis.

> **TIP**
>
> What is the gradient of the x-axis?

7   The curve with equation $y = x^3 + 3$ has two tangents parallel to the line with equation $y = 12x - 1$. Find the coordinates of the two points.

8   The curve with equation $y = ax^3 - 4x + 1$ is parallel to the line $y = 50x - 1$ at the point with x-coordinate 3.

   a   Find the gradient of the curve at the point with x-coordinate 4.

   b   Show that the tangent at the point with x-coordinate -3 is also parallel to the same line.

> **REFLECTION**
>
> Did you make any mistakes in this work?
>
> If so, what did you do to review the mistakes and understand what you did wrong?

Equations of tangents

In Chapter 10 you learnt how to find the equation of a line when you know both its gradient and the coordinates of a point on the line. You can use the same method to find the equation of a tangent to a curve at a specific point.

You can find the gradient of the tangent by differentiating the equation and using the x-coordinate of the point where the tangent is drawn. You can find a point on the line by using the given x-coordinate and substituting it into the equation of the curve to find the y-coordinate.

WORKED EXAMPLE 27

Find the equation of the tangent to the curve with equation $y = 3x^2 - 4x + 1$ at the point with x-coordinate 2.

Answer

If $x = 2$ then:

$$\begin{aligned} y &= 3(2)^2 - 4(2) + 1 \\ &= 12 - 8 + 1 \\ &= 5 \end{aligned}$$

Substitute $x = 2$ into the equation to find the y-coordinate.

So the tangent passes through the point (2, 5).

$$\frac{dy}{dx} = 6x - 4$$

Find the gradient of the tangent by differentiation.

So the gradient = $6(2) - 4 = 8$

Substitute $x = 2$.

The equation will be of the form $y = 8x + c$.

You need to find the equation of a line with gradient 8, passing through the point with coordinates (2, 5).

When $x = 2$, $y = 5$, so

$5 = 8 \times 2 + c$

Substitute values for x and y and solve for c.

$\Rightarrow c = -11$

So the equation of the tangent is $y = 8x - 11$.

Exercise 18.14

1   Find the equation of the tangent of each curve at the given point.

   a $y = x^2$ at the point with coordinates (3, 9)

   b $y = x^2$ at the point with x-coordinate -2

   c $y = x^3 + x^2$ at the point with x-coordinate 4

   d $y = 3x^3 - 2x + 1$ at the point with x-coordinate 1.5

   e $y = \frac{1}{4}x^2 + \frac{1}{5}x$ at the point with x-coordinate $\frac{1}{2}$

2   A curve has equation $y = 2x^2 + 3x - 2$. The tangent to the curve at $x = 4$ meets the x-axis at the point A. Find the coordinates of the point A.

3   A curve has equation $y = -3x^3 + x - 4$. The tangent to this curve at the point where $x = 1$ meets the x-axis at the point A and the y-axis at the point B. Find the area of triangle OAB.

4   The tangents to the curve with equation $y = x^3 - 3x$ at the points A and B with x-coordinates -1 and 4 respectively meet at the point C. Find the coordinates of the point C.

Turning points

Earlier in this chapter you learnt that you can use the method of completing the square to find the points at which a quadratic curve is highest or lowest.

You will now learn how use differentiation to do the same thing, and then compare the answer that you get from completing the square.

Think about the curve with equation $y = x^2 - 4x + 1$. The diagram shows the curve with a tangent drawn at the lowest point.

Note that the gradient of the tangent is zero. Any point where the gradient of a quadratic curve is zero is known as a stationary point. If the point is also either a maximum or minimum point then we call it a turning point.

If the gradient of the tangent is zero at this point, then so is $\dfrac{dy}{dx}$.

So, $\dfrac{dy}{dx} = 2x - 4$

$\qquad = 0$

$\Rightarrow x = 2$

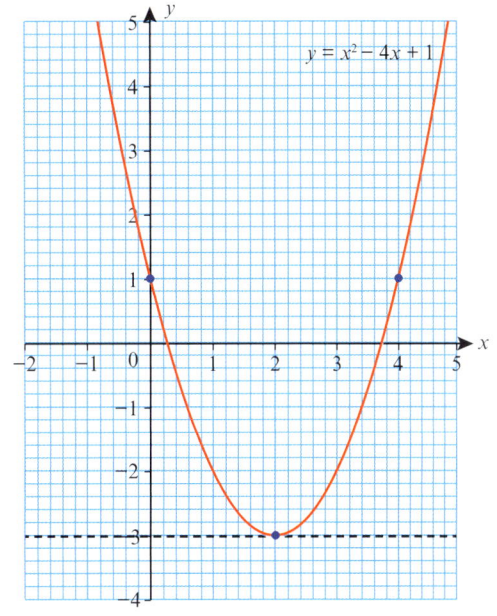

MATHEMATICAL CONNECTIONS

Turning points are just one type of stationary point. Another type of stationary point is a point of inflexion (sometimes written as inflection). If you study mathematics beyond Cambridge IGCSE level, you will learn more about these points. You could do some research to find out what a point of inflexion is and what happens to the gradient on either side of a point of inflexion.

Substitute this x-value into the original equation to find the coordinates of the turning point:

$y = 2^2 - 4 \times 2 + 1$

$\quad = 4 - 8 + 1 = -3$

You can see that the point $(2, -3)$ is the lowest point of the graph. The value -3 is known as the minimum value of y.

If you complete the square to check the answer, you can see that

$y = x^2 - 4x + 1$

$\quad = (x - 2)^2 - 3$

This confirms that the minimum value of y is -3 and that this occurs when $x = 2$, exactly as you found by differentiation.

Maximum and minimum points

In the previous example the turning point was the minimum point on the curve. However, sometimes the turning point is a maximum point. You need to be able to tell which is which. There are several methods you can use to do this.

Using the shape of the graph

It is easy to see which points are maxima (the plural of *maximum*) and minima if you use the shape of the curve to help you.

In the case of $y = x^2 - 4x + 1$ the coefficient of x^2 is positive, which means that the curve is ∪ shaped. The turning point must be a minimum as it is lower than the rest of the curve.

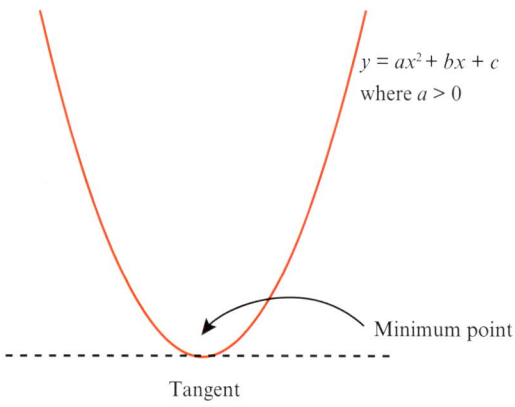

$y = ax^2 + bx + c$
where $a > 0$

Minimum point

Tangent

If the coefficient of x^2 is negative then the curve is ∩ shaped, and the turning point is now a maximum.

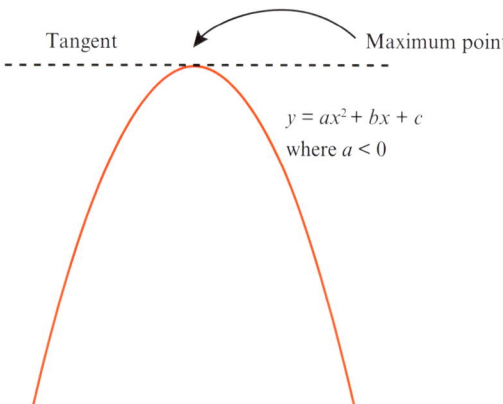

Tangent   Maximum point

$y = ax^2 + bx + c$
where $a < 0$

Finding the gradient either side of the turning point

You can test find the gradient of other points on the graph by substituting different values for x.

In the case of $y = x^2 - 4x + 1$, the gradient is equal to $\dfrac{dy}{dx} = 2x - 4$ and the turning point is at $x = 2$.

Substitute $x = 1.9$ and $x = 2.1$ to find the gradient on either side of the turning point:

At $x = 1.9$, $\dfrac{dy}{dx} = 2 \times 1.9 - 4 = -0.2$. The curve is sloping downwards.

At $x = 2.1$, $\dfrac{dy}{dx} = 2 \times 2.1 - 4 = 0.2$. The curve is sloping upwards.

This shows that the curve is sloping downwards to the left of the turning point and upwards on the right, so the turning point must be a minimum point.

Using the second derivative

A third method is to differentiate the function a second time. This gives the second derivative and you write this as $\dfrac{d^2 y}{dx^2}$. The second derivative gives the rate of change of the gradient, so it tells you whether the gradient is increasing or decreasing at any point x.

If the value of the second derivative at the turning point is:

- positive, the gradient is increasing and the turning point is a minimum point
- negative, the gradient is decreasing and the turning point is a maximum point.

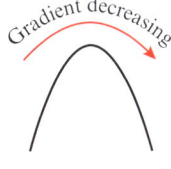
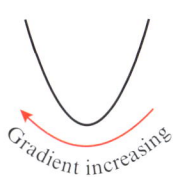

For $y = x^2 - 4x + 1$, you know that $\dfrac{dy}{dx} = 2x - 4$ and differentiating a second time gives $\dfrac{d^2 y}{dx^2} = 2$. This is positive for all values of x, which means the gradient is always increasing and so the turning point is a minimum point.

WORKED EXAMPLE 28

Find the coordinates of the two turning points on the curve with equation $y = 2x^3 - 3x^2 + 1$.

Explain which point is a maximum and which point is a minimum.

Answer

First find the turning points by differentiation:

$\dfrac{dy}{dx} = 6x^2 - 6x$

At a turning point:

$6x^2 - 6x = 0$

$\Rightarrow x^2 - x = 0$

$\Rightarrow x(x - 1) = 0$

$\Rightarrow x = 0$ or $x = 1$

WORKED EXAMPLE 28 CONTINUED

When $x = 0$, $y = 0 - 0 + 1 = 1$, so there is a turning point at $(0, 1)$.

When $x = 1$, $y = 2 \times 1^3 - 3 \times 1^2 + 1 = 0$, so there is a turning point at $(1, 0)$.

Method 1 – using the shape of the curve

Now remind yourself what the graph of a cubic equation looks like. There are two possibilities:

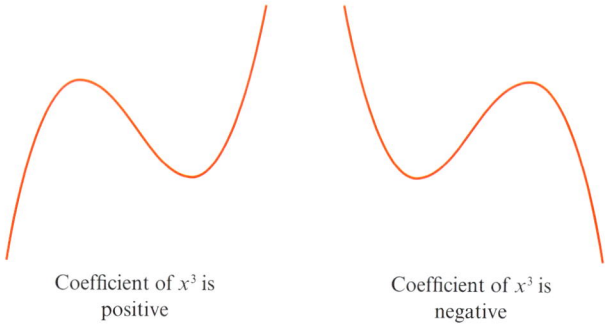

Coefficient of x^3 is
positive

Coefficient of x^3 is
negative

Given that the coefficient of x^3 is positive, the left graph must be the correct one. Notice that the maximum point lies on the left, with a lower x-coordinate, and the minimum point lies on the right, with the higher x-coordinate. So $(0, 1)$ is a maximum and $(1, 0)$ is a minimum.

Method 2 – using the value of the gradient either side of the turning point

For $(0, 1)$ find the gradient at -0.1 and 0.1:

At -0.1, $\dfrac{dy}{dx} = 6 \times (-0.1)^2 - 6 \times (-0.1) = 0.06 + 0.6 = 0.66$ so the curve slopes upwards.

At 0.1, $\dfrac{dy}{dx} = 6 \times (0.1)^2 - 6 \times (0.1) = 0.06 - 0.6 = -0.54$ so the curve slopes downwards.

So $(0, 1)$ is a maximum point.

For $(1, 0)$ find the gradient at 0.9 and 1.1:

At 0.9, $\dfrac{dy}{dx} = 6 \times (0.9)^2 - 6 \times (0.9) = 4.86 - 5.4 = -0.54$ so the curve slopes downwards.

At 1.1, $\dfrac{dy}{dx} = 6 \times (1.1)^2 - 6 \times (1.1) = 7.26 - 6.6 = 0.66$ so the curve slopes upwards.

So $(1, 0)$ is a minimum point.

WORKED EXAMPLE 28 CONTINUED

Method 3 – using the second derivative

$\frac{dy}{dx} = 6x^2 - 6x$, so differentiating a second time gives $\frac{d^2y}{dx^2} = 12x - 6$

For $(0, 1)$, $\frac{d^2y}{dx^2} = 12 \times 0 - 6 = -6$

This is negative, so $(0, 1)$ is a maximum point.

For $(1, 0)$, $\frac{d^2y}{dx^2} = 12 \times 1 - 6 = 6$

This is positive, so $(1, 0)$ is a minimum point.

Sketching cubic functions

Earlier in this chapter you learnt that you can sketch a parabola if you know certain features of the graph. You can also sketch the graphs of cubic functions of the form $y = ax^3 + bx^2 + cx + d$ if you know the following features:

- The basic shape and orientation of the graph. Cubic graphs have two basic shapes depending on whether $a > 0$ or $a < 0$.

- The y-intercept. This is determined by substituting $x = 0$ into the equation.

- The x-intercepts. When the cubic equation is given in factor form, that is, $y = (x + a)(x + b)(x + c)$, you can let $y = 0$ and solve for x. A cubic graph may have three, two or one x-intercepts.

- The turning point(s) of the graph. To find the turning points of a cubic function you need to use differentiation and work out whether they are maximum or minimum points by considering the shape of the graph.

Exercise 18.15

1   Find the turning point or points on the following curves and explain whether each point is a maximum or a minimum.

a $y = x^2 - 4x + 1$ b $y = x^2 + 6x - 4$ c $y = -x^2 + 8x - 2$

d $y = 3x^2 - 12x + 4$ e $y = -2x^2 + 4x - 3$ f $y = x^2 + 3x - 1$

g $y = -5x^2 + 3x + 4$ h $y = x^3 - 12x - 1$ i $y = -x^3 + 6x^2 + 3$

j $y = x(x - 4)$ k $y = (x - 5)(x + 5)$ l $y = x(2x - 3)$

m $y = x(2x^2 - 21x + 72)$ n $y = x^2(3 - x)$

2   Use the turning points you worked out in question 1 and what you already know about curved graphs to sketch the graphs in parts (m) $y = x(2x^2 - 21x + 72)$ and (n) $y = x^2(3 - x)$.

APPLY YOUR SKILLS

3 The height, h metres, of a ball above the ground is given by the formula $h = 7t - 5t^2$ at time t seconds after the ball is thrown upwards.

    a Find $\dfrac{dh}{dt}$.

    b Find the greatest height of the ball above the ground.

4 The population of bacteria in a pond is p thousand, d days after the pond is filled. It is known that $p = d^3 - 12d^2 + 45d$. Find the highest population of bacteria in the pond in the first four days after it is filled.

5 A manufacturer makes open-topped boxes by taking a 2 m × 1 m sheet of metal, cutting x m × x m squares out of the corners and folding along the dotted lines shown in the diagram.

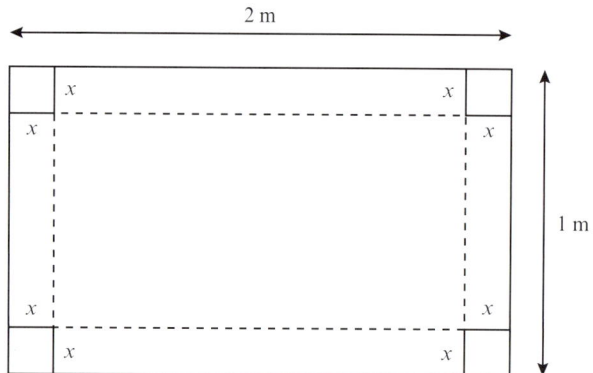

    a Show that the volume of the box produced is given by $V = x(2 - 2x)(1 - 2x)$.

    b Explain why x must be less than 0.5 m

    c Find the value of x that will give the maximum possible volume of the box.

TIP

Notice that h has taken the place of y and t has taken the place of x. The method is the same, only the letters have changed.

MATHEMATICAL CONNECTIONS

You will need to use the quadratic formula or complete the square to solve a quadratic equation in this question. You learnt how to do this in Chapter 14.

LINK

Maxima and minima are used in many situations. For example, if you have a fixed amount of material to make a box and want to maximise the volume, you would make a cubic box. Similarly, if you want a pond with fixed perimeter but with greatest surface area, you would make a circular pond. Both of these things can be calculated using differentiation.

SUMMARY

Do you know ...?

The graph of a quadratic equation is a recognisable curve called a parabola.
A reciprocal equation is an equation of the form $y = \dfrac{a}{x}$ or $xy = a$.
The graph of a reciprocal equation is a two-part curve called a hyperbola.
You can use graphs to solve equations by finding the value of x or y at different points on the graph. You can find the solution to simultaneous equations using the points of intersection of two graphs.
Linear, quadratic, cubic and reciprocal terms can occur in the same equation. It is possible to draw graphs of these curves by constructing a table of values and then plotting the points.
An exponential equation has the form $y = ab^x + c$. These equations produce steep curved graphs.
You can draw a tangent to a curve and use it to find the gradient of the curve at the point where the tangent touches it.
You can differentiate functions to find gradients and stationary (turning) points.

Are you able to ...?

construct a table of values for quadratic and reciprocal equations
plot the graph of a parabola from a table of values
sketch the graph of a parabola using its characteristics
find turning points by completing the square
plot the graph of a hyperbola from a table of values
use quadratic graphs to solve equations
construct tables of values and draw graphs for cubic equations and simple sums of linear and non-linear terms
construct a table of values and draw the graph of an exponential equation
sketch graphs of cubic, reciprocal and exponential functions using their characteristics
use cubic graphs to solve equations
estimate the gradient of a curve by drawing a tangent to the curve
differentiate functions of the form ax^n
find the equation of the tangent to a curve
find turning points using differentiation and work out whether they are maximum or minimum points.

Practice questions

1 **a** Write the equation for each of the graphs A, B, C and D. [4]

b Write down the coordinates of the intersection of:

    i A and B [1]

    ii C and D. [1]

c Find the coordinates satisfy the equations of B and D at the same time. [2]

d Determine which graph has an x-intercept of $-\dfrac{1}{2}$. [1]

e Determine which graph is symmetrical about the y-axis. [1]

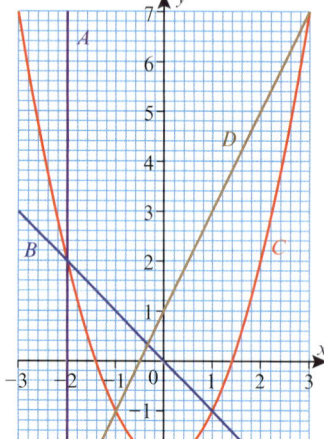

2 **a** The table shows some corresponding values of $y = x^2 + 3$. Copy and complete the table by filling in the missing values.

x	−2	−1.5	−1	−0.5	0	0.5	1	1.5	2
y		5.25	4	3.25	3		4	5.25	7

[2]

b Plot the graph of $y = x^2$ and the graph of $y = x^2 + 3$ for $-3 \leqslant x \leqslant 3$ on a grid. [3]

c Work out whether the two curves ever meet. Explain your answer. [3]

d By drawing a suitable straight line on the same grid, solve the following equations.

    i $x^2 = 6$ [3]

    ii $x^2 + 3 = 6$ [3]

3 Answer the whole of this question on graph paper.

x	0.6	1	1.5	2	2.5	3	3.5	4	4.5	5
y	p	−5.9	−3.7	−2.3	−1.1	0.3	1.9	3.8	q	r

Some of the values of $y = \dfrac{x^3}{12} - \dfrac{6}{x}$ are shown in the table. Values of y are given correct to 1 decimal place.

a Find the values of p, q and r. [2]

b Using a scale of 2 cm to represent 1 unit on the x-axis and 1 cm to represent 1 unit on the y-axis, draw the graph of $y = \dfrac{x^3}{12} - \dfrac{6}{x}$ for $0.6 \leqslant x \leqslant 5$. [4]

c From the graph, find the value of x (correct to 1 decimal place) for which $\dfrac{x^3}{12} - \dfrac{6}{x} = 0$. [2]

d Draw the tangent to the curve at the point where $x = 1$ and estimate the gradient of the curve at this point. [4]

4   Six sketch graphs are shown here.

i
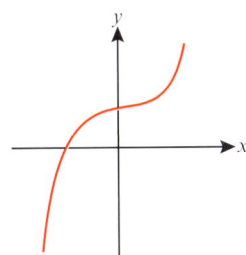

ii
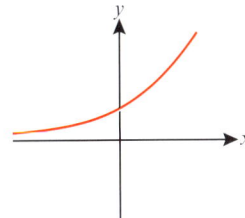

iii
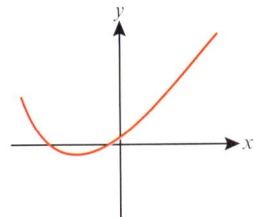

iv
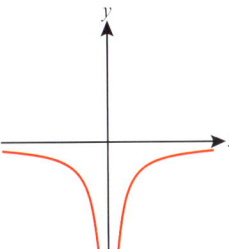

v
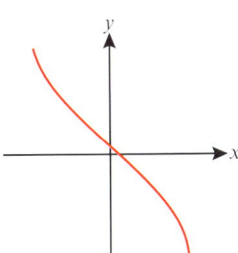

vi
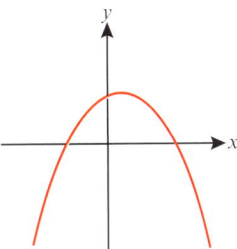

Match the graphs to the following equations.

a $y = 1 + x - 2x^2$ [2]

b $y = 3^x$ [2]

c $y = x^3 + x^2 + 1$ [2]

d $y = -\dfrac{16}{x^2}$ [2]

5   a   In a chemical reaction, the mass, M grams, of a chemical is given by the

formula $M = \dfrac{160}{2^t}$, where t is the time, in minutes, after the start.

A table of values for t and M is given.

t (min)	0	1	2	3	4	5	6	7
M (g)	p	80	40	20	q	5	r	1.25

   i   Find the values of p, q and r.   [2]

   ii   Draw the graph of M against t for $0 \le t \le 7$. Use a scale of 2 cm to
          represent one minute on the horizontal t-axis and 1 cm to represent 10
          grams on the vertical M-axis.   [4]

   iii Draw a suitable tangent to your graph and use it to estimate the rate of
          change of mass when $t = 2$.   [3]

b   The other chemical in the same reaction has mass m grams, which is given
       by $m = 160 - M$. Find the value of t for which the two chemicals have
       equal mass.   [4]

6 Solve these simultaneous equations. Give your answers to 2 decimal places.

$y = 2x^2 - 3x - 1$

$3y - x = 6$ [5]

7 A quadratic curve has equation $y = 3x^2 + 6x - 1$.
   - **a** Write the equation of the curve in the form $y = a(x + p)^2 + q$. [3]
   - **b** Write down the equation of the line of symmetry of the curve. [1]
   - **c** Write down the coordinates of the minimum point on the curve. [1]

8 A curve has equation $y = 3x^2 + 2x + 1$.
   - **a** Find the y-coordinate of the point with x-coordinate 2. [2]
   - **b** Find $\dfrac{dy}{dx}$. [2]
   - **c** Find the gradient of the curve at the point with x-coordinate 2. [2]
   - **d** Find the equation of the tangent to the curve at the point with x-coordinate 2. [3]
   - **e** Find the coordinates of the point where the tangent to the curve at $x = 2$ meets the x-axis. [2]

9 The *normal* to a curve at a given point is the straight line that passes through the point, but is perpendicular to the tangent at that point.

Find the equation of the normal to the curve $y = (x - 3)^2$ at the point with x-coordinate 5. [5]

10 A rectangle has fixed perimeter $4a$ metres.
   - **a** If the rectangle measures x m by y m, find y in terms of x. [2]
   - **b** Find the area of the rectangle in terms of x. [1]
   - **c** Show that the rectangle has maximum area when it is a square. [4]

SELF ASSESSMENT

Can you answer yes to all of these questions?

If not, write down what you need to do to change your answer.
- Did I understand all of the questions?
- Did I know what to do to answer them?
- Did I follow the instructions correctly?
- Was my work clear and organised?
- Did I perform procedures accurately?
- Was I able to use my calculator efficiently?
- Could I interpret results in the context of the given problem?
- Were my solutions correct?
- If I made mistakes, could I work out what I did wrong?

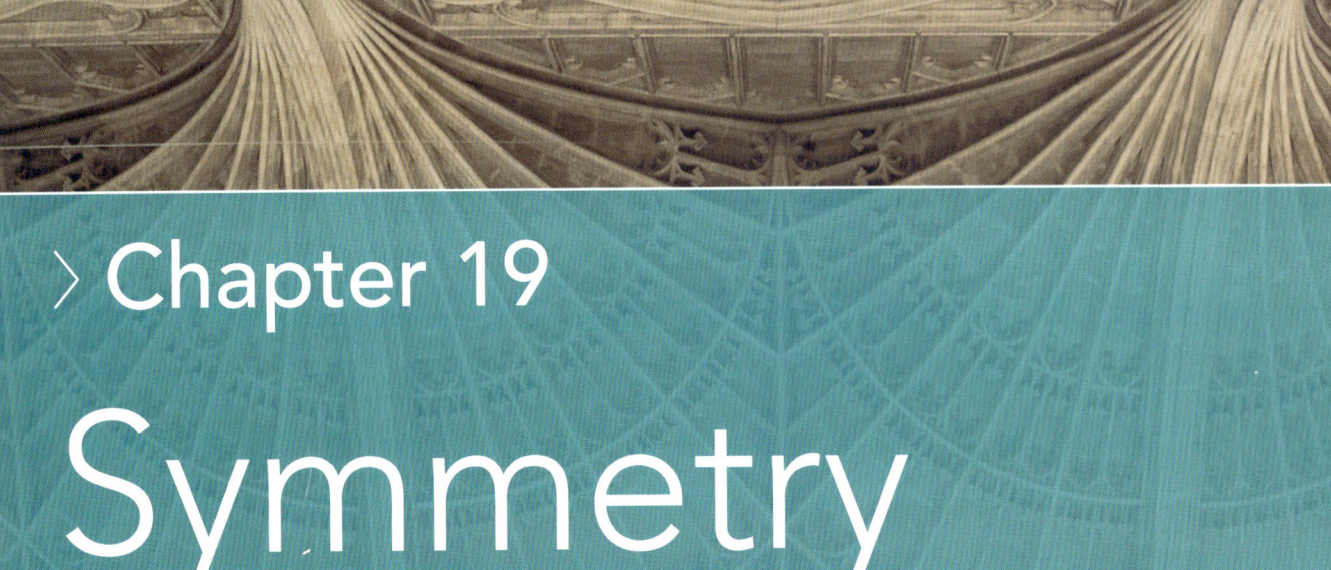

> # Chapter 19

Symmetry

The vaulted ceiling of the building in the photo on the previous page has symmetry. Where is the mirror line on the ceiling? How many other examples of symmetry can you find in the ceiling's features?

Shapes or objects that can be divided into two or more parts which are identical in shape and size are said to be symmetrical. Symmetry is found in both two-dimensional shapes and three-dimensional objects.

Natural objects sometimes look symmetrical but when you examine them closely you can see that the two halves are not identical. If you put a mirror on one half of your own face, you will see this very clearly.

In this chapter you are going to learn more about line symmetry and turning, or rotational, symmetry, in both two-dimensional shapes and three-dimensional objects. You will also explore the symmetry properties of circles and learn how these are used in geometrical proofs.

KEY WORDS

alternate segment

axis of symmetry

centre of rotation

cyclic quadrilateral

line symmetry

perpendicular bisector

plane symmetry

rotational symmetry

subtended angle

GETTING STARTED

1   Explain why this shape has can be said to have symmetry even though it has no mirror line.

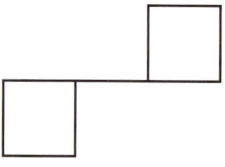

2   Sugata and Naledi were given some coloured and white squares and told to make a symmetrical 3 × 3 design. This is what they each did:

Sugata    Naledi

a   How many lines of symmetry are there in Sugata's design?

b   How can you move two coloured squares in Sugata's design to make a pattern with only one line of symmetry?

c   How many lines of symmetry are there in Naledi's design?

d   How can you move one coloured square in Naledi's design to make a pattern with two lines of symmetry?

e   How can you use three yellow and six white squares to make a design with no lines of symmetry?

f   Use one colour and a 3 × 3 square to make a pattern that has four lines of symmetry.

19.1 Symmetry in two dimensions

There are two types of symmetry in two-dimensional shapes:

- **line symmetry**
- **rotational symmetry**.

Line symmetry

If a shape can be folded so that one half fits exactly over the other half, it has line symmetry (also called reflection symmetry).

Triangle A is symmetrical. The dotted line divides it into two identical parts.

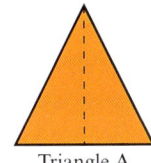

Triangle A

Triangle B is not symmetrical. You cannot draw a line which will divide it into two identical halves.

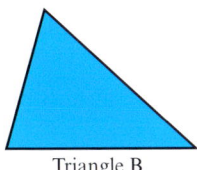

Triangle B

If you place a mirror on the dividing line on shape A, the view in the mirror will be that of the whole triangle. The line is called the line of symmetry or mirror line of the shape.

> **LINK**
>
> Molecular symmetry is an important concept in chemistry. When a molecule has symmetry, it means that certain parts of it can be interchanged with other parts without changing the identity of the molecule.
>
> For example, if you rotate a water molecule by 180° about an axis passing through the central O atom (between the two H atoms) it will look the same as before.
>
>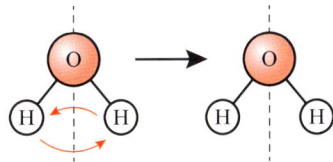
>
> Knowing the symmetry properties allows chemists to predict or explain the properties of molecules using a branch of mathematics called group theory.

> **MATHEMATICAL CONNECTIONS**
>
> You will deal with line symmetry on the Cartesian plane when you deal with reflections about a line in Chapter 23.

Shapes can have more than one line of symmetry:

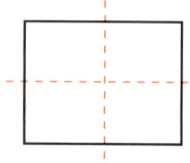

2 lines of symmetry

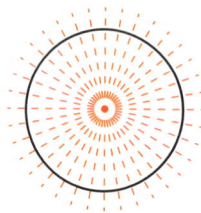

3 lines of symmetry

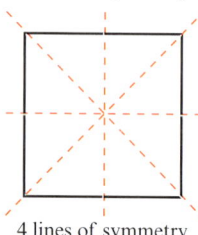

4 lines of symmetry

Infinite number of
lines of symmetry

Exercise 19.1

1   Which of the broken lines in these figures are lines of symmetry? Check with a
small mirror or trace and fold the shape if you are not sure.

a   Parallelogram

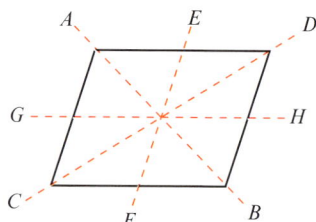

b   Ellipse

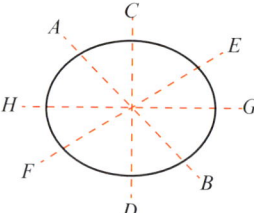

c   Rectangle

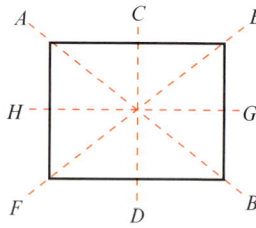

d   Isosceles trapezium

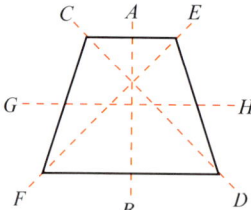

e   Rhombus

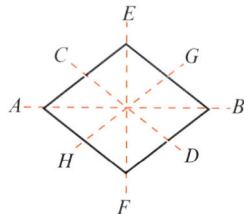

f   Torus

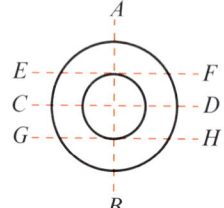

g   L-shape

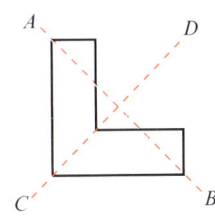

h   Regular pentagon

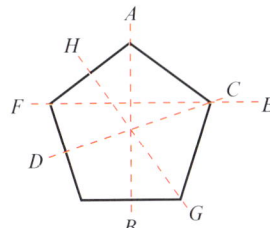

2   Sketch the following polygons and investigate to see how many lines of symmetry each one has. Copy and complete the table to summarise your results.

Shape	Number of lines of symmetry
Square	
Rectangle	
Equilateral triangle	
Isosceles triangle	
Scalene triangle	
Kite	
Parallelogram	
Rhombus	
Regular pentagon	
Regular hexagon	
Regular octagon	

3   Copy these figures and draw in all possible lines of symmetry.

a

b

c

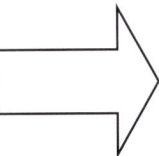

d

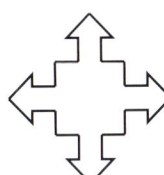

e

f

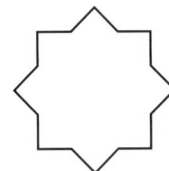

APPLY YOUR SKILLS

4   The children in a primary school class made shapes for a class pattern by cutting out a design drawn on the corner of a folded piece of paper.

a   Draw the shapes that will be produced by each of these cut outs.

i 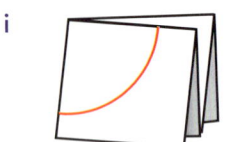   ii 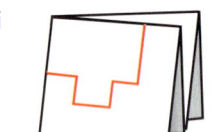   iii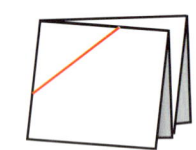

b   Show the lines of symmetry on each shape using dotted lines.

i 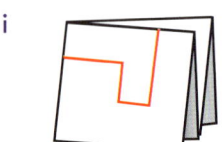   ii    iii

5   Find and draw the badges of five different makes of motor vehicle. Indicate the lines of symmetry on each drawing.

> **TIP**
>
> Think carefully about how the paper is folded. The diagram shows that it is folded into four.

Rotational symmetry

A rotation is a turn. If you rotate a shape through 360°, keeping its centre point in a fixed position, and it fits onto itself exactly at various positions during the turn, then it has rotational symmetry. The number of times it fits onto itself during a full revolution is its order of rotational symmetry.

MATHEMATICAL CONNECTIONS

You will deal with rotational symmetry on the Cartesian plane when you deal with rotations in Chapter 23.

The diagram shows that a square fits onto itself four times when it is turned through 360°. The dot in the centre of the square is the **centre of rotation**. This is the point around which it is turning. The star shows the position of one corner of the square as it turns.

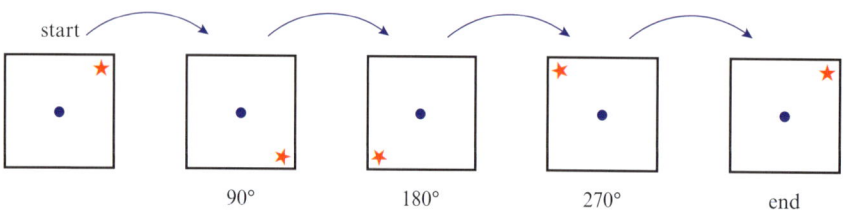

The square fits exactly onto itself four times in a rotation, when it has turned through 90°, 180°, 270° and 360°, so its order of rotational symmetry is 4. Remember it has to turn 360° to get back to its original position.

> **TIP**
>
> If you have to turn the shape through a full 360° *before* it fits onto itself then it does *not* have rotational symmetry.

Exercise 19.2

1 State the order of rotational symmetry of each of the following polygons. The dot represents each centre of rotation.

a

b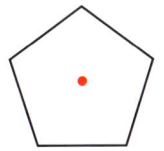

c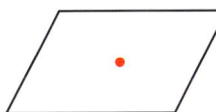

d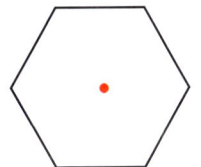

e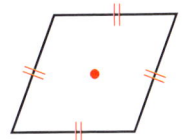

f

g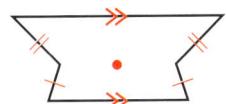

h

INVESTIGATION

2 This table shows how many lines of symmetry there are in six regular polygons.

Regular polygon	Lines of symmetry	Order of rotational symmetry
Triangle	3	
Quadrilateral	4	
Pentagon	5	
Hexagon	6	
Octagon	8	
Decagon	10	

a Draw each shape and investigate its rotational symmetry. Sometimes it helps to physically turn the shape to see how many times it fits onto itself in a revolution.

b Copy and complete the table by filling in the order of rotational symmetry for each polygon.

c Describe how line symmetry and rotational symmetry are related in regular polygons.

d What pattern can you see relating line symmetry, order of rotational symmetry and number of sides in a regular polygon?

APPLY YOUR SKILLS

3 Refer back to the motor vehicle badges you drew in Exercise 19.1 (question 5). For each one, state its order of rotational symmetry.

4 Using a computer, print out the capital letters of the alphabet. (You can choose whichever font you like). Which letters have:

   a only one line of symmetry?

   b two or more lines of symmetry?

   c rotational symmetry of order 2 or more?

5 Alloy rims for tyres are very popular on modern cars. Find and draw five alloy rim designs that you like. For each one, state its order of rotational symmetry.

SELF ASSESSMENT

How well do you understand the work on symmetry?

1 Look back over your completed exercises.

2 Complete these sentences to summarise what went well:

   a The things that went well were …

   b I am good at …

   c I am proud of …

   d The best bit of my work was …

3 How could you improve your work? Complete these sentences about your own work:

   a To improve my work I need to …

   b Next time I work on symmetry I must remember to …

   c I think I could improve if I focussed on …

19.2 Symmetry in three dimensions

There are two types of symmetry in three-dimensional shapes:

- **plane symmetry**

- rotational symmetry.

Plane symmetry

A plane is a flat surface. If you can cut a solid in half along a plane so that each half is the mirror image of the other, then the solid has plane symmetry.

This diagram of a cuboid shows that it can be cut three different ways to make two identical halves.

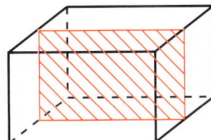 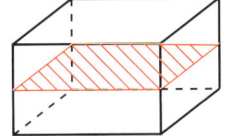 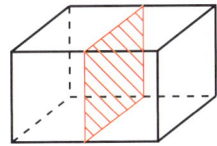

The shaded area on each diagram represents the plane of symmetry (this is where you would cut it).

Can you see that a sphere technically has an infinite number of planes of symmetry? It is symmetrical about any plane that passes through its centre.

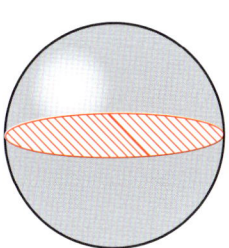 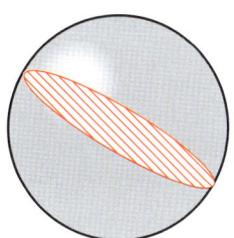

LINK

If you look at an electricity pylon from the air it is clear that it has more than one plane of symmetry. This helps the pylon to stay balanced.

Exercise 19.3

1   Here are two of the planes of symmetry in a cube:

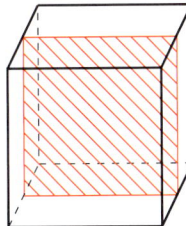 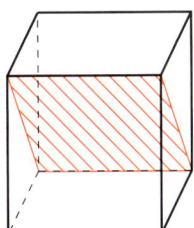

A cube has nine possible planes of symmetry. Make sketches to show the other seven planes.

2 How many planes of symmetry does each of the following solids have?

a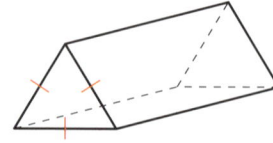

b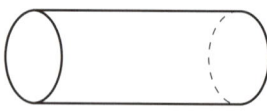

c

d

e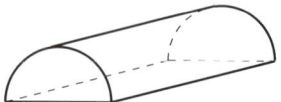

f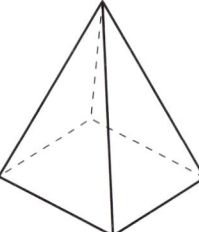

g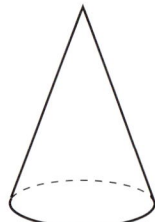

h

i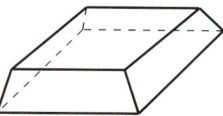

Rotational symmetry

Imagine a rod through a solid shape. The rod forms an axis for the shape to turn around. If you rotate the shape around the axis and it looks the same at different points on its rotation, then the shape has rotational symmetry. The rod is then the **axis of symmetry**.

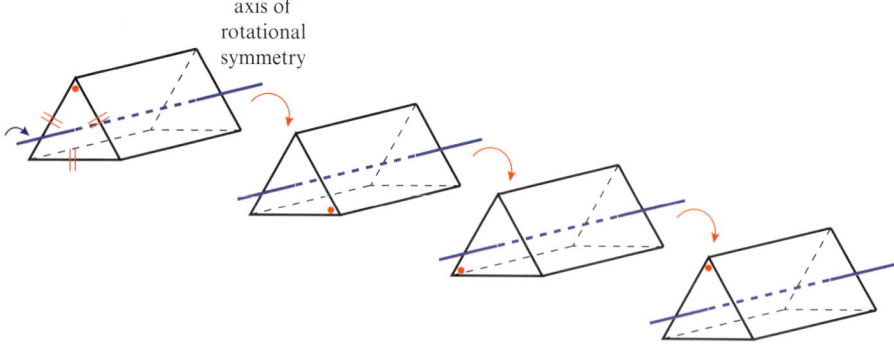

The triangular prism looks the same in three positions during a rotation, when it has turned 120°, 240° and 360° around the axis. The dot shows the position of one of the vertices during the turn.

Exercise 19.4

1   This diagram shows three possible axes of symmetry through a cuboid. For each one, state the order of rotational symmetry.

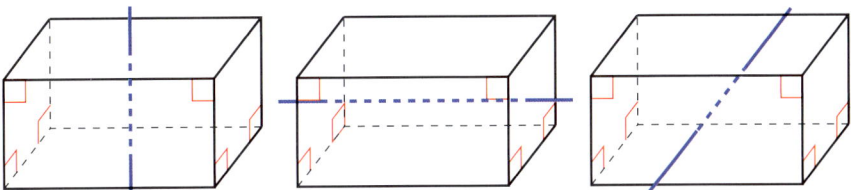

2   For each solid shown, determine the order of rotational symmetry for rotation about the given axis.

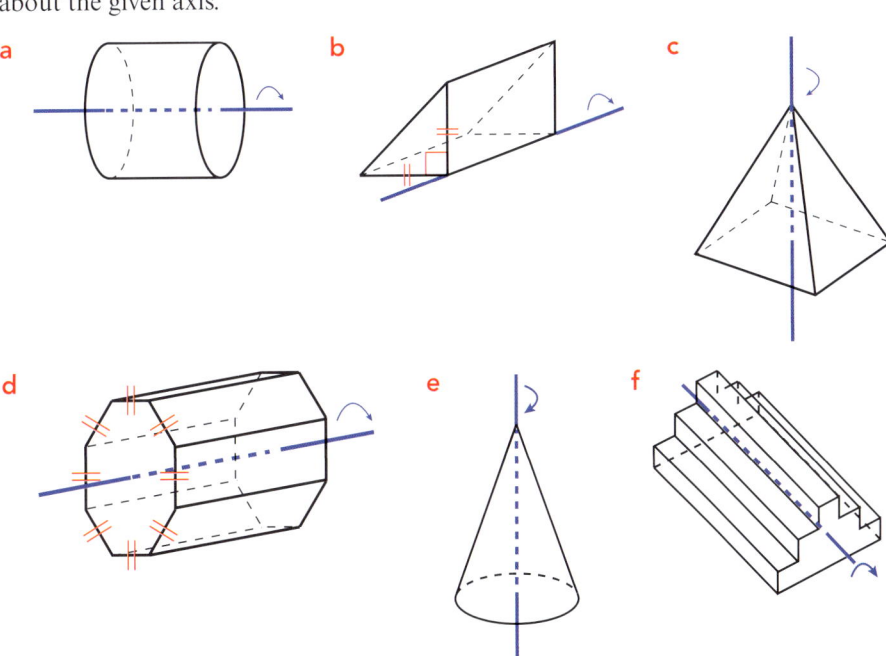

a   b   c

d   e   f

REFLECTION

•   Did you struggle in any way to visualise the three-dimensional symmetries?
•   What did you do to make it easier for yourself?

19.3 Symmetry properties of circles

A circle has line symmetry about any diameter and it has rotational symmetry about its centre. From these facts a number of results can be deduced:

1   The **perpendicular bisector** of a chord passes through the centre.

2   Equal chords are equidistant from the centre, and chords equidistant from the centre are equal in length.

3   Two **tangents** drawn to a circle from the same point outside the circle are equal in length.

LINK

The Earth rotates about an axis of symmetry. Where the Earth's axis meets the Earth's surface you will find the Geographical North and South Poles.

The perpendicular bisector of a chord passes through the centre

The perpendicular bisector of chord AB is the locus of points equidistant from A and B.

But centre O is equidistant from A and B (OA and OB are radii of circle with centre O).

$\therefore O$ must be on the perpendicular bisector of AB.

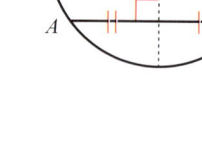

This result can be expressed in other ways:

*   The perpendicular from the centre of a circle to a chord meets the chord at its midpoint.

*   The line joining the centre of a circle to the midpoint of a chord is perpendicular to the chord.

You can use this fact to find the lengths of chords and the lengths of sides of right-angled triangles drawn between the centre and the chord.

WORKED EXAMPLE 1

Chord AB is drawn in a circle with a radius of 7 cm. If the chord is 3 cm from the centre of the circle, find the length of the chord correct to 2 decimal places.

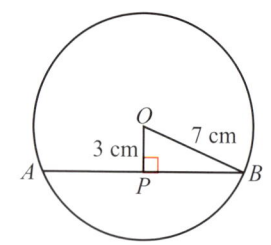

Answer

$PB^2 = OB^2 - OP^2$ (Rearrange Pythagoras' theorem)

$ = 7^2 - 3^2$

$ = 49 - 9$

$ = 40$

$\therefore PB = \sqrt{40}$

Chord $AB = 2 \times \sqrt{40} = 12.65$ cm

Equal chords are equidistant from the centre and chords equidistant from the centre are equal in length

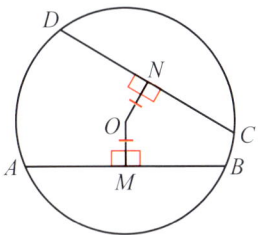

If chords AB and CD are the same length, then $OM = ON$, and vice versa.

This is true because triangle OAM is congruent to triangle ODN and because the circle has rotational symmetry about its centre, O.

When you are asked for the distance from a point to a line, it is always the perpendicular distance which is expected. This is the shortest distance from the point to the line.

> **TIP**
>
> Think about how you could you prove triangle $OAM \equiv$ triangle ODN; remember OA and OD are radii of the circle.

WORKED EXAMPLE 2

O is the centre of the circle, radius 11 cm.

AB and CD are chords, $AB = 14$ cm.

If $OX = OY$, find the length of OY correct to 2 decimal places.

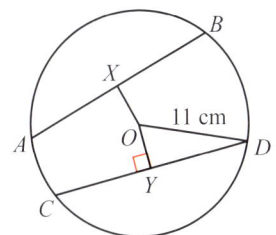

Answer

Since $OX = OY$, chords are equidistant so,
$AB = CD = 14$ cm

$CY = YD = 7$ cm (OY is the perpendicular bisector of CD)

Angle $OYD = 90°$

$$OY^2 = OD^2 - YD^2 \text{ (Pythagoras)}$$
$$= 11^2 - 7^2$$
$$= 121 - 49$$
$$= 72$$
$$\therefore OY = \sqrt{72} = 8.49 \text{ cm}$$

Two tangents drawn to a circle from the same point outside the circle are equal in length

A and B are the points of contact of the tangents drawn from P.

The result is $PA = PB$.

In addition:

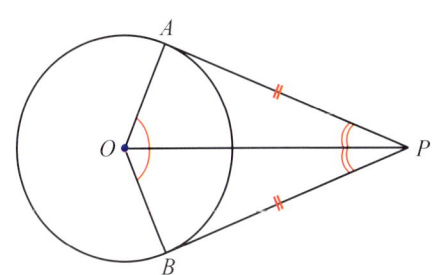

- the tangents subtend equal angles at the centre
  (i.e. angle $POA =$ angle POB)

- the line joining the centre to the point where the tangents meet bisects the angle between the tangents.
  (i.e. angle $OPA =$ angle OPB).

You can show the two tangents are equal in length by proving that triangle OAP is congruent to triangle OBP, but in order to do this you need to use the 'tangent perpendicular to radius' property that you will learn about in Section 19.4.

WORKED EXAMPLE 3

Find the lengths of x and y in this diagram correct to 2 decimal places where appropriate.

Answer

$NM = PM = 25$ cm (equal tangents)

$\therefore x = 25$ cm

$y^2 = x^2 + NO^2$ (Pythagoras)

$\quad = 25^2 + 12^2$

$\quad = 625 + 144$

$\quad = 769$

$y = \sqrt{769} = 27.73$ cm

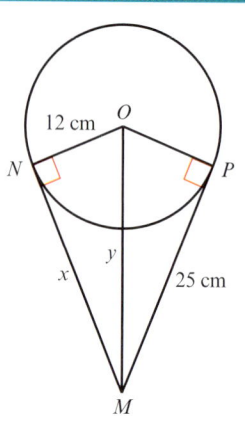

WORKED EXAMPLE 4

Find the size of angles x and y in this diagram.

Answer

Angle $OCB = 90°$ (OC perpendicular to tangent CB)

$\therefore y = 180° - 90° - 30°$ angle sum of triangle

$\quad y = 60°$

$y = x = 60°$ (tangents subtend equal angles at centre)

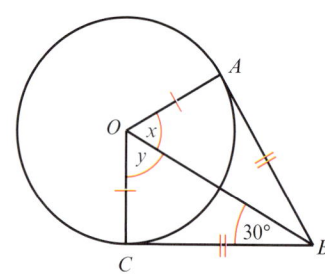

Exercise 19.5

1   Calculate the length of the chord AB in each of the following circles. (In each case, X is the midpoint of AB.)

a
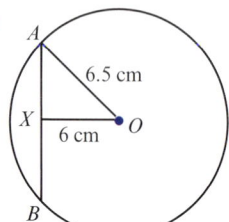

b
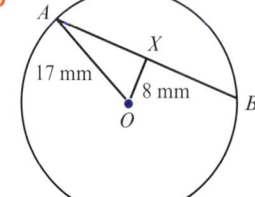

c
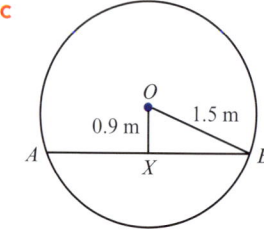

2   *P* is a point inside a circle whose centre is *O*. Describe how to draw the chord that has *P* as its midpoint

3   In the diagram, *AB* and *AD* are tangents to the circle. *ABC* is a straight line.

Calculate the size of angle *x*.

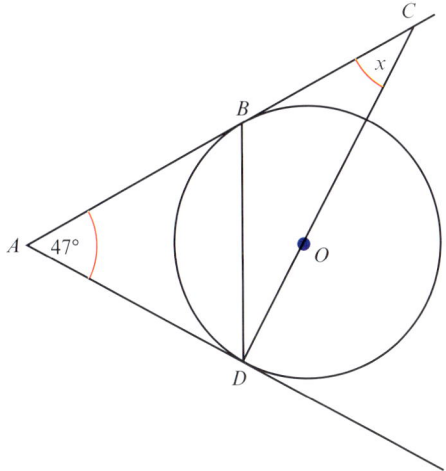

4   A circle with a radius of 8.4 cm has a chord 5 cm from its centre. Calculate the length of the chord correct to 2 decimal places.

5   In this diagram, find the length of *AO* and the area of quadrilateral *AOCB*.

BA and BC are tangents to the circle.

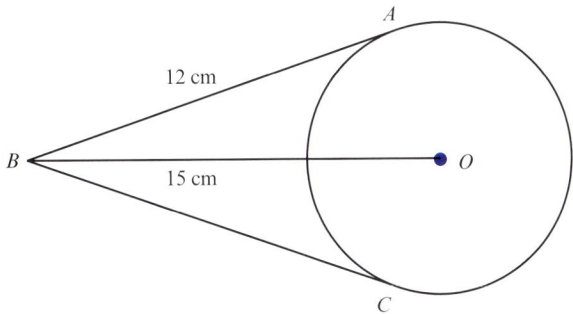

6   A straight line cuts two concentric circles at *A*, *B*, *C* and *D* (in that order).

Prove that *AB* = *CD*.

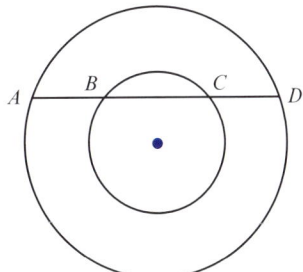

7 Apply what you have learned about circle properties to calculate the diameter of each circle. Give approximate answers to 3 significant figures. Show all your working and give reasons for any deductions.

a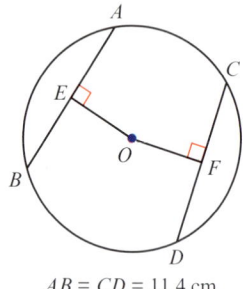

$AB = CD = 11.4$ cm
$OF = 6.5$ cm

b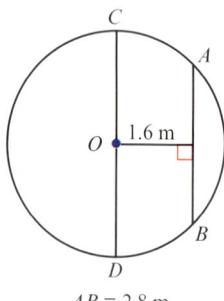

$AB = 2.8$ m

c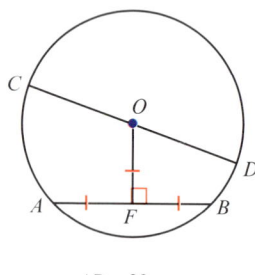

$AB = 22$ mm

8 Mahindra makes badges by sticking an equilateral triangle onto a circular disc as shown.
If the triangle has sides of 15 cm, find the diameter of the circular disc.

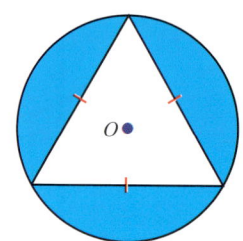

19.4 Angle relationships in circles

Circles have many useful angle properties that you can use to solve problems.

Useful properties of circles

The angle in a semicircle is a right angle (90°)

Read through Worked example 5 to see how to work out the size of an angle in a semicircle.

WORKED EXAMPLE 5

AB is the diameter of a circle. *C* is the centre.
D is any point on the circumference.
Remember that all radii of a circle are equal.
Work out the size of angle *ADB*.

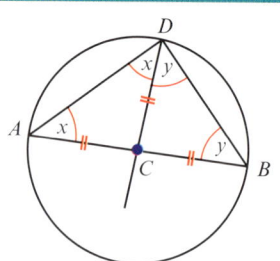

Answer

$AC = CB = CD$ (radii of circle)

$\therefore$ triangle *ACD* and triangle *BCD* are isosceles.

$\therefore$ angle CAD = angle $ADC = x$

and angle CDB = angle $DBC = y$

But $2x + 2y = 180°$ (sum of angles in triangle *ABD*)

$\therefore x + y + 90°$

so angle $ADB = 90°$

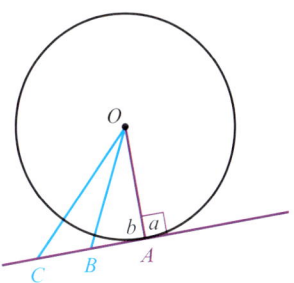

The angle between the tangent and radius is 90°

Look at the diagram carefully.

A tangent touches a circle at one point only.

If you draw lines from the centre to points on the tangent, you can see that the shortest possible line is a radius. (*OA*).

You already know that the shortest distance from a point to a line is the perpendicular distance from the point to the line.

So, the radius is perpendicular to the tangent.

It follows that angles *a* and *b* are right angles.

TIP

OC and *OB* (and any other lines from the centre to the tangent) extend beyond the circle and are therefore longer than any radius.

LINK

The hammer throw event involves movement in a circle.

When the athlete stops the circular movement, the hammer moves in a direction tangential to the circular motion. The athlete has to think about this before letting go or the hammer will end up in the nets.

Exercise 19.6

1 Calculate the size of the lettered angles in each diagram. Show your working and give reasons for any deductions.

a
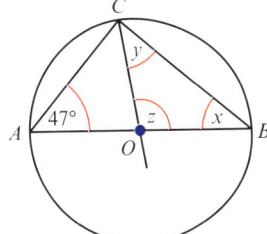

b
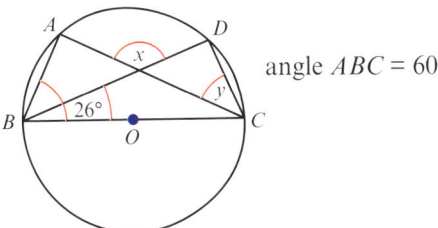
angle *ABC* = 60°

c
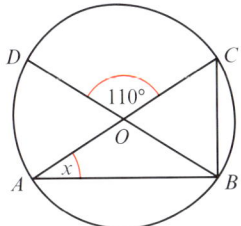

d
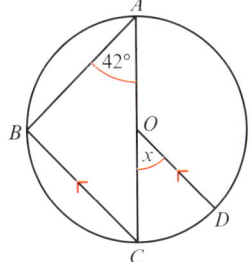

2 Calculate the value of *x* in each diagram. Show your working and give reasons for any deductions.

a

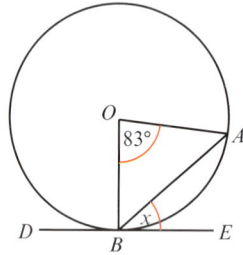

b

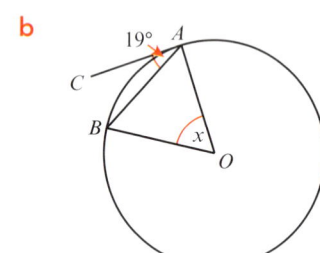

3 In the diagram, *BCF* and *BAE* are the tangents to the circle at *C* and *A* respectively.

AD is a diameter and angle *ABC* = 40°.

a Explain why triangle *ABC* is isosceles.

b Calculate the size of:

   i angle *CAB*

   ii angle *DAC*

   iii angle *ADC*.

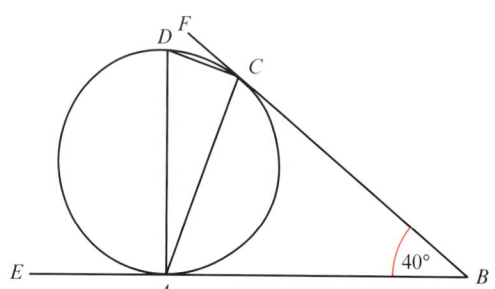

PEER ASSESSMENT

- Work in pairs to teach each other how to solve the problems in question 2.
- One person should teach part (a), the other should teach part (b).
- Once you have taught your partner how to solve the problem, ask them to give you feedback on how well you explained the work to them.

Further circle theorems

The angle at the centre of a circle is twice the angle at the circumference

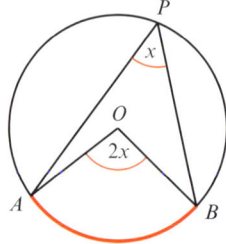
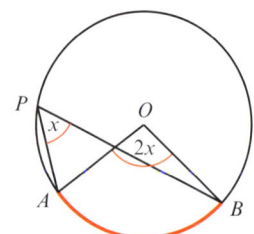
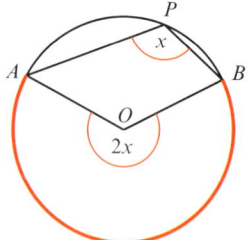

AB is an arc of a circle with centre *O*. *P* is a point on the circumference, but not on the arc *AB*. The angle at the centre theorem states that:

angle *AOB* = 2 × angle *APB*

As you saw before, this is also true when AB is a semicircular arc. The angle at the centre theorem states that the angle in a semicircle is 90°. This is because, in this case, angle AOB is a straight line (180°).

Angles in the same segment are equal

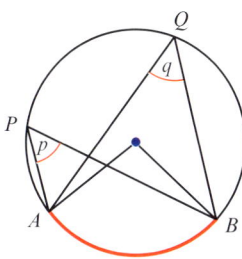 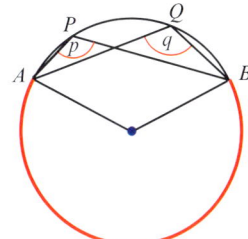

In these two diagrams, $p = q$. Each of the angles p and q is half the angle subtended by the arc AB at the centre of the circle.

The opposite angles of a cyclic quadrilateral add up to 180°

A **cyclic quadrilateral** is one that has all four vertices touching the circumference of a circle.

Look at the diagrams and follow the working to see why why the opposite angles add up to 180°.

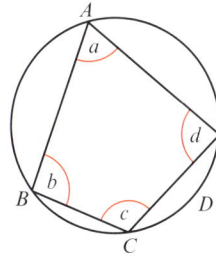 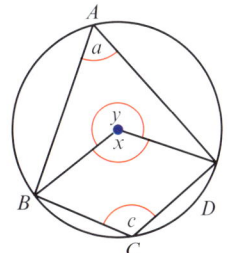

$x = 2a$ (angle at centre theorem, minor arc BD)

$y = 2c$ (angle at centre theorem, major arc BD)

$\therefore x + y = 2a + 2c$

But $x + y = 360°$ (angles round a point)

$\therefore a + c = 180°$

By a similar argument:

$b + d = 180°$

Each exterior angle of a cyclic quadrilateral is equal to the interior angle opposite to it

Worked example 6 shows why this is the case.

TIP

You may sometimes see 'cyclic quadrilateral' written as 'cyclical quadrilateral'.

A common error is to see the following as a cyclic quadrilateral:

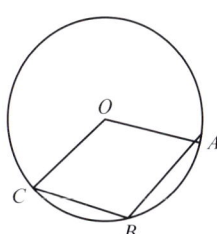

You must check that *all four* vertices sit on the circumference of the circle.

WORKED EXAMPLE 6

Prove that $x = a$.

Answer

x + angle $BCD = 180°$ (angles on a straight line)

a + angle $BCD = 180°$ (opposite interior angles of a cyclic quadrilateral)

$x = a$

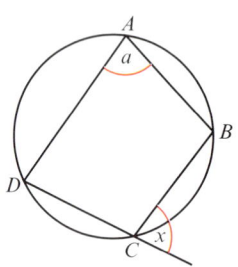

Exercise 19.7

1 Find the size of each lettered angle in these sketches. When it is marked, O is the centre of the circle.

a

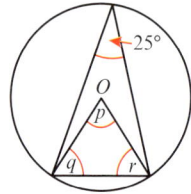

b

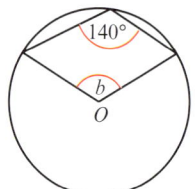

c

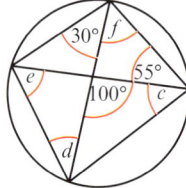

d

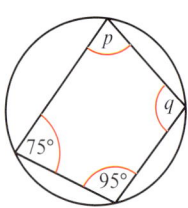

e

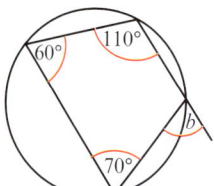

f

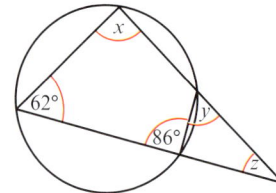

g

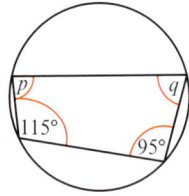

2 In the diagram SAT is the tangent to the circle at point A. The points B and C lie on the circle and O is the centre of the circle. If angle $ACB = x$, express, in terms of x, the size of:

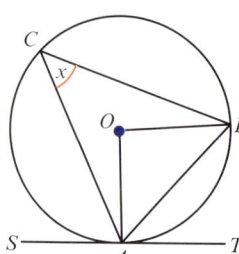

a angle AOB

b angle OAB

c angle BAT.

3 Find the size of each lettered angle in these sketches.

When it is marked, *O* is the centre of the circle.

a

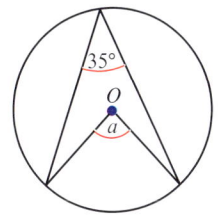

b

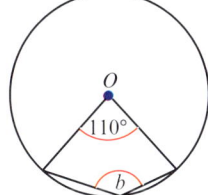

c

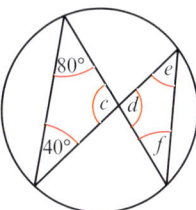

4 In the diagram, *TA* and *TB* are the tangents from *T* to the circle whose centre is *O*. *AC* is a diameter of the circle and angle $ACB = x$.

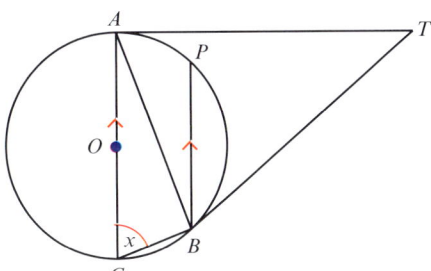

a Find angle *CAB* in terms of x.

b Find angle *ATB* in terms of x.

c The point *P* on the circumference of the circle is such that *BP* is parallel to *CA*. Express angle *PBT* in terms of x.

5 The diagram shows two chords, *AC* and *BD*, drawn in a circle. The chords intersect at the point *X*.

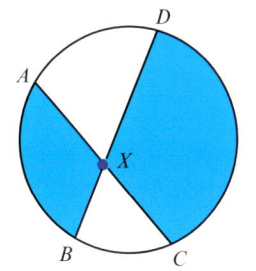

a Use angle properties to show that triangle *AXD* is similar to triangle *BXC*.

b Use the fact that the two triangles are similar to show that:

$AX \times CX = BX \times DX$

> **TIP**
>
> This is called the intersecting chords theorem.

Alternate segment theorem

You already know that where a tangent and diameter of a circle meet they form a right angle. The diameter will divide the circle into two semicircles.

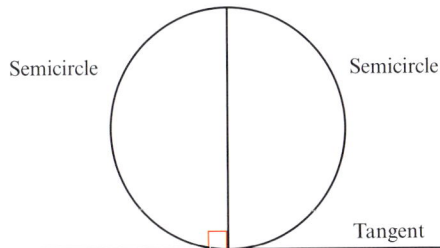

Semicircle   Semicircle

Tangent

You also know that a diameter of any circle is a chord that passes through the centre of the circle. When a chord meets a tangent but does *not* pass through the centre, the circle is divided into a major segment and a minor segment. The point at which the tangent and chord meet is called the point of contact.

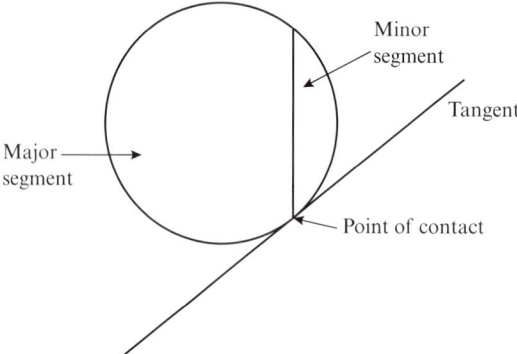

You can draw two possible angles between the tangent and this chord. One crosses the major segment and the other crosses the minor segment.

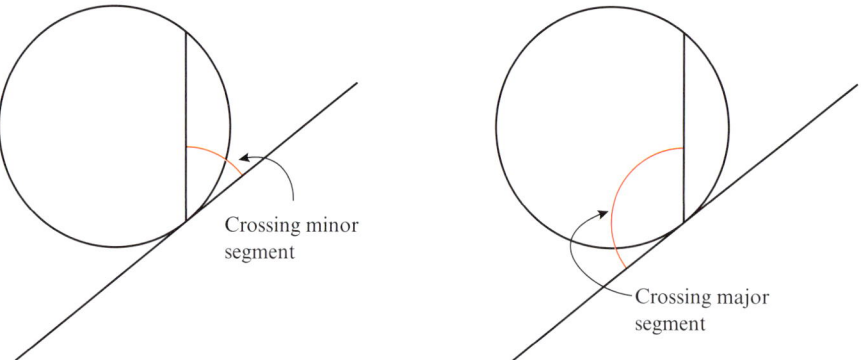

The segment that the angle does *not* cross is called the **alternate segment**.
Draw an angle in the alternate segment.

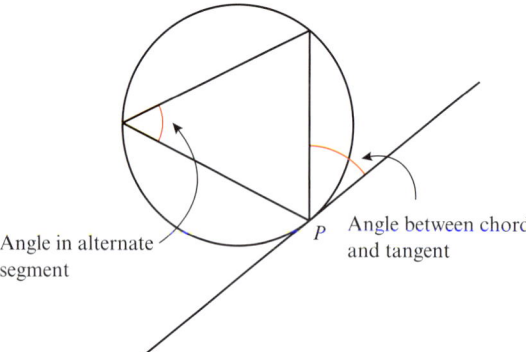

INVESTIGATION

Understanding the alternate segment theorem

1   **a**   Follow these instructions.

   - Draw three large circles.
   - Draw a tangent to each circle, taking care to be as accurate as possible – your line should only touch the circle once.
   - Draw a chord so that it meets the tangent.
   - Draw an angle between the tangent and chord. You can choose either angle.
   - Work out which segment is the alternate segment and draw an angle in it.
   - Measure, as accurately as you can, both the angle in the alternate segment and the angle between the tangent and the chord.

   b   What do you notice?

   The alternate segment theorem states that the angle between the tangent and chord is always equal to the angle in the alternate segment. The diagram shows which angles are equal to which:

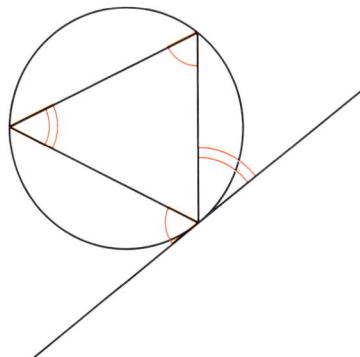

2   How do you prove the alternate segment theorem?

This is an interesting proof because it will use some of the theorems that you already know.

Begin by drawing the circle, chord, tangent, angle and angle in the alternate segment. Call the angles x and y respectively and label the point where the chord meets the tangent P.

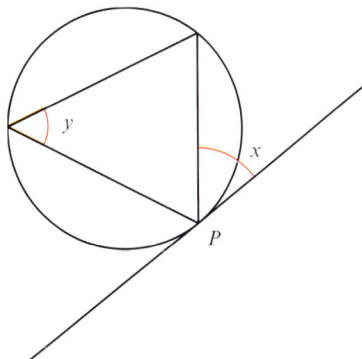

INVESTIGATION CONTINUED

Draw in lines *PA* and *AB* as indicated on this diagram. Note that *PA* goes through the centre of the circle.

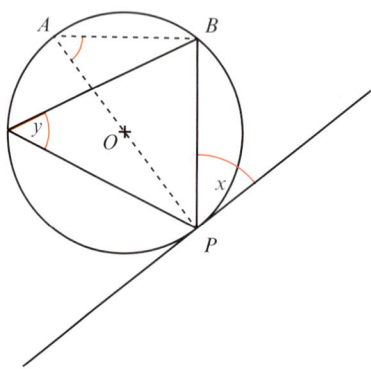

a   Explain why angle *PAB* is equal to *y*.

b   What type of triangle is *PAB*? Why?

c   What does this tell you about the size of angle *APB*?

d   Use the angle between a diameter and a tangent to show that *x* = *y*.

Now that you have seen how the theorem works, you can apply it like the others you know to solve problems.

WORKED EXAMPLE 7

Find the unknown angle *x* in the diagram.

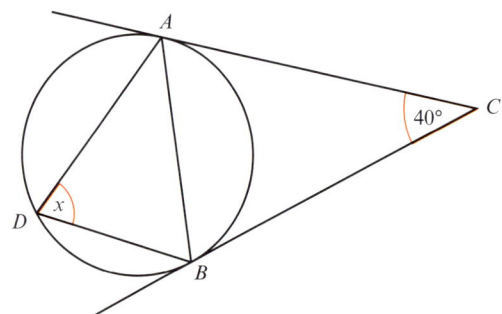

Answer

Angles in a triangle add to 180°.

∴ *ABC* + *BAC* + 40° = 180°

Both *AC* and *BC* are tangents to the circle so triangle *ABC* is isosceles.

ABC + *BAC* + 40° = 180°

∴ *ABC* = *BAC* = 70°

By the alternate segment theorem, angle *ABC* = angle *ADB* = 70°.

So *x* = 70°

Exercise 19.8

1   Find the angle x in each of the following. Give full reasons for your answers.

a

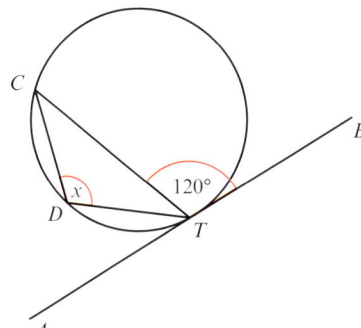

b

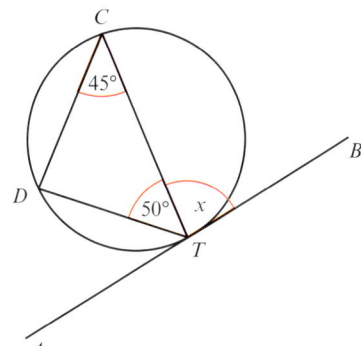

c

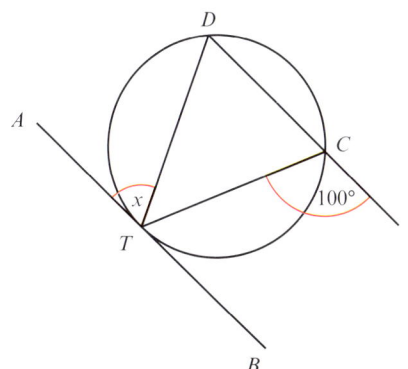

d

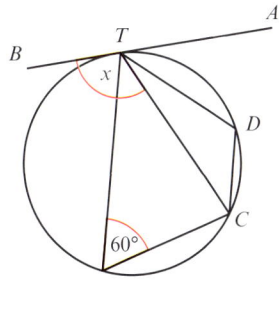

e

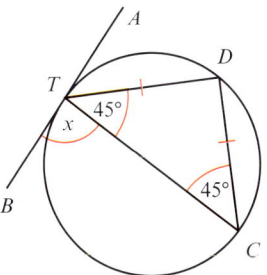

f

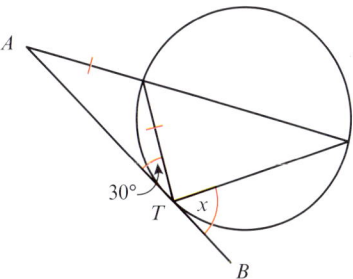

2 Prove that *CD* is a diameter of the circle.

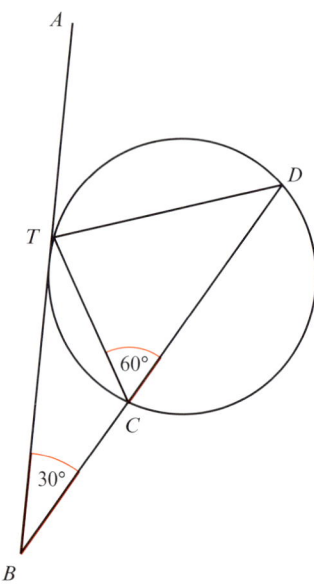

3 Given that *O* is the centre of the circle prove that $2x - y = 90°$

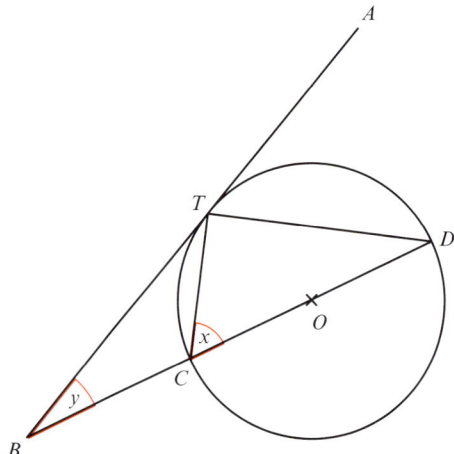

4 Find the unknown angle *x*.

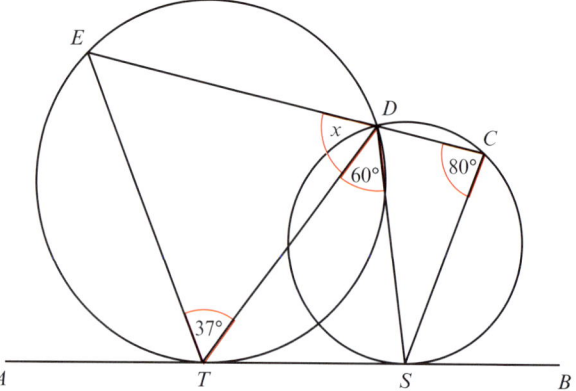

SUMMARY

Do you know ...?

Shapes can have more than one line of symmetry. The number of lines of symmetry of a regular polygon corresponds with the number of sides the shape has.

The order of rotational symmetry tells you the number of times a shape fits onto itself in one rotation.

When a shape can be cut along a plane to form two solid parts that are mirror images of each other then it has plane symmetry.

If a three-dimensional shape is rotated around an axis and it looks the same at one or more positions during a complete revolution then it has rotational symmetry.

The perpendicular bisector of a chord passes through the centre of a circle.

Equal chords are equidistant from the centre and chords equidistant from the centre are equal in length.

Two tangents drawn to a circle from a point outside the circle are equal in length.

The angle in a semi-circle is a right angle.

The angle between a tangent and the radius of a circle is a right angle.

The angle subtended at the centre of a circle by an arc is twice the angle subtended at the circumference by the arc.

Angles in the same segment, subtended by the same arc, are equal.

Opposite angles of a cyclic quadrilateral add up to 180°.

Each exterior angle of a cyclic quadrilateral is equal to the interior angle opposite to it.

The alternate segment theorem states that the angle between the tangent and chord is always equal to the angle in the alternate segment.

Are you able to ...?

recognise rotational and line symmetry in two-dimensional shapes

find the order of symmetry of a two-dimensional shape

recognise rotational and line symmetry in three-dimensional shapes

use the symmetry properties of polygons and circles to solve problems

calculate unknown angles in a circle using its angle properties

use the symmetry properties of circles to solve related problems.

Practice questions

1 Which of the following figures have both line and rotational symmetry?

a 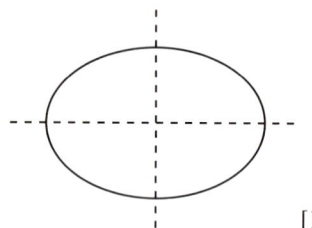 [1]

b 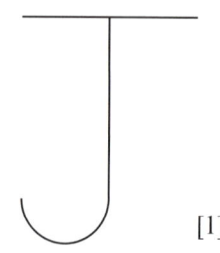 [1]

c 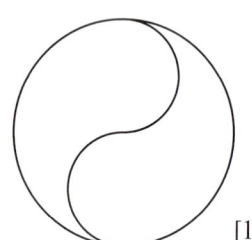 [1]

d 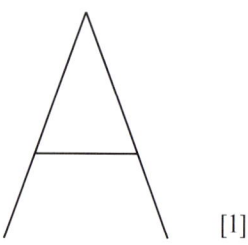 [1]

e 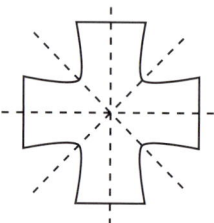 [1]

2 State the order of rotational symmetry in this figure.

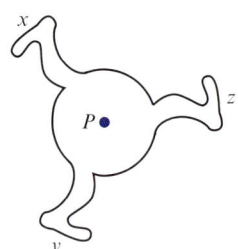 [1]

3 Draw two copies of the square grid.

a On your first grid, add three more crosses, so that the pattern has line symmetry, but no rotational symmetry. [2]

b On your second grid add three more crosses, so that the pattern has rotational symmetry, but no line symmetry. [2]

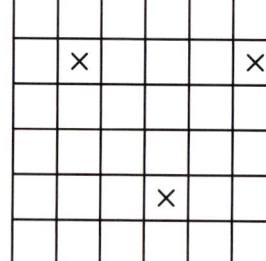

4 RST is a tangent to the circle with centre O. PS is a diameter. Q is a point on the circumference and PQT is a straight line.

Angle $QST = 37°$.

Write down the values of a, b, c and d. [6]

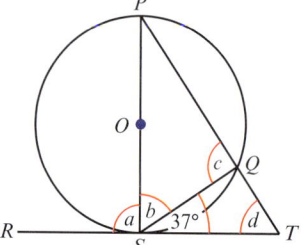

5 The diagram shows a prism with regular cross-section.

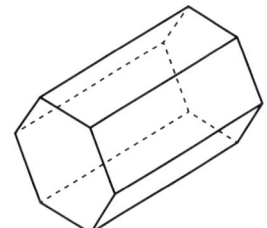

   a One axis of symmetry passes through both end faces. Find the order of rotational symmetry about this axis. [1]

   b Find the total number of axes of symmetry. [2]

   c Find the total number of planes of symmetry. [2]

6 The diagram shows a circle with two tangents PX and XQ. The tangents intersect at the point X and meet the circle at P and Q respectively.

If the centre of the circle is O, and the angle POQ is 150°, calculate the angle PXQ.

Give clear reasons for each step of your working. [4]

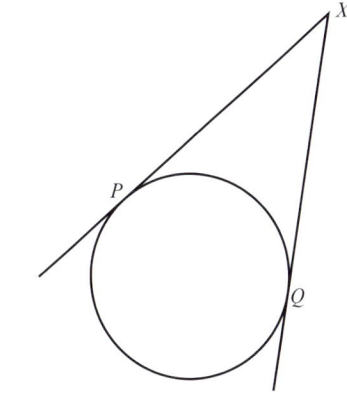

7 The diagram shows a circle and quadrilateral $OABC$, where O is the centre of the circle and A, B and C all lie on the circumference.

Find the value of x, showing full reasoning. [4]

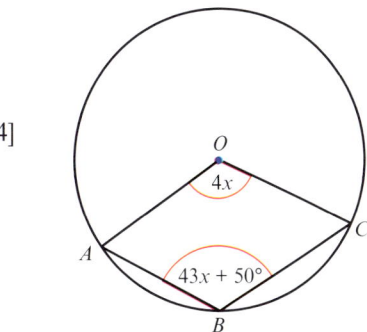

8 P, Q, R and S are points on the circumference of a circle with centre O. AB and CB are tangents to the circle at P and Q respectively.

Find the size of the following angles, giving reasons.

   a angle QSP [2]   **b** angle SQP [3]

   c angle PBQ [2]   **d** angle QRS [2]

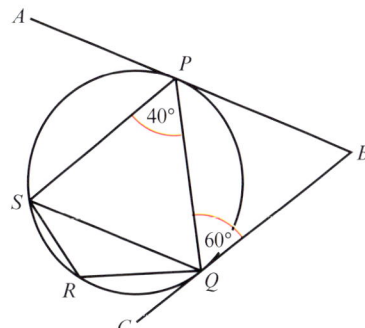

9   The diagram shows two chords, AC and BD, that intersect at the point X.

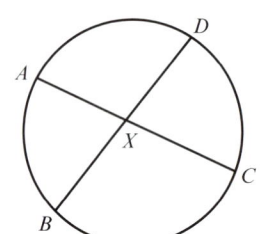

a   Explain why Angle BXA is equal to angle DXC.   [1]

b   Explain why angle XAB is equal to angle XDC.   [1]

c   Explain why triangles ABX and DCX are similar.   [2]

d   Show that $(AX)(CX) = (BX)(DX)$.   [3]

This result is called the intersecting chords theorem.

10   A, B, C and D are points on the circle, centre O. Angle $BOD = 86°$.

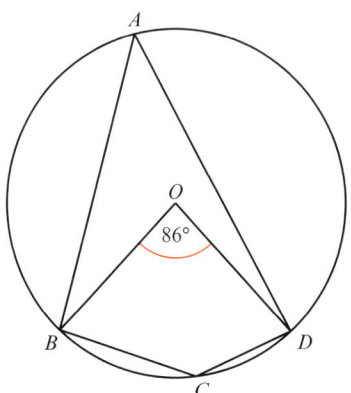

a   i   Work out the size of angle BAD.   [2]

   ii   Give a reason for your answer.   [1]

b   i   Work out the size of angle BCD.   [2]

   ii   Explain your answer fully.   [1]

SELF ASSESSMENT

Mark your answers to the practice questions.

Complete these statements in your book.

- I now know …
- I need to know more about …
- These things went well …
- I could do better if I …

> Chapter 20

Histograms and cumulative frequency diagrams

Look at the three histograms on the display screen in the photo below. How is a histogram similar to a bar chart? How is it different? The shape of a histogram allows you see where most of the measurements are located and how spread out they are. Describe the distribution of the data values in the dark blue histogram at the bottom left of the screen.

KEY WORDS

cumulative
   frequency

cumulative
   frequency curve

frequency density

histogram

percentiles

We live in an age of big data, which makes it possible to understand almost anything that happens by collecting and analysing data associated with that event. The data that is collected is often represented visually to make it easier for people to interpret and understand it. You are going to learn how to use and interpret histograms and cumulative frequency diagrams to make sense of large groups of continuous data, sorted into different intervals.

GETTING STARTED

1   The table shows the number of passengers carried by a taxi each trip for one weekend.

Number of passengers (x)	Frequency (f)	fx
1	12	p
2	5	q
3	6	r
4	9	s
	t	52

a   What does fx mean in the third column?

b   How do you work out the values of p, q, r and s?

c   What is the value of t?

d   What does the value 52 at the bottom of the third column represent?

e   Use the formula mean = $\dfrac{\text{sum of } fx}{\text{total frequency}}$ to work out the mean number of passengers.

f   What is the mode of this data set?

g   What is the median number of passengers?

2   Imagine you are an online tutor and a student brings this diagram to the lesson and asks you to explain what it is and how to draw it. What would you tell them?

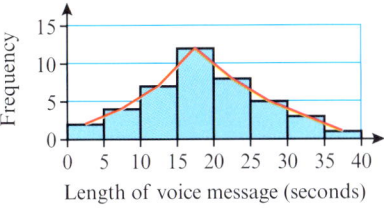

20.1 Histograms

A **histogram** shows the distribution of continuous, grouped data. Look at this histogram showing the ages of adult patients admitted to hospital with a diagnosis of pneumonia.

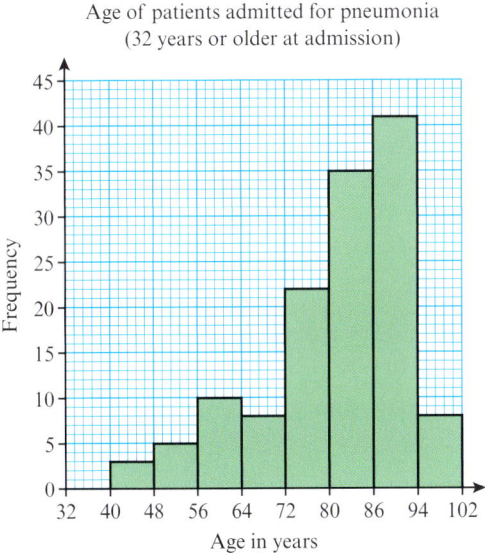

In this case, the class interval is 8 years. The shape of the graph shows that most patients admitted to hospital for pneumonia tend to be older (70 years or more) and that fewer middle-aged adults are admitted to hospital with pneumonia. You can read the number of patients in each class from the frequency axis.

LINK

Histograms are one of the most useful tools in epidemiology. They are used to organise and display a large set of measurements or numerical data in a simple way, so they are often used to display data related to public health events. The class intervals may show characteristics such as age, body temperature, exposure time and other factors relevant to the event.

This histogram shows data grouped in unequal intervals. You can see that the first interval (0 km/h ≤ v < 50 km/h) is much larger than the others.

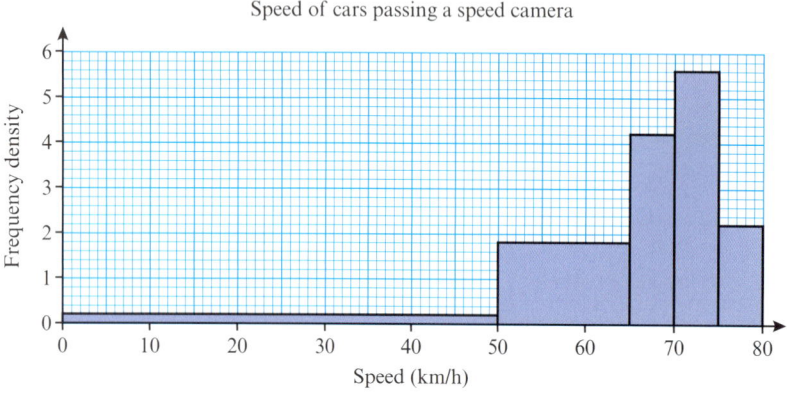

On a histogram with unequal class intervals:

- The horizontal scale is continuous and each column of the graph is drawn above a particular class interval.

- The frequency of the data is shown by the *area* of the bars. Frequency density is shown against the vertical axis.

Working with unequal class intervals

When the class intervals are not equal you cannot use the height of each bar to work out the frequency. Instead, you need to use the area of each bar.

When the class intervals are unequal you use the vertical scale to show the **frequency density**:

$$\text{Frequency density} = \frac{\text{frequency}}{\text{class width}}$$

Frequency density takes into account the frequency relative to the size of the class interval and is used for comparing data in different-sized intervals.

MATHEMATICAL CONNECTIONS

You worked with grouped data in Chapter 4.

TIP

By rearranging the formula, you can see that frequency is equal to the area of a bar. You can use this to help you read frequencies from the histogram. Many questions are based on this principle.

WORKED EXAMPLE 1

Here is a table showing the heights of 25 plants. Draw a histogram to show these results.

Height in cm	Number of plants
$5 \leq h \leq 15$	4
$15 < h \leq 20$	8
$20 < h \leq 25$	7
$25 < h \leq 40$	6

WORKED EXAMPLE 1 CONTINUED

Answer

First work out the frequency density by adding columns to your frequency distribution table like this:

Height (h) in cm	Number of plants	Class width	Frequency density (frequency ÷ class width)
$5 \leqslant h \leqslant 15$	4	10	$\dfrac{4}{10} = 0.4$
$15 < h \leqslant 20$	8	5	$\dfrac{8}{5} = 1.6$
$20 < h \leqslant 25$	7	5	$\dfrac{7}{5} = 1.4$
$25 < h \leqslant 40$	6	15	$\dfrac{6}{15} = 0.4$

TIP

The heights in cm are the class intervals. The number of plants is the frequency.

Next draw the axes. You will need to decide on a suitable scale for both the horizontal and the vertical axes.

Once you have done this, draw the histogram, paying careful attention to the scales on the axes.

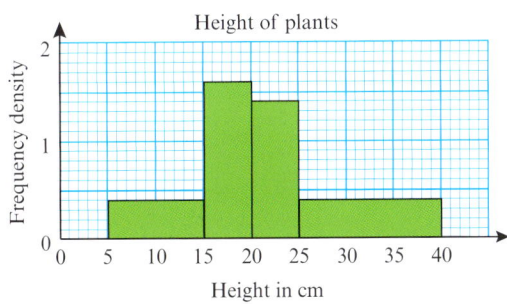

TIP

If you plotted the data against frequency instead of frequency density (see histogram), it looks like there are more plants in the 25–40 class compared to the 5–10 class but actually, their frequency densities are the same (see histogram in Worked example 1). The larger size of interval is misleading here, so we use frequency density as it is a better way to compare frequencies in classes of different sizes.

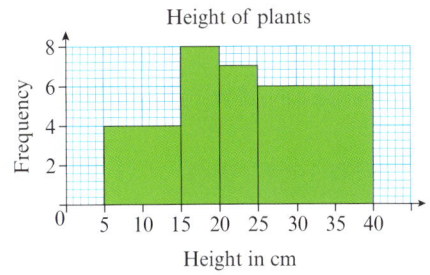

Exercise 20.1

1 140 people at a school fund-raising event were asked to guess how many sweets were in a large glass jar. Those who guessed correctly were put into a draw to win the sweets as a prize. The table shows the guesses.

No. of sweets (n)	Frequency (f)
$100 \leqslant n \leqslant 200$	18
$200 < n \leqslant 250$	18
$250 < n \leqslant 300$	32
$300 < n \leqslant 350$	31
$350 < n \leqslant 400$	21
$400 < n \leqslant 500$	20

    a Use the table to calculate the frequency density for each class.

    b Construct a histogram to display the results. Use a scale of 1 cm = 100 sweets on the horizontal axis and a scale of 1 cm = 0.2 units on the vertical axis.

2 The table shows the masses of young children visiting a clinic. Draw a histogram to illustrate the data.

Mass in kilograms (m)	Frequency
$6 \leqslant m \leqslant 9$	9
$9 < m \leqslant 12$	12
$12 < m \leqslant 18$	30
$18 < m \leqslant 21$	15
$21 < m \leqslant 30$	18

3 The table shows the distribution of the masses of the actors in a theatre group. Draw a histogram to show the data.

Mass in kilograms (m)	Frequency
$60 \leqslant m \leqslant 63$	9
$63 < m \leqslant 64$	12
$64 < m \leqslant 65$	15
$65 < m \leqslant 66$	17
$66 < m \leqslant 68$	10
$68 < m \leqslant 72$	8

APPLY YOUR SKILLS

4   An online tutor told a student that 'a histogram is similar to a stem-and-leaf diagram'.

   a   What do you think this means?

   b   How are these two types of diagrams similar?

   c   Give an example of when a histogram is more useful than a stem-and-leaf diagram and another example of when a stem-and-leaf diagram is more useful than a histogram.

5   A group of personal trainers at a gym were given fitness tests where their percentage body fat was calculated. The fitness assessor drew this histogram of the results.

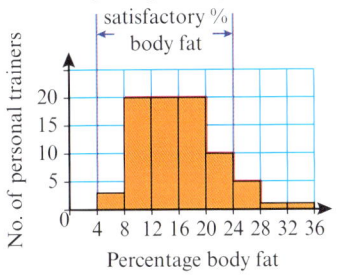

   a   How many personal trainers were tested?

   b   How many personal trainers had body fat levels within the satisfactory limits?

   c   How many personal trainers had levels which were too high?

   d   Why do you think there is no bar in the 0–4 category?

   e   Would you expect a similar distribution if you tested a random selection of people in your community? Give a reason for your answer.

6   The histogram shows the ages of people using the fitness centre at the Sports Science Institute after 5 p.m. in the evening.

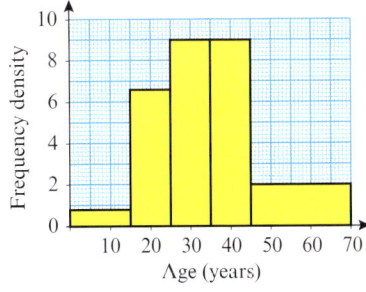

APPLY YOUR SKILLS CONTINUED

a Copy and complete the frequency table for this data.

b How many people aged between 15 and 35 used the fitness centre after 5 p.m.?

Age (*a*) in years	Frequency
$0 \leqslant a \leqslant 15$	
$15 < a \leqslant 25$	
$25 < a \leqslant 35$	
$35 < a \leqslant 40$	
$40 < a \leqslant 70$	

7 A traffic officer used a computer program to draw this histogram showing the average speed (in km/h) of a sample of vehicles using a highway. The road has a minimum speed limit of 50 km/h and a maximum speed limit of 125 km/h.

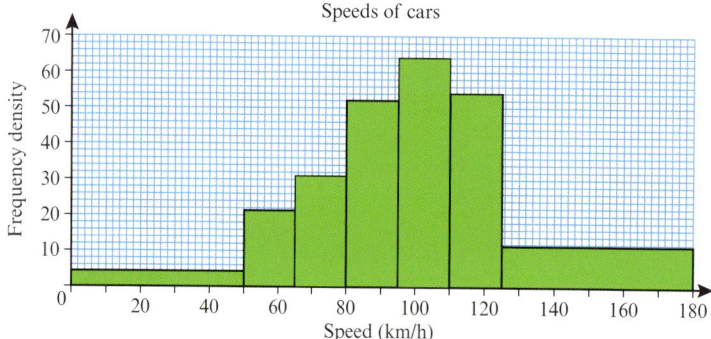

Speeds of cars

a Is it easy to see how many vehicles travelled above or below the speed limit? Give a reason for your answer.

b The traffic officer claims the graph shows that most people stick to the speed limit. Is this correct? Give a reason for your answer.

c The traffic superintendent wants to know exactly how many vehicles travel below or above the speed limit.

   i Reconstruct this frequency table. Round frequencies to the nearest whole number.

Speed in km/h (*s*)	Frequency	Class width	Frequency density
$0 \leqslant s \leqslant 50$			4.8
$50 < s \leqslant 65$			21.3
$65 < s \leqslant 80$			33.3
$80 < s \leqslant 95$			52
$95 < s \leqslant 110$			64
$110 < s \leqslant 125$			54.6
$125 < s \leqslant 180$			11.6

   ii How many vehicles were below the minimum speed limit?

d What percentage of vehicles in this sample were exceeding the maximum speed limit?

APPLY YOUR SKILLS CONTINUED

8   The unfinished histogram and table give information about the heights, in centimetres, of the senior students at a High School.

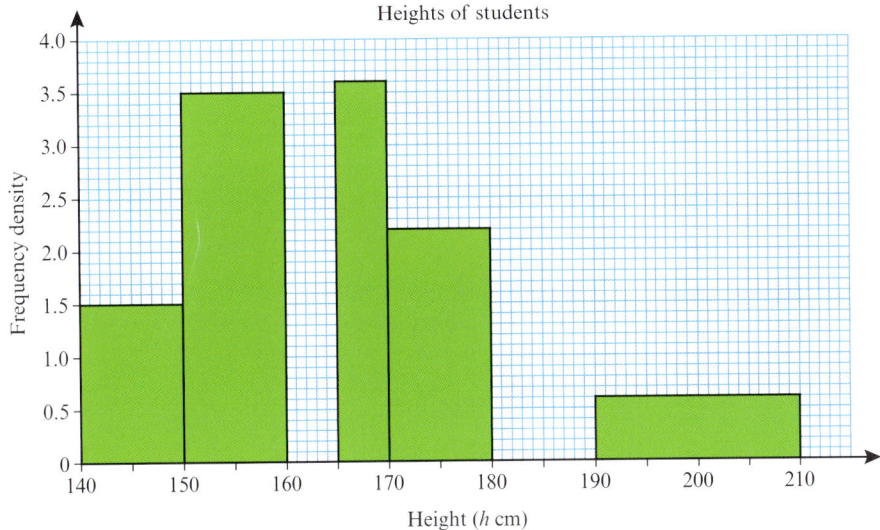

Height (h cm)	Frequency
$140 \leqslant h \leqslant 150$	15
$150 < h \leqslant 160$	
$160 < h \leqslant 165$	20
$165 < h \leqslant 170$	
$170 < h \leqslant 180$	
$180 < h \leqslant 190$	12
$190 < h \leqslant 210$	

a   Use the histogram to complete the table.

b   Use the table to complete the histogram.

c   State the modal group.

d   Work out an estimate for the percentage of senior students at the High School that are above the height of 155 cm.

INVESTIGATION

9 **a** Work with a partner to collect data about how long it takes a sample of students to type this text message correctly.

> Dear customer. Your order number 1234567890 is ready at the Z-max pickup point. For directions and unique QR code login to your account using this link: http://my account.

- Your sample size should be at least 12 students. Include yourselves in the sample.
- Decide how you will measure and record the data.
- Carry out your investigation.

b Choose suitable uneven intervals for the data and draw a frequency distribution table.

c Choose an appropriate scale and draw a histogram to show the distribution.

d Write short notes to summarise what your histogram shows.

SELF ASSESSMENT

How well do you understand the work on histograms with unequal intervals?

1 Read the statements.

A	I can draw and read a frequency table with unequal, non-overlapping intervals.
B	I can accurately construct a histogram with unequal intervals.
C	I can calculate frequency density for each interval using the frequency and class width.
D	I can interpret data shown on a histogram.

Write the letters A to D in your exercise book. Draw an emoji to show how you feel about each statement.

2 Write a short statement next to each emoji explaining why you chose it.

20.2 Cumulative frequency

Sometimes you may be asked questions such as:

- How many people type fewer than 20 words per minute?
- How many cars were travelling above 100 km/h?
- How many students scored less than 50% on the test?

- In statistics you can use a **cumulative frequency** table or a **cumulative frequency curve** to answer questions about data up to a particular class boundary. You can also use the cumulative frequencies to estimate and interpret the median and the value of other positions of a data set.

Cumulative frequency tables

Cumulative frequency is a 'running total' of the scores or results (the frequency in each group). The cumulative frequency gives the number of results which are less than, or equal to, a particular class boundary. This table shows how many students got a particular mark out of 10 (the frequency of each result) as well as the cumulative frequency.

TIP

Cumulative means 'increasing as more is added'. In daily use we might use the word 'accumulating' to mean the same thing.

Score out of 10	Frequency (f)	Cumulative frequency
3	4	4
4	5	4 + 5 = 9
5	3	9 + 3 = 12
6	3	12 + 3 = 15
7	5	20
8	7	27
9	2	29
10	1	30
Total	**30**	

- Each entry in the cumulative frequency column is calculated by adding the frequency of the current class to the previous cumulative frequency (or by adding all the frequencies up to and including the current class).
- The last figure in the cumulative frequency column must equal the sum of the frequencies because all results will be below or equal to the highest result.

WORKED EXAMPLE 2

The heights of plants were measured during an experiment. The results are summarised in the table.

Height (h cm)	Frequency
$0 < h \leqslant 5$	20
$5 < h \leqslant 10$	40
$10 < h \leqslant 15$	60
$15 < h \leqslant 25$	80
$25 < h \leqslant 50$	50
Total	**250**

a   Draw a cumulative frequency table for this distribution.

b   Determine which class interval contains the median height.

WORKED EXAMPLE 2 CONTINUED

Answers

a

Height (h cm)	Frequency	Cumulative frequency
$0 < h \leqslant 5$	20	20
$5 < h \leqslant 10$	40	60
$10 < h \leqslant 15$	60	120
$15 < h \leqslant 25$	80	200
$25 < h \leqslant 50$	50	250
Total	250	

b $15 < h \leqslant 25$ The heights are given for 250 flowers, so the median height must be the mean of the height of the 125th and 126th flower. If you look at the cumulative frequency you can see that this value falls into the fourth height class (the 125th and 126th are both greater than 120 but less than 200).

MATHEMATICAL CONNECTIONS

Cumulative frequency curves allow you to estimate the median when there is a large number of data and you don't want to arrange the raw data in order.

Cumulative frequency curves

When you plot the cumulative frequencies against the upper boundaries of each class interval you get a cumulative frequency curve. Cumulative frequency curves can be used to estimate other values.

Cumulative frequency curves are also called ogive curves or ogives because they take the shape of narrow pointed arches called ogees.

TIP

You must plot the cumulative frequency at the upper end point of the class interval. Do not confuse this section with the midpoint calculations you use to estimate the mean in frequency tables.

WORKED EXAMPLE 3

The examination marks of 300 students are summarised in the table.

Mark	Frequency
1–10	3
11–20	7
21–30	13
31–40	29
41–50	44
51–60	65
61–70	70
71–80	49
81–90	14
91–100	6

WORKED EXAMPLE 3 CONTINUED

a Draw a cumulative frequency table.

b Construct a cumulative frequency graph to show this data.

c Calculate an *estimate* for the median mark.

Answers

a

Mark	Frequency	Cumulative frequency
1–10	3	3
11–20	7	10
21–30	13	23
31–40	29	52
41–50	44	96
51–60	65	161
61–70	70	231
71–80	49	280
81–90	14	294
91–100	6	300

b

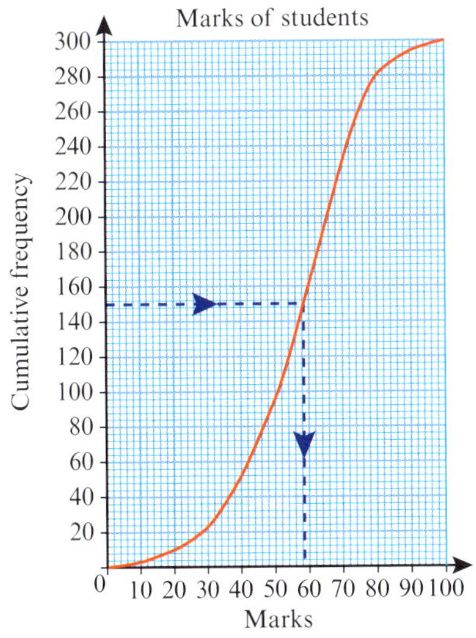

c The median is the middle value. You can find the middle value by dividing the total frequency by 2:

$\frac{300}{2} = 150$, so the median mark is the 150th result.

Draw a line from the 150th student (on the vertical axis) parallel to the marks (horizontal) axis. Drop a perpendicular from where this line cuts the graph. Read the value from the horizontal axis.

The median mark is 58.

WORKED EXAMPLE 4

This cumulative frequency curve shows the journey times to school for different students.

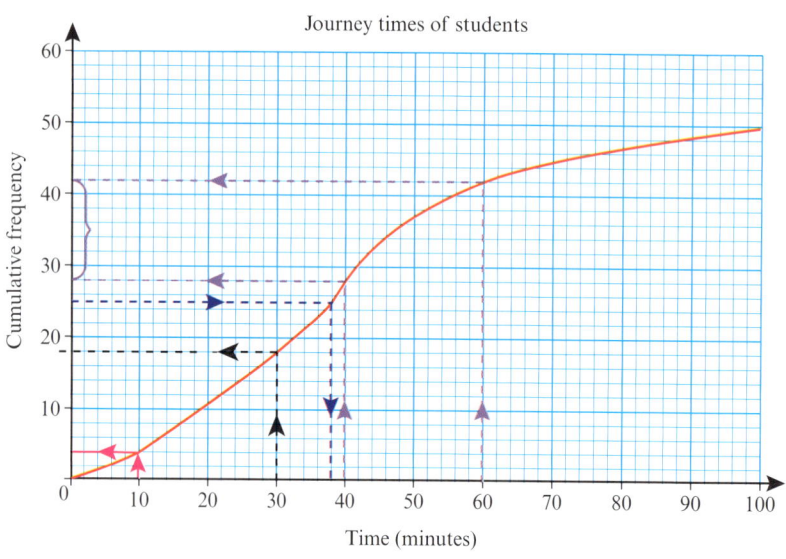

Use the curve to find or estimate:

a the total number of students

b the median journey time

c the number of students who took less than 10 minutes to get to school

d the number of students who had journey times greater than 30 minutes

e the number of students who took between 40 minutes and one hour to get to school.

Answers

a 50   The top of the curve is at 50, so this is the total frequency.

b 38 $\frac{50}{2} = 25$, so the median is the 25th result; drop a perpendicular from where the line cuts the graph.

c 4   Read off the cumulative frequency at 10 minutes.

d $50 - 18 = 32$ The cumulative frequency at 30 minutes is 18. Subtract this from the total frequency.

e $42 - 28 = 14$ Subtract the cumulative frequency at 40 minutes from that at 60 minutes.

WORKED EXAMPLE 5

Twenty bean seeds were planted for a biology experiment. The heights of the plants were measured after three weeks and recorded in the table.

Heights (h cm)	$0 < h \leqslant 3$	$3 < h \leqslant 6$	$6 < h \leqslant 9$	$9 < h \leqslant 12$
Frequency	2	5	10	3

a Find an estimate for the mean height.

b Draw a cumulative frequency curve and find an estimate for the median height.

Answers

a You will need the midpoints of the classes to find an estimate of the mean, and you need the cumulative frequency to find an estimate of the median, so you must add more columns to the table. Don't forget to label the new columns.

Heights (h cm)	Midpoint (x)	Frequency (f)	Frequency × midpoint (fx)	Cumulative frequency
$0 < h \leqslant 3$	1.5	2	3	2
$3 < h \leqslant 6$	4.5	5	22.5	7
$6 < h \leqslant 9$	7.5	10	75	17
$9 < h \leqslant 12$	10.5	3	31.5	20
Total		$\Sigma f = 20$	132	

Estimated mean height $= \dfrac{132}{20} = 6.6$ cm $\left(\text{mean} = \dfrac{\text{total } fx}{\text{total } f} \right)$

> **MATHEMATICAL CONNECTIONS**
>
> You learnt how to estimate the mean using grouped data in Chapter 12.

> **TIP**
>
> The symbol Σ is the Greek letter capital 'sigma'. It is used to mean 'sum'. So, Σf simply means, 'the sum of all the frequencies'.

b

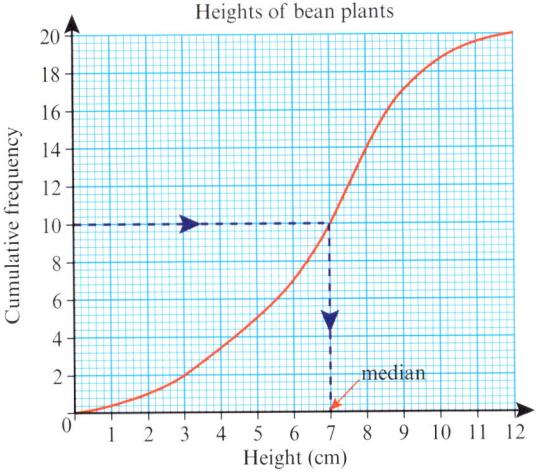

Heights of bean plants

$\dfrac{20}{2} = 10$, so the median height is the 10th value.

Median height $= 7.0$ cm

Exercise 20.2

1   The heights of 25 plants were measured and the results are summarised in the table.

Height (h) in cm	$5 < h \leqslant 16$	$16 < h \leqslant 20$	$20 < h \leqslant 25$	$25 < h \leqslant 40$
Number of plants	3	7	10	5

   a   Draw a cumulative frequency table for this distribution.

   b   In which interval does the median plant height lie?

   c   Draw the cumulative frequency curve and use it to estimate, to the nearest centimetre, the median plant height.

2   The table shows the amount of money, $\$x$, spent on books by a group of students.

Amount spent	No. of students
$0 < x \leqslant 10$	0
$10 < x \leqslant 20$	4
$20 < x \leqslant 30$	8
$30 < x \leqslant 40$	12
$40 < x \leqslant 50$	11
$50 < x \leqslant 60$	5

   a   Calculate an estimate of the mean amount of money per student spent on books.

   b   Use the information in the table above to find the values of p, q and r in the cumulative frequency table.

Amount spent ($\$x$)	$x \leqslant 10$	$x \leqslant 20$	$x \leqslant 30$	$x \leqslant 40$	$x \leqslant 50$	$x \leqslant 60$
Cumulative frequency	0	4	p	q	r	40

   c   Using a scale of 1 cm to represent 10 units on each axis, draw a cumulative frequency diagram.

   d   Use your diagram to estimate the median amount spent.

3   The cumulative frequency table shows the distribution of the masses of the children attending a clinic.

Mass (m) in kilograms	Cumulative frequency
$0 < m \leqslant 10$	12
$0 < m \leqslant 20$	26
$0 < m \leqslant 30$	33
$0 < m \leqslant 40$	41
$0 < m \leqslant 50$	46
$0 < m \leqslant 60$	50

a   Draw a cumulative frequency diagram. Use a horizontal scale of 1 cm = 10 kg and a vertical scale of 0.5 cm = 5 children.

b   Estimate the median mass.

c   How many children had a mass of 45 kg or more?

Quartiles

In Chapter 12 you found the range (the biggest value − the smallest value) to see how dispersed various sets of data were. However, the range is easily affected by outliers (extreme or unusual values), so it is not always the best measure of how the data is spread out.

You can divide the data shown on a cumulative frequency curve into quartiles to find the interquartile range, which is more representative than the range because it is not affected by extreme values.

This cumulative frequency curve the marks obtained by 64 students in a test.

> **TIP**
>
> Describing how 'dispersed' data is, is the same as describing how 'spread out' it is. So we can say that the range is a 'measure of dispersion' or a 'measure of spread'.

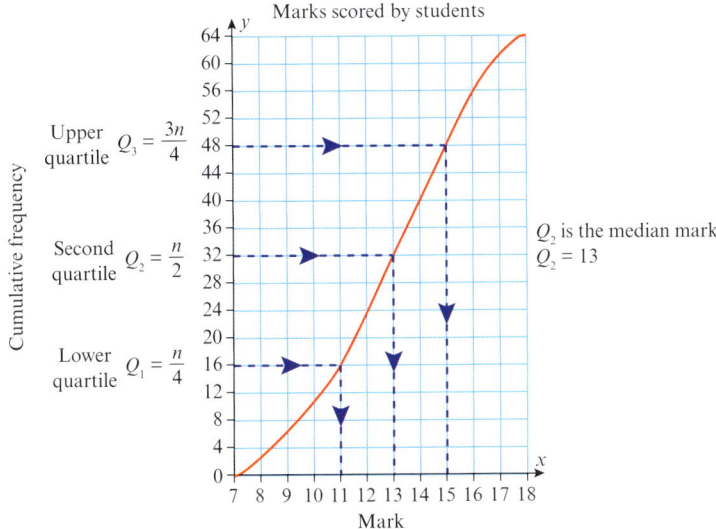

Marks scored by students

Upper quartile $Q_3 = \dfrac{3n}{4}$

Second quartile $Q_2 = \dfrac{n}{2}$

Lower quartile $Q_1 = \dfrac{n}{4}$

Q_2 is the median mark
$Q_2 = 13$

When finding the positions of the quartiles from a cumulative frequency curve you do not use the $\dfrac{(n+1)}{4}$, $\dfrac{(n+1)}{2}$ and $\dfrac{3}{4}(n+1)$ rules that you met for discrete data in Chapter 12. Instead, you use: $\dfrac{n}{4}$, $\dfrac{n}{2}$ and $\dfrac{3n}{4}$.

Looking at the curve, you can see that:

- 48 students scored less than 15 marks. 15 marks is the upper quartile or third quartile Q_3.
- 32 students scored less than 13 marks. 13 marks is the second quartile Q_2, or median mark.
- 16 students scored less than 11 marks. 11 marks is the lower quartile or first quartile Q_1.

> **TIP**
>
> Whole number values are being used in this example to make it easier to understand. Usually your answers will be estimates and they will involve decimal fractions.

MATHEMATICAL CONNECTIONS

Revise the work you did on quartiles and the interquartile range in Chapter 12 if you need to.

The interquartile range

The interquartile range (IQR) is the difference between the upper and lower quartiles: $Q_3 - Q_1$.

In effect, this is the range of the middle 50% of the scores, or the median of the upper half of the values minus the median of the lower half of the values.

In the example about marks scored by students, the IQR = $15 - 11 = 4$.

Because the interquartile range does not use any extreme small or large values it is considered a more reliable measure of spread than the range.

WORKED EXAMPLE 6

The percentage scored by 1000 students on an exam is shown on this cumulative frequency curve.

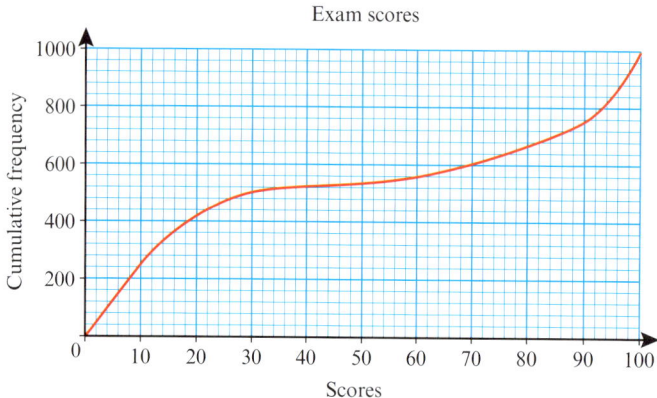

Use the cumulative frequency curve to find an estimate for:

a   the median score   **b**   the lower quartile

c   the upper quartile   **d**   the interquartile range.

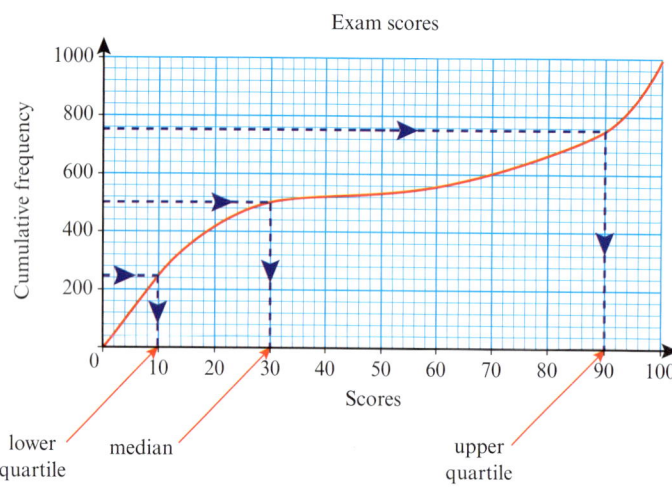

WORKED EXAMPLE 6 CONTINUED

Answers

a $n = 1000$

So the position of Q_2 on the vertical axis is $\dfrac{n}{2} = \dfrac{1000}{2} = 500$.

Draw the lines on the graph.

Estimate the median from the horizontal axis as 30 marks.

b $n = 1000$

So the position of Q_1 on the vertical axis is $\dfrac{n}{4} = \dfrac{1000}{4} = 250$.

An estimate for the lower quartile, from the horizontal axis is 10 marks

c $n = 1000$

So the position of Q_3 on the vertical axis is $\dfrac{3n}{4} = \dfrac{3 \times 1000}{4} = 750$.

An estimate for the upper quartile, from the horizontal axis is 90 marks.

d $\begin{aligned} IQR &= Q_3 - Q_1 \\ &= 90 - 10 \\ &= 80 \text{ marks} \end{aligned}$

Percentiles

When you are dealing with large amounts of data, such as examination results for the whole country, or the average height and mass of all children in different age groups, it is useful to divide the data into even smaller groups called **percentiles**.

To find the position of a percentile use the formula $\dfrac{pn}{100}$, where p is the percentile you are looking for and n is how much data you have (the total frequency).

Using the data set in Worked example 6:

The position of the 10th percentile on the cumulative frequency axis is:

$P_{10} = \dfrac{10 \times 1000}{100} = 100$

The position of the 85th percentile on the cumulative frequency axis is:

$P_{85} = \dfrac{85 \times 1000}{100} = 850$

Remember that 100 and 850 are only the *positions* of the 10th and 85th percentile. To find the actual values of the percentiles you need to use the cumulative frequency graph.

TIP

The position of percentile p is the value at p percent $= \dfrac{p}{100} \times n$.

WORKED EXAMPLE 7

The cumulative frequency curve shows the test results of 200 candidates who have applied for an internship at a media company. Only those who score above the 80th percentile will be invited for an interview. What is the lowest score that can be obtained to be offered an interview?

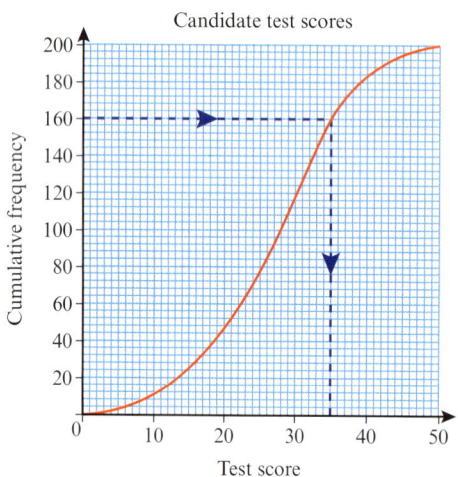

Candidate test scores

Answer

80% of 200 is 160.

So, the value of P80 is a test score of 35. (Read off the graph where the curve is 160.)

Only those candidates who scored above 35 marks on the test will be invited for an interview.

Exercise 20.3

1   The lengths of 32 metal rods were measured and recorded on this cumulative frequency curve. Use the graph to find an estimate for:

   a   the median

   b Q_1

   c Q_3

   d   the IQR

   e   the 40th percentile.

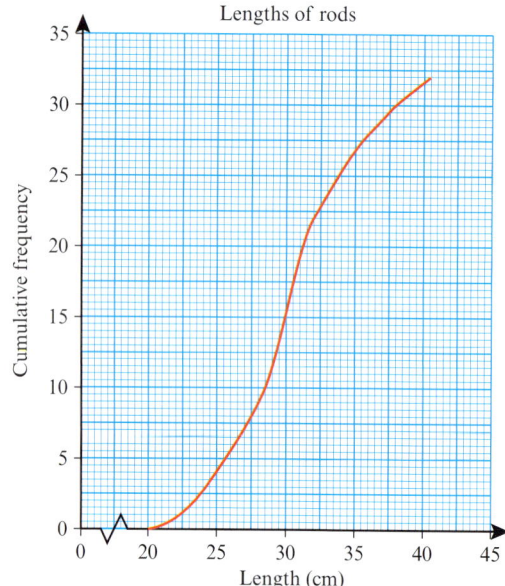

Lengths of rods

2   This cumulative frequency curve compares the results 120 students obtained on
    two maths papers.

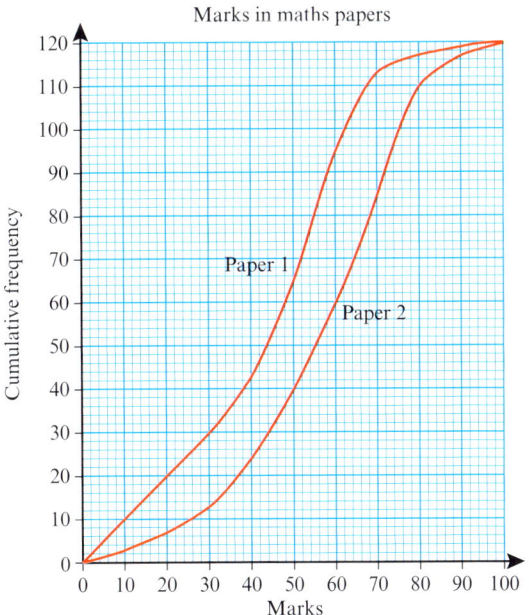

Marks in maths papers

a   For each paper, use the graph to find:
    i   the median mark
    ii   the IQR
    iii   the 60th percentile.
b   What mark would you need to get to be above the 90th percentile on each paper?

3   This cumulative frequency curve shows the masses of 500 12-year-old children (in kg).

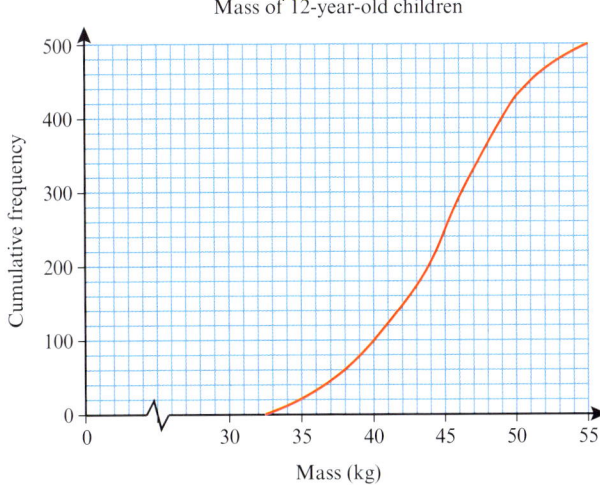

Mass of 12-year-old children

a   Use the graph to work out:
    i   the median mass of the 12-year-olds
    ii   how many children have a mass between 40 kg and 50 kg.
b   What percentage of these children will not be allowed to go on an amusement
    park ride if the upper mass limit for the ride is 51 kg?

4   This cumulative frequency table gives the speeds of 200 cars travelling on the highway from Kuala Lumpur Airport into the city.

Speed (s) in km/h	Cumulative frequency
$s \leqslant 60$	2
$60 < s \leqslant 70$	8
$70 < s \leqslant 80$	24
$80 < s \leqslant 90$	45
$90 < s \leqslant 100$	96
$100 < s \leqslant 110$	123
$110 < s \leqslant 120$	171
$120 < s \leqslant 130$	195
$130 < s \leqslant 140$	200
Total	200

a   Draw a cumulative frequency curve to show this data. Use a scale of 1 cm per 10 km/h on the horizontal axis and a scale of 1 cm per 10 cars on the vertical axis.

b   Use your curve to estimate the median, Q_1 and Q_3 for this data.

c   Estimate the IQR.

d   The speed limit on this stretch of road is 120 km/h. What percentage of the cars were travelling above the speed limit?

SUMMARY

Do you know …?

Histograms are specialised bar graphs used for displaying continuous and grouped data.

If the class widths are unequal, the bars are not equally wide and the vertical axis shows the frequency density.

$$\text{Frequency density} = \frac{\text{frequency per class interval}}{\text{class width}}$$

Cumulative frequency is a running total of the class frequencies up to each upper class boundary.

When cumulative frequencies are plotted they give a cumulative frequency curve or ogive.

The curve can be used to estimate the median value in the data.

The data can be divided into four equal groups called quartiles. The interquartile range is the difference between the upper and lower quartiles ($Q_3 - Q_1$).

Large amounts of data can be divided into percentiles, which divide the data into 100 equal groups. If a score of 20 out of 25 is at the 82nd percentile it means that 82% of the scores are below 20.

Are you able to …?

interpret and construct histograms with unequal intervals
construct a table to find the frequency density of different classes
calculate cumulative frequencies
plot and draw a cumulative frequency curve
use a cumulative frequency curve to estimate the median
find quartiles and calculate the interquartile range
estimate and interpret percentiles.

Practice questions

1   A researcher took a questionnaire to 64 households. The grouped frequency table shows the time taken (t minutes) by various home owners to complete a questionnaire.

Time taken (t) in minutes	No. of home owners
$0 \leqslant t \leqslant 2$	2
$2 < t \leqslant 3$	18
$3 < t \leqslant 4$	25
$4 < t \leqslant 6$	12
$6 < t \leqslant 9$	5
$9 < t \leqslant 15$	2

Using a scale of 1 cm to represent 2 minutes, construct a horizontal axis for $0 \leqslant t \leqslant 15$.

Using a vertical scale of 1 cm per 2 units, draw a histogram to represent this data.   [5]

2 Juri looks for young trees in a large garden and measures their heights in centimetres. The results are shown in the partially completed table and histogram.

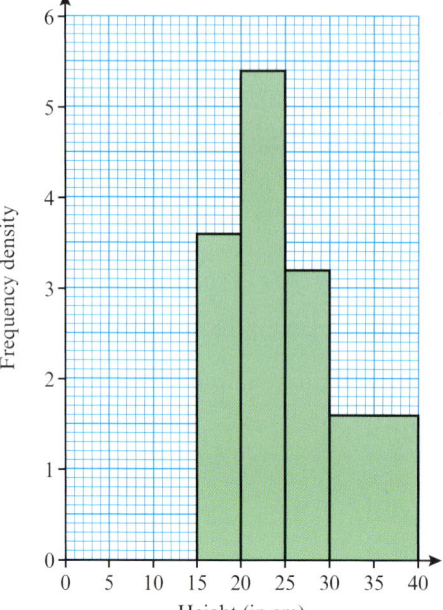

Height (h cm)	Frequency
$0 < h \le 10$	4
$10 < h \le 15$	12
$15 < h \le 20$	18
$20 < h \le 25$	
$25 < h \le 30$	
$30 < h \le 40$	

a Copy and complete the histogram using information from the table. [4]

b Copy and complete the table using information from the histogram. [4]

c Estimate the mean height of the young trees Juri measured. [3]

3 The table shows the ages, in complete years, of the 80 people taking part in a cookery competition in 2023.

Age in years	0 to 29	30 to 39	40 to 49	50 to 59	60 to 69	70 to 89
Frequency	2	18	27	18	12	3

a Explain why the upper class boundary for the first group is 30 not 29.5. [1]

b Construct a cumulative frequency table for this data and draw a cumulative frequency curve. [6]

c Use your curve to estimate the median age of people who took part in the competition. [2]

d Use your curve to estimate the interquartile range of the ages of people who took part in the competition. [2]

e Use your curve to estimate the percentage of people taking part who were aged 65 or more. [2]

SELF ASSESSMENT

Use this scale to rate your work in each of the following categories.

4 Excellent	3 Accomplished	2 Proficient	1 Still developing

- Interpreting questions and making connections.
- Level of understanding
- Ability to show working clearly.
- Use of mathematical processes and techniques.
- Correct solutions.

Past paper questions

1

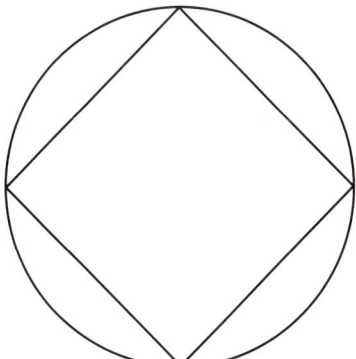

  a   Write down the order of rotational symmetry of this diagram.

[1]

  b   On the diagram, draw all the lines of symmetry. [Using Figure 1 in the Unit 5 Past Paper Questions Resource Sheet.]

[2]

Cambridge IGCSE Mathematics (0580) Paper 11 Q3, June 2021

2   Nazaneen changes $6500 into 5798 euros at a bank.

    Work out the exchange rate the bank uses.

[1]

Cambridge IGCSE Mathematics (0580) Paper 11 Q8, June 2021

3   Annie invests $8300 at a rate of 5.6% per year compound interest.

    Calculate the value of her investment at the end of 6 years.

[2]

Cambridge IGCSE Mathematics (0580) Paper 11 Q18, June 2021

4 a   On each shape, draw all the lines of symmetry. [Using Figure 2 in the Unit 5 Past Paper Questions Resource Sheet.]

    i

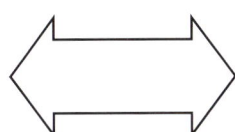

[1]

    ii

[2]

b Write down the name of a quadrilateral that has

- rotational symmetry of order 2

and

- exactly two lines of symmetry.

[1]

Cambridge IGCSE Mathematics (0580) Paper 11 Q19, June 2019

5 **a** Complete the table of values for $y = 7 + 2x - x^2$. [Using Figure 3 in the Unit 5 Past Paper Questions Resource Sheet.]

x	−2	−1	0	1	2	3	4
y	−1			8	7		−1

[2]

b On a copy of the grid, draw the graph of $y = 7 + 2x - x^2$ for $-2 \leqslant x \leqslant 4$. [Using Figure 4 in the Unit 5 Past Paper Questions Resource Sheet.]

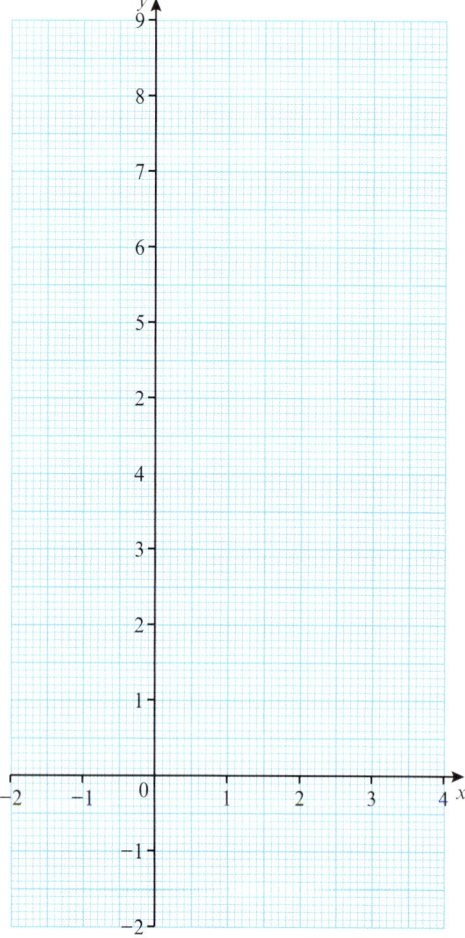

[4]

c Write down the equation of the line of symmetry of the graph.

[1]

d Use your graph to solve the equation $7 + 2x - x^2 = 0$.

[2]

Cambridge IGCSE Mathematics (0580) Paper 31 Q4, June 2020

6 Here is part of the menu for Jamie's café.

```
                    Menu
                              Price ($)
         Tea                     2.35
         Coffee                  3.40
         Lemonade                1.80
         Cake                    4.45
         Biscuit                 0.85
```

a Sue has one tea and one cake.

Calculate how much she pays.

[1]

b Derrick has one coffee and two biscuits.

How much change does he receive from a $10 note?

[2]

c Harriet works at the café for 34 hours each week.

She is paid $8.25 for each hour.

   i Work out the amount she is paid each week.

[1]

   ii One week she works 8 hours extra.

     The extra hours are paid at 1.5 times her usual rate of $8.25 for each hour.

     Work out the total amount she is paid for that week.

[2]

d Peter works these hours each week at the café.

Day	Time
Monday	08 30 to 16 00
Tuesday	10 00 to 17 00
Thursday	08 30 to 16 30
Saturday	08 00 to 18 30

Work out the number of hours he works in one week.

[2]

e   Jamie buys a clock for the café from Japan for 9395 yen.

The exchange rate is $1 = 110.27 yen.

Work out the cost of the clock in dollars, correct to the nearest cent.

[3]

f   Jamie invests $12 000 at a rate of 5% per year compound interest.

Calculate the value of his investment at the end of 3 years.

[3]

Cambridge IGCSE Mathematics (0580) Paper 31 Q1, June 2019

7

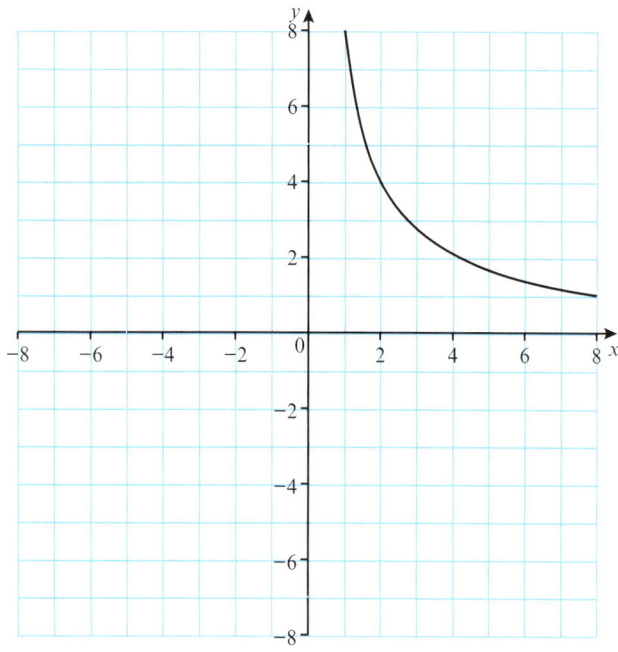

The diagram shows the graph of $y = \dfrac{k}{x}$ for $1 \leqslant x \leqslant 8$.

a   Use the graph to find the value of x when $y = 4$.

[1]

b   i   Show that $k = 8$.

[1]

ii   Calculate the value of y when $x = 250$.

[1]

c   i   Complete this table of values for $y = \dfrac{8}{x}$. [Using Figure 5 in the Unit 5 Past Paper Questions Resource Sheet.]

x	−8	−4	−2	−1
y				

[2]

   ii   On the grid, draw the graph of $y = \dfrac{8}{x}$ for $-8 \leqslant x \leqslant -1$. [Using Figure 6 in the Unit 5 Past Paper Questions Resource Sheet.]

[3]

d   Write down the equation on each line of symmetry of the graph.

[2]

Cambridge IGCSE Mathematics (0580) Paper 31 Q5, June 2021

8   a

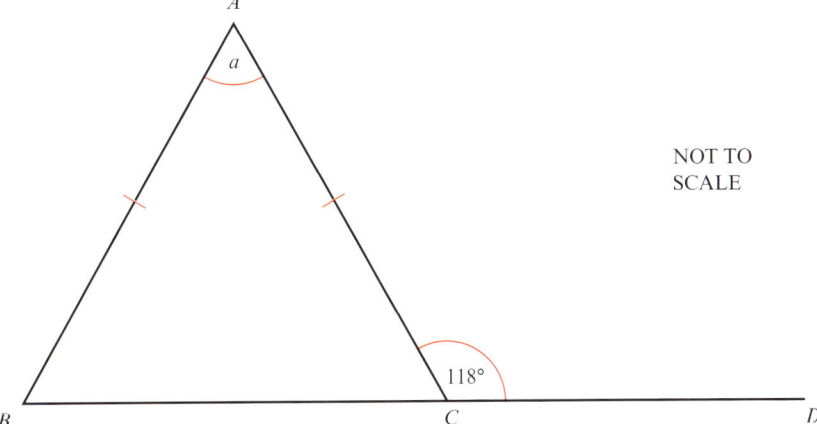

NOT TO SCALE

ABC is an isosceles triangle.

BCD is a straight line.

Find the value of *a*.

[2]

b   Find the size of one interior angle of a regular 10-sided polygon.

[3]

c

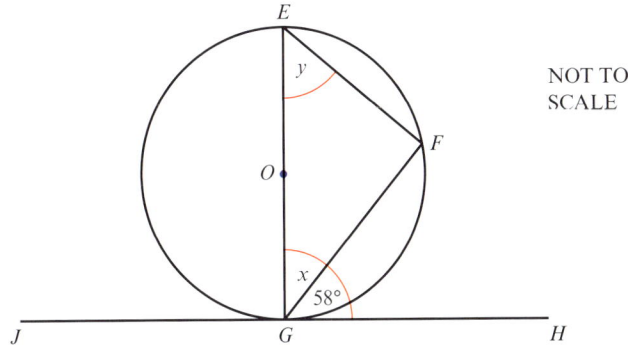

NOT TO SCALE

The points *E*, *F* and *G* lie on the circumference of a circle, centre *O*.

JGH is a tangent to the circle.

Find the value of *x* and the value of *y*.

[2]

d

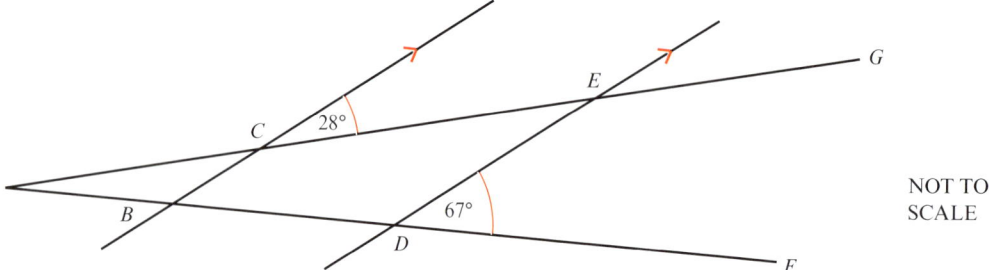

NOT TO
SCALE

In the diagram *AG* and *AF* are straight lines.

Lines *BC* and *DE* are parallel.

Find angle *CED* and give a reason for your answer.

[2]

e

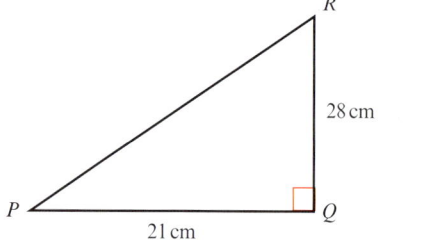

NOT TO
SCALE

28 cm

21 cm

Calculate *PR*.

[2]

Cambridge IGCSE Mathematics (0580) Paper 31 Q4, June 2019

 9 **a** The diagram shows a rectangle with length 7*a* and width 2*a*.

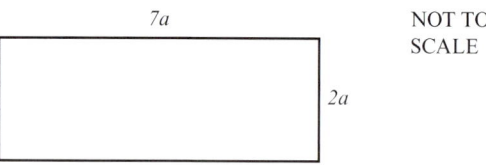

7*a*

NOT TO
SCALE

2*a*

Write an expression, in its simplest form, for

i   the perimeter,

[2]

ii   the area.

[2]

b The nth term of a sequence is $n^2 + 5$.

Find the first three terms of this sequence.

[2]

c i Copy and complete the table of values for $y = \dfrac{12}{x}$, $x \neq 0$.

x	−6	−4	−3	−2	−1		1	2	3	4	6
y	−2	−3					12				2

[3]

ii On the grid, draw the graph of $y = \dfrac{12}{x}$ for $-6 \leqslant x \leqslant -1$ and $1 \leqslant x \leqslant 6$.

[Using Figure 7 in the Unit 5 Past Paper Questions Resource Sheet.]

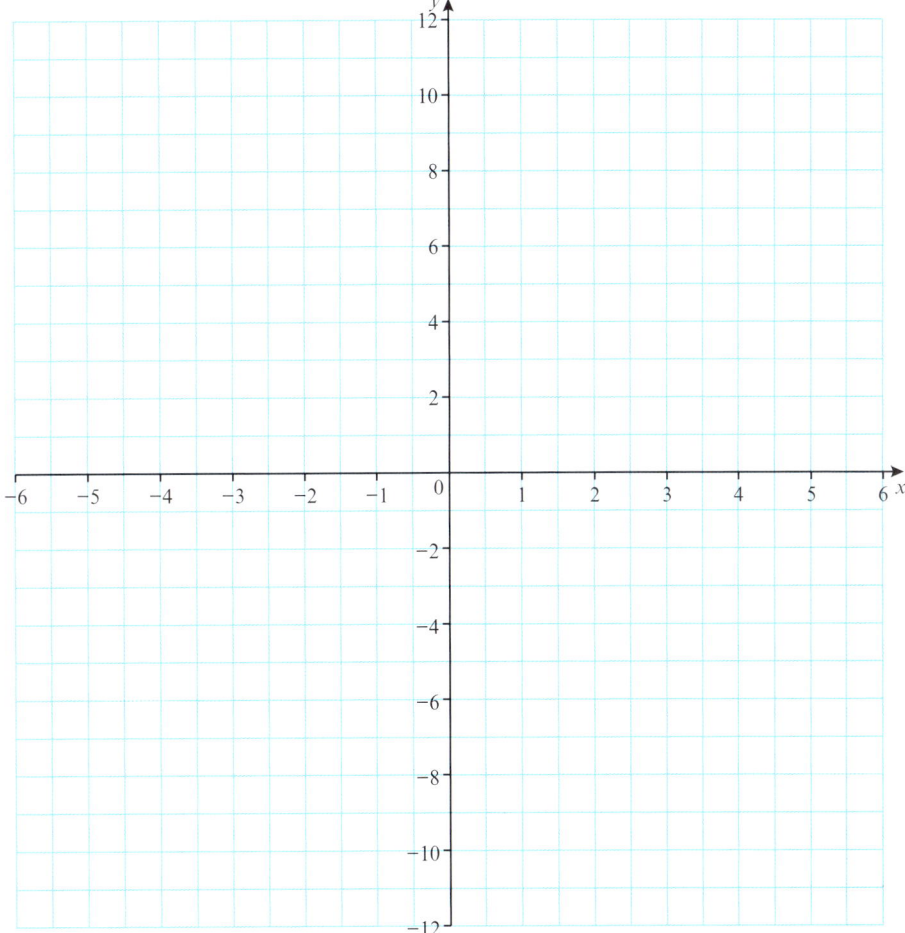

[4]

iii On the grid, draw the line $y = 8$. [Using Figure 7 in the Unit 5 Past Paper Questions Resource Sheet.]

[1]

iv Use your graph to solve $\dfrac{12}{x} = 8$.

[1]

Cambridge IGCSE Mathematics (0580) Paper 31 Q5, June 2019

10

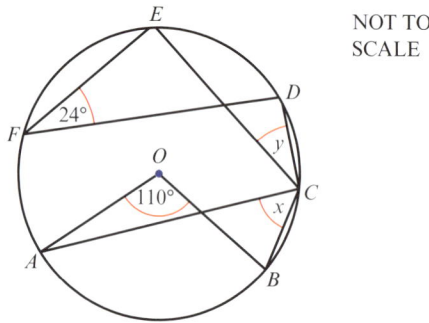

NOT TO SCALE

Points A, B, C, D, E and F lie on a circle, centre O.

Find the value of x and the value of y.

[2]

Cambridge IGCSE Mathematics (0580) Paper 21 Q10, June 2020

11 The curve $y = x^2 - 2x + 1$ is drawn on a grid.

A line is drawn on the same grid.

The points of intersection of the line and the curve are used to solve the equation $x^2 - 7x + 5 = 0$.

Find the equation of the line in the form $y = mx + c$.

[1]

Cambridge IGCSE Mathematics (0580) Paper 21 Q20, June 2020

12 a The table shows information about the mass, in kilograms, of each of 50 children.

Mass (k kg)	$0 < k \leqslant 10$	$10 < k \leqslant 25$	$25 < k \leqslant 35$	$35 < k \leqslant 40$	$40 < k \leqslant 50$
Frequency	3	19	21	5	2

i Complete the cumulative frequency table.
[Using Figure 8 in the Unit 5 Past Paper Questions Resource Sheet.]

Mass (k kg)	$k \leqslant 10$	$k \leqslant 25$	$k \leqslant 35$	$k \leqslant 40$	$k \leqslant 50$
Cumulative frequency					

[2]

ii   On a copy of the grid, draw a cumulative frequency diagram to show this information.
[Using Figure 9 in the Unit 5 Past Paper Questions Resource Sheet.]

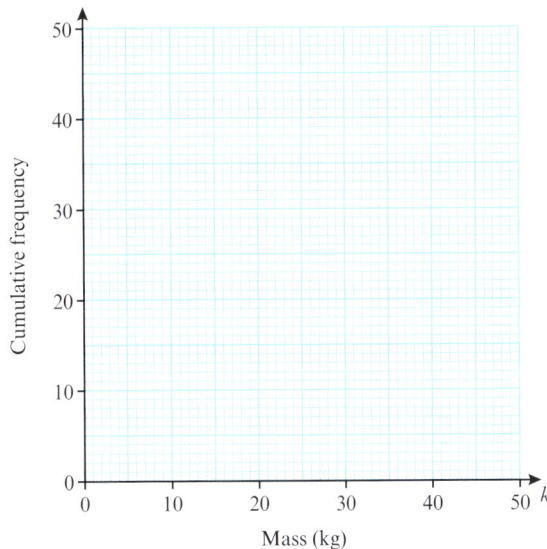

[3]

iii Use your diagram to find an estimate of the number of children with a mass of 32 kg or less.

[1]

Cambridge IGCSE Mathematics (0580) Paper 41 Q8a, June 2021

13 a i   On the axes, sketch the graph of $y = \sin x$ for $0° \leqslant x \leqslant 360°$.
[Using Figure 10 in the Unit 5 Past Paper Questions Resource Sheet.]

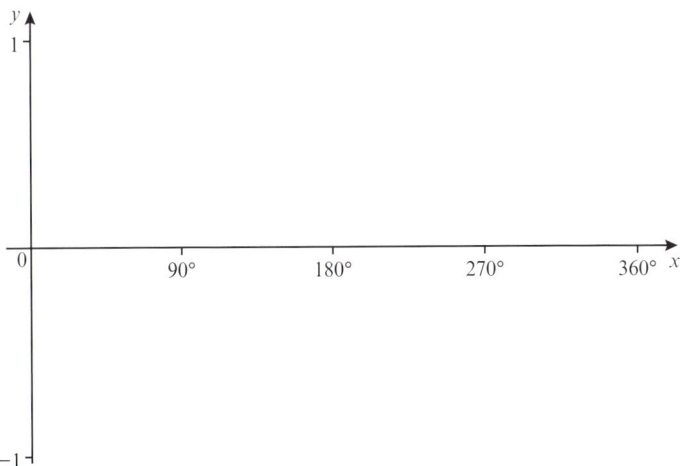

[2]

ii   Describe fully the symmetry of the graph of $y = \sin x$ for $0° \leqslant x \leqslant 360°$.

[2]

b Solve $4 \sin x - 1 = 2$ for $0° \leqslant x \leqslant 360°$.

[3]

c **i** Write $x^2 + 10x + 14$ in the form $(x + a)^2 + b$.

[2]

ii On a copy of the axes, sketch the graph of $y = x^2 + 10x + 14$, indicating the coordinates of the turning point. [Using Figure 11 in the Unit 5 Past Paper Questions Resource Sheet.]

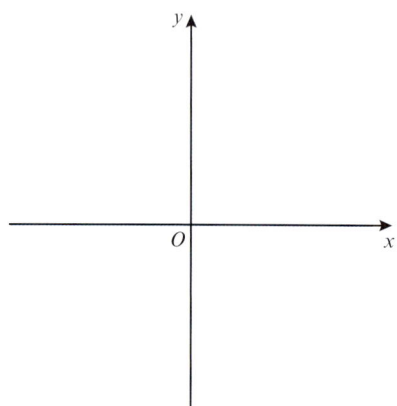

[3]

Cambridge IGCSE Mathematics (0580) Paper 41 Q8, June 2020

14 The table shows some values for $y = x^3 + 3x^2 + 2$.

x	−3.5	−3	−2.5	−2	−1.5	−1	−0.5	0	0.5	1	1.5
y	−4.1		5.1	6	5.4	4	2.6		2.9		12.1

a Complete the table. [Using Figure 12 in the Unit 5 Past Paper Questions Resource Sheet.]

[3]

b On a copy of the grid, draw the graph of $y = x^3 + 3x^2 + 2$ for $-3.5 \leqslant x \leqslant 1.5$.
[Using Figure 13 in the Past Paper Questions Resource Sheet.]

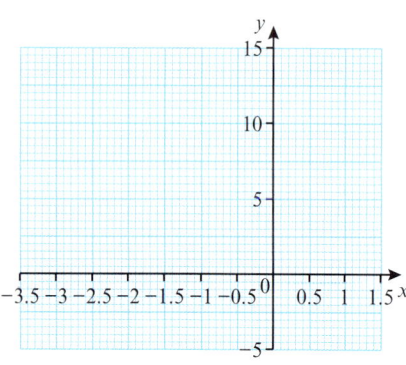

[4]

c Use your graph to solve the equation $x^3 + 3x^2 + 2 = 0$ for $-3.5 \leqslant x \leqslant 1.5$.

[1]

d By drawing a suitable straight line, solve the equation $x^3 + 3x^2 + 2x + 2 = 0$ for $-3.5 \leqslant x \leqslant 1.5$.

[2]

e For $-3.5 \leqslant x \leqslant 1.5$, the equation $x^3 + 3x^2 + 2 = k$ has three solutions and k is an integer.

Write down a possible value of k.

[1]

Cambridge IGCSE Mathematics (0580) Paper 41 Q2, June 2019

15 a The price of a book increases from $2.50 to $2.65.

Calculate the percentage increase.

[3]

b Scott invests $500 for 7 years at a rate of 1.5% per year simple interest.

Calculate the value of his investment at the end of the 7 years.

[3]

c In a city the population is increasing exponentially at a rate of 1.6% per year.

Find the overall percentage increase at the end of 20 years.

[2]

d The population of a village is 6400.

The population is decreasing exponentially at a rate of r% per year.

After 22 years, the population will be 2607.

Find the value of r.

[3]

Cambridge IGCSE Mathematics (0580) Paper 41 Q8, June 2019

16 a The test scores of 14 students are shown.

21   21   23   26   25   21   22   20   21   23   23   27   24   21

i Find the range, mode, median and mean of the test scores.

[6]

ii A student is chosen at random.

Find the probability that this student has a test score of more than 24.

[1]

b Petra records the score in each test she takes.

The mean of the first n scores is x.

The mean of the first $(n - 1)$ scores is $(x + 1)$.

Find the nth score in terms of n and x.

Give your answer in its simplest form.

[3]

c During one year the midday temperatures, $t\,°C$, in Zedford were recorded.

The table shows the results.

Temperature (t°C)	$0 < t \leqslant 10$	$10 < t \leqslant 15$	$15 < t \leqslant 20$	$20 < t \leqslant 25$	$25 < t \leqslant 30$
Number of days	50	85	100	120	10

i Calculate an estimate of the mean. [4]

ii Complete the histogram to show the information in the table.
[Using Figure 14 in the Unit 5 Past Paper Questions Resource Sheet.]

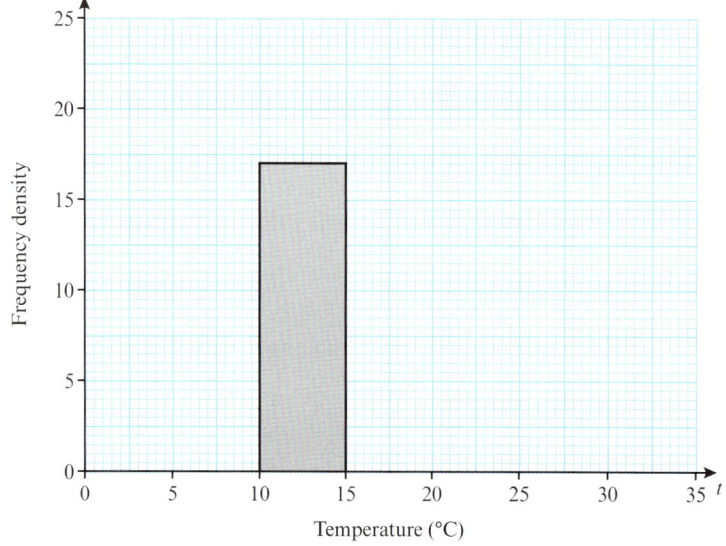

[4]

Cambridge IGCSE Mathematics (0580) Paper 41 Q4, June 2019

17 a Simplify $\dfrac{x^2 - 25}{x^2 - x - 20}$

[3]

b Write as a single fraction in its simplest form.

$$\frac{x + 5}{x} + \frac{x + 8}{x - 1}$$

[3]

c A curve has equation $y = 2x^3 - 4x^2 + 6$.

    i Find $\dfrac{\mathrm{d}y}{\mathrm{d}x}$, the derived function of y.

                                                 [2]

    ii Calculate the gradient of the curve $y = 2x^3 - 4x^2 + 6$ at $x = 4$.

                                                 [2]

    iii Find the coordinates of the two stationary points on the curve.

                                                 [4]

Cambridge IGCSE Mathematics (0580) Paper 41 Q7, June 2021

> Unit 5 Project

Attractive tablecloths

A café owner has designed tablecloths for Monday to Friday. Each cloth has as many colours as possible but they must have some symmetry.

The 5 by 5 tablecloths below each satisfy a different symmetry rule.

Monday's 5 by 5 tablecloth has just 1 vertical line of symmetry.

Design some tablecloths of other odd by odd sizes with just 1 line of symmetry.

Check you agree that a 7 by 7 tablecloth can have at most 28 colours.

Can you find a way of working out the maximum number of different colours that can be used on an *n* by *n* tablecloth (where *n* is odd), following Monday's rule?

Tuesday's 5 by 5 tablecloth has rotational symmetry of order 4, and no lines of symmetry.

Design some tablecloths of other odd by odd sizes with rotational symmetry of order 4, and no lines of symmetry.

Check you agree that a 7 by 7 tablecloth can have at most 13 colours.

Can you find a way of working out the maximum number of different colours that can be used on an *n* by *n* tablecloth (where *n* is odd), following Tuesday's rule?

Wednesday's 5 by 5 tablecloth has 2 lines of symmetry (horizontal and vertical), and rotational symmetry of order 2.

Design some tablecloths of other odd by odd sizes with 2 lines of symmetry, and rotational symmetry of order 2.

Check you agree that a 7 by 7 tablecloth can have at most 16 colours.

Can you find a way of working out the maximum number of different colours that can be used on an *n* by *n* tablecloth (where *n* is odd), following Wednesday's rule?

Thursday's 5 by 5 tablecloth has 2 (diagonal) lines of symmetry and rotational symmetry of order 2.

Design some tablecloths of other odd by odd sizes with 2 (diagonal) lines of symmetry and rotational symmetry of order 2.

Check you agree that a 7 by 7 tablecloth can have at most 16 colours.

Can you find a way of working out the maximum number of different colours that can be used on an *n* by *n* tablecloth (where *n* is odd), following Thursday's rule?

Friday's 5 by 5 tablecloth has 4 lines of symmetry and rotational symmetry of order 4.

Design some tablecloths of other odd by odd sizes with 4 lines of symmetry and rotational symmetry of order 4.

Check you agree that a 7 by 7 tablecloth can have at most 10 colours.

Can you find a way of working out the maximum number of different colours that can be used on an n by n tablecloth (where n is odd), following Friday's rule?

GO FURTHER...

On Saturdays and Sundays, the café owner uses tablecloths with an even number of squares. Investigate the number of colours that are needed for different types of symmetric n by n tablecloths where n is even.

Chapter 21

Ratio, rate and proportion

IN THIS CHAPTER YOU WILL:

- record relationships using ratio notation

- find one quantity when the other is given

- divide amounts in a given ratio

- make sense of scales on maps, models and plans

- read and interpret rates

- calculate average speed

- use and interpret distance–time and speed–time graphs

- solve problems using distance–time and speed–time graphs

- understand what is meant by direct and inverse proportion

- solve problems involving proportionate amounts

- use algebra to express direct and inverse proportion.

The photo shows architect Jean Nouvel with plans and a model of the Louvre Abu Dhabi Museum on Saadiyat Island. The model is an approximately 1 : 90 scaled version of the real building. What does that tell you about the size of the real building?

KEY WORDS

direct proportion

inverse proportion

rate

ratio

speed

A ratio compares amounts in a particular order. The amounts are expressed in the same units and are called the terms of the ratio. A ratio is usually written in the form $a : b$. Actual measurements are not given in a ratio, what is important is the proportion of the amounts. Ratio is used when working with scale on maps, models and plans.

A rate compares two different quantities and the units of both are given in the rate. For example, speed is often given in kilometres per hour; this is a rate which compares distance travelled to the time taken.

GETTING STARTED

1   Simplify each ratio.

   a   600 : 400   b   32 : 72   c   60 cm to 2 metres

2   The sectors in this pie chart are in the ratio 1 : 2 : 3 : 4.

   a   Calculate the angle at the centre of each sector.

   b   What percentage of the whole does sector C represent?

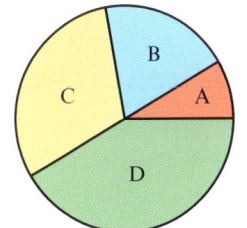

3   a   Discuss where you might see each of these rates and describe what is being measured.

   - $/metre squared   • litres/day   • $/hour   • metres/second
   - Runs/over   • bpm   • kg/metre squared   • $/£

   b   List at least three more examples of rates used in daily life.

TIP

Rates are often used in daily life. When we write a rate such as kilometres per hour, we use the abbreviation km/h. The / means 'per'.

4   Quantity y is directly proportionate to quantity x. When y is 12, x is 3.

   a   Work out the values a to e in the table.

   b   What rule connects quantity y and quantity x in this proportion?

x	3	a	5	c	1.5	e
y	12	4	b	48	d	14

21.1 Working with ratio

A **ratio** is a numerical comparison of amounts. The order in which you write the amounts is very important. For example, if there is one teacher for every 25 students in a school, then the ratio of teachers to students is $1 : 25$.

We normally write ratios in the form $1 : 25$, but when we work with them, it is sometimes useful to express the ratio as a fraction.

Think about the teacher to student ratio $1 : 25$. This means there is 1 teacher for every 25 students.

You can write this as $\frac{1}{25}$. This fraction compares the number of teachers with the number of students. It means that there is $\frac{1}{25}$ as many teachers as there are students.

So, if there are 150 students you can use the fraction to work out how many teachers there are:

$$\frac{1}{25} = \frac{?}{150}$$

$$\frac{1}{25} \text{ of } 150 = 6$$

So, for 150 students there will be 6 teachers.

$\frac{6}{150}$ is equivalent to $\frac{1}{25}$ and this matches the ratio $1 : 25$.

When you write two quantities as a ratio, you must make sure they are both in the same units. For example, the ratio of $20\,c$ to \$1 is not $20 : 1$, it is $20 : 100$ because there are 100 cents in a dollar.

> **TIP**
>
> When you say a ratio, you use the word 'to', so you say $5 : 2$ as '5 to 2'.

Writing ratios in simplest form

Ratios are in their simplest form when you write them using the smallest whole numbers possible. The ratio of $20 : 100$ above is not in its simplest form. You can simplify ratios in the same way that you simplify fractions:

$$\frac{20}{100} = \frac{2}{10} = \frac{1}{5} \text{ so } 20 : 100 = 1 : 5$$

If a breakfast cereal has 200 grams of rice for every 300 grams of wheat and 500 grams of corn, the ratio of rice to wheat to corn is $200 : 300 : 500$. To find the simplest form, divide each part of the ratio by 100 to get $2 : 3 : 5$.

WORKED EXAMPLE 1

A painter mixed eight litres of white paint with three litres of red paint to get pink paint.

What is the ratio of:

a   red paint to white paint?

b   white paint to the total amount of paint in the mixture?

c   red paint to the total amount of paint in the mixture?

WORKED EXAMPLE 1 CONTINUED

Answers

a   3 litres to 8 litres = 3 : 8

b   8 litres white out of a total of 11 litres so 8 : 11 is the required ratio

c   3 litres red out of a total of 11 litres so 3 : 11 is the required ratio

LINK

Ratios are commonly used in food science to compare the ingredients in food and to give dietary guidelines. Scientists may also use a measure called the protein efficiency ratio to determine the quality of proteins in food. Scientists have found that the carbohydrate : protein ratio in a meal can affect brain function, mood and metabolism in adults.

WORKED EXAMPLE 2

To make concrete, you mix cement, sand and gravel in the ratio 1 : 2 : 4.

a   What is the ratio of cement to gravel?

b   What is the ratio of sand to gravel?

c   What is the ratio of gravel to the total amount of concrete?

d   What fraction of the concrete is cement?

Answers

a   Cement to gravel is 1 : 4

b   Sand to gravel is 2 : 4 = 1 : 2

c   Concrete = 1 + 2 + 4 = 7 parts
    ∴ gravel is 4 parts to 7, so 4 : 7 is the required ratio

d   Concrete = 1 + 2 + 4 = 7
    ∴ cement = $\frac{1}{7}$

Exercise 21.1

1   Write each of the following as a ratio:

   a   nine children to nine adults

   b   one litre to five litres

   c   25 minutes to 3 minutes

   d   18 seconds to one minute

   e   15 c to $1

   f   two millimetres out of every centimetre

   g   10 bags of sand for every 4 bags of gravel and 8 bags of cement.

2 A packet of sweets contains 12 red and 5 yellow sweets. What is the ratio of:

    a   red to yellow sweets?   **b**   yellow to red sweets?

3 Look at these two rectangles.

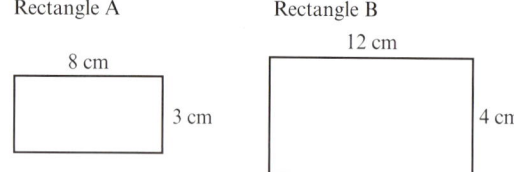

Rectangle A   Rectangle B

8 cm   12 cm

3 cm   4 cm

Express the following relationships as ratios:

    a   length of rectangle A to length of rectangle B

    b   width of rectangle A to width of rectangle B

    c   perimeter of rectangle A to perimeter of rectangle B

    d   area of rectangle A to area of rectangle B.

4 The table gives the mean life expectancy (in years) of some African animals.

Animal	Life expectancy (years)
Tortoise	120
Parrot	50
Elephant	35
Gorilla	30
Lion	15
Giraffe	10

Find the ratio of the life expectancies of:

    a   giraffe to tortoise   **b**   lion to gorilla   **c**   lion to tortoise

    d   elephant to gorilla   **e**   parrot to lion   **f**   parrot to tortoise.

5 What is the ratio of:

    a   a millimetre to a centimetre?   **b**   a centimetre to a metre?

    c   a metre to a centimetre?   **d**   a gram to a kilogram?

    e   a litre to a millilitre?   **f**   a minute to an hour?

6 Express the following as ratios in their simplest form.

    a   25 litres to 50 litres   **b**   25c to $2.00

    c   75 cm to 2 m   **d**   600 g to five kilograms

    e   15 mm to a metre   **f**   2.5 g to 50 g

    g   4 cm to 25 mm   **h**   400 ml to 3ℓ

INVESTIGATION

7   These diagrams show the aspect ratio of the screen on different devices.

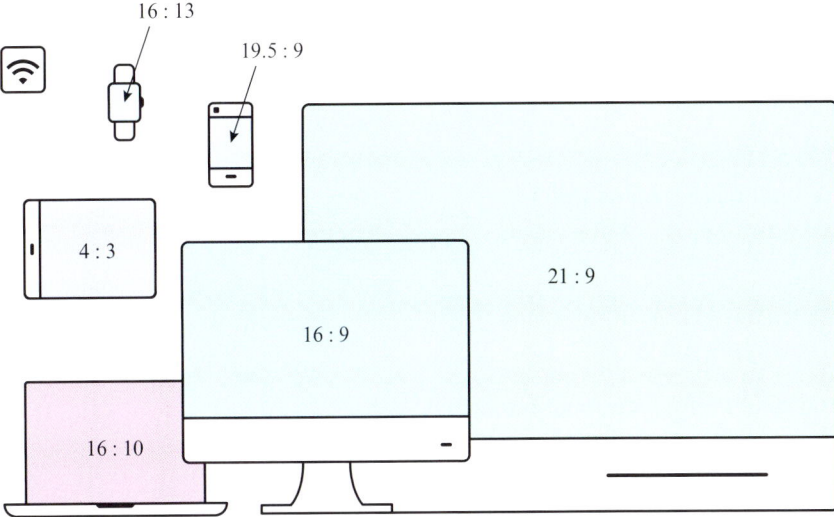

a   Find out what is compared in an aspect ratio.

b   Some of the aspect ratios are not given in their simplest form. Which of these are not in their simplest form? What would they be in simplest form?

c   If a tablet screen has an aspect ratio of 4 : 3 and the screen is 18 cm wide, how long is the screen?

d   Measure the length and width of the screens on some devices, for example phones, computers or television screens. Do the measurements match any of these aspect ratios? If not, what is the aspect ratio?

Equivalent ratios

Equivalent ratios are basically the same as equivalent fractions. If you multiply or divide the terms of the ratio by the same number (except 0) you get an equivalent ratio. Equivalent ratios are useful when you need to solve problems involving a missing amount.

MATHEMATICAL CONNECTIONS

You dealt with common factors in Chapter 1 and you learnt about the reciprocals of fractions in Chapter 5.

WORKED EXAMPLE 3

For each of the following ratios find the missing value.

a $1:4 = x:20$

b $4:9 = 24:y$

Answers

Method 1: multiplying by a common factor.

a $1:4 = x:20$ $20 \div 5 = 4$, so $20 = 4 \times 5$

$1:4 = 5:20$ 1 must be multiplied by 5 as well.

$\overset{\times\,?}{\overparen{1:4}} = x:20$ Work out what 4 is multiplied by to get 20.

$\overset{\times\,5}{\overparen{1:4}} = 5:20$ $20 \div 5 = 4$, so $20 = 4 \times 5$

$\underset{\times\,5}{\underparen{1:4}} = 5:20$ For an equivalent ratio, you must multiply 1 by 5 as well.

b $4:9 = 24:y$ $24 \div 4 = 6$, so $4 \times 6 = 24$

$4:9 = 24:54$ 9 must be multiplied by 6 as well.

Method 2: cross multiplying fractions.

a $\dfrac{1}{4} = \dfrac{x}{20}$ Write the ratios as fractions.

$x = 1 \times \dfrac{20}{4}$ Solve the equation by multiplying both sides by 20.

$x = 5$

b $\dfrac{4}{9} = \dfrac{24}{y}$ Write each ratio as a fraction.

$\dfrac{9}{4} = \dfrac{y}{24}$ Take the reciprocal of the fractions (turn them upside down) to get **y** at the top and make the equation easier to solve.

$\dfrac{9 \times 24}{4} = y$ Solve the equation by multiplying both sides by 24.

$\dfrac{216}{4} = y$

$y = 54$

REFLECTION

Two methods are shown for finding missing values in equivalent ratios. Which method made most sense to you? Why?

You learnt that if $\dfrac{a}{b} = \dfrac{c}{d}$ then the cross-products ad and bc are equal.

Do you understand why this works or do you just follow the rule?

Exercise 21.2

1 Find the unknown values in the following equivalent ratios. Use whichever method you find easiest.

  a $2:3 = 6:x$ **b** $6:5 = y:20$ **c** $12:8 = 3:y$ **d** $27:x = 9:2$

  e $3:8 = 66:x$ **f** $1:5 = 13:y$ **g** $x:25 = 7:5$ **h** $40:9 = 800:y$

  i $3:7 = 600:y$ **j** $2:7 = 30:x$ **k** $1.5:x = 6:5$ **l** $\frac{1}{6}:\frac{1}{3} = 2:y$

2 Use the equation (cross multiplying fractions) method to find the unknown values in the following equivalent ratios.

  a $x:20 = 3:4$ **b** $12:21 = x:14$ **c** $2:5 = 8:y$ **d** $3:5 = x:4$

  e $1:10 = x:6$ **f** $8:13 = 2:y$ **g** $4:5 = x:7$ **h** $5:4 = 9:y$

3 Say whether these statements are true or false. If a statement is false, explain why it is false.

  a   The ratio $1:6$ is the same as the ratio $6:1$.

  b   The ratio $1:6$ is equivalent to $3:18$.

  c   The ratio $20:15$ can be expressed as $3:4$.

  d   If the current ratio of a mother's age to her daughter's age is $8:1$, and the daughter is nine, then the mother is 48 years old.

  e   If Mr Smith's wages are $\frac{5}{8}$ of Mr Jones' wages, then the ratio of their wages is $20:32$.

APPLY YOUR SKILLS

4 An alloy is a mixture of metals. Most of the gold used in jewellery is an alloy of pure gold and other metals which are added to make the gold harder. Pure gold is 24 carats (ct), so 18 carat gold is an alloy of gold and other metals in the ratio $18:6$. In other words, $\frac{18}{24}$ parts pure gold and $\frac{6}{24}$ other metals.

  a   A jeweller makes an 18 ct gold alloy using three grams of pure gold. What mass of other metals does she add?

  b   An 18 ct gold chain contains four grams of pure gold. How much other metal does it contain?

  c   What is the ratio of gold to other metals in 14 ct gold?

  d   What is the ratio of gold to other metals in 9 ct gold?

5 An alloy of 9 ct gold contains gold, copper zinc and silver in the ratio $9:12.5:2.5$.

  a   Express this ratio in simplest form.

  b   How much silver would you need if your alloy contained six grams of pure gold?

  c   How much copper zinc would you need to make a 9 ct alloy using three grams of pure gold?

6 An epoxy glue comes in two tubes (red and black), which have to be mixed in the ratio 1 : 4 (red : black).

  a If you measure 5 ml from the red tube, how much do you need to measure from the black tube?

  b How much would you need from the red tube if you used 10 ml from the black tube?

7 A brand of pet food contains meat, cereal and fats in the ratio 2 : 9 : 1. During one shift, the factory making the pet food used 3500 kg of meat. What mass of cereal did they use?

Dividing a quantity in a given ratio

Ratios can be used to divide or share quantities. There are two ways of solving problems like these.

Method 1: find the value of one part. This is the unitary method.

1 Add the values in the ratio to find the total number of parts involved.

2 Divide the quantity by the total number of parts to find the quantity per part (the value of one part).

3 Multiply the values in the ratio by the quantity per part to find the value of each part.

Method 2: express the shares as fractions. This is the ratio method.

1 Add the values in the ratio to find the total number of parts involved.

2 Express each part of the ratio as a fraction of the total parts.

3 Multiply the quantity by the fraction to find the value of each part.

WORKED EXAMPLE 4

Share $24 between Jess and Anne in the ratio 3 : 5.

Answer

Method 1

3 + 5 = 8	There are 8 parts in the ratio.
24 ÷ 8 = 3	This is the value of 1 part.
Jess gets $9	Jess gets 3 parts: 3 × 3 = 9
Anne gets $15	Anne gets 5 parts: 5 × 3 = 15

Method 2

3 + 5 = 8 — There are 8 parts in the ratio.

Jess gets $\frac{3}{8}$ of $24 = $\frac{3}{8} \times 24$ = $9

Anne gets $\frac{5}{8}$ of $24 = $\frac{5}{8} \times 24$ = $15

Express each part as a fraction of the total parts and multiply by the quantity.

Exercise 21.3

1 Divide:

   a   200 in the ratio 1 : 4

   b   1500 in the ratio 4 : 1

   c   50 in the ratio 3 : 7

   d   60 in the ratio 3 : 12

   e   600 in the ratio 3 : 9

   f   38 in the ratio 11 : 8

   g   300 in the ratio 11 : 4

   h   2300 in the ratio 1 : 2 : 7.

2 Fruit concentrate is mixed with water in the ratio of 1 : 3 to make a fruit drink. How much concentrate would you need to make 1.2 litres of fruit drink?

3 Jo shares 45 marbles with Ahmed in the ratio 3 : 2. How many marbles does each person get?

4 $200 is to be shared amongst Annie, Andrew and Amina in the ratio 3 : 4 : 5. How much will each person receive?

5 A line 16 cm long is divided in the ratio 3 : 5. How long is each section?

6 A bag of N:P:K fertiliser contains nitrogen, phosphorus and potassium in the ratio 2 : 3 : 3. Work out the mass of each ingredient if the bags have the following total masses:

   a   one kilogram

   b   five kilograms

   c   20 kilograms

   d   25 kilograms.

> **TIP**
>
> The capital letters N:P:K on fertiliser bags are the chemical symbols for the elements. The ratio of chemicals is always given on packs of fertiliser.

7 The lengths of the sides of a triangle are in the ratio 4 : 5 : 3. Work out the length of each side if the triangle has a perimeter of 5.4 metres.

8 A rectangle has a perimeter of 120 cm. The ratio of its length to its width is 5 : 3. Sketch the rectangle and label the lengths of each side.

9 In a group of 3200 elderly people, the ratio of people using a walking aid to people not using a walking aid is 3 : 5. Calculate how many people in the group use a walking aid.

10 a Show that the ratio area : circumference for any circle is $r : 2$, where r is the radius of the circle

   b   Find the ratio volume : surface area for a sphere of radius r, giving your answer as simply as possible

> **REFLECTION**
>
> Did you use the unitary method or the ratio method most in this exercise? Why?
>
> Are there problems or situations where one method is more efficient than the other? Explain your answer.

21.2 Ratio and scale

Scale drawings (maps and plans) and models such as the one of the Louvre Museum in Abu Dhabi (shown at the start of this chapter), are the same shape as the real objects but they are generally smaller.

Scale is a ratio. It can be expressed as 'length on drawing : real length'.

The scale of a map, plan or model is usually given as a ratio in the form $1 : n$. For example, the architects who designed the new Louvre building for Abu Dhabi made a 6 m wide scale model of the domed roof using aluminium rods to test how light would enter the dome. The scale of the model was $1 : 33$.

A scale of $1 : 33$ means that a unit of measurement on the model must be multiplied by 33 to get the length (in the same units) of the real building. So, if the diameter of the dome in the model was 6 m, then the diameter of the real dome is $6\,\text{m} \times 33 = 198\,\text{m}$.

Expressing a ratio in the form $1 : n$

All ratio scales must be expressed in the form $1 : n$ or $n : 1$.

To change a ratio so that one part = 1, you need to divide both parts by the number that you want expressed as 1.

WORKED EXAMPLE 5

Express $5 : 1000$ in the form $1 : n$.

Answer

$5 : 1000 = \dfrac{5}{5} : \dfrac{1000}{5}$ Divide both sides by 5, i.e. the number that you want expressed as 1.

$ = 1 : 200$

WORKED EXAMPLE 6

Express $4\,\text{mm} : 50\,\text{cm}$ as a ratio scale.

Answer

$4\,\text{mm} : 50\,\text{cm} = 4\,\text{mm} : 500\,\text{mm}$ Express the amounts in the same units first.

$\phantom{4\,\text{mm} : 50\,\text{cm}} = 4 : 500$

$\phantom{4\,\text{mm} : 50\,\text{cm}} = \dfrac{4}{4} : \dfrac{500}{4}$ Divide by 4 to express in the form $1 : n$.

$\phantom{4\,\text{mm} : 50\,\text{cm}} = 1 : 125$

WORKED EXAMPLE 7

Write $22 : 4$ in the form $n : 1$.

Answer

$22 : 4 = \dfrac{22}{4} : \dfrac{4}{4}$ Divide both sides by 4, i.e. the number that you want expressed as 1.

$ = 5.5 : 1$ In this form you may get a decimal answer on one side.

MATHEMATICAL CONNECTIONS

Scale drawings were discussed in more detail in Chapter 15.

Some scale drawings, such as diagrams of cells in Biology, are larger than the real items they show. In an enlargement the scale is given in the form $n : 1$ (where $n > 1$).

TIP

The form $1 : n$ or $n : 1$ may give a ratio with decimal values.

Solving scale problems

There are two main types of problems involving scale:
- calculating the real length of an object given its scaled length
- calculating the scaled length of an object given its real length.

In both cases you will be told one of the lengths and the scale, expressed as 'length on the diagram : real length'.

You can write the scale as fractions and cross-multiply to find the unknown length.

WORKED EXAMPLE 8

The scale of a map is $1:25\,000$.

a   What is real distance between two points that are 5 cm apart on the diagram?

b   Express the real distance in kilometres.

Answers

a   Map distance : real distance = $1:25\,000$ — Substitute the map distance and use x to represent the unknown real distance.

So, $5\,\text{cm}:x\,\text{cm} = 1:25\,000$

$$\frac{5}{x} = \frac{1}{25\,000}$$

Write the ratios as fractions.

$5 \times 25\,000 = x$

Cross multiply to find the real distance.

$x = 125\,000$

∴ Real distance = $125\,000$ cm — The units in your answer will the same units as the map distance units.

b $1\,\text{km} = 100\,000\,\text{cm}$ — From part (a) you know the real distance is $120\,000$ cm.

$125\,000\,\text{cm} \div 100\,000$ — You know that 1 km = 100 000 cm.

$= 1.25\,\text{km}$ — So convert the real distance to km.

WORKED EXAMPLE 9

A dam wall is 480 m long. How many centimetres long will it be on a map with a scale of $1:12\,000$?

Answers

Map length : real length = $1:12\,000$ — Substitute the real length and use x to represent the unknown map length.

So, $x\,\text{m}:480\,\text{m} = 1:12\,000$

$$\frac{x}{480} = \frac{1}{12\,000}$$

Write the ratios as fractions.

$$x = \frac{480}{12\,000}1$$

Cross multiply to find the map length.

$x = 0.04$

∴ map distance = 0.04 m — 1 m = 100 cm so multiply by 100 to convert the answer to cm.

$= 4\,\text{cm}$

WORKED EXAMPLE 10

A biology book shows a diagram of a flea drawn to a scale of 12 : 1. If the flea in the diagram is 25 mm long, how long is the real flea? Give your answer correct to 2 decimal places.

Answer

Diagram length : real length = 12 : 1

So, 25 mm : x mm = 12 : 1

$$\frac{25}{x} = \frac{12}{1}$$

$$25 = 12x$$

$$\frac{25}{12} = x$$

$$2.08 = x$$

∴ real length = 2.08 mm (2 d.p.)

Substitute the length on the diagram and use x to represent the real length.

Write the ratios as fractions and solve for x.

Round your answer to 2 decimal places.

Exercise 21.4

1   Write each of the following scales as a ratio in the form:

   i   1 : n **ii** n : 1

   a   1 cm to 2 m   **b**   2 cm to 5 m   **c**   4 cm to 1 km

   d   5 cm to 10 km   **e**   3.5 cm to 1 m   **f**   9 mm to 150 km

2   A scale diagram of a shopping centre is drawn at a scale of 1 : 400. Find the real distance in metres of the following lengths measured on the diagram.

   a   1 cm   **b**   15 mm   **c**   3.5 cm   **d**   12 cm

3   A map has a scale of 1 : 50 000. How long will each of these real lengths be on the map?

   a   60 m   **b**   15 km   **c**   120 km   **d**   75.5 km

4   A rectangular hall is 20 m long and 50 m wide. Draw scale diagrams of this hall using a scale of:

   a   1 : 200   **b**   4 mm to 1 m.

5   An insect drawn at a scale of 5 : 1 is 2.75 cm long. What is the actual length of the insect in millimetres?

6   A scale drawing of an 8.2 mm long electronic component shows the component as 9.84 cm long. What scale was used for the drawing?

APPLY YOUR SKILLS

7 This image shows a section through the stem of a pondweed plant. The image is magnified 80 times. What is the actual width of the stem from A to B?

8 Use this map to find the straight-line distance between:

  a New Delhi and Bengaluru   **b** Mumbai and Kolkata

  c Srinagar and Nagpur.

APPLY YOUR SKILLS CONTINUED

9 This floor plan of a house is drawn to a scale of 1 : 150.

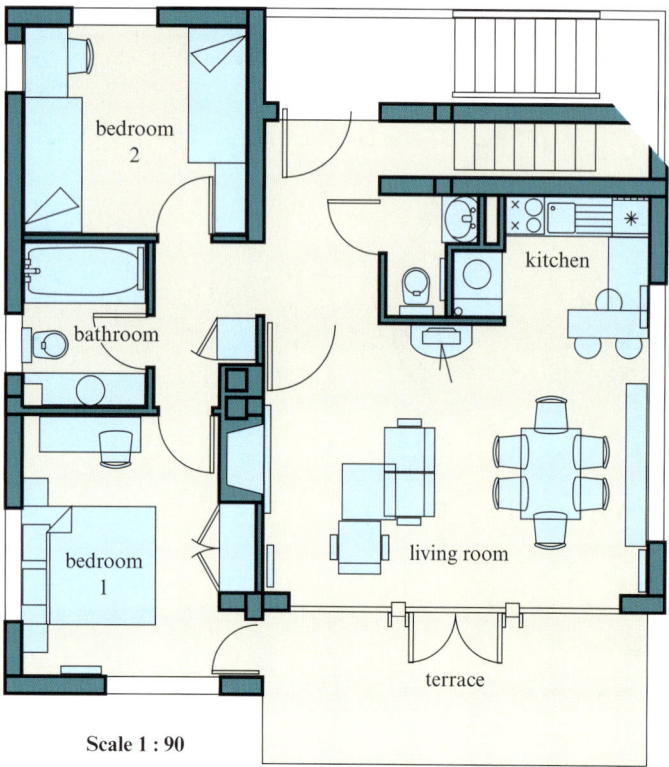

Scale 1 : 90

a What is the real distance in metres represented by 1 cm on the plan?

b Calculate the real length in metres of:

    i the length of living room

    ii the width of the living room

    iii the length of the bath

    iv the width of the terrace.

c What is the real area of:

    i bedroom 1?

    ii bedroom 2?

    iii the terrace?

d Calculate how much floor space there is in the bathroom (in m²). (Include the toilet in the floor space.)

e Calculate the cost of tiling the bathroom floor if the tiles cost $25.99 per square metre and the tiler charges $15.25 per square metre for laying the tiles.

TIP

Remember to measure from inside wall to inside wall.

TIP

Work out the actual size of *each* length before you calculate the area.

Copy the headings and complete a learning log for the work on ratio.

Learning log for: Ratio	
I learnt …	
I still need to learn more about …	
My next steps will be …	
I need some help with …	
In general, I feel _____ about this section of work.	

21.3 Rates

A **rate** compares two different quantities. In a rate, the quantity of one thing is usually given in relation to one unit of the other thing. For example, 750 ml per bottle, 60 km/h or 100 people per square kilometre (km^2). You must give the units of *both* quantities in a rate.

Rates can be simplified just like ratios. When a rate is in simplest form, the first quantity is expressed per one unit of the second, so, for example, 60 km per hour is in simplest form, but 120 km per 2 hours is not. You solve rate problems in the same ways that you solve ratio and proportion problems.

WORKED EXAMPLE 11

492 people live in an area of 12 km^2. Express this as a rate in its simplest terms.

Answer

492 people in 12 km^2

$= \dfrac{492}{12}$ people per km^2 Divide by 12 to get a rate per unit.

$= 41$ people/km^2 Don't forget to write the units.

INVESTIGATION

Population density

Population density is a rate that specifies the numbers of people, animals or plants in a given area (normally per square kilometre).

1   Work in pairs to answer these questions about population density.

     a   Which are the most and least densely populated areas in the world?

     b   Suggest why some places are densely populated while others are not.

     c   Why do social scientists usually look at population distribution as well as population density when they study different populations?

INVESTIGATION CONTINUED

2 In biology, scientists often state that where conditions for an organism are favourable, the population density will be high, and that where conditions are unfavourable, the population density will be low because organisms will die out or move away.

    a Find an environmental example to support this hypothesis.

    b Do you think this hypothesis is true for human populations? Explain your answer, giving examples.

3 How is population density data useful in the following areas?

    a Ecology

    b Epidemiology

    c Infrastructure planning

Average speed

You need to be able to work with speed, distance and time quantities to solve problems.

Average **speed** is one of the most commonly used rates. We talk about average speed because usually a vehicle will change speed during a journey. The driver might slow down, speed up or stop at an intersection. We use the total distance covered over time to calculate the average speed. The average speed is given as a rate comparing the units of distance to the units of time. For example, metres per second, kilometres per hour or miles per hour.

> **TIP**
>
> A rate like km/h may sometimes be written kph (the 'p' stands for 'per').

You can use the distance–time–speed triangle to help you solve problems related to distance, time or speed.

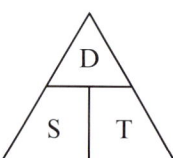

If you cover the letter of the quantity you need to find, then the remaining letters in the triangle give you the calculation you need to do (a multiplication or a division). For example:

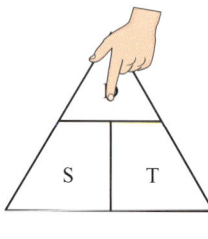

$$D = S \times T$$

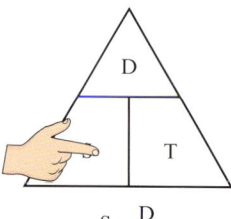

$$S = \frac{D}{T}$$

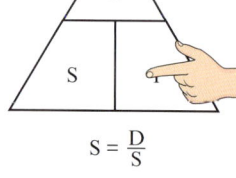

$$S = \frac{D}{S}$$

WORKED EXAMPLE 12

A bus travels 210 km in three hours, what is its average speed in km/h?

Answer

Speed = $\dfrac{D}{T}$

Distance = 210 km, time = 3 h

∴ speed = $\dfrac{210}{3}$

= 70 km/h

Its average speed is 70 km/h.

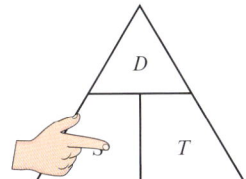

TIP

When you see the phrases 'how fast', 'how far' or 'for how long' you know you are dealing with a speed, distance or time problem.

LINK

Nurses and other medical support staff work with ratio and rates when they calculate medicine doses, convert between units of measurement and set the patients' drips to supply the correct amount of fluid per hour.

WORKED EXAMPLE 13

I walk at 4.5 km/h. How far can I walk in $2\frac{1}{2}$ hours at the same speed?

Answer

Distance = $S \times T$

Speed = 4.5 km/h, time = 2.5 h

∴ distance = 4.5 × 2.5 = 11.25 km

I can walk 11.25 km.

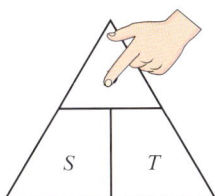

WORKED EXAMPLE 14

How long will it take to cover 200 km at a speed of 80 km/h?

Answer

Time = $\dfrac{D}{S}$

Distance = 200 km, speed = 80 km/h

∴ time = $\dfrac{200}{80}$ = 2.5

It would take $2\frac{1}{2}$ hours.

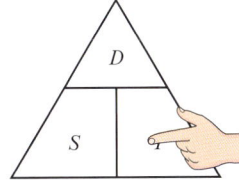

Exercise 21.5

APPLY YOUR SKILLS

1 Express each of these relationships as a rate in simplest form.

   a 12 kg for $5   **b** 120 litres for 1000 km

   c $315 for 3 nights   **d** 5 km in 20 min

   e 135 students for 5 teachers   **f** 15 hours spent per 5 holes dug

2 A quarry produces 1200 t of crushed stone per hour. How much stone could it supply in:

   a an eight-hour shift?   **b** five eight-hour shifts?

3 Water leaks from a pipe at a rate of 5 ℓ/h. How much water will leak from the pipe in:

   a a day?   **b** a week?

4 A machine fills containers at a rate of 135 containers per minute. How long will it take to fill 1000 containers at the same rate?

5 Two friends walk at 4.25 km/h. How far will they walk in three hours?

6 How far will a train travelling at 230 km/h travel in:

   a $3\frac{1}{2}$ hours?   **b** 20 minutes?

7 A plane flies at an average speed of 750 km/h. How far will it fly in:

   a four hours?   **b** 25 minutes?

8 How long will it take to travel 200 km at:

   a 75 km/h?   **b** 80 km/h?   **c** 45 km/h?

   d 120 km/h?   **e** 4 m/min?

9 A train left Cairo at 9 p.m. and travelled 880 km to Aswan, arriving at 5 a.m. What was its average speed?

10 A runner completed a 42 km marathon in two hours 15 minutes. What was their average speed?

11 In August 2009, Usain Bolt of Jamaica set a world record by running 100 m in 9.58 seconds.

   a Translate this speed into km/h.

   b How long would it take him to run 420 m if he could run it at this speed?

21.4 Kinematic graphs

Kinematics is the study of how objects move. A kinematic graph may show how far an object moves over time or how its speed changes with time.

Distance–time graphs

Graphs that show the connection between the distance an object has travelled and the time taken to travel that distance are called distance–time graphs or travel graphs. On such graphs, time is normally shown along the horizontal axis and distance on the vertical axis.

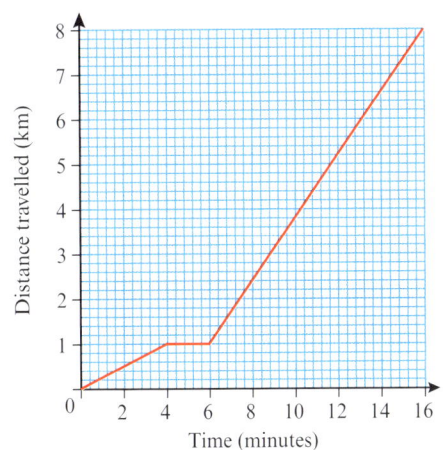

> **TIP**
>
> In travel graphs time is an independent variable and it is always shown on the x-axis.

Look at the graph. Can you see that it shows the following journey:

- a cycle ride for 4 minutes from home to a bus stop 1 km away
- a 2 minute wait for the bus
- a 7 km journey on the bus that takes 10 minutes.

The line of the graph remains horizontal while the person is waiting for the bus because they don't get any further from the starting point. The steeper the line, the faster the person is travelling.

> **MATHEMATICAL CONNECTIONS**
>
> You learned how to read and draw line graphs in Chapter 4.

WORKED EXAMPLE 15

Ashraf's school is 4 km from home and it takes 40 minutes to walk to school. One morning he leaves at 7 a.m. After 15 minutes, he realises he has left his boots at home, so he runs back in 10 minutes. It takes him three minutes to find the boots. He then runs to school at a constant speed. The graph shows his journey.

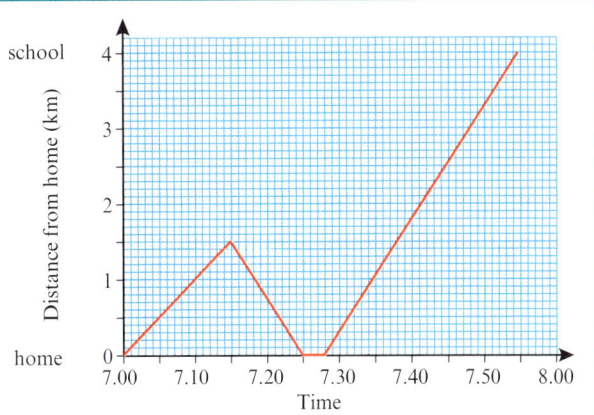

WORKED EXAMPLE 15 CONTINUED

a How far had he walked before he remembered his boots?

b What happens to the graph as he returns home?

c What does the horizontal line on the graph represent?

d How fast did he run in m/min to get back home?

Answers

a Ashraf walked 1.5 km before he remembered his boots.

b The graph slopes downwards (back towards 0 km) as he goes home.

c The horizontal part of the graph corresponds with the three minutes at home.

d He runs 1.5 km in 10 minutes, an average speed 150 m/min.

Exercise 21.6

APPLY YOUR SKILLS

1 This distance–time graph represents Monica's journey from home to the library and back again.

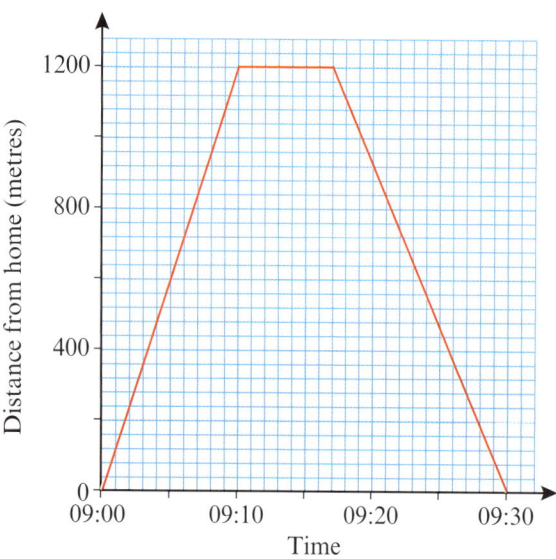

a How far was Monica from home at 09:06 hours?

b How many minutes did she spend at the library?

c At what times was Monica 800 m from home?

d On which part of the journey did Monica travel faster: going to the library or returning home?

2   Omar left school at 16.30. On his way home, he stopped at a
friend's house before going home on his bicycle. The graph shows
this information.

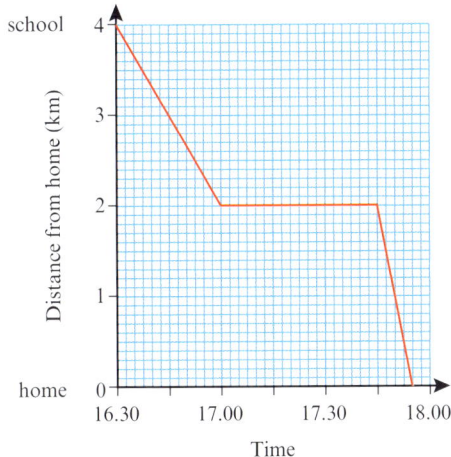

a   How long did he stay at his friend's house?

b   At what time did Omar arrive home?

c   Omar's brother left school at 16.45 and walked home using the same
route as Omar. If he walked at 4 km per hour, work out at what time
the brother passed Omar's friend's house.

3   Neo left home and cycled the 10 km to the library in 45 minutes.

He spent $1\frac{1}{2}$ hours in the library. He then took 40 minutes to cycle home.

a   Draw a distance–time graph to represent this information.
Use a scale of 1 cm per 20 minutes and 1 cm per 2 km.

b   How long did it take Neo to cycle 4 km after leaving home?

c   How long did it take Neo to cycle 4 km after leaving the library?

4   A swimming pool is 25 m long. Jasmine swims from one end to the other
in 20 seconds. She rests for 10 seconds and then swims back to the
starting point. It takes her 30 seconds to swim the second length.

a   Draw a distance–time graph for Jasmine's swim.

b   How far was Jasmine from her starting point after 12 seconds?

c   How far was Jasmine from her starting point after 54 seconds?

Speed in distance–time graphs

The steepness gradient of a graph gives an indication of speed.

•   A straight line on a graph indicates a constant speed. Any change in the angle of
the line indicates a change of speed.

- The steeper the graph, the greater the speed.

- An upward slope and a downward slope represent movement in opposite directions.

The distance–time graph shown is for a person who walks, cycles and then drives for three equal periods of time. For each period, speed is given by the formula:

$$\text{speed} = \frac{\text{distance travelled}}{\text{time taken}}$$

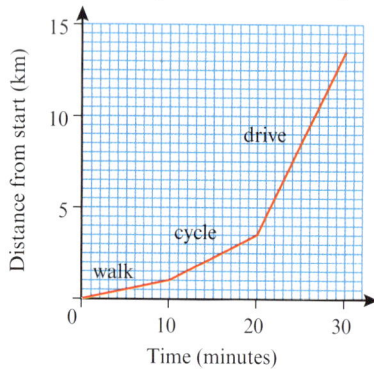

Different steepnesses for different speeds

Speed is a rate of change. A straight line from the origin shows a constant rate of change and you can use the formula $\dfrac{\text{change in } y}{\text{change in } x}$ to find the rate of change.

If the gradient changes along the graph, the speed will be different for different time periods.

The gradient precisely describes the steepness of a line.

In the diagram, the steepness of line AB is measured by: $\dfrac{\text{increase in } y\text{-coordinate}}{\text{increase in } x\text{-coordinate}}$

This is the same as $\dfrac{\text{rise}}{\text{run}}$ or gradient of a straight line graph.

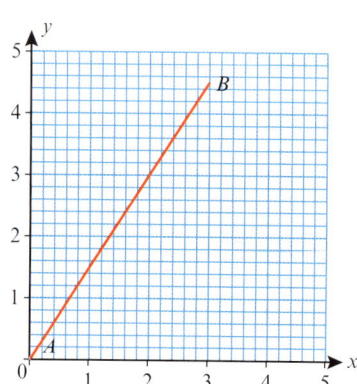

A positive gradient means that as x increases y also increases. On a distance–time graph, the y value indicates distance from the starting point, so a positive gradient means the object is moving away from the starting point. A zero gradient means the y-value is not changing, so the object is not moving. A negative gradient means that as x increases the y-value decreases, so the object is moving back towards the starting point.

For a distance–time graph:

$$\frac{\text{change in } y\text{-coordinate (distance)}}{\text{change in } x\text{-coordinate (time)}} = \frac{\text{distance travelled}}{\text{time taken}} = \text{speed}$$

Therefore, the gradient of the graph tells you the speed of the object and its direction of motion. This is known as the velocity of the object.

Here is another example:

The travel graph represents a car journey.
The horizontal sections have zero gradient
(so the car was stationary during these times).

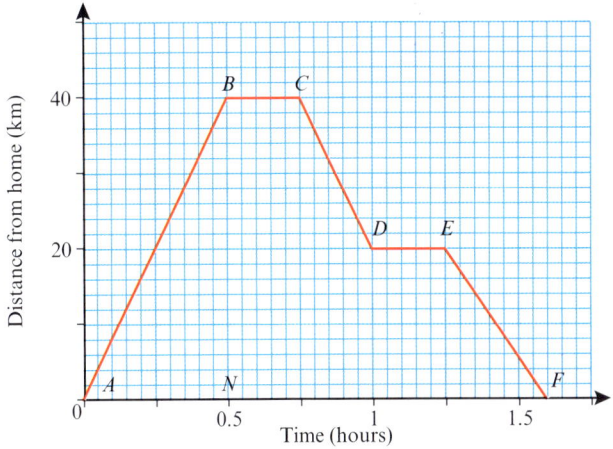

For section AB, the gradient is positive:

$$\text{Gradient} = \frac{NB}{AN} = \frac{40 - 0}{0.5} = 80\,\text{km/h}$$

$\therefore$ the velocity was 80 km/h in the direction away from home.

For section CD, the gradient is negative:

$$\text{Gradient} = \frac{20 - 40}{0.25} = -80\,\text{km/h}$$

$\therefore$ the velocity was -80 km/h.

For section EF the gradient is negative:

$$\text{Gradient} = \frac{0 - 20}{0.35} = -57.1\,\text{km/h}$$

$\therefore$ the velocity was -57.1 km/h.

MATHEMATICAL CONNECTIONS

You learned how to calculate the gradient of a straight line graph in Chapter 10.
Remember the gradient of a line is:

*   positive if the line slopes up from left to right
*   negative if the line slopes down from left to right.

TIP

When the velocity is positive, the direction of motion is away from home. When the velocity is negative, the direction is towards home.

Exercise 21.7

INVESTIGATION

1   **a**   Clearly describe what is happening in each of the distance–time graphs below.

b   Suggest a possible real-life situation that would produce each graph.

i

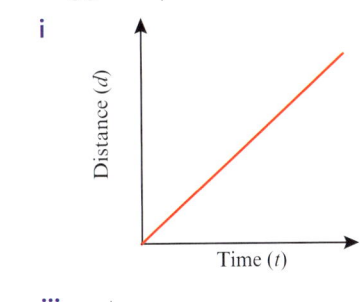

ii

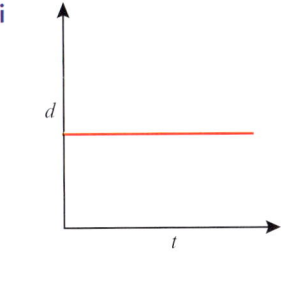

iii

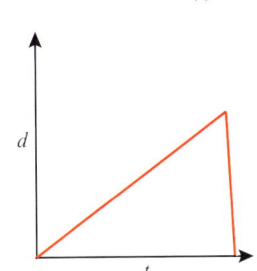

iv

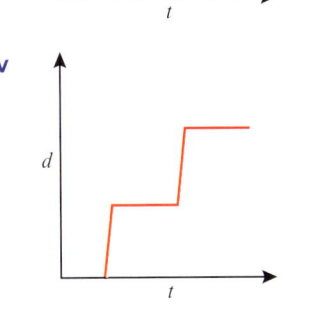

INVESTIGATION CONTINUED

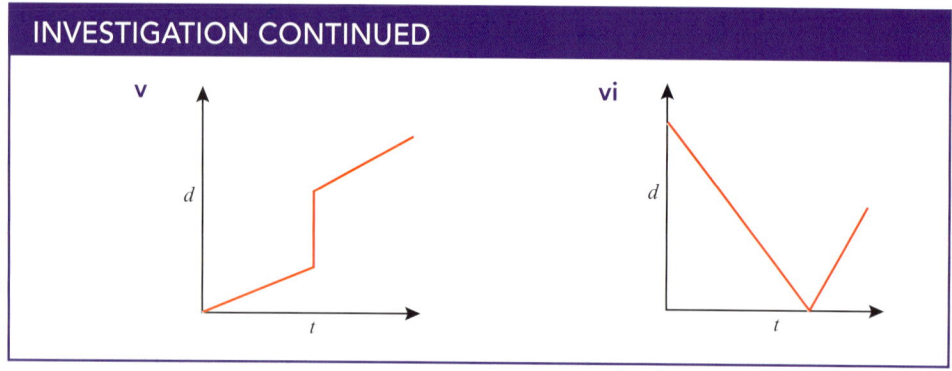

2 The graph shows Andile's daily run.

   a For how many minutes does Andile run before taking a rest?

   b Calculate the speed in km/h at which Andile runs before taking a rest.

   c For how many minutes does Andile rest?

   d Calculate the speed in m/s at which Andile runs back home.

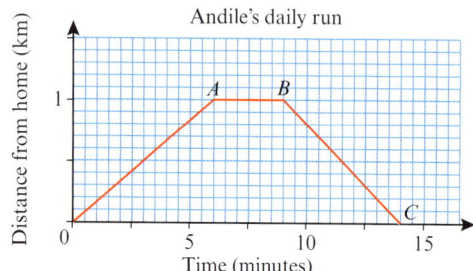

3 This graph shows the movement of a taxi in city traffic during a 4-hour period.

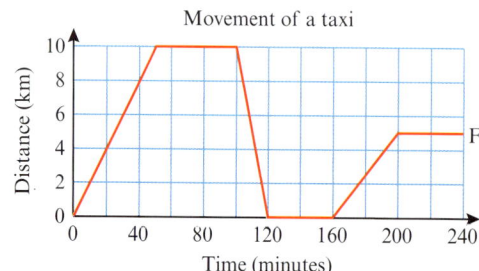

   a Clearly and concisely describe the taxi's journey.

   b For how many minutes was the taxi waiting for passengers in this period? How can you tell this?

   c What was the total distance travelled?

   d Calculate the taxi's average speed during:

      i   the first 20 minutes

      ii   the first hour

      iii from 160 to 210 minutes

      iv   for the full period of the graph.

4   The distance–time graph represents Ibrahim's journey from home to school one morning.

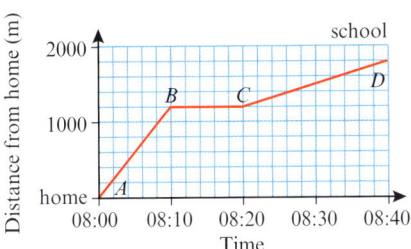

   a   How far was Ibrahim from home at 08:30 hours?

   b   How fast, in m/s, was Ibrahim travelling during the first 10 minutes?

   c   Describe the stage of Ibrahim's journey represented by the line *BC*.

   d   How fast, in m/s, was Ibrahim travelling during the last 20 minutes?

5   This is a real distance–time graph showing distance from the ground against time for a helicopter as it takes off and flies away from an airport.

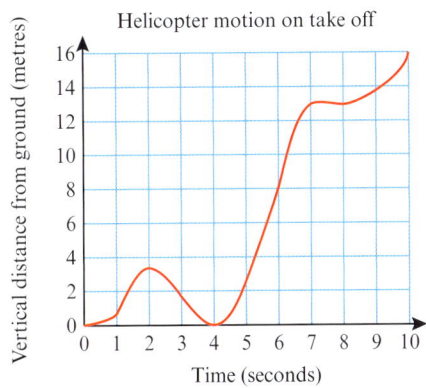

   a   Make up five mathematical questions that can be answered from the graph.

   b   Exchange questions with another student and try to answer each other's questions.

Speed–time graphs

In certain cases, the speed (or velocity) of an object may change. An increase in speed is called acceleration; a decrease in speed is called deceleration. A speed–time graph shows speed (rather than distance) on the vertical axis.

This graph shows a train journey between two stations.

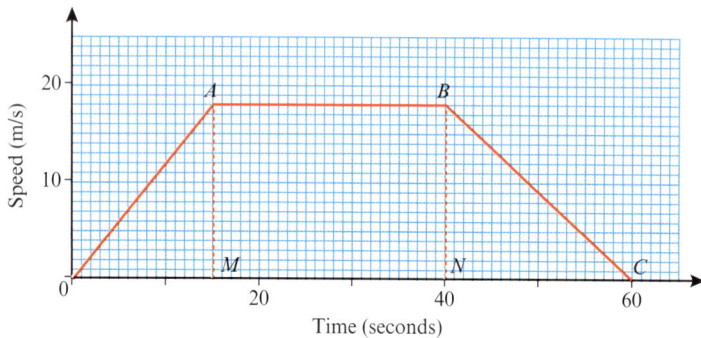

- The train starts at zero speed.

- The speed increases steadily reaching 18 m/s after 15 seconds.

- The train travels at a constant speed (horizontal section) of 18 m/s for 25 seconds.

- The train then slows down at a steady rate till it stops.

- The entire journey takes 60 seconds.

Look at the first part of the journey again.

The speed increased by 18 m/s in 15 seconds.

$\dfrac{18 \text{ m/s}}{15 \text{ seconds}}$ is the gradient of the line representing the first part of the journey.

This is a rate of 1.2 m/s every second. This is the rate of acceleration. You write this as 1.2 m/s^2 (or m/s/s).

For a speed–time graph, the gradient = acceleration.

A positive gradient (acceleration) is an increase in speed.

A negative gradient (deceleration) is a decrease in speed.

Distance travelled in a speed–time graph

You already know that distance = speed × time. On a speed–time graph, this is represented by the area of shapes under the sections of graph. You can use the graph to work out the distance travelled.

> ### TIP
> You may sometimes see m/s written as m s^{-1} and m/s^2 written as m s^{-2}.

MATHEMATICAL CONNECTIONS

You worked with distance, time and speed earlier in this chapter. Make sure you remember how to use and manipulate the formulae.

WORKED EXAMPLE 16

This speed–time graph represents the motion of a particle over a period of five seconds.

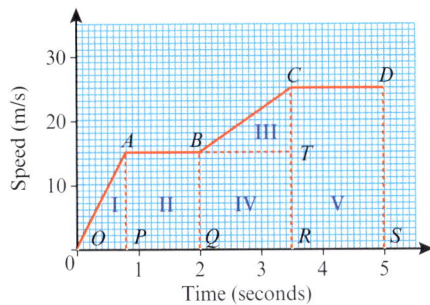

a   During which periods of time was the particle accelerating?

b   Calculate the particle's acceleration 3 seconds after the start.

c   Calculate the distance travelled by the particle in the 5 seconds.

Answers

a   The particle was accelerating in the period 0 to 0.8 seconds (section *OA*) and in the period 2 to 3.5 seconds (section *BC*).

b   The gradient is constant between 2 and 3.5 seconds so acceleration was also constant in that period. So, the acceleration 3 seconds after the start is:

$$\frac{25 - 15 \,(\text{m/s})}{3.5 - 2 \,(\text{s})} = \frac{10}{1.5} = 6.7 \text{ m/s}^2$$

c   Distance travelled = area under graph

$$= \text{area I} + \text{area II} + \text{area III} + \text{area IV} + \text{area V}$$

$$= \frac{1}{2}(0.8 \times 15) + (1.2 \times 15) + \frac{1}{2}(1.5 \times 10) + (1.5 \times 15) + (1.5 \times 25)$$

$$= 6 + 18 + 7.5 + 22.5 + 37.5$$

$$= 91.5$$

The distance travelled is 91.5 m.

MATHEMATICAL CONNECTIONS

The areas under a straight line graph will always be polygons. Apply the area formulae you learnt in Chapter 7 to calculate the area of the shapes under the graphs.

Units are important

When you calculate acceleration and distance travelled from a speed–time graph, the unit of speed on the vertical axis must involve the same unit of time as on the horizontal axis. In the example above the speed unit is metres per second and, on the horizontal axis, time is also measured in seconds. These units are compatible.

If the units of time are not the same, convert the unit on one of the axes to a compatible unit.

WORKED EXAMPLE 17

The diagram shows the distance–time graph for a short car journey. The greatest speed reached is 60 km/h. The acceleration in the first two minutes and the deceleration in the last two minutes are constant.

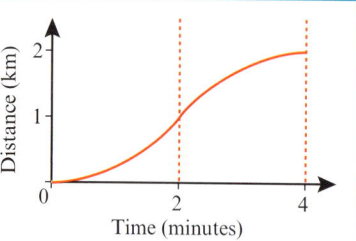

a   Draw the speed–time graph of this journey.

b   Calculate the average speed, in km/h, for the journey.

Answers

a

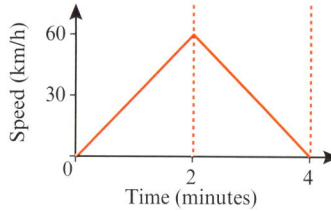

Since the acceleration and deceleration are both constant, the speed–time graph consists of straight lines.
The greatest speed is 60 km/h.

b   Average speed = $\dfrac{\text{total distance}}{\text{total time}}$

     $= \dfrac{2\,km}{(4\text{ minutes})}$

     $= \dfrac{2 \times 15}{60\,(\text{minutes})}$

     $= 30\,km/h$

Units of speed are more commonly m/s or km/h so the units need changing.

Multiply top and bottom by 15 to get 60 minutes (= 1 hour) on the bottom.

Calculate to give answer in km/h.

Exercise 21.8

1   Study this speed–time graph.

    a   What is the speed at:

      i   9.00?

      ii   9.30?

      iii   10.00?

      iv   10.40?

    b   Describe what is happening from 10.00 to 10.30.

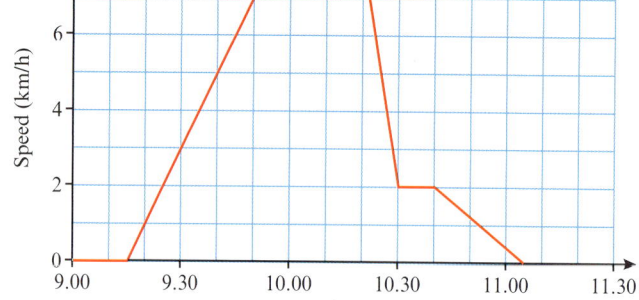

    c   What distance was travelled from:

      i   9.15 to 9.30?   ii   10.20 to 10.30?   iii   9.00 to 11.30?

    d   Calculate the average speed for the whole journey.

2 The graph below shows the speed, in m/s, of a car as it comes to rest from a speed of 10 m/s.

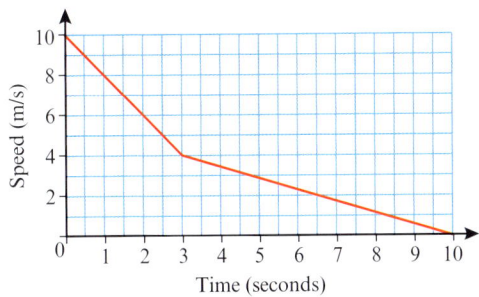

a Calculate the rate at which the car is slowing down during the first three seconds.

b Calculate the distance travelled during the 10 second period shown on the graph.

c Calculate the average speed of the car for this 10 second period.

3 The diagram below is the speed–time graph for a car journey.

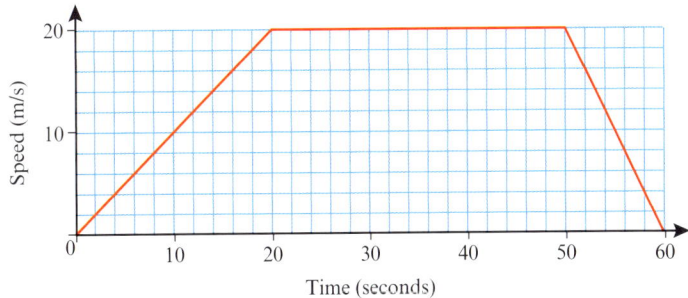

a Calculate the acceleration during the first 20 seconds of the journey.

b Calculate the distance travelled in the last 10 seconds of the journey.

c Calculate the average speed for the whole journey.

21.5 Proportion

Quantities increase or decrease in proportion if multiplying (or dividing) one quantity by a value results in multiplying (or dividing) the other quantity by the same value. In other words, there is a constant ratio between the corresponding elements of two sets.

Direct proportion

When two quantities are in **direct proportion** they increase or decrease at the same rate. In other words, the ratio of the quantities is equivalent (in general terms, $a : b = c : d$). If there is an increase or decrease in one quantity, the other will increase or decrease in the same proportion.

LINK

Home economists, chefs and food technologists use proportional reasoning to mix ingredients, convert between units or work out the cost of a dish.

Here are some examples of quantities that are in direct proportion:

Speed (km/h)	0	45	60	75	90	120
Distance covered in an hour (km)	0	45	60	75	90	120

Distance = speed × time, so the faster you drive in a set time, the further you will travel in that time.

Number of items	0	1	2	3	4
Mass (kg)	0	2	4	6	8

If one item has a mass of 2 kg, then two of the same item will have a mass of 4 kg and so on. The more you have of the same item, the greater the mass will be.

Number of hours worked	0	1	2	3
Amount earned ($)	0	12	24	36

The more hours you work, the more you earn.

Graphs of directly proportional relationships

If you draw the graph of a directly proportional relationship you will get a straight line that passes through the origin.

Of course, the converse (opposite) of this is also true. When a graph is a straight line that passes through the origin, one quantity is directly proportional to the other.

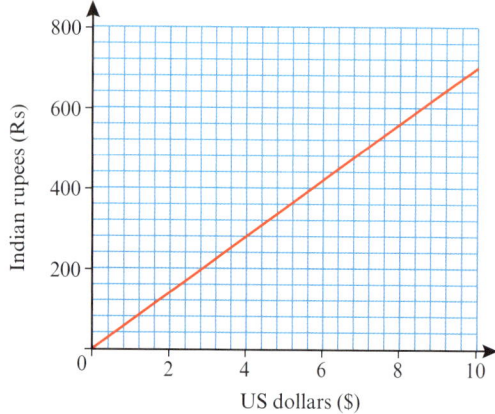

This graph shows the amount of Indian rupees you would get for different amounts of US dollars at an exchange rate of US$1 : Rs 75. Exchange rates are a good example of quantities that are in direct proportion.

LINK

When a liquid cools, the rate at which the temperature decreases is directly proportional to the difference between the temperature of the liquid and the temperature of the surroundings.

Exercise 21.9

1   Which of these could be examples of direct proportion?

   a   The length of the side of a square and its area.

   b   The ages and heights of students.

   c   The amount of money collected in a sponsored walk if you are paid 5c per kilometre.

   d   The time it takes to cover different distances at the same speed.

   e   The heights of objects and the lengths of their shadows.

   f   The amount of petrol used to travel different distances.

   g   The number of chickens you could feed with 20 kg of feed.

   h   The height of the tree and the number of years since it was planted.

   i   The area of the sector of a circle and the angle at the centre.

2   This graph shows two variables that are directly proportional to each other.

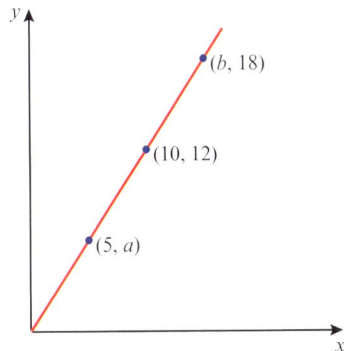

   a   Find the values of a and b.

   b   What equation describes this relationship?

Calculating with direct proportion

The unitary method is useful for solving a range of problems involving proportion. Using this method, you start by finding the value of one unit of the quantity, for example the price of one cupcake or the amount of rupees you would get for one dollar.

WORKED EXAMPLE 18

Five bottles of perfume cost $200. What would 11 bottles cost?

Answer

Unitary method

5 bottles cost $200

1 bottle costs $200 ÷ 5 = $40

11 bottles cost 11 × $40 = $440

WORKED EXAMPLE 18 CONTINUED

You can also solve this problem using the ratio method.

$\dfrac{5}{200} = \dfrac{11}{x}$ Write out each part as a fraction.

$\dfrac{200}{5} = \dfrac{x}{11}$ Take the reciprocal of both ratios (turn them upside down) to make it easier to solve the equation.

$\dfrac{200 \times 11}{5} = x$

$x = \$440$

> **MATHEMATICAL CONNECTIONS**
>
> You used the unitary method and the ratio method to solve ratio problems earlier in this chapter.

Exercise 21.10

1   Four soft drinks cost $9. How much would you pay for three?

2   A car travels 30 km in 40 minutes. How long will it take to travel 45 km at the same speed?

3   If a clock gains 20 seconds in four days, how much time does it gain in two weeks?

4   Six identical drums of oil weigh 90 kg in total. How much will 11.5 identical drums weigh?

5   An athlete runs 4.5 kilometres in 15 minutes. How far can they run in 35 minutes at the same speed?

APPLY YOUR SKILLS

6   To make 12 muffins, you need:

240 g flour

48 g sultanas

60 g margarine

74 ml milk

24 g sugar

12 g salt

   a   How much of each ingredient will you need to make 16 muffins?

   b   Express the amount of flour to margarine in this recipe as a ratio.

7   A vendor sells frozen yoghurt in 250 g and 100 g tubs. It costs $1.75 for 250 g and 80 cents for 100 g. Which is the better buy?

8   A car uses 45 litres of fuel to travel 495 km.

   a   How far can the car travel on 50 ℓ of fuel at the same rate?

   b   How much fuel will the car use to travel 190 km at the same rate?

> **TIP**
>
> Familiarise yourself with the language used in word problems involving proportion. This will help you recognise proportion problems in other contexts.

APPLY YOUR SKILLS CONTINUED

9   This graph shows the directly proportional relationship between lengths in metres (metric) and lengths in feet (imperial).

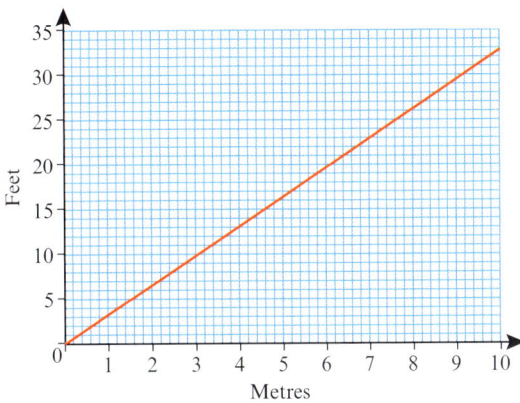

a   Use the graph to estimate how many feet there are in four metres.

b   Which is longer:

   i   four metres or 12 feet?

   ii   20 feet or 6.5 metres?

c   Mr Bokomo has a length of fabric 9 m long.

   i   What is its length to the nearest foot?

   ii   He cuts and sells 1.5 m to Ms Johannes and 3 ft to Mr Moosa. How much is left in metres?

d   A driveway was originally 18 feet long. It was resurfaced and extended to be one metre longer than previously. How long is the newly resurfaced driveway in metres?

Inverse proportion

In **inverse proportion**, one quantity decreases in the same proportion as the other quantity increases. Think about this in terms of money. If you have $20 to spend on pens, the number of pens you can buy depends on the price.

Price $	1	2	4	10
Number you can buy	20	10	5	2

In other words, as the price increases, the number of pens you can buy decreases. Looking at the table, you can see that as price doubles, the number of pens halves. The product of the price and the number you can buy for $20 is always 20.

The graph of an inversely proportional relationship is half of a hyperbola ($y = \frac{a}{x}$ where a is positive) and not a straight line.

This graph shows how the volume of air in a syringe changes when the pressure on the air is increased. You can see from the graph that this is an inverse relationship. As the pressure increases, the volume of air in the syringe decreases.

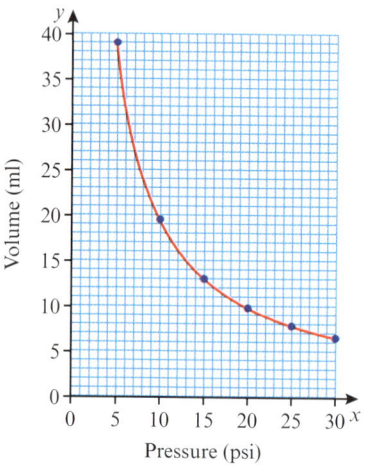

LINK

You may have learnt about the relationship between gas volume and increased pressure when you studied Boyle's law in science.

WORKED EXAMPLE 19

A person travelling at 30 km/h takes 24 minutes to get home from work. How long will the journey take if they travel at 36 km/h?

Answer

30 km/h takes 24 minutes.

So, 1 km/h would take 30 × 24 minutes.

∴ at 36 km/h it will take $\dfrac{30 \times 24}{36}$

= 20 minutes.

This is inverse proportion; as one value decreases the other increases.

To get 1 km/h you divide the speed by 30, so multiply the time by 30.

To get 36 km/h you multiply the speed by 36, so divide the time by 36.

WORKED EXAMPLE 20

A peson working six hours per day can complete a job in four days. How many hours per day will they need to work to complete the job in three days?

Answer

For 4 days it takes 6 hours per day

∴ 1 day would take 4 × 6 hours = 24 hours per day

3 days would take $\dfrac{24}{3}$ = 8 hours per day.

Exercise 21.11

1 Sanjay has a 50 m long piece of rope.

    a How many pieces can he cut it into if the length of each piece is:

        i 50 cm?   **ii** 200 cm?   **iii** 625 cm?

    b He cuts the rope into 20 equal lengths. What is the length of each piece?

2   A hurricane disaster centre has a certain amount of clean water. The length of time the water will last depends on the number of people who come to the centre. Calculate the missing values in this table.

No. of people	120	150	200	300	400
Days the water will last	40	32			

3   It takes six people 12 days to paint a building. Work out how long it would take at the same rate using:

a   9 people   **b**   36 people.

4   An airbus usually flies from Mumbai to London in 11 hours at an average speed of 920 km/h. During some bad weather, the trip took 14 hours. What was the average speed of the plane on that flight?

5   A journey takes three hours when you travel at 60 km/h. How long would the same journey take at a speed of 50 km/h?

21.6 Direct and inverse proportion in algebraic terms

We can use generalised equations to represent direct and inverse relationships between two quantities, x and y, using k to represent a constant value.

Direct proportion

If the values of two variables are always in the same ratio, we say that the variables are in direct proportion. If the variables are P and Q, you write this as $P \propto Q$ and you read it as 'P is *directly* proportional to Q'.

$P \propto Q$ means that $\frac{P}{Q}$ is constant. That is, $P = kQ$, where k is a constant.

If the constant is 2, then $P = 2Q$. This means that whatever Q is, P will be double that.

You can also write this as $\frac{P}{Q} = 2$.

Inverse proportion

If the product of the value of two variables is constant, the variables are said to be inversely proportional. If the variables are P and Q, you can write $PQ = k$, where k is a constant. This means that 'P is inversely proportional to Q'.

$PQ = k$ can also be written as $P = \frac{k}{Q}$.

So P is inversely proportional to Q can be written as $P \propto \frac{1}{Q}$.

> **MATHEMATICAL CONNECTIONS**
>
> A question might ask you to find a proportion equation and then find unknowns by solving it. Recap how to solve equations in Chapter 6.

WORKED EXAMPLE 21

y is directly proportional to x^3 and when $x = 2$, $y = 32$.

a   Write this relationship as an equation.

b   Find the value of y when $x = 5$.

Answers

a $y \propto x^3$, which means (as an equation) $y = kx^3$.

   When $x = 2$, $x^3 = 2^3 = 8$

   $\therefore 32 = 8k$

   $\therefore k = \dfrac{32}{8} = 4$ and $y = 4x^3$

b   If $x = 5$, then

   $y = 4x^3 = 4 \times 5^3 = 500$

> **TIP**
>
> The relationship between quantities is usually described in words and you will need to add the $\propto$ symbol in your working, as in these examples. The word 'direct' is not always used but if quantities are in inverse (or indirect) proportion this is explained.

WORKED EXAMPLE 22

F is inversely proportional to d^2 and when $d = 3$, $F = 12$.
Find the value of F when $d = 4$.

Answer

$F \propto \dfrac{1}{d^2}$, which means (as an equation) $F = \dfrac{k}{d^2}$.

When $d = 3$ and $F = 12$, $12 = \dfrac{k}{3^2} = \dfrac{k}{9}$

$\therefore k = 12 \times 9 = 108$

So, $F = \dfrac{108}{d^2}$

If $d = 4$, then $F = \dfrac{108}{d^2} = \dfrac{108}{4^2} = 6.75$

WORKED EXAMPLE 23

Some corresponding values of the variables p and q are shown in the table.
Are p and q directly proportional?

p	2.8	7	11.2	16.8
q	2	5	8	12

Answer

Compare each pair in turn:

$\dfrac{2.8}{2} = 1.4 \qquad \dfrac{7}{5} = 1.4 \qquad \dfrac{11.2}{8} = 1.4 \qquad \dfrac{16.8}{12} = 1.4$

All the values are the same.

So, the values are directly proportional, $p = 1.4q$.

WORKED EXAMPLE 24

x	3	4	5	6
y	12			

Copy and complete this table of values for:

a $y \propto x$ **b** $y \propto \dfrac{1}{x}$

Answers

a $y \propto x$ means $y = kx$ Write the relationship as an equation.

$12 = 3k$ Solve the equation for k.

$\therefore k = 4$ and $y = 4x$ Substitute the value of k into original equation.

x	3	4	5	6
y	12	16	20	24

b $y \propto \dfrac{1}{x}$ means $xy = k$ Write the relationship as an equation.

$\therefore k = 3 \times 12 = 36$ and $y = \dfrac{36}{x}$ Use a value of x and corresponding value of y, to solve the equation for k.

x	3	4	5	6
y	12	9	7.2	6

WORKED EXAMPLE 25

The speed of water in a river is determined by a water-pressure gauge. The speed (v m/s) is directly proportional to the square root of the height (h cm) reached by the liquid in the gauge. Given that $h = 36$ when $v = 8$, calculate the value of v when $h = 18$.

Answer

$v \propto \sqrt{h}$ means that $v = k\sqrt{h}$ where k is constant.

When $v = 8$, $h = 36$ and so $8 = k\sqrt{36} = 6k$

It follows that $k = \dfrac{4}{3}$ and the formula connecting v and h is $v = \dfrac{4\sqrt{h}}{3}$.

When $h = 18$, $v = \dfrac{4\sqrt{18}}{3} = 5.66$ (to 3 s.f.)

Exercise 21.12

1   $y = kx$. When $y = 24$, $x = 16$. Calculate:

   a   the value of k **b** y when $x = 10$ **c** x when $y = 12$.

2 Some corresponding values of p and q are given in the table. Are p and q inversely proportional? Justify your answer.

q	2	5	8	12
p	75	30	20	15

3 For each of the following, y is inversely proportional to x. Write an equation expressing y in terms of x if:

   a $y = 0.225$ when $x = 20$ **b** $y = 12.5$ when $x = 5$

   c $y = 5$ when $x = 0.4$ **d** $y = 0.4$ when $x = 0.7$

   e $y = 0.6$ when $x = 8$.

4 y is inversely proportional to x^3. If $y = 80$ when $x = 4$, find:

   a   the constant of proportionality   **b**   the value of y when $x = 8$

   c   the value y when $x = 6$ **d**   the value of x when $y = 24$.

5 Given that y is inversely proportional to x^2, complete the table.

x	0.1	0.25	0.5	
y			1	64

6 Given that y is inversely proportional to $\sqrt{x}$, complete the table.

x	25	100		
y	10		26	50

7 x and y are known to be proportional to each other. When $x = 20$, $y = 50$. Find k, if:

   a $y \propto x$ **b** $y \propto \dfrac{1}{x}$ **c** $y \propto x^2$

8 F is inversely proportion to p^3. When $F = 108$, $p = 2$.

   a   Find a formula for F in terms of p.

   b   Calculate p when F is 13.5

   c   Find F when p is 3.

9 A is directly proportional to r^2 and when $r = 3$, $A = 36$. Find the value of A when $r = 10$.

10 l is inversely proportional to d^3. When $d = 2$, $l = 100$. Find the value of l when $d = 5$.

11 An electric current I flows through a resistance R. I is inversely proportional to R and when $R = 3$, $I = 5$. Find the value of I when $R = 0.25$.

12 Corresponding values of *s* and *t* are given in the table.

s	2	6	10
t	0.4	10.8	50

Which of the following statements is true?

a $t \propto s$ **b** $t \propto s^2$ **c** $t \propto s^3$

13 It takes 4 people 10 hours to plaster a section of a building. How long will it take 8 people to do the same job working at the same rate?

14 In an industrial experiment it is found that the force, *f*, needed to break a concrete beam varies inversely with the length, *l*, of the beam. If it takes 50 000 newtons to break a concrete beam 2 metres long, how many newtons will it take to break a beam that is 6 metres long?

15 A submarine crew discovers that the water temperature (°C) varies inversely with the depth to which they submerge (km). When they were at a depth of 4 km, the water temperature was 6 °C.

   a What will the water temperature be at a depth of 12 km?

   b What depth do they need to reach for the water temperature to be −1 °C?

16 Variable *P* varies directly with variable *m* and inversely with variable *n*.
If $P = 24$ when $m = 3$ and $n = 2$, find *P* when:

   a $m = 5$ **b** $n = 8$

17 A cyclist's speed over a fixed distance is inversely proportional to the time it takes to complete the ride. Due to poor weather on one ride, the cyclist's speed decreases by 20%. By what percentage will their time increase on this ride?

TIP

Sometimes you may see 'varies as' written instead of 'is directly proportional to'. Similarly, 'varies inversely with' means 'is inversely proportional to'.

SUMMARY

Do you know …?

A ratio is a comparison of two or more quantities in a set order. Ratios can be expressed in the form $a:b$ or $\frac{a}{b}$. Ratios have no units.

Ratios can be simplified by multiplying or dividing both quantities by the same number. This method produces equivalent ratios.

Map scales are good examples of ratios in everyday life. The scale of a map is usually given in the form $1:n$. This allows you to convert map distances to real distances using the ratio scale.

A rate is a comparison of two different quantities. Usually a rate gives an amount of one quantity per unit of the other. Rates must include the units of the quantities.

Speed is one of the most common rates of change. Speed = distance ÷ time.

Kinematic graphs are used to show relationships between:
- distance and time (distance–time graph)
- speed and time (speed–time graph)

and to solve problems in these areas.

SUMMARY CONTINUED

The gradient of a distance–time graph shows how the speed changes over time.
Proportion is a constant ratio between two sets of numbers.
When quantities are in direct proportion they increase or decrease at the same rate.
When quantities are inversely proportional, one increases as the other decreases.
Algebraic expressions can be used to represent direct and indirect (inverse) proportion and to solve problems related to these concepts. The symbol for proportion is $\propto$.

Are you able to …?

simplify ratios and find the missing values in equivalent ratios
divide quantities in a given ratio
convert measurements on maps, plans and other scale diagrams to real measurements and vice versa
express relationships between different quantities as rates in their simplest form and solve problems relating to rates
read and interpret kinematic graphs • by calculating average speed • by calculating acceleration and deceleration from a graph and finding the distance travelled using the area under a linear speed–time graph
solve problems involving direct and indirect proportion
express direct and inverse proportion in algebraic terms
solve direct and inverse proportion problems using algebraic methods.

Practice questions

1   Manos and Raja make $96 selling handcrafts. They share the income in the ratio 7 : 5. How much does Raja receive?   [3]

2   Silvia makes a scale drawing of her bedroom using a scale of 1 : 25. If one wall on the diagram is 12 cm long, how long is the wall in her room?   [3]

3   Mrs James bakes a fruit cake using raisins, currants and dates in the ratio 4 : 5 : 3. The total mass of the three ingredients is 4.8 kilograms. Calculate the mass of:

   a   the raisins   [4]

   b   the dates.   [1]

4   A recipe for dough uses three parts wholemeal flour for every four parts of plain flour. What volume of wholemeal flour do you need if you use 12 cups of plain flour?   [3]

5 Three children play a card game. At the start of the game the cards are distributed amongst Amelia, Bahram and Celeste in the ratio 4 : 6 : 5. At the end of the game the cards are distributed in the ratio 6 : 10 : 9.

    a Work out which player has the same number of cards at the start and end of the game. Explain your reasoning. [3]

    b Calculate the percentage change in the number of cards Celeste has, between the start and end of the game. State whether this change is an increase or a decrease. [2]

    c Work out the minimum number of cards used in the game. Show your reasoning carefully. [3]

6 A special microscope enlarges images to 90 000 times their actual size. The microscope is used to photograph a bacterium for a textbook and the new image is 118 mm long. Find the actual length of the bacterium, giving your answer:

    a in metres, using standard form [3]

    b in micrometres. [2]

7 The speed–time graph represents the journey of a train between two stations. The train slowed down and stopped after 15 minutes because of engineering work on the railway line.

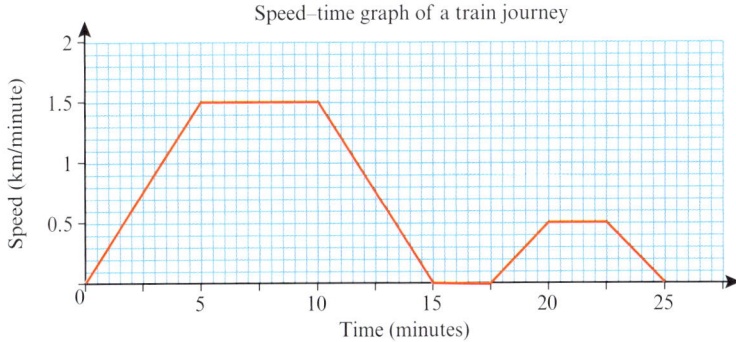

Speed–time graph of a train journey

    a Calculate the greatest speed, in km/h, that the train reached. [1]

    b Calculate the deceleration of the train as it approached the place where there was engineering work. [2]

    c Calculate the distance the train travelled in the first 15 minutes. [3]

    d For how long did the train stop at the place where there was engineering work? [1]

    e What was the speed of the train after 19 minutes? [2]

    f Calculate the distance between the two stations. [3]

8 The distance, d metres, travelled by an acorn falling from a tree is directly proportional to the square of the time, t seconds, for which it falls.

The acorn takes 3 seconds to fall 20 metres.

a Find a formula connecting d and t. [3]

b Find the distance fallen after 4 seconds. [2]

c Find the time taken to fall 3.5 m. [2]

9 The six graphs show six different relationships between variables x and y.

A
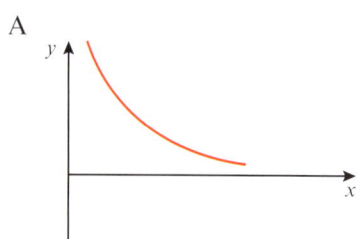

B
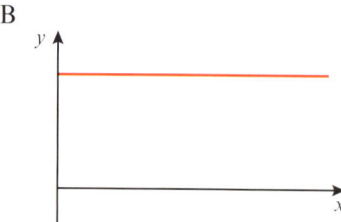

C
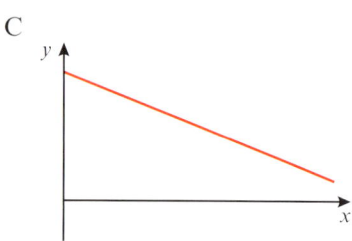

D
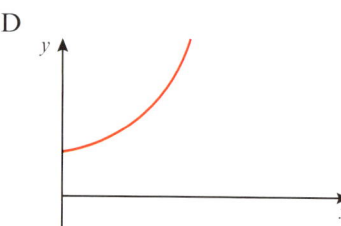

E
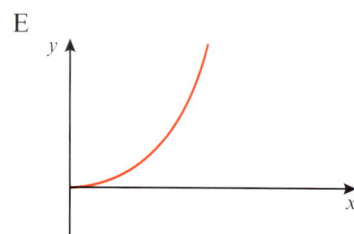

F
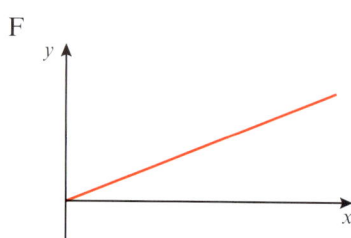

a State which graph shows y and x in direct proportion. Explain your answer. [2]

b State which graph shows that y is constant. Explain your answer. [2]

c State which graph could show that y is directly proportional to the square of x. [2]

d State which graph could show that y is inversely proportional to x. Explain your answer. [2]

e State which graph could show that y is inversely proportional to the cube of x. Explain your answer. [2]

f State possible equations for any graphs that were not answers in parts (a)–(e). [2]

10 The extension of a spring, x (measured in metres), is directly proportional to the mass, m (measured in kilograms), attached to the end. The extension of the spring is 30 cm when the mass is 5 kg.

   a   Find an equation connecting x with m.   [3]

   b   Find x if $m = 12$ kg.   [2]

   c   Find m if $x = 0.54$ m.   [2]

You are now given that the potential energy stored, E (measured in joules), in the spring is proportional to the square of the extension, x. When the extension is h metres, the energy stored is P joules.

   d   Find an equation connecting E and x (your answer will contain terms in P and h).   [3]

   e   Find the mass attached to the spring if the potential energy is 49 P joules.   [3]

11 The resistance, R, of a fixed length of wire is inversely proportional to the square of the diameter, d mm, of the wire. When the diameter is 4 mm, the resistance is 0.096 ohms.

   a   Find a formula for R in terms of d.   [3]

   b   Find the resistance when the diameter is 6 mm, giving your answer to 3 significant figures.   [2]

   c   Rearrange your answer to part (a) to find a formula for d in terms of R.   [3]

   d   Find the diameter required for a resistance of 3×10^{-5} ohms.   [2]

   e   Find the resistance when both the resistance and diameter have the same value. Give your answer to 3 significant figures.   [2]

SELF ASSESSMENT

You can get good marks in mathematics by clearly showing your working and methods even if you get the final answer incorrect.

Evaluate your answers to the practice questions.

- Did you show your working?

- Is your working clearly laid out and systematic?

- Does your working show that you understood the question and give evidence that you know how to answer it?

- Do you think you would get part marks for any questions where you got the incorrect answer? Support your opinion.

Chapter 22

More equations, formulae and functions

IN THIS CHAPTER YOU WILL:

- make your own equations and use them to solve worded problems
- construct and transform more complex formulae
- use function notation to describe simple functions and their inverses
- form composite functions.

Formulae can be used to describe very simple things as well as complicated situations. They can be used to calculate the area of a shape, to decide where best to strike a board to break it or how to launch a rocket into space.

Many real-ife calculations rely on formulae. For example, working out how much it will cost to tile rooms of different sizes, converting measurements from one system to another, calculating dosage of medicines for different ages and masses, and calculating how inflation rates will affect profit and loss. Knowing how to work with formulae and how to rearrange them to make the value you are interested in the subject can save you time and money.

In this chapter you will work with more complicated formulae and equations. You will need to be able to rearrange formulae to solve related problems.

You will also revise what you know about functions and learn how to use a more formal mathematical notation to describe functions and their inverses. You will also work with composite functions.

KEY WORDS

composite function

function

function notation

GETTING STARTED

1   A driver's education manual says that you can work out a safe following distance (d) between vehicles that are travelling at s kilometres per hour using the formula $d = \frac{s}{10} + 2$, where d is measured in vehicle lengths.

    a   What does this mean in words?

    b   How many vehicle lengths should a truck driver leave between the truck and the vehicle in front of it at a speed of 90 km per hour?

    c   At what speed is 3 vehicle lengths a safe following distance?

    d   How does an increase in speed affect the safe following distance?

2   The cost of adding a new USB port and cable to a system is $\$C$ when the length of the cable is y metres and $C = 4.5 + 1.8y$.

    a   What do you think 4.5 represents in this formula?

    b   What is the meaning of coefficient 1.8?

    c   How long is the cable when the total cost is $26.55?

3   The diagram shows the height (h) of a tower.
QR is 5 m shorter than RS and PQ is 2 m shorter than QR.

    a   Write a formula for calculating h, the total height PS.

    b   Make a the subject of your formula.

    c   What is the height of the tower when $a = 7.5$ metres?

    d   If the tower is 18 m tall, what is the height PQ?

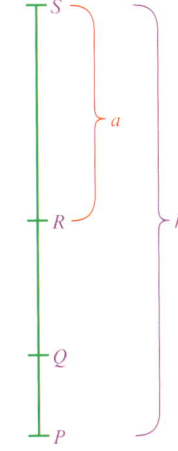

22.1 Setting up equations to solve problems

You already know that you can translate word problems into equations using variables to represent unknown quantities. You can then solve the equation to find the solution to the problem.

Working through the problems in Exercise 22.1 will help you remember how to set up equations that represent the sum, difference, product and quotient of quantities and use these to solve problems.

MATHEMATICAL CONNECTIONS

You used algebra to write expressions and simple equations in Chapter 2. Read through that section again if you have forgotten how to do this.

Exercise 22.1

1   For each statement, write an equation in terms of x and then and solve it.
    a   A number multiplied by four gives 32.
    b   If a certain number is multiplied by 12 the result is 96.
    c   A number added to 12 gives 55.
    d   The sum of a number and 13 is 25.
    e   When six is subtracted from a certain number, the result is 14.
    f   If a number is subtracted from nine the result is -5.
    g   The result of dividing a number by seven is 2.5.
    h   If 28 is divided by a certain number, the result is four.

2   Represent each situation using an equation in terms of y. Solve each equation to find the value of y.
    a   A number is multiplied by three, then five is added to get 14.
    b   When six is subtracted from five times a certain number, the result is 54.
    c   Three times the sum of a number and four gives 150.
    d   When eight is subtracted from half of a number, the result is 27.

3   Solve each problem by setting up an equation.
    a   When five is added to four times a certain number, the result is 57. What is the number?
    b   If six is subtracted from three times a certain number the result is 21. What is the number?
    c   Four more than a number is divided by three and then multiplied by two to give a result of four. What is the number?
    d   A number is doubled and then six is added. When this is divided by four, the result is seven. What is the number?

TIP

Translating information from words to diagrams or equations is a very useful problem-solving strategy.

TIP

Computer programmers work with many different formulae. Their work often relies on taking an input and manipulating it to get the required output. If you use a spreadsheet you will follow a similar process, using variables to calculate results for values entered into cells on the sheet.

4   An artist places three photos so they are centred in a frame as shown. The photos are congruent and each one is *r* cm wide and *s* cm high. The other dimensions are shown on the diagram.

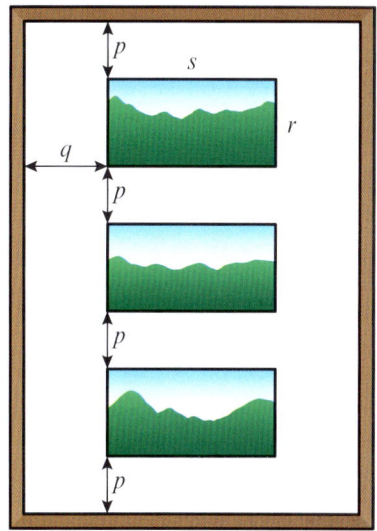

   a Write an expression for:

      i the width of the inside of the frame

      ii the height of the inside of the frame.

   b What is the total area of:

      i the three photographs

      ii the area inside the frame not covered by the photographs?

5   A military helicopter flies to inspect an oil platform *x* km away. The helicopter flies directly to the ship at a speed of 320 km/h and directly back at a speed of 240 km/hr.

   a Write an equation to calculate the total flying time (*t*) hours.

   b Calculate the flying time in minutes when the oil platform is 120 km away.

REFLECTION

Reflect on your work in this exercise.

• Which ideas in this work make most sense to you? Why?

• Did you struggle at all? If so, how did you overcome this?

• Why do you think we are studying this objective?
  How will you use what you have mastered here?

Solving more complex problems

The problems you solved in Exercise 22.1 involved simple algebraic manipulation. You need to be able to set up equations to solve any problem. To do this, you need to read and make sense of the written problem, represent the situation as an equation and then solve it.

To solve problems by setting up equations:

• Read the problem carefully, paying attention to the words used.

• Decide what you need to find and what information is already given. It might help to draw a bar model to represent the problem.

• Ask yourself if there is anything to be assumed or deduced from the given information. For example, if the problem mentions equal lengths and widths of a room can you assume the room is a rectangle? Or, if you are working with a pack of cards, can you assume it is a standard pack with 52 cards?

• Consider whether there is a formula or mathematical relationship that you can use to connect the information in the problem. For example, if you are asked to find the distance around a round swimming pool, you can use the formula $C = \pi d$, or if the problem involves time, distance and speed, you can use the distance–time–speed triangle to form an equation.

WORKED EXAMPLE 1

My mother was 26 years old when I was born. Now, she is three times as old as I am. What are our ages now?

Answer

Let my age now be x.

∴ my mother's age now is 3x.　　　　She is 3 times as old as me.

The difference in ages is 26 years, so:　　Mother will always be 26 years older.

$3x - x = 26$

∴　$2x = 26$

∴　　$x = 13$

My age now is 13. My mother's age now is 39.

WORKED EXAMPLE 2

The longest sides of a parallelogram are five times longer than its shorter sides. If it has a perimeter of 9.6 m, what are the lengths of the long and short sides?

Answer

Let the shorter side be x metres.
∴ the longer side is 5x.

The longer side is five times the shorter side.

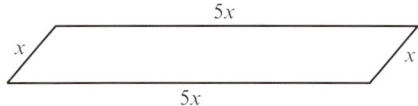

It is often helpful to draw a sketch.

$5x + x + 5x + x = 9.6 \, \text{m}$

∴　　　$12x = 9.6 \, \text{m}$

Perimeter is the sum of the sides.

∴　　　$x = \dfrac{9.6}{12} = 0.8 \, \text{m}$

So, the shorter side is 0.8 m and the longer side is 5 × 0.8 = 4 m.

TIP

Always say what the variables represent.

INVESTIGATION

Heart rates

In medicine, cardiac output (C) is the amount of blood (millilitres) that your heart pumps through your body in a minute. You can work out your own cardiac output using the equation $C = V \times R$. V represents the stroke volume, which is the amount of blood your heart pumps each time it beats, and R represents your heart rate, the number of times your heart beats in a minute.

1　Explain why C, V and R are all rates.

2　Work with a partner to determine your own resting heart rate (R). You can do this by taking each other's pulses for 10 seconds and using that to the number of heart beats per minute. If you have a fitness device, it may work out your resting heart rate for you.

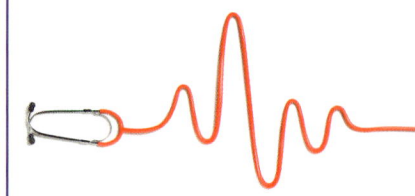

INVESTIGATION CONTINUED

3   a   Use a mean stroke volume of 80 ml/beat and your own heart rate to determine your cardiac output.

   b   Zef has a heartrate of 55 beats per minute and a stroke volume of 92 cm^3. How does Zef's cardiac output compare with yours?

   c   Najwa has the same cardiac output as Zef with a stroke volume of 59 cm^3. Calculate Najwa's heart rate.

4   Given that $C = V \times R$ is a directly proportionate relationship, describe what happens to your cardiac output for both an increase and a decrease in heart rate.

5   Heart specialists sometimes have to consider the resistance of blood flow through a particular blood vessel. They use the formula $R = \dfrac{1}{r^4}$ to work this out. In this formula, R is the resistance of the blood flow and r is the radius of the blood vessel it flows through.

   a   What type of relationship is this? Why?

   b   A muscular artery has a diameter of 10 mm, the venae cavae vein has a diameter of 15 mm and an arteriole has a diameter of 2 mm. Calculate R for each type of blood vessel (ignore the units).

   c   What happens to the resistance of blood flow as vessel diameter decreases?

   d   Why is narrowing of the arteries a health concern? (You may need to do some research to answer this fully.)

Exercise 22.2

1   A parent is three times as old as their child. If the parent is 31 years older than the child, what are their ages?

2   Jess and Silvia have 420 marbles between them. If Jess has five times as many marbles as Silvia, how many do they each have?

3   Soumik has $5 less than Kofi. If they have $97.50 altogether, how much does each person have?

4   Two competition winners are to share a prize of $750. If one winner receives twice as much as the other, how much will they each receive?

5   A grandparent is six times as old as their grandchild. If the grandparent was 45 when the grandchild was born, how old is the grandchild?

6   A rectangle with perimeter 74 cm is 7 cm longer than it is wide. What is the length of each side?

7   Smitville is located between Jonesville and Cityville. Smitville is five times as far away from Cityville as it is from Jonesville. If the distance between Jonesville and Cityville is 288 km, how far is it from Jonesville to Smitville?

8   Amira is twice as old as Pam. Nine years ago, their combined age was 18. What are their present ages?

> **TIP**
>
> Remember to follow the basic steps in problem-solving when you are faced with a word problem.

9   Jabu left town A at 6.00 a.m. and drove at an average speed of 80 km/h to town B. At 8.30 a.m., Sipho left town A to travel to town B and drove at an average speed of 100 km/h. At what time will Sipho catch up with Jabu?

10 Remi took 40 minutes to complete a journey. He travelled half the distance at a speed of 100 km/h and the other half at 60 km/h. What distance did Remi travel to complete the journey?

SELF ASSESSMENT

Complete your own 3 : 2 : 1 summary to assess your understanding of writing equations and using them to solve problems.

Use these sentence stems:

3 things I learned are:

2 questions I had were:

1 thing I understood really quickly was:

> **TIP**
>
> Refer back to Chapter 2 if you need some ideas for completing a 3 : 2 : 1 self assessment.

Deriving quadratic equations

To solve some word problems you might need to derive and solve a quadratic equation. Before you can solve the equation you must write the word problem using equations. You may need to use geometry, number facts, probability or any other appropriate techniques that relate to the topic you are working with.

WORKED EXAMPLE 3

The product of two consecutive integers is 42. Form and solve a quadratic equation to find both possible pairs of integers.

Answer

Use the letter n to represent the smaller of the two numbers. Then the larger of the two numbers is $n + 1$.

The product of the two number is 42, so

$n(n + 1) = 42$

$\Rightarrow n^2 + n = 42$

$\Rightarrow n^2 + n - 42 = 0$

$\Rightarrow (n + 7)(n - 6) = 0$

$\Rightarrow n = -7 \quad \text{or} \quad n = 6$

If $n = -7$, then $n + 1 = -6$.

Check: -7 and -6 are consecutive integers and $-6 \times -7 = 42$.

If $n = 6$, then $n + 1 = 7$.

Check: 6 and 7 are consecutive integers and $6 \times 7 = 42$.

So the pairs of integers are 6, 7 and $-7, -6$.

> **TIP**
>
> You might have spotted the solution 6, 7 without using algebra, but writing a quadratic equation means you will definitely find *all* the solutions.

WORKED EXAMPLE 4

The length of a rectangle is 2 cm greater than its width. The area of the rectangle is 15 cm². Find its perimeter.

Answer

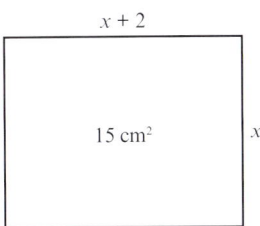

Always draw a diagram to show the information and to help you visualise the situation.

The area is the length × width, so

$x(x + 2) = 15$

$\Rightarrow x^2 + 2x = 15$

$\Rightarrow x^2 + 2x - 15 = 0$

$\Rightarrow (x + 5)(x - 3) = 0$

$\Rightarrow x = -5 \quad \text{or} \quad x = 3$

Use x to represent the width of the rectangle. This means that the length will be x + 2

x is the width of the rectangle, so it cannot be a negative number. This means x must be 3.

The dimensions of the rectangle are 3 cm × 5 cm.

Its perimeter = 3 + 5 + 3 + 5 = 16 cm

WORKED EXAMPLE 5

A right-angled triangle has height h cm and base b cm. The hypotenuse of the triangle has length $\sqrt{13}$ cm. If the area of the triangle is 3cm² find the possible values for b and h.

Answer

Use the formula for the area of a triangle:

$\dfrac{1}{2}bh = 3$

$\Rightarrow bh = 6$

$\Rightarrow \quad h = \dfrac{6}{b} \qquad$ [1]

Now use Pythagoras' theorem and the fact that the hypotenuse has length $\sqrt{13}$ cm:

$b^2 + h^2 = 13 \qquad$ [2]

Substitute [1] into [2]:

$b^2 + \left(\dfrac{6}{b}\right)^2 = 13$

$\Rightarrow b^2 + \dfrac{36}{b^2} = 13$

TIP

Where possible, make one unknown the subject of the equation, so that it can be substituted into any later equation.

WORKED EXAMPLE 5 CONTINUED

Solve the equation to find the values of b and substitute into [1] to find the values of h:

$$(b^2)^2 + 36 = 13b^2$$
$$\Rightarrow (b^2)^2 - 13(b^2) + 36 = 0$$
$$\Rightarrow (b^2 - 9)(b^2 - 4) = 0$$
$$\Rightarrow b = 3 \text{ or } 2$$
$$\Rightarrow h = 2 \text{ or } 3$$

Exercise 22.3

1 A number is 3 more than another number and the product of these two numbers is 40. Find the possible pairs of numbers.

2 A ball starts to roll down a slope. If the ball is d metres from its starting point at time t seconds and $d = t^2 + 3t$, find the time when the ball is 10 m from its starting point.

3 The nth term of the sequence

| 1 | 3 | 6 | 10 | 15 | .... |

is $\dfrac{n(n+1)}{2}$, where n is the position of each term in the sequence.

Use algebra to find the position of the number 78.

TIP

This is the sequence of triangular numbers.

4 The sum of two integers is 11 and the product of the same two integers is 28. Use algebra to show that the two integers must be 4 and 7.

5 The base of a triangle is 2 cm longer than its perpendicular height. If the area of the triangle is 24 cm², find the height of the triangle.

6 A trapezium has area 76 cm². The parallel sides differ in length by 3 cm, and the shorter of the two is equal in length to the perpendicular height of the trapezium. Find the distance between the two parallel sides of the trapezium.

7 The number of diagonals of a convex polygon with n sides is $\frac{1}{2}n(n-3)$.

    a How many sides does a polygon with 54 diagonals have?

    b Show that it is not possible for a polygon to have 33 diagonals.

TIP

A rectangle that can be divided up in this way is known as a golden rectangle and the positive solution of the equation that you have solved is known as the Golden Ratio. It is a very, very special number in mathematics and is important in the arts and sciences as well as mathematics.

8 The diagram shows a rectangle that has been divided into a square and a smaller rectangle. The smaller rectangle is similar to the larger one.

    a Show that $x^2 - x - 1 = 0$.

    b Solve this equation, giving your answers to 2 decimal places.

    c Explain why one of your solutions does not work in this case.

    d Find the perimeter of the rectangle.

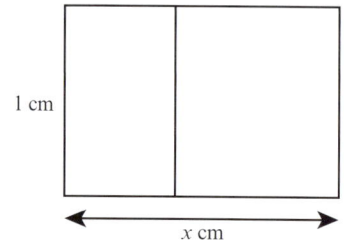

9 A ball is thrown from a building and falls $3t + 5t^2$ metres in t seconds. After how many seconds has the ball fallen 6 m?

10 The product of three consecutive integers is 30 times the smallest of the three integers. Find the two possible sets of integers that will satisfy this condition.

11 The square of a number is 14 more than 5 times the number. Find the two possible numbers for which this is true.

12 A rectangle has sides of length x cm and y cm. If the perimeter of the rectangle is 22 cm and the area of the rectangle is 24 cm², use algebra to find the dimensions of the rectangle.

13 A stone is thrown up into the air from ground level. If the height of the stone is $16t - 5t^2$ in t seconds, for how long will the stone be more than 8 metres above the ground?

14 The cube of a number is 152 more than the cube of another number that is 2 smaller. What are the two possible numbers for which this is true?

15

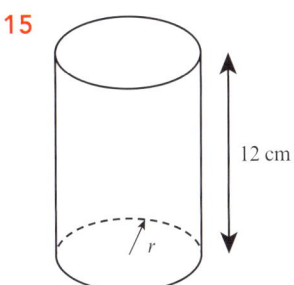

12 cm

r

The diagram shows an open-topped cylinder with radius r cm and height 12 cm. If the outer surface area of the cylinder is 81π cm², find the radius of the cylinder.

16 The product of two consecutive integers is 11 more than 3 times their sum. Use algebra to find the two pairs of integers that meet these conditions.

22.2 Using and rearranging formulae

You already know that the variable which is written alone on one side of the '=' sign (usually the left) of a formula is called the subject of the formula. For example, in the formula for finding the circumference of a circle, $C = \pi d$, C is the subject of the formula. This means that it is very easy to find the value of C if you know the diameter of the circle.

In some situations it is more helpful to have a different variable as the subject, so you will need to rearrange the formula.

To change the subject of a formula:

* expand to get rid of any brackets if necessary

* use inverse operations to isolate the variable required.

WORKED EXAMPLE 6

Solve for h if $A = 2\pi r(r + h)$.

Answer

$$A = 2\pi r(r + h)$$
$$A = 2\pi r^2 + 2\pi rh \qquad \text{Expand to remove the brackets.}$$
$$A - 2\pi r^2 = 2\pi rh \qquad \text{Subtract to isolate the term with } h \text{ in it.}$$
$$\frac{(A - 2\pi r^2)}{2\pi r} = h \qquad \text{Divide to get rid of } 2\pi r \text{ on the right-hand side.}$$
$$h = \frac{(A - 2\pi r^2)}{2\pi r} \qquad \text{Express the formula in terms of } h.$$

TIP

If you are told to solve for x, or find x, it means the same as 'make x the subject of the formula'.

Formulae containing squares and square roots

Some formulae have squared terms and square roots. You need to remember that a squared number has both a negative and a positive root when you solve these equations.

TIP

$\sqrt{x}$ means the *positive* square root only, so $\sqrt{9}$ is equal to 3.

However, if $x^2 = 9$ then $x = \pm\sqrt{9} = \pm 3$. You must use $\pm$ when undoing a square.

WORKED EXAMPLE 7

Make x the subject of the formula $ax^2 = b$.

Answer

$$ax^2 = b$$
$$x^2 = \frac{b}{a} \qquad \text{Divide both side by } a.$$
$$x = \pm\sqrt{\frac{b}{a}} \qquad \text{Take square root of both sides to get } x.$$

WORKED EXAMPLE 8

Given $r = \sqrt{\dfrac{A}{\pi}}$ express the formula in terms of A.

Answer

$$r = \sqrt{\frac{A}{\pi}}$$
$$r^2 = \frac{A}{\pi} \qquad \text{Square both sides to get rid of the square root.}$$
$$\pi r^2 = A \qquad \text{Multiply each side by } \pi.$$
$$A = \pi r^2$$

Exercise 22.4

1   Make x the subject of each formula.

   a $m = x + bp$ **b** $n = pr - x$ **c** $4x = m$ **d** $ax^2 - b = c$

   e $d - 2b = mx + c$ **f** $\dfrac{x}{y} = 3b$ **g** $m = \dfrac{p}{x}$ **h** $\dfrac{mx}{n} = p$

   i $m = \dfrac{2x}{k}$ **j** $p = \dfrac{20}{x}$

2   Solve for x.

   a $m = 3(x + y)$ **b** $c = 4(t - x)$ **c** $y = 3(x - 5)$

   d $r = 2r(3 - x)$ **e** $m = 4c(x - y)$ **f** $a = \pi r(2r - x)$

3   Express each formula in terms of the variable given in brackets.

   a $E = mc^2$ (m) **b** $I = \dfrac{PRT}{100}$ (R) **c** $k = \dfrac{1}{2}mv^2$ (m)

   d $A = \dfrac{h(a + b)}{2}$ (b) **e** $V = \dfrac{Ah}{3}$ (h) **f** $V = \dfrac{\pi r^2 h}{3}$ (h)

4   Make x the subject of each formula.

   a $m = ax^2$ **b** $x^2 - y = m$ **c** $m = n - x^2$ **d** $\dfrac{x^2}{y} = a$

   e $a = \dfrac{bx^2}{c}$ **f** $a = x^2 - b^2$ **g** $m = \dfrac{n}{x^2}$ **h** $\sqrt{xy} = m$

   i $a = \sqrt{5x}$ **j** $y = \sqrt{x - z}$ **k** $y = \sqrt{x} - z$ **l** $a = b + \dfrac{c}{\sqrt{x}}$

   m $a - b\sqrt{x} = m$ **n** $\sqrt{3x - 1} = y$ **o** $a = \sqrt{y - 2x}$ **p** $y = \dfrac{a}{\sqrt{4x - b}}$

TIP

When you have several calculations like this it is quicker to rearrange the formula before substituting in each value.

5   The formula for converting temperatures from Celsius to Fahrenheit is $F = 32 + \dfrac{9C}{5}$. Find the temperature in degrees C to the nearest degree when F is:

   a   100   **b**   212   **c**   32

6 You can find the area of a circle using the formula $A = \pi r^2$. If $\pi = 3.14$, find the radius r, of circular discs of metal with the following areas (A):

a 14   **b** 120   **c** 0.5

Formulae where the subject appears in more than one term

When the variable that is to be the subject occurs more than once, you need to collect the like terms and factorise before you can express the formula in terms of that variable.

MATHEMATICAL CONNECTIONS

You learnt how to factorise in Chapter 6.

WORKED EXAMPLE 9

Given that $m = 6 - \dfrac{12}{p}$, make p the subject of the formula.

Answer

$$m = 6 - \frac{12}{p}$$

$$mp = 6p - 12 \qquad \text{Multiply both sides by } p \text{ to remove the fraction.}$$

$$mp - 6p = -12 \qquad \text{Collect like terms.}$$

$$p(m - 6) = -12 \qquad \text{Factorise.}$$

$$p = \frac{-12}{(m - 6)} \text{ or } \frac{12}{6 - m}$$

Exercise 22.5

1 Express each of these formulae in terms of a.

a $x + a = ax + b$ **b** $L = Ba + (1 + C)a$ **c** $b = \dfrac{a}{a - 5}$

d $y = \dfrac{a + x}{a - x}$ **e** $y = \dfrac{a + 3}{1 + a}$ **f** $ma^2 = na^2 + 2$

2 Einstein developed the formula $E = mc^2$ when he worked on relativity. Express this formula in terms of c.

3 Pythagoras' theorem can expressed as $a^2 + b^2 = c^2$. Express this in terms of a.

4 In each of these formulae, make y the subject.

a $\dfrac{x}{3} = \dfrac{y}{2} - 1$ **b** $x = \dfrac{y + c}{3}$

c $\dfrac{x + z}{3} = \dfrac{y + z}{4}$ **d** $a = b - \dfrac{3y}{2}$

5 Given that $y = \dfrac{a}{a + 2}$, express this formula in terms of a.

6 A circle sector has an area (A) of $\dfrac{1}{2}r^2\theta$. Rearrange the formula to find the radius in terms of A and θ.

7 Given that $\dfrac{y}{x} = \dfrac{kx}{z^2}$, express this formula in terms of x.

APPLY YOUR SKILLS

8   In physics, the kinetic energy (E) of a particle can be found using the formula $E = \frac{1}{2}mv^2$, where m is the mass and v is the velocity of the particle.

   a   Find E when $m = 8$ and $v = 3.5$.

   b   Show how you could rearrange the formula to find v.

9   The volume (V) of a cylinder is found using the formula $V = \pi r^2 h$, where r is the radius and h is the height of the cylinder.

   a   Find the volume, correct to the nearest cm^3, of a cylinder with a radius of 0.8 m and height of 1 m.

   b   Rearrange the formula to make r the subject.

10 You can use the formula $A = \frac{\pi d^2}{4}$ to find the area (A) of a circle, where d is the diameter of the circle.

   a   Find the area of a circle of diameter 1.2 m.

   b   Use the formula $A = \pi r^2$ to find the area of the same circle.

   c   Express the formula $A = \frac{\pi d^2}{4}$ in a way that would allow you to find the diameter of the circle when the area is known.

11 A cylindrical iron tank that is h m tall with a radius of r m is placed on a concrete base. The top of the tank and the curved surface are to be coated with a sealant to prevent rust.

   a   Using h and r, write a formula for the surface area to be painted.

   b   1 litre of sealant covers 6 square metres of surface. Modify the surface area formula you found in (a) to work out how many litres of sealant are needed for the tank.

   c   Calculate the amount of sealant you would need to cover a tank that is 2.3 metres high with a radius of 1.7 metres.

REFLECTION

What strategies, skills and procedures did you use to complete this exercise?

Which were the most effective? Why?

22.3 Functions and function notation

A **function** is a rule or set of instructions for changing one number (the input) into another number (the output). If y is a function of x, then the value of y depends on the values you use for x. In a function, there is only one possible value of y for each value of x.

Function notation

Function notation is a mathematical way of writing equations (functions). Function notation is widely used in computer applications and also in technical fields.

You already know that a function can be represented in a number of ways. For example, you can show the function $y = 4x - 1$ using:

- a function machine (flow diagram):

  Input $\rightarrow$ $\boxed{\times 4}$ $\rightarrow$ $\boxed{-1}$ $\rightarrow$ output

- a mapping diagram:

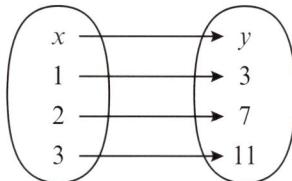

- a table of values:

x	1	2	3
y	3	7	11

- a set of x and y-values (coordinates):

  $\{(1, 3), (2, 7), (3, 11), (4, 15)\}$

  In set notation this is written as $\{(x, y): y = 4x - 1\}$

- a graph:

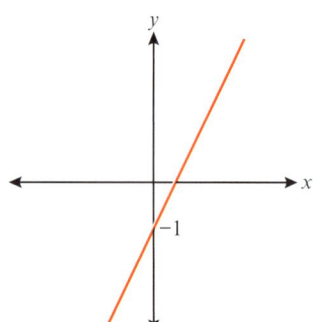

When you write the equation $y = 4x - 1$ in function notation it becomes

$f(x) = 4x - 1$.

You read f(*x*) as, 'the function of *x*' or 'f of *x*'.

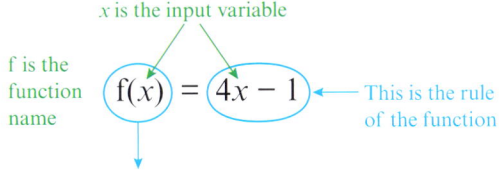

f is the function name

x is the input variable

$f(x) = 4x - 1$

This is the rule of the function

f(*x*) is the output variable

> **TIP**
>
> In function notation you leave out the *y* and replace it with the notation f(*x*). So, if 'f' is a function and '*x*' is an input, then f(*x*) is the output when f is applied to *x*.

If f(*x*) = 4*x* − 1, then f(5) means the value of the function when *x* = 5.

In other words, f(5) = 4 × 5 − 1 = 19.

Similarly, f(−2) = 4 × −2 − 1 = −9.

The number 4*x* − 1 is sometimes called the image of *x* (under function f).

When a problem involves two or more functions, you use different letters to represent them. For example, you could have:

g(*x*) = *x*² − 2*x* + 3 and h(*x*) = 5*x* − 3

You can show the steps you take to work out the value of any function f(*x*) using a simple flow diagram. For example, you can represent the function h(*x*) = 5*x* − 3 as:

$x \rightarrow \boxed{\times 5} \rightarrow \boxed{-3} \rightarrow 5x - 3$

The function j(*x*) = 5(*x* − 3) can be represented as:

$x \rightarrow \boxed{-3} \rightarrow \boxed{\times 5} \rightarrow 5(x - 3)$

Note that the flow charts show the same operations but, as they are done in a different order, they produce different results.

INVESTIGATION

Shadow maths

1   What does it mean mathematically when we say 'the length of your shadow is a function of your height and the time of day'?

2   Investigate how you can use mathematical functions involving the length of a shadow and time to determine the height of tall objects such as trees or buildings. Share your ideas and findings with your group.

WORKED EXAMPLE 10

Given that $f(x) = x^2 - 3x$ and $g(x) = 4x - 6$, find the value of:

a $f(6)$ b $f(-3)$ c $g\left(\dfrac{1}{2}\right)$ d $g(6)$

Answers

a $f(6) = 6^2 - 3(6) = 36 - 18 = 18$

b $f(-3) = (-3)^2 - 3(-3) = 9 + 9 = 18$

c $g\left(\dfrac{1}{2}\right) = 4\left(\dfrac{1}{2}\right) - 6 = 2 - 6 = -4$

d $g(6) = 4(6) - 6 = 24 - 6 = 18$

WORKED EXAMPLE 11

Given $h(x) = 9 - x^2$,

Find:

i $h(0)$ ii $h(3)$ iii $h(9)$ iv $h(-9)$

Answers

i $h(0) = 9 - (0)^2 = 9 - 0 = 9$

ii $h(3) = 9 - (3)^2 = 9 - 9 = 0$

iii $h(9) = 9 - (9)^2 = 9 - 81 = -72$

iv $h(-9) = 9 - (-9)^2 = 9 - 81 = -72$

WORKED EXAMPLE 12

$f(x) = 3 + 2x$

Solve the equation $f(x) = 6$.

Answer

$3 + 2x = 6$ The functions are equivalent.

$2x = 6 - 3$

$2x = 3$

$x = 1.5$

WORKED EXAMPLE 13

Given the functions $f(x) = x^2$ and $g(x) = x + 2$,

a   solve the equation $f(x) = g(x)$

b   solve the equation $4g(x) = g(x) - 3$.

WORKED EXAMPLE 13 CONTINUED

Answers

a
$$f(x) = g(x)$$
$$x^2 = x + 2 \qquad \text{The functions are equivalent.}$$
$$x^2 - x - 2 = 0$$
$$(x - 2)(x + 1) = 0 \qquad \text{Factorise.}$$
$$\text{So, } x = 2 \text{ or } x = -1$$

b
$$4g(x) = g(x) - 3$$
$$3g(x) = -3 \qquad \text{Subtract } g(x) \text{ from both sides.}$$
$$g(x) = -1 \qquad \text{Divide both sides by three.}$$
$$x + 2 = -1 \qquad \text{Replace } g(x) \text{ with } x + 2.$$
$$x = -3$$

Domain and range

A function is defined by a rule that provides the output values for corresponding input values.

The domain (D) of a function is the set of input values. These are the possible values for the independent variable (the x-values).

The range (R) is the set of output values from the rule. These are the y-values, which are dependent on the variable input.

There may be restrictions on the domain. For example, if you are working with time or distance, the input values cannot be negative. Restrictions on the domain may be given with the function. For example $y = 2x + 3$ where $x > 1$. This tells you that you are only interested in values of y where x is greater than 1, so the domain is $x > 1$.

TIP

Remember:

* You cannot divide by 0.

* The square root of a negative number is not a real number.

* The square root sign ($\sqrt{\ }$) refers to the positive square root only.

WORKED EXAMPLE 14

Determine the domain and range of each function.

a $y = \sqrt{2x - 1}$

b $y = \dfrac{3x}{2x + 1}$

Answers

a $y = \sqrt{2x - 1}$

Domain: y will not be a real number if $(2x - 1)$ is negative.

$$2x - 1 \geqslant 0 \qquad \text{(must be positive)}$$

WORKED EXAMPLE 14 CONTINUED

$2x \geqslant 1$

$x \geqslant \dfrac{1}{2}$ So, x values must be greater than or equal to $\dfrac{1}{2}$.

Domain: $\left\{x : x \geqslant \dfrac{1}{2}\right\}$

Range: The $\sqrt{}$ sign means only positive square roots.

So, y must be 0 or greater than 0.

Range: $\{y : y \geqslant 0\}$

b $y = \dfrac{3x}{2x + 1}$

y will be undefined if $(2x + 1) = 0$

$2x + 1 = 0$

$2x = -1$

$x = -\dfrac{1}{2}$

Domain: $\left\{x : x \neq -\dfrac{1}{2}\right\}$

To find the range we need to work out for which values of y, x will be undefined.

$2xy + y = 3x$ Rearrange the equation

$2xy - 3x = -y$

$x(2y - 3) = -y$ Factorise

So, $x = \dfrac{-y}{2y - 3}$ Make x the subject

x is undefined if $(2y - 3) = 0$,

$3 = 2y$

$y = \dfrac{3}{2}$

Range: $\left\{y : y \neq \dfrac{3}{2}\right\}$

Exercise 22.6

1 For each function, calculate:

  i f(2)   **ii** f(−2)   **iii** f(0.5)   **iv** f(0)

  a f(x) = 3x + 2   **b** f(x) = 5x − 2   **c** f(x) = 2x − 1

  d f(x) = 2x^2 + 3   **e** f(x) = x^2 − 2x **f** f(x) = x^3 − 2

2 f(x) = 4x − 1, find:

  a f(−1)   **b** f(0)   **c** f(1.5)   **d** f(−4)

3   $f(x) = x^2 - 4$, find:

   a $f(2)$ **b** $f(0)$ **c** $f(-3)$ **d** $f(0.25)$

4   Given the functions $f(x) = x^3 - 8$ and $g(x) = 3 - x$, find the value of:

   a $f(2)$ **b** $f(-1)$ **c** $g(5)$ **d** $g(-2)$

5   Given the function $h(x) = 4x^2$, find:

   a $h(2)$ **b** $h(-2)$ **c** $h\left(\dfrac{1}{2}\right)$

6   $f(x) = 3x - 1$

   Solve the equation $f(x) = 3$.

7   $h(x) = \dfrac{1}{x} + 1$

   Solve the equation $h(x) = 4$.

8   $g(x) = \sqrt{4x + 1}$ and $g(x) = 5$

   a   Solve the equation $g(x) = 5$.

   b   State the domain and range of the function.

9   Given the functions $f(x) = x^2 - x$ and $g(x) = x^2 - 3x - 12$,

   a   solve the equation $f(x) = 6$ **b**   solve the equation $f(x) = g(x)$.

10 Given $f(x) = 2x$, find:

   a $f(a)$ **b** $f(a + 2)$ **c** $f(4a)$ **d** $4f(a)$

11 $f(x) = \dfrac{4 + x}{x}$ $(x \neq 0)$

   a   Calculate $f\left(\dfrac{1}{2}\right)$, simplifying your answer.

   b   Solve $f(x) = 3$.

12 $f(x) = (2x + 1)(x + 1)$, find:

   a $f(2)$ **b** $f(-2)$ **c** $f(0)$

Composite functions

A **composite function** is a combination of two or more functions. If you have two functions, the composite function is the result of making the output of the first function, the input of the second function. You can think of this as:

Input → [function 1] → output of function 1 → [function 2] → output

Look at these two functions: $f(x) = 2x + 1$ and $g(x) = x^2$.

You can apply function f followed by function g to find the composite function. For the input $x = 4$:

   $f(4) = 2(4) + 1 = 8 + 1 = 9$ (9 is the result of the first function.)

   $g(9) = 9^2 = 81$ (The function g has been applied to the result.)

You can write what has been done as $g[f(4)] = 81$. However, normally the square brackets are left out and you just write $gf(4) = 81$.

gf(x) is a composite function.

The order of the letters in a composite function is important:

gf(4) ≠ fg(4)

gf(x) means do f first then g, but fg(x) means do g first then f.

So, the function closest to the x is applied first.

You can also find an algebraic expression for the composite function gf(x):

f(x) = 2x + 1   (2x + 1 is the result of the first function.)

g(2x + 1) = (2x + 1)^2

$\qquad\quad$ = 4x^2 + 4x + 1   (The function g has been applied to the result.)

So, gf(x) = 4x^2 + 4x + 1 and gf(4) = 4 × 4^2 + 4 × 4 + 1 = 64 + 16 + 1 = 81

WORKED EXAMPLE 15

Given f(x) = 2x − 1 and g(x) = x^2 + 6, find:

a   fg(x)   **b**   ff(x)

Answers

a   fg(x) = 2(x^2 + 6) − 1   Input g(x) into f(x).

$\qquad$ = 2x^2 + 12 − 1

$\qquad$ = 2x^2 + 11

$\quad$ fg(x) = 2x^2 + 11

b   ff(x) = 2(2x − 1) − 1   Input f(x) into f(x).

$\qquad$ = 4x − 2 − 1

$\qquad$ = 4x − 3

$\quad$ ff(x) = 4x − 3

WORKED EXAMPLE 16

Given the functions f(x) = x^2 − 2x and g(x) = 3 − x, find the value of:

a   gf(4)   **b**   fg(4)   **c**   ff(−1)   **d**   gg(100)

Answers

a   gf(4) = g[f(4)] = g[16 − 8] = g[8] = 3 − 8 = −5

b   fg(4) = f[g(4)] = f[3 − 4] = f[−1] = (−1)^2 − 2(−1) = 1 + 2 = 3

c   ff(−1) = f[f(−1)] = f[1 + 2] = f[3] = 9 − 6 = 3

d   gg(100) = g[g(100)] = g[3 − 100] = g[−97] = 3 − (−97) = 3 + 97 = 100

Exercise 22.7

1 For each pair of functions, write down the composite functions fg(x) and gf(x).

    a   f(x) = x + 6   **b**   f(x) = $2x^2 - 3x + 1$

         g(x) = x - 3   g(x) = $5x$

    c   f(x) = $3x^2 - 4x + 2$ **d**   f(x) = $\dfrac{4x}{3}$

         g(x) = $3x$ - 2   g(x) = $x^2 - 9$

2 Given f(x) = $2x$ and g(x) = $-x$, find:

    a   fg(x)   **b**   fg(2)   **c**   ff(4)   **d**   gf(1)

3 Given f(x) = $3x$ + 1 and h(x) = $6x^2$, find:

    a   ff(x)   **b**   fh(x)   **c**   hh(−2)   **d**   hf(−2)   **e**   hf$\left(\dfrac{2}{5}\right)$

4 Given the functions g(x) = $x^2 + 1$ and h(x) = $2x + 3$, find the values of:

    a   gh(1)   **b**   hg(1)   **c**   gg(2)   **d**   hh(5)

5 Find gh(4) and hg(4) if g(x) = $\dfrac{1}{x}$ and h(x) = $\dfrac{1}{x+1}$.

6 Given f(x) = $8 - x^2$ and g(x) = $x^2 - 8$, find:

    a   fg(x)   **b**   gf(x)   **c**   ff(x)   **d**   gg(x)

7 Given f(x) = $2x$ − 5 and g(x) = $\dfrac{1}{x}$, evaluate:

    a   f(−10)   **b**   g$\left(\dfrac{2}{3}\right)$ **c**   gf$\left(\dfrac{5}{70}\right)$ **d**   gf(4)   **e**   ff(0)

8 If f(x) = x^4 and g(x) = $\sqrt{(x^2 + 36)}$, evaluate:

    a   fg(x)   **b**   gf(x)   **c**   ff(0)   **d**   gg(−2)

9 Given that f(x) = $-x$, g(x) = $x - 1$ and h(x) = $\dfrac{1}{x+2}$, show why it is not possible to evaluate hgf(1).

Inverse functions

The inverse of any function (f) is the function that will do the opposite of f. In other words, the function that will undo the effects of f. So, if f maps 4 onto 13, then the inverse of f will map 13 onto 4.

In effect, when f is applied to a number and the inverse of f is applied to the result, you will get back to the number you started with.

In simple cases, you can find the inverse of a function by inspection. For example, the inverse of $x \rightarrow x + 5$ must be $x \rightarrow x - 5$ because subtraction is the inverse of addition; to undo add five you have to subtract five.

Similarly, the inverse of $x \rightarrow 2x$ is $x \rightarrow \dfrac{x}{2}$, because to undo multiply by two you have to divide by two.

The inverse of the function (f) is written as f^{-1}.

So, if $f(x) = x + 5$, then $f^{-1}(x) = x - 5$

and, if $g(x) = 2x$, then $g^{-1}(x) = \dfrac{x}{2}$.

Some functions do not have an inverse. Think about the function $x \rightarrow x^2$. This is a function because for every value of x, there is only one value of x^2. The inverse (in other words, the square root) is not a function because a positive number has two square roots, one negative, and one positive.

> ### MATHEMATICAL CONNECTIONS
>
> You briefly worked with inverse functions in trigonometry in Chapter 15.

Finding the inverse of a function

There are two methods of finding the inverse:

- **Method 1:** using a flow diagram.

  In this method you draw a flow diagram for the function and then work out the inverse by 'reversing' the flow to undo the operations in the boxes.

- **Method 2:** reversing the mapping.

  In this method you use the fact that if f maps x onto y, then f^{-1} maps y onto x. To find f^{-1} you have to find a value of x that corresponds to a given value of y.

Worked examples 17–20 show how to find the inverse for two functions, first using method 1 and then using method 2.

> ### WORKED EXAMPLE 17
>
> Find the inverse of $f(x) = 3x - 4$.
>
> **Answer**
>
> Using method 1, the flow diagram, you get: f : input $\rightarrow \boxed{\times 3} \rightarrow \boxed{-4} \rightarrow$ output
>
> Reversing the diagram gives: f^{-1} : output $\leftarrow \boxed{\div 3} \leftarrow \boxed{+4} \leftarrow$ input
>
> Let x be the input to f^{-1} : $\dfrac{x+4}{3} \leftarrow \boxed{\div 3} \leftarrow \boxed{+4} \leftarrow x$
>
> So, $f^{-1}(x) = \dfrac{x+4}{3}$

> ### WORKED EXAMPLE 18
>
> Given $g(x) = 5 - 2x$, find $g^{-1}(x)$.
>
> **Answer**
>
> Using method 1, the flow diagram, you get: g : input $\rightarrow \boxed{\times(-2)} \rightarrow \boxed{+5} \rightarrow$ output
>
> Reversing the diagram gives: g^{-1} : output $\leftarrow \boxed{\div(-2)} \leftarrow \boxed{-5} \leftarrow$ input
>
> Let x be the input to g^{-1} : $\dfrac{x-5}{-2} \leftarrow \boxed{\div(-2)} \leftarrow \boxed{-5} \leftarrow x$
>
> So, $g^{-1}(x) = \dfrac{x-5}{-2} = \dfrac{5-x}{2}$

WORKED EXAMPLE 19

Find the inverse of the function f(x) = 3x − 4.

Answer

Using method 2, reversing the mapping.

$y = 3x - 4$	Suppose the function maps x onto y (y is the subject).
$y + 4 = 3x$	Make x the subject of the formula, so that y maps onto x.
$x = \dfrac{y + 4}{3}$	

You know that f⁻1 maps y onto x, so $f^{-1}(y) = \dfrac{y + 4}{3}$

This is usually written in terms of x so, $f^{-1}(x) = \dfrac{x + 4}{3}$

WORKED EXAMPLE 20

Given g(x) = 5 − 2x, find g⁻¹(x).

Answer

Let $y = 5 - 2x$	This means g maps x onto y.
$2x = 5 - y$	Make x the subject of the formula, so that y maps onto x.
$x = \dfrac{5 - y}{2}$	

g⁻¹ maps y onto x, so $g^{-1}(y) = \dfrac{5 - y}{2}$

This is usually written in terms of x so, $g^{-1}(x) = \dfrac{5 - x}{2}$

Exercise 22.8

1   Find the inverse of each function.

a $f(x) = 7x$

b $f(x) = \dfrac{1}{7x^3}$

c $f(x) = x^3$

d $f(x) = 4x + 3$

e $f(x) = \dfrac{1}{2}x + 5$

f $f(x) = \dfrac{x + 2}{2}$

g $f(x) = 3(x - 2)$

h $f(x) = \dfrac{2x + 9}{2}$

i $f(x) = \dfrac{2(x + 1)}{4 - x}$

j $f(x) = x^3 + 5$

k $f(x) = \sqrt{3x + 8}$

l $f(x) = \dfrac{x + 1}{x - 1}$

2   Given the function $g(x) = \dfrac{x}{3} - 44$, find $g^{-1}(x)$.

3   For each function, find:

i $f^{-1}(x)$

ii $ff^{-1}(x)$

iii $f^{-1}f(x)$

a $f(x) = 5x$

b $f(x) = x + 4$

c $f(x) = 2x - 7$

d $f(x) = x^3 + 2$

e $f(x) = \sqrt{2x - 1}$

f $f(x) = \dfrac{9}{x}$

g $f(x) = x^3 - 1$

4 For each pair of functions, determine whether g(x) is the inverse of f(x).

    a   f(x) = 2x − 6

           g(x) = $\dfrac{x}{2}$ + 3

    b   f(x) = 12x

           g(x) = $\dfrac{x}{12}$

    c   f(x) = 3x + 2

           g(x) = x + $\dfrac{3}{2}$

    d   f(x) = x^3 − 2

           g(x) = $\sqrt[3]{x + 2}$

5 Given the function h(x) = 2(x − 3), find the value of:

    a $h^{-1}(10)$
    b $hh^{-1}(20)$
    c $h^{-1}h^{-1}(26)$

6   f(x) = $\dfrac{1}{2}x$ + 5 and g(x) = 4x − $\dfrac{2}{5}$

    a   Solve f(x) = 0.

    b   Find $g^{-1}(x)$.

    c   Solve f(x) = g(x) giving your answer correct to 2 decimal places.

    d   Find the value of:

         i $gf^{-1}(-2)$
         ii $f^{-1}f(3)$
         iii $f^{-1}g^{-1}(4)$

SUMMARY

Do you know …?

When you set up your own equations to represent problems you need to state what the variables stand for.
You can rearrange formulae to make any of the variables the subject. This is called changing the subject of the formula. It may also be called solving the formula for (x) or expressing the formula in terms of (x).
A function is a rule for changing one variable into another.
Functions are written using notation of f(x) = x + 2.
You can use a flow diagram to represent the steps in a function.
A composite function is a function of a function. The order of a composite function is important fg(x) means do g first then f.
An inverse function is function that undoes the original function. It is the reverse of the function.

Are you able to …?

set up your own equations and use them to solve worded problems
change the subject of formula
set up and rearrange more complicated formulae such as those that contain squares, square roots or where the subject appears in more than one term
read, understand and use function notation to describe simple functions
form composite functions such as gf(x) and ff(x)
find the inverse of a function using a flow diagram
find the inverse of a function by reversing the mapping.

Practice questions

1   Six litres of white paint are mixed with three litres of blue paint. Blue paint costs \$2 per litre more than white paint. The total price of the mixture is \$24. Find the price of the white paint.   [4]

2   A trader has a mixture of 5c and 10c coins. He has 50 coins in all, with a total value of \$4.20. How many of each coin does he have?   [4]

3   Lana cycles at 12 km/h from her home to the station and immediately boards a train. The average speed of the train for the rest of the journey is 48 km/h and the total distance travelled through the whole journey is 64 km. The total time for the journey is 1 hour and 50 minutes.

   a   If Lana cycles for T hours to get to the station, find the distance to the station in terms of T.   [2]

   b   Write 1 hour 50 minutes in hours, giving your answer as an improper fraction.   [1]

   c   Find the time taken to complete the train journey and the distance travelled by train, both in terms of T.   [3]

   d   Find T and hence calculate the distance Lana cycled to the station.   [3]

4   A rectangle with area 117 cm^2 has perimeter 44 cm. Work out the dimensions of the rectangle.   [5]

5   Two consecutive integers are n and $n + 1$. The sum of their squares is 545. Find the smaller of the two integers.   [5]

6   In 2021, a competition prize of £30 was divided equally between x friends. In 2022, the same competition prize was divided equally between $x + 4$ friends. In 2022, each person received £2 less than each person in 2021.

   a   Show that $x^2 + 4x - 60 = 0$.   [4]

   b   Find the total number of people who received prize money in 2021 and 2022.   [3]

7   The rectangle and triangle have the same area. All dimensions are given in cm. Find the perimeter of the triangle.

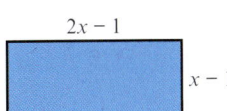
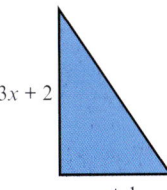

$2x - 1$

$x - 1$ $3x + 2$

$x + 1$ [6]

8   Rearrange $\sqrt{x} + \dfrac{1}{\sqrt{x}} = \dfrac{1}{\sqrt{x}\sqrt{y}}$ to make x the subject.   [3]

9   Rearrange $y = \dfrac{\sqrt{x} + z}{\sqrt{x} - z}$ to make x the subject.   [4]

10   f and g are the functions f$(x) = x - 5$ and g$(x) = 5 - x$. Are each of the following statements true or false?

   a   f^{-1} = g   [2]   **b**   g$^{-1}: x \to 5 - x$ [2]

   c   fg$: x \to -x$ [2]   **d**   fg = gf   [2]

11 $f(x) = 3x^2 - 3x - 4$ and $g(x) = 4 - 3x$

    a   State the value of $f(-2)$.   [1]

    b   Solve the equation $f(x) = -3$.   [3]

    c   Solve the equation $f(x) = 0$, giving your answer correct to 2 decimal places.   [3]

    d   Solve the equation $g(x) = 2g(x) - 1$.   [3]

    e   Find $g^{-1}(x)$.   [2]

    f   Find and simplify $fg(x) - 4gf(x)$.   [4]

    g   Solve $gg(x) = 17$.   [4]

    h   Find and simplify $ff(x) - (f(x))^2$.   [4]

12 $f(x) = \dfrac{1 - x}{1 + x}$

    a   Show that $ff(x) = x$.   [3]

    b   Write down $f^{-1}(x)$.   [1]

    c   Find $fffff(x)$.   [3]

13 $f(x) = 3 - 4x$

    a   Find $f(-1)$.   [1]

    b   Find $f^{-1}(x)$.   [1]

    c   Find $ff^{-1}(4)$.   [1]

14 $f(x) = \dfrac{5}{2x - 1}$

    Solve the equation $f(x) = -2$.   [4]

SELF ASSESSMENT

Use the table to rate your understanding of the mathematical concepts needed in this section.

My work shows that I ...	Rating
understand all of the mathematical concepts needed to solve these problems	4
understand most of the mathematical concepts needed to solve these problems	3
understand some of the mathematical concepts needed to solve these problems	2
have limited understanding of the mathematical concepts needed to solve these problems	1

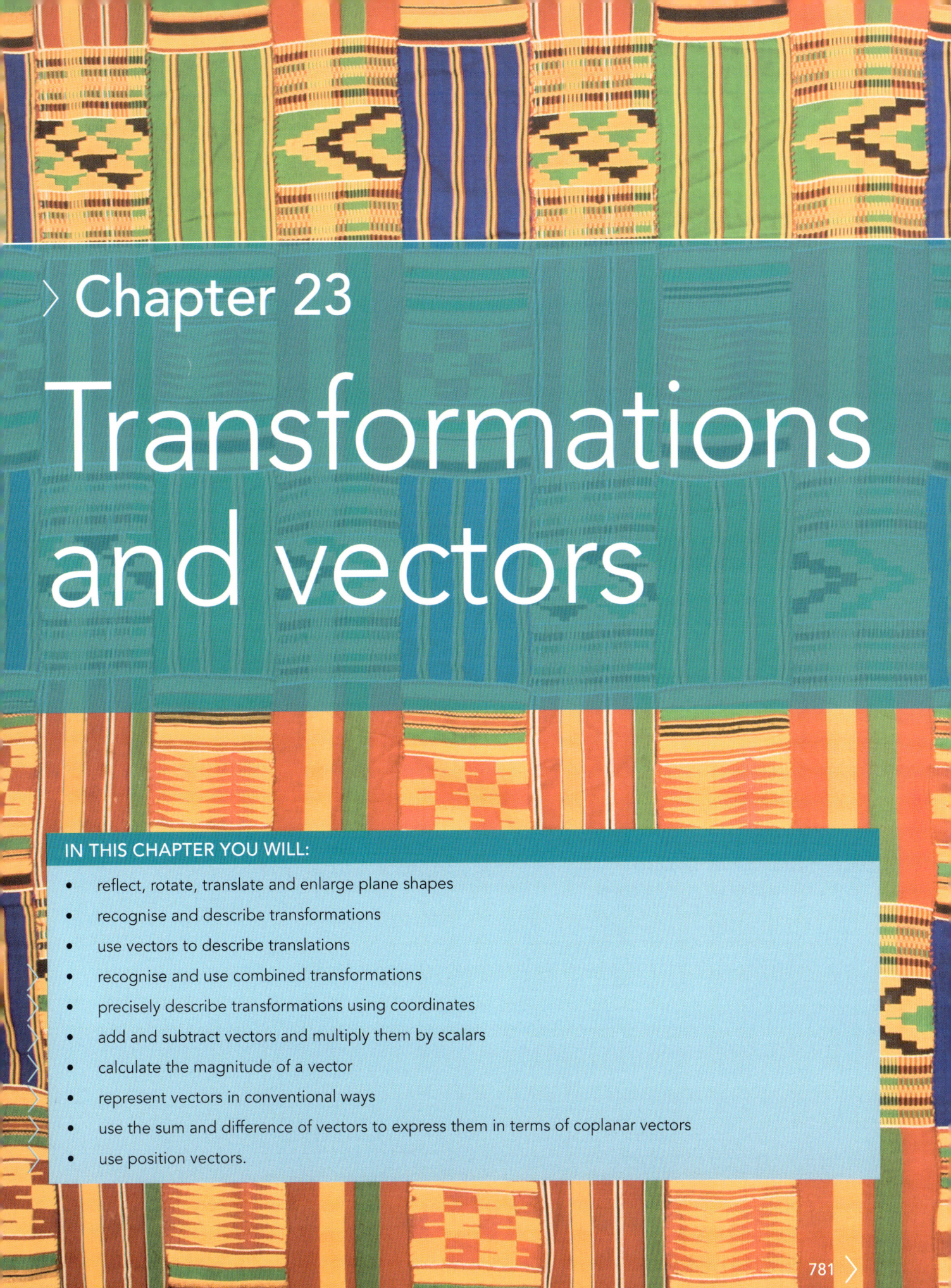

> Chapter 23

Transformations and vectors

The photograph on the previous page shows traditional kente cloth from Ghana. The fabric designer has repeated shapes by moving them and turning them in regular ways. You may remember that a change in the position or size of a shape is called a transformation. Choose one or two of the shapes and tell your partner how they have been transformed in this fabric design.

Transformation geometry deals with moving or changing shapes in set ways. You are going to revise what you know about transformations, use vectors, and work with more precise mathematical descriptions of transformations.

KEY WORDS

column vector

enlargement

magnitude

reflection

rotation

scalar

transformation

translation

vector

GETTING STARTED

1 The red shape (A) in each diagram is the object. The blue shape (A') is the image of the red shape after a

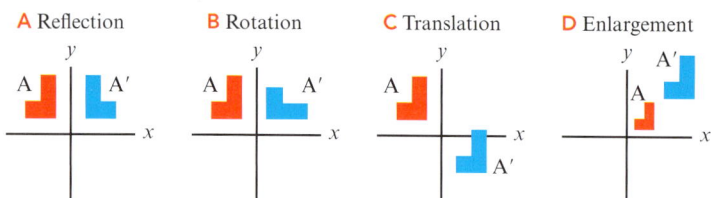

A Reflection   **B** Rotation   **C** Translation   **D** Enlargement

a Describe how A moved or changed in each transformation.

b Match each diagram to the correct mathematical name for the transformation. Choose from the box.

translation	enlargement	reflection	rotation

c In which transformation(s) is the object and its image:
  i congruent?   **ii** similar?

2 You have learnt how to describe movement using a column vector $\begin{pmatrix} x \\ y \end{pmatrix}$.

The top number (x) represents horizontal movement and the bottom number (y) represents vertical movement.

a Copy this table. Use the words right, left, up and down to complete it.

	Direction of movement	
	x	**y**
If number is positive		
If number is negative		

b Write a column vector to describe the translation from A to B.

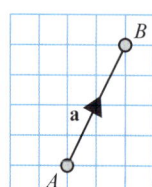

c Draw your own sketch to show the vectors $MN = \begin{pmatrix} -3 \\ -2 \end{pmatrix}$ and $PQ = \begin{pmatrix} -3 \\ 4 \end{pmatrix}$.

23.1 Simple plane transformations

Transformation means change. In mathematics, a transformation is a change in the position or size of an object (or point). In this section you will deal with four types of transformations:

- **reflection** (a flip or mirror image)

- **rotation** (a turn)

- **translation** (a slide movement)

- **enlargement** (making the object larger or smaller).

A transformation produces an image of the original object in a new position or at a different size. A point, P, on the object is labelled as P' on the image.

Reflections, rotations and translations change the position of an object, but they do not change its size. So, the object and its image are congruent. If you place the object and its image on top of each other, they coincide exactly.

When you enlarge an object, you change its size. The object and its image are similar. In other words, the lengths of corresponding sides on the image are in the same proportion as on the object and the corresponding angles on the object and its image are equal.

Reflection

A reflection is a mirror image of the shape. The line of reflection is called the mirror line. Corresponding points on the object and the image are the same distance from the mirror line. These distances are always measured perpendicular to the mirror line. (In other words, the mirror line is the perpendicular bisector of the distance between any point and its image.) You can see this on the following diagrams.

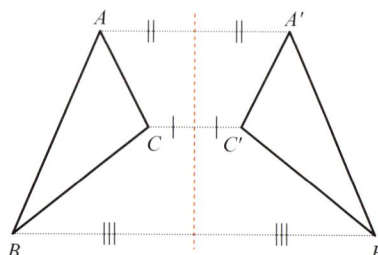

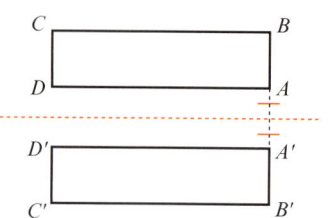

To fully define a reflection, you need to give the equation of the mirror line.

Properties of reflection

- A point and its image are equidistant from the mirror line (m) after reflection about the line m.

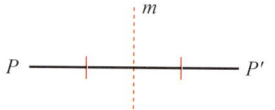

- The mirror line bisects the line joining a point and its image at right angles.

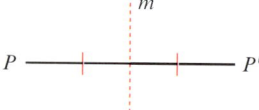

- A line segment and its image are equal in length. $AB = A'B'$.

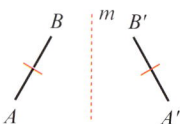

- A line and its image are equally inclined to the mirror line. angle AOM = angle $A'OM$.

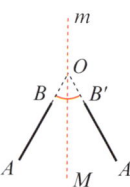

- Points on the mirror line are their own images and are invariant.

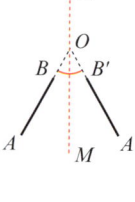

- Under reflection, a figure and its image are congruent.

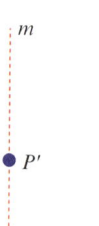

TIP

Note that we usually draw the mirror line as a dashed line.

TIP

You need to be able to work with reflections in horizontal and vertical lines only.

TIP

Invariant means a point, or a line, remains unchanged in its position and size.

WORKED EXAMPLE 1

Reflect triangle *ABC* about the mirror line.

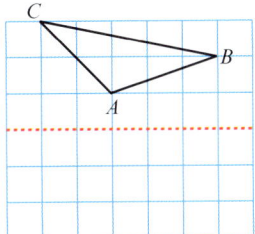

Answer

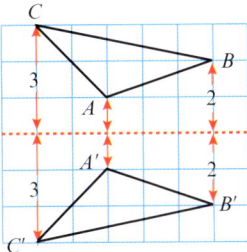

In the diagram, *A* is 1 unit from the mirror line, so its image *A′* is also 1 unit from the mirror line. Point *B* is 2 units from the mirror line, so its image *B′* is also 2 units from the mirror line. This is also true for *C* and its image *C′*.

The reflection of a straight line is a straight line. So, to obtain the reflection of triangle *ABC*, join *A′* to *B′*, *B′* to *C′* and *C′* to *A′*.

> **TIP**
>
> When the mirror line is one of the grid lines it is simple to reflect any point. You count the squares from the point to the mirror line and the reflection is the same distance the other side of the mirror line.

WORKED EXAMPLE 2

A shape and its reflection are shown on the grid.

a   Draw the mirror line.

b   What is the equation of the mirror line?

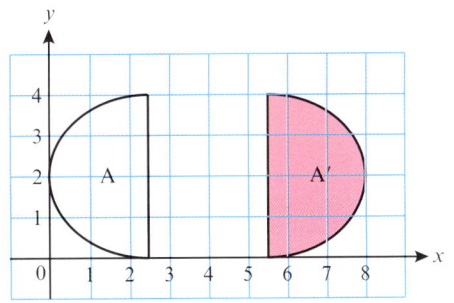

Answers

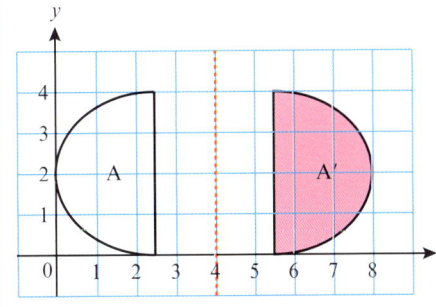

a   The mirror line must be the same distance from corresponding points on A and A′.

b   The mirror line is parallel to the *y*-axis. The *x*-value of any point on it is 4, so the equation of the line is *x* = 4.

> **TIP**
>
> The mirror line is the perpendicular bisector of the line joining any point and its image.

WORKED EXAMPLE 3

Shape A is the object.

a Reflect shape A in the y-axis.
Label the image B.

b Reflect shape A and shape B in the x-axis.
Label the images A′ and B′ respectively.

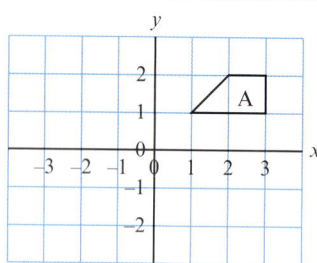

Answers

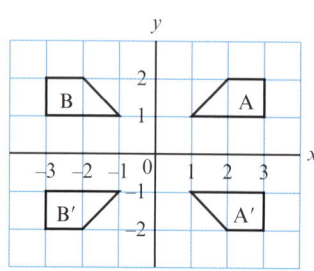

a The y-axis ($x = 0$) is the mirror line.

b The x-axis ($y = 0$) is the mirror line.

Exercise 23.1

1 Copy the shapes and the mirror lines onto squared paper. Draw the image of each object.

a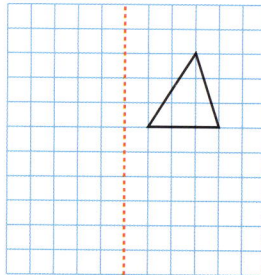
b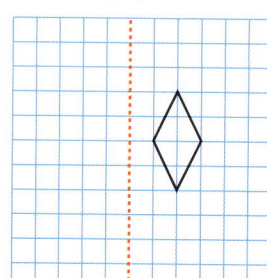
c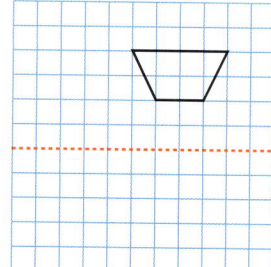

2 Copy the axes and shapes onto squared paper.
For each diagram:

i draw the mirror line

ii give the equation of the mirror line.

a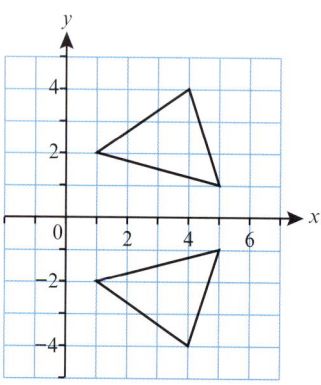
b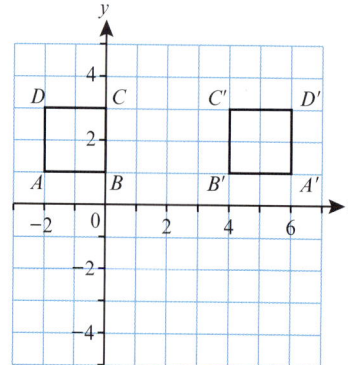
c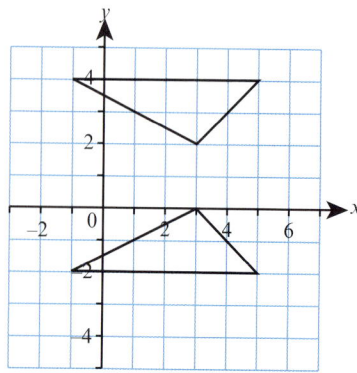

3   Copy the axes and the shape onto squared paper.

   a   Reflect polygon *ABCDE* in the *y*-axis.

   b   Give the coordinates of point *B* after reflection (*B'*).

   c   Which point on the shape *ABCDE* is invariant? Why?

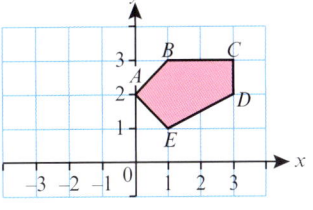

4   Copy the axes and the shape onto squared paper.

   a   Reflect the shape in the line *x* = 1. Label the image *P'Q'R'S'*.

   b   Reflect *P'Q'R'S'* in the line *y* = 2. Label the image *P"Q"R"S"*.

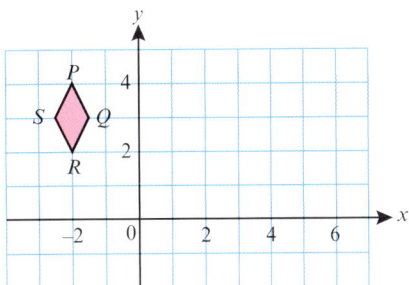

5   Copy the axes and the diagram onto squared paper.

   a   Draw the image of triangle *DEF* when reflected in the *y*-axis. Label it *D'E'F'*.

   b   Give the coordinates of point *F* before and after reflection.

   c   Reflect triangle *DEF* in the line *y* = 1. Label the image *D"E"F"*.

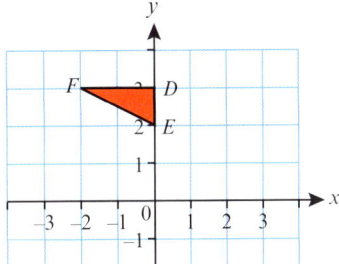

Rotation

A rotation is a turn around a fixed point. Rotation occurs when an object is turned around a given point. Rotation can be clockwise or anti-clockwise. The fixed point is called the centre of rotation and the angle through which the shape is rotated is called the angle of rotation.

In this diagram, the object has been rotated 90° clockwise about the centre of rotation (a vertex of the object).

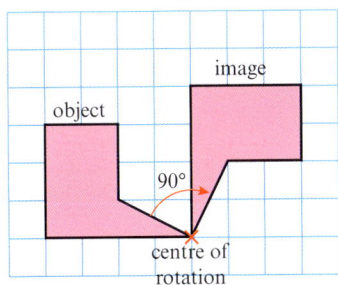

Properties of rotation

- A rotation through 180° is a half turn; a rotation through 90° is a quarter turn.

- A point and its image are equidistant from the centre of rotation.

- Each point of an object moves along the arc of a circle whose centre is the centre of rotation. All the circles are concentric:

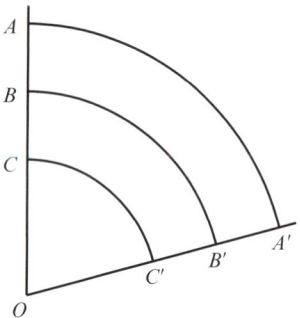

MATHEMATICAL CONNECTIONS

You dealt with rotation when you studied rotational symmetry in Chapter 19.

- Only the centre of rotation is invariant.

- The object and the image are congruent after rotation.

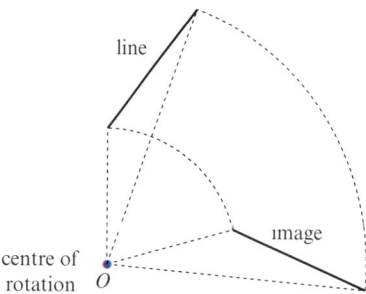

- The perpendicular bisector of a line joining a point and its image passes through the centre of rotation.

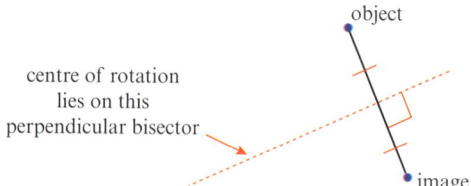

- A line segment and its image are equal in length.

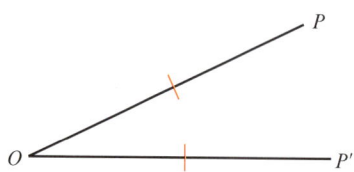

To describe a rotation you need to give:

- the centre of rotation
- the amount of turn (90°, 180° or 270°)
- the direction of the turn (clockwise or anti-clockwise).

You can use thin paper or tracing paper to help you with rotations:

1   Trace the shape and label the vertices.

2   Place the tracing over the object.

3   Use the point of a pair of compasses or pen to hold the paper at the point (centre) of rotation.

4   Turn the paper through the given turn.

5   The new position of the shape is the image.

TIP

The centre of rotation will normally be the origin (0, 0), a vertex of the shape or the midpoint of a side of the shape. The amount of turn will normally be a multiple of 90°.

WORKED EXAMPLE 4

Rotate this shape 90° clockwise about:

a   the origin (label the image $A'B'C'D'$)

b   point A (label the image $A''B''C''D''$).

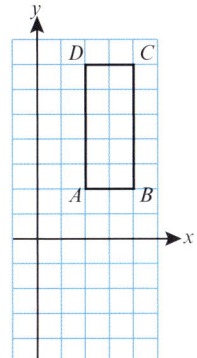

Answers

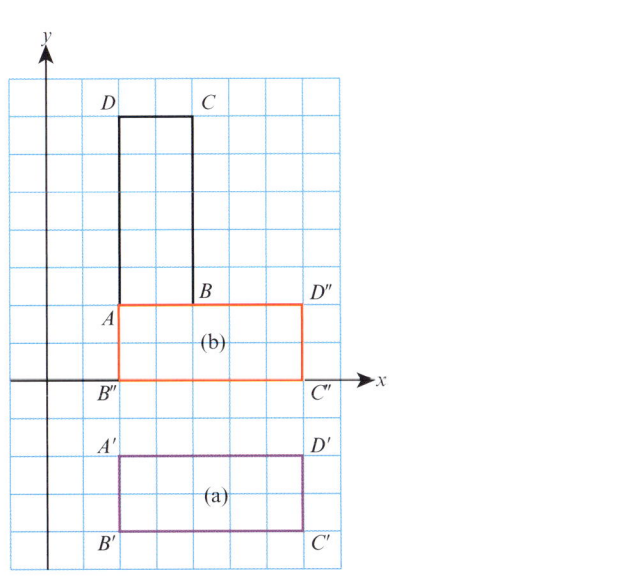

Exercise 23.2

1   Copy the diagrams in parts (a) to (c).

Draw the images of the given triangle under the rotations described.

a

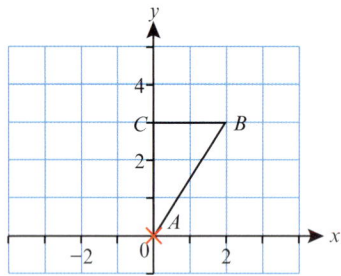

b

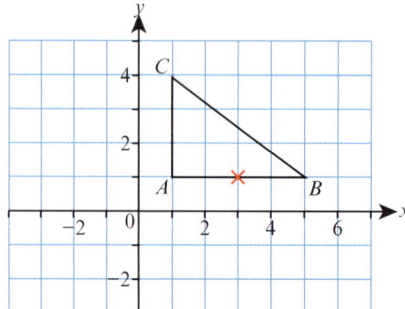

c

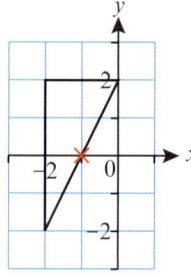

Centre of rotation (0, 0); angle of rotation 90° anti-clockwise.

Centre of rotation (3, 1); angle of rotation 180°. (Note that (3, 1) is the midpoint of *AB*.)

Centre of rotation (−1, 0); angle of rotation 180°.

2   Shapes A to E and their images are shown on the grid. For each shape, fully describe each rotation.

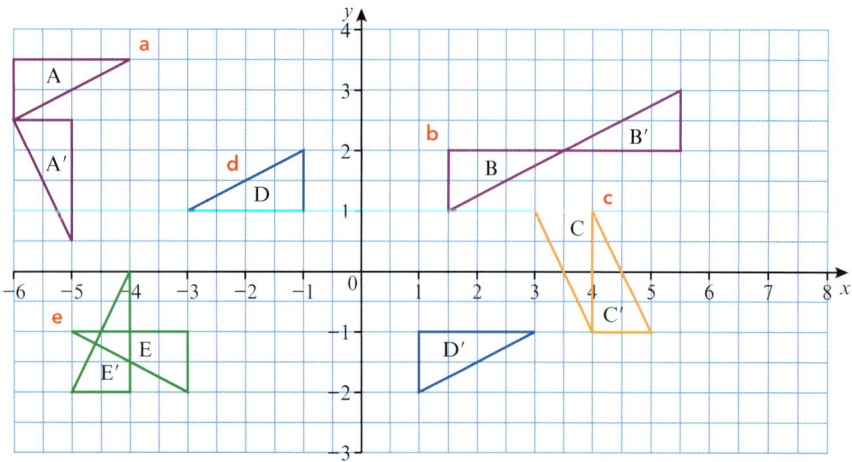

> **TIP**
>
> To fully describe a rotation, you must give the centre of rotation as well as the angle and direction of the rotation.

3   Fully describe the rotation that maps triangle *ABC* onto triangle *A′B′C′* in each case.

a

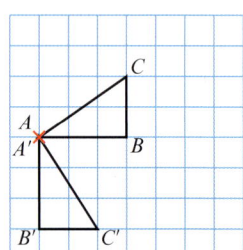

b

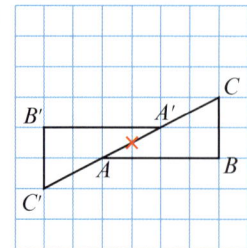

c

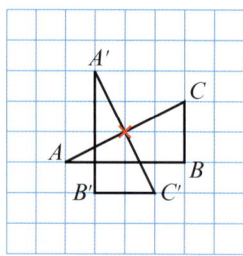

APPLY YOUR SKILLS

4   Kofi wants to rearrange the furniture in a room. This scale diagram shows the original layout of the room.

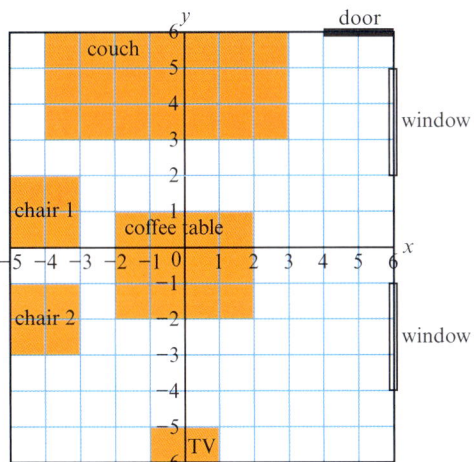

Is it possible for Kofi to rotate all the furniture through point (0, 0) by the following amounts and for the furniture still to fit into the room?

a   90° clockwise

b   90° anti-clockwise

c   180° clockwise

REFLECTION

Identifying the reasons for mistakes

Research shows that mistakes are often related to misconceptions or misunderstanding and that simply finding and correcting mistakes does not help to prevent similar mistakes in the future.

* Identify any mistakes you made in this exercise.
* Analyse why you made these mistakes. Decide if you were careless or whether you misunderstood any of the concepts.
* Suggest one thing you will do so that you don't make similar mistakes in the future.

Translation

A translation, or slide, is the movement of an object over a specified distance along a line. The object is not twisted or turned. The movement is indicated by positive or negative signs according to the direction of movement along the axes of a plane. For example, movements to the left or down are negative and movements to the right or up are positive.

You can describe a translation using a **column vector**: $\begin{pmatrix} x \\ y \end{pmatrix}$. This means a movement of x units in the x-direction (left or right) and a movement of y units in the y-direction (up or down). So, for example, a translation of $\begin{pmatrix} 2 \\ -3 \end{pmatrix}$ means the object moves two units to the right and three units down.

In this diagram, the triangle T is translated to five positions. Each translation is described below the diagram:

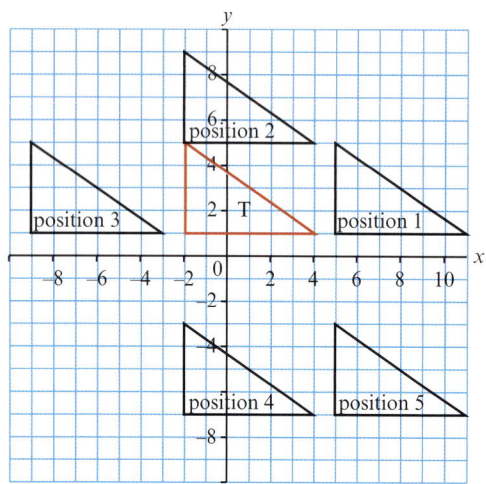

<table>
<tr><td>MATHEMATICAL
CONNECTIONS</td></tr>
</table>

MATHEMATICAL CONNECTIONS

You will deal with vectors in more detail later in this chapter.

Position 1 $\begin{pmatrix} 7 \\ 0 \end{pmatrix}$

Position 2 $\begin{pmatrix} 0 \\ 4 \end{pmatrix}$

Position 3 $\begin{pmatrix} -7 \\ 0 \end{pmatrix}$

Position 4 $\begin{pmatrix} 0 \\ -8 \end{pmatrix}$

Position 5 $\begin{pmatrix} 7 \\ -8 \end{pmatrix}$

Properties of translation

- A translation moves every point in an object the same distance in the same direction, so you can describe the translation of the whole object by describing the translation of any one point.

- To specify the translation, give both the distance and direction of the translation using a column vector $\begin{pmatrix} x \\ y \end{pmatrix}$.

- No part of the object is invariant.

- The object and the image are congruent.

TIP

Be careful when writing column vectors. There is no dividing line, so they should *not* look like fractions. Write $\begin{pmatrix} 3 \\ 8 \end{pmatrix}$ rather than $\left(\frac{3}{8}\right)$; they mean different things.

Exercise 23.3

1 Draw sketches to illustrate the following translations:

    a a square translated 6 cm to the left

    b a triangle translated 5 cm to the right.

2 Write column vectors to describe the translations from A to B and from A to C in each of the following diagrams.

a

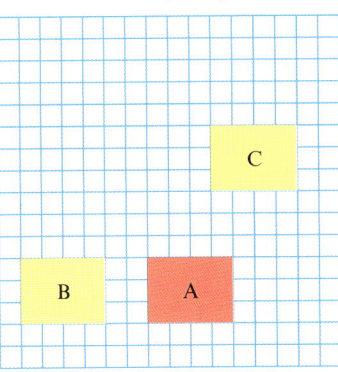

b

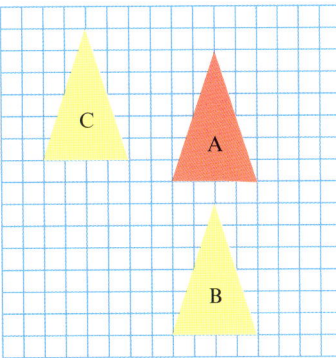

c

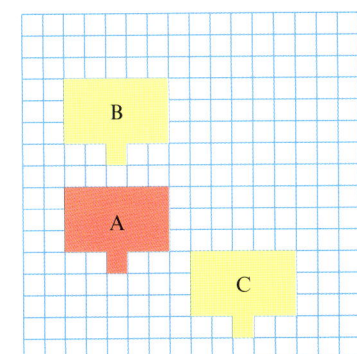

3 Copy the diagram onto squared paper. Translate the triangle ABC:

    a three units to the right and two units down

    b three units to the left and two units down

    c three units up and one unit to the left

    d three units down and four units right.

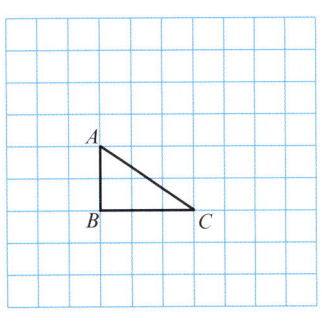

> **TIP**
>
> The phrase 'under the translation $\begin{pmatrix} 2 \\ -3 \end{pmatrix}$' means the same as 'after translating using the vector $\begin{pmatrix} 2 \\ -3 \end{pmatrix}$.

4 On squared paper, draw x- and y-axes and mark the points $A(3, 5)$, $B(2, 1)$ and $C(-1, 4)$.

    a Draw triangle $A'B'C'$, the image of triangle ABC under the translation $\begin{pmatrix} 2 \\ -3 \end{pmatrix}$.

    b Draw triangle $A''B''C''$, the image of ABC under the translation $\begin{pmatrix} 4 \\ 1 \end{pmatrix}$.

5 Triangle XYZ with $X(3, 1)$, $Y(2, 6)$ and $Z(-1, -5)$ is transformed onto triangle $X'Y'Z'$ by a translation of $\begin{pmatrix} 4 \\ -2 \end{pmatrix}$. Determine the coordinates of X', Y' and Z'.

6 A rectangle $MNOP$ with vertices $M(1, 6)$, $N(6, 6)$, $O(6, 3)$ and $P(1, 3)$ is transformed by the translation $\begin{pmatrix} -3 \\ 2 \end{pmatrix}$ to produce rectangle $M'N'O'P'$.

a Represent this translation accurately on a set of axes.

b Give the coordinates of the vertices of the image.

Enlargement

When you enlarge a shape, you make it bigger (or smaller). In an enlargement the lengths of sides on the object are multiplied by a constant scale factor (k) to form the image. The sizes of angles do not change during an enlargement, so the object and its image are similar. To find the scale factor, you use the ratio of corresponding sides on the object and the image:

$$\text{Scale factor} = \frac{\text{image length}}{\text{original length}}$$

MATHEMATICAL CONNECTIONS

'Scale factor' was introduced in Chapter 11. It is the multiplier that tells you how much one shape is larger than another.

If the scale factor is given, you can find the lengths of corresponding sides by multiplication.

This diagram shows a square which has been enlarged by a scale factor of 1.5.

This means that $\dfrac{\text{side } B}{\text{side } A} = 1.5$.

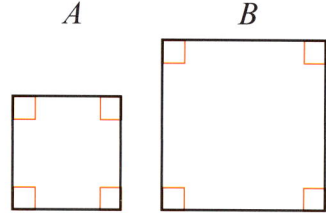

When an object is enlarged from a fixed point, it has a centre of enlargement. The centre of enlargement determines the position of the image. Lines drawn through corresponding points on the object and the image will meet at the centre of enlargement. You can see this in the diagram below.

You can determine the scale factor by comparing any two corresponding sides, for example:

$$\frac{A'B'}{AB} = \frac{2}{1} = 2,$$

or by comparing the distances of two corresponding vertices from the origin, for example:

$$\frac{OC'}{OC} = 2$$

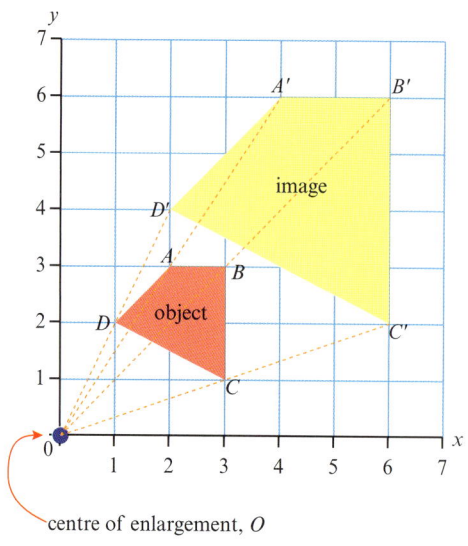

LINK

When you pinch an image on a phone screen to make it bigger you are transforming the image by enlargement.

Properties of enlargement

- The centre of enlargement can be anywhere (inside the object, outside the object or on a vertex or line).

- A scale factor greater than 1 enlarges the object whilst a scale factor between 0 and 1 reduces the size of the object, although this is still described as an enlargement.

- An object and its image are similar (not congruent) with sides in the ratio $1 : k$ where k is the scale factor.

- Angles of the object are invariant.

> **TIP**
>
> Remember, similar shapes are the same shape but not the same size. Congruent shapes are the same size.

WORKED EXAMPLE 5

The figure shows quadrilateral $ABCD$ and its image $A'B'C'D'$ under an enlargement. Find the centre of enlargement and the scale factor.

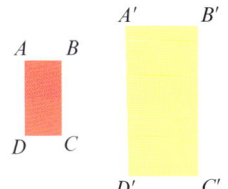

Answer

Join the point A and its image A'.

Extend AA' in both directions. Similarly, draw and extend BB', CC' and DD'.

The point of intersection of these lines is the centre of enlargement, O.

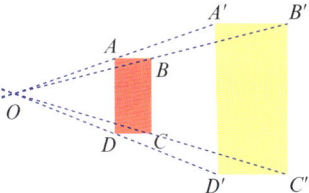

$OA = 25\,\text{mm}$ Measure OA and OA'.

$OA' = 50\,\text{mm}$ OA' is twice as long as OA.

Scale factor $= \dfrac{50}{25} = 2$

WORKED EXAMPLE 6

Draw the image of rectangle $ABCD$ with O as the centre of enlargement and a scale factor of 2.

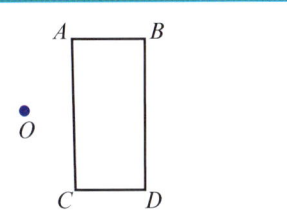

WORKED EXAMPLE 6 CONTINUED

Answer

Join *OA*. Continue (produce) the line beyond *A*.

Measure *OA*.

Multiply the length of *OA* by 2.

Mark the position of *A'* on the produced line so that *OA'* = 2*OA*.

Repeat for the other vertices.

Join *A'B'C'D'*.

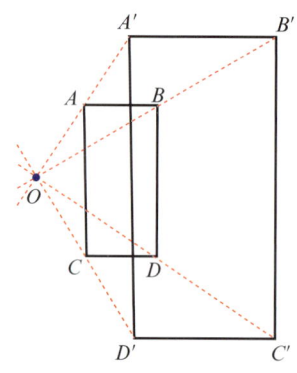

WORKED EXAMPLE 7

Draw *A'B'C'D'*, the image of *ABCD* under an enlargement by a scale factor of $\frac{1}{3}$ through the origin.

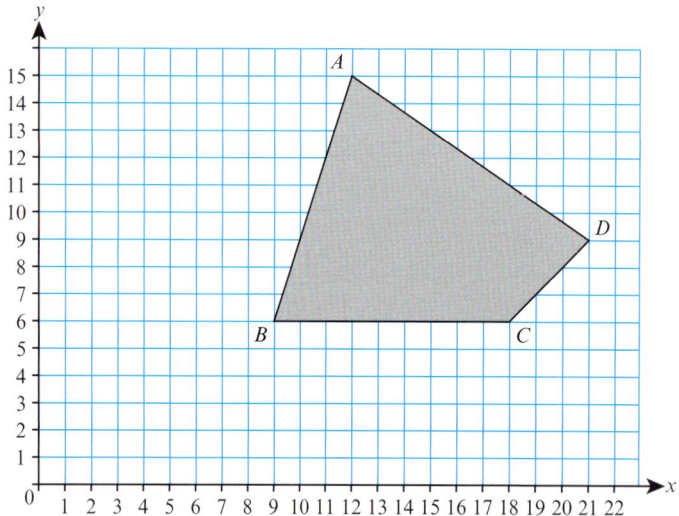

Answer

A scale factor of $\frac{1}{3}$ means the image will be smaller than the object.

Determine the coordinates of each vertex on the image. You can do this by multiplying the (*x*, *y*) coordinates of the vertices on the object by $\frac{1}{3}$.

A = (12, 15), so *A'* = (4, 5)   *B* = (9, 6), so *B'* = (3, 2)

C = (18, 6), so *C'* = (6, 2)   *D* = (21, 9), so *D'* = (7, 3)

Plot the point and draw and label the enlargement.

continued …

TIP

You can also measure the length of the line from the origin to each vertex on the object and divide those lengths by 3 to determine the position of each vertex on the image. This method is useful when the diagram is not on a coordinate grid.

WORKED EXAMPLE 7 CONTINUED

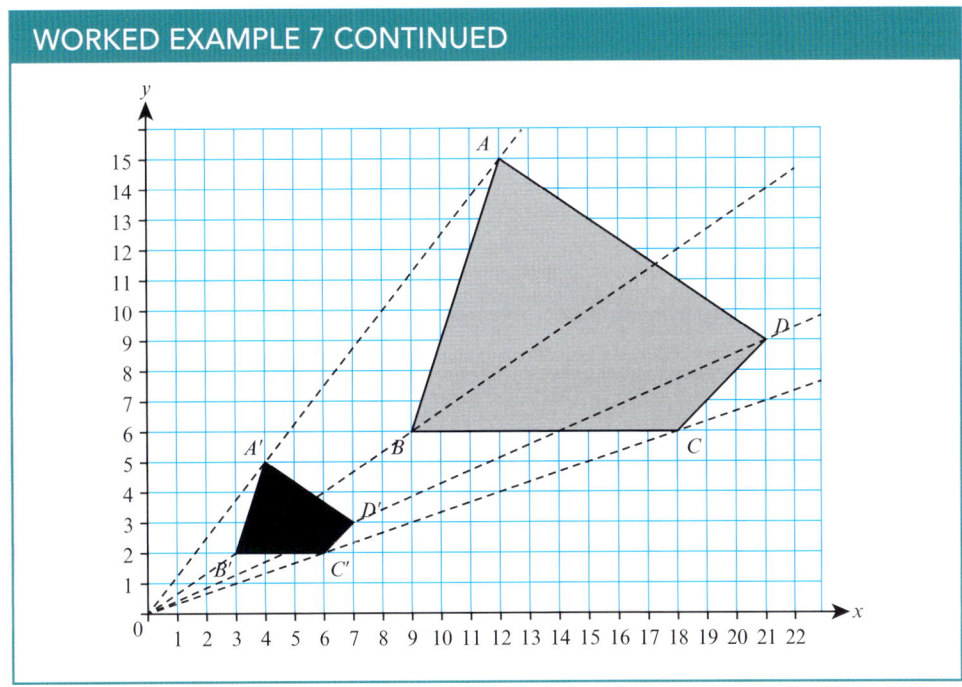

Exercise 23.4

1   For each enlargement, give the coordinates of the centre of enlargement and the
    scale factor of the enlargement.

a

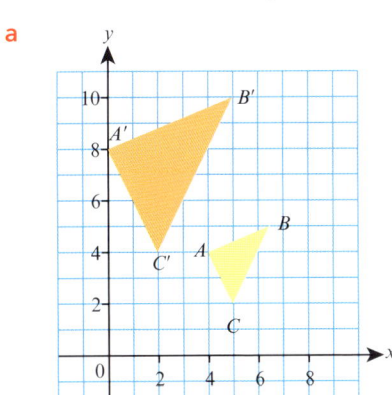

b

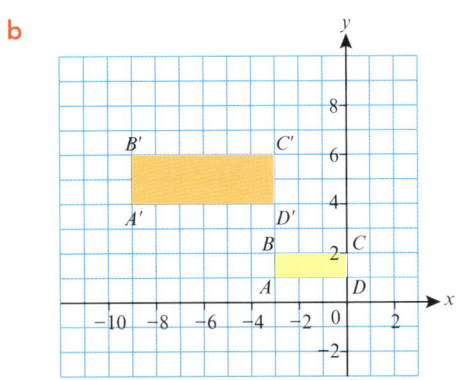

c

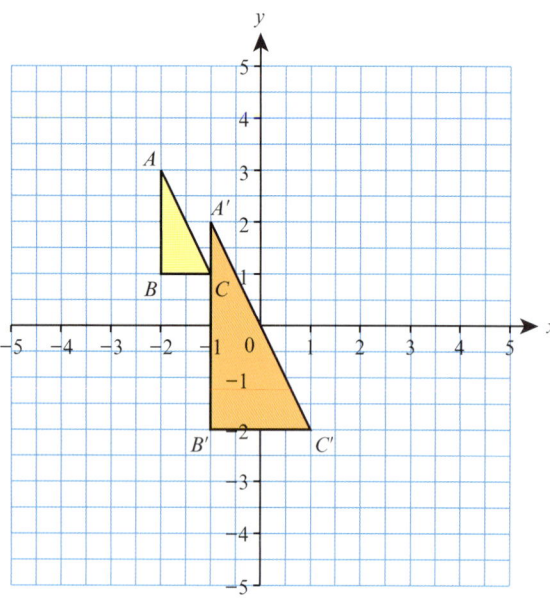

d

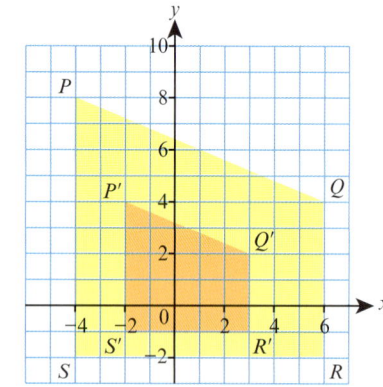

2   Copy the axes and shapes onto squared paper. Using the origin as the centre of enlargement, and a scale factor of 3, draw the image of each shape under enlargement.

a

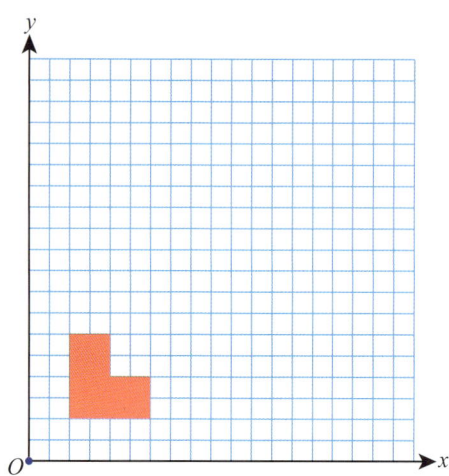

b

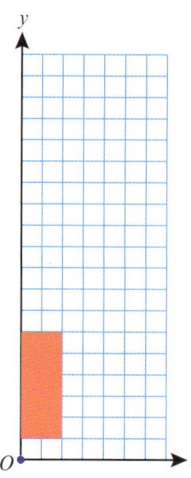

3 Copy the axes and shape onto squared paper. Draw the image of triangle *ABC* under an enlargement by a scale factor of 2 and centre of enlargement *P*(2, 1).

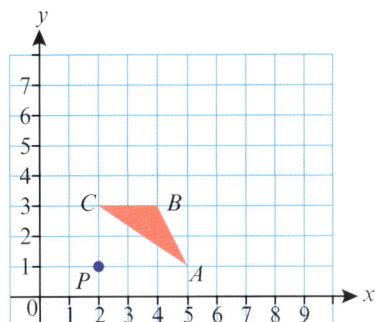

4 Triangle *G'H'I'* is the image of triangle *GHI* under an enlargement. Find the scale factor of the enlargement and the coordinates of the centre of enlargement.

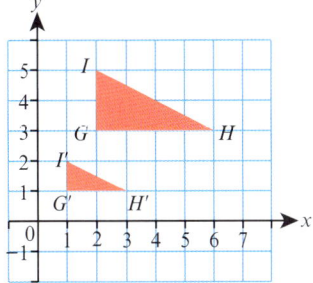

5 In the diagram, square *P'Q'R'S'* is the image of square *PQRS* under an enlargement. Find the scale factor of the enlargement and the coordinates of the centre of enlargement.

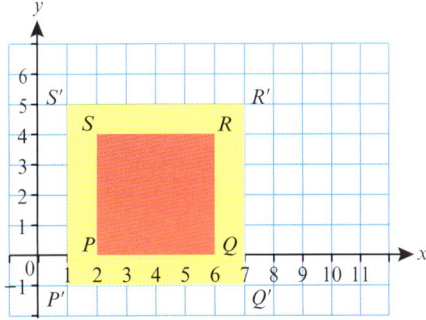

6 Draw the enlargement of object *ABCD* with a scale factor of $\frac{1}{4}$ and centre of enlargement at (0, 0).

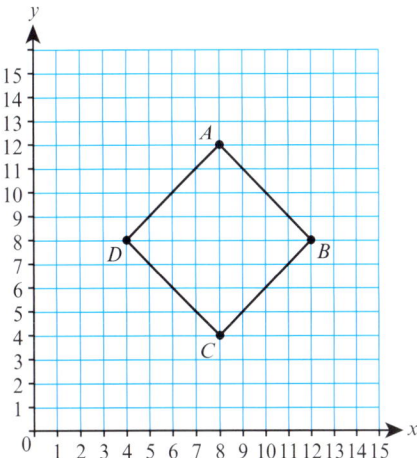

APPLY YOUR SKILLS

7   A designer uses computer software to enlarge and reduce pictures.

   a   A picture is 10 cm long and 6 cm wide. If it is enlarged to be 16 cm long, how wide will it be?

   b   If the designer triples the width of the picture, what will happen to its length?

   c   Is it possible to enlarge the picture by increasing the length and leaving the width the same? Give a reason for your answer.

   d   The designer is asked to reduce the picture so it is a quarter of its original size. What will the new dimensions be?

8   A rectangular painting is 240 mm by 180 mm. The artist wants to make a reduced colour copy of the painting to put into a small silver frame. The display area of the frame is 18 cm by 13.5 cm.

   a   What scale factor should the artist use to make the copy?

   b   How many times smaller is the area of the picture in the frame than the area of the original painting?

INVESTIGATION

9   Look carefully at this design.

   a   Discuss the transformations you can see in the design.

   b   Explain mathematically what you would do to fill in the next row of the pattern.

Work with a partner.

Discuss how you would mark each other's drawn enlargements.

Make a short list of the things you would check to make sure the enlargement was correct.

Use your list to assess your partner's drawing.

Provide feedback telling them what they could improve.

23.2 Further transformations

In addition to the transformations you have already dealt with, you need to be able to reflect an object through any line, rotate an object about any point and use negative scale factors for enlargements. The properties of the object and its image under these transformations are the same as those you already learned.

WORKED EXAMPLE 8

Reflect shape A in the line $y = x$.

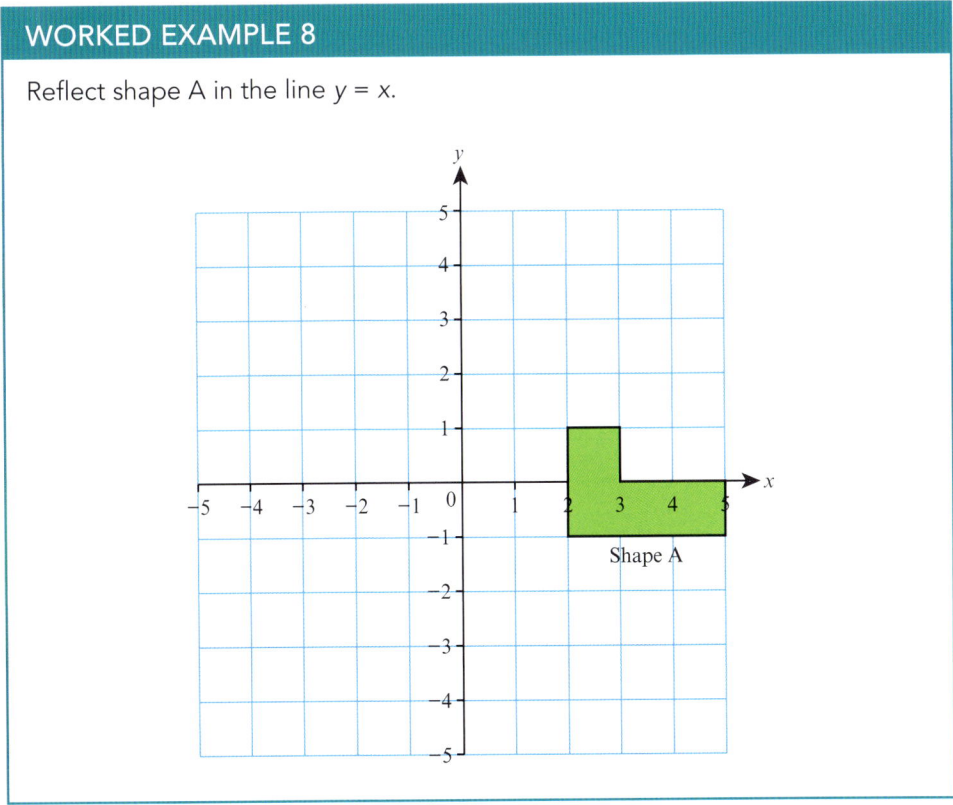

WORKED EXAMPLE 8 CONTINUED

Answer

Draw the line $y = x$.

Apply the rules you know for reflecting shapes to draw the image A'.

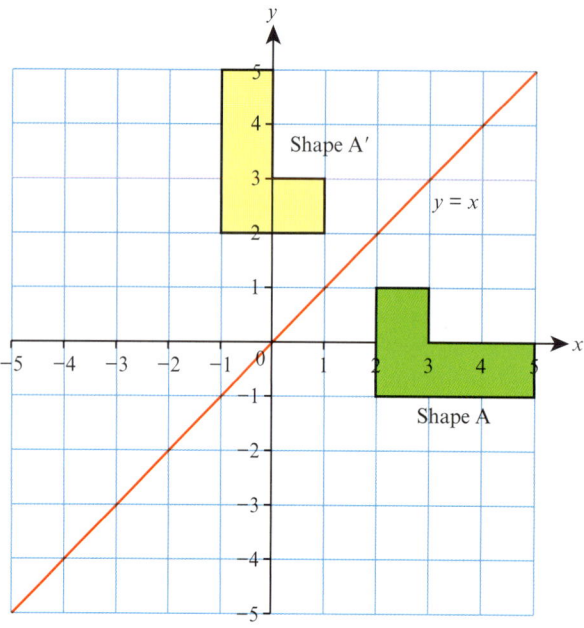

WORKED EXAMPLE 9

Sketch triangle A with vertices at (1, 1), (5, 1) and (5, 4). Rotate this shape 180° about the point (5, 5).

Answer

Plot the points and join them to draw triangle A.

Mark the centre of rotation.

Draw the image and label it A'.

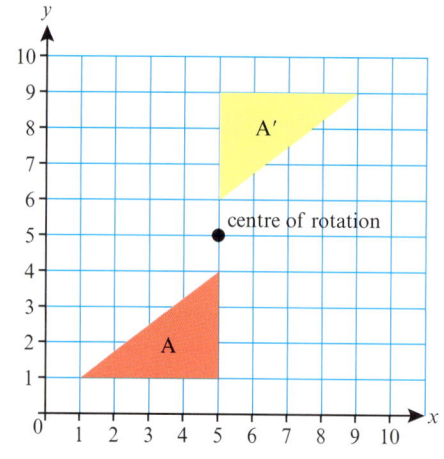

WORKED EXAMPLE 10

Enlarge rectangle *ABCD* by a scale factor of –2 with the origin as a centre of enlargement.

Answer

Multiply each set of coordinates by –2.

A(1, 4), so A'(–2, –8)

B(3, 4), so B' (–6, –8)

C(3, 1), so C'(–6, –2)

D(1, 1), so D'(–2, –2)

Plot the points.

Make sure you label them correctly.

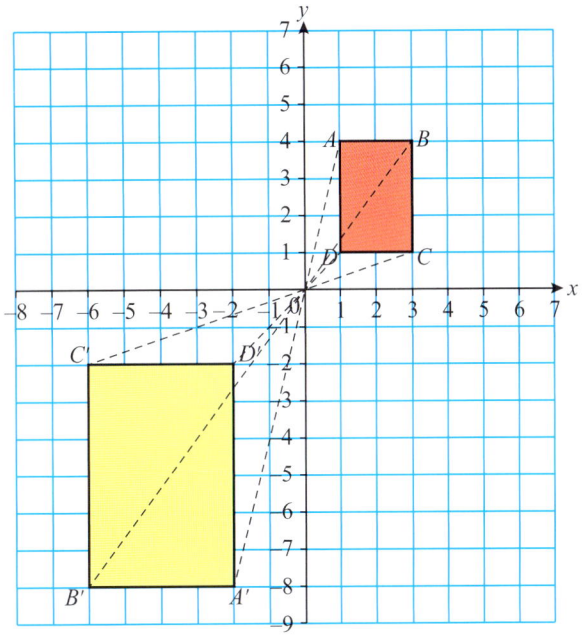

TIP

Drawing in the rays from each vertex allows you to check the points on the image are in line with the corresponding ones on the object.

If a point and its image are on opposite sides of the centre of enlargement, then the scale factor is negative.

Combining transformations

You've already seen that an object can undergo a single transformation to map it to an image. An object can also undergo two transformations in succession. For example, it could be reflected in the *x*-axis and then rotated through a quarter turn, or it could be rotated and then reflected in the *y*-axis. Sometimes a combined transformation can be described by a single, equivalent transformation.

The following capital letters are conventionally used to represent different transformations:

M   Reflection (remember the M is for mirror!)

R   Rotation

T   Translation

E   Enlargement

WORKED EXAMPLE 11

For the shape P shown in the diagram, let T be the translation $\begin{pmatrix} 2 \\ 1 \end{pmatrix}$ and let M be the reflection in the y-axis.

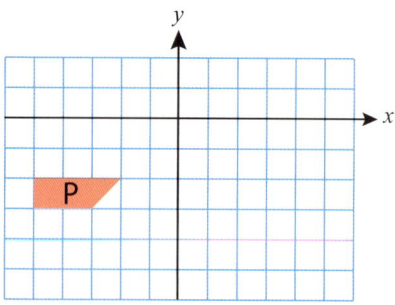

a Draw the image P′ after the transformation MT(P).

b Draw the image P″ after the transformation TM(P).

c What single transformation maps P′ onto P″?

Answer

a MT(P) means do T first then do M.

Use a pencil. Do the first transformation and (faintly) draw the shape. Do the second transformation, draw the image.

Label it correctly.

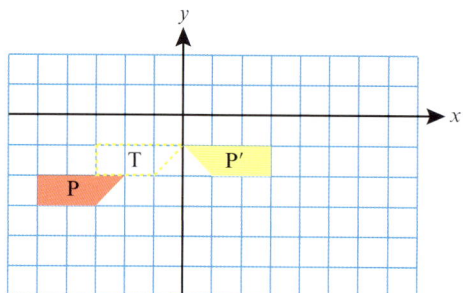

b TM(P) means do M first then do T.

Use a pencil. Do the first transformation and (faintly) draw the shape. Do the second transformation, draw the image.

Label it correctly.

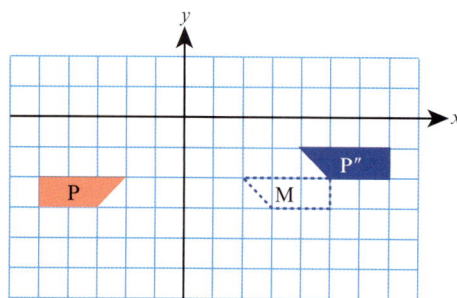

c P′ can be mapped to P″ by the translation $\begin{pmatrix} 4 \\ 0 \end{pmatrix}$.

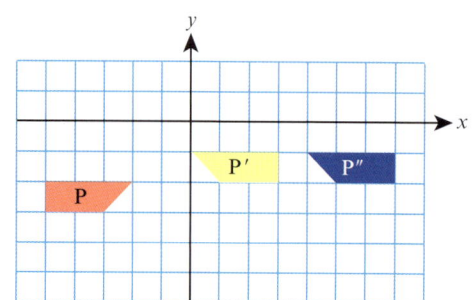

Exercise 23.5

1   For each pair of reflected shapes, give the equation of the mirror line.

   a

   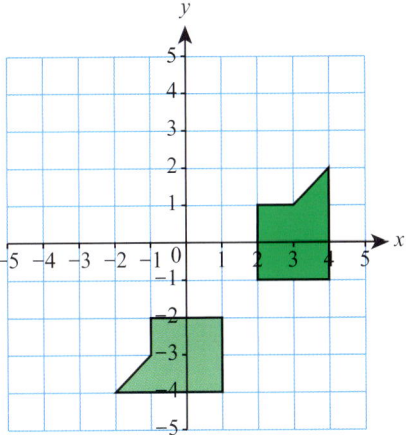

   b

   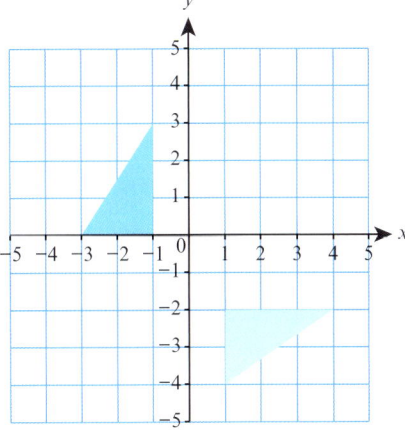

   c

   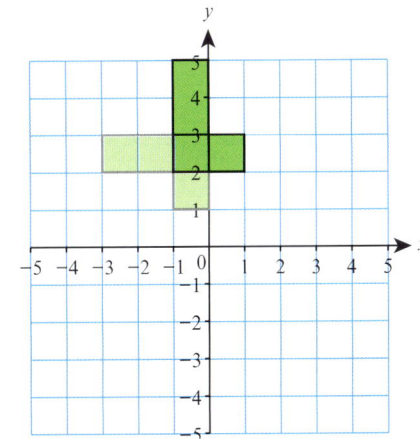

2   Draw each shape on a coordinate grid and perform the given rotation.

   a   Rotate the triangle ABC 90° anticlockwise about the point $(-2, 2)$.

   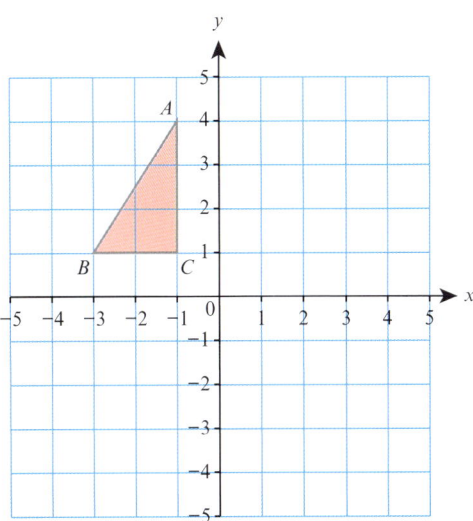

b Rotate object *ABCDEF* 180° about the point (1, −1).

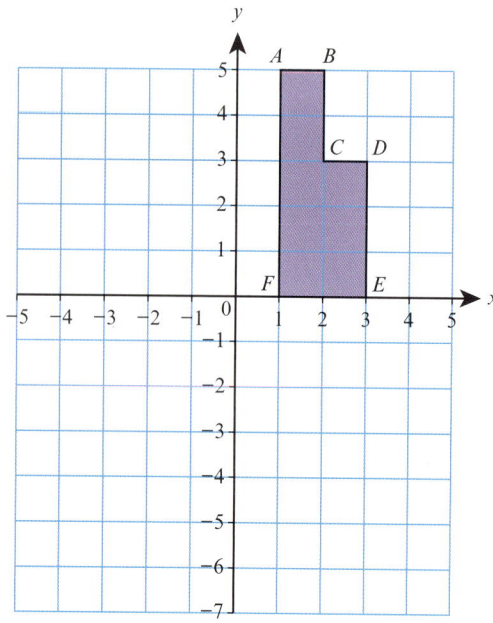

3 Draw the image of each shape under the given transformation on the same set of axes.

a Reflect shape A in the line $y = -x - 2$.

b Rotate shape B 90° anticlockwise around point (2, 4).

c Reflect shape C in the line $y = -3$ and then rotate it 270° clockwise about the point (−1, −1).

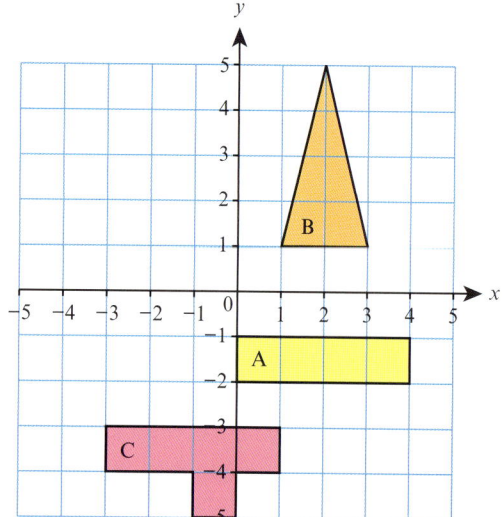

4 Copy the axes and shape onto squared paper. Draw the image of triangle *DEF* under an enlargement with a scale factor of −3 and centre of enlargement *P*(2, 0).

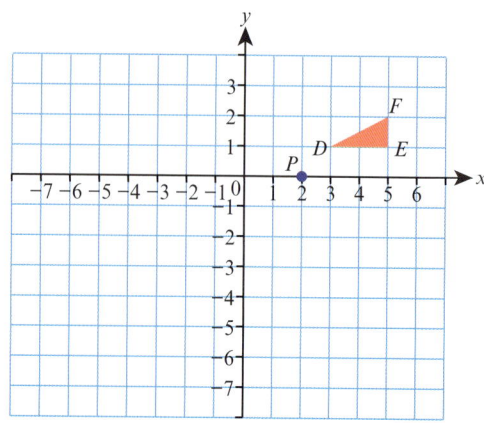

5 Enlarge the given shape by a scale factor of −1. Use the origin as the centre of enlargement.

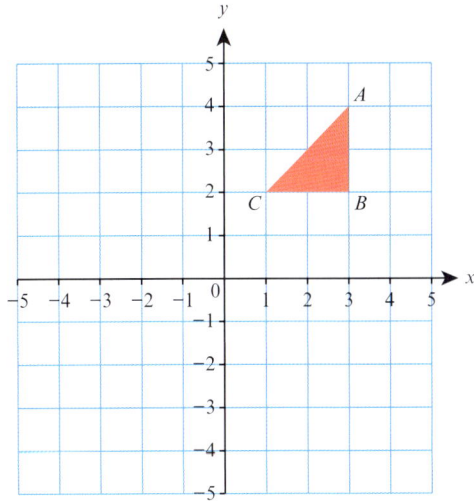

6 Enlarge shape *DEFG* by a scale factor of −2 with (−1, −2) as the centre of enlargement.

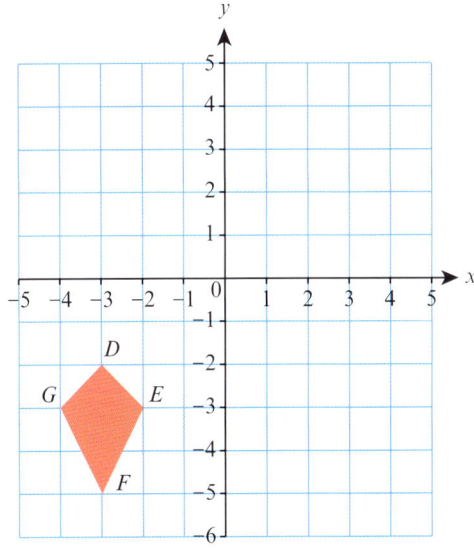

7 Enlarge the object shown by a scale factor of −1.5 using the point (1, 0) as the centre of enlargement.

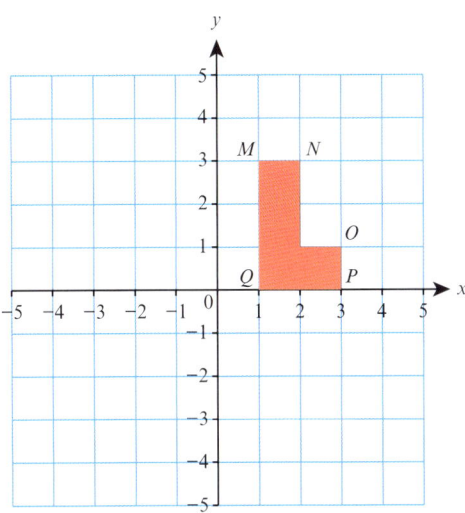

8 Enlarge the shape by a scale factor of $-\frac{1}{2}$ using the origin as the centre of enlargement.

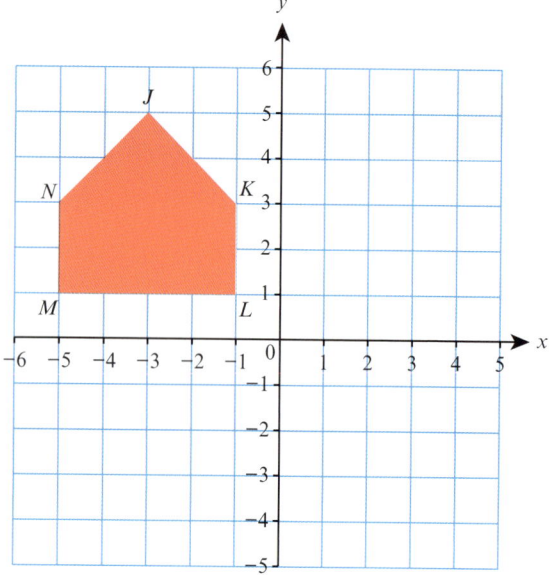

9 Triangle ABC maps onto $A'B'C'$ after an enlargement by a scale factor of 2 from the centre of enlargement (2, 5). $A'B'C'$ is then mapped onto $A''B''C''$ by reflection in the line $x = 1$.

Copy the diagram and draw and label the image:

a $A'B'C'$ b $A''B''C''$.

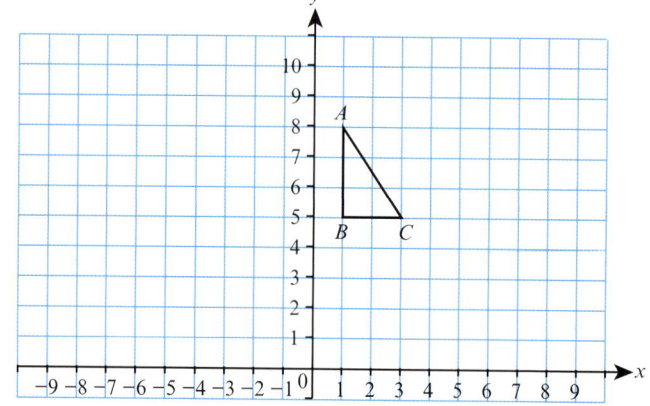

10 A square $MNOP$ maps onto $M'N'O'P'$ after an enlargement by a scale factor of 1.5 with the centre of enlargement (3, 4). $M'N'O'P'$ is then rotated 180° about the point (0, 6) to give the image $M''N''O''P''$. Copy the diagram and show the position of both $M'N'O'P'$ and $M''N''O''P''$.

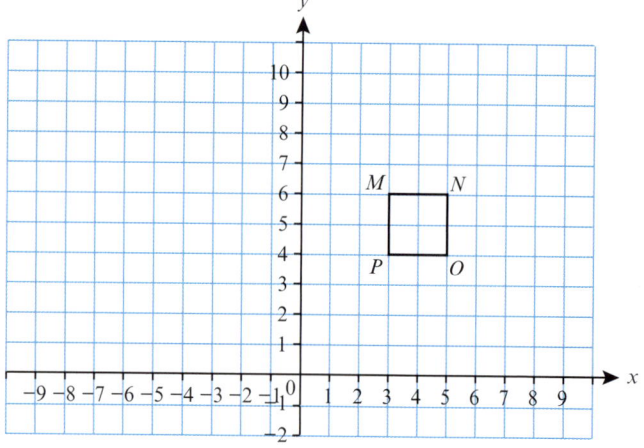

23.3 Vectors

Some quantities are best described by giving both a **magnitude** (size) and a direction. For example, a wind speed of 35 km/h from the southeast or an acceleration upwards of $2\,m/s^2$. Force, velocity, displacement and acceleration are all **vector** quantities.

Other quantities such as time, temperature, speed, mass and area can be described by only giving their magnitude (they don't have a direction). These quantities are called **scalars**.

A vector is an ordered pair of numbers that you can use to describe a translation. The ordered pair gives both magnitude and direction.

Vector notation

Vectors can be represented by a directed line segment as shown in the diagrams. Note that the notation is either a small letter with a wavy line beneath it or a bold letter: e.g. a or **a**.

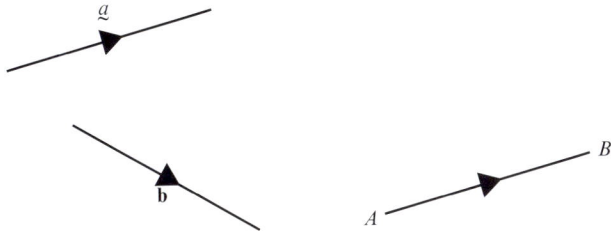

Vectors can also be represented by a named line such as AB. In such cases, the vector is denoted by $\overrightarrow{AB}$. The order of letters is important because they give the direction of the line. $\overrightarrow{AB}$ is not the same as $\overrightarrow{BA}$.

Writing vectors as number pairs

Vectors can also be written as a column vector using number pair notation. Look at line PQ in the diagram.

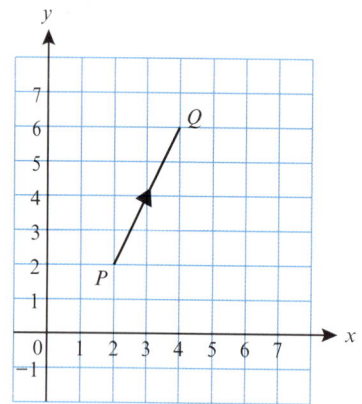

This line represents the translation of P to Q. The translation is two units in the positive x-direction and four units in the positive y-direction. You can write this as the ordered pair $\begin{pmatrix} 2 \\ 4 \end{pmatrix}$.

You can therefore write $\overrightarrow{PQ} = \begin{pmatrix} 2 \\ 4 \end{pmatrix}$.

WORKED EXAMPLE 12

Express $\overrightarrow{RS}$ and $\overrightarrow{LM}$ as column vectors.

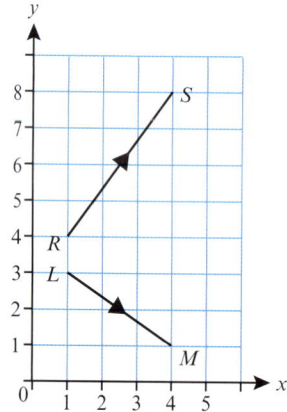

Answer

$\overrightarrow{RS} = \begin{pmatrix} 3 \\ 4 \end{pmatrix}$ Translation from R to S is three units right and four up.

$\overrightarrow{LM} = \begin{pmatrix} 3 \\ -2 \end{pmatrix}$ Translation from L to M is three units right and two down.

WORKED EXAMPLE 13

Draw the column vectors $\begin{pmatrix} 1 \\ 3 \end{pmatrix}$ and $\begin{pmatrix} -2 \\ -4 \end{pmatrix}$.

Answer

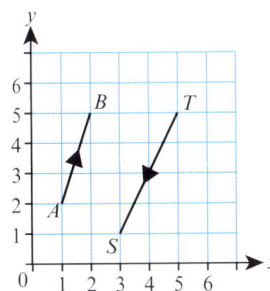

Start at any point, for example A, and move one right and three up to B. Join the points and indicate the direction using an arrow.

Start at any point, for example T, and move two left and then four down to S. Join the points and indicate the direction using an arrow.

Using vectors to describe a translation

You have already seen that column vectors can be used to describe translations.

In this diagram, triangle ABC is translated to triangle $A'B'C'$. All points on the object have moved two units to the right and three units up, so the column vector that describes this translation is $\begin{pmatrix} 2 \\ 3 \end{pmatrix}$.

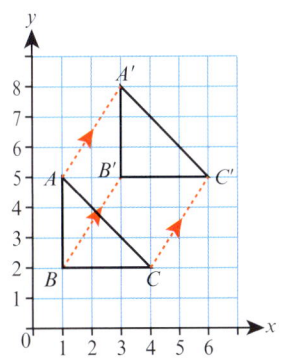

WORKED EXAMPLE 14

Square R is translated to square S.
Find the column vector for the translation.

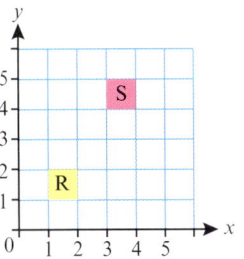

Answer

The column vector is $\begin{pmatrix} 2 \\ 3 \end{pmatrix}$.

Use one vertex of the object and the same vertex in its image to work out the translation.

Exercise 23.6

1   Write a column vector for each of the vectors shown on the diagram.

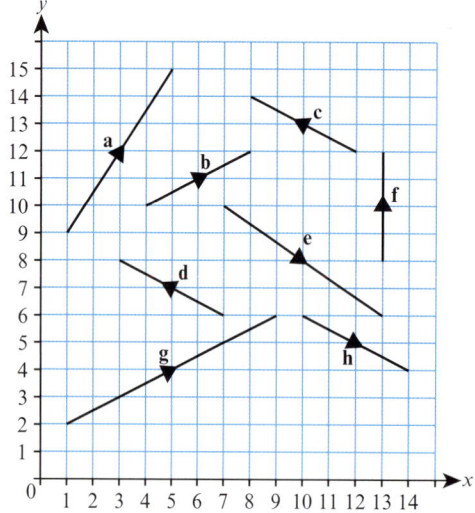

2   Represent these vectors on squared paper.

a $\overrightarrow{AB} = \begin{pmatrix} 5 \\ 2 \end{pmatrix}$ b $\overrightarrow{CD} = \begin{pmatrix} 2 \\ 2 \end{pmatrix}$ c $\overrightarrow{PQ} = \begin{pmatrix} -1 \\ 3 \end{pmatrix}$ d $\overrightarrow{RS} = \begin{pmatrix} 0 \\ 3 \end{pmatrix}$

e $\overrightarrow{TU} = \begin{pmatrix} -2 \\ 0 \end{pmatrix}$ f $\overrightarrow{MN} = \begin{pmatrix} -2 \\ -4 \end{pmatrix}$ g $\overrightarrow{KL} = \begin{pmatrix} 0 \\ -5 \end{pmatrix}$ h $\overrightarrow{VW} = \begin{pmatrix} -3 \\ -3 \end{pmatrix}$

i $\overrightarrow{EF} = \begin{pmatrix} 4 \\ 0 \end{pmatrix}$ j $\overrightarrow{JL} = \begin{pmatrix} -3 \\ -2 \end{pmatrix}$ k $\overrightarrow{MP} = \begin{pmatrix} -5 \\ 0 \end{pmatrix}$ l $\overrightarrow{QT} = \begin{pmatrix} -4 \\ 2 \end{pmatrix}$

3   In the diagram, $ABCD$ is a parallelogram.

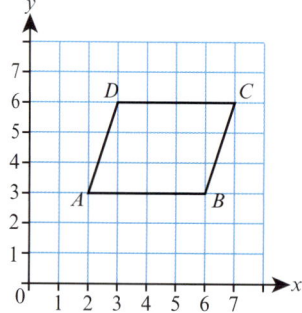

a   Write column vectors for the following:

   i $\overrightarrow{AB}$ and $\overrightarrow{DC}$

   ii $\overrightarrow{BC}$ and $\overrightarrow{AD}$.

b   What can you say about the two pairs
    of vectors?

4   In the diagrams below, shapes A, B, C, D, E and F are mapped onto images A′,
    B′, C′, D′, E′ and F′ by translation. Find the column vector for the translation in
    each case.

a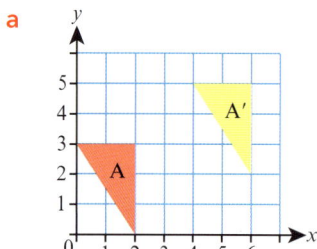

b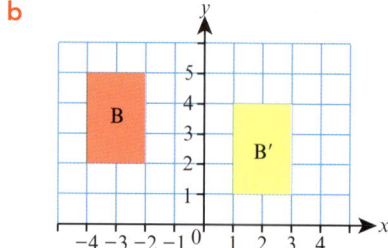

c

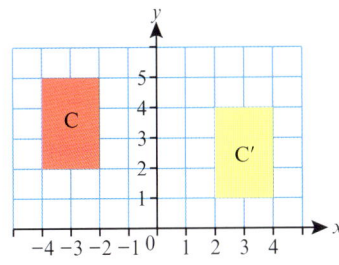

d

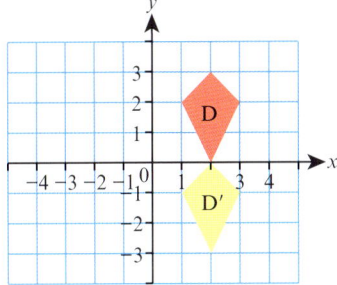

e

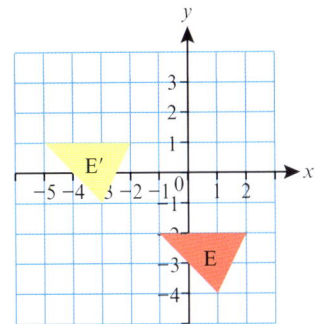

f

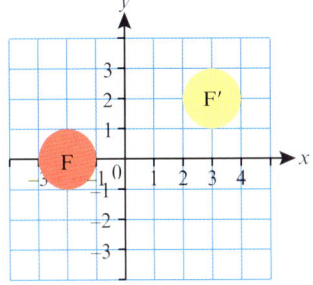

Equal vectors

Equal vectors have the same size (magnitude) and direction. As vectors are usually independent of position, they can start at any point. The same vector can be at many places in a diagram.

In the diagram, $\overrightarrow{AB}$, $\overrightarrow{CD}$, $\overrightarrow{XY}$, $\overrightarrow{LM}$ and $\overrightarrow{RS}$ are equal vectors.

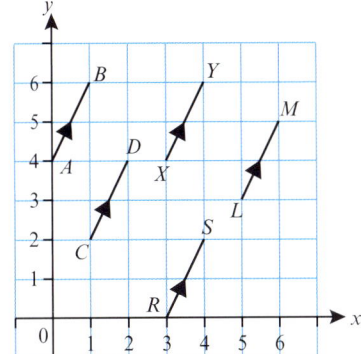

$$\overrightarrow{AB} = \overrightarrow{CD} = \overrightarrow{XY} = \overrightarrow{LM} = \overrightarrow{RS} = \begin{pmatrix} 1 \\ 2 \end{pmatrix}$$

When equal vectors share a common point, for example when $\overrightarrow{AB} = \overrightarrow{BC}$ you can deduce that that the points A, B and C all lie on a straight line. When points lie on a straight line, they are collinear.

Multiplying a vector by a scalar

Look at the diagram. Vector $\overrightarrow{AC}$ is twice as long as vector $\overrightarrow{AB}$.

You can say:

$\overrightarrow{AC} = 2\overrightarrow{AB} = 2\begin{pmatrix} 2 \\ 1 \end{pmatrix} = \begin{pmatrix} 4 \\ 2 \end{pmatrix}.$

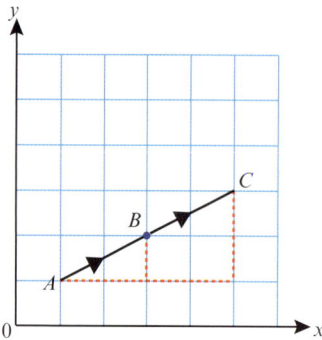

Here is another example.

A force, represented by vector **f**, is needed to move a 1 kg concrete block.

If you want to move a 2 kg concrete block, you need to apply twice the force. In other words, you would need to apply **f** + **f** or 2**f**.

A force of 2**f** has the same direction as **f**, but it has twice its magnitude.

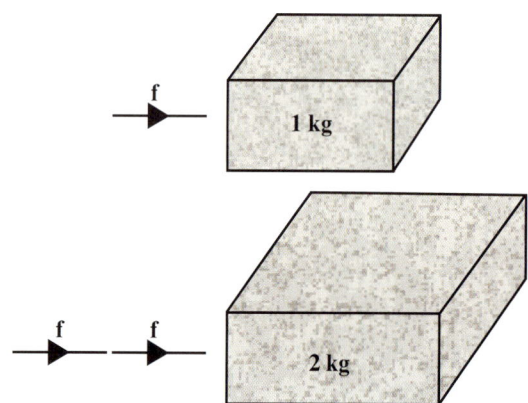

Multiplying any vector $\begin{pmatrix} x \\ y \end{pmatrix}$ by a scalar k, gives $k\begin{pmatrix} x \\ y \end{pmatrix} = \begin{pmatrix} kx \\ ky \end{pmatrix}.$

Vector **a** multiplied by 2 is the vector 2**a**. Vector 2**a** is twice as long as vector **a**, but they have the same direction. In other words, they are either parallel or in a straight line.

If $\mathbf{a} = \begin{pmatrix} 3 \\ 2 \end{pmatrix}$ then $2\mathbf{a} = 2\begin{pmatrix} 3 \\ 2 \end{pmatrix} = \begin{pmatrix} 6 \\ 4 \end{pmatrix}.$

Vector **a** multiplied by −1 is the vector −**a**, which is opposite in direction to **a**, but with the same magnitude as **a**.

WORKED EXAMPLE 15

If $\mathbf{u} = \begin{pmatrix} 8 \\ -4 \end{pmatrix}$, find $\frac{1}{4}\mathbf{u}$.

Answer

$$\frac{1}{4}\mathbf{u} = \frac{1}{4}\begin{pmatrix} 8 \\ -4 \end{pmatrix} = \begin{pmatrix} \frac{1}{4} \times 8 \\ \frac{1}{4} \times -4 \end{pmatrix} = \begin{pmatrix} 2 \\ -1 \end{pmatrix}$$

> **TIP**
>
> When k is positive, $k\mathbf{a}$ is in the same direction as $\mathbf{a}$ and k times as long. When k is negative, then $k\mathbf{a}$ is opposite in direction to $\mathbf{a}$ but still k times as long.

WORKED EXAMPLE 16

If $\mathbf{v} = \begin{pmatrix} -3 \\ 2 \end{pmatrix}$, find $-5\mathbf{v}$.

Answer

$$-5\mathbf{v} = -5\begin{pmatrix} -3 \\ 2 \end{pmatrix} = \begin{pmatrix} -5 \times -3 \\ -5 \times 2 \end{pmatrix} = \begin{pmatrix} 15 \\ -10 \end{pmatrix}$$

Exercise 23.7

1   If $\mathbf{a} = \begin{pmatrix} 3 \\ -7 \end{pmatrix}$, calculate:

    a $3\mathbf{a}$ **b** $\frac{1}{2}\mathbf{a}$ **c** $-2\mathbf{a}$ **d** $-\mathbf{a}$ **e** $-\frac{3}{4}\mathbf{a}$ **f** $1.5\mathbf{a}$

APPLY YOUR SKILLS

2   The diagram shows a rectangular metal burglar bar. Each section of the burglar bar can be represented by a vector. Sections can also be compared in terms of vectors. So, for example, $\overrightarrow{AJ} = 3\overrightarrow{AD}$. Copy and complete these comparisons:

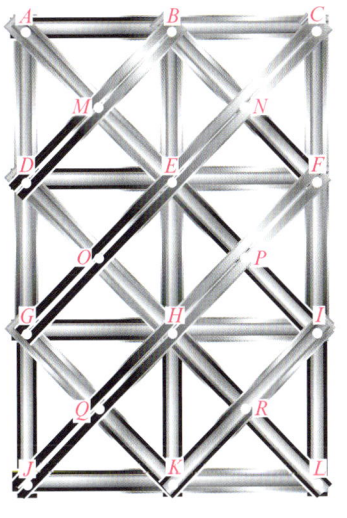

    a $\overrightarrow{DF} = \underline{}\overrightarrow{JK}$ **b** $\overrightarrow{JQ} = \underline{}\overrightarrow{JF}$

    c $\overrightarrow{HP} = \underline{}\overrightarrow{HF}$ **d** $2\overrightarrow{GO} = \underline{}\overrightarrow{GC}$

    e $3\overrightarrow{DG} = \underline{}\overrightarrow{CL}$ **f** $6\overrightarrow{BE} = \underline{}\overrightarrow{CL}$

> **TIP**
>
> Given that $\overrightarrow{AJ} = 3\overrightarrow{AD}$ and A is common to both vectors, points A, D and J are collinear.

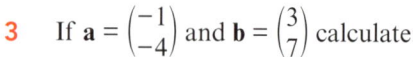
3 If $\mathbf{a} = \begin{pmatrix} -1 \\ -4 \end{pmatrix}$ and $\mathbf{b} = \begin{pmatrix} 3 \\ 7 \end{pmatrix}$ calculate:

a $-2\mathbf{a}$

b $3\mathbf{b}$

c $\frac{3}{2}\mathbf{b}$

d $-\frac{3}{4}\mathbf{a}$

e $-1.5\mathbf{a}$

f $-12\mathbf{b}$

g $-\frac{3}{2}\mathbf{a}$

h $-\frac{5}{9}\mathbf{b}$

Adding vectors

In the diagram, point A is translated to point B and then translated again to end up at point C. However, if you translated the point directly from A to C, you end up at the same point. In other words, $\overrightarrow{AB} + \overrightarrow{BC} = \overrightarrow{AC}$.

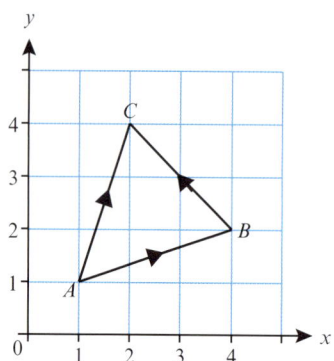

You can represent each translation as a column vector:

$$\overrightarrow{AB} = \begin{pmatrix} 3 \\ 1 \end{pmatrix}, \quad \overrightarrow{BC} = \begin{pmatrix} -2 \\ 2 \end{pmatrix}, \quad \overrightarrow{AC} = \begin{pmatrix} 1 \\ 3 \end{pmatrix}$$

You know that $\overrightarrow{AB} + \overrightarrow{BC} = \overrightarrow{AC}$, so:

$$\begin{pmatrix} 3 \\ 1 \end{pmatrix} + \begin{pmatrix} -2 \\ 2 \end{pmatrix} = \begin{pmatrix} 1 \\ 3 \end{pmatrix}$$

So, to add the vectors, you add the corresponding x- and y-coordinates:

$$\begin{pmatrix} x_1 \\ y_1 \end{pmatrix} + \begin{pmatrix} x_2 \\ y_2 \end{pmatrix} = \begin{pmatrix} x_1 + x_2 \\ y_1 + y_2 \end{pmatrix}$$

This is called the 'nose to tail' method or the triangle law.

LINK

Airline pilots need to consider vectors when landing in a crosswind. The plane can be controlled to move relative to the air, but the air is often also moving in a different direction relative to the ground. The combination of the aircraft and air velocities is important when the pilot determines how to steer the aircraft onto a runway.

Subtracting vectors

Think again about the three vectors:

$$\overrightarrow{AB} = \begin{pmatrix} 3 \\ 1 \end{pmatrix}, \quad \overrightarrow{BC} = \begin{pmatrix} -2 \\ 2 \end{pmatrix}, \quad \overrightarrow{AC} = \begin{pmatrix} 1 \\ 3 \end{pmatrix}$$

Subtracting a vector is the same as adding its negative, so:

$$\overrightarrow{AC} - \overrightarrow{AB} = \overrightarrow{AC} + \left(-\overrightarrow{AB} \right)$$

The diagram shows the result of adding $\overrightarrow{AC}$ and $-\overrightarrow{AB}$ 'nose to tail'. This shows that vector $\overrightarrow{AC} - \overrightarrow{AB}$ is the same as vector $\overrightarrow{BC}$.

So, $\overrightarrow{AC} - \overrightarrow{AB} = \overrightarrow{BC}$

$$\begin{pmatrix} 1 \\ 3 \end{pmatrix} - \begin{pmatrix} 3 \\ 1 \end{pmatrix} = \begin{pmatrix} -2 \\ 2 \end{pmatrix}$$

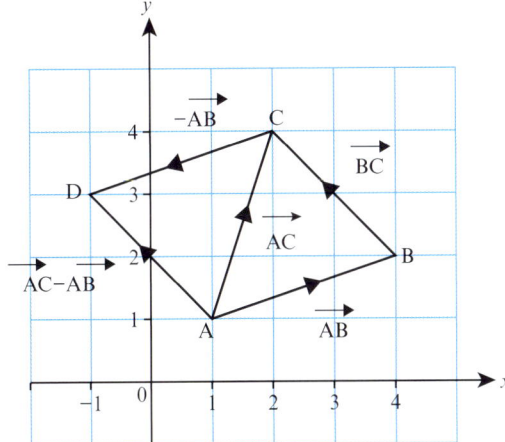

To subtract the vectors, you subtract the corresponding x- and y-coordinates:

$$\begin{pmatrix} x_1 \\ y_1 \end{pmatrix} - \begin{pmatrix} x_2 \\ y_2 \end{pmatrix} = \begin{pmatrix} x_1 \\ y_1 \end{pmatrix} + \begin{pmatrix} -x_2 \\ -y_2 \end{pmatrix} = \begin{pmatrix} x_1 - x_2 \\ y_1 - y_2 \end{pmatrix}$$

> **TIP**
>
> You could also use the fact that vector $-\overrightarrow{AB}$ is the same size as $\overrightarrow{AB}$ but in the opposite direction, so $-\overrightarrow{AB} = \overrightarrow{BA}$.
>
> This means that $\overrightarrow{AC} - \overrightarrow{AB} = \overrightarrow{AC} + \overrightarrow{BA}$
>
> If you rearrange the vectors, you can apply the nose to tail rule method and add them:
>
> $$\overrightarrow{AC} - \overrightarrow{AB} = \overrightarrow{BA} + \overrightarrow{AC} = \overrightarrow{BC}$$

WORKED EXAMPLE 17

In the figure, the various line segments represent vectors.

Find in the figure directed line segments equal to the following:

a $\overrightarrow{AE} + \overrightarrow{EC}$

b $\overrightarrow{DB} + \overrightarrow{BE}$

c $\overrightarrow{AD} + \overrightarrow{DB} + \overrightarrow{BC}$

d $\overrightarrow{CB} + \overrightarrow{BE} + \overrightarrow{EA} + \overrightarrow{AD}$

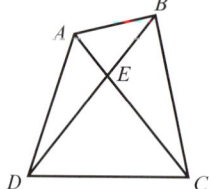

TIP

Any section of a line joining two points is called a line segment.

Answers

a $\overrightarrow{AE} + \overrightarrow{EC} = \overrightarrow{AC}$

b $\overrightarrow{DB} + \overrightarrow{BE} = \overrightarrow{DE}$ (If you travel from D to B and then from B to E, you have gone back on yourself and ended up at E, which is the same as travelling from D to E.)

c $\overrightarrow{AD} + \overrightarrow{DB} + \overrightarrow{BC} = \overrightarrow{AC}$ ($\overrightarrow{AD} + \overrightarrow{DB} = \overrightarrow{AB}$ and $\overrightarrow{AB} + \overrightarrow{BC} = \overrightarrow{AC}$

$\therefore \overrightarrow{AD} + \overrightarrow{DB} + \overrightarrow{BC} = \overrightarrow{AC}$)

d $\overrightarrow{CB} + \overrightarrow{BE} + \overrightarrow{EA} + \overrightarrow{AD} = \overrightarrow{CE} + \overrightarrow{EA} + \overrightarrow{AD} = \overrightarrow{CA} + \overrightarrow{AD} = \overrightarrow{CD}$

WORKED EXAMPLE 18

If $\mathbf{a} = \begin{pmatrix} 3 \\ 4 \end{pmatrix}$ and $\mathbf{b} = \begin{pmatrix} 2 \\ -1 \end{pmatrix}$ find the column vectors equal to:

a $\mathbf{a} + \mathbf{b}$ b $\mathbf{a} - \mathbf{b}$ c $3\mathbf{a}$ d $\mathbf{a} + 4\mathbf{b}$ e $2\mathbf{a} - 3\mathbf{b}$

Answers

a $\mathbf{a} + \mathbf{b} = \begin{pmatrix} 3 \\ 4 \end{pmatrix} + \begin{pmatrix} 2 \\ -1 \end{pmatrix} = \begin{pmatrix} 3 + 2 \\ 4 - 1 \end{pmatrix} = \begin{pmatrix} 5 \\ 3 \end{pmatrix}$

b $\mathbf{a} - \mathbf{b} = \begin{pmatrix} 3 \\ 4 \end{pmatrix} - \begin{pmatrix} 2 \\ -1 \end{pmatrix} = \begin{pmatrix} 3 - 2 \\ 4 + 1 \end{pmatrix} = \begin{pmatrix} 1 \\ 5 \end{pmatrix}$

c $3\mathbf{a} = 3\begin{pmatrix} 3 \\ 4 \end{pmatrix} = \begin{pmatrix} 3 \times 3 \\ 3 \times 4 \end{pmatrix} = \begin{pmatrix} 9 \\ 12 \end{pmatrix}$

d $\mathbf{a} + 4\mathbf{b} = \begin{pmatrix} 3 \\ 4 \end{pmatrix} + 4\begin{pmatrix} 2 \\ -1 \end{pmatrix} = \begin{pmatrix} 3 + 8 \\ 4 + (-4) \end{pmatrix} = \begin{pmatrix} 11 \\ 0 \end{pmatrix}$

e $2\mathbf{a} - 3\mathbf{b} = 2\begin{pmatrix} 3 \\ 4 \end{pmatrix} - 3\begin{pmatrix} 2 \\ -1 \end{pmatrix} = \begin{pmatrix} 6 \\ 8 \end{pmatrix} - \begin{pmatrix} 6 \\ -3 \end{pmatrix} = \begin{pmatrix} 0 \\ 11 \end{pmatrix}$

WORKED EXAMPLE 19

$OACB$ is a parallelogram in which
$\overrightarrow{OA}$ = **a** and $\overrightarrow{OB}$ = **b**.

M is the midpoint of BC and N is the
midpoint of AC.

a   Find in terms of **a** and **b**:

   i $\overrightarrow{OM}$ **ii** $\overrightarrow{MN}$

b   Show that $\overrightarrow{OM} + \overrightarrow{MN} = \overrightarrow{OA} + \overrightarrow{AN}$.

Answers

a   **i** $\overrightarrow{OM} = \overrightarrow{OB} + \overrightarrow{BM}$

   $\overrightarrow{OB}$ = **b**

   M is the midpoint of BC, so $\overrightarrow{BM} = \frac{1}{2}\overrightarrow{BC} = \frac{1}{2}\mathbf{a}$

   $\therefore \overrightarrow{OM} = \mathbf{b} + \frac{1}{2}\mathbf{a}$

   ii $\overrightarrow{MN} = \overrightarrow{MC} + \overrightarrow{CN} = \frac{1}{2}\overrightarrow{BC} + \frac{1}{2}\overrightarrow{CA}$

   $\frac{1}{2}\overrightarrow{BC} = \frac{1}{2}\mathbf{a}$ and $\frac{1}{2}\overrightarrow{CA} = -\frac{1}{2}\overrightarrow{AC} = -\frac{1}{2}\overrightarrow{OB} = -\frac{1}{2}\mathbf{b}$

   So, $\frac{1}{2}\overrightarrow{BC} + \frac{1}{2}\overrightarrow{CA} = \frac{1}{2}\mathbf{a} - \frac{1}{2}\mathbf{b}$

   $\qquad\qquad\qquad = \frac{1}{2}(\mathbf{a} - \mathbf{b})$

b $\overrightarrow{OM} + \overrightarrow{MN} = \left(\mathbf{b} + \frac{1}{2}\mathbf{a}\right) + \left(\frac{1}{2}\mathbf{a} - \frac{1}{2}\mathbf{b}\right)$

   $= \mathbf{a} + \frac{1}{2}\mathbf{b}$

   $\overrightarrow{OA} + \overrightarrow{AN} = \mathbf{a} + \frac{1}{2}\mathbf{b}$

   $\therefore \overrightarrow{OM} + \overrightarrow{MN} = \overrightarrow{OA} + \overrightarrow{AN}$

WORKED EXAMPLE 20

Show that points $P(2, 4)$, $Q(8, 6)$ and $R(11, 7)$ are collinear.

Answers

$\overrightarrow{PQ} = \mathbf{q} - \mathbf{p}$ $\overrightarrow{QR} = \mathbf{r} - \mathbf{q}$

$= \begin{pmatrix} 8 \\ 6 \end{pmatrix} - \begin{pmatrix} 2 \\ 4 \end{pmatrix} = \begin{pmatrix} 6 \\ 2 \end{pmatrix}$ $= \begin{pmatrix} 11 \\ 7 \end{pmatrix} - \begin{pmatrix} 8 \\ 6 \end{pmatrix} = \begin{pmatrix} 3 \\ 1 \end{pmatrix}$

But $\begin{pmatrix} 6 \\ 2 \end{pmatrix} = 2\begin{pmatrix} 3 \\ 1 \end{pmatrix}$, so $\overrightarrow{PQ} = 2\overrightarrow{QR}$ and $\overrightarrow{PQ}$ is parallel to $\overrightarrow{QR}$.

Point Q is common to $\overrightarrow{PQ}$ and $\overrightarrow{QR}$, so P, Q and R are collinear.

Exercise 23.8

1 $\mathbf{p} = \begin{pmatrix} 4 \\ -2 \end{pmatrix}$ and $\mathbf{q} = \begin{pmatrix} -1 \\ -3 \end{pmatrix}$.

Express in column vector form:

a $3\mathbf{p}$ b $\mathbf{p} + \mathbf{q}$

2 Given that $\mathbf{a} = \begin{pmatrix} 4 \\ -2 \end{pmatrix}$ and $\mathbf{b} = \begin{pmatrix} -4 \\ 3 \end{pmatrix}$, express $2\mathbf{a} - \mathbf{b}$ as a column vector.

3 If $\mathbf{a} = \begin{pmatrix} 8 \\ 10 \end{pmatrix}$, $\mathbf{b} = \begin{pmatrix} 4 \\ -2 \end{pmatrix}$ and $\mathbf{c} = \begin{pmatrix} 0 \\ -1 \end{pmatrix}$, calculate:

a $\mathbf{a} + \mathbf{b}$ b $2\mathbf{a} - 2\mathbf{b}$ c $\mathbf{b} - \mathbf{a}$ d $\frac{1}{2}\mathbf{b} - \mathbf{c}$

e $\mathbf{a} - 2(\mathbf{b} - \mathbf{c})$ f $2\mathbf{a} - \mathbf{c}$ g $\frac{1}{2}(2\mathbf{a} + \mathbf{b})$ h $\mathbf{c} + \frac{1}{2}(\mathbf{b} - \mathbf{a})$

4 *OACB* is a parallelogram in which

$\overrightarrow{OA} = 2\mathbf{p}$ and $\overrightarrow{OB} = 2\mathbf{q}$.

M is the midpoint of *BC* and *N* is the midpoint of *AC*.

Find in terms of **p** and **q**:

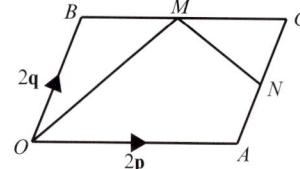

a $\overrightarrow{AB}$ b $\overrightarrow{ON}$ c $\overrightarrow{MN}$

5 In triangle *XYZ*, $\overrightarrow{XY} = \mathbf{x}$ and $\overrightarrow{YZ} = \mathbf{y}$ and $WZ = \frac{1}{4}(XZ)$.
Find in terms of **x** and **y**:

a $\overrightarrow{XZ}$ b $\overrightarrow{XW}$ c $\overrightarrow{YW}$

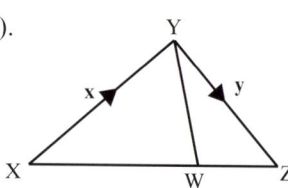

6 In the diagram, *BCE* and *ACD* are straight lines.

$\overrightarrow{AB} = 2\mathbf{a}$ and $\overrightarrow{BC} = 3\mathbf{b}$. The point *C* divides *AD* in the ratio $2 : 1$ and divides *BE* in the ratio $3 : 1$.
Express the following vectors in terms of **a** and **b**.

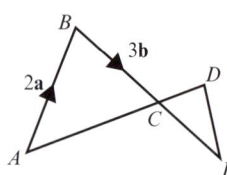

a $\overrightarrow{AC}$ b $\overrightarrow{CD}$ c $\overrightarrow{CE}$ d $\overrightarrow{ED}$

TIP

Remember: success criteria are sometimes called 'what I'm looking for'.

The magnitude of a vector

The magnitude of a vector is its length. You use the notation $|\overrightarrow{AB}|$ or $|\mathbf{a}|$ to write the magnitude of a vector ($\overrightarrow{AB}$).

You can use Pythagoras' theorem to calculate the magnitude of a vector.

In general, if $\overrightarrow{AB} = \begin{pmatrix} x \\ y \end{pmatrix}$ then $|\overrightarrow{AB}| = \sqrt{x^2 + y^2}$.

TIP

The magnitude of a vector is sometimes called the modulus.

WORKED EXAMPLE 21

Find the magnitude of the vector $\overrightarrow{AB} = \begin{pmatrix} 3 \\ -4 \end{pmatrix}$.

Answer

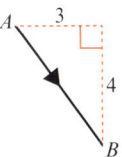

Draw $\overrightarrow{AB}$ as the hypotenuse of a right-angled triangle.

$AB^2 = 3^2 + 4^2$ (Pythagoras' theorem)

$AB^2 = 9 + 16$

$AB^2 = 25$

$AB = 5$

$\therefore |\overrightarrow{AB}| = 5$ units

WORKED EXAMPLE 22

If $\mathbf{a} = \begin{pmatrix} -5 \\ 12 \end{pmatrix}$ find $|\mathbf{a}|$.

Answer

$|\mathbf{a}| = \sqrt{(-5)^2 + (12)^2}$

$\quad = \sqrt{169}$

$\quad = 13$

Position vectors

A vector that starts from the origin (O) is called a position vector.

In this diagram, point A has the position vector $\overrightarrow{OA}$ or $\mathbf{a}$.

If $\mathbf{a} = \begin{pmatrix} 3 \\ 2 \end{pmatrix}$ then the coordinates of point A will be (3, 2).

Because the coordinates of the point A are the same as the components of the column vector $\begin{pmatrix} 3 \\ 2 \end{pmatrix}$ you can use position vectors to find the magnitude of any vector.

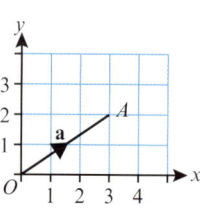

WORKED EXAMPLE 23

The position vector of A is $\begin{pmatrix} 3 \\ 2 \end{pmatrix}$ and the position vector of B is $\begin{pmatrix} -2 \\ 4 \end{pmatrix}$.

Find the vector $2\overrightarrow{AB}$.

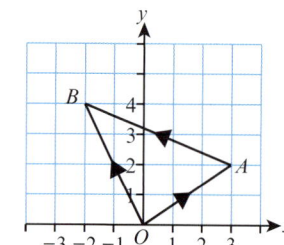

Answer

$\overrightarrow{OA} = \begin{pmatrix} 3 \\ 2 \end{pmatrix}$ and $\overrightarrow{OB} = \begin{pmatrix} -2 \\ 4 \end{pmatrix}$

$\overrightarrow{AB} = \overrightarrow{AO} + \overrightarrow{OB} = -\overrightarrow{OA} + \overrightarrow{OB} = \overrightarrow{OB} - \overrightarrow{OA}$

$\qquad = \begin{pmatrix} -2 \\ 4 \end{pmatrix} - \begin{pmatrix} 3 \\ 2 \end{pmatrix} = \begin{pmatrix} -5 \\ 2 \end{pmatrix}$

So, $2\overrightarrow{AB} = 2\begin{pmatrix} -5 \\ 2 \end{pmatrix} = \begin{pmatrix} -10 \\ 4 \end{pmatrix}$.

Alternative method:

You could also find the column vector for $\overrightarrow{AB}$ by counting the movements parallel to the x-axis followed by those parallel to the y-axis.

Movement parallel to x-axis = −5 units. Movement parallel to the y-axis = 2 units.

$\overrightarrow{AB} = \begin{pmatrix} -5 \\ 2 \end{pmatrix}$

TIP

$\overrightarrow{AB}$ = **b** − **a**, where **a** and **b** are the position vectors of A and B.

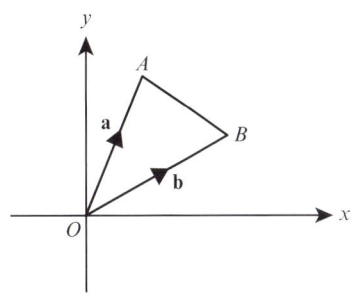

WORKED EXAMPLE 24

If A is point (−1, −2) and B is (5, 6), find $\left|\overrightarrow{AB}\right|$.

Answer

$\overrightarrow{OA} = \begin{pmatrix} -1 \\ -2 \end{pmatrix}$ and $\overrightarrow{OB} = \begin{pmatrix} 5 \\ 6 \end{pmatrix}$.

$\overrightarrow{AB} = \overrightarrow{AO} + \overrightarrow{OB} = -\overrightarrow{OA} + \overrightarrow{OB}$

$$= \begin{pmatrix} -(-1) + 5 \\ -(-2) + 6 \end{pmatrix} = \begin{pmatrix} 6 \\ 8 \end{pmatrix}$$

$\left|\overrightarrow{AB}\right| = \sqrt{6^2 + 8^2} = \sqrt{36 + 64} = \sqrt{100} = 10$

Exercise 23.9

1   Calculate the magnitude of each vector. Give your answers to 2 decimal places where necessary.

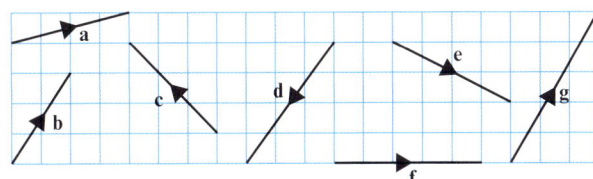

2   Find the magnitude of the following vectors. Give your answers to 2 decimal places where necessary.

   a $\mathbf{a} = \begin{pmatrix} 5 \\ 9 \end{pmatrix}$ b $\overrightarrow{MN} = \begin{pmatrix} 7 \\ 11 \end{pmatrix}$ c $\mathbf{x} = \begin{pmatrix} -3 \\ 4 \end{pmatrix}$ d $\overrightarrow{PQ} = \begin{pmatrix} -6 \\ -8 \end{pmatrix}$

3   O is the point (0, 0), P is (3, 4), Q is (−5, 12) and R is (−8, −15).
   Find the values of:

   a $\left|\overrightarrow{OP}\right|$ b $\left|\overrightarrow{OQ}\right|$ c $\left|\overrightarrow{OR}\right|$

4 Points A, B and C have position vectors $\overrightarrow{OA} = \begin{pmatrix} 4 \\ 2 \end{pmatrix}$, $\overrightarrow{OB} = \begin{pmatrix} -1 \\ 3 \end{pmatrix}$ and $\overrightarrow{OC} = \begin{pmatrix} 6 \\ -2 \end{pmatrix}$.

    a Write down the coordinates of A, B and C.

    b Write down the vectors $\overrightarrow{AB}$, $\overrightarrow{CB}$ and $\overrightarrow{AC}$ in column vector form.

5 Find the magnitude of:

    a the vector joining the points $(-3, -3)$ and $(3, 5)$

    b the vector joining the points $(-2, 6)$ and $(3, -1)$.

> **TIP**
>
> If a question on vectors does not provide a diagram, it may help if you draw one yourself.

APPLY YOUR SKILLS

6 Vector **b** shows the velocity (in km/h) of a car on a highway. The sides of each square on the grid represent a speed of 20 km/h. Find the speed at which the car was travelling.

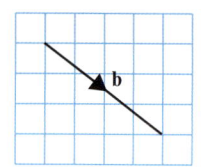

7 Vector **v** represents the velocity in km/h of a person jogging. The sides of each block on the grid represent a speed of 1 km/h. Calculate the speed at which the person was jogging.

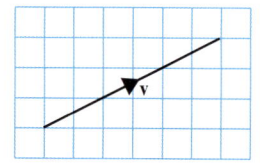

---

8 In the diagram $\overrightarrow{OA} = \mathbf{a}$ and $\overrightarrow{OB} = \mathbf{b}$.

Also $\overrightarrow{AC} = 2\mathbf{a}$ and $\overrightarrow{AD} = 3\mathbf{b} - \mathbf{a}$.

    a Write $\overrightarrow{AB}$ in terms of $\mathbf{a}$ and $\mathbf{b}$.

    b $\overrightarrow{OD} = n\mathbf{b}$ where n is a whole number. Find n.

    c Prove that OAB and OCD are similar triangles.

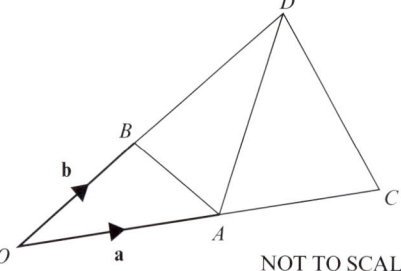

NOT TO SCALE

9

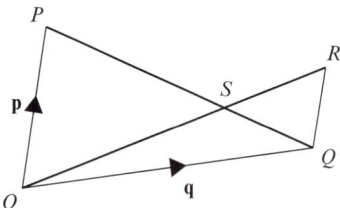

In the diagram $\overrightarrow{OP} = \mathbf{p}$, $\overrightarrow{OQ} = \mathbf{q}$, $QR = \frac{1}{2} OP$ and $SQ = \frac{1}{3} PQ$.

RQ is parallel to OP.

Find in terms of $\mathbf{p}$ and $\mathbf{q}$:

    a $\overrightarrow{PQ}$ **b** $\overrightarrow{PS}$ **c** $\overrightarrow{OS}$ **d** $\overrightarrow{OR}$

10 *OATB* is a parallelogram. *M*, *N* and *P* are midpoints of *BT*, *AT* and *MN* respectively. *O* is the origin and the position vectors of *A* and *B* are **a** and **b** respectively. Find in terms of **a** and/or **b**:

  a $\overrightarrow{MT}$ **b** $\overrightarrow{TN}$ **c** $\overrightarrow{MN}$

  d the position vector of *P*, giving your answer in simplest form.

11 Line *MN* has endpoints *M*(3, 2) and *N*(7, 14). What are the coordinates of point *P*, which divides *MN* in the ratio 1 : 3?

12 In this triangle, *M* is the midpoint of *AB* and the ratio *ON* : *NA* is 1 : 2.

Find in terms of **a** and **b** in its simplest form:

  a $\overrightarrow{AB}$

  b $\overrightarrow{AM}$

  c $\overrightarrow{ON}$

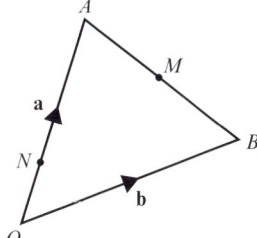

13 In this quadrilateral *OABC*, *AB* is parallel to *OC* and the ratio *OC* to *AB* is 2 : 3. $\overrightarrow{OA} = \mathbf{a}$ and $\overrightarrow{OB} = \mathbf{b}$.

N is the midpoint of *OB*.

M is a point on *AB* such that $\overrightarrow{AM} = \frac{1}{3}\overrightarrow{AB}$.

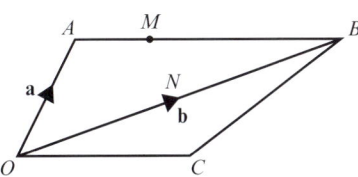

  a Find, in terms of **a** and **b**, in its simplest form:

    i $\overrightarrow{AB}$ **ii** $\overrightarrow{AM}$ **iii** $\overrightarrow{MN}$ **iv** $\overrightarrow{NC}$

  b Explain why the vectors $\overrightarrow{MN}$ and $\overrightarrow{NC}$ shows that *M*, *N* and *C* lie on a straight line.

DISCUSSION

Perpendicular vectors

Work with a partner. You will need a ruler and squared paper.

1 Draw three different pairs of vectors that are perpendicular to each other.

2 Use your diagrams to find a general rule for determining whether two vectors are perpendicular.

SUMMARY

Do you know …?

A transformation involves a change in the position and/or size of a shape.
A reflection is a mirror image, a rotation is a turn, a translation is a slide and an enlargement is an increase in size.
To fully describe a reflection you need to give the equation of the mirror line.
To fully describe a rotation you need to give the angle and centre of rotation.
To describe a translation you can use a column vector $\begin{pmatrix} x \\ y \end{pmatrix}$.
To describe an enlargement you need to give the scale factor and the centre of enlargement.
A vector has both magnitude and direction. You can add and subtract vectors but you cannot multiply or divide vectors. You can multiply a vector by a scalar.
The magnitude of a vector $\begin{pmatrix} x \\ y \end{pmatrix} = \sqrt{x^2 + y^2}$. You write the magnitude as $\left\lvert \overrightarrow{XY} \right\rvert$ or $\lvert \mathbf{x} \rvert$.
A position vector is a vector that starts at the origin.

Are you able to …?

reflect points and plane figures about horizontal and vertical lines
rotate plane figures about the origin, vertices of the object and midpoints of the sides
translate shapes using a column vector
construct enlargements of simple shapes using the scale factor and centre of enlargement
recognise and describe single transformations
recognise and describe combined transformations
add and subtract vectors and multiply vectors by a scalar
calculate the magnitude of a vector
use position vectors to find the magnitude of vectors.

Practice questions

1   The diagram shows a triangle, labelled A.

   On a grid of squared paper, draw accurately the following transformations:

   a   the reflection of triangle A in the
         y-axis, labelling it triangle B   [2]

   b   the rotation of triangle A through
         180° about the point (4, 3),
         labelling it triangle C   [2]

   c   the enlargement of triangle A,
         scale factor of 2, centre (4, 5),
         labelling it triangle D.   [2]

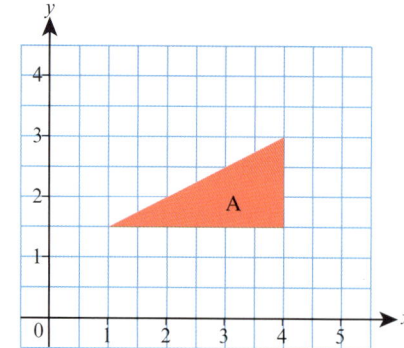

2   Describe fully the transformations of the shaded triangle E onto triangles A, B, C and D in the diagram.

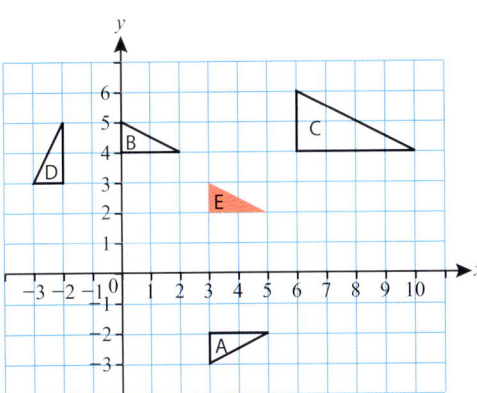

[8]

3   $\mathbf{m} = \begin{pmatrix} 3 \\ -4 \end{pmatrix}$ and $\mathbf{n} = \begin{pmatrix} -2 \\ 1 \end{pmatrix}$.

   a   Find:
      i $\mathbf{m} + \mathbf{n}$ [2]   ii $3\mathbf{n}$ [2]
   b   Draw the vector $\mathbf{m}$ on a grid or on squared paper.   [2]

4   Triangle ABC is mapped onto triangle $A'B'C'$ by an enlargement.
   a   Find the centre of the enlargement.   [2]
   b   What is the scale factor of the enlargement?   [2]

5   a   Write down the column vector of the translation that maps rectangle R onto rectangle S.   [2]

   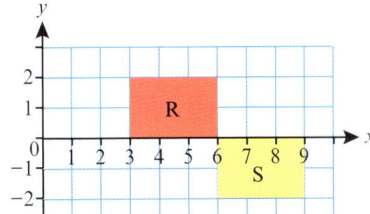

   b   Describe fully another single transformation (not a translation) that would also map rectangle R onto rectangle S.   [2]

   c   i   Copy the diagram onto a grid.
         Enlarge R with centre of enlargement $A(10, 2)$ and scale factor of 2.   [2]

      ii   Write down the ratio area of the enlarged rectangle to the area of rectangle R in its simplest terms.   [2]

6   Triangle P has vertices at the point $A(2, 11)$, $B(2, 8)$ and $C(5, 7)$. Triangle Q has vertices at the point $A'(4, 10)$, $B'(4, 16)$ and $C'(10, 8)$.

   a   Draw both triangles on the same grid.   [2]

   b   Find the centre of enlargement.   [2]

   c   Find the scale factor of the enlargement.   [2]

   d   Find the scale factor of areas of the triangles.   [2]

7   $\overrightarrow{OA} = \mathbf{a}$ and $\overrightarrow{OB} = \mathbf{b}$.

   a $\overrightarrow{OC} = \mathbf{a} + 2\mathbf{b}$. Make a copy of the diagram and label the point C on your diagram.   [2]

   b $D = (0, -1)$. Write OD in terms of $\mathbf{a}$ and $\mathbf{b}$.   [2]

   c   Calculate $|\mathbf{a}|$ giving your answer to 2 decimal places.   [2]

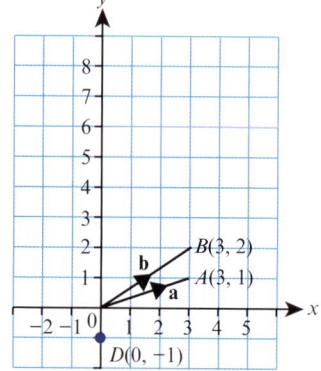

8

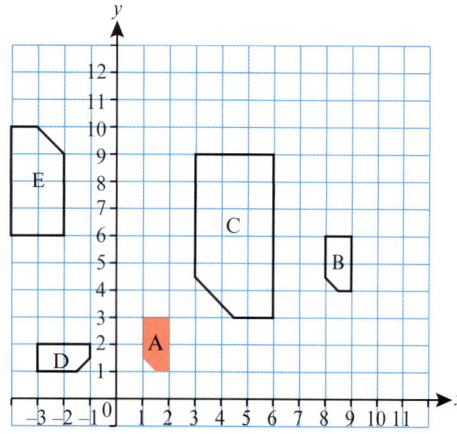

   a   In each case, describe fully the transformation that maps A onto:

       i   B   [2]   ii   C   [2]   iii   D   [2]   iv   E   [2]

   b   State which shapes have an area equal to that of A.   [1]

9   Answer the whole of this question on a sheet of graph paper.

   a   Draw axes from −6 to +6, using a scale of 1 cm to represent 1 unit on each axis.

       i   Plot the points $A(5, 0)$, $B(1, 3)$ and $C(-1, 2)$ and draw triangle ABC.   [1]

       ii Plot the points $A'(3, 4)$, $B'(3, -1)$ and $C'(1, -2)$ and draw triangle $A'B'C'$.   [1]

   b   i   Draw and label the line l in which triangle $A'B'C'$ is a reflection of triangle ABC.   [2]

       ii Write down the equation of the line l.   [2]

10

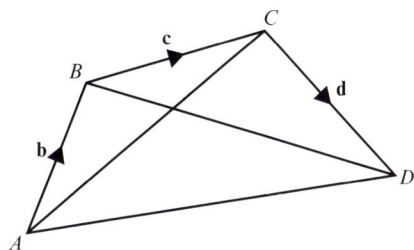

The diagram shows quadrilateral *ABCD*, with

$\overrightarrow{AB} = \mathbf{b}$, $\qquad \overrightarrow{BC} = \mathbf{c}$, $\qquad \overrightarrow{CD} = \mathbf{d}$

Find, in terms of **b**, **c** and **d**:

a $\quad \overrightarrow{AC}$ [1]

b $\quad \overrightarrow{AD}$ [1]

The line *AC* is extended to pass through a point *E*, such that $AE = 2 \times AC$.
$\overrightarrow{DE}$ is parallel to $\overrightarrow{AB}$ and $DE = 2AB$.

c $\quad$ Show that $\mathbf{c} = \mathbf{b} + \mathbf{d}$. [3]

d $\quad$ Show that *ABCD* is a trapezium. [3]

SELF ASSESSMENT

Mark your answers to the practice questions.

Complete these statements in your book.

- I now know …
- I need to know more about …
- These things went well …
- I could do better if I …

Chapter 24

Probability using tree diagrams and Venn diagrams

IN THIS CHAPTER YOU WILL:

- use tree diagrams and Venn diagrams to show all possible outcomes of combined events
- calculate the probability of simple combined events using tree diagrams and Venn diagrams
- use tree diagrams, Venn diagrams and two-way tables to calculate conditional probability.

The probability of getting heads when you toss one coin is 0.5. But what is the probability of getting heads only when you toss two, three or 20 coins at the same time?

Probability is an important branch of mathematics, but understanding probability is also important in real life, especially for understanding risk and relative risk. For example, if you are told that carrying a particular gene doubles your chances of getting a serious disease, it is important to think about what the probability was in the first place. For example, does doubling the probability mean you have a 2 in 1 000 000 chance of getting the disease rather than a 1 in 1 000 000 chance? Because in that case, the probability has doubled, but it is still very low.

In this chapter, you are going to use diagrams to show possible outcomes and calculate the probability of combined events to deepen your understanding of probability concepts.

KEY WORD

conditional probability

GETTING STARTED

1 Here are four statements about probability.

   a Read each statement carefully and decide whether it is correct or not.

   b Explain your decisions to a partner.

Statement A	Statement B	Statement C	Statement D
Tomorrow it will either be sunny or not sunny. The probability that it will be sunny is 0.5.	In a true or false test with 20 questions, you are certain to get 10 correct if you just guess.	If you roll a fair dice four times, you are more likely to get four different numbers than four sixes in a row.	If you toss a coin five times in a row and the first four tosses are heads your next toss is more likely to be tails.

2 Look at this Venn diagram.

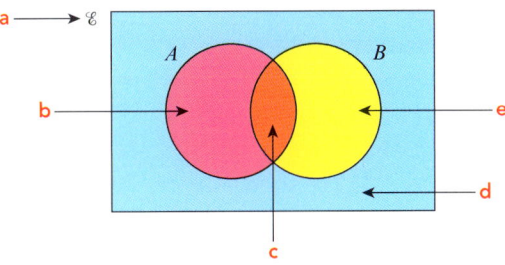

   What do the letters **a**, **b**, **c**, **d** and **e** represent?

3 Look at the three statements in the box.

$n(A)$	$A \cup B$	$A \cap B$

   a What does each one mean?

   b How would you work out each one from a Venn diagram?

24.1 Using tree diagrams to show outcomes

In Chapter 8 you used sample space diagrams to show the sample space and all possible outcomes for statistical experiments.

If you roll a dice and flip a coin, the sample space diagram could look like this:

Coin \ Dice	1	2	3	4	5	6
Heads	H1	H2	H3	H4	H5	H6
Tails	T1	T2	T3	T4	T5	T6

These outcomes can also be shown on a tree diagram:

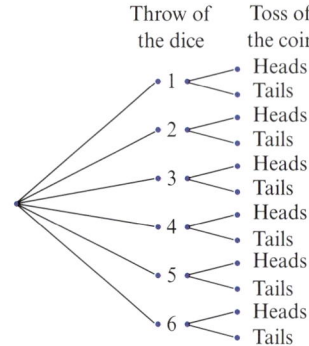

On a tree diagram the outcomes are written at the end of the branches.

Think about the event 'getting all heads' when you toss a coin three times in a row. You cannot show all the possible outcomes for this on a possibility diagram, but you can show them on a tree diagram as in Worked example 1.

WORKED EXAMPLE 1

When you toss a coin you can either get heads or tails. Draw a tree diagram to show the possible outcomes for tossing a coin three times. Use H for heads and T for tails.

Answer

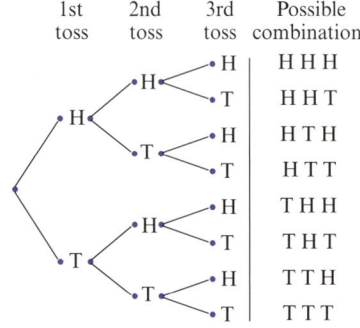

Draw a dot for the first toss.

Draw and label two branches, one H and one T.

Repeat this at the end of each branch for the second and third coin toss.

Exercise 24.1

1 Sunil has a bag containing three coloured counters: red, blue and green.

   a Draw a tree diagram to show the possible outcomes when one counter is drawn from the bag at random, then returned to the bag before another counter is drawn at random.

   b How many possible outcomes are there for the two draws?

   c How many outcomes produce two counters of the same colour?

   d How many outcomes contain at least one blue counter?

   e How many outcomes do not contain the blue counter?

2 Four cards marked A, B, C and D are in a container. A card is drawn, the letter noted, and then it is replaced. Another card is then drawn and the letter noted to make a two-letter combination.

   a Draw a tree diagram to show the sample space in this experiment.

   b How many outcomes are in the sample space?

   c What is the probability of getting the letter combination BD?

24.2 Calculating probability from tree diagrams

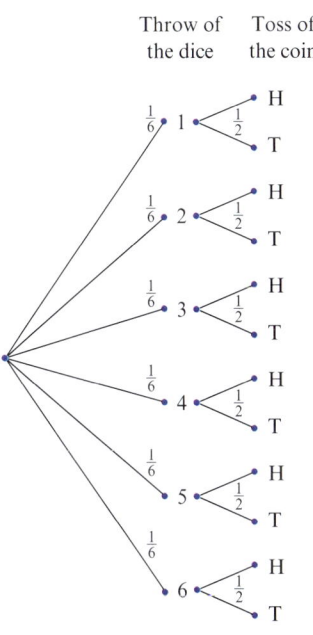

Throw of the dice   Toss of the coin

MATHEMATICAL CONNECTIONS

For independent events $P(A$ and then $B) = P(A) \times P(B)$.

For mutually exclusive events $P(A$ or $B) = P(A) + P(B)$.

Read through Chapter 8 again if you have forgotten this.

Here is the tree diagram showing possible outcomes for throwing a dice and tossing a coin at the same time (H is used for head and T is used for tail).

This is the same diagram as the one at the start of Section 24.1, but now the probability of each outcome is written by the side of each branch.

LINK

One particular kind of study of tiny particles is called *quantum mechanics*. This looks at the probability of finding particles in particular places at particular times.

The probability of combined events on a tree diagram

To find the probability of one particular combination of outcomes:

- multiply the probabilities on consecutive branches, for example the probability of throwing a 5 and getting an H is $\frac{1}{6} \times \frac{1}{2} = \frac{1}{12}$.

To find the probability when there is more than one favourable combination or when the events are mutually exclusive:

- multiply the probabilities on consecutive branches

- add the probabilities (of each favourable combination) obtained by multiplication, for example, throwing 1 or 2 and getting an H is

$$\left(\frac{1}{6} \times \frac{1}{2}\right) + \left(\frac{1}{6} \times \frac{1}{2}\right) = \frac{1}{12} + \frac{1}{12} = \frac{2}{12} = \frac{1}{6}$$

When you are interested only in specific probabilities, you can draw a tree diagram that only shows the favourable outcomes. For example, if you wanted to find the probability of getting a number <5 and H in the above experiment, you might draw a tree diagram like this one:

$P(<5 \text{ and } H) = \frac{4}{6} \times \frac{1}{2} = \frac{1}{3}$

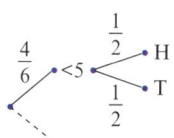

Throw of   Toss of
the dice   the coin

> **MATHEMATICAL CONNECTIONS**
>
> You learnt in Chapter 8 that mutually exclusive events cannot both happen together.

> **TIP**
>
> There are four numbers on a dice that are less than 5. As they are equally likely to occur, the probability of scoring < 5 is $\frac{4}{6} = \frac{2}{3}$.

WORKED EXAMPLE 2

Two coins are tossed together. Draw a tree diagram to find the probability of getting:

a   two tails

b   one head and one tail.

Answers

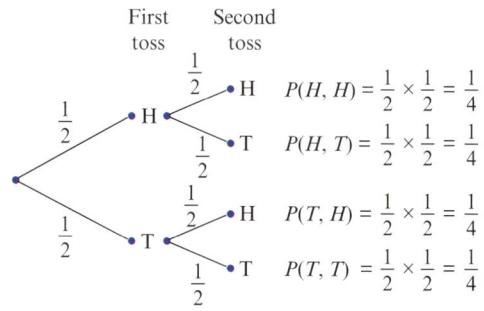

$P(H, H) = \frac{1}{2} \times \frac{1}{2} = \frac{1}{4}$

$P(H, T) = \frac{1}{2} \times \frac{1}{2} = \frac{1}{4}$

$P(T, H) = \frac{1}{2} \times \frac{1}{2} = \frac{1}{4}$

$P(T, T) = \frac{1}{2} \times \frac{1}{2} = \frac{1}{4}$

a $P(TT) = P(T \text{ on 1st toss}) \times P(T \text{ on 2nd toss})$

$$= \frac{1}{2} \times \frac{1}{2} = \frac{1}{4}$$

b $P(HT \text{ or } TH) = P(HT) + P(TH)$

$$= \left(\frac{1}{2} \times \frac{1}{2}\right) + \left(\frac{1}{2} \times \frac{1}{2}\right) = \frac{1}{4} + \frac{1}{4} = \frac{1}{2}$$

WORKED EXAMPLE 3

This tree diagram shows all possible combinations of male and female calves for a cow after three pregnancies.

This assumes that each pregnancy produces one calf and that the outcomes, male or female, are equally likely.
Find the probability that:

a at least one calf is female

b two of the calves are female

c the first and last born calves are the same sex.

1st calf	2nd calf	3rd calf	Possible combinations
			M M M
			M M F
			M F M
			M F F
			F M M
			F M F
			F F M
			F F F

Answers

a $P(\text{at least one female}) = 7\left(\frac{1}{2} \times \frac{1}{2} \times \frac{1}{2}\right)$

$= 7 \times \frac{1}{8}$

$= \frac{7}{8}$

All outcomes except MMM have at least one female. This makes seven outcomes. As each outcome is $\frac{1}{2} \times \frac{1}{2} \times \frac{1}{2}$ you can simply multiply this by 7.

b $P(\text{two are female}) = \frac{3}{8}$

There are three out of eight outcomes where there are two females.

c $P(\text{first and last same sex}) = \frac{4}{8} = \frac{1}{2}$

FFF, FMF, MFM and MMM have the first and last with the same sex. The probability for each combination is $\frac{1}{8}$, so you can add the favourable combinations to give $\frac{4}{8}$.

Exercise 24.2

1 An unbiased coin is tossed twice. Draw a tree diagram to show the outcomes and use it to find the probability of the two tosses giving the same results.

2 A bag contains eight blue marbles and two red marbles. Two marbles are drawn at random. The first marble is replaced before the second is drawn.

    a Draw a tree diagram to show all possible outcomes.

    b What is the probability of getting:

      i two red marbles?

      ii one red marble and one blue marble?

      iii two blue marbles?

3 A bag contains 12 beads. Five are red and the rest are white. Two beads are drawn at random. The first bead is replaced before the second is drawn.

    a Represent the possible outcomes on a tree diagram.

    b Find the probability that:

      i both beads are red

      ii both beads are white.

4   This tree diagram shows the probability of getting heads and tails when a biased coin is tossed twice.

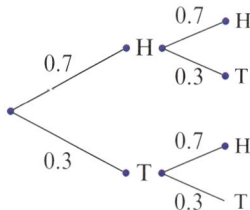

Find the probability of getting:

a   two heads

b   two tails

c   tails on the first toss and heads on the second toss

d   only one tail

e   at least one tail.

5   Yossi wants to buy two new pets; he will buy them a week apart. He prefers birds to cats, but only slightly, and decides that so long as he buys them as chicks and/or kittens, it does not matter what combination he gets. The tree diagram represents the combination of two pets he might buy.

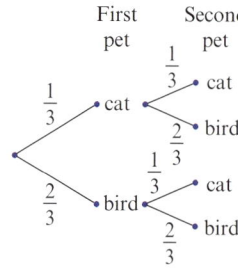

a   How many possible combinations of pets could he buy?

b   What is the probability that he buys a cat and a bird?

c   What is the probability that he buys two cats?

d   Based on these probabilities, what combination is Yossi most likely to buy?

LINK

Probability has huge implications in health and medicine. The probability that medical tests for different diseases are accurate is very high, but it is rarely 100% and an incorrect test result can have really serious implications.

REFLECTION

Research findings suggest that to be successful at maths in school, natural talent is much less important than working hard, preparing well and having confidence.

- What does this suggest about personal perseverance and struggle?

- How can you use this research finding to improve your own results?

Frequency trees

Frequency trees are organisational tools that show the actual frequency of events. The branches of the tree show the choices or decisions. The actual numerical data for each path is shown at the intersection of the branches.

1   A health care worker is interested in whether patients know the difference between having COVID-19 and a cold.

Out of 83 patients, 31 believed they had a cold and 52 believed they had COVID-19.

The health care worker started to record the data like this:

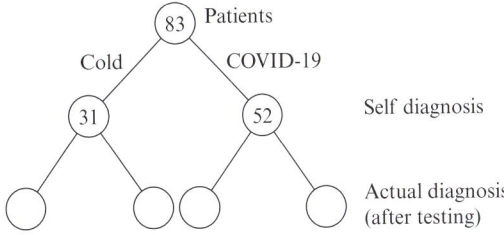

It turned out that only 32 of the patients who believed they had COVID-19 actually had COVID-19 and 13 of the patients who said they had a cold actually had COVID-19.

   a   Redraw the frequency tree and add this data to it.

   b   How does this diagram help you to make sense of complicated probabilities?

   c   What is the difference between a frequency tree and a tree diagram?

2   **a**   How could you show this data using a two-way table?

   b   Which is clearer and easier to understand: the diagram or the table? Why?

3   Assuming the data is representative:

   a   What is the probability that a patient who thinks they have COVID-19 will actually have COVID-19?

   b   What percentage of people who thought they had a cold actually had COVID-19?

24.3 Calculating probability from Venn diagrams

You used Venn diagrams to show the relationships between sets in Chapter 9. Now you are going to use Venn diagrams to solve probability problems.

This Venn diagram shows the results of a survey in which people were asked whether they watch programme A or programme B. Study the diagram and read the information to see how to determine probabilities from a Venn diagram.

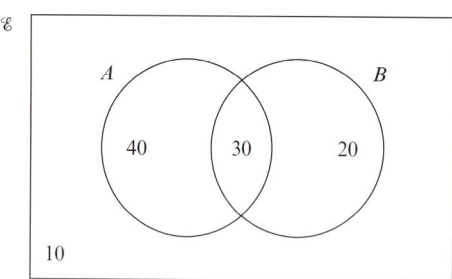

$\mathscr{E}$ means the universal set. In probability this is the sample space, or set of all possible outcomes. In this example the sample space is $40 + 30 + 20 + 10 = 100$ people.

$n(A)$ means the number of elements in set A.

$n(A) = 40 + 30 = 70$

$P(A)$ means the probability that an element is in set A. You can write this as the number of elements in set A as a fraction of the sample space.

Remember to include the elements in the intersection in set A.

$P(A) = \dfrac{70}{100} = \dfrac{7}{10}$ or 0.7

$A \cap B$ is the intersection of sets A and B. It is the elements shared by A and B. You write the probability of the two events happening as $P(A$ and $B)$. This is the same as $P(A \cap B)$, the probability that an element is in both set A and set B. The word 'and' is a clue that the probability is found in the intersection of the sets.

$n(A \cap B) = 30$, so $P(A \cap B) = \dfrac{30}{100} = \dfrac{3}{10}$ or 0.3

$A \cup B$ is the union of sets A and B. It is the elements in both sets, with none repeated. You write the probability of either event A happening or event B happening as $P(A$ or $B)$. This is the same as $P(A \cup B)$, the probability that an element is found either in set A or in set B. The word 'or' is a clue that the probability is found in the union of the sets.

$n(A \cup B) = 40 + 30 + 20 = 90$, so $P(A \cup B) = \dfrac{90}{100} = \dfrac{9}{10}$ or 0.9

When a question contains words like 'is not' or 'neither' it is a clue that you are looking for the complement of a set. For example, 'What is the probability that a person watches neither of the two programmes?' In the Venn diagram this is everything outside of $A \cup B$. So, P(neither A nor B) is $1 - P(A \cup B)$.

TIP

$1 - P(A \cup B)$ is the same as $P(A \cup B)'$. The complement of $A \cup B$.

WORKED EXAMPLE 4

In a survey, 25 people were asked to say if they liked fruit and if they liked vegetables.

15 people said they liked vegetables and 18 said they liked fruit.

Assuming that everyone surveyed liked fruit or vegetables or both, draw a Venn diagram and use it to work out the probability that a person chosen at random from this group will like:

a   both fruit and vegetables   **b**   either fruit or vegetables

Answers

Start by defining the sets and writing the information in set language.
Use letters to make it quicker and easier to refer to the sets.

$\mathcal{E}$ = {number of people surveyed}, $n(\mathcal{E})$ = 25

F = {people who like fruit}, so $n(F)$ = 18

V = {people who like vegetables}, so $n(V)$ = 15

$n(F) + n(V)$ = 18 + 15 = 33

But the total number of people surveyed was only 25.

33 − 25 = 8, so 8 people must have said they liked both fruit and vegetables.

$n(F \cap V)$ = 8

Once you've defined the sets, you can draw the diagram.

You don't know the names of the people surveyed, so you have to work with the number of people in each set.

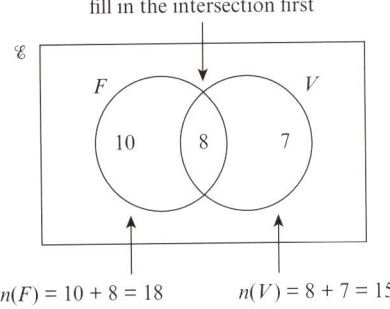

fill in the intersection first

$n(F) = 10 + 8 = 18$ $n(V) = 8 + 7 = 15$

a   After you have drawn the diagram, calculate the probability.

In words:

$P(\text{Person likes both}) = \dfrac{\text{number of people who like both}}{\text{number of people surveyed}} = \dfrac{8}{25} = 0.32$

In set language:

$P(F \text{ and } V) = \dfrac{n(F \cap V)}{n(\mathcal{E})} = \dfrac{8}{25} = 0.32$

b $P(F \text{ or } V) = \dfrac{10}{25} + \dfrac{8}{25} + \dfrac{7}{25} = \dfrac{25}{25} = 1$

This is the same as $F \cup V$.

MATHEMATICAL CONNECTIONS

In Chapter 9 you saw that numbers in Venn diagrams can represent either the *elements* in a set or the *number of elements* in a set. In probability, you will usually work with the number of elements in the set.

WORKED EXAMPLE 5

In a survey, 30 people were asked whether they used the bus, metro or E-hailing providers for public transport. The survey found that 16 people use the bus, 10 use the metro, 8 use E-hail providers, 3 people use all three types, 4 use the bus and the metro only, 3 use the metro and E-hail providers only and 4 use the bus and E-hail providers only.

a Draw a Venn diagram to show the results.

b How many of the people surveyed do not use any of three types of transport?

c If a person was chosen at random, calculate:

    i P(bus and metro)   **ii** P(bus only)   **iii** P(not bus, metro or E-hail).

Answers

a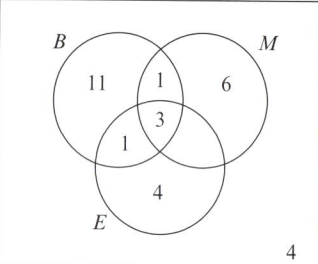

b This is the number of elements outside the three sets = 4.

c **i** $P(B \text{ and } M) = \dfrac{4}{30} = \dfrac{2}{15}$

    ii $P(B \text{ only}) = \dfrac{11}{30}$

    iii $P(\text{not } B, M \text{ or } E) = \dfrac{4}{30} = \dfrac{2}{15}$

Exercise 24.3

1 Use the Venn diagram to determine the following probabilities.

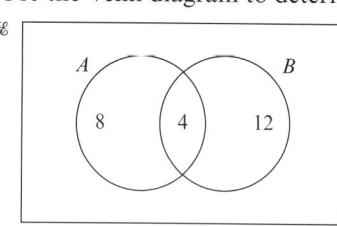

  a $P(A)$ **b** $P(B)$ **c** $P(A \text{ and } B)$

  d $P(\text{not } B)$ **e** $P(A \text{ or } B)$

2 Zora owns 20 T-shirts. Six are long-sleeved and four are black. Only one of the long-sleeved T-shirts is black. Draw a Venn diagram and use it to find the following probabilities:

  a P(T-shirt is not black)

  b P(T-shirt is long sleeved but not black)

  c P(T-shirt is neither black nor long-sleeved).

3   Twenty students walked into a classroom. 13 of these students were wearing headphones and 15 were typing messages on their phones. 4 students were not wearing headphones nor typing messages on their phones.

   a   Draw a Venn diagram to show this information.

   b   What is the probability that a student was both wearing headphones and typing on their phone when they walked into class?

4   In a class of 28 students, 12 take physics, 15 take chemistry and 8 take neither physics nor chemistry.

   a   Draw a Venn diagram to show the information.

   b   What is the probability that a student chosen at random from this class:

   i   takes physics but not chemistry?

   ii   takes physics or chemistry?

   iii   takes physics and chemistry?

5   In a group of 130 students, 56 play the piano and 64 play the violin. 27 of the students play both instruments.

   a   Draw a Venn diagram to show this information.

   b   Use your Venn diagram to find the probability that a student chosen at random from this group:

   i   plays the violin

   ii   plays either the piano or the violin

   iii   plays both instruments

   iv   plays neither instrument.

6   A survey is carried out to discover which brand of cat food cats enjoy.
24 cats are tested to see whether they like Fluffy or Bouncer.
Some of the results are shown in the Venn diagram. The Venn diagram is not complete, but shows how many cats liked each brand.

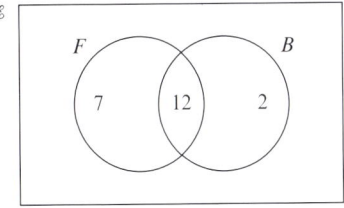

$\mathscr{E}$ = {all cats tested}
F = {cats who like Fluffy}
B = {cats who like Bouncer}

   a   How many cats like both Fluffy and Bouncer?

   b   How many cats do not like either food?

   c   Write down the value of n($F \cup B$).

   d   Write down the value of n($F \cap B$).

   e   A tested cat is selected at random. What is the probability that this cat likes Bouncer?

   f   A cat that likes Fluffy is chosen at random. What is the probability that this cat also likes Bouncer?

7   A study tested three medications: Painstop (P), Nopain (N) and Gopain (G) to see how effective they were at relieving migraine pain. During the study, 80 participants tried all three medications. These are the results:

Reported relief when using:	Number of participants
Painstop only	11
Nopain only	9
Gopain only	8
Painstop and Gopain	21
Nopain and Gopain	18
Painstop and Nopain	15
At least one medication	68

a   Draw a Venn diagram to show this information.

b   How many people got pain relief from all three medications?

c   How many people experienced pain relief from Painstop and Gopain, but not from Nopain?

d   What is the probability that a randomly chosen participant experienced no pain relief from any of the medications?

8   This Venn diagram shows the number of students who study Biology (B), Physics (P) and Chemistry (C) in a group of 130 high school student. 74 of the students study Biology and 49 of the students study Physics.

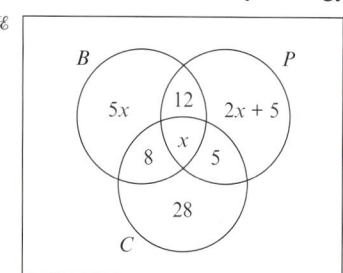

a   Determine the value of x.

b   Calculate:

   i $n(B \cup P)$ ii $n(C \cap B)$ iii $n(B' \cap C')$

c   Determine P(B and C).

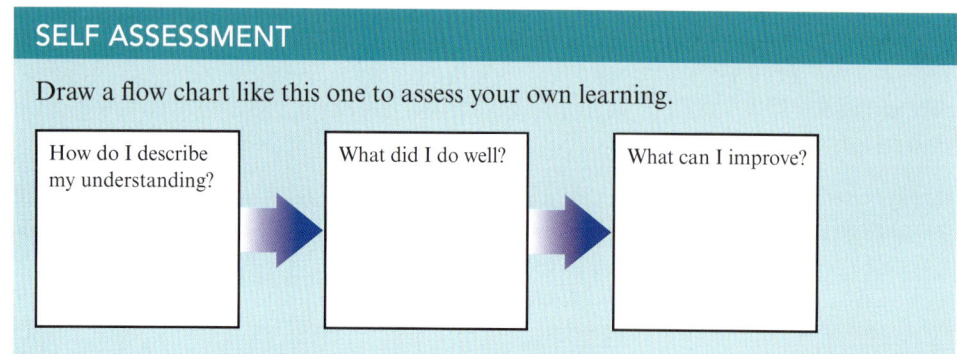

SELF ASSESSMENT

Draw a flow chart like this one to assess your own learning.

| How do I describe my understanding? | → | What did I do well? | → | What can I improve? |

TIP

Look back to Chapter 1 if you need some suggestions for sentence stems to get started.

24.4 Conditional probability

If the probability of an event depends on the outcome of a previous event then the probability is said to be conditional.

For two events A and B, $P(B$ given that A has happened) refers to the conditional probability of B happening given that A has already happened.

The way that you work out the **conditional probability** depends on whether the events are independent or not.

Independent events

Imagine you roll two normal six-sided dice.

The first dice lands on a 6. What is the probability of the second dice also landing on 6?

These two events are independent. The score on the second dice is not affected by the outcome of the first.

If two events A and B are independent, it is always true that

$P(B$ given that A has happened$) = P(B)$,

so in this case, the probability of getting a 6 with the second dice is $\frac{1}{6}$.

Dependent events

If two events A and B are dependent, the first event does affect the probability of the second event.

For example, suppose you have an apple, an orange and a banana and you choose two of the fruits at random. If you choose the apple first, you can only choose between the orange and the banana for your second fruit. The options for your second fruit are dependent on what you chose first because now you only have two fruits left to choose from.

To find the probability of B given that A has happened, use the rule:

$$P(B \text{ given that } A \text{ has happened}) = \frac{P(A \text{ and } B)}{P(A)}$$

When you deal with Venn diagrams, this rule can be written in set language as:

$$P(B \text{ given that } A \text{ has happened}) = \frac{P(A \cap B)}{P(A)}$$

You can use tree diagrams and Venn diagrams to help you solve problems involving conditional probability.

> **TIP**
>
> When you are using a tree diagram always check whether the probability of an event changes because of the outcome of a previous event. Questions involving conditional probability often contain the instructions 'without replacement' or 'one after the other'.

WORKED EXAMPLE 6

A bag contains 21 balls. There are 12 blue balls and 9 green balls. Without looking, two balls are removed one after the other, without replacing them.

a Draw a tree diagram to represent the situation.

b Find the probability that:
  i both balls are blue (BB)
  ii both balls are green (GG)
  iii one ball is green and the other is blue.

c A third ball is taken at random. What is the probability that:
  i all three balls are blue?
  ii at least one of the balls is green?

Answers

a

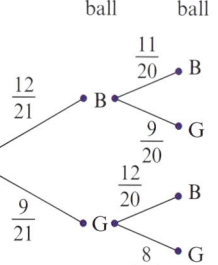

This is an example of conditional probability. You cannot choose the same ball twice, so for the second set of branches there are only 20 balls left. If the first ball is blue, there are only 11 blue balls left but still 9 green balls . If the first ball is green, there are only 8 green balls left, but still 12 blue. In each case the numerator of one branch has changed but the numerators still add up to the value of the denominator (as this has also changed).

b **i** $P(BB) = \dfrac{12}{21} \times \dfrac{11}{20} = \dfrac{11}{35}$

  ii $P(GG) = \dfrac{9}{21} \times \dfrac{8}{20} = \dfrac{6}{35}$

  iii $P(BG) + P(GB) = \dfrac{12}{21} \times \dfrac{9}{20} + \dfrac{9}{21} \times \dfrac{12}{20} = \dfrac{18}{35}$

  The blue and green can be chosen in either order.

c

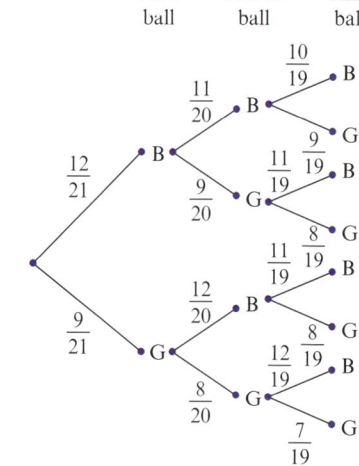

You may find it helpful to add a third set of branches to the diagram, but, if you can see the pattern of the probabilities on the branches, you can just show the arithmetic.

  i $P(BBB) = \dfrac{12}{21} \times \dfrac{11}{20} \times \dfrac{10}{19} = \dfrac{22}{133}$

  ii $P(\text{at least one green}) = 1 - P(\text{all blue})$

  $= 1 - \dfrac{22}{133} = \dfrac{111}{133}$

  (Sometimes it is faster to work out the probabilities that you don't want and subtract the result from 1.)

WORKED EXAMPLE 7

In a group of 50 students, 36 students work on tablet computers, 20 work on laptops and 12 work on neither of these.

A student is chosen at random. What is the probability that this student:

a   works on a tablet and a laptop computer?

b   works on at least one type of computer?

c   works on a tablet given that he or she works on a laptop?

d   does not work on a laptop, given that he or she works on a tablet?

Answers

Start by identifying the sets and drawing a Venn diagram.

T = {students who work on tablets} $n(T) = 36$

L = {students who work on laptops} $n(L) = 20$

$50 - 12 = 38$, so there are 38 students in T and L combined.

$36 + 20 = 56$, but there are only 38 students in T and L combined.

$56 - 38 = 18$, so 18 students work on both $(T \cap L)$.

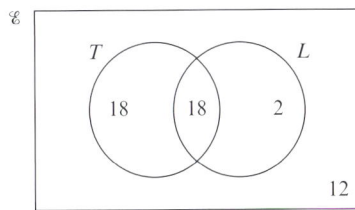

a $P(\text{works on both}) = P(T \cap L) = \dfrac{18}{50} = \dfrac{9}{25}$

b $P(\text{works on at least one}) = 1 - P(\text{works on neither}) = 1 - \dfrac{12}{50} = \dfrac{38}{50} = \dfrac{19}{25}$

c $P(T \text{ given that } L \text{ has happened}) = \dfrac{P(L \text{ and } T)}{P(L)} = \dfrac{n(L \cap T)}{n(L)}$

$\qquad\qquad = \dfrac{18}{20} = \dfrac{9}{10}$

d $P(\text{Not } L \text{ given } T \text{ has happened}) = \dfrac{P(L' \text{ and } T)}{P(T)} = \dfrac{18}{36} = \dfrac{1}{2}$

TIP

$P(T$ given that L has happened) is dependent on students already using a laptop, so the probability is calculated using the total number of students who use a laptop not the total number of students. $n(T$ and $L)$ is the number of students in the intersection of the two sets.

WORKED EXAMPLE 8

A group of Grade 10 and Grade 11 students were asked which device they used most often to access the internet. The data is given in the table.

	Phone	Tablet	PC
Grade 10	200	330	120
Grade 11	250	320	80

WORKED EXAMPLE 8 CONTINUED

a What is the probability a randomly chosen student uses a phone to access the internet, given that the student is in Grade 11?

b A student is in Grade 10. What is the probability that the student uses a PC to access the internet?

c If a randomly chosen student uses a tablet to access the internet, what is the probability they are in Grade 11?

Answers

	Phone	Tablet	PC	Total
Grade 10	200	330	120	**650**
Grade 11	250	320	80	**650**
Total	**450**	**650**	**200**	

Add totals to the table so that you can use them to calculate probabilities.

a

	Phone	Tablet	PC	Total
Grade 10	200	330	120	**650**
Grade 11	<u>250</u>	320	80	**650**
Total	**450**	**650**	**200**	

You know the student is in Grade 11, so you only need to look at the values for Grade 11.

250 out of the 650 students in Grade 11 use a phone to access the internet.

$$P(\text{Phone user given Grade 11}) = \frac{250}{650} = \frac{5}{13}$$

b $P(\text{PC user given Grade 10}) = \dfrac{120}{650} = \dfrac{12}{65}$

This time you need to look at the Grade 10 values.

c $P(\text{Grade 11 given they use a tablet}) = \dfrac{320}{650} = \dfrac{32}{65}$

You know the student uses a tablet so use the values in the tablet column.

650 students use a tablet and 320 are in Grade 11.

TIP

Conditional probability involves finding something using something that you know already. So for $P(A$ given that B has happened$)$, A is the event of interest, and B is the event that we assume has occurred.

Exercise 24.4

1 A card is randomly selected from a pack of 52 playing cards, and its suit is recorded. The card is not replaced. Then a second card is chosen and the suit recorded.

    a Draw a tree diagram to represent this situation.

    b Use the tree diagram to find the probability that:

        i both cards are hearts

        ii both cards are clubs

        iii the first card is red and the second card is black

        iv both cards are hearts given that the first card is a heart.

2 Mohammed has four scrabble tiles with the letters A, B, C and D on them. He draws a letter at random and places it on the table, then he draws a second letter and a third, placing them down next to the previously drawn letter.

    a Draw a tree diagram to show the possible outcomes.

    b What is the probability that the letters he has drawn spell the following words?

        i   CAD   **ii**   BAD   **iii**   DAD

    c What is the probability that he will not draw the letter B?

    d What is Mohammed's chance of drawing the letters in alphabetical order?

3 In a group of 25 people, 15 like coffee (C), 17 like tea (T) and 2 people like neither. Using an appropriate diagram, calculate the probability that a person will:

    a like coffee

    b like coffee given that they like tea.

4 100 teenagers went on a computer camp. 80 of them learned coding and 42 learned animation techniques. Each student did at least one of these activities.

    a Draw a Venn diagram to show how many teenagers did both activities.

    b A teenager is randomly selected. Find the probability that he or she:

        i   learned coding but not animation techniques

        ii   learned animation techniques given that he or she learned coding.

5 At computer camp, students from two different schools (A and B) were asked which device they preferred to use to play computer games. The data is given in the table.

Device preferred / School	School A	School B
Smartphone	52	48
Gaming console	37	23
PC	48	35

Give your answers as decimals correct to 3 decimal places if necessary.

    a What is the probability that any student chosen at random prefers to use a gaming console?

    b Given that the student prefers using a gaming console, what is the probability they are from school A?

    c What is the probability that a student from school A prefers using a PC to play games?

    d What is the probability that a student who either prefers a smartphone or a console attends school B?

6 There are $2n$ black counters and $2n + 1$ green counters in a bag. If two counters are randomly drawn, one after the other, show that the probability of getting two counters the same colour is $\dfrac{2n}{n + 1}$.

APPLY YOUR SKILLS

7 Clarissa is having a baby. She wants the baby to have a first and a second name. The names she is considering are Onyx, Shae, Kai and Avery.

   a Draw a tree diagram to show all possible combinations of names for the baby.

   b If Clarissa chooses two names at random, what are the chances that the baby will be called Kai Avery?

   c What is the chance of the baby being named Avery Shae?

8 Sindi, Lee, Marita, Roger, Bongile and Simone are the six members of a school committee. The committee needs to choose a chairperson and a treasurer. One person cannot fill both positions.

   a Draw a tree diagram to show how many ways there are of choosing a chairperson and a treasurer.

   b If the chairperson and treasurer are chosen at random, what is the probability of choosing Sindi as chairperson and Lee as treasurer?

9 A cleaner accidentally knocked the name labels off three students' lockers. The name labels are Raju, Sam and Kerry. The tree diagram shows the possible ways of replacing the name labels.

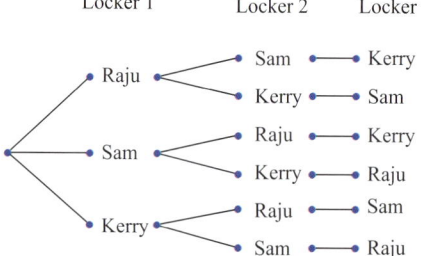

   a Draw a tree diagram to show the possible ways of replacing the name labels. Write the probabilities next to each branch.

   b Are these events conditional or independent? Why?

   c How many correct ways are there to match the name labels to the lockers?

   d How many possible ways are there for the cleaner to label the lockers?

   e If the cleaner randomly stuck the names back onto the lockers, what are the chances of getting the names correct?

10 In a group of 120 students, 25 are in the sixth form and 15 attend maths tutorials.

Four of the students are sixth formers who attend maths tutorials.

What is the probability that a randomly chosen student who attends maths tutorials will be in the sixth form?

APPLY YOUR SKILLS CONTINUED

11   A climatologist reports that the probability of rain on Friday is 0.21. If it rains on Friday, there is a 0.83 chance of rain on Saturday, if it doesn't rain on Friday, the chance of rain on Saturday is only 0.3.

   a   Draw a tree diagram to represent this situation.

   b   Use your diagram to work out the probability of rain on:
      i   Friday and Saturday
      ii   Saturday.

12   Look at this tree diagram drawn by a weather forecaster.

   What does it tell you about the weather for the next two days in this place? (Make sure you include probabilities as part of your answer).

13   Mahmoud enjoys windsurfing. On any given day, the probability that there is a good wind is $\frac{3}{4}$. If there is a good wind, the probability that he will go windsurfing is $\frac{5}{8}$. If there is not a good wind, the probability that he will go windsurfing is $\frac{1}{16}$.

   a   Copy this tree diagram. Write the probabilities next to each branch.

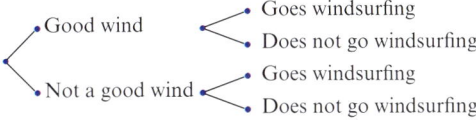

   b   What is the probability that there is good wind and Mahmoud goes windsurfing?

   c   Find the probability that, whatever the wind, Mahmoud does not go windsurfing.

   d   If Mahmoud goes windsurfing, the probability that he has to wait for a strong enough wind so he can move is $\frac{1}{2}$. Calculate the probability that, whatever the wind, Mahmoud spends some time waiting for a strong enough wind to move.

SUMMARY

Do you know …?

The sample space is all the possible outcomes of a statistical experiment.
When an event has two or more stages it is called a combined event.
Tree diagrams and Venn diagrams are useful for organising the outcomes of different stages in an event. They are particularly useful when there are more than two stages because a sample space diagram can only show outcomes for two events.
The outcomes are written at the ends of branches on a tree diagram. The probability of each outcome is written next to the branches as a fraction or decimal.
For independent events you find the probability by multiplying the probabilities on each branch of the tree.
When events are mutually exclusive, you need to add the probabilities obtained by multiplication.
The probability that an event happens, given that another event has already happened, is called conditional probability.

Are you able to …?

draw a tree diagram to organise the outcomes for simple combined events
find the probability of each branch of a tree diagram
calculate the probability of events using tree diagrams
draw a Venn diagram to represent sets of information and use it to calculate probabilities
use tree diagrams and Venn diagrams to determine conditional probability.

Practice questions

1 A school cafeteria offers the following choices for lunch:

Each student can choose a starter, a main course and a dessert.

Starter	Main	Dessert
Soup	Curry	Lassi
Salad	Roti	Ice Cream
	Fish	
	Vegetarian	

   a Draw a tree diagram to show all the possible choices for a three-course lunch. [3]

   b What is the probability that a student will choose soup, curry and ice-cream? [3]

2 The Venn diagram shows data about the subjects taken by 250 students in an International School.

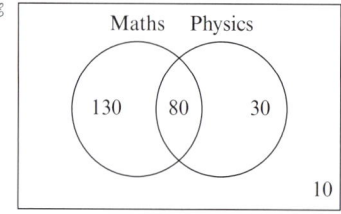

   a How many of the students do not take maths or physics? [1]

   b What is the probability that a student chosen at random will take maths? [3]

   c Calculate the probability that a student chosen at random will take maths or physics. [3]

3   15 people stand in a room. 5 have blue eyes, 4 have brown eyes and 6 have green eyes.

   a   Two people are chosen at random to leave the room.
   Find the probability that:

      i   at least one of them has green eyes   [3]

      ii   they do not have the same eye colour.   [3]

   b   A third person now leaves the room.
   Find that probability that exactly one of the people who has left the room
   has brown eyes.   [3]

4   In a group of 140 students, 103 study maths and 37 study music. 25 students study neither maths nor music.

   a   Draw a Venn diagram to show the information.   [4]

   b   Calculate $P(\text{music})$ using your diagram.   [2]

   c   Calculate the probability that a student chosen at random will study
   music, given that he or she studies maths.   [3]

5   The universal set for a Venn diagram is the set of 26 letters of the Roman
   alphabet. $A = \{$letter in the word 'Abibliophobia'$\}$
   $B = \{$first 8 letters of the alphabet$\}$
   $C = \{$letters in the phrase 'afraid to run out of reading material'$\}$

   a   Draw a Venn diagram to show this information.   [4]

   b   List the following sets:

      i $A \cap B \cap C$ [2]

      ii $(A \cup B) \cap C$ [2]

      iii $A \cap (B \cup C)'$ [2]

6   In a group of 59 children, some like to watch Hoggle, Goggle or Smoggle (or some
   combination of these TV programmes). 4 children watch all three, 3 watch Goggle
   and Smoggle, but not Hoggle, 9 watch Hoggle and Smoggle, but not Goggle, and 7
   watch Hoggle and Goggle, but not Smoggle. The number who watch only Smoggle
   or none of the programmes is two fewer than the number who watch only Hoggle
   or only Goggle. Using a Venn diagram, work out how many watch Hoggle only or
   Goggle only.   [6]

7   A bag contains n white tiles and five black tiles. The tiles are all equal in shape
   and size. A tile is drawn at random and is not replaced. A second tile is then drawn.

   a   Find:

      i   the probability that the first tile is white   [2]

      ii   the probability that both the first and second tiles are white.   [2]

   b   You are told that the probability of drawing two white tiles is $\dfrac{7}{22}$.
   Show that $3n^2 - 17n - 28 = 0$.   [3]

   c   Solve the equation, $3n^2 - 17n - 28 = 0$, and hence find the probability
   that exactly one white and exactly one black tile is drawn.   [5]

Past paper questions

> **TIP**
>
> Unit 6 Past Paper Questions Resource Sheet is available on Cambridge GO.

1

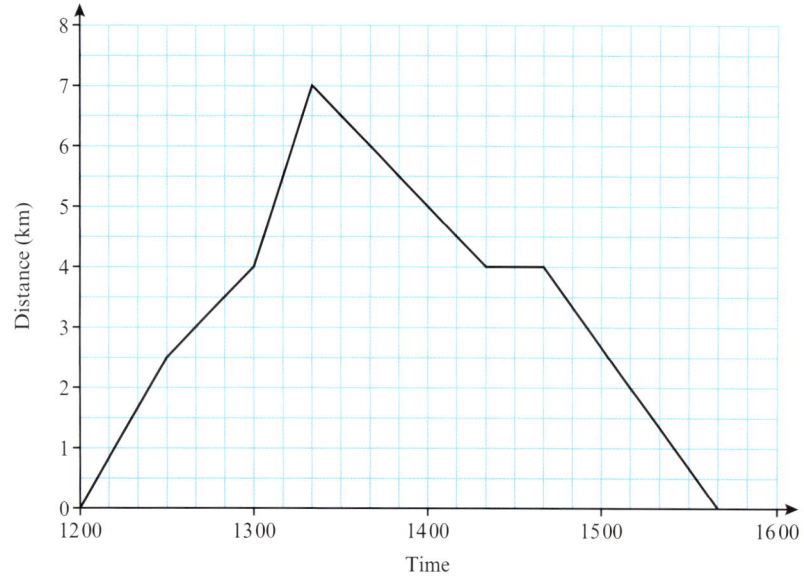

The travel graph shows a student's journey.

a Explain what is happening between 14 20 and 14 40.

[1]

b Copy and complete the statement.

The student is travelling fastest between the times … and … because …….

[2]

Adapted from Cambridge IGCSE Mathematics (0580) Paper 11 Q6, June 2021

2 a $\mathscr{E} = \{1, 2, 3, 4, 5, 6, 7, 8, 9, 10, 11, 12\}$

$E = \{x: x \text{ is an even number}\}$

$M = \{x: x \text{ is a multiple of } 3\}$

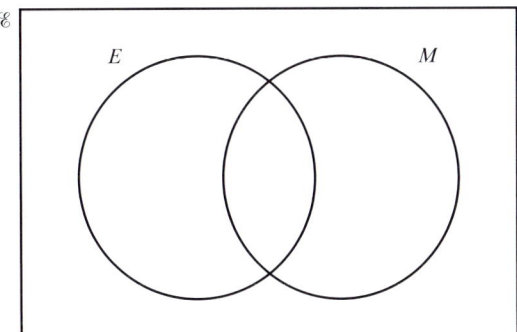

    i   Complete the Venn diagram. [Using Figure 1 in the Unit 6 Past Paper Questions Resource Sheet.]

[2]

    ii   Write down n($E \cup M$).

[1]

    iii   A number is chosen at random from the universal set $\mathscr{E}$.

        Write down the probability that the number is in the set $E \cap M$.

[2]

b   Meg says that an even number cannot be a prime number.

    Is she correct?

    Give a reason for your answer.

[1]

Cambridge IGCSE Mathematics (0580) Paper 31 Q9, June 2021

3   There is a straight road between town A and town B of length 130 km.

    Maxi travels from town A to town B.

    Pippa travels from town B to town A.

    Both travel at a constant speed of 40 km/h.

    Maxi leaves 30 minutes before Pippa.

    Work out how far from A they will be when they pass each other.

[4]

Cambridge IGCSE Mathematics (0580) Paper 11 Q22, June 2021

4 The diagram shows three triangles, *A*, *B* and *C*, on a 1 cm² grid.

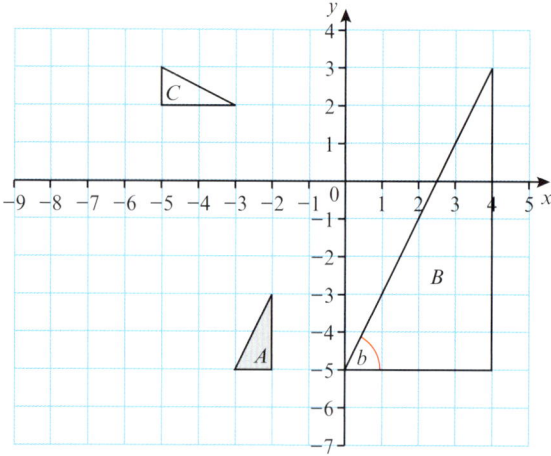

a Describe fully the **single** transformation that maps

   i triangle *A* onto triangle *B*,

                                                                              [3]

   ii triangle *A* onto triangle *C*.

                                                                              [3]

b On the grid, draw the image of

   i triangle *A* after a translation by the vector $\begin{pmatrix} -5 \\ 4 \end{pmatrix}$,

                                                                              [2]

   ii triangle *A* after a reflection in the line *x* = −4.5.
     [Using Figure 2 in the Unit 6 Past Paper Questions Resource Sheet.]

                                                                              [2]

c The diagram also shows an angle *b* in triangle *B*.

   Use trigonometry to show that angle *b* is 63.4°, correct to 1 decimal place.

                                                                              [2]

d Two new triangles, *D* and *E*, are made from triangle *B*, as shown in the diagram.

   Are all three triangles similar?

   Give a reason for your answer.

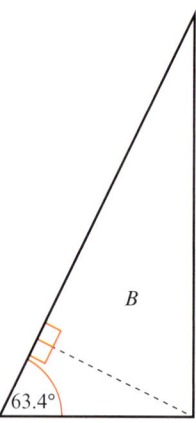
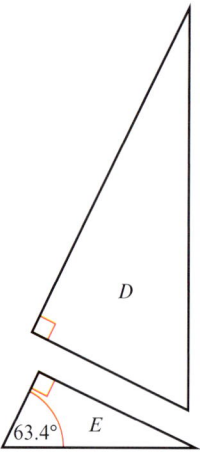

                                                                              [2]

Cambridge IGCSE Mathematics (0580) Paper 31 Q6, June 2021

5 Gabriela designs the seating layout for a new theatre.

There are three sections of seats, A, B and C.

a Section A has 152 seats.

Section B has 12.5% more seats than Section A.

Section C has $\frac{3}{8}$ of the number of seats in Section A.

    i Show that the number of seats in Section B is 171.

                                                                  [1]

    ii Show that the total number of seats is 380.

                                                                 [2]

b Write down and simplify the ratio of the number of seats in each section A : B : C.

                                                                 [2]

c In Section A:
- There are 12 seats in the front row.
- Each row has 2 more seats than the row in front of it.

Work out the number of rows for the 152 seats in Section A.

                                                                 [2]

d For a concert in the theatre, the ticket prices are in the ratio

A : B : C = 9 : 7 : 4.

A ticket for Section C costs $6.

    i Show that a ticket for Section B costs $10.50.

                                                                  [1]

    ii Find the cost of a ticket for Section A.

                                                                  [1]

    iii The table shows the number of tickets sold in each section.

Section	Number of tickets sold
A	120
B	136
C	30

Calculate the total amount received from the ticket sales.

                                                                    [3]

    iv The concert costs $4500 to organise.

Calculate the amount received from the ticket sales as a percentage of the $4500.

                                                                    [1]

Cambridge IGCSE Mathematics (0580) Paper 31 Q1, June 2020

6

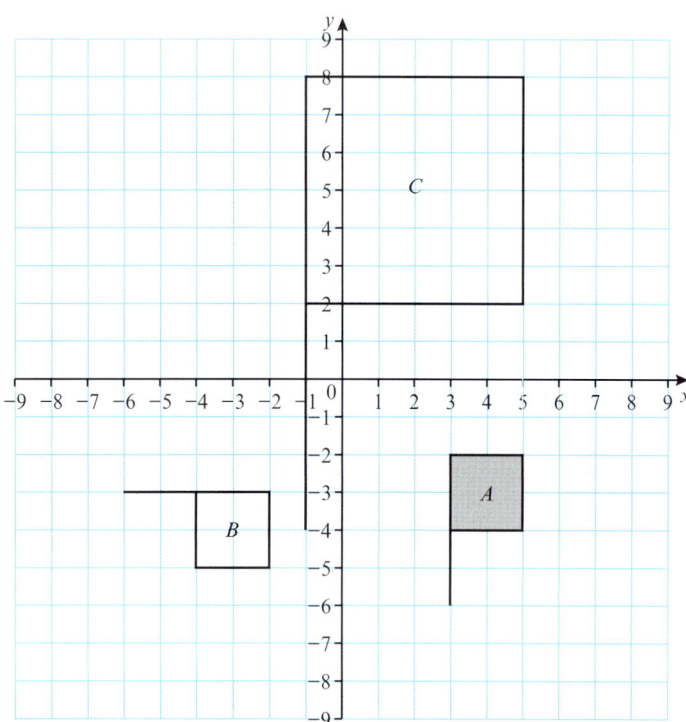

a   Describe fully the **single** transformation that maps shape *A* onto shape *B*.

[3]

b   Describe fully the **single** transformation that maps shape *A* onto shape *C*.

[3]

c   On the grid, draw the image of shape *A* after a translation by the vector $\begin{pmatrix} 3 \\ 1 \end{pmatrix}$.

[Using Figure 3 in the Unit 6 Past Paper Questions Resource Sheet.]

[2]

d   On the grid, draw the image of **shape *B*** after a reflection in the line *y* = 1.
[Using Figure 3 in the Unit 6 Past Paper Questions Resource Sheet.]

[2]

Cambridge IGCSE Mathematics (0580) Paper 31 Q7, June 2019

7   Work out.

a $\begin{pmatrix} 6 \\ -5 \end{pmatrix} + \begin{pmatrix} 8 \\ -1 \end{pmatrix}$

[1]

b $3 \begin{pmatrix} -4 \\ 7 \end{pmatrix}$

[1]

Cambridge IGCSE Mathematics (0580) Paper 11 Q9, June 2021

8 *y* is directly proportional to the square root of (*x* − 3).

When *x* = 28, *y* = 20.

Find *y* when *x* = 39.

[3]

Cambridge IGCSE Mathematics (0580) Paper 21 Q14, June 2021

9

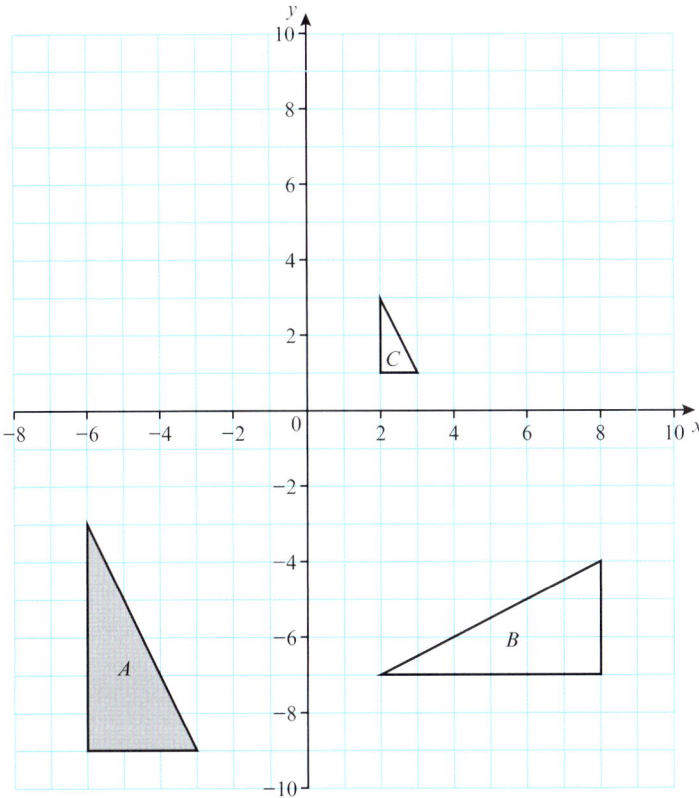

a Describe fully the **single** transformation that maps
   i   triangle *A* onto triangle *B*,

[3]

   ii triangle *A* onto triangle *C*.

[3]

b On the grid, draw the image of triangle *A* after a translation by the vector $\begin{pmatrix} 2 \\ 10 \end{pmatrix}$.
   [Using Figure 4 in the Unit 6 Past Paper Questions Resource Sheet.]

[2]

Cambridge IGCSE Mathematics (0580) Paper 21 Q10, June 2021

10

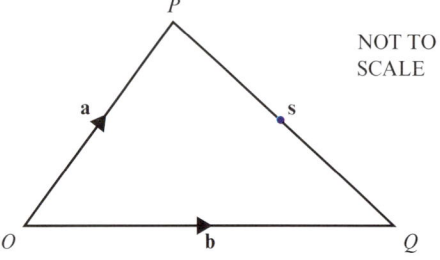

NOT TO SCALE

S is a point on *PQ* such that *PS* : *SQ* = 4 : 5.

Find $\overrightarrow{OS}$, in terms of **a** and **b**, in its simplest form.

[2]

Cambridge IGCSE Mathematics (0580) Paper 21 Q18, June 2021

11

| 1 | | 2 | | 3 | | 4 | | 5 |

The diagram shows five cards.

Two of the cards are taken at random, without replacement.

Find the probability that both cards show an even number.

[2]

Cambridge IGCSE Mathematics (0580) Paper 21 Q11, June 2019

12 a $f(x) = 4x + 3$ $g(x) = 5x - 4$

$fg(x) = 20x + p$

Find the value of *p*.

[2]

b $h(x) = \dfrac{5x - 1}{3}$

Find $h^{-1}(x)$.

[3]

Cambridge IGCSE Mathematics (0580) Paper 21 Q14, June 2020

13   *m* is inversely proportional to the square of $(p - 1)$.

When $p = 4$, $m = 5$.

Find *m* when $p = 6$.

[3]

Cambridge IGCSE Mathematics (0580) Paper 21 Q16, June 2020

14 a i $\mathbf{m} = \begin{pmatrix} 5 \\ 7 \end{pmatrix}$

Find 3**m**.

[1]

ii $\overrightarrow{VW} = \begin{pmatrix} 10 \\ -24 \end{pmatrix}$

Find $\left| \overrightarrow{VW} \right|$.

[2]

b

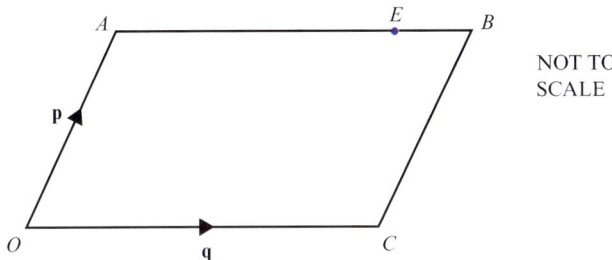

NOT TO SCALE

OABC is a parallelogram.

$\overrightarrow{OA} = \mathbf{p}$ and $\overrightarrow{OC} = \mathbf{q}$

E is the point on *AB* such that *AE* : *EB* = 3 : 1.

Find $\overrightarrow{OE}$, in terms of **p** and **q**, in its simplest form.

[2]

Cambridge IGCSE Mathematics (0580) Paper 21 Q17, June 2020

15 a In 2018, Gretal earned $32 000.

i She paid tax of 24% on these earnings.

Work out the amount she paid in tax in 2018.

[2]

ii In 2019, Gretals's earnings increased by 7%.

Work out her earnings in 2019.

[2]

b Gretal invests $5000 at a rate of 2% per year compound interest.

Calculate the value of her investment at the end of 3 years.

[2]

c One month, Gretal spent a total of $360 on presents.

She spent $\frac{1}{5}$ of this total on presents for her parents.

She spent $\frac{2}{3}$ of the remaining money on presents for her friends.

She spent the rest of the money on presents for her sisters.

Calculate the percentage of the $360 that she spent on presents for her sisters.

[4]

d Arjun earned $36 515 in 2019.

This was an increase of 9% on his earnings in 2018.

Work out his earnings in 2018.

[2]

e Arjun and Gretal each pay rent.

In 2018, the ratio of the amount each paid in rent was Arjun : Gretal = 5 : 7.

In 2019, the ratio of the amount each paid in rent was Arjun : Gretal = 9 : 13.

Arjun paid the same amount in rent in both 2018 and 2019.

Gretal paid $290 more in rent in 2019 than she did in 2018.

Work out the amount Arjun paid in rent in 2019.

[4]

Cambridge IGCSE Mathematics (0580) Paper 41 Q1, June 2020

16 The diagram shows the speed–time graph for the first 180 seconds of a train journey.

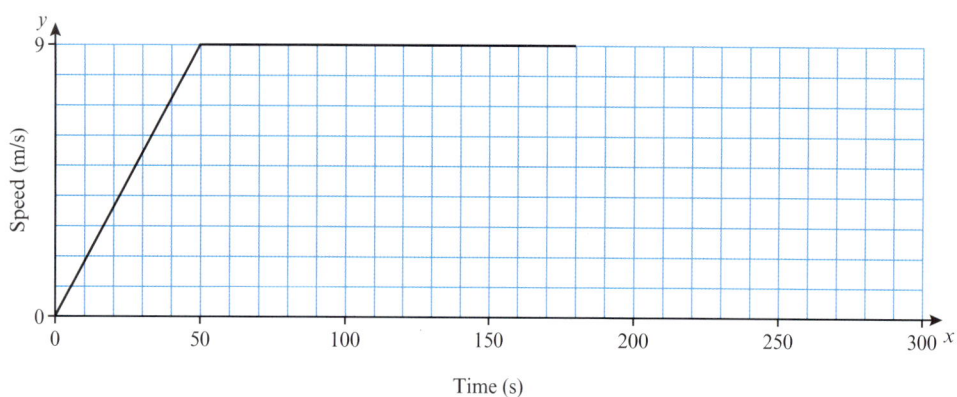

a Find the acceleration, in m/s², of the train during the first 50 seconds.

[1]

b After 180 seconds, the train decelerates at a constant rate of 1944 **km/h²**.

Show that the train decelerates for 60 seconds until it stops.

[2]

c   Complete the speed–time graph.
     [Using Figure 5 in the Unit 6 Past Paper Questions Resource Sheet.]

                                                                              [1]

d   Calculate the average speed of the train for the whole journey.

                                                                              [4]

Cambridge IGCSE Mathematics (0580) Paper 41 Q2, June 2021

17 a   On the Venn diagram, shade the region $P' \cup Q$.
             [Using Figure 6 in the Unit 6 Past Paper Questions Resource Sheet.]

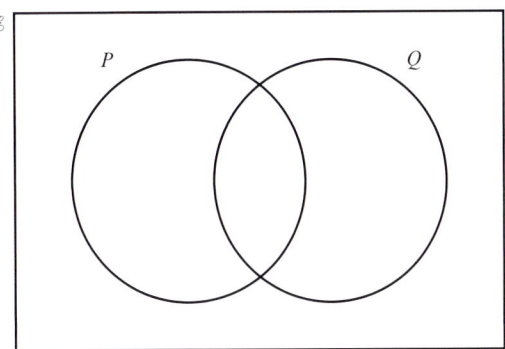

                                                                              [1]

b   There are 50 students in a group.

     34 have a mobile phone (M).

     39 have a computer (C).

     5 have no mobile phone and no computer.

     Complete the Venn diagram to show this information.
     [Using Figure 7 in the Unit 6 Past Paper Questions Resource Sheet.]

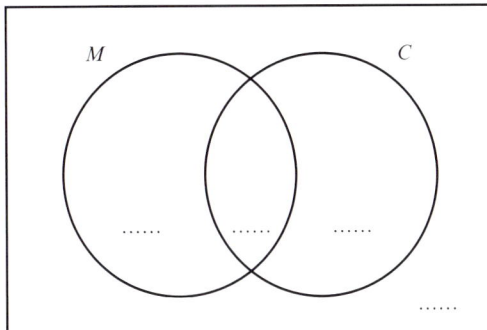

                                                                              [2]

c The Venn diagram shows the number of students in a group of 30 who have brothers (B), sisters (S) or cousins (C).

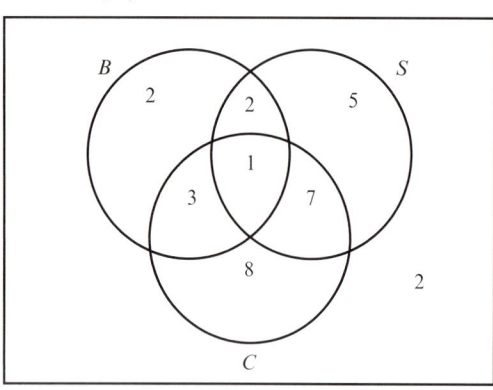

i Write down the number of students who have brothers.

[1]

ii Write down the number of students who have cousins but do not have sisters.

[1]

iii Find n$(B \cup S \cup C)'$.

[1]

iv Use set notation to describe the set of students who have both cousins and sisters but do not have brothers.

[1]

v One student is picked at random from the 30 students.

Find the probability that this student has cousins.

[1]

vi Two students are picked at random from the students who have cousins.

Calculate the probability that both these students have brothers.

[3]

vii One student is picked at random from the 30 students.

Event A This student has sisters.

Event B This student has cousins but does not have brothers.

Explain why event A and event B are equally likely.

[1]

Cambridge IGCSE Mathematics (0580) Paper 41 Q6, June 2021

18 a $s = ut + \frac{1}{2}at^2$

    i Find s when $t = 26.5$, $u = 104.3$ and $a = -2.2$.

    Give your answer in standard form, correct to 4 significant figures.

                                 [4]

    ii Rearrange the formula to write a in terms of u, t and s.

                                 [3]

b

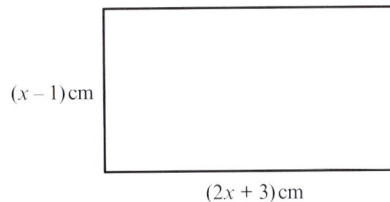
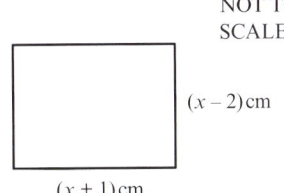

NOT TO SCALE

$(x-1)$cm $(x-2)$cm

$(2x+3)$cm $(x+1)$cm

The difference between the areas of the two rectangles is $62\,\text{cm}^2$.

    i Show that $x^2 + 2x - 63 = 0$.

                                 [3]

    ii Factorise $x^2 + 2x - 63$.

                                 [2]

    iii Solve the equation $x^2 + 2x - 63 = 0$ to find the difference between the perimeters of the two rectangles.

                                 [2]

Cambridge IGCSE Mathematics (0580) Paper 41 Q7, June 2019

19

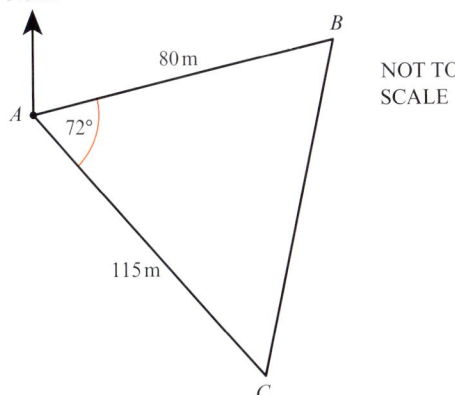

North

B

80 m

NOT TO SCALE

A

72°

115 m

C

The diagram shows the positions of three points A, B and C in a field.

a Show that BC is 118.1 m, correct to 1 decimal place.

                                 [3]

b Calculate angle ABC.

[3]

c The bearing of C from A is 147°.

Find the bearing of

   i A from B,

[3]

   ii B from C.

[2]

d Mitchell takes 35 seconds to run from A to C.

Calculate his average running speed in kilometres per hour.

[3]

e Calculate the shortest distance from point B to AC.

[3]

Cambridge IGCSE Mathematics (0580) Paper 41 Q7, June 2020

20 $f(x) = 7x - 2$ $g(x) = x^2 + 1$ $h(x) = 3^x$

  a   Find $gh(2)$.

[2]

  b   Find $f^{-1}(x)$.

[2]

  c $gg(x) = ax^4 + bx^2 + c$

      Find the values of a, b and c.

[3]

  d   Find x when $hf(x) = 81$.

[3]

Cambridge IGCSE Mathematics (0580) Paper 41 Q9, June 2019

21   The heights, h metres, of the 120 boys in an athletics club are recorded.

The table shows information about the heights of the boys.

Height (h metres)	$1.3 < h \leqslant 1.4$	$1.4 < h \leqslant 1.5$	$1.5 < h \leqslant 1.6$	$1.6 < h \leqslant 1.7$	$1.7 < h \leqslant 1.8$	$1.8 < h \leqslant 1.9$
Frequency	7	18	30	24	27	14

a **i** Write down the modal class.

[1]

ii Calculate an estimate of the mean height.

[4]

b **i** One boy is chosen at random from the club.

Find the probability that this boy has a height greater than 1.8 m.

[1]

ii Three boys are chosen at random from the club.

Calculate the probability that one of the boys has a height greater than 1.8 m
and the other two boys each have a height of 1.4 m or less.

[4]

c **i** Use the frequency table at the start of the question to complete the cumulative frequency table.

Height (h metres)	$h \leqslant 1.4$	$h \leqslant 1.5$	$h \leqslant 1.6$	$h \leqslant 1.7$	$h \leqslant 1.8$	$h \leqslant 1.9$
Cumulative frequency	7	25				

[2]

ii On the grid, draw a cumulative frequency diagram to show this information.
[Using Figure 8 in the Unit 6 Past Paper Questions Resource Sheet.]

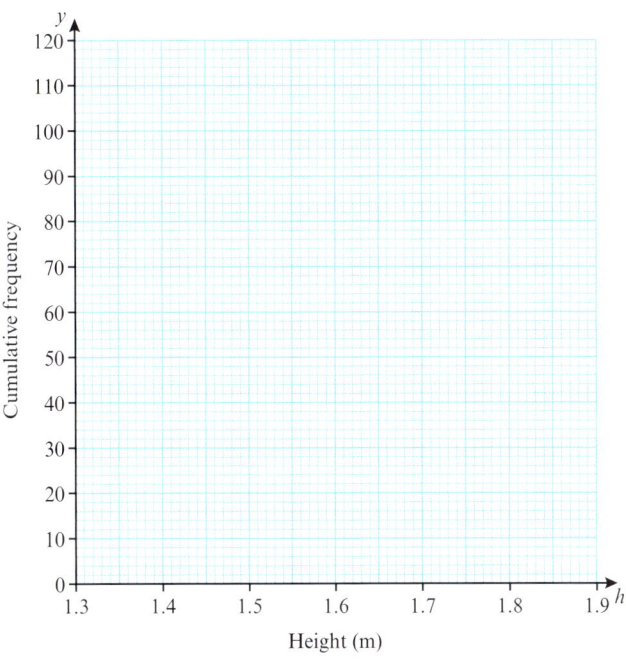

[3]

d Use your diagram to find an estimate for

    i the median height,

[1]

    ii the 40th percentile.

[2]

Cambridge IGCSE Mathematics (0580) Paper 41 Q2, June 2020

› Glossary

Key words

adjacent: a 'shorter' side of a right-angled triangle that is 'next to' an angle other than the right angle.

alternate angles: a pair of angles on opposite sides of the transversal between two parallel lines.

alternate segment: when an angle is drawn between a tangent and a chord the alternate segment is the segment that the angle does not cross.

apex: in a pyramid, the apex is the point, above the base, at which all the sloping sides meet.

asymptote: a line that a graph approaches but never intersects.

axis of symmetry: a line that divides a plane shape into two symmetrical halves or a 'rod' about which a solid can rotate and still look the same in different positions.

base: when working with indices, the base is the number that is being raised to a power.

bearing: an angle indicating the direction of travel between two points. The bearing begins from the 'North' direction and is measured clockwise round to the line joining start point and destination.

bias: something that affects the chance of an event occurring in favour of a desired outcome.

bivariate data: two measurements, relating to an investigation, taken at the same time.

categorical data: non-numerical data.

centre of rotation: the point around which a plane shape can rotate and show the same shape in different positions.

class interval: the group into which numeral data has been placed.

coefficient: in a term which is a mixture of numbers and letters, the coefficient is the number that is multiplying the letters.

co-interior angles: a pair of angles between the parallel lines on the same side of a transversal.

column vector: number pair notation used to describe a vector as the movement between two points: x units in the x-direction (left or right) and y units in the in the y-direction (up or down) e.g. $\begin{pmatrix} x \\ y \end{pmatrix}$. See also vector.

combined events: one event followed by another event.

common denominator: a common value that two or more fractions need to be converted to in order to be able to add and/or subtract fractions.

complement (of a set): set of objects that are not in a set, but which are part of the larger universal set.

complementary angles: two angles that add to give 90°.

completing the square: writing a quadratic expression in the form $a(x + b)^2 + c$.

composite function: applying a function to a value and then another function to that result.

composite number: integer with more than two factors i.e. it has more factors than just 1 and itself.

compound interest: interest paid on interest already earned and not just the original capital.

conditional probability: the probability of an event assuming that another has occurred.

congruent: shapes that are identical in both shape and size.

consecutive: following one after the other.

constant term: a term in an equation or expression that has a fixed numerical value.

continuous data: data that can take any value in a range, such as height or weight.

conversion: changing one quantity or unit into its equivalent in another unit.

correlation: the relationship between bivariate data.

corresponding angles: a pair of angles in the same position at each intersection.

cosine ratio: for a given angle (other than the right-angle) in a right-angled triangle, the cosine ratio is the length of the side adjacent to the angle divided by the hypotenuse of the triangle.

cosine rule: a formula connecting the three sides of a triangle and one of the angles.

cost price: the price that a trader pays for goods.

cube number: a cube number is the result obtained when a number is multiplied by itself and then multiplied by itself again.

cube root: the number which, when multiplied by itself and then by itself again, gives the cube.

cumulative frequency: a 'running total' of the frequencies.

cumulative frequency curve: a curve formed using the cumulative frequencies as the vertical axis value.

cyclic quadrilateral: a quadrilateral whose vertices all exactly touch the circumference of a circle.

denominator: the number on the bottom of a fraction.

dependent variable: a variable whose value depends on the value of another variable.

derivative of function: the derivative of function (or derivative) of a function is another function that gives the rate of change at any point on a graph.

difference between two squares: a method of factorising (putting into brackets) one squared term subtracted from another.

differentiation: the process of finding a derived function, which tells you the gradient of the function at a point on the curve.

direct proportion: when two quantities increase or decrease at the same rate.

discount: the amount by which an original selling price is reduced.

discrete data: data that can only take certain (usually integer) values.

element: an item in a set, sometimes called a member of the set.

empty set: a set with no elements.

enlargement: a transformation of a shape that keeps the ratio of corresponding sides the same but increases or decreases the lengths of the sides.

equation of a line: a formula that shows how the x-coordinate is related to the y-coordinate, for any point on a line.

equivalent fraction: the result of multiplying (or dividing) the top and bottom of a fraction by the same value.

event: the outcome that is being tested for in a probability 'experiment'.

exact value: precise or accurate value, not an approximation.

expand: multiply the terms inside a bracket by the term multiplying the bracket. (This includes multiplying one bracket by another.)

experimental probability: the chance of an event happening, calculated by running an 'experiment' many times.

exponent: another word for power or index, indicating how many times a base number is multiplied by itself.

exponential: a function formed when the variable is in the index.

expression: a group of terms linked by operation signs.

extrapolation: a value determined by continuing a line of best fit beyond the plotted data.

face: a plane shape that forms part of a solid.

factor: a number that divides exactly into another number with no remainder.

factorisation: to rewrite an expression using brackets.

formula: a general 'rule' expressed algebraically (such as how to find the area of a shape).

frequency density: the frequency of a class divided by the width of the class.

function: a set of rules or instructions for changing one number (an input) into another (an output).

function notation: an alternative mathematical way of writing equations.

gradient: the steepness of a line (or the steepness of a tangent drawn at a point on a curve).

grouped data: the collection of individual data values into convenient groups. Used especially for continuous data.

histogram: a specialised graph used to illustrate grouped continuous data.

hyperbola: a graph defined by the equation $xy = k$, where k is a constant. (Also called reciprocal graphs.)

hypotenuse: the longest side of a right angled triangle.

independent events: events where the outcome is not affected/influenced by what has occurred before.

index: another word for power or exponent, indicating how many times a base number is multiplied by itself.

index notation: a method of writing number using a base number and a power, for example $2 \times 2 \times 2 = 2^3$.

integer: any of the negative and positive whole numbers, including zero.

interest: the amount charged for borrowing, or earned for investing, money.

interest rate: the percentage charged for borrowing, or earned for investing, money. (Usually an annual rate.)

interquartile range: the difference between the upper and lower quartiles.

intersection: the intersection of two sets is the set of elements that are found in both sets (the overlapping or shared elements).

inverse function: a function that does the opposite of the original function.

inverse proportion: when one quantity decreases in the same proportion as another quantity increases.

irrational number: a (decimal) number that does not terminate or recur and cannot be written as a fraction.

line of best fit: a trend line drawn onto a scatter graph that passes as close to as many data points as possible.

line symmetry: a line that divides a plane shape into two halves so that one half is the mirror image of the other. (See also axis of symmetry.)

linear equation: a linear equation has no terms with a power in x greater than one.

linear inequalities: similar to linear equations but using $<$, $>$, $\leq$ or $\geq$.

loss: when goods are sold for less than they were bought, the loss is the cost price less the selling price.

lower bound: the exact smallest value that a number (given to a specified accuracy) could be.

lower quartile: the value of data at the 25th percentile.

lowest terms: an equivalent fraction where the numerator and denominator are the smallest allowable whole numbers. Also called simplest form.

magnitude: the size (of a vector) irrespective of direction.

maximum: a turning point or vertex on a graph whose y-coordinate is greater than points immediately to its left and right.

mean: an average that uses all the data.

median: an average, the middle value of data when it is arranged in increasing order.

metric: the metric system uses measurements that are fractions or multiples of metres.

midpoint: exactly halfway between the ends of a line segment.

minimum: a turning point or vertex on a graph whose y-coordinate is lower than points immediately to its left and right.

mixed number: a number with a whole number part and a fraction part.

modal class: for grouped data, a class that has the highest frequency.

mode: an average, the most frequently occurring value in a set of data.

multiple: the result of multiplying a number by an integer.

mutually exclusive events: events that cannot happen at the same time.

negative correlation: a trend, in bivariate data, where, as one value increases, the other value decreases.

net: the plane shape formed from the faces of a solid when it is 'unfolded'.

numerator: the number on the top of a fraction.

numerical data: data that is in the form of numbers.

opposite: a 'shorter' side of a right-angled triangle that is 'opposite' an angle other than the right angle.

outcomes: the possible results of an 'experiment'.

parabola: the graph of a quadratic relationship.

parallel (lines): lines that are the same distance apart along their length.

percentile: the value of data at a specified position (the data must be arranged in increasing order).

perpendicular: at right angles to each other.

perpendicular bisector: a line that cuts exactly through the middle of another line, making an angle of 90° with it.

plane symmetry: a flat surface that cuts a solid into two halves so that one half is the mirror image of the other.

positive correlation: a trend in bivariate data where as one value increase, so does the other.

power: another word for exponent or index, indicating how many times a base number is multiplied by itself.

prime factor: a prime number that divides exactly into another number with no remainder.

prime number: a whole number greater than 1 which has only two factors: the number itself and 1.

principal: the initial amount of money invested or borrowed.

probability: a measure of how likely an event is to happen.

profit: when goods are sold for more than they were bought, the profit is the selling price less the cost price.

projection: the image of a line on a plane such that the angle between the angle and the image is the smallest possible.

quadratic equation: an equation that contains a quadratic expression.

quadratic expression: an expression where one term has a variable squared (and no variable with a higher power).

qualitative data: another name for categorical data.

quantitative data: another name for numerical data.

range: a measure of the spread of data. The difference between the highest value and the lowest value.

rate: a comparison of two different quantities.

ratio: a comparison of amounts in a particular order.

rational number: a number that can be expressed as a fraction in the form $\frac{a}{b}$ where a and b are integers and $b \neq 0$.

rationalising the denominator: expressing the denominator of any fraction as a rational number by removing any surds.

reciprocal: the fraction obtained when the values of the numerator and denominator are interchanged. (See also hyperbola.)

recurring decimal: a decimal that continues to infinity repeating itself at regular intervals.

reflection: a transformation that creates an image by reflecting points in a given line.

region: a region in a plane that satisfies a set of linear inequalities.

relative frequency: the experimental probability of an event happening.

rotation: a transformation that creates an image by rotating points by a given angle about a fixed point.

rotational symmetry: symmetry by turning a shape about a fixed point so that it looks the same in different positions.

sample space: all the possible outcomes of an event or combination of events.

sample space diagram: a list or diagram that shows all the equally likely outcomes of an 'experiment'.

scalar: a quantity that has size (magnitude) but not direction.

scale: a ratio that indicates how much smaller (or larger) a drawing is from the original object.

scale factor: the multiplying factor for the sides of a shape that is enlarged from an original.

scatter diagram: a diagram that plots pairs of bivariate data to help determine if there is any correlation between them.

selling price: the price that a trader sells goods for.

sequence: a number pattern or list of numbers in a particular order.

set: a list or collection of objects that share a characteristic.

set builder notation: a way of describing what elements are in a set without having to list them all.

similar: plane objects that have the same shape and proportion but are different in size.

simple interest: interest that is calculated only on the original amount borrowed or invested.

simplest form: an equivalent fraction where the numerator and denominator are the smallest allowable whole numbers. Also called lowest terms.

simultaneous: at the same time (or in the same position).

sine ratio: for a given angle (other than the right-angle) in a right-angled triangle, the sine ratio is the length of the side opposite to the angle divided by the hypotenuse of the triangle.

sine rule: in any triangle, the ratio of the sine of an angle to the length of the side opposite the angle is always the same.

slant height: in a cone, the slant height is the shortest distance from a point on the circumference of the base to the apex.

solution: the value obtained from solving an equation.

speed: a rate that compares distance travelled in a given time.

square number: the product obtained when an integer is multiplied by itself.

square root: a number that, when multiplied by itself, gives a square.

standard form: a shorthand method of writing very large or very small numbers.

stationary point: a point on a graph where it stops increasing or decreasing.

stem-and-leaf diagram: a type of bar graph made by arranging numerical data in a display, the first part of the numbers forms the stem and the last part forms the leaves.

subject: the variable written by itself (usually to the left of the '=' sign).

subscript notation: a method of writing the nth term as u_n (u sub n)

subset: a set whose elements are all also members of another set.

subtended angle: an angle formed at the meeting of two given lines.

supplementary angles: two angles that add to give 180°.

surd: the irrational root of a number, for example, $\sqrt{2}$.

surface area: the total area of the faces of a three-dimensional solid.

tangent ratio: for a given angle (other than the right-angle) in a right-angled triangle, the tangent ratio is the length of the side opposite to the angle divided by the side adjacent to the angle.

term (in algebra): part of an expression.

term (in sequences): any of the numbers in a sequence.

terminating decimal: any decimal that has a fixed number of decimal places.

theoretical probability: the chance of an event happening, calculated if it is known that the possible outcomes are equally likely.

transformation: a change in the position of a point or line following a given rule.

translation: a transformation that creates an image of a point by 'sliding' it along a plane.

trial: an 'experiment' to determine the value of an outcome.

turning point: a point on a graph where it changes direction. Usually a maximum or minimum point.

two-way table: a table that summarises the data from two or more sets of data.

union: the union of two sets is the set of all the elements in the combined sets.

universal set: the set that contains all the elements you are dealing with.

upper bound: the largest value that a number (given to a specified accuracy) could be.

upper quartile: the value of data at the 75th percentile.

variable: a letter in a formula or equation that can have different values.

vector: a quantity that has direction as well as size.

Venn diagram: a pictorial method for illustrating the elements and interconnections of sets.

vertically opposite: a pair of equal angles formed when two straight lines cross.

vertices: the points where two or more edges of a plane shape meet.

volume: the amount of space contained inside, or occupied by a solid object.

zero correlation: no apparent linear relationship between two sets of data.

> Index